AF580132

REMBRANDT'S

Religious Prints

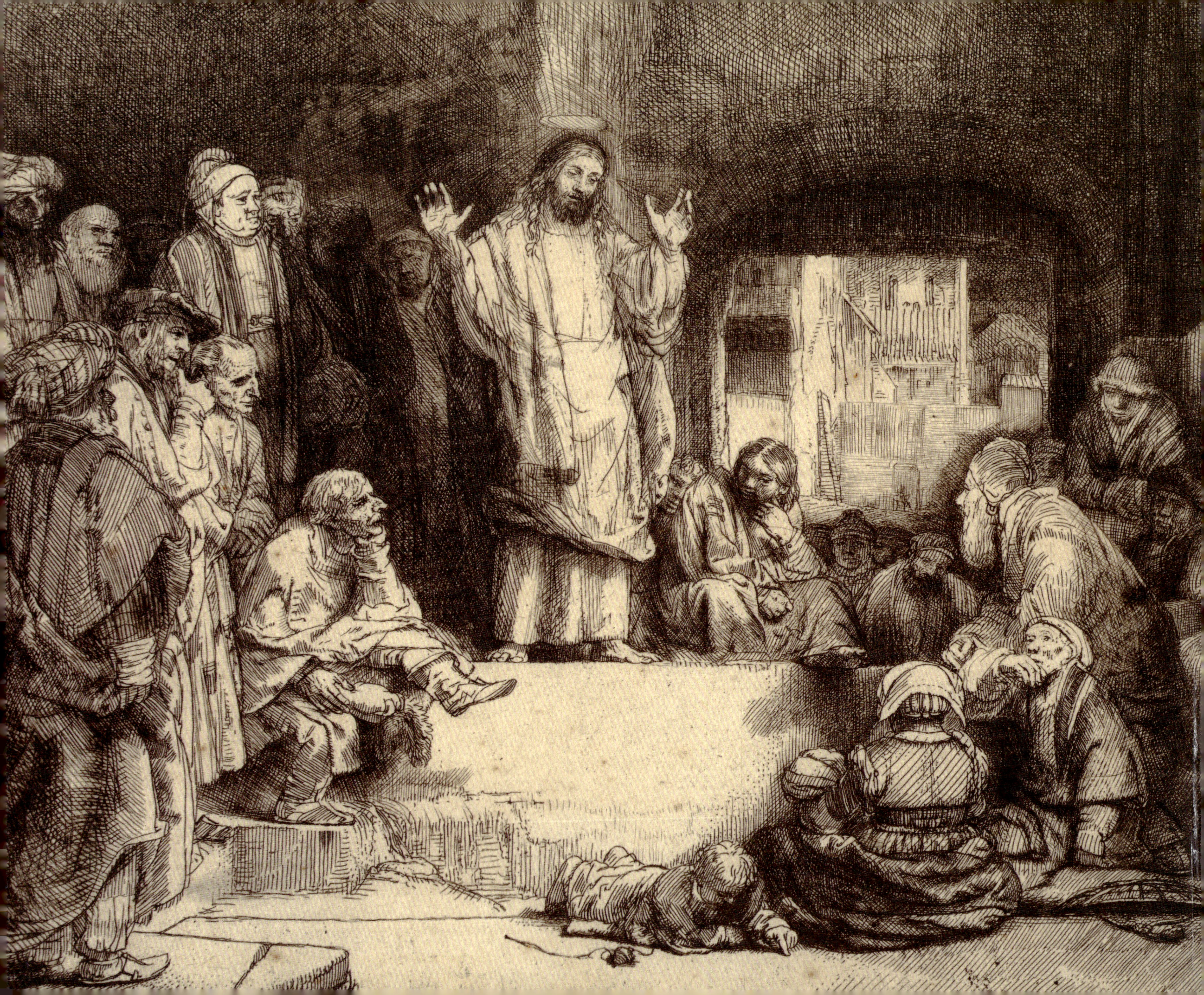

The Feddersen Collection
at the Snite Museum of Art

REMBRANDT'S *Religious Prints*

CHARLES M. ROSENBERG

INDIANA UNIVERSITY PRESS
WITH THE SNITE MUSEUM OF ART,
UNIVERSITY OF NOTRE DAME

This book is a publication of

Indiana University Press
Office of Scholarly Publishing
Herman B Wells Library 350
1320 East 10th Street
Bloomington, Indiana 47405 USA

iupress.indiana.edu

This book is printed on acid-free paper.

Manufactured in China

Library of Congress Cataloging-in-Publication Data

Names: Snite Museum of Art, author. | Rosenberg, Charles M., author. | Rembrandt Harmenszoon van Rijn, 1606–1669.
Title: Rembrandt's religious prints : the Feddersen collection at the Snite Museum of Art / catalog by Charles M. Rosenberg.
Description: Bloomington, Indiana : Indiana University Press, 2017. | Includes bibliographical references and index.
Identifiers: LCCN 2017004816 (print) | LCCN 2017008806 (ebook) | ISBN 9780253025876 (cl) | ISBN 9780253025906 (eb)
Subjects: LCSH: Rembrandt Harmenszoon van Rijn, 1606–1669—Catalogues raisonnés. | Bible—Illustrations—Catalogs. | Christian art and symbolism—Netherlands—Modern period, 1500-—Catalogs. | Feddersen, Jack, 1913–1990—Art collections—Catalogs. | Feddersen, Alfrieda, 1912–1995—Art collections—Catalogs. | Etching—Private collections—Indiana—Notre Dame—Catalogs. | Snite Museum of Art—Catalogs.
Classification: LCC NE2054.5.R4 A4 2017 (print) | LCC NE2054.5.R4 (ebook) | DDC 759.9492—dc23
LC record available at https://lccn.loc.gov/2017004816

1 2 3 4 5 22 21 20 19 18 17

CONTENTS

PREFACE AND ACKNOWLEDGMENTS

The literature on Rembrandt's art in general, and prints in particular, is vast and constantly growing. Two recent publications in the field have been particularly useful in the preparation of this catalog. The first is Shelley Perlove and Larry Silver's magisterial consideration of Rembrandt's works with religious themes, *Rembrandt's Faith: Church and Temple in the Dutch Golden Age* (2009). The authors' discussion of the iconography of these works is thorough and provocative. Their perceptive interpretations demand serious attention and are therefore addressed in numerous entries throughout this catalog. The second significant recent work is the set of volumes dedicated to Rembrandt's prints in *The New Hollstein Dutch and Flemish Etchings, Engravings and Woodcuts, 1450–1700* series (2013), compiled by Erik Hinterding and Jaco Rutgers, and edited by Ger Luijten. The individual entries by Hinterding and Rutgers include a wealth of information concerning the various states of individual prints, the location of existing impressions, and the history of Rembrandt's copperplates, a number of which still survive. In addition, the authors of the *New Hollstein* volumes have proposed revisions to the previously accepted dating of several works, including a number of those discussed in this catalog. Since their chronology is based not only on stylistic considerations, but also on the more objective criterion of the history of watermarks, it has been adopted here.

The "tombstone" header for each print in this catalog records the numbers assigned to the work in four standard catalogs of Rembrandt's prints: Adam von Bartsch ("B."), *Catalogue raisonné de toutes les estampes qui forment l'oeuvre de Rembrandt*, 1797; Arthur Hind ("H."), *A Catalogue of Rembrandt's Etchings*, 1923; Ludwig Münz ("Mz."), *A Critical Catalogue of Rembrandt's Etchings*, 1952; and Erik Hinterding and Jaco Rutgers, the *New Hollstein* volumes on Rembrandt cited above ("NHD").

Adam von Bartsch arranged his material by subject matter: self-portraits; Old Testament and New Testament subjects; saints; allegorical and "fancy" subjects; beggars; nudes, and "free" and mythological subjects; landscapes; portraits of men and studies of unidentified men; studies of women; and miscellaneous subjects. This is the order that is followed in the Snite Museum catalog, which includes one self-portrait and subjects from the Old and New Testaments. However, since Bartsch did not usually list different examples of the same subject, for example the Flight into Egypt, in chronological order, and since it is useful to consider how Rembrandt's treatment of a theme changed over time, entries in this catalog have been arranged first by subject and then by date. As a result, there are some deviations from the order found in Bartsch's catalog.

The titles of Rembrandt's prints are primarily descriptive. This tradition dates back to the seventeenth century, specifically to the sales catalogs of print dealers such as Clement de Jonghe.[1] Two of Rembrandt's religious prints (*"La petite Tombe"* [cat. no. 41, B. 67] and the *Hundred Guilder Print* [cat. no. 48, B. 74]) bear titles which are not specifically related to their content but which were informally adopted in the seventeenth century and have subsequently become the standard.[2] The titles in this catalog are those used by Christopher White and Karel Boon in their illustrated catalogue raisonné[3] and which have most recently been utilized by Hinterding and Rutgers in the Rembrandt volumes in *The New Hollstein* catalog. With very few exceptions, initial articles, e.g., "a" and "the," have been omitted.

Plate dimensions are taken from Hinterding and Rutgers's *New Holstein* catalog, as is the number of states for each plate. Unless otherwise noted, all prints are on laid paper.

Finally, a project of this scope is not the result of a single individual's work. Over the years, I have benefited from the assistance and expertise of many people, including John Feddersen, Ann Feddersen, David Tunick, Armin Kunz, Julia Quinn, Emily Kretschmer, Eric Huston, Elizabeth Murphy, Paul Crenshaw, Larry Silver, Gary Schwartz, Eva Frojmovic, Roger Kuin, John van Engen, Randall Zachman, Gary Dunham, Carol Kennedy, Nancy Lightfoot, Stephen Spiro, Charles Loving, Rebeka Cerevolo, and Cheryl Snay. I am grateful for all of their contributions. Above all, I should like to thank Carol Weiss Rosenberg for her inestimable contributions to this catalog. This project might never have been completed without her patience, editorial acumen, and astute critical insights.

This catalog is published in part with generous support from the Fritz and Mildred Kaeser Endowment for Liturgical Art.

Charles M. Rosenberg
Notre Dame, Indiana

Notes

1. D[ieuwke] de Hoop Scheffer and K[arel] G. Boon, "De inventaislijst van Clement de Jonghe en Rembrandts etsplaten," *Kroniek van het Rembrandthuis* 25 (1971): 1–17.

2. See individual catalog entries for these two prints for a discussion of these titles.

3. Christopher White and Karel G. Boon, *Rembrandt's Etchings: An Illustrated Critical Catalogue* (Amsterdam: Van Gendt; New York: Abner Schram, [1970]).

CHRONOLOGY OF REMBRANDT'S LIFE AND RELIGIOUS PRINTS

This is a chronology of all of Rembrandt's religious prints, including those that are not part of the Feddersen collection. If there is no catalog number after the print title, it is not part of the collection.

1606 Rembrandt Harmenzoon van Rijn is born on July 15 in Leiden to Harmen Gerritszoon van Rijn, a miller, and Neeltgen (Cornelia) Willemsdochter van Zuytbrouck, a baker's daughter.

1613–19 Attends Latin school in Leiden.

1621–3 Serves apprenticeship with Jacob Isaacz. van Swanenburgh in Leiden.

1624 Serves six-month apprenticeship with Pieter Lastman in Amsterdam.

1625 Becomes an independent master in Leiden, possibly sharing space with Jan Lievens.

1626 *Circumcision* (cat. no. 22), Rembrandt's first etching.
The Rest on the Flight into Egypt

1628 Takes on his first pupil, Gerrit Dou.
St. Jerome Kneeling: Large Plate
The Flight into Egypt: A Sketch

1629 *St. Paul in Meditation*
The Blindness of Tobit: A Sketch
St. Peter and St. John at the Gate of the Temple: Roughly Etched

1630 Begins collaborating with Jan Georg van Vliet, an engraver.
Rembrandt's father dies.
Christ Disputing with the Doctors: Small Plate (cat. no. 37)
Presentation in the Temple with the Angel: Small Plate (cat. no. 25)
Circumcision: Small Plate (cat. no. 23)

1631 Establishes himself in Amsterdam, living in the house of Hendrik Uylenburgh, art dealer and purveyor of artists' materials.
Beheading of St. John the Baptist (cat. no. 64)

1632 Paints *The Anatomy Lesson of Dr. Nicholas Tulp.*
St. Jerome Praying: Arched
Raising of Lazarus: Larger Plate (cat. no. 46)
Holy Family (cat. no. 35)

1633 *The Good Samaritan* (cat. no. 62)
Flight into Egypt: Small Plate (cat. no. 27)
The Descent from the Cross: The First Plate
Descent from the Cross: The Second Plate (cat. no. 55)

1634 Marries Saskia Uylenburgh.
Becomes a citizen of Amsterdam.
Joseph's Coat Brought to Jacob (cat. no. 12)
Angel Appearing to the Shepherds (cat. no. 19)
St. Jerome Reading
Christ and the Woman of Samaria among Ruins (cat. no. 44)
Joseph and Potiphar's Wife (cat. no. 13)
Christ at Emmaus: Small Plate (cat. no. 59)
The Tribute Money (cat. no. 42)

1635 *Christ Driving the Money Changers from the Temple* (cat. no. 43)
Stoning of St. Stephen (cat. no. 67)
St. Jerome Kneeling in Prayer, Looking Down
Crucifixion: Small Plate (cat. no. 52)
Christ before Pilate: Large Plate (cat. no. 50)

1636 *Return of the Prodigal Son* (cat. no. 63)

1637 *Abraham Caressing Isaac* (cat. no. 5)
Abraham Casting Out Hagar and Ishmael (cat. no. 4)

1638 *Joseph Telling His Dreams* (cat. no. 11)
Adam and Eve (cat. no. 2)
The Little Jewish Bride (Saskia as St. Catherine)
Self-Portrait in a Velvet Cap with Plume (cat. no. 1)

1639 Buys what is now known as "Rembrandt's House" on Sint Anthoniebreestraat.
Death of the Virgin (cat. no. 69)

1640 *Beheading of John the Baptist* (cat. no. 65)
Presentation in the Temple: Oblong Print (cat. no. 26)

1641 Titus is born, Rembrandt's only child by Saskia to survive past infancy.
Triumph of Mordecai (cat. nos. 14 and 15)
Baptism of the Eunuch (cat. no. 68)
Virgin and Child in the Clouds (cat. no. 34)
Angel Departing from the Family of Tobias (cat. no. 18)
Three Oriental Figures (Jacob and Laban?) (cat. no. 70)
Christ Crucified between the Two Thieves: Oval Plate (cat. no. 53)

1642 Paints *The Nightwatch*, a militia company group portrait.
Saskia dies.
The Descent from the Cross: A Sketch
Raising of Lazarus: Small Plate (cat. no. 47)
The Virgin with the Instruments of the Passion
St. Jerome in a Dark Chamber

1644 *The Rest on the Flight into Egypt: A Night Piece* (cat. no. 32)

1645 *Christ Carried to the Tomb* (cat. no. 57)
Abraham and Isaac (cat. no. 6)
St. Peter in Penitence
Rest on the Flight into Egypt: Lightly Etched (cat. no. 33)

1648 *Hundred Guilder Print* (cat. no. 48)
St. Jerome beside a Pollard Willow

1649 Sued for breach of promise by his former housekeeper and Titus's dry nurse, Geertje Dircx.

1651 *Flight into Egypt: A Night Piece* (cat. nos. 28 and 29)
Blindness of Tobit: Larger Plate (cat. no. 17)

1652 *Christ Disputing with the Doctors: A Sketch* (cat. no. 38)
David in Prayer (cat. no. 16)
Agony in the Garden (cat. no. 49)
Flight into Egypt: Altered from Seghers (cat. no. 31)

1653 *Christ Crucified between the Two Thieves: "The Three Crosses"* (cat. no. 51)
St. Jerome Reading in an Italian Landscape

1654 Housekeeper and mistress Hendrickje Stoffels censured by the Church Council.
Hendrickje gives birth to Rembrandt's daughter, Cornelia.
Christ Returning from the Temple with His Parents (cat. no. 40)
Flight into Egypt: Crossing a Brook (cat. no. 30)
Virgin and Child with the Cat and the Snake (cat. no. 36)
Adoration of the Shepherds: With the Lamp (cat. no. 20)
Circumcision in the Stable (cat. no. 24)
Christ Seated Disputing with the Doctors (cat. no. 39)
Christ at Emmaus: Larger Plate (cat. no. 60)
Entombment (cat. no. 58)
Presentation in the Temple in the Dark Manner
Descent from the Cross by Torchlight (cat. no. 56)

1655 Auctions off some of his collection.
Abraham's Sacrifice (cat. no. 7)
Four Illustrations to Menasseh ben Israel's *Piedra gloriosa* (cat. nos. 8, 9, and 10)
Christ Presented to the People: Oblong Plate (cat. no. 51)

1656 Declares bankruptcy and his possessions are inventoried for auction.
Abraham Entertaining the Angels (cat. no. 3)
Christ Appearing to the Apostles (cat. no. 61)

1656–58 Rembrandt's property is auctioned off.

1657 *Christ Preaching ("La petite Tombe")* (cat. no. 41)
St. Francis beneath a Tree Praying
Adoration of the Shepherds: A Night Piece (cat. no. 21)
Christ and the Woman of Samaria: An Arched Print (cat. no. 45)

1658 Titus and Hendrickje form a company with Rembrandt as their sole employee. They sell his work as a way of protecting him from his creditors.

1659 *Peter and John Healing the Cripple at the Gate of the Temple* (cat. no. 66)

1660 Titus and Hendrickje formalize their art-dealing relationship.

1663 Hendrickje dies.

1668 Titus marries and then dies seven months later.
Titus's daughter, Titia, is born.

1669 Rembrandt dies on October 4. He is buried at the Westkerk, Amsterdam.

ABBREVIATIONS

Ash and Fletcher Nancy Ash, Shelley Fletcher, and J. P. Filedt Kok. *Watermarks in Rembrandt's Prints.* Washington, DC: National Gallery of Art, 1998.

B. Adam von Bartsch and Edme-François Gersaint. *Catalogue raisonné de toutes les estampes qui forment l'oeuvre de Rembrandt, et ceux de ses principaux imitateurs, composé par les Sieurs Gersaint, Helle, Glomy et P. Yver.* Vienna: Chez A. Blumauer, 1797.

Basan Pierre François Basan. *Recueil de quatre-vingt estampes originales, dessinées et gravées par Rembrandt.* Paris: Chez Basan, Rue et hotel Serpente, no. 14, [1789], from Hinterding, *Copperplates.*

Ben. Otto Benesch and Eva Benesch. *The Drawings of Rembrandt.* 6 vols. London: Phaidon, 1973.

Bredius Abraham Bredius and Horst Gerson. *Rembrandt: The Complete Edition of the Paintings.* London: Phaidon, 1969.

Briquet C.-M. [Charles-Moise] Briquet. *Les filigranes: dictionnaire historique des marques du papier.* Hildesheim, Germany: George Olms Verlag, 1991.

G. and Gersaint Edme-François Gersaint. *Catalogue raisonné de toutes les pièces qui forment l'oeuvre de Rembrandt.* Paris: Chez Hochereau, 1751; London, 1752.

H. Arthur Mayger Hind. *Rembrandt's Etchings: An Essay and a Catalogue, with Some Notes on the Drawings.* 2nd ed. London: Metheun; New York: Scribner, 1923; reprint, New York: Da Capo Press, 1967.

HD F[riedrich] W[ilhelm] H[einrich] Hollstein. *Hollstein's Dutch and Flemish Etchings, Engravings, and Woodcuts, ca. 1450–1700.* Amsterdam: M. Hertzberger, 1949–2006.

HG F[riedrich] W[ilhelm] H[einrich] Hollstein. *Hollstein's German Etchings, Engravings, and Woodcuts, 1400–1700.* Amsterdam: M. Hertzberger, 1954–.

Hinterding, *Copperplates* Erik Hinterding. *The History of Rembrandt's Copperplates: With the Catalogue of Those That Survive.* Zwolle, Netherlands: Waanders, 1995.

Hinterding, *Lugt Catalogue* Erik Hinterding. *Rembrandt Etchings from the Frits Lugt Collection.* 2 vols. Bussum, Netherlands: Thoth; Paris: Fondation Custodia, 2008.

Lieure Jules Lieure. *Jacques Callot.* 8 vols. New York, NY: Collectors Editions, 1969.

Lugt Frits Lugt. *Les marques de collections de dessins & d'estampes; marques estampillées et écrites de collections particulières et publiques. Marques de marchands, de monteurs et d'imprimeurs. Cachets de vente d'artistes décédés. Marques de graveurs apposées après le tirage des planches. Timbres d'édition. Etc. Avec des notices historiques sur les collectionneurs, les collections, les ventes, les marchands et éditeurs, etc.* 4 vols. Amsterdam: Vereenigde drukkerijen, 1921. Accessed July 18, 2014. http://www.marquesdecollections.fr/.

Mz. and Münz, *Critical Catalogue* Ludwig Münz. *A Critical Catalogue of Rembrandt's Etchings and the Etchings of His School Formerly Attributed to the Master: With an Essay on Rembrandt's Technique and Documentary Sources.* 2 vols. London: Phaidon, 1952.

NHD *The New Hollstein Dutch & Flemish Etchings, Engravings and Woodcuts, 1450–1700.* Roosendaal, Netherlands: Koninklijke van Poll in cooperation with the Rijksprentenkabinet, Rijksmuseum, 1993–1994, and Ouderkerk aan den Ijssel, Netherlands: Sound & Vision Publishers, 1996–.

Rembrandt's Faith Shelley Karen Perlove and Larry Silver. *Rembrandt's Faith: Church and Temple in the Dutch Golden Age.* University Park: Pennsylvania State University Press, 2009.

Rembrandt's Journey Clifford S. Ackley, Ronni Baer, Thomas Rassieur, and William W. Robinson. *Rembrandt's Journey: Painter, Draftsman, Etcher.* Exh. cat. Boston: MFA Publications, 2003.

RRP, *Corpus* Rembrandt van Rijn and Rembrandt Research Project. *A Corpus of Rembrandt Paintings: Stichting Foundation Rembrandt Research Project.* 6 vols. The Hague: Nijhoff; Dordrecht: Springer, 1982–2015.

S Seidlitz, Woldemar von. *Kritisches Verzeichnis der Radierungen Rembrandts, zugleich eine Anleitung zu deren Studium.* Leipzig: E. A. Seeman, 1895.

TIB Adam von Bartsch. *The Illustrated Bartsch.* New York: Abaris Books, 1978–2012.

Tümpel, *Rembrandt legt* Christian Tümpel and Astrid Tümpel. *Rembrandt legt die Bibel aus. Zeichnungen und Radierungen aus dem Kupferstichkabinett der Staatlichen Museen Preussischer Kulturbesitz Berlin.* Exh. cat. Berlin: Verlag Bruno Hessling, 1970.

White and Boon Christopher White and Karel G. Boon. *Rembrandt's Etchings: An Illustrated Critical Catalogue.* 2 vols. Amsterdam: Van Gendt; New York: Abner Schram, 1970.

REMBRANDT'S

Religious Prints

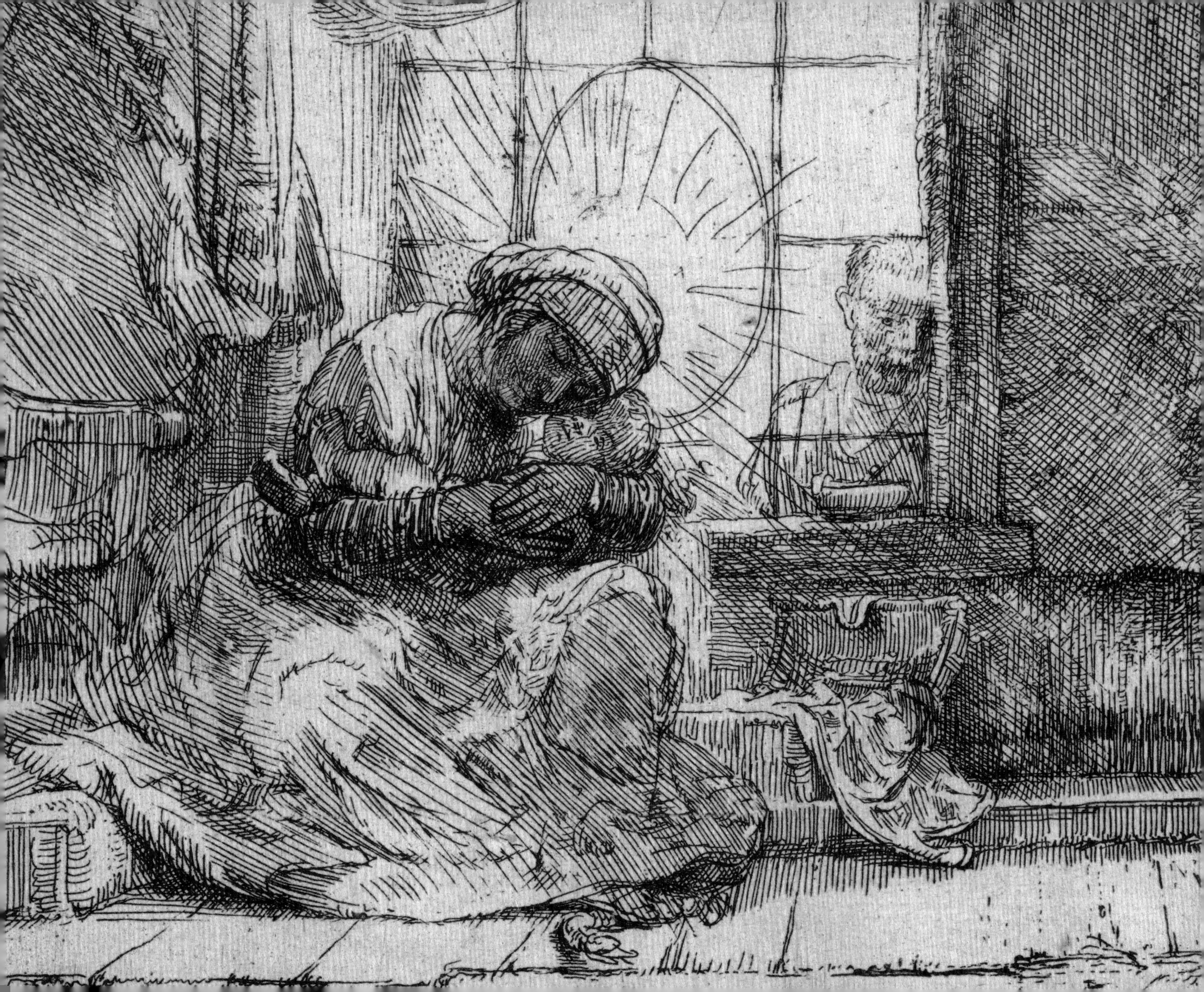

JACK AND ALFRIEDA FEDDERSEN: BUILDING A COLLECTION

Julia Quinn and Charles M. Rosenberg

In 1991, the University of Notre Dame's Snite Museum of Art received seventy remarkable Rembrandt etchings as a bequest from Jack and Alfrieda Feddersen, avid art collectors and longtime residents of Elkhart, Indiana. In the late 1960s, the Feddersens began to focus their attention exclusively on Rembrandt's etchings devoted to religious subjects, and over the course of sixteen years, they assembled an impressive group of biblical narrative prints. Surviving invoices, as well as interviews with family members, business associates, and the staff of the Snite Museum of Art,[1] have shed light on the Feddersens' objectives and have addressed such questions as how they came to focus on Rembrandt's religious prints, in particular; what motivated them to donate these etchings to the Snite Museum; and how the works they owned fit into the overall tradition of connoisseurship and collecting with regard to Rembrandt's prints.

Prints, including woodcuts, engravings, and etchings, are portable, relatively inexpensive works of art, and they have been collected in quantity since at least the late fifteenth century.[2] Initially produced as devotional objects, talismans, textual illustrations, workshop models, or practical sources of ornament, prints were collected for both religious and utilitarian purposes. In the course of the seventeenth century, these works of art began to be prized and collected not only as objects of devotion or important sources of information about the natural world, history, religion, politics, and art, but also as aesthetic objects in their own right.

In the seventeenth century, prints were stored in cabinets, mounted on walls like paintings, or, much more commonly, pasted down in albums.[3] Typically, the contents of these albums were organized by subject or artist,[4] a reflection of the utilitarian vision of the medium and a perception of these collections as educational resources.[5] In the early seventeenth century, collectors strove to amass encyclopedic collections, motivated in part by the same intellectual principles that resulted in the formation of the universal, microcosmic collections of natural oddities and manmade artifacts known as cabinets of curiosities.[6] Perhaps the most famous example of an encyclopedic print collection is the one that was assembled by Abbé Michel de Marolles (1600–81). Between 1644 and 1666, Marolles put together what must certainly have been the largest collection of prints: more than 123,400 impressions gathered together in 400 large volumes and 120 small ones. These volumes were organized according to more than seventy different subjects, topics that ranged from maps to clocks to gardening to dances to the lives of saints. About one-third of the volumes were dedicated to artists.[7] Marolles also recorded the number of impressions he possessed by each artist. He owned 224 works by Rembrandt.[8]

Rembrandt himself owned a significant collection of prints that were gathered in albums and stored in boxes and baskets. Although these certainly served as an important visual resource, it is also likely that he collected them for their intrinsic aesthetic and historical value. An inventory taken at the time of Rembrandt's bankruptcy in 1656[9] listed thirty-four albums containing graphic works by or after a wide variety of artists, including Lucas van Leyden, Titian, Raphael, Federico Barocci, Mantegna, Brueghel, Cranach, Antonio Tempesta, Maarten van Heemskerck, the Carracci, Hendrick Goltzius, Rubens, and others. Historians Roelof van Gelder and Jaap van der Veen estimated that on average, an album of prints held about 115 sheets. Based on this figure and the recording of loose prints and works included in albums of drawings,[10] van Gelder and van der Veen estimated Rembrandt's collection at over 4,000 prints.[11]

As art historian William Robinson noted, a new type of collector began to emerge by the middle of the seventeenth century, one who focused more on issues of process, invention, and quality, rather than on sheer numbers and breadth of coverage.[12] Driven by a connoisseur's aesthetic, this kind of refined collector was interested in questions of inking,[13] types of support,[14] variations in states,[15] and the clarity and integrity of individual impressions.[16] Some collected the works of only a few artists, seeking to acquire complete sets of the highest-quality examples of all of their works. Artist biographer Arnold Houbraken (1660–1719) acknowledged this passion for creating a comprehensive collection in his remarks about the popularity of Rembrandt's etchings during the late seventeenth century:

> The rage for his works was then so great that anyone who did not own both the little *Juno* [B. 112] with and without her crown, or the little *Joseph* [B. 37] with and without the dark throne, and others besides, was not considered a true lover of art. Yes, everyone wanted *The Woman by the Stove* [B. 197], one of the least of his works, with and without the white bonnet, with and without the stove key even though, as if it were not important enough for him to be bothered with it, he allowed it to be sold through his son Titus.[17]

According to Robinson, the Dutch art dealer Jan Pieterz Zomer (1641–1724) exemplified this shift in attitude toward print collecting as an end in itself. Zomer collected works by a variety of artists, but focused his efforts on Rembrandt, seeking to collect all of his prints in every state. After fifty years of collecting, he had acquired 428 prints by the artist. Even more significant, perhaps, was the fact that "Zomer's values were those of the print connoisseur. It was the beauty of the work of art that motivated him, not a thirst for universal knowledge."[18]

Rembrandt has always been admired for his inventiveness and skill as a printmaker,[19] and his works were widely prized and passionately collected even during his own lifetime. In 1660, Sicilian nobleman Don Antonio Ruffo commissioned the Italian artist Guercino to paint a companion piece for Rembrandt's portrait of Alexander the Great. In his correspondence with Ruffo, Guercino expressed his admiration for Rembrandt based on his acquaintance with the Dutch artist's prints: "As for the particulars of the half-length figure by Rembrandt which is in the possession of your Excellency, it cannot be other than perfection, because I have seen a number of his printed works which have appeared in these parts; they are very beautiful, engraved in good taste and in a good manner . . . I frankly consider him to be a great virtuoso."[20]

Filippo Baldinucci (1625–97), a Florentine ducal bureaucrat, amateur artist, and author who wrote a history of etching and engraving that included a biography of Rembrandt,[21] was very critical of the artist as a painter, but he begrudgingly expressed his respect for him as a printmaker:

> The way in which this artist truly distinguished himself was in a certain most bizarre manner which he invented for etching on copper plates. This manner too was entirely his own, neither used again by others nor seen again: with certain scratches of varying strength and irregular and isolated strokes, a deep chiaroscuro of great strength nevertheless springing forth out of the whole. And it must be conceded that in this particular branch of engraving [drypoint] Rembrandt was much more highly esteemed by the professors of art than in his painting.[22]

Houbraken's 1718 biography of Rembrandt also remarked upon the artist's unique methods:

> He [Rembrandt] has produced many witty Histories, Figures, little Portraits and numerous male and female heads with his needle, many of which are etched on copper, which have been circulated thanks to the press and to the delight of lovers of art.
>
> He had his own particular manner of preparing and handling his etched plates, something he never shared with his pupils. It is not possible to know how it was done, and thus the invention has gone to the grave with its inventor.[23]

Rembrandt's etchings were as popular in England as on the continent. Charles Rogers (1711–84), a self-educated customhouse official whose prodigious collection of prints included works by Rembrandt,[24] published a volume dedicated to the history of the art of drawing in which he included a biography of the artist.[25] His fulsome praise of Rembrandt and his etchings indicates the esteem in which the printmaker was held in England during the Georgian period.

> He [Rembrandt] expressed his inimitable Coloring even in his Prints. In general painters etch only their historical compositions; but very few, except Van Dyk [*sic*] and Rembrandt, have attempted Portraits. Rembrandt etched them with the same judgment that he painted them; every Line is spirited, and represents the touch of his pencil; nothing can exceed the effects of his Chiaro-scuro: a light and free Point went over his outlines and his hatchings, but with a Taste and Air of Facility which make us think that he did this work very quick, and without much trouble. Others have arranged their strokes, and cut their copper with greater labor; but he alone has dispensed with such fatigue, and has had the art of expressing Flesh, and producing Tints with a dry Point: the Effect of a beautiful tout-ensemble was his end, and he has attained it.
>
> ... The Prints of no Master have been more eagerly desired, or purchased at greater prices, than those of Rembrandt. The Freedom of his Etching, the Force of his light and shadow, and the perfect Nature expressed in his Portraits, have charms for the Artist, the Connoisseur, and the Gentleman. Zealous Collectors are not satisfied with having the best of his works, but are uneasy 'till they become possessed of Impressions from all his plates.[26]

John Barnard (1709–84) was another of the great eighteenth-century English print collectors with a passion for Rembrandt. Barnard, the independently wealthy son of a British financier, was described by Dutch scholar and collector Frits Lugt as one of the best judges of art of his epoch. In his magisterial work on collectors' marks,[27] Lugt said that among all of the English marks, Barnard's was the most revered. "The sheets from his [Barnard's] collection are always the choicest, both in terms of quality and condition. . . . The perfect taste of this collector was almost never at fault, and consequently his initials . . . on a sheet ensures that . . . a better impression [of a print] is virtually not to be found."[28] According to the 1798 catalog of the posthumous sale of Barnard's print collection, the foundation of his collection of Rembrandt etchings came from the holdings of Willem Six, a nephew of Jan Six, one of Rembrandt's most important patrons.[29] The catalog lists 425 individual sheets by Rembrandt, including an impression of the very rare fifth state of *The Three Crosses* (*Christ Crucified between the Two Thieves* [B. 78, cat. no. 54]). This impression may have been purchased by Thomas Major (1714/20–99), an English engraver known primarily for his landscapes and views of ancient ruins.[30] His collection of prints and drawings, including twenty-eight etchings by Rembrandt, was sold in London in January 1801. It is quite likely that *The Three Crosses* was purchased at this sale by George Hibbert (1757–1837). Hibbert, an extremely wealthy merchant and member of Parliament who made his money in shipping, particularly to and from the West Indies,[31] was also an inveterate bibliophile and collector of prints. In April and May 1809, his collection of almost 10,000 prints was sold at auction in London by a Mr. T. Philipe. Hibbert's largest holdings were of original etchings by Rembrandt and prints after Rubens. The former were sold in 306 lots of one or more impressions, and the latter in 388 lots. The impression of the fifth state of *The Three Crosses* was sold on the thirteenth day of the sale, and it is this impression that Jack Feddersen ultimately purchased from Harrods in London almost 170 years later. It was an acquisition that linked four discerning collectors over the centuries.

In assembling their collection during the latter part of the twentieth century, the Feddersens faced a daunting task. High-quality Rembrandt prints not only were in great demand and consequently quite expensive, but also were quite rare. Many of the best impressions were already in museums or private collections that had been assembled long ago. As a result, the easiest and most affordable way to begin a Rembrandt collection would have been to purchase posthumous impressions of lesser quality, examples of which were and are still readily available. A few years ago, David Tunick, president of David Tunick Inc., a gallery specializing in old master prints from which the Feddersens purchased nine Rembrandt prints, stated that "90% of what is on the market is junk."[32] He said that although poor-quality impressions were still procurable, it was quite difficult to build a collection of medium to high quality during the period in which the Feddersens collected. Yet, despite these challenges, Jack and Alfrieda Feddersen were able to build an outstanding collection in less than two decades. Each print under consideration for possible purchase was inspected by Jack Feddersen and was subject to return if it did not meet his standards.

Surviving invoices for all but three of the prints—*Flight into Egypt: Small Plate* (B. 52, cat. no. 27), *Flight into Egypt: Crossing a Brook* (B. 55, cat. no. 30), and *Christ Returning from the Temple with His Parents* (B. 60, cat. no. 40)—have made it possible to construct a chronology of the collection's creation and growth for the first time. Correspondence between Jack Feddersen and various art dealers still exists, and interviews with Stephen Spiro, the former John D. Reilly Curator of Western Arts at the Snite Museum; Dean Porter, director emeritus of the museum; David Tunick; and John and Ann Feddersen, two of the donors' children, have also provided valuable insights into the way in which the Feddersens acquired and shaped their collection.

Although Jack and Alfrieda Feddersen lived in Elkhart, Indiana, neither was originally from the area. Alfrieda was born in Springfield, Illinois. Jack Feddersen was born in Clinton, Iowa, and attended Wartburg College for two years before transferring to the University of Illinois. After earning his bachelor's, Jack went on to get a master of business administration degree from New York University, where he wrote a thesis on band instruments. He sent his research to the Selmer Company, a manufacturer of musical instruments based in Elkhart,[33] and in 1940, he was hired as the company's advertising director. In 1945, Jack was elected executive vice president of the company, and in 1960, the same year in which he married Alfrieda, he became president. Alfrieda became active in the Elkhart Symphony Club and Elkhart Concert Club, while Jack continued to play a leadership role at the Selmer Company until he retired in 1974. The Feddersens purchased nearly all of their Rembrandt prints after his retirement. Jack Feddersen passed away in 1990, and Alfrieda died in 1995.

Although the Feddersens were always interested in art, they did not have any specific goals in mind when they began to collect. Jack Feddersen, a self-taught artist, developed a particular interest in drawing and printmaking. At first, he gravitated toward modern prints and drawings, purchasing works by Miró, Picasso, and Toulouse-Lautrec, as well as images by artists from the Elkhart area. In general, he tended to favor black-and-white prints over colored ones. Then, looking to expand the scope of their print collection, the Feddersens purchased their first three Rembrandt prints—*Christ and the Woman of Samaria among Ruins* (B. 71, cat. no. 44), *Faust* (B. 270),[34] and *Stoning of St. Stephen* (B. 97, cat. no. 67)—on November 15, 1966, from the New York art gallery Associated American Artists. They were immediately attracted to the artist's unique, innovative style, and over time, this attraction became a passion. "I think that was really the start of his etching collection," said their son John Feddersen. "Before, [Jack's] collection hadn't had much direction. Once he got going on the Rembrandts, he wanted to know everything about them."

Soon after these initial purchases, the Feddersens chose to focus exclusively on Rembrandt prints inspired by biblical subjects. Their decision to concentrate on collecting the works of a single artist and theme was not unusual. According to David Tunick, identifying a specific area of interest has been a common practice among modern collectors of Rembrandt prints. It brings a particular focus to a collection and, given the scarcity of available fine impressions and the range of different images and prints Rembrandt created, it provides the collector with a more attainable goal. The Feddersens decided that Jack would be in charge of researching and purchasing the prints, while Alfrieda would organize receipts, invoices, and correspondence. Over time, John Feddersen recalled, his father acquired and read over one hundred books on Rembrandt, etching, printmaking, and the art of the print, in order to educate himself as a buyer. "He had an idea of what he wanted. With the Rembrandt etchings, there are a lot of problems of making sure the advertised etching is what they say it is." As for subject matter, the Feddersens decided that the biblical narratives were the best examples of Rembrandt's ambitious and expressive style. In addition, religious subjects were especially appealing because Alfrieda Feddersen was a very devout Episcopalian. After the family purchased a print, Alfrieda would locate the corresponding Bible verse and keep a copy in her files.

The Feddersens originally purchased prints from only a few art dealers in the United States. Jack would often travel to a gallery and, once he had established a personal relationship with the owner, would buy prints from the gallery's catalog on approval. Eventually, he widened his search for quality prints, seeking out prospects with galleries and dealers in England and Germany, as well as in the United States. The fact that on several occasions Jack Feddersen returned impressions that were not to his satisfaction attests to his high standards. On April 12, 1978, Feddersen wrote a letter of disapproval to the art gallery of Craddock & Barnard:

> I am disappointed in item 184, the angel departing from the family. Your catalogue describes this as being in "perfect condition." However, there is a light discoloration about 2mm × 3mm in size, above the left foot of the angel. Also, on [the] recto there is a brown stain about 5mm in diameter (see photo herewith).[35]

He received a response six days later:

> Dear Mr. Feddersen, I do not remember any spots on it, but your photograph certainly does show a very tiny one . . . as far as I can judge from your photograph the tiny spot which it shows would have no more than a trifling effect on its value. Nevertheless you have been a very good customer and I do not want you to feel dissatisfied.[36]

On another occasion, in response to Feddersen's displeasure with the condition of a print, Craddock & Barnard's representative wrote:

> Dear Sir, Thank you for your letter of December 11th. . . . We are sorry to read that you did not find the catalogue description full enough. I have asked Mr. Barnard about it and he says he did not mention the thin spot as it was a natural flaw in the paper, a sweat mark, as far as he can remember. If you are dissatisfied with the condition of the print we would feel much happier if you return it.[37]

Jack did, in fact, return the print. He had developed an eye for detail and was quite thorough in examining prospective purchases. "He rejected a lot of prints," John Feddersen said. "He'd say, 'this one has a gray wash,' or something. He was very discerning."

Other times, Jack Feddersen had representatives travel on his behalf to inspect specific impressions. This is especially true of the prints that the Feddersens purchased from London art galleries. Records of their correspondence indicate that a representative usually traveled to inspect a print, and then, if the impression under consideration was deemed suitable, had it shipped to Elkhart, typically on a ten-day approval, so that the Feddersens could see the work for themselves.

This was the method by which the Feddersens acquired the extremely rare fifth-state impression of *The Three Crosses* (B. 78, cat. no. 54) discussed above, one of the gems of their collection. The fifth state of this etching is considered by Rembrandt scholars to be one of the artist's greatest works. It is also one of the rarest, with only three other examples known to exist.[38] Jack Feddersen began investigating the print in 1972, recording the names of the galleries that had sold the fourth state in recent years and the range of prices that the print had fetched. On October 26, 1976, Harrods' fine arts department contacted the Feddersens to see if they would be interested in the gallery's fifth-state impression of *The Three Crosses*. For nearly three months, Jack Feddersen corresponded with his representative in London, and in a letter dated November 17, 1976, he relayed specific instructions:

> There are only a few impressions of this state in the world. . . . I would appreciate it if you would see . . . Harrod's [*sic*] fine arts department and take a look at *The Three Crosses* and let me know how it looks to you . . . a sparkling impression or just ordinary? Any folds, tears, repairs, etc.? Also, please note whether or not Christ's loin cloth has a "tail" on it as in one of the enclosed photo[s] . . . I[t] would be very helpful if you could scribble me a few lines about this. We have around 30 Rembrandts now, but they seem to get scarcer every month, at least good specimens.[39]

After receiving word from his London representative on December 1, 1976, that the impression was excellent, Jack responded on December 23, 1976:

> Your letter contained exactly the kind of information I needed . . . it sounds like a good impression . . . between studying etching information, my phonograph record collection, household and yard chores, a bit of traveling, etc. I manage to keep quite a busy life.[40]

The Feddersens purchased the print on January 24, 1977, subject to approval.

After the print arrived, David Tunick expressed skepticism about its authenticity, for he felt certain that no example of the fifth state of *The Three Crosses* was available on the market. Because he was convinced that it must be a fake, Tunick immediately flew out to Elkhart to inspect the print himself. Tunick's suspicions proved unfounded, and after examining the print himself, he declared that the Feddersens had, indeed, acquired an elusive fifth-state impression. John Feddersen recalled that the meeting was a memorable one: "Tunick was a great expert . . . for me it was kind of funny: Here's this big guy and my dad is acting like he knows more than he does!"

Jack Feddersen surprised David Tunick again in June 1977, during a visit to the dealer's gallery in New York City. He told Tunick that he owned three of the four Rembrandt illustrations for a Spanish book, *Piedra gloriosa*: *The Image Seen by Nebuchadnezzar* (B. 36a, cat. no. 8), *David and Goliath* (B. 36c, cat. no. 9), and *Daniel's Vision of Four Beasts* (B. 36d, cat. no. 10). What distinguished Feddersen's impressions was the fact that they were printed on vellum, instead of on Japanese or European paper. Tunick wrote back regarding the fourth illustration that Rembrandt had made for the book, *Jacob's Ladder*, which the Feddersens' collection lacked.

> Dear Mr. Feddersen: The B. 36B, *Jacob's Ladder*, which Elizabeth called you about, turned out to be on Japan, not vellum. Are you absolutely certain that the three you have are on vellum and not Japan? I have never seen them on vellum and would love to, as they must be extraordinary.[41]

Jack Feddersen replied:

> Dear Mr. Tunick: Regarding the 3 prints from a Spanish book, I am certain they are on vellum. Dr. Joachim,[42] of the Chicago Art Institute, like you, said he had never seen them on vellum.[43]

Perhaps the closest relationship the Feddersens developed with a dealer was the one they had with Tunick. After acquiring *Abraham Entertaining the Angels* (B. 29, cat. no. 3) from Tunick's gallery on October 3, 1975, the Feddersens purchased eight other prints from him. They also often employed him as a consultant, exchanging letters throughout the 1970s and early 1980s. According to Tunick, the Feddersens were some of his first customers to specialize in collecting Rembrandt etchings, specifically biblical prints. "[Old master prints] involve real connoisseurship stuff and Mr. Feddersen had some of that, I remember, and he cared. That was why he wanted to know if his prints were any good."

On one occasion, the Feddersens sent Tunick to examine prints at an art gallery in Edina, Minnesota. The dealer visited on October 9, 1978, and made notes on all forty-five prints that the gallery was offering. The reviews were underwhelming, with Tunick making such judgments as, "very late, not good . . . damage in upper right hand corner . . . unbelievably awful . . . good impression, [but] terrible condition . . . late reproduction . . . drags at all corners . . . worst impression ever." Tunick called the Feddersens to tell them, "no . . . [the prints are a] hunk of junk." Feddersen made a similar note in his own files: "David Tunick went to East Saint Paul and examined these prints, says 'forget it.' Very poor prints." Needless to say, none of the works in question was purchased.[44]

Jack sent Tunick "wish lists," and Tunick often wrote to Feddersen to tell him about works that his gallery had recently acquired, prints that he offered to put on hold for the Feddersens' approval before advertising them for sale. Jack sent one of his last wish lists to Tunick in late 1979 or early 1980, with a note attached: "As you can see from the above, we are rounding out our collection of Old and New Testament subjects."[45]

In 1981, the Feddersens loaned sixty-four of their prints to the University of Notre Dame's Snite Museum of Art, which had opened the previous fall. An exhibition of the etchings ran from January 18 through March 29. In the foreword to the accompanying catalog, Dr. Dean Porter, then director of the Snite Museum, wrote, "This [collection] is truly quite an accomplishment considering the state of today's art market in fine old master prints. A close scrutiny of the works on view quickly reveals that this is one of the more important private collections of Rembrandt etchings in North America."[46]

The long-term loan and exhibition of the prints was seminal, for it helped to attract other high-quality exhibitions and donations to the newly established museum. The Feddersens continued to collect through 1982, adding six more etchings to their holdings. During a luncheon with Dr. Porter and curator Stephen Spiro, they offered to make the Snite Museum the permanent home for the collection. The Feddersens were listed as anonymous donors until 1992, at which time their identity was publicly acknowledged. Although the Feddersens had maintained an association with the Art Institute of Chicago, they did not offer their etchings to that venerable institution. In fact, they had always intended to keep their collection in Northern Indiana. Although the family did not have any formal ties to Notre Dame before they donated their Rembrandt prints to the university, "[Jack] thought Notre Dame would be the best place to share the prints," John Feddersen said. "The big goal was that he wanted them to be available for the general public . . . Notre Dame offered the perfect situation: a competent art museum that would display them on a regular basis." Spiro concurred: "[The Feddersens] were really proud of the collection; they really wanted to share the collection. . . . If they gave it to someplace like the Art Institute of Chicago, which has such a fabulous Rembrandt collection, it would not have been the main focus." To ensure that the prints would always be available to the public, the Feddersens drafted a deed of gift that required that the entire collection be displayed regularly. However, the delicate nature of these artworks, which are especially sensitive to light, necessitates that their exposure be limited.

The patient, diligent, and informed manner in which Jack and Alfrieda Feddersen went about acquiring their art resulted in the creation of one of the most notable modern collections of Rembrandt biblical prints. The quality of their collection has been surpassed by few others in the second half of the twentieth century. The generous gift of these etchings to Notre Dame's Snite Museum has meant that these great works, so lovingly and painstakingly acquired, are now available to both the general public and the university's faculty and students, offering direct access to the graphic works of one of the world's most renowned artists.

Notes

1. These interviews took place in 2006 as part of University of Notre Dame senior Julia Quinn's research project into the history of the Feddersens' collection of Rembrandt etchings. All of the information based on conversations with Jack Feddersen's son, John, and his daughter, Ann; art dealer David Tunick; and Snite Museum of Art personnel was obtained during these interviews.

2. David Landau and Peter Parshall have noted that the Nuremberg physician, humanist, and historian Hartmann Schedel (1440–1514) is documented as having owned several hundred prints. Landau and Parshall, *The Renaissance Print: 1470–1550* (New Haven, CT: Yale University Press, 1994), 64.

3. Antony Griffiths, "The Archaeology of the Print," in *Collecting Prints and Drawing in Europe, c. 1500–1750*, ed. Christopher Blake, Caroline Elam, and Genevieve Warwick (Aldershot, UK: Ashgate, 2003), 9–27. Rembrandt kept much of his own prodigious collection of prints and drawings in albums.

4. William W. Robinson, "'This Passion for Prints': Collecting and Connoisseurship in Northern Europe during the Seventeenth

Century," in Clifford S. Ackley, *Printmaking in the Age of Rembrandt*, (Boston: Boston Museum of Fine Arts, 1981), xxxi–xxxv.

5. John Evelyn (1620–1706), the author of a seventeenth-century history and guide to the art of engraving, *Sculptura; or, the History and Art of Chalcography, and Engraving in Copper* (London: Printed by J.C. for G. Beedle and T. Collins, 1662), asserted that "this Art . . . above all other whatsoever, [is suited] to insinuate all sorts of Notions and things into Children, and be made an Instrument of Education superior to all those Abstracted termes and secondary intentions wherewith Masters commonly torment and weary their tender and weak Capacities" (138).

According to seventeenth-century French engraver and art critic Roger De Piles (1635–1709), the persistent study of prints refined a person's judgment and educated him in the fine arts. Robinson, "'This Passion for Prints,'" xxiv.

6. Evelyn, *Sculptura*, 135–37, quoted a discourse delivered in 1644 by the Abbé Michel de Marolles (see text, below), one of the most prodigious collectors of prints of all times, in which the abbé spoke of his motivation for acquiring prints as a "curiosity" and praised his extraordinary collection as superior to "a World of other trifling Collections."

7. Marolles's discourse quoted in Evelyn lists all of the different categories into which his albums were sorted. Evelyn, *Sculptura*, 136.

8. For Marolles's collection, see Robinson, "'This Passion for Prints,'" xxxvii–xxxix. King Louis XIV of France purchased Marolles's collection in its entirety, at which point the abbé began collecting all over again. By 1672, he had managed to amass an entirely new collection of well over 111,000 impressions.

9. Walter Strauss and Marjon van der Meulen, eds. and trans., *The Rembrandt Documents* (New York: Abaris, 1979), doc. 1656/12. The albums were kept in the so-called art chamber (*Kunstcaemer*). Prints by Schongauer, Holbein, Hans Brosamer, Israhel van Meckenem, and Jan Georg van Vliet were stored in boxes (items number 237 and 277), while prints by Rembrandt, Wenceslaus Hollar, Hieronymus Cock, and others, were kept in an "East Indian basket" (item number 235). There were three framed prints by unnamed artists in the "antechamber of the art room" (*Voorvertrek voor de Kunstcaemer*).

It is curious that no prints by Dürer are listed in the 1656 inventory, since Rembrandt is known to have purchased a significant numbers of graphic works by this German artist at auction. These included multiple copies of Dürer's *Life of the Virgin* and two copies of one of Dürer's Passions. It is possible that Rembrandt bought all of these prints for resale and that he no longer owned any of them in 1656. Strauss and van der Meulen, *The Rembrandt Documents*, doc. 1638/2, February 9, 1638.

10. Strauss and van der Meulen, *The Rembrandt Documents*, doc. 1656/12:

> Item 201: One [album] of large size filled with drawings and prints by various masters
> Item 202: One [album] of larger size with drawings and prints by various masters
> Item 203: One [album] filled with curious drawings in miniature as well as woodcuts and engravings on copper of various costumes.

11. Bob van den Boogert, ed., *Rembrandt's Treasures*, exh. cat. (Zwolle, Netherlands: Waanders, 1999), 25, box 5, and 58.

12. Robinson, "'This Passion for Prints,'" xli–xliii.

13. Rembrandt manipulated the amount of ink left on the plate in a very sophisticated manner, often creating quite different-looking impressions drawn from a single state. See, for example, the discussion of *Entombment* (B. 86, cat. no. 58) in this catalog.

14. By Rembrandt's time, a wide variety of types of paper was available, from coarse cartridge or oatmeal paper to much finer Japanese and Indian papers and European laid papers. The kind of paper that Rembrandt used for a particular impression has sometimes offered clues to historians seeking to determine the date of a work. Laid papers, in particular, often bear watermarks that can provide clues as to the city, shop, and date of production. For a full discussion of watermarks found on Rembrandt's prints, see Erik Hinterding, *Rembrandt as an Etcher: The Practice of Production and Distribution*, 3 vols. (Ouderkerk aan den Ijssel, Netherlands: Sound and Vision Publishers, 2006).

15. Rembrandt's etchings exist in anywhere from a single state to as many as nine different states. Some of the changes in a plate were minor, but some were transformative. The identification of the states of a plate can be complicated by the artist's inking habits (e.g., a lightly inked impression that makes it appear as though lines have been eliminated may be mistaken for a variation in the plate itself, and hence as a separate state) and, even more significant, by the continued use of Rembrandt's plates after his death. Some late states

of a work may be the result of changes introduced by a subsequent owner of the plate. These late variations often represent attempts to repair or reinforce a worn plate.

16. Impressions printed early on in the life of a plate are preferable to those pulled later, because in the course of printing, fine details are often worn away as the pressure of the press gradually flattens the surface of a plate.

17. Arnold Houbraken, "Life of Rembrandt," in Joachim von Sandrart, Filippo Baldinucci, Arnold Houbraken, and Charles Ford, *Lives of Rembrandt,* (London: Pallas Athene, 2007), 89–91. The biography was originally published in Houbraken's *De groote schouburgh der Nederlantsche konstschilders en schilderessen: waar van 'er vele met hunne beeltenissen ten tooneel een verschynen, en hun levensgedrag en konstwerken beschreven worden: zynde een vervolg op Het Schilderboek van K. v. Mander.* (Amsterdam: Weduwe des Autheurs, 1718–21).

18. Robinson, "'This Passion for Prints,'" xl.

19. Joseph Maberly, writing in the middle of the nineteenth century, commented on the rising cost of Rembrandt prints and noted that "there has never, indeed, been a time when this artist [Rembrandt] was not highly prized; he has endured while others have passed away. . . . No one, who is unshackled by prepossessions, can well refuse to concur in the opinion that a rage for the works of Rembrandt is more to the credit of the taste of the age, than a rage for the works of Hollar, or any such engraver." *The Print Collector: An Introduction to the Knowledge Necessary for Forming a Collection of Ancient Prints* (New York: Dodd, Mead, 1885; 1st ed., London: Saunders and Otley, 1844), 54.

20. Strauss and van der Meulen, *The Rembrandt Documents,* doc. 1660/7.

21. Filippo Baldinucci, *Comminciamento e progresso dell'arte d'intagliare in rame colle vita de' più eccellenti maestri della stessa professione* (Florence: Stamperia di P. Matini, 1686). This was the first history of etching and engraving.

22. Filippo Baldinucci, "Life of Rembrandt," in *Lives of Rembrandt,* 41.

23. Houbraken, "Life of Rembrandt," 88–89.

24. More than 160 prints in 85 lots either by or based on Rembrandt were offered for sale at the auction of Rogers's collection in March 1799. "Eighth Day's Sale, Dutch School, Rembrandt," *Catalogue of the Capital and Extensive Collection of Prints, and Books of Prints of Charles Rogers . . .* (London: G. Hayden, 1799), 53–57. This catalog also includes a brief biography of Rogers, i–iv.

25. Charles Rogers, *A Collection of Prints in Imitation of Drawings: To Which Are Annexed Lives of Their Authors with Explanatory and Critical Notes by Charles Rogers Esq. F.R.S. and S.A.L.*, 2 vols., London: Printed by J. Nichols, successor to Mr. Bowyer, and sold by John Boydell, engraver, No. 93, Cheapside. Benjamin White, at Horace's Head, Fleet-Street. Peter Molini, in Oxendon-Street, Hay-Market, 1778. Rogers's eclectic biography of Rembrandt can be found in 2:214–19.

26. Rogers, *A Collection*, 2:217–18. For a superb example of Rembrandt's etched portraits, see his *Self-Portrait in a Velvet Cap with Plume* (B. 20, 1638, cat. no. 1).

27. Since at least the eighteenth century, some collectors have indicated their ownership of a drawing or print by stamping, embossing, or writing their initials or some personal symbol on the front or back of a sheet.

28. Lugt, 1419.

29. Lugt, 1539, "Jan Six."

30. Majors was employed as the chief engraver of seals and had the distinction of becoming the first associate engraver of the Royal Academy in 1770.

31. Biographies of George Hibbert can be found at http://www.georgehibbert.com (accessed October 21, 2013) and at the Legacies of British Slave-Ownership site, http://www.ucl.ac.uk/lbs/person/view/16791 (accessed October 21, 2013), since Hibbert was known to have been a vocal supporter of the slave trade.

32. David Tunick conversation with Julia Quinn.

33. The Selmer Company is now the Conn-Selmer Company

34. This print is no longer part of the collection.

35. Jack F. Feddersen to Ruth Mahin of Craddock & Barnard, April 12, 1978. From the personal files of Jack F. Feddersen, Elkhart, Ind. Feddersen is probably referring to Rembrandt's print of *Angel Departing from the Family of Tobias* (B. 43, cat. no. 18).

36. Ruth Mahin of Craddock & Barnard to Jack F. Feddersen, April 18, 1978. From the personal files of Jack F. Feddersen, Elkhart, Ind.

37. Craddock & Barnard, London, to Jack F. Feddersen, January 3, 1979. From the personal files of Jack F. Feddersen, Elkhart, Ind.

38. This figure comes from the entry (274) in the NHD volumes on Rembrandt.

39. Jack F. Feddersen to Fred (?), November 17, 1976. From the personal files of Jack F. Feddersen, Elkhart, Ind.

40. Jack F. Feddersen to Fred (?), December 23, 1976. From the personal files of Jack F. Feddersen, Elkhart, Ind.

41. David Tunick to Jack F. Feddersen, June 16, 1977. From the personal files of Jack F. Feddersen, Elkhart, Ind.

42. Harold Joachim was curator of prints and drawings at the Art Institute of Chicago from 1958 until his death in 1983.

43. Jack F. Feddersen to David Tunick, June 22, 1977. From the personal files of Jack F. Feddersen, Elkhart, Ind.

44. David Tunick, conversation with Julia Quinn; and Jack Feddersen, from the personal files of Jack F. Feddersen, Elkhart, Ind.

45. From the personal files of Jack F. Feddersen, Elkhart, Ind.

46. Snite Museum of Art, *Rembrandt Etchings from a Private Collection, Biblical Subjects: The Old and New Testaments*, Catalogue from the Exhibition of January 8–March 29, 1981 (Notre Dame, IN: Snite Museum of Art, 1981).

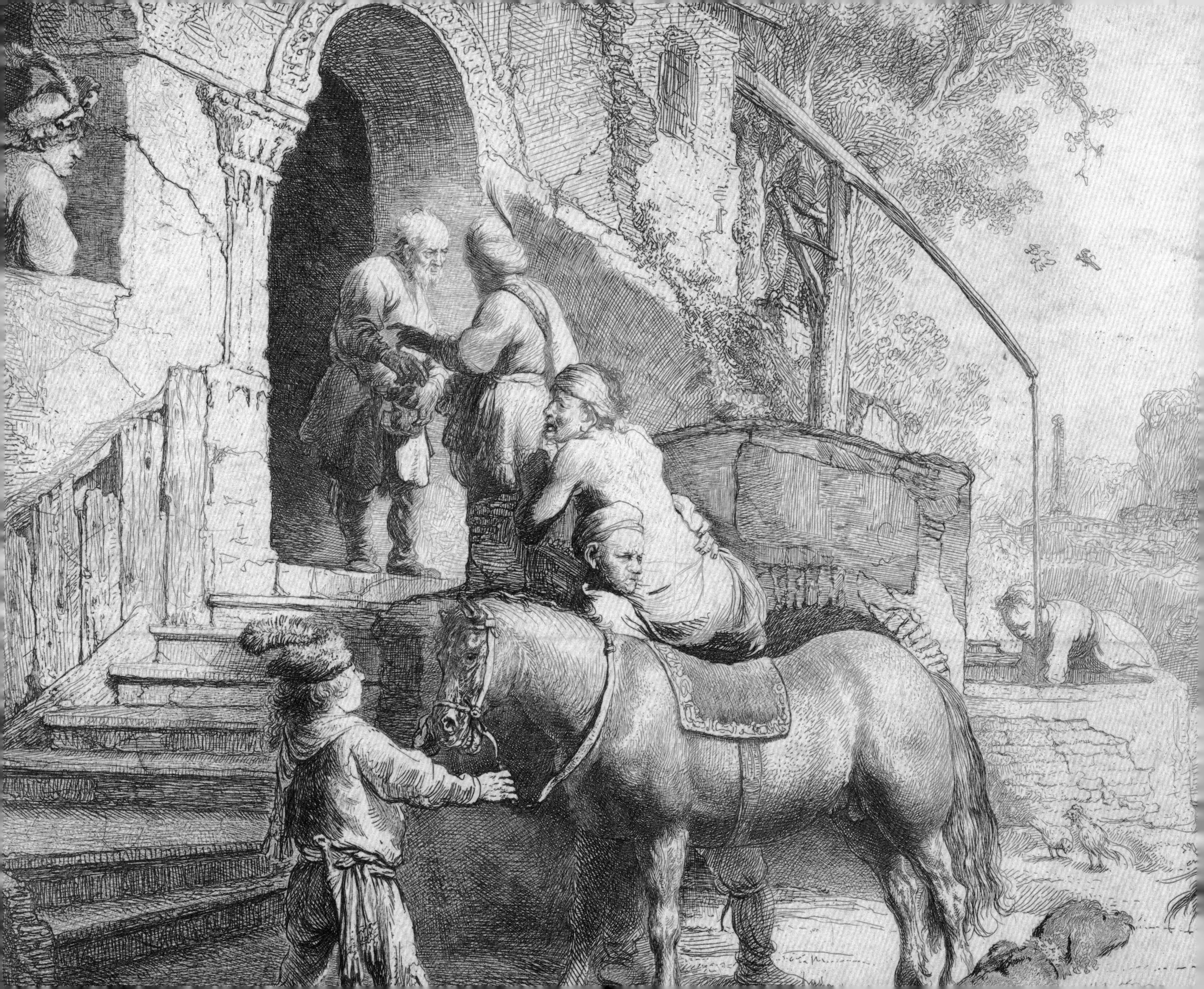

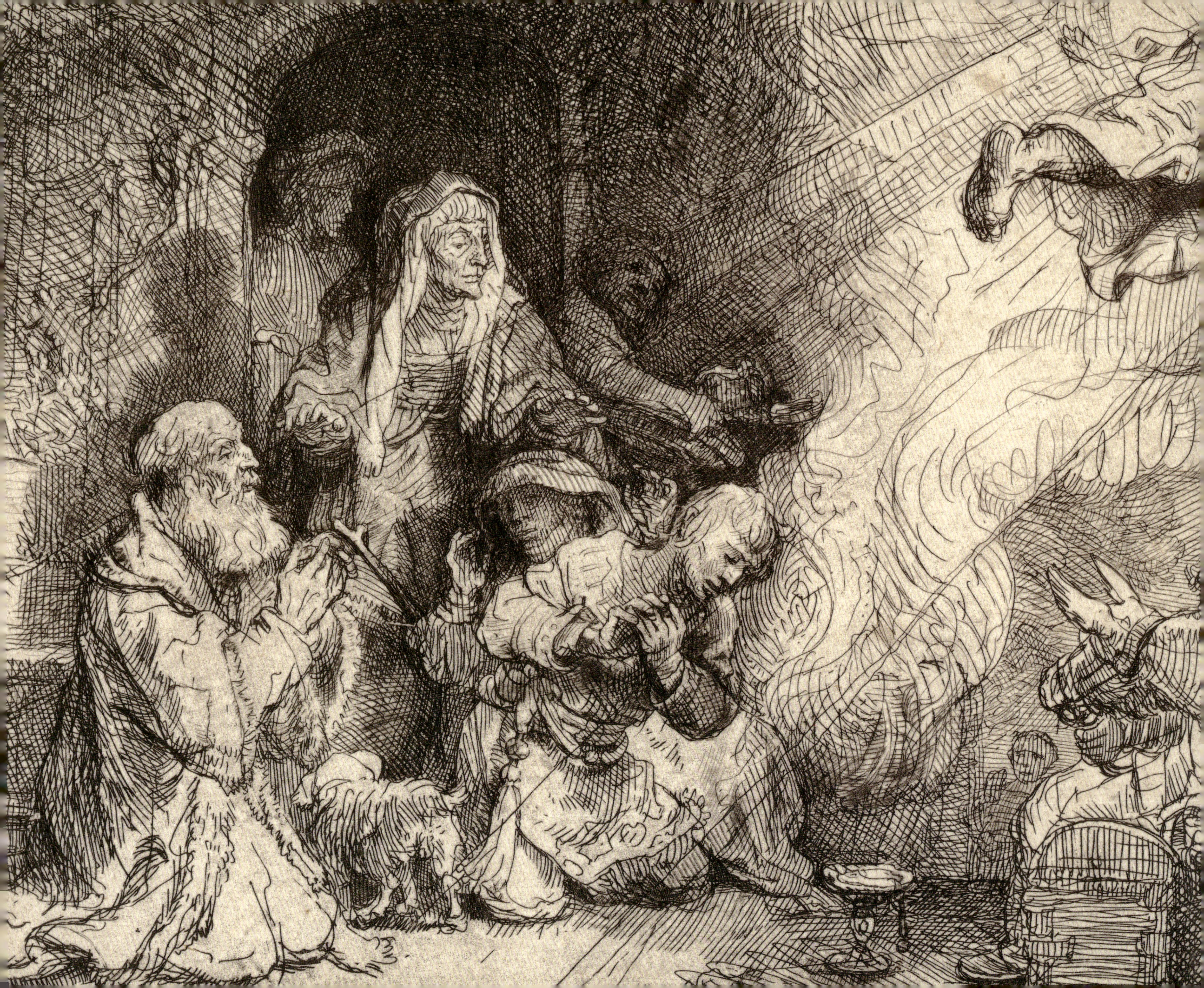

REMBRANDT'S RELIGIOUS PRINTS

Charles M. Rosenberg

Rembrandt Harmenszoon van Rijn was born in the university town of Leiden on July 15, 1606, the ninth of ten children.[1] His father, Harmen Gerrittsz. van Rijn, was a miller, and his mother, Neeltgen Willemsdochter van Zuytbrouck, was the daughter of a baker. The barley mill that his father owned was located on the edge of Leiden overlooking the Rhine river, and the mill, known as the *Rijn*, may well have been the source of Rembrandt's patronymic.

Rembrandt's father was a member of the Dutch Reformed Church. Although the artist's mother was Catholic, his parents were wed in the Reformed Church,[2] and their intermarriage suggests that neither was particularly devout.[3] One of the main characteristics of the Dutch Republic, in general, and Holland, in particular, during the late sixteenth and seventeenth centuries, was a philosophy of religious tolerance. Although the Reformed Church was the dominant religion, it was not the official state religion, so Lutherans, Mennonites, Catholics, Anabaptists, and even Jews were all allowed to practice their faith in private, as long as their observances did not interfere with the practices of Dutch Calvinists.[4] This does not mean that religious beliefs were never a source of conflict, particularly when combined with politics. During the early seventeenth century, a dispute between two theology professors at the University of Leiden over predestination and original sin blossomed into a virulent controversy that encompassed broader questions concerning the relationship of the church and the state and also the conduct of the war with Spain.[5] What became known as the Remonstrant/Counter-Remonstrant controversy engulfed the entire Dutch Republic, and Leiden was especially affected because its university faculty in religion was actively engaged in the dispute.[6] As a boy, Rembrandt would certainly have witnessed the public turmoil that resulted from this divisive dispute.[7] Later, a number of Rembrandt's patrons were allied with the more liberal Remonstrant faction, which suggests that Rembrandt himself may have been sympathetic to their position.

Rembrandt's own religious orientation is unclear. When he and Saskia Uylenburgh wed in 1634, they were married in the Reformed Church.[8] Their children, in turn, were baptized in the faith, and, as late as 1669, Rembrandt stood as godfather at the baptism of his granddaughter, Titia. In order to serve in this capacity, he would have been required to be one who "professed the pure teaching," that is, the doctrines of the Reformed Church. Despite this, the late seventeenth-century Italian historian and biographer Filippo Baldinucci claimed that Rembrandt was a Mennonite, an allegation based on information from a former Rembrandt pupil.[9] Although some of Rembrandt's earliest patrons were Mennonites, and some of his wife's relatives adhered to that religion, there is no independent evidence that he ever espoused this faith.[10] In fact, Rembrandt's clients were drawn from a broad confessional spectrum, which included Mennonite and conservative Reformed preachers and theologians, and at least one Jewish rabbi.[11] Ultimately, it seems likely that, as W.A. Visser 't Hooft concludes, Rembrandt was a Protestant, but one who remained independent of any particular confessional orientation or system.[12]

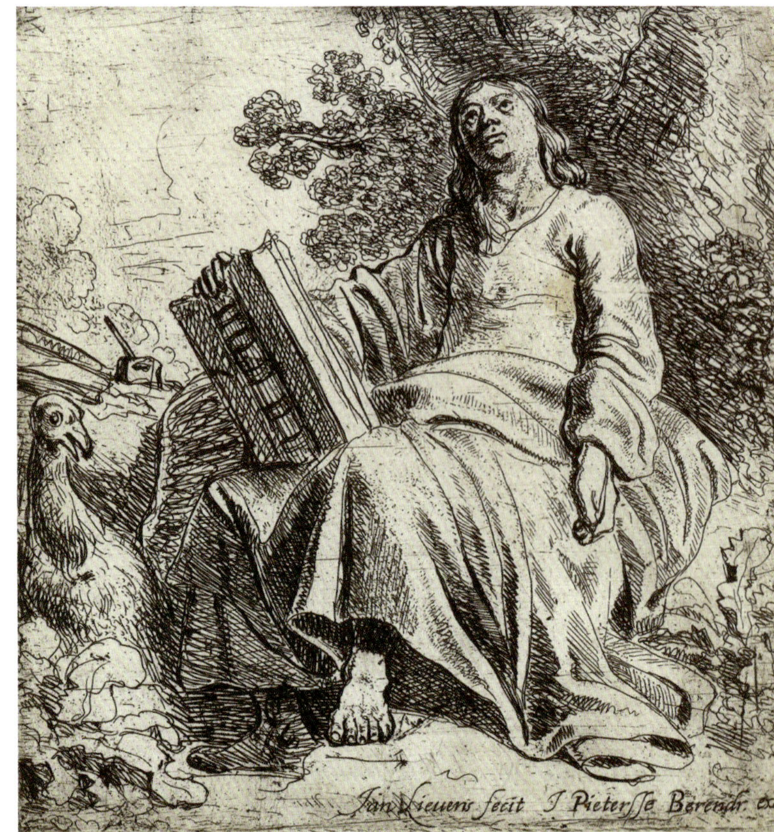

FIGURE 1. Jan Lievens, *St. John on Patmos*, etching, 1625–26. *Rijksmuseum, Amsterdam.*

According to a brief biography of the artist, written in 1641 by bookseller and historian Jan Jansz Orlers,[13] when Rembrandt was a boy, he attended the Latin School in Leiden. The school's curriculum was designed to prepare students for the university and a career in law, theology, or medicine. Consequently, Latin language and literature were the most important subjects, though students were also taught some Greek, mathematics, logic, and theology.[14] How much of this curriculum Rembrandt actually absorbed is unknown.[15] Still, the image of Rembrandt as an unschooled and rustic artist only capable of reading "Netherlandish"—a view promoted by seventeenth-century artist and biographer Joachim von Sandrart[16]—is certainly inaccurate. As many scholars have observed, this biographer's view was probably motivated by an aversion to what Sandrart, an academic artist, saw as Rembrandt's anticlassical and unrestrained style and plebian origins.

The fact that Rembrandt attended Latin School indicates that his parents must have hoped that he would go on to university and pursue a professional career.[17] In fact, on May 20, 1620, he was listed as having registered for the university.[18] However, there is no evidence that he ever actually enrolled.[19] Instead, in about 1621, Rembrandt began a three-year apprenticeship with Jacob Isaacz. van Swanenburgh (1571–1638), one of Leiden's foremost history painters.[20] Although van Swanenburgh would certainly have taught Rembrandt the rudiments of painting, the master's somewhat old-fashioned style did not have much of an impact on his pupil. After completing his apprenticeship with van Swanenburgh, Rembrandt moved briefly to Amsterdam, where he spent six months in the shop of Pieter Lastman (1583–1633).[21] Lastman, a Catholic who was also a successful history painter, had a much larger influence on the young Rembrandt's artwork. Echoes of this master's clear, planar compositions, enamel colors, theatrical narrative strategies, and delight in anecdotal detail appear in Rembrandt's early history paintings.

By 1625, however, Rembrandt was back in Leiden, ready to begin his career as a master in his own right. It has been suggested that when he returned to Leiden, Rembrandt shared studio space with another precocious young painter, Jan Lievens (1607–74).[22] Whether or not the two ever actually shared studio space, it is quite clear that in the late 1620s and very early 1630s there was something of a rivalry between these ambitious young artists.[23]

Very shortly after his return to Leiden, Rembrandt began his career as a printmaker. The reason for his foray into what was for him a new medium is not known. Art historian Thomas Rassieur suggested that the Haarlem-based printer and publisher Jan Pietersz. Berendrecht, whose name appears on one of Rembrandt's

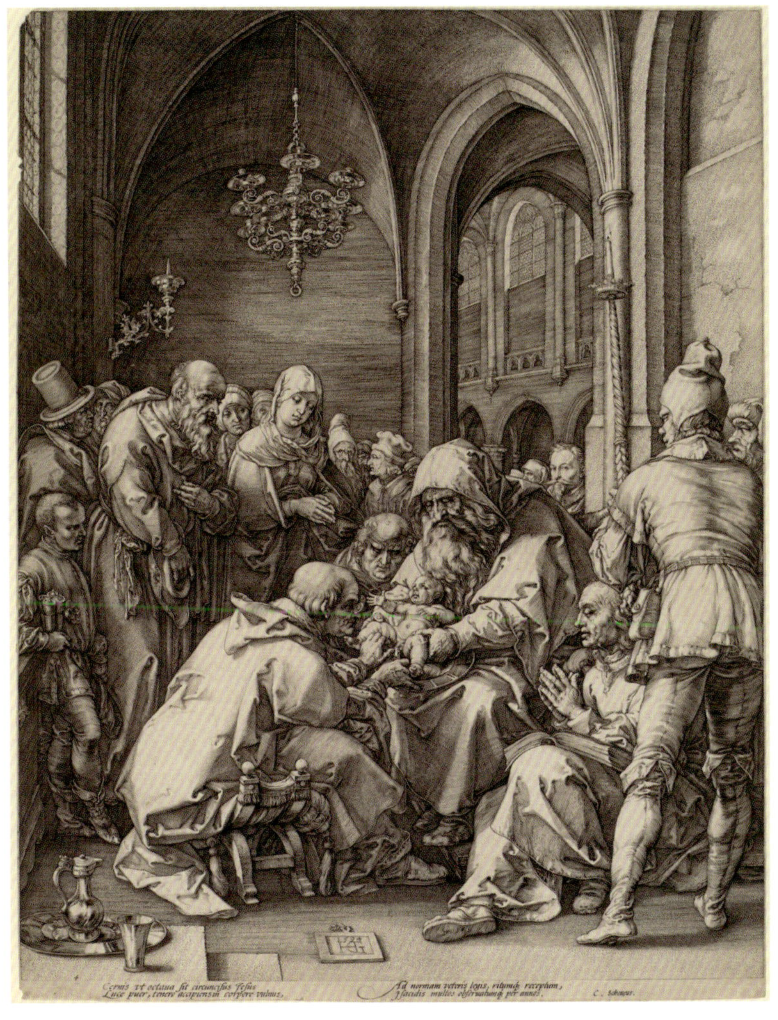

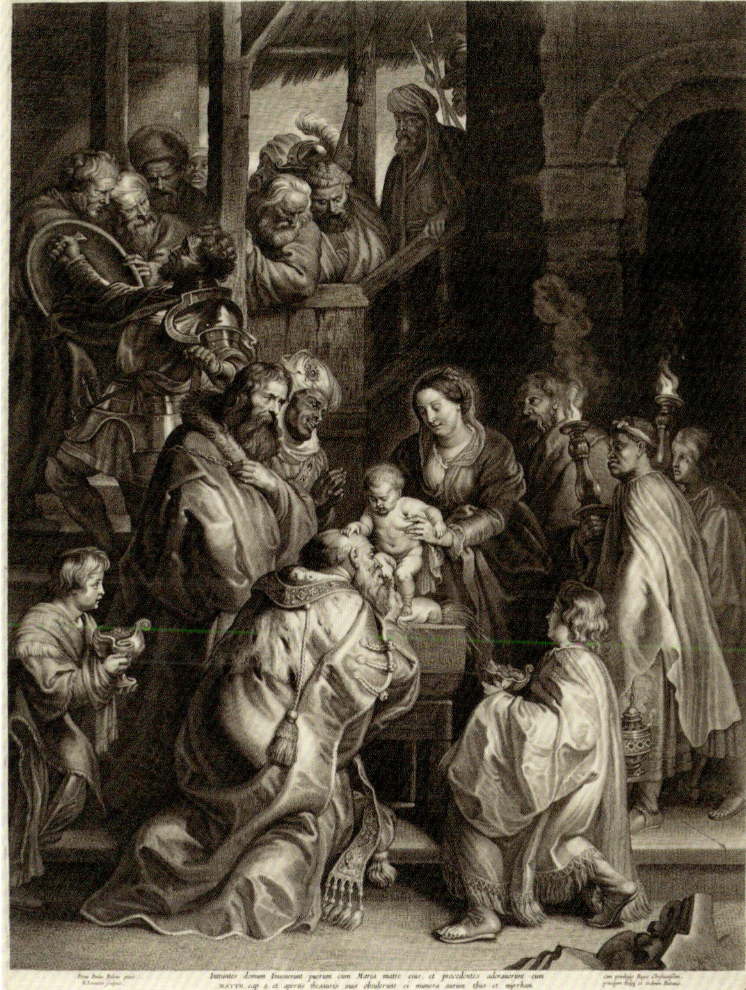

FIGURE 2. Hendrick Goltzius, *The Circumcision*, engraving, 1594. *Photo: Courtesy of the National Gallery of Art, Washington, DC.*

FIGURE 3. Nicolaas Lauwers after Rubens, *The Adoration of the Magi*, engraving, c. 1620. *Photo: Courtesy of the National Gallery of Art, Washington, DC.*

very first prints, *Circumcision* (S. 398, c. 1626, cat. no. 22), might have been instrumental in this choice.[24] Rassieur proposed that the artist might have learned the art of etching during a brief residency in Berendrecht's shop in Haarlem. In this regard, it is worth noting that Jan Lievens seems to have made his first etchings at about the same time and that one of his earliest prints, *St. John on Patmos* (fig. 1),[25] also bears Berendrecht's name as the publisher. Whether this means that Rembrandt and Lievens spent time together or separately in the Haarlem printer's shop learning the printmaking process, or whether Berendrecht introduced them both to the medium during a trip either to or through Leiden en route to The Hague, or whether both young artists were actually motivated by something or someone else, remains an open question.[26] Whatever the case, it is clear that Rembrandt's engagement with the medium began to intensify in 1629, a circumstance that has led Roelof van Straten to conclude that the artist must have purchased his first printing press in that year.[27]

Although the etching of the *Circumcision* from about 1626 lacks the sophisticated handling of light and modeling techniques that would characterize the artist's later prints, it is remarkably finished and technically adept for an early effort. The degree of skill evinced by the etching suggests that Rembrandt may have produced the work with the technical assistance or supervision of a much more experienced printmaker, possibly within Berendrecht's shop. In terms of its sources and details, the etching seems to anticipate the approach to composition and narrative which would characterize the artist's religious prints throughout his career, and for this reason, it can serve as an instructive starting point for an analysis of Rembrandt's etchings. In creating the *Circumcision*, Rembrandt appears to have drawn on a number of visual sources, including an original engraving of the same subject (1594) (fig. 2) by Hendrick Goltzius (one of Goltzius's so-called Meisterstiche, or masterpieces), and a reproductive engraving done around 1620 by Nicolaas Lauwers after Peter Paul Rubens's *Adoration of the Magi* in Brussels (fig. 3).[28]

Although Rembrandt often borrowed motifs, poses, and details of architecture and costume from his sources, he tended to reinterpret them in his own fashion.[29] In a discussion of the difficulty of tracing Rembrandt's sources, art historian Svetlana Alpers suggested that the artist did not follow the classically inspired Renaissance tradition of emulation and quotation pursued by masters such as Rubens. Artists working in the earlier tradition overtly cited works of art drawn from the existing canon as a means of defining their place within the established history of painting and of exploiting the expressive content of their sources. In contrast, according to Alpers, Rembrandt sought to disguise his sources,[30] pursuing the kind of technique that the painter, etcher, and writer Philips Angel (ca. 1618–64) described in a 1642 oration based on the theoretical writings of the early seventeenth-century artist, art theorist, and biographer Karel van Mander (1548–1606):

> Someone . . . might ask whether it is not justified to borrow from other masters? I grant that this is permissible, yes, for otherwise it would be in direct contravention of the teaching of K[arel] van Mander in his *Grondt der edel vrij schilderkonst*, ch. i, verse 46, where it is permitted, with arguments. . . . The aforementioned spirit [van Mander] said, "Well-boiled turnips make good soup." By this he meant that someone who wishes to borrow something should do so in such a subtle way that he incorporates it in his own work so sweetly and fluently that it escapes notice.[31]

Alpers also noted that Rembrandt often borrowed from somewhat "obscure" sources, that is, from works outside the canon, a strategy motivated by a desire to avoid inherited stereotypes and to encourage the viewer to regard individual figures as expressive actors in a uniquely staged drama.[32] Although this may hold true for some of his works,[33] it is apparent that Rembrandt also drew on more significant and presumably well-known examples, probably with the expectation that connoisseurs and collectors would regard his etchings favorably when they were viewed alongside his sources. Indeed, it is difficult to imagine that a connoisseur would not have compared Rembrandt's 1626 *Circumcision* with the quite famous example by Goltzius. Other prints also evoked celebrated models: *Triumph of Mordecai* (B. 40, c. 1641, cat. nos. 14 and 15) and *Christ Presented to the People: Oblong Plate* (B. 76, 1655, cat. no. 51) with prints of the same subjects by Lucas van Leyden; the *Descent from the Cross: The Second Plate* (B. 81 II, 1633, cat. no. 55) with Lucas Vorsterman's reproductive engraving after Rubens's *Descent from the Cross*; *Virgin and Child in the Clouds* (B. 61, 1641, cat. no 34) with one or more of the variations on Federico Barocci's *Virgin and Child in the Clouds*; and *Death of the Virgin* (B. 99, 1639, cat. no. 69) with examples by Martin Schongauer and Albrecht Dürer.[34] The perceptive viewer who compared Rembrandt's etchings with these earlier examples might ultimately discern the compositional and thematic connections, but he would also become aware of the ways in which Rembrandt had recast each subject as his own.

In addition, in at least one instance, Rembrandt may well have counted on a viewer's recognition of his source as a means of deepening the symbolic import of an etching. In his *Christ at Emmaus: Larger Plate* (B. 87, 1654, cat. no. 60), echoes of the poses of Christ and the apostles in an engraved copy of Leonardo's *Last Supper* would have suggested a theological parallel between the two biblical events, reinforcing the Eucharistic implications of the miracle at Emmaus.

Rembrandt also drew on other artists' works for some of the exotic costumes and armaments with which he embellished his prints and paintings. For example, two of the costumes in his etching of the 1626 *Circumcision*, those of the mohel[35] and the seated observer on the right, were probably inspired by specific sources: the ermine collar of the seated elder recalls the one worn by the kneeling magus in Rubens's *Adoration of the Magi* in Brussels, while the priestly miter and cope of the mohel may have been drawn from Adriaen Collaert's engraving of the Circumcision after a design by Johannes Stradanus published in Antwerp in 1585–95 (fig. 4).[36]

Rembrandt's fascination with fanciful clothing and accoutrements went beyond these types of visual sources, however. He amassed an extensive, eclectic array of wardrobe items and accessories of his own. The 1656 inventory of his possessions lists an impressive collection of weapons and armor that could be used as props for both his paintings and his prints: Japanese and Croatian helmets; a Turkish powder horn; sixty pieces of Indian hand weapons, arrows, shafts, javelins, and bows; five antique helmets and shields; twenty pieces including halberds, swords, and Indian fans; five cuirasses; and more.[37] A number of these items made appearances in Rembrandt's etchings: the saber and arrow-filled quiver hanging on the tomb wall in *Raising of Lazarus: Larger Plate* (B. 73, c. 1632, cat. no. 46); the weapons, helmets, and armor of the soldiers in *Christ before Pilate: Large Plate* (B. 77, 1636, cat. no. 50); the pot helmet worn by one of St. Stephen's tormentors in *Stoning of St. Stephen* (B. 97, 1635, cat. no. 67); and the lance carried by the mounted soldier in *Baptism of the Eunuch* (B. 98, 1641, cat. no. 68). In addition to this wide-ranging collection, Rembrandt owned a "book filled with curious drawings in miniature, as well as woodcuts and engravings on copper of various [folk] costumes."[38] The "curious drawings" were probably Mughal or Persian miniatures, one of which served as a compositional source for Rembrandt's late print of *Abraham Entertaining the Angels* (B. 29, 1656, cat. no. 3). Some of the other woodcuts and engravings in this album were probably taken from the numerous and enormously popular costume books that began to appear in Europe in the second half of the sixteenth century.[39] In addition, on the streets of Amsterdam, one of the largest, most prosperous, and cosmopolitan cities in all of Europe, Rembrandt would have been able to observe a wide range of national costumes and ethnic types.

The artist's awareness and utilization of these rich resources is evident in the way he incorporated Moorish figures in his paintings and prints[40] and also appropriated the costumes of Ashkenazi and Sephardic Jews.[41] Like many of his contemporaries, Rembrandt took a particular interest in Turkish, or "Oriental," dress, not only

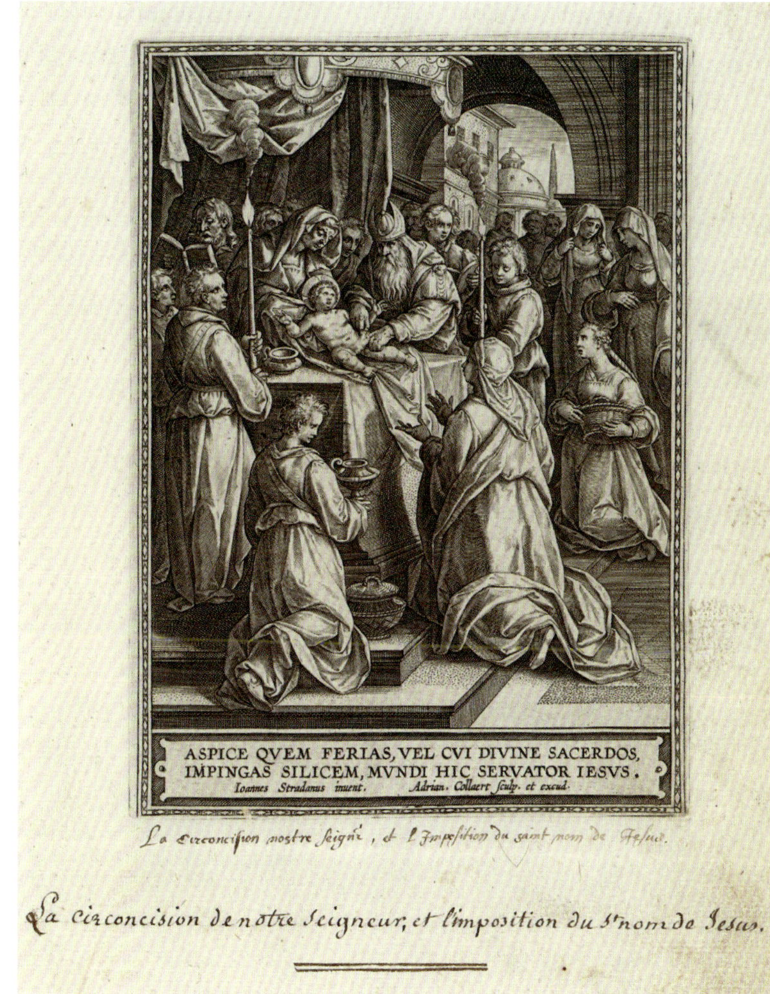

FIGURE 4. Adriaen Collaert after Johannes Stradanus, *The Circumcision*, engraving, c. 1589. *Yale University Art Gallery, New Haven, Connecticut, Everett V. Meeks, B.A. 1901 Fund.*

because it was exotic, but also because it was thought to represent the clothing that would have been worn in the Holy Land in biblical times.[42] Biblical patriarchs dressed in turbans and caftans lent an aura of authenticity to Old and New Testament scenes. Rembrandt did not limit himself to reproducing authentic costumes, however; he was just as likely to clothe figures in creations of his own devising,[43] for in addition to authenticity, he and his contemporaries valued originality and variety. These were qualities that were prized in history painting, and they were characteristics for which Rembrandt was highly praised.[44]

The architectural backgrounds of Rembrandt's etchings also reflect the artist's use of earlier sources, leavened by his own inventions. Rubens's *Adoration of the Magi*, for example, appears to have inspired the architectural background of Rembrandt's early print of the Circumcision. Both works include an ascending staircase parallel to the picture plane; figures who observe the main action from this staircase; and a darkened, barrel-vaulted corridor on the left. The juxtaposition of a shallow space with what was called a *doorsein* or *perspect*—that is, a "look through" or vista—was recommended by contemporary art theorists such as Karel van Mander and Samuel van Hoogstraten (1627–78), and was employed as a common compositional strategy by Dutch artists, including Rembrandt, throughout the seventeenth century.[45] The pairing of the staircase and barrel-vaulted corridor in Rembrandt's 1626 *Circumcision* represents a very rudimentary example of this compositional type.

In his later prints and paintings,[46] he employed this approach in a much more sophisticated manner and to much greater effect. For example, Rembrandt staged the main action of the etching *Presentation in the Temple with the Angel: Small Plate* (B. 51, 1630, cat. no. 25) in a patch of sunlight in the Temple. He then expanded this foreground space with two contrasting perspects: a brilliantly lit series of towering, domed spaces with a second-story gallery on the left, and a deeply shadowed view of a broad flight of stairs on the right, where three small figures kneel before an enthroned priest and standing elders pose on a landing above them. The massive curtains that hang from the ceiling over this landing have been parted so that a triangle of white light casts the assembled priests into silhouette, a detail that harmonizes with the moment of revelation taking place below. The diminutive size of the figures in both enframed vistas suggests the enormous scale of these secondary spaces, a technique that contributes to the overall sense of the majesty of the temple and the significance of the event taking place within it.

In another example, *Presentation in the Temple: Oblong Print* (B. 49, c. 1639, cat. no. 26), the encounter between the Holy Family and Simeon is set in a vaulted chamber illuminated by both divine and natural light. Once again, the background is split in two, with each side defined by a large stone archway. The right side is shrouded in darkness, which makes it unclear whether the arch enframes a blank wall, a niche, or an unlit corridor. In contrast, the arch on the left offers a view into a series of large, sunlit chambers where an assembly of Jewish elders has congregated. Here, as in *Presentation with an Angel*, the effect of the perspect is one of visual contrast and scale.

In the etching *Christ Driving the Money Changers from the Temple* (B. 69, 1635, cat. no. 43), Rembrandt expanded the main action by adding two secondary scenes behind Christ's violent expulsion of the sinners from the Temple. In the right background, a woman kneels before an assembly of lavishly dressed priests and Temple elders who are seated or standing under a billowing baldachin. This secondary scene depicts a session of the Sanhedrin, the council of twenty-three men that met daily to deal with religious matters and that would ultimately sanction the arrest and crucifixion of Jesus. On the left side, an archway opens into a second deep space, this one composed of a series of tall, brightly illuminated, vaulted chambers reminiscent of the nave of a Romanesque church. In this ecclesiastical space, two lightly sketched Jews converse with one another, while a third turns to walk back farther into the distance. Here, as in the two *Presentation* etchings from the 1630s, the effect is to reinforce the size and majesty of the Temple.

The view into a deep valley on the right side of *Abraham's Sacrifice* (B. 35, 1655, cat. no. 7) serves a somewhat different function. Abraham, Isaac, and the angel, the large, central figures, are at the front of the image. At the right, just over the edge of the mountainside, are the donkey and servant who were left behind when father and son made their final ascent on Mount Moriah. Finally, two tiny figures can be seen walking in the valley far below. The diminutive size of these men reveals the distance that Abraham and Isaac have traveled and the height of the mountain that they have climbed, while the servant and donkey, which look back down the mountain, remind the viewer of the origins of the journey and also emphasize the isolation of the patriarch and his son during their test of faith.

The vista behind the main figures in *Peter and John Healing the Cripple at the Gate of the Temple* (B. 94, 1659, cat. no. 66) provides a panoramic view into the Priests' Court of the Temple[47] and delineates numerous details of the biblical site. The Temple is surrounded by a vast double cloister that includes the "Solomonic" sanctuary porch; the two "brazen columns" that were erected at the entry to the porch;[48] an elevated holocaust altar; and an enormous circular building, possibly part of the citadel of Antonia.[49] In this case, the background not only identifies the site of the miracle taking place, but also expands the narrative by anticipating the next part of the biblical story, that is, Peter's preaching to the masses who will be drawn to Solomon's porch when word reaches them of the cripple's miraculous cure.[50] The conjoined spaces and vistas in the background of Rembrandt's prints also serve another purpose, one that is particularly apposite for the intimacy of the print medium: they invite the viewer to explore the invented spaces and to enjoy and contemplate the meaning of what is to be discovered there.[51]

The introduction of secondary observers into the backgrounds and margins of Rembrandt's religious prints—such as the two men standing on the staircase, watching the act of circumcision in the 1626 print—is another compositional device that the artist used repeatedly throughout his career, one that, like the landscapes, architecture, and vistas, encourages the viewer to contemplate the image's central theme while closely examining secondary details. These figures provide variety, expand the narrative, serve as emotional or dramatic foils, or act as surrogates—either sympathetic or skeptical—for the viewer. In *Abraham Entertaining the Angels* (B. 29, cat. no. 3), for example, the depiction of Sarah standing in the shadows brings to mind the biblical account of her disbelief when the three visitors prophesy that she will bear a son in her dotage, while the image of the young Ishmael drawing his bow as he turns away from God and his messengers not only identifies him as a hunter, but also presages the child's future banishment into the wilderness and his fate and that of his descendants as exiles from the covenant. The figures of Esther and Ahasuerus, seated in the balcony in *Triumph of Mordecai* (B. 40, cat. no. 14), recall the circumstances that preceded Mordecai's condemnation, exoneration, and triumph, and Haman's disgrace and punishment. In *Adoration of the Shepherds: With the Lamp* (B. 45, 1654, cat. no. 20), the worshipful family of peasants leaning over the edge of the stall while gazing down at Mary and the infant Jesus presents a paradigm of piety for the viewer and, within the context of the print, an earthly mirror for the Holy Family itself.

In a number of the biblical prints, peripheral Jewish figures provide a skeptical chorus and exemplify the intransigence of those who resisted Jesus's message. These men include the dubious elders who gaze down at the miracle of a child confounding the scholars in the Temple in *Christ Seated Disputing with the Doctors* (B. 64, 1654, cat. no. 39) and *Christ Disputing with the Doctors: A Sketch* (B. 65, 1652, cat. no. 38); the Jew who looks on with disdain while another speaks into his ear as Peter and John confront the lame beggar at the temple gate in *Peter and John Healing the Cripple at the Gate of the Temple* (B. 94, cat. no. 66);[52] and the elderly Jews standing and seated at the edges of *Presentation in the Temple: Oblong Print* (B. 49, cat. no. 26) and *The Tribute Money* (B. 68, c. 1635, cat. no. 42), who observe and discuss what is transpiring before them.

The manner in which the auxiliary characters in Rembrandt's tableaux contribute to and expand upon the central narrative of his works varies. The apostles coming up the hill from Sychar in both versions of *Christ and the Woman of Samaria* (B. 70 and B. 71, 1658 and 1634, cat. nos. 45 and 44) extend the story beyond the immediate encounter between Christ and the Samarian woman by anticipating the disciples' puzzled reaction to Christ's generosity of spirit. In *Abraham Casting Out Hagar and Ishmael* (B. 30, 1637, cat. no 4), the inclusion of the maliciously grinning Sarah leaning out of the window and the young Isaac peering out from the safety of Abraham's house, not only reminds one of the reason why the patriarch banished his concubine and her son, but also contrasts Sarah's look of jealous self-satisfaction with Abraham's reluctance and Hagar's and Ishmael's sorrow. The mournful pose of Jacob's wife leaning over her distraught husband in *Joseph's Coat Brought to Jacob* (B. 38, c. 1633, cat. no. 12), both expands the emotional scope of the moment and makes Jacob's overt grief even more poignant. In *Angel Departing from the Family of Tobias* (B. 43, 1641, cat. no. 18), the maidservants looking out of the window and standing in the shadows of the doorway of Tobias's home represent unenlightened curiosity and serve as foils to the reactions of those who have experienced and understood the epiphanic revelation taking place before them. In *Hundred Guilder Print* (B. 74, c. 1648, cat. no. 48), it is the mass of characters—the well-dressed Pharisee with his knob-headed walking stick, the contemplative young man seated beside a clutch of chattering elders, the excited child dragging his mother toward Jesus, the multitude of the lame and the sick, the exotic Moor, and the turbaned rider leaning over the back of a camel, all gathered around the glowing image of Christ reaching out to a mother and child—who flesh out the scene, creating a provocative, multiple-layered narrative epitomizing the universal nature of those who are touched by Christ as a teacher and a healer of body and soul. Finally, the small detail of Pilate's wife looking out a window in the background of *Christ Presented to the People: Oblong Plate* (B. 76, cat. no. 51) recalls her troubled dreams and admonition to her husband to have nothing to do with "this just man." The evocation of these prophetic words highlights the ominous, unjust, but foreordained nature of the suffering that "this just man" has been condemned to endure.

Animals also serve as auxiliary "characters" in Rembrandt's religious narratives. From the cows and sheep that join the shepherds in panicked flight at the explosive appearance of the annunciate angel in *Angel Appearing to the Shepherds* (B. 44, 1634, cat. no. 19) to the trumpeting elephant in the background of the etching of *Adam and Eve* (B. 28, 1638, cat. no. 2), their presence is sometimes traditional and sometimes extraordinary.[53] They may serve symbolic or narrative functions, add humor, or simply contribute a sense of variety. When Rembrandt depicted the chaos wrought by Christ's impassioned assault on the money changers and merchants in the Temple (B. 69, cat. no. 43), for example, he gave the scene comic relief by adding flapping fowl, wide-eyed bolting cows, and yapping dogs caught up in the excitement. In *Virgin and Child with the Cat and the Snake* (B. 63, 1654, cat. no. 36), the cat that gazes at the serpent caught under Mary's foot may be a sign of domesticity, but it may also have a theological significance relating to the defeat of Satan. In this latter capacity, the watchful feline would serve as what Susan Donahue Kuretsky has called a *parergon*, that is, a "secondary motif added to enrich a main theme . . . employed by Renaissance artists as a means of promoting contemplation and mediating the viewer's access to sacred figures and stories."[54]

Dogs are fairly common in Rembrandt's etchings. In fact, they appear in fifteen of his religious prints. These canine companions serve as both mundane embellishments and *parerga*. Some of them act indecorously: the scratching dog that ignores Simeon's miraculous recognition of the Messiah in the *Presentation in the Temple with the Angel: Small Plate* (B. 49, cat. no. 26), the pup that licks its genitals in *Joseph Telling His Dreams* (B. 37, 1638, cat. no. 11), and the infamous hound that defecates in the foreground of *The Good Samaritan* (B. 90, 1633, cat. no. 62). Some of these animals snarl, dash about, and even endanger their masters in their excitement: the barking dogs in the crowd in *Triumph of Mordecai* (B. 40, cat. no. 14), a pup that prances down the steps in *Abraham Casting Out Hagar and Ishmael* (B. 30, cat. no. 4), the dog that scampers around the feet of the Holy Family as they return from the Temple (B. 60, 1654, cat. no. 40), another one that races alongside the departing disciples in the early states of *Christ Crucified between the Two Thieves: "The Three Crosses"* (B. 78, c. 1653–55, cat. no. 54), and the shaggy pet that almost trips his blind master as the elderly man shuffles toward the door in *Blindness of Tobit: Larger Plate* (B. 42, 1651, cat. no. 17). Other dogs simply sit or stand about, sometimes watching the central action, but often ignoring it. In *Angel Departing from the Family of Tobias* (B. 43, cat. no. 18), the small terrier turns its back on the miracle of Raphael's departure; in *Hundred Guilder Print* (B. 74, cat. no. 48), a slender dog sitting on the ground pays no attention to Christ's sermon; in *Christ at Emmaus: Small Plate* (B. 88, 1634, cat. no. 59), the mangy mutt seems far more interested in a possible scrap from the table than in the epiphany being played out around it; and in *Baptism of the Eunuch* (B. 98, cat. no. 68), a mournful, long-eared hound peeks out from behind the Moorish servant and gazes off into the distance, with no concern for the sacred ritual being performed nearby.[55]

The number of domestic and exotic animals that appear in Rembrandt's works is remarkable.[56] Whether or not they were meant to bear some symbolic significance, it is clear that one of the functions of cats, dogs, chickens, and cows was to forge connections between the ancient biblical events portrayed and viewers' everyday experiences.

After Rembrandt began to make etchings, his skill as a printmaker improved rather rapidly, and by 1630, he was producing religious images in which there was a much greater subtlety in the use of line and hatching to define figures and depict the distribution of light and shadow in space. This can be seen in the three small-scale prints from 1630 that portray events from Christ's childhood: *Circumcision: Small Plate* (B. 48, cat. no. 23); *Presentation in the Temple with the Angel: Small Plate* (B. 51, cat. no. 25); and *Christ Disputing with the Doctors: Small Plate* (B. 66, cat no. 37). These prints and the religious images that followed were clearly intended to appeal to an audience that included both art connoisseurs,[57] who could appreciate them as collector's items, and the devout, who might value them as meditational aids and biblical illustrations. Rembrandt was familiar with the interests of both of these audiences.[58]

Although the fact that Rembrandt frequently reworked his plates is certainly evidence of a desire to perfect his images through a process of continuous refinement and/or repair,[59] the reworking also resulted in the production of a number of different states, which could then be collected individually by connoisseurs bent on acquiring the complete printed oeuvre of the artist. Arnold Houbraken suggested rather cynically that the small alterations that Rembrandt introduced from state to state were, in fact, a marketing strategy:

> Doing this [printing a plate as the image progressed from sketch to finished creation, thereby creating a series of different states] brought him great fame and no small profit, as did the trick of making minor alterations, or adding small and unimportant details to his prints, by means of which they could be resold as new designs. The rage for his works was then so great that anyone who did not own both the little *Juno* [B. 112] with and without her crown, or the little *Joseph* [*Telling His Dreams*, B. 37, cat. no. 11] with and without the dark throne, and other besides, was not considered a true lover of art.[60]

The number of changes that Rembrandt introduced from state to state varied widely. Some were very minor alterations, typically the addition of areas of hatching, often in drypoint, in order to increase the density of shadow. Other modifications were more significant, ranging from actually cutting down the plate[61] to burnishing out or replacing entire figures[62] to even more dramatic and substantive changes.[63]

Rembrandt also varied individual impressions by experimenting with different methods of applying ink to his plates and by printing on different types of paper. As Thomas Rassieur observed,[64] during the 1630s and early 1640s, Rembrandt and his assistants followed the accepted practice of wiping his plates as thoroughly as possible before printing so that virtually no excess ink remained on the unbitten surface of the plate. The goal was to create a uniform edition of consistent, clear images. However, beginning in the mid-1640s, Rembrandt's strategy changed. He began to leave a film of ink on the plate, creating a surface or plate tone that essentially transformed some impressions into virtual monoprints. Probably one of the most dramatic examples of this practice was *Entombment* (B. 86, cat. no. 58) from around 1654. During this print's evolution through four states, the shadows in the tomb became progressively denser. None of the surviving first-state impressions shows any significant plate tone. By contrast, the second and third states were very frequently printed with a very heavy surface tone, so that in some instances (figs. 5 and 6), it is almost impossible to discern the nature of the architectural surroundings or even most of the figures.[65] Obviously, these individual variations arose in part from Rembrandt's engagement with the printing process, but they also created variations that would have intrigued the connoisseur/collector, if not the audience that bought prints chiefly for didactic or devotional purposes.

In the mid-1640s, Rembrandt started to experiment with various types of support for his prints. According to Rassieur, the Dutch East India Company imported about four thousand sheets of Japanese paper into Amsterdam between 1644 and 1645.[66] Starting in 1647, Rembrandt began to use this newly available paper. Japanese paper was made from various types of vegetable fibers, including the inner bark of the gampi, mitsumata, and mulberry trees, and it varied in thickness, transparency, and color.[67] How well the paper absorbed ink depended on its source materials and its density. Although it was more expensive than competing European papers, Japanese paper was a support that had unique visual and textural

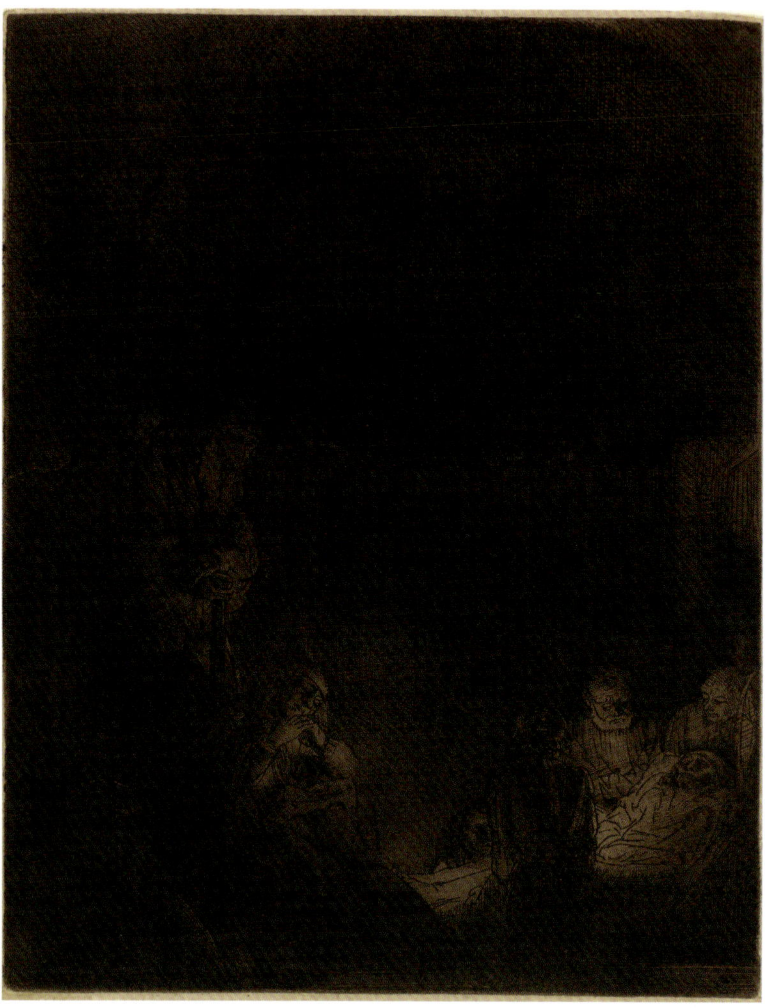

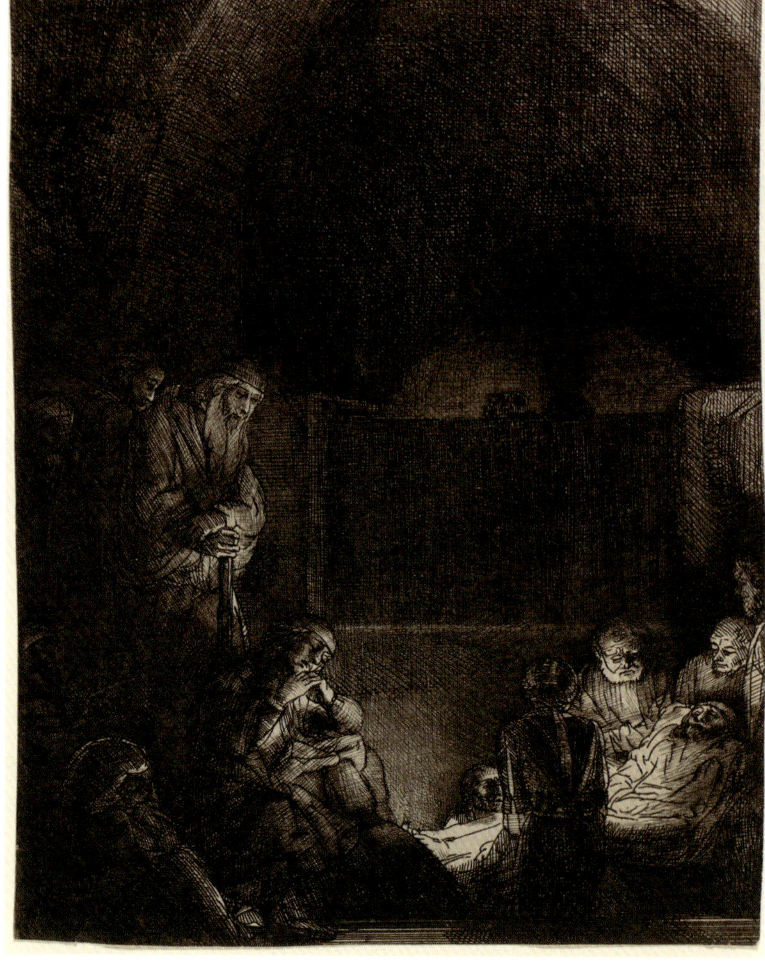

FIGURE 5. Rembrandt, *The Entombment*, State II, etching and drypoint, c. 1654. *Photo: Courtesy of the National Gallery of Art, Washington, DC.*

FIGURE 6. Rembrandt, *The Entombment*, State III, etching and drypoint, c. 1654. *Photo: Courtesy of the National Gallery of Art, Washington, DC.*

qualities that Rembrandt must have appreciated, since after 1647, he used it to print at least some impressions of each new plate.[68] In addition, there can be little doubt that the artist knew that etchings printed on this exotic paper could be marketed as unique objects whose rarity would have a special appeal for connoisseurs. These same considerations must have been behind the artist's decision to begin producing some impressions on vellum. Vellum, a fine and expensive form of parchment made from the skins of young calves, had been used for manuscripts since antiquity. Because of its association with the production of singular, precious objects, it was also used to produce luxury editions of printed books as early as the fifteenth century.[69] However, since vellum does not absorb ink, it is not normally employed as a support for etchings or engravings. Because there is a tendency for the ink to spread or smudge during the printing process, it is virtually impossible to produce clear and consistent images. For an artist who was interested in making each impression unique, however, as Rembrandt seems to have been, this would not have been a serious problem. He began printing small editions of new works on vellum at about the same time he started to utilize Japanese paper.[70]

Several of Rembrandt's prints, works that were clearly intended for display, stand out as exemplars of his technical brilliance. These include the *Hundred Guilder Print* (B. 74, cat. no. 48), a complex image that carried the coloristic potential of black ink and white paper to unparalleled heights; and *Christ Presented to the People: Oblong Plate* (B. 76, cat. no. 51) and *Christ Crucified between the Two Thieves: "The Three Crosses"* (B. 78, cat. no. 54), two prints done entirely in drypoint on an unprecedented scale. Connoisseurs would have valued such works as virtuoso demonstrations of the artist's abilities in the print medium.

Between 1631 and 1636, Rembrandt collaborated with Leiden printmaker Jan Georg van Vliet.[71] Van Vliet made a number of modest and often rather dry and pedestrian engravings after biblical paintings and *tronies* designed by Rembrandt.[72] More significant than van Vliet's derivative work, however, was the role he played in the production of two of Rembrandt's largest prints, *Descent from the Cross: The Second Plate* (B. 81 II, 1633, cat. no. 55) and *Christ before Pilate: Large Plate* (B. 77, 1635–36, cat. no. 50). Rembrandt's etching of *Descent from the Cross: The Second Plate* is based on a painting of the same subject that he had produced for Stadtholder Frederik Hendrik, prince of Orange.[73] It is the only known example of the artist actively sponsoring a reproductive image of one of his paintings. An inscription in the lower margin of the etching states that the print was published "with privileges," that is, with a copyright. In the third state of the etching, an additional inscription identifies the art dealer Hendrik Uylenburgh as the print's publisher. In the case of the even larger *Christ before Pilate*, Rembrandt first produced a full-scale painting of the composition *en brunaille* and then, it appears, turned it over to van Vliet to transfer the image to an etching plate.[74] The composition in the small number of extant impressions of the first state of this print, signed and dated *Rembrandt f. 1635* in the plate, lacks the core grouping of Pilate and the Jews in front of him, which suggests that Rembrandt later reclaimed the plate from van Vliet and completed it, adding those figures.[75] The second completed state is signed and dated the following year, 1636. Like the earlier *Descent*, it makes the claim that it was published with privileges. The scale of these two etchings (*Christ before Pilate* and *Descent*), the collaborative role of van Vliet, the reproductive nature of *Descent*, and the references to "privileges," clearly recall the method by which Peter Paul Rubens disseminated his images by producing a series of carefully supervised reproductive engravings published with privileges. For Rubens, these prints were a means of enhancing his reputation while retaining his claims to authorship. There is no doubt that Rembrandt was familiar with Rubens's practice, and it seems likely that he had a similar outcome in mind. It is quite possible that these projects were an undertaking suggested by Uylenburgh, an entrepreneurial dealer who would certainly have seen the economic potential of such an enterprise. However, it is also worth noting that during the period when *Christ before Pilate* and *Descent* were produced, the artist was working for the prince of Orange and the court at The Hague. Rembrandt may have chosen to produce these extraordinary etchings as a means of advertising his association with the court and of elevating himself to the level of international status and prestige enjoyed by Rubens, the ultimate court painter. Nonetheless, Rembrandt did not continue to create works of this scope. His flirtation with collaboration ended with the production of his etching of *Christ before Pilate*.

As noted above, prints with religious themes were prized not only for their aesthetic qualities, but also as didactic or devotional objects. There was a long tradition of justifying the creation of and exposure to religious images by characterizing them as "bibles of the illiterate" that instructed viewers in sacred history, engaged their emotions, and imprinted biblical stories in their memories.[76] In the sixteenth century, Martin Luther invoked this tradition in the 1529 edition of his polemical pamphlet *Passional Christi und Antichristi*, which was illustrated with woodcuts by Lucas Cranach the Elder. In the preface to this tract, Luther declared that the pictures that he had commissioned were "most suitable for children and the simple-minded, who would better recall sacred history when moved by images and parables."[77] This notion of the instructive, mnemonic, and affective power of images remained an important rationale for the production and collection of religious paintings and prints throughout the sixteenth and seventeenth centuries.

Although Roman Catholics were forbidden to worship in public in the Netherlands, they maintained clandestine house churches that were adorned with altars and altarpieces. Protestants, including

Dutch Calvinists, banned images from their houses of worship, but were not doctrinally opposed to the display of religious images in public, secular settings as moral and political exemplars, and also in private, where images could serve as complements to, and reminders of, the word of God. Old Testament scenes, for example, decorated such public buildings as the Amsterdam Town Hall, where they could evoke commonly drawn parallels between the history of the Jews and the history of the Dutch provinces and serve as models for town officials and ordinary citizens.[78] In terms of personal ownership of religious images, private inventories of Dutch seventeenth-century collections show that although there was a decline in the number of religious paintings in private homes (as a percentage of total holdings) from the first to the second half of the seventeenth century, both Old and New Testament subjects were enthusiastically collected by Protestants and Catholics alike.[79] The depiction of biblical events and personages served several functions. As dramatic narratives, they offered artists an opportunity to portray ancient and exotic figures in scenarios that often involved conflict and intrigue. On a more spiritual level, they made sacred history and its moral and spiritual lessons seem present and real. In addition, Old Testament scenes could be interpreted typologically, that is, as prefigurations of the New Testament, manifestations of the promise and fulfillment of God's plan, and visual demonstrations of the miraculous.

In the sixteenth and seventeenth centuries, religious prints were typically produced in series that focused on the individual lives of such Old Testament figures as Abraham, David, Joseph, Tobit, or Esther, as well as on New Testament themes such as Christ's childhood, the Passion, and the parables. Although some of these prints might be directed toward a specific religious group—Catholic, Dutch Reformed, Remonstrant, Mennonite, or Lutheran—they were more commonly produced with the aim of appealing to an ecumenical and diverse pan-European audience. Biblical series were often printed with brief accompanying texts, sometimes in as many as four different languages,[80] which either identified the biblical passage being illustrated or explicated its allegorical or moral message. These series were commonly brought together in what has been termed "picture bibles," where they could serve as visual accompaniments to the spoken or written word.[81] These bound collections of biblical scenes were enormously popular during this period.[82]

Except for two sets of prints produced in 1654,[83] it appears that Rembrandt's religious etchings were created as individual sheets, not as series. Purchasers of individual prints may have hung them on a wall, stored them loose in a cabinet, or pasted them down into an album or even a Bible. Because collectors tended to group prints by artist and/or subject, Rembrandt's etchings may well have been gathered together with other artists' prints with religious themes. In any case, it is clear that Rembrandt's etchings, like the picture bibles, were intended to appeal to a popular appetite for religious images that could be perused in private for instruction and/or delight. Although Rembrandt's Old and New Testament prints were original in their particulars and execution, they adhered closely enough to biblical texts to fulfill the ostensive didactic and mnemonic purposes traditionally expected of sacred images. The emotional spectrum of his etchings—ranging from the maternal and paternal tenderness of the Virgin and Joseph toward their son to the intense physical and emotional suffering of Christ and the faithful in the Passion, and from the anguish of a father forced to banish his child to the overwhelming amazement of a spiritual epiphany—imbues the artist's works with the kind of affective qualities that would be expected in religious images. Unlike paintings with a religious theme that might be created for a specific site or individual, Rembrandt's etchings—which circulated not only in the Netherlands, but also throughout Europe[84]—had an audience that was as broad as the public that purchased contemporary picture bibles.

Conscious of the confessional diversity of the market, Rembrandt, like many of his contemporaries, generally practiced what has been referred to as "pragmatic ecumenism,"[85] creating images whose implications would have been acceptable to spectators viewing them from different religious perspectives. Sometimes, his diplomacy walked a fine line: the representation of God in *Abraham Entertaining the Angels* (B. 29, cat. no. 3) might have offended a strict follower of the doctrines of the Dutch Reformed Church, given Calvin's injunction against anthropomorphic representations of the deity;[86] and the devotional image of the *Virgin and Child in the Clouds* (B. 61, 1641, cat. no. 34), a work that glorifies Mary in her role as Queen of Heaven, would seem to have been directed more toward a Catholic audience than a Protestant one.[87] In general, however, Rembrandt seems to have steered a carefully neutral course.[88] This delicate balance can be seen in two other Marian images, the large print of *Death of the Virgin* (B. 99, cat. no. 69) and the more intimate etching of *Virgin and Child with the Cat and the Snake* (B. 63, cat. no. 36). The Death of the Virgin was a theme that had particular resonance for Catholic audiences, because Mary's bodily assumption following her death denoted her special status as divine intercessor. For this reason, numerous authors have identified Rembrandt's print as an image specifically intended for a Catholic clientele.[89] Certainly, the intrusion of heaven and a group of angels into the space of the Virgin's bedchamber would seem to support such a conclusion. However, as Marijn Schapelhouman[90] and also Shelley Perlove and Larry Silver[91] observed, Rembrandt eliminated some elements in his composition and incorporated others in a way that would have made the image acceptable to Protestants, as well. In particular, he eliminated references to items specific to Catholic Last Rites, such as the aspergillum and candles, objects that had been prominently displayed in Martin Schongauer's and Dürer's depictions of the Virgin's death.[92] Rembrandt also accentuated the earthly side of Mary, emphasizing her age and corporeality and even including an attending physician.[93] As Perlove and Silver suggested, these elements associated the image with the broader Christian tradition of "the good death," a concept that would have been familiar to Catholics and Protestants alike.[94]

Rembrandt's etching of *Virgin and Child with the Cat and the Snake* is another example of the manner in which the artist finessed the religious implications of a devotional image. Holm Bevers suggested that the etching's medieval iconography and Marian focus indicate that it was specifically directed toward a Catholic audience.[95] However, the etching also exemplifies Calvinist principles. While acknowledging Mary's sanctity, Calvin also emphasized her humility and low estate and contrasted these attributes with the queenly status accorded to her by the Catholic Church. The fact that in Rembrandt's print the Virgin has eschewed what appears to be a canopied throne in the corner of the room and is seated instead with her child upon a low step exemplifies the qualities extolled by Calvin.

Despite Rembrandt's skill at producing work with a broad appeal, the course of his career as a printmaker was not always an easy one. It is difficult to ascertain precisely what impact Rembrandt's personal and financial vicissitudes had on his work, but it does appear that private woes, the practical effects of his economic circumstances, and the conditions under which he worked were influential, particularly as regarded his etchings. He produced the greatest number of etchings (seven of them with religious themes) between 1629 and 1631.[96] As noted above, he probably acquired his own etching press at the beginning of this period or perhaps the year before, and it is likely that his burst of productivity was prompted both by having a press close at hand and by his desire to explore and exploit the etching process, particularly as a form of reproducible drawing. By contrast, there was a sharp decline in Rembrandt's overall production of prints in 1632 and in 1633,[97] a decrease that may have been due to two factors. First, it is likely that this is the period when Rembrandt moved permanently to Amsterdam and that during the move he did not have ready access to his press. Second, he was extraordinarily busy and productive as a painter during this period, for he was beginning to work on a prestigious series of paintings of the Passion for Stadtholder Frederik Hendrik, and was also producing numerous portraits,[98] including his first major group portrait, *The Anatomy Lesson of Dr. Tulp*. It is not unreasonable to assume that at this juncture, Rembrandt decided to focus his energies on developing his successful career as a portraitist and history painter, and devote less time to etching. During this same period, he and van Vliet were also experimenting with collaborative print production.

When Rembrandt married Saskia Uylenburgh in 1634, they initially lived with Saskia's uncle Hendrik Uylenburgh, but by 1636, they were living on their own in a house on the Amstel river,

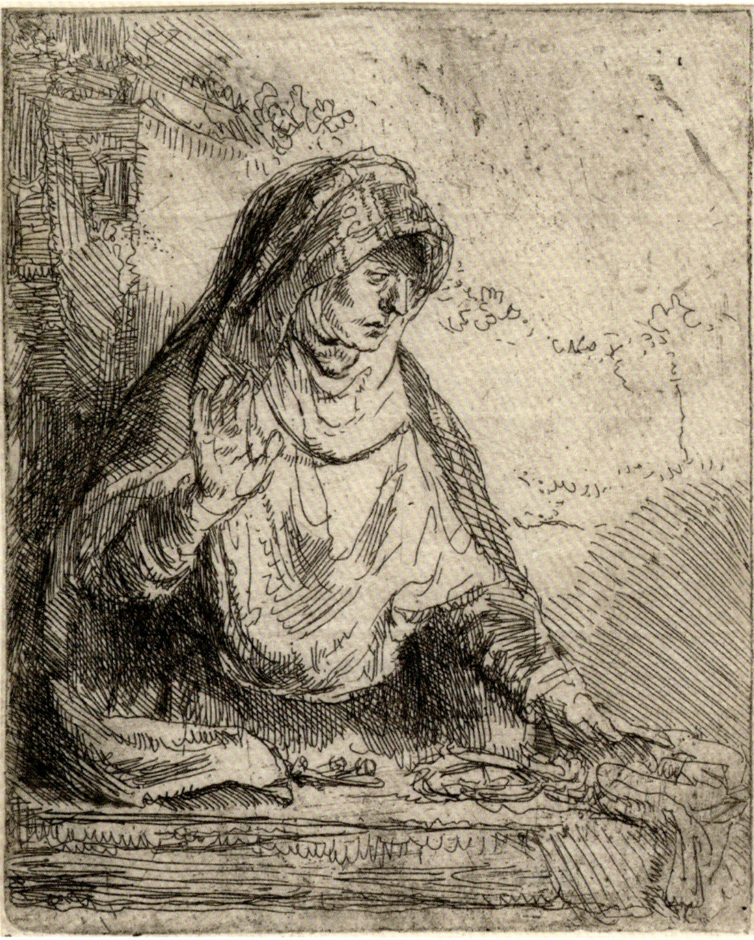

FIGURE 7. Rembrandt, *Virgin with the Instruments of the Passion*, etching and drypoint, c. 1642. *The Pierpont Morgan Library & Museum, New York, New York, RvR 132. Photography by Janny Chiu.*

in Amsterdam. The following year, the couple moved to another rental property on the banks of the river beside what was known as "the Sugar bakery." They lived there until 1639, when Rembrandt purchased a substantial house on Sint Antoniebreestraat.[99] In 1641, most of the artist's paintings were commissioned portraits, including one of the most prestigious of his career, the group portrait popularly known as *The Nightwatch*,[100] portraying the Amsterdam militia company of Frans Banning Cocq. That year, Rembrandt also significantly increased his production of prints, creating eighteen new etchings, one-third of which depicted religious subjects.[101] One of these is the visionary devotional image of the *Virgin and Child in the Clouds* (B. 61, cat. no. 34). In contrast to the images of the Virgin that inspired this print, there is a certain wistful sadness to Rembrandt's Mary.[102] Rembrandt's son, Titus, was born in September 1641. None of Saskia and Rembrandt's first three children had survived beyond its second month, and it is conceivable that this image of the Virgin and Child reveals the couple's anxiety about the survival of their own newborn son.

Titus survived, but on June fourteenth of the following year, 1642, Rembrandt's beloved wife, Saskia, died. The loss of his wife seems to have affected his work. Beyond the completion of *The Nightwatch*, there is only one other painting, a self-portrait, that is universally accepted as having been produced by Rembrandt in that year.[103] By contrast, he created ten new prints in 1642, including four with religious themes. It is not known which of these preceded and which followed Saskia's illness and death, but two of the etchings from that year seem to reflect Rembrandt's darkening state of mind: *The Virgin with the Instruments of the Passion* (B. 85, fig. 7)[104] and *Saint Jerome in a Dark Chamber* (B. 105, fig. 8). The depiction of Mary contemplating the instruments of her son's torment and death was inspired by medieval Catholic images of the Mater Dolorosa, but it is steeped in a more internalized, quietly contemplative melancholy than traditional examples of the genre. The representation of Jerome, dressed in heavy robes and lost in profound contemplation of a text open before him in a room shrouded in Stygian gloom, is unlike any other Rembrandt images of the saint, all of which are set outdoors.[105] The skull carefully placed on a shelf behind Jerome is a traditional attribute of the saint, but the light from the window that dimly illuminates this symbol of death gives it a haunting presence that makes it emblematic.[106] Like *The Virgin with the Instruments of the Passion*, the St. Jerome etching is a meditation on loss and mortality.

In 1642, Rembrandt also made his second etching of the Raising of Lazarus (*Raising of Lazarus: Small Plate*, B. 72, 1642, cat. no. 47). The scene, in which a peaceful-looking Jesus and a group of onlookers gaze at the dead man rising from his grave, may reflect Rembrandt's preoccupation with death, burial, and the afterlife. This print differs in tone from his earlier etching of the subject, which is rendered in a more dramatic and emotionally strident fashion. The following year, 1643, was one of Rembrandt's least productive. There are only a handful of paintings from that year and only two prints,[107] neither of which has a religious subject.

Rembrandt seems to have recovered his enthusiasm for etchings by 1645, producing ten prints, four of them dealing with religious subjects. Two of these, *Rest on the Flight into Egypt: Lightly Etched* (B. 58, 1645, cat. no. 33) and *Abraham and Isaac* (B. 34, 1645, cat. no. 6), seem to signal a new spirit of investigation regarding the technical and expressive possibilities of intaglio print media. Traditionally, printmakers sought (and still seek) to create clear and crisp images in which the black etched or engraved lines stand out clearly against the white of the paper. In *Rest on the Flight into Egypt: Lightly Etched*, Rembrandt departed from this tradition and dramatically reduced the contrast between figure and ground by manipulating the etching process. He exposed the plate to acid for a relatively short period of time, so that the lines that resulted were shallow and consequently held little ink. The outcome was a print with a silvery gray tonality that, as Christopher White observed, has the quality of a metalpoint drawing.[108] In terms of the contents of the etching, White also noted a new sense of relaxed intimacy in the way in which the scene was represented. Particularly striking is the delight that Joseph seems to take in his child.[109] It is easy to imagine that the relationship reflected the warmth that Rembrandt felt for his own young son.

Rembrandt also engaged in a more limited form of technical experimentation in *Abraham and Isaac*, utilizing drypoint as a much more important element in the print's descriptive modeling and relief. Drypoint is potentially less durable than etching, but it offers an even more direct translation of the artist's hand and a different, potentially more velvety, line. Rembrandt's exploration of this medium would reach its peak in the early 1650s with *Christ Presented to the People: Oblong Plate* (B. 76, cat. no. 51) and *Christ Crucified between the Two Thieves: "The Three Crosses"* (B. 78, cat. no. 54), but he had already begun to investigate the technique's potential in *Abraham and Isaac*. The story of Abraham was very popular in the Netherlands during the sixteenth and seventeenth centuries, and scenes from the Old Testament account of the patriarch's life were

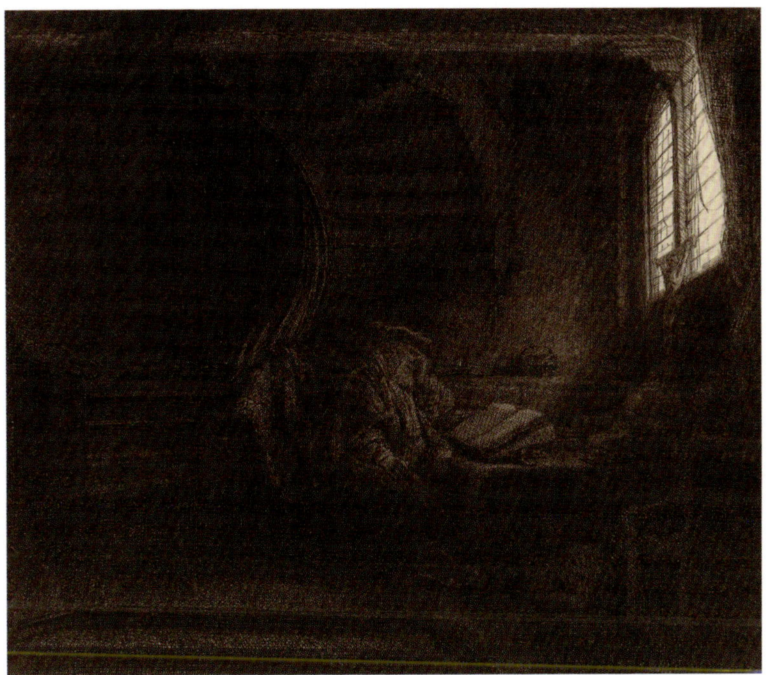

FIGURE 8. Rembrandt, *St. Jerome in a Dark Chamber*, etching and drypoint, 1642. *Photo: Courtesy of the National Gallery of Art, Washington, DC.*

regularly portrayed in both paintings and print series. Rembrandt himself created five prints focusing on Abraham.[110] However, his focus in *Abraham and Isaac* signaled a departure from traditional depictions of the story. Representations of the particular moment that Rembrandt chose to depict in *Abraham and Isaac*—Abraham's response to his son's query about the impending sacrifice (Genesis 22:5–8)—are at best extremely rare,[111] and the unusual nature of the subject matter would certainly have enhanced its appeal for connoisseurs and the devout alike. The print also represents a clear example of Rembrandt's interest in depicting the prelude to or consequence of a momentous event, leaving it to the viewer to conjure up the more climactic moment itself. In this way, Rembrandt's *Abraham and Isaac* signaled a shift in emphasis from narrative action to psychological interaction.[112] The scene also represents a poignant moment of intimacy between an anguished father and his innocent son, one that may mirror the artist's own thoughts on the challenges of parenthood.

The burst of creative energy that began in 1645 reached its climax around 1648 with the *Hundred Guilder Print* (B. 74, cat. no. 48).

This etching, which employs engraving and extensive passages of drypoint in order to achieve its remarkably subtle coloristic effects, also eschews dramatic action. Instead, it focuses on the reactions of a cross section of humanity—young and old, rich and poor, male and female—to Christ's words. Although this subject would have appealed to a broad spectrum of buyers, impressions that were printed on vellum and the newly available Japanese paper were clearly meant to attract wealthy collectors. The very fact that, as the etching's nickname suggests, impressions sold for the remarkable sum of one hundred guilders[113] indicates that this print provided a lucrative source of income for the artist at a time when demand for his paintings appears to have been waning.[114]

There was a dramatic change in Rembrandt's home life in 1649. In that year, Hendrickje Stoffels, a young woman from Bredevort in the province of Gelderland, entered his employ as a housekeeper.[115] Geertje Dircx, a trumpeter's widow who had been employed as Titus's nurse following Saskia's death in 1642, had become the artist's mistress, but with Hendrickje's arrival, the older woman's relationship with Rembrandt changed drastically. Hendrickje replaced her as the artist's mistress, and Geertje did not react well to this change. She moved out of Rembrandt's house and took him to court. Claiming that Rembrandt had promised to marry her and had had sexual relations with her several times, Geertje demanded that he support her by giving her 200 guilders immediately, and then 160 guilders per annum, beginning in 1650. The Chamber of Marital affairs upheld her claims on October 23, 1649.[116] The matter did not end there: probably as a way of avoiding his obligations to his former mistress, Rembrandt undertook to have Geertje declared mentally unstable in July 1650, and was apparently successful in making his case against her and having her committed to an institution.[117] Whether or not these upheavals in his personal life were the reason for the decline in his output, Rembrandt produced no documentable paintings or prints in 1649.

Between 1650 and 1652, Rembrandt purchased several large batches of paper and began printing and reprinting his plates in more significant numbers than he had before.[118] However, this process stopped abruptly in 1653. That year, Rembrandt created only four prints,[119] almost completely ceased reprinting his earlier plates, and produced only one dated painting. Paul Crenshaw, following the lead of S. A. C. Dudok van Heel, suggested that this disruption might have been caused by renovations to Rembrandt's house and that of his neighbor, Daniel Pinto. Shifts in the foundations of both houses required significant structural work, particularly in the area of a common wall. The noise and dust produced by this project may well have disrupted the artist's ability to work in his home, and because of growing financial difficulties, Rembrandt probably found himself unable to afford a separate studio.[120] Payments due on his mortgage, costly repairs to the house on Breestraat, and bad investments in an overseas shipping venture had all begun to erode what few financial resources Rembrandt had.[121] In 1654, in an attempt to recover his economic footing, he took out a series of sizable loans,[122] and sometime between 1653 and 1656, it seems that he sold a significant number of his earlier etching plates, possibly to Amsterdam publisher and print seller Clement de Jonghe.[123] Ultimately, he was forced to declare bankruptcy.[124]

Perhaps because of his economic troubles, Rembrandt returned to printmaking in 1654. In that year, he produced eleven new etchings, ten of which had religious themes, the most he had ever done in a single year. These ten prints can be grouped into two series. One is dedicated to Christ's childhood: *Adoration of the Shepherds: With the Lamp* (B. 45, cat. no. 20), *Circumcision in the Stable* (B. 47, cat. no. 24), *Flight into Egypt: Crossing a Brook* (B. 55, cat. no. 30), *Virgin and Child with the Cat and the Snake* (B. 63, cat. no. 36), *Christ Seated Disputing with the Doctors* (B. 64, cat. no. 39), and *Christ Returning from the Temple with His Parents* (B. 60, cat. no. 40). The other deals with moments from the Passion and its aftermath: *Presentation in the Temple in the Dark Manner* (B. 50), *Descent from the Cross by Torchlight* (B. 83, cat. no. 56), *Entombment* (B. 86, cat. no. 58), and *Christ at Emmaus: Larger Plate* (B. 87, cat. no. 60).[125] As noted above, Rembrandt had not previously produced print series, even though these were very common and popular in both the sixteenth and seventeenth centuries.[126] According to art historian Erik Hinterding, the artist may have adopted this more traditional approach in 1654 for economic reasons, hoping to reach a broader public beyond that of the collectors of the single-leaf art prints that he had typically produced in the past.[127]

The series dedicated to Christ's childhood conveys not only the profound spiritual import of the events portrayed, but also a powerful sense of tenderness and Rembrandt's compassionate view of humanity. Within this series, Joseph's role as the earthly father and nurturer of his son, already visible in *Rest on the Flight into Egypt: Lightly Etched* from 1645, seems to occupy an even more prominent place. In the *Adoration of the Shepherds: With the Lamp*, for example, Mary lifts her cloak to display the peacefully sleeping Christ child nestled in her lap to a group of reverently attentive shepherds, while Joseph, no longer simply a passive observer, rises from his seat on an overturned barrow, looks toward the shepherds, and spreads out his arms, a proud husband and earthly father presenting his wife and child to the adoring faithful. In *Circumcision in the Stable*, Joseph doesn't simply stand to one side and watch the ceremony as he had done in the artist's earlier representations of the scene; now, he actually holds his son on his lap and gazes down lovingly at the boy as the *mohel* prepares to perform the biblical ritual. In *Virgin and Child with the Cat and the Snake*, the primary focus of the print is on the bond between a mother and her child. A pensive Joseph, relegated to the role of wistful observer, stands outside the room where Mary embraces her child. There may well be a theological significance to Joseph's exclusion from the Virgin's chamber, but on an emotional level, his expression seems to convey the love and longing of a father who can never experience the unique connection that exists between a mother and her newborn infant.

Finally, in *Christ Returning from the Temple with His Parents*, Rembrandt depicted the journey of the family back to Nazareth after Christ's disputation with the doctors in the Temple. Although the Gospel of Luke maintains that Jesus remained the obedient son of Mary and Joseph after the family returned to Nazareth following the boy's disappearance to dispute with the elders in the Temple,[128] Jesus's confrontation with the Temple scholars is an important moment in the synoptic Gospels, for it marks the first time that the boy, acknowledging his destiny, acts independently and questions the authority of the Old Law. The depiction of the journey back home, which is Joseph's final appearance in the Gospels and which had not been pictorially represented before, gave Rembrandt the opportunity to examine the reactions of each of the protagonists to this pivotal moment, for as the biblical texts state, Mary and Joseph were upset and puzzled by their child's actions and explanation. In the etching, Jesus, a twelve-year-old boy on the cusp of becoming a young man,[129] walks between his mother and father. Bathed in light, he turns toward Mary and gazes up at or beyond her. She seems distracted, lost in thought, and Jesus holds her hand in his so that he can lead her. Joseph, holding a thin walking stick in his left hand, moves resolutely forward. His broad-brimmed hat casts a shadow on his face, and the elderly patriarch seems, like Mary, to be trying to understand his son's words and what has happened. While Joseph's expression suggests his psychological separation from his son, he is still physically quite close to the boy. He asserts his place as Jesus's father by firmly grasping the boy's left hand with his right, even as Jesus turns away toward his mother and gazes heavenward.

Although no chronology has been established for the etchings that Rembrandt produced in 1654, it is possible that the childhood series was not only a meditation on particular biblical narratives, but also a conscious or unconscious reflection of the artist's own circumstances. In addition to his financial problems, Rembrandt's life was complicated by his relationship with his mistress, Hendrickje Stoffels. The fact that they were living together out of wedlock came to the attention of the Church Council in Amsterdam, and in late June 1654, Hendrickje was summoned to account for her behavior. By the time she actually made her appearance before the council in late July, she was pregnant with Rembrandt's child. The elders on the council condemned her as a whore, forbade her access to Communion, and ordered her to repent.[130] Her daughter, Cornelia, was born three months later. All of these circumstances—Rembrandt's perilous economic situation, Hendrickje's pregnancy, and the birth of Cornelia, along with the threats to the stability of their home occasioned by the actions of the Church Council—may well have encouraged Rembrandt to reflect in an even deeper way on the nature of family, the relationship between a newborn child and its mother, and the affections and responsibilities of fathers, themes that can all be discerned in the childhood series.[131] In addition, Rembrandt's son Titus, who turned twelve in 1654, was the same age as Jesus in the *Christ Seated Disputing with the Doctors* and *Christ Returning from the Temple with His Parents*. It is not difficult to imagine that the latter print could have been influenced by Rembrandt's own experience with an adolescent beginning to assert his independence.

In 1655, Rembrandt created four small Old Testament illustrations for Rabbi Menasseh ben Israel's visionary text *Piedra gloriosa* (B. 36 A–D, cat. nos. 8, 9, and 10). This was an anomalous undertaking for two reasons. First, it is one of the very few book illustration projects that the artist ever undertook; second, the mystical tenor of three of the four prints is quite contrary to Rembrandt's down-to-earth approach to biblical themes. However, the artist was probably sympathetic to the rabbi's chiliastic vision, and although it is unlikely that this was a very lucrative commission, it is possible that Rembrandt undertook the project because he needed the income. The fact that impressions survive of the undivided plate (one with all four images together on a single sheet), printed on Japanese paper or vellum,[132] suggests that the etchings were sold not only to individuals intending to cut them apart and bind them together with the printed text, but also to collectors of single-leaf art prints who might have been willing to pay a higher price.

In this same year, Rembrandt created his second large-scale print executed entirely in drypoint, *Christ Presented to the People: Oblong Plate* (B. 76, cat. no. 51). This print went through eight different states, with radical changes introduced in the fourth, sixth, and seventh states. The sheer size of the print (Rembrandt's second largest) and the fact that a number of impressions were printed on Japanese paper or vellum meant that it could be sold as a luxury item to collectors. In addition, as noted above, although changes in the plate may have been motivated in part by the deterioration of the drypoint lines, each new state could be marketed as a separate print. This was an efficient and economical way of expanding the scope of available stock, an important consideration given Rembrandt's financial circumstances and the fact that it seems that he was no longer in possession of his earlier plates.

In 1656, Rembrandt formally declared bankruptcy. The following year, as a means of protecting the family's remaining assets and the artist's future earnings from his creditors, Titus and Hendrickje formed a company, with Rembrandt as their sole employee. Four of the five etchings that the artist may have produced under this new arrangement had religious themes.[133] One of these was *Christ Preaching*, also known as *La petite Tombe* (B. 67, c. 1657, cat. no. 41).[134] Thematically, this print is related to the *Hundred Guilder Print*, although it is considerably smaller and much more restricted in the range of its characters and its layers of meaning. Directly in front of Jesus, a young boy provides a telling contrast to the attentive crowd of the faithful and skeptical who have come to hear Christ's words. This child has put aside his toy top and lies stretched out on the ground, with his feet extended toward Jesus. He ignores Christ's preaching and absent-mindedly draws in the dirt with his finger.[135] Inserting this figure into the foreground of the image added a typically realistic, contemporary note to an otherwise reverent scene, and the small, naturalistic detail undoubtedly resonated with both the artist's and the viewers' own experiences of the nature of young boys, who might not always be raptly attentive in church and would much rather be playing with their tops or idly scratching about in the ground than listening to sermons.

The nickname of this print, *La petite Tombe*, can be traced back as far as the seventeenth century, when it was recorded in the 1679 inventory of plates owned by Clement de Jonghe.[136] In a brief biography of the Amsterdam painter and art dealer Pieter de la Tombe, Arnold Houbraken specifically stated that the print's sobriquet referred to Pieter's brother, the book dealer and collector and seller of prints Nicolaes de la Tombe. It seems likely that Nicolaes owned the plate before it passed into the hands of Clement de Jonghe, and may even have commissioned the work.[137] If *Christ Preaching* was created specifically for Nicolaes de la Tombe, then the print would be the only known example—aside from the four illustrations for the *Piedra gloriosa*—of Rembrandt producing a religiously themed print on commission. Rembrandt had other associations with the de la Tombe family. Most notably, he and either Pieter or Jacob de la Tombe were joint owners of a painting of *Christ and the Woman of Samaria* by Moretto da Brescia.[138] Rembrandt produced an etching of *Christ and the Woman of Samaria*: *An Arched Print* (B. 70, cat. no. 45) in 1657, around the same time that he created *Christ Preaching*. Aspects of the *Woman of Samaria* print have been associated with the Moretto painting of the same subject,[139] which raises the possibility that the etching could have been produced as a second de la Tombe commission, one intended not to reproduce, but rather to invoke, the jointly owned painting.[140] Unfortunately, one can only speculate as to the reasons—aesthetic, economic, or even compassionate, given the artist's financial straits—that might have motivated members of the de la Tombe family to commission these works by the master printmaker.

In 1659, Rembrandt returned to a subject that he had depicted at the very beginning of his career as a printmaker, creating a new version of *Peter and John Healing the Cripple at the Gate of the Temple* (B. 94, cat. no. 66). This was the last of his prints to focus on a religious theme.[141] The technical, compositional, and narrative distance between Rembrandt's two representations of the miracle is remarkable. In both prints, the main focus of the composition is the encounter between the apostles and the beggar, not the miracle itself, and the three central figures are set into the immediate foreground. The protagonists and the view behind them are enframed by an arch, although in the earlier etching (B. 95, 1629) (fig. 9), this is only an architectural fragment. In the later version, the sophistication and breadth of the setting and the narrative have been radically expanded. The confusing and jumbled architectural background of the crudely rendered early etching has been replaced by a carefully structured view into the Temple courtyard constructed from a series of planes linked through the receding diagonal of the majestic façade of the Temple porch. In the later print, the presence of two skeptical witnesses in the left foreground, dressed in clothing similar to that worn by seventeenth-century Jews, would have struck a chord with viewers concerned about contemporary relations with Jews, an issue that had both theological and political implications.[142] The later etching is remarkable for the specificity of its setting, not just in comparison with the 1629 print, but also in regard to Rembrandt's religious prints in general.[143] As noted above, there is a wealth of architectural detail: the arcaded walls of the courtyard, the broad pyramidal staircase, the basin-shaped holocaust altar, two free-standing columns, the embroidered baldachin, and a massive circular tower. The decision to depict all of these particulars may have been motivated by the specificity of the biblical account of the miracle, which clearly states that it took place at the "Beautiful Gate" and that Peter then preached at "Solomon's Porch," but it is also possible that Rembrandt was responding to a broader contemporary interest in the geography of the Temple on the part of theologians and the larger Christian and Jewish communities.[144] Connoisseurs and the devout alike might have taken pleasure in passing through the Beautiful Gate into the courtyard and perusing "familiar" Temple landmarks.

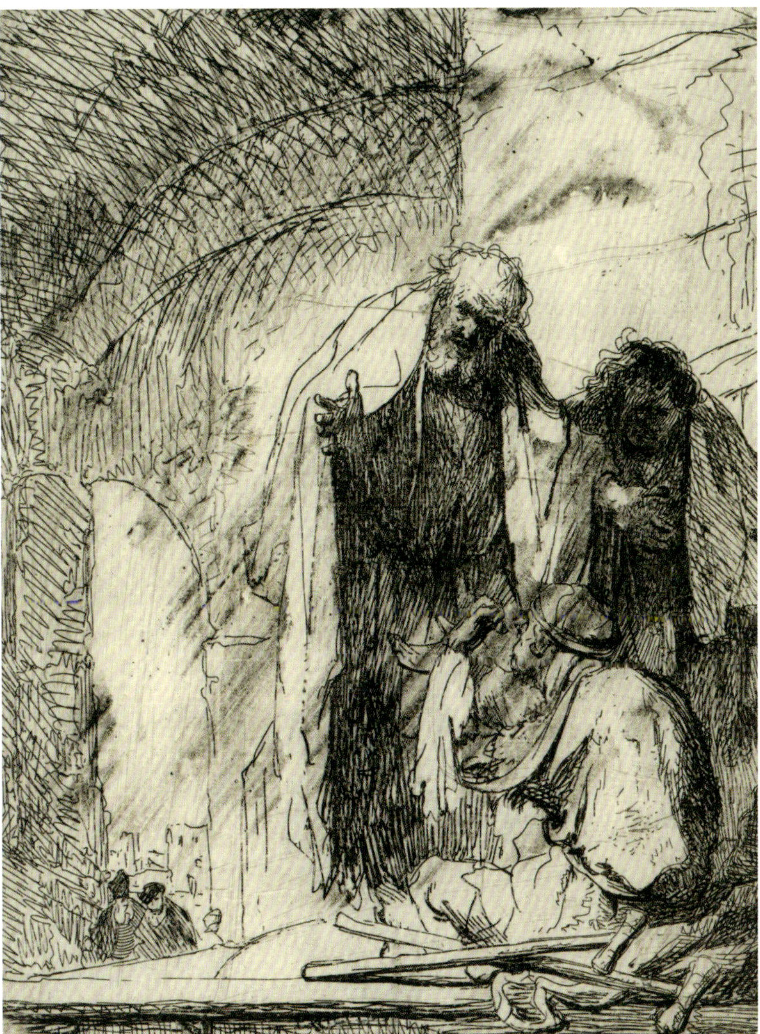

FIGURE 9. Rembrandt, *St. Peter and St. John Healing the Cripple at the Temple Gate*, etching, c. 1629. *Rijksmuseum, Amsterdam.*

Rembrandt's religious prints stand as evidence of the artist's extraordinary skill as a technician and as a testament to his genius as a teller of tales. From the joyous epiphany of the coming of the Messiah to the anguish of the betrayal of a father (Jacob) by his children, from the choirs of angels waiting to receive the Virgin into heaven to the dog who defecates in the road by an ancient inn (*The Good Samaritan*), Rembrandt's etchings offer a window into the nature of faith, aspiration, and human experience, ranging from the ecstatically divine to the worldly and mundane. Ultimately, these prints—modest, intimate, fragile objects—are great works of art that, like all masterpieces, reward the patient viewer with fresh insights and discoveries at each new encounter.

Notes

1. The baptismal records for Rembrandt have never been located, so there is no archival evidence of when he was born. The specific date of his birth comes from the biography of the artist that Arnold Houbraken wrote in *De groote schouburgh der Nederlantsche konstschilders en schilderessen* [The great theater of Netherlandish painters and paintresses], (Amsterdam: Weduwe des Autheurs, 1718–21).

2. Willem Adolph Visser 't Hooft, *Rembrandt and the Gospel* (New York: Meridian Books, 1960), 61.

3. Rembrandt's family probably belonged to what Jelle Bosma has called the "great floating middle," that is, Calvinists with only a loose relationship to the Reformed Church. After having been baptized, they attended services only occasionally, and were not actually church members. In contemporary terms, these individuals were called *liefhebbers van de gereformeerde religies,* or "favorers of the Reformed religion." Jelle Bosma, "Preaching in the Low Countries, 1450–1650," in *Preachers and People in the Reformations and Early Modern Period*, ed. Larissa Taylor (Leiden: Brill, 2001), 349. The sixteenth-century English traveler Fynes Moryson actually commented on the somewhat laissez-faire attitude of the Dutch populace in religious matters. Writing in 1593 about Sunday observances in Leiden, Moryson wrote, "I often observed at tymes of divine service, much more people to be in the markett place than in the church." Quoted in Christine Kooi, *Liberty and Religions: Church and State in Leiden's Reformation, 1572–1620* (Leiden: Brill, 2000), 125.

4. In 1632, English traveler James Howell commented on the confessional variety and tolerance that he observed in Amsterdam: "I believe in this street where I lodge there be well near as many religions as there are houses; for one neighbor knows not, nor cares not much what religion the other is of, so that the number of conventicles exceed the number of churches here." Quoted in Volker Manuth, "*'Are you a Mennonite, Papist, Arminian, or Beggar?'* Art, Religion and Rembrandt," in *Rembrandt, Quest of a Genius*, ed. Ernst de Wetering, exh. cat. (Zwolle, Netherlands: Waanders Publishers: Amsterdam: Museum het Rembrandtshuis, 2006), 66.

Leiden was no exception to this confessional diversity. Christine Kooi has estimated that in 1620, about 30% of the city's population were Dutch Reformed, 10% Walloon Reformed, and 11% Roman Catholic. Lutherans, although a considerably smaller and poorer minority, were actually able to construct their own church in 1618. The number of Roman Catholics increased after the conclusion of the war with Spain in 1648. It is estimated that they represented 15% of the population in 1656. Kooi, *Liberty and Religions*, 178, 187–88, and 194.

For a discussion of the religious variety that characterized the Dutch Republic in the seventeenth century, including the presence of a significant Jewish community, see *Rembrandt's Faith*, chapter 1, "A Religious Stew. " On the limited nature of this religious tolerance, see Xander van Eck, "Painting and Religious Toleration in the Golden Age," in *Traits of Tolerance: Religious Tolerance in the Golden Age*, ed. Xander van Eck, Beverly Jackson, and Ruud Priem (Zwolle, Netherlands: W Books, 2013), 49–50.

5. For a discussion of what was known as the Remonstrant/Counter-Remonstrant controversy and its consequences, see Jonathan Israel, *The Dutch Republic: Its Rise, Greatness and Fall, 1477–1806* (Oxford: Clarendon Press, 1995), 393–95 and 421–65.

6. For a discussion of the impact of the Remonstrant controversy in Leiden, see Christine Kooi, chapter 5, "The Second Generation Conflict: Arminians and Gomarists," in *Liberty and Religion*, esp. 140–58; and Ingrid W. L. Moerman, "Leiden, City in Holland," in Roelof van Straten, *Young Rembrandt: The Leiden Years, 1606–1632* (Leiden: Foleor, 2005), 250–51.

7. Gary Schwartz, *Rembrandt: His Life, His Paintings* (London: Penguin, 1991), passim. For possible references to this conflict in Rembrandt's own work, see the discussion of *Stoning of St. Stephen* (B. 97, 1635) in catalog entry number 67. Visser 't Hooft (*Rembrandt and the Gospel*, 64) has noted that in 1637, Rembrandt also painted a portrait of Eleazar Swalmius, who was a strong supporter of the Counter-Remonstrant position.

8. Rembrandt and Saskia were wed in Sint Annaparochie, in Friesland. B. P. J. Broos, "Review of Walter L. Strauss; Marjon van der Meulen, *The Rembrandt Documents*," *Simiolus: Netherlands Quarterly for the History of Art* 12, no. 4 (1981–82): 253–54.

9. Filippo Baldinucci, "Life of Rembrandt," from *Cominciamento, e progresso dell'arte dell'intagliare in rame, colle vite di molti de' più eccellenti maestri della stessa professione* [The origins and progress of the art of engraving on copper, with the lives of many of the most excellent masters of this same profession] (Florence: Stamperia di P. Matini, 1686), in Joachim von Sandrart, Filippo Baldinucci, and Arnold Houbraken, *Lives of Rembrandt*, introd. Charles Ford (London: Pallas Athene, 2007), 40.

10. Visser 't Hooft laid out the arguments against Rembrandt's membership in the Mennonite Church in *Rembrandt and the Gospel*, chapter 5. In contrast, Jacob Rosenberg (*Rembrandt: Life & Work* [London: Phaidon, 1964], 180–84) argued for a distinctly Mennonite orientation in Rembrandt's religious works, while still advising against considering "his art as based exclusively upon their creed."

11. Xander van Eck, "Painting and Religious Toleration," 34–37.

12. Visser 't Hooft, *Rembrandt and the Gospel*, 70.

13. The biography appears in Orlers's *Description of the City of Leiden* [*Beschrijvinge der stad Leyden*] (Leiden, 1641). The text is available in translation in Walter Strauss and Marjon van der Meulen, eds. and trans., *The Rembrandt Documents* (New York; Abaris, 1979), doc. 1641/8.

14. Ingrid W. L. Moerman, "Leiden: The City and Its Inhabitants in Rembrandt's Time," in Roelof van Straten, *Young Rembrandt*, 282.

15. From the inventory of Rembrandt's personal possessions conducted in 1656 in conjunction with his bankruptcy, it seems that the artist owned about two dozen books, including a Bible; a German edition of Josephus's *Jewish Wars* and *Jewish Antiquities* illustrated by Tobias Stimmer; Dürer's four books on proportion; Bernardino da Gallipoli's treatise on the plan of, and buildings in, the Holy Land and Jerusalem with illustrations by Jacques Callot; and translations of Ovid's *Metamophoses*, Homer's *Odyssey*, and works by Livy and others. For a more extensive discussion of Rembrandt's library, see Amy Golanhy, *Rembrandt's Reading: The Artist's Bookshelf of Ancient Poetry and History* (Amsterdam: Amsterdam University Press, 2003).

16. Joachim von Sandrart, "Life of Rembrandt," from Joachim von Sandrart and Jochen Becken,*Teutsche Academie der edlen Bau-, Bild- und Mahlerey-Künste* [*The German Academy of the Noble Art of Architecture, Sculpture, and Painting*] (Nuremberg, 1675), in Sandrart, Baldinucci, and Houbraken, *Lives of Rembrandt*, 29.

17. On the relationship between the Latin School and the university, and information regarding the kind of education that Rembrandt would have received at school, see Golanhy, *Rembrandt's Reading*, 51–58.

The eighteenth-century biographer and artist Arnold Houbraken claimed that Rembrandt's "particular inclination for drawing made [his parents] change their minds [about his future]." Although this sounds formulaic, there may also be a measure of truth in this assertion. Houbraken, "Life of Rembrandt," in Sandrart, Baldinucci, and Houbraken, *Lives of Rembrandt*, 51.

18. Strauss and van der Meulen, *The Rembrandt Documents*, doc. 1620/1. Leiden University, founded in 1575, was the oldest university in the Republic. It offered degrees in theology, jurisprudence, and medicine. For a very brief history of the university, see the discussion by Moerman, "Leiden, City in Holland," 241–42.

19. Roelof van Straten suggested that this was simply a "pre-enrollment" for Latin School students. Van Straten, *Young Rembrandt*, 21.

20. Van Swanenburgh, who was Catholic, had been trained by his father, Isaac Claesz. van Swanenburgh, but had also spent more than twenty-five years in Italy, studying first in Venice and then in Rome. He finally settled in Naples in about 1608. Except for a brief trip back to the Netherlands, he remained in Naples until 1617, when he returned to Leiden. His art, which does not reflect contemporary early Italian Baroque trends, is characterized by a late form of Boschian fantasy and recollected views of Rome painted after his return to the Netherlands. Rudolf E. O. Ekkart, "Swanenburg [*sic*], van," *Grove Art Online, Oxford Art Online*, Oxford University Press, accessed August 22, 2014, http://www.oxfordartonline.com.proxy.library.nd.edu/subscriber/article/grove/art/T082554pg2.

The term "history painting" refers to narrative works that depict scenes from the Bible, classical mythology, literature, or history. This category of art is distinct from paintings representing genre scenes, portraits, landscapes, or still lifes.

21. Pieter Lastman was born in Amsterdam in 1583, and was trained by Mannerist painter Gerrit Pietersz. Sweelinck. In 1602, Lastman, a Catholic, traveled to Rome, where he lived until 1607. Then he returned to Amsterdam, where he remained until he died. Lastman was known as one of the foremost painters of small history paintings with subjects drawn from the Bible, secular history, and mythology. B. P. J Broos, "Lastman, Pieter (Pietersz.)," in *From Rembrandt to Vermeer: 17th-Century Dutch Artists*, ed. Jane Turner, Grove Dictionary of Art (New York: St. Martin's Press, 2000), 192–96.

22. Jan Lievens was born in Leiden in 1607. A child prodigy, he entered the shop of painter Joris van Schooten at the age of eight. After completing his apprenticeship with van Schooten, Lievens moved to Amsterdam, where he studied with Pieter Lastman. He then returned to Leiden in 1619 and began his career as an independent master specializing in history painting and portraiture. Lievens left Leiden in 1632, settling first in England and then, in 1635, in Antwerp, where he perfected a new style influenced by the Flemish Baroque paintings of Rubens and van Dyck. Lievens joined the artist's guild in Antwerp and continued to work as a history painter and portraitist. In 1643, he moved back to Amsterdam, where he remained until his death, in 1674. William W. Robinson, "Lievens (Lievensz.), Jan," in *From Rembrandt to Vermeer*, ed. Turner, 198–204.

23. On the early associations and rivalry between Rembrandt and Lievens, see Mariët Westerman, *Rembrandt* (London: Phaidon, 2000), 38–42, and Stephanie Dickey, "Lievens and Printmaking," in Arthur Wheelock Jr., *Jan Lievens: A Dutch Master Rediscovered*, exh. cat. (London and New Haven, CT: Yale University Press; Washington, DC: National Gallery of Art, 2008), 56–59. Roelof van Straten (*Young Rembrandt*, 86–87 and 234–35) thinks it unlikely that the two artists shared a studio, although he does believe that there was a close association between them, particularly after 1628, when they lived virtually around the corner from one another.

Rembrandt and Lievens depicted a number of the same subjects. Both made paintings of the capture of Samson (1628); painted and graphic versions of the Raising of Lazarus (produced between 1630 and 1631), including Rembrandt's *Raising of Lazarus: Larger Plate* (B. 73, cat. no. 46); and paintings of Christ on the Cross (1631), the latter presumably produced in competition for a lucrative commission from Frederik Hendrik, prince of Orange and Stadtholder of Holland. For a discussion of this competition and illustrations of all of these paintings and prints, see Gary Schwartz, *Rembrandt: His Life, His Paintings*, 78–90.

24. Thomas Rassieur in *Rembrandt's Journey*, 70–72. On Berendrecht as a printer and publisher, see Elizabeth Wyckoff, "Innovation and Popularization: Printmaking and Print Publishing in Haarlem during the 1620s," PhD diss., Columbia University, 1998, 139–93. See also catalog entry 22 on *Circumcision* (S. 398, c. 1626).

25. HD 9.

26. Van Straten suggested that Rembrandt might have been inspired by the painter and experienced etcher Jacob de Gheyn III (1596–1641). De Gheyn resided in The Hague and was a close friend of Constantijn Huygens, secretary to Stadtholder Frederik Hendrik. Van Straten, *Young Rembrandt*, 84.

27. In support of his hypothesis, van Straten noted that the prints that Rembrandt made before 1629 are only known to have existed in a single state, whereas prints made in that year and thereafter normally appear in several states and in much greater numbers, suggesting easy access to a press. Van Straten, *Young Rembrandt*, 124–25.

An examination of Rembrandt's rate of production also supports this idea. The number of prints that he produced increased from two in 1627 to nine in 1628. Production rose to fifteen prints in 1629, and as many as 41 in 1630, the largest number he ever produced. Erik Hinterding, *Rembrandt as an Etcher: The Practice of Production and Distribution*, vol. 1 (Ouderkerk aan den IJssel, Netherlands: Sound and Vision Publishers, 2006), fig. 28.

28. For a fuller description of these and other sources, see *Circumcision* (S. 398, cat. no. 22).

29. The art historical tradition of unraveling Rembrandt's sources is documented in B. P. J. Broos's *Index to the Formal Sources of Rembrandt's Art* (Maarssen, Netherlands: Schwartz, 1977).

30. Svetlana Alpers, *Rembrandt's Enterprise: The Studio and the Market* (Chicago: University of Chicago Press, 1988), 73–74.

31. Philips Angel, "In Praise of Painting," trans. Michael Hoyle; introd. and commentary Hessel Miedema, *Simiolus: Netherlands Quarterly for the History of Art* 24, no. 2/3 (1996): 243.

32. Alpers, *Rembrandt's Enterprise*, 74.

33. For example, it is unlikely that contemporary collectors would have recognized Rubens's kneeling magus and curious elders as sources for Rembrandt's seated assistant and onlookers

in *Circumcision*, or that they would have identified Mantegna's rare engraving of the Madonna and Child as the source for Mary and her son in *Virgin and Child with the Cat and the Snake* (B. 32, 1654, cat. no. 36), or been aware of the citation of the equestrian figure from the reverse of Pisanello's medal of Gianfrancesco Gonzaga in the fourth state of *Christ Crucified between the Two Thieves: "The Three Crosses"* (B. 78, 1653–55, cat. no. 54).

34. For each of these comparisons, see the entries for the Rembrandt prints in this catalog.

35. A *mohel* is a Jewish male who performs a circumcision.

36. NHD 195 (Johannes Stradanus). There was an established tradition of representing Hebraic priests in costumes that mirrored those of the Catholic priesthood. See, for example, Israhel van Meckenem's engraving of *The Presentation in the Temple with the Circumcision* (HG 57, c. 1490–1500) and Albrecht Altdorfer's *Circumcision* from his series The Fall and Redemption of Man (HG, woodcuts, 11, c. 1513–15).

37. Strauss and van der Meulen, *The Rembrandt Documents*, doc. 1656/12, Items 157, 158, 184, 313, 320, 339, and 342.

38. Ibid., doc. 1656/12, Item 204.

39. According to Bronwen Wilson (*The World in Venice: Print, the City, and Early Modern Identity* [Toronto, ON: University of Toronto Press, 2005], 292n3), the first printed collection of costumes was produced by Enea Vico. His *Diversarum gentium aetatis habitus*, which appeared in Venice in 1558, contained 70 engravings of Spanish costumes and 29 prints of costumes from other countries. This was quickly followed by François Deserps's *Recueil de la diversité des habits qui sont présent en usage tant ès pays d'Europe, Asie, Affrique et Iles sauvages* (Paris: Richard Breton, 1562). Deserps's collection included 121 woodcuts of costumes drawn from France, Holland, Flanders, England, Poland, Hungary, America, India, Persia, Egypt, Turkey, Greece, Arabia, and Africa. This compendium was followed by examples published in Nuremberg, Frankfurt, Cologne, and Antwerp. Some of these concentrated on specific regions or countries. Probably the best known example, however, is Cesare Vecellio's *De gli habiti antichi, et moderni di diverse parti del mondo* (Venice: Damian Zenaro, 1590; rept. New York: Dover, 1977). Vecellio's was an encyclopedic collection. According to Karl Küp ("Some Early Costume Books," in Küp, *Costume, Gothic & Renaissance: Some Early Costume Books* [New York: New York Public Library, 1937], 7), what really differentiates this compendium from its predecessors is its historical approach to the subject. Vecellio offers examples drawn from the Middle Ages through to the end of the sixteenth century. Three hundred fifty-nine full-page woodcut illustrations are given over to the costumes of Western Europe, and fifty-nine are devoted to Asia and Africa.

40. See, for example, the Moorish figures in *Beheading of John the Baptist* (B. 92, 1640, cat. no. 65), *Baptism of the Eunuch* (B. 98, 1641, cat. no. 68), and *Hundred Guilder Print* (B. 74, c. 1649, cat. no. 48).

41. On the representation of contemporary Jewish costumes in Rembrandt's work, see *Rembrandt's Faith*, 53–54, 214–15 (which specifically deals with Jewish costumes in *Presentation in the Temple: Oblong Print* [B. 49, c. 1639–41, cat. no. 26]), and 307 (where the authors discuss Rembrandt's knowledge of contemporary Jewish ritual dress in the context of the *Entombment* [B. 86, 1654, cat. no. 58]).

42. For this assumption and its reflection in Rembrandt's biblical prints, see Marieke de Winkel, *Fashion and Fancy: Dress and Meaning in Rembrandt's Paintings* (Amsterdam: Amsterdam University Press, 2006), 255–59, and the entry in this catalog for *Three Oriental Figures [Jacob and Laban?]* (B. 118, 1641, cat. no. 70). As de Winkel observes (260), Ottoman dress did not have to be drawn from life since it was often incorporated in costume books. (See note 39, above.) For example, Nicolas de Nicolay published numerous engravings of Turkish costumes in his 1568 account of his travels in the East. Nicolas de Nicolay, *Les quatre premiers livres des navigations et pérégrinations orientales* (Lyon: Guillaume Roville, 1568; rept. Antwerp: Guillaume Silvius, 1576).

43. See, for example, Rembrandt's *Self-Portrait in a Velvet Cap with Plume* (B. 20, 1638, cat. no. 1), the headdresses worn by the priestly figure standing beside Mary's bed in *Death of the Virgin* (B. 99, 1639, cat. no. 69), the appearance of the eldest "angel" in *Abraham Entertaining the Angels* (B. 29, 1656, cat. no. 3), the costume of the mounted soldier in *Baptism of the Eunuch* (B. 98, 1641, cat. no. 68), and the clothing of Joseph of Arimathea in *Descent from the Cross: The Second Plate* (B. 81 II, 1633, cat. no. 55).

44. Paraphrasing Karel van Mander, the seventeenth-century Dutch dramatist Cornelis Biens asserted that a successful history painting should show figures in a variety of poses and "adorned with manifold garments." Quoted in de Winkel, *Fashion and Fancy*, 193.

Arnold Houbraken ("Life of Rembrandt," 60) specifically praised Rembrandt for the inventiveness he demonstrated in constantly rethinking biblical subjects while repeatedly altering the "characterisation, posture and *details of costume*" (emphasis added) of his actors. Cited by de Winkel, *Fashion and Fancy*, 191.

45. For a discussion of this compositional structure and its application by Dutch artists in the seventeenth century, see Martha Hollander, *An Entrance for the Eyes: Space and Meaning in Seventeenth-Century Dutch Art* (Berkeley: University of California Press, 2002). For a discussion of the terms *doorsein* and *perspect*, particularly in the writings of van Mander and Hoogstraten, see Hollander, 9–47. According to Hollander, the term *perspect* was used primarily for architectural interiors and views, while *doorsein* was used to describe landscape vistas, as well as architecturally enframed views.

46. Rembrandt's paintings of *The Supper at Emmaus* (c. 1628, RRP, *Corpus*, A16) and *The Repentant Judas Returning the Thirty Pieces of Silver* (1629, RRP, *Corpus*, A15) are early examples of this compositional strategy.

47. The identification of this space as the Priests' Court was made by Perlove and Silver, *Rembrandt's Faith*, 257.

48. 1 Kings 7:21: "And he set up the pillars in the porch of the temple: and he set up the right pillar, and called the name thereof Jachin: and he set up the left pillar, and called the name thereof Boaz."

49. *Rembrandt's Faith*, 259.

50. Acts 3:11–12. "Now as the lame man who was healed held on to Peter and John, all the people ran together to them in the porch which is called Solomon's, greatly amazed. So when Peter saw it, he responded to the people."

51. There are numerous other examples where a *perspect* or vista expands the narrative or clarifies the temporal or historical location of the scene. See, for example, *Triumph of Mordecai* (B. 40, 1641, cat. no. 14), the two versions of *Christ and the Woman of Samaria* (B. 70, 1657, cat. no. 45, and B. 71, 1634, cat. no. 44), *Raising of Lazarus: Small Plate* (B. 72, 1642, cat. no. 47), *Christ Carried to the Tomb* (B. 84, 1645, cat. no. 57), and *Return of the Prodigal Son* (B. 91, 1636, cat. no. 63). The background of *Abraham Casting Out Hagar and Ishmael* (B. 30, 1637, cat. no. 4) serves a different kind of function. Here, the contrast between Abraham's dwelling on the left side and the empty opening on the right echoes the emotional and psychological distinction between the safety of home and the uncertainty of exile.

52. Michael Zell identified the two Jews as contemporary figures who are distinguished by their costumes from the biblical figures around them. *Reframing Rembrandt: Jews and the Christian Image in Seventeenth-Century Amsterdam* (Berkeley: University of California Press, 2002), 158–59. This distinction was also noted by Perlove and Silver, *Rembrandt's Faith*, 261.

53. There do not appear to be any direct precedents for the singular appearance of the elephant in *Adam and Eve*. For a discussion of the elephant, see the catalog entry on *Adam and Eve* (B. 28, 1638, cat. no. 2). By contrast, oxen are traditionally included in scenes of the Annunciation to the Shepherds and the Adoration of the Shepherds. They are appropriate for the setting of these stories and potentially symbolic.

54. Susan Donahue Kuretsky, "Rembrandt's Cat," in *Aemulatio. Imitation, Emulation and Invention in Netherlandish Art from 1500 to 1800: Essays in Honor of Eric Jan Sluijter*, ed. Anton W. A. Boschloo, Jacquelyn N. Couttre, Stephanie S. Dickey, and Nicolette C. Sluijter-Seijffert (Zwolle, Netherlands: Waanders Publishers, 2011), 271.

55. Some historians (cf. Perlove and Silver, *Rembrandt's Faith*, 213, 317, and 440n177) have interpreted Rembrandt's dogs as representing carnality and/or unconverted Jews and nonbelievers. The fact that the dogs tend to ignore or even confront God's messengers in Rembrandt's prints and paintings makes this interpretation plausible, despite other connotations of dogs as paragons of loyalty and virtue.

56. The ubiquity of sometimes unruly dogs in seventeenth-century Holland is attested to by the existence of a church employee called a "dog-whipper," or *Hondeslager*. If dogs were interrupting a sermon by barking or fighting, it was the *Hondeslager*'s job to drive the animals from the church. It seems that the animals' presence was otherwise tolerated, even in sacred spaces. On the role of the dog-whipper or "dog-butcher" in Leiden, see Moerman, "Leiden: The City and Its Inhabitants," 281.

57. During the course of his lifetime, Rembrandt produced a total of about three hundred prints. Of these, eighty-one dealt specifically with religious subjects. The majority of these prints were of narrative scenes drawn from the Old and New Testaments, while the remainder were devotional images of the Holy Family (B. 62, 1632, cat. no. 35), the Virgin Mary (B. 61, 1641, cat. no. 34; B. 63, 1654, cat. no. 36; and B. 85), and Saints Jerome and Francis. Two other prints are ambiguous, *Three Oriental Figures* (B. 118, 1641, cat. no. 70), which

has also been identified as *Jacob and Laban*, and *The Little Jewish Bride* (B. 342), which has more recently been identified as *Saskia as St. Catherine*.

58. For Rembrandt's concern with the marketplace in general, see Alpers, *Rembrandt's Enterprise*, esp. chapter 4, "Freedom, Art, and Money." Baldinucci ("Life of Rembrandt," 46) commented on Rembrandt's desire to maintain the value of his prints:

> Since it seemed to him that his prints did not sell at the prices which he felt they deserved, he imagined that he had found a method of increasing the desire of them universally. Hence at intolerable expense he had them bought back all over Europe, wherever he could find them, at any price. Among others he bought one for 50 scudi at a sale by auction in Amsterdam, a *Raising of Lazarus*, and this he did while himself possessing the copper-plate engraved [*sic*] by his own hand.

59. Images on plates that were lightly etched or utilized a significant degree of drypoint line could break down after repeated printings, which meant that some plates required reinforcement or repair. Although most of the "repair states" were probably produced after Rembrandt's death, this was not always the case, and in fact, it has been suggested that one of the motivations for his radical reworkings of *Christ Presented to the People: Oblong Plate* (B. 76, 1655, cat. no. 51) and *Christ Crucified between the Two Thieves: "The Three Crosses"* (B. 78, 1653–55, cat. no. 54) was the deterioration of the plates. Erik Hinterding, Ger Luijten, and Martin Royalton-Kisch, *Rembrandt the Printmaker*, exh. cat. (Chicago and London: Fitzroy Dearborn Publishers, 2000), cat. 78, 319–20, and *Rembrandt's Journey*, 257.

60. Houbraken, "Life of Rembrandt," 89–91.

61. This type of alteration was not very common. An early example of Rembrandt cutting down a plate was the change he made between the second and third states of *Christ Disputing with the Doctors: Small Plate* (B. 66, 1630, cat. no. 37). According to White and Boon, the plate measured 10.8 × 7.8 cm in the first two states, but then was reduced on three sides so that it measured only 8.9 × 6 cm. This resulted in the removal of two figures on the right side and Rembrandt's signature at the bottom. A late, equally dramatic example of this type of change, one that was probably motivated by practical considerations, was the removal of 2½ centimeters from the top of the plate between the third and fourth states of *Christ Presented to the People: Oblong Plate* (B. 76, cat. no. 51). In its original format, the plate, which measured 38.3 × 45.5 cm, was so large that Rembrandt was forced to paste a strip onto the top of each sheet of Japanese paper on which the impression was printed in order to accommodate the image. The reduction in the size of the plate meant that he was able to print the etching on a single sheet.

62. See, for example, the changes between states IV and V and between VI and VII in *Raising of Lazarus: Larger Plate* (B. 73, 1632, cat. no. 46), and those between states V and VI in *Christ Presented to the People: Oblong Plate* (B. 76, cat. no. 51).

63. The clearest example of major alterations made to a plate can be found in the compositional and conceptual transformations made in reworking *Christ Crucified between the Two Thieves: "The Three Crosses"* (B. 78, cat. no. 54) between states III and IV.

64. Thomas Rassieur, "Looking over Rembrandt's Shoulder: The Printmaker at Work," in *Rembrandt's Journey*, 56.

65. This observation concerning the use of plate tone in *Entombment* is based on the description of the surviving impressions cataloged in the New Hollstein volume dedicated to Rembrandt (NHD 284). The impression in the Snite Museum was taken from the fourth and final state of the plate. Interestingly, it has very little evidence of plate tone.

66. Rassieur, "Looking over Rembrandt's Shoulder," 55.

67. Deborah La Camera, Rhona Macbeth, and Kimberly Nichols, "Materials and Technique," in *Rembrandt's Journey*, 336.

68. Rassieur, "Looking over Rembrandt's Shoulder," 55. None of the prints in the Feddersen collection is on Japanese paper.

69. Of the forty surviving copies of the Gutenberg Bible, for example, twelve are on vellum, and the remainder on paper. "British Library, Treasures in Full, Gutenberg Bible, Making the Bible, 9. How Many," accessed August 22, 2014, http://www.bl.uk/treasures/gutenberg/howmany.html.

70. The three illustrations from Menassah ben Israel's *Piedra gloriosa* of 1655 in the Feddersen collection (B. 36 A, C, and D, cat. nos. 7, 8, and 9) are printed on vellum. According to the entry in the New Hollstein Rembrandt volume, most of the surviving examples of these etchings are on vellum or Japanese paper, suggesting that they were intended for luxury editions of the *Piedra gloriosa* or to be purchased as separate collector's items.

71. Van Vliet is also known variously as Johannes van Vliet, Jan Gillisz. van Vliet, and Jan Joris van Vliet. The most complete discussion of the relationship between van Vliet and Rembrandt is

the catalog of an exhibition held in Amsterdam at the Rembrandthuis in 1996. Christiaan Schuckman, Martin Royalton-Kisch, and Erik Hinterding, *Rembrandt and Van Vliet: A Collaboration on Copper* (Amsterdam: Museum het Rembrandthuis, 1996). See also *Christ before Pilate: Large Plate* (B. 77, 1635, cat. no. 50), note 8, in this catalog.

72. Van Vliet engravings after Rembrandt include three biblical narratives dated 1631 (*Lot and His Daughters* [HD 1], *The Baptism of the Eunuch* [HD 12], and *St. Jerome Kneeling in Prayer* [HD 13]); an undated *Old Woman Reading* (HD 18); a *Portrait of Rembrandt,* dated 1634 (HD 14); and several *tronies,* i.e., character heads, dated 1633 and 1634 (HD 15–26). All of these prints identify Rembrandt as the designer and van Vliet as the engraver in the plate. Rembrandt is identified through his monogram, RHL, a form of signature that he abandoned in 1632 after he moved permanently to Amsterdam.

Van Vliet also did reproductive prints after Jan Lievens (HD 2 and 3) and Joris van Schooten (HD11).

73. RRP, *Corpus,* A65.

74. RRP, *Corpus,* A89.

75. See the entry for *Christ before Pilate: Large Plate* (B. 77, 1635, cat. no. 50) for an illustration of the first, incomplete, state of this composition.

76. The locus classicus of this argument is two letters written by Pope Gregory the Great to Serenus, the bishop of Marseilles, around 600 AD. Gregory's statements served as the foundation for the more refined arguments that appear in the thirteenth-century writings of Saints Thomas Aquinas and Bonaventure. For a discussion of the arguments marshaled in defense of religious images, see David Freedberg, *The Power of Images: Studies in the History and Theory of Response* (Chicago and London: University of Chicago Press, 1989), 162–67; and Herbert L. Kessler, "Gregory the Great and Image Theory in Northern Europe during the Twelfth and Thirteenth Centuries," in *A Companion to Medieval Art,* ed. Conrad Rudolph (Blackwell Publishing, 2006), Blackwell Reference Online, accessed September 10, 2014, http://www.blackwellreference.com/subscriber/tocnode.html?id=g9781405102865_chunk_g97814051028658.

77. Martin Luther, *Werke,* 10/II, 458, "Umb der kinder und eifeltigen willen, welche durch bildnis und gleichnis besser bewegt weden, die Göttlichen geschicht zu behalten," cited in Max Engammare, "Les Figures de la Bible. Le destin oublié d'un genre littéraire en image (XVIe–XVIIe siècles)," *Mélanges de l'Ecole française de Rome. Italie et Méditerranée,* 106, no. 2 (1994): 561.

78. See Simon Schama, *The Embarrassment of Riches: An Interpretation of Dutch Culture in the Golden Age* (New York: Knopf, 1987), 93–125; and Peter van der Coelen, "Netherlandish Printmakers and the Old Testament," in Peter van der Coelen, *Patriarchs, Angels and Prophets: The Old Testament in Netherlandish Printmaking from Lucas van Leyden to Rembrandt,* exh. cat. (Amsterdam: Rembrandt Information Centre, 1996), 8.

79. John Michael Montias, "Works of Art in Seventeenth-Century Amsterdam: An Analysis of Subjects and Attributions," in *Art in History/History in Art, Studies in Seventeenth-Century Dutch Culture,* ed. David Freedberg and Jan de Vries (Santa Monica, CA: Getty Center for the History of Art and the Humanities, 1991), tables 2, 5, 6a, and 6b.

80. Cornelis Danckerts's *Icones Biblicae praecipuas sacrae Scripturae historias eleganter et graphice representantes,* illustrated with images engraved by Matthäus Merian the Elder and published in Amsterdam between 1648 and 1659, included inscriptions in Latin, French, German, English, and Dutch. Engammare, "Les Figures de la Bible," 552–54.

81. On "picture bibles" see Engammare, "Les Figures de la Bible," 549–91, and van der Coelen, "Netherlandish Printmakers and the Old Testament," 15–23.

82. The pan-European popularity of "picture bibles" is attested to by the publication history of *Quadrins historiques de la Bible,* a picture bible with illustrations by French printmaker Bernard Salomon. Between 1553 and 1558, the book was published in seven different editions, each in a different language: French, English, Spanish, German, Italian, Dutch, and Latin. Ultimately, the *Quadrins historiques* went through twenty-six editions. Engammare, "Les Figures de la Bible," 551–52, and van der Coelen, "Netherlandish Printmakers and the Old Testament," 15–16.

83. See the discussion of the childhood of Christ and Passion/Post-Passion series from 1654, below.

84. There is ample evidence of the international scope of Rembrandt's clientele. In 1660, for example, Italian painter Guercino wrote to Sicilian aristocrat and collector Don Antonio Ruffo, "I have seen a number of his [Rembrandt's] printed works which have appeared in these parts; they are very beautiful, engraved in good taste and in good manner." Two years later, the English writer/

diarist John Evelyn praised "the incomparable Reinbrand [*sic*] whose Etchings and gravings are of a particular spirit." Holm Bevers, "Rembrandt as an Etcher," in Bevers, Peter Schatborn, and Barbara Welzel, *Rembrandt: The Master and His Workshop*, vol. 2, *Drawings and Etchings* (New Haven, CT: Yale University Press, 1991), 160.

85. The term "pragmatic ecumenism" was coined by Willem Frijhoff to describe "the ease of social intercourse" among individuals from different faiths that prevailed in Holland, particularly in the seventeenth century. Xander van Eck applied the term to the confessional neutrality that artists such as Rembrandt displayed in their work and used to attract a diverse clientele. Van Eck, "Painting and Religious Toleration," 34–42.

86. Manuth, "*'Are you a Mennonite, Papist, Arminian, or Beggar?'* Art, Religion and Rembrandt," 70.

87. Holm Bevers in Bevers, Schatborn, and Welzel, *Rembrandt: The Master and His Workshop*, vol. 2, *Drawings and Etchings*, 270.

88. For a discussion of Rembrandt's modifications of Catholic iconography as a means of making his religious prints acceptable to a Protestant audience, see Catherine Scallen, "Rembrandt's Reformation of a Catholic Subject: The Penitent and the Repentant St. Jerome," *Sixteenth Century Journal* 30, no. 1 (1999): 71–88.

89. See, for example, Catherine Scallen, "Rembrandt, Emulation and the Northern Tradition," in *In Detail: New Studies of Northern Renaissance Art in Honor of Walter S. Gibson*, ed. Laurinda S. Dixon (Turnhout, Belgium: Brepols, 1998), 142; Barbara Welzel, "The Death of the Virgin," in Bevers, Schatborn, and Welzel, *Rembrandt: The Master and His Workshop*, vol. 2, *Drawings and Etchings*, 203; and *Rembrandt's Faith*, 45.

90. Marijn Schapelhouman, "Death of the Virgin," in Hinterding, Luijten, and Royalton-Kisch, *Rembrandt the Printmaker*, 162–64.

91. *Rembrandt's Faith*, 47–48.

92. See the entry for *Death of the Virgin* (cat. no. 69) for a fuller discussion of Rembrandt's sources.

93. Schapelhouman, 164: "In one detail Rembrandt's reading is unlike all previous ones: his Mary is no blissfully smiling, youthful apparition, but a sick old woman. The earnest-faced physician taking her pulse is likewise wholly original."

94. *Rembrandt's Faith*, 48–49.

95. Holm Bevers, "The Virgin and Child with the Snake," in Bevers, Schatborn, and Welzel, *Rembrandt: The Master and His Workshop*, vol. 2, *Drawings and Etchings*, 270.

96. The total number of etchings produced in this period may be somewhat inflated, since a large number of these etchings are small figure studies that are essentially sketches, rather than fully realized, more complex narrative compositions, portraits, or landscapes.

97. Although there was a decline in the absolute number of prints that Rembrandt produced in 1632–33, his production of religious etchings increased. After creating only one religious print in 1631, he made three in 1632, and four in 1633, including his first etching of an Old Testament subject, the highly dramatic *Joseph's Coat Brought to Jacob* (B. 38, 1633, cat. no. 12).

98. There are at least fifteen individual portraits from this two-year period.

99. It is probably not coincidental that one of Rembrandt's most aggressively self-confident self-portraits, *Self Portrait Leaning on a Stone Sill* (B. 21), was produced in the same year that he purchased this house. Like the purchase of the house, this self-portrait, which was influenced by portraits done by artistic giants Raphael and Titian, was an assertion of the artist's professional and material success.

100. According to art historian Egbert Havercamp-Begemann (*Rembrandt: The Nightwatch* [Princeton, NJ: Princeton University Press, 1982], 14–15), the commission for *The Nightwatch* (RRP, *Corpus*, 146) must have been awarded sometime before December 1640, with the painting being completed by mid-1642, the date that appears on the painting itself. In 1641, in addition to working on *The Nightwatch*, Rembrandt painted a double portrait of the Mennonite preacher Cornelius Claesz. Anslo and his wife, Aeltje Gerritsdr. Schouten (RRP, *Corpus*, 143); and single portraits of Nicolaes van Bambeeck (RRP, *Corpus*, 144), Agatha Bas (RRP, *Corpus*, 145), and Saskia (RRP, *Corpus*, 142).

101. In 1638, the year before he moved into his new house on Sint Antoniebreestraat, Rembrandt produced only five prints, including two Old Testament subjects, *Joseph Telling His Dreams* (B. 37, cat. no. 11) and *Adam and Eve* (B. 28, cat. no. 2), and the ambiguous *The Little Jewish Bride (Saskia as St. Catherine)* (B. 342). In 1639, he created eight prints, but only one of them, *Death of the Virgin* (B. 99, cat. no. 69), depicted a religious subject. In 1640, the number of etchings dropped back to five, including two religious subjects, *Beheading of John the Baptist* (B. 92, cat. no. 65), and *Presentation in the Temple: Oblong Print* (B. 49, cat. no. 26). The six prints with religious subjects that were produced in 1641 included *Christ Crucified between the Two Thieves: Oval Plate* (B. 79, cat. no. 53), *Angel Departing from the*

Family of Tobias (B. 43, cat. no. 18), *Virgin and Child in the Clouds* (B. 61, cat. no. 34), *Triumph of Mordecai* (B. 40, cat. no. 14), *Baptism of the Eunuch* (B. 98, cat. no. 68), and *Three Oriental Figures (Jacob and Laban?)* (B. 118, cat. no. 70).

102. This aura of melancholy is not without precedent, since tradition held that the Virgin had the gift of prophecy and thus knew the fate of her son, even at the moment of his birth. However, the Virgin in the etching of the *Virgin and Child in the Clouds* by Federico Barocci and prints based on it do not evince this same sense of sadness. For a fuller discussion of Rembrandt's sources, see the discussion in catalog entry 34.

103. RRP, *Corpus*, 146. The portrait is in the collection at Windsor Castle.

104. Although this print has been dated as late as the 1650s by some scholars, Erik Hinterding's research into the watermark history of surviving impressions of the etching make the 1642 date a virtual certainty. NHD 207 (Rembrandt).

105. For Rembrandt's other images of St. Jerome, see Scallen, "Rembrandt's Reformation of a Catholic Subject," 71–88.

106. According to Eugene F. Rice, Albrecht Dürer was the first to introduce the image of the skull into representations of St. Jerome in his study. Rice, *St. Jerome in the Renaissance* (Baltimore, MD: Johns Hopkins University Press, 1985), 111–12.

107. *The Three Trees* (B. 212) and *The Hog* (B. 157).

108. Christopher White, *Rembrandt as an Etcher: A Study of the Artist at Work*, 2nd ed. (New Haven, CT: Yale University Press, 1999), 50. White noted that contrary to conclusions of earlier historians, the effect was not likely to have been the result of an error on the part of an artist who had made close to 200 prints prior to 1645, but rather a calculated aesthetic decision.

109. In Rembrandt's etching of *Holy Family* from 1632 (B. 62, cat. no. 35), Joseph seems much more remote. In *Rest on the Flight into Egypt: A Night Piece* from 1644 (B. 57, cat. no. 32), Joseph is the watchful guardian of his wife and son, but it is not until *Rest on the Flight into Egypt: Lightly Etched* (B. 58, 1645, cat. no. 33) that Rembrandt conveys so eloquently a father's pleasure in contemplating his wife and son. White (*Rembrandt as an Etcher*, 51) suggested that the aura of contentment that is visible in the 1645 etching may be a reflection of the arrival of Geertje Dircx, a bugler's widow, who was hired as Titus's nursemaid and became Rembrandt's mistress. Geerjte's devotion to Titus is attested to by the fact that she made him one of her principal heirs in the will that she drew up in 1648 (Strauss and van der Meulen, *Rembrandt Documents*, 1648/2).

110. *Abraham Casting Out Hagar and Ishmael* (B. 30, 1637, cat. no. 4), *Abraham Caressing Isaac* (B. 33, 1637, cat. no 5), *Abraham and Isaac* (B. 34, 1645, cat. no. 6), *Abraham's Sacrifice* (B. 35, 1655, cat. no.7), and *Abraham Entertaining the Angels* (B. 29, 1656, cat. no. 3).

111. According to Petra Jeroense and Astrid Tümpel, this dialogue between Isaac and Abraham appears in medieval representations of the story of Abraham's sacrifice. Unfortunately, I was unable to locate a single example in a search of the online Princeton Index of Christian Art database. There are, however, a handful of depictions of Abraham and Isaac ascending the mountain that have been proposed as precedents for Rembrandt's print, e.g., Lucas van Leyden's woodcut (NHD, 187) and Georg Pencz's engraving from his series dedicated to the life of Abraham (HG 4). Jeroense and Tümpel, "Abraham and Isaac before the Sacrifice," in van der Coelen, *Patriarchs, Angels and Prophets*, 79. As Perlove and Silver (*Rembrandt's Faith*, 86) have observed, the image of Isaac carrying a bundle of wood up the mountain was represented in the *Biblia pauperum,* where it was typologically paired with Christ bearing the Cross. See *The Bible of the Poor* [Biblia Pauperum], *a Facsimile Edition of the British Library Blockbook C.9d.2*, trans. and commentary Albert C. Labriola and John W. Smeltz (Pittsburgh, PA: Duquesne University Press, 1990), plate .d. and 38, 80, and 123.

112. This shift was observed by Perlove and Silver. *Rembrandt's Faith*, 87–88, citing Julius Held, "Das gesprochene Wort bei Rembrandt," in *Neue Beiträge zur Rembrandt-Forschung*, ed. Otto von Simson and Jan Kelch (Berlin: Gebr. Mann, 1973), 111–25. Rembrandt had investigated a different aspect of the relationship between Abraham and his son about a decade earlier, in *Abraham Caressing Isaac* (cat. no. 5). Although this tender print may represent the prelude to Abraham's banishment of Hagar and Ishmael, the etching—like *Abraham and Isaac*—does not in itself depict a dramatic moment. Instead, it examines the loving relationship between a troubled elderly patriarch and his childishly gleeful son. The composition purposefully avoids any allusions to the miraculous nature of Isaac's conception (*Abraham Entertaining the Angels*) or the impending spiritual agony of Abraham's choices (*Abraham Casting Out Hagar and Ishmael*), in favor of a touchingly human moment.

113. Most prints sold for only a few stuivers. By comparison, each of the members of the militia portrayed in *The Nightwatch* paid 100 guilders for the privilege of appearing in the painting. There were 20 stuivers to the guilder. For representative prices of prints in the early seventeenth century, see Nadine Orenstein, *Hendrick Hondius and the Business of Prints in Seventeenth-Century Holland* (Rotterdam: Sound and Vision Interactive, 1996), 130–31, and Ilja M. Veldman, *Images for the Eye and Soul: Function and Meaning in Netherlandish Prints (1450–1650)* (Leiden: Primavera Pers, 2006), 272. For the cost of Rembrandt's prints in his own day, see Hinterding, *Rembrandt as an Etcher,* 1:59–65.

114. As an indication of the decline in his fortunes as a painter, there is no documentary evidence of portraits being made by Rembrandt in 1648 or 1649. According to Jan Jansz. Orlers, it was the artist's reputation as a portraitist that had established Rembrandt's career in Amsterdam, and these commissions would have been the artist's most reliable source of income. Strauss and van der Meulen, *The Rembrandt Documents,* doc. 1641/8.

115. It is not possible to document precisely when Hendrickje entered Rembrandt's household, but it was certainly before June 15, 1649, because she claimed to have witnessed an agreement between Rembrandt and Geertje Dircx, Titus's nurse and Rembrandt's paramour, on that date. Strauss and van der Meulen, *The Rembrandt Documents,* doc. 1649/4.

116. All of the court proceedings are available in Strauss and van der Meulen, *The Rembrandt Documents,* under the year 1649.

117. For the documents concerning Geertje's confinement and eventual release, see Strauss and van der Meulen, *The Rembrandt Documents,* docs. 1650/5, 1655/2, 1656/4, and 1656/5.

118. Hinterding, *Rembrandt as an Etcher,* 1:124.

119. Rembrandt had made ten prints in 1652, including four with religious themes: *Christ Disputing with the Doctors: A Sketch* (B. 65, cat. no. 38), *David in Prayer* (B. 41, cat. no. 16), *Agony in the Garden* (B. 75, cat. no. 49), and *Flight into Egypt: Altered from Seghers* (B. 56, cat. no. 31). In 1653, he made only two religious prints, *Christ Crucified between the Two Thieves: "The Three Crosses"* (B. 78, cat. no. 54), and the less experimental, more modest-sized print of *St. Jerome Reading in an Italian Landscape* (B. 104).

120. Paul Crenshaw, *Rembrandt's Bankruptcy* (New York: Cambridge University Press, 2006), 48–51. Rembrandt's troubles with his neighbor, Daniel Pinto, who rented storage space in the artist's cellar, are documented in Strauss and van der Meulen, *The Rembrandt Documents,* docs. 1653/9, 1654/3, and 1654/8.

121. The deterioration of Rembrandt's financial circumstances is thoroughly analyzed in Crenshaw, *Rembrandt's Bankruptcy.*

122. These loans are discussed in Crenshaw, *Rembrandt's Bankruptcy,* 51–56.

123. Rassieur, "Looking over Rembrandt's Shoulder," 54. Based on watermark dating, Erik Hinterding suggests the somewhat later date of 1656 for the sale of Rembrandt's plates to de Jonghe. Hinterding, *Rembrandt as an Etcher,* 1:143. None of the surviving impressions of these earlier prints is on paper used by Rembrandt after 1653.

124. Many historians have noted the absence of any etching plates in the 1656 inventory of the artist's possessions recorded prior to the *cessio bonorum,* or bankruptcy sale. Several theories have been offered for their absence, including the possibility of a prior sale of the plates, or even outright deception. It should be noted, however, that none of the tools of Rembrandt's trade as a painter and printmaker is mentioned in the inventory. It includes no brushes, easels, burins, plates, or presses. It seems possible that these objects were excluded from the bankruptcy proceedings because they were professional necessities, tools that the artist would need in order to earn a living in the future. Paul Crenshaw concurs with this suggestion (personal communication August 13, 2014).

125. On these series, see White, *Rembrandt as an Etcher,* 88–97; and Ernst van de Wetering, "Remarks on Rembrandt's Oil-Sketches for Etchings," in Hinterding, Luijten, and Royalton-Kisch, *Rembrandt the Printmaker,* 44–47.

126. On various Old Testament series, see Peter van Coelen, "Netherlandish Printmakers and the Old Testament," in van Coelen, *Patriarchs, Angels and Prophets,* 8–28.

127. Hinterding, *Rembrandt as an Etcher,* 1:134–35. It should be noted, however, that the manner in which Rembrandt manipulated the surface tone in printing *Entombment* (see discussion above) suggests that he intended to appeal to collectors of art prints, as well.

128. Luke 2:51.

129. According to Jewish Law, a boy assumes adult responsibilities at the age of thirteen.

130. On the meaning of the term "whore" in the seventeenth century and the nature of the punishment that Hendrickje received,

see Lotte van de Pol, *The Burgher and the Whore: Prostitution in Early Modern Amsterdam* (Oxford: Oxford University Press, 2011), 4–5, and 106.

131. Rembrandt's lifelong interest in young children is evident in his drawings. For examples of the artist's drawings of children, see the discussion in Martin Royalton-Kisch, *Drawings by Rembrandt and His Circle in the British Museum* (London: British Museum Press, 1992), cat. nos. 16, 17, and 60; and Seymour Slive, *Rembrandt Drawings* (Los Angeles: J. Paul Getty Museum, 2009), chapter 7. Rembrandt's engagement with family life may be a reflection of contemporary Dutch concerns about the education and well-being of their children. See Schama, *The Embarassment of Riches*, chapter 7, "In the Republic of Children."

132. See the entry for the illustrations in NHD 288.

133. Although the dating of some of these prints is uncertain, it is generally agreed that the etchings produced in 1657 include *Christ Preaching ("La petite Tombe")* (B. 67, cat. no. 41), *St. Francis beneath a Tree Praying* (B. 107), *Adoration of the Shepherds: A Night Piece* (B. 46, cat. no. 21), and *Christ and the Woman of Samaria: An Arched Print* (B. 70, cat. no. 45).

134. The dating of this print is somewhat problematic. White and Boon dated it to c. 1652, while Münz dated it later, to c. 1656, citing its similarity to the dated print of *Christ and the Woman of Samaria: An Arched Print*. More recently, Hinterding proposed a date of c. 1657, based on his examination of the watermarks on surviving impressions of the print (Hinterding, *Rembrandt as an Etcher*, 1:140–41). A large number of impressions of this etching were printed on Japanese paper, and hence cannot be dated by watermark.

135. See catalog entry 41, *Christ Preaching*, for a discussion of the possible symbolic meaning of this figure.

136. It is called "La tombisch plaaten" in the 1679 inventory of Rembrandt plates in the possession of Clement de Jonghe, and "la Tombisch printje" in Houbraken's short biography of painter and book and art dealer Pieter de la Tombe (1593–1674). Hinterding, *Rembrandt's Copperplates*, 15–16.

137. Hinterding, *Lugt Catalogue*, 141.

138. Rembrandt and Pieter de la Tombe were recorded as joint owners of the painting *The Samaritan Woman*, which was rather optimistically attributed to Giorgione in the 1656 bankruptcy inventory. However, as Crenshaw and others have observed (*Rembrandt's Bankruptcy*, 177n140), a petition was filed in 1658 on behalf of Jacob de la Tombe, who had died in 1656, for his portion of the proceeds from the sale of the painting. The implication is that Pieter's brother Jacob was also an owner (or the co-owner in lieu of his brother Pieter). The petition was granted, and Pieter de la Tombe collected the sum on behalf of his deceased brother (Strauss and van der Meulen, *The Rembrandt Documents*, docs. 1656/12, item no. 109, and 1658/26–28). This painting has been identified as one by Moretto da Brescia that is today in the Accademia Carrara, Bergamo.

139. See the comments in Münz, *Critical Catalogue*, 2:169, who doubts the connection of the Moretto painting and the Rembrandt print, but cites W. H. Valentiner's earlier association of the two; and Hinterding, *Lugt Catalogue*, 147–48, who sees some similarities.

140. In its first state, which is signed and dated 1657, *Christ and the Woman of Samaria* was printed from a plate that has almost the same dimensions as *Christ Preaching*, although in the case of the *Woman of Samaria*, the top two-fifths of the plate is left blank. The plates measure 20.5 × 16 cm and 15.5 × 20.7 cm respectively. Whether the correspondence in the size of the plates was simply a coincidence engendered by the materials that Rembrandt had available to him, or whether it occurred because the two plates were supplied to the artist by Nicolaes de la Tombe in conjunction with a two-part commission, cannot be determined.

141. It is not known why Rembrandt ceased to produce religious prints at the very end of his life, a time at which an aging artist might seem amenable to studying biblical texts for the comfort or promise they could provide. It is possible that there was a practical reason: the artist and his "employers," Hendrickje and Titus, may have sensed a decline in the market for this kind of subject matter. There is some evidence that this was the case. In Michael Montias's survey of categories of paintings in private inventories in Amsterdam, the percentage of works with Old and New Testament and other religious subjects declined from 24.9% in the period 1620–49 to 11.3 % in the period 1650–79. Montias, "Works of Art in Seventeenth-Century Amsterdam," table 2.

It appears that Rembrandt began to court a different kind of audience with his final etchings. In 1658, the year before he produced his final religious print, the artist made four etchings of the female nude (*Woman Sitting Half Dressed beside a Stove* [B. 197], *Woman at the Bath with a Hat beside Her* [B. 199], *Woman Bathing Her Feet at a Brook* [B. 200], and *Negress Lying Down* [B. 205]), a subject that he had depicted only three times before (*Naked Woman Seated on a*

Mound [B. 198], *Diana at the Bath* [B. 201], and *Jupiter and Antiope: The Smaller Plate* [B. 204] all three dated to c. 1631). He returned to this subject again in 1659, with *Jupiter and Antiope: The Larger Plate* (B. 203), and finally, in 1661, with *Woman with the Arrow* (B. 202), his penultimate print. This series of female nudes, otherwise unprecedented in the artist's oeuvre, certainly seems to signal a conscious shift in Rembrandt's intended audience from those drawn to biblical subjects toward collectors with more humanistic or voyeuristic tastes. For a discussion of Rembrandt's nudes, see Eric Jan Sluijter, *Rembrandt and the Female Nude* (Amsterdam: Amsterdam University Press, 2006) and Volker Manuth, "'As stark naked as one could possibly be painted . . .': The Reputation of the Nude Female Model in the Age of Rembrandt," in Julia Lloyd Williams, *Rembrandt's Women* (Munich: Prestel Verlag, 2001), 48–53.

142. See cat. no. 66 (*Peter and John Healing . . .*) for the millenarianist interpretation of the Jews. See also Shelley Perlove, "An Irenic Vision of Utopia: Rembrandt's 'Triumph of Mordecai' and the New Jerusalem," *Zeitschrift für Kunstgeschichte* 56, no. 1 (1993): 38–60, for a further discussion of the millennialist philosemitic movement and its reflection in Rembrandt's print of *The Triumph of Mordecai*.

143. Although Perlove and Silver (*Rembrandt's Faith*, passim) often try to use architectural markers to identify the particular spaces in which images such as *The Presentation of the Christ in the Temple* take place, Rembrandt's biblical settings tend to be more generic than specific.

144. On contemporary reconstructions of the Solomonic and Herodian Temples, see the catalog entry on the 1659 *Peter and John Healing the Cripple at the Gate of the Temple* (cat. no. 66) and *Presentation in the Temple with the Angel: Small Plate* (cat. no. 25). See also *Rembrandt's Faith*, 202–5, and 257–59.

CATALOG

1. *Self-Portrait in a Velvet Cap with Plume*

B. 20 (H. 156, Mz. 22, NHD 170)[1]
Etching
1638 (signed *Rembrandt f. 1638* in plate, but only "*R*" visible on the Snite Museum impression)
State III of IV
Sheet: 13.4 × 10.3 cm, trimmed to plate mark
On mat: *B 20 3/3; Self-portrait in a velvet cap*

Provenance:
International Art Associates Ltd., Park Forest, IL, 1972
Feddersen, Elkhart, IN, 1991
Snite Museum of Art
Acc. No.: 1991.025.001

Plate survives:
Private collection, USA

During the course of a career that spanned over forty years, Rembrandt produced more than seventy painted, drawn, and etched self-portraits,[2] by far the largest number created by any seventeenth-century artist. Throughout most of the nineteenth and twentieth centuries, these extraordinary images were interpreted as reflections of an unusually introspective artist's lifelong investigation of his own mental and spiritual state.[3] They were seen as marking out a journey of self-discovery from brash youth to successful middle age to weary and worldly wise senescence. More recently, the practical and theatrical nature of these images has also been recognized. Rembrandt's self-portraits now tend to be interpreted as "expression studies" or representations that were carefully crafted to appeal to a market of sophisticated amateurs and collectors, rather than as examples of an artist's self-examination and inner reflection.[4] In Rembrandt's time, there was a growing demand for portraits of famous individuals, especially artists,[5] and an image such as the Snite Museum's *Self-Portrait in a Velvet Cap with Plume* would certainly have appealed to this market. The print is a true tour de force, a rich illustration of the artist's skill at rendering etched lines in such a way as to depict and distinguish such textures as velvet, fur, hair, embroidery, feathers, and more.[6]

A number of examples of this self-portrait survive, suggesting that the original edition may have been fairly substantial.[7] Rembrandt signed and dated the plate (*Rembrandt f 1638*), but only a faint "R" from this original signature is visible in the upper left corner of the Snite Museum etching. The absence of the date and the artist's full signature implies that the Snite Museum's print, though of good quality, is probably a late impression.

The question of whether or not this etching was intended to be read primarily as a self-portrait or as an exotic character study or *tronie*[8] for which Rembrandt served as his own model remains open. However, the identity of the sitter in the etching has been acknowledged ever since the very first catalog of the artist's graphic work was published by Edme-François Gersaint in 1751, for the figure clearly bears Rembrandt's distinctive features: a broad face with a rounded jawline; a low, furrowed brow above intense, narrow eyes set close to the bridge of a fleshy nose; thin lips; and a short, spherical chin, which, along with a bit of jowl, can be discerned beneath the curls of his beard. The figure also sports Rembrandt's characteristic bushy mane of hair,[9] which in this case peeks out

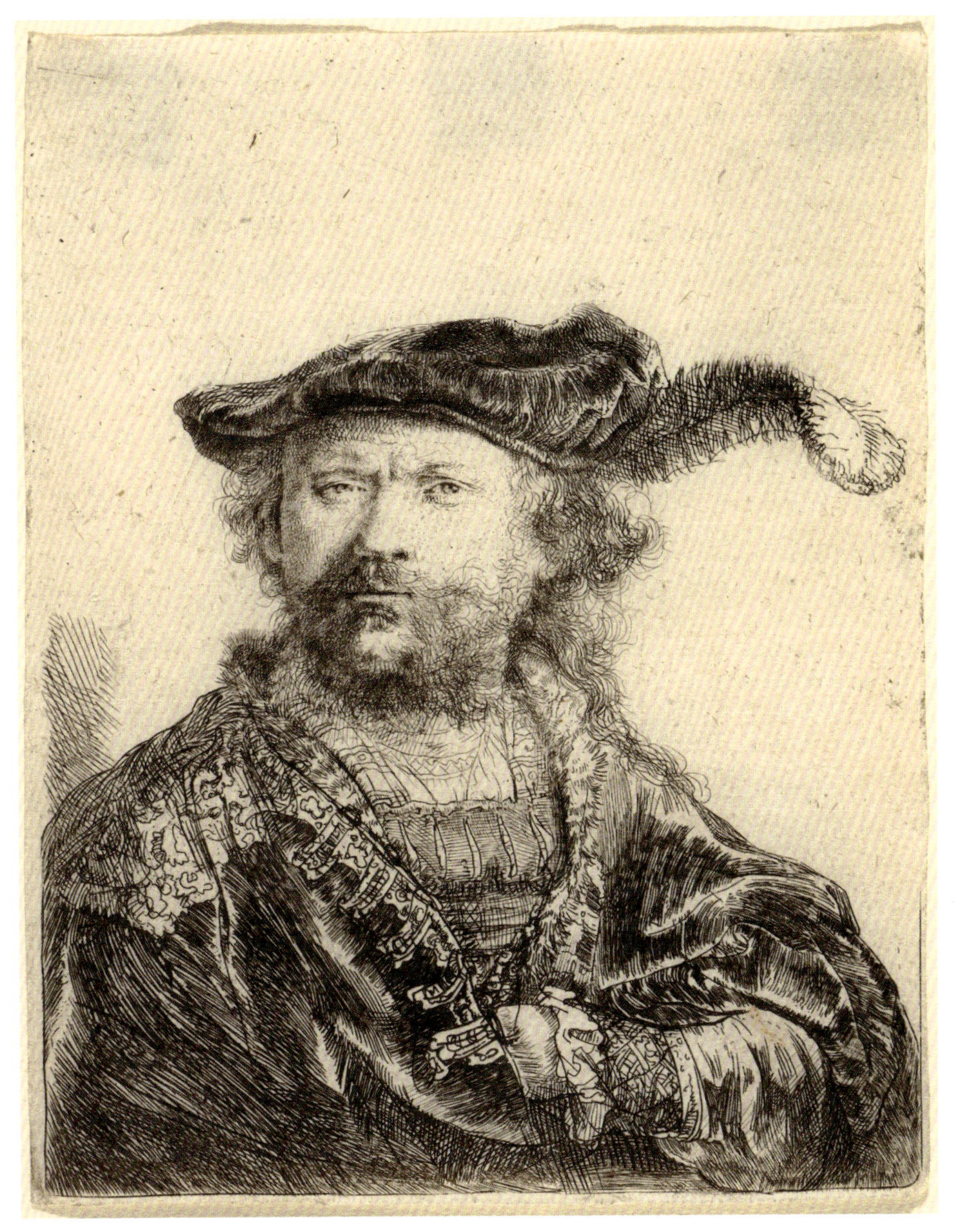

PLATE 1

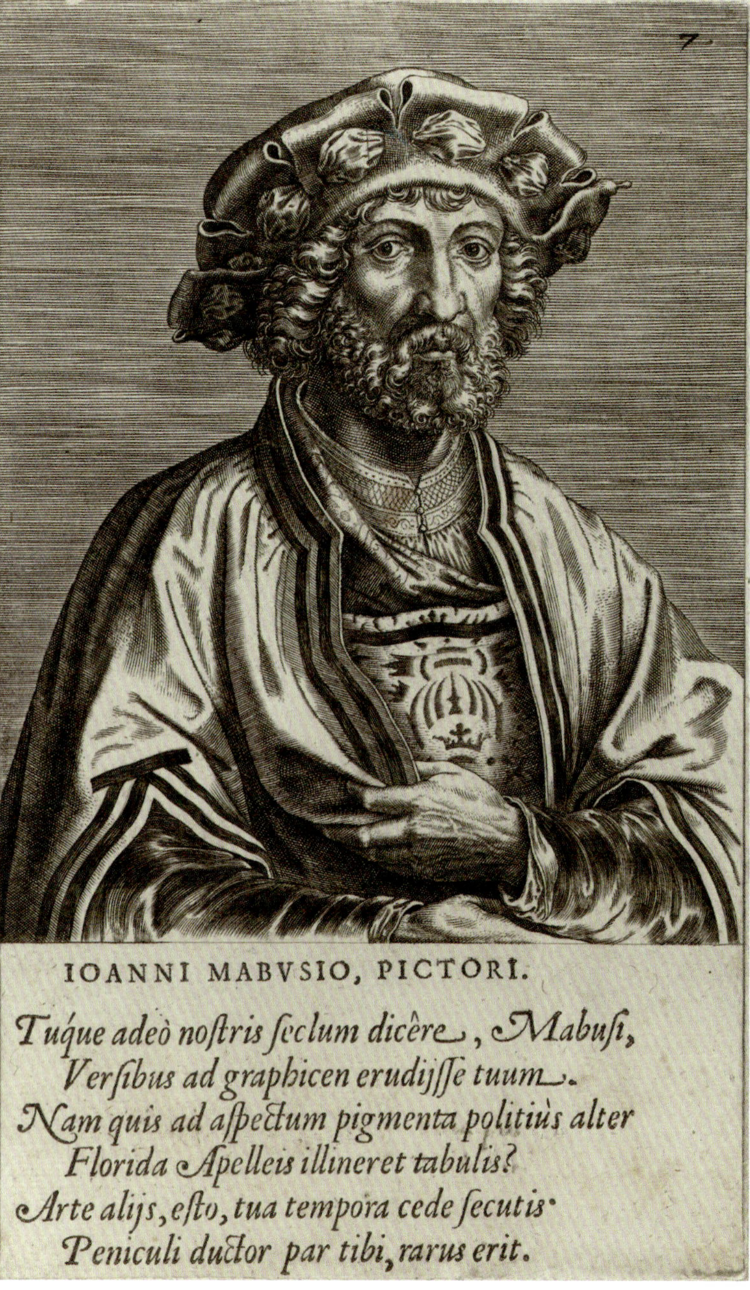

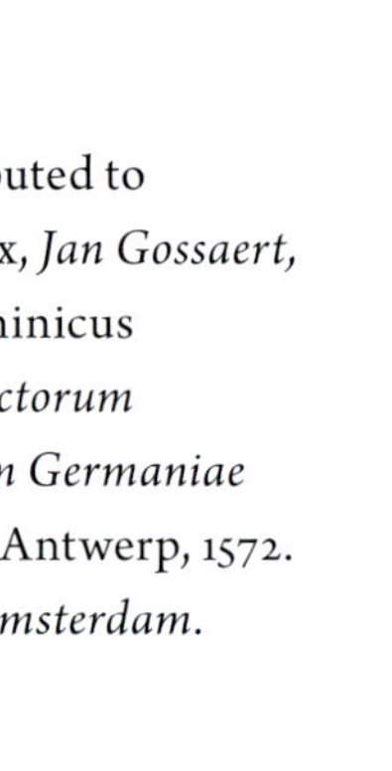

FIGURE 1. Attributed to Johannes Wierix, *Jan Gossaert, Mabuse,* in Dominicus Lampsonius, *Pictorum aliquot celebrium Germaniae inferiors effigies,* Antwerp, 1572. *Rijksmuseum, Amsterdam.*

from under a soft, flat, velvet cap adorned with a showy plume. One long lock of hair creates a *liefdelok,* or lovelock, which falls over the artist's left shoulder. According to Marieke de Winkel, this unusual hairstyle was cultivated by members of the aristocracy. Condemned by Calvinist preachers as an example of extravagant vanity, it rarely appeared in seventeenth-century Dutch male portraits except in those of "foreign officers and members of the international court of Frederik, Elector Palatine."[10] Although Rembrandt depicted himself with lovelocks in a few other, more youthful, self-portraits,[11] it is unlikely that he actually wore his hair in this fashion at the time of the 1638 etching. Instead, he probably added this fashionable detail, along with an uncharacteristically scraggly beard,[12] as a means of defining the character that he had chosen to portray.

Rembrandt's lavish and anachronistic costume also contributes to the artist's adopted persona. He wears a satin, fur-lined cloak edged with frogging and embellished with a decorative patch on the right shoulder. A few links of a heavy chain are just barely visible beside the left lapel of his mantle. Beneath his cloak, he wears a blouse with decorative stitching, a patterned scarf, and a jerkin ornamented with vertical slashing. The artist's body is turned at a slight angle to the picture plane, while his head is turned slightly in the opposite direction, even as his gaze directly engages the viewer. These contrasts help create a sense of alertness. Finally, Rembrandt's right arm is hidden beneath the folds of his garments, while his other arm is crossed over his body, with the left hand tucked beneath the right lapel of his cloak, folding in the fur edging of the cloak in the process.

Two earlier portraits have been proposed as possible sources for Rembrandt's decidedly old-fashioned costume.[13] Thomas Döring[14] suggested that the artist was inspired by an engraved portrait of the sixteenth-century Flemish painter Jan Gossaert (fig. 1). This image was published in 1572 in Dominicus Lampsonius's well-known late sixteenth-century collection of portraits of Northern Renaissance artists, *Portraits of Some Very Famous Flemish Painters.*[15] De Winkel, on the other hand, connected Rembrandt's self-portrait with an early seventeenth-century engraving by Hendrik Hondius, after a print by the sixteenth-century Flemish engraver and painter Lucas van Leyden. Lucas's print, which is dated 1519 (fig. 2), is a typical *memento mori* image depicting a young man wearing a cloak and plumed hat and holding a skull.[16] Hondius's engraving (fig. 3), which was published in the 1610 revision of Lampsonius's collection as a portrait of Lucas van Leyden, eliminates the plumes from the

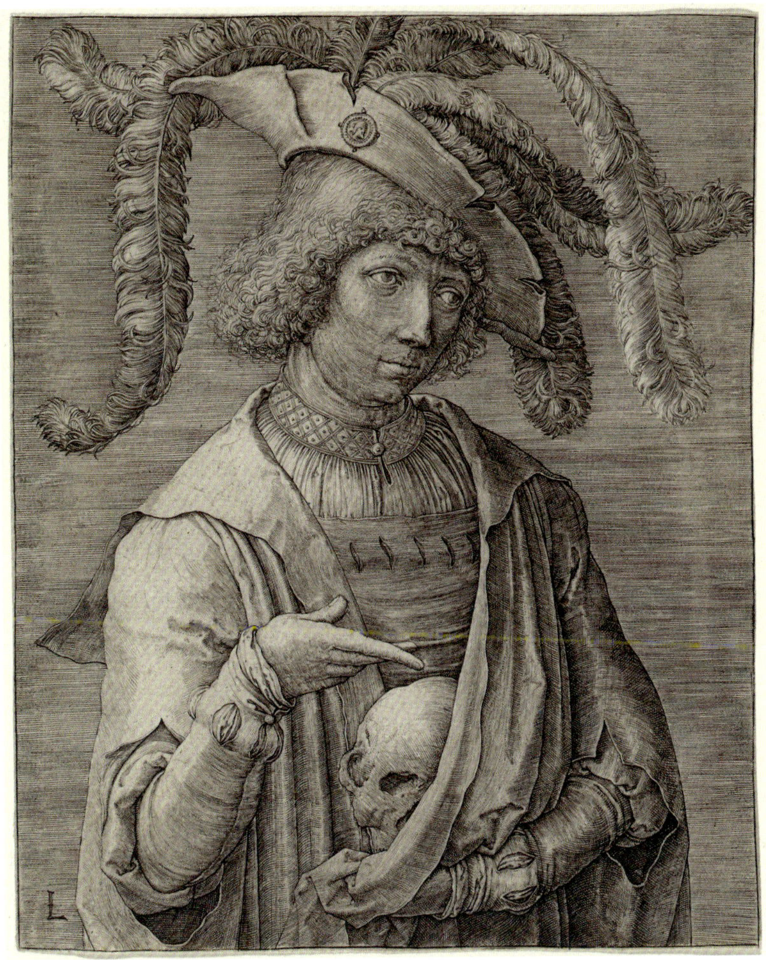

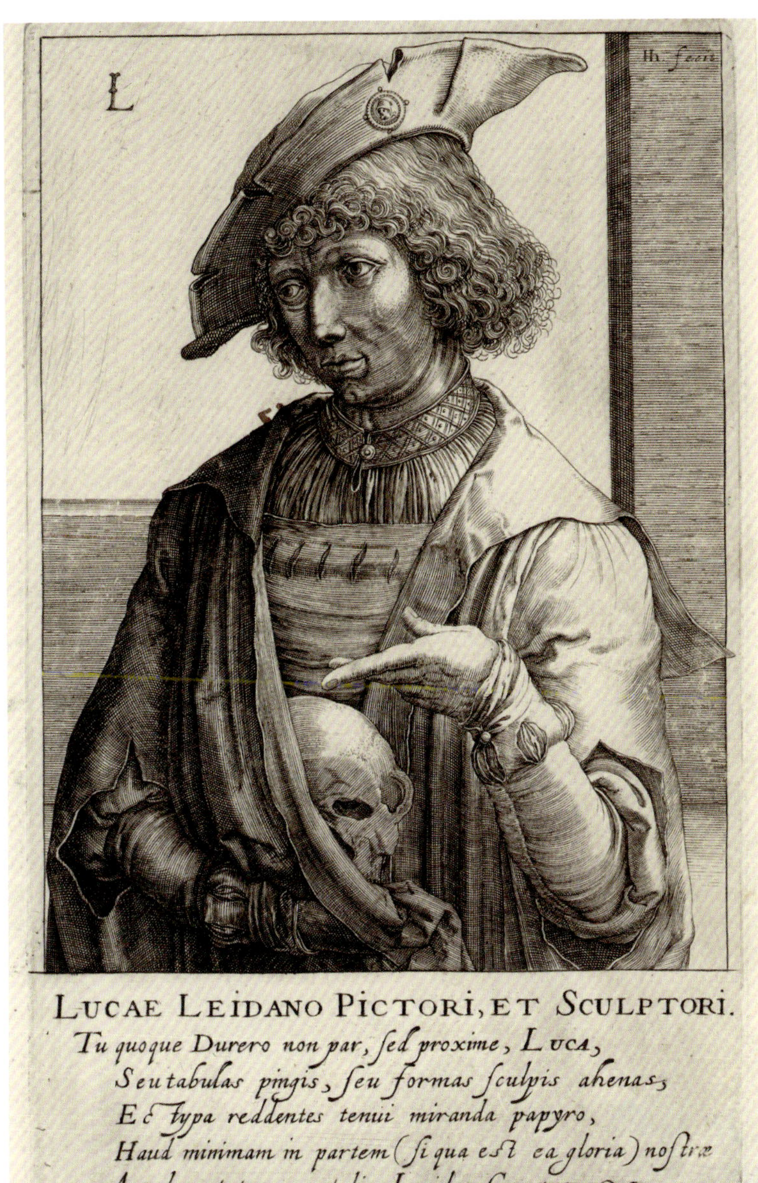

FIGURE 2. Lucas van Leyden, *Young Man with a Skull*, engraving, 1519. *Photo: Courtesy of the National Gallery of Art, Washington, DC.*

FIGURE 3. Hendrik Hondius, *Lucas van Leyden*, in Dominicus Lampsonius, *Pictorum aliquot celebrium Germaniae inferiors effigies*, Antwerp, 1610. *Rijksmuseum, Amsterdam.*

young man's hat, but otherwise duplicates the figure's appearance, including his voluminous cloak, slashed jerkin, and cross-stitching on the collar of his shirt. Although some elements of costume in the Rembrandt print can be associated with these sources, Stephanie Dickey proposed yet another interpretation of these anachronistic details, one that appears more likely. In her view, Rembrandt did not seek to identify himself with any specific sixteenth-century Northern work of art, but rather with the historical genre of artist portraiture in general.[17] Rembrandt's interest in the art of his predecessors is well documented. He bought prodigiously at auction, amassing a large collection of prints and other works on paper, which he then regularly mined for motifs and compositional ideas.[18] Nonetheless, Rembrandt's 1638 self-portrait appears to be a unique and sophisticated form of "metier" print in which he claimed his place in the historical tradition of artists such as Albrecht Dürer, Lucas van Leyden, and others, whose portraits celebrated Northern painters and printmakers.[19]

The Snite Museum etching offers additional insights into Rembrandt's ambitions and his times. The overall elegance of Rembrandt's costume, his courtly lovelocks, and the chain just barely

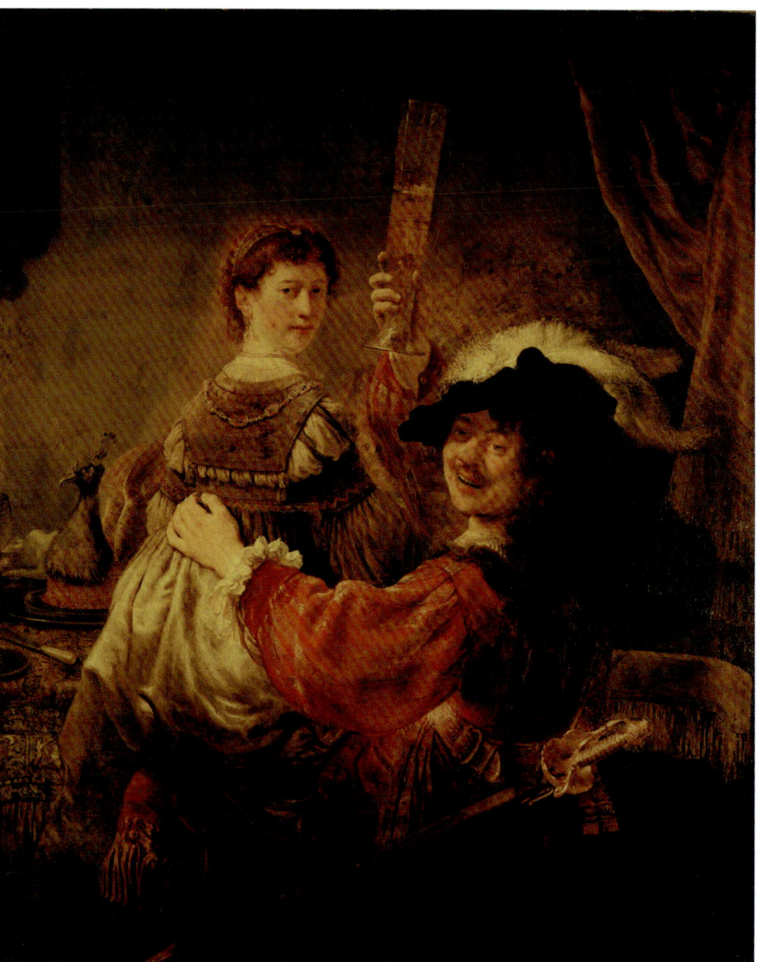

FIGURE 4. Rembrandt, *Self-Portrait with Saskia in the Guise of the Prodigal Son and the Harlot*, oil on canvas, c. 1635. *Gemäldegalerie Alte Meister, Staatliche Kunstsammlungen, Dresden. Photo: Erich Lessing/Art Resource, New York.*

visible beneath his cloak all invest the sitter with an aristocratic air. In addition, certain details of his costume and pose would have had specific connotations. Golden chains, for example, were awarded to artists in recognition of their virtue and *ingenium*, or creative talent. Titian, Rubens, and Anthony van Dyck all received gold chains from imperial or royal patrons, and all three artists painted self-portraits in which they depicted themselves wearing these signal badges of aristocratic honor.[20] Even though Rembrandt never received such an award, several of his self-portraits show him wearing a golden chain.[21] The self-portraits representing Rembrandt in this guise, including the Snite Museum etching, may be related to the artist's association with the House of Orange. During the period in which Rembrandt produced the 1638 etching, he was also completing the final two paintings in a Passion cycle that had been commissioned by Stadtholder Frederik Hendrik of Orange for the prince's gallery in The Hague. This series, begun in the early 1630s, proceeded in fits and starts until its completion in 1639. Although the final two paintings, *The Resurrection* and *The Entombment*, were the last commissions that Rembrandt would receive from the prince, it is not unreasonable to suggest, as Stephanie Dickey has, that, in 1638–39, the artist might well have harbored hopes of attaining some sort of more permanent, or at least continuing, relationship with the court.[22] Cutting an aristocratic figure in his self-portraits from the late thirties could have been Rembrandt's way of asserting his aspirations.

The plumed cap the artist wears has also prompted various interpretations. Perry Chapman and others have posited that although the beret was essentially a normal part of studio attire, it might also have been selected in order to suggest intellectual prowess, since professors and students at the University of Leiden also wore berets, as did philosophers in Rembrandt's paintings.[23] In this same vein, Hans-Joachim Raupp observed that the ostrich plume that adorns the figure's "bonnet" could have been a reference to poetry. In Cesare Ripa's well-known sixteenth-century iconographical handbook, *Iconologia*, a feathered hat was one of the attributes of *Capriccio*, or fantastic invention, and Samuel van Hoogstraten, one of Rembrandt's pupils, described a master artist's "Muse of poetical invention" as wearing plumes in her hair.[24] In this context, then, the artist's cap could have been an allusion to Rembrandt's creative powers.

A very different interpretation of the plumed beret can be derived from its inclusion in Rembrandt's painted self-portrait in the guise of the prodigal son, a few years earlier (c. 1635) (fig. 4).[25] In this work, the hat is clearly associated with intemperance. This same association has been made in regard to the artist's erotic print *The French Bed* (B. 186, 1641). In this etching, a feathered cap exactly like the one depicted in the Snite Museum etching is prominently displayed on the post of the eponymous bed in which a couple is energetically engaged in copulation. Eddy de Jongh suggested that the plumed beret's placement in this context was emblematic, and that it was based on a long tradition that associated caps and feathers with intemperate, amorous behavior.[26]

The fact that Rembrandt's left hand is tucked inside his cloak may also have had symbolic overtones.[27] According to Susan Koslow, the gesture of hiding one's hands in one's bosom was commonly interpreted in seventeenth-century Dutch art as a sign of sloth or idleness.[28] Such interpretations, however, are contingent on context and historical circumstances.[29] For example, artists were also known to employ the hidden-hand gesture to signify the phlegmatic or melancholic humors.[30] Even if the gesture in the Snite Museum's etching alludes to the sitter's idleness, Rembrandt and his contemporaries may have been putting a virtuous spin on what might otherwise have seemed a vice: Dickey suggested that the pose may imply abstention from manual labor in favor of the pursuit of leisure or *otium*, a state conducive to poetic inspiration and characteristic of the intelligentsia and of the aristocratic class to which Rembrandt may have aspired.[31]

Rembrandt's *Self-Portrait in a Velvet Cap with Plume*, then, is a multifaceted image, open to a variety of interpretations. As a *tronie*, or portrait-like exemplar, the figure decked out in an antique costume and posed in a somewhat provocative and unusual manner would have appealed to the contemporary taste for exotic character studies. As a self-portrait, the etching would have held additional connotations, identifying Rembrandt with the grand tradition of Northern painters/printmakers while also affirming his unique creative inventiveness and social aspirations.

Notes

1. This entry depends heavily on my earlier published discussion of this print. Charles M. Rosenberg, "A Rembrandt Self-Portrait and *Tronie*," in *Face to Face*, exh. cat. (Notre Dame, IN: Snite Museum of Art, 2003), 6–11.

2. Rembrandt's self-portraits include at least forty paintings and thirty-one etchings. Ernst van de Wetering, "The Multiple Functions of Rembrandt's Self Portraits," in *Rembrandt by Himself*, ed. Christopher White and Quentin Buvelot, exh. cat. (London, The Hague, and New Haven, CT: dist. by Yale University Press, 1999), 10.

3. Jakob Rosenberg, *Rembrandt: Life & Work* (London: Phaidon, 1964), 37, "[Rembrandt's self-portraits show] a gradual change from outward description and characterization to the most penetrating self-analysis and self-contemplation. . . . Rembrandt seems to have felt that he had to know himself if he wished to penetrate the problem of man's inner life." Cited in Van de Wetering, "Multiple Functions," 18.

H. Perry Chapman's *Rembrandt's Self-Portraits: A Study in Seventeenth-Century Identity* (Princeton, NJ: Princeton University Press, 1990) is a more recent discussion of this subject. Although Chapman is also interested in discerning some measure of self-revelation in Rembrandt self-portraits, she is generally more concerned with placing the images into a larger social and art historical context.

4. Rembrandt's very earliest etched self-portraits show the artist assuming exaggerated expressions, e.g., *Self-Portrait, Wide-eyed* (B. 320), *Self-Portrait with Angry Expression* (B. 10), and *Self-Portrait Smiling* (B. 316), all from 1630. These may have served the artist and, later, his pupils as visual references for depicting the emotional tenor of figures in their history paintings. This is probably not the case with works from the mid-1630s on. On Rembrandt's earliest self-portraits, see H. Perry Chapman, "Reclaiming the Inner Rembrandt: Passion and the Early Self-Portraits," in *The Passions in the Arts of the Early Modern Netherlands; De Hartstochten in de Kunst in de vroegmoderne Nederlanden,* edited by Stephanie S. Dickey and Herman Roodenburg, *Nederlands Kunsthistorisch Jaarboek* 60 (Zwolle, Netherlands: Waanders Uitgeverij, 2010), 233–61.

5. The interest in portraits of artists had already manifested itself in a number of different ways. In the sixteenth century, for example, Giorgio Vasari added woodcut portraits to the second edition of his collection of artists' biographies, *Le vite de' più eccellenti pittori, scultori, e architettori* (Florence: Giunti, 1568). In 1572, Hieronymus Cock's widow published her husband's collection of twenty-three portraits of famous Netherlandish painters, along with Latin epigrams written by Dominicus Lampsonius (*Pictorum aliquot celebrium Germaniae inferiors effigies*, Antwerp). Cock's portraits were reissued with embellishments in the early seventeenth century by Theodore Galle (*Illustrium quos Belgium habuit Pictorum effigies*, Antwerp, no date) and Hendrick Hondius (*Pictorum aliquot celebrium praecipuae Germaniae effigies*, The Hague: Officina Henrici Hondii, 1610). Probably the most ambitious example in the first half of the seventeenth century of an artist producing a collection

of portraits to be engraved was Anthony van Dyck's *Iconography*, a collection of eighty portrait engravings done after drawings by van Dyck. The collection included not only images of princes, statesmen, generals, and men of learning, but fifty-two portraits of artists and amateurs. In 1645, after the artist's death, Gilles Hendricx published these portraits in Antwerp under the title *Icones/ Principum/ Virorum Doctorum/ Pictorum Chalcagraphorum/ Statuariorum nec non Amattorum . . . /ab/ Antonio van Dyck Pictore ad vivum expressae.* On Vasari's second edition of *Le Vite*, see Patricia Rubin, *Giorgio Vasari: Art and History* (New Haven, CT: Yale University Press, 1995), chapter 5. On the various series published by Cock, Galle, and Hondius, see Sarah Meiers, "Portraits in Print: Hieronymus Cock, Dominicus Lampsonius, and 'Pictorum aliquot celebrium Germaniae inferioris effigies,'" *Zeitschrift für Kunstgeschichte* 69, no. 1 (2006): 1–16, with earlier bibliography. On van Dyck's *Iconography*, see Ger Luijten, "The *Iconography*: Van Dyck's Portraits in Print," in *Anthony van Dyck as a Printmaker,* ed. Carl Depauw and Ger Luijten (Antwerp: dist. by Rizzoli, 1999), 75–91, and Stephanie S. Dickey, "Van Dyck in Holland: The Iconography and Its Impact on Rembrandt and Jan Lievens," in *Van Dyck 1599–1999: Conjectures and Refutations,* ed. Hans Vlieghe (Turnhout, Belgium: Brepols, 2001), 289–302.

6. Although Rembrandt provided no backdrop for this figure, and the portrait doesn't manifest the kind of expressive contrasts of light and shadow characteristic of many of his dramatic works, he still took care to indicate how the light was falling by rendering the sitter's left cheek brighter than the right, using light crosshatching at the far left of the composition in order to indicate the figure's shadow, and manipulating the play of light and shadow across the various textures of the sitter's apparel.

7. NHD lists sixty examples of this print in public and private collections. Gordon W. Nowell-Usticke, *Rembrandt's Etchings: States and Values* (Narbeth, PA: Livingston Publishing, 1967), lists the print as fairly common (C1).

8. The word *tronie* literally means a head or a face. As a genre, *tronien* were portrait-like bust-length representations of imaginary figures that were often decked out in exotic or historical costumes and that embodied some particular quality such as piety or bellicosity, youth or old age. It was not at all unusual for an artist to base such a painting or print on a particular model, but the main content of the resulting image was not intended to be a portrait, merely portrait-like. On the nature of *tronien,* see Van de Wetering, "Multiple Functions," 21. The possibility that the etching might have been intended as a *tronie* of "a richly dressed, exotic figure from a past age" was suggested by Peter Schatborn in White and Buvelot, *Rembrandt by Himself,* cat. 49, 166.

9. Stephanie S. Dickey also noted that Rembrandt's bushy hair could be interpreted as a sign of the sitter's creativity: "Wild hair was an emblematic attribute of Pictura, signifying creative 'fire, fury and pride.'" *Rembrandt Portraits in Print* (Amsterdam: John Benjamins Publishing, 2004), 173n36.

10. Marieke de Winkel, "Costume in Rembrandt's Self-Portraits," in White and Buvelot, *Rembrandt by Himself,* 62. For the condemnation of this hairstyle by Calvinist preachers, see Simon Schama, *Rembrandt's Eyes* (New York: Alfred Knopf, 1999), 8.

11. See, for example, Rembrandt's painted self-portrait with a leather gorget in Nuremberg from about 1629, and the etched self-portrait with a soft, brimmed hat (B. 7, 1631), reproduced in White and Buvelot, *Rembrandt by Himself,* cat. 14a and 32.

12. In the etching *Self-Portrait Leaning on a Sill* (B. 21), done the following year, 1639, Rembrandt portrayed himself sporting a neatly trimmed van Dyck beard. In the Dresden Gemäldegalerie *Self Portrait with a Bittern,* also from 1639 (RRP, *Corpus,* A 133), Rembrandt wears only a mustache. White and Buvelot, *Rembrandt by Himself,* cat. 50.

13. In contemporary inventories, figures depicted in old-fashioned or historical garb were referred to as being *antycks* or *à l'antique.* De Winkel, "Costume," 67.

14. Thomas Döring, *Ansichten vom Ich. 100 ausgewählte Blatter der Sammlung Künstler sehen sich selbst. Graphische Selbstbildnisse des 20. Jahrhunderts* (Braunschweig, Germany: Herzog Anton-Ulrich Museum, 1997), 11–12, cited in White and Buvelot, *Rembrandt by Himself,* 74n49.

15. See note 5, above.

16. De Winkel, "Costume," 70. For a discussion of the Lucas van Leyden print, see Ellen S. Jacobowitz and Stephanie Loeb Stepanek, *The Prints of Lucas van Leyden and His Contemporaries* (Washington, DC: National Gallery of Art, 1983), cat. 73.

17. Stephanie Sowa Dickey, "Prints, Portraits and Patronage in Rembrandt's Work around 1640," PhD diss., New York University, 1994, 120–22. Dickey's observation was made in regard to Rembrandt's etched self-portrait of 1639, but it can clearly be applied with equal validity to the Snite Museum image of 1638. For a discussion of the portrait types that were used in Cock's 1572 publication and by

Hondius in his later revision, see Hans-Joachim Raupp, *Untersuchengen zu Künstlerbildnis und Künstlerdarstellung in den Niederlanden im 17. Jahrhundert* (Hildesheim, Germany: Olms, 1984), 18–30.

18. On Rembrandt's collecting habits, see Filippo Baldinucci, "Life of Rembrandt," from *Cominciamento, e progresso dell'arte dell'intagliare in Rame, colle vite di molti de' più eccellenti maestri della stessa professione* [The origins and progress of the art of engraving on copper, with the lives of many of the most excellent masters of this same profession] (Florence: Stamperia di P. Matini, 1686), in Joachim von Sandrart, Filippo Baldinucci, and Arnold Houbraken, *Lives of Rembrandt,* intro. Charles Ford (London: Pallas Athene, 2007), 44–45; Bob van den Boogert, ed., *Rembrandt's Treasures,* exh. cat. (Zwolle, Netherlands: Waanders, 1999); and Ger Luijten, "Rembrandt the Printmaker: The Shaping of an *Oeuvre,*" in Erik Hinterding, Ger Luijten, and Martin Royalton-Kisch, *Rembrandt the Printmaker,* exh. cat. (Chicago and London: Fitzroy Dearborn Publishers, 2000), 11–23; Paul Crenshaw, *Rembrandt's Bankruptcy* (New York: Cambridge University Press, 2006), chapter 5; and the essay by Julia Quinn and Charles Rosenberg, "Jack and Alfrieda Feddersen: Building a Collection," in this catalog.

19. This kind of allusion is exactly the sort of reference that the class of sophisticated collectors or "lovers of the art of painting" would have recognized and appreciated. These connoisseurs and collectors were expected to be familiar not only with the current art scene, but with the history of art, as well. They would presumably have been acquainted with the tradition of engraved historical portraits in general, and Cock's and Hondius's collections in particular. On the character of this collecting public, see Van de Wetering, "Multiple Functions," 22–23, and "The Miracle of Our Age: Rembrandt through the Eyes of His Contemporaries," in Albert Blankert, *Rembrandt: A Genius and His Impact,* exh. cat. (Melbourne: National Gallery of Victoria; Canberra: National Gallery of Australia; Zwolle, Netherlands: Waanders, 1997), 58–68.

20. On the significance of the chain, see Chapman, *Rembrandt's Self-Portraits,* 50–54.

21. See, for example, White and Buvelot, *Rembrandt by Himself,* cat. nos. 26, 35–37, 53, 57, and 59.

22. Dickey, "Prints," 113–14.

23. Chapman, *Rembrandt's Self-Portraits,* 49.

24. Raupp, *Untersuchengen,* 177. Although Ripa's *Iconologia* wasn't translated into Dutch until 1644, it is generally agreed that this iconographic handbook, first published in 1593, was known to artists throughout Europe by the early seventeenth century. Samuel van Hoogstraten's verse celebration of the arts, *Inlyding tot de hoge Schoole der Schilderkonst* [Introduction to the academy of painting], was published in 1678.

25. *Rembrandt and Saskia in the Scene of the Prodigal Son in the Tavern,* c. 1635 (RRP, *Corpus,* A111). Gemäldegalerie Alte Meister, Dresden.

26. Eddy de Jongh and Ger Luijten, *Mirror of Everyday Life: Genre Prints in the Netherlands 1550–1700,* trans. Michael Hoyle (Amsterdam: Rijksmuseum; Ghent: Snoeck-Ducaju & Zoon, 1997), 284: "Roemer Visscher speaks of men who 'triumphantly place Cupid's feathered hat on their lecherous heads.' He uses the word 'cap' as a synonym for amorousness and love, as did many other writers in the sixteenth and seventeenth centuries."

27. The hand tucked inside a cloak is a very uncharacteristic gesture for seventeenth-century Dutch portraits. Seymour Slive's catalogue raisonné of the paintings of Frans Hals, for example, provides very few examples of figures posed with their hands tucked into their clothing (Seymour Slive, *Frans Hals* [London: Phaidon, 1970–74]). There are only two painted portraits of Rembrandt by either the artist or his shop that depict him with his hand tucked into his waistcoat (White and Buvelot, *Rembrandt by Himself,* cat. nos. 56 and 57). In both the Cock and the Hondius portrait collections, the portrait of Lambert Lombard depicts the artist with his hand tucked into his cloak, but he is the only artist so pictured. The Cock and Hondius images are reproduced at http://www.courtauld.org.uk/netherlandishcanon/lampsonius/image-tombstone/21b.html (accessed January 6, 2014).

28. Susan Koslow, "Frans Hal's *Fisherboys*: Exemplars of Idleness," *Art Bulletin* 57, no. 3 (September 1975): 418–32.

29. On the contextual nature of gestures, see Keith Thomas, "Introduction," in Jan Bremmer and Herman Roodenburg, *A Cultural History of Gesture* (Ithaca, NY: Cornell University Press, 1992), 1–14. On the dangers of taking a dictionary approach to symbolic objects, in general, see E. H. Gombrich, "The Aims and Limits of Iconography," in *Symbolic Images* (Oxford: Clarendon Press, 1972), 1–22.

30. Koslow, "Frans Hals," 432, and White and Buvelot, *Rembrandt by Himself,* cat. 49, 166. By the end of the seventeenth century, the gesture had even come to stand for an admirably restrained and controlled temperament.

31. Dickey, "Prints," 118, and *Rembrandt Portraits in Print,* 94.

2. *Adam and Eve*

B. 28 (H 159, M. 177, NHD 168)
Etching
Signed and dated in the plate: *Rembrandt.F.1638*
State II of II
Sheet: 16.2 × 11.6 cm, trimmed to the plate mark
Verso: in graphite, *M. 193 / 26949 / B.28II / Stiglmeier / B. 28; 53; DFZ*

Provenance:
[Johann] Stiglmeier (19th century) (Lugt 2315)
J. A. Novak (1842–1918) (Lugt 1949)
Christie's, New York, NY, May 10, 1982, lot 64[1]
Feddersen, Elkhart, IN, 1991
Snite Museum of Art
Acc. No.: 1991.025.067

The plate does not survive.

Rembrandt's 1638 etching of *Adam and Eve* grew out of a long tradition of graphic representations of the Fall, works that included Albrecht Dürer's masterful engraving of 1504 (fig. 1), more than half a dozen early sixteenth-century engraved and woodcut examples by Lucas van Leyden,[2] and Marcantonio Raimondi's early sixteenth-century engraving after Raphael (fig. 2). It is likely that when Rembrandt decided to create his own *Adam and Eve*, he set out to create a print that would rival the works of these illustrious predecessors.[3]

Three preparatory drawings in pen and ink, one in Philadelphia (fig. 3)[4] and two on a sheet in Leiden (fig. 4),[5] focus on the relationship between Adam and Eve and elucidate the process by which Rembrandt developed his composition. In the Philadelphia sketch, which is presumably the earlier of the two sheets, Adam and Eve sit facing one another, with Eve seated slightly higher than her mate. She extends her right arm, offering Adam an apple, and he reacts rather forcefully, throwing up his hands in a gesture of shock or surprise as he gazes at the proffered fruit. The placement of Adam's legs is rather unusual. His right leg is bent at the knee and placed slightly closer to the picture plane than Eve's, on her left, while his left leg is thrown out straight beyond her, on her right, a pose that seems to be without precedent and that has obvious sexual overtones.[6] Lucas van Leyden's 1506 engraving (fig. 5) is generally accepted as the source of the two figures' positions, that is, seated and facing one another, albeit in a more innocent pose. In Lucas's print, Adam and Eve are separated by the Tree of the Knowledge of Good and Evil, with a simian-looking Satan perched on the branches above. Eve turns toward Adam, offering him an apple with her right hand, while she holds a second piece of fruit in her left. It is unclear whether she is showing this second apple to Adam, to the viewer, or to both. Adam's response is somewhat ambiguous; his hands are open and his upper torso is turned toward Eve, but his eyes glance furtively away, as if he is concerned about being discovered. His reaction to temptation is not as dramatic as it is in Rembrandt's Philadelphia drawing.

Rembrandt's two studies on the sheet in Leiden are closer to the final appearance of his 1638 etching. As in the Philadelphia sketch, Rembrandt concentrated on the interaction between Adam

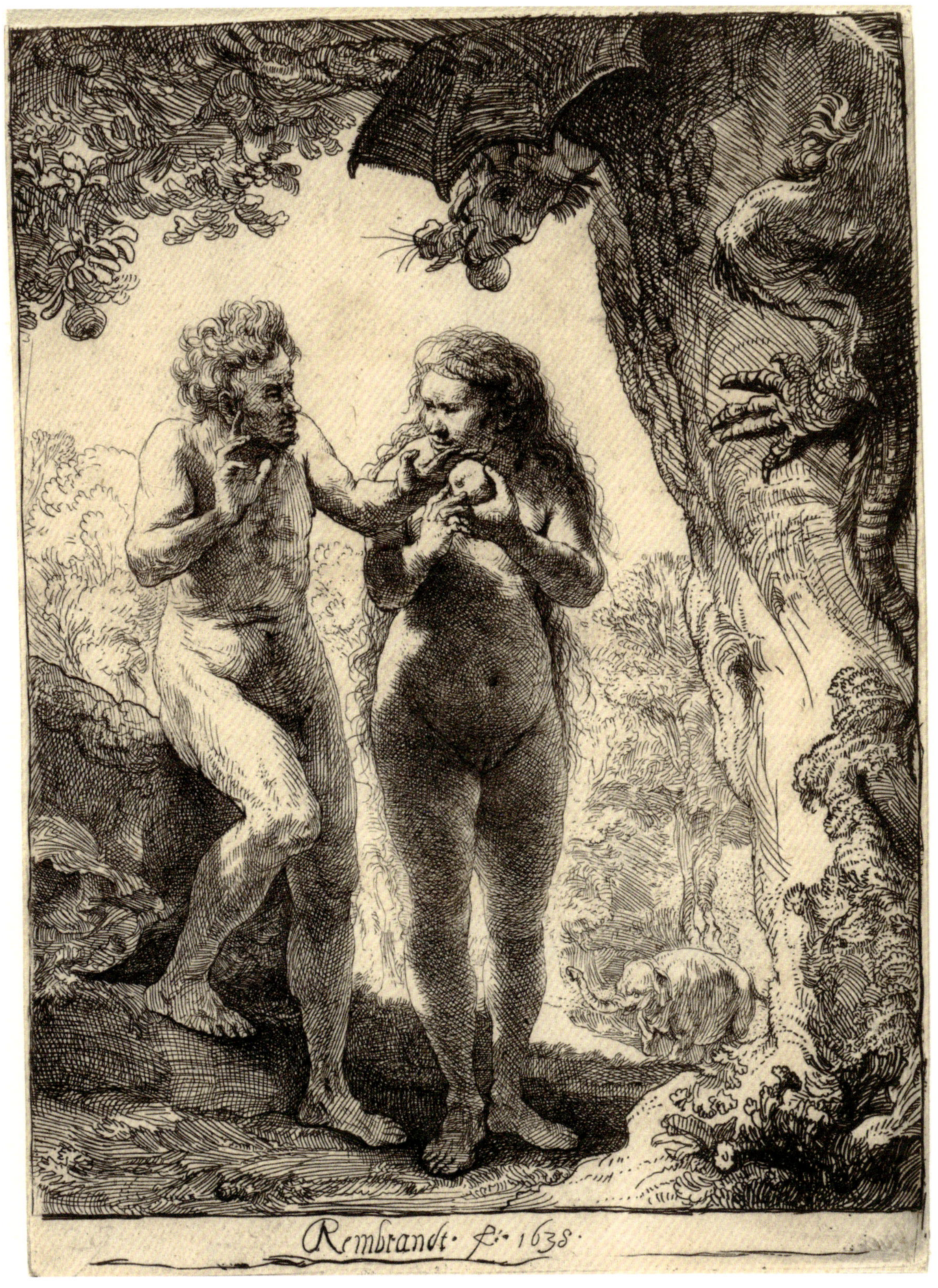

PLATE 2

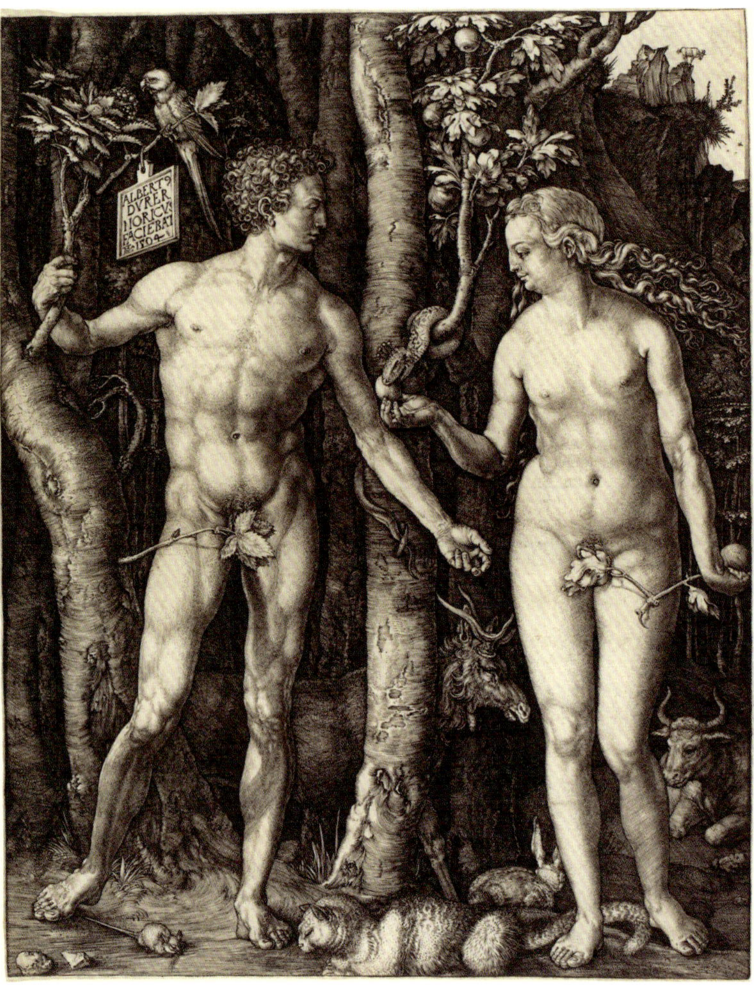

FIGURE 1. Albrecht Dürer, *Adam and Eve*, engraving, 1504. *Photo: Courtesy of the National Gallery of Art, Washington, DC.*

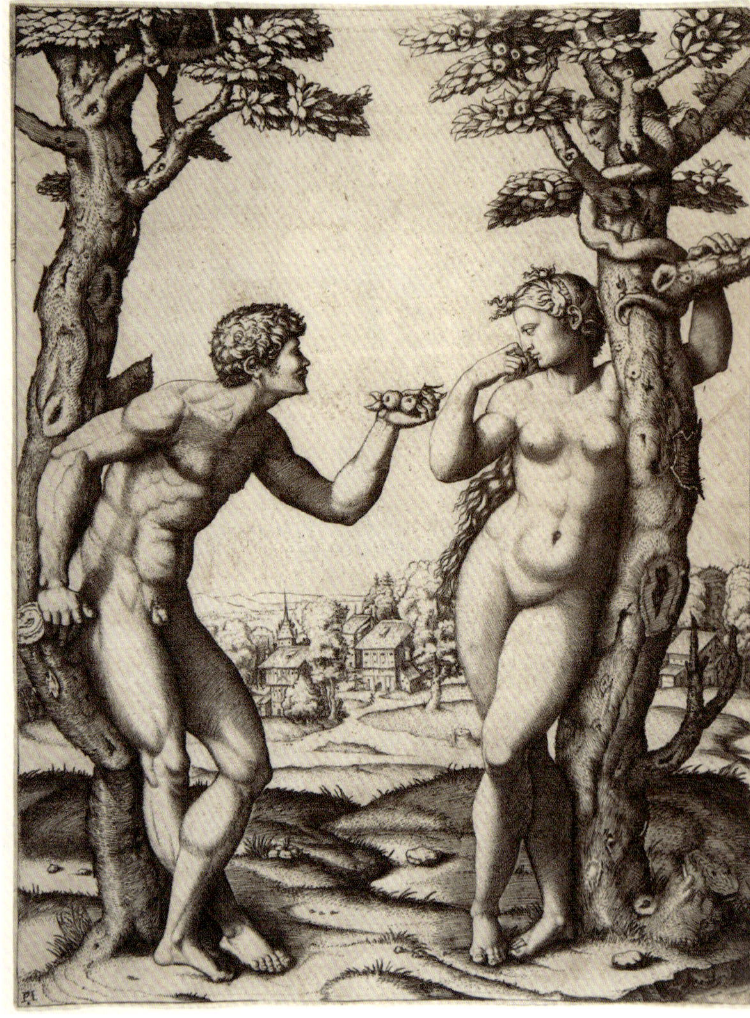

FIGURE 2. Marcantonio Raimondi after Raphael, *Adam and Eve*, engraving, c. 1510–20. *The Metropolitan Museum of Art, New York, New York, Joseph Pulitzer Bequest.*

and Eve, but both figures are now standing, rather than seated. In the sketch on the left side of the page, Eve is at her most aggressive and seductive. As she leans forward, she turns toward Adam, looking at him provocatively and offering him the forbidden fruit with her right hand, while reaching toward his genitals with her left. Here, the sexuality that was implied in the Philadelphia sketch has become explicit. Adam stands slightly higher than Eve, with his legs spread apart and his upper torso leaning back toward the right, away from the seductress, although his head is bent forward, toward Eve, or perhaps the apple. His gestures are difficult to read; he may be about to place his right hand on Eve's left arm, or he may be reaching for the fruit. His left hand is ambiguous, as well. He may be warding off Eve's advances, indicating his reluctance to participate in her transgression, or he may be reaching out hesitantly toward the apple. In the cursory sketch in the lower right corner of the Leiden sheet, Adam is depicted in essentially the same pose, but Eve's actions are noticeably less aggressive and provocative. In addition, her expression, as she looks toward Adam, seems more quizzical. Her arms are now folded in front of her, and Adam appears to be placing his right hand on top of her hands. In this sketch, Adam's gesture seems clearer. As he looks down into Eve's face, he holds up his left hand, palm forward, as if to reject her offering or to tell her to stop.

In Rembrandt's 1638 etching, the relationship of Adam and Eve recalls that of the quick sketch at the bottom of the Leiden sheet. Both figures are completely nude. As Adam approaches Eve, he appears to be moving down from a slight rise at the left side of the composition, with his right leg bent and his right foot resting on an earthen "step." His straight left leg is planted firmly on the ground, on the lower plane on which Eve stands. Although Adam is taller than Eve, his head is hunched forward as he turns toward her,[7] with the result that their eyes are nearly on the same level. Adam's face has a rustic, rather primitive, appearance. His upper torso, the front of which is cast into shadow, is turned toward the viewer, even as his head, capped by a crown of flame-like hair, is turned almost in full profile as he contemplates Eve. His expression is serious, perhaps concerned or questioning, and his lips are slightly parted, as if he were speaking. As in the preliminary sketches, Adam's forward right arm is bent and his hand is raised, palm forward, with his right index finger pointing upward, in a gesture that may indicate the presence of God. This can also be read as a rhetorical gesture alluding to Adam's admonition to Eve that she must heed God's warning and shun the fruit of the Tree.[8] Adam's left arm is extended so that his open hand hovers just beyond the fruit that Eve cups in her left hand, in front of her breasts. The nature of his gesture is ambiguous: Is Adam reaching for the apple, or is he trying to prevent Eve's fall from grace? Eve's right hand is poised in front of her, with two fingers resting on the apple, further focusing the viewer's attention on the dramatic center of the composition.

Although Eve's breasts are hidden by her hands and the dimpled fruit, there is no modesty about her pose. As she stands before the viewer, her toes pointing outward and her rounded abdomen, heavy hips, and genitalia fully exposed, she serves as the visual and psychological fulcrum of the composition at the critical moment in the story. Eve, who seems to be on the point of partaking of the forbidden fruit, casts a cunning glance at Adam as she attempts to involve him, too, in a conspiracy of disobedience. Although most of Eve's body is in shadow, her face and the forbidden fruit are brightly illuminated. As she turns her head to look at Adam, she reveals coarse features, small eyes, and fleshy lips turned upward at the corners in a sly smile. Her look is both calculating and piercing. The front of her hair

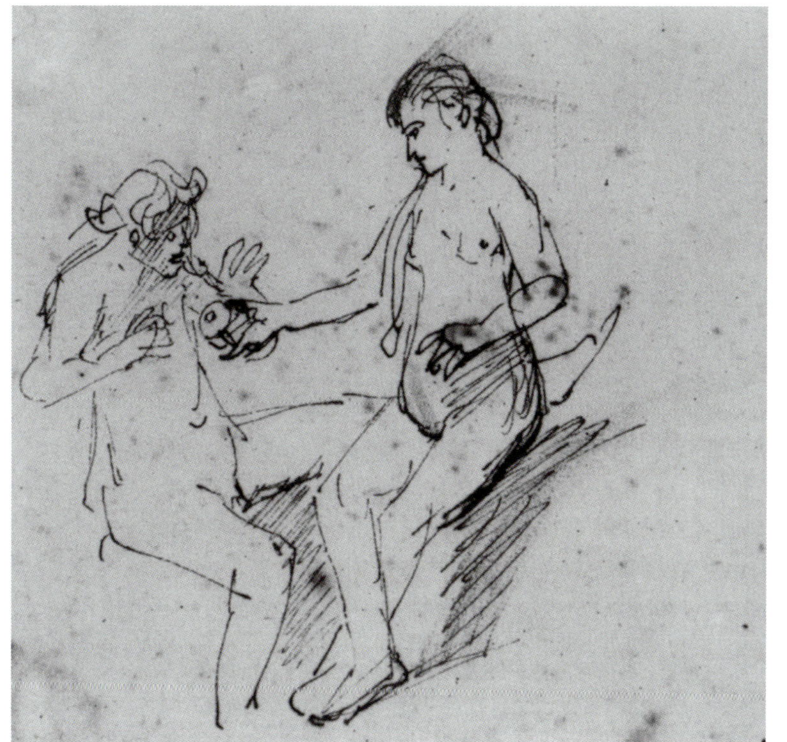

FIGURE 3. Attributed to Rembrandt, *Adam and Eve*, pen and ink, Ben. 163. *Formerly Felix Collection, Philadelphia, Pennsylvania. Photo © 1988 Christie's Images Limited.*

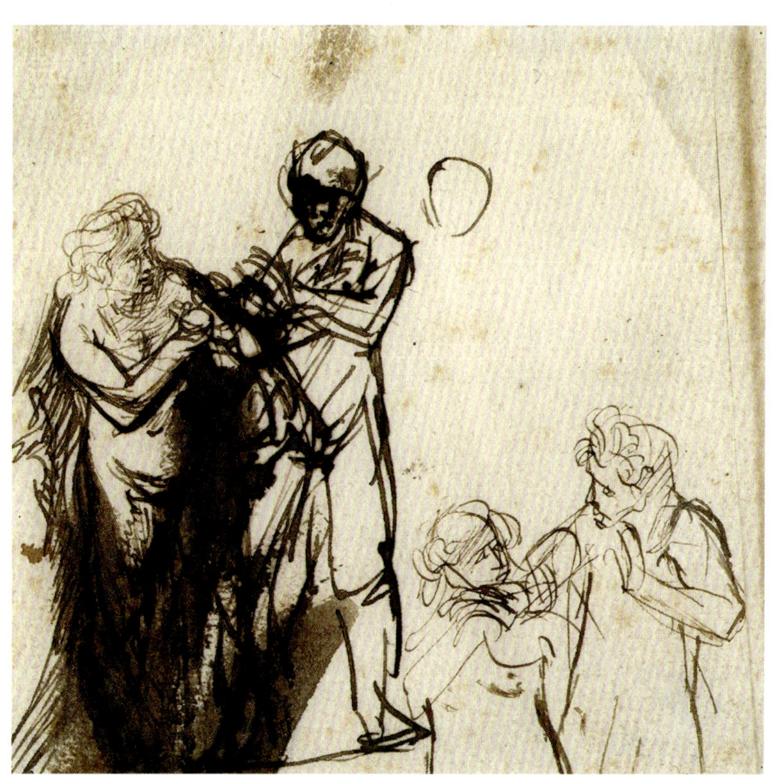

FIGURE 4. Rembrandt, *Adam and Eve*, pen and ink, Ben. 164. *Prentenkabinet der Rijksuniversiteit, Leiden, Inv. Nr. AW 1097.*

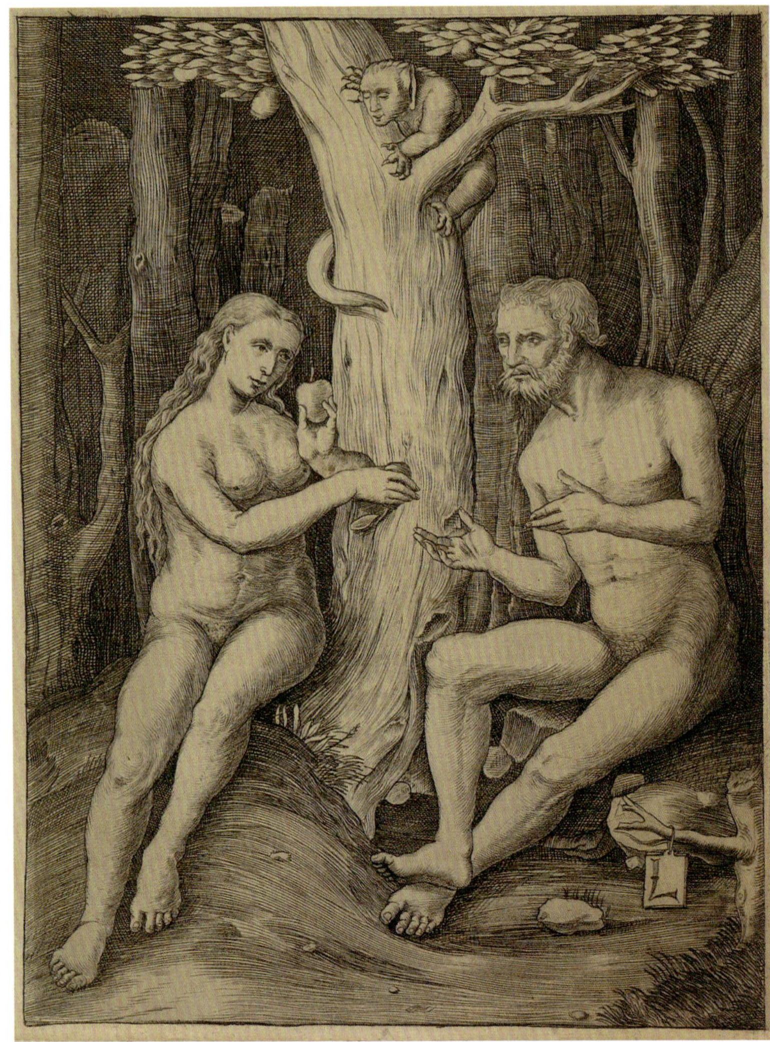

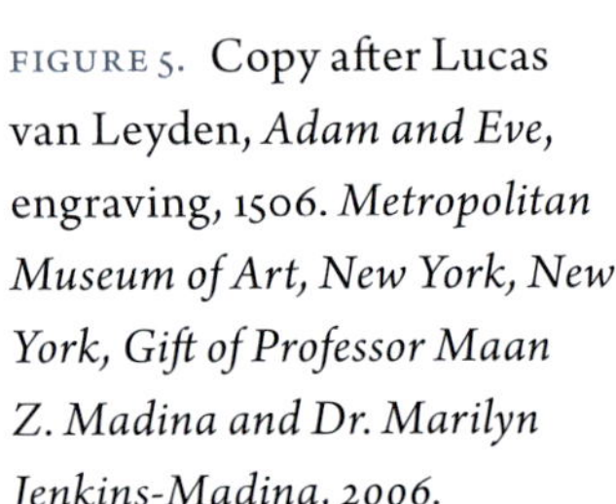

FIGURE 5. Copy after Lucas van Leyden, *Adam and Eve*, engraving, 1506. *Metropolitan Museum of Art, New York, New York, Gift of Professor Maan Z. Madina and Dr. Marilyn Jenkins-Madina, 2006.*

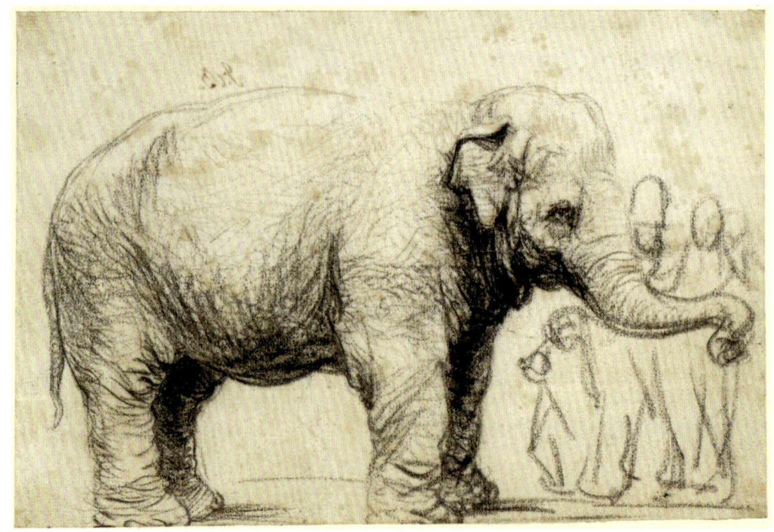

FIGURE 6. Rembrandt, *Elephant (Hansken)*, black chalk and charcoal, Ben. 459, c. 1637. *British Museum, London. Photo: © The Trustees of the British Museum/Art Resource, New York.*

is elaborately braided above her forehead, while the rest cascades loosely down her back, an odd combination of order and abandon.

A massive tree, presumably the Tree of the Knowledge of Good and Evil, closes off the composition on the right side. Its branches reach out to form an arch over the couple, while Satan, depicted as a grotesque, winged dragon, clings to its trunk. The demon glares down at the couple below, its horned snout, hanging jowls, and piercing eyes forming a malevolent mask of evil. The apple that hangs from his mouth alludes to his role in the Fall.

Adam and Eve, the tree, and the serpent are all placed on a relatively narrow, high shelf of land, close to the picture surface, which locates the action directly in front of the viewer. Beyond these figures, however, is a vista that stretches out below them, revealing a brightly lit image of the soon-to-be-lost Paradise. The most prominent element in this otherwise uninhabited distant landscape is a trumpeting elephant. Although this creature may have been included in the composition as a representative of all of God's innocent creatures in Paradise before the Fall, it seems an unusual choice, even for one of Rembrandt's exotic biblical scenes. However, Rembrandt may have had a personal reason for selecting this particular animal. The elephant's appearance in the etching followed Rembrandt's encounter with a touring elephant named "Hansken" a year earlier, an experience that clearly fascinated the artist, for he made four chalk sketches of the beast (fig. 6).[9]

Over the years, Rembrandt's etching has elicited a great deal of discussion. In the early eighteenth century, Arnold Houbraken was particularly critical of the artist's handling of Adam and Eve. He contrasted them with the idealized figures in Dürer's famous print, saying that they should be "depicted after the most consummate beauty," and that one should "not gape at and even less, follow, such a misshapen portrayal of Adam and Eve, as one finds in the prints of Rembrandt van Rijn; to his shame and to the praise of Dürer, it has to be said that the latter in the springtime of art, already early in the fifteenth century, published a more perfect print."[10]

Edme-François Gersaint was also critical of the artist's handling of the figures, stating that "because Rembrandt was not at all skillful in drawing the nude, this piece is rather inaccurate, and the heads are quite unpleasant."[11] By contrast, modern historians have read the earthiness of Rembrandt's figures not as reflecting a lack of skill or decorum, but as symbolic, suggesting that Adam's and Eve's imperfections reflect the ugliness of incipient sin or even their fate after the Fall, revealing their mortality, their animal nature, or both.[12] Unlike Dürer's and Marcantonio Raimondi's idealized figures, Rembrandt's Adam and Eve exhibit the gradual softening and sagging of flesh that is often attendant on aging, a process that prefigures Adam and Eve's fate.[13]

The moment represented in Rembrandt's print is rather ambiguous. It appears that Eve has not yet tasted the apple and that Adam may be trying to prevent her from doing so. Yet their poses, Eve's demeanor, and the maturity of their flesh indicate that their decline from innocence has already begun, especially since the Satanic dragon casts a shadow across her body. Perhaps in the artist's eye, the mere anticipation and acceptance of committing an act of disobedience has been sufficient to doom the two. While the unselfconsciousness of their stances and sexuality could be evidence of their continuing innocence, the sly expression on Eve's face is eloquent. She seems fully aware of what she is about to do.[14] This overall commingling of ambiguity, anticipation, and insight is very much in harmony with Rembrandt's interest in matters of human psychology.

Several authors have commented on the placement and appearance of Satan in the print. Most notably, Christian Tümpel suggested that the demonic dragon derives from Dürer's print of *The Harrowing of Hell* from the engraved *Passion* of 1512 (fig. 7). While Dürer's serpent does differ from the typical snake or snake-tailed creature depicted in images of the Garden of Eden, Rembrandt's dragon is much grander and more fanciful.[15] In *The Harrowing*, even as Dürer's Adam and Eve are threatened by a dragon-like demon perched atop the ruined archway that is the entrance into hell, Christ reaches down to help another damned soul rise up out of the depths. With that scenario in mind, Tümpel interpreted Rembrandt's variation on Dürer's dragon as more than simply an homage to the venerable printmaker. He has suggested that

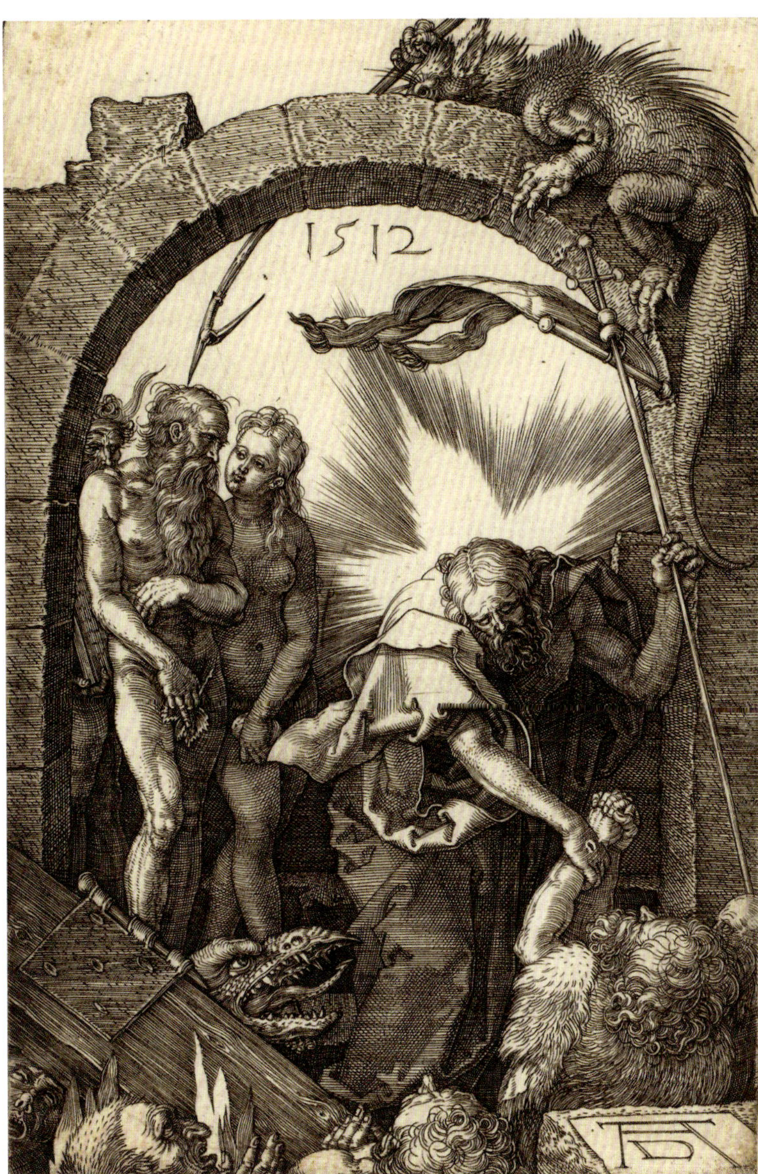

FIGURE 7. Albrecht Dürer, *The Harrowing of Hell*, engraving, 1512. *Photo: Courtesy of the National Gallery of Art, Washington, DC.*

Rembrandt included the reference in order to remind viewers of the earlier image's implication that redemption through Christ would follow the Fall, thus assuring mankind's salvation.[16] Shelley Perlove and Larry Silver connected Rembrandt's representation of Satan in the form of a dragon to a biblical passage, noting that in Revelation 12:9, the devil is referred to as "the great dragon," and philosopher, theologian, and poet Hugo Grotius used the same term in the Passion play that he produced in 1618.[17]

The trumpeting elephant in the background of this print has also garnered a fair degree of attention and provides another source of ambiguity in the etching, for it has been variously interpreted as signifying innocence and, conversely, the devil. Dürer included a number of different birds and animals in his engraving of Adam and Eve, creating a menagerie that, according to Erwin Panofsky, was symbolic of the four humors and, by extension, their perfect balance in mankind before the Fall. Rembrandt's elephant is also generally interpreted as having an emblematic purpose. Leonard Slatkes traced the popular lore associated with elephants back to Pliny and the so-called *Physiologus* and bestiary traditions of antiquity and the Middle Ages. In these sources, elephants were considered particularly chaste and virtuous creatures. For example, "the pair of Elephants is like to Adam and Eve. Adam and his wife, as long as they lived in the plenty of Paradise, were innocent of all carnal desire." Elephants were also seen as the natural enemy of snakes and, by extension, of dragons, malevolent creatures thought to lie in wait for elephants in order to ensnare them in their coils and suffocate them.[18] This struggle in the wild was interpreted as an allegory of satanic entrapment: "The Devil, who is the most enormous of all reptiles, is like this dragon. . . . He lies hidden round the paths on which [the foolish] saunter, because their way to heaven is encumbered by the knowledge of their sins, and he strangles them to death."[19] In this context, Rembrandt's inclusion of the elephant may be seen as a reference to the strength of virtue as a defense against sin.

A different interpretation of the elephant is that it is a wild beast that must be tamed, or restrained from sinning. Perlove and Silver noted that in the commentary on the Book of Job in the Dutch State Bible,[20] the behemoth to whom God refers in Job 40:10–18 is specifically identified as an elephant, "the chief piece of the ways of God." In the commentary, the docility of the elephant is described as a demonstration of God's power to tame savagery. Similarly, in a popular late sixteenth-century German biblical bestiary written by Hermann Frey, the elephant was likened to Satan being restrained by God. Finally, Perlove and Silver observed that Calvin specifically stated that Adam and Eve should have looked to the animals for instruction in the ways of God and that "only God can tame humankind's propensity for sin."[21] In light of these interpretations, Rembrandt's elephant could have had a number of different symbolic functions for contemporary viewers: as a symbol of virtue, as a harbinger of the imminent end of mankind's time in Paradise and the advent of Death, and as a reminder that God could tame not only animals, but also human beings, rescuing sinners from the snares of a reptilian or dragon-like Satan.[22]

Notes

1. Purchased on behalf of Jack Feddersen by Theodore B. Donson at Christie's New York sale of Old Master and modern prints, lot 64, on May 10, 1982.

2. NHD, engravings, 3 and 7–10; woodcuts, 175 and 181.

3. In February 1638, Rembrandt attended an auction of the estate of Gommer Spranger. The prints that Rembrandt purchased and saw at this sale may have inspired him to create the *Adam and Eve*. At the Spranger auction, the artist purchased a sizable number of woodcuts and engravings by both Albrecht Dürer and Lucas van Leyden. He also purchased a copy of a *Passion* by Dürer ("*d'passi van Alborduer f. 16:—:—*"). Given the high price that Rembrandt paid for the *Passion*, 16 guilders, it seems likely that it was Dürer's engraved *Passion* of 1512. The image of Satan as a dragon in Rembrandt's *Adam and Eve* has been linked to *The Harrowing of Hell* from this engraved *Passion*. See below for a discussion of this relationship.

Also sold at the Spranger auction was a single copy of Dürer's *Adam and Eve*. This engraving was purchased by Johannes de Renialme for 2 guilders 12 stuivers. ("*1 Adam ende Eva van Albord[uer] f 2:12:—*"). De Renialme was a merchant and art dealer who, according to Michael Montias, became one of Rembrandt's preferred dealers. Montias, *Art at Auction in 17th-Century Amsterdam* (Amsterdam: Amsterdam University Press, 2002), 137.

The information on the Spranger sale is from *The Montias Database of 17th Century Dutch Art Inventories* (accessed June 29, 2015, http://research.frick.org/montias/home.php). Rembrandt's purchase of the *Passion* is recorded as Montias inv. no. 305.0082. De Renialme's purchase of the *Adam and Eve* is recorded as Montias inv. no. 305.0067.

4. Ben. 163.

5. Ben. 164.

6. On the sexual implications of the so-called "slung leg motif," see Leo Steinberg, "Michelangelo's Florentine *Pietà:* The Missing Leg," *Art Bulletin* 50, no. 2 (1968): 343–53.

7. Adam's hunched position resembles that of the figure in the Philadelphia sketch.

8. Shelley Perlove and Larry Silver (*Rembrandt's Faith*, 72–73) have drawn attention to the fact that Adam's finger is also near his ear, highlighting the faculty of hearing and the need to recall God's spoken admonition.

9. Ben. 457–60. This "hardy beast" toured Europe for over twenty years during the second quarter of the seventeenth century and was apparently on display in the Netherlands as early as 1630. Leonard Slatkes, "Rembrandt's Elephant," *Simiolus: Netherlands Quarterly for the History of Art* 11, no. 1 (1980):7.

Somewhat earlier, in 1611, in an engraved profile view of Amsterdam by Claes Jansz. Visscher (HD 125) and Herman Allertsz. Coster depicted an elephant as one of a number of objects brought from Dutch Guinea to Amsterdam. This may indicate that there was a more widespread familiarity with this exotic creature. Boudewijn Bakker and Erik Schmitz, *Het aanzien van Amsterdam* (Amsterdam: Thoth, 2007), plate I.

10. Quoted in Eric Jan Sluijter, *Rembrandt and the Female Nude* (Amsterdam: Amsterdam University Press, 2006), 291.

11. Edme-François Gersaint, *Catalogue raisonné* (Paris: Chez Hochereau, 1751), cat. 34, 22: "Comme Rembrandt n'était point habile à dessiner le nu, ce morceau est assez incorrect, et les têtes sont tout-à-fait désagréables."

12. See, for example, *Rembrandt's Journey*, 164–65: "Rembrandt's pair are more primitive and earthy [than Dürer's]. Past the first flush of youth, they are distinctly naked and dominated by the pull of gravity. Their vulnerable physical appearance . . . seems already to reflect the consequences of the transgressions they are in the very act of committing." Shelly Perlove and Larry Silver linked the flawed appearance of the bodies to Calvinist comments on the fate of mankind. In particular, they noted the distinction between the human and spiritual bodies that is made in the gloss on 1 Corinthians 5:45 in the Dutch State Bible: "Humankind received from the first Adam a natural or animal body, so also by the second Adam, namely Christ, we shall obtain a spiritual body." They conclude that "Rembrandt may have intended to portray the miserable, corrupted bodies of the first human beings in their 'animal condition.'" *Rembrandt's Faith*, 75. Eric Jan Sluijter suggested that their imperfect bodies could "be understood as eulogizing God's Creation" illustrating the diversity of the world. Sluijter, *Rembrandt and the Female Nude*, 292.

13. In contrast to the critical evaluation of Rembrandt's Eve, Christopher White likened her to the artist's drawing of the beautiful Cleopatra in the Getty Collection (Ben. 137). As Peter Krüger noted, these female nudes actually represent the emergence of a new, more classical and sensuous female type for Rembrandt. Christopher White, *Rembrandt as an Etcher: A Study of the Artist at Work*, 2nd ed. (New Haven, CT: Yale University Press, 1999), 198–99; and Peter Krüger, "'Adam und Eva'—Radierung. Eine Aemulatio mit Dürer," *Jahrbuch der Berliner Museen*, N.F. 35 (1993): 217.

14. Sluijter noted that in the seventeenth century, female genitals were exposed only in prints that were intended to be pornographic. He suggested that their display would have emphasized Eve's role as the seductress "because of the then current notion—stemming from antiquity—of the female genitals as insatiably hungry for the male seed." Sluijter, *Rembrandt and the Female Nude*, 289.

15. Although representations of the serpent as a winged dragon with feet are unusual, there is medieval precedent for this typology. Henry Ansgar Kelly, "The Metamorphoses of the Eden Serpent during the Middle Ages and Renaissance," *Viator* 2 (1971): 306.

16. Tümpel, *Rembrandt legt*, cat. 1.

17. *Rembrandt's Faith*, 70–71.

18. Slatkes, "Rembrandt's Elephant," 12.

19. Ibid., 13.

20. The *Staatenbijbel*, or State Bible, is the Dutch translation of the Bible first ordered by the government of the Dutch Republic in 1637, the year before Rembrandt's etching of Adam and Eve was completed.

21. *Rembrandt's Faith*, 73–74.

22. Shelley Perlove summarizes her interpretation of the print thus: "The message implicit in Rembrandt's print is that only God, who tames the wild elephant, can curb Adam and Eve's enslavement to sin and transform their 'weak' and 'dishonored' flesh into a spiritual body of 'power' and 'glory.'" "The Ferocious Dragon and the Docile Elephant: The Unleashing of Sin in Rembrandt's *Garden of Eden*," in *Religion, the Supernatural and Visual Culture in Early Modern Europe*, ed. Jennifer Spinks and Dagmar Eichberger (Leiden: Brill, 2015), 299.

3. *Abraham Entertaining the Angels*

B. 29 (H. 286, Mz. 185, NHD 295)
Etching and drypoint
Signed and dated in the plate: *Rembrandt f. 1656*
State I of I
Sheet: 16.5 × 13.6 cm, plate mark 15.9 × 13.1 cm
Verso: upper left corner, stamp in ink, *G.B.* in a circle (Lugt 1138c, George Biörklund); upper right corner in graphite, *Duvat* (?); lower left corner in graphite, *71.80*; center bottom in graphite, *c30280/ B29 only state/ H286 only state.*

Provenance:
George Biörklund (1887–after 1968)[1]
David Tunick Inc., New York, NY, 1975
Feddersen, Elkhart, IN, 1991
Snite Museum of Art
Acc. No.: 1991.025.002

Plate survives:
National Gallery, Washington, DC (inv. 1997.85.1.a), with a landscape attributed to Flemish painter Peeter Gysels on its reverse.

In Genesis 18:1–15, the Jewish patriarch Abraham receives a visit from three mysterious strangers who are eventually revealed to be God and two of his angels. The story of this encounter was a popular subject for artists,[2] and there were already numerous depictions of Abraham Entertaining the Angels before Rembrandt created his own etched version in 1656.[3] As recounted in Genesis, the three visitors appeared one day while Abraham was seated outside his tent near a grove of terebinth trees in Mamre. Abraham went to meet the men, bowed before them, and invited them to sit in the shade of a tree and share his hospitality. Once the strangers had settled themselves, Abraham went into his tent and told his wife, Sarah, to make cakes to serve to them. He took a calf from his herd and had it prepared for his guests, along with butter and milk. After the visitors had finished their meal, one of them inquired about Sarah, who was still in the tent. He then informed Abraham that the patriarch and his barren, aged wife were going to have a son. Sarah, who was ninety years old at the time, laughed at the prospect. When the speaker, whom the Bible reveals was God, asked Sarah why she had laughed, she became frightened and denied that she had done so. After this exchange, the three visitors rose and, accompanied by Abraham, went to look out over the city of Sodom. In Genesis 19, it is revealed that the two strangers accompanying God were angels.

In Rembrandt's interpretation of the story, the physical setting of the narrative diverges from the biblical account. Instead of sitting under a tree near Abraham's tent, the men gather together on a raised terrace in front of the door to Abraham's house, a substantial stone building with a rose vine climbing up it.[4] Although a grove of trees is visible in the distance, the terebinth trees mentioned in the Bible and prominently depicted in earlier representations are absent. Sarah has an enigmatic expression as she stands listening in the shadowy interior of the house, partly hidden by the door, which is ajar. Abraham, looking old and weary, is at the right, standing below the terrace where his guests are kneeling or sitting cross-legged on a fringed carpet. His head bowed, he bends slightly

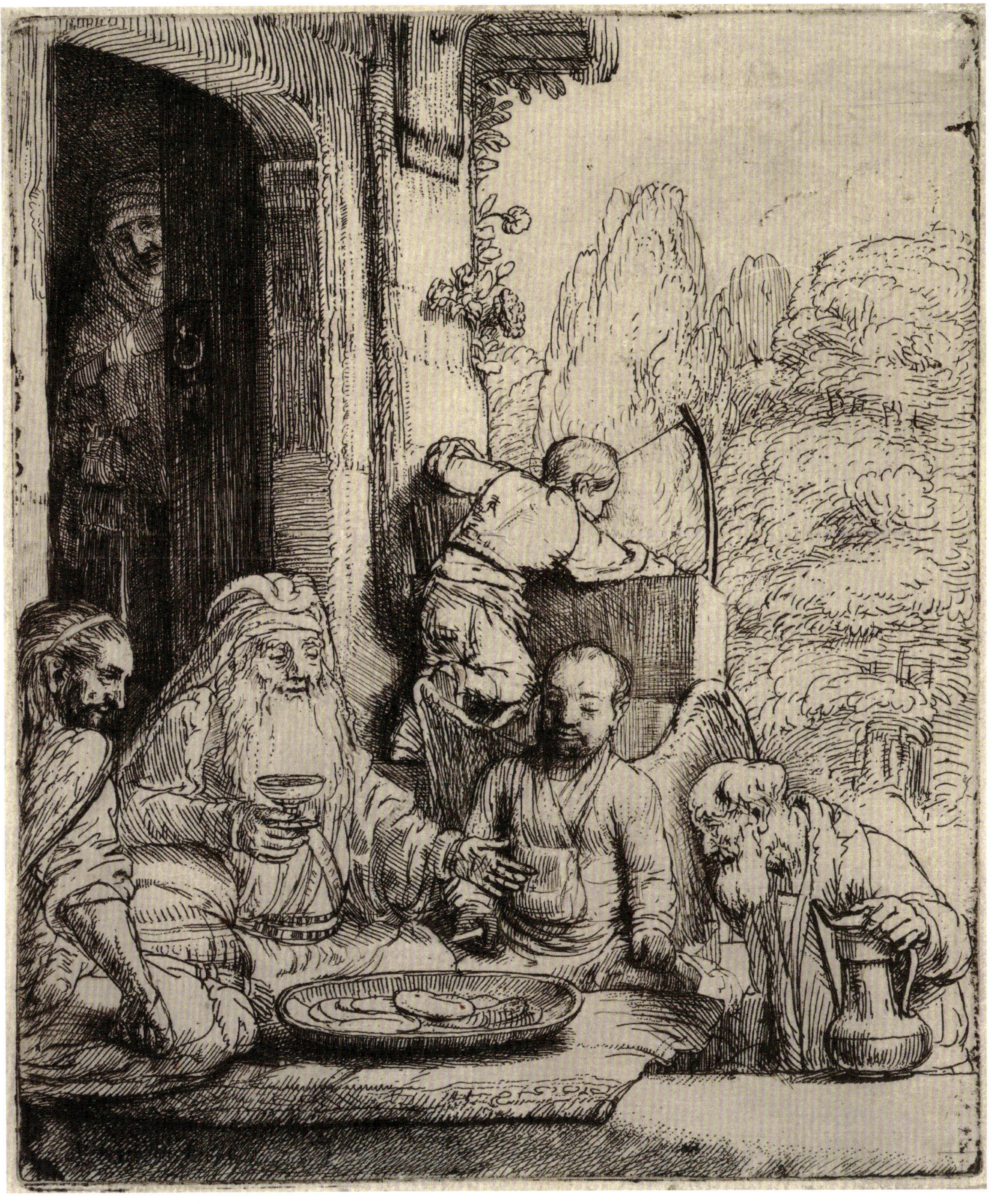

PLATE 3

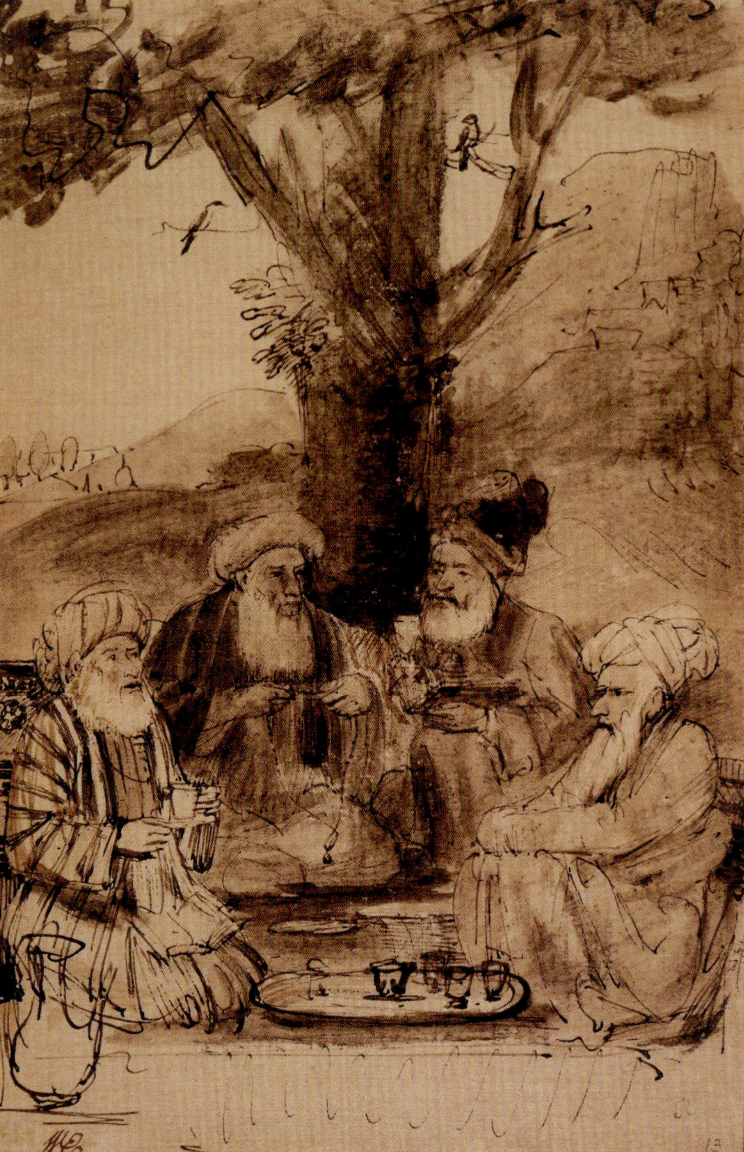

FIGURE 1. Rembrandt, *Four Orientals Seated beneath a Tree*, pen and brown ink with brown and gray wash, c. 1654–56, Ben. 1187. *British Museum, London. Photo: © Trustees of the British Museum/ Art Resource, New York.*

forward, in a pose that suggests deference and a readiness to serve. He grips a large ewer in his left hand, ready to refill the cup that the guest at the center holds out before him. A simple repast of flat round cakes has been set out on a large platter in front of the strangers.

The physiognomy of each of the guests is distinctive. The slender, muscular figure at the left has short, sparrow-like wings folded over his shoulders. He has Semitic features and a dark, close-cropped beard. His long hair, which hangs down his back, is held back away from his face by a fillet.[5] The visitor at the center of the group, commonly identified as God,[6] is clearly the focal point of the scene by virtue of his size, dress, and gesture, as well as the light that illuminates his headdress, face, and long white beard. He is noticeably larger and older than his companions. He is also the only man whose head is covered. The cloth of his headdress is gathered on top of his head and hangs down his back. He holds a cup in his right hand and gestures toward Abraham with his left, as he addresses him. The third visitor is clearly identified as an angel by the large, open wings spread out behind him. He is more compact than his fellow angel, and his balding head, Asian features, and small beard distinguish him from the others.

One final figure appears in the print: a young boy with his back to the men and his face in partial profile to the viewer leans over a stone parapet and aims his bow down toward the valley below. This is clearly meant to be Abraham's eldest son, Ishmael, born to Sarah's handmaiden Hagar and identified in the Bible as an archer.[7] There seems to be no precedent for Ishmael's inclusion in the scene.

It has long been recognized that Rembrandt's composition was inspired by a Mughal [Indian] miniature depicting four oriental dignitaries seated in the shade of a tree, drinking tea.[8] Around 1655, Rembrandt did a pen and ink sketch after this miniature (fig. 1).[9] He may have studied the scene in order to invest his own composition with a more authentic "Eastern" aura in regard to such details as God's apparel and the staging of the scene, and he may even have subscribed to the view that Mughal art actually provided a window into the customs and costumes of biblical times.[10]

The popularity of the story of Abraham Entertaining the Angels was based on its obvious Christological implications: the three strangers, for example, have traditionally been glossed as a manifestation of the three persons of the Trinity; the sharing of food and drink has been viewed as an allusion to the Eucharist; and the announcement of the impending birth of a child to the 100-year-old Abraham and 90-year-old Sarah has been interpreted as an antetype for the annunciation of the miraculous birth of the

Christ child.[11] The platter of round flat cakes and the manner in which the central figure holds his chalice certainly suggest a sacramental moment.[12]

Images of Abraham and the angels dating from the Early Christian period through the Renaissance typically represented the visitors as three identical or very similar figures, sometimes with wings and sometimes without.[13] Rembrandt's etching deviates from this tradition, not only in treating each of the visitors as an individual, but also in clearly differentiating God from his two angelic companions. Erik Hinterding suggested that this print might, in fact, be the first visual instance in which these distinctions occur, and notes that the Dutch State Bible of 1637 specifically described Abraham's visitors as consisting of two angels and the Lord himself.[14]

Michiel Roscam Abbing suggested that this print should more accurately be titled "The Annunciation of the Birth of Isaac."[15] The quizzical expression on Sarah's face seems to indicate that she is taken aback by the prophecy that she will bear a child. If, indeed, Rembrandt has portrayed this prophetic moment, then the etching is about an event that is critical not only for the future of the Jews, for whom Sarah's future son, Isaac, will fulfill Abraham's covenant with God and carry out God's plan for their progeny, but also, as noted above, as a foreshadowing of the annunciation of the miraculous birth Jesus.[16] The fact that Sarah is hidden in darkness may suggest that she is not yet a believer and is skeptical of the stranger's prophecy that her wish for a son will actually be granted.[17]

The inclusion of Ishmael is one of the most intriguing and unusual aspects of this print. The fact that his back is turned toward Abraham and his visitors suggests his exclusion from the event and may also allude to his future exile. The presence of the young lad alone at play near his elders, men who are conferring about weighty matters that will dramatically affect him, lends a certain degree of poignancy to the picture. All that Ishmael has known is about to change. Viewers of Rembrandt's print who knew their Bible would recognize this outwardly peaceful scene as one filled with history-altering consequences.[18]

Michael Zell interpreted Ishmael's role in the context of the millenarian prophecies that were being circulated by Rabbi Menasseh ben Israel and the theologian and philosemite Paul Felgenhauer in the mid-seventeenth century. In particular, Zell, following Felgenhauer, suggested that the etching's concept of Abraham as the progenitor of two lineages—Ishmael's and Isaac's—makes it a harbinger of a "utopian rapprochement between Jews and Christians."[19] However, as Shelley Perlove and Larry Silver observed, the fact that Ishmael has turned away from the gathering suggests not harmonious convergence, but, rather exclusion.[20] It seems clear that the print is fundamentally centered on the prophecy of the eventual completion of the Old Testament covenant with Abraham (foreshadowing the New Testament covenant of Christianity), rather than the reconciliation of multiple covenants.

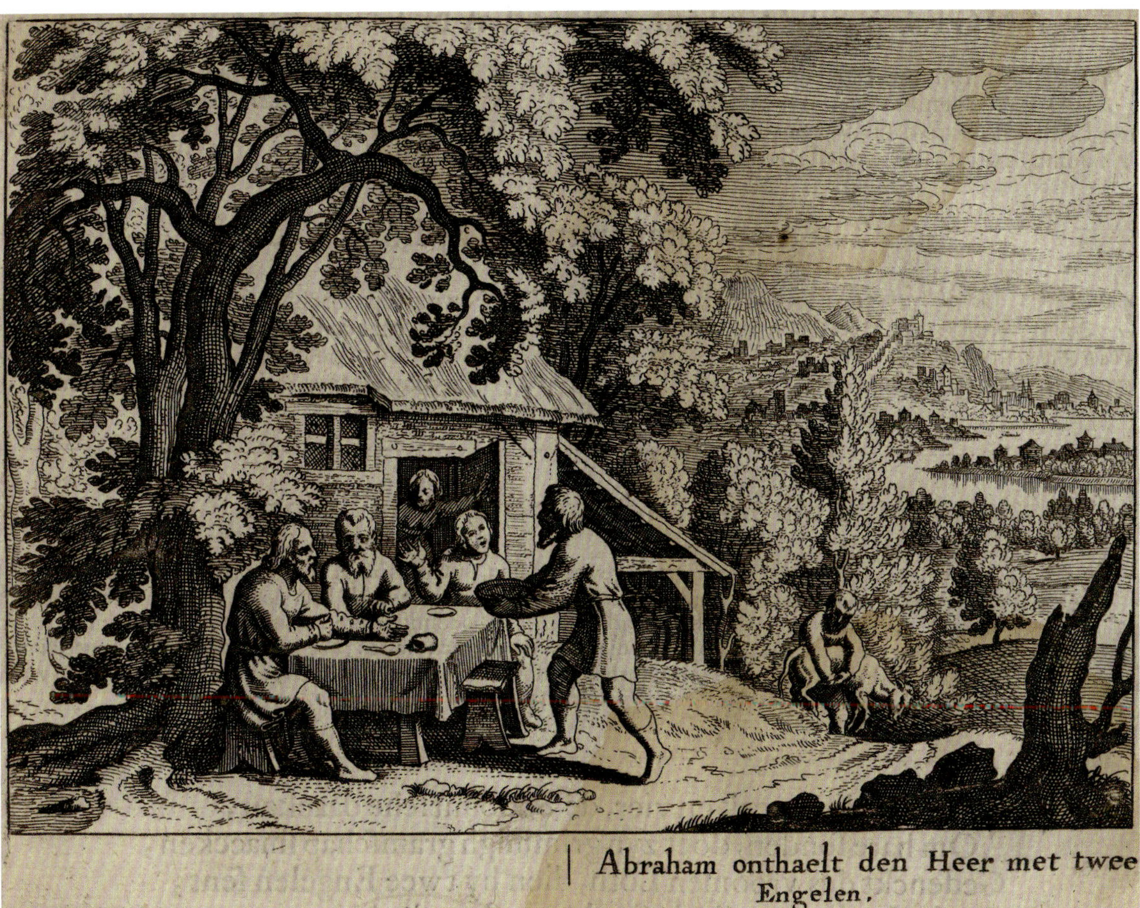

FIGURE 2. Matthäus Merian, *Abraham Entertaining the Angels*, etching, *Icones Biblicae*, Frankfurt, 1627. *Folger Shakespeare Library, Washington, DC.*

Notes

1. George Biörklund, a Swedish engineer, was a distinguished collector of Rembrandt prints and the author, with Osbert H. Barnard, of *Rembrandt's Etchings: True and False: A Summary Catalogue in a Distinctive Chronological Order and Completely Illustrated by George Biörklund* (Stockholm: n.p., 1955; 2nd ed. with essay by Barnard, New York: n.p., 1968). The Snite Museum's impression of *Abraham Entertaining the Angels* is illustrated on page 115 of Biörklund's catalog. Two impressions of this print from George Biörklund's collection were sold at auction in Bern, Switzerland, on June 4, 1957. The Snite impression may be one of these. Klipstein & Kornfeld, *Kupferstiche, Radierungen und Holzschnitte alter Meister: Teile der Sammlung Atherton Curtis, Doubletten der Albertina und anderer Museen, verschiedene Privatsammlungen, darunter die Sammlungen Dr. R. und George Björklund; Versteigerung in Bern, 4. Juni 1957 durch Klipstein et Kornfeld vorm. Gutekunst et Klipstein. Auktion 85* (Bern: Gutekunst & Klipstein, 1957), 47: "241a. Rembrandt Harmensz van Rijn. 209. Abraham, die Engel bewirtend. BB 56-B. Prachtvoller Druck mit Grat und mit rauhen Plattenrändern von bester Erhaltung.—Dabei ein weiteres Exemplar."

2. In the sixteenth and early seventeenth centuries, the biblical story was commonly incorporated in series depicting the story of Abraham. See, for example, engravings by Georg Pencz (HG 2, 1543), Cornelis Massijs (HD 1, c. 1545), and Claes Cornelisz. Moeyaert (HD 5, 1615–55). It also appears as an illustration of Genesis 18, after Maerten de Vos, in *Thesaurus sacrarum historiarum Veteris Testamenti* . . . ([Antwerp]: Gerard de Jode, 1585); in a series of "Annunciations" designed by Hendrick Goltzius (NHD 416, 1586); and as an illustration for Genesis 18 in Matthäus Merian's *Icones Biblicae* (Frankfurt: Merian, 1627) (fig. 2).

3. *Abraham Entertaining the Angels* (1656) was the last of four etchings that Rembrandt made illustrating critical moments in Abraham's life. The others are *Abraham Casting Out Hagar and Ishmael* (B. 30, 1637, cat. no. 4); *Abraham and Isaac* (B. 34, 1645, cat. no. 6); and *Abraham's Sacrifice* (B. 35, 1655, cat. no. 7). This sequence of prints did not follow the biblical chronology of events.

4. Artists normally represented Abraham's dwelling as a house, rather than as a tent. See the examples cited in note 2, above.

5. Emanuel Winternitz ("A Rabbi with Wings: Remarks on Rembrandt's Etching 'Abraham Entertaining the Angels,'" *Metropolitan Museum Journal* 12 [1977]: 104–5) suggested that this angel bears the features of Rabbi Menasseh ben Israel, the author of the Messianic treatise *Piedra gloriosa*, which Rembrandt illustrated in 1655 (see cat. nos. 8, 9, and 10). He based the identification on a comparison with Rembrandt's portrait of Menasseh (B. 269, 1636). However, there seems to be no resemblance.

6. The long-bearded visitor's appearance and clothing are very similar to those of Rembrandt's representation of God in the artist's illustration of Daniel's apocalyptic vision of the four beasts in Menasseh ben Israel's *Piedra gloriosa* (B. 36D, 1655, cat. 10).

7. Genesis 21:20, "[Ishmael] grew up; he lived in the wilderness, and became an expert with the bow."

8. This source was first identified by Heinrich Glück in 1933, and it has been accepted ever since. The original miniature, which was probably in Rembrandt's own collection, is today part of the decorations in the Millionenzimmer in Schönbrunn Palace, Vienna. Michael Zell, *Reframing Rembrandt: Jews and the Christian Image in Seventeenth-Century Amsterdam* (Berkeley: University of California Press, 2002), 239n79.

9. British Museum, London, Ben. 1187.

10. Leonard Slatkes proposed that Rembrandt's interest in Persian and Mughal miniatures was motivated by his belief "that even relatively contemporary Persian and Moghul miniatures transmitted the social customs and dress of biblical days, and he used a variety of these elements to add a note of historical veracity to his work." Slatkes then went on to cite *Abraham Entertaining the Angels* as the best-known example of Rembrandt borrowing compositional elements from these sources. Slatkes, *Rembrandt and Persia* (New York: Abaris Books, 1983), 25.

Rembrandt did choose to portray Abraham and his guests eating al fresco, but given the artist's interest in the Mughal miniature, it is curious that he didn't depict them sitting under a tree, as described in *Genesis* and shown in the miniature.

11. Shelley Perlove and Robert Baldwin, *Impressions of Faith: Rembrandt's Biblical Etchings* (Dearborn: University of Michigan-Dearborn, Mardigian Library, 1989), cat. 14, 68. It is also worth noting that Hendrick Goltzius illustrated the scene of Abraham Entertaining the Angels in his series of "Annunciations." See note 2, above.

12. In addition, Shelley Perlove and Larry Silver (*Rembrandt's Faith*, 81) suggested that the unleavened bread on the plate might be

related to Luther's claim that Abraham gave the angels unleavened bread "because leaven represent iniquity, lust, hypocrisy, uncleanness, false doctrine in religion, and legalism."

13. One clear, earlier exception to this tradition is Matthäus Merian's illustration in the *Icones Biblicae* (1625–30) (fig. 2). Merian's three wingless figures represent the three ages of man. See note 2, above.

14. Erik Hinterding, *Lugt Catalogue*, cat. 19, 71.
Michael Zell observed that there is an oil painting by Rembrandt from 1646 (Aurora Art Fund, New York) that follows the older tradition of showing all three figures as angels, but that also clearly distinguishes one of the visitors by means of scale and light. Zell, *Reframing*, 177.

15. Cited in Zell, *Reframing*, 176.

16. The roses that grow along the edge of Abraham's house may be another Marian reference, since they are a well-known attribute of the Virgin.

17. *Rembrandt's Faith*, 81.

18. In similar fashion, the winged angels in the representation foreshadow events to come. Abraham's placement below the level of the visitors may indicate not only his deference to the strangers who are his guests, but also—to the informed viewer—his status vis-à-vis these particular guests. According to the biblical account, Abraham was not aware of the identity of his guests when he served them, but many artists, including Rembrandt, adorned them with wings in order to reveal their true nature, thereby reminding viewers of the repercussions of this encounter. The etching is one of a number of prints in which the artist includes figures or details that anticipate future biblical events. See, for example, *The Descent from the Cross: The Second Plate* (B. 81 II, 1633, cat. no. 55).

19. Zell, *Reframing*, 182.

20. *Rembrandt's Faith*, 82.

4. *Abraham Casting Out Hagar and Ishmael*

B. 30 (H. 149, Mz. 174, NHD 166)
Etching and drypoint
Signed and dated in the plate: *Rembrandt f. 1637*
State I of I
Sheet: 13.3 × 10.4; cm plate mark: 12.5 × 9.5 cm

Provenance:
Craddock & Barnard, London, 1978
Feddersen, Elkhart, IN, 1991
Snite Museum of Art
Acc. No.: 1991.025.003

The plate does not survive.

The story of Abraham and Sarah's maidservant, Hagar, recounted in the book of Genesis, is complex and tragic. Although God had appeared to the childless Abraham in a vision and promised him that he would have a son and that his descendants would be as numerous as the stars in the heavens, Sarah, his wife, remained barren. Finally, Sarah asked Abraham to take her Egyptian bondswoman, Hagar, as his second wife, so that he could have a child with her. However, once Hagar became pregnant by the eighty-six-year-old patriarch, Sarah became jealous and fearful for her position and began to mistreat her servant. Hagar, fearing for her life, fled into the desert, but the angel of the Lord appeared and told her that she must return to Abraham and bear him a son, whom she would name Ishmael. Hagar returned, and Ishmael was born. Thirteen years later, when Abraham was ninety-nine, God came to him again and said that he would bless Sarah and she would bear Abraham a son. The patriarch laughed at the prospect of siring a child at his age, and he asked God to establish a covenant with Ishmael, instead. God refused, saying that although Ishmael would prosper and have many children, the Lord's covenant was to be with Sarah's son, who would be named Isaac, "he will laugh." Shortly thereafter, three strangers (God and two angels, in disguise) came to visit Abraham and prophesied that Sarah would bear him a son.[1] Despite Sarah's skepticism, God's promise was fulfilled; when Abraham was one hundred years old and Sarah ninety, Sarah miraculously gave birth to their son, Isaac.

Once Isaac was weaned, Sarah watched him at play with Ishmael. When Ishmael mocked her son, Sarah began to fear for her child's inheritance, so she came to Abraham and told him to banish Hagar and Ishmael. Abraham was very displeased, but God returned and told him to do as Sarah said, and consoled Abraham by telling him that Ishmael would become the father of a great nation "because he is your offspring." Therefore, "Abraham rose up early in the morning, and took bread, and a bottle of water, and gave it unto Hagar, putting it on her shoulder, and [gave her] the child, and sent her away: and she departed, and wandered in the wilderness of Beersheba."[2]

Rembrandt's etching depicts the elderly, bearded, sumptuously dressed Abraham poised at the entrance to his house, with Sarah and Isaac behind him, at the left, and the now-banished Hagar and Ishmael, departing, at the right side of the composition.[3] Hagar, overcome with grief, turns away, covering her face in sorrow. The water skin that Abraham has provided for her journey hangs from her belt.[4] The print is structured so that the space is closed off on the left side, where Abraham's house stands, and opens up on the right,

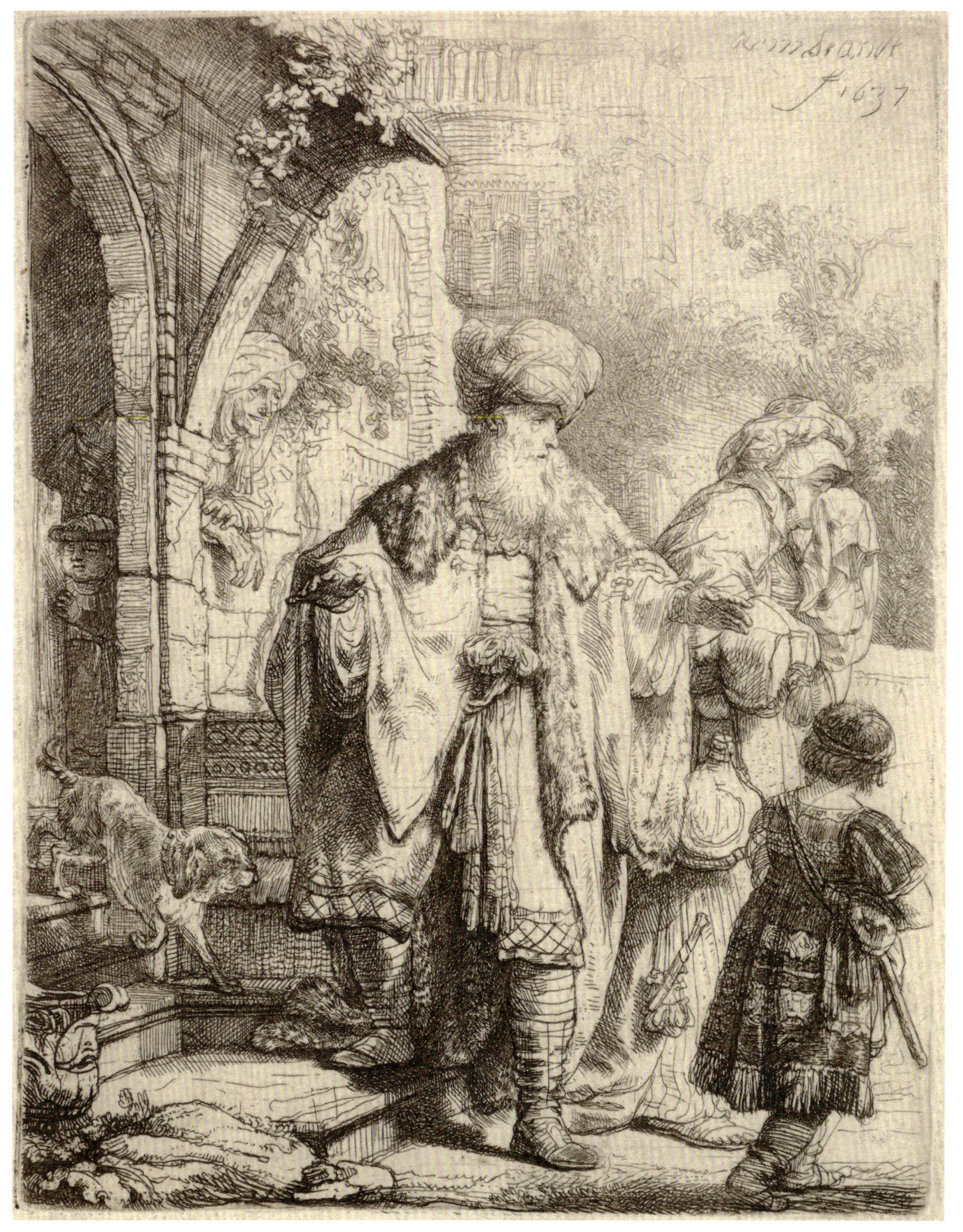

PLATE 4

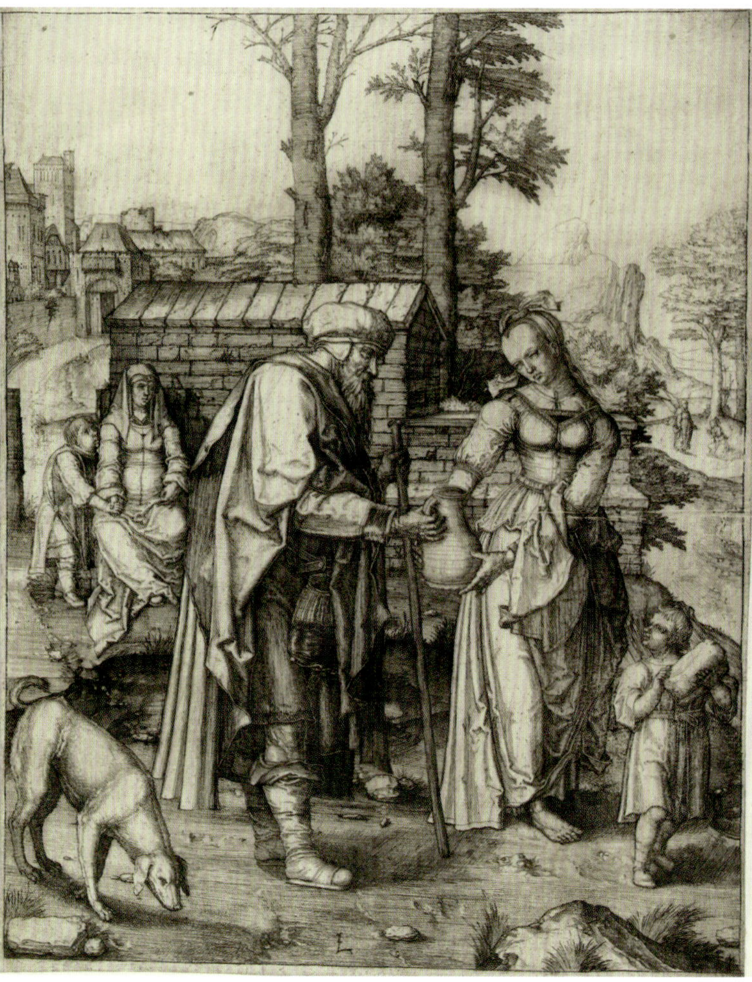

FIGURE 1. Lucas van Leyden, *Abraham Dismissing Hagar,* engraving, 1506. *Rijksmuseum, Amsterdam.*

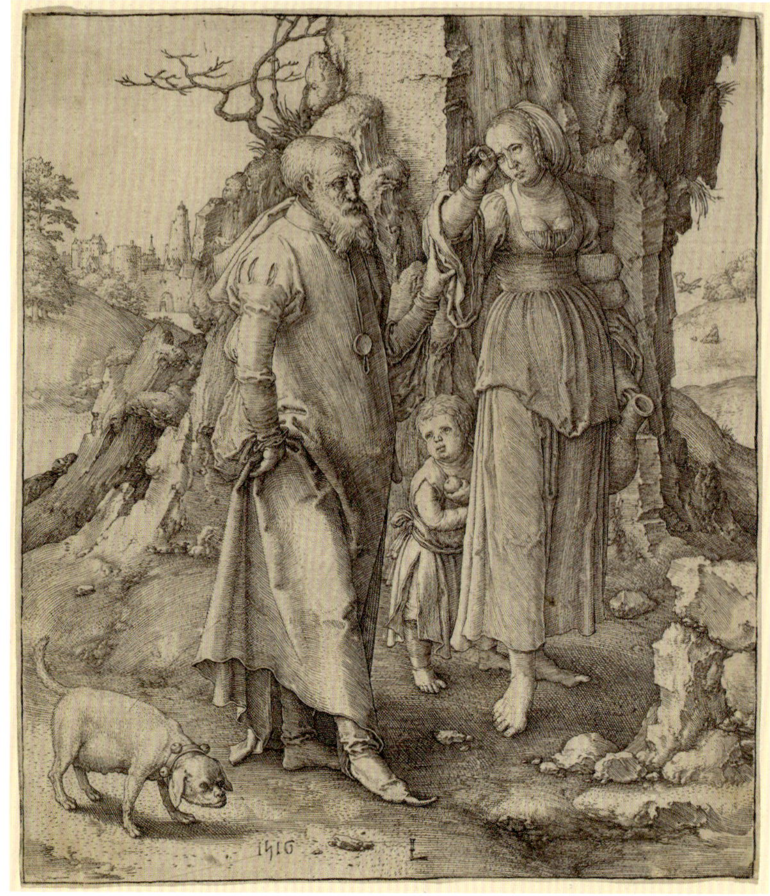

FIGURE 2. Lucas van Leyden, *Abraham Dismissing Hagar,* engraving, 1516. *Photo: Courtesy of the National Gallery of Art, Washington, DC.*

toward a lightly sketched landscape. A strong diagonal descends from the upper left corner, through Abraham's gesture, and down to the figure of Ishmael, in the lower right corner. These compositional devices reinforce the theme of exile, visually driving the despondent Hagar and her son out into the undefined "wilderness of Beersheba" and barring their return. Although Abraham's body faces out toward the viewer, his pose, gesture, and expression signal conflicting emotions. His right foot is turned back toward the doorway, where it rests on the threshold, suggesting a movement back toward the house. His left foot, though, is turned slightly outward, in the direction of Hagar and Ishmael. Abraham's arms are outspread, with his right hand extended out toward the viewer and his left hand stretching out in the direction of the banished maidservant and her son. He has turned his back on Hagar, and his outstretched arm appears to separate mother and child as he reaches out toward Ishmael, the child whom he had asked the Lord to bless. Abraham's head is turned toward the departing pair and the path they will take. He looks down with a troubled expression. Although he is bending to the will of his wife as commanded by God, Rembrandt's Abraham still evinces a very human sense of uncertainty.[5]

Ishmael is seen from behind as he moves toward his mother. His attire is unusually elegant for the child of a servant, a departure from the way in which he is traditionally represented.[6] His hair is bound with a fillet, and a knife and pouch hang from his belt. Rembrandt's decision to dress the exiled boy in so fine a manner may have been motivated by more than the artist's abiding interest in exotic clothing. First, in keeping with the prophecy that Ishmael would be the father of a great and numerous people, though not of the Jews, Rembrandt may have intended the boy's costume to differentiate him from both Abraham and Isaac. Second, Hagar and Ishmael's banishment, though clearly part of God's plan, was also engendered by Sarah's fear that Ishmael might share in her son's inheritance.[7] Ishmael's lavish attire may have been meant to suggest that Abraham's generosity toward the boy had fanned the flames of Sarah's jealousy.

The elderly Sarah watches her rivals' departure as she leans out the window of her home, an expression of pleasure on her lined face. It has been suggested that Sarah's smile may allude to her joy at having a son of her own,[8] but it may also imply a sense of spiteful triumph over her rival.[9] Isaac is just barely visible as he stands beside his mother, peering out of the shadowy doorway with narrowed eyes and a sour expression on his pudgy face. The last figure in the print is a small dog, which comes prancing down the steps of the house toward Abraham. His pose, like that of his master, expresses divided loyalties, for it is not clear whether the dog is coming to stand by Abraham or to follow Ishmael out into the wilderness.[10]

The tale of Abraham's expulsion of Hagar and Ishmael was fairly popular in the Netherlands in the seventeenth century.[11] Joost van den Vondel, for example, included the episode in his 1620 poem "Abraham the Faithful Father," and Jacob Cats referred to the story in his 1625 treatise on marriage, *Houwelyck*, in the section on the proper conduct and treatment of a wife. For Vondel, Abraham's actions were proof of his faith, while for Cats, Abraham's eventual submission to Sarah's insistence that Hagar be banished was taken as evidence that a woman may be assertive and have a say in the running of the household. The theme of the expulsion was also represented with some regularity in both paintings and prints. Three representations of the story have been cited as possible sources for Rembrandt's etching: an engraving by Georg Pencz from about 1543 (fig. 3),[12] a painting in Hamburg by Rembrandt's teacher Pieter Lastman, dating from 1612 (fig. 4),[13] and a lost version of the subject by Lastman. Rembrandt's composition has been likened to the Pencz engraving because of the manner in which the figures

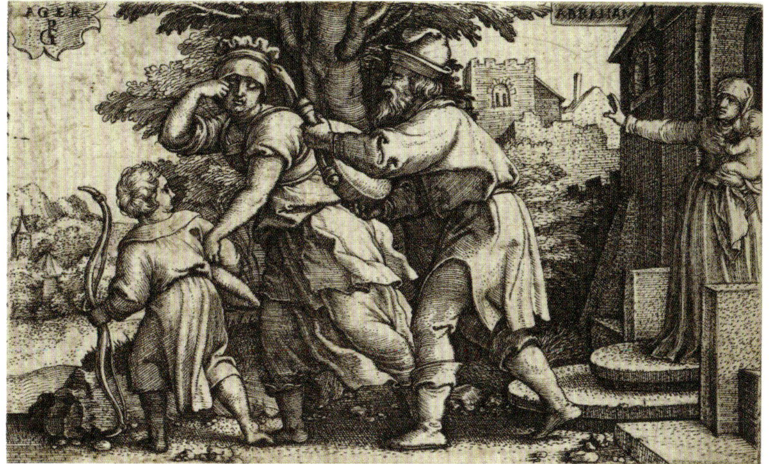

FIGURE 3. Georg Pencz, *Abraham Casting Out Hagar and Ishmael*, engraving, c. 1543. *Metropolitan Museum of Art, New York, New York, Bequest of Phyllis Massar, 2012.*

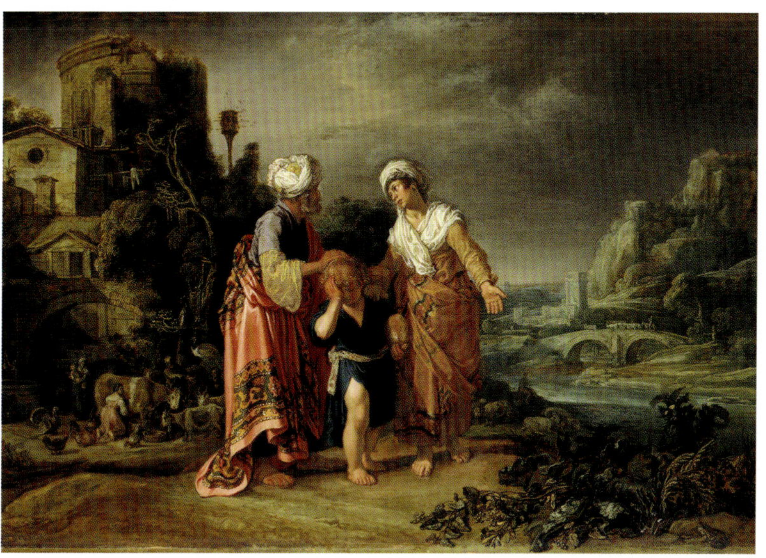

FIGURE 4. Peter Lastman, *Abraham Casting Out Hagar and Ishmael*, 1612. *Hamburger Kunsthalle, Hamburg. Photo: bpk/Hamburger Kunsthalle/Elke Walford/Art Resource, New York.*

move in an almost processional line from one side of the print to the other, from Abraham's house to the wilderness. However, Rembrandt's figures are more tightly grouped, and Abraham's pose suggests a much more palpable sense of uncertainty. Rembrandt was familiar with Lastman's painting,[14] and the fact that both works evince a concern with Abraham's emotional reaction has led some historians to see a connection between the painting and the etching.[15] Lastman's Abraham actually places a hand on Ishmael's head as if to bless the weeping child. Nonetheless, Rembrandt's composition differs significantly from both Lastman's painting and

Pencz's engraving in the manner in which it reinforces not only the narrative but also the emotional turmoil of the moment.

The story of Hagar's banishment was glossed by St. Paul in Galatians 4:21–23.[16] Paul reads the story as an allegory that distinguishes between the old covenant of the law and the new covenant born of promise. Hagar, a slave whose son was born of the flesh, represents the earthly Jerusalem and the Old Law, while Sarah, a free woman whose son was born of God's promise, represents the heavenly Jerusalem and grace.

Martin Luther framed his discussion of Abraham's dilemma, his conflict with Sarah, and the expulsion of Hagar and Ishmael in terms of the nature of marriage as a form of spiritual life, as a means of distinguishing between those who were the true heirs of God's covenant and those who were not—the latter including not only Jews and Turks, but also "papists"—and of demonstrating the necessity of obeying God's will.[17] Luther discussed Abraham's actions in very human terms, acknowledging the personal cost of the patriarch's decision, calling it a tragedy and asserting that Abraham "did not do this without a very great struggle and a very heavy sorrow. . . . But he sent his very dear wife away with loud sobs and many tears."[18] Although Rembrandt's Abraham is not as demonstrative as the figure described by Luther, the artist's etching does convey a sense of the sorrow experienced by both the patriarch and Hagar. John Calvin did not dwell on the subject of Abraham's emotions as Luther did, but Calvin's commentary did make many of the same points. He held up Abraham's actions as an example of his total submission to God,[19] and he asserted that the story of the two sons illustrated not only the distinction between Jews and Christians, and between law and grace, but also, within the context of the Church itself, between those who were true followers of Christ and those who claimed to be. In particular, like Luther, Calvin identified the offspring of Isaac as true believers, committed to piety and humility, and those of Ishmael—also identified as "papists"—with the corrupters of the faith.[20]

Contemporary Christians viewing Rembrandt's image would have understood the distinctions drawn by Paul between the new covenant, which they themselves embraced, and the old. For a Dutch Reformed Calvinist, the print would have evoked not only the Pauline allegory, but also Luther's and Calvin's distinctions between true believers and corrupters of the faith. Furthermore, as Perlove and Silver have noted, within the contentious world of Dutch Calvinism itself, the story of the banishment of Hagar could also have been read as a reformist allegory, illustrating the return of the Church to its pristine state through the exercise of God's will.[21]

There is one additional chapter in the story of this print and its audience. In 1637, the year when the etching was made, Rembrandt was involved in a dispute with Samuel d'Orta, a Jewish Portuguese painter residing in Amsterdam. Rembrandt had apparently sold d'Orta the plate of *Abraham Casting Out Hagar and Ishmael*, and as part of the transaction, had agreed not to sell any of the impressions of the etching that he retained. It is possible that Rembrandt violated this agreement, because records show that d'Orta saw fit to summon witnesses before a notary on December 17, 1637, so that they could testify regarding the arrangement.[22] This incident attests to the existence of an extraordinarily early market for Rembrandt's plates, one presumably based on the assumption that the purchaser could make a profit by continuing to produce impressions from it. It is also noteworthy that the buyer was Jewish. Rembrandt's house on Breestraat was near the Jewish quarter in Amsterdam. He painted and etched portraits of Jewish sitters, and in 1655 he was engaged to produce four illustrations for the visionary treatise *Piedra gloriosa*, written by Amsterdam Rabbi Menasseh ben Israel.[23] Clearly, Dutch Jews were one of the audiences for Rembrandt's prints,[24] and for them, an etching that portrayed the story of the expulsion of Hagar and Ishmael would certainly have been read as an unambiguous reaffirmation of God's covenant with the Jews.

Notes

1. This is the subject of Rembrandt's 1656 etching of *Abraham Entertaining the Angels* (B. 29, cat. no. 3).
2. Genesis 21:14.
3. This was the first of four etchings that Rembrandt made that depicted incidents from Abraham's life.
4. Rembrandt took liberties with the biblical text, which describes Hagar carrying the bread and water on her shoulder.

5. Hela Baudis also linked the theme of the print to what she termed an "everyday dilemma," a man caught between two women. In this context she noted that some years later, Rembrandt would find himself in just such a dilemma, caught between his son Titus's nurse, Geertje Dircx, and the younger housemaid, Hendrickje Stoffels. Hela Baudis, cat. 12, "Die Verstossung der Hagar—1637," in Hela Baudis, Kornelia Röder, Horst Janssen, and Kornelia von Berswordt-Wallrabe, *Rembrandt fecit: 165 Rembrandt-Radierungen aus der Sammlung des Staatlichen Museums Schwerin: Ausstellung vom 28. Mai bis 6. August 1995*, exh. cat. (Schwerin, Germany: Das Museum, 1995), 30.

6. There are numerous other sixteenth- and seventeenth-century depictions of this dramatic incident, but in none of them is Ishmael portrayed in such an elegant costume. For earlier examples, see the illustrations in Christine Petra Sellin, *Fractured Families and Rebel Maidservants: The Biblical Hagar in Seventeenth-Century Dutch Art and Literature* (New York: Continuum, 2006).

7. The commentary in the Dutch State Bible states that "it appears that Ishmael, doubtless through the instigation or instruction of his mother, had also boasted of his right as the firstborn and the inheritance of Abraham's goods." (*Dort Study Bible*, vol. 1, trans. Theodore Haak [Pella, IA: Inheritance Publications, 2003], 97).

8. Genesis 21:6, "God hath made me to laugh."

9. Shelley Perlove and Larry Silver (*Rembrandt's Faith*, 86) drew attention to Sarah's unprecedented expression. She is considerably more serious in Lucas van Leyden's 1506 (fig. 1) (NHD 17) and Georg Pencz's c. 1543 (fig. 3) (HG 3) engravings of the theme. Perlove and Silver interpreted her smile as reflecting not only the biblical text regarding her laughter when God told her that she would bear a son, and her feeling of triumph, but also "the spiritual joy of the covenant now fulfilled in Isaac."

10. A review of Rembrandt's oeuvre makes it clear that he didn't need any excuse or model for including a dog in a composition as a domestic detail, even in the case of sacred subjects, but in this instance, the motif of the dog may have been suggested by Lucas van Leyden's engravings of the *Banishment of Hagar and Ishmael* of 1506 or 1516 (figs. 1 and 2) (NHD 17 and 18). In both of Lucas's engravings, the hangdog attitude of the animal and its placement beside Abraham may have been meant to reflect the patriarch's emotional state. Rembrandt's dogs usually serve the purpose of providing a homey touch to a scene, but in this etching, the dog's uncertain destination echoes the ambiguity of Abraham's pose.

11. The examples provided in the text are drawn from Christine Petra Sellin's study of the theme of Hagar in the Netherlands in the seventeenth century (cited in note 6, above).

12. HD 3.

13. Hamburger Kunsthalle, Hamburg, Inv. 191.

14. Rembrandt copied Lastman's central group of Abraham, Hagar, and Ishmael in a black chalk drawing that is now in the Albertina Museum, Vienna. Ben. 447, c. 1637.

15. Tümpel, *Rembrandt legt*, cat. 6; Astrid Tümpel and Peter Schatborn, *Pieter Lastman: leermeester van Rembrandt: The Man Who Taught Rembrandt*, exh. cat. (Zwolle, Netherlands: Waanders Uitgevers; Amsterdam: Museum het Rembrandthuis, 1991), 67–69; and, Hinterding, *Lugt Catalogue*, cat. 20, 73. Hinterding also cites a print by Jacob Matham after a painting by Abraham Bloemaert from 1603 (NHD 2 [Jacob Matham]) as a possible source.

16. The commentary on Genesis 21:14 in the 1629 Dutch State Bible cites St. Paul's gloss.

17. Luther, *Lectures on Genesis, Chapters 21–25*, in *Luther's Works*, vol. 4, trans. by George Schick (St. Louis: Concordia Publishing House, 1964), 21–42.

18. Ibid., 37.

19. Calvin, *Commentary on Genesis*, 1:422, Commentary on Genesis 21:14, "This is the true test of faith and piety, when the faithful are so far compelled to deny themselves, that they even resign the very affections of their original nature, which are neither evil nor vicious in themselves, to the will of God." Accessed February 21, 2013, http://www.ccel.org/ccel/calvin/calcom01.pdf.

20. Ibid., 421–22.

21. *Rembrandt's Faith*, 86. Perlove and Silver draw attention to the specific use of the Expulsion of Hagar as an emblem for the purgation of the Church and its return to a pristine state as explained in *De Grooten Emblemata Sacra* (Amsterdam, 1654), written by the Waterlander Mennonite Jan Philipsz. Schabaelje.

22. Walter L. Strauss and Marjon van der Meulen, eds. and trans., *The Rembrandt Documents* (New York: Abaris, 1979), doc. 1637/7. The documents include the testimony of only one of the witnesses to the agreement. Unfortunately, it is not known whether Rembrandt actually sold any of the impressions of the print that

he kept after he sold the plate to d'Orta, or how the situation was ultimately resolved.

23. See the discussion of Rembrandt's illustrations for Menasseh ben Israel's *Piedra gloriosa* in this catalog (B. 36A, C, and D; cat. nos. 8, 9, and 10).

24. Steven Nadler discussed Rembrandt's Jewish clientele in general in the first chapter of *Rembrandt's Jews* (Chicago: University of Chicago Press, 2003). He also made specific observations regarding Jews collecting prints of Jewish history and scenes from the Bible (81). It has also been suggested that another one of Rembrandt's prints, *Abraham and Isaac* (B. 34, cat. no. 6), was produced for a Jewish Portuguese client, though without any direct evidence. Christian Tümpel, "Religious History Painting," in Albert Blankert, et al., *Gods, Saints and Heroes, Dutch Painting in the Age of Rembrandt*, exh. cat. (Washington, DC: National Gallery of Art; Detroit: Detroit Institute of Arts; Amsterdam; Rijsmuseum, 1980), 54n29.

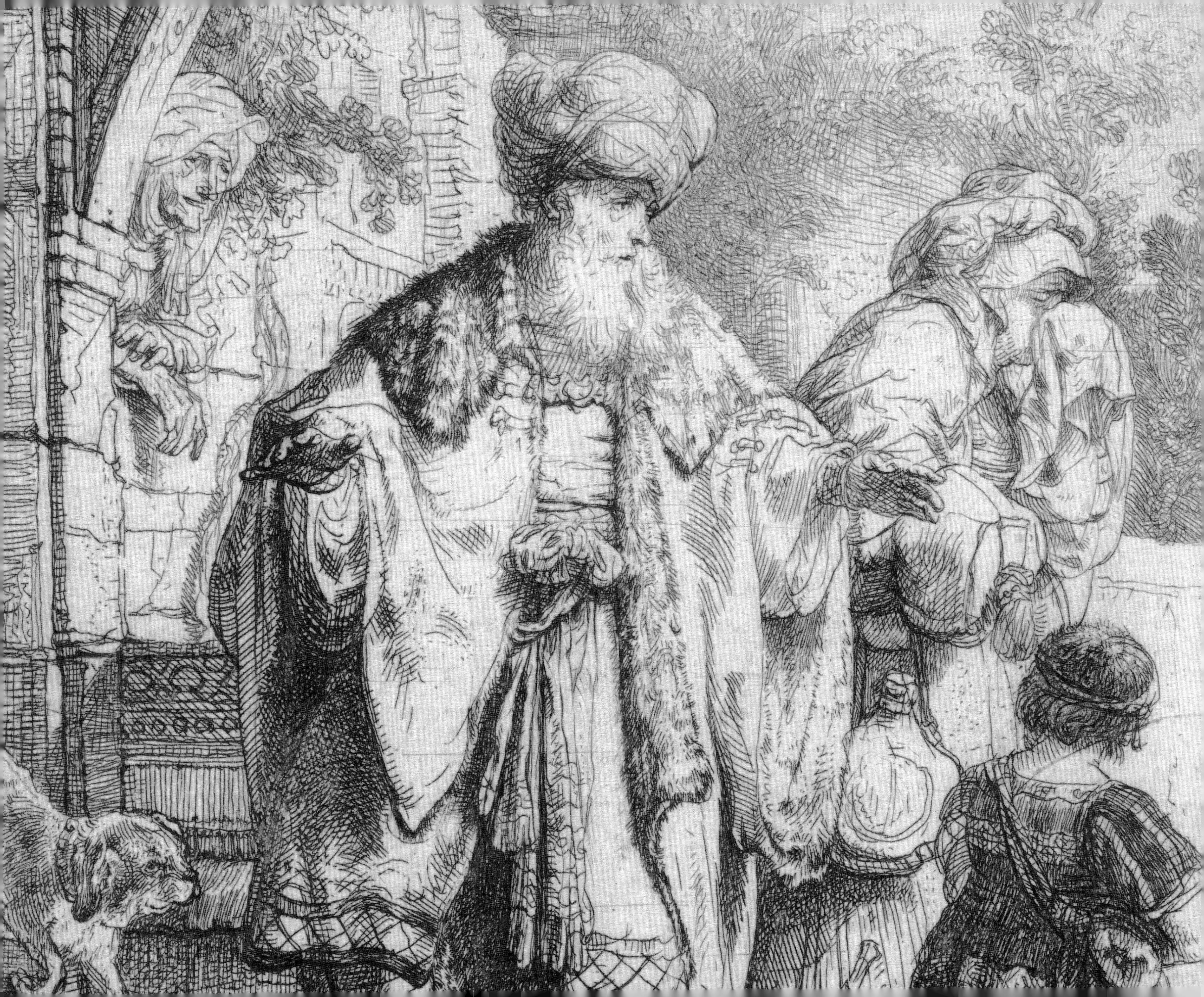

5. *Abraham Caressing Isaac (or Jacob Caressing Benjamin)*

B. 33 (H. 148, Mz. 176, NHD. 165)
Etching
Signed in the plate: *Rembrandt f.*
c. 1637/38
State III of IV
Sheet: 11.5 × 8.6 cm, trimmed inside the plate mark
Verso: lower left corner in graphite: *H8995 / B33*

Provenance:
Harrods, London, 1980
Feddersen, Elkhart, IN, 1991
Snite Museum of Art
Acc. No.: 1991.025.004

Plate survives:
Museum of Fine Arts, Boston (inv. 1993.91)

The precise subject of Rembrandt's charming print of a seated elderly man cradling a smiling young boy between his knees has been a matter of some controversy.[1] The etching is generally assumed to be the work that is described in Clement de Jonghe's 1679 inventory of Rembrandt's surviving plates as "Father Abraham Playing with His Son,"[2] and the long robe and soft flat hat worn by the bearded elderly man makes his identification as an Old Testament patriarch very likely. In the Rembrandt catalogs of Bartsch, Hind, Münz, White and Boon, and Hinterding, the two protagonists were also identified as Abraham and Isaac.[3] However, as early as 1893, an alternative title for the print was proposed. In a footnote to a brief article on Rembrandt's etchings, Albrecht Jordan suggested that the print should be renamed "Jacob and Benjamin," based on a similar pair of figures in a Rembrandt drawing of the elderly Jacob listening to a youthful Joseph recounting his dreams.[4]

This idea was subsequently taken up by Christian Tümpel, who labeled the print "Jacob Caressing Benjamin" and interpreted it as a reference to the biblical story of Jacob's refusal to allow his youngest and most beloved son to leave famine-stricken Canaan in order to travel with his brothers to Egypt, to purchase grain.[5] Jacob and his sons did not know that their brother Joseph, presumed dead, not only had survived, but had become governor of Egypt. When the travelers arrived in Egypt, Joseph recognized them as the siblings who had plotted against him, sold him into slavery, and reported him dead, but they did not realize that this was the man whom they had betrayed, and he did not reveal his true identity to them. Joseph called them before him and accused them of being spies. They protested their innocence and explained that they had traveled to Egypt simply to buy grain and then return to their father and youngest brother, in Canaan. Joseph, feigning disbelief, imprisoned them for three days. Then, he declared that he would consider them honest men if they returned to Canaan and came back to Egypt with their youngest brother. Until that time, however, one of them, Simeon, would have to remain in prison as a hostage. The other brothers returned to Canaan with the grain that they had purchased and told Jacob what had transpired. At first, their father refused to consider letting Benjamin go with them, saying "My son shall not go down with you, for his brother [Joseph] is dead, and he only [Benjamin] is left [of the children of Rachel]. If harm should befall him on the journey that you are to make, you would bring down my gray hairs with sorrow to Sheol [the land

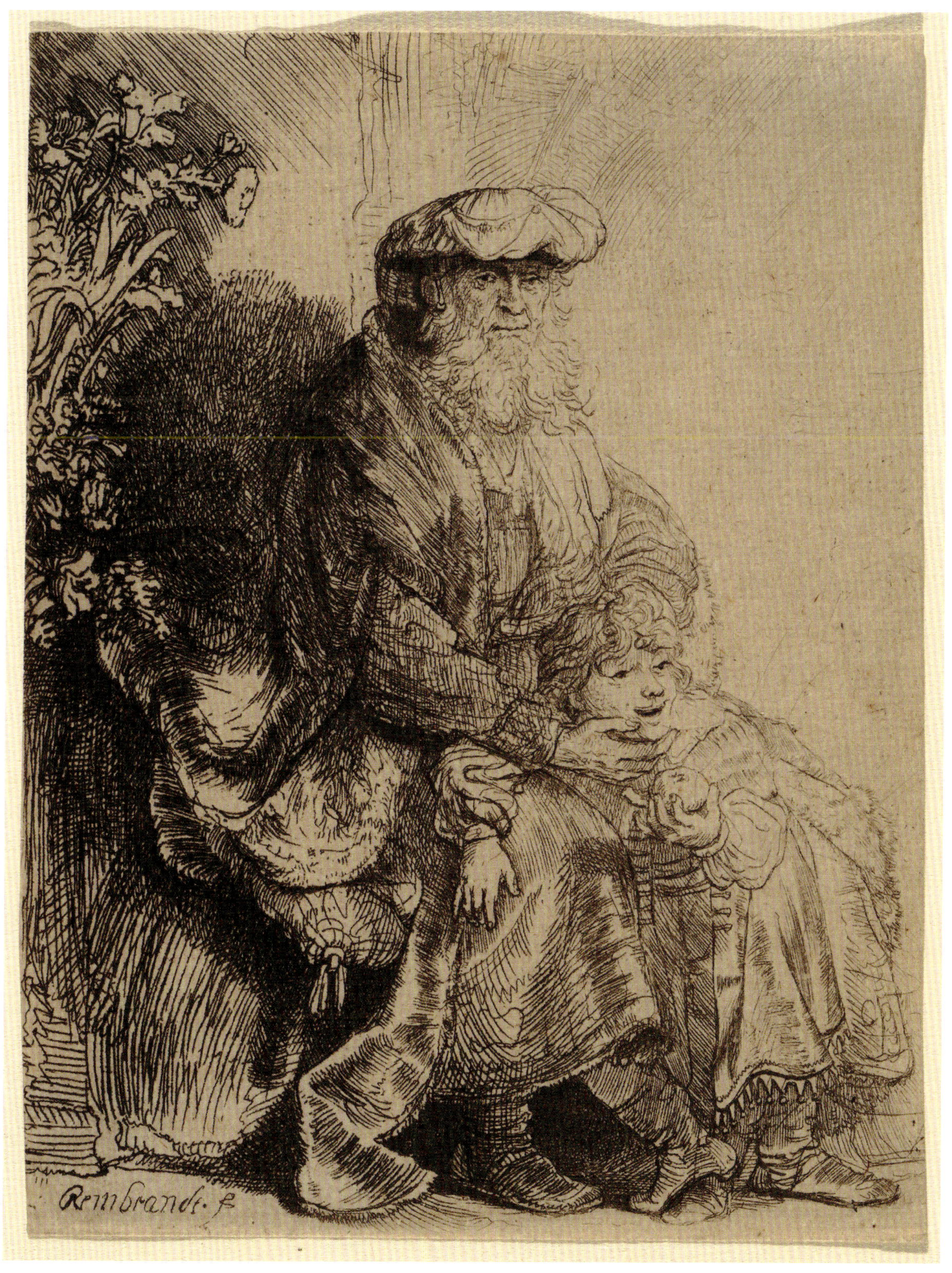

PLATE 5

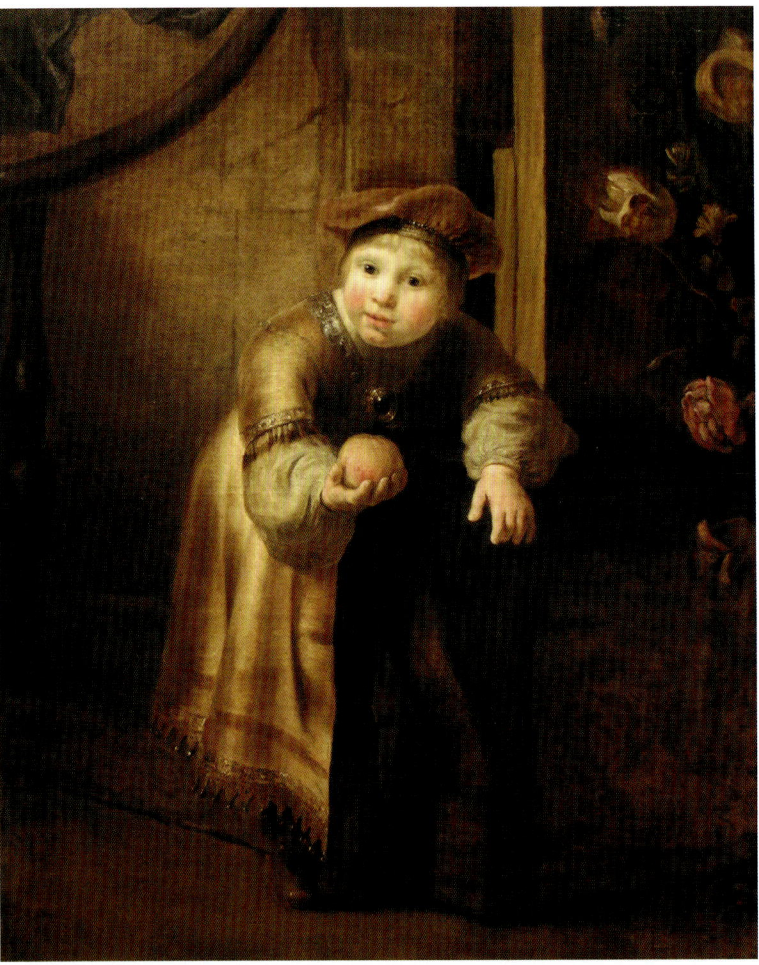

FIGURE 1. Attributed to Govaert Flinck, *Young Boy with an Apple*, oil on canvas, c. 1638–45. *Collection of the Bass Museum of Art, Miami, Florida, Gift of John and Johanna Bass.*

of the dead].” Once all of the imported grain had been consumed, Jacob instructed his sons to return to Egypt to purchase more, but they reminded him that they were not to return without Benjamin. Again, Jacob was very reluctant to agree, but finally, after his son Judah promised to stand as surety for the safety of his youngest son, the elderly patriarch acquiesced.[6]

Focusing on the tender, expressive content of Rembrandt's print, Tümpel interpreted the etching as an example of the artist's practice of excerpting moments from larger narratives as a means of eliciting emotional responses. For someone familiar with the biblical tale, the somber patriarch and merry child could have served to evoke the entire story of Joseph and his brothers. Tümpel's hypothesis was accepted by Petra Jeroense,[7] Clifford Ackley,[8] and, most recently, Shelley Perlove and Larry Silver.[9] In support of this interpretation of the print, Perlove and Silver drew attention to the apple in the boy's left hand. They suggested that the piece of fruit symbolized Benjamin's place as a favored son, “the apple of his father's eye,” a phrase that would have invested the print with a “covenantal” context, because in the Dutch State Bible commentary on Deuteronomy, God's people, “Jacob's line of inheritance,” were described as “the apple of his [the Lord's] eye,” led and instructed by God.

Wayne Franits[10] and Johannes Nieuwstraten,[11] on the other hand, offered alternative interpretations of the grinning child with a piece of fruit, ones that supported the original interpretation of the pair as Abraham and Isaac. Franits associated the image with a story that first appeared in a medieval compilation of moral tales intended to be used by clergy in sermons. In this story, a king tested the obedience of his two sons by offering each of them a piece of apple. The boy who accepted the food without question was judged to be the more trustworthy and obedient and was, therefore, made his father's heir. Franits observed that this story was later invoked by Luther as a prototype for Isaac's absolute obedience to his father, Abraham, when the boy was about to be offered up as a sacrifice. Franits also noted that since Luther referred to the test as a “game,” or “sport,” the original title in the De Jonghe catalog, “Father Abraham Playing with His Son,” might well be the right one. This descriptive title may account for the child's whimsical expression, while the sober stare of the elderly patriarch indicates that he understands the serious implications of the “game.” Nieuwstraten related the print to a painting (fig. 1) attributed to either Ferdinand Bol or Govaert Flinck, both pupils of Rembrandt.[12] The painting shows the young Isaac holding a piece of fruit and standing with his legs crossed, an image that, as Franits observed, was clearly derived from the Rembrandt etching. Nieuwstraten also drew attention to two paintings by the mid-seventeenth-century Dutch artist Jan Victors in which Abraham's preference for Isaac over Ishmael, the patriarch's son by Hagar, is symbolized by the piece of fruit that the chosen boy is holding.[13] Interpreted in this fashion, Rembrandt's print could allude to Abraham's troubling decision to choose Isaac, his miraculously conceived son, over

Ishmael, his firstborn, as his heir. Such a scenario could account for both Isaac's somewhat self-satisfied grin and Abraham's look of serious reflection.[14] Regardless of whether the etching depicts Abraham and Isaac or Jacob and Benjamin, the print's primary appeal remains its sensitive rendering of the sober paternal figure and the energetic, mischievous child.

Despite the fact that the boy is nestled against the elder man's legs and the man cradles the child's chin in his hand, there is no direct communication between the two figures; they do not look at one another, and the man doesn't react to the boy's gaiety. The result is the strange sort of detachment that is characteristic of some later family groupings in Rembrandt's oeuvre.[15] If the figures are Jacob and Benjamin or Abraham and Isaac, however, this impassiveness is understandable, because in each case, the father's distracted detachment from the child is the result of his anxiety about a future of which the child is unaware.

The date of this print is yet another matter of speculation. Some art historians, including Münz, White and Boon, and Hinterding, dated the etching to about 1637–38, whereas others, notably Ackley, as well as Perlove and Silver, suggested a date closer to 1645. Hinterding's arguments, which are based on the rapidity of the artist's strokes and the appearance of certain motifs, are more convincing.[16]

Notes

1. Remarking on the elusive nature of the subject matter in many of Rembrandt's works, Joseph Koerner wrote, "The history of the naming of Rembrandt's works could then be interpreted less as the steady progress toward an indisputable and fully identified oeuvre than as a symptom of something at the heart of Rembrandt's art: the artist's paintings seem often to resist being named, or at least they seem to withhold clues that would finally confirm the rightness of a title." "Rembrandt and the Epiphany of the Face," *RES: Anthropology and Aesthetics* 12 (Autumn 1986): 13.

2. D[ieuwke] de Hoop Scheffer and K[arel] G. Boon, "De inventaislijst van Clement de Jonghe en Rembrandts etsplaten," *Kroniek van het Rembrandthuis* 25 (1971): 8, cat. 25, "Vaeder Abraham speelend met zijn soon."

3. All of these authors have entitled the print "Abraham Caressing Isaac," and this is the title that the etching bears in the Snite Museum's collection. For the history of this title, see Hinterding, *Lugt Catalogue*, 76n1. Hinterding noted that Gersaint, in his 1751 catalog, identified the work as a genre piece. The patriarch's costume would seem to argue against this characterization.

4. Albrecht Jordan, "Bemerkungen zu Rembrandt's Radierungen," *Repertorium für Kunstwissenschaft* 16 (1893): 301n4. The drawing, Ben. 526, is in the Albertina Museum in Vienna.

5. Tümpel, *Rembrandt legt,* cat. 20.

6. Genesis 42–43.

7. Petra Jeroense, cat. 21, in Peter van der Coelen, ed., *Patriarchs, Angels & Prophets: The Old Testament in Netherlandish Printmaking from Lucas van Leyden to Rembrandt*, exh. cat. (Amsterdam: Rembrandt Information Centre, 1996), 96–97.

8. *Rembrandt's Journey*, 20–22 and 131–32, cat. 64.

9. *Rembrandt's Faith*, 100–101.

10. Wayne Franits, "On the Subject Matter of Rembrandt's Etching, B. 33," *Marsyas* 21 (1981–82): 13–16.

11. J[ohannes] Nieuwstraten, "Het werkelijke onderwerp van Aert de Gelders 'Heilige Familie' te Berlijn," *Oud Holland* 112 (1998): 157–68.

12. The painting is currently in the Bass Museum, Miami, Florida.

13. Nieuwstraten, "Het werlijke," figs. 3 and 4. One of the two paintings, *The Expulsion of Hagar and Ishmael,* is in the State Hermitage Museum, St. Petersburg. The other, *Abraham's Feast Celebrating the Weaning of Isaac with Ishmael Mocking Isaac*, was sold at auction in Brussels in 1929. Its current location is unknown.

14. It is clear that Rembrandt was interested in the relationship between Abraham and his son. He addressed the subject of Abraham casting out Hagar and Ishmael in a signed and dated print from 1637 (B. 30, cat. no. 4), a work probably from around the same time as B. 33. He also made an etching of Abraham and Isaac on the road to Mount Moriah (B. 34, 1645, cat. no. 6)

15. Cf. the isolation of the members of the Holy Family in *Adoration of the Shepherds: A Night Piece* (B. 46, c. 1656–57, cat. no. 21) and *Adoration of the Shepherds: With the Lamp* (B. 45, 1654, cat. no. 20).

16. Hinterding, *Lugt Catalogue*, 74–76.

6. Abraham and Isaac

B. 34 (H. 214, Mz. 180, NHD 224)
Etching and burin
Signed and dated in the plate: *Rembrandt f. 1645*
State I of II
Sheet: 15.7 × 13.0 cm, trimmed to the plate mark

Provenance:
Associated American Artists Inc., New York, NY, 1978
Feddersen, Elkhart, IN, 1991
Snite Museum of Art
Acc. No.: 1991.025.005

Plate survives:
Private collection, Lilian, Netherlands.

Rembrandt's etching of *Abraham and Isaac* depicts the moment in Genesis 22:5–8 when Isaac, unaware of the role that he is meant to play in God's test of his father, expresses his confusion about the sacrifice that God has commanded Abraham to perform on a mountain in Moriah:

> And Abraham took the wood of the burnt offering, and laid it upon Isaac his son; and he took in his hand the fire and the knife; and they went both of them together. And Isaac spoke unto Abraham his father, and said "My father." And he said: "Here am I, my son." And he said: "Behold the fire and the wood; but where is the lamb for a burnt-offering?" And Abraham said: "God will provide Himself the lamb for a burnt-offering, my son." So they went both of them together.

Although prior images of the moment when Isaac questions his father are rare, there is a pair of images that Rembrandt could have drawn on for his etching. A woodcut by Lucas van Leyden (fig. 1) portrays both the journey of Abraham and Isaac to the mountain and—off in the distance—the sacrifice of Isaac; and a print after Maerten de Vos (f. 1603) focuses on the sacrifice of Isaac, but also depicts the journey to Moriah (fig. 2).[1] However, Rembrandt's sparse image differs significantly from both of these earlier examples. He chose to isolate just one element of the drama, the poignant moment in which the father, committed to carrying out God's decree, answers his son as they pause on their way up the mountainside. Rembrandt's print was probably the first work of art to depict this event by itself.[2]

Every item necessary for carrying out the sacrifice is evident in the etching: at Abraham's side is the knife with which he intends to slay his son; Isaac is holding the wood upon which his body will be burned as an offering; and behind Abraham is the smoking pot in which he has carried the fire with which he will ignite the sacrificial pyre.

The elderly patriarch is dressed in a long belted tunic beneath a fur-lined cloak. A chain—just barely visible—hangs diagonally across his chest. He wears a turban whose trailing cloth hangs down at his left and is draped over his right shoulder from behind. Isaac's costume is richly ornamented and detailed. As Abraham leans forward toward his son, he raises his left hand and extends the index finger upward, a gesture that can connote both God's presence and the act of speaking. Meanwhile, Abraham's right hand reaches across his chest and clutches his garment above his heart, an action that some have read as signifying his inner turmoil and anguish.[3] These two gestures sum up Abraham's conflict as he is

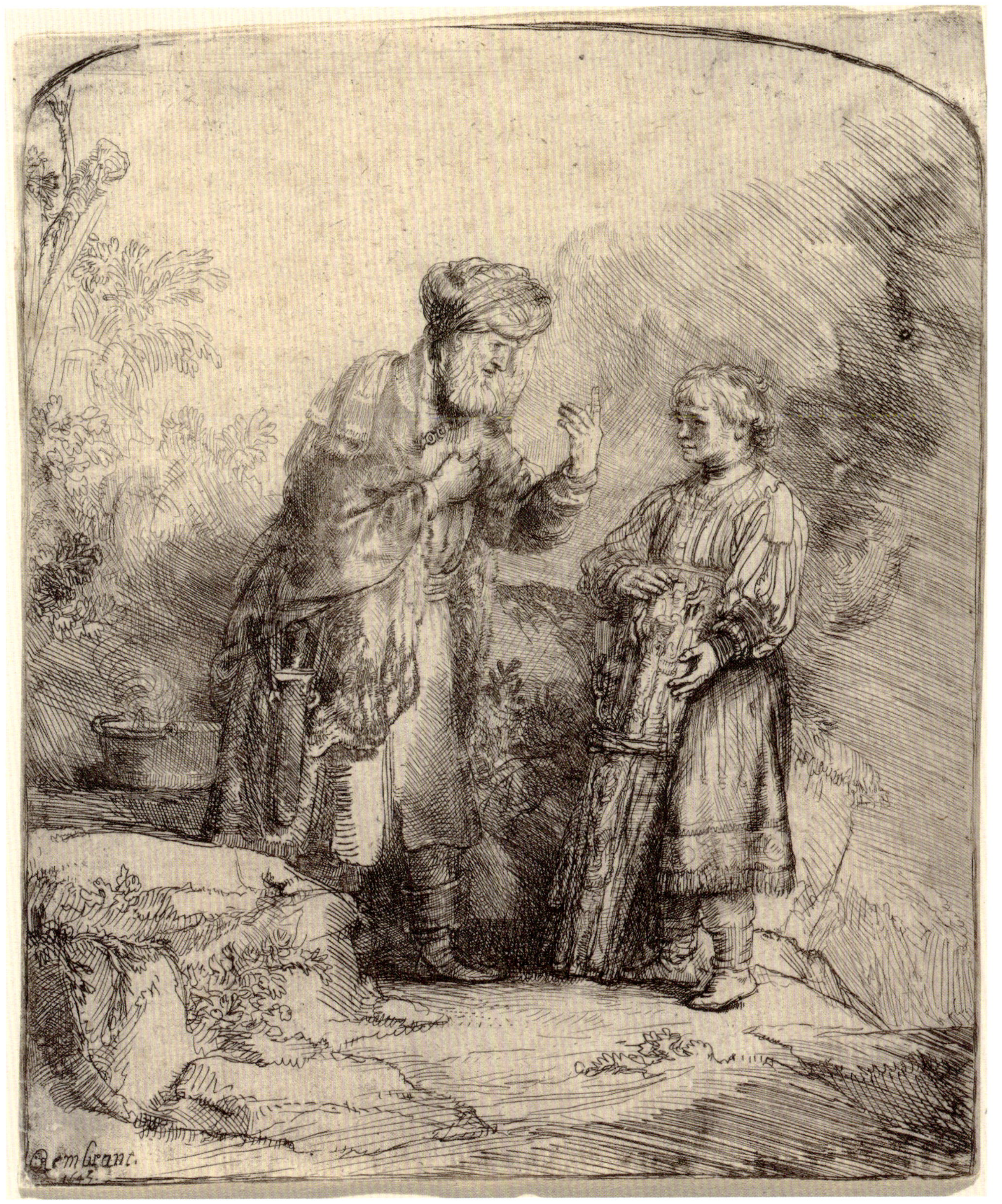

PLATE 6

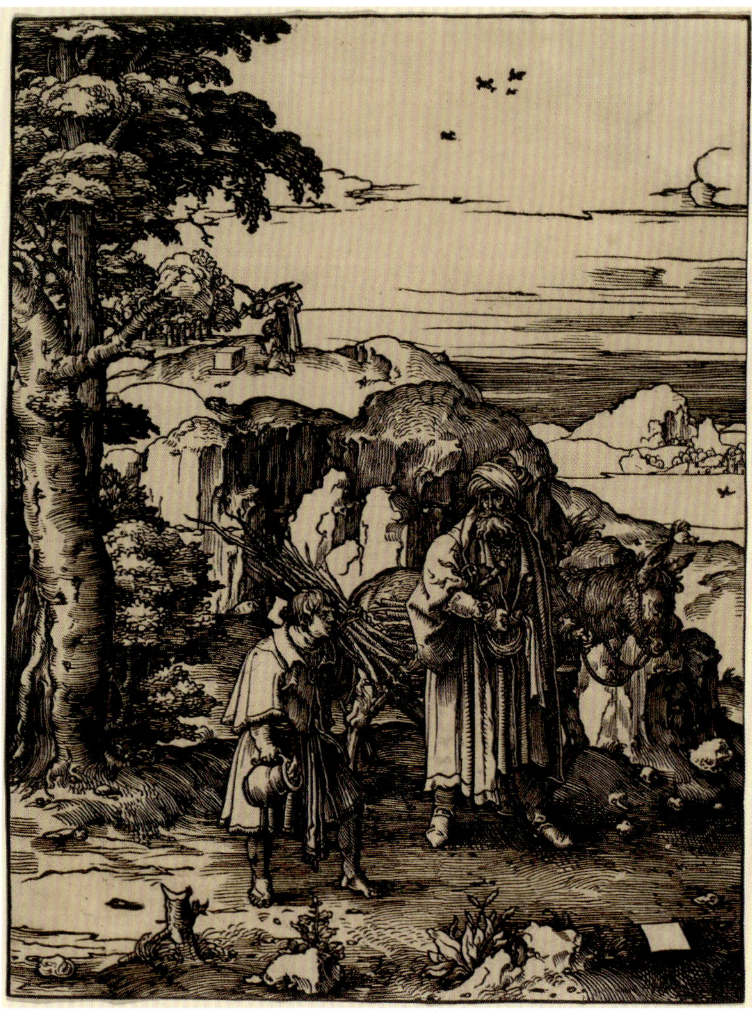

FIGURE 1. Lucas van Leyden, *Abraham and Isaac,* woodcut, c. 1517–19. *Photo: Courtesy of the National Gallery of Art, Washington, DC.*

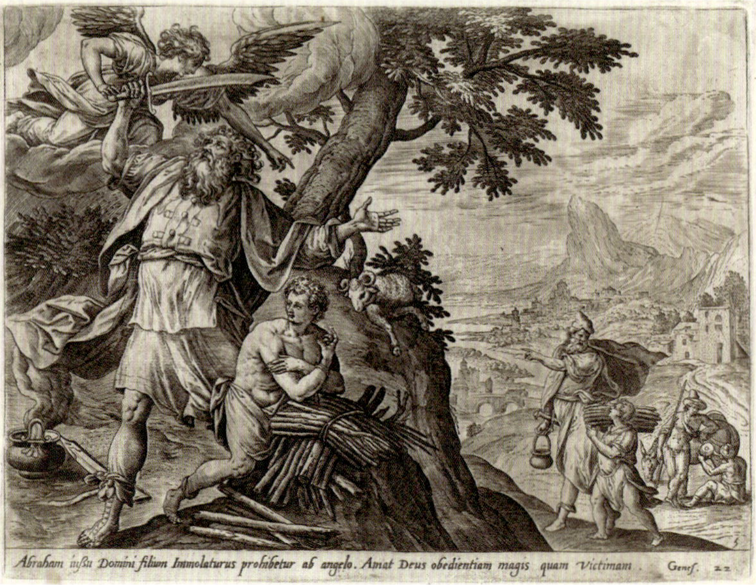

FIGURE 2. After Maerten de Vos, *Sacrifice of Isaac with Abraham and Isaac Ascending Mount Moriah,* etching and engraving, from *Thesaurus sacrarum historiarum veteris testamenti,* 1585. *Rijksmuseum, Amsterdam.*

torn between his obligations to his heavenly Father and those to his beloved son. Isaac stands passively before his father. His shrouded eyes are focused on Abraham's face,[4] and he appears to be listening intently to his father's words, but he betrays no emotion. It seems that the youthful and vulnerable-looking Isaac has meekly accepted his father's assurance that "God will provide."

Christian Tümpel has suggested that it was characteristic of Rembrandt to have chosen to represent not the climactic moment in the story—the angel staying Abraham's hand as he prepares to slay his son—but, rather, the suspenseful interval that preceded and anticipated it.[5] In typical fashion, Rembrandt chose to highlight the psychological essence of the tale. In the biblical text, when God calls to Abraham, the patriarch responds, "Here I am." God gives Abraham his orders, and his obedient servant immediately sets out to fulfill his terrible charge. In the passage illustrated by Rembrandt, Abraham responds to another call, this time from his son, who is puzzled about the purpose of their journey. Once again, Abraham accepts the responsibility of answering. He tells his son, "Here am I, my son." Thus, Rembrandt's depiction speaks to Abraham's willingness to acknowledge and accept the duties put before him: his obedience to God and his responsibilities as a parent. Isaac, in turn, accepts his filial duty to obey his father.

In addition to the knife, kindling, and fire, two more aspects of the scene prefigure sacrifices to come: the first is a low, flat rock. Prominently placed in the left foreground, it suggests the surface of an altar on which an offering could take place. The second detail, the bundle of wood, establishes a link between the Old Testament and the New: Abraham's acceptance of the command to sacrifice Isaac was commonly viewed as an antetype for God's sacrifice of his own son, and the wood that the boy bore up the mountain was specifically equated with the cross that Christ carried up to Golgotha.[6]

Several authors have observed that the location of this scene on Mount Moriah seems to follow the account that appears in Flavius Josephus's first-century *Jewish Antiquities,* book 1, 13. The Roman historian asserted not only that Isaac queried his father at the site of the sacrifice itself, but that this was the very place where the Temple would one day be built. Both Calvin and the Dutch State Bible subscribed to this belief.[7] The possibility that Rembrandt drew on Josephus's text as a source has led some critics to suggest that the creation of this print was influenced by a Sephardic Jew and possibly even produced for a Jewish client. However, Rembrandt himself owned a copy of a German translation of *Jewish Antiquities*[8] and it is therefore possible that he consulted this text on his own.[9]

Notes

1. This painting was sold at Christie's *Important Sale of Old Master Pictures* as sale 6405, lot 22, on December 13, 2000. Erik Hinterding has drawn attention to an anonymous engraving of this painting, *Lugt Catalogue*, cat. 22.

2. Tümpel, *Rembrandt legt*, cat. 8.

3. Shelley Perlove and Robert Baldwin, *Impressions of Faith: Rembrandt's Biblical Etchings* (Dearborn: University of Michigan-Dearborn, Mardigian Library, 1989), 17. Christopher White (*Rembrandt as an Etcher: A Study of the Artist at Work*, 2nd ed. [New Haven, CT: Yale University Press, 1999], 52) characterizes Rembrandt's rendering of Abraham as the image of "a father fighting his conscience."

4. Perlove and Baldwin (*Impressions of Faith*, 17–18) have suggested that Isaac's darkened eyes indicate his blindness to the physical world and his "blind" obedience to his father. One might draw the same conclusion about "blind obedience" in regard to Abraham's dark, sunken eyes in Rembrandt's etching of *Abraham's Sacrifice* (B. 35, 1655, cat. no. 7). These types of connotations cannot be universally applied to the figures in Rembrandt etchings, however. Cf. *Joseph Telling His Dreams* (B. 37, 1638, cat. no. 11), in which the young boy's eyes are also deeply shadowed.

5. Tümpel, *Rembrandt legt*, cat. 8. It should also be noted that Rembrandt made an etching of the much more common subject of the angel saving Isaac from the knife, *Abraham's Sacrifice* (B. 35, 1655, cat. no. 7), ten years after completing the print of Abraham and Isaac standing on the mountainside.

6. As Perlove and Silver have noted, in the *Biblia pauperum*, the image of Christ bearing the cross is paired with that of Isaac carrying the wood. *Rembrandt's Faith*, 86.

7. *Rembrandt's Faith*, 87.

8. Flavius Josephus's *Jewish Antiquities* with woodcut illustrations by Tobias Stimmer, one of the few books in Rembrandt's possession, was listed in the 1656 inventory of the artist's house. Amy Golhany, *Rembrandt's Reading: The Artist's Bookshelf of Ancient Poetry and History* (Amsterdam: Amsterdam University Press, 2003), 78. The Stimmer illustrations do not include an image of Isaac querying Abraham.

9. Perlove and Baldwin, *Impressions*, 17, citing Albert Blankert, *God, Saints & Heroes, Dutch Painting in the Age of Rembrandt*, exh. cat. (Washington, DC: National Gallery of Art; Detroit: Detroit Institute of Arts; Amsterdam: Rijksmuseum, 1980), 54n29.

7. *Abraham's Sacrifice*

B. 35. (H. 283, Mz. 184, NHD 287)
Etching and drypoint
Signed and dated in the plate: *Rembrandt f. 1655* (d and 6 reversed)
State I of I
Sheet: 16.2 × 13.8 cm; plate mark: 15.6 × 13.1 cm
Verso: in graphite, *m/a/ 1/6/ 39/ DTMKBB / 18* *
On mount: *David Tunick Inc. / 12 East 80th Street / New York, NY 10021*

Provenance:
Israel Museum, Jerusalem
David Tunick Inc., New York, NY, 1977
Feddersen, Elkhart, IN, 1991
Snite Museum of Art
Acc. No.: 1991.025.006

The plate does not survive.

Rembrandt's 1655 etching of *Abraham's Sacrifice* is a classic example of the psychological complexity and studied intensity that characterize the artist's late style. Twenty years earlier, in 1635, Rembrandt had created a more tumultuous painted version of the subject (fig. 1).[1] In this earlier work, the artist had conceived of the story's climactic moment in broad, theatrical terms, deploying strong tenebristic lighting, along with dramatic gestures and expressions, in order to create an explosive confrontation between Abraham and the angel who forcibly intervenes to prevent him from sacrificing his son. In the painting, the three actors—Isaac, Abraham, and the angel—are pushed close to the picture surface. Laid out in a tight, ascending S-curve, they almost completely fill the shallow space. Isaac, dressed only in a loincloth, lies in the foreground at the base of the composition, his naked torso and neck illuminated by a brilliant light. His hands are bound behind his back and his legs are drawn up under him as he lies on his back atop the bundle of sticks meant to be his sacrificial pyre. Isaac's face is covered by Abraham's hand, and his head is pushed back forcibly in such a way that his view is obstructed and his throat is bared, emphasizing his vulnerability. The angel, at the peak of the linked arc of figures, emerges from a dark and roiling sky. As he looks down at Isaac's bared throat, he grasps Abraham's wrist with his right hand and gestures upward toward heaven with his left, indicating that he is the heavenly spirit who has come to convey God's message that since Abraham had shown his obedience to God, Isaac will be spared.[2] At the center of the composition, the startled elderly Abraham looks up at the angel. As the angel grabs Abraham's wrist, the knife falls from his grasp.

In contrast to this earlier work, the 1655 etching depicts the three protagonists as joined together in a single, tight-knit group. The dramatic sense of the moment of rescue that characterized the painting has been replaced by a more restrained and static vision. Isaac, a wiry adolescent, kneels on a raised shelf of earth, his body bent over a draped shape that could be construed as either a covered altar stone or his father's robed knee. In the print, the youth's hands are not bound. His body appears tense with anticipation, but he does not resist his fate. This kind of interpretation of Isaac's acquiescence, which derives from Josephus's account of the sacrifice,[3] was commended by Calvin as a model of faith.[4]

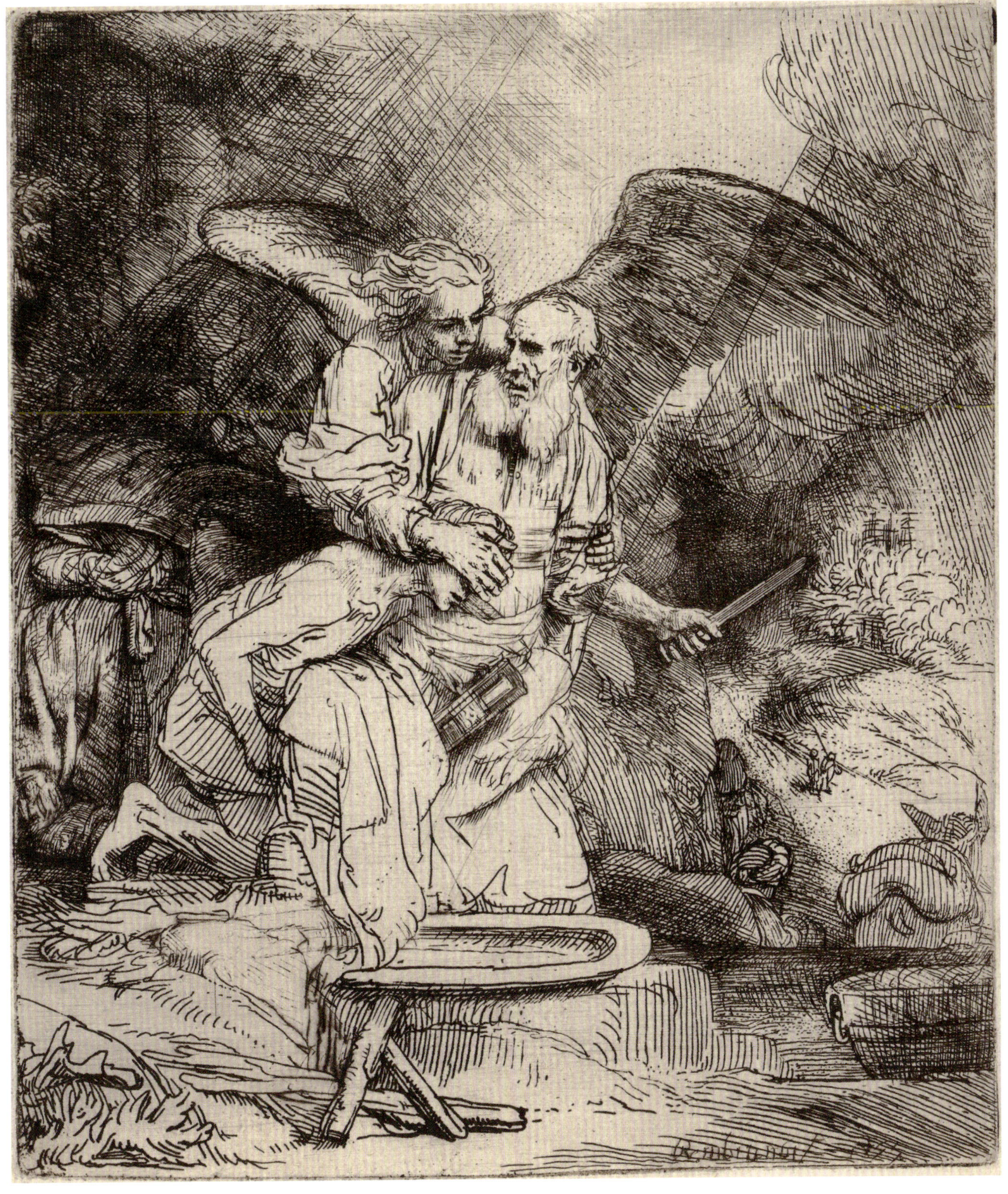

PLATE 7

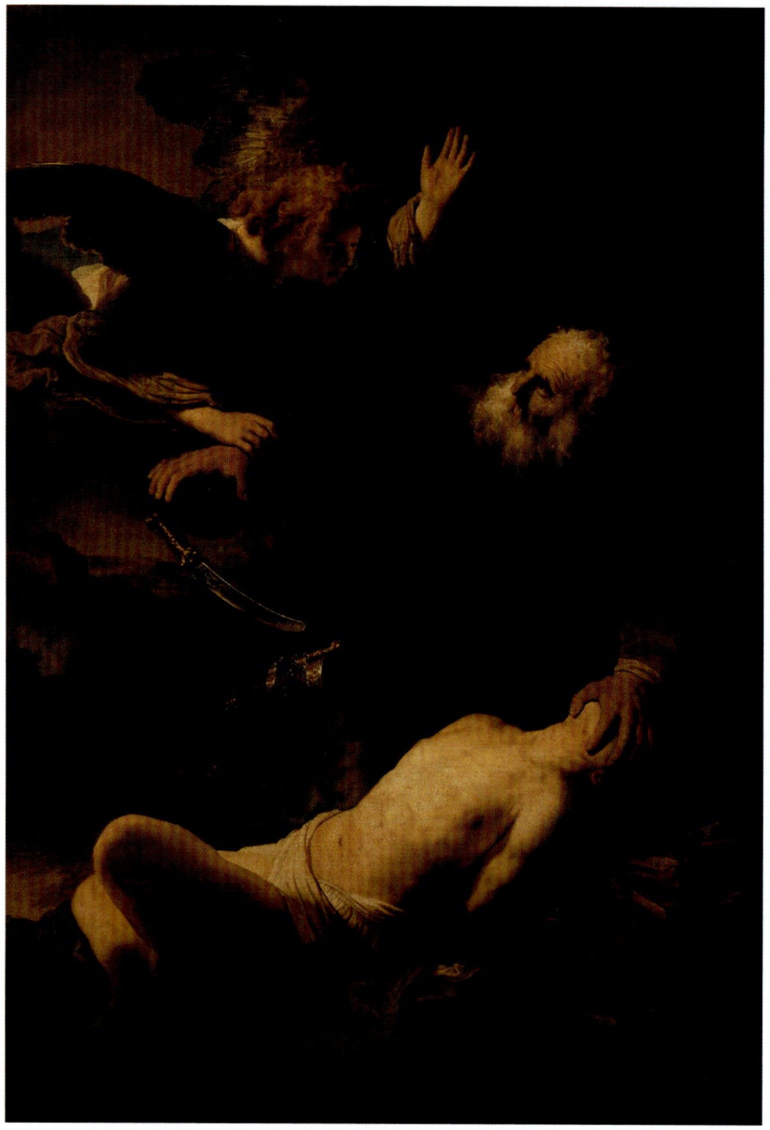

FIGURE 1. Rembrandt, *Abraham's Sacrifice*, oil on canvas, 1635. *The State Hermitage Museum, St. Petersburg. © The State Hermitage Museum/ Photography by Vladimir Terebenin.*

In Rembrandt's print, Abraham has methodically prepared for the sacrifice. He has removed his cloak and turban and set them aside on the rocks to his right, and he has set out the objects he will need to accomplish his task. Yet, as he proceeds, he is clearly torn. He brandishes a knife with his left hand and simultaneously draws the boy toward him with the other hand, covering Isaac's eyes and cradling his son's head against his own body. The violence and tension that characterized the painted version of the tale are gone. Rather than thrusting Isaac's head back against the hard ground, Abraham embraces him. As Jakob Rosenberg observed, Abraham's gesture is "infinitely more human than the one in the earlier version."[5] The tenderness between father and son in this late etching is typical of Rembrandt's deepening interest in exploring familial relationships. In fact, some have seen this as a reflection of the artist's close relationship with his own son, Titus.[6] Some critics have even gone so far as to suggest that the etching's depiction of Isaac actually resembles images of Titus.[7]

As in the painted version, Abraham turns to look back over his shoulder toward the angel, who has arrived just in time to prevent the sacrifice. The patriarch's eyes are black hollows, a detail that has been interpreted as symbolic of the patriarch's blind faith.[8] This reading accords with Calvin's interpretation of the story. In particular, Calvin noted that the patriarch, although confused and distraught, acted both freely and in accordance with God's will, passing what was an extraordinary divine test.[9] According to Calvin, Abraham's trial should be taken to heart by all, for it was an extreme example of every man's fate, in which "each [person] will be tried by God, according to the measure of his faith."[10] Abraham's dark, haunted eyes, reminiscent of the deep-set gaze of his son in the 1645 etching of Abraham and Isaac before the sacrifice (B. 34, cat. no. 6), can also be interpreted as an external expression of the internal pain suffered by a father preparing himself to sacrifice his own son—a foreshadowing of God's own future sacrifice.

The angel has descended down a shaft of light that splits the symbolic darkness of the rocky mountainside, at the left, and the billowing clouds and sunlit valley, at the right. His left wing is spread out gracefully to the side, as though it is ready to enfold Abraham and his son.[11] In a gesture quite unlike that of the earlier, painted version, the angel leans over Abraham's shoulder, embracing and comforting him;[12] God's emissary seems to restrain the patriarch not so much by force as by persuasion and tenderness. The message of the heavenly spirit, with its emphasis on faith, obedience, and mercy, is very much in harmony with Calvinist principles.

The setting of the 1655 etching includes many more details than that of the 1635 painting. For example, the print includes the ram that, the Bible relates, will eventually take Isaac's place as a sacrifice.[13] This ram is just barely visible beneath the angel's folded right wing. Rembrandt's cross-hatching has nearly obscured the animal, so that the viewer, like Abraham, does not initially realize that the beast is nearby. The etched version of the tale also includes secondary actors. A bit farther down the mountain, below Abraham and Isaac at the right, are the servant and donkey that accompanied them to Moriah. Beyond these figures and still farther below, two additional figures can be discerned in the bright valley that stretches out into the distance. These tiny, barely delineated travelers, ignorant of the miracle occurring nearby, have been interpreted by some as representing the unbelievers who remain ignorant of God's true ways.[14]

In the right foreground of the *Sacrifice* is the pot with fire that Abraham carried up the mountainside, and in the center, three sticks lean against a flat rock that holds a large shallow basin set out to catch Isaac's blood. These sticks, which had been destined to feed the fire on which Abraham's son would be immolated, evoke not only Isaac's intended sacrifice, but also Christ's future crucifixion on a cross of wood. The association of Isaac and Christ was a common typological reading of the Abraham and Isaac story, and the large platter on the altar stone reinforces this reading through its Eucharistic implications.[15] It is probably no coincidence that Rembrandt chose to place *three* sticks prominently at the foreground of the print. The three are arranged in a triangle, the apex of which points up toward the miraculous event above them, a drama of willing sacrifice and last-minute redemption being enacted by a father, a son, and a holy emissary sent by God.

Notes

1. *Abraham's Sacrifice*, c. 1635, the State Hermitage Museum, St. Petersburg (RRP, *Corpus*, A108). Two free copies of the painting, attributed to Rembrandt's pupils, are located in Munich and the Louvre.

2. Genesis 22:12.

3. Barbara Welzel, "Abraham's Sacrifice," in Holm Bevers, Peter Schatborn, and Barbara Welzel, *Rembrandt: The Master and his Workshop*, vol. 2, *Drawings and Etchings*, exh. cat. (New Haven, CT: Yale University Press, 1991), 278–80. Josephus, *Jewish Antiquities*, 1, 13, 232: "Now Isaac was of such a generous disposition as became a son of such a father, and was pleased with this discourse; and said 'that he was not worthy to be born at first, if he should reject the determination of God and of his father, and should not resign himself up readily to both their pleasures; since it would have been unjust if he had not obeyed, even if his father alone had so resolved.' So he went immediately to the altar to be sacrificed."

4. Shelley Perlove and Robert Baldwin, *Impressions of Faith: Rembrandt's Biblical Etchings* (Dearborn: University of Michigan-Dearborn, Mardigian Library, 1989), 18.

5. Jakob Rosenberg, *Rembrandt: Life and Work* (London: Phaidon, 1964), 176.

6. Titus was fourteen at the time this print was made, about the age of Rembrandt's Isaac.

7. Münz, *Critical Catalogue*, vol. 2, cat. 184, 90; and Perlove and Baldwin, *Impressions of Faith*, 20. Michael Zell suggested that it is the angel's face that resembles Titus (Zell, *Reframing Rembrandt: Jews and the Christian Image in Seventeenth-Century Amsterdam* [Berkeley: University of California Press, 2002], 186).

8. Christopher White, *Rembrandt as an Etcher: A Study of the Artist at Work*, 2nd ed. (New Haven, CT: Yale University Press, 1999), 104; and David R. Smith, "Toward a Protestant Aesthetics: Rembrandt's 1655 *Sacrifice of Isaac*," *Art History* 8 (1985): 295.

9. In Calvin's view, Abraham had proven his loyalty to God. "He was unwilling to measure, by his own understanding, the method of fulfilling the promise, which he knew depended on the incomprehensible power of God. It remains for everyone to apply this example to himself." Cited in Zell, *Reframing*, 190–91.

10. Quoted in Perlove and Baldwin, *Impressions of Faith*, 20. On the desirability of using Abraham as a model of faithful obedience, see the quote in note 9.

11. A number of historians have observed that Rembrandt altered the position of the angel's right wing, burnishing out details and bringing it in closer to his body.

12. Rembrandt used a similar motif of the embracing angel in his etching of *Agony in the Garden* (B. 75, 1652, cat. no. 49). The angel who restrains and the angel who supports can both be seen as representing God's compassionate love.

13. Genesis 22:13. The ram was added to the Munich and Louvre copies of the Hermitage painting.

14. Tümpel, *Rembrandt legt*, cat. 9.

15. David R. Smith denied that any such Christological meaning was intended, citing Calvin's dismissal of these sorts of traditional typological associations as unnecessary (Smith, "Toward a Protestant Aesthetics," 293). By contrast, Perlove (Perlove and Baldwin, *Impressions of Faith*, 19) noted that "Rembrandt's allusion to the Eucharist in *Abraham's Sacrifice* wholly conforms to the Calvinist view of Communion as a celebration of the covenant, the Word of God." She also suggested that the cloth that drapes the rock upon which Isaac is leaning invokes the image of the "corporal," making the reference to the Eucharist even more compelling.

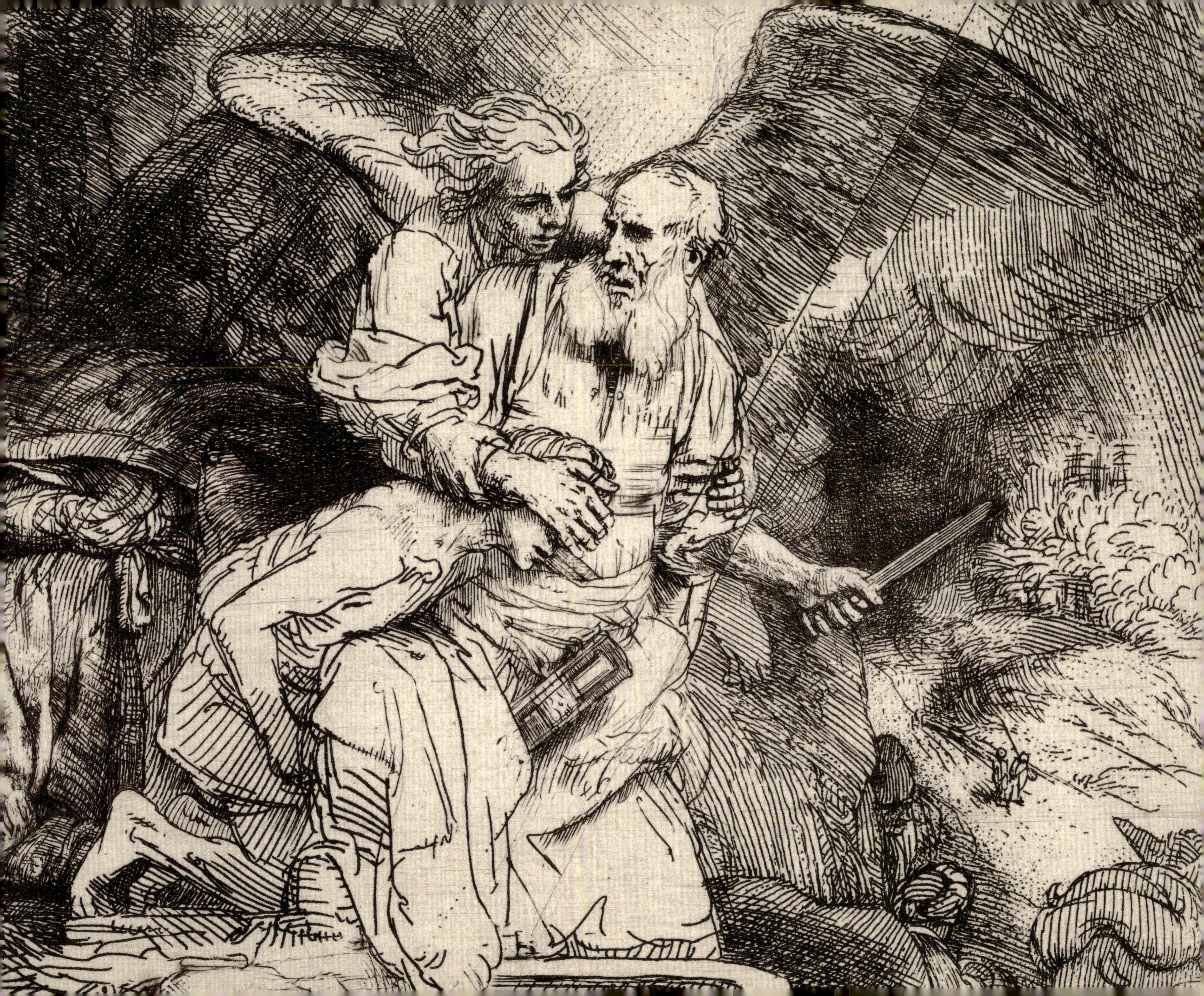

8–10. Illustrations for Samuel Menasseh ben Israel, *Piedra gloriosa o de la Estatua de Nebuchadnesar*, Amsterdam, 1655

8. *The Image Seen by Nebuchadnezzar*

B. 36 A (H. 284 A, Mz. 183, NHD 288a)
Etching, drypoint, and burin
Signed and dated in plate: *Rembrandt f. 1655*
State II of V
Sheet: vellum, irregularly trimmed: 10.0 × 6.5 cm
Recto: in brown ink, upper right corner: *82*

Provenance:
P. & D. Colnaghi & Co. Ltd., London, 1976
Feddersen, Elkhart, IN, 1991
Snite Museum of Art
Acc. No.: 1991.025.007

The plate does not survive.

9. *David and Goliath*

B. 36 C (H. 284 C, Mz. 183, NHD 288c)
Etching, drypoint, and burin
Signed and dated in plate: *Rembrandt f. 1655*
State II of V
Sheet: vellum, irregularly trimmed: 10.1 × 7.2 cm
Recto: in brown ink, upper right corner: *80*

Provenance:
P. & D. Colnaghi & Co. Ltd., London, 1976
Feddersen, Elkhart, IN, 1991
Snite Museum of Art
Acc. No.: 1991.025.008

The plate does not survive.

10. *Daniel's Vision of the Four Beasts*

B. 36 D (H. 284 D, Mz. 183, NHD 288d)
Etching, drypoint, and burin
Signed and dated in plate: *Rembrandt f. 1655*
State II of IV
Sheet: vellum, irregularly trimmed: 10.2 × 7.4 cm

Provenance:
P. & D. Colnaghi & Co. Ltd., London, 1976
Feddersen, Elkhart, IN, 1991
Snite Museum of Art
Acc. No.: 1991.025.009

The plate does not survive.

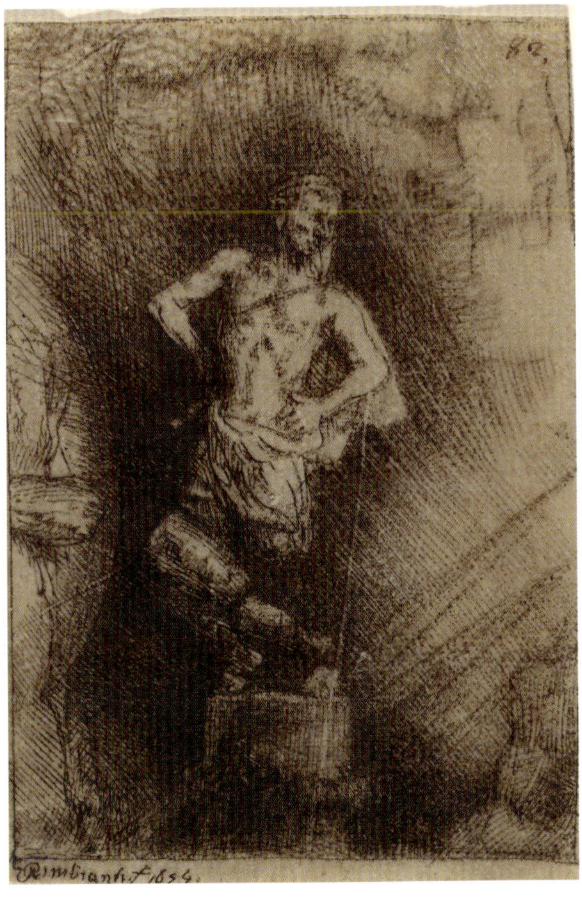

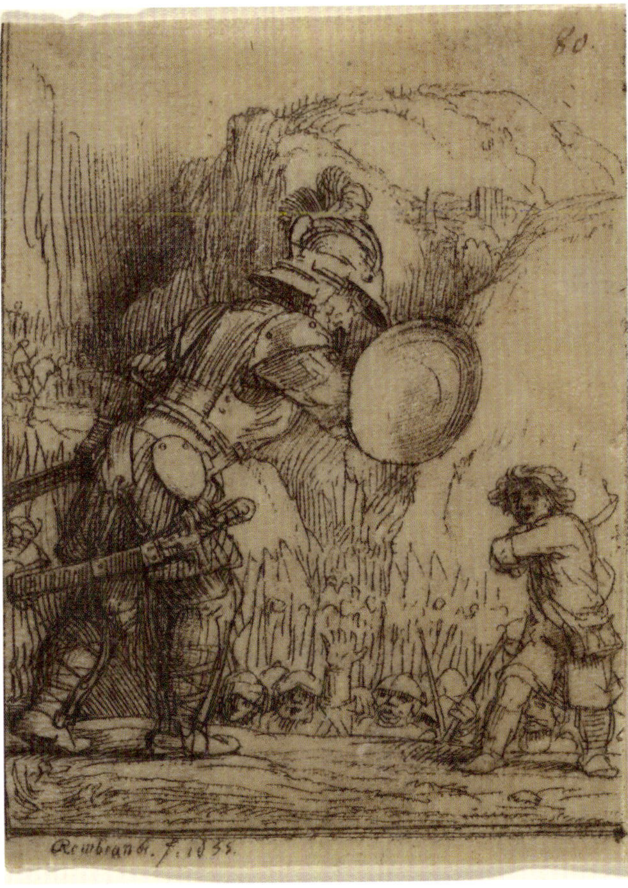

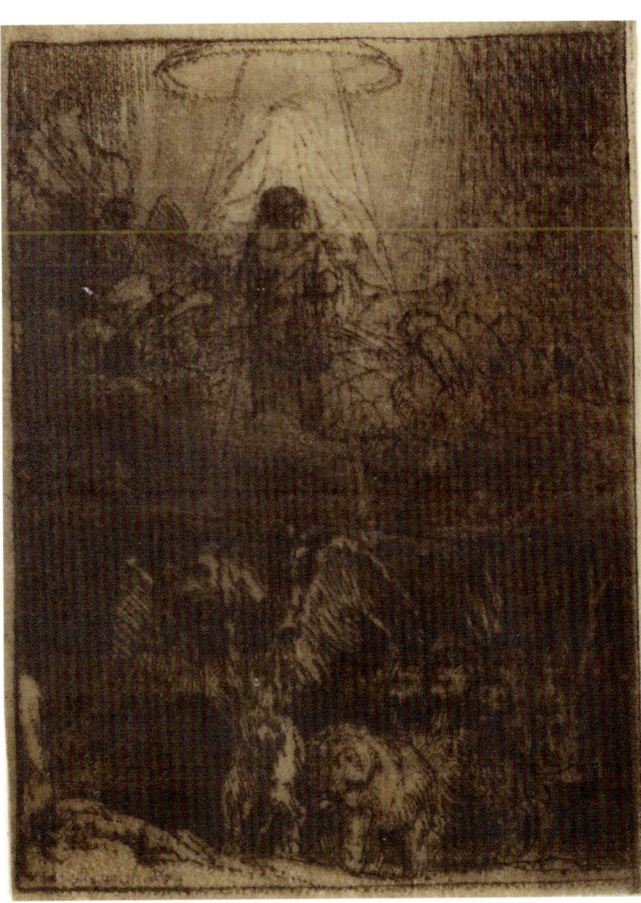

PLATES 8–10

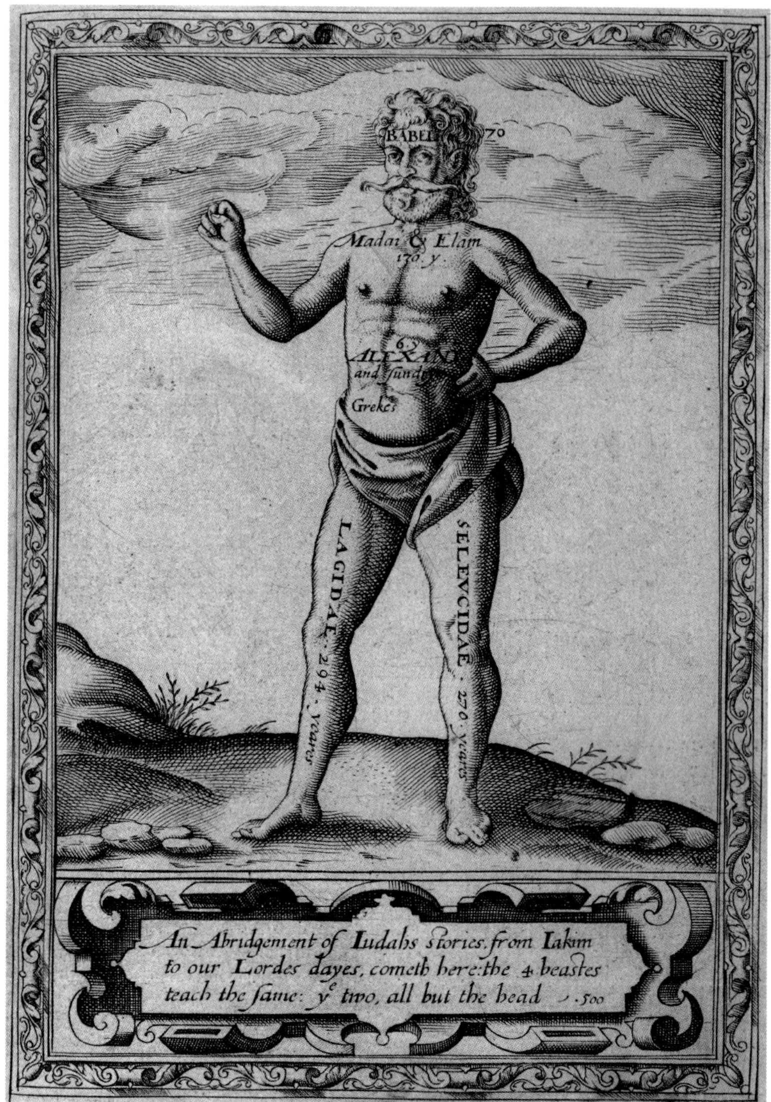

FIGURE 1. William Rogers, *The Image Seen by Nebuchadnezzar,* from Hugh Broughton's *A Concent of Scripture,* London, c. 1590. *Folger Shakespeare Library, Washington, DC.*

In 1655, Rembrandt was commissioned to create four prints to serve as illustrations for Rabbi Samuel Menasseh ben Israel's messianic treatise *Piedra gloriosa o de la Estatua de Nebuchadnesar* (The Glorious Stone, or the Statue of Nebuchadnezzar),[1] a book dedicated to Isaac Vossius, a Dutch scholar and bibliophile.[2] Three of the subjects, *The Image Seen by Nebuchadnezzar, Jacob's Ladder,*[3] and *David and Goliath,* were derived from biblical stories linked by the titular "glorious stone," while the fourth etching was inspired by *Daniel's Vision of the Four Beasts.* These prints were an unusual commission for Rembrandt for two reasons: First, up until this time, he had made only two book illustrations, *The Ship of Fortune* (B. 111), for Elias Herckmans's rambling irenic history of the world seen through the lens of navigation, *Der Zee-Vaert Lof* (In Praise of Navigation), published in 1634;[4] and *Medea, or the Wedding of Jason and Creusa* (B. 112), a print that served as the title page for Jan Six's verse drama *Medea,* published in 1648. Second, although the individual illustrations for Menasseh's treatise were based on biblical passages, three of the four subjects were mystical and overtly symbolic, qualities that are somewhat antithetical to Rembrandt's predilection for representing the earthy and quotidian even in images illustrating the most profound biblical events. In spite of these limitations, however, Rembrandt was able to create etchings that evidently satisfied his patron's wishes.[5]

There is no record as to how Rembrandt came to receive this commission. In Henri van de Waal's seminal article on these etchings, the art historian suggested that Menasseh ben Israel might have been motivated by financial considerations.[6] Rembrandt and the rabbi were neighbors who had probably known each other for twenty years,[7] and it is possible that the artist charged Menasseh a favorable price for the four small illustrations.[8] In accepting the commission, Rembrandt may also have been motivated by his acquaintance with the rabbi, his recognition of the significance of the project for Menasseh's messianic millenarianism, and the artist's own straitened economic circumstances.[9]

Piedra gloriosa takes as its starting point the Book of Daniel's account of Nebuchadnezzar's dream, in which a colossal statue of gold, silver, brass, iron, and clay was destroyed by a stone "cut out without hands."[10] According to Menasseh, the stone that shattered the symbolic statue was the Messiah, who would one day come to sweep away the earthly kingdoms represented by the colossus. Menasseh went on to identify this same "glorious stone" as the rock upon which Jacob slept when he had his vision of the angels ascending and descending a ladder to heaven,[11] and the stone with which David slew Goliath.[12] The culmination of Menasseh's messianic vision of history past and future is found in Daniel's apocalyptic dream of the four beasts that rise out of the sea and of the son of man who comes "with the clouds of heaven" before the Ancient of Days (God) and who is given eternal dominion over the earth.[13] These four prophetic events and visions are the subjects of Rembrandt's etchings.

In creating the illustrations for *Piedra gloriosa*, Rembrandt drew upon four sources: biblical texts, visual precedents, Menasseh's advice, and his own imagination. Ludwig Münz proposed that the etchings of *The Image Seen by Nebuchadnezzar* and *Daniel's Vision of the Four Beasts* were inspired by illustrations from Matthäus Merian's well-known picture Bible.[14] Otto Benesch and Henri van de Waal, however, suggested another source: illustrations by William Rogers for the British Hebrew scholar Hugh Broughton's *A Concent of Scripture*, published in London around 1590.[15] Ultimately, however, Rembrandt's rendering of these two themes remains unique. His wiry-framed, somewhat awkwardly composed colossus posed on a columnar base in front of a shadowy, stony cave-like background is quite unlike the rather stiff interpretations of the Nebuchadnezzar image in Broughton and Merian (figs. 1 and 2). Similarly, Rembrandt's rendering of Daniel's vision of the four beasts emerging out of the darkness is more fanciful, naturalistic, and textually accurate than earlier illustrations. In illustrating Daniel's "four winds of the heaven blowing upon the great sea," Merian drew lines emerging

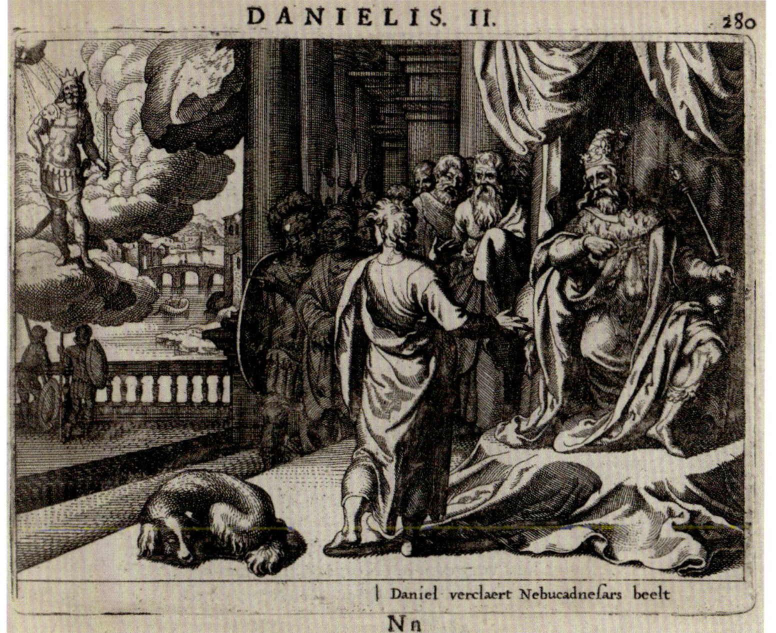

FIGURE 2. Matthäus Merian, *The Image Seen by Nebuchadnezzar*, from *Iconum biblicarum*, Frankfurt, 1627. *Folger Shakespeare Library, Washington, DC.*

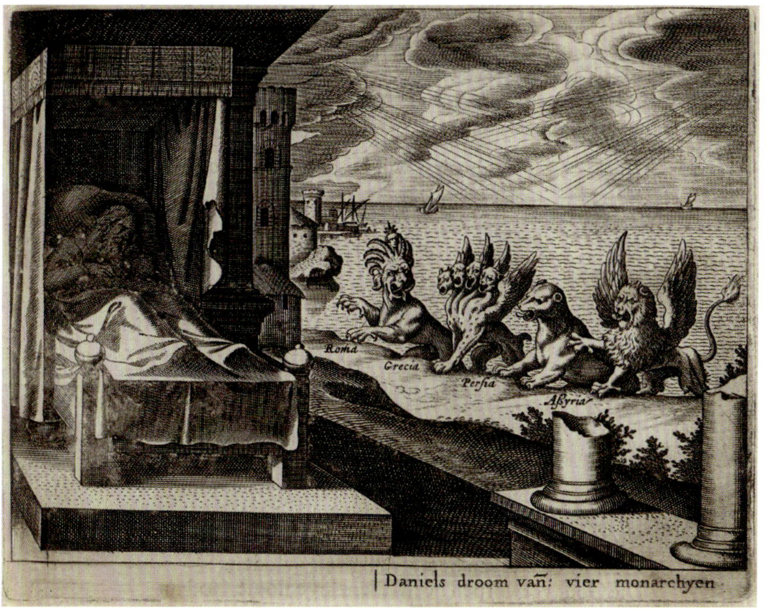

FIGURE 3. Matthäus Merian, *Daniel's Vision of the Four Beasts*, from *Iconum biblicarum*, Frankfurt, 1627. *Folger Shakespeare Library, Washington, DC.*

from the clouds (fig. 3), whereas Rembrandt created traditional wind gods, small children expelling air from their inflated cheeks. Although only their heads are visible, these children display an energy that transforms the earlier, static image into a picture that

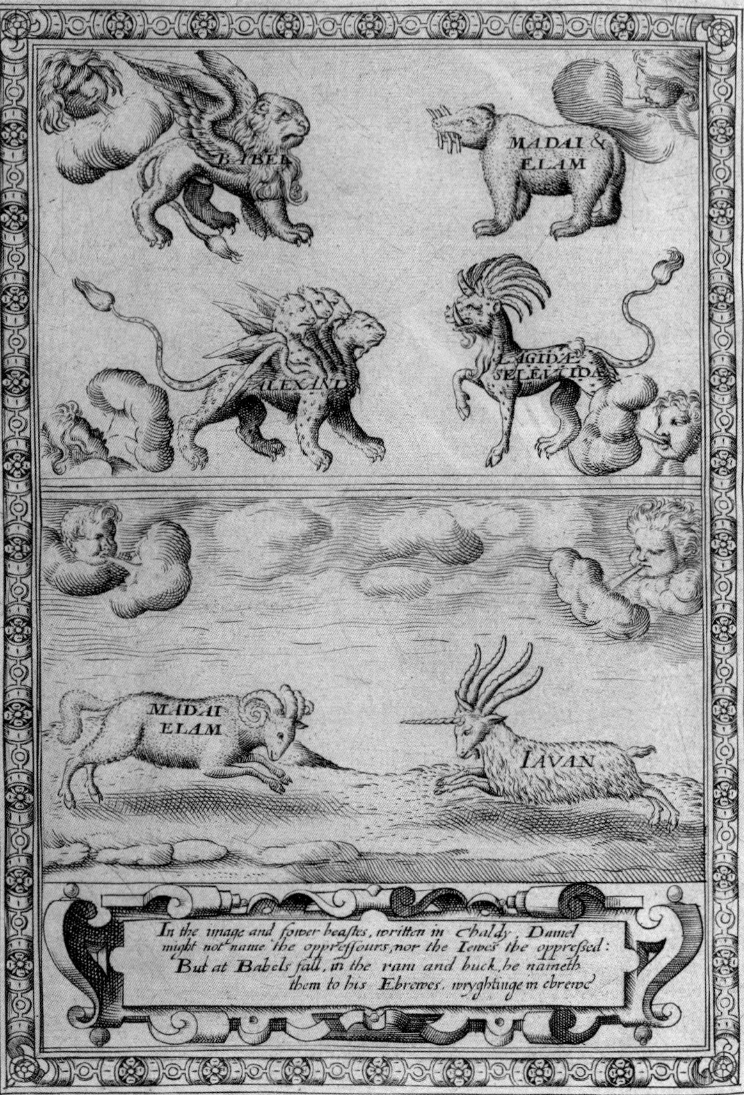

FIGURE 4. William Rogers, *Daniel's Vision of the Four Beasts*, from Hugh Broughton's *A Concent of Scripture*, London, c. 1590. *Folger Shakespeare Library, Washington, DC.*

is much more lively and whimsical. Rembrandt's version of the bear with three bones in its mouth is highly naturalistic, looking as if it had been rendered from life. His interpretation of the lion with the wings of an eagle raised up on its feet like a man is much closer to the biblical text than the depictions of winged lions that appear in *A Concent of Scripture* (fig. 4) and Merian's picture Bible. Rogers and Merian both depicted a beast walking on all fours, an animal that closely resembles traditional images of the lion of St. Mark, rather than the creature in Daniel's vision. By contrast, Rembrandt's hybrid animal is the stuff of nightmares, rearing up on its hind legs and raising its front legs above its head. Baring its claws, the looming, ominous creature leads a frightening apocalyptic procession. Finally, in rendering the fourth beast, the most purely imaginary creature, Rembrandt followed both the original biblical text and Menasseh ben Israel's description. Rejecting the traditional version of this creature as a spiky-crested, Caliban-faced monster with claws or trotters, Rembrandt gave the apparition the head of a wild boar, a detail derived from Menasseh's text,[16] and also the multiple horns and the distinctive small horn with eyes and a mouth that spoke "great words," as described in the Book of Daniel. The artist's conflation of Daniel's dream of the four beasts with the prophet's messianic vision of the man appearing before the Ancient of Days is unique. In the upper portion of the etching, the young Messiah stands before an old bearded man (God) bathed in brilliant white light, while down below, frightening creatures emerge from the darkness. Drawing the two visions together into one image, Rembrandt reinforced Menasseh's mystical millenarianism, an innovation presumably undertaken with his patron's encouragement.

As Michael Zell observed, Rembrandt's interpretation of the story of David and Goliath deviates from Menasseh's description of the illustration in his prefatory address to the reader.[17] In this text, Menasseh states that the picture shows David standing over the fallen giant, an image that is meant to echo the crushed colossus in Nebuchadnezzar's vision. Instead, Rembrandt chose to depict a more dramatic moment in the narrative, the actual confrontation between the Philistine giant and the diminutive shepherd boy. Goliath, clad in armor and holding a shield in his right hand and a spear in his left,[18] leans forward toward David. The biblical hero, by contrast, is portrayed as a young boy with a mop of unruly hair.[19] His body coiled, David looks directly up at the giant towering above him, but Rembrandt has left the outcome of the encounter unresolved. It is possible that David is about to fling a stone toward Goliath, but it is also possible that he has already hurled the fateful missile at his opponent and that the arm holding the sling, following through on the trajectory, has wrapped itself around his body. Hordes of soldiers can be seen in the background, watching the battle. Their reactions are muted, except for one figure in the foreground who raises an arm as he looks up at Goliath. Christian Tümpel suggested that in creating this etching, Rembrandt drew on Tobias Stimmer's woodcut illustration of the battle in the *Neue Künstliche Figuren Biblischer Historien* published in Basel in 1576 (fig. 5).[20] A more likely inspiration would have been Stimmer's illustration (fig. 6) in the German edition of Flavius Josephus's collected works, of which Rembrandt owned a copy.[21] Although the figures in this work have a different orientation, David, whose back is turned toward the viewer, shows a somewhat similar coiled posture. Still more intriguing is the fact that Stimmer's Goliath is not attacking, but is actually off-balance, as if he were about to fall backward and to his right, even though there is still a stone in David's sling that has not yet been flung. In Rembrandt's print, Goliath is clearly leaning forward toward his opponent, but it is unclear whether he is advancing to attack or is about to topple over. He seems to be gazing not at David, but down at the ground. Similarly, the gesture of the soldier in the background with his arm raised can be interpreted either as a motion urging the Philistine giant onward or as a shocked reaction at Goliath's unexpected defeat. This kind of ambiguity, which allows the viewer to consider multiple possibilities in an image simultaneously, is typical of Rembrandt's approach to illustrating biblical narratives.

Another element that distinguishes Rembrandt's prints of these subjects from his predecessors is his use of light and shadow. The images that represent dreams or visions emerge from the darkness, with light only in the upper, heavenly reaches of the etchings of Daniel's vision and Jacob's dream. In the scene of David and Goliath, Rembrandt used parallel lines and cross-hatching to darken the area around the malevolent giant, but silhouetted David against a white background and even described a kind of halo of light behind his head.

Initially, Rembrandt etched all four of the illustrations on a single plate, from which he then pulled proofs. Later, he cut the plate into four individual pieces so that each image could be printed

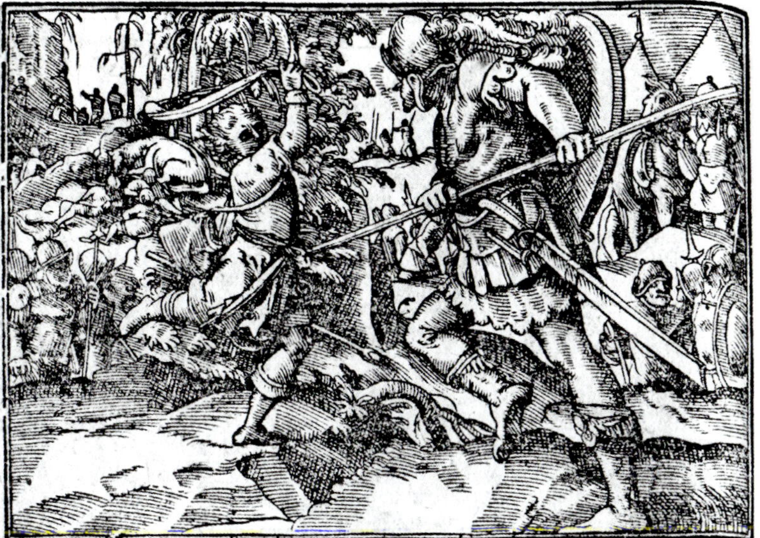

FIGURE 5. Tobias Stimmer, *David and Goliath*, from *Neue Künstliche Figuren Biblischer Historien*, Basel, 1576. *Image courtesy of Concordia Seminary Library Special Collections, St. Louis, Missouri.*

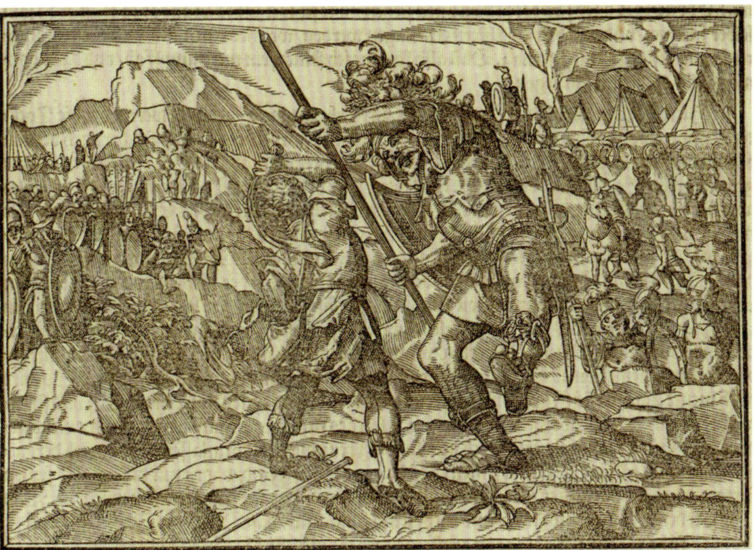

FIGURE 6. Tobias Stimmer, *David and Goliath*, from Falvius Josephus and Conrad Lautenbach, *Flavii Josephi Des Hochberühmten Jüdischen Geschichteschreibers Historien . . .*, Strasburg, 1574. *Rare Books and Special Collections, Hesburgh Libraries, University of Notre Dame, Notre Dame, Indiana.*

separately. The impressions were then sold individually or else trimmed and stubbed into the binding of a copy of Menasseh's book.[22] The three *Piedra gloriosa* illustrations in the Snite Museum's Feddersen collection are printed on vellum, a more costly and more prestigious support than paper. Rembrandt's decision to print some of the early states this way is in keeping with his predilection for experimentation during the 1650s.[23] Although impressions printed

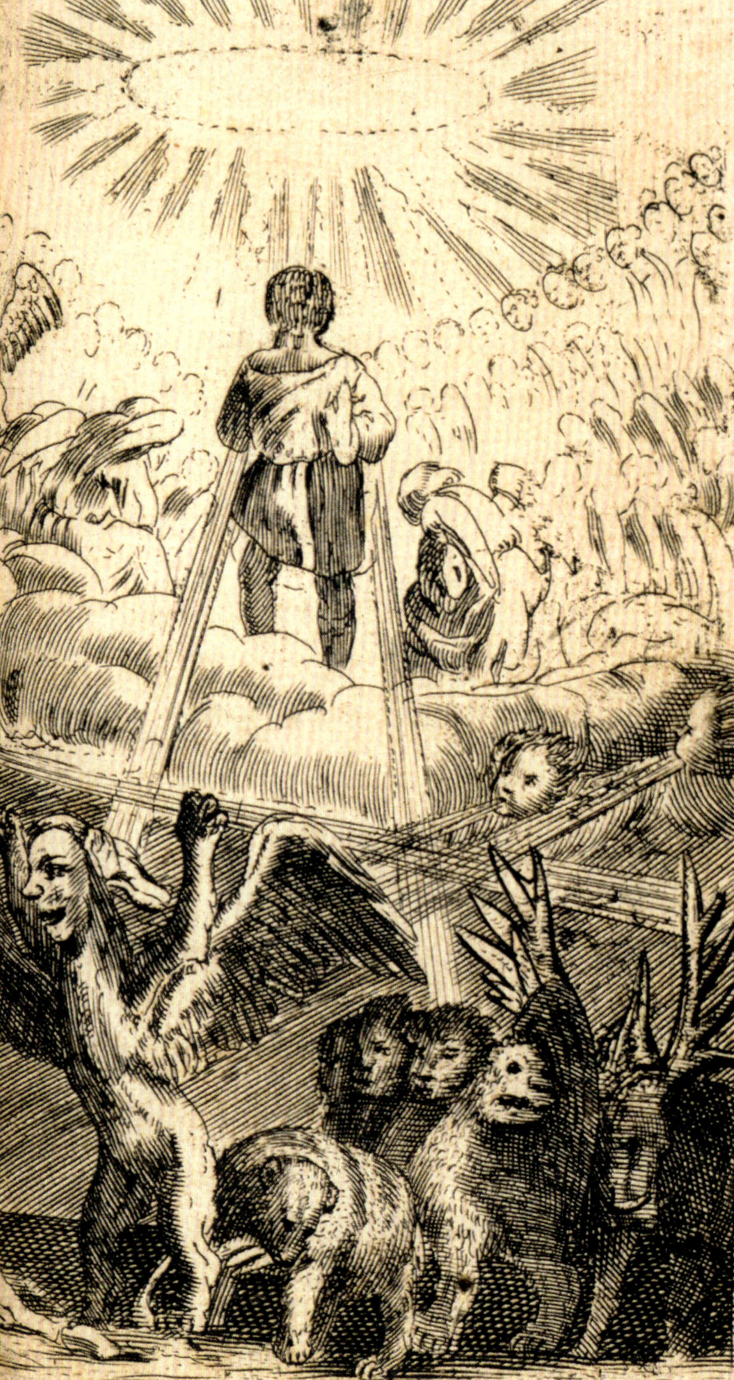

FIGURE 7. Shalom Italia (?), *Daniel's Vision of Four Beasts,* from Menasseh ben Israel, *Piedra gloriosa,* c. 1657. *Courtesy of the Library of the Jewish Theological Seminary, New York, New York.*

on vellum could theoretically have been bound into a copy of *Piedra gloriosa,* it is more likely that they were intended to be sold to collectors as a series. Impressions of any of the four *Piedra gloriosa* etchings on vellum, all of which were created before the plate was cut up, are relatively rare. Vellum's hard surface does not absorb ink in the same way that paper does, and as a result, impressions printed on this support can smear during the printing process, resulting in a reduction in legibility and detail, as seen in the Snite Museum impressions.

It seems likely that in a relatively short period of time, Rembrandt's plates became too worn to be used effectively. As a result, his etchings were replaced by engraved copies, possibly produced by the Jewish engraver Shalom Italia.[24] These illustrations are fairly accurate reproductions of the final states of Rembrandt's original etchings, with one notable exception. Contrary to the Old Testament injunction against visual representations of God, Rembrandt had included an image of the "Ancient of Days" in his representation of Daniel's messianic vision. Although this must have been acceptable to Menasseh ben Israel, since the image is included in the presentation copy which Menasseh gave to Isaac Vossius, it would nonetheless have been quite controversial within the Hebraic community at large.[25] It was probably in response to the provocative nature of Rembrandt's etching that when Shalom Italia (?) went to copy it after Menasseh's death, he omitted the figure representing God and left only the suggestive haloed cone of light to suggest his presence (fig. 7).[26]

Notes

1. The full text of *Piedra gloriosa* is available online, accessed February 26, 2013, http://permalink.opc.uva.nl/item/001251080.

2. Eric Jorink and Dirk van Miert. *Isaac Vossius (1618–1689): Between Science and Scholarship* (Leiden: E. J. Brill, 2012).

3. The Snite Museum does not own an impression of *Jacob's Ladder* (B. 36 B).

4. This poem was illustrated with eighteen etchings, only one of which was by Rembrandt. Herman de la Fontaine Verwey, "Rembrandt as a Book-Illustrator," *Quaerendo* 3, no. 1 (1971): 7.

5. Henri van de Waal published a copy of *Piedra gloriosa* from the Leiden University library (Shelfmark 1370 G 13) that was originally owned by Isaac Vossius, the man to whom the tract was dedicated. The Vossius copy, which included Rembrandt's illustrations, is in its original binding with some uncut pages. As van de Waal observes, Menasseh clearly accepted Rembrandt's images, for they were present in what must have been the copy that Menassah himself presented to Vossius. Henri van de Waal, "Rembrandt's Etchings for Menasseh Ben Israel's *Piedra gloriosa*," in van de Waal, *Steps Towards Rembrandt: Collected Articles 1937–1972*, ed. R. H. Fuchs (Amsterdam: North-Holland, 1974), 118.

6. Van de Waal, "Rembrandt's Etchings," 116.

7. It appears that around 1635, while creating *Belshazzar's Feast*, Rembrandt used Menasseh's published description of the miraculous inscription on the wall as a guide for his painting. See Michael Zell, *Reframing Rembrandt: Jews and the Christian Image in Seventeenth-Century Amsterdam* (Berkeley: University of California Press, 2002), 59–65; and Steven Nadler, *Rembrandt's Jews* (Chicago: University of Chicago Press, 2003), 123–28.

It has been suggested that the 1636 *Portrait of a Man* in an oval (B. 269) is a likeness of Menasseh ben Israel, although this idea is not universally accepted. See, for example, Kornelia Röder, "Samuel Manasseh [*sic*] ben Israel—1636," cat. 131, in Hela Baudis, Kornelia Röder, Horst Janssen, and Kornelia von Berswordt-Wallrabe, *Rembrandt fecit: 165 Rembrandt-Radierungen aus der Sammlung des Staatlichen Museums Schwerin: Ausstellung vom 28. Mai bis 6. August 1995*, exh. cat. (Schwerin, Germany: Das Museum, 1996), 131, for an identification of the figure as Menasseh; and Stephanie S. Dickey, *Rembrandt Portraits in Print* (Amsterdam: John Benjamins Publishing, 2004), 20, for the contrary view.

8. Martin Royalton-Kisch, quoting H. T. Cartensen, noted that the 400 guilders that Rembrandt was promised for an etched portrait of Otto van Kattenburg (never realized) would have been more than twice Menasseh ben Israel's annual salary of 150 guilders. Even though the four small etchings would presumably have been less demanding than an etched portrait rendered from life, Rembrandt's fee under normal circumstances might have been beyond Menasseh's means. However, given Rembrandt's financial difficulties in the mid-1650s, it is certainly possible that the artist took on this unusual commission for economic reasons. Royalton-Kisch, "Four illustrations to a Spanish book, 1655," cat. 79, in Erik Hinterding, Ger Luijten, and Martin Royalton-Kisch, *Rembrandt the Printmaker*, exh. cat. (Chicago and London: Fitzroy Dearborn Publishers, 2000), 324n4. For a discussion of Rembrandt's economic troubles, see Paul Crenshaw, *Rembrandt's Bankruptcy* (New York: Cambridge University Press, 2006), and Charles M. Rosenberg, "Rembrandt's Religious Prints," in this catalog. The 400 guilders price is quoted in a document from 1655 concerning Rembrandt's proposed purchase of a house owned by Kattenburg in Amsterdam. Walter Strauss and Marjon van der Meulen, eds. and trans., *The Rembrandt Documents* (New York: Abaris, 1979), doc. 1655/7 and 1655/8.

9. Samuel Menasseh ben Israel (1604–57) was an important figure not only because of his place within the Jewish community in Amsterdam, but also because of his ties with a sizable group of European Christian theologians. He was born in the Portuguese colony of Madeira in 1604 to *converso* parents. In fear of the Inquisition, his family left Madeira, first traveling to France and then settling in Amsterdam around 1610. A precocious student and gifted orator, Samuel was chosen in 1622 to be one of the rabbis of the Sephardic congregation of Neve Shalom and to teach in its elementary school. In 1627, he founded the first Hebraic press in Amsterdam. His reputation beyond the synagogue was such that he was asked to teach Hebrew to the children of some of the most prominent families in Amsterdam. Menasseh was well acquainted with many of the most important Dutch intellectuals and liberal theologians of his day, including Simon Episcopius, first rector of the Remonstrant seminar; and Gerard Johan Barlaeus and Johann Vossius, who were professors at the Amsterdam Athenaeum. Johann Vossius was the brother of Isaac Vossius, to whom the *Piedra gloriosa* was dedicated. Because Menasseh shared messianic and millennialist beliefs with these and other contemporary Protestant theologians and was, therefore, willing to engage in public dialogue with them, he had a difficult relationship with some members of the Jewish community and felt that he never really received the respect he deserved. Menasseh's most famous publications were the *Conciliador*, published between 1632 and 1651, a four-volume work in which he sought to reconcile apparent contradictions in the Bible, and *Esperança de Israel* (*Hope of Israel*), published in 1650, a tract in which he linked contemporary reports of the discovery of the lost tribes of Israel in South America by *converso* traveler and explorer Aaron Levi de Montezinos with

biblical prophecies of the coming of the Messiah. Menasseh died in Amsterdam in 1657 after a tragically unsuccessful trip to England undertaken to try to convince Cromwell and the British Parliament to readmit Jews to the British Isles. For additional biographical information on Menasseh ben Israel, see Cecil Roth, *A Life of Menasseh Ben Israel, Rabbi, Printer, and Diplomat* (Philadelphia: Jewish Publication Society of America, 1934); van de Waal, "Rembrandt's Etchings," 113–16; and Nagler, *Rembrandt's Jews*, 104–43.

For a discussion of the Dutch millenarianism movement and Rembrandt's association with it and its "philosemitic" adherents, see Shelley Perlove, "An Irenic Vision of Utopia: Rembrandt's 'Triumph of Mordecai' and the New Jerusalem," *Zeitschrift für Kunstgeschichte* 56, no. 1 (1993): 38–60; Perlove, "Awaiting the Messiah: Christians, Jews and Muslims in the Late Work of Rembrandt," *Bulletin of the University of Michigan Museum of Art* 11 (1996): 84–113; and Zell, *Reframing Rembrandt*, passim.

10. Daniel 2:31–35:

> Thou, O king, sawest, and behold a great image. This great image, whose brightness was excellent, stood before thee; and the form thereof was terrible. This image's head was of fine gold, his breast and his arms of silver, his belly and his thighs of brass, his legs of iron, his feet part of iron and part of clay. Thou sawest till that a stone was cut out without hands, which smote the image upon his feet that were of iron and clay, and brake them to pieces. Then was the iron, the clay, the brass, the silver, and the gold, broken to pieces together, and became like the chaff of the summer threshing floors; and the wind carried them away, that no place was found for them: and the stone that smote the image became a great mountain, and filled the whole earth.

11. Genesis 28:10–13:

> And Jacob went out from Beersheba, and went toward Haran. And he lighted upon a certain place, and tarried there all night, because the sun was set; and he took of the stones of that place, and put them for his pillows, and lay down in that place to sleep. And he dreamed, and behold a ladder set up on the earth, and the top of it reached to heaven: and behold the angels of God ascending and descending on it. And, behold, the Lord stood above it, and said, I am the Lord God of Abraham thy father, and the God of Isaac: the land whereon thou liest, to thee will I give it, and to thy seed.

12. Samuel 17:48–49.

> And it came to pass, when the Philistine arose, and came, and drew nigh to meet David, that David hastened, and ran toward the army to meet the Philistine. And David put his hand in his bag, and took thence a stone, and slang it, and smote the Philistine in his forehead, that the stone sunk into his forehead; and he fell upon his face to the earth.

13. Daniel 7:2–14:

> Daniel spake and said, I saw in my vision by night, and, behold, the four winds of the heaven strove upon the great sea. And four great beasts came up from the sea, diverse one from another. The first was like a lion, and had eagle's wings: I beheld till the wings thereof were plucked, and it was lifted up from the earth, and made [to] stand upon the feet as a man, and a man's heart was given to it. And behold another beast, a second, like to a bear, and it raised up itself on one side, and it had three ribs in the mouth of it between the teeth of it: and they said thus unto it, Arise, devour much flesh. After this I beheld, and lo another, like a leopard, which had upon the back of it four wings of a fowl; the beast had also four heads; and dominion was given to it. After this I saw in the night visions, and behold a fourth beast, dreadful and terrible, and strong exceedingly; and it had great iron teeth: it devoured and brake in pieces, and stamped the residue with the feet of it: and it was diverse from all the beasts that were before it; and it had ten horns. I considered the horns, and, behold, there came up among them another little horn, before whom there were three of the first horns plucked up by the roots: and, behold, in this horn were eyes like the eyes of man, and a mouth speaking great things. I beheld till the thrones were cast down, and the Ancient of days did sit, whose garment was white as snow, and the hair of his head like the pure wool: his throne was like the fiery flame, and his wheels as burning fire. A fiery stream issued and came forth from before him: a thousand thousands ministered unto him, and ten thousand

times ten thousand stood before him: the judgment was set, and the books were opened. I beheld then because of the voice of the great words which the horn spake: I beheld even till the beast was slain, and his body destroyed, and given to the burning flame. As concerning the rest of the beasts, they had their dominion taken away: yet their lives were prolonged for a season and time. I saw in the night visions, and, behold, one like the Son of man came with the clouds of heaven, and came to the Ancient of days, and they brought him near before him. And there was given him dominion, and glory, and a kingdom, that all people, nations, and languages, should serve him: his dominion is an everlasting dominion, which shall not pass away, and his kingdom that which shall not be destroyed.

14. Münz, *Rembrandt's Etchings*, vol. 2, cat. 183, 89–90, with illustrations from Merian's picture Bible of Daniel's vision and the representation of God in heaven from *Revelation* 4. Matthäus Merian, Pieter Hendricksz. Schut, and Nicolaes Visscher, *Bybel printen: vertoonende de voornaemste Historien der Heylige Schrifture . . .* (Amsterdam: Visscher, 1660). These same illustrations were used in *Iconum Biblicarum*, first published in Frankfurt, Germany, in 1627.

15. Otto Benesch, *Artistic and Intellectual Trends from Rubens to Daumier as Shown in Book Illustrations*, (Cambridge, MA: Harvard College Library, 1943), 23–25; and van de Waal, "Rembrandt's Etchings," 117–18. The engravings in Hugh Broughton's *A Concent of Scripture* may be the more likely source for the *Images Seen by Nebuchadnezzar*, since the colossal statue in Broughton is nude except for a loincloth, whereas the figure in Merian's illustration is clothed in armor. Rembrandt's colossus does have one arm akimbo in the same manner as Merian's statue, although it is the opposite arm.

16. Shana Stuart, cited in Zell, *Reframing*, 78. The text in the "Address to the Reader" in *Piedra gloriosa* reads, "Finalmente en la quarta, las 4 bestias, y entre ellas aquel javali [boar] diez cuernos, y otro pequeno con boca y ojos."

17. Zell, *Reframing*, 75. The text in the "Address to the Reader" in *Piedra gloriosa* reads, "En la tercera, David derribando aquel gigante Golias postado a sus pies, que tanto al natural, representa la misma encumbrada Estatua."

18. The spear is hidden by Goliath's body, but the end of its shaft is visible. It is the dark, narrow rectangle parallel to and above the sword that hangs from the giant's belt. It was traditional to show Goliath dressed in armor, holding a spear, as described in 1 Samuel 17:4–7: "And there went out a champion out of the camp of the Philistines, named Goliath, of Gath, whose height was six cubits and a span. And he had a helmet of brass upon his head, and he was armed with a coat of mail; and the weight of the coat was five thousand shekels of brass. And he had greaves of brass upon his legs, and a target of brass between his shoulders. And the staff of his spear was like a weaver's beam; and his spear's head weighed six hundred shekels of iron."

19. David's physiognomy and wild hair evoke youthful self-portraits by Rembrandt. The etching dates from the time between Rembrandt's companion Hendrickje's condemnation by the Church (1654) and Rembrandt's sale of his property due to financial ruin (1656), circumstances that would make it understandable if the artist viewed himself as another "David" at the mercy of powerful forces beyond his control.

20. Tümpel, *Rembrandt legt*, cat. 39.

21. Amy Golahny has identified the entry "Flavius Josephus in High German profusely illustrated by Tobias Stimmer," item number 284 in the 1656 bankruptcy inventory of Rembrandt's possessions, as Flavius Josephus and Conrad Lautenbach's *Flavii Josephi Des Hochberühmten Jüdischen Geschichtschreibers Historien Und Bücher: Von Alten Jüdischen Geschichten Zwentzig Sambt Eynem Von Seinem Leben: Vom Jüdischen Krieg Und Der Statt Jerusalem Unnd Des Gantzen Lands Zerstörung Siben: Von Der Juden Altem Herkommen Wider Apionem Gramfiaticum Zwey: Von Meysterschafft Der Vernunfft Und Der Machabeer Marter Eyns: Alles Aus Dem Griechischen Exemplar*, Strassburg, 1574. Amy Golahny, *Rembrandt's Reading: The Artist's Bookshelf of Ancient Poetry and History* (Amsterdam: Amsterdam University Press, 2003), 164.

22. The prints are stubbed into the binding of the presentation copy of *Piedra gloriosa* in the Leiden University Library (personal communication from John Frankhuizen, Librarian, Universiteitsbibliotheek, Leiden, February 28, 2013). The illustrations were also tipped into the copy now in the Cambridge University Library (personal communication from Liam Sims, Rare Books Specialist, Cambridge University Library).

23. The NHD records impressions not only on vellum, but also on Japanese paper.

24. The NHD lists only six examples of *The Image Seen by Nebuchadnezzar,* and only four to six of each of the other prints in the series, as printed on vellum.

Because of issues of wear, engravings rather than etchings were usually used for book illustrations. The etched line is much less durable. The drypoint technique that Rembrandt employed in the illustrations for *Piedra gloriosa* would have made the images deteriorate even more quickly. G. W. Nowell-Usticke (*Rembrandt's Etchings, States and Values* [Narbeth, PA: Livingston Publishing, 1967]) classified every state of all four of these etchings as virtually unobtainable. WorldCat lists fewer than a dozen copies of *Piedra gloriosa,* which implies a very restricted run. Unfortunately, the catalog does not specify whether the copies are illustrated with Rembrandt's etchings or engraved copies of them possibly produced by Shalom Italia. Shalom Italia, an Ashkenazi Jew, was born in Lisbon and trained in Mantova and Venice before arriving in Amsterdam in 1641.

25. It would also have been offensive to a strict follower of the Dutch Reformed Calvinism, since Calvin forbade the creation of images of God.

26. Christian Tümpel, *Rembrandt mit Selbstzeugnissen und Bilddokumenten* (Reinbeck bei Hamburg: Rowohlt, 1977), 80.

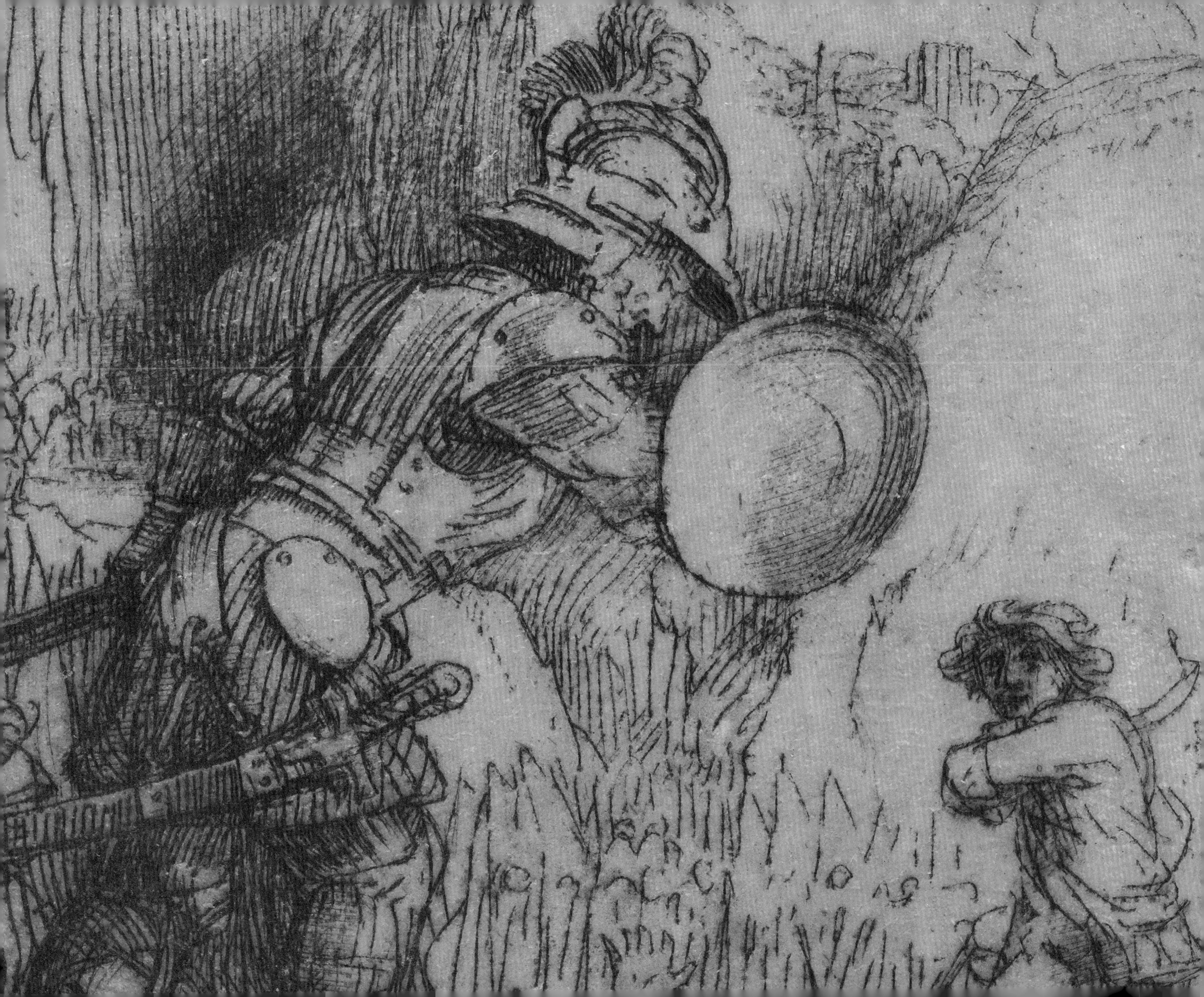

11. *Joseph Telling His Dreams*

B. 37 (H. 160, Mz. 175, NHD 167)
Etching
Signed and dated in the plate: *Rembrandt f. 1638*
State III of VI
Sheet: 11.0 × 8.3 cm, trimmed to the plate mark
Verso: in graphite, *63248; Scott coll, 3me état; HW*; and in sepia ink: +

Provenance:
Scott Collection (?)
Harold James Lean Wright (1885–1961) (?)
Craddock & Barnard, London, 1978
Feddersen, Elkhart, IN, 1991
Snite Museum of Art
Acc. No.: 1991.025.010

Plate survives:
Private collection, USA

Joseph Telling His Dreams is the third of three small-scale etchings from the 1630s in which Rembrandt illustrated episodes from Joseph's life.[1] Although the dream-telling episode precedes the other two prints in terms of their biblical chronology, it is the last of the three scenes that the artist chose to represent. Rembrandt's youthful Joseph is in the midst of describing one of his prophetic dreams to his father and brothers, presumably the dream in which he saw the sun, the moon, and eleven stars bowing down to him (Genesis 37:9). In the biblical account, Jacob, taken aback by the implications of this vision, responds by rebuking his son, asking him if the dream meant that he, Joseph's mother,[2] and the boy's brothers "would come to bow ourselves to the ground before you?"[3] Joseph's eleven brothers were already jealous of him, not only because he was their father's favorite, but because he had already told them of another dream in which he appeared to reign over them. In that earlier dream, sheaves of grain that his brothers had gathered bowed down to Joseph's sheaf. The dream-telling incident that Rembrandt portrayed is central to the account of Joseph's life, not only because it deals with one of the foundations of the brothers' resentment, but also because it establishes Joseph's gifts as an oneiromancer and prefigures his future triumph in Egypt and his status as a leader chosen by God.

In the print, the young Joseph sits at the center of a tightly packed vertical composition. The handsome boy with long curling locks leans forward and gestures as he turns his head slightly to his right, looking toward the seated figure of his aged, bearded father. Joseph's frontal pose makes it seem as though the viewer is included in this privileged group of witnesses, closing the circle established by the assembled members of Jacob's family. Jacob sits back in his chair and grips one of its arms as he looks at his son. On the floor at the lower left corner of the print, near the patriarch's seat, are a small box and a little fire fed by a few sticks of wood.[4] Beside the fire, a dog lies at Jacob's feet and licks itself indecorously.[5] One of Joseph's brothers, an imposing figure wearing a turban and sporting a large mustache, stands behind Jacob. Seven more of Joseph's brothers are crowded together, standing behind him or seated at a table at the right side of the composition. Each of these men has a unique appearance, and each reacts to Joseph's story in his own way.[6] Rembrandt clearly saw this vignette as an opportunity to

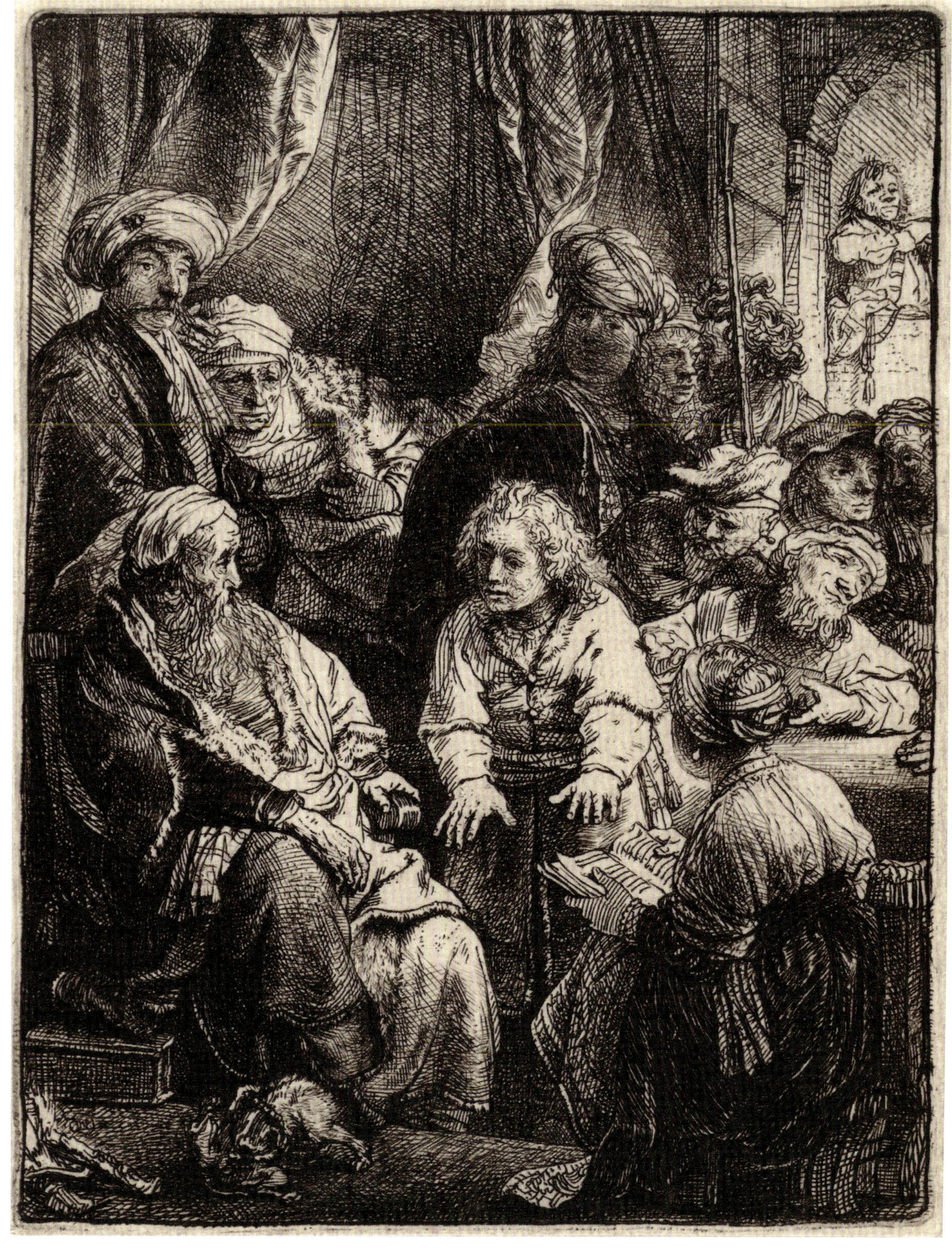

PLATE 11

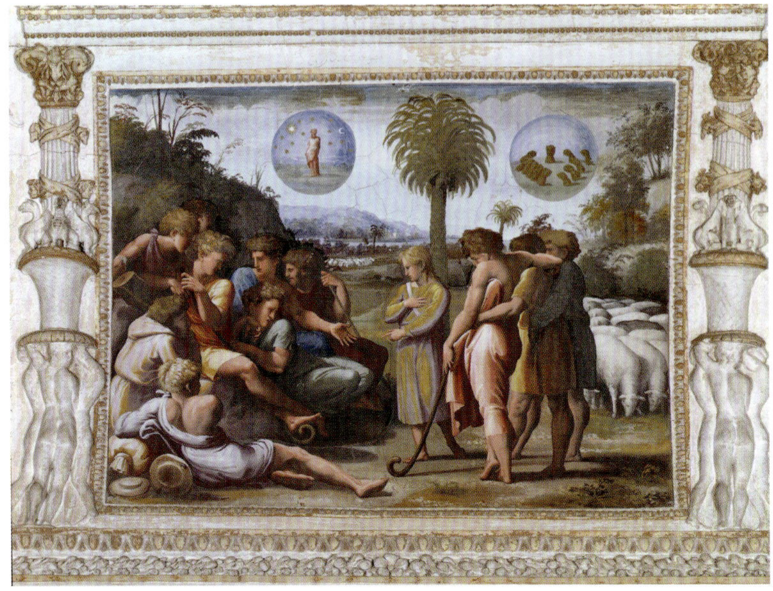

FIGURE 1. Raphael, *Joseph Telling His Dreams*, c. 1518–19, Loggia, Vatican. *Photo: Scala/Art Resource, New York.*

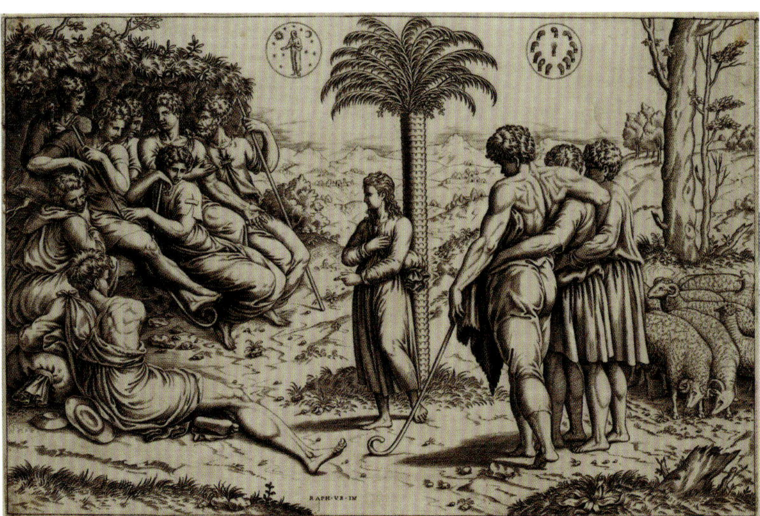

FIGURE 2. Circle of Marcantonio Raimondi after Raphael, *Joseph Telling His Dreams*, engraving, c. 1530–5. *Museum of Fine Arts, Budapest.*

display his prowess at depicting a wide variety of emotions, ranging from skepticism to anxiety to surprise. A ninth young man, engaged in putting on or taking off his waistcoat, is visible through an arched doorway in the deep right background.[7]

In addition to Jacob and his sons, there are two women in the composition. An elderly woman reclining in a curtained bed leans forward and listens intently to Joseph's account of his dream, while a younger woman, seated with her back toward the viewer, looks up from her reading to hear what the boy is saying. The identity of these women is not clear. The elderly woman may represent Joseph's mother, Rachel, or his stepmother, Leah,[8] and some have suggested that the younger woman is Joseph's stepsister, Dinah.[9] The inclusion of these two women represents a significant deviation from the biblical account, though it is not completely without visual precedent. The women may have been introduced into Rembrandt's etching not only to broaden the sense of family in a domestic setting, but also, in the case of the younger woman, to provide potential female clients with a role model, encouraging them to pause in their own daily routines, as the print's young *repoussoir* figure has, in order to contemplate this divinely inspired revelation.

At the time that Rembrandt created this etching, there were three traditional ways in which the story of Joseph recounting his dreams had been represented. One type was invented by Raphael as part of the Old Testament cycle that he and his shop painted in the loggia of the Vatican palace around 1518–19 (fig. 1), which was subsequently reproduced in engravings by a number of other artists, including an artist in the circle of Marcantonio Raimondi (in the 1530s) (fig. 2); Nicolas Beatrizet (1541); and Sisto Badalocchio and Giovanni Lanfranco (1607); and in an etching by Orazio Borgianni (1615). In Raphael's composition, Joseph stands at the center of a landscape with large palm tree behind him, a detail that presumably prefigures his symbolic martyrdom at the hands of his brothers.[10] Joseph recounts his dreams to his brothers, who sit or stand on either side of him as their sheep graze contently nearby. Representations of Joseph's two dreams (the sheaves bowing down to a central sheaf; the sun, moon, and stars) float in the sky above the figures. Jacob is notably absent from the scene.[11]

A second pictorial variation moves the story inside and focuses on the dialogue between Joseph and his father. This type is exemplified by a small vertical format engraving of the story done by Heinrich Aldegrever, one of the so-called Little Masters, in 1532 (fig. 3).[12] In Aldegrever's print, a more mature, fashionably dressed Joseph stands before his seated father and three of his brothers. Joseph raises his left hand and points upward with his thumb in a rhetorical gesture of address. Jacob reacts to the account of his son's dream by gesturing toward himself, while one of Joseph's brothers

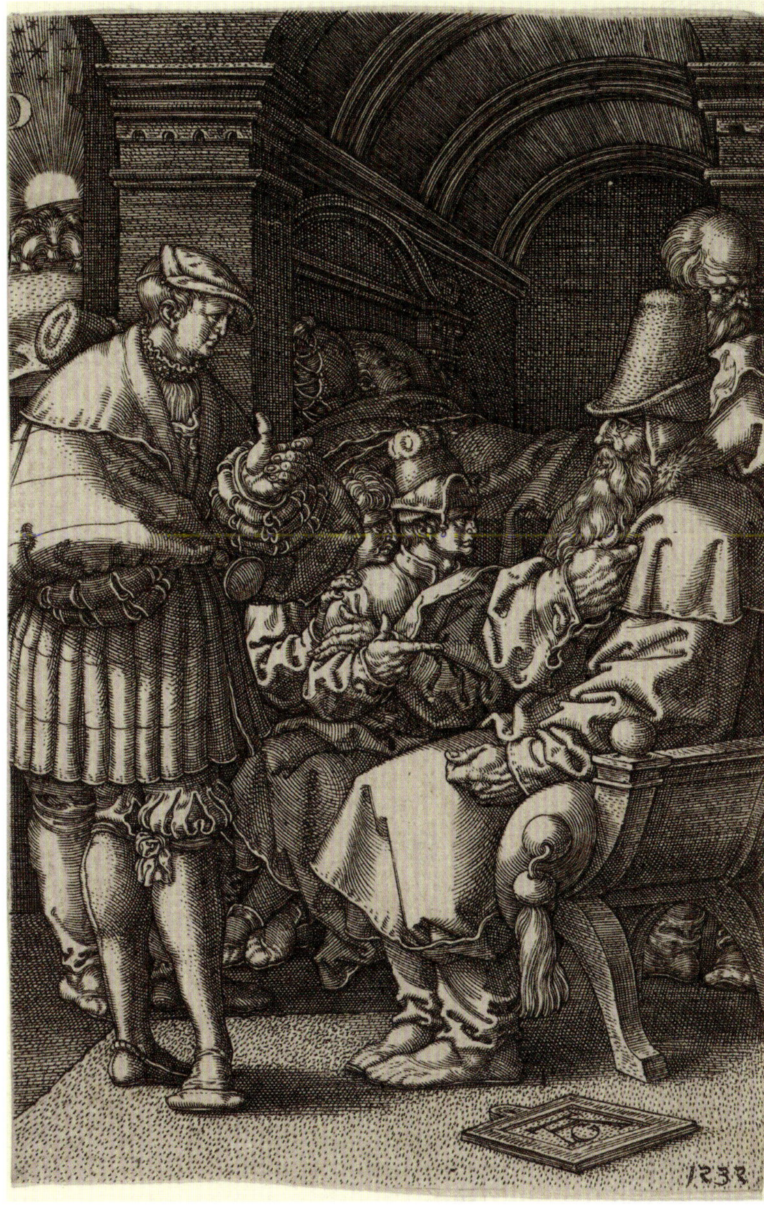

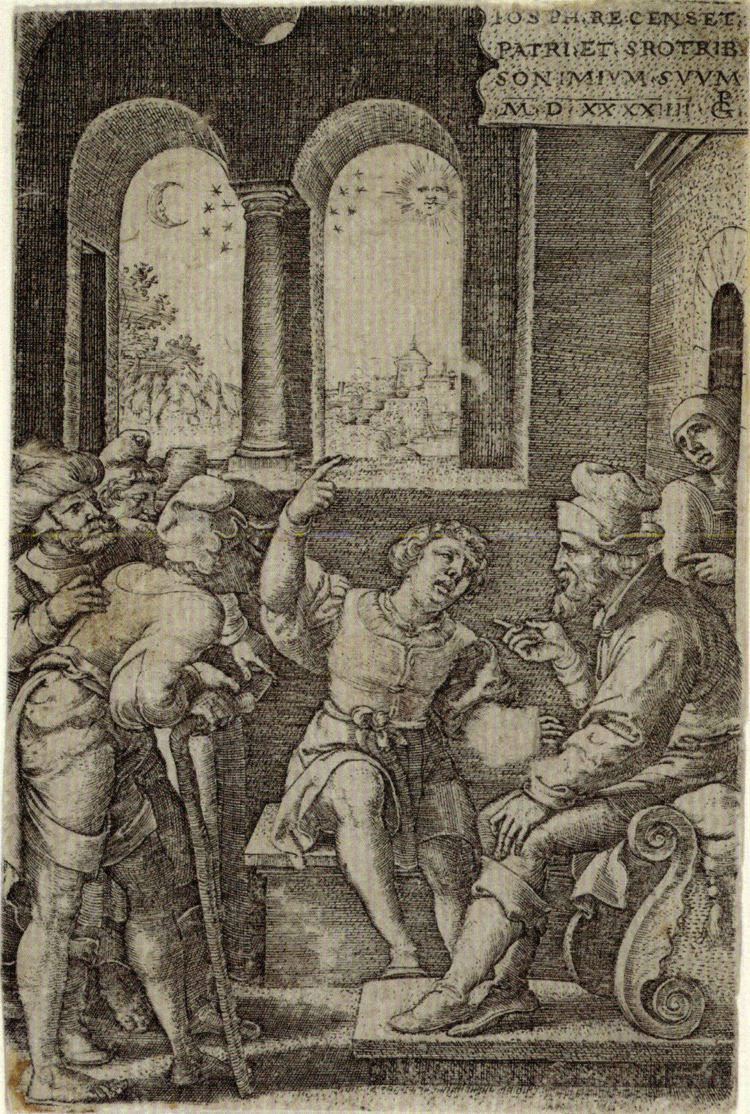

FIGURE 3. Heinrich Aldegrever, *Joseph Telling His Dreams*, engraving, 1532. *The Metropolitan Museum of Art, New York, New York, Gift of Edwin De T. Bechtel, 1949.*

FIGURE 4. Georg Pencz, *Joseph Telling His Dreams*, engraving, 1544. *The Metropolitan Museum of Art, New York, New York, Bequest of Grace M. Pugh, 1985.*

points directly toward Jacob. The scene is set in front of a vaulted bedchamber in which a sleeping figure lies in a massive bed. It has been suggested that this sleeping figure is a second representation of Joseph, showing him in the act of dreaming.[13] The symbolic bowing sheaves and the sun, moon, and stars that float above the landscape in Raphael's version can be seen through a narrow arched opening on the left side of Aldegrever's print. It is generally agreed that in his own rendition, Rembrandt borrowed the constricted interior setting and the detail of the figure in bed from Aldegrever, even though Rembrandt's curtained bed is considerably more imposing and the figure in it is awake and listening to Joseph's story. In 1544, George Pencz made a print that is another variation of this indoor type (fig. 4). A seated, centrally placed, younger Joseph is shown pointing up toward two large arched windows through which the dream visions can be seen. Joseph is actively addressing his father, who is seated on the right side of the room. Jacob, who also appears

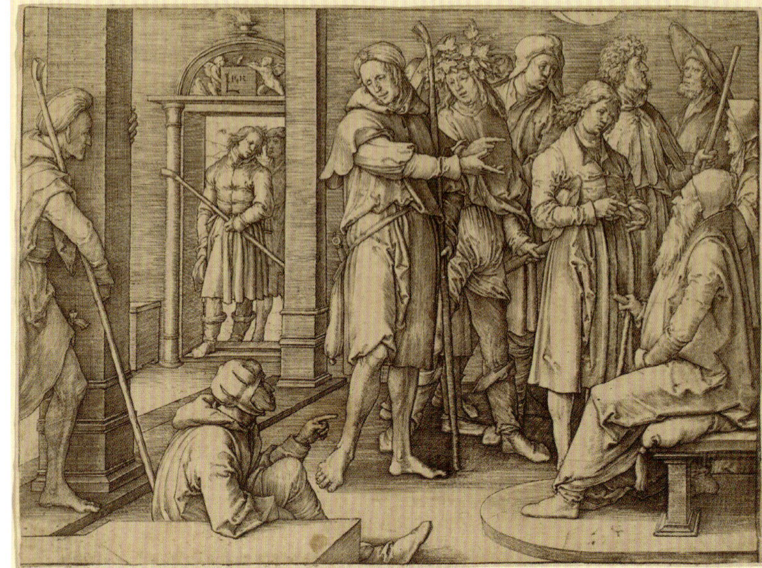

FIGURE 5. Lucas van Leyden, *Joseph Telling His Dreams*, engraving, 1512. *Photo: Courtesy of the National Gallery of Art, Washington, DC.*

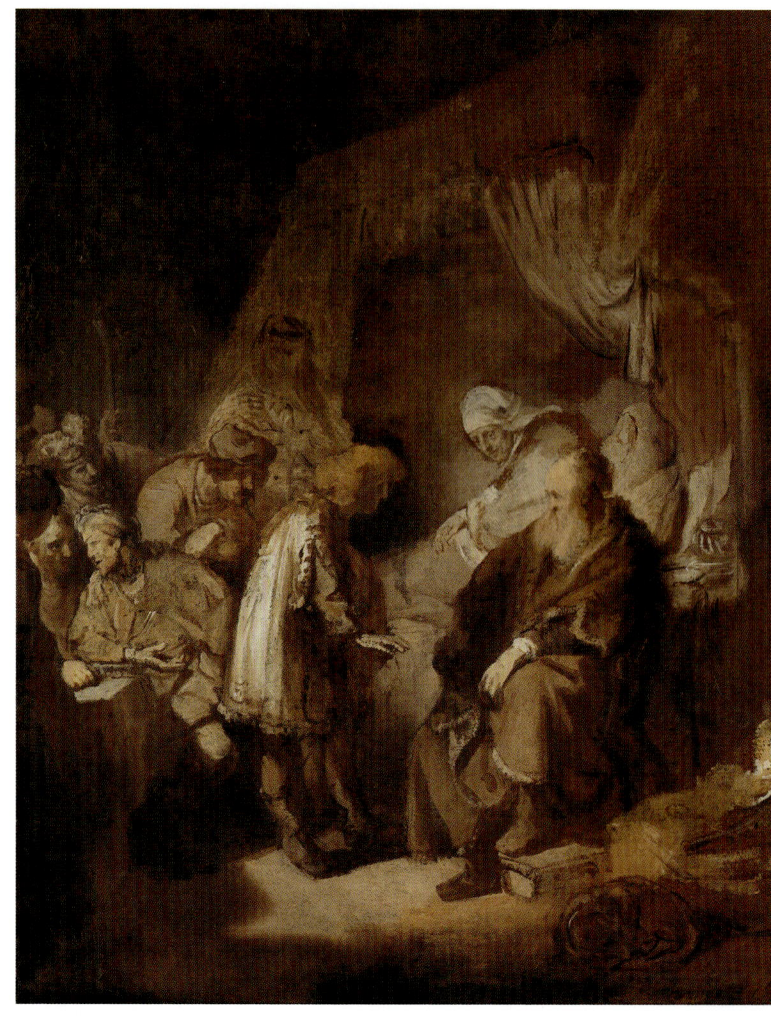

FIGURE 6. Rembrandt, *Joseph Telling His Dreams, en brunaille* oil on paper laid on cardboard, 1633. *Rijksmuseum, Amsterdam.*

to be speaking, stares at his animated son and lifts his right hand to point to the boy. Four of Joseph's brothers look on from the left side of the print, while a pensive woman standing halfway through an arched doorway behind Jacob also gazes at Joseph.[14]

The third typology is represented by Lucas van Leyden's version of the story (fig. 5),[15] which also clearly influenced Rembrandt's interpretation of the subject. In an engraving from 1512, which is also set in an interior space, Joseph is shown standing close to Jacob, who is seated at the right side of the composition. The young boy, gesturing in a typically rhetorical manner, recounts his dream to his father, who listens intently. Nine of Joseph's brothers have gathered around, listening to the boy's prophetic dream and discussing it among themselves, while the remaining two brothers enter the room through a doorway at the upper left side of the composition. An elderly woman wearing a bonnet and headscarf can be seen at the right, standing behind Jacob. Lucas's version differs from the other, later, examples. It is also clearly different in format and mood from Rembrandt's 1638 etching, but the two works do share a number of features, attesting to Rembrandt's familiarity with the sixteenth-century engraving: all of the brothers are present in an interior setting, and each one wears a different costume and reacts in his own way to the prophetic vision; the seated, elderly Jacob listens to Joseph without showing any overt emotion or reaction; an elderly woman, possibly Rachel or Leah, is clearly a participant; and all overt representations of the dreams themselves have been eliminated.[16] Furthermore, Rembrandt's print reverses the positions of the chief actors in Lucas's image, that is, the main group of brothers and also the figures who observe the action from brightly lit spaces at a remove from the main action—in one case, in an alcove or chamber, and in the other, in a doorway. Such a reversal might be the natural result of an image being printed from a plate designed to resemble Lucas's composition.

Around 1633–34, a few years before he made his etching, Rembrandt did a considerably larger oil-on-paper sketch *en brunaille* of this same subject (fig. 6).[17] The oil sketch and the print share a number of elements, including the elderly woman in bed in the background, the dog, and the passive pose of Jacob. However, there are also significant differences. Not only is the oil sketch larger; the space in which the dream telling takes place is more spacious. Consequently, the sketch *en brunaille* lacks the sense of intimacy that prevails in the etching. Furthermore, Joseph is posed in such a way that he looks directly toward his seated father, rather than facing slightly outward toward the viewer. As a result, the viewer of the *brunaille* sketch is more of an observer of the drama, and less of a participant.

The story of Joseph was a popular subject for prints in the sixteenth century, not only because it afforded artists an opportunity for narrative invention, but also because the tribulations of the biblical hero made him a perfect antetype for Christ.[18] In his commentary on Genesis, John Calvin was explicit in drawing a parallel between the prophet and Jesus: "In the person of Joseph, a lively image of Christ is presented."[19] Joseph's prophetic dreams were also of critical importance for Calvin, because they revealed the presence of God's preordained plan, thereby demonstrating the workings of Divine Providence.[20] It was characteristic of Rembrandt that he did not choose to depict the contents of the dreams as most of his predecessors had. He often eschewed overt symbolism in his artworks, preferring instead to depict the human drama of biblical narratives. He focused on the acts of telling and listening, and in this context, he cast Jacob as engaged, but somewhat skeptical.[21] Rembrandt's particular interest in Jacob's pose and expression is confirmed by a separate red-chalk study of a seated old man[22] that survives in a private collection (fig. 7). This sketch served as the basis for the Jacob figure in the oil *brunaille* rendition and, almost without alteration, in the etching, as well. The depiction of a quiet, attentive Jacob is also in keeping with Calvin's reading of the story and its significance, for he believed that Jacob recognized the divine source of Joseph's dreams, and expressed skepticism only in order to avoid dissension with his other sons, who were blinded to the truth due to the "virus of envy."[23] From Calvin's perspective, Jacob should never have turned away from the truth. In a Calvinist context, then, Rembrandt's print was not only an illustration of a biblical tale and an expression of human drama, but also an admonition to listen closely to the word of God as it is revealed, to meditate upon it, to accept his divine plan, and to uphold God's truth even in the face of dissension.[24] Such a message might have been particularly germane in the theologically fractious environment that prevailed in seventeenth-century Holland.

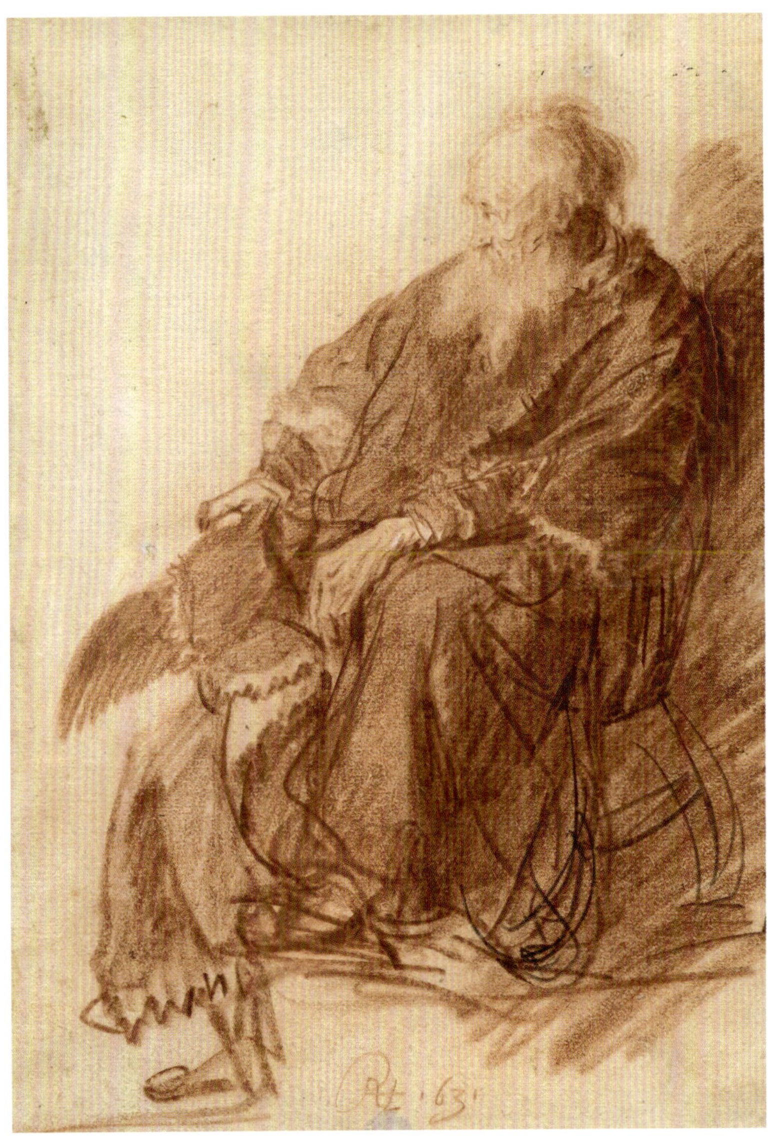

FIGURE 7. Rembrandt, *Bearded Old Man Seated in an Armchair,* Ben. 20, red and black chalk, 1631, private collection. *Photo: Alex Jamison.*

Notes

1. Around 1633, Rembrandt had depicted the tragic scene in which Joseph's bloodied coat was brought to Jacob (B. 38, cat. no. 12), and in the following year, he made an etching of the salacious but moralizing story of Joseph and Potiphar's wife (B. 39, cat. no. 13). Although the prints are relatively close in size, there is no indication that Rembrandt conceived of these three works as a series.

2. Since Joseph's mother, Rachel, had died, Jacob can only be referring to Joseph's stepmother, Leah.

3. Genesis 37:10.

4. The open fire suggests that the room is cold, and the box may be a foot warmer. Although Jacob does not use it as such in this rendition of the scene, Rembrandt's Jacob in his *en brunaille* sketch of the event, now in the Rijksmuseum in Amsterdam, rests one foot on a similar box. The "box" in the etching may also be read as the edge of a platform beneath Jacob's chair.

5. There have been a few attempts to interpret the significance of this dog. For example, Perlove and Silver (*Rembrandt's Faith*, 95), suggested that it represents the self-gratification and greed of Joseph's brothers. However, the dog's presence may simply be an example of Rembrandt's tendency to incorporate amusing and sometimes scatalogical details into otherwise serious compositions. See, for example, the defecating dog in the foreground of *The Good Samaritan* (B. 90, 1652, cat. no. 62). In any event, the presence of a dog curled up at his master's feet enhances the domestic atmosphere of the etching.

6. Perlove and Silver (*Rembrandt's Faith*, 96) drew special attention to the shepherd's staff that one of the brothers holds. They interpreted this detail as identifying the brother as Judah, and the staff as prefiguring the scepter that the tribe of Judah would retain in its role as leader of the Jews until the coming of Messiah (Genesis 49:10). However, since all of the visual versions of the story of Joseph recounting his dreams cited below in both the text and the notes of this catalog entry depict at least one of the brothers holding a crook or shepherd's staff, it seems more likely that the staff simply identifies Jacob's sons as herders.

7. It is interesting to note that Rembrandt indicated the presence of a tenth brother by placing a disembodied hand resting on the table at the extreme right side of the composition and by directing the gaze of the bearded brother seated behind the table off to the right, toward the unseen figure.

8. When Jacob, in response to Joseph's dream, asks, "Shall we then wholly come, I and your *mother* [emphasis added] and your brothers, in order to bow ourselves down to the ground before you" (Genesis 37:10), the commentary in the Dutch State Bible offers three possibilities for the "mother" invoked in the passage: Leah, Rachel, or Rachel's maidservant (and Jacob's concubine), Bilhah. Rachel, however, had already died. Evidently, the Dutch State Bible construed the woman to be Jacob's consort, but not necessarily Jacob's mother or mother-in-law.

9. The story of Dinah, the daughter of Jacob and Leah, is told in Genesis 34. Her rape by Shechem, the son of Hamor, prince of the city of Shechem, was avenged by two of her brothers, Simeon and Levi, against the wishes of their father. There is no really satisfactory explanation as to why she would have been included in this scene, although Perlove and Silver (*Rembrandt's Faith*, 96) hypothesized that she might have been placed there as a reminder of the wrathful tendencies of Joseph's brothers, whose jealousy would later turn them against the young visionary.

10. The palm, emblematic of the East and ancient biblical times, was also associated with martyrdom, and could have reminded viewers of later events in Joseph's life. Because Joseph's brothers brought his coat, stained with animal blood, to his father, Jacob believed that his son had been killed. The eventual revelation that Joseph was still alive has been compared to the miracle of Christ's death and resurrection. Cf. the discussion of John Calvin in the text below.

11. This typology would have been well-known in the Netherlands. A simplified woodcut variation of the composition was used to decorate the title page of a slender "biblical reader" called the *Story of Joseph*, published by Jan van Waesberghe in Rotterdam in 1617. See Peter van der Coelen, "The History of Joseph," cat. 72, in van der Coelen, *Patriarchs, Angels and Prophets: The Old Testament in Netherlandish Printmaking from Lucas van Leyden to Rembrandt*, exh. cat. (Amsterdam: Rembrandt Information Centre, 1996), 174.

12. The Aldegrever print is one of a series of four prints dedicated to the life of Joseph (HD 18–21).

13. Christian Tümpel and Petra Jeroense, "Joseph Telling his Dreams, 1638," cat. 17, in van der Coelen, *Patirarchs, Angels and Prophets*, 90.

14. In a 1629 engraving, Nicolaes de Bruyn (NHD 21.II) set the scene in a courtyard. In his print, the dream images are visible above a low wall in the background, and all of Joseph's brothers are present. What distinguishes de Bruyn's version from the others is the prominence of an older woman, presumably Rachel or Leah, who is framed by the very young boy and his elderly father.

15. Lucas van Leyden, like Aldegrever after him, did a series of five engravings of the life of Joseph (NHD 19–23), as well as a separate woodcut of Jacob being shown Joseph's bloody cloak (NHD 188, c. 1517).

16. The significance of the Aldegrever and Lucas van Leyden prints for Rembrandt's conception of the story has been noted by numerous historians. See B. P. J. Broos, *Index to the Formal Sources of Rembrandt's Art* (Maarssen, Netherlands: Schwartz, 1977), under B. 37; and Christian Tümpel, *Rembrandt legt,* cat. 14.

17. The *en brunaille* sketch, which measures 55.8 × 38.7 cm., is now in the Rijksmuseum, Amsterdam. It has been hypothesized that this painting was intended to serve as a model for a large-scale engraving to be executed by the professional printmaker Jan Georg van Vliet. Around the same time, in 1634, Rembrandt produced a similar *en brunaille* sketch for the print of *Christ before Pilate: Large Plate* (B. 77, cat. no. 50) that was engraved by van Vliet and published "with privileges" by Hendrik Uylenburgh in 1635. The *en brunaille* sketch of *Christ before Pilate,* which is in the British Museum, measures 54.5 cm × 44.5 cm. For a discussion of both of these sketches, see Ernst van Wetering, "Remarks on Rembrandt's Oil-Sketches for Etchings," in Erik Hinterding, Ger Luijten, and Martin Royalton-Kirsch, *Rembrandt the Printmaker,* exh. cat. (Chicago and London: Fitzroy Dearborn Publshers, 2000), 36–56.

18. The Joseph story was also a very popular subject for sixteenth- and seventeenth-century Northern dramatists, including Hugo Grotius and Joost van den Vondel. See James A. Parente Jr., *Religious Drama and the Humanist Tradition: Christian Theater in Germany and in the Netherlands 1500–1680* (Leiden: E. J. Brill, 1987), 110–31.

19. John Calvin, *Commentaries on Genesis,* 2:224, Commentary on Genesis 37:6, accessed July 25, 2014, http://www.ccel.org/ccel/calvin/calcom02.pdf.

20. Ibid., 2:260, accessed July 14, 2014, http://www.ccel.org/ccel/calvin/calcom02.pdf: "God revealed in dreams what he would do, that afterwards it might be shown that nothing had happened fortuitously: but that what had been fixed by celestial decree, was at length . . . carried forward through circuitous windings to its completion." In sum, "in this history we have . . . a most beautiful example of Divine Providence."

21. Unlike the biblical version, Josephus's account of Jacob's reaction to Joseph's dream (*Jewish Antiquities,* 2, 2, 15–16) puts a positive spin on the father's response: "Now Jacob was pleased with the dream: for, considering the prediction in his mind and shrewdly and wisely guessing at its meaning, he rejoiced at the great things thereby signified."

22. Ben. 20.

23. John Calvin, *Commentaries on Genesis,* 225, Commentary on Genesis 37:10, accessed July 17, 2014 http://www.ccel.org/ccel/calvin/calcom02.pdf: "For Moses, making a distinction between him [Jacob] and his sons, says that *they* breathed nothing but the *virus* of envy; while *he* revolved in his own mind what this might mean; which could not have happened unless he had been affected with reverence." Calvin continues, "I do not doubt that he feignedly reproved his son, from a desire to appease contention. Nevertheless, this method of pretending to be adverse to the truth, when we are endeavouring to appease the anger of those who rage against it, is by no means approved by God."

24. A similar message of ethical probity and loyalty to one's master (God), this time in regard to resisting temptation,was the subtext of the story of Joseph and Potiphar's wife, which Rembrandt represented in an earlier etching (B. 39, 1634, cat. no. 13).

12. Joseph's Coat Brought to Jacob

B. 38 (H. 104, Mz. 172 NHD 122)
Etching, with touches of drypoint
Signed in the plate: *Rembrandt/van Rijn fe.*[1]
c. 1633
State II of II
Sheet 11.1 × 8.0 cm; plate mark 10.7 × 8.0 cm
Verso: in graphite, *B38; H8330*

Provenance:
Harrods, London, 1980
Feddersen, Elkhart, IN, 1991
Snite Museum of Art
Acc. No.: 1991.025.011

Plate does not survive.

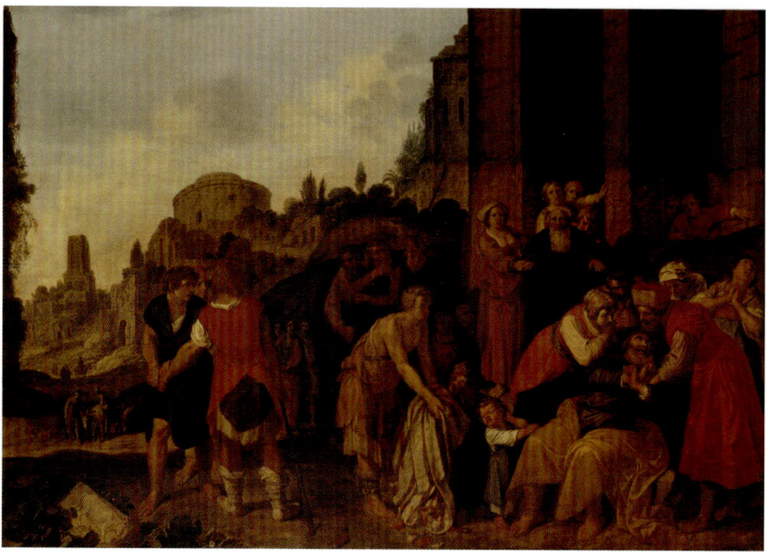

FIGURE 1. Jacob Pynas, *Joseph's Coat Brought to Jacob*, oil on panel, 1618. *The State Hermitage Museum, St. Petersburg, Russia. Photo: © The State Hermitage Museum/ Photography by Vladimir Terebenin.*

Rembrandt's etching of *Joseph's Coat Brought to Jacob* is the earliest of three etchings of similar size dating from the 1630s in which the artist depicted different episodes from Joseph's life. The story of Joseph's bloodied coat and his brothers' plot against him is recounted in Genesis 37:18–34. Joseph's brothers, jealous of Joseph's place in their father's affections and angered by the dreams he had described, in which they had to pay homage to him, plotted against him. After discussing whether or not to kill their brother, they compromised by throwing him into a pit. However, when a group of Midianites passed by on the way to Egypt, Joseph's siblings decided to sell their brother to the merchants, instead of leaving him to perish. In order to explain Joseph's disappearance, the siblings devised a plan to make their father, Jacob, believe that Joseph was dead. After slaying one of the goats that they were tending, they dipped Joseph's many-colored coat—a gift from Jacob to Joseph—in the animal's blood. When Jacob was presented with the bloody garment, he recognized it as Joseph's and concluded that his son had been torn to pieces by wild beasts. Overcome by grief, Jacob "rent his clothes and put sackcloth upon his loins and mourned for his son many days."

Although Rembrandt's interest in the story of Joseph is confirmed by the existence of two later prints in which he depicted other events in the young man's life, the authorship of this particular print has been called into question. A perceived lack of subtlety in

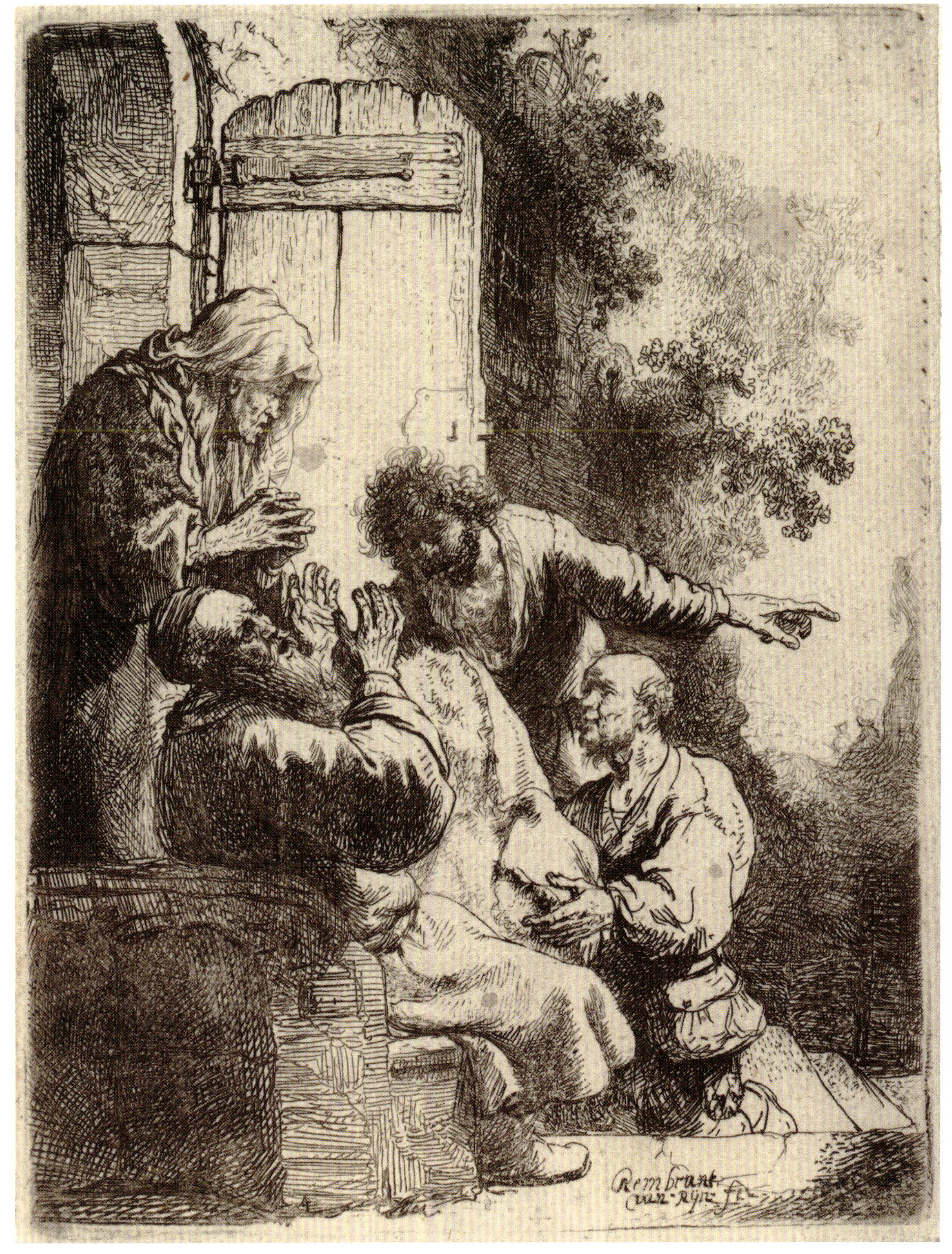

PLATE 12

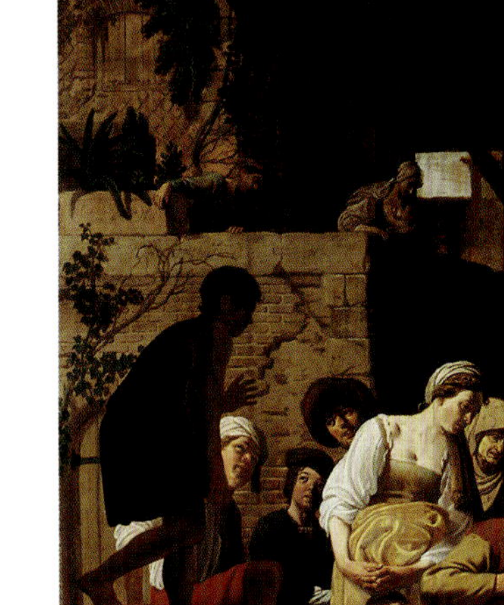

FIGURE 2. Claes Cornelisz. Moeyaert, *Joseph's Coat Brought to Jacob*, oil on panel, 1624. *Muzeum Sztuki, Lodz, Poland.*

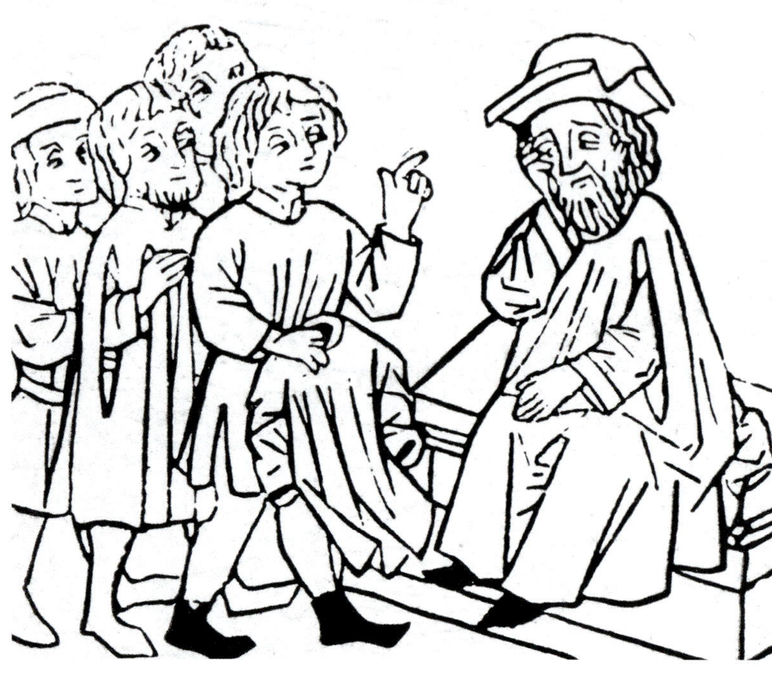

FIGURE 3. Anonymous German, *Joseph's Coat Brought to Jacob*, woodcut, *Biblia pauperum*, c. 1462.

transitions from light to shadow, as well as the schematic quality of the cross-hatching on Jacob's stone bench, caused some early Rembrandt scholars to question exactly what role Rembrandt played in the creation of this etching. Rembrandt's authorship was rejected by Hans Singer and Dimitri Rovinski without further attribution, while C. H. Middleton and Woldemar von Seidlitz attributed the print to Jan Georg van Vliet.[2] Unlike these historians, Ludwig Münz saw the master's hand in the etching, but suggested that Rembrandt had developed the print in two stages. Münz dated the first stage (of which there are no extant impressions) to c. 1629, and the second to 1632–33. According to Münz, Rembrandt was assisted by pupils when he reworked the plate.[3] Petra Jeroense[4] concurs with Münz's view that assistants played a role in the creation of the etching. Arthur M. Hind[5] and most modern scholars, including Christopher White and Karel Boon, J. P. Filedt Kok,[6] and Erik Hinterding,[7] on the other hand, have concluded that Rembrandt was the sole author of the etching. The dating of the print is based on stylistic considerations and the manner in which it is signed. Rembrandt used his patronymic "van Rijn" only during the period of 1632–33.

There are not many earlier depictions of the biblical episode in which Joseph's bloodied cloak is presented to Jacob.[8] The two most notable Dutch painted versions are by Jan Pynas[9] (fig. 1) and Claes Cornelisz. Moeyaert[10] (fig. 2). Both of these paintings, however, represent a moment in the biblical account that takes place slightly later than the one highlighted in Rembrandt's etching. Rembrandt portrays Jacob's dramatic initial reaction to the "evidence" of his son's death, whereas the paintings illustrate Jacob's grief afterward, when "all his sons, and all his daughters, rose up to comfort him."[11] In the two paintings, Jacob is surrounded by members of his family and curious onlookers. Rembrandt, however, chose to follow the graphic tradition represented by the woodcut illustrations that appeared in fifteenth-century editions of the *Biblia pauperum*[12] (fig. 3), a more sophisticated woodcut by Lucas van Leyden (fig. 4) from around 1517,[13] and an early seventeenth-century biblical

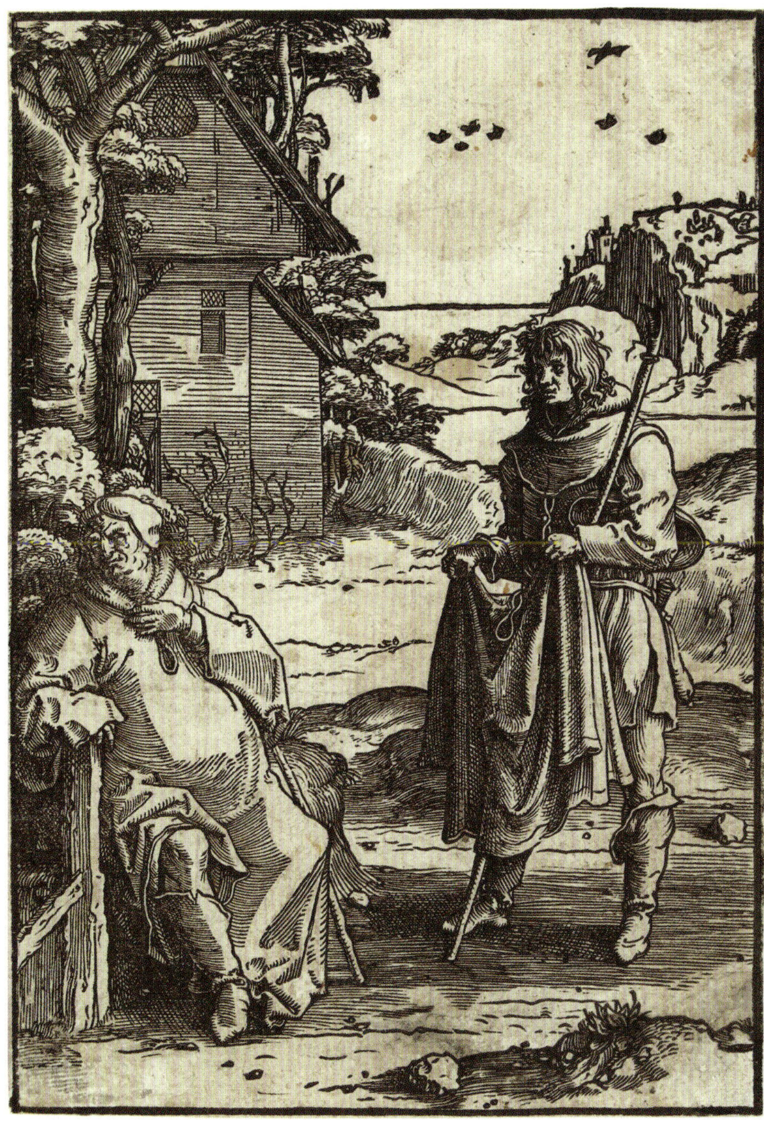

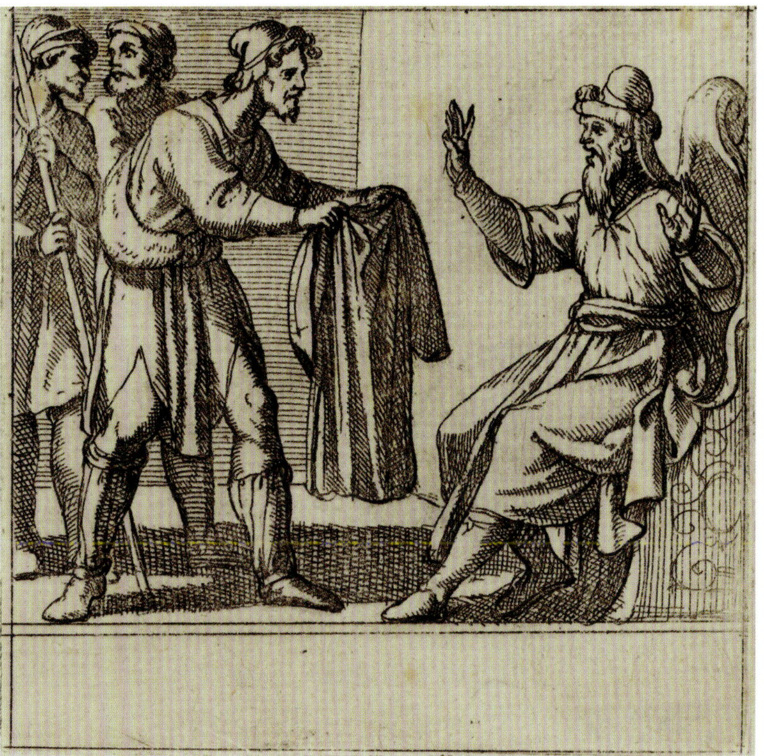

FIGURE 4. Lucas van Leyden, *Joseph's Coat Brought to Jacob*, woodcut, c. 1517. *Rijksmuseum, Amsterdam.*

FIGURE 5. Antonio Tempesta, *Joseph's Coat Brought to Jacob*, etching, c. 1620. *Museum of Fine Arts, Budapest.*

illustration engraved by Antonio Tempesta[14] (fig. 5). These examples focus on the moment in which Jacob is first shown the bloodied cloak, and the number of actors is accordingly many fewer than in the paintings. In fact, in the Lucas van Leyden print, there are only two figures, Jacob and a shepherd holding up the cloak. None of these earlier images communicates Jacob's agony as strongly as Rembrandt's version. In fact, the emotional power of that etching is one of the strongest arguments in favor of Rembrandt's authorship.

The print focuses on four characters: Jacob; an elderly woman who is presumably Leah;[15] and the two men who show the bloodied coat to Jacob. All four are grouped together on the threshold of a rustic house. There has been some disagreement as to whether the men proffering the coat are Jacob's sons or emissaries sent by them. Donna Hunter and Shelley Perlove have proposed that the men presenting the bloodstained coat are Jacob's sons: Reuben, a figure with wildly tousled hair and a face cast into shadow, who stands and points, and Judah, a balding man with a purse hanging conspicuously from his belt, who kneels at Jacob's feet.[16] The familiarity with which the standing man leans into Jacob's space as the old man grieves might indicate that this is, indeed, one of Jacob's sons, not an unrelated messenger. As the man speaks to Jacob, he gestures broadly back to his left, presumably indicating the place where the coat was found. His gesture also directs the viewer's attention to two barely visible men standing in the distant landscape, one in light, and one in shadow. If the two young men hovering near Jacob are messengers, then the men in the distance could be two of the brothers who dispatched them. Another possibility is that the far-off figures, one of them wearing a turban and the other a flat hat, are two of the merchants to whom Joseph was sold.

Jacob's distraught reaction to the bloodied coat's significance is extraordinarily moving. He throws his arms up in a classic gesture of despair,[17] tosses his head back, and seems to wail with grief. As he recoils from the cloak that signifies his son's death, it is as if he has received a physical blow. He looks up toward the heavens as if to protest—or appeal—to God. By contrast, in a curious reversal of the norms of gendered emotion,[18] the elderly woman standing behind him is rather restrained in her reaction to the news. She leans forward, looking not at Jacob but at the coat, and brings her outstretched hands together as she begins to speak. There is no clear precedent for including Jacob's wife Leah—Joseph's stepmother—as a witness to this painful deception.[19] Indeed, her inclusion in the scene seems to be Rembrandt's own invention, possibly in order to provide an emotional contrast to Joseph's father. Her odd calmness makes the image of Jacob's inconsolable grief all the more powerful.

Notes

1. This is the only plate signed with Rembrandt's full name.

2. Petra Jeroense, in Peter van der Coelen, ed., *Patriarchs, Angels and Prophets: The Old Testament in Netherlandish Printmaking from Lucas van Leyden to Rembrandt*, exh. cat. (Amsterdam: Rembrandt Information Centre, 1996), cat. 18, 93. For more on van Vliet, see the discussion of *Christ before Pilate: Large Plate* in this catalog (B. 77, 1636, cat. no. 50).

3. *Critical Catalogue*, 1:335, note for plate 191: "Originally about 1629, reworked about 1632–33 with the help of pupils."

4. See note 2, above.

5. *Rembrandt's Etchings: An Essay and a Catalogue, with Some Notes on the Drawings*, 70: "[Carel] Vosmaer doubted, and van Vliet's name was suggested by Middleton, but with little foundation."

6. J. P. Filedt Kok, *Rembrandt Etchings and Drawings in the Rembrandt House* (Maarssen, Netherlands: Gary Schwartz, 1972), 47: "In view of the subtle and meticulous execution . . . and the correspondence with Rembrandt's work of around 1632, this [the participation of pupils] seems most unlikely."

7. *Lugt Catalogue*, cat. 26, 90: "It is true that the authenticity was debated in the past, but since the beginning of the twentieth century there has been almost unanimous agreement that Rembrandt alone was responsible for this work."

8. Although there were few visual precedents for Rembrandt's print, the story of Joseph was well known in his day and was the subject of theatrical productions.

9. The Jan Pynas painting, signed and dated 1618, is now in the State Hermitage Museum, St. Petersburg, Russia.

10. The Claes Cornelisz. Moeyaert painting, signed and dated 1624, is now in the Muzeum Sztuki, Lodz, Poland.

11. Genesis 37:35. It is possible that the painted versions were based on the account in Josephus's *Jewish Antiquities*, which states that "when they had done so [dipped the coat in goats' blood], they came to the old man. . . . Then they said they had not seen Joseph, nor knew what mishap had befallen him; but that they had found his coat bloody and torn to pieces." Josephus, *Jewish Antiquities*, 2, 3, 4.

12. In the *Biblia pauperum*, the image was paired with representations of Judas betraying Christ before the High Priests or the Jews' Renunciation of Jesus. Ellen S. Jacobowitz and Stephanie Loeb Stepanek, *The Prints of Lucas van Leyden and His Contemporaries* (Washington, DC: National Gallery of Art, 1983), 190.

13. NHD 4. See also Jacobowitz and Stepanek, *The Prints of Lucas van Leyden*, cat. 70. It does not seem to have any direct connection with Lucas's engraved Joseph series. See the discussion of *Joseph Telling His Dreams* in this catalog (B. 37, 1638, cat. no. 11).

14. TIB 65. Numerous authors have suggested that Tempesta's engraving is the visual source for the stone throne on which Rembrandt's Jacob is seated. However, Jacob's seat in Rembrandt's etching bears a greater resemblance to the heavy seat in the 1517 Lucas van Leyden print than to the more lyrical thrones in the Tempesta image and in prints of the subject by Pierre Eskrich (1565) and Petrus Furnius (1572).

15. Perlove and Silver (*Rembrandt's Faith*, 98) unequivocally identify the elderly woman as Leah, while Hinterding (*Lugt Catalogue*, 90) calls her "Joseph's mother," i.e., Rachel. For a discussion of the inconsistency in the biblical chronology surrounding Rachel's death, see the discussion of *Joseph Telling His Dreams* in this catalog (B. 37, cat. no. 11).

16. The biblical text is not clear regarding whether Jacob's sons brought or sent Joseph's cloak to their father. Although almost all

of the earlier visual examples of this episode include a shepherd's staff, an attribute of Joseph's brothers, Rembrandt's image does not include one. Josephus, however, explicitly states that it was the brothers themselves who brought the coat to Jacob. (See note 11, above). Donna Hunter, in Shelley Perlove and Robert Baldwin, *Impressions of Faith: Rembrandt's Biblical Etchings* ([Dearborn: University of Michigan-Dearborn, Mardigian Library, 1989], cat. 2, 24) identifies the two figures as Reuben and Judah because they are specifically named earlier in the biblical tale and in Josephus's account of the plot to kill Joseph and then, later, to sell him into slavery. The standing figure is identified as Reuben because his face is cast into shadow, an indication of his deception, while the kneeling figure is identified as Judah, whose purse is symbolic of greed.

17. Tempesta's Jacob also raises his arms, but his gesture appears to be more a rhetorical pose than a convincing somatic expression of shock and sorrow. In a move that seems defensive, rather than distraught, he appears to be trying to repel or block the terrible news that he believes is being conveyed to him.

18. In the early modern period, women were typically considered to be less in control of their emotions than men.

19. Although an older woman does appear amid the oddly unemotional throng of people surrounding Jacob in Moeyaert's painting, she has not been singled out as a principal character in the drama.

13. *Joseph and Potiphar's Wife*

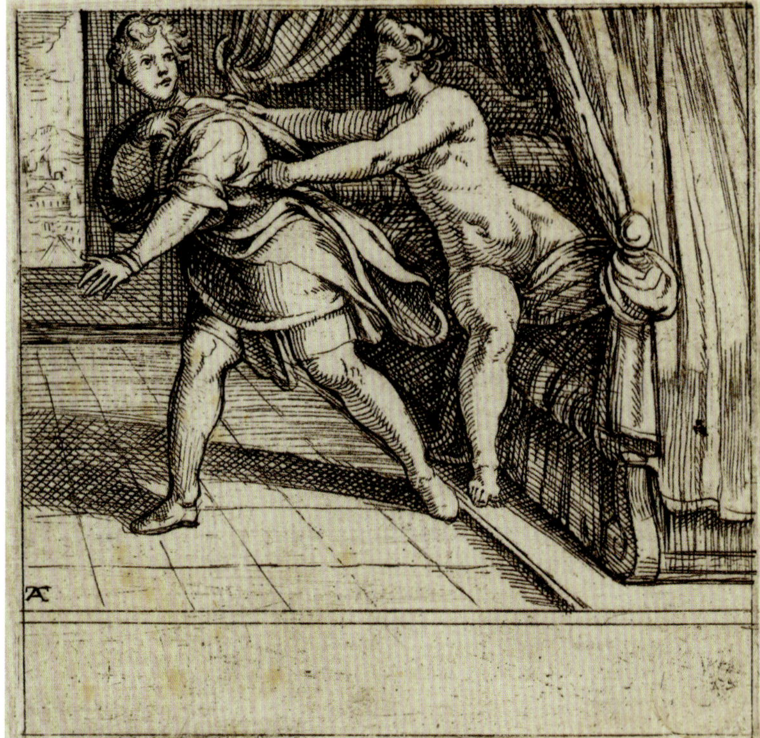

B. 39 (H. 118, Mz. 173, NHD 128)
Etching
Signed and dated in the plate: *Rembrandt f. 1634*
State IV of IV
Sheet: 9.0 × 11.5 cm, trimmed to the plate mark
Verso: in graphite, *H7803 B39*
Nineteenth-century impression on wove paper, Basan workshop

Provenance:
Harrods, London, 1980
Feddersen, Elkhart, IN, 1991
Snite Museum of Art
Acc. No.: 1991.025.012

Plate survives:
On long-term loan to Museum het Rembrandthuis, Amsterdam.

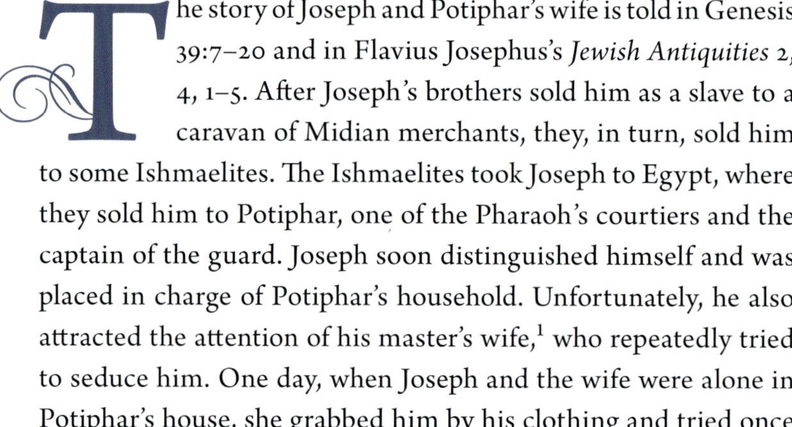

FIGURE 1. Antonio Tempesta, *Joseph and Potiphar's Wife*, etching, c. 1622. *Museum of Fine Arts, Budapest.*

The story of Joseph and Potiphar's wife is told in Genesis 39:7–20 and in Flavius Josephus's *Jewish Antiquities* 2, 4, 1–5. After Joseph's brothers sold him as a slave to a caravan of Midian merchants, they, in turn, sold him to some Ishmaelites. The Ishmaelites took Joseph to Egypt, where they sold him to Potiphar, one of the Pharaoh's courtiers and the captain of the guard. Joseph soon distinguished himself and was placed in charge of Potiphar's household. Unfortunately, he also attracted the attention of his master's wife,[1] who repeatedly tried to seduce him. One day, when Joseph and the wife were alone in Potiphar's house, she grabbed him by his clothing and tried once again to persuade him to join her in bed. Joseph refused her advances and ran out of the house, leaving his garment behind. Thwarted in her lascivious ambitions, Potiphar's wife took her revenge by accusing Joseph of attempting to lie with her. She presented his abandoned garment as proof, and Potiphar, believing his wife's tale, had Joseph thrown into prison. As the story is told in Genesis, Joseph was able to resist the seductress because he was loyal to his master. Josephus's account also credits Joseph's loyalty to Potiphar, but places even greater emphasis on a second factor, the biblical hero's self-control, that is, his ability to overcome his own passions.

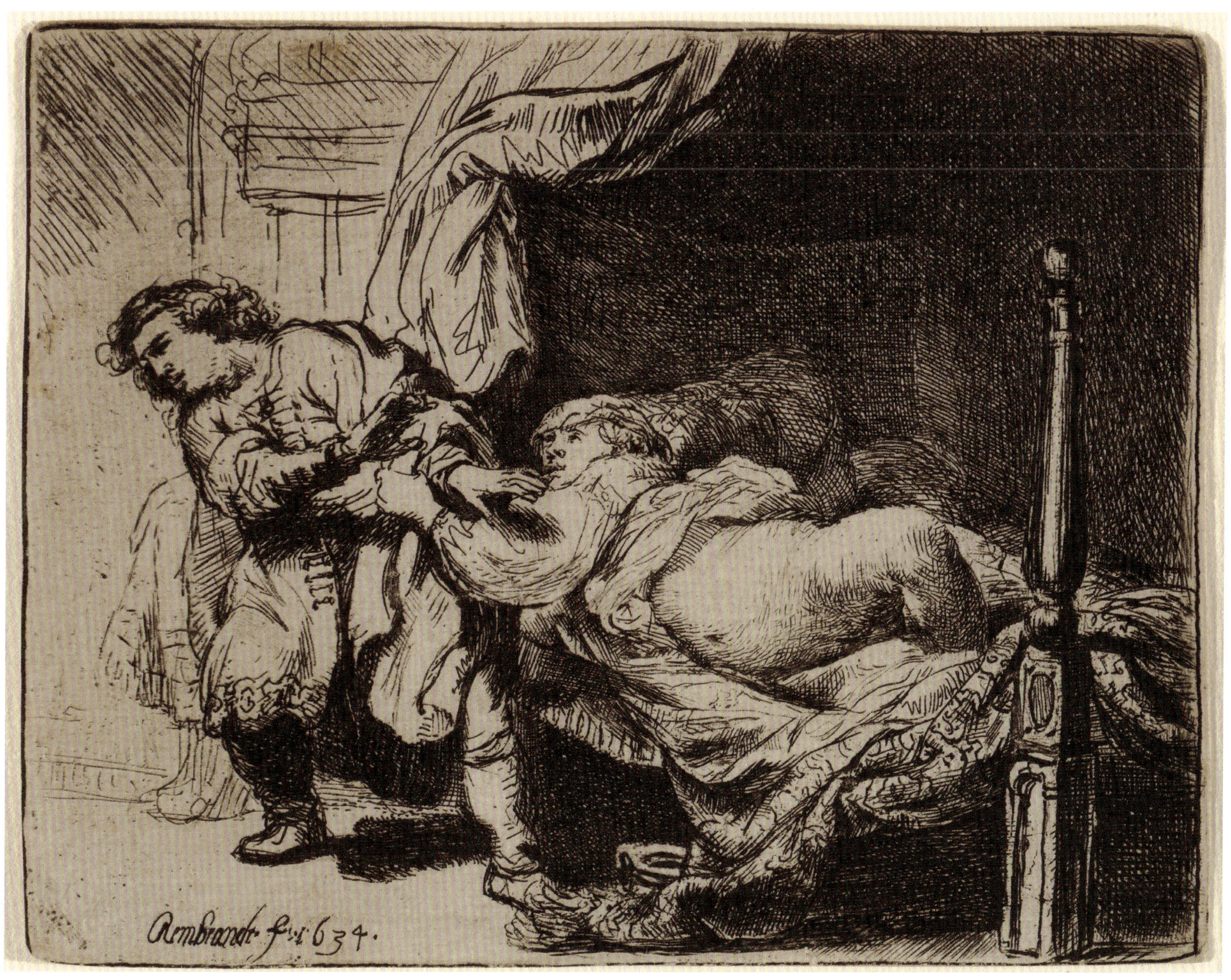

PLATE 13

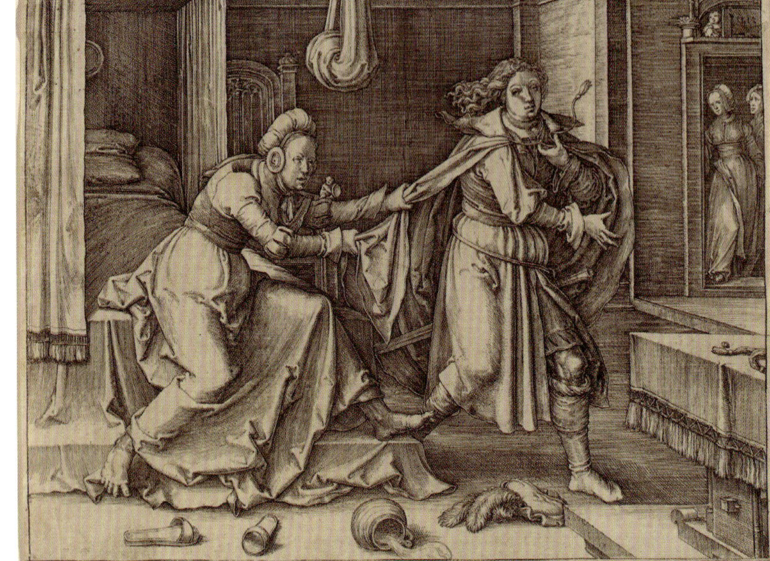

FIGURE 2. Lucas van Leyden, *Joseph and Potiphar's Wife*, engraving, 1512. *Photo: Courtesy of the National Gallery of Art, Washington, DC.*

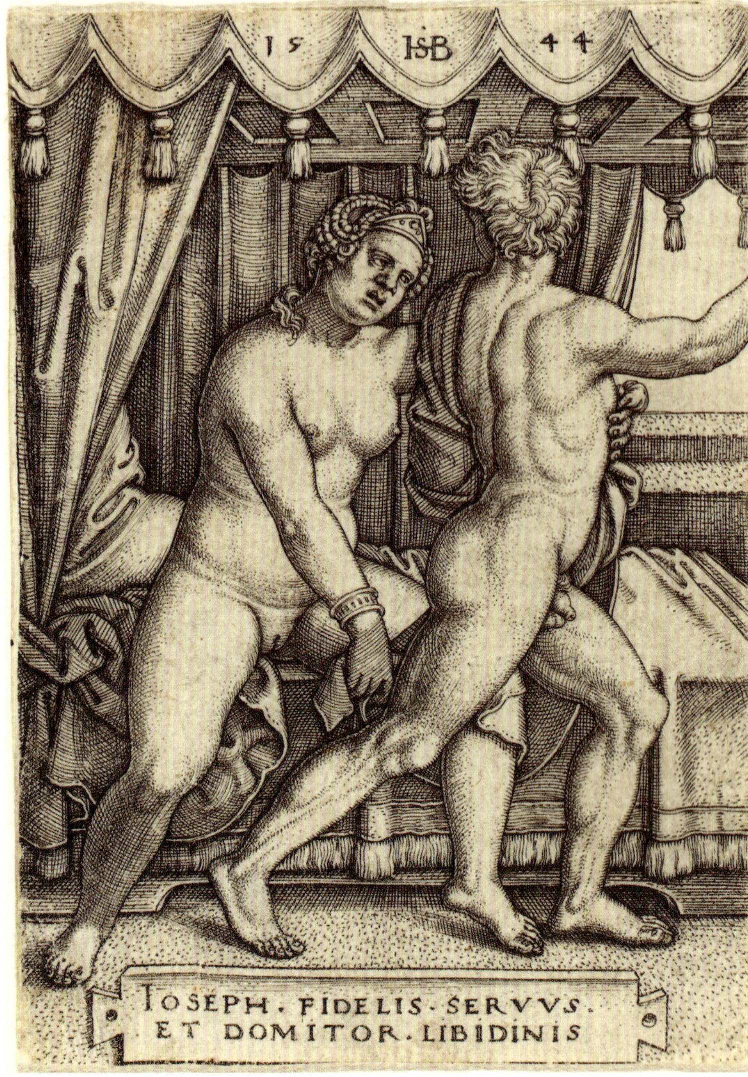

FIGURE 3. Hans Sebald Beham, *Joseph and Potiphar's Wife*, engraving, 1544. *Photo: Courtesy of the National Gallery of Art, Washington, DC.*

In Flavius Josephus's analysis, then, the story offers a more strongly gendered vision, with male rationality triumphing over female passion.[2]

Rembrandt's tiny print presents a rather earthy and erotic depiction of the attempted seduction. Based on Antonio Tempesta's small etching from about 1600[3] (fig. 1), the scene in Rembrandt's etching is set in a constricted space dominated by a large canopied bed. Potiphar's wife reclines on top of the disheveled mattress, twisting her body toward Joseph, who turns away from the half-naked woman. She holds onto Joseph's cloak in an effort to pull him toward her, but he resists, and his rejection and disapproval are clearly communicated in his posture and gestures.[4]

The fleshiness of Potiphar's wife exemplifies Rembrandt's typically unidealized representation of the female body, an approach that he first began to develop in a number of etchings and drawings of female models around 1631–32,[5] and the unmediated character of the seductress's body casts her as naked, rather than nude.[6] The temptress's chemise has ridden up to her waist in such a way that she shamelessly displays her belly, legs, and pudenda to the viewer.[7] A large, shiny, phallic bedpost dominates the right foreground,[8] while a bedpan is just visible under the bed, beyond the discarded coverlet. This last detail, which may derive from an engraving by Lucas van Leyden[9] (fig. 2), is a typically Rembrandtesque touch of mundane realism, albeit one fraught with sexual innuendo.

Rembrandt's use of white light and dark shadow leaves no doubt as to which part of the chamber is the focal point of this scene. Although the artist undoubtedly created these contrasts for dramatic effect, it is also apparent that Joseph, a man of integrity, is figuratively, as well as literally, fleeing from darkness into the light. Indeed, several authors have observed that the print suggests a symbolic distinction between virtue (Joseph, in full light) and vice (Potiphar's wife, silhouetted against the dark shadows of the canopied bed).[10]

Representations of Joseph and Potiphar's wife were fairly popular in the early Modern period because of the biblical story's moral lessons and erotic connotations.[11] For example, it was used by Hans Brosamer as an illustration of the ninth commandment, "Thou shalt not covet thy neighbor's wife," in the 1550 edition of Martin Luther's *Catechismus für die gemeine Pfarrherr und Prediger*,[12] and by Harmen Jansz. Müller in an engraving after Maarten van Heemskerck, as an illustration of the same commandment in the series of the Ten Commandments published by Hieronymus Cock in 1566.[13] In addition to being represented in the Joseph cycle engraved by Lucas van Leyden, the scene also appeared in illustrated editions of the Old Testament and Josephus's *Jewish Antiquities*,[14] and as an independent biblical and/or moralizing narrative. An intriguing example of the last category is a very small engraving by Hans Sebald Beham (fig. 3), which bears the inscription "IOSEPH. FIDELIS. SERVUS/ ET DOMITOR LIBIDINIS" ("Joseph, the faithful servant and conqueror of lust").[15] This inscription focuses not only on Joseph's loyalty to his master, but also on his ability to resist temptation and to control his passions, the two qualities that are specifically emphasized in Josephus's framing of the story. The Beham print is somewhat unusual in that both of the protagonists are nude. Its even more visually explicit sexual nature challenges the viewer to emulate Joseph and overcome the temptations of lust. While Rembrandt's blatantly erotic representation of Potiphar's wife's body may have been simply a way of appealing to a male audience, it may also have been intended to serve a moralizing function, challenging the male viewer to avoid temptation by averting his eyes as Joseph does, and controlling his own passions.

The print in the Snite Museum's collection appears to have been heavily reworked in a manner that coarsened the lines and muddied the shadows, particularly in and around the figure of Joseph. These changes suggest that the plate was altered by a hand other than Rembrandt's, and the fact that the Museum's copy was printed on wove paper confirms that this example is a late, posthumous impression in which the printer has reinforced the original plate, which had become worn.[16]

Notes

1. In the Bible, the seductress is referred to only as "his master's wife." In the Islamic tradition and in later Jewish retellings of the tale, however, she is known as Zuleika.

2. "He demonstrated that wisdom was able to govern the uneasy passions of life" (Josephus, *Jewish Antiquities*, 2, 4, 1), and "So she made known her wicked inclinations, and spoke to him about lying with her. However, he rejected her pleas, not thinking it agreeable to religion to yield so far to her, as to do what would tend to the affront and injury of him that purchased him, and had given him so great honors " (Josephus, *Jewish Antiquities*, 2, 4, 2).

3. TIB 71. Tümpel, *Rembrandt legt*, cat. 18. The overall configuration of the space, the disposition of the bed, and the aggressiveness of Potiphar's wife all suggest a connection between Tempesta's print and Rembrandt's rendition of the scene. There are marked differences, however: In contrast to Rembrandt's version, the Tempesta etching portrays a seductress who is a much more idealized, completely nude figure. She sits upright on the bed, with one foot planted on the floor, as if ready to chase after her prey. The clothing that Tempesta's Joseph wears has an antique look, whereas Rembrandt's Joseph wears more contemporary clothing. Tempesta's Joseph gazes back toward the seductress as he strides off, but Rembrandt's Joseph turns resolutely away as he wrenches himself free of the woman's grasp. In the Tempesta etching, the doorway is more completely described than in Rembrandt's print, and a sliver of a landscape is visible through the opening.

4. Shelley Perlove and Larry Silver (*Rembrandt's Faith*, 99) noted that Rembrandt's Joseph consciously avoids looking at Potiphar's wife's exposed body and does not meet her gaze. They associated this detail with Calvin's comment that the wife gazed at Joseph and strove to seduce him "by her 'impure and dissolute look,' so that her eyes were as 'torches to inflame the heart with lust.'" For Calvin, this event illustrated the dangers of sight.

5. Cf. Rembrandt's etchings of *A Naked Woman Seated on a Mound* (B. 198), *Diana at the Bath* (B. 201), and *Jupiter and Antiope:*

The Small Plate (B. 204). Otto Benesch dated a handful of drawings of female nudes to the same period (Ben. 191–193).

6. The terms "naked" and "nude" as used here derive from Kenneth Clark's *The Nude: A Study in Ideal Form* (New York: Pantheon, 1956), which held that "nudes" are idealized and, therefore, more distant from real experience, whereas "naked" figures represent the human body as it actually is.

7. This is an anomalous representation of Potiphar's wife, because ordinarily, in artworks in which her body is exposed, she is either uncovered from the waist up or completely naked.

8. The phallic nature of the bedpost is made even more explicit in Rembrandt's later erotic etching known as *The French Bed*, or *Leidikant* (B. 186, 1646).

9. Lucas van Leyden's engraving of *Joseph Escaping from Potiphar's Wife* (NHD 20, 1512) was one of five prints that he dedicated to the story of Joseph. In his composition, a pair of discarded slippers (a traditional symbol of sexuality), a plumed hat, and a chamber pot are arrayed on the bedroom floor in front of Potiphar's wife. The chamber pot, a vessel that can have sexual associations, has been overturned, and it lies with its mouth toward the viewer, its contents spilling out on to the floor.

10. See, for example, comments by Petra Jeroense, "Joseph and Potiphar's Wife, 1634," in Peter van Coelen, *Patriarchs, Angels and Prophets: The Old Testament in Netherlandish Printmaking from Lucas van Leyden to Rembrandt*, exh. cat. (Amsterdam: Rembrandt Information Centre, 1996), cat. 19, 94.

11. Clifford Ackley, in *Rembrandt's Journey*, cat. 97, 165.

12. HG 384.

13. NHD 73 [Heemskerck].

14. A woodcut print illustration of Joseph and Potiphar's wife based on a design by Tobias Stimmer (HG 412) appears in the German edition of Josephus's *Jewish Antiquities*. Rembrandt owned a copy of this edition of Josephus's *Jewish Antiquities*.

15. HG 15. Contrary to tradition, in this version the genitals of both Joseph and Potiphar's wife are exposed.

16. In a communication on file in the Registrar's Office at the Snite Museum of Art, art historian Clifford Ackley indicated that he believed this to be a late impression, printed after Rembrandt's death. The Snite Museum owns a second, higher-quality original impression of the second state of this etching (cat. no. A2, acc. no. 1981.107). This seventeenth-century impression was given to the Snite by Dr. and Mrs. Norval Green.

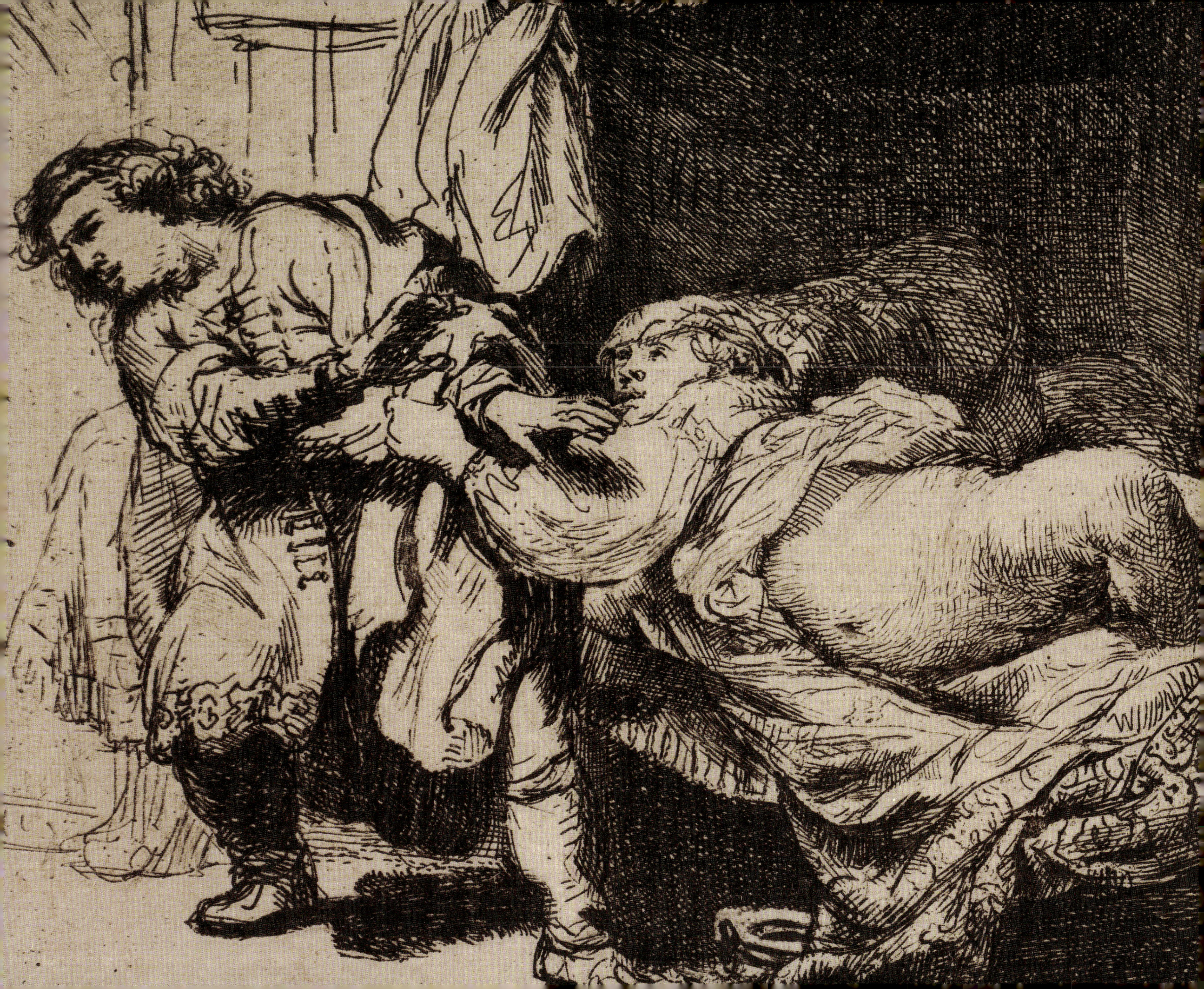

14–15. Triumph of Mordecai

14. Triumph of Mordecai

B. 40 (H. 172, Mz. 178, NHD 185)
Etching and drypoint
c. 1641[1]
State III of IV[2]
Sheet: 17.4 × 21.5 cm, trimmed to the plate mark
Watermark: Fragment at top left: . . . *4 WR.*
Verso: in red chalk at left corner, unidentified initials.
Bottom, in graphite, from the left: *180*/L / *104*(inverted)/ *L. 30.19.7737/ B. N° 40 Belle/ T* or *I hunans* (?)[3]/ *D 163/ No. 40*

Provenance:
Associated American Artists Inc., New York, NY, 1976
Feddersen, Elkhart, IN, 1991
Snite Museum of Art
Accession no.: 1991.025.013

The plate does not survive.

15. Triumph of Mordecai (Counterproof)

Counterproof
Sheet: 17.4 × 21.5 cm, trimmed to the plate mark.
Recto: bottom left, collector's stamp: joined script capital *IM* and *IV* in a circle (?) (not in Lugt)
Verso: in graphite, *G.T./ No. 39 Rev./ Mead 10^{v}/5/ counterproof*

Provenance:
Associated American Artists Inc., New York, NY, 1976
Feddersen, Elkhart, IN, 1991
Snite Museum of Art
Accession no.: 1991.025.014

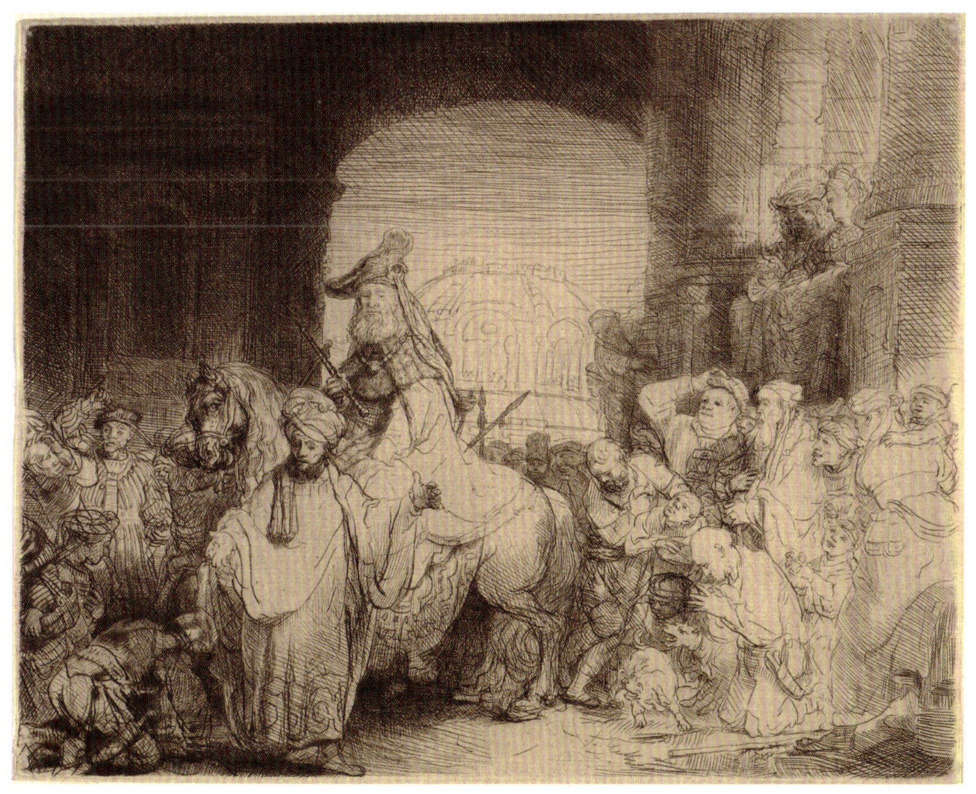

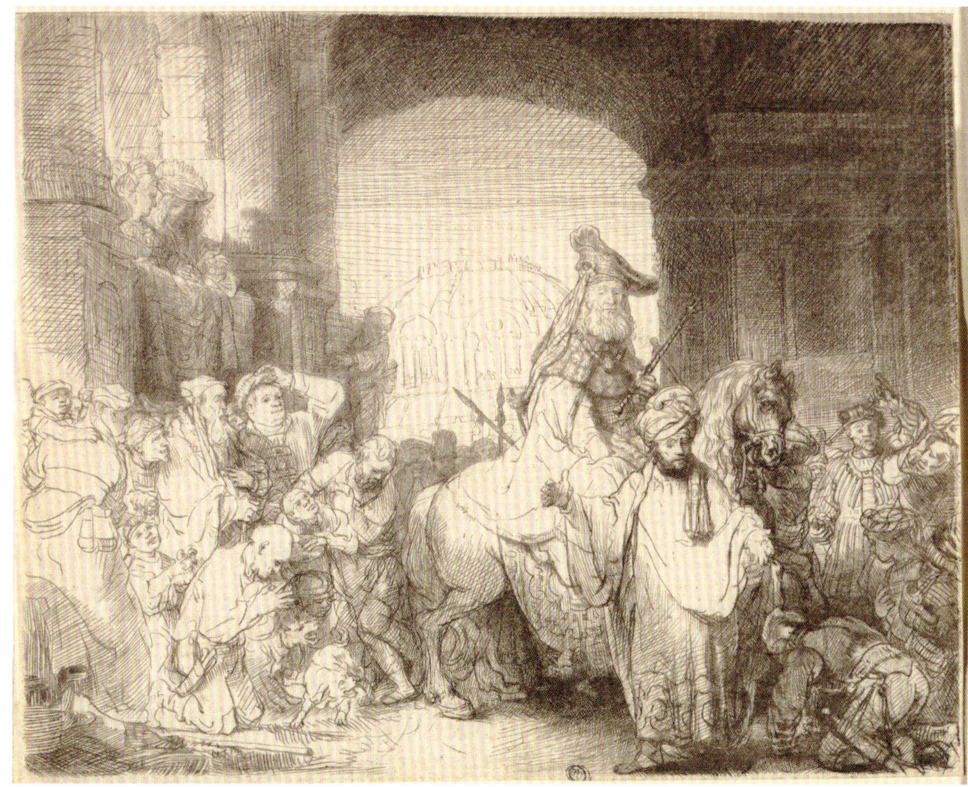

PLATE 14–15

The theme of Rembrandt's *Triumph of Mordecai* is taken from the Old Testament Book of Esther. According to the biblical account, the beautiful young Jewess Esther, an orphan who had been raised as a ward of her uncle Mordecai, was chosen by Ahasuerus, king of the Persian Empire, as his new queen. One evening, Mordecai, who was sitting vigil by the palace gates, overheard two of Ahasuerus's guardsmen plotting against the king. Mordecai informed Esther, and she, in turn, told the king. As a result, the two conspirators were apprehended and hanged. Shortly after Esther had become queen, the king decided to elevate a member of his court, Haman, "above all of the princes who were with him."[4] Ahasuerus decreed that all of his servants and subjects must now bow down to Haman. When Haman encountered Mordecai near the gate, however, Mordecai refused to bow down, since Jews bow only to God. This infuriated Haman, who decided to punish Mordecai by hanging him and all the other Jews in the kingdom. When Mordecai learned of this plan, he sent a note to his ward, telling her of Haman's plot. Esther, who had never told the king that she was Jewish, hesitantly agreed to try to intercede on behalf of her people. Dressed in her most splendid garments, the young queen appeared before the king even though he had not summoned her, an offense for which she could have been executed. Ahasuerus, dazzled by Esther's beauty, not only granted her an audience, but promised to fulfill any wish she might have. Esther's only request was that her husband and Haman attend a special banquet that she was planning.

The night before the meal, Ahasuerus was restless and decided to have the chronicles of his reign read to him. When the account of Mordecai's revelations concerning the plot against the king was read, Ahasuerus asked if Mordecai had been rewarded. He was told that he had not. Later, when Haman came to the palace, Ahasuerus asked him how he thought one should honor someone who had delighted the king. Haman, thinking that it was he who was to be honored, replied, "For the man whom the king delights to honor, let royal robes be brought which the king has worn, and the horse which the king has ridden, and on whose head a royal crown is set; and let the robes and the horse be handed over to one of the king's most noble princes; let him array the man whom the king delights to honor, and let him conduct the man on horseback through the open square of the city, proclaiming before him: 'Thus shall it be done to the man whom the king delights to honor.'"[5] Hearing this, Ahasuerus instructed Haman to bestow these honors on "Mordecai the Jew, who sits at the king's gate." Haman obeyed: "[He] took the robes and the horse, and he arrayed Mordecai and made him ride through the open square of the city, proclaiming, 'Thus shall it be done to the man whom the king delights to honor.'"[6] At the banquet, that evening, Esther revealed to Ahasuerus that she was a Jew. She then told him of Haman's plans and asked the king to spare her life and the lives of her people. When Ahasuerus discovered that Haman was the author of the plot to slay the Jews, he condemned his minister to be hanged from the very gallows that Haman had prepared for Mordecai's execution.

Although the episode of Mordecai's triumphant ride through the city square and Haman's resulting humiliation was rarely illustrated in the North,[7] two earlier Dutch examples of this theme served as visual sources for Rembrandt. Lucas van Leyden had done an engraving of the subject in 1515[8] (fig. 1) and Pieter Lastman, Rembrandt's teacher in Amsterdam, had done a small oil painting of the event in 1617[9] (fig. 2). The Rembrandt print includes two figures at the right side of the composition that were clearly inspired by Lucas van Leyden's engraving: the kneeling man holding his hat in front of him, and the man behind this figure, who is in the process of tipping his hat. Lastman's influence may be seen in the classical form of the architecture in Rembrandt's print, including the centralized temple placed in the background,[10] certain details of Mordecai's costume,[11] and the emergence of the figures from shadow into light.[12] In the final analysis, however, Rembrandt's conception of the event is significantly different from those of his predecessors. In both of the earlier versions, the triumph proceeds from left to right, with figures emerging out of what must be construed as the palace gate. Rembrandt rotated the architecture ninety degrees, so that the monumental opening of the gate is now behind the figures. As a result, the distant temple and the mounted Mordecai are enframed by—and associated with—an archway of light. In addition, the artist included Ahasuerus and Esther as observers, placing them on a low draped balcony on the right side of the composition, above the curious and respectful crowd.[13] Some have suggested that the king and queen bear the features of Rembrandt[14] and his wife, Saskia, but the resemblance is minimal. The barking dogs and the expansive crowd of men, women, and children exhibiting a variety of reactions serve as a contrast to the calm figure of the aged Mordecai, who gazes out at the viewer with serene dignity.

By altering the direction of the procession as it had been portrayed by Lucas and Lastman, Rembrandt added drama to the scene, orchestrating it in such a way that Haman and Mordecai appear to be moving out of the square and into the space of the viewer. Although Mordecai remains the dominant figure in the composition, the changed orientation of the procession places a new emphasis on Haman by bringing him forward, into the light,[15] and placing him at the very front edge of the space. The body language of the humiliated minister speaks volumes about his state of mind. Although Haman's outstretched arms[16] make way for and introduce the honoree, and his open mouth suggests that he is obeying the royal injunction that he proclaim, "Thus shall it be done to the man whom the king delights to honor" as he leads Mordecai through the square, his eyes are downcast and his expression is one of consternation. The result is that Rembrandt has placed the evildoer front and center, emphasizing a dramatic psychological moment and making sure that the viewer is witness to Haman's reversal of fortunes.

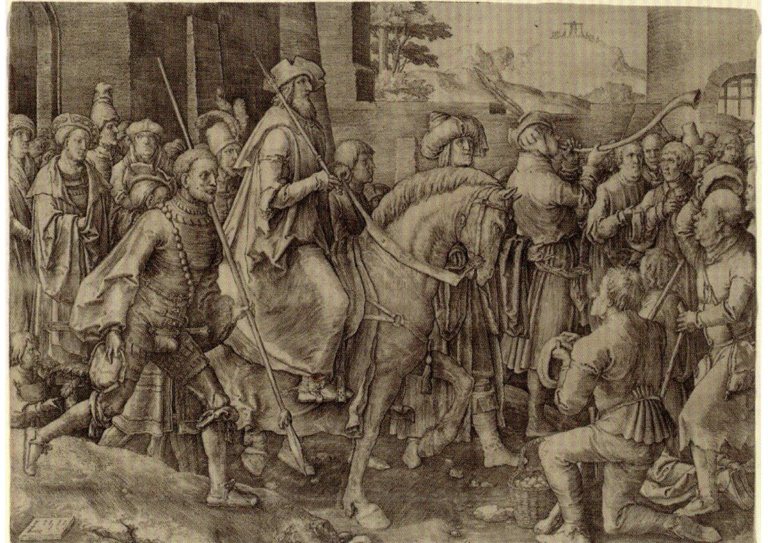

FIGURE 1. Lucas van Leyden, *The Triumph of Mordecai*, engraving, 1515. *Photo: Courtesy of the National Gallery of Art, Washington, DC.*

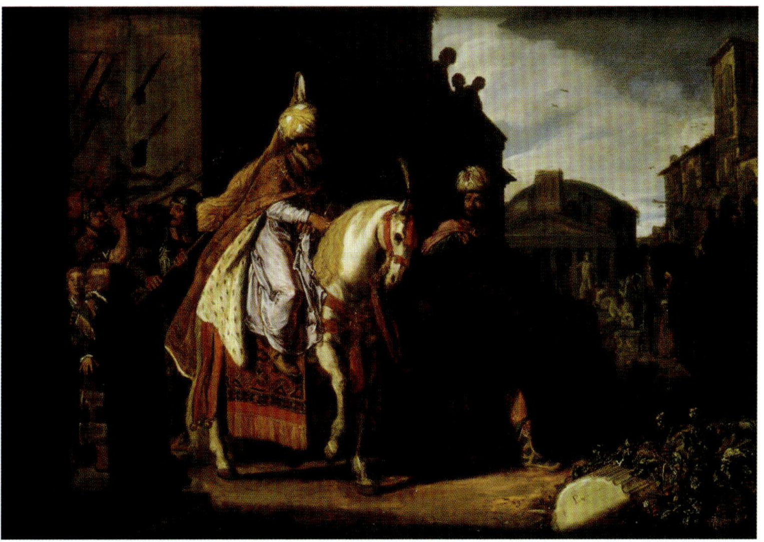

FIGURE 2. Peter Lastman, *The Triumph of Mordecai*, oil on panel, 1617. *Museum het Rembrandthuis, Amsterdam.*

The events related in the Book of Esther had a special resonance for the Dutch in Rembrandt's day. The reason that Mordecai, Esther, and their Jewish compatriots were living in Susa was that they, along with the king of Judah and his soldiers, had been taken captive by Nebuchadnezzar, the Akkadian king and destroyer of the Temple in Jerusalem. Hence, Mordecai's ordeal and the subjugation of the Jewish people in Persia were seen as exemplary of the historical sufferings of the Jews in exile under the dominion of despotic foreign rulers. The Jews' escape from Haman's treachery as a result of the heroic actions of Mordecai and Esther was seen as an example of God's intervention on behalf of his chosen people. During the seventeenth century, the inhabitants of the rebellious Dutch northern provinces were fighting for freedom from what they saw as Spanish tyranny and Catholic persecution,[17] which made them inclined to identify with the struggles of the Israelites. In addition, in purely allegorical terms, Haman's downfall had long been interpreted as an exemplar of the way in which those who suffer from the sin of pride are brought low.[18]

According to Steven Nadler, the tale of Esther "appears as a theme in the literature and the visual arts of the Netherlands in the seventeenth century more often than anywhere else at any other time in history"[19] because of its appeal to both the Dutch regent class, for political reasons, and the Sephardic Jews residing in the Netherlands, who celebrated the holiday of Purim by reading the entire Book of Esther (the *megillah*), masquerading,[20] and performing Purim plays. Although it is clear that Esther's courageous actions and the execution of Haman were the main focus of many of the Dutch literary and visual retellings of the story, Mordecai's role was not neglected. In fact, in 1630, the Middelburg writer and poet Johannes de Swaef published a prose account of the story that focused on Mordecai as a patriotic paradigm: *Mardachai, ofte Christelijcken Patriot* (Mordecai, or the Christian patriot).[21] For all of these reasons, Rembrandt's print, with its emphasis on both the wicked, hubristic Haman and the dignified, triumphant Mordecai, would have had far-reaching appeal.[22]

The etching is quite sophisticated in its descriptive techniques. Rembrandt used dense masses of cross-hatching in the architecture of the gateway, and thin spidery lines in the spectral temple in the background, creating a broad range of light and shadow. In addition, if one accepts the consensus date of 1641 for this print, it is one of the earliest works in which drypoint, particularly in the delineation of many of the figures, played a major role in Rembrandt's oeuvre.[23] The Snite Museum's impression is a relatively late one, which means that it has lost some of the work's subtler embellishments. Nonetheless, some of the velvety effects produced by the drypoint burr can still be discerned in the edging of Mordecai's cloak and in the large fur collar.

The museum also owns a counterproof of this print, an impression drawn from a still-wet original impression. This process re-reverses the image, so that the counterproof depicts what appears on the plate itself. Erik Hinterding and Jaco Rutgers[24] list ten known counterproofs of the *Triumph of Mordecai* in their catalog. This is an unusually large number of such prints to have been made, particularly for an image that exists in only a single state.[25] The function of Rembrandt's counterproofs is not at all clear.[26] In the case of this print, however, given the number of examples that survive, it does not seem likely that Rembrandt intended them to serve exclusively as working proofs. It is more likely that he intended them for the marketplace. Also, given that one of the major differences between Rembrandt's conception of the Triumph of Mordecai and Lucas van Leyden's version was the direction of the procession, Rembrandt may have wished to provide connoisseurs or collectors with an image that would make it easier to compare and contrast the two prints.

Notes

1. According to Erik Hinterding (*Lugt Catalogue*, cat. 27, 93), the watermark found on impressions of the "Triumph" suggests a later date of about 1646.

2. The entry in NHD for this print identifies two earlier states and one later, posthumous state. There are only three impressions and no counterproofs of the two earlier states, suggesting that they are anomalies never intended for circulation.

3. On the Associated American Artists bill of sale, this is recorded as "Trainus (?)."

4. Esther 3:1.

5. Esther 6:7–9.

6. Esther 6:11.

7. Although images of the story of Esther enjoyed a certain popularity in the Netherlands, the particular scene that Rembrandt chose to represent was rarely depicted. Erik Forssman made this

observation ("der Triumph des im persischen Exil lebenden Juden Mardochai offenbar seltener herausgelöst worden") in his study "Rembrandt's Radierung 'Der Triumph des Mardochai,'" *Zeitschrift für Kunstgeschichte* 39, no. 4 (1976): 298. As Forssman noted, when the figure of Mordecai in triumph does appear, it is normally in the background of a representation of another part of the story. See, for example, the engraving from 1564 by Philip Galle after a drawing by Maarten van Heemskerck. The engraving, which focuses on Ahasuerus consulting with Haman, is one of a series of eight prints dedicated to the *Book of Esther* (NHD 55 [Philip Galle]). Astrid Tümpel, "The History of Esther," cat. 39, in Peter van der Coelen, *Patriarchs, Angels & Prophets: The Old Testament in Netherlandish Printmaking from Lucas van Leyden to Rembrandt*, exh. cat. (Amsterdam: Rembrandt Information Centre, 1996), 124–26. Rembrandt's decision to focus on the triumph of Mordecai is very much in harmony with the artist's abiding interest in the virtue of humility.

8. NHD 32. See also Ellen S. Jacobwitz and Stephanie Loeb Stepanek, *The Prints of Lucas van Leyden and Contemporaries*, exh. cat. (Washington, DC: National Gallery of Art, 1983), cat. 48, for a political interpretation of the Lucas van Leyden print.

9. The painting is located in the Museum het Rembrandthuis, Amsterdam. Around 1635, Rembrandt did a pen and wash drawing after the Lastman painting (Ben. 1). This study, which was destroyed during the Second World War, was a faithful copy of Lastman's composition.

10. There are, however, significant differences between the architecture in Rembrandt's print and that of Lastman's painting. On the left side of Rembrandt's etching, there is a raised niche flanked by pilasters supporting an entablature with a projecting cornice from which springs a massive barrel vault. This motif appears to derive not from Lastman's painting, but rather from the architecture in Raphael's *School of Athens*, a source that Rembrandt could have known from a mid-sixteenth-century engraving by Giorgio Ghisi (B. 24) after the painting. In addition, whereas Lastman's centralized temple was clearly inspired by the Pantheon, which Lastman would have seen during his residence in Rome, Rembrandt invented a very different kind of structure. As Shelley Perlove pointed out, Rembrandt's low-domed building, with its gallery of two-light arched windows separated by heavy buttresses, seems closer to sixteenth- and seventeenth-century reconstructions of the Temple in Jerusalem. This latter type already appears in what is generally acknowledged to be a preparatory drawing for the print. The drawing is now in Lviv, Ukraine. Shelley Perlove, "An Irenic Vision of Utopia: Rembrandt's 'Triumph of Mordecai' and the New Jerusalem," *Zeitschrift für Kunstgeschichte*, 56, no. 1 (1993): 41–42.

11. Similarities in Mordecai's attire include the chain that he wears (a detail derived from Josephus's account of the story, per Perlove, "An Irenic Vision," 45–46), and the manner in which a piece of cloth attached to the back of Mordecai's hat falls down over his shoulder (Forssman, "Rembrandt's Radierung," 301). The hats themselves, however, are quite different in style. Whereas Lastman's Mordecai wears a turban topped by a tall, thin projection from which the fabric flows, Rembrandt gave his Mordecai a rather fanciful flat hat set at a jaunty angle. This variation may have been intended to distinguish Persian from Jew.

12. Petra Jeroense, "The Triumph of Mordecai," cat. 41, in Coelen, *Patriarchs*, 127.

13. See the discussion of Rembrandt's use of secondary observers in the essay by Charles M. Rosenberg, "Rembrandt's Religious Prints," in this catalog.

14. For a self-portrait of Rembrandt from 1638, see cat. no. 1.

15. Although Rembrandt often adheres to the artistic tradition of casting light on the virtuous and obscuring the wicked in darkness, this etching shines a light on Haman's shame.

16. Numerous historians have recognized elements of the etching that echo some of the compositional devices that Rembrandt utilized in his painting *The Nightwatch* of about the same time (1640–42), including the juxtaposition of the excited crowd against a stabilizing architectural backdrop, and Haman's rhetorical gesture, particularly the manner in which his hand seems to break the surface of the print in the same way as Captain Banning Cocq's left hand does in *The Nightwatch*. Whether or not these parallels were meant to imply some sort of symbolic link between Mordecai and the heroic militiamen of the painting remains an open question. Egbert Haverkamp-Begemann, "Rembrandt's *Night Watch* and the *Triumph of Mordecai*," in *Album Amicorum J. G. van Gelder*, ed. Josua Bruyn, J. A. Emmons, E. De Jongh, and D. P. Snoep (The Hague: Nijhoff, 1973), 5–8.

17. Steven Nadler, *Rembrandt's Jews* (Chicago: University of Chicago Press, 2003), 98. See also Simon Schama, *The Embarrassment of Riches: An Interpretation of Dutch Culture in the Golden Age* (Berkeley: University of California Press, 1987), 97 ff.

18. In the *Purgatorio*, for example, Dante placed Haman among those who were guilty of the sin of pride (*Purgatorio*, xvii, 25–30).

19. Nadler, *Rembrandt's Jews*, 100.

20. Purim masquerades reflected the Book of Esther's lessons that things are not always as they seem, particularly in regard to politics and/or God's works.

21. Nadler (*Rembrandt's Jews*, 101) incorrectly identified this author as Johannes de Saef, rather than Swaef. The work was published in Middleburg under the pseudonym Nehemia Publicola. For a brief biography of de Swaef and a bibliography of his work, see A. J. van der Aa, *Biographisch woordenboek der Nederlanden*. Vol. 17, part 2 (Haarlem: J. J. van Brederode, 1874), 1089.

22. Perlove also suggested that the print would have carried specific millenarial implications, visible in what she interprets as an image of the restored Temple and the repentant and converted Jewish masses at the End of Days. "With Mordecai cast in the role of godly patriot, this work seems to enunciate a yearning for both temporal victory and eternal peace." Perlove, "An Irenic Vision," 58–60.

For a discussion of millenarianism and Rembrandt's association with the millenarianist Rabbi Menasseh ben Israel, see Illustrations for Samuel Menasseh ben Israel, *Piedra gloriosa o de la Estatua de Nebuchadnesar*, cat. nos. 8, 9, and 10, esp. note 9.

23. Regarding the technical significance of this print, see Christopher White, *Rembrandt as an Etcher: A Study of the Artist at Work*, 2nd ed. (New Haven, CT: Yale University Press, 1999), 45–47; and Marijn Schapelhouman, "The Triumph of Mordecai," cat. 44, in Erik Hinterding, Ger Luijten, and Martin Royalton-Kisch, *Rembrandt the Printmaker*, exh. cat. (Chicago and London: Fitzroy Dearborn Publishers, 2000), 195–96.

24. NHD 185.

25. If a plate were being carried through a number of different states, it would be natural for an artist to pull counterproofs at various stages of the creative process so as to retain a record of the plate's changing appearance. If only one state of a print was being made, however, this sort of record would not be necessary. According to Marie-Christine Seigneur, about eighty of Rembrandt's prints are known to have counterproofs. "On Counterproofs," *Print Quarterly* 21 (2004):117.

26. It has been suggested that counterproofs may have been retained by the artist to use as models in his workshop. This would still not explain the extraordinarily large number of counterproofs for this plate. Josua Bruyn, cited in Marie-Christine Seigneur, "On Counterproofs," 121–123.

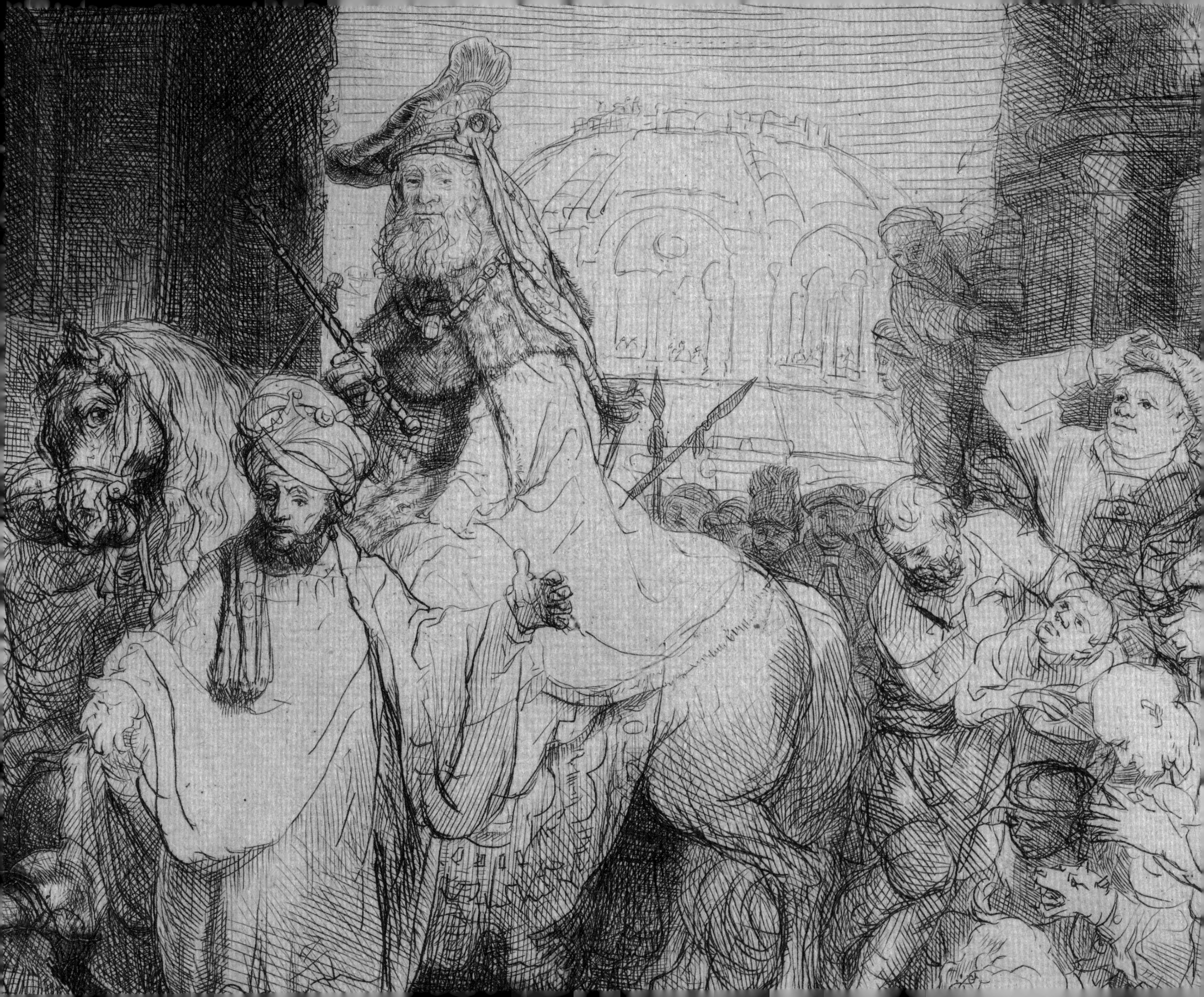

16. David in Prayer

B. 41 (H. 258, Mz. 232, NHD 268)
Etching and drypoint
Signed and dated in the plate: *Rembrandt f. 1652.*
State I of III
Sheet: 14.5 × 9.5 cm, plate mark 14.3 × 9.3 cm
Verso: collector's stamp, LL in a circle in red ink (Lugt 4796, Leslie E. Lancy); bottom, in graphite from left: *B 48 II/David im Gebet(at)/I.3 (Z) ol*

Provenance:
Leslie E. Lancy, Ellwood, PA (1911–96)
David Tunick Inc., New York, NY, 1977
Feddersen, Elkhart, IN, 1991
Snite Museum of Art
Acc. No.: 1991.025.015

Plate survives:
The Israel Museum, Jerusalem

At first glance, Rembrandt's etching of a man kneeling in prayer beside his bed appears to be a timeless, intimate domestic scene. The large harp lying in the foreground of the print, however, identifies the praying figure as the biblical King David. The prominence of the harp makes it clear that in this print, Rembrandt chose to emphasize David's role as a singer of psalms, rather than as a legendary biblical hero and warrior.[1]

Although the image is unusual, it is not without precedent. Lucas van Leyden created two images of David at prayer (figs. 1 and 2),[2] which may have inspired Rembrandt's etching. Nonetheless, there are some marked differences between the two artists' works. Lucas placed David outdoors, and in each case gave him not only a harp, but also a scepter. In addition, each of Lucas's images includes a celestial figure hovering in the clouds above, one bearing two arrows and the other, dressed in priestly garb, holding an arrow and an orb. The inclusion of a scepter and harp in these prints identifies David as both the king of Israel and a psalmist, while the figure bearing arrows is associated with plague imagery. As numerous critics have noted, the reference to pestilence that appears in the Lucas prints recalls the plague visited upon the people of Israel as a result of David's sins, as recounted in 2 Samuel 24:10–17.[3]

Near the end of his life, David confessed to the Lord that he had done wicked and foolish things. In response, God gave him a choice of punishments: three years of famine, three years of pursuit by David's enemies, or three days of plague. David chose the last option, but when he saw the terrible price that his choice had made the people of Israel pay—the death of 70,000 men—he prayed to God, "Lo, I have sinned. And I have done wickedly; but these sheep, what have they done? Let thy hand, I pray thee, be against me and against my father's house."[4] God, who had already decided that he had exacted a heavy enough price, stayed the hand of the angel of death.[5]

The biblical basis for Rembrandt's *David in Prayer* is not as clear as that of the Lucas van Leyden prints, and this has led to diverse interpretations of Rembrandt's etching. Hans Rotermund suggested that the print should be labeled "David's Penance," and interpreted the composition as an illustration of David's fruitless

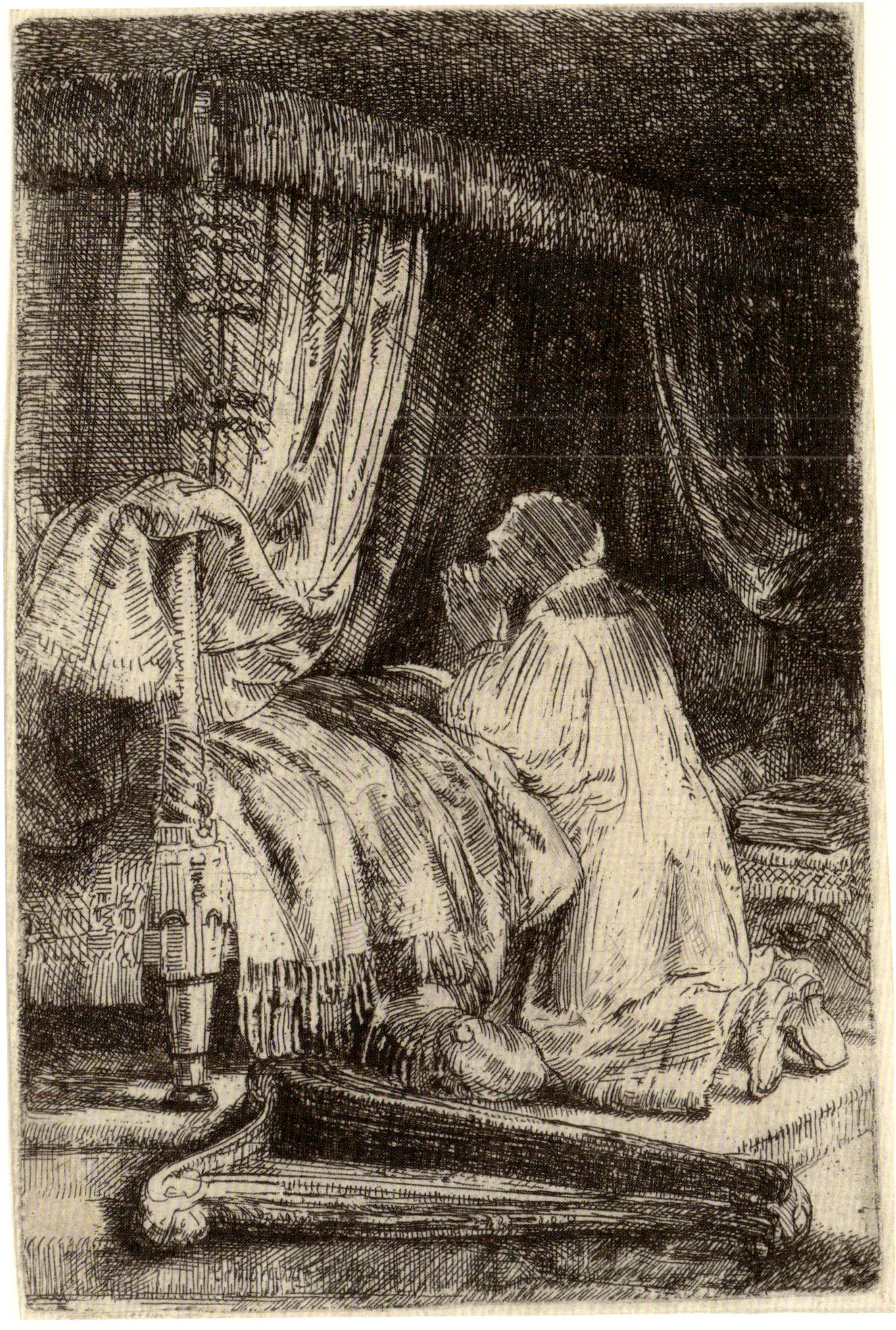

PLATE 16

FIGURE 1. Lucas van Leyden, *David in Prayer*, engraving, c. 1507. *Photo: Courtesy of the National Gallery of Art, Washington, DC.*

FIGURE 2. Lucas van Leyden, *David in Prayer*, engraving, 1520. *The Metropolitan Museum of Art, New York, New York, Harris Brisbane Dick Fund.*

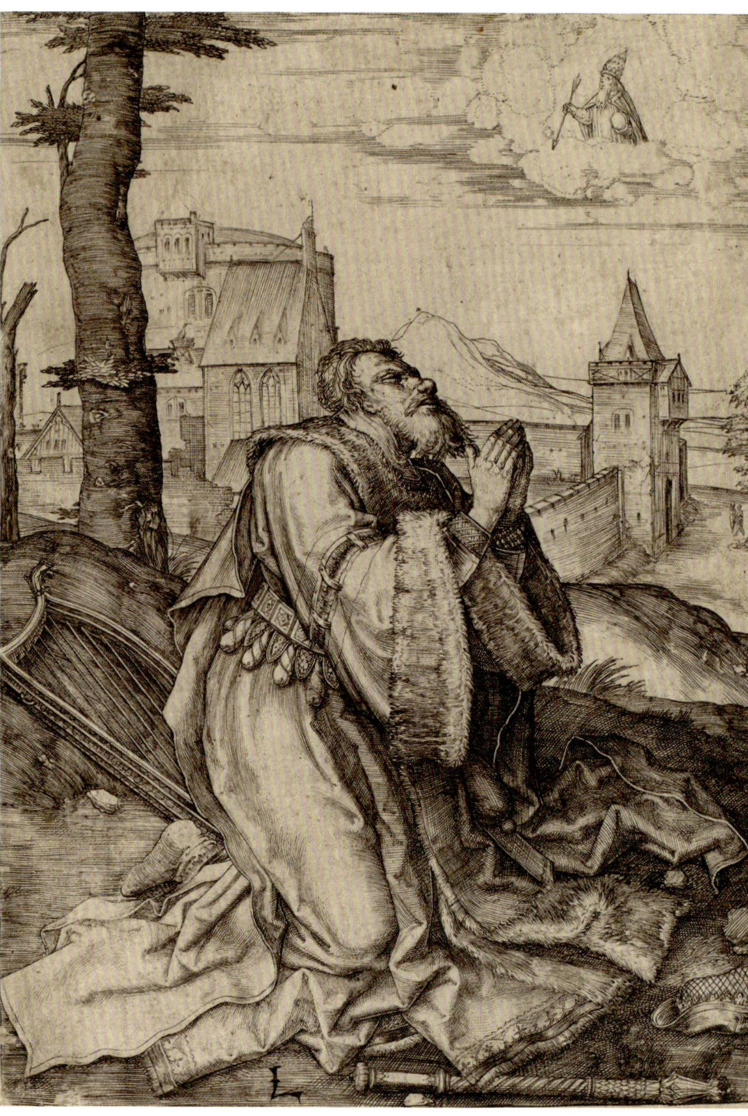

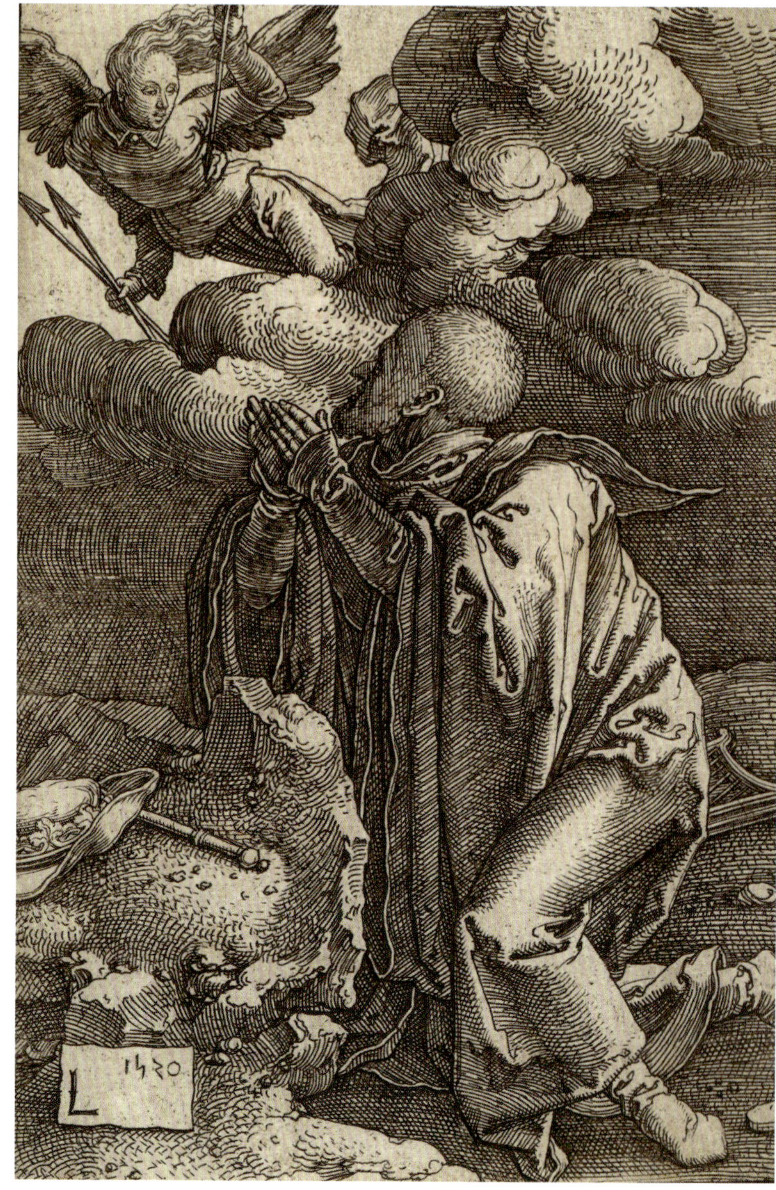

prayers for the life of his first son, who was conceived in an adulterous affair with Bathsheba (2 Samuel 12:15–17).[6] For Martin Dieker, the fact that the scene takes place in a bedchamber is evidence that this was, indeed, the incident that inspired the image.[7] Others have read the print more generically as an illustration of Psalm 51, the so-called Penitential Psalm.[8] As Perlove and Silver pointed out, the French and the Flemish both had a tradition of illustrating this psalm with an image of David praying, although these images typically represented the king kneeling in prayer outdoors, as in the Lucas van Leyden prints.[9]

Rembrandt's choice of an interior setting seems to be unique. It creates a much greater sense of intimacy than the Lucas van Leyden scenes of David praying in a stark landscape, and it contributes to a sense of the penitent sinner as Everyman, engaged in personal communion with God.[10] At the same time, the way in which the poet-king leans into the shadowed recess of his canopied bed transforms the darkness into a hallowed space, one that Catholic viewers may have perceived as tantamount to a confessional. Despite the fact that Rembrandt included details that project warmth and domesticity (David's slippers and the rug and cushion on which he kneels), the sumptuousness of the canopied bed and bedclothes makes it clear that this is the chamber of a wealthy man. The etching, then, is a glimpse of humility in a regal setting, with an eye to contemporary Dutch décor.

Although the harp lying on the floor would seem to serve as an impediment to anyone wishing to enter the room and disturb David at prayer, Rembrandt employed light as a means of inviting the viewer into the chamber. Highlights lead the eye from the nearby curtains, bedpost, and coverlet on the left to the shining robes of the kneeling figure at center-right. David's pose can even be interpreted as an invitation to other "congregants" to join him in prayer,[11] kneeling "behind" him. In this way, the print is an ideal devotional object.

In characteristic fashion, Rembrandt also made light a major symbolic component in the scene. David's head and hands are shrouded in deep, flat shadows relieved only by a sliver of light that falls along the edges of his fingers, across the nape of his neck, and, most significant, on the edge of his face, seen in profile. The implication is that as David kneels and clasps his hands in a gesture of fervent contrition, his prayers will be heard by a merciful God whose light will ultimately illuminate the penitent soul and forgive the repentant sinner.[12]

Notes

1. In 1655, Rembrandt depicted David as a youth fighting Goliath in one of four prints made to illustrate Rabbi Menasseh ben Israel's *Piedra Gloriosa*. Cf. cat. no. 9 (B. 36C).

2. NHD 28 (c. 1507) and NHD 29 (1520).

3. Ellen S. Jacobowitz and Stephanie Loeb Stepanek, *The Prints of Lucas van Leyden and His Contemporaries*, exh. cat. (Washington, DC: National Gallery of Art, 1983), cat. 76, 202.

4. 2 Samuel 24:17.

5. Jacobwitz and Stepanek pointed out that this specific passage was cited by Erasmus in *Concerning the Immense Mercy of God* as exemplary of divine Mercy. It should also be noted that the image of David in prayer with an angel bearing three arrows was used more generically as an illustration of the Penitential Psalms in late medieval and early Renaissance Books of Hours. Roger S. Wieck, *Time Sanctified: The Book of Hours in Medieval Art and Life* (New York: George Braziller, 1988), 99.

6. Hans Rotermund, trans. Shierry M. Weber, *Rembrandt's Drawings and Etchings for the Bible* (Philadelphia: Pilgrim Press, 1969), 100.

7. Cited in Petra Jeroense and Astrid Tümpel, "David in Prayer," cat. 32, in Peter van der Coelen, *Patriarchs, Angels & Prophets: The Old Testament in Netherlandish Printmaking from Lucas van Leyden to Rembrandt*, exh. cat. (Amsterdam: Rembrandt Information Centre, 1996), 114n3.

8. Münz, *Critical Catalogue*, vol. 2, cat. 182, 88. From Psalm 51:1–2: "Have mercy upon me, O God, according to thy loving kindness: according unto the multitude of thy tender mercies blot out my transgressions. Wash me thoroughly from mine iniquity, and cleanse me from my sin."

9. *Rembrandt's Faith*, 125. See also Wieck, *Time Sanctified*, 98–99.

10. Per Shelley Perlove and Robert Baldwin, *Impressions of Faith: Rembrandt's Biblical Etchings*, Dearborn: University of Michigan-Dearborn, Mardigian Library, 1989, 62: "The intimacy of the scene brings to mind the Protestant ideal of a personal relationship between man and deity, without the need of an intercessor."

11. Perlove and Silver (*Rembrandt's Faith*, 126) noted that as the author of the penitential psalms, David was considered "the model penitent."

12. According to Jeroense and Tümpel, "David in Prayer," cat. 32, 114, "His [David's] face is enlightened."

17–18. Images from the Apocryphal Book of Tobit

17. Blindness of Tobit: Larger Plate

B. 42 (H. 252, Mz. 181, NHD 265)
Etching with touches of drypoint
Signed and dated in the plate: *Rembrandt f. 1651*
State II of II
Sheet: 16.1 × 12.9 cm, trimmed to the plate mark
Verso: in graphite, center script *D*

Provenance:
Harrods, London, 1980
Feddersen, Elkhart, IN, 1991
Snite Museum of Art
Acc. No.: 1991.025.016

The plate does not survive.

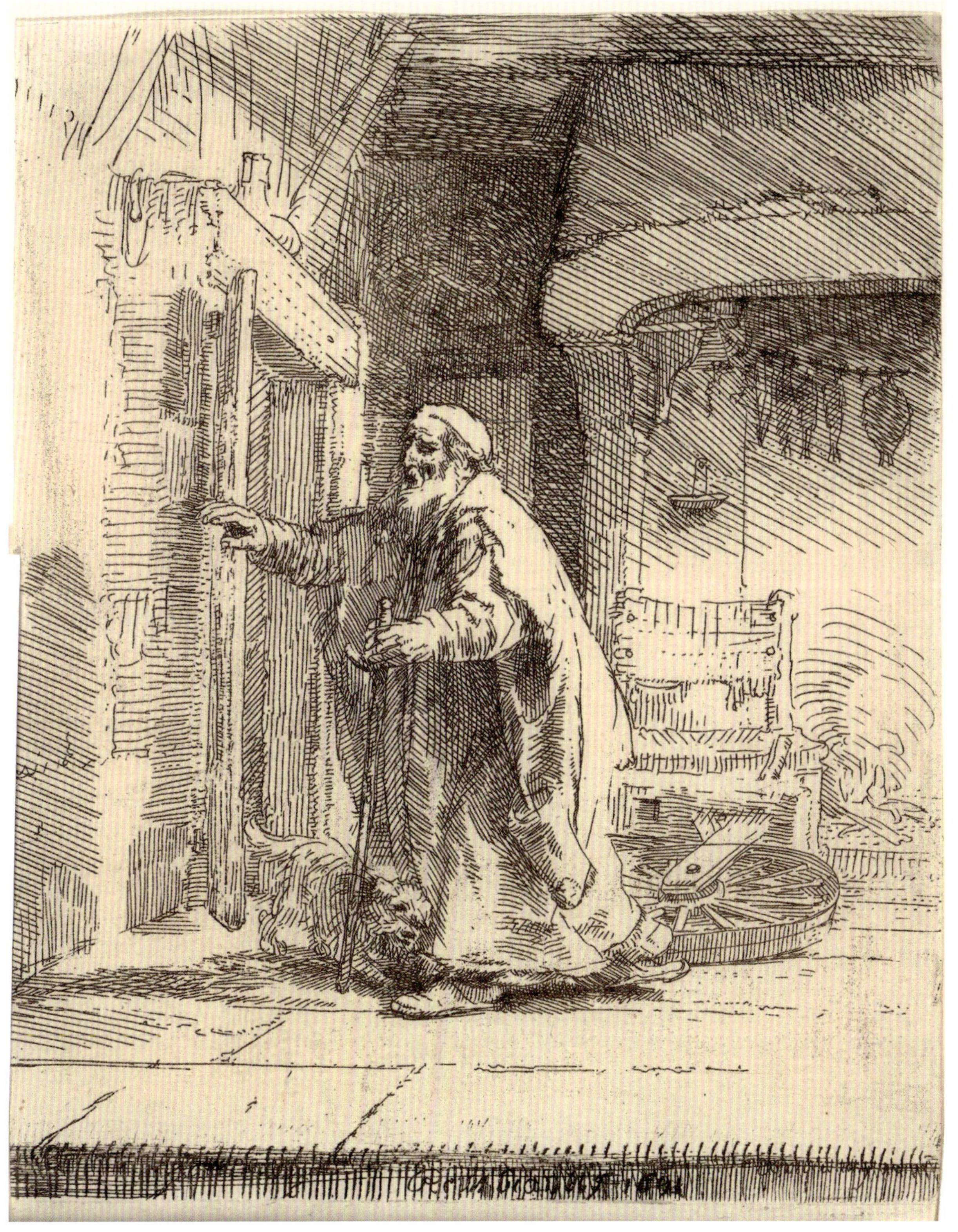

PLATE 17

18. Angel Departing from the Family of Tobias

B. 43 (H. 185, Mz. 179, NHD 189)
Etching and drypoint
Signed and dated in the plate: *Rembrandt f. 1641*
State II of IX
Sheet: 10.8 × 15.7 cm; plate mark 10.3 × 15.4 cm
Verso: in graphite, *ll: 110*

Provenance:
Craddock & Barnard, London, 1978 (cat. 136, no. 184)
Feddersen, Elkhart, IN, 1991
Snite Museum of Art
Acc. No.: 1991.025.017

Plate survives:
Museum of Fine Arts, Boston.

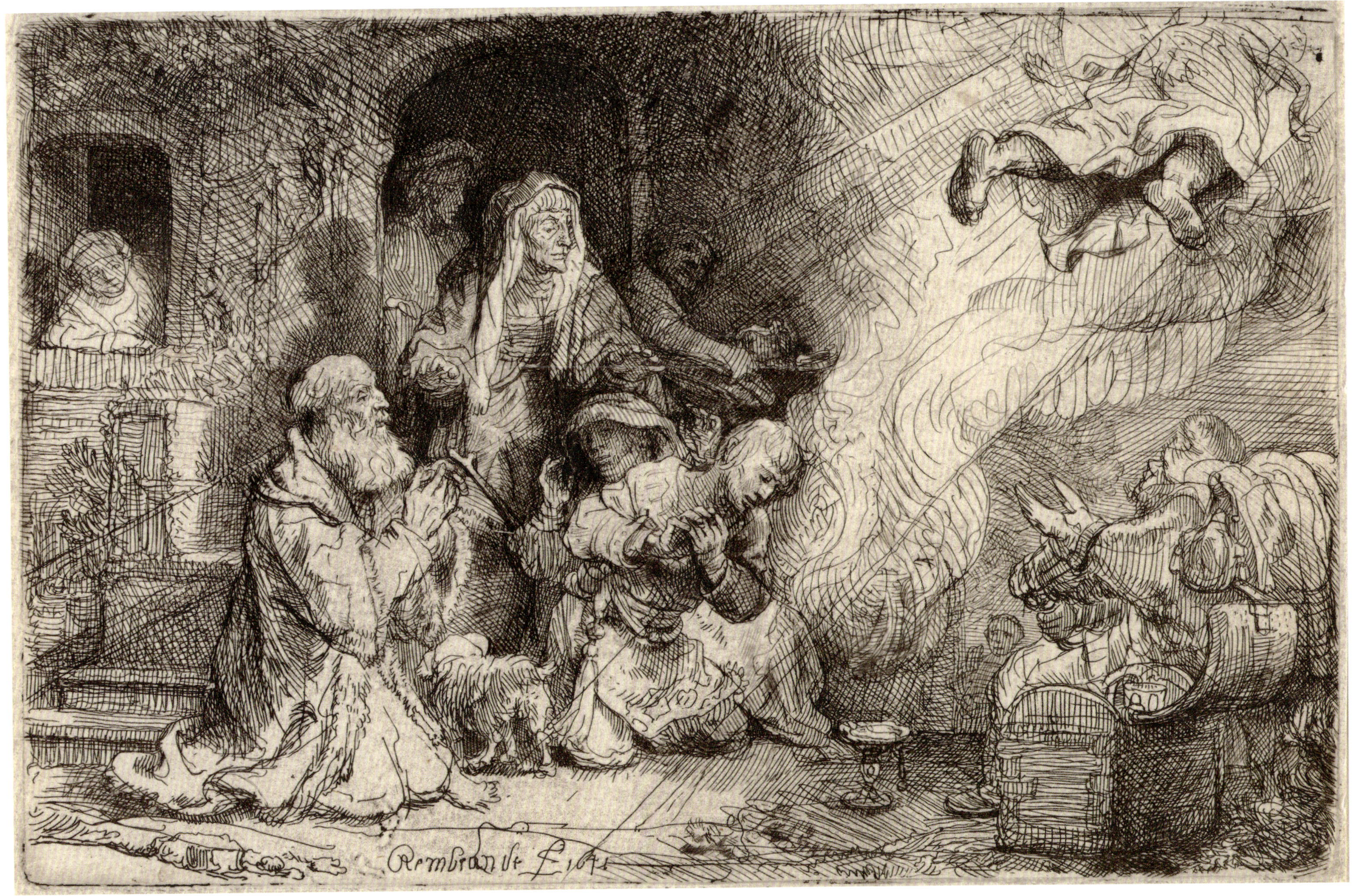

PLATE 18

The narrative moments depicted in Rembrandt's *Blindness of Tobit* (1651) and *Angel Departing from the Family of Tobias* (1641) derive from the apocryphal Book of Tobit. Tobit, who along with his fellow Jews had been captured by the King of Assyria and exiled to Nineveh, was a pious man who continued to adhere to Jewish law even while in captivity. When King Sennacheribe discovered that Tobit had been providing honorable burials for fellow Jews who had been executed by the state, he confiscated all of Tobit's goods, leaving him, his wife, Anna, and their son, Tobias, poverty-stricken. To make matters worse, one evening Tobit fell asleep outside his house and sparrow dung fell into his eyes, blinding him.

Tobit had once been a man of means, serving as an agent for Sennacheribe's predecessor, and he had deposited a considerable sum as a bond with a man with whom he was doing business in the land of Media. Now blind and impoverished, Tobit decided to reclaim this money. He summoned Tobias and asked him to find a companion to travel with him to Media, to recover the bond. When Tobias set out to seek a companion, he encountered the archangel Raphael, who pretended to be "Azariah," a distant relative of Tobit's. Raphael offered to act as Tobias's companion and guide. Tobias introduced "Azariah" to his father, who approved of his son's choice. Raphael, Tobias, and Tobias's dog set out on their journey, and at the end of the first day, they camped beside the Tigris River. When Tobias went down to the water to bathe, a large fish leaped out and tried to devour him. Raphael assured the young man that he had nothing to fear and instructed him to capture the fish. The creature proved to have magical and medicinal powers.

When Tobias and the angel reached Media, they collected the money owed to Tobit, but before returning home to Nineveh, "Azariah" suggested that they visit the house of a relative, Raguel. The angel told Tobias that Raguel had a daughter, Sarah, and that as her nearest living kinsman, Tobias had the right to take her as his bride. When Tobias asked for Sarah's hand, Raguel readily consented, and then Tobias, Sarah, and the angel Raphael departed for Nineveh. Just before they arrived, Raphael instructed Tobias to make a paste from the gall of the miraculous fish so that he could apply the ointment to his father's eyes.

Tobit's wife, Anna, had been standing watch, waiting for their son's return. When she saw him coming, she gave Tobit the good news and then rushed out to meet her son in the courtyard of their home. According to the Book of Tobit, "Then Tobit got up and came stumbling out through the courtyard door."[1] After a joyous reunion with his parents, Tobias applied the miraculous paste to his father's eyes, restoring Tobit's sight. Tobit held a great marriage celebration for Tobias and Sarah. Afterward, Tobit asked his son how he should reward the man who had accompanied the youth on his journey. Tobias suggested that "Azariah" should be paid not only his wages, but also half of the wealth that they had brought back with them from Media. His father agreed, but before they could carry out this plan, Tobias's companion called them aside. He advised them to live righteously, to pray and fast, and to give alms. He then revealed his true identity as the archangel Raphael. "The two of them [Tobit and Tobias] were shaken; they fell face down, for they were afraid. But he [Raphael] said to them, 'Do not be afraid; peace be with you. . . . So now get up from the ground, and acknowledge God. See, I am ascending to him who sent me. Write down all these things that have happened to you.' And he ascended. Then they stood up, and could see him no more."[2]

The Book of Tobit is now considered part of the Apocrypha, although it was accepted as a canonical text by the Catholic Church at the Council of Trent in 1546.[3] Calvin rejected the book outright because no original Hebrew version of it survived, but at the 1618 Synod of Dortr, the Dutch Reformed Church accepted the tale as authentic, despite its being outside the biblical canon. Although the Book of Tobit was included in the Dutch State Bible of 1637, there was no commentary on the text, and the book was actually excluded from the 1657 English translation of the Dutch Bible.[4]

Despite the doubts that surrounded the authenticity of the Book of Tobit, painted and graphic images inspired by the tale—particularly representations of Tobias and the angel Raphael[5] and of Tobias healing his father—were fairly common both north and south of the Alps, from the fifteenth through the seventeenth centuries. Maarten van Heemskerck (1498–1574), Georg Pencz (1500–1550), Cornelis Massys (c. 1510–56/57), Moses van Uyttenbroeck (1595/1600–1645/46), and Claes Cornelisz. Moeyaert (1590/91–1655) all created print series dedicated to Tobit. As Julius S. Held and others have pointed out, the story of Tobit seems to have had a special appeal for Rembrandt, not only because of its religious lessons, but quite possibly for personal reasons, as well. His own father may have lost his sight, and the idea of becoming blind would certainly have been daunting for a man whose livelihood and passion for making art depended on his ability to see.[6]

Rembrandt made two etched versions of *The Blindness of Tobit*. The very rare early example, *The Blindness of Tobit: A Sketch* (B. 153) (fig. 1), is normally dated to around 1629. It is so closely related to Rembrandt's images of beggars that there has been some confusion as to whether this is actually a representation of Tobit or simply a generic sketch of a blind man.[7] The 1629 print shows a bent and aged figure groping his way toward an open doorway. Dressed in rags and wearing a high soft hat of the kind that Rembrandt often used to identify beggars, the old man shuffles forward toward the door. As he leans on a stick held in his left hand, his right hand reaches out in front of him so that he can feel his way. In the second state of this print, three shadowy figures, presumably Anna, Tobias, and the archangel Raphael, can be seen at a distance through the open door. By the fourth state of the etching, however, these figures have vanished within a dense web of cross-hatching.

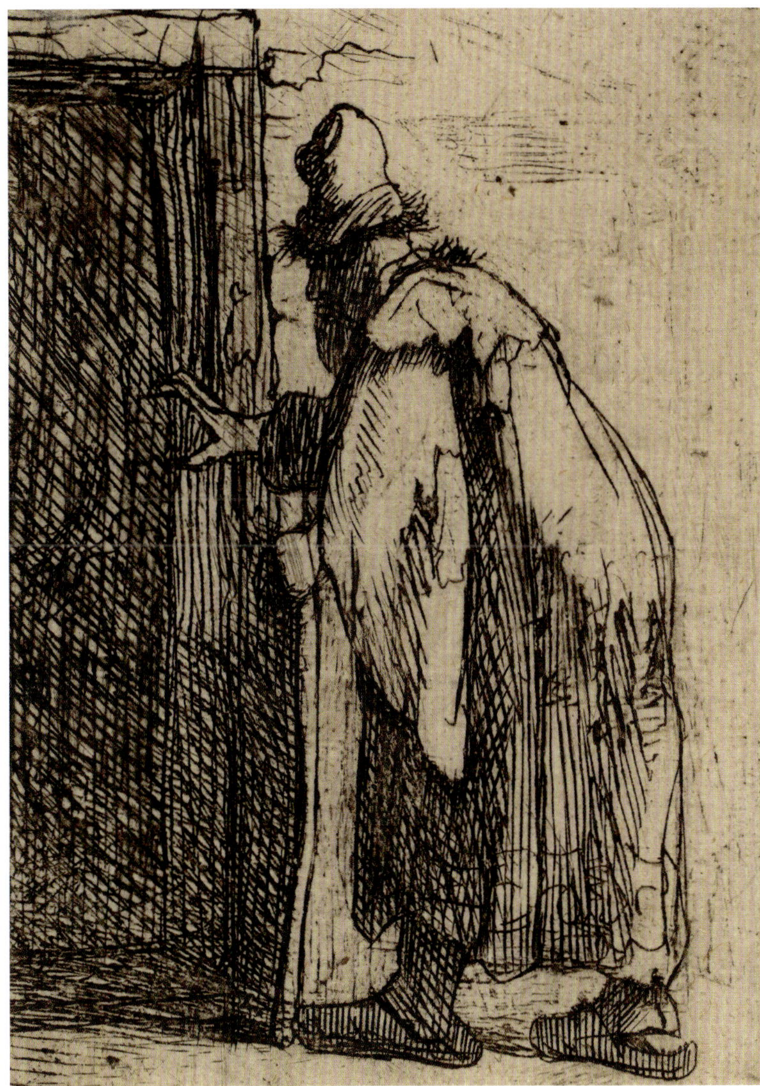

FIGURE 1. Rembrandt, *The Blindness of Tobit*, State VII, etching, c. 1629. *Photo: Courtesy of the National Gallery of Art, Washington, DC.*

In contrast to the loose, graphic quality of the 1629 print, the 1651 version (B. 42, cat. no. 17) was carried out in Rembrandt's more disciplined mature style, one in which shadows are described by a system of very regular parallel lines with minimal cross-hatching. The quality of the line itself in this later example is also rather

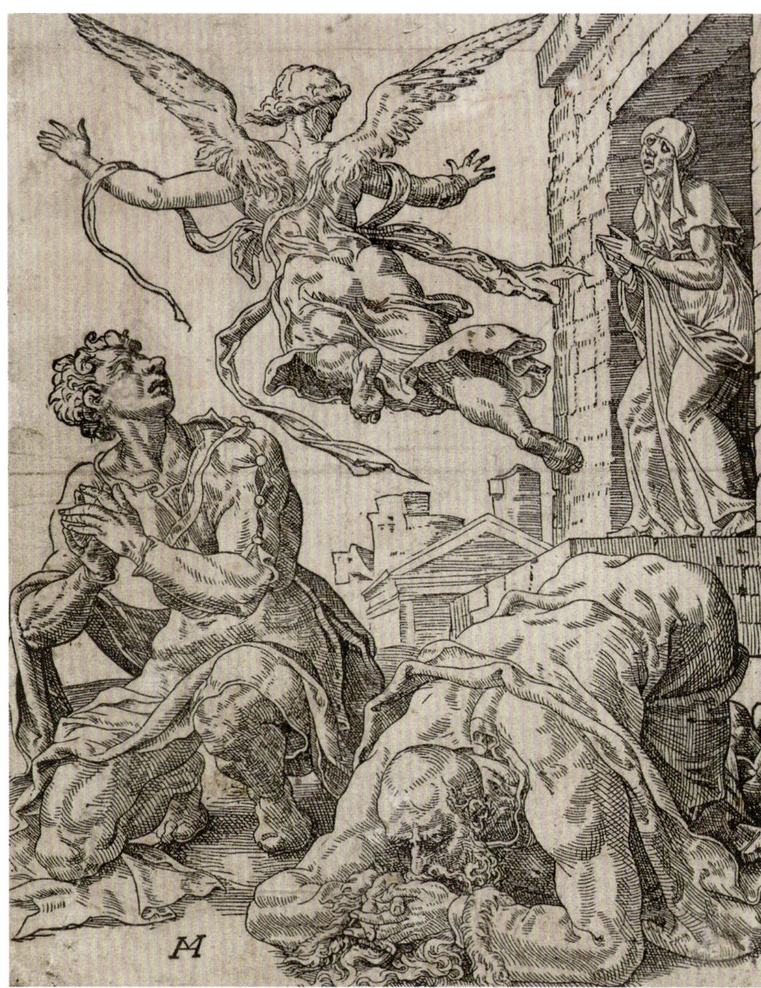

FIGURE 2. Dirck Volkerstz. Coornhert after Maarten van Heemskerck, *The Angel Departing from the Family of Tobias*, woodcut, c. 1550. *Museum Boijmans Van Beuningen, Rotterdam. Photo: Studio Tromp, Rotterdam.*

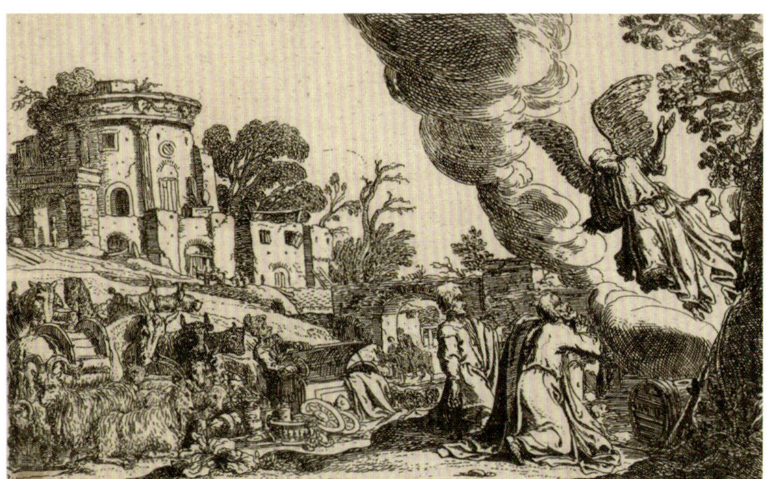

FIGURE 3. Claes Cornelisz. Moeyaert, *The Angel Departing from the Family of Tobias*, etching, c. 1630. *Rijksmuseum, Amsterdam.*

tightly controlled. The setting of the second print is much more completely described than that of the 1629 version. Tobit, having risen in haste from his chair to greet his returning son, has knocked over a spinning wheel,[8] a symbol of his wife's domestic labors. Behind the chair is a large fireplace in which fish have been hung to dry over a blazing fire. These fish may indicate Tobit's poverty, as Erik Hinterding has suggested,[9] but they may also have symbolic overtones, providing an allusion to the miraculous fish that will soon restore Tobit's sight, both literally and figuratively, adding Christological significance to a humble domestic detail.

As in the earlier etching, Tobit steps forward toward an open door, his right hand outstretched, his left grasping a slender staff.[10] In contrast to the early states of the 1629 print, however, nothing can be seen through the doorway; the viewer's attention is focused solely on Tobit and the room he is intent on leaving. The old man's way is impeded by a small terrier—presumably the dog that accompanied Tobias and Raphael on their journey—which rushes in to greet its master. Since in Rembrandt's time dogs could be symbolic of the "unsaved," this dog's obstruction of Tobit's progress toward Raphael may have had metaphorical overtones, as well.[11]

Light from the blazing fire falls on Tobit's back, projecting a clear shadow onto the wall to the left of the door. This detail exemplifies Rembrandt's special interest in cast shadows, which he employed for a variety of effects in both paintings and prints.[12] In the case of *Blindness of Tobit*, it has been suggested that the location of the shadow alerts the viewer to the fact that Tobit is actually going to miss the doorway. The position of Tobit's right arm and hand show that he has indeed veered off course. The scene may indicate an old blind man's helplessness, or it could simply be Rembrandt's conception of a father's joyful haste as he rushes out to embrace his beloved son. Despite the fact that the light in the room emanates from the hearth behind Tobit, his face, with its dramatic dark eye sockets signifying blindness, is bathed in light, suggesting that the old man is about to be illuminated both literally, by the daylight that awaits him outside the house, and metaphorically, as he moves toward enlightenment.

Rembrandt's 1641 etching of *Angel Departing from the Family of Tobias*, created ten years earlier than *Blindness of Tobit*, illustrates the conclusion of the story of Tobit's encounter with the archangel Raphael. Dutch artists Heemskerck (fig. 2), Uyttenbroeck, and Moeyaert (fig. 3) all included depictions of this moment—Raphael's departure—at the end of their Tobit cycles. In addition, Rembrandt's mentor, Pieter Lastman, created at least one painted version of this dramatic scene,[13] and, in 1637, Rembrandt also made a painting of the angel departing (fig. 4).[14] The apocryphal text states that Raphael called Tobit and Tobias aside before he revealed himself to them, but in visual representations the cast of characters witnessing this epiphany was sometimes enlarged to include Anna and/or a single servant. This is the case, for example, with Heemskerck's woodcut, in which Tobit and Tobias are placed directly in front of Tobit's house, with a prayerful Anna standing in the doorway behind them.

In Rembrandt's painted version of the scene, he followed Heemskerck's example and then added Tobias's wife, Sarah, as well. Raphael flies off into a burst of light with his body splitting apart a funnel of dark, roiling clouds as he rises dramatically upward and away from the viewer.[15] As he departs, the angel turns his head so as to look back down at the members of Tobit's family, assembled together at the threshold of the house. The choice of Raphael's unusually dramatic pose and the location of the miraculous revelation directly in front of Tobit's house were clearly influenced by Heemskerck's woodcut, and there is an additional similarity: in the foreground, Tobit, kneeling, bows down in a gesture of submission and humility, with his head close to the ground, as if overwhelmed by the transformation taking place before him. Tobias, slightly behind his father, also kneels, but his torso is upright. Unlike his father, the young man gazes up at the departing angel. Rembrandt's women also react to Raphael's revelation in different ways. Anna drops her cane in shock and turns away from the angel, while the younger woman, Sarah, clasps her hands in prayer and gazes imploringly up at Raphael. The small terrier cowering at the feet of the women and barking at the man flying off into the air may be construed literally as the family's pet and guardian of the house, perturbed at the startling actions of a stranger, or, read figuratively, as a representative of those who do not comprehend or believe in miraculous events even when they occur before them.

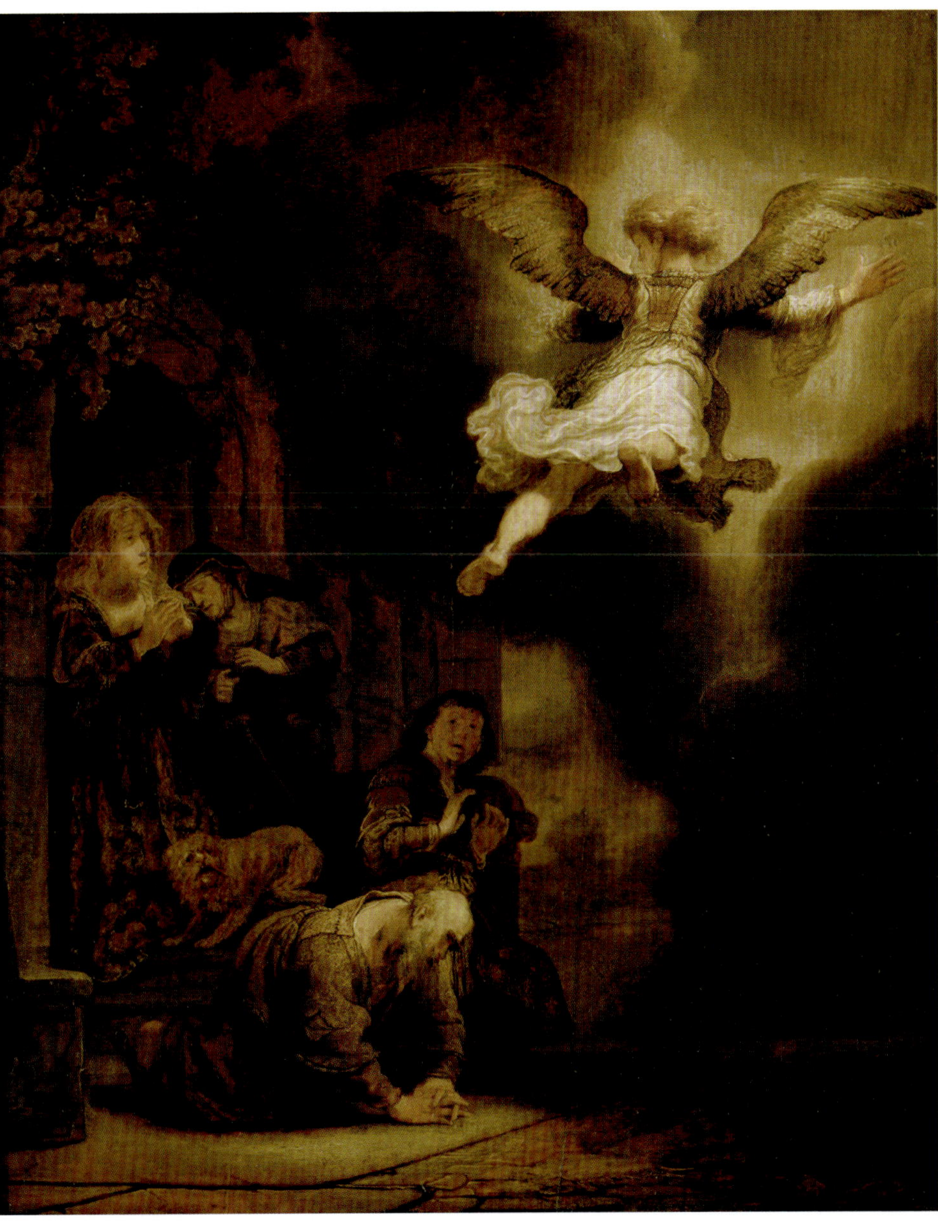

FIGURE 4. Rembrandt, *The Angel Departing from the Family of Tobit*, oil on canvas, 1637. *Louvre, Paris. Photo: Erich Lessing/Art Resource, New York.*

In Rembrandt's etched version of the angel departing, the vertical format of the painting has been transformed into a horizontal composition and the setting, cast of characters, and props have been significantly expanded. Raphael still flies away from the viewer into a vortex of light, but his pose has been made even more theatrical. The light, no longer a nimbus, appears as a shaft of strong, parallel lines, with billowing white clouds behind them. The upper edge of the print cuts Raphael off at the waist so that only the dramatically foreshortened lower half of the archangel is visible: the soles of his feet, his calves, and the lower portion of his windblown robes.[16]

Rembrandt anchored the lower right corner of the composition by adding an open chest, a donkey laden with goods, and a seated servant who looks upward at Raphael.[17] In addition, a new element was introduced midway between this grouping and Tobit's family: conspicuously placed between the chest and the kneeling father and son is a chalice with a necklace draped over its edge. The chest, chalice, and jewelry are emblems of the wealth that Tobias brought back with him and that he and Tobit wished to share with "Azariah." The image of the archangel Raphael literally rising above these riches creates a visual dichotomy between spiritual and earthly concerns, and recalls the angel's instruction to give alms. Shelly Perlove and Larry Silver suggested that the prominently displayed chalice might also serve as a reference to the Passion.[18]

Rembrandt's etched version of Raphael's departure does not reflect Heemskerck's print as closely as his earlier painting did. As Tobit and his family cluster together in a tight triangle on the threshold of the house, the four figures reverse the reactions they exhibited in the painted version of this dramatic moment. This time, Tobit and Anna look directly toward the departing Raphael, while Tobias gazes down, and Sarah turns away. All four figures are illuminated by the light emanating from heaven, with Tobit and Anna casting shadows onto the steps and wall behind them. Five other figures witness this miracle: the man seated beside the casket, three household servants, and a diminutive, barely noticeable figure in shadow, seen at a distance, just below the end of the donkey's nose. This man raises his right arm in amazement. Even the donkey is affected; it turns its head toward the supernatural scene and stares at its master, Tobias, and at the space where Raphael had just been standing.

Two of the servants flank Anna. The one to her right seems unaffected by what is happening, but the one to Anna's left recoils in shock, spilling the contents of a large salver. These two figures are in shadow, suggesting their lack of direct involvement in the miracle before them. The fifth figure, a servant girl, has emerged from the dark interior of the house and is peering out an open window at the extreme left side of the composition. Although the shaft of light from the departing angel falls below her window, her clothing is illuminated and she casts a shadow on the wall or shutter beside her. The light that falls on her face is not as bright as that which falls on her clothes, possibly indicating that this servant is present at the miracle, but does not fully partake of it.[19] The final participant in Rembrandt's print is the family's dog. Unlike the cowering dog in Rembrandt's painting, this terrier turns away from the scene and ambles back toward the house, ignobly presenting his hindquarters to the viewer and symbolically rejecting the grace that the angel had brought from the heavenly father to the faithful and pious earthly father and son, Tobit and Tobias.

Notes

1. The Book of Tobit, 11:10, in *The New Oxford Annotated Apocrypha*, 3rd ed. (Oxford: Oxford University Press, 2007), 26.

2. Ibid., 27.

3. Susan Donahue Kuretsky, "Rembrandt at the Threshold," in *Rembrandt, Rubens, and the Art of Their Time: Recent Perspectives*, ed. Roland E. Fleisher and Susan Clare Scott (University Park: Penn State University Press, 1997), 66.

4. Gary Schwartz, *Rembrandt: His Life, His Paintings* (London: Penguin, 1991), 181; and *Rembrandt's Faith*, 148.

5. The particular popularity of this image may have derived from its appeal to travelers, possibly as an apotropaic image or talisman used to ward off harm. A notable example of the Tobias/Raphael theme was Hercules Seghers's etching of the subject. Rembrandt acquired the original plate for Seghers's print and reworked it into an image of the Flight into Egypt. (See the discussion of *Flight into Egypt: Altered from Seghers*, B. 56, cat. no. 31.)

6. Julius Held stated that "Rembrandt illustrated the Book of Tobit more often than any other biblical text of comparable length." Although Held made no claim to having made an exhaustive survey, he stated that approximately fifty-five drawings, paintings, and etchings relate to this subject. Held offered several reasons why the story might have appealed to Rembrandt. In addition to the hypothesis that as an artist, Rembrandt might have been anxious about the possibility of becoming blind, Held also considered a possible

Mennonite influence. Rembrandt may have been familiar with the tenets of the Mennonite sect, members of which had a special regard for the story of Tobit and referred to each other as "brother" and "sister," as did the characters in the Book of Tobit. Held noted that Mennonites considered the Book of Tobit a model of Christian education, since it emphasized Tobit's patience, piety, and charity, as well as concepts of sexual morality, e.g., Tobit's directive that one should marry a woman of one's own people. Julius S. Held, "Rembrandt and the Book of Tobit," in Held, *Rembrandt's* Aristotle *and Other Rembrandt Studies* (Princeton, NJ: Princeton University Press, 1969), 104–29.

7. Hinterding, *Lugt Catalogue,* cat. 126, 294. In NHD, Hinterding and Rutgers suggests that the first state, which exists in a unique impression in the Amsterdam Rijksmuseum print cabinet (RP-P-OB-376), is the only original. All subsequent states, which are 0.4 cm narrower, would have been pulled from the original plate after it had been trimmed on the left side. The Snite Museum does not own a copy of this print.

8. As Hinterding noted, the spinning wheel is not mentioned in any source. It does, however, appear in a painting of Tobit of about 1635 attributed to Rembrandt's first pupil, Gerrit Dou. Hinterding, *Lugt Catalogue,* cat. 29, 97. Dou's painting, which is in a private collection in the United States, is reproduced in Ernst van de Wetering, Bernhard Schnackenburg, and Ed de Heer, *The Mystery of the Young Rembrandt* (Wolfratshausen, Germany: Edition Minerva, 2001), cat. 67.

9. Hinterding, *Lugt Catalogue,* cat. 29, 97.

10. Ludwig Münz (*Critical Catalogue,* vol. 2, cat. 181, 87–88) suggested that Tobit's pose was derived from the figure of Elymas, a Jewish sorcerer who was blinded, in Raphael's tapestry of *The Blinding of Elymas* (Acts 13:11). There is an early sixteenth-century print after the Raphael image by Agostino Veneziano (TIB 43).

11. The dog that accompanied Tobias and the angel is mentioned very briefly in the Dutch State Bible. However, unlike the account in the Latin Vulgate version of the Book of Tobit, which describes the dog as scampering on ahead and jumping on Tobit in its excitement, the Dutch State Bible version states only that the dog accompanied the two travelers. A dog appears with some regularity in the depictions of the story of Tobit. See Petra Jeroense, "The Homecoming of Tobit," cat. 49, in *Patriarchs, Angels & Prophets: The Old Testament in Netherlandish Printmaking from Lucas van Leyden to Rembrandt*, ed. Peter van der Coelen, exh. cat. (Amsterdam: Rembrandt Information Centre, 1996), 140; and *Rembrandt's Faith*, 150. Perlove and Silver interpret the dog as representing Judaism, a faith that causes Tobit to stumble in his quest for the truth (*Rembrandt's Faith*, 153).

Dogs appear in a number of Rembrandt's etchings, not only as representatives of the unsaved, but also, sometimes, as comic relief, introduced as unselfconscious foils to the sacred, as a means of bringing a biblical and/or spiritual subject down to earth. See the discussion of dogs in Charles M. Rosenberg, "Rembrandt's Religious Prints," in this catalog.

12. See also the discussion of the *Hundred Guilder Print* (B. 74, cat. no. 48) and *Christ Presented to the People: Oblong Plate* (B. 76, cat. no. 51).

13. Statens Museum for Kunst, Copenhagen, 1620.

14. The painting is in the Louvre, Paris.

15. The print by Claes Cornelisz. Moeyaert (HD 20) also portrays the angel as surrounded by light and separated from Tobit and his son (fig. 3).

16. This truncation calls to mind images of the Ascension in which only Christ's feet are visible as he rises into the clouds. See, for example, the sixteenth-century Ascension from the *Fall and Redemption of Man* cycle by Albrecht Altdorfer (HG, woodcuts, 37).

17. Claes Cornelisz. Moeyaert's print (see note 15, above) also includes an open casket, a donkey, and an attendant, although they are not grouped together as they are in the Rembrandt print. This similarity was noted by Christian Tümpel, *Rembrandt legt,* cat. 34, who suggested that Moeyaert's print was directly related to the painting of the subject by Lastman (now in Copenhagen) (see note 13 above). Although the Moeyaert print is undated, it is considered to be an early work by the artist, done between 1620 and 1635. Moeyaert was a noted history painter in Amsterdam, and his work was most certainly known to Rembrandt. Konrad Renger, *Graphik in Holland,* exh. cat. (Munich: Staatliche Graphische Sammlung, 1982), 59.

18. *Rembrandt's Faith*, 156.

19. Susan Kuretsky suggested that in the reactions of the figures witnessing Raphael's departure, Rembrandt marked out a progression from perception (the servants), to enlightenment (Tobias's family), to union with God (the angel). Kuretsky, "Rembrandt at the Threshold," 67.

19. *Angel Appearing to the Shepherds*

B. 44 (H. 120, Mz. 199, NHD 125)
Etching
Signed and dated in the plate: *Rembrandt f. 1634*
State III of VI
Sheet: 26.2 × 21.8 cm, trimmed to the plate mark
Fragment of watermark: three circles and inverted 4
Verso: in black ink, upside down *aprilEnaht1816* (Lugt 810, "Enaht," Thomas Thane) / top left in brown ink *26/*

Provenance:
Thomas Thane, 1816
Craddock & Barnard, London, 1977
Feddersen, Elkhart, IN, 1991
Snite Museum of Art
Acc. No.: 1991.025.018

Plate survives:
Private collection, USA

Rembrandt's 1634 *Angel Appearing to the Shepherds* is one of the artist's most dramatic etchings. Art historian Clifford Ackley once described it as "a wonderful amalgam of soaring operatic grandeur and earthy Dutch realism."[1]

Theologically, the biblical story of the annunciation to the shepherds was traditionally interpreted as the announcement to the Jews that the Messiah had been born.[2] Throughout the later Middle Ages and the Renaissance, the subject was occasionally included as a secondary scene in representations of the Nativity or the Adoration of the Shepherds.[3] Even more common was its inclusion in Books of Hours, where representations of the subject often accompanied the prayers for Prime or Terce in the Hours of the Virgin.[4]

Although the text in Luke 2:8–14 clearly describes the event as taking place at night[5] and characterizes the shepherds as terrified by the startling arrival of an angelic messenger,[6] medieval and Renaissance artists rarely focused on these two dramatic elements. Over the course of the sixteenth century, however, this changed. The growing popularity of the theme as an independent subject may have been due, in part, to the opportunity that it gave artists to depict the miracle as a nocturnal scene and to represent animated peasants and animals.

The Italian painter Jacopo Bassano (1510–92) was influential in this development. He created at least two versions of the Angel Appearing to the Shepherds, both of which are night scenes.[7] These compositions became known in the Netherlands when they were circulated as engravings done by Dutch artist Johannes Sadeler I (1550–1600)[8] and his nephew Aegidius Sadeler II (1570–1629).[9] Inspired by Aegidius's print, Abraham Bloemaert (1564–1651) created his own version of the theme, which in turn was the source of an engraving by Jan Pieterz. Saenredam in 1599.[10] Johannes Sadeler I also engraved two versions of the subject based on drawings by Maerten de Vos (1532–1603), one dated 1579 (fig. 1)[11] and the other 1587 (fig. 2).[12] Although Johannes Sadeler's prints are quite different, one element unites them: the artist's emphasis on the reactions of the shepherds. In particular, in the 1587 engraving, also called *The Annunciation to the Shepherds with a Choir of Angels*, the diminutive shepherds respond with genuine shock and fear to the

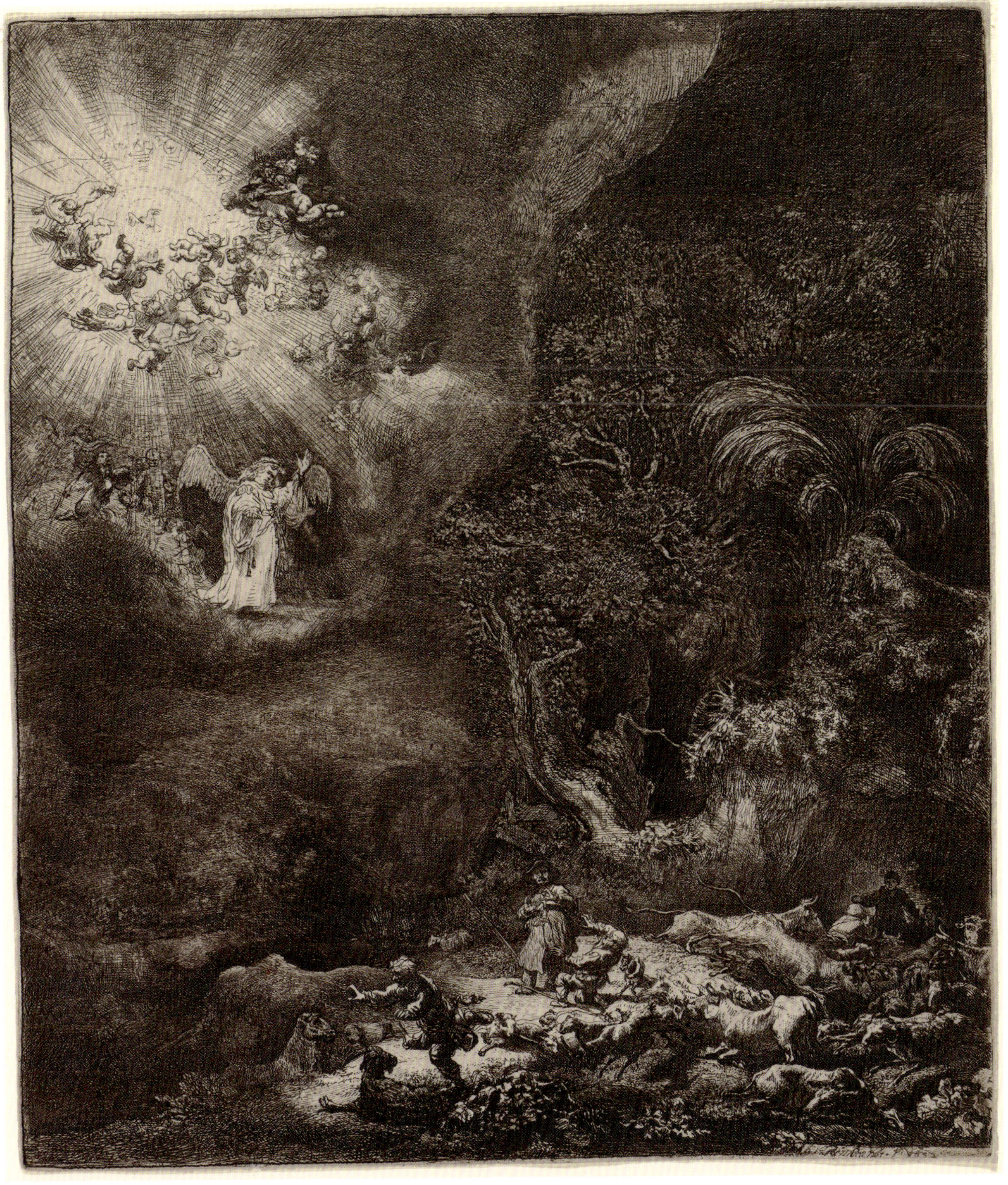

PLATE 19

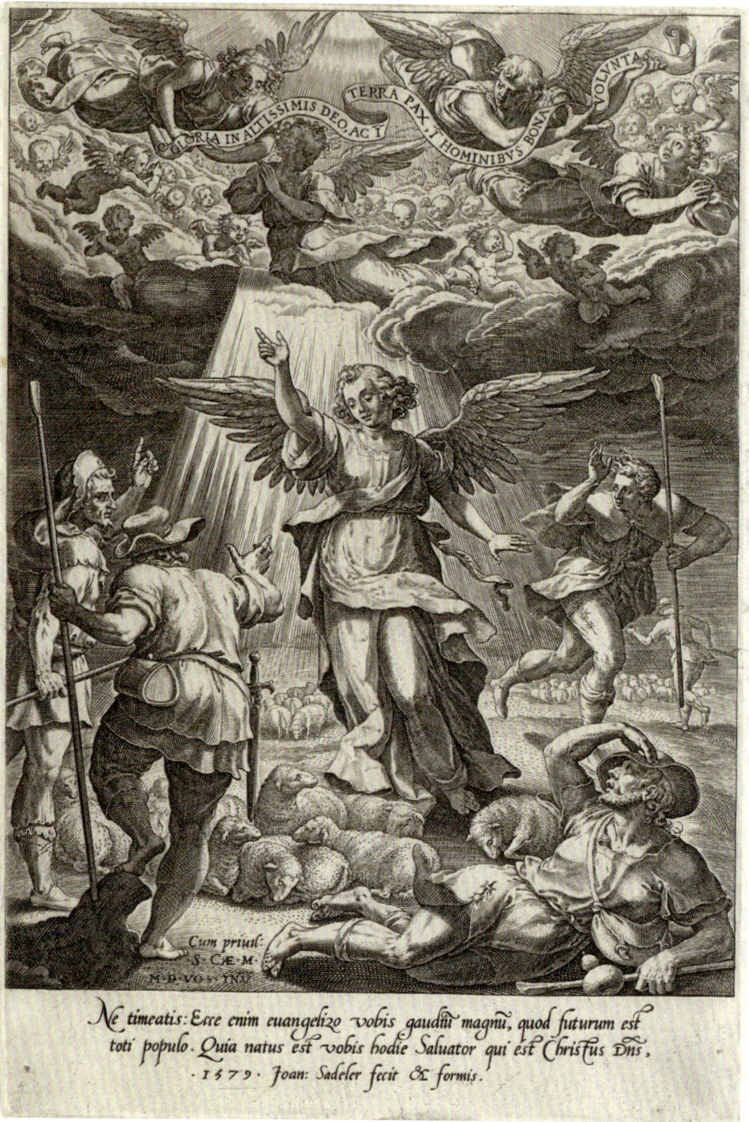

FIGURE 1. Johannes Sadeler after Maerten de Vos, *The Annunciation to the Shepherds*, engraving, 1579. *Rijksmuseum, Amsterdam.*

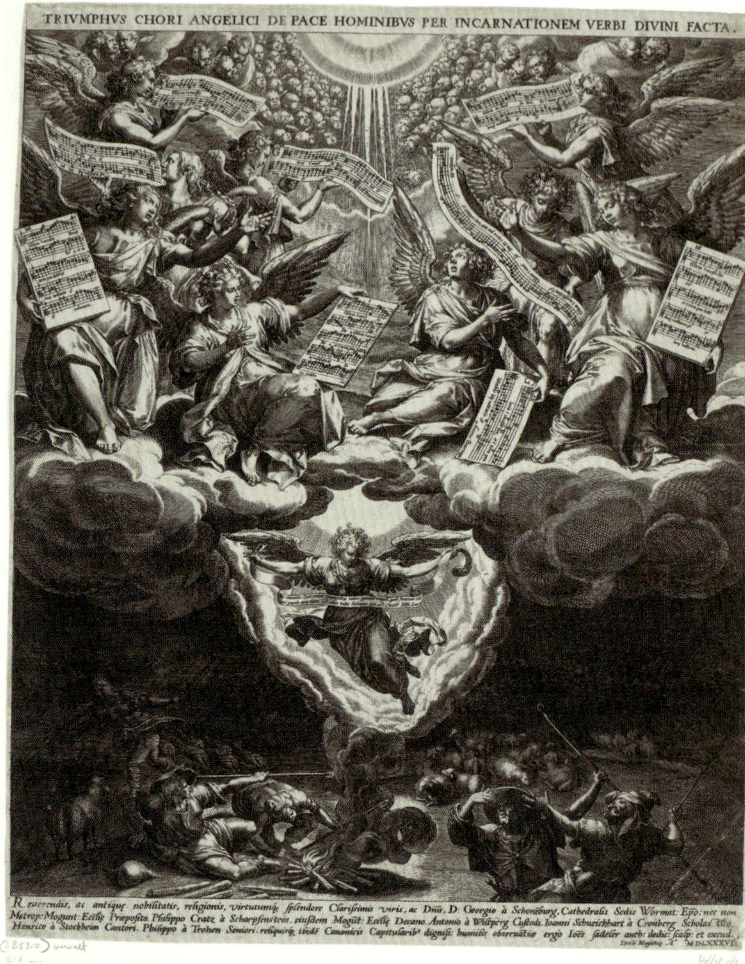

FIGURE 2. Johannes Sadeler I after Maerten de Vos, *The Annunciation to the Shepherds*, engraving, 1587. *Rijksmuseum, Amsterdam.*

appearance of the heavenly vision. One of the peasants and some of the animals actually seem to flee in terror. It may be this engraving that inspired Rembrandt's print.

Rembrandt's etching represents an important moment in the artist's development as a printmaker.[13] Measuring almost 10½ inches by 8½ inches, the sheet is one of the largest prints he had made to date. Even more significant, however, is the fact that it was his first etched nocturnal landscape. Rembrandt used the work as an opportunity to create a dramatic display of chiaroscuro, investigating a broad array of lighting effects, including the explosive vortex of light emanating outward from the dove of the Holy Spirit, the pool of light that is shed on the clearing where the shepherds and their herd had been dozing in darkness only a few moments earlier, and the barely visible glow of a distant campfire (and its reflection) tucked into the deep, slumbering landscape at the left. The first, unfinished, state of this print[14] reveals that Rembrandt initially concentrated on carefully articulating the diagonal swath of densely shadowed landscape on the right and in the distance. He only lightly sketched in the overtly dramatic elements, that is, the figures of the angel and cherubs at the upper left and the shepherds and their herd at the lower right. As Christopher White observed, this would have given the appearance of light areas emerging out of a basically dark ground.[15] It certainly suggests that this dialogue between shadow and light was of considerable importance to the artist. In order to create the full range of light effects that the composition demanded, Rembrandt also expanded his range of techniques, enhancing the etched shadows in the second and third states of the print with additional cross-hatching by means of burin and drypoint needle. The result is a display of technical virtuosity.

Like Maerten de Vos, Rembrandt depicted the scene from a high point of view, one that relegated the figures of the shepherds and their herds of cattle and sheep to the bottom quarter of the sheet. In Rembrandt's composition, only one figure actually gazes up toward the heavens: a shepherd kneeling in the center of the pool of divine light. This figure hears the angel's message and acknowledges its meaning. Another shepherd looks down at the kneeling figure before him, leans back, and raises his hands in puzzled amazement. Both of these shepherds have dropped their staffs, and in Rembrandt's image, the rods are frozen in midair, emphasizing the sudden, transitory nature of the miraculous event. For a modern viewer, this telling detail evokes the image of a flash photograph. All of the other actors, bestial and human, react to the explosive and unexpected divine intrusion into their pastoral world with curiosity or fear, and Rembrandt seems to have taken particular delight in rendering the somewhat comical, startled reactions of the cows, sheep, and one of the shepherds who take to their heels in panicked flight, a natural reaction to a supernatural event.[16]

Unlike de Vos, Rembrandt chose not to fill a large portion of the scene with an elaborate choir of angels. Instead, he confined the dove of the Holy Spirit; the calm, white, shimmering angel standing on a shelf of clouds; and the accompanying throng of tumbling cherubim to the upper left-hand corner of the sheet. The remainder of the composition consists of a complex landscape made up of the dense, dark thicket of bushes and trees at the right and a deep vista with what appears to be a view of the Dutch countryside at the left.[17] There was nothing extraordinary about setting a biblical scene in a familiar, contemporary environment, but in this instance, Rembrandt also provided a reference to the traditional Middle Eastern location of the biblical tale by placing an exotic palm tree in the midst of the woods at the right.

Notes

1. Clifford Ackley, *Printmaking in the Age of Rembrandt*, exh. cat. (Boston: Boston Museum of Fine Arts, 1981), cat. 80, 129.

2. St. Augustine, *Sermons on Christmas and Epiphany*, ed. Thomas Comerford Lawler, (Westminister, MD: Newman Press, 1952), 170.

3. A few of the best known examples of images of the Annunciation to the Shepherds together with scenes of the Nativity appear on the monumental pulpits by Nicola and Giovanni Pisano in Pisa (Baptistery and Cathedral), Pistoia (San Andrea), and Siena (Cathedral); and in the predella of Gentile da Fabriano's *Strozzi Adoration* (Uffizi, Florence). As an adjunct to depictions of the Adoration of the Shepherds, images of the Annunciation to the Shepherds appear in the background of the main panel of Hugo van der Goes's *Portinari Altarpiece* (Uffizi, Florence), and Albrecht Dürer's *Small Woodcut Passion* (TIB, woodcuts, 20).

4. Roger S. Wieck, *Time Sanctified: The Book of Hours in Medieval Art and Life* (New York: George Braziller, 1988), 60. Among the most famous examples are the illuminations in the *Hours of Jeanne d'Evreux* (The Cloisters, Metropolitan Museum of Art, New York, acc. no. 54.1.2, f. 62), the *Hours of Jeanne de Navarre* (Bibliothèque nationale, Paris, ms. n.a. Latin 3145, f. 53), the *Très Riches Heures du Duc de Berry* (Musée Condé, Chantilly, France, ms. 65, f. 48); the *Belles Heures du Duc de Berry* (The Cloisters, Metropolitan Museum of Art, New York, acc. no. 54.1.1a, b, f. 52r), and the *Rohan Hours* (Bibliothèque nationale, Paris, ms. Latin 9471, f. 85v).

5. Gentile da Fabriano's *Nativity* in the *Strozzi Adoration* predella sets the scene at night.

6. In some images, a shepherd's dog is seen to react to the celestial visitor. See, for example, the *bas-de-page* vignette in the *Hours of Jeanne d'Evreux*, f. 62.

7. Accademia di San Luca, Rome; and National Gallery of Art, Washington, DC.

8. HD 180. This version is also a nocturne, but the restrained reactions of the shepherds and their dog and flock to the appearance of a luminous angel in the night sky are diametrically opposite to those evinced in Rembrandt's version.

9. HD 31 [Aegidius II].

10. HD 24.

11. HD 163 [Johannes Sadeler I].

12. HD 188 [Johannes Sadeler I].

13. Christopher White (*Rembrandt as an Etcher: A Study of the Artist at Work*, 2nd ed. [New Haven, CT: Yale University Press, 1999], 32) describes this as a technical watershed for the artist.

14. London, British Museum, F,4.80.

15. White, *Rembrandt as an Etcher*, 33.

16. Rembrandt also included a seated goat in the very front of the print. Goats have long been associated with iniquity. In Jesus's prophecy of the Last Judgment, according to Matthew (25:31–46), the goat is specifically identified with those who are cursed. It is possible that Rembrandt wished to draw a distinction between those who hear the message of the birth of the Messiah and will be saved and those who ignore it and will be damned.

There are a few examples of the Annunciation to the Shepherds that include goats. In these earlier manuscript illuminations, the goat is usually set apart from the rest of the flock. It feeds on a vine or bush, and ignores the miracle that is taking place. See, for example, the illumination in the *Belles Heures of Jean, Duc de Berry* cited in note 4, above.

17. David R. Smith has noted that Rembrandt uses two powerful strategies to differentiate between heaven and earth, "divine majesty and human fallibility." The former is filled with light while the latter is enveloped in darkness, and the former is dominated by centripetal forces while the latter is shattered by centrifugal forces. For Smith, this is a visual trope that he likens to the juxtaposition of opposites in metaphysical poetry. David R. Smith, "Rembrandt's Metaphysical Wit: *The Three Trees* and *The Omval*," *Word & Image: A Journal of Verbal/Visual Inquiry* 21, no. 1 (2005), 8.

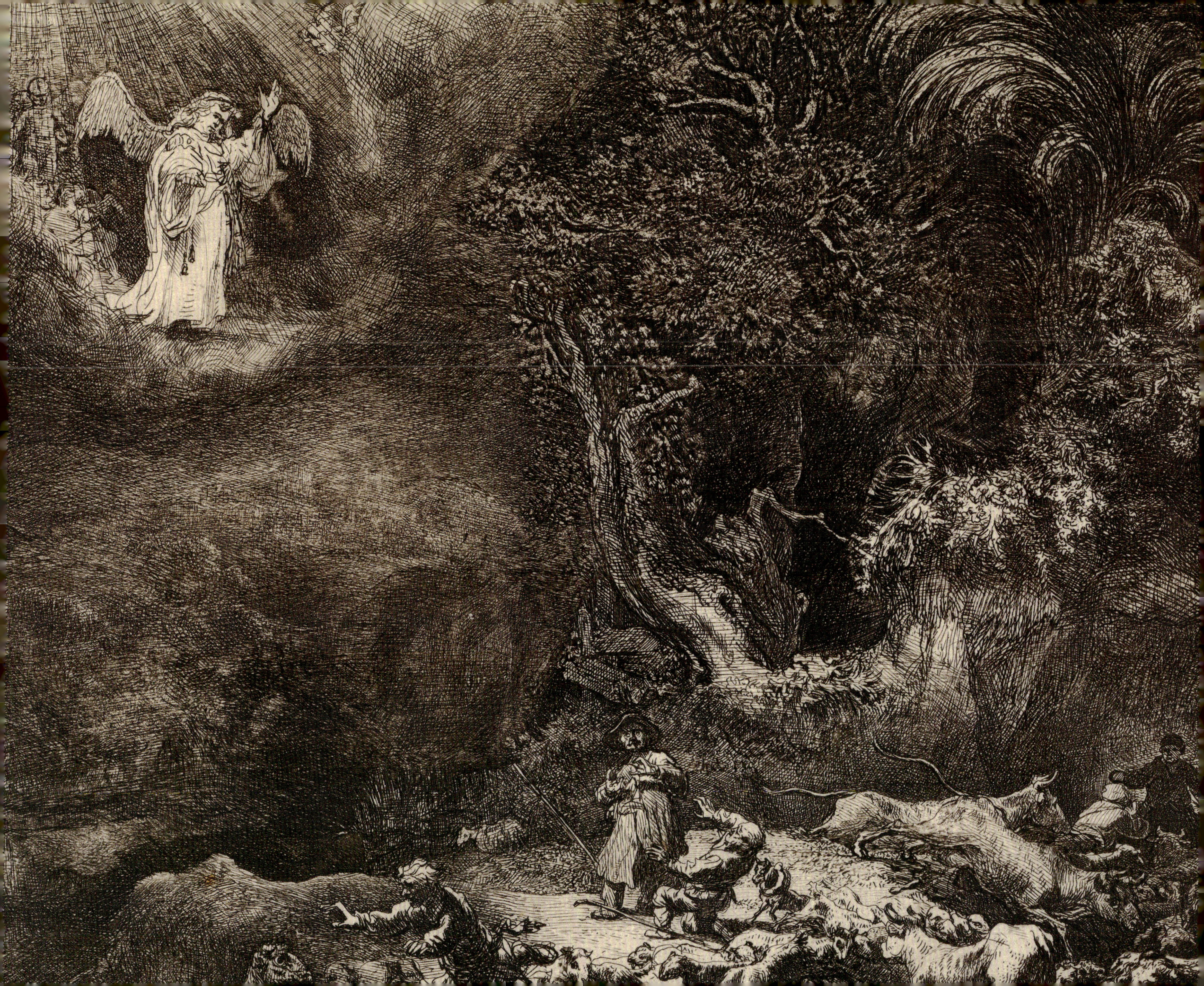

20–21. Adoration of the Shepherds

20. Adoration of the Shepherds: With the Lamp

B. 45 (H. 273, Mz. 226, NHD 279)
Etching
Signed in the plate: *Rembrandt f.*
c. 1654
State II of III
Sheet: 11.9 × 14.1 cm; plate mark: 10.5 × 12.9 cm
Verso: in graphite, bottom center: *La Nativité (B. 45)*

Provenance:
International Art Associates Ltd., Park Forest, IL, 1979 (?)
Feddersen, Elkhart, IN, 1991
Snite Museum of Art
Acc. No.: 1991.025.019

Plate survives:
Private collection, Germany.

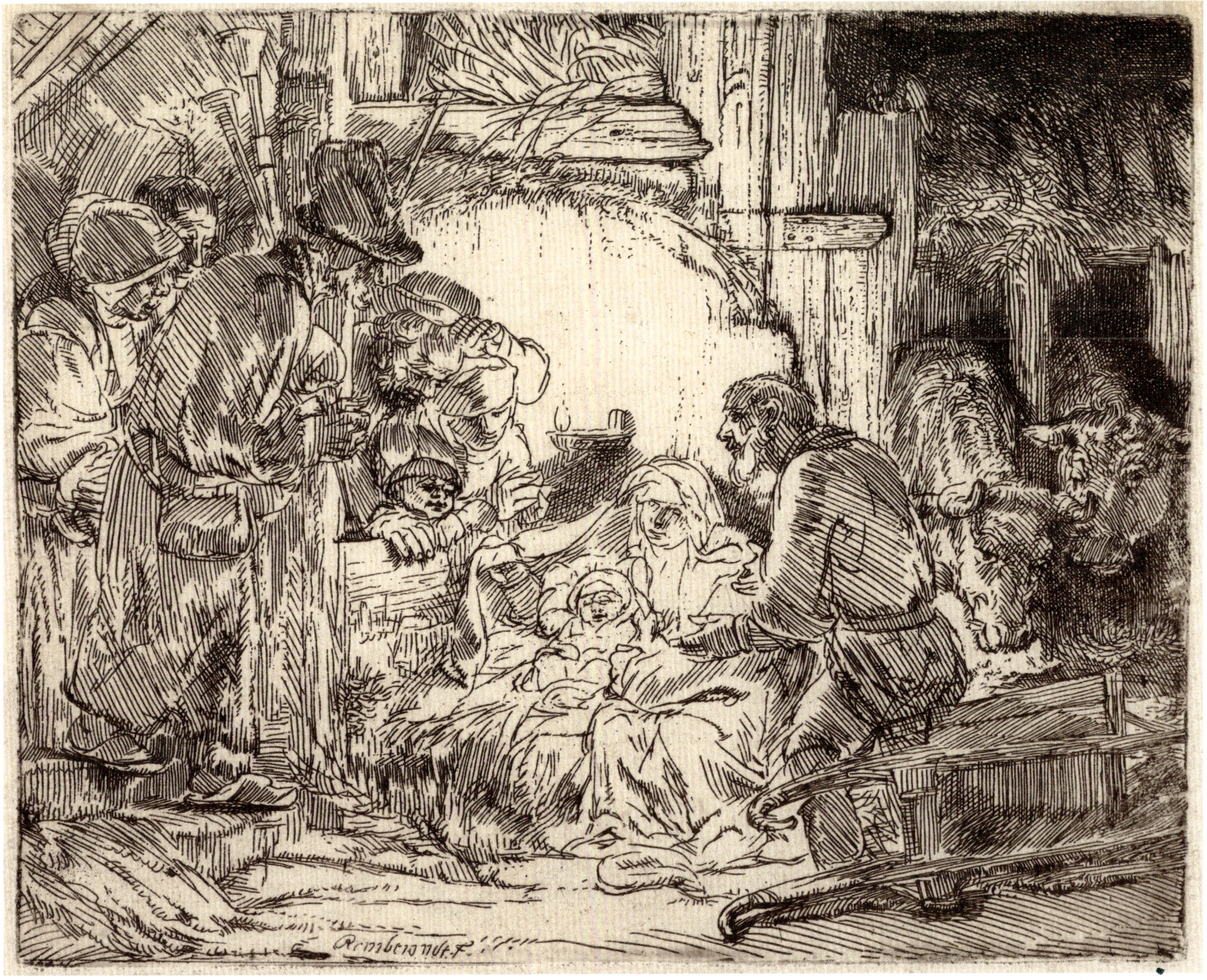

PLATE 20

21. Adoration of the Shepherds: A Night Piece

B. 46 (H. 225, Mz. 237, NHD 300)
Etching, drypoint, and engraving
c. 1656–57[1]
State VIII of IX
Sheet: 14.8 × 19.8 cm, trimmed to the plate mark
Verso: collector's stamp, LL in a circle in red ink (Lugt 4796, Leslie E. Lancy); in graphite, *B. 46*

Provenance:
Karl + Faber, Munich, May 23, 1969
C. G. Boerner, Dusseldorf, Germany, 1970[2]
Leslie E. Lancy, Ellwood, PA (1911–96)
David Tunick Inc., New York, NY, 1977
Feddersen, Elkhart, IN, 1991
Snite Museum of Art
Acc. No.: 1991.025.020

Plate survives:
Private collection (Kornfeld), Switzerland.

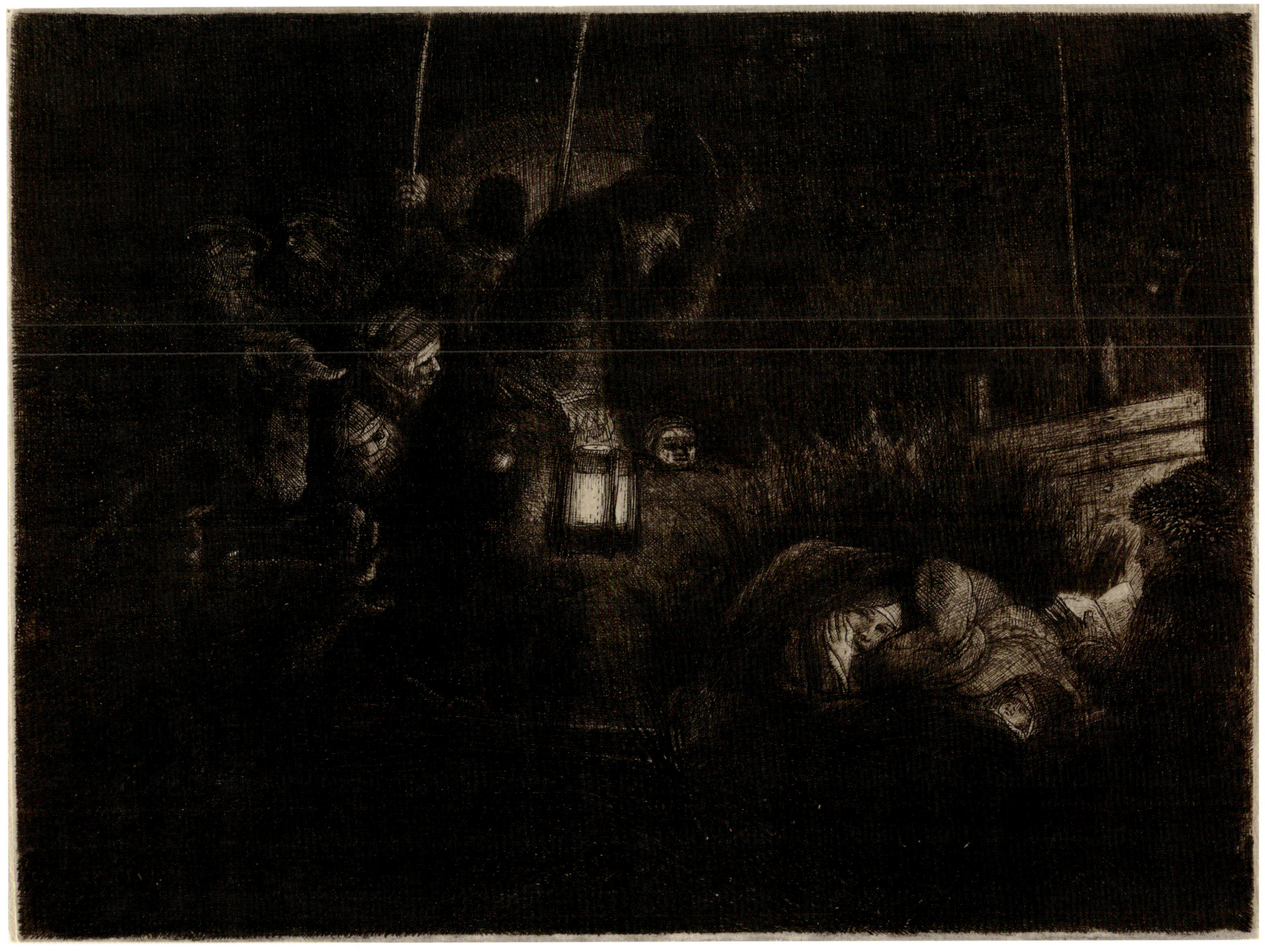

PLATE 21

*A*doration of the Shepherds: With the Lamp was one of six horizontal etchings that Rembrandt created in 1654 depicting scenes from the infancy and youth of Christ.[3] Four of these prints dealt with topics that the artist had already treated one or more times before (the Adoration of the Shepherds, the Circumcision, the Flight into Egypt, and Christ Disputing with the Doctors), while two of them involved new subjects for the artist (*Virgin and Child with the Cat and the Snake* and *Christ Returning from the Temple with His Parents*). These six prints appear to form a thematic series, one that reflects Rembrandt's continuing engagement not just with New Testament subjects, in general, but with images of the Holy Family, in particular.

In the *Adoration of the Shepherds: With the Lamp*, light plays a transcendent role. At the center of the composition, Mary sits on a low mound of straw. Her curled left hand lies on her lap beside the peacefully sleeping infant Jesus, whose head rests on a pillow propped up against his mother's chest. The baby is swaddled and his head is covered, with the result that only his face is visible. As Mary leans slightly to her right, toward the child, she spreads out a portion of the hanging drapery of her headdress above Jesus like a canopy. It is not clear whether she has just pulled the cloth back, so as to reveal the child to the shepherds and, consequently, to the viewer of the etching, or if she is pulling the cloth forward, so as to shield the child from the brilliant light and the peasants who have gathered at the left. Both Mary and Jesus are rendered in a very economical manner. Shadows are kept to a minimum, with the figures described almost exclusively by means of simple contour lines. This method of rendering the Holy Family provides quite a contrast to the extensive descriptiveness of the other figures and objects in the print. A small oil lamp sits near Mary and Jesus, but it is clear that its tiny flame is not the source of the bright semicircle of light surrounding it. Instead, the brilliant aura of light can be read as the spiritual illumination that has entered the world with the birth of the Christ.[4] Although the wall of light is *behind* Mary and Jesus, they are also brightly lit from the front, defining them as a source of divine illumination.

An elderly Joseph stands just to the left of his wife, facing the curious, reverent shepherds. Knees flexed, he leans forward with his arms before him, as if to welcome the visitors and present the child to them. Light falls only on the portions of his body and face closest to Mary and the sleeping child, as if it is reflected from them. Just behind him, close to the picture plane, a rustic hand barrow lies on its side. It appears that Joseph has just risen, after having used the barrow as an improvised seat.

At the right edge of the print, two oxen stand in narrow, densely shadowed stalls. The one closest to the Virgin and Child is partially illuminated by the central light in which the Holy Family is bathed, while the other beast is almost completely enshrouded in darkness. The inclusion of the two oxen, rather than the more customary symbolic ox and ass, suggests that Rembrandt was more interested in rendering an authentic contemporary setting than in adhering closely to traditional iconography.

Rembrandt departed from visual tradition in his selection of the peasant types who have come to view the child. Three shepherds, two women, and a child crowd into the stable, filling the left third of the image. An elderly, emaciated peasant wearing a tall, brimmed hat over a fitted cap is holding a bagpipe, a traditional attribute of rustics. He wears the sabots that would have been typical peasant footwear, and, as he cranes forward to look, he pauses with one foot on each of the two low steps leading down to the stable floor. An elderly woman with African features stands behind and to the left of the bagpiper, her hands folded in front of her. A bareheaded man is just visible behind her. All of the figures have bundled up to keep warm. Rembrandt's inclusion of figures representing a range of ages (old, young, and middle-aged) and types (male and female, European and African) expands the scope of his *Adoration* so that the baby Jesus is presented not solely to the Jews, in keeping with traditional representations of the event, but to a more universal Family of Man.[5]

In a prime viewing spot, right up against the low wooden partition that separates the onlookers from the Holy Family, is a tight-knit group of father, mother, and child. This trio both mirrors and contrasts with the sacred family. The bearded, middle-aged father leans forward, with his right hand, which grasps the top of the partition, resting beside his young child's cheek. As he raises his left hand to his head, framing his wife's head with his arm, he draws his family into an encircling embrace. His somewhat younger wife leans forward as well, gazing down directly at the sleeping Christ Child. Finally, their young son, nestled between them, peers over the barrier, smiling sweetly as he looks at the holy infant. The prominent placement of a young peasant family so close to the Holy Family suggests the paradigmatic role of Mary, Joseph, and Jesus in inspiring others to emulate them in both spiritual matters and the domestic sphere of human interactions.[6]

Although Catholicism was banned as a state religion in Rembrandt's time, it was still the faith of the largest religious minority within the Dutch Republics. While Protestant theological principles are a natural interpretive frame for most of Rembrandt's biblical prints, a number of works, such as the *Virgin and Child in the Clouds* (B. 61, 1641, cat. no. 34) and the *Virgin and Child with the Cat and the Snake* (B. 63, 1654, cat. no. 36), indicate that Rembrandt was clearly conscious of his Catholic clientele, as well. Given his theologically diverse public, it would not be unreasonable to assume that he produced some prints, quintessentially market-dependent objects, with those differing theological beliefs in mind. Furthermore, if Rembrandt wished to cultivate an international audience for his work, he would undoubtedly have sought to incorporate elements that would resonate with collectors in such institutionally Catholic countries as Flanders and Italy. In this context, the manner in which Rembrandt composed the *Adoration of the Shepherds: With the Lamp* seems to reflect Catholic traditions more than Calvinist ones. The Virgin appears to present the Christ Child to the viewer in a sacred space as if he were the Eucharist displayed on a church altar, and the cloth that she holds aloft evokes the ritual of the corporal. Finally, the fence behind which the shepherds gather is like an altar rail behind which one of the "congregants" folds her hands in prayer.

Around the same time that Rembrandt created the etched *Adoration of the Shepherds: With the Lamp*, he made a print of the same subject in a somewhat larger format, *Adoration of the Shepherds: A Night Piece* (B. 46, cat. no. 21).[7] Both etchings followed the visual tradition of setting the scene in a stable. However, the *Night Piece* is a virtuoso example of a nocturnal interior scene, and Rembrandt appears to have been interested as much in investigating the emotive possibilities of darkness as in elucidating the significance of the biblical theme. In order to achieve the nocturnal effects in this work, Rembrandt made extensive use of both drypoint needle and burin, in addition to etching the plate. He reworked the image through eight separate states,[8] often deepening the darkness and the image's sense of intimacy and mystery. As a result, the stable becomes enveloped in a shroud of dense, velvety darkness. The few areas of light (the lantern, the reflection of its glow on the Virgin's face, and a spray of light at the right) become dramatic highlights.

The composition of *Adoration of the Shepherds: A Night Piece* is broadly divided into two parts, with the Holy Family on the right side and the shepherds, with their companions and livestock, on the left. In contrast to the *Adoration of the Shepherds: With the Lamp*, the details of the setting are very difficult to decipher, since they are cloaked in darkness.[9]

Joseph, huddled in shadow, is seated on the ground at the far right edge of the composition. Since he is specifically mentioned in the biblical account of the Adoration of the Shepherds, he is often included in compositions depicting the event. Rembrandt's etching is unusual, however, in that as Joseph looks up at the gathering of shepherds, he looks out over the pages of an open book, a work that is so brightly illuminated that the light reflects up into

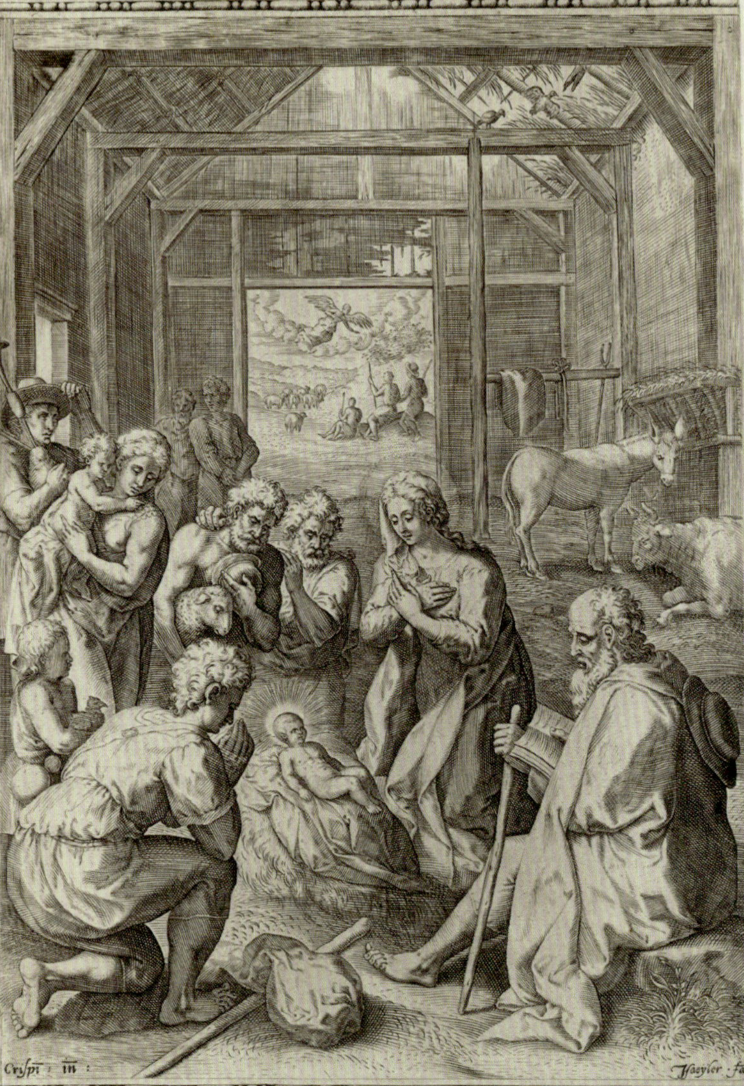

FIGURE 1. Johannes Sadeler I after Crispijn van den Broeck, *The Adoration of the Shepherds*, engraving, f. 1600. *Albertina, Vienna.*

his face, drawing the viewer's eye. It appears that the peasants' arrival interrupted Joseph as he was reading, either to himself or to Mary. Although there was a tradition of depicting Joseph in the act of reading in images of the Holy Family,[10] depictions of the Adoration of the Shepherds rarely represented him in this way. In selecting this motif, Rembrandt may well have been inspired by an etching of the Adoration by Johannes Sadeler I after a drawing by Crispijn van den Broeck (fig. 1).[11] The inclusion of the open book identifies Joseph as a literate, even learned, man, not the simple, buffoonish carpenter that he was sometimes portrayed as in the late Middle Ages. This new, more cultured image of Joseph emerged in the course of the later fifteenth and sixteenth centuries, along with a new cult of the saint.[12] The book may also distinguish Joseph as a devout man, one who spent time reading the Old Testament. According to Anthony Blunt, the particular emphasis on Joseph as a learned man owed its popularity to the writings of the Italian theologian Isidoro Isolani, whose tract on the gifts of Joseph was published in Pavia in 1522.[13] Isolani tied the concept of a learned Joseph to his role as counselor, nurturer, and educator of Christ.[14] Rembrandt, then, may have incorporated this motif in order to appeal to potential Catholic patrons who would have understood the broader theological implications of Joseph in such a role. In addition, the view of Joseph as Jesus's paternal guide would have been compatible with Rembrandt's own broader interest in family relationships, especially the connection between fathers—even surrogate fathers, in Joseph's case—and sons.[15]

In the nocturne, Mary and the sleeping Christ Child are nestled under a cocoon of covers beside Joseph, who is hunched up against the winter cold. Densely etched and drawn black lines suggesting grasses or grain surround the sleeping figures, creating a kind of nest. The light from the brightly shining lantern borne by one of the shepherds is the most prominent focal point of the composition, and the lamp dimly illuminates the faces of Mary, Jesus, and Joseph.[16] Mary's face, closest to the lantern, is the brightest; less light falls on the child's face, and still less on Joseph's. This gradation of illumination suggests that Rembrandt was focusing on light as both a physical emanation and a spiritual one. The lantern also illuminates the face of the man raising his hat, as well as the features of the woman and child peering out from behind him. As with the Holy Family, it is the woman who is most brightly illuminated, while there is less light on the child, and the least on the father.

In addition to the shepherds, two of whom hold tall staffs, there are two women, two children, and a pair of cows, which are just barely visible in the darkness. The range of ages and types of the peasants represented in the print suggests the universality of the epiphany that Rembrandt also proclaimed in his *Adoration of the Shepherds: With the Lamp.*

The symbolic use of light that characterized *Adoration of the Shepherds: With the Lamp* and the first state of *Adoration of the Shepherds: A Night Piece* was gradually abandoned in the course of the *Night Piece*'s evolution in favor of an almost obsessive interest in creating a nocturne. Rembrandt was quite possibly motivated not just by the personal, technical challenge, but also by the market: the dramatic effect of this kind of composition demonstrated an artist's skill, and seventeenth-century collectors prized works of this sort as an independent category of print.[17]

Notes

1. The date of the final version has been a matter of some discussion. Until fairly recently, the consensus was that the print was completed around 1652. This is the date given to the print by Hind, White and Boon, and Tümpel (*Rembrandt legt*, cat. 42). However, Ludwig Münz (*Critical Catalogue*, vol. 2, cat. 237) proposed a later date of around 1656–57, based on stylistic grounds. This suggestion has been supported by Erik Hinterding's investigation of the chronology of watermarks on Rembrandt prints. See Ger Luijten in Erik Hinterding, Ger Luijten, and Martin Royalton-Kisch, *Rembrandt the Printmaker*, exh. cat. (Chicago and London: Fitzroy Dearborn Publishers, 2000), 280; and Clifford Ackley and Thomas Rassieur in *Rembrandt's Journey*, cat. 153, 232.

2. Illustrated in Boerner catalog *Neue Lagerliste 53 (1969)*, no. 77.

3. Although this print is undated, it is generally agreed—on the basis of both style and content—that it dates from 1654 and is part of Rembrandt's "childhood of Christ" series. On the six horizontal prints as a series, see Ernst van de Wetering, "Remarks on Rembrandt's Oil-Sketches for Etchings," in Hinterding, Luijten, and Royalton-Kisch, *Rembrandt the Printmaker*, 46–47. The other five prints in the group are *Circumcision in the Stable* (B. 47, cat. no. 24), *Flight into Egypt: Crossing a Brook* (B. 55, cat. no. 30), *Christ Returning from the Temple with His Parents* (B. 60, cat. no. 40), *Christ Seated Disputing with the Doctors* (B. 64, cat. no. 39), and *Virgin and Child with the Cat and the Snake* (B. 63, cat. no. 36). These prints are thematically related, stylistically coherent, and, except for *Adoration of the Shepherds*, of similar proportions.

4. There is a long tradition of depicting the brilliant spiritual light of Christ as overwhelming the natural light of a candle (usually held by St. Joseph). This trope derives from the writings of St. Bridget of Sweden, but by the seventeenth century, the motif of the Child's holy presence illuminating the darkness had simply become part of the visual tradition. For a very early Northern example, see Geertgen tot Sint Jans, *The Nativity at Night*, c. 1490 (National Gallery, London). For an example that is more contemporary with Rembrandt's work, see Gerrit van Honthorst, *The Adoration of the Shepherds*, 1622 (Wallraf-Richartz Museum, Cologne).

5. Although it is traditional to represent the three ages of man in depictions of the Adoration of the Magi, this is not common in images of the Adoration of the Shepherds.

Regarding images of the Annunciation to the Shepherds and the Adoration of the Shepherds as traditionally representing the epiphany of the Jews, see the discussion of *Angel Appearing to the Shepherds* (B. 44, 1634, cat. no. 19). For possible implications of the inclusion of an African woman in this scene, see the discussion of the *Baptism of the Eunuch* (B. 98, 1641, cat. no. 68).

6. Although the theme of the Holy Family as a model for all Christians may have had its most immediate resonance in the arena of Catholic theological discourse (Cynthia Hahn, "'Joseph Will Perfect, Mary Enlighten, and Jesus Save Thee': The Holy Family as Marriage Model in the Mérode Triptych," *Art Bulletin* 68 [1986]: 54–66), David R. Smith observed that one of the principal messages of Calvinist theology was the extraction of personal meaning from biblical events. Smith, "Towards a Protestant Aesthetics: Rembrandt's 1655 *Sacrifice of Isaac*," *Art History* 8, no. 3 (1985): 294. The peasant family bearing witness to this sacred moment could have encouraged the Calvinist viewer to "participate" as well, drawing inspiration from the Holy Family as a model for domestic life and responsibilities.

7. Although *Adoration of the Shepherds: A Night Piece* is also a representation of Jesus as an infant, it is not considered part of the childhood series, because it is a nocturne and differs in style from the other etchings.

8. In agreement with Adam von Bartsch's analysis, White and Boon listed eight states, apparently attributing all eight to Rembrandt himself. Of these eight, the first four states exist in very small numbers (only eleven total examples survive), suggesting that they

were pulled while the print was still a work in progress. States IX–XI are posthumous.

9. In the first state of the print (Christopher White, *Rembrandt as an Etcher: A Study of the Artist at Work*, 2nd ed. [New Haven, CT: Yale University Press, 1999], fig. 92), it is clearer that this "backdrop" is made up of sheaves of wheat or straw. By the second state (ibid., fig. 93), however, this type of discursive detail has begun to become indistinct as darkness falls over the print.

10. Joseph is shown reading, for example, in Rembrandt's own *Holy Family* of c. 1631–32 (B. 62, cat. no. 35), and Münz (*Critical Catalogue*, 109) has identified this print as the source for Rembrandt's figure in *Adoration of the Shepherds: A Night Piece*. See below for an alternative source.

I should like to thank Jonathan Umglaub and Margaret Goehring for drawing my attention to examples of Joseph reading in Holy Family images by Andrea del Sarto (*Madonna del Sacco*, SS. Annunziata, Florence) and Joos van Cleve (Vienna, London, and New York). Max J. Friedländer catalogs nine separate examples of the Joos van Cleve *Holy Family with Saint Joseph Reading* (*Early Netherlandish Painting*, trans. Heinz Norden, vol. 9, pt. 1 [New York: Praeger, 1973], cat. 66). I am also particularly indebted to Carolyn C. Wilson for her insightful comments on this motif: Carolyn C. Wilson, *St. Joseph in Italian Renaissance Society and Art: New Directions and Interpretations* (Philadelphia: St. Joseph's University Press, 2001); ibid., "St. Joseph as *Custos* in the *Summa* of Isidoro Isolani and in Italian Renaissance Art," in *Saint Joseph Studies: Papers in English from the Seventh and Eighth International St. Joseph Symposia Malta 1997 and El Salvador 2001*, ed. Larry Toschi, OJS (Santa Cruz, CA: Guardian of the Redeemer Books, 2002), 89–120; and ibid., "*Sanctus Joseph Nutritor Domini*: A Triptych Attributed to Jan Gossaert Considered as Evidence of Early Hapsburg Embrace of St. Joseph's Cult," in *Święty Józef-Patron na nasze czasy. Akta X Międzynarodowego Kongresu Józefologicznego; Saint Joseph: Patron for Our Times. Proceedings of the Tenth International Josephological Congress, Kalisz, Poland, September 27–October 4, 2009* (Kalisz, Poland: Centrum Józefologiczne, 2010): 499–524.

11. HD 186.

12. On the distinction between the medieval and Renaissance views of Joseph, see Carolyn C. Wilson, *St. Joseph*, passim, and John C. Hand, *Joos van Cleve: The Complete Paintings* (New Haven, CT: Yale University Press, 2001), 54–56.

13. Isidoro Isolani, *Summa de donis Sancti Ioseph* (Pavia, 1522). Anthony Blunt, *Nicolas Poussin* (New York: Bollingen Foundation, 1967), 1:182–83.

14. See the discussions of *Holy Family* (B. 62, 1632, cat. no. 35) and *Rest on the Flight into Egypt: Lightly Etched* (B. 58, 1645, cat. no. 33) for other examples in which this interpretation of Joseph seems applicable. Carolyn C. Wilson (*St. Joseph*) also suggested that images of Joseph with a book may refer to his fulfillment of the prophecy of the Incarnation and of him as both patriarch and apostle.

15. See, for example, his sympathetic renderings of Abraham in his role as father in *Abraham Caressing Isaac* (B. 33, 1637, cat. no. 5) and *Abraham and Isaac* (B. 34, 1645, cat. no 6).

16. It is interesting that Rembrandt chose to make the towering lantern-bearing shepherd the initial focal point of the print. The bright lantern draws the eye, and it is not until one follows the line of the shepherd's posture and gaze that one turns one's attention to the Holy Family, down below.

17. On nocturnes and the tradition of collecting them, see William W. Robinson, "'This Passion for Prints': Collecting and Connoisseurship in Northern Europe during the Seventeenth Century," in Clifford Ackley, *Printmaking in the Age of Rembrandt*, exh. cat. (Boston: Boston Museum of Fine Arts, 1981), xlv–xlvi; Catherine Scallen, "Rembrandt's Nocturne Prints," *On Paper* 1 (January–February 1997): 13–17; and Adriaan Waiboer and Michiel Franken, *Northern Nocturnes: Nightscapes in the Age of Rembrandt* (Dublin: National Gallery of Ireland, 2005).

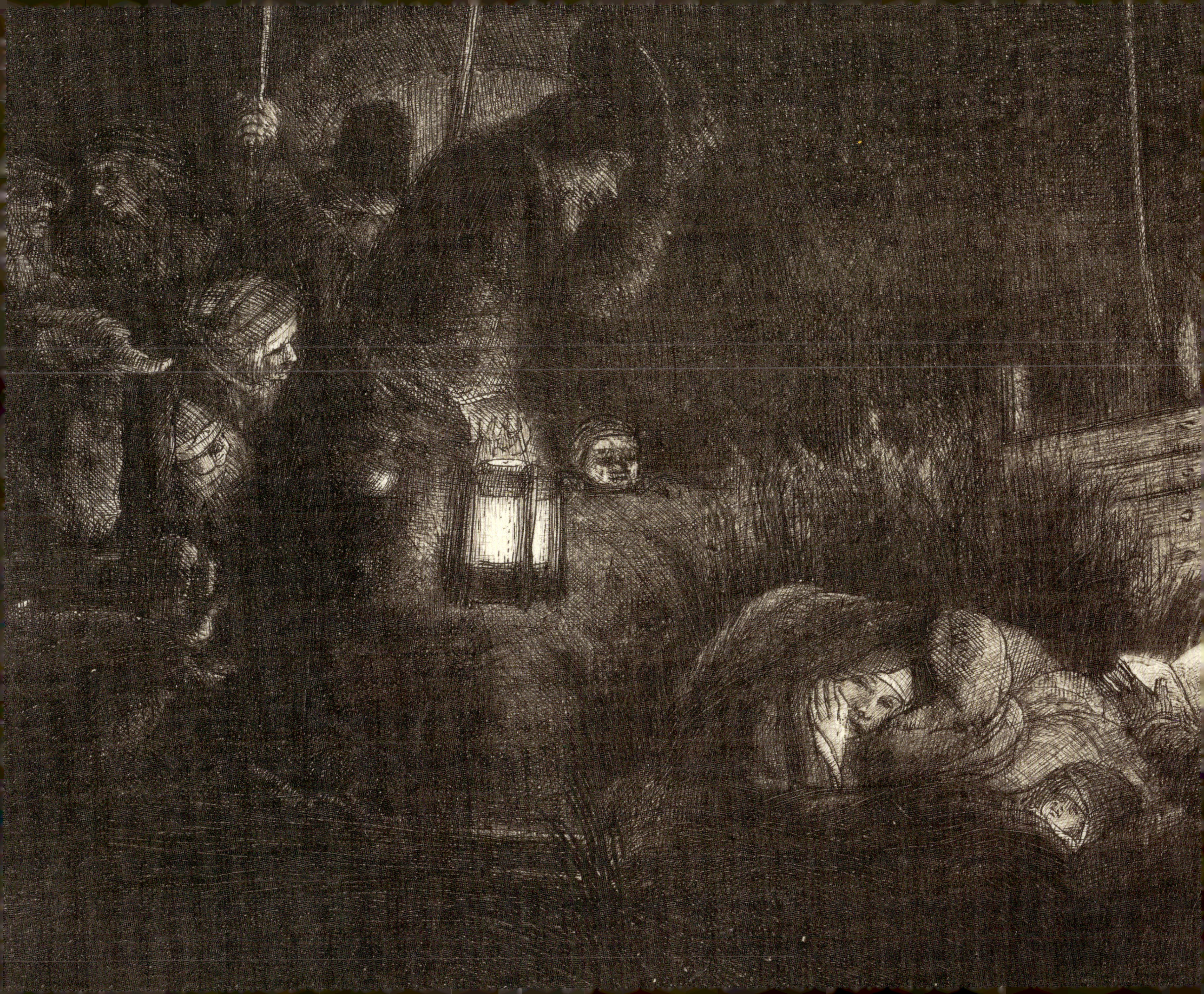

22–24. The Circumcision

22. Circumcision

S. 398 (H. 388 [rejects as work of Rembrandt], Mz. 187, NHD 1)
Etching
c. 1626
State III of III
Sheet: 21.4 × 16.5 cm, trimmed to the plate mark
Recto: in the lower margin at left, *Rembrant fecit*; right, *I.P. Berendrech ex.*
Verso: in brown ink, middle right, *P*

Provenance:
Kennedy Galleries Inc., New York, NY, 1976
Feddersen, Elkhart, IN, 1991
Snite Museum of Art
Accession No.: 1991.025.066

The plate does not survive.

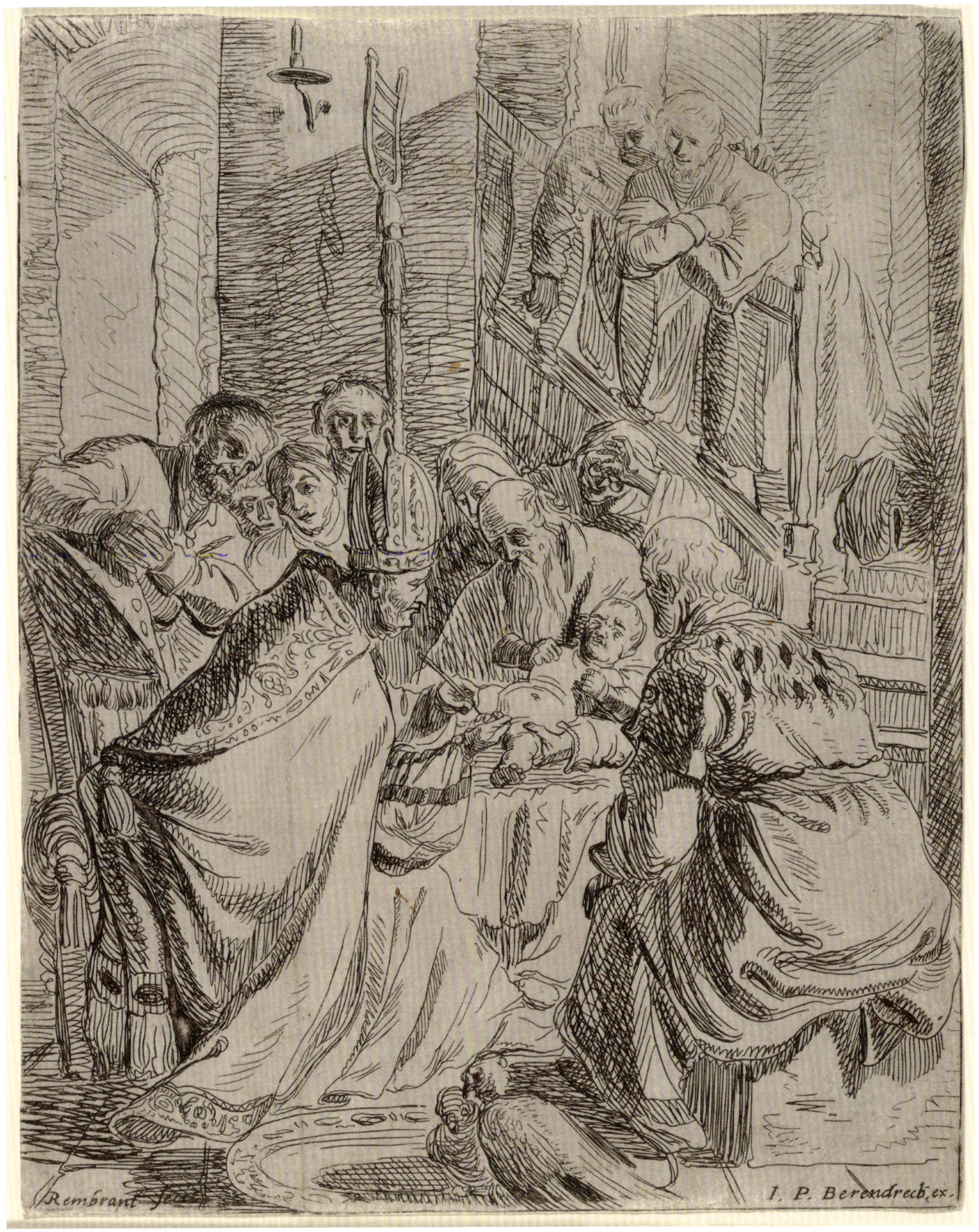

PLATE 22

23. Circumcision: Small Plate

B. 48 (H. 19 [1630]; Mz. 194 [1632/33], NHD 55)
Etching and drypoint
c. 1630
State I of I
Sheet: 9.3 × 6.7 cm; plate mark: 8.8 × 6.4 cm
Verso: blue ink, collectors stamp RYKS/MUSM (Lugt 2165); in graphite, *M153+*; upper right, *23758*; upper left, *T2*

Provenance:
Rijksmuseum, Amsterdam, second half of the nineteenth century
Craddock & Barnard, London, 1975
Feddersen, Elkhart, IN, 1991
Snite Museum of Art
Acc. No.: 1991.025.022

The plate does not survive.

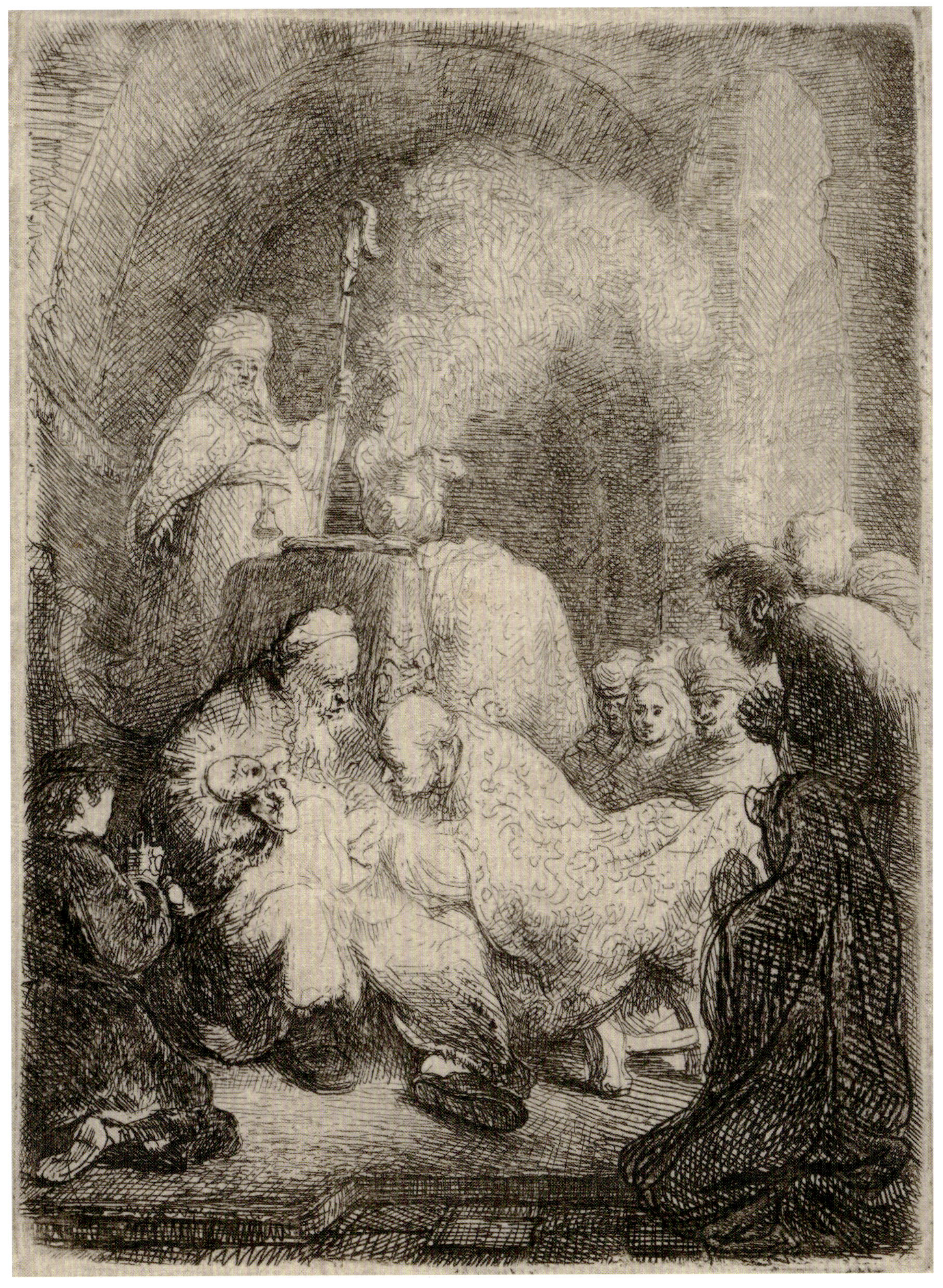

PLATE 23

24. *Circumcision in the Stable*

B. 47 (H. 274, Mz. 227, NHD 280)
Signed and dated in the plate: *Rembrandt f. 1654*
Etching
State II of V
Sheet: 9.5 × 14.4 cm, trimmed to the plate mark.
Verso, in graphite, in center: *47*; along the bottom edge: *C. 2 303 /a20426/B47/ 48/ c. 5527*

Provenance:
Kennedy Galleries Inc., New York, NY, 1976 (Kennedy Gallery cat. 26)
Feddersen, Elkhart, IN, 1991
Snite Museum of Art
Acc. No.: 1991.025.021

Plate survives: Rijksprentenkabinett, Amsterdam.

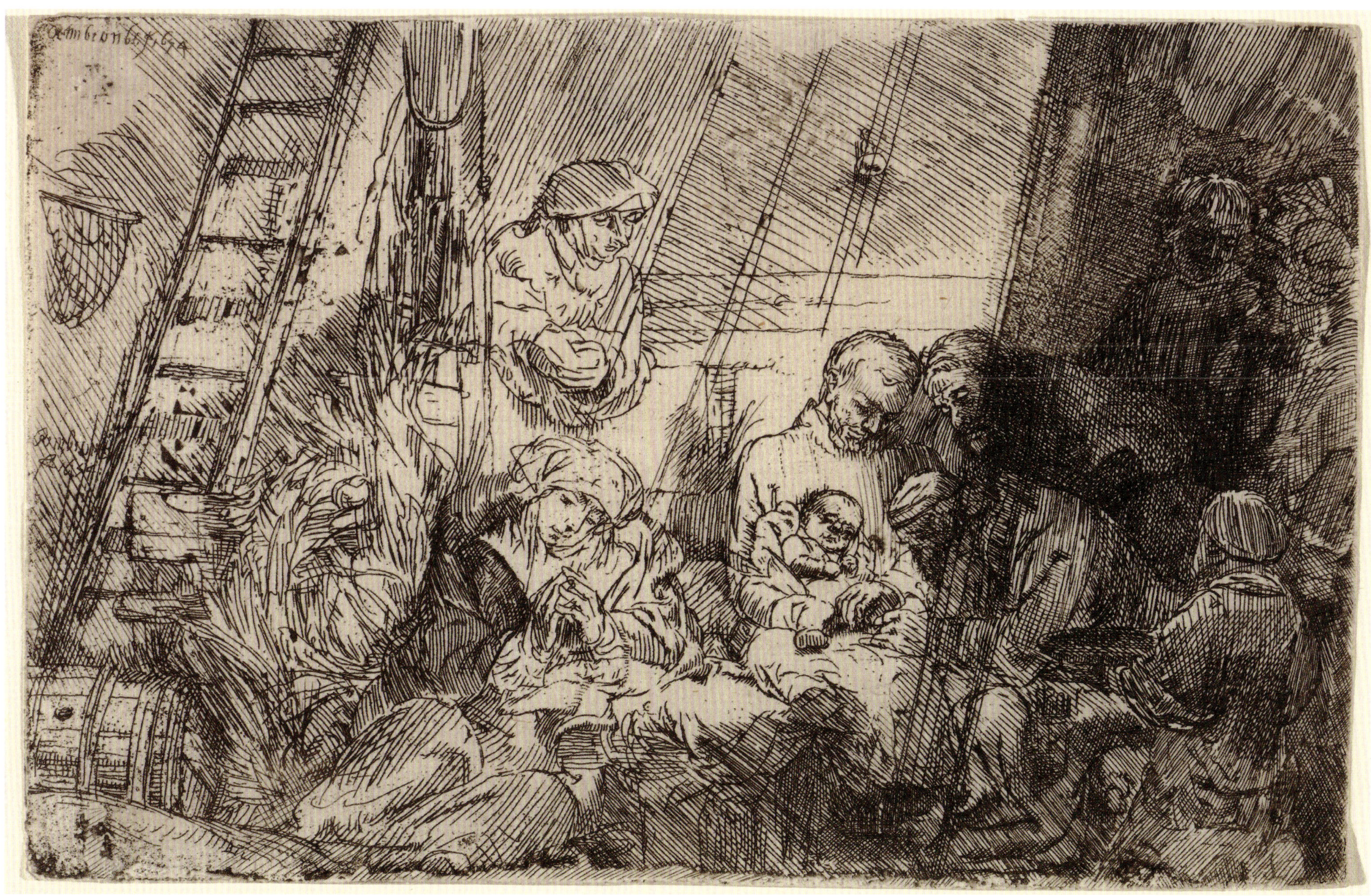

PLATE 24

In Genesis 17:10–14, God informs Abraham that all males must be circumcised on the eighth day after they are born, an act that would serve as a sign of the covenant between God and the Jewish people. In accordance with this biblical decree, the Christ Child was circumcised on the eighth day after his birth (Luke 2:21), and was given the name Jesus, for at the time of the Annunciation, the Angel Gabriel had told Mary, "thou shalt . . . bring forth a son, and shalt call his name Jesus" (Luke 1:31). Interpreting the passage in Luke 2:21, Calvin asserted that "by undergoing circumcision, Christ acknowledged himself to be the slave of the law, that he might procure our freedom [from the ritual]."[1] This was the rationale by which the Hebraic ritual of circumcision was replaced by the sacrament of Baptism, and the Old Law and the covenant of the flesh were replaced by the New Law and the covenant of faith.[2]

Rembrandt made several prints depicting the ritual of Jesus's circumcision. The first of these (S. 398), possibly the artist's earliest etching, dates to around 1626, that is, before Rembrandt left Leiden and moved permanently to Amsterdam. Here, the infant Jesus rests against the arm of an elderly, balding man with a very long beard, the *sandak*.[3] Because of the ambiguous manner in which Rembrandt manipulated the hatching beneath the child, it is not clear whether Jesus is resting on the *sandak*'s lap or on an altar table directly before him. There are precedents for both possibilities in representations of the Circumcision, and the ambiguity in Rembrandt's print may be felicitous, since in Hebrew tradition, the lap of the person holding the child at the time of its circumcision is considered analogous to the altar in the Temple itself. The infant Jesus's hands appear to be clenched, and he looks apprehensive as he gazes up at the face of a second elder. This man, seated with his back toward the viewer, leans in toward the child. He is more elegantly dressed than the central figure, and on his shoulders he wears some sort of fringed or fur-trimmed shawl suggestive of a Jewish prayer shawl, or tallit.

The act of circumcision is being carried out by a mohel[4] who wears an embroidered cope and a tall, horned hat like a bishop's miter. This kind of ecclesiastical costume for the mohel is not without visual precedent. The mohel in a woodcut illustration of the Circumcision in a *Passional* done by Virgil Solis and published in Nuremberg in 1552 wears a similar hat, as does the mohel in an engraving by Adriaen Colleart after a design by Johannes Stradanus for a series dedicated to the Life of the Virgin that was published in Antwerp between 1585 and 1595.[5] In Rembrandt's etching, Joseph and Mary probably stand to the left, behind the mohel's chair. Joseph clasps his hands in front of him and stares down at his son, while Mary averts her eyes and looks up toward her husband. Among the other figures who crowd in around the central grouping is a young man who holds a staff with a ladder-like finial. The rod, a symbol of priestly authority, likely belongs not to the young man, but to one of the elders. It is yet another detail that reinforces the ecclesiastical aura of the event. Two other figures stand behind the tight-knit central group: an elderly woman peers over the right shoulder of the man holding the Christ Child and an oddly cadaverous figure who appears to be holding a pince-nez in front of her eyes looks over the *sandak*'s other shoulder. The intensity of their gazes testifies to their status as witnesses of this seminal event.

Since the rite of circumcision was conceived of as a Jewish "sacrament," representations of Christ's circumcision were typically set in a noble ecclesiastical space,[6] and this seems to be the case here, as well. A short flight of steps with a balustered railing leads up to a diagonal stairway that rises behind the central figures, and two men lean over the railing in casual poses, one resting his arm around the shoulders of the other as they gaze down at the scene below.[7] A sconce with a single candle projects out of the wall above the Virgin and Joseph, and a barrel-vaulted passageway opens up behind the couple.[8]

A large salver with two turtledoves occupies the center foreground of the composition, and this detail links the etching with the next landmark episode in Jesus's life, the Presentation of the Christ Child. The ritual of presentation, which was to take place forty days after the birth of a child, required the family to give an offering to the Temple: a lamb or, if the family was too poor, two turtledoves. The conflation of elements of the Circumcision and Presentation is not without visual precedent.[9]

As art historian Roelof van Straten has observed, Rembrandt appears to have drawn inspiration for this etching from a reproductive engraving after Peter Paul Rubens's *Adoration of the Magi*[10] (see Rosenberg, "Rembrandt's Religious Prints," this catalog, fig. 3) done by Nicolaas Lauwers in about 1620.[11] The arched opening on the left side of both compositions, the staircase populated with onlookers, and the similarity of the costumes of Rubens's kneeling magus and that of Rembrandt's seated observer attest to the Dutch artist's familiarity with the earlier engraving.[12] Rembrandt's conversion of the Adoration of the Magi into a Circumcision would have masked the artist's dependence on the earlier model.

The authenticity of Rembrandt's print has been a matter of some dispute, despite the fact that the plate was signed "Rembrant" [*sic*] in the second and third states.[13] The image was omitted from Adam von Bartsch's catalogue raisonné, although it did appear in the first edition of Edme-François Gersaint's 1751 catalog.[14] Woldemar von Seidlitz[15] and Arthur M. Hind[16] rejected the etching as a work by Rembrandt, while Leonard Slatkes attributed the print to Jan Lievens,[17] an attribution that was seconded by Roelof van Straten.[18] However, in addition to Gersaint, a number of scholars, including Ludwig Münz,[19] Christopher White and Karel Boon,[20]

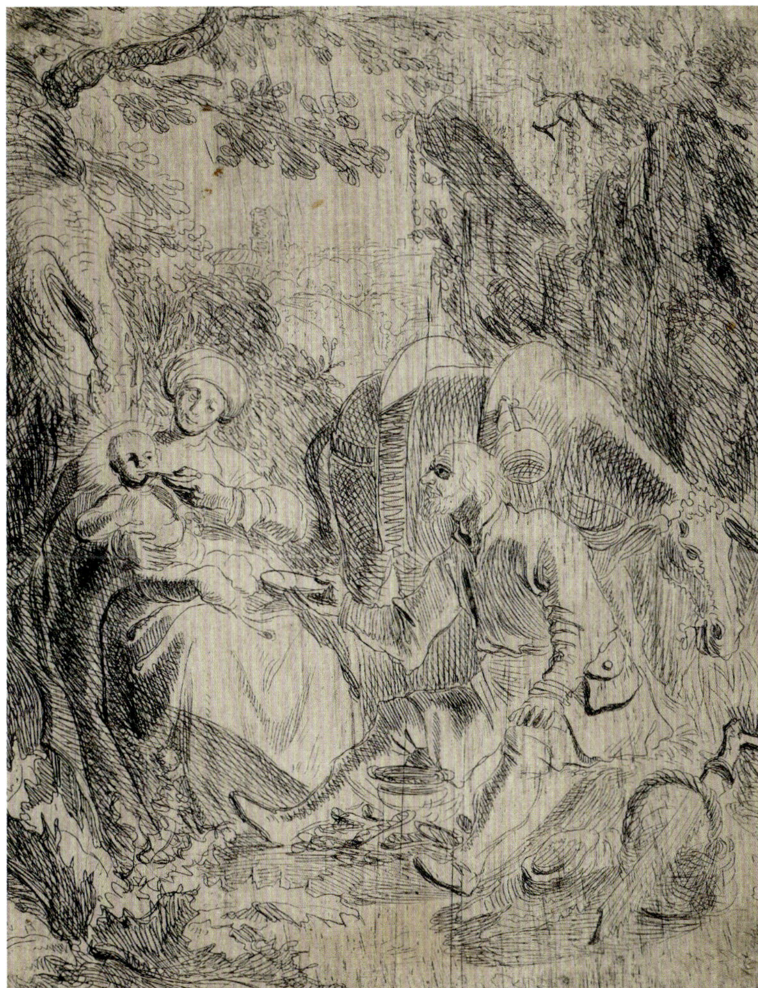

FIGURE 1. Rembrandt, etching, *Rest on the Flight into Egypt*, c. 1626. *Photo: © Trustees of the British Museum.*

Ger Luijten,[21] Thomas Rassieur,[22] and Shelley Perlove and Larry Silver,[23] have concluded that the print is, indeed, a work by Rembrandt. Comparison of *Circumcision* with Lievens's virtually contemporary print of *St. John on Patmos*[24] (Rosenberg, "Rembrandt's Religious Prints," this catalog, fig. 1) shows some similarities, particularly in the reinforcement of the contours and the calligraphic approach to the medium. Nonetheless, as several historians have pointed out, the point of view in the *St. John* is considerably lower, giving the figure a greater sense of monumentality, and the modeling techniques are subtler. Furthermore, Lievens employed a form of stippling to create the lightest of his shadows, a technique that

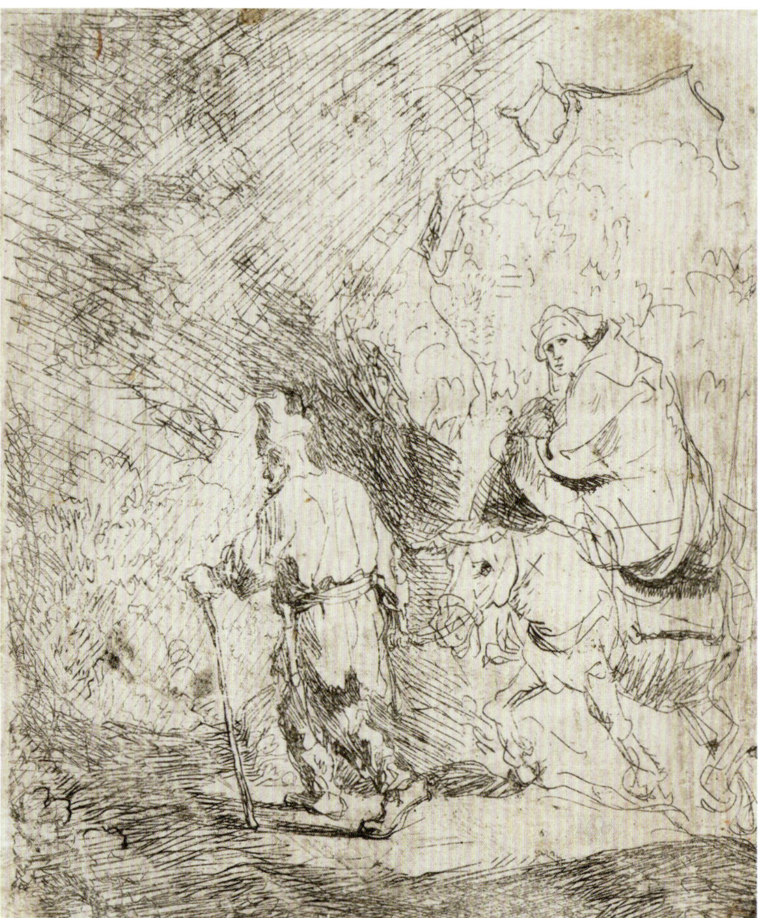

FIGURE 2. Rembrandt, *The Flight into Egypt*, etching, c. 1628. *Rijksmuseum, Amsterdam.*

is absent from Rembrandt's etching. While *Circumcision* appears to be somewhat more finished than two other early etchings by Rembrandt, *Rest on the Flight into Egypt* (B. 59, c. 1626) (fig. 1) and *The Flight into Egypt* (B. 54, c. 1628) (fig. 2), it still clearly reveals the inexperience of the artist as a printmaker. Shadows are constructed by means of a wide variety of types of hatching, but are distributed in an inconsistent manner.[25] As a result, the lighting is dramatic, but not very logical. There are also problems with the rendering of figures and with the rather bizarre architectural perspective.

This is the only one of Rembrandt's early prints to have a signature, but even more significant, it is one of only three prints in the artist's entire oeuvre to bear the name of a publisher, in this case, I. P. Berendrech.[26] Jan Pietersz. Berendrecht was an entrepreneurial printer and art dealer. Originally from Haarlem, he was a founding member of the book trades guild in that city. In addition to *Circumcision*, Berendrecht published about 150 prints in the second and third decades of the seventeenth century, including works by Willem Buytewech, Lievens, and Esaias van de Velde. Sometime in the early 1630s, he moved to The Hague, where he died around 1645.[27] The extent of Berendrecht's influence on Rembrandt is a matter of conjecture. It is not known whether the publisher was responsible for the young artist's first attempts at etching or if Rembrandt undertook the project on his own. Lievens's role is also a mystery.[28] In a brief biography of Lievens, Jan Jansz. Orlers reports that when the precocious artist was about ten years old, he copied the prints of Willem Buytewech.[29] Since Berendrecht was one of Buytewech's publishers, it is possible that Lievens became acquainted with the entrepreneurial Haarlem printer after seeing his name on Buytewech's etchings and that Lievens, in turn, introduced Rembrandt to Berendrecht. Lievens's *St. John on Patmos* (Rosenberg, "Rembrandt's Religious Prints," fig. 1), which was also published by Berendrecht, is normally dated 1625–26, that is, a bit earlier than *Circumcision*.[30] One thing that complicates the history of *Circumcision* is the existence of an impression on a type of paper that Rembrandt used around 1641. This would imply that Rembrandt either retained the plate or recovered it from Berendrecht at some point, possibly when the publisher left Haarlem for The Hague.[31] Why Rembrandt would have printed such a juvenile plate at a much later date remains a mystery.

Rembrandt's second representation of the circumcision of the Christ Child (*Circumcision: Small Plate*, B. 48, cat. no. 23) was created around 1630, in the same miniaturist style that the artist employed in the contemporary *Presentation in the Temple with the Angel: Small Plate* (B. 51, cat. no. 25) and *Christ Disputing with the Doctors: Small Plate* (B. 66, cat. no. 37).[32] As in Rembrandt's earlier depiction (cat. no. 22), the circumcision takes place in the Herodian Temple, but the setting in the new image is more intimate than the one in the 1626 etching. Rembrandt's handling of shadows, considerably more subtle than his first version, ranges from the silvery tones of reflected light in the chamber that can be seen through an arch in the right background to the dense, almost solid black shadows on the backs of the figures kneeling at the front corners. On the whole, Rembrandt's rendering of forms is more convincing, and his characters' gestures and expressions are more natural, than those in his first print of the subject. He was no longer treating etching as a form of drawing, but was working in a more pictorial language.

In the center of the composition, a rather rotund, bearded elder holds the squalling Christ Child on his lap. The figures are bathed in light, and an aureola surrounds the infant's head. This overt sign of Jesus's divinity is decidedly at odds with the child's very human response to the actions of the bald, coped mohel who leans forward over him to carry out his task.[33] Behind this central trio is a large draped altar table with a portable incense burner and salver. Smoke billows out of the mouth of the censer and up into the dark vaults of the mysterious surrounding architecture.[34] Although the use of perspective is not as disjointed as it is in the setting of the earlier print, this interior is still somewhat mystifying. According to Perlove and Silver, the burner and smoke recall the incense that was regularly burned on the altar outside of the Holy of Holies, or Oracle, in the ancient Temple. Rembrandt's inclusion of these details appears to locate the scene within the Temple and directly outside of the Oracle. Perlove and Silver also associated the burning incense with the return of the divine fire that had filled the original Solomonic Temple, but that was absent from the Herodian Temple until the return of the Messiah and the salvific sacrifice of Christ.[35]

Standing on the platform behind the altar is a turbaned and coped High Priest. He holds a staff in his left hand, a sign of his authority.[36] Unlike the curious ladder-crowned staff in the earlier etching of the Circumcision (cat. no. 22), this one has the typical shape of a shepherd's crook or priestly crozier. Hanging from the sash that encircles the man's substantial waist is a bell, a decorative element that recalls Old Testament raiment as described in Exodus: bells and golden pomegranates adorned Moses's robes, and bells were prescribed for Aaron's robes so that their sound would announce his approach when he came before the Lord in the Holy of Holies.[37]

A small crowd of Jewish men and women kneel behind the mohel, witnessing Jesus's entry into a covenant with God. The young man kneeling in the left corner clasps some sort of vessel before him as he looks toward the child. Perlove and Silver identified the item as a mortar and pestle, but it could also be a vessel to receive the sacred foreskin, or a container of wine, which would have been customary at sacred events and might have been used to soothe the baby before the surgery.[38] In the corner opposite the young man, Mary kneels and Joseph stands beside her, his hands clasped together as he bends forward in an attitude of prayer. Mary's face is hidden in shadow, but Joseph's posture and the expression on his face evince concern for the baby who is at the heart of the ritual.

Rembrandt's third and final etching depicting Jesus's circumcision, *Circumcision in the Stable* (B. 47, cat. no. 24), shifts the setting significantly, from the grandeur of the Herodian Temple to the humble surroundings of a stable in Bethlehem. This change may reflect Rembrandt's acquaintance with historical Jewish practices. According to Jewish law, a woman could not enter the Temple until forty days after she had given birth. Since the circumcision had to take place on the eighth day after Jesus's birth, Mary could not have attended the ritual if it had taken place in the Temple. By changing the venue to the stable in Bethlehem, Rembrandt created an image that not only focused more on the humble circumstances of the Holy Family, but also adhered more closely to historical Jewish practice.[39]

Circumcision in the Stable, which is signed and dated twice, was one of the six etchings from 1654 that Rembrandt devoted to Christ's childhood. Joseph, bathed in light, sits on a low draped platform as he holds the sleeping Christ Child on his lap.[40] Like the bearded elder in the *Circumcision* of c. 1626, one hand clasps Jesus's thigh, in order to restrain the child. There is a tenderness in Joseph's gaze that reflects an intimacy between father and son that does not appear in the earlier versions of the Circumcision but that is apparent in the other infancy prints from 1654. Mary, who is seated on the floor to Jesus's right, leans on the edge of the platform, her eyes cast down and her hands folded in prayer, the very image of pious humility. Behind the Virgin, an older peasant woman leans over a low wooden rail, her hands clasped in front of her as she gazes down at the child and the mohel who is performing the operation. In costume and pose, she resembles the woman standing at the far left of another of the 1654 etchings, *Adoration of the Shepherds: With the Lamp*. Emerging from the deep shadows in the right quadrant of the print, the mohel and a bearded onlooker lean over the child, intent on the rite that they are performing. Standing behind the mohel and the bearded observer, three other men look on and converse among themselves, while in the lower right-hand corner of the composition, a turbaned man, seen from the rear, kneels or sits in the foreground, holding a salver out in front of him, perhaps to receive the blood and foreskin of Christ. It is impossible to gauge the man's age; he may be the counterpart of the young assistant in the 1630 print who kneels at the left side of the composition.

In typical fashion, Rembrandt used light and shadow in a dramatically symbolic way. Although there is a tiny candle and sconce on the back wall of the stable, it sheds no light. Instead, the radiance that illuminates the Holy Family and the pious woman behind the Virgin seems to rain down from the heavens above, signaling the presence of the divine. The light just barely reaches the heads of the mohel and his assistant, but otherwise, they and the other male figures in the stable are seen through a screen of darkness, an indication that they have not yet received the "light."[41] This screen of shadows, created by heavy parallel strokes, separates the viewer from the male observers. The heaviest lines, those that descend in front of the mohel and his assistant, create a dense shaft of shadow that echoes the incline of a ladder at the left of the print, as well as the slanted beams of light that illuminate the sacred family and the female attendant standing behind the Virgin.

At the far left side of the print, midway between Rembrandt's two signatures, a net dangles from a round rim.[42] Nearby, a pile of hay or sheaves of wheat hides the base of a large, truncated, vertical beam. The adjacent ladder, which presumably leads to a loft, passes close to the top of this beam. As Frank Robinson has noted, the ladder and beam serve as a symbolic allusions to the Crucifixion and the future Passion of Christ.[43] The large barrel and mass of straw or wheat that lie at the base of the ladder may simply be anecdotal details, or they may also serve as references to the sacramental wine and wafer of the Eucharist.[44]

Notes

1. John Calvin, *Commentary on a Harmony of the Evangelists, Matthew, Mark, and Luke*, 1:121–22, accessed August 5, 2011, http://www.ccel.org/ccel/calvin/calcom31.pdf. Commentary on Luke 2:21:

> 21. *That the child might be circumcised.* As to circumcision in general, the reader may consult the Book of Genesis, (17: 10). At present, it will be sufficient to state briefly what applies to the person of Christ. God appointed that his Son should be circumcised, in order to subject him to the law; for circumcision was a solemn rite, by which the Jews were initiated into the observance of the law. Paul explains the design, when he says, that Christ was "made under the law, to redeem them that were under the law" (Galatians 4: 4–5).
>
> By undergoing circumcision, Christ acknowledged himself to be the slave of the law, that he might procure our freedom. And in this way not only was the bondage of the law abolished by him, but the shadow of the ceremony was applied to his own body, that it might shortly afterwards come to an end. For though the abrogation of it depends on the death and resurrection of Christ, yet it was [as] a sort of prelude to it, that the Son of God submitted to be circumcised.

2. On the typological parallel between circumcision and baptism, see Tümpel, *Rembrandt legt*, cat. 44. See also John Calvin, *Institutes of the Christian Religion* (1536–59); chapter 16, sec. 4:

> For circumcision was for the Jews their first entry into the church because it was a token to them to which they were assured of adoption as the people and household of God, and they in turn professed to enlist in God's service. In like manner, we are also consecrated to God through baptism, to be reckoned as his people, and in turn we swear fealty to him. By this it appears incontrovertible that baptism has taken the place of circumcision to fulfill the same office among us.

Quoted in Larry Silver and Shelley Perlove, "Rembrandt's Protestant Joseph," in *Joseph of Nazareth through the Centuries*, ed. Joseph F. Chorpenning, OSFS (Philadelphia: St. Joseph's University Press, 2011), 185.

3. The *sandak* was the man who was given the honor of holding the male child during the circumcision. He served as a sort of

godfather for the boy and was thought to have a special spiritual bond with the child. *Rembrandt's Faith*, 196 and 417n126.

4. The only qualification for the mohel, the individual who carries out a circumcision, is that he be a Jewish male. Rembrandt's mohel is left-handed, a feature that could be the result of the reversal that occurs when printing from a plate, or, possibly, a compositional stratagem to make the operating hand visible to the viewer, given the figure's position in the grouping.

5. Virgil Solis, woodcut, *Circumcision*, from a *Passional* published by Valentin Geissler in Nuremberg, 1552 (HG 2.49 [Book illustrations]); and Adriaen Colleart after Johannes Stradanus, engraving, from the series *Beatae Virginis Mariae*, 1585–95 (NHD 195 [Johannes Stradanus]).

6. See, for example, Albrecht Dürer, woodcut, *The Circumcision*, from his *Life of the Virgin*, c. 1505 (TIB, woodcuts, 88); Albrecht Altdorfer, woodcut, *Circumcision*, from his series *The Fall and Redemption of Man*, c. 1513 (HG, woodcuts, 11); Wolfgang Huber, woodcut, *Circumcision*, 1515–30 (HG 3); Hans Schäufelein (1500–1540), woodcut, *Circumcision* (HG, woodcuts, 10); Virgil Solis, woodcut, *Circumcision*, from the *Passional* published by Valentin Geissler in Nuremberg, 1552 (as in note 5 above); Hendrick Golztius, engraving, *Circumcision*, one of the "masterpieces" from his *Early Life of the Virgin*, 1594 (NHD 11) (Rosenberg, "Rembrandt's Religious Prints," fig. 2); and Adriaen Collaert after Johannes Stradanus, engraving, from the series *Beatae Virginis Mariae*, 1585–95 (as in note 5 above).

During the time of Second Temple, an infant's circumcision would have been performed in the home, not in a temple. Furthermore, Romeyn de Hooghe's drawing of a circumcision from 1668 shows the ritual taking place in a domestic setting. William H. Wilson, "'The Circumcision,' A Drawing by Romeyn de Hooghe," *Master Drawings* 13, no. 3 (Autumn 1975): pls. 22–23. I am grateful to Prof. Eva Frojmovic for drawing this article to my attention.

However, according to Johann Buxtorf in the seventeenth century the ritual could be performed in "the Synagogue, or the common School, or in some private Conclave." Johann Buxtorf, *The Jewish Synagogue, or, An Historical Narration of the State of the Jewes, at This Day Dispersed over the Face of the Whole Earth . . . / Translated out of the Learned Buxtorfius . . . by A.B., M.A. of Q. Col. in Oxford* (London, 1663), 46. Cf. also the discussion of Rembrandt's 1654 etching of *Circumcision in the Stable*, below (B. 47, 1654, cat. no. 24).

7. This is one of a number of etchings in which Rembrandt included spectators—behind a wall or fence, or on a balcony, or peering out of a window. See the discussion of Rembrandt's subsidiary observers in Rosenberg, "Rembrandt's Religious Prints."

8. Stairways and/or a barrel-vaulted passageway appear in other later Rembrandt etchings set in or near the Temple in Jerusalem, as well. See, for example, *Circumcision: Small Plate* (B. 48, 1630, cat. no. 23) and *Presentation in the Temple with the Angel: Small Plate* (B. 51, 1630, cat. no. 25).

9. See, for example, Israhel van Meckenem's *Presentation in the Temple* from the *Life of the Virgin* of 1490–1500, where the circumcision is represented in the background (HG 57).

10. Circa 1620, Musée royaux des Beaux-Arts de Belgique, Brussels.

11. Roelof van Straten, *Young Rembrandt. The Leiden Years, 1606–1632* (Leiden: Foleor, 2005), 37. Van Straten attributes the *Circumcision* to Jan Lievens.

12. Rembrandt may also have been inspired by Goltzius's *Circumcision* (as in n. 6 above). Goltzius's print was one of six dedicated to the early life of the Virgin that became known as "The Masterpieces," not only because of their quality, but also because of their relationship to the work of master printmakers Lucas van Leyden and Albrecht Dürer. Goltzius's prints, which were well known and widely collected, elicited an unusual measure of attention from Karel van Mander in his 1604 *Schilder-boek* (Book of painters), and it may have been because of the print's fame that Rembrandt turned to the Goltzius *Circumcision* as a model. On Goltzius as a printmaker, see *Hendrik Goltzius (1558–1617): Drawings, Prints and Paintings*, exh. cat. (Zwolle, Netherlands: Waanders; Amsterdam: Rijksmuseum; New York: Metropolitan Museum of Art; Toledo, OH: Museum of Art, 2003), cat. 75.3.

Ludwig Münz (*Critical Catalogue*, vol. 2, cat. 187) suggested that an engraving of the circumcision by Johannes Sadeler I (HD 166) after a design by Maerten de Vos (1579–82) was a source for Rembrandt's print.

13. The misspelling may have been an error on the part of the publisher of the print, Jan Pietersz. Berendrecht, who may have added Rembrandt's name to the plate after the artist consigned it to him.

14. Gersaint, cat. 48 (cited in White and Boon, 165).

15. Woldemar von Seidlitz, *Kritisches Verzeichnis der Radierungen Rembrandts* (Leipzig: E. A. Seeman, 1895), cat. 398.

16. Hind, cat. 388, "The authenticity of this execrable plate, manifestly a work by the same calligraphic hand as the *Rest on the Flight* (307), has been recently defended by Dr. Jan Six. . . . The gulf between these meaningless scrawls and authentic early work of the larger and rougher type . . . is, in my opinion, too great to justify the acceptance of Gersaint's tradition."

17. Leonard Slatkes, "Review of C. White and K. Boon, *Rembrandt's Etchings*, and C. White, *Rembrandt as an Etcher*," *Art Quarterly* 36 (1973): 252–53.

18. Roelof van Straten, "Rembrandt's 'Earliest Prints' Reconsidered," *Artibus et historiae* 23, no. 45 (2002): 167–77. Holm Bevers, "Rembrandt as an Etcher," in Bevers, Peter Schatborn, and Barbara Welzel, *Rembrandt: The Master and His Workshop*, vol. 2, *Drawings and Etchings*, exh. cat. (New Haven, CT: Yale University Press, 1991), 161, seems to take a neutral stance in the matter, stating that while the print is usually categorized as a Rembrandt, "its authenticity is by no means certain."

19. *Critical Catalogue*, vol. 2, cat. 187.

20. White and Boon, S. 398, "Prints not mentioned by Bartsch," "Rejected by Hind and all earlier cataloguers, except for Gersaint, but now generally accepted as the work of Rembrandt."

21. Ger Luijten, "Rembrandt the Printmaker: The Shaping of an Oeuvre," in Erik Hinterding, Ger Luijten, and Martin Royalton-Kisch, *Rembrandt the Printmaker*, exh. cat. (Chicago and London: Fitzroy Dearborn Publishers, 2000), 13.

22. Thomas Rassieur in *Rembrandt's Journey*, cat. 7, 70–72.

23. *Rembrandt's Faith*, 188–91.

24. HD 9.

25. Ed de Heer has suggested that Rembrandt's "free and open etching style" may have been influenced by the work of Willem Buytewech and Moses van Uyttenbroeck or the Italian artist Antonio Tempesta. Ed de Heer, "The Circumcision," cat. 40, in Ernst van de Wetering, Bernhard Schnackenburg, and Ed de Heer, *The Mystery of the Young Rembrandt*, exh. cat. (Kassel, Germany: Staatliche Museen; Amsterdam: Rembrandthuis; Wolfratshausen, Germany: Edition Minerva, 2001), 250. Rembrandt may have been familiar with Buytewech's work because Berendrecht published works by both artists. See below in this entry.

26. The other two prints that include the publisher's name are *Descent from the Cross: The Second Plate* (B. 81 II, state III, cat. no. 55), published by Hendrik Uylenburgh; and *The Three Crosses* (B. 78, state V, cat. no. 54), published posthumously by Frans Carelse.

27. For Berendrecht's activity as a printer, see Elizabeth Wyckoff, "Innovation and Popularization: Printmaking and Print Publishing in Haarlem during the 1620s," PhD diss., Columbia University, New York, 1998, 139–91. Roelof van Straten, who doubts Rembrandt authorship of this print, noted that since Berendrecht lived in Haarlem in the 1620s but also sold prints in The Hague, the publisher would have passed through Leiden on his travels and quite possibly could have met Lievens and Rembrandt and directly solicited prints from the two young artists. Van Straten, *Young Rembrandt*, 293–94. See also the discussion in Rosenberg, "Rembrandt's Religious Prints."

28. On Jan Lievens's activity as a printmaker, see Stephanie S. Dickey, "Lievens and Printmaking," in Arthur Wheelock Jr., *Jan Lievens: A Dutch Master Rediscovered* (London and New Haven, CT: Yale University Press; Washington, DC: National Gallery of Art, 2008), 54–67.

29. Buytewech's *Holy Family* of about 1615 (HD 5) exists in two states. The first state was printed without the artist's or publisher's name. In the second state, Buytewech's monogram appears in one corner and Berendrecht's name in the other. This is similar to the difference between the first and second states of Rembrandt's *Circumcision*. On Buytewech's activities as an etcher, see Egbert Haverkamp-Begemann, "The Etchings of Willem Buytewech," in Carl Zigrosser, *Prints* (New York: Holt, Rinehart, and Winston, 1962), 55–81.

30. There are two other possible connections among these men: Constantijn Huygens, the stadtholder's secretary, who resided in The Hague, was certainly familiar with the art of both Rembrandt and Lievens by 1629. He may have known Berendrecht, who rented space in 1623 in the Binnenhof in The Hague during the annual kermis market. In addition, Petrus Scriverius, one of Rembrandt's patrons, resided in Leiden, but also had ties to Haarlem and The Hague. Wyckoff, "Innovation and Popularization," 158.

31. Hinterding, *Copperplates*, 13n33, citing a discovery by Theo Laurentius.

32. Both the *Presentation in the Temple with the Angel: Small Plate* (B. 51, cat. no. 25) and *Christ Disputing with the Doctors: Small*

Plate (B. 66, cat. no. 37) are signed and dated 1630. There is general agreement that *Circumcision: Small Plate* was completed a little later than *Christ Disputing with the Doctors.* Ludwig Münz (*Critical Catalogue,* vol. 2, 93, cat. no. 194) related the use of the burin in *Circumcision: Small Plate* to the slightly later *Raising of Lazarus: Larger Plate* (B. 73, cat. no. 46), and accordingly suggested a date of 1632–33. On the question of dating, see the discussion in Hinterding, *Lugt Catalogue,* 1:108–10.

Clifford Ackley suggested that the three small prints of similar dimensions constitute a series dedicated to the Childhood of Christ. *Rembrandt's Journey,* 102–3.

33. It is also possible that the infant's reaction is a reference to the pain that Jesus endured at the beginning of his life, as well as at the end, on behalf of mankind. On the import of Jesus's circumcision, see Calvin's remarks, quoted in note 1, above.

34. The architecture is reminiscent of the barrel-vaulted setting in Dürer's *Circumcision* from his woodcut *Life of the Virgin,* c. 1505 (TIB, woodcuts, 88).

35. *Rembrandt's Faith,* 192–94.

36. Perlove and Silver (*Rembrandt's Faith,* 95–96, and 190) suggested that this staff and the one in the 1626 *Circumcision* allude to the scepter of Judah (Genesis 49:10), which was prophesied to remain with the House of Judah until the ruler of all nations (the Messiah) would come to take it away.

37. *Rembrandt's Faith,* 193–94.

38. Perlove and Silver (*Rembrandt's Faith,* 192) identified the boy as a young Levite who was assisting at the Temple service. According to Johan Buxtorf, a number of youths accompanied and assisted the mohel during the ceremony. Two of these youths carried goblets of wine, one a basin of sand, and one a basin of balsam oil. Buxtorf, *The Jewish Synagogue,* 46.

39. Christian Tümpel pointed out that the change represented a closer reading of the biblical text specifying the injunction against women returning to the temple until forty days after giving birth. Tümpel, *Rembrandt legt,* cat. 46. He also noted a possible precedent for shifting the venue of the circumcision: an engraving by Anton Wierix that sets the scene in front of a cave (HD 136 [the Wierix Family]).

Arthur Wheelock Jr. suggested that the change was also meant to emphasize the "contrast between the humility of the Christian Messiah and the hieratic ceremony of the Jewish Law." Cited in Michael Zell, *Reframing Rembrandt: Jews and the Christian Image in Seventeenth-Century Amsterdam* (Berkeley: University of California Press, 2002), 131.

Rembrandt's increased familiarity with contemporary and historical Jewish customs may have resulted from his acquaintance with Rabbi Menasseh ben Israel and the philosemitic movement in Amsterdam during this period in his life. See the discussion of Rembrandt's illustrations for Menasseh's *Piedra Gloriosa,* published in 1655 (B. 36 A, C, and D, cat. nos. 8, 9, and 10).

40. In this image, Joseph has been accorded the honor of serving as *sandak,* perhaps in recognition of his role as Jesus's earthly mentor and protector. See note 3, above. Although representations of Joseph as the *sandak* are rare, Rembrandt's incorporation of this motif is not without precedent. See, for example, the engraving of the Circumcision set in an ecclesiatical space by Pieter van der Borcht II from an edition of the *Horae Beatissima Virginis Mariae ad usum Romanum,* printed in Antwerp in 1570 by Cristophe Plantin, British Museum inv. no. 1875,0710.104.

41. Christian Tümpel, *Rembrandt: Images and Metaphors* (London: Haus Books, 2006), 226.

42. As far as I have been able to determine, no one has commented on, or offered an explanation for, the presence of this net. I have been unable to find comparable nets in images of barn interiors in seventeenth-century Dutch and Flemish paintings and prints, be they religious or secular.

43. Frank Robinson, "Puns and Plays in Rembrandt's Etchings," *Print Collector's Newsletter* 11, no. 5 (November–December 1980): 166–67.

44. If this allusion to the wine and host of the Eucharist was intentional, it would probably have been subtle enough so as not to offend Protestant sensibilities. Rembrandt did not normally engage in this sort of "medieval" symbolism, but the beam and ladder certainly seem to fit into this more archaic tradition. *Virgin and Child with the Cat and the Snake* (B. 63, cat. no. 36), another of the etchings in the Childhood of Christ series of 1654, also exhibits this type of symbolism, and the same may be true of *Christ at Emmaus: Larger Plate* from the Passion/post-Passion series of the same date (B. 87, cat. no. 60).

25–26. Presentation in the Temple

25. Presentation in the Temple with the Angel: Small Plate

B. 51 (H. 18, Mz. 191, NHD 54)
Etching
Signed and dated in the plate: *RHL 1630*
State II of II
Sheet: 10.1 × 7.8 cm, trimmed to the plate mark
Collector's mark: front lower left corner,
George Hibbert (Lugt 2849)
Verso: in graphite, *D57/B51*; left bottom corner, *50*

Provenance:
George Hibbert (1757–1837)[1]
Helmut H. Rumbler Kunsthandlung,
Frankfurt-am-Main, Germany, 1976
Feddersen, Elkhart, IN, 1991
Snite Museum of Art
Acc. No.: 1991.025.024

The plate does not survive.

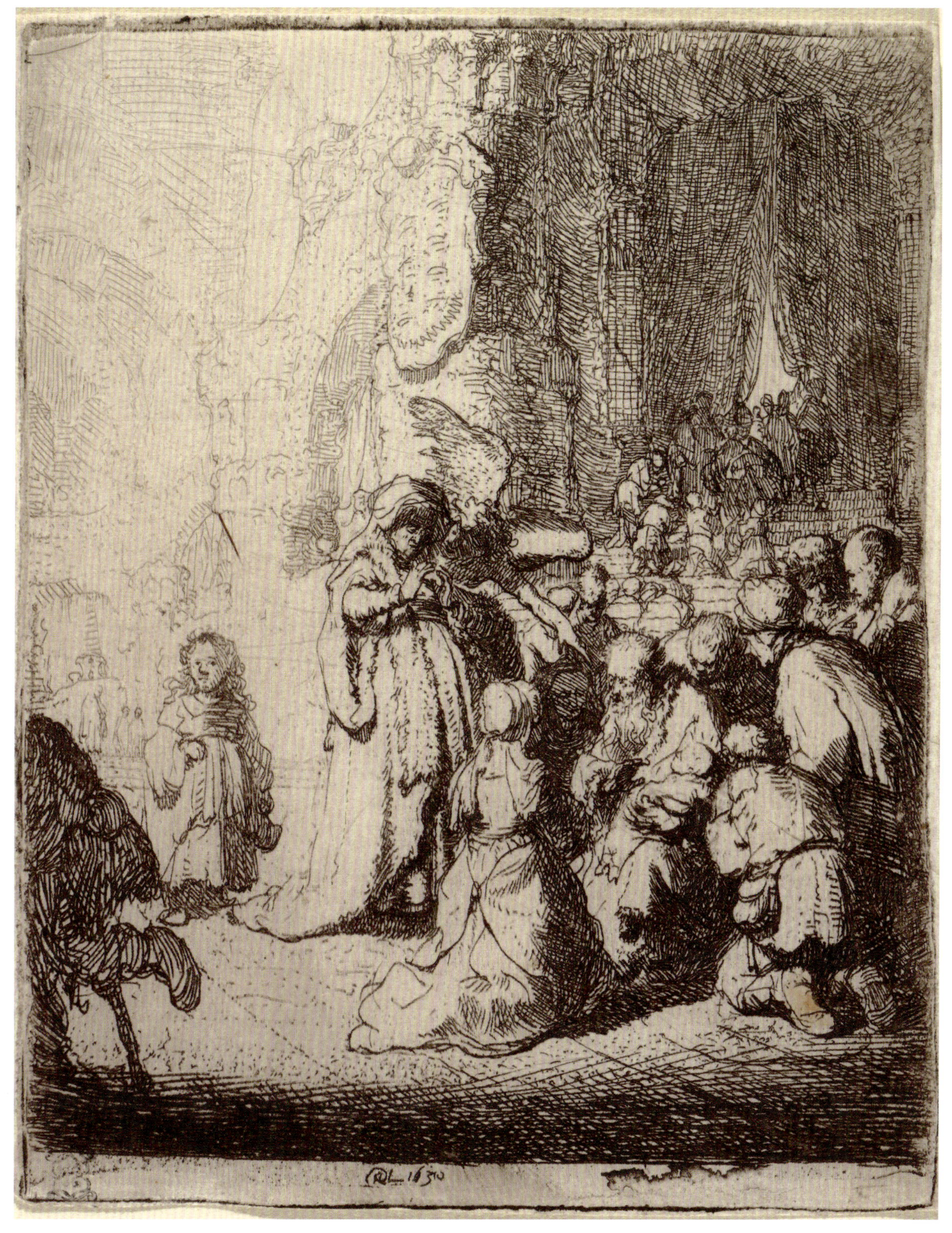

PLATE 25

26. Presentation in the Temple: Oblong Print

B. 49 (H. 162, Mz. 210, NHD 184)
Etching and drypoint
c. 1639–41
State undescribed of V
Sheet: 21.3 × 29.0 cm, trimmed to the plate mark
Verso: in graphite, *1603/ B49*; lower right corner, *74534*
Late impression

Provenance:
London Arts Gallery, London, 1971
Feddersen, Elkhart, IN, 1991
Snite Museum of Art
Acc. No.: 1991.025.023

Plate survives:
Museum het Rembrandthuis, Amsterdam.

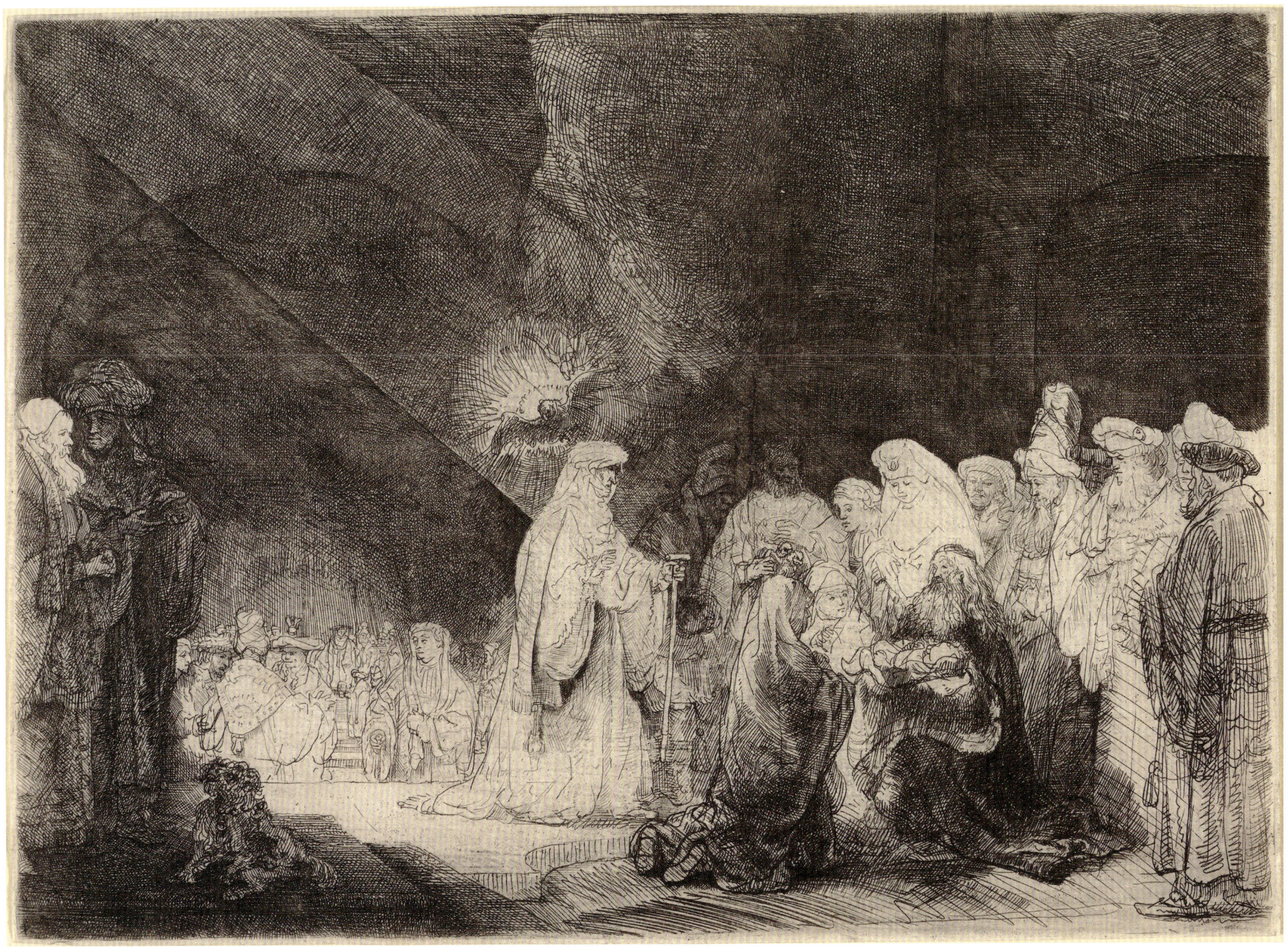

PLATE 26

According to the Gospel of Saint Luke,[2] after the Virgin had completed a period of purification following the birth of Jesus, she and Joseph brought their son to the Temple in Jerusalem to be presented there in accordance with Jewish law. They also brought an offering of two doves. On that same day, the Holy Ghost spoke to Simeon, a man who was "just and devout," and instructed him to go to the Temple, as well. God had previously informed Simeon that he would not die before he saw the Messiah. When Simeon encountered Mary, Joseph, and Jesus at the Temple, he recognized the infant's identity. He took the Holy Child in his arms and recited a hymn of praise to the Lord, saying that he could now die in peace, for he had seen God's salvation. Simeon then blessed the Holy Family and told Mary about her son's destiny and her future sorrow. At that moment, the prophetess Anna, an elderly widow who had spent all the days of her widowhood in prayer, fasting, and service within the Temple, came upon the group and, recognizing Christ, also bore witness to the coming of the Messiah. After these encounters with Simeon and Anna, the Holy Family completed the required rituals at the Temple and returned to their home in Nazareth.

Rembrandt depicted the Presentation in the Temple a number of times throughout the course of his career, in both paintings and prints. His earliest example, a painting from about 1627–28[3] (fig. 1), was created while he was still residing in Leiden. Only Mary, Joseph, Simeon, Anna, and the Christ Child are represented. Gathered together in an intimate group, they are placed relatively close to the picture plane, dominating the composition. The space behind these figures is defined by a fragmentary view of the Temple's architecture—a shadowy railing and the base of an enormous column with an extinguished lamp attached to it. Light from unseen mullioned windows illuminates the left side of the column and the back wall, leaving the right side of the space in deep shadow. The elderly Simeon, who has the traditional long beard of a biblical patriarch, kneels on the floor. As he cradles the Christ Child in the crook of his left arm, he addresses Mary, who kneels in pious solemnity before him. Joseph, seen from the back, in silhouette, also kneels in prayer. The aged prophetess Anna stands behind the Virgin and raises her arms in an expressive gesture of prayer and epiphany. Divine light appears to emanate from the infant Jesus, illuminating the figures before him. The child's luminous glow contrasts with the natural light from the windows and the darkness that pervades the hidden interior of the Temple.[4] In this painting, Rembrandt deviated from the traditional manner in which the Presentation had been represented in the fifteenth through seventeenth centuries. Artists such as Israhel van Meckenem,[5] Albrecht Dürer,[6] Tobias Stimmer,[7] and Johannes Wierix[8] created more overtly sacramental interpretations, typically including an altar in the composition and identifying Simeon as a priest. By paring the scene down to its barest minimum,[9] Rembrandt encouraged a more focused reflection on the notion of divine revelation and humble piety and, probably with his Dutch Calvinist clientele in mind, avoided the overt Eucharistic references that the juxtaposition of the infant Jesus (the body of Christ) with a priest and an altar might naturally evoke.

The Snite Museum's *Presentation in the Temple with the Angel: Small Plate* (B. 51, cat. no. 25), an etching from 1630, represents a significant expansion of the earlier, painted composition. This print is one of three etchings from the same period with approximately the same dimensions. The others are *Circumcision: Small Plate* (B. 48, c. 1630, cat. no. 23) and *Christ Disputing with the Doctors: Small Plate* (B. 66, 1630, cat. 37). In all three prints, the young Christ is shown within the confines of the Temple. Although not necessarily conceived of as a series, these etchings effectively map out the early steps of Jesus's spiritual maturation, from adherence to the laws of the Old Covenant (circumcision and the dedication of the firstborn to the Temple[10]), to the recognition of Jesus as the Messiah (Simeon and Anna), to his active assumption of his role as the Christ ("I must be about my Father's business," he explains to Mary and Joseph when they find him disputing with the scholars at the Temple).[11]

In the 1630 etching of the Presentation, Mary and Joseph are seen from behind as they kneel, facing the seated Simeon. The pouch that hangs from Joseph's belt is a reminder of the five shekels that, according to Jewish law, he was required to pay to redeem his firstborn son from the Temple.[12] The rough soles of his shoes and the patches on his clothing suggest the Holy Family's humble status. As in the painting of 1627–28, Simeon speaks directly to Mary. This time, he cradles the diminutive child in his left arm. An enigmatic female figure dressed in black and cloaked in shadow is just visible kneeling beside them. The aged Anna, dressed in a heavy cloak, her head covered by a hood with long fur lappets, looms large as she stands to one side of the central group. Her hands are tented in prayer as she gazes piously down at the Christ Child. Hovering in the air beside her is a winged angel who whispers in the prophetess's ear and points to the infant Jesus. This is an unprecedented motif, and one that confers an exceptional status on Anna, especially since no one else appears to be aware of the angel's presence.[13] A young girl holding a basket stands slightly behind the prophetess. The child pays no attention to the ceremony taking place nearby, but stares, instead, at a lame man who is leaving the scene, hobbling away with the help of his crutch. This crippled beggar, shrouded in shadow, is cut off at the left edge of the plate, which has prompted some observers to suggest that Rembrandt trimmed a larger plate on which he had included the full figure. Clifford Ackley proposed that this strange figure might foreshadow Christ's future ministry and his healing of the lame.[14] A small cluster of turbaned and bareheaded men press in around Simeon, trying to see the child in his arms, and some of them seem to be debating the significance of what they see and hear. These figures contrast sharply with the

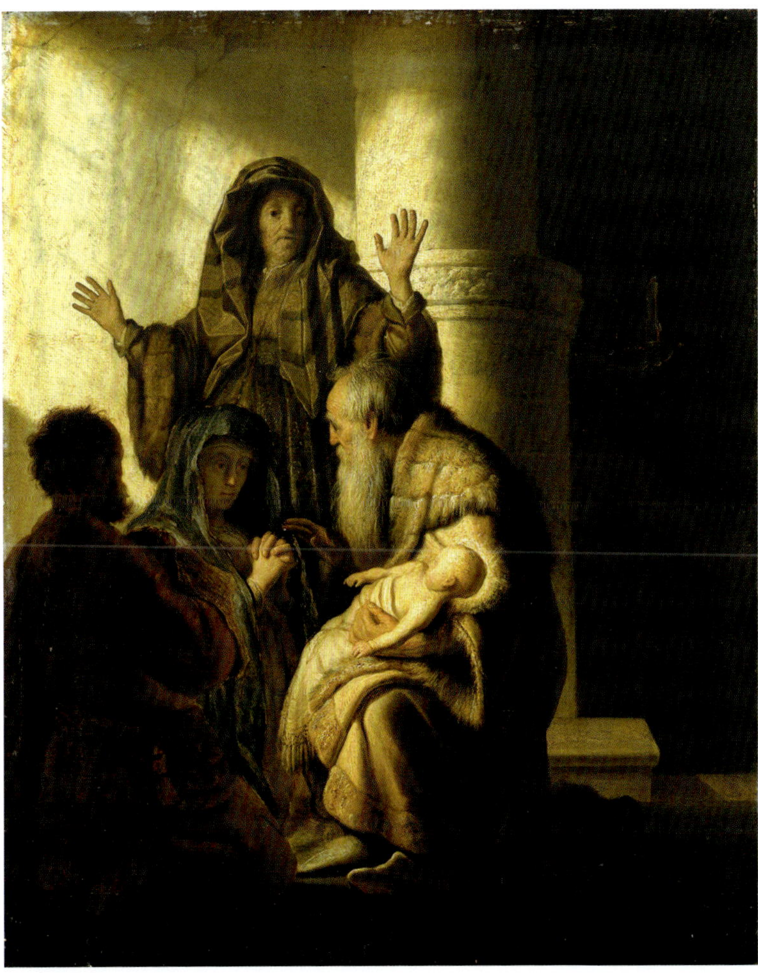

FIGURE 1. Rembrandt, *The Presentation in the Temple*, oil on panel, c. 1627–28. *Hamburger Kunsthalle, Hamburg. Photo: Elke Walford/ Art Resource, New York.*

divinely inspired Anna, who knows with certainty what she is witnessing.

The background opens up into two very deep vistas divided by a massive column adorned with an ornate shield, a sign of the Temple's wealth.[15] The column and the large, standing figure of Anna create a strong vertical axis near the center of the print, dividing the light and dark areas. The space at the left, a virtually empty chamber framed by soaring vaults and arcuated galleries partially open to the sky, is filled with an almost blinding light that washes out the articulation of individual components of the room. The shadowy space at the right, equally monumental, is peopled with numerous figures on a massive flight of stairs that rises up toward a chamber at the top. The immense black curtains that conceal the entrance

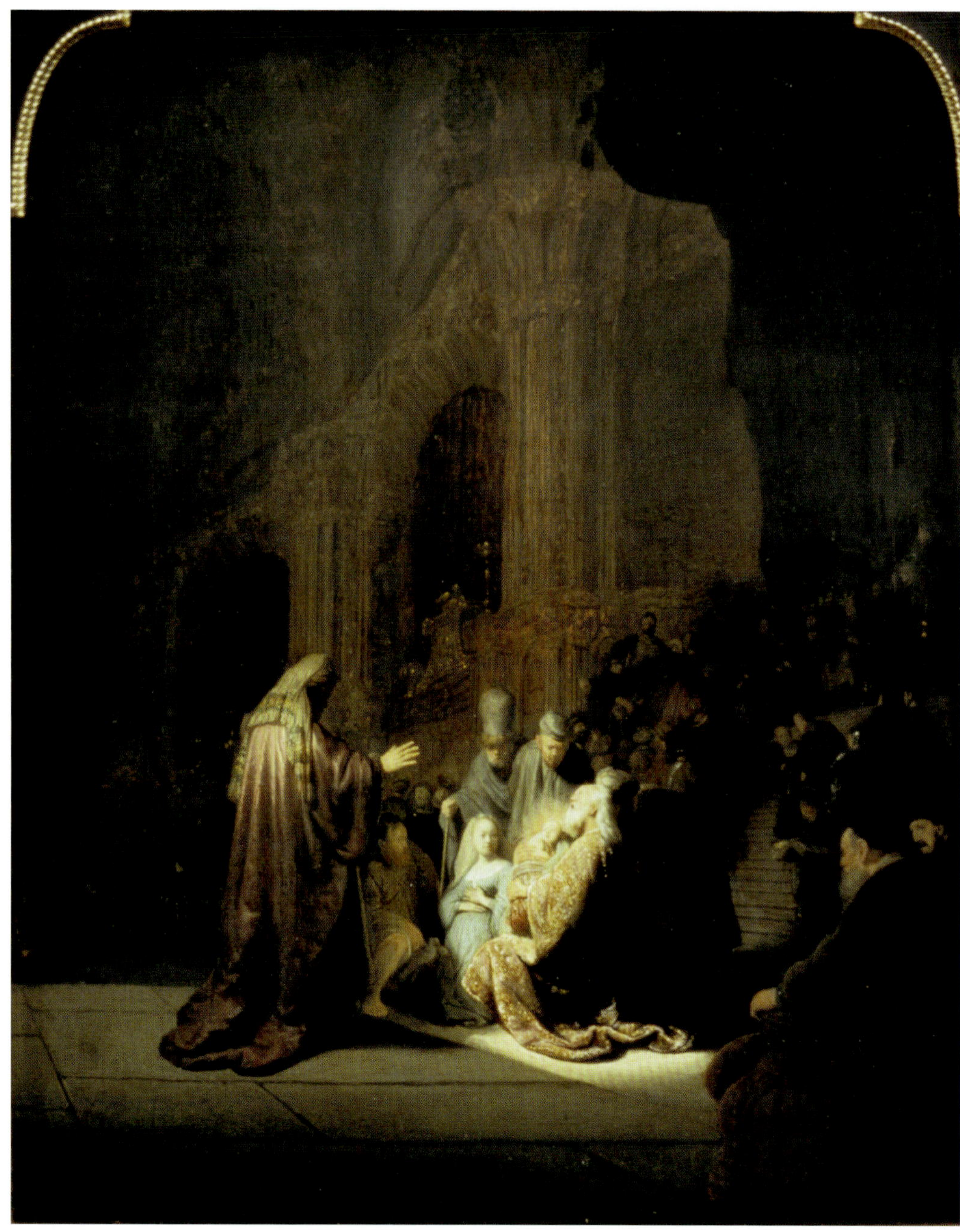

FIGURE 2. Rembrandt, *Presentation in the Temple*, oil on panel, 1631. *Mauritshuis, The Hague. Photo: Kavaler/Art Resource, New York.*

to the upper chamber have been parted just a bit. These curtains, one of the many "veils" that covered the gates and doorways of the Temple,[16] may allude specifically to the veil that closed off the Holy of Holies, a space that is now symbolically opened by the Incarnation. According to scripture, it was only when Christ was sacrificed upon the cross that the curtains would be fully opened so that believers could see the "spiritual mysteries of the Gospel."[17] A few worshippers kneel on the steps at the top of the stairway leading up to the curtains, and a corpulent priest wearing massive robes and a high turban is seated above them. He is flanked by one priest who stands nearby and other priests and elders making their way up to the sanctuary.[18] Some of them wear tall turbans, and others wear head coverings that evoke the miters worn by the Catholic priests of Rembrandt's time.

The etching's juxtaposition of the Holy Family, Simeon, and Anna in the foreground, with the priests and worshippers in the background, draws a clear distinction between the Holy Spirit's divine revelation to a pious man and an ancient woman and the elaborate rituals of the Temple priesthood. It is a distinction that is consistent with Calvin's commentary on Luke 2:36. In his remarks, Calvin drew particular attention to the fact that the Holy Spirit chose to reside in Simeon and Anna because of their piety and holiness, but not in the priests, scribes, and rulers who were surrounded by great splendor and dazzling—but meaningless—magnificence.[19] For the Calvinist viewer, Rembrandt's print would have been perceived as contrasting the truth of the new covenant with the elaborate rituals and laws of the old, as well as pitting the pious simplicity of the Reformed Church against what Calvin condemned as the pomp and "empty titles" of the Roman Catholic priesthood. Rembrandt's distinction between contemporary dress (the distracted young girl and the figures involved in the presentation ceremony) and his imagined "biblical" costumes also emphasizes the contrast between the New Covenant and the Old.

After creating the 1630 etching, Rembrandt returned to the theme of the Presentation almost immediately, painting another version of the encounter in 1631 (fig. 2).[20] As Perlove and Silver noted, this work represents a different moment in the story, the *Nunc Dimittis*, or Song of Simeon, in which the elderly seer praises God for allowing him to see the coming of the Messiah.[21] Illuminated by a symbolic ray of light, the kneeling Simeon, dressed in gold brocade, holds the Christ Child in his arms and gazes upward. His mouth is open as he addresses God directly. The Virgin, dressed in a light blue, belted tunic, kneels beside him, looking toward her son. Joseph, barefoot, squats beside her, holding the pair of doves mandated in Leviticus. Standing at the group's left, where she is seen from behind, Anna is once again a towering presence as she extends her arms in prayer or amazement. She is dressed in elaborate priestly robes and a high turban. Two elderly men dressed in drab, gray robes stand behind the Virgin. One looks down at Simeon and Jesus, while the other, wearing a high, bulbous hat and leaning on a slender stick, looks out toward Anna. Two bearded men, one elderly, and one younger, sit on a bench in the right foreground. The elderly Jew looks at Simeon and the Holy Family, while his companion turns toward him as if to comment on what they are witnessing.[22] A tall, ornate arcade made up of immense piers wrapped in slender colonettes serves as a backdrop for the scene. A broad staircase with figures standing on its steps can be seen in the right background. Although there are priestly figures at the top of the staircase as in the 1630 etching, the figures on the steps in the painting have turned to look down at Simeon and Anna, rather than at the priests, above. The main focus of the painting is a celebration of the moment of revelation that is represented not only through Simeon's expression and Anna's gesture, but also symbolically, by means of a shaft of light that illuminates them both literally and figuratively.

Rembrandt's next depiction of the Presentation and Simeon's song of praise was a second etching, *Presentation in the Temple: Oblong Print* (B. 49, cat. no. 26), an unsigned work usually dated to about 1640. This large etching, also in the Snite Museum's collection, reprises the theme of Simeon's address to the Virgin that had been the focus of the artist's first two representations of the subject. Simeon, dressed in dark robes and wearing a skullcap, kneels, holding Jesus out in front of him in both arms as if offering the child to Mary. The Virgin, kneeling in front of Simeon, is seen from behind. The manner in which the child is being presented to his mother evokes images of the Virgin receiving her crucified son's body at the foot of the cross, an association that imbues this image with a strong sense of pathos that is consonant with Simeon's prophecy of Christ's future tribulations and sacrifice and Mary's sorrows.[23] Joseph, his face obscured by shadow, holds two doves as he stands at Simeon's right. Other men, wearing exotic robes and high or flat

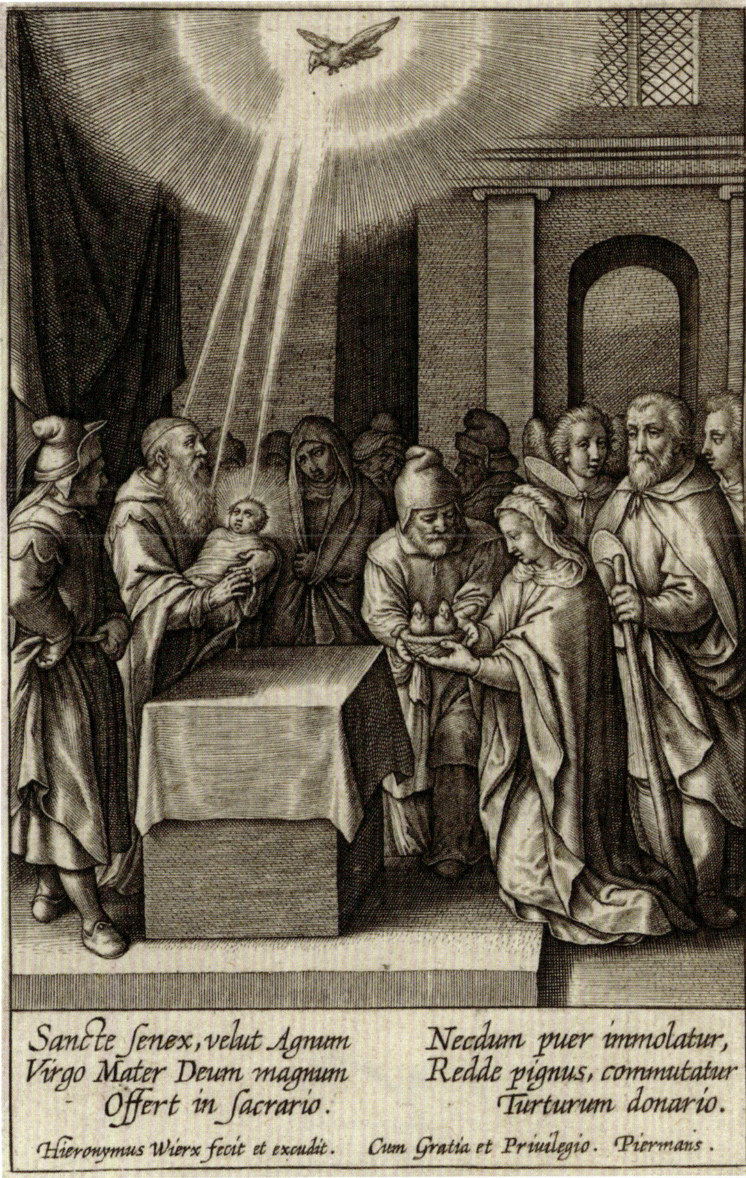

FIGURE 3. Hieronymus Wierix, *The Presentation of the Christ Child*, engraving, f. 1619. *Rijksmuseum, Amsterdam.*

Eastern turbans that reflect both imaginary and seventeenth-century Jewish attire,[24] stand close to Simeon and the Virgin, watching the seer and the child. At the left edge of this group is the tall figure of Anna, who is dressed in a long robe, turban, and striped prayer shawl, or *tallit*. She holds a walking stick in her raised left hand as she lifts her right hand in a gesture of astonishment or awe. Beams of light pour in from the upper left corner, falling on Anna

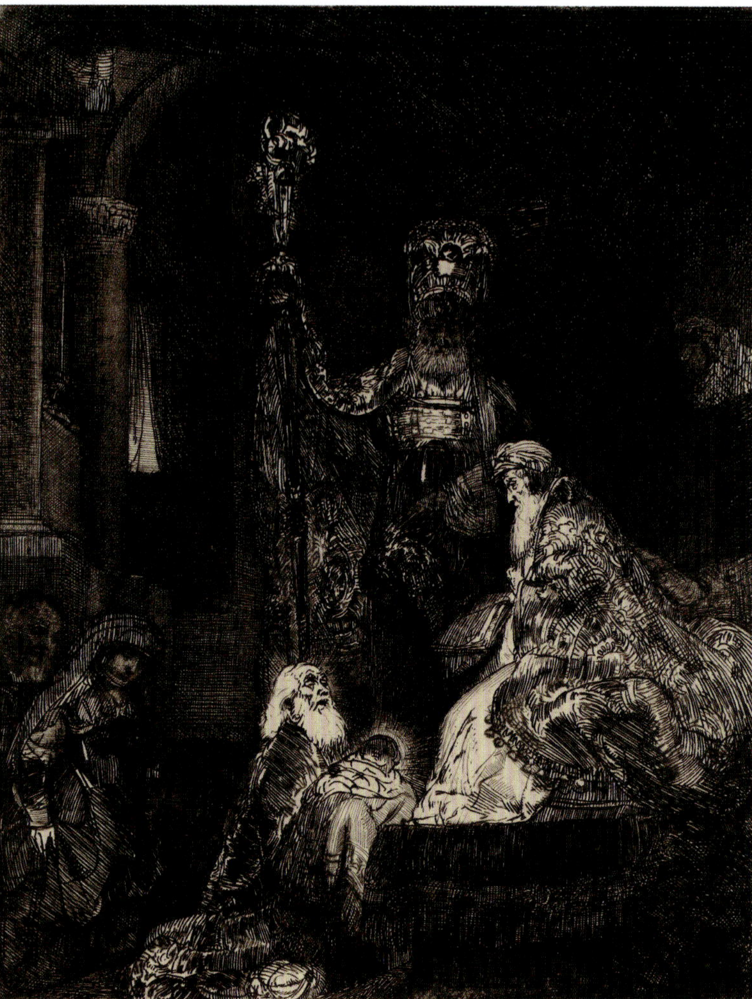

FIGURE 4. Rembrandt, *The Presentation in the Temple in the Dark Manner*, etching and drypoint, B. 50, c. 1654. *Photo: Courtesy of the National Gallery of Art, Washington, DC.*

and Simeon and the figures standing behind him, especially a tall woman with a high headdress. As in the smaller print (cat. no. 25), a woman kneels beside Mary and Simeon. The light that illuminates this woman must be reflected from the Holy Child, since her back is turned toward the shaft of heavenly rays. This kneeling woman, all in white, has replaced the kneeling woman in black in the 1630 etching, a figure that is almost obscured by shadow.

Hovering above the prophetess's head are two doves, one of which is very prominent and radiates light as a halo, and one of which is partially hidden behind the first dove's aura. This motif of two doves is without precedent. In an engraving of the Presentation by Hieronymus Wierix[25] (fig. 3) from a series dedicated to the Life of the Virgin, created at the end of the second decade of the seventeenth century, a single dove emits three distinct rays of light that are beamed down in laser-like fashion upon Simeon and the Christ Child. In that image, the dove's presence signals Simeon's and Jesus's sanctity and acts as an overt reference to Luke's statement that Simeon had been drawn to the Temple by the Holy Spirit.[26] Joseph and Mary, meanwhile, are offering two other doves to Simeon, at the altar. In Wierix's print, the sacrificial implications of the scene are made explicit by an accompanying inscription that states that the Virgin Mother offers the Lamb of God to the holy old man [Simeon] in the Temple, but "before the boy is sacrificed," a pledge is paid, and doves are presented to the high priest.[27] Although Rembrandt's print, like Wierix's, evokes Christ's future sacrifice, Wierix's engraving does not provide a precedent for Rembrandt's second airborne dove or for Anna's prominence in the etching. Perlove and Silver suggested that of Rembrandt's two doves, the dimmer one may represent the Old Testament, "the covenant of works rooted in God's goodness," and the brighter one may represent the New Covenant, the one that flows from "God's grace."[28] Unfortunately, since the authors do not elaborate on this interpretation of the two birds or why the doves are so obviously associated with Anna, the birds' presence remains a mystery.

In the far left foreground of Rembrandt's etching, the two Pharisees who had been seated discussing Simeon's song in the artist's 1631 painting reappear as standing figures at the far left. At their feet, one of the artist's ubiquitous dogs is busy scratching itself in a thoroughly indecorous way, exposing its genitals. Perlove and Silver suggested that the dog might allude to "carnal Israel," which is bound by the covenant of the flesh and not the spirit.[29] Whether or not it has symbolic import, the animal serves to distract the young boy[30] sandwiched between Anna and Joseph in much the same way that the departing beggar drew the attention of the young girl in the earlier Presentation print (cat. no. 25). The boy, peering around from behind the prophetess in order to watch the dog, is oblivious to the miraculous moment of revelation that is playing out before him.

Like the background in the 1630 etching, the space behind the foreground frieze of characters in the later print is split in two by a massive column. One side of the background is cast into darkness and the other is brightly lit.[31] On the right side, a low arch suggests a continuation of the space into a deeper plane but, because of the density of the shadows across and beneath the arch, the space appears flat and shallow. By contrast, on the left side, a second low arch opens into a sunken, well-lit cavernous chamber. Here, groups of Jews stand about conversing among themselves, unaware of, or uninterested in, what is transpiring nearby and, therefore, by implication, not yet enlightened. In the final analysis, the print's biblical source and the overall message of this etching are clear: the recognition of Jesus as the Messiah and the prophecy that he, along with his mother, will suffer for the salvation of mankind. However, a number of iconographical anomalies—the two doves in flight, the dog, and the use of light and shadow—render this work enigmatic.

Rembrandt created one final print of this subject in about 1654 (B. 50) (fig. 4) (not in the Snite Museum collection). This etching, which focuses on Simeon's song once again, draws an even greater distinction between the splendid, but ultimately empty, rituals of the Old Covenant and the simple piety of the elderly holy man. Simeon appears to be presenting the Christ Child directly to an imposing seated priest as the humble Joseph and Mary and a shadowy figure at the right look on. Behind this ensemble, a towering priestly figure with a large staff looks down at the ceremony from on high. These figures are set against a backdrop of Stygian darkness that invests the print with an aura of mystery appropriate to the miraculous revelation of God's living presence in the world of man.

Notes

1. This print was probably sold at an auction of Rembrandt prints from the collection of George Hibbert that took place on May 1, 1809, the thirteenth day of a fifteen-day sale. It was most likely either item 43 or 44 in the sale catalog. The first of these two impressions sold for eight shillings, and the second for one pound one shilling. Although the Duke of Buckingham and the dealer William Eisdaile purchased Rembrandt prints at the sale, the purchaser of the two items in question remains unknown. *Catalogue of a Superb Assemblage of Prints and Books of Prints, Formed by a Gentleman of Distinguished Taste and Judgment . . . Which Will Be Sold by Auction under the Direction of Mr. T. Philipe . . . Monday the 17th of April, 1809, and Fourteen following Days (Sundays Excepted),* (London: n.p., 1809), n.p., "13th Day [May 1, 1809]. Rembrandt. "43 One—the little Presentation, with the angel, *fine and rare* __ 51" [in left margin: "—8—," i.e., 8 shillings]. "44 One—DITTO—BRILLIANT __ 51" [in left margin: "1.1—," i.e., 1 pound 1 shilling]. Accessed August 9, 2013, http://gallica.bnf.fr/ark:/12148/bpt6k990277p/f116.image.r =Catalogue%20of%20a%20Superb%20Assemblage%20of %20Prints,%20formed%20by%20a%20Gentleman%20of %20Distinguished%20taste.langEN.

2. Luke 2:22–39. What Luke describes as the presentation of the Christ Child in the Temple may actually be a conflation of two different Old Testament rituals relating to the birth of a Jewish male child. The first, specified in Numbers 18:16, is the father's repurchase of his firstborn son from the Temple for five shekels, the *Pidyon Ha'ben,* thirty days after the child is born. The second ritual is a purification offering made by the mother as specified in Leviticus 12:1–8. A woman who gives birth to a male child is considered unclean for forty days. During that period, she may not enter the sanctuary nor touch anything that is holy. Once the forty days have passed, the new mother must make an offering to the priest of a lamb and a dove or, if she is unable to bring a lamb, then two doves, after which she may once again enter the sanctuary.

3. RRP, *Corpus,* A12, Kunsthalle, Hamburg. The painting, which was done in oil on panel, measures 55.4 × 23.7 cm.

4. It is conceivable that Rembrandt, always cognizant of the symbolic effects of light and shadow, meant to draw a contrast between the extinguished lamp in the Temple, which was the center of the Old Faith, and the radiance emanating from above (admitted by the windows) and from the Christ Child himself, the embodiment of the New Faith.

5. *Presentation in the Temple,* from a series of *The Life of the Virgin,* engraving, 1490–1500 (HG 57).

6. *Presentation in the Temple,* from *The Life of the Virgin,* woodcut, 1503–5 (TIB, woodcuts, 88).

7. *Presentation in the Temple,* woodcut, 1583, one of eleven illustrations for Peter Canisius, *Commentariorum de verbi dei Corruptelis Tomi duo,* Ingolstadt: David Sartorius, 1573 (HG 1076).

8. *Presentation in the Temple,* engraving, 1602–3 (HD 78 [the Wierix Family]).

9. At the very end of his life, Rembrandt returned to this theme in an even more succinct manner in a drawing in the *album amicorum* of Jacobus Heyblocq (1661, Ben. 1057, The Hague) and a painting of Simeon in the Temple (Bredius 600; Nationalmuseum, Stockholm) that was probably commissioned by Dirck van Cattenburgh around 1661 and that was left incomplete at the time of the artist's death. Walter Strauss and Marjon van der Meulen, eds. and trans., *The Rembrandt Documents* (New York: Abaris, 1979), doc. 1658/22, 426. In the tightly enframed, rough, pen-and-wash drawing, the Virgin and St. Joseph gaze down at Simeon, who is singing his canticle of praise, the *Nunc Dimittis*. Broadly drawn rays of light illuminate the trio. In the painting, Simeon is shown in half-length, with the Christ Child lying across his outstretched arms. Simeon's mouth is open as he praises the Lord. The prophetess Anna peers over his shoulder at the infant. These figures fill the canvas, and the background is essentially undefined. On the *Nunc Dimittis*, see *Rembrandt's Faith*, 197. On both the drawing and the painting, see ibid., 327–31.

10. See note 2.

11. Luke 2:49.

12. See note 2, regarding the ritual of the *Pidyon Ha'ben*.

13. Perlove and Silver (*Rembrandt's Faith*, 200) suggested that the appearance of the angel in this print, and the doves in the later oblong print of the Presentation (see the discussion of cat. no. 26 in the text, below), refer to the fulfillment of a prophecy in Malachi 3:1 concerning the coming of the Messiah. In their view, the angel alludes to the return of the gift of prophecy to the Temple, the *afflatus* or divine breath that had been present in the time of Solomon, but that was absent from the Herodian Temple until the incarnation.

14. *Rembrandt's Journey*, 63. Although it is possible that the crippled man was included in order to suggest Christ's future ministry, it seems odd that Rembrandt would have truncated a symbolic figure in that way. Perlove and Silver (*Rembrandt's Faith*, 205) suggested that the man is a leper who had come to the Temple to be purified, and that Rembrandt's image sets up an ironic juxtaposition of the leper, who is seeking to be purified by a false priesthood, and the Virgin, who is seeking purification in accordance with Old Testament law, although she actually has no need of it, given the virgin birth of her son. The identification of the figure as a leper is based on Perlove and Silver's assumption that Rembrandt's composition offered sufficient clues for a sophisticated viewer to identify the specific location of the encounter with Simeon in what would have been the Court of Women adjacent to the Nicanor Gate. The crippled man, then, would have been exiting from the nearby Lepers' Chamber, where ritual bathing occurred.

If, indeed, the site of Rembrandt's *Presentation* can be identified, this would demonstrate the artist's engagement with a broader seventeenth-century interest in the reconstruction of the Temple, a subject documented by Perlove and Silver (*Rembrandt's Faith*, 201–5) and manifest in the writings of John Lightfoot (*Descriptio Templiu Hierosolymitani Praesertium quale erat tempore Servatoris Nostris*, 1650), Rabbi Jehudah Leon (*Afbeeldinge van den Tempel Salomonis*, 1644), and Constantijn L'Empereur de Oppyck (*Maseket middot mittalmud bavli = hoc est, Talmudis Babylonici codex Middoth sive De Mensuris temple, unà cum versione Latina*, 1630). However, it is also clear that Rembrandt did not seek to create archaeologically exact settings for his religious dramas; rather, he projected an aura of historical authenticity by citing familiar aspects of the geography of the Holy Land, in general, and the plan and appearance of the Temple, in particular. See also the discussions of Rembrandt's settings in Rosenberg, "Rembrandt's Religious Prints," in this volume, and in the entry on *Peter and John Healing the Cripple at the Gate of the Temple* (B. 94, cat. no. 66), in this catalog.

15. A similar, almost contemporary, use of the escutcheon in Rembrandt's painting of *The Repentant Judas* (RRP, *Corpus*, A15, 1629, Mulgrave Castle, Yorkshire, England) is interpreted in this manner by Perlove and Silver (*Rembrandt's Faith*, 235).

16. Maimonides stated that there were thirteen veils hung over the Temple's gates or passageways. Cited in *Rembrandt's Faith*, 205.

17. Ibid., 205.

18. See also Rembrandt's 1635 etching of *Christ Driving the Money Changers from the Temple* (B. 69, cat. no. 43) for a similar representation of the priests on the steps of the Temple.

19. Calvin, *Commentary on a Harmony of the Evangelists, Matthew, Mark, and Luke*, 1:142, Commentary on Luke 2:36:

> *And there was Anna, a prophetess.* Luke mentions not more than two persons who received Christ; and this is intended to teach us, that whatever belongs to God, however small it may *be*, ought to be preferred by us to the whole world. The scribes and priests, no doubt, were then surrounded by great splendor; but, as the Spirit of God, whose *presence* was not at all enjoyed by those rulers, dwelt in *Simeon* and *Anna*, those

> two persons are entitled to greater reverence than an immense multitude of those whose pride is swelled by nothing but empty titles. For this reason, the historian mentions Anna's *age,* gives her the designation of *prophetess,* and, thirdly, bears a remarkable testimony to her piety, and to the holiness and chastity of her life. These are the qualities that justly give to men weight and estimation. And certainly none are led astray by the dazzling and empty magnificence of outward show, but those who are drawn, by the vanity of their own minds, to take pleasure in being deceived.

Accessed July 18, 2014, http://www.ccel.org/ccel/calvin/calcom31.pdf.

20. RRP, *Corpus,* A36, Mauritshius, The Hague. This painting, which is oil on panel, measures 60.9 × 47.8 cm.

21. *Rembrandt's Faith,* 205–7.

22. On Rembrandt's use of observers in his religious works, see Rosenberg, "Rembrandt's Religious Prints."

23. Perlove and Silver (*Rembrandt's Faith,* 216) also observed that the three women clustered around Simeon and Mary recall the three Marys at the Crucifixion and at Christ's sepulcher.

24. See *Rembrandt's Faith,* 214, regarding the costumes of the Jews in this print. Perlove and Silver suggested that Anna is wearing a *tallit,* or prayer shawl. Clifford Ackley (*Rembrandt's Journey,* 63) saw the garments of the Jews as less contemporary and more invented, in order "to evoke the ancient Near East of the Bible." This observation underscores the print's divergence from Rembrandt's 1630 etching. The women of the new covenant are no longer dressed in contemporary clothing, but are clothed in long robes and capes. Mary's simple garb differs markedly from the dress and bonnet in which she was pictured in the earlier etching.

25. HD 799 (the Wierix Family).

26. Luke 2:27: "And he came by the Spirit into the temple."

27. "Sancte senex, velut Agnum Virgo Mater Deum magnum offert in sacrario. Necdum puer immolator, redde pignis, commutatur turturum donario."

28. *Rembrandt's Faith,* 214.

29. Ibid., 213.

30. This young boy, who appears to be carrying a large, closed book (the Old Testament?) and who has a pouch hanging from his belt, may be Anna's servant or attendant. He, as well as the more prominently featured young girl carrying a basket in the 1630 etching (perhaps a different conception of an assistant for Anna), may represent the innocence of childhood, though the fact that the children ignore the history-making events nearby suggests that they may represent unawakened souls or even folly, instead. For another example of a distracted child in Rembrandt's etchings, see *Christ Preaching* (B. 67, 1657, cat. no. 41).

31. Rembrandt appears to have subverted some of the symbolic conventions of light and darkness here, since those in the left background, the unenlightened, are illuminated, while Simeon is garbed in dark robes (in the second state Rembrandt made the seer's robes even darker), Mary is in shadow, and Joseph's face is so dark that it almost melts into the murky chamber behind him. On the other hand, the two Pharisees at the far left exemplify traditional conventions of lighting: The face of the figure who pays attention to the holy ritual is illuminated, whereas that of his companion, who turns away to make a comment, is in darkness.

27–31. The Flight into Egypt

27. Flight into Egypt: Small Plate

B. 52 (H. 105, Mz. 195, NHD 117)
Etching
Signed and dated in the plate: *Rembrandt · inventor et fecit · 1633*
State IV of IV
Sheet: 9.2 × 6.4 cm, trimmed to the plate mark
Verso: in graphite, *74/57II/B52*

Provenance:
Theodore B. Donson Ltd., New York, NY, 1980
Feddersen, Elkhart, IN, 1991
Snite Museum of Art
Acc. No.: 1991.025.025

The plate does not survive.

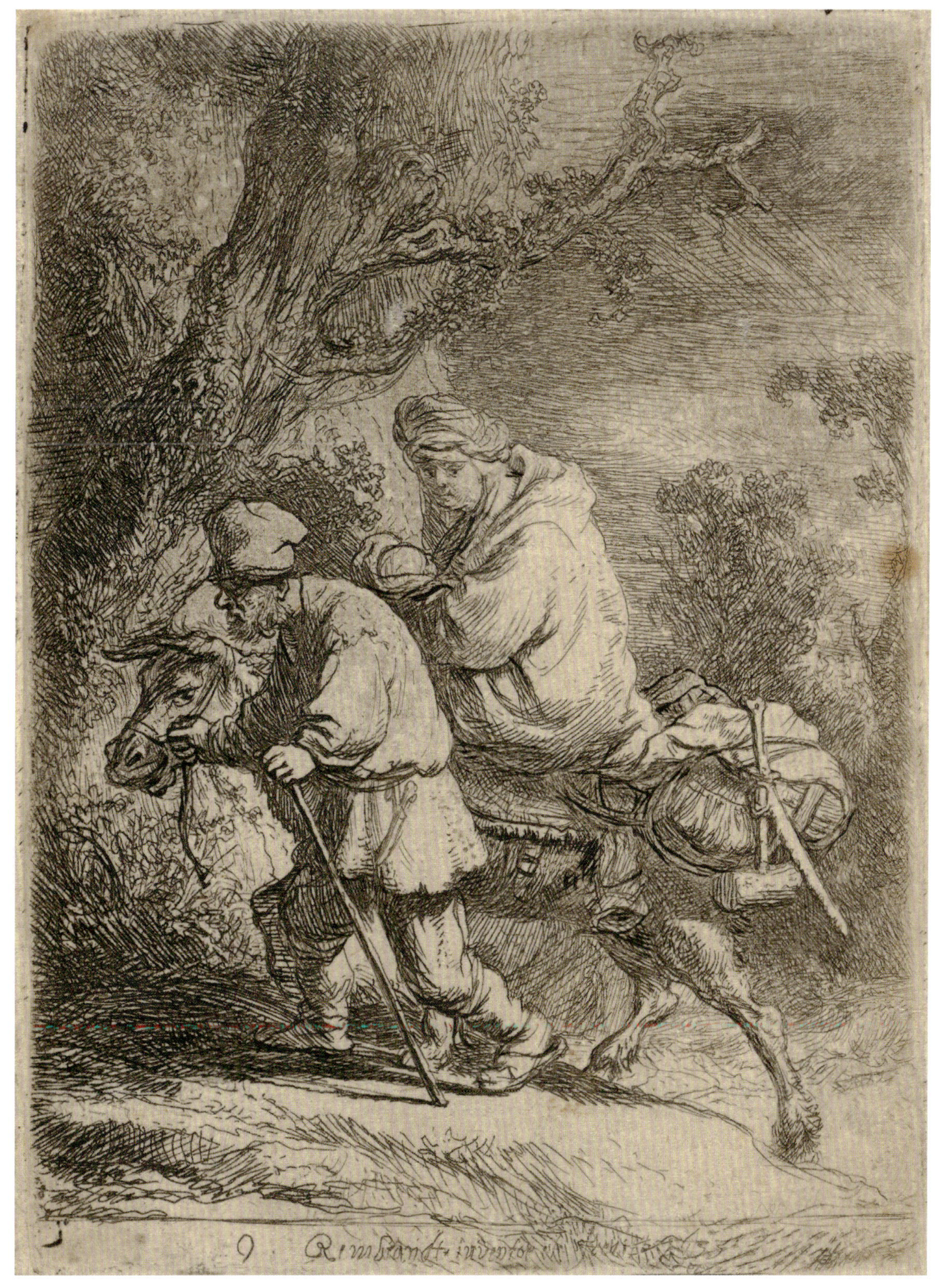

PLATE 27

28. *Flight into Egypt: A Night Piece*

B. 53 (H. 253, Mz. 221, NHD 262)
Etching and drypoint
Signed and dated in the plate: *Rembrandt f. 1651* ("6" is reversed)
State IV of X
Sheet: 12.7 × 11.0 cm, trimmed to the plate mark
Verso: in graphite, *8501018/121752.2/ 2L*

Provenance:
Kennedy Galleries Inc., New York, NY, 1976
Feddersen, Elkhart, IN, 1991
Snite Museum of Art
Acc. No.: 1991.025.026

Plate survives: Artemis Collection, London (1993).

29. *Flight into Egypt: A Night Piece (Basan)*

B. 53 (H. 253, Mz. 221, NHD 262)
State IX of X
Basan *recueil*—1385, c. 1810
Sheet: 13.2 × 11.2 cm; plate mark: 12.7 × 11.0 cm

Provenance: See cat. no. 28
Acc. No.: 1991.025.027

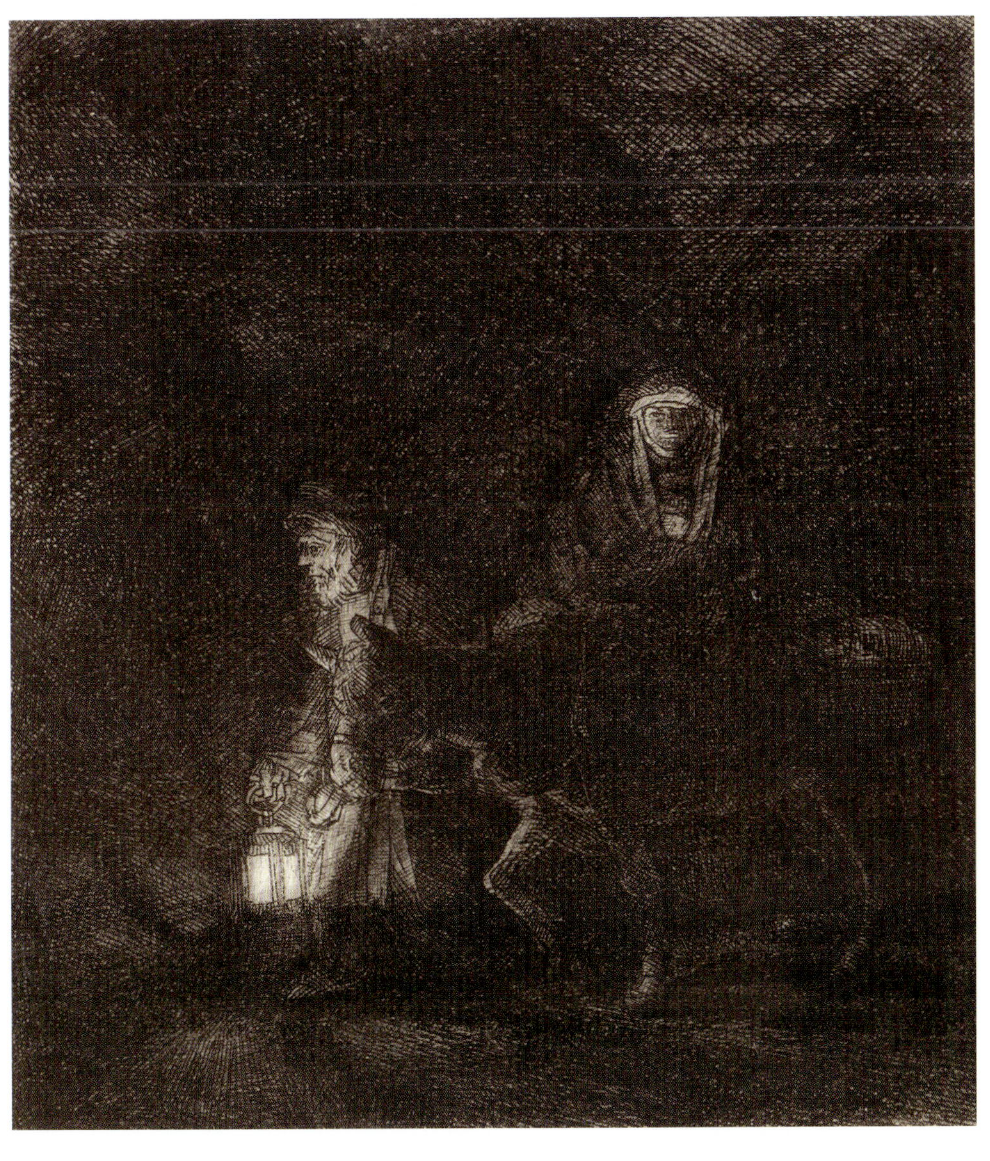

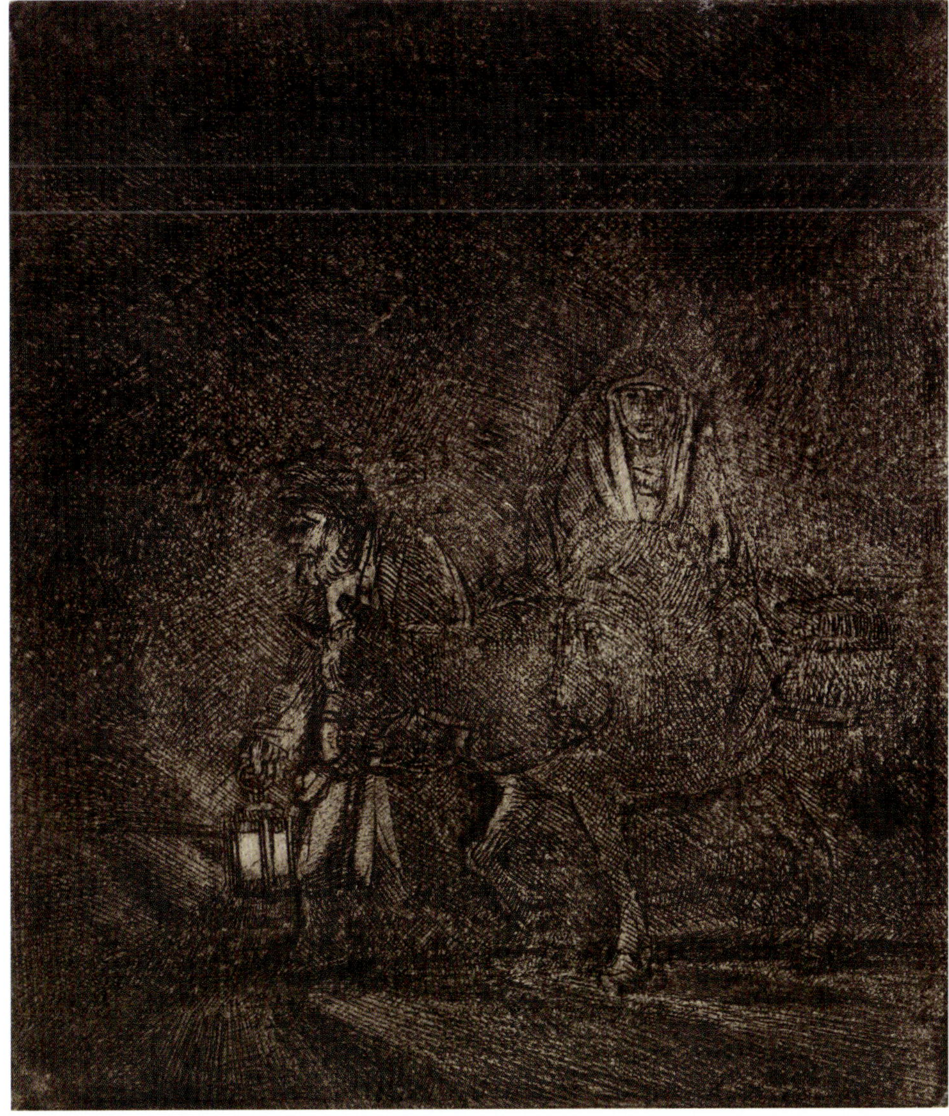

PLATE 28–29

30. *Flight into Egypt: Crossing a Brook*

B. 55 (H. 276, Mz. 228, NHD 277)
Etching, burin, and drypoint
Signed and dated in the plate: *Rembrandt f. 1654*
State I of I
Sheet: 9.3 × 14.4 cm, trimmed to the plate mark
Verso: in graphite, center, *B55*; lower right, *FEO* lower left, *A96843*

Provenance:
Sotheby Parke-Bernet, New York, NY, May 8, 1975, lot 553
Feddersen, Elkhart, IN, 1991
Snite Museum of Art
Acc. No.: 1991.025.028

Plate survives:
Private collection, Switzerland.

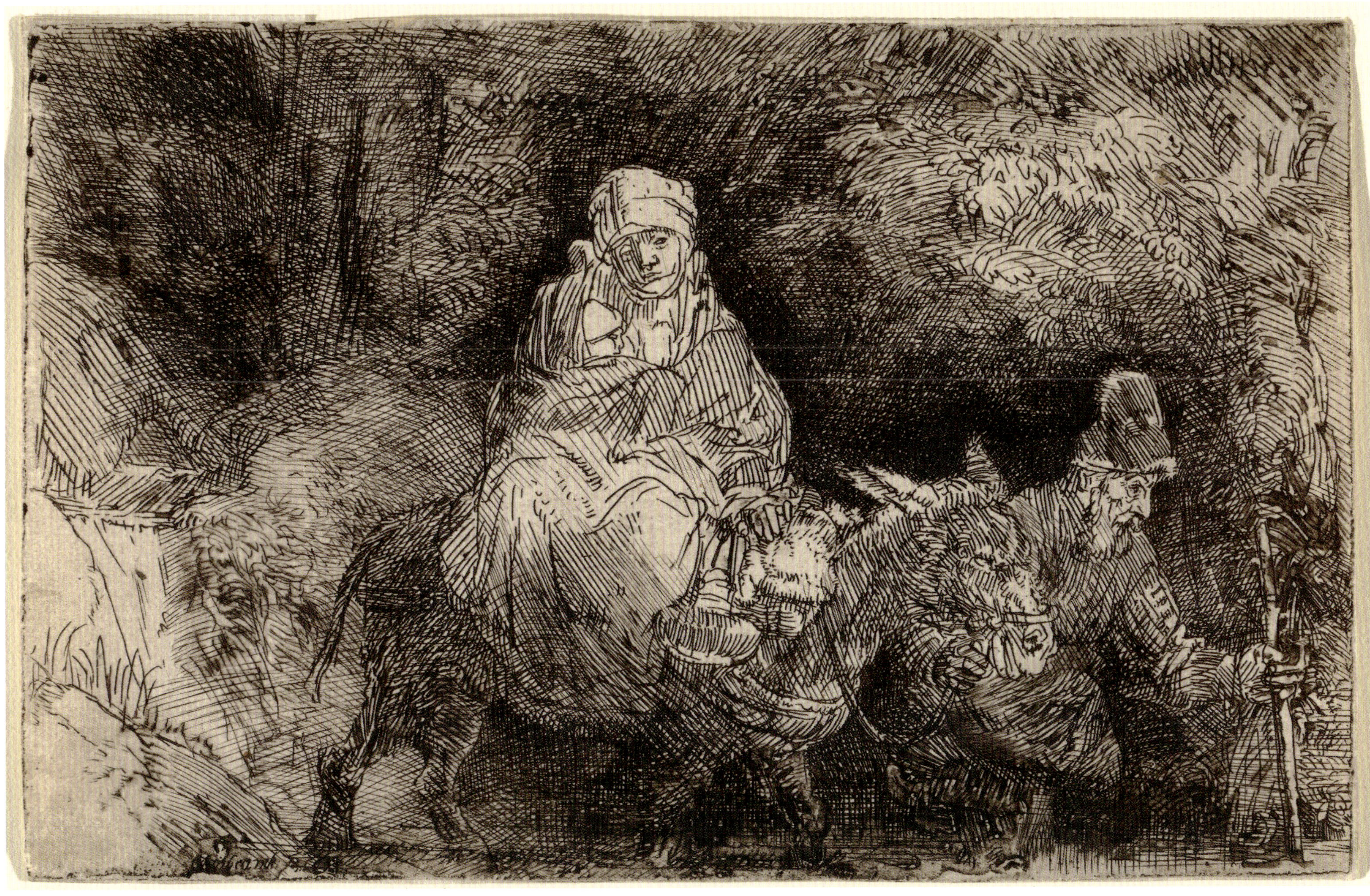

PLATE 30

31. Flight into Egypt: Altered from Seghers

B. 56 (H. 266, Mz. 216, NHD 271)
Etching, burin, and drypoint, reinforced with black ink
c. 1652
State V of VI (State I is by Hercules Seghers)
Sheet: 28.9 × 32.7 cm; plate mark: 21.2 × 28.4 cm
Watermark: Similar to Ash and Fletcher, IHS.A.a

Provenance:
Harrods, London, 1980 (Illustrated in Harrods catalog)
Feddersen, Elkhart, IN, 1991
Snite Museum of Art
Acc. No.: 1991.025.029

The plate does not survive.

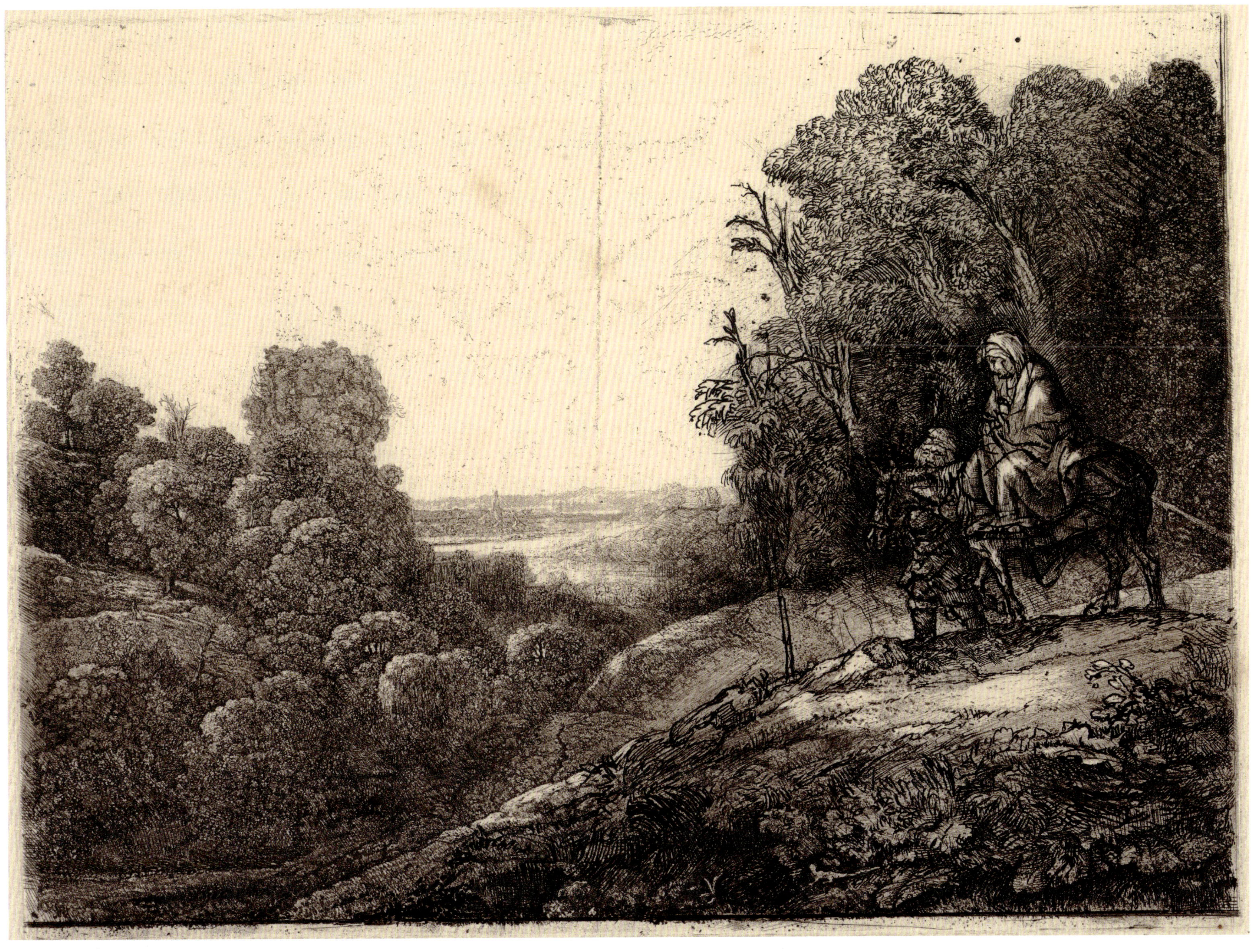

PLATE 31

The story of the Holy Family's flight into Egypt is related in a very brief passage in Matthew 2:12–14. After the Magi came to greet the newborn child in Bethlehem, an angel appeared to Joseph in a dream and warned him of Herod's plan to kill all male children of age two and under. When the angel urged Joseph to take his son and wife and flee to Egypt, Joseph took the dream to heart. Although it was the middle of the night, Joseph, Mary, and Jesus immediately left Bethlehem and set off for Egypt.

The Holy Family's flight to, and sojourn in, Egypt was seen as fulfilling the prophecy of Hosea (11:1) that they would abide there: "When Israel was a child I loved him, out of Egypt I called my son."[1] This journey was a popular subject in Renaissance and Baroque art. It was depicted in the Hours of the Virgin, often accompanying prayers for Vespers;[2] in series dedicated to the life of Christ, the life of the Virgin, and the sorrows of the Virgin;[3] and as stand-alone images.[4]

Rembrandt represented the Flight into Egypt at least five times. In all of these prints he followed the traditional mode of depicting the subject: the Virgin and Child are seated on a donkey, which Joseph is leading through a landscape. The first example (B. 54) (cat. nos. 22–24, fig. 2), a work that is not represented in the Snite Museum's Feddersen Collection, dates from around 1628 and was one of the artist's earliest etchings. As is typical of Rembrandt's first experiments in this medium, the composition and technique are rather awkward. The artist tried to translate the calligraphic qualities of a pen and ink drawing directly onto the plate, and the result was a lack of linear control and definition. The figures are crudely sketched; the lighting is indistinct, with shadows indicated in broad linear strokes; and the details of the landscape are barely described. The donkey bearing the Virgin ascends a shallow incline on the right of the composition as Mary, seen from the back as she rides sidesaddle, looks over her left shoulder, a pose that reveals her face to the viewer. The Virgin cradles the sleeping child in her arms. Joseph, seen from the rear as he walks off toward the left, leans on a walking stick while leading the donkey onward toward their destination.

In 1633, Rembrandt returned to the subject, executing a considerably smaller and much more artfully rendered print. This miniature version of The Flight (B. 52, cat. no. 27) is barely 3½ inches high, making it one the smallest of the artist's religious prints. It is signed and dated in the bottom margin, naming Rembrandt as both the inventor of the composition and the maker of the print. This is unusual, since Rembrandt typically included only his name or monogram on his plates, along with a date. As Ludwig Münz has pointed out, however, this was the period during which the artist was collaborating with printmaker Jan Georg van Vliet on a very large etching, *Descent from the Cross* (B. 81 II, cat. no. 55), a work that roughly reproduced the artist's painting of the same subject.[5] It may be because of this collaboration that Rembrandt was particularly sensitive about the often divided roles of designer and printmaker, and decided to employ a signature that left no doubt as to who was the sole author of the tiny print.[6]

In this small etching, as in the earlier example, Joseph leads a donkey bearing Mary and the infant Jesus up a slight incline toward a dense, dark wood. The donkey looks up toward his master in a quizzical fashion, as the grizzled, elderly carpenter, leaning on a slender walking stick and holding onto the onager's bridle, plods forward. Joseph's back and thin neck are bent, suggesting his weariness. Mary, wrapped in a voluminous cloak and wearing a turban, rides sidesaddle, with her body seen in profile. Her infant son, held in her left arm, is tucked into her cloak, and as she turns her head to look at him, she reveals a tender, maternal gaze. Behind her, on the donkey's rump, sits a large bundle, presumably the family's earthly goods, along with a carpenter's saw and mallet, the tools of Joseph's trade.[7] The landscape, which includes a gnarled tree, bushes, grasses, and weeds, is much more fully described than in Rembrandt's 1628 example, as is the time of day. As in the earlier print, light comes from the right, and Joseph and his walking stick cast sharp shadows on the ground. In the small print, however, the sky has darkened, and Rembrandt has filled the heavens with silver and black shadows spotted with small bubbles of starlight.

Around 1651, Rembrandt took up the story of the Flight once more, this time creating a true nocturne (B. 53, cat. no. 28). It has been suggested that in doing so, the artist was inspired by Hendrik Goudt's 1613 reproductive engraving of Adam Elsheimer's small oil painting on copper of this subject (fig. 1).[8] However, as Christopher White noted, whereas Goudt embedded his figures in an expansive landscape, Rembrandt focused solely on the Holy Family. Also, Goudt's Joseph walks beside the donkey's flank, rather than leading the way.[9] Rembrandt's nocturne progressed through a number of different stages as he worked on the plate. The shroud of night gradually closed in on the figures, until in the sixth and final state, shadow overwhelmed light.[10] In order to achieve an extraordinary level of blackness, Rembrandt not only employed etching, drypoint needle, and burin to create a dense web of hatching; he also left a prominent veil of ink on the plate. The only area that he wiped completely clean was the glowing lantern that Joseph holds as he leads the Holy Family through the enveloping darkness. The light from this lantern barely penetrates the night, selectively illuminating Joseph, the forward leg and the muzzle of the donkey, and, still more faintly, the cowled head and face of Mary. Each of the individual glass panes of Joseph's lantern sheds a fan of light upon the ground, while the metal frames that anchor the panes cast bars of shadow that form the image of a cross beneath Joseph's forward foot. The print is a dramatic example of the artist's tenebristic, nocturnal style.

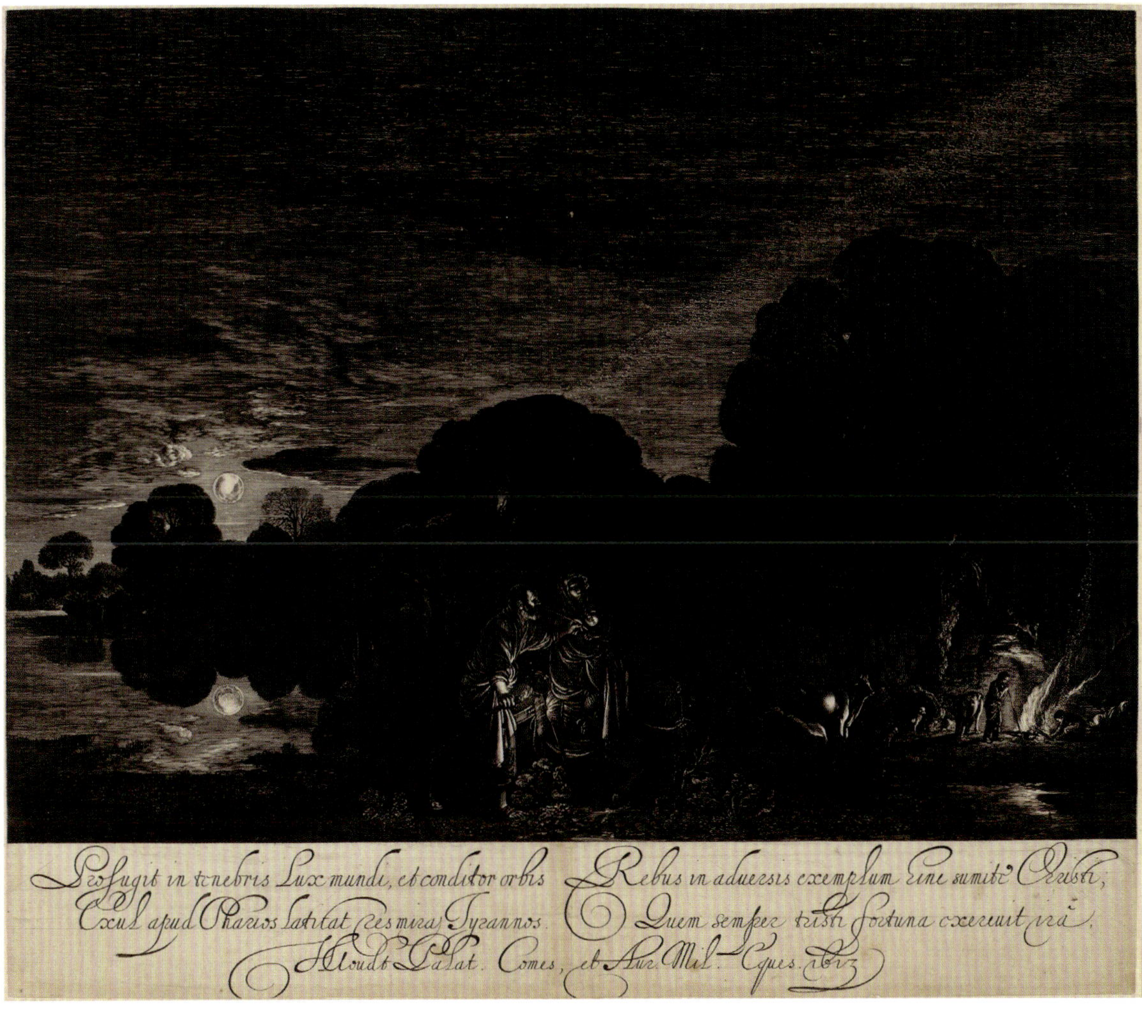

FIGURE 1. Hendrik Goudt after Adam Elsheimer, *Flight into Egypt*, engraving and etching, 1613. *Photo: Courtesy of the National Gallery of Art, Washington, DC.*

The Snite Museum also owns an impression of the Basan edition of this print, pulled from a Rembrandt plate that appears to have been heavily reworked. The history of Rembrandt's copper plates, of which eighty-one survive, has been traced by Erik Hinterding.[11] He reported that the fate of Rembrandt's plates is unclear until the eighteenth century, when a large number of them surfaced at the 1767 auction of the estate of print dealer Pieter de Haan. At least seventy-five plates, as well as numerous impressions, were sold at this auction. Fifty-six of these plates were purchased by

Amsterdam art dealer Pierre Fouquet on behalf of Claude-Henri Watelet, a Parisian writer, art critic, and engraver.[12] By the time he died, Watelet had accumulated eighty-one of Rembrandt's plates. All of these were eventually purchased by Pierre-François Basan, a Parisian print dealer and publisher who was known for producing albums of reproductive engravings after works by well-known European masters.[13] Between 1789 and 1797, Basan published a collection, or *recueil*, devoted to Rembrandt prints, utilizing the plates that he had purchased, and he commissioned reproductive copies of a handful of rarer examples. After the dealer's death, his son Henri-Louis Basan took up the project anew, reworking some of the plates and publishing his own *Recueil Rembrandt* around 1807. The "Basan" Snite example of the nocturnal Flight print exhibits a coarse reinforcement of the contours of the Holy Family and the donkey, as well as crude highlights and a uniform treatment of the background, indicating that this work probably resulted from a later reworking of Rembrandt's plate, possibly by Basan père or fils.

Around 1653, Rembrandt created another rendition of the Flight into Egypt (B. 56, cat. no. 31) by reworking a plate that had already been etched by Dutch painter and printmaker Hercules Seghers (1589/90–1633/38). This plate had originally borne an image of Tobias and the Angel in a landscape.[14] Seghers was one of the most inventive printmakers of his generation, creating what Samuel van Hoogstraten referred to as "printed-paintings,"[15] that is, etchings that were printed on canvas and finished with oils. Even in his more conventional prints, he experimented with colored inks and different types of paper. Seghers was also one of the first printmakers to customarily leave a veil of ink on the surface of his plates, making every impression that he printed unique. Rembrandt often used this technique during the second half of his career. The circumstances surrounding the artist's acquisition of Seghers's plate of Tobias and the Angel are unknown, as is Rembrandt's motivation for reworking another artist's plate. This appears to be the only time that he did so. There is no doubt, though, that he admired Seghers's work. At the time of his bankruptcy three years later, in 1656, an inventory of his possessions showed that Rembrandt owned eight of the artist's landscape paintings.[16]

In the process of converting Seghers's composition into a depiction of the Flight into Egypt, Rembrandt left much of the original landscape intact, although he did reduce the slope of the foreground hill and open up the view of a deep river valley at the center of composition. His most significant change, however, was burnishing out the relatively large figures of Tobias and the Angel Raphael and replacing them with the diminutive figures of Joseph, Mary, Jesus, and the donkey, all of which he rendered primarily in drypoint. Rembrandt also filled in some of the space with additional foliage above the Holy Family and at the lower right foreground. Curiously, traces of the original Seghers composition can still be discerned. For example, as numerous historians have noted, remnants of the angel's wings are visible in the upper right corner of the group of trees behind the Holy Family. Whether these vestiges were an intentional, tacit acknowledgment of the origins of the plate or merely a technical oversight is unknown. However, given the many different states and subtle changes that this plate underwent, it seems unlikely that the persistence of the shadowy wing and other remnants from Seghers's work was simply accidental.

Rembrandt's final representation of the Flight into Egypt (B. 55, cat. no. 30) was an etching that he made in 1654 as part of a group of prints dedicated to Christ's childhood.[17] This is the only version in which the family proceeds from left to right, rather than from right to left. In this final print dealing with the Flight into Egypt, the artist continued his investigation of nocturnal effects, although less dramatically than in the 1651 version (cat. no. 28). A halo of darkness surrounds the Holy Family as the figures move out of the shadowy depths of a dense forest, down a rocky slope, and across a brook. The broad triangular structure of the composition contributes to a sense of stately, slow-paced movement through the space. A very elderly Joseph, cut off at the lower margin of the plate, is up to his knees in the murky water. Despite his fatigue, he manages to plant his walking stick before him and persevere on his perilous journey through the night. The most prominent figures in this image are the Virgin and Child, placed at the center of the composition and gently bathed in moonlight, with Mary's brightly lit headdress defining the peak of the triangle formed by the central figures. Although her head is slightly inclined in the direction of the child resting in her right arm, beneath the folds of her copious cloak, Mary's melancholy face is visible as her sleepy eyes peer out toward the viewer. The intimacy and tenderness that pervade this etching are very much in harmony with the emotional tenor of the other prints in Rembrandt's 1654 childhood series.

Notes

1. See, for example, Calvin's commentary on Matthew 2:15 in his *Commentary on a Harmony of the Evangelists, Matthew, Mark, and Luke*, 1:145–46, accessed July 18, 2014, http://www.ccel.org/ccel/calvin/calcom31.pdf.

2. See, for example, Jean Pucelle, *Hours of Jeanne d'Evreux* (The Cloisters, Metropolitan Museum of Art, New York, acc. no. 54.1.2, f. 83r); Jacquemart de Hesdin, *Brussels Hours* (Bibliothèque Royale de Belgique, Brussels, ms. 11060, f. 106); Boucicaut Master, *Boucicaut Hours* (Musée Jacquemart-André, Paris, ms. 2, f. 90v); and the Limbourg Brothers, *Belles Heures* (The Cloisters, Metropolitan Museum of Art, New York, acc. no. 54.1.1 a,b, f. 63r).

3. See, for example, Albrecht Dürer's woodcut illustration from his *Life of the Virgin* of c. 1504 (TIB, woodcuts, 89); Anonymous *Sorrows of the Virgin* (British Museum, 1864,0514.262); Jacob Cornelisz. van Oostsanen, *Large Passion*, Brussels, 1513 (HD 40); Hans Sebald Beham, *Sorrows of the Virgin*, 1520–30 (HG 888β); and Jan Collaert II after Johannes Stradanus, in *Beatae Virginis Mariae*, published in Antwerp in 1585–95 (NHD 198 [Johannes Stradanus]). The theme also appears in the Netherlandish mid-fifteenth-century woodblock edition of the *Biblia Pauperum* now in the British Museum (1845,0809.6).

4. The story was a particularly popular subject for paintings, although not as popular as the Rest on the Flight. See, for example, Jacopo Bassano, *Flight into Egypt*, c. 1544–45, Norton Simon Museum, Los Angeles, CA.

5. Münz, *Critical Catalogue*, vol. 2, cat. 195.

6. The etching of the *Descent from the Cross: The Second Plate* is signed *Rembrandt f. 1633*.

7. The representation of carpenter's tools is unusual in this context, though not completely without precedent. See, for example, the illustration of *The Flight Into Egypt* by Jan Wierix after a design by Pieter van der Borcht in the 1571 edition of Benito Arias Montano, *Humanae Salutis Monumenta* (HD 11.A.79 [the Wierix Family, Book Illustrations]). In the Wierix print, a basket filled with carpenter's tools hangs from a long saw that Joseph rests on his right shoulder.

8. See, for example, Münz, *Critical Catalogue*, vol. 2, cat. 221.

9. Christopher White, *Rembrandt as an Etcher: A Study of the Artist at Work*, 2nd ed. (New Haven, CT: Yale University Press, 1999), 71–72.

10. This is clearly illustrated in White, *Rembrandt as an Etcher*, figs. 86–91. A similar process can be seen in the various states of Rembrandt's *Adoration of the Shepherds: A Night Piece* (B. 46, cat. no. 21), of about 1652.

11. Hinterding, *Copperplates*.

12. On Claude-Henri Watelet, see Jean de Cayeaux, "Watelet et Rembrandt," *Bulletin de la société de l'histoire de l'art français* (1965): 131–61.

13. On Pierre-François Basan and his sons Antoine-Simon-Ferdinand and Henri-Louis, see Pierre Casselle, "Pierre-François Basan, marchand d'estampes à Paris (1723–1797)," *Paris et Ile-de-France* 33 (1982): 99–185.

14. For information about Hercules Seghers as a printmaker, see Egbert Haverkamp-Begemann, K. G. Boon, and J. Verbeek, *Hercules Seghers, the Complete Etchings* (Amsterdam: Scheltema & Holkema, 1973). Seghers's print of *Tobias and the Angel* is known in only two impressions, both printed in greenish ink on white paper. This print was produced in the 1620s. It is reproduced in *Rembrandt's Journey*, fig. 114.

15. *Rembrandt's Journey*, 183.

16. Walter Strauss and Marjon van der Meulen, eds. and trans., *The Rembrandt Documents* (New York: Abaris, 1979), doc. 1656/12.

17. The other five prints that are part of the childhood series are the *Adoration of the Shepherds: With the Lamp* (B. 45, cat. no. 20), *Circumcision in the Stable* (B. 47, cat. no. 24), *Christ Seated Disputing with the Doctors* (B. 64, cat. no. 39), *Christ Returning from the Temple with His Parents* (B. 60, cat. no. 40), and *Virgin and Child with the Cat and the Snake* (B. 63, cat. no. 36).

32–33. The Rest on the Flight into Egypt

32. *Rest on the Flight into Egypt: A Night Piece*

B. 57 (H. 208, Mz. 337 [as Ferdinand Bol], NHD 216)
Etching and drypoint with heavy plate tone
c. 1644
State V of IX
Sheet: 9.4 × 6.1; plate mark: 9.2 × 5.9 cm
Verso: in graphite: *921*; collector's stamp, LL in a circle in red ink (Lugt 4796, Leslie E. Lancy), fragment of a stamp, script *D* (probably Richard Dawnay, 10th Viscount Downe, [Lugt 719a?])

Provenance:
Richard Dawnay, 10th Viscount Downe (1903–65) (?)
Sotheby's & Co.(?), London, November 26, 1970, lot 61[1]
Leslie E. Lancy, Ellwood City, PA (1911–96)
David Tunick Inc., New York, NY, 1977
Feddersen, Elkhart, IN, 1991
Snite Museum of Art
Acc. No: 1991.025.030

Plate survives, heavily reworked:
Private collection, the Netherlands.

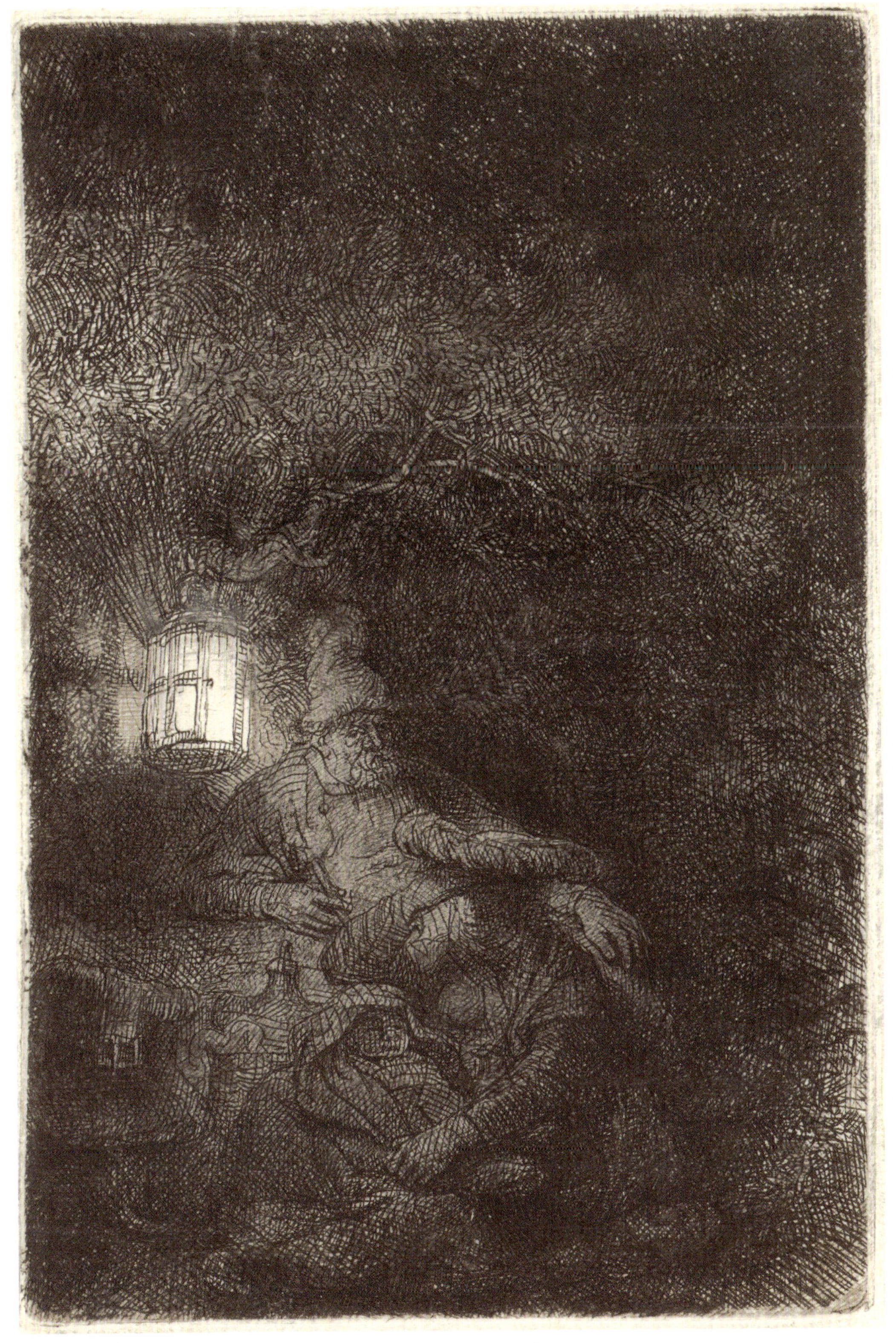

PLATE 32

33. *Rest on the Flight into Egypt: Lightly Etched*

B. 58 (H. 216, Mz. 219, NHD 227)
Etching and drypoint
Signed and dated in the plate: *Rembrandt f. 1645*
State I of I
Sheet: 13.0 × 11.5 cm, trimmed to the plate mark
Fragment of watermark: three balls
Verso: in graphite, *B58/ 49/ B58 only state/40/ C. 5316/ C. 40620*

Provenance:
P. & D. Colnaghi & Co. Ltd., London, 1976
Feddersen, Elkhart, IN, 1991
Snite Museum of Art
Acc. No.: 1991.025.031

The plate does not survive.

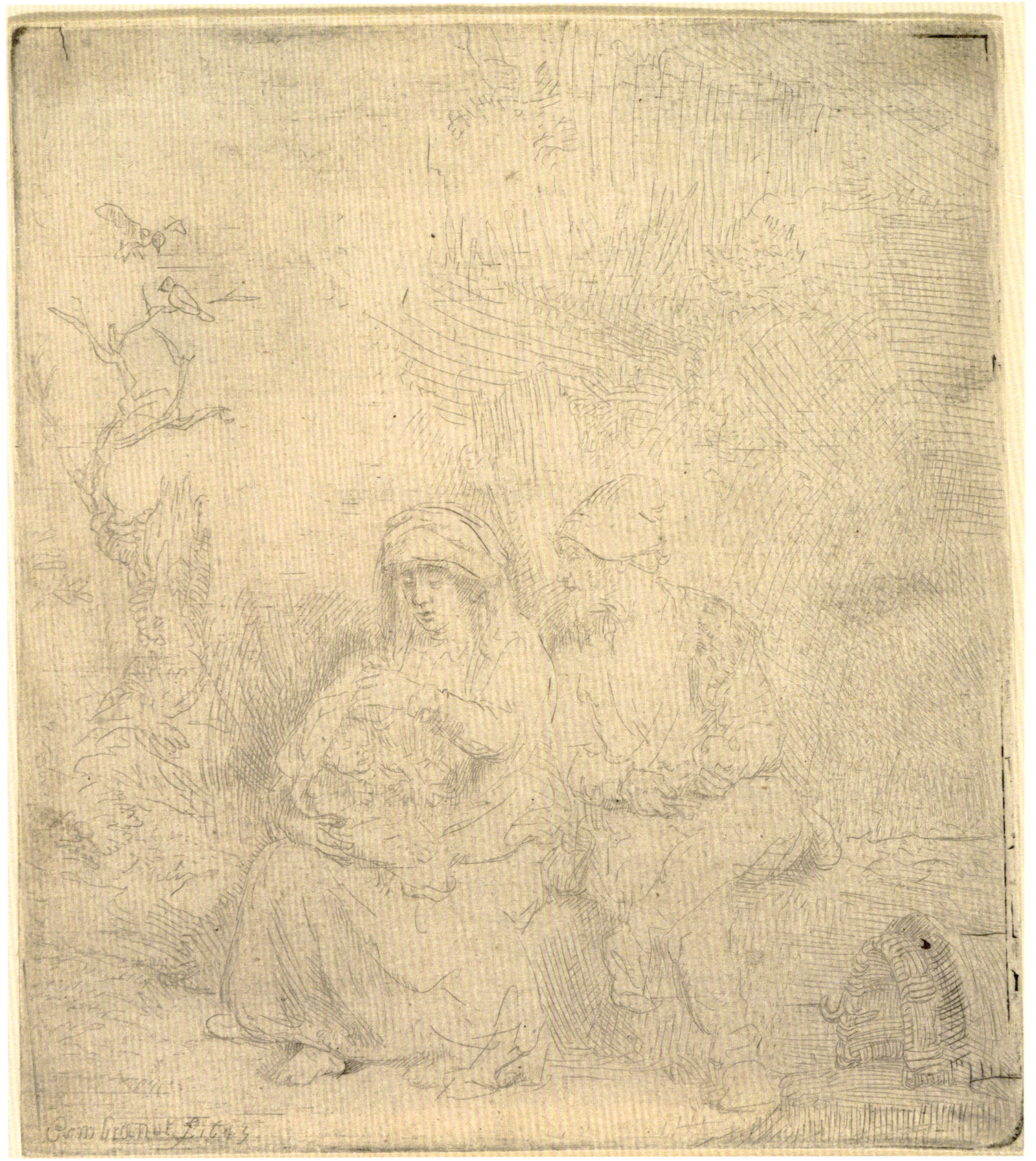

PLATE 33

FIGURE 1. Lucas van Leyden, *Rest on the Flight into Egypt*, engraving, c. 1506. *Rijksmuseum, Amsterdam.*

The story of the Holy Family's Rest on the Flight into Egypt does not appear in any of the synoptic gospels, but is related in the apocryphal Gospel of Pseudo-Matthew:[2] On the third day of the journey into Egypt, the Virgin Mary, worn out from the heat of the desert, spied a palm tree and asked Joseph if they could rest for a while in its shade. Joseph immediately led the donkey carrying Mary and Jesus over to the tree. The account goes on to describe two miracles performed by the infant Christ: the miracle of the date palm and the miracle of the freshwater spring.

Rembrandt depicted the Rest on the Flight into Egypt several times, and it is the subject of one of his earliest etchings (B. 59, c. 1626, not in the Snite collection) (cat. no. 22–24, fig. 1). In that rather naively composed and crudely executed print, possibly inspired by Lucas van Leyden's 1506 version of the same subject (fig. 1),[3] the Holy Family sits within a rocky landscape, with the Virgin and Child at the left, beneath a gnarled tree.[4] The outline of a tower can be seen in the distance, behind them. Mary, who wears a thick turban, cradles Jesus in her right arm and feeds him from a spoon as he stares straight ahead. Behind the baby's head, a circular halo emits rays of light. Joseph, a wizened old man with a full beard, is seated on the ground below Mary. He leans forward, holding out a bowl toward the mother and child as he stares fixedly at them through darkened, almost masklike eyes. Joseph's legs are extended on either side of a small fire that is warming the little bowl or pot he is tending. At his left, in the right foreground, a long saw with a carved handle lies atop a wicker basket with a braided handle, and a broad-brimmed hat sits on the ground nearby.[5] Behind Joseph, the family's lop-eared donkey, still bearing its saddle and a flask, munches contentedly on some grass. All of the figures, man and

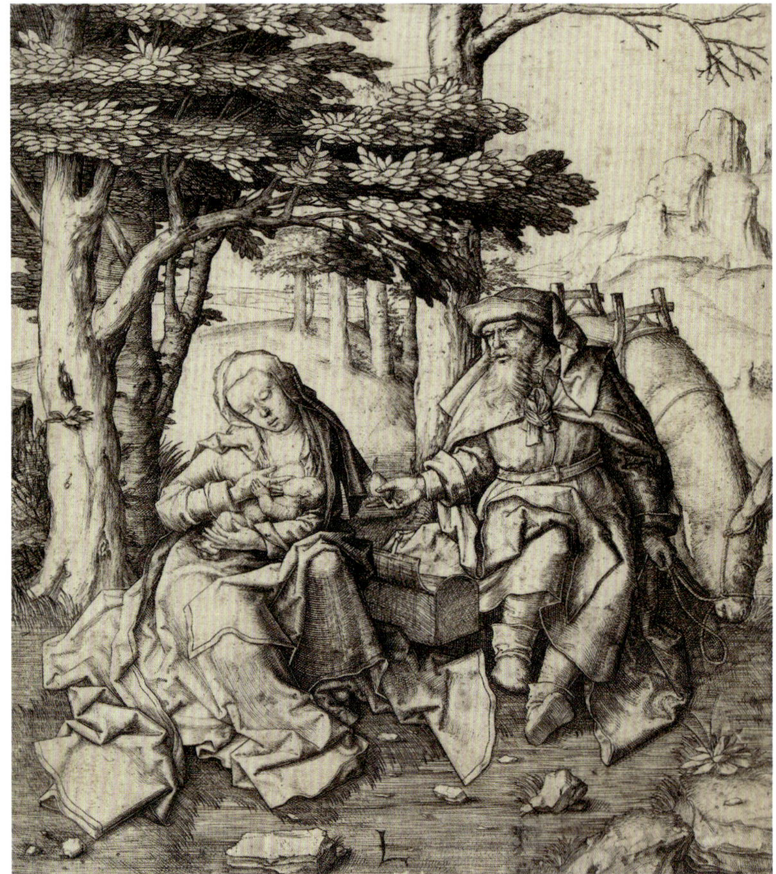

beast, seem at peace. This print is an extremely youthful work, displaying none of the subtlety of line and modeling that characterize the artist's more mature compositions.

The early etching, like the two later Rembrandt prints of the subject, does not include any references to the miracles associated with the Rest on the Flight into Egypt. This decision may have been influenced by the Dutch Reformed Church's rejection of apocryphal sources, although a number of other artists also chose not to depict the miracles. Instead, all three prints focus on an intimate moment, creating a vision of the Holy Family as an ideal model of marital domesticity and tranquility. The 1626 etching is quite unusual in that Joseph is not simply offering a dish of food to the Christ child, but also appears to be in charge of the cooking.[6] Conceptually, however, this motif reinforces one of the most common themes of the Rest on the Flight into Egypt: the role of Joseph as earthly protector of the Virgin and Child and, specifically, as the *nutritoris domini*, or provider for Christ.[7] The Snite Museum's two later prints of the Rest on the Flight into Egypt also highlight Joseph's role as protector and provider, though in a less overt fashion.

In the very small etching *Rest on the Flight into Egypt: A Night Piece* (B. 57, cat. no. 32), which has been dated to around 1644, Rembrandt created a unique interpretation of the scene. Because the account in pseudo-Matthew describes Mary as longing for respite from the sun and seeking shelter in the shade of a palm tree, the scene is usually represented as taking place in daylight. In this print, however, Rembrandt ignored not only the miracles associated with the tree, but also the time of day. This decision may have been influenced by the account in the Gospel of St. Matthew, which relates that the Holy Family fled by night,[8] and by Hendrik Goudt's well-known etched and engraved reproduction of Adam Elsheimer's nocturnal *Flight into Egypt*.[9] By staging the scene at night, Rembrandt was able to demonstrate his skill as an etcher while also appealing to the seventeenth-century taste for nocturnes.[10]

In Rembrandt's *Night Piece*, the Holy Family has settled down in—or at the edge of—a dense forest. A glowing lantern illuminates a watchful Joseph and also sets the canopy of leaves above his head magically aglow with twinkling light. In the Snite Museum impression, Rembrandt not only worked the entire surface of the plate except for the lantern, but also left significant plate tone on everything but the luminous white of the lantern panes. Mary and the sleeping child are seated on the ground below Joseph, a sign of the Virgin's humility. Beside them is a saddlebag and a basket with its cover ajar, revealing clothing or the baby's linens, a domestic detail.

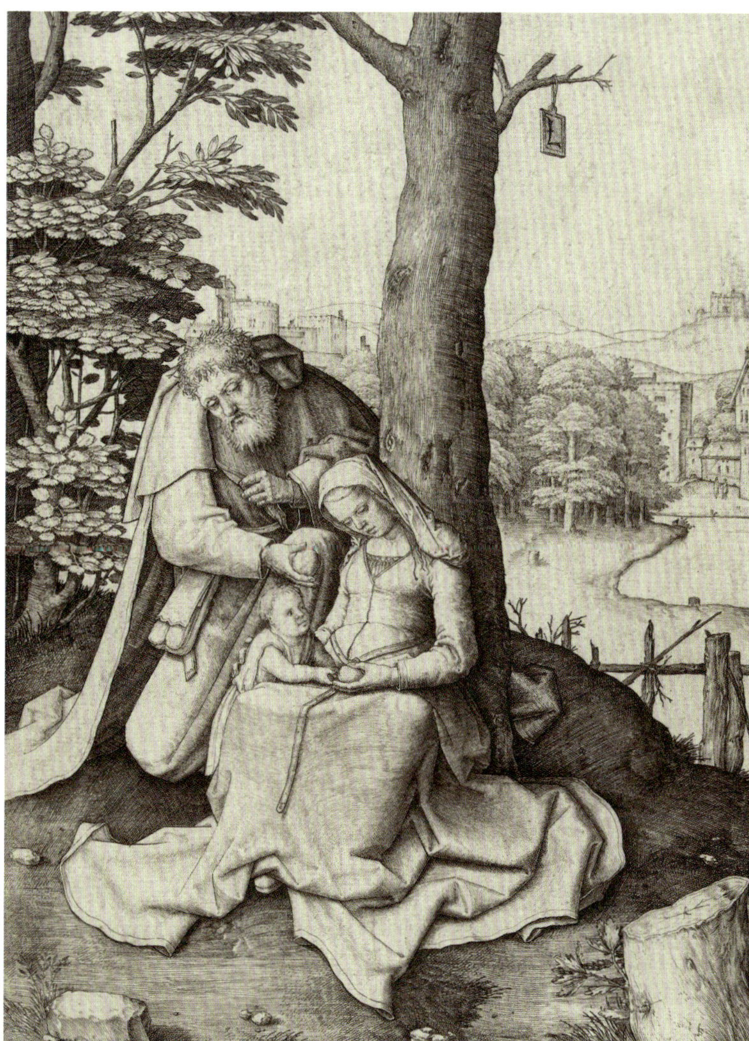

FIGURE 2. Lucas van Leyden, *Rest on the Flight into Egypt*, engraving, c. 1509. *Rijksmuseum, Amsterdam.*

Mary, who wears an unusual, very broad, flat turban, is resting, perhaps even dozing. She props up her weary head with her right hand and lays her left hand protectively across her sleeping child. Fashion historian Marieke de Winkel identified Mary's hat as part of the traditional costume of seventeenth-century Gypsy women. In Rembrandt's time, it was believed that Gypsies came from Egypt and that their clothing reflected ancient Egyptian attire.[11] This was the kind of exotic flourish that would have appealed to Rembrandt, a collector of unusual costumes, for it was a way of depicting "authentic" biblical apparel. Joseph sits with his back to a tree trunk, which is illuminated by the lantern he has hung from a nearby tree branch. His right hand holds the end of what may be a walking stick, and his left hand rests on his extended left leg. Although aged and tired, he remains awake, the vigilant guardian of his little family. Rembrandt has offered clues to Joseph's role as protector: in the glow of the lantern, he is the dominant figure, the one most brightly illuminated, and his large left hand, also brightly lit, echoes the curve of Mary's back as if to shelter and support her. He gazes out into the night with a pensive expression.

The Snite Museum's impression of this print represents the fifth state of nine. In comparison to earlier states, the shadows have been darkened, while the pattern of the foliate canopy above the Holy Family has been more clearly defined. In the next state, Rembrandt would add the front part of a braying donkey in the shadowy area at the far right, reinforcing the identity of this intimate scene as the Rest on the Flight into Egypt.

The second Snite Museum example of the subject, *Rest on the Flight into Egypt: Lightly Etched* (B. 58, cat. no. 33), is signed and dated 1645. As scholars have observed, Rembrandt's technique—the shallow lines, gray ink, and emphasis on drawn contours—gives this etching a shimmering, ghostly quality similar to that of a metalpoint drawing.[12] In this very simple composition, Joseph and Mary are seated on a low bank that runs parallel to the picture surface.[13] The Virgin, who is barefoot and dressed in a plain hooded cloak and voluminous dress,[14] holds the sleeping infant in her arms. Raising the edge of the shawl in which she has wrapped the child, Mary gazes solemnly down at his face. In both this print and the 1644 etching, Jesus is asleep, which increases the sense of his vulnerability and need for protection. Joseph, seated beside Mary with his legs crossed, leans in toward the Virgin, gazing tenderly over her shoulder at the napping child. Joseph holds a knife in one hand and an apple or pear in the other, a clear allusion to his role as the *nutritoris domini*.[15] Although the donkey does not appear in this etching, its presence is indicated by the wicker-and-wood saddle that sits on the ground to Joseph's left. Behind the Holy Family, an open pattern of parallel lines and light cross-hatching at the right side of the print suggest a hazy background of trees and/or rocks behind the figures, but it does not define the space in detail beyond the foreground plane, and hence does not distract from the focus on the Holy Family.

At the left side of the etching, a bird is perched on the branch of a barren, blasted tree. Another bird flies toward it, possibly holding a bit of straw in its mouth, presumably to help build a nest. Shelley Perlove and Larry Silver linked the broken-off tree trunk and the branch growing out of it with the prophetic passage in Isaiah 1:1 that foretold the birth of the Messiah from the line of David: "And there shall come forth a small branch out of the stem of Jesse that is hewn down and a shoot out of is roots shall bring forth fruit."[16] However, the barrenness of the tree and its branch makes this association somewhat questionable. Perlove and Silver also identify the two birds with Mary and Joseph. In their view, the bird that has settled on the branch is associated with Mary, who holds the branch (the Christ Child) in her arms, while the one fluttering above is linked to Joseph, the unenlightened Jew who has not yet committed himself to Christ.[17] This somewhat esoteric interpretation seems less likely than one offered by Clifford Ackley, who construed the avian pair as simply representing the theme of familial harmony.[18] It would not have been difficult for viewers to draw a parallel between the bird in flight hovering over the one in the tree, and Joseph as protector of and provider for Mary and Jesus. Furthermore, Ackley's interpretation is more in keeping with seventeenth-century descriptions of the Holy Family as an exemplar of marital perfection, an allusion that would undoubtedly have been familiar to Catholic and Protestant audiences alike.

It is possible that, as Christopher White suggested,[19] Rembrandt's own personal circumstances caused him to return to the subject of the Rest on the Flight into Egypt in the two prints of the mid-1640s, many years after his first etching of the theme. Rembrandt's wife, Saskia, died in 1642, shortly after giving birth to their only surviving child, Titus. Around this time, Geertje Dircx entered Rembrandt's household, probably during Saskia's pregnancy, and remained there to care for Titus after Saskia's death. Geertje eventually became Rembrandt's mistress. Although she was later supplanted in his affections by Hendrikje Stoffels and was forced to leave the artist's house, it seems very likely that in the mid-1640s, Rembrandt was enjoying a comfortable and relatively tranquil domestic situation. As Titus grew from infant to toddler, Rembrandt's experience of the pleasures and responsibilities of fatherhood may have informed and enriched his depictions of Joseph, Christ's earthly protector, in these tender familial scenes.[20]

Notes

1. Illustrated in Sotheby's & Co., *Catalogue of the Collection of Rembrandt Etchings Formed by the 10th Viscount Downe (1903–1965)*, Part 1, 26 November 1970, lot 61.

2. *The Gospel of Pseudo-Matthew*, in J. K. Elliott, *The Apocryphal New Testament: A Collection of Apocryphal Christian Literature in an English Translation* (Oxford: Clarendon Press, 1993), 95.

3. Richard Verdi has suggested that this print is based on an engraving by Lucas van Leyden from about 1506 (NHD 38) (fig. 1). Verdi, *Rembrandt's Themes: Life into Art* (New Haven, CT: Yale University Press, 2014), 40.

Rembrandt's 1626 *Rest on the Flight* dates from about the same time as the museum's etching of *Circumcision* (S. 398, cat. no. 22).

4. Although the tale in Pseudo-Matthew features a palm tree, the trees depicted in Rembrandt's prints of the episode are more typical of species found in the artist's northern clime, which was not unusual for representations of the subject.

5. Since Joseph was a carpenter by trade, the saw serves as an identifying attribute.

6. Ludwig Münz (*Critical Catalogue*, cat. 186) associated this print with an early fifteenth-century Austrian or Bohemian woodcut now in the Albertina Museum in Vienna. For an illustration and discussion of this early woodcut, see Peter Parshall and Rainer Schoch, *Origins of European Printmaking: Fifteenth-Century Woodcuts and Their Public* (Washington, DC: National Gallery of Art, in association with Yale University Press, New Haven, CT, 2005), cat. 29, 133–35. Popular fourteenth- and fifteenth-century Northern Nativity and Adoration plays sometimes portrayed Joseph as a buffoon who was ridiculed for performing tasks that women usually did. Later, as the cult of Joseph grew, he came to be regarded as a model husband in his role as the wholly human member of the earthly trinity. Although he is occasionally shown offering food to the Virgin, as he does in the Lucas van Leyden engravings of 1506–1509 (NHD 38 and 85) (figs. 1 and 2) and in Rembrandt's own later lightly etched *Rest* (cat. no. 33), Joseph was rarely depicted in the act of cooking, because the earlier negative associations with woman's work lingered. Rembrandt's etching was an exception. For a discussion of the German miracle plays and the image of Joseph, see Sheila Schwartz, "The Iconography of the Rest on the Flight into Egypt" (PhD diss., New York University, 1975), 80–84. For the history of the cult of St. Joseph, see Francis L. Filas, SJ, *Joseph: The Man Closest to Jesus: The Complete Life, Theology and Devotional History of St. Joseph* (Boston: St. Paul Editions, 1962), chapters 23 and 24.

7. For the theme of Joseph as *nutritoris domini*, see Schwartz, "The Iconography of the Rest," 62–67 and 92–95. In liturgical calendars from the fourteenth century on, March 19 has frequently been designated as the day of "*Sancti Joseph nutritoris domini.*" Ibid., 63n13.

8. Matthew 2:14.

9. The print, HD 3, is dated 1613.

10. On nocturnes and the tradition of collecting them, see William W. Robinson, "'This Passion for Prints': Collecting and Connoisseurship in Northern Europe during the Seventeenth Century," in Clifford Ackley, *Printmaking in the Age of Rembrandt*, exh. cat. (Boston: Boston Museum of Fine Arts, 1981), xlv–xlvi; Catherine Scallen, "Rembrandt's Nocturne Prints," *On Paper* 1 (January–February 1997): 13–17; and Adriaan Waiboer and Michiel Franken, *Northern Nocturnes: Nightscapes in the Age of Rembrandt* (Dublin: National Gallery of Ireland, 2005).

11. Marieke de Winkel, *Fashion and Fancy: Dress and Meaning in Rembrandt's Paintings* (Amsterdam: Amsterdam University Press, 2006), 266–67.

12. Christopher White (*Rembrandt as an Etcher: A Study of the Artist at Work*, 2nd ed. [New Haven, CT: Yale University Press, 1999], 50) likened Rembrandt's *Rest on the Flight into Egypt: Lightly Etched* to a metalpoint drawing and cited the only two other examples of the artist's etchings that are similar in technique, *St. Peter in Penitence* (B. 96, 1645) and *The Old Man in Meditation Leaning on a Book* (B. 147, c. 1645) (not in the Snite Museum collection). White's view that Rembrandt created this effect on purpose, and not, as some historians have speculated, by mistake, seems reasonable.

To produce a metalpoint drawing, the artist draws on prepared paper or parchment, using a stylus made of lead, tin, silver, or even gold. The result is a very fine and delicate line that, in the case of lead, tin, or silver, darkens over time but remains relatively faint, particularly in comparison with drawings done in chalk or ink. Modeling is created by means of hatching.

13. In this version of the scene, Rembrandt strays even further from the story, since the only tree in the area is blighted, offering no shelter or respite from the sun, and the Holy Family is not seated beneath the tree.

14. Mary's costume is a major departure from the Virgin's exotic attire in Rembrandt's *Rest on the Flight into Egypt: A Night Piece* (cat. no. 32) from the previous year. Also, although Mary is barefoot, Joseph is shod, perhaps an acknowledgment that on this journey, he is walking, whereas Mary and the baby are riding. The disparity also helps to emphasize Mary's vulnerability and Joseph's role as the protector.

15. It has been suggested that this print was influenced by Lucas van Leyden's two engravings of the Rest on the Flight into Egypt from c. 1506–1509 (NHD 38 and 85) (figs. 1 and 2). In both images, Joseph holds out a piece of fruit. This motif of Joseph offering nourishment continued to appear in artworks, including, for example, Cornelius Cort's engraving after a composition by Bernardino Passeri from 1576 (NHD 39).

Given the association of an apple or pear with the Garden of Eden, the fruit can also be construed as an allusion to the roles of Christ and the Virgin as the new Adam and Eve. *Rembrandt's Faith*, 173.

16. *Rembrandt's Faith*, 173.

17. Ibid., 174. Perlove and Silver also suggested that the expression on Mary's face alludes to her prescient knowledge of the death of her son, whereas Joseph's smiling visage identifies him as the unenlightened Jew who is unaware of Christ's fate.

18. *Rembrandt's Journey*, cat. 111, 181.

19. White, *Rembrandt as an Etcher*, 50–51.

20. On the Dutch fascination with the education of children, see Simon Schama, *The Embarrassment of Riches: An Interpretation of Dutch Culture in the Golden Age* (Berkeley: University of California Press, 1987), chapter 7, "In the Republic of Children."

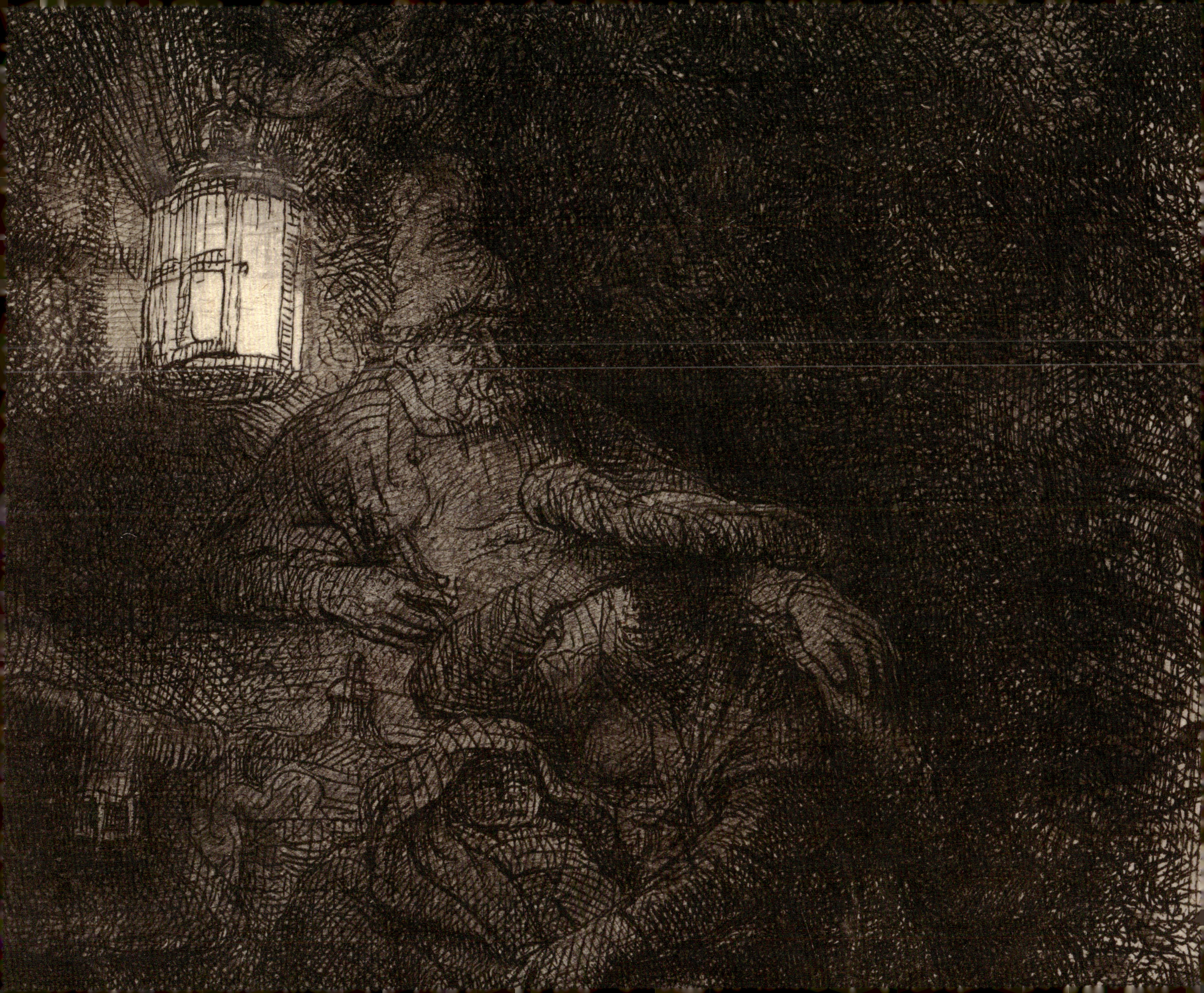

34. *Virgin and Child in the Clouds*

B. 61 (H. 186, Mz. 212, NHD 188)
Etching and drypoint
Signed and dated in the plate: *Rembrandt f. 1641*
State I of I
Sheet: 16.8 × 10.6 cm, trimmed to the plate mark
Fragment of watermark on right middle: cross on three circles
Verso: in graphite, lower left corner: *42* in a circle; bottom center: *B61*only*/c. 1634/OTMML'*; lower right: *XL* . . . . with line above/ *n. 46*; collectors' stamps on verso: National Picture Gallery, Budapest (Lugt 2000); Charles Delanglade (Lugt 660); and unidentified blind stamp

Provenance:
National Picture Gallery, Budapest (stamp used until 1906)
Charles Delanglade, Marseille, France (1870–1952)
David Tunick Inc., New York, NY, 1977
Feddersen, Elkhart, IN, 1991
Snite Museum of Art
Acc. No.: 1991.025.032

The plate does not survive.

Rembrandt's etching of the *Virgin and Child in the Clouds* is a free variation on a print by the Italian artist Federico Barocci from about 1581 (B. 2)[1] (fig. 1). As is typical of Barocci's devotional images, the Virgin in his etching displays a sense of gentle sweetness. She holds her infant son tenderly upon her lap, clasping her hands around his waist and gazing fondly at him with a smile upon her lips. The cherubic nude Jesus looks down and to his left, as if acknowledging an unseen donor or saint. His left hand toys with the cloth of his mother's cloak, while his right hand is raised in a traditional gesture of blessing. Rembrandt's print differs from the Barocci model in a number of significant ways: He eliminated the cherubs' heads that Barocci tucked into the upper corners of his composition; transformed the crisply drawn halo around Mary's head into a broader emanation of light; gave Jesus a separate aura of rays; moved the figures down and to the left, filling the space beside them with dark masses of clouds; and, most notably, altered the Virgin's expression and her relationship with the now swaddled Christ Child who lies across her lap. Barocci's Mary holds the infant Jesus in a more upright position, facing outward, as if she is presenting him to the viewer. Rembrandt's Mary looks off into the distance, away from her child, with an unfocused expression of wistfulness.[2]

Devotional images of the Virgin and Child in heaven were not uncommon in the Renaissance and Baroque periods. With their focus on the celestial and maternal aspects of Mary, these images were primarily intended to appeal to a Catholic audience,[3] and Rembrandt's print would certainly have suited this clientele. However, as several authors have noted, Rembrandt's deviations from Barocci's model rendered the print acceptable to both Catholic and Protestant clients. As such, the etching is a clear example of Rembrandt's confessional and commercial practicality. The artist recognized the desirability of cultivating a market for his prints beyond the confines of Protestant Amsterdam,[4] and typically framed his religious images in such a manner that they could be appreciated not only aesthetically, but also spiritually, by Christian viewers of different persuasions. In the case of the *Virgin and Child*

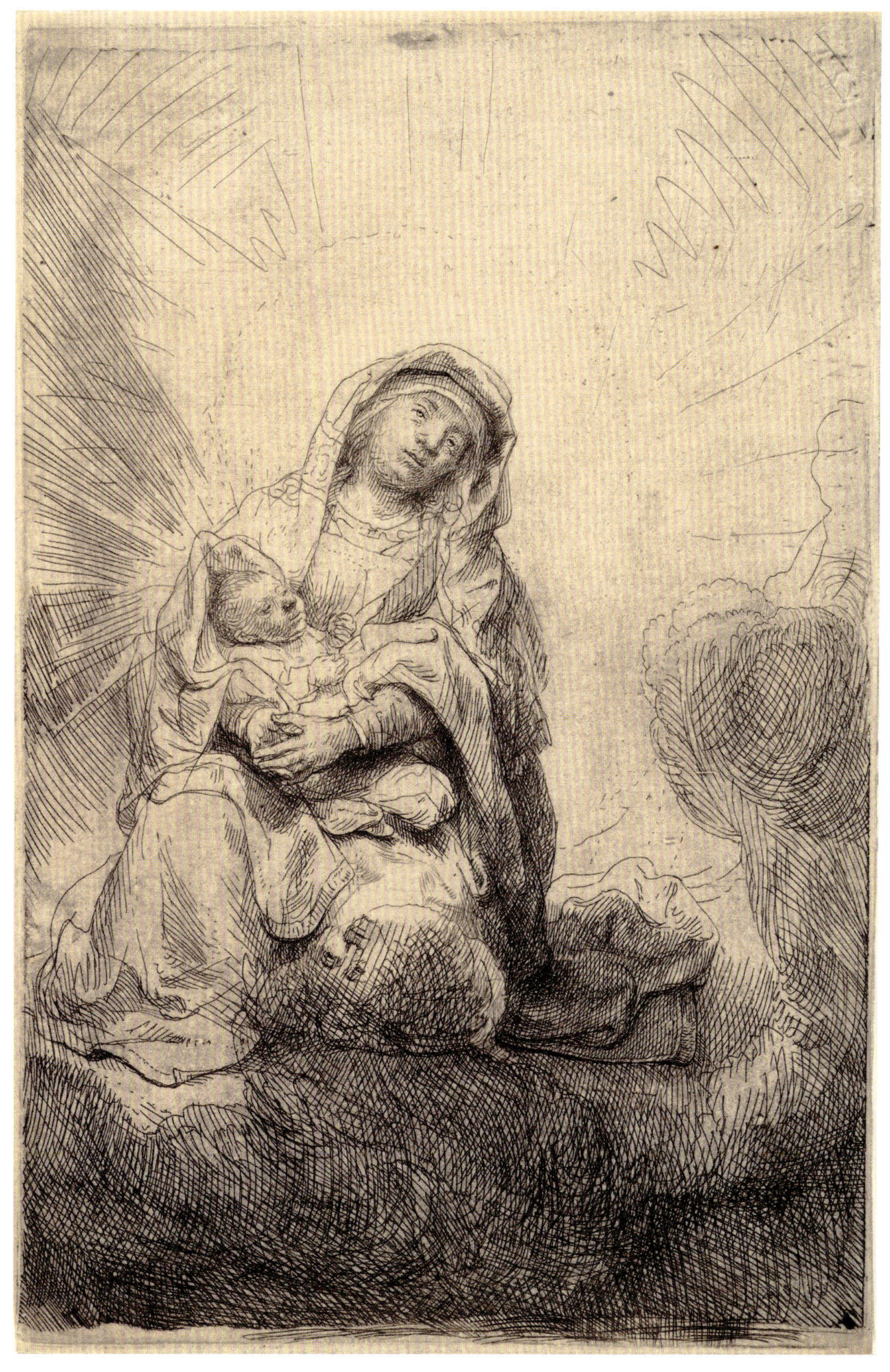

PLATE 34

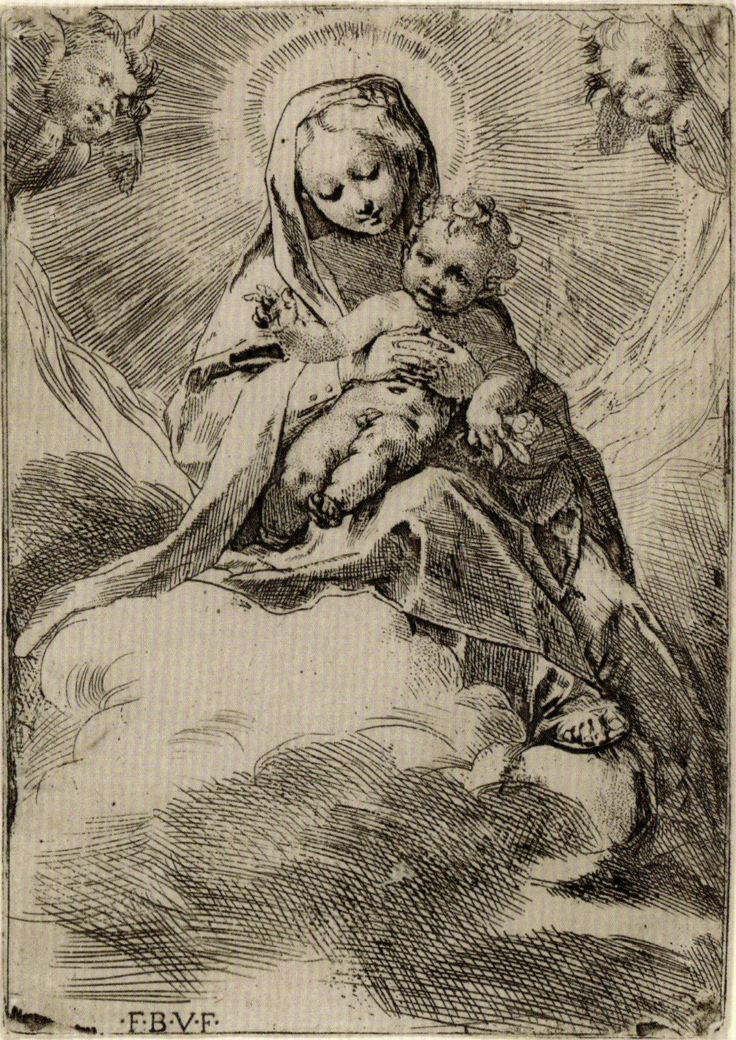

FIGURE 1. Federico Barocci, *Virgin and Child in the Clouds*, etching, c. 1581. *Yale University Art Gallery, New Haven, Connecticut, Everett V. Meeks, B.A. 1901 Fund.*

in the Clouds, he changed the point of view of the spectator so that Mary and her son are viewed more directly, thereby reducing the "regal" aura of the elevated Virgin. In addition, Rembrandt's Virgin and Child are less idealized.[5] Christ's gestures are more natural and childlike; he is no longer the precocious, priestly figure envisioned by Barocci.[6] Mary's solid, draped, triangular figure dominates the space, but the addition of myriad rays emanating from the child's head, along with the alteration of Mary's halo from a prominent circle with radiating rays to an undefined aura of light behind her, serves to emphasize Christ's divinity, rather than his mother's sanctity. These modifications cast Mary as a more down-to-earth model of motherhood.

One curious detail in Rembrandt's print is the existence of an upside-down face near the Virgin's left knee. It has been proposed that this is a remnant from a previous work that was begun and then abandoned. According to Ludwig Münz and others,[7] it is possible that Rembrandt began working on the plate, etched the face, became dissatisfied with what he had done, turned the plate upside down, and created a new image, that of the Virgin and Child in the Clouds. Why he would have left such a noticeable *pentimento* when he could easily have removed it before printing the plate is a mystery. An alternative explanation is that the face represents the head of a cherub who is helping to support the mass of clouds or the Virgin and Child. In fact, a careful examination of the clouds just to the left of the anomalous face reveals the outline of a feathered wing. If Rembrandt was, indeed, inspired by Barocci's *Mother and Child in the Clouds* as he began work on his own rendition of the subject, he might have been toying with the idea of including cherubim in the composition, as Barocci and others had done. A number of other examples of the Virgin and Child in the Clouds depicted angels and cherubim in the clouds below and surrounding the seated figures.[8] The disembodied head could be a remnant of this conception.

Notes

1. Rembrandt's dependence on the Barocci print was already recognized at the beginning of the twentieth century. B. P. J. Broos, *Index of the Formal Sources of Rembrandt's Art* (Maarssen, Netherlands: Schwartz, 1977), 77–78. An entry in Rembrandt's 1656 bankruptcy inventory (Walter Strauss and Marjon van der Meulen, *The Rembrandt Documents* [New York: Abaris, 1979], doc. 1656/12, item 195: *Een dito* [Book] *met kopere printen van Vani* [Vanni] *en anderen als meede Barotius* [Barocci]) confirms that he owned a volume that included prints by or after Barocci.

Barocci was not a prolific graphic artist. Only four Barocci prints are known, of which the *Virgin and Child in the Clouds*, normally dated to c. 1581, may well be the first. That etching, which shows a remarkable degree of skill, particularly for a first effort, was quite popular. It was copied not only by Rembrandt, but also by Johannes Sadeler I (1575), Agostino Carracci (1582), and Raffaello Schiaminossi (1613).

Other less likely sources for Rembrandt's print are Dürer's woodcut print of the *Virgin and Child on a Crescent Moon* (1511, TIB, woodcuts, 76), which appeared on the title page of the German artist's *Life of the Virgin*, and a print of the same subject by Jan van de Velde II, after a composition by Willem Buytewech (1615–41) (HD 13).

2. If Ludwig Münz (*Critical Catalogue*, vol. 2, cat. 212, 99) and Willem Adolph Visser 't Hooft (*Rembrandt and the Gospel* [New York: Meridian Books, 1960], 44–45) are correct in identifying this print as the one described in the De Jonghe inventory of Rembrandt plates as the "Sorrowful Mary with the Child," then the sober character of this etching was recognized by the artist's near contemporaries. Recently, Peter Black (Black and Erma Hermans, *Rembrandt and the Passion*, exh. cat. [Munich: Prestel Verlag, 2012], 82) noted that 1641, the year in which this print was created, was the year that Rembrandt's son Titus was born, and that "the print might represent a prayer for Titus' survival." That connection might help to explain Mary's somber, unfocused gaze. Indeed, since Rembrandt and Saskia had lost a son and two daughters at a tender age, the artist might have been particularly sensitive to a mother's fears for her child, especially a woman whose son was destined to die before his time, a fact that Mary knew, since she had been forewarned by Simeon at the time of Jesus's presentation at the Temple. See the entries in this catalog for *Presentation in the Temple with the Angel: Small Plate* (B. 51, cat. no. 25) and *The Presentation in the Temple: Oblong Print* (B. 49, cat. no. 26).

3. For the Catholic context of this print, see *Rembrandt's Faith*, 50–52.

4. On Rembrandt as a proto-capitalist, see Svetlana Alpers, *Rembrandt's Enterprise: The Studio and the Market* (Chicago: University of Chicago Press, 1988), passim. For a discussion of the artist's "pragmatic ecumenism" see Charles M. Rosenberg, "Rembrandt's Religious Prints," in this catalog.

5. Münz (*Critical Catalogue*, vol. 1, 28) described the Virgin as having "the face of a young woman, very human and full of pain, and without any beautification." He even went so far as to suggest that Mary could have been based on Saskia, Rembrandt's wife, when she was suffering during her final illness. This interpretation may be overly romantic. Nonetheless, Mary's half-closed eyes and her pose, as she leans back to the right, counterbalancing the weight of the child she is supporting, suggest that she is at least weary, if not actually ill.

6. Rembrandt's more naturalistic rendering of the Christ Child is not particularly flattering. In fact, Kenneth Clark (*Rembrandt and the Italian Renaissance* [New York: New York University Press, 1966], 28) described the child as a "plain little Dutch pygmy infant."

7. See also, for example, the entry by Marijn Schapelhouman in Erik Hinterding, Ger Luijten, and Martin Royalton-Kisch, *Rembrandt the Printmaker*, exh. cat. (Chicago and London: Fitzroy Dearborn Publishers, 2000), cat. 43, 193: "Rembrandt made a false start when he embarked on this print, and an upside-down face is visible in Mary's knee. Evidently, the artist soon realized that the head was too small and poorly positioned in the picture plane. Without erasing the traces of his initial design he turned the plate 180 degrees and started afresh."

8. See, for example, Simone Cantarini's virtually contemporary Virgin and Child in the clouds with angels (1630–48) (TIB 19), and Vespasiano Strada's etching of the Virgin and Child seated in the clouds with the head of an angel below and two cherubim in the upper corners (1600–1622) (TIB 11). In yet another example, an anonymous print (1620–60, British Museum, Reg. no. U,3.96) after a composition by Guido Reni depicts a Virgin of Sorrows who is seated in the clouds with her hands folded in her lap and her eyes cast upward, with seven swords pointing at her head and several cherubim at her feet.

35. *Holy Family*

B. 62. (H. 95, Mz., 193, NHD 114)
Etching
Signed in the plate: *RL* [*RHL?*]
c. 1632
State I of I
Sheet: 9.7 × 7.4 cm; plate mark: 9.6 × 7.0 cm
Verso: in graphite, *Crichton/August/1842*, lower left and lower right, *D.61*, bottom center, *c.40139*, upper center, *G/C*

Provenance:
Crichton (?)
P. & D. Colnaghi & Co. Ltd., London, 1976
Feddersen, Elkhart, IN, 1991
Snite Museum of Art
Acc. No.: 1991.025.033

The plate does not survive.

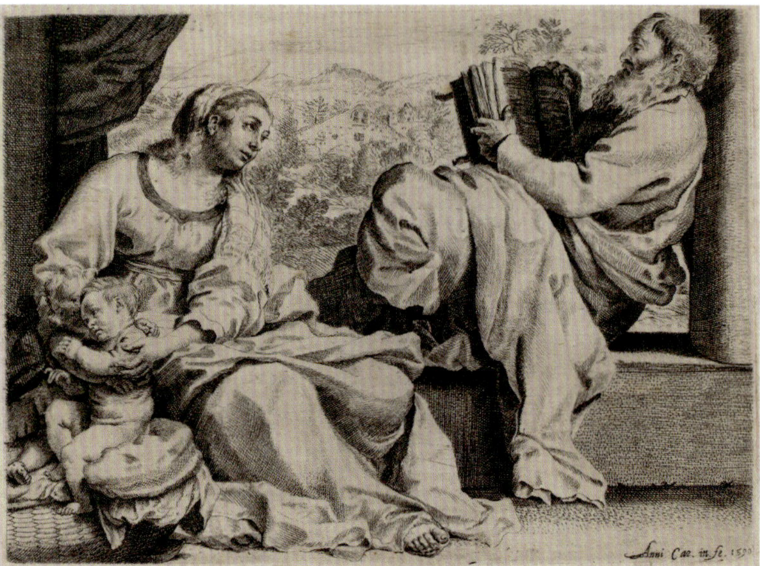

FIGURE 1. Annibale Carracci, *The Holy Family with St. John*, etching and engraving, 1590. *Photo: Courtesy of the National Gallery, Washington, DC.*

Rembrandt's *Holy Family* is a very small etching that has no specific narrative source.[1] Rather, it is a devotional image that, as it blurs the boundaries between simple domesticity and spiritual presence, elicits an intimate emotional response through its representation of common daily experiences.

The print was probably inspired by Annibale Carracci's etching of c. 1590, *Holy Family with St. John the Baptist* (fig. 1),[2] which in turn appears to owe a debt to Andrea del Sarto's 1525 painting of the *Madonna of the Sack* (fig. 2).[3] The fresco was reproduced in an engraving by Giovanni Battista de' Cavalieri in 1573 (fig. 3). Whereas Carracci and del Sarto situated the Holy Family in a somewhat formal environment, Rembrandt portrayed Mary, Joseph, and Jesus as a typical seventeenth-century Dutch family enjoying a peaceful moment in a more informal setting. The Virgin is seated on a low step in the foreground. The baby, cradled in her right arm, reclines upon her lap. In the Carracci and del Sarto models, Mary holds onto an active toddler, but in Rembrandt's etching, she is depicted as a mother offering her breast to her dozing son. Lost in a quiet state of reverie, the Virgin looks out and down, beyond the Christ Child, with an unfocused, contemplative gaze. An open sewing basket sits on the step just to the Virgin's left, a sign of Mary's exemplary domesticity and probity.[4] Characteristically, Rembrandt

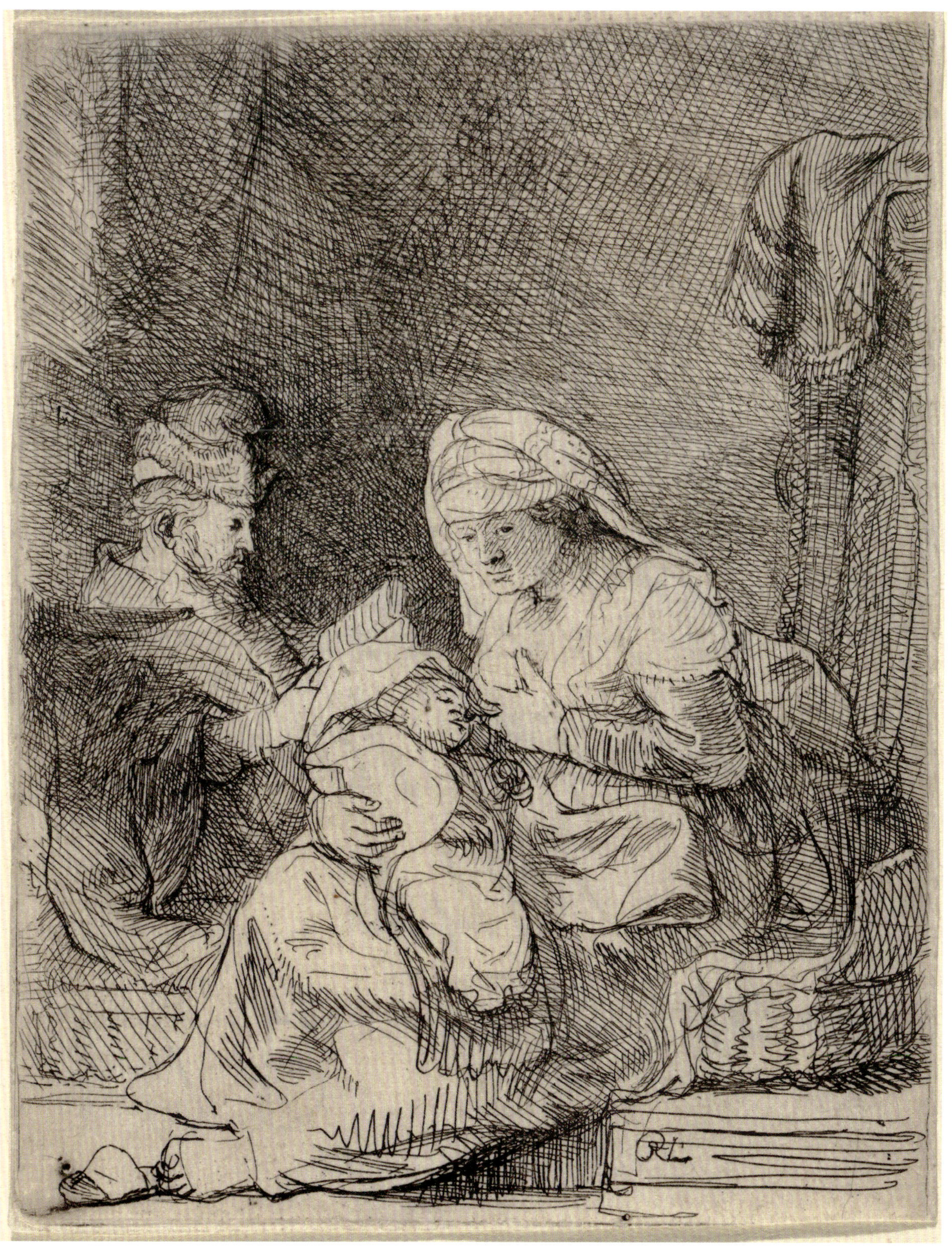

PLATE 35

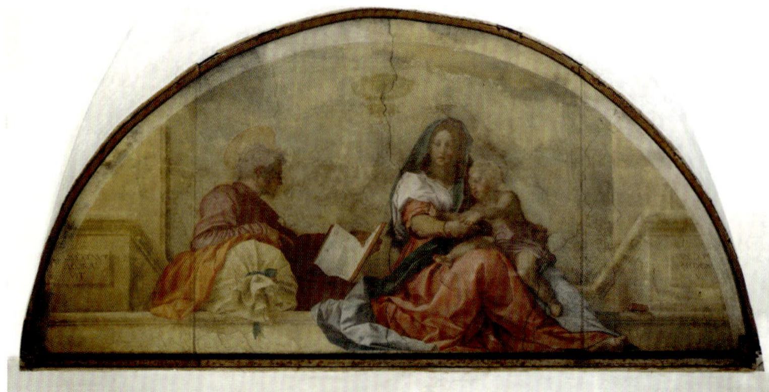

FIGURE 2. Andrea del Sarto, *The Madonna of the Sack*, 1525. *Chiostro delle morte, SS. Annunziata, Florence, Italy. Photo: Scala/Art Resource.*

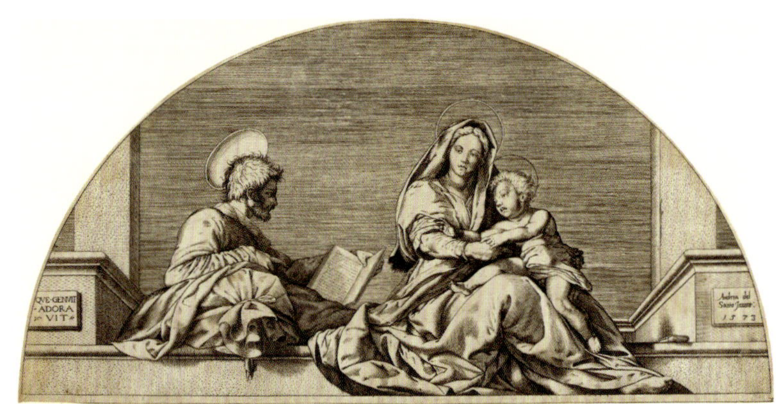

FIGURE 3. Giovanni Battista de' Cavalieri after Andrea del Sarto, *The Madonna of the Sack*, engraving, 1573. © *The Fitzwilliam Museum, Cambridge, England.*

added another casual, homey detail as a means of humanizing the divine: one of Mary's slippers has slid off, and her bare left foot peeks out from beyond her gown.[5] The Virgin's pose—resting on a low step near the floor as she feeds her child—fits comfortably into a long tradition of images that emphasize Mary's humility and her maternal character as the nurturer of Christ.[6]

As Mary tends to her baby, Joseph sits behind her, with the two appearing to inhabit separate worlds dictated by traditional male/female roles. Shown in profile, Joseph is absorbed in reading a small book that he holds open on his lap. He provides a contrast to Carracci's Joseph, who props up an enormous tome, and del Sarto's Joseph, who holds his book out as if to display it to the viewer. The representation of a literate Joseph, the "pious Jew who spends his time studying the Torah,"[7] may be a reference to his dual roles as a teacher and earthly protector of Christ and as a prophet.[8] Larry Silver and Shelley Perlove suggested that Joseph's subordinate position in the etching indicates that as an unconverted Jew, he is not yet fully enlightened.[9] However, although the right side of his body is cast into shadow, Joseph's head, shoulder, and hand, as well as the book that he holds, are all brightly illuminated, suggesting, perhaps, that he has actually become "enlightened" by the words that he reads and the Word incarnate.[10] Nonetheless, it is clear that of the three figures in the triangular grouping, mother and child hold center stage by virtue of their placement, size, and illumination. The very obvious Marian emphasis in this etching would probably have appealed to a Catholic audience, while the very human figures depicted in their contemporary dress and setting with its obvious emphasis on Marian humility would have made the print attractive to a Calvinist clientele as well.

There appears to be a curtain behind and to the left of Joseph, suggesting that the Holy Family is seated in front of, or within, a shallow alcove. Closing off the composition at the right side is an upended wicker couch called a *bakermat*. The shawl or rug draped over the top of it contributes to the composition's aura of casual intimacy and domesticity. The anachronistic *bakermat* would have been a familiar piece of furniture for many seventeenth-century viewers, for this particular type of couch was commonly used by nursing mothers in contemporary Amsterdam.[11]

Notes

1. On the theme of the Holy Family in Rembrandt's paintings and prints, see Joan Mary Hogan, "The Iconography of Rembrandt's Depiction of the Holy Family (in a Domestic Setting)," MA diss., Queens University, Kingston, ON, 2008. A brief discussion of the etching appears on 28–29.

2. TIB 11. The Carracci print has been cited as a source by numerous authors, including Ludwig Münz, *Critical Catalogue*, 1:40–41 and fig. 50. It is also quite close in format and spirit to Simone Cantarini's almost-contemporary etching of *The Holy Family with Rosary* (TIB 13).

3. Andrea del Sarto's fresco, located in the so-called Cloister of the Dead attached to the Servite pilgrimage church of SS. Annunziata in Florence, was painted in 1525.

4. According to Wayne Franits, "Genre paintings of maidens occupied with needlework . . . conveyed virtuous associations revolving around probity and proper training." Franits, *Paragons of Virtue: Women and Domesticity in Seventeenth-Century Dutch Art* (Cambridge, UK: Cambridge University Press, 1993), 22. The basket may carry other symbolic significance, as well. According to a tradition derived from the Protoevangelium of James, when Mary was a young girl residing in the Temple, she was chosen to be one of the virgins to weave the purple veil for the Temple because of her humility. Since the great Temple veil came to symbolize the Incarnation, images of the Virgin sewing or weaving evoked not only her status and humility, but also the destiny of her son. In addition, the cloth draped over the edge of the basket may be both a piece of handiwork and an allusion to the shroud that one day would cover Jesus's body as he was carried to the tomb. On the passional significance of images of the sewing Virgin and the sewing basket, see John F. Moffitt, "Mary as a 'Prophetic Seamstress' in Siglo de Oro Sevillian Painting," *Wallraf-Richartz-Jahrbuch* 54 (1993): 141–61. For a further discussion of the tradition of the Virgin as the weaver of the Temple veil, see *Virgin and Child with the Cat and the Snake*, B. 63, cat. no. 36.

5. A seventeenth-century viewer might also have read an erotic subtext into the discarded slipper, for it is a motif that had sexual connotations from at least the fifteenth century on. See, for example, the discarded slippers in Israhel van Meckenem, *Couple Seated on a Bed*, c. 1495–1503, from his series "Scenes from Daily Life" (HG 508); Lucas van Leyden's *Joseph and Potiphar's Wife* (NHD 20, 1512); and the discarded shoe in Rembrandt's own *Joseph and Potiphar's Wife* (B. 39, 1634, cat. no. 13), as well as the shoe in the front of Rembrandt's pornographic etching *The Monk in the Cornfield* (B. 187, c. 1646). For a discussion of this motif in the seventeenth century, see Eddy de Jongh, "Erotica in vogelperspectief, De dubbelzinnigheid van een reeks 17de eeuwse genrevoorstellingen," *Simiolus: Netherlands Quarterly for the History of Art* 3 (1968–69): 36–37.

6. On these themes, see Millard Meiss, "The Madonna of Humility," *Art Bulletin* 18, no. 4 (1936): 435–64; and Beth Williamson, *The Madonna of Humility: Development, Dissemination & Reception, c. 1340–1400* (Woodbridge, UK: Boydell, 2009), and "Liturgical Image or Devotional Image? The London 'Madonna of the Firescreen,'" in *Objects, Images, and the Word,* ed. Colum Hourihane (Princeton, NJ: Princeton University Press, 2003), 298–318.

7. Larry Silver and Shelley Perlove, "Rembrandt's Protestant Joseph," in *Joseph of Nazareth through the Centuries,* ed. Joseph F. Chorpenning, OFSF (Philadelphia: St. Joseph's University Press, 2011), 191.

8. For a discussion of the motif of Joseph reading, see the entry on *Adoration of the Shepherds: A Night Piece* (B. 46, 1657, cat. no. 21). For information about Joseph's role as the *nutritoris domini*, see the entries for *Rest on the Flight into Egypt: A Night Piece* (B. 57, c. 1644, cat. no. 32, note 6) and *Rest on the Flight into Egypt: Lightly Etched* (B. 58, 1645, cat. no. 33).

9. See note 7, above.

10. For a discussion of other, earlier, Italian examples where Joseph's body is in shadow and his head is illuminated, see Carolyn C. Wilson, *St. Joseph in Italian Renaissance Society and Art: New Directions and Interpretations* (Philadelphia: St. Joseph's University Press, 2001), 63–64. Among other things, Wilson points out the trope of Joseph as "the shadow of God the Father," the protector of the hidden God.

11. *Rembrandt's Journey,* cat. 56, 124.

36. *Virgin and Child with the Cat and the Snake*

B. 63 (H. 275, Mz. 229, NHD 278)
Etching
Signed and dated in the plate: *Rembrandt f. 1654*
State I of IV
Sheet: 9.5 × 14.5 cm, trimmed to the plate mark
Watermark: fragment of foolscap (unidentifiable)
Verso: in graphite, *B63I/c. 27775*

Provenance:
David Tunick Inc., New York, NY, 1977
Feddersen, Elkhart, IN, 1991
Snite Museum of Art
Acc. No.: 1991.025.034

Plate survives:
Victoria and Albert Museum, London (inv. E655-1993).

The *Virgin and Child with the Cat and the Snake* is one of a group of six prints from 1654 that relate to Christ's childhood.[1] Unlike the other etchings in this series, this print does not represent a particular biblical text or event. Instead, it has a more symbolic, devotional theme, one with theological implications. Mary is the main focus of the scene, which is set in a seventeenth-century domestic interior. Seated on a low step,[2] she holds her son tightly in her arms, pressing her cheek against his in a warm, maternal embrace, as if to keep him safe from danger. Her left foot, visible beneath the hem of her voluminous cloak, presses down upon the back of a hissing, struggling snake. A cat, crouching on a mat beside her, stares intently at the writhing serpent. In the left back corner of the room is a canopied alcove that contains a substantial wooden Savonarola chair with a cushion on it, and on the right side of the chamber is a large hearth with a blazing fire. The area immediately in front of the hearth has been reworked, suggesting that Rembrandt had originally placed a figure or object there, before changing his mind.[3] A small, open coffer filled with linens rests on the floor immediately to the Virgin's left. The back wall of the chamber behind her is dominated by a large window with a curtain drawn to one side.[4] An oval pane of glass in the center of this window forms a sort of naturalistic halo behind Mary's head, a halo that Rembrandt enhanced with a spray of lightly etched rays. Joseph stands outside the chamber, gazing in at the cozy scene. He looks downward, toward the small lamp or bowl sitting on a corner of the sill in front of him or at the chest of linens on the floor. His exclusion from the chamber casts him as an outsider and reinforces Mary's status as the Virgin.[5] On the opposite side of the room, in the center foreground, directly in front of the Virgin and child, a single step indicates an open stairway leading toward what must be a cellar, below.[6]

As numerous authors have observed, the representation of the Virgin and Child in what appears to be a contemporary Dutch home connects this print with a well-established tradition of Northern late medieval and Renaissance devotional images.[7] Rembrandt's uncharacteristically overt symbolism also seems to echo these traditions. The Savonarola chair set under a canopy, for example, serves as a reference to the throne that Mary occupies as the Queen of Heaven.[8] Mary's pose is drawn from an Andrea Mantegna print

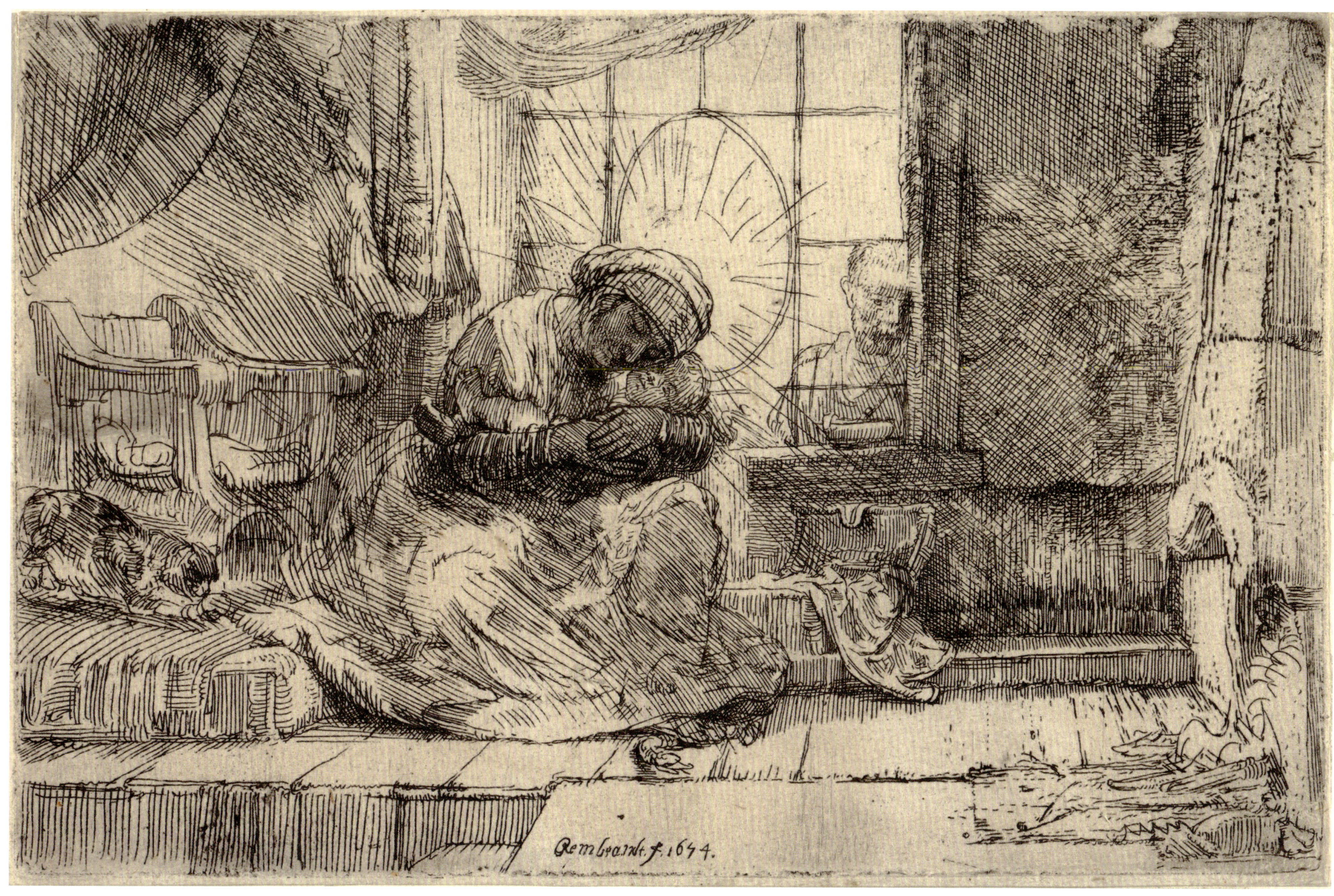

PLATE 36

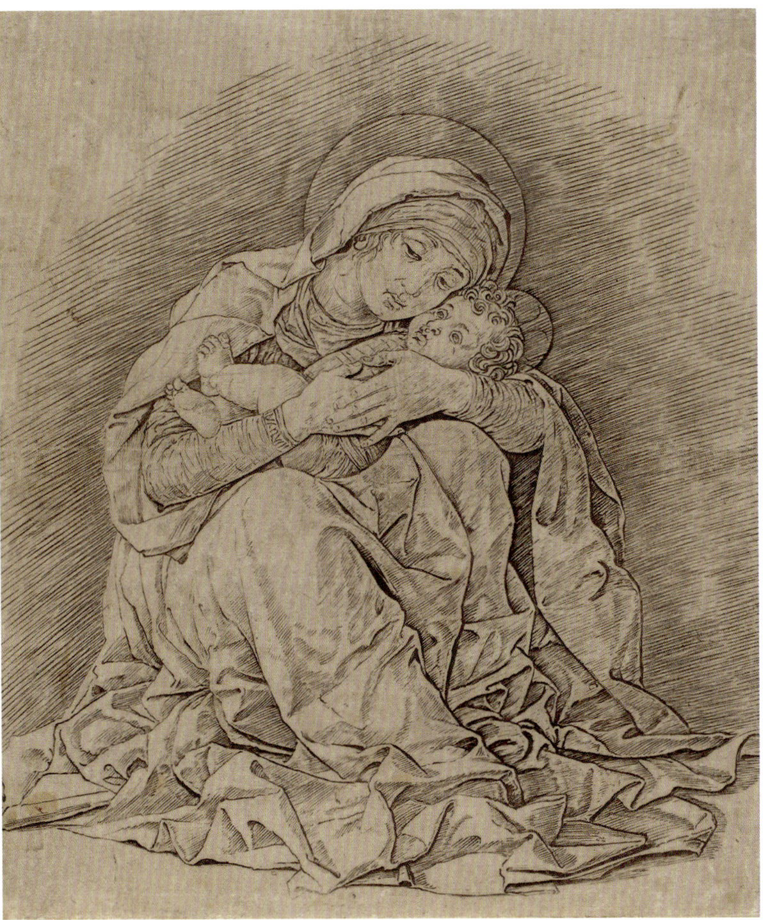

FIGURE 1. Mantegna, *Madonna and Child*, engraving, 1470s. *Photo: Courtesy of the National Gallery of Art, Washington, DC.*

of *The Madonna and Child* (fig. 1), one of the clearest examples of Rembrandt's acquaintance with Italian Renaissance sources,[9] but in contrast to the undefined setting of Mantegna's Madonna, Rembrandt's Mary is seated upon a low step, a position that emphasizes her role as a paradigm of humility.

The small, open chest of linens to Mary's left is a common attribute of the Virgin,[10] and for seventeenth-century viewers, it would have had a number of associations. Needlework, sewing, and weaving were common indications of such feminine virtues as obedience and diligence.[11] When associated with Mary, these occupations could allude not only to generic feminine virtues, but also specifically to her piety, humility, and selection by God.[12] They may also have served to reinforce the Virgin's identity as the new Eve, since Mary's pursuit of feminine labors showed her fulfilling a woman's postlapsarian destiny to toil alongside man.[13] Given Mary's somber expression and Joseph's mournful and meditative gaze, the small chest of linens may also have been meant to evoke the Passion in general, and Christ's shroud in particular. In this context, the fire burning in the hearth, ostensibly a homey domestic detail, may be a reference to the burnt offerings of the Old Law that would be replaced by Christ's sacrifice and the New Law.

The hissing viper trapped beneath the Virgin's foot is a traditional symbol of evil and sin in general, and Satan in particular. In the context of the prophetic punishment of the serpent in Genesis 3:15 ("I will put enmity between you and the woman, and between your seed and her seed; he shall bruise your head, and you shall bruise his heel"),[14] the image of Mary stepping on a snake or serpentine basilisk became another link to her identity as the new Eve, the woman who would reopen the gates of Paradise. The passage in Genesis promised the defeat of Satan, a prophecy that was fulfilled by Christ, the seed of Mary. According to historian Michael Zell, this motif is actually key to understanding the entire 1654 series of etchings dedicated to Jesus's childhood, for it emblematically announced Christ's fulfillment of the Mosaic prophecy and his role as redeemer.[15]

The significance of the cat has been a matter of some discussion. A number of scholars identified it as a symbol of evil, in part because of the cat's traditional association with witches and demons.[16] More recently, however, Susan Donahue Kuretsky sought to redeem Rembrandt's feline, noting that these domesticated animals were also identified as loyal homebodies that, though capable of mischief, were guardians of the hearth.[17] In support of the cat's benevolent role in the etching, Kuretsky quoted Colin Eisler's observation that St. Augustine likened the Incarnation of Christ to a trap for the Devil, "much as a cat catches a mouse." In the context of this etching, then, Rembrandt's cat, which seems ready to attack the serpent, the embodiment of evil, may be seen as a defender of virtue against Satan, rather than a demonic presence intent on threatening the Virgin and her child.[18] Finally, Kuretsky proposed yet another function for Rembrandt's cat, a purpose that relates to other potentially symbolic details in the etching. She identified the cat as a *parergon*, an anecdotal embellishment that is included in a narrative in order to enrich the main theme and that, if properly employed, encourages "attentive viewing of the scene as a whole and closer focus on its main figures."[19] In this context, the cat has "been integrated into the life of . . . [its] owners in a way that enhances the snugness and warmth of the Holy Family's domestic world while symbolically providing it with spiritual protection."[20]

Mary's prominence within the scene and the fact that her depiction was derived from a well-known devotional image by Andrea Mantegna, along with Rembrandt's use of unusually dense, almost medieval symbolism in this etching, have suggested to some scholars that the print was directed primarily toward a Catholic audience.[21] It seems likely, however, that this work was intended to have a broad confessional appeal. On a purely emotional level, the etching's attraction derives from its description of a tender, intimate relationship between a mother and her child, a quality that probably drew Rembrandt to the Mantegna print as a source in the first place. For a Catholic audience, the Marian theme would certainly have had a strong spiritual appeal. At the same time, Dutch Reformists would have responded to the etching's emphasis on Mary's humility and her image as a woman and mother, rather than as the more distant, mystical "Queen of Heaven." Although a canopied "throne" is present in the Virgin's chamber, Rembrandt chose to seat Mary upon a low step, instead. Calvin, in his commentary on Luke 1:48, drew a sharp distinction between his view of the Virgin and that of the Catholic Church. He was emphatic in his praise of Mary's humility and low estate, and virulent in his criticism of those who "adorn her with their empty devices" and "heap up an abundance of magnificent and very presumptuous titles, such as, 'Queen of Heaven, Star of Salvation, Gate of Life, Sweetness, Hope, and Salvation.'"[22] For the Dutch Calvinist viewer, Rembrandt's print would have illustrated precisely this distinction.

Notes

1. For a list of the other prints in this series, see *Adoration of the Shepherds: With the Lamp* (B. 45, cat. no. 20), esp. note 3.

2. Mary's humble seat on a low step is reminiscent of Rembrandt's etching of the Holy Family of c. 1631–32 (B. 62, cat. no. 35), as are the basket with linens or sewing and the arrangement (in reverse) of the central figures of the Virgin and Child, with Joseph behind them.

3. J. Q. Van Regteren Altena suggested that Rembrandt might have originally included Joseph in the room, but then removed him. Quoted in J. P. Filedt Kok, *Rembrandt Etchings and Drawings in the Rembrandt House: A Catalogue* (Maarssen, Netherlands: Schwartz, 1972), 60.

4. Leonard Slatkes, "Review of C. White and K. Boon, *Rembrandt's Etchings*, and C. White, *Rembrandt as an Etcher*," *Art Quarterly* 36 (1973): 258. Slatkes noted that a window through which light passes without breaking it is a traditional symbol for Mary's virginity. Millard Meiss, "Light as Form and Symbol in Some Fifteenth-Century Paintings," *Art Bulletin* 27, no. 3 (September 1945):176, cited Bernard of Clairvaux as one of the sources of this metaphor: "Just as the brilliance of the sun fills and penetrates a glass window without damaging it, and pierces its solid form with imperceptible subtlety, neither hurting it when entering nor destroying it when emerging: thus the word of God, the splendor of the Father, entered the virgin chamber and then came forth from the closed womb."

Slatkes also suggested that the absence of any obvious door in the room may have been meant to identify it as a sealed chamber, another symbol of Mary's purity.

5. I am not convinced by Perlove and Silver's contention (*Rembrandt's Faith*, 67 and 181–83) that Joseph's placement outside the chamber looking in through the window identifies him as the yet-unenlightened Jew awaiting conversion, one who can see God and God's plan only "through a glass darkly." The fact that the curtain that would have obstructed his view of the room has been pulled aside may be a symbol of revelation.

Perhaps Joseph, like Mary, who cradles her infant protectively, is reflecting on what is to come, since Simeon warned them of Jesus's sacrifice when he met them at the time of the baby's presentation at the Temple. (For a discussion of the Presentation, see the entries on the Presentation in the Temple in this catalogue [cat. nos. 25 and 26].) This would explain Joseph's sorrowful expression. For the relationship between the raised curtain and the Calvinist theme of revelation, specifically in respect to Rembrandt's *Holy Family with a Curtain* in the Gemäldegalerie in Kassel, Germany (RRP, *Corpus*, V6), which depicts a similar domestic image of the Holy Family, see John Moffitt, "Rembrandt, Revelations and Calvin's Curtains," *Gazette des Beaux-Arts* 113/114 (April 1987): 175–84.

6. The fact that Joseph stands outside the window indicates that the room is on the ground floor. The stairway and wooden platform of the floor are similar to those in Rembrandt's *Christ at Emmaus: Larger Plate* (B. 87, cat. no. 60), which was also done in 1654.

7. Slatkes, "Review of C. White and K. Boon, *Rembrandt's Etchings*," 257–58; Catherine B. Scallen, "Rembrandt, Emulation and the Northern Print Tradition," in *In Detail: New Studies of Northern Renaissance Art in Honor of Walter S. Gibson*, ed. Laurinda S. Dixon (Turnhout, Belgium: Brepols, 1998), 142; and Hinterding, *Lugt Catalogue* cat. 49, 134.

8. Holm Bevers, "Rembrandt as an Etcher," in Bevers, Peter Schatborn, and Barbara Welzel, *Rembrandt: The Master and His Workshop*, vol. 2, *Drawings and Etchings* (New Haven, CT: Yale University Press, 1991), 269.

9. Mantegna, *Madonna and Child,* TIB 8. This source was already recognized in the late nineteenth century by Hofstede de Groot. See B. P. J. Broos, *Index to the Formal Sources of Rembrandt's Art*. It has often been noted that Rembrandt adopted Mantegna's technique of modeling in this and other prints in the 1654 youth-of-Christ series, using long parallel strokes to describe shadows.

10. A similar basket appears in *Holy Family* (B. 62, cat. no. 35). Probably the best known example of the Virgin with a sewing basket is Correggio's *Madonna della Cesta* (c. 1524) in the National Gallery, London.

11. Wayne Franits, *Paragons of Virtue: Women and Domesticity in Seventeenth-Century Dutch Art* (Cambridge: Cambridge University Press, 1993), 21.

12. According to St. Jerome, as quoted in Jacobus da Voragine's *Golden Legend* (trans. Granger Ryan and Helmut Ripperger [New York and London: Longmans, Green, 1941], Sept. 8, "Feast of the Nativity of the Virgin Mary," 523), after the Virgin entered the Temple at the age of three, she set for herself a daily regimen: "From dawn to the third hour she devoted herself to prayer, from the third to the ninth hour she worked at weaving, and from the ninth hour she prayed until an angel appeared, bringing her food." After her betrothal to Joseph, Mary continued to pursue her vocation of weaving, but now for an even higher purpose. In the eighth chapter of the *Gospel of Pseudo-Matthew*, it is recounted that after the betrothal, the high priest Abithar allowed five other virgins to accompany Mary to Joseph's house, to live with her there until Joseph was willing to acknowledge her as his wife. While there, Mary and her companions were asked to make a new veil for the Temple in Jerusalem. Their specific tasks were chosen by lot, and Mary drew the task of weaving the most precious materials, the sacred purple and scarlet. Although Mary's selection was purportedly random, it was believed that because she was the humblest and most deserving of the women, the task she drew was the result of God's will and a sign of her destiny. *The Gospel of Pseudo-Matthew*, trans. Alexander Walker, chapter 8, in *Anti-Nicene Fathers*, ed. Philip Shaff, vol. 8, accessed February 18, 2013, http://www.ccel.org/ccel/schaff/anf08.pdf.

That the story of the Virgin and the Temple veil was still alive in the seventeenth century is attested to by a print from a series of twenty-six plates dedicated to the Life of the Virgin done by Hieronymus Wierix before 1619. The engraving shows the young Mary and four other young girls sewing as two angels attend them (HD 791 [the Wierix Family]). In the Annunciation from the same series, a basket filled with cloth is clearly visible on the floor beside the Virgin, who is interrupted in her reading by the appearance of the angel Gabriel (HD 792 [the Wierix Family]). See also *Holy Family* (B. 62, cat. no. 35), note no. 4.

13. As David Ekserdjian (*Correggio* [New Haven, CT: Yale University Press, 1997]) noted in his comment on Correggio's *Madonna della Cesta*, there is a tradition of depicting Mary and Joseph at work. This is exemplified in Albrecht Dürer's woodcut of the *Holy Family in Egypt* (TIB, woodcuts, 90) from his *Life of the Virgin*. On the tradition of the Virgin working as a seamstress in Egypt to help support the family, see Robert W. Gaston, "Prospero Fontana's Holy Family with Saints," *Art Bulletin of Victoria* 19 (1978): 32–35.

The idea that Eve's fall condemned women to work, and specifically to spin, is quite old. For example, it is memorialized in the fourteenth-century English rhyme "When Adam delve and Eve span / Who was then a gentleman?" (cited in Ekserdjian, *Correggio*, 148). In Cennino Cennini's early fifteenth-century treatise on painting, he specifically identified digging and spinning as the labors of Adam and Eve.

There are also several prints in Hieronymus Wierix's seventeenth-century *Life of the Infant Jesus* series in which the Holy Family is shown at work, with Mary specifically engaged in sewing, knitting, or spinning (HD 486, HD 488, HD 490, and HD 495 [the Wierix Family]).

14. According to Hinterding, *Lugt Catalogue*, 135n1, the connection between Rembrandt's print and this passage in Genesis was first made in 1836, though at that point without additional interpretive comment.

15. Michael Zell, *Reframing Rembrandt: Jews and the Christian Image in Seventeenth-Century Amsterdam* (Berkeley: University of California Press, 2002), 129.

16. See, for example, Bevers, "Rembrandt as an Etcher," 270: "The cat too must be intended as an embodiment of evil, and of Satan, who dwelt, according to popular superstition, in the chimney." It could be argued, then, that the cat is gazing not at the snake, but at the fireplace (its home) across the room. On the tradition of the cat in art and the ambiguous attitude toward its meaning, see Suzana Sebkova Thaller, "Il gatto nell'arte tardo Medioevo e del Rinascimento," in *Gatti nell'arte: il magico e il quotidiano: 3 giugno–19 luglio 1987, Palazzo Barberini, Galleria nazionale d'arte antica* (Rome: Multigrafica, 1987), 27–34.

17. Susan Donahue Kuretsky, "Rembrandt's Cat," in *Aemulatio. Imitation, Emulation and Invention in Netherlandish Art from 1500 to 1800: Essays in Honor of Eric Jan Sluijter*, ed. Anton W. Boschloo, Jacquelyn N. Couttre, Stephanie S. Dickey, and Nicolette C. Sluijter-Seijffert (Zwolle, Netherlands: Waanders, 2011), 269–70.

18. Also in defense of Rembrandt's cat, Kuretsky ("Rembrandt's Cat," 271) cited Edward Topsell (*The Histoire of Four Footed Beastes and Serpents*, London, 1607), who asserted that cats "are immune to serpent poison," a quality that makes them the perfect opponents of Satanic serpents.

19. Kuretsky, "Rembrandt's Cat," 271. Although the concept of *parerga* is a classical concept, Kuretsky noted that Rembrandt's contemporaries were cognizant of it. In particular, she cited the comments of seventeenth-century humanist scholar Franciscus Junius the Younger on the proper use of the *parerga*, which he explains in his treatise on ancient art, *De pictura veterum*. This treatise was first published in Latin in 1637, but was translated into Dutch only four years later.

20. Kuretsky, "Rembrandt's Cat," 271. A cat occasionally appears in images of the Annunciation. In this context, it is probably intended to suggest the peaceful domesticity of the Virgin's chamber, which is being disrupted by Gabriel's miraculous appearance. See, for example, Federico Barocci's etching after his own painted *Annunciation* (B. 2).

A cat also appears in an unusual 1581 engraving of the Holy Family in Egypt by Johannes Sadeler I after a composition by Maerten de Vos (Sadeler, HD 169; de Vos, HD 265). This scene is set in a typical Dutch interior. The Virgin, seated on a wicker couch known as a *bakermat,* is intent on feeding the Christ Child, who is seated on her lap. Nearby, angels attend to various domestic chores, with one of them drying a diaper in front of the fire in the hearth on the left side of the composition. Joseph, hard at work trimming a wooden beam, can be seen through a large window at the back of the room. The seated cat in the foreground of the engraving, immediately in front of the Virgin and child, has chosen the optimal spot to enjoy the warmth of the fire. Although the cat may serve as a symbolic guardian of hearth and home, it is equally likely that it is simply a familiar, domestic detail, adding to the tranquil aura of the scene.

21. See, for example, Bevers, "Rembrandt as an Etcher," 270: "These works [this print and *Virgin in the Clouds* (B. 61, cat. no. 34)], must have been intended for members of the Catholic merchant class who were also to be found in Protestant Holland."

22. Calvin, *Commentary on a Harmony of the Evangelists, Matthew, Mark, and Luke*, 1:64–65, Commentary on Luke 1:48, accessed July 18, 2014, http://www.ccel.org/ccel/calvin/calcom31.pdf.

37–39. Christ Disputing with the Doctors

37. Christ Disputing with the Doctors: Small Plate

B. 66 (H. 20, Mz.190, NHD 53)
Etching
Signed and dated in the plate in states I and II: *RHL 1630*
State III of VII
Sheet: 8.9 × 6.8 cm, trimmed to within plate mark on the left side, 8.7 × 6.7 cm
Verso: in graphite, *B66/H8549*

Provenance:
Harrods, London, 1980
Feddersen, Elkhart, IN, 1991
Snite Museum of Art
Acc. No.: 1991.025.037

Plate survives:
Private collection of I. de Bruijn van der Leeuw, Muri (missing since 1961).

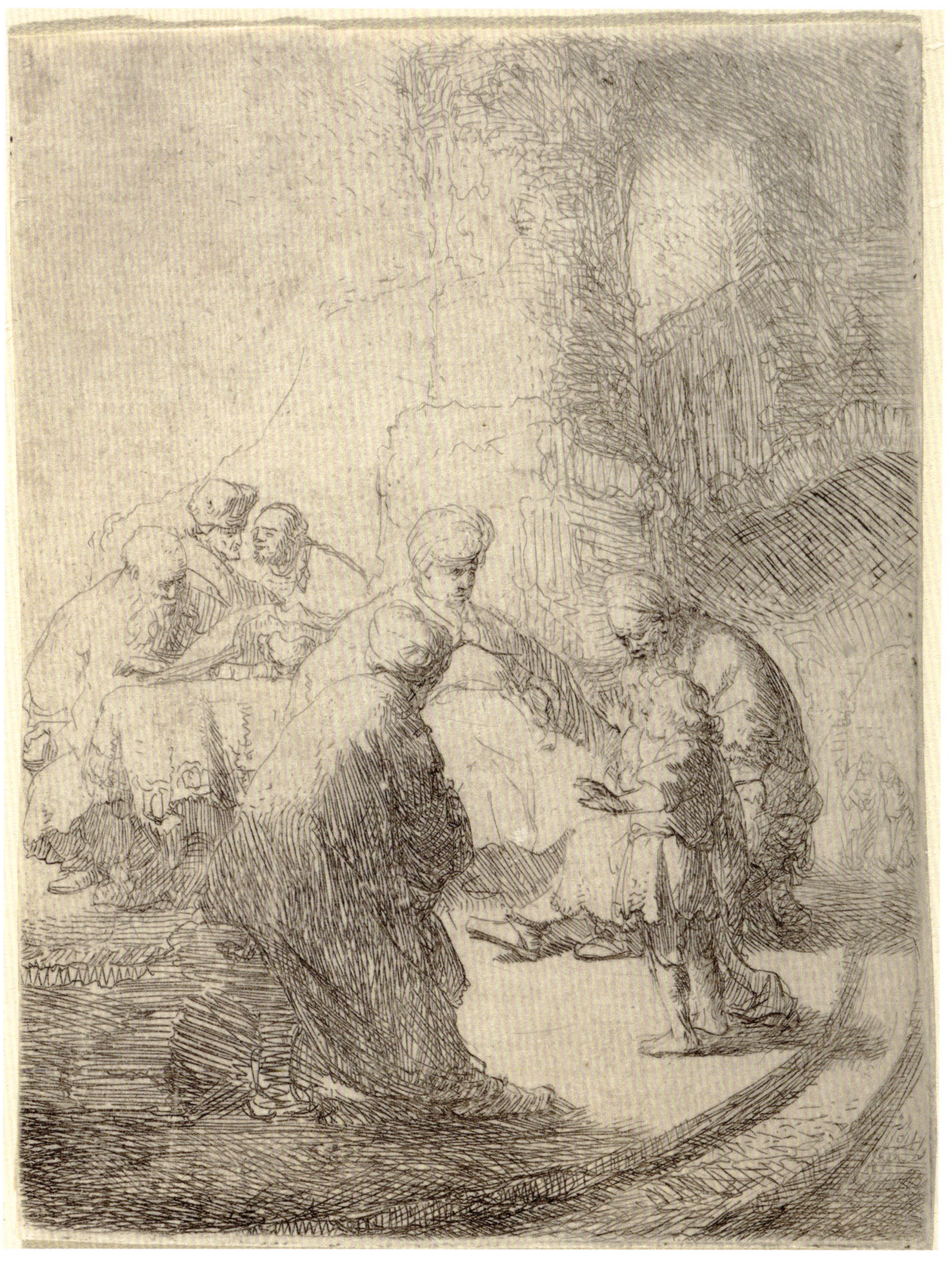

PLATE 37

38. Christ Disputing with the Doctors: A Sketch

B. 65 (H. 257, Mz. 222, NHD 267)
Etching and drypoint
Signed and dated in the plate: *Rembrandt f. 1652*
State I of II
Sheet: 13.2 × 21.7 cm; plate mark 12.6 × 21.4 cm
Verso: in graphite, *B65ii/ c. 14656*

Provenance:
Associated American Artists Inc., New York, NY, 1974
Feddersen, Elkhart, IN, 1991
Snite Museum of Art
Acc. No.: 1991.025.036

The plate does not survive.

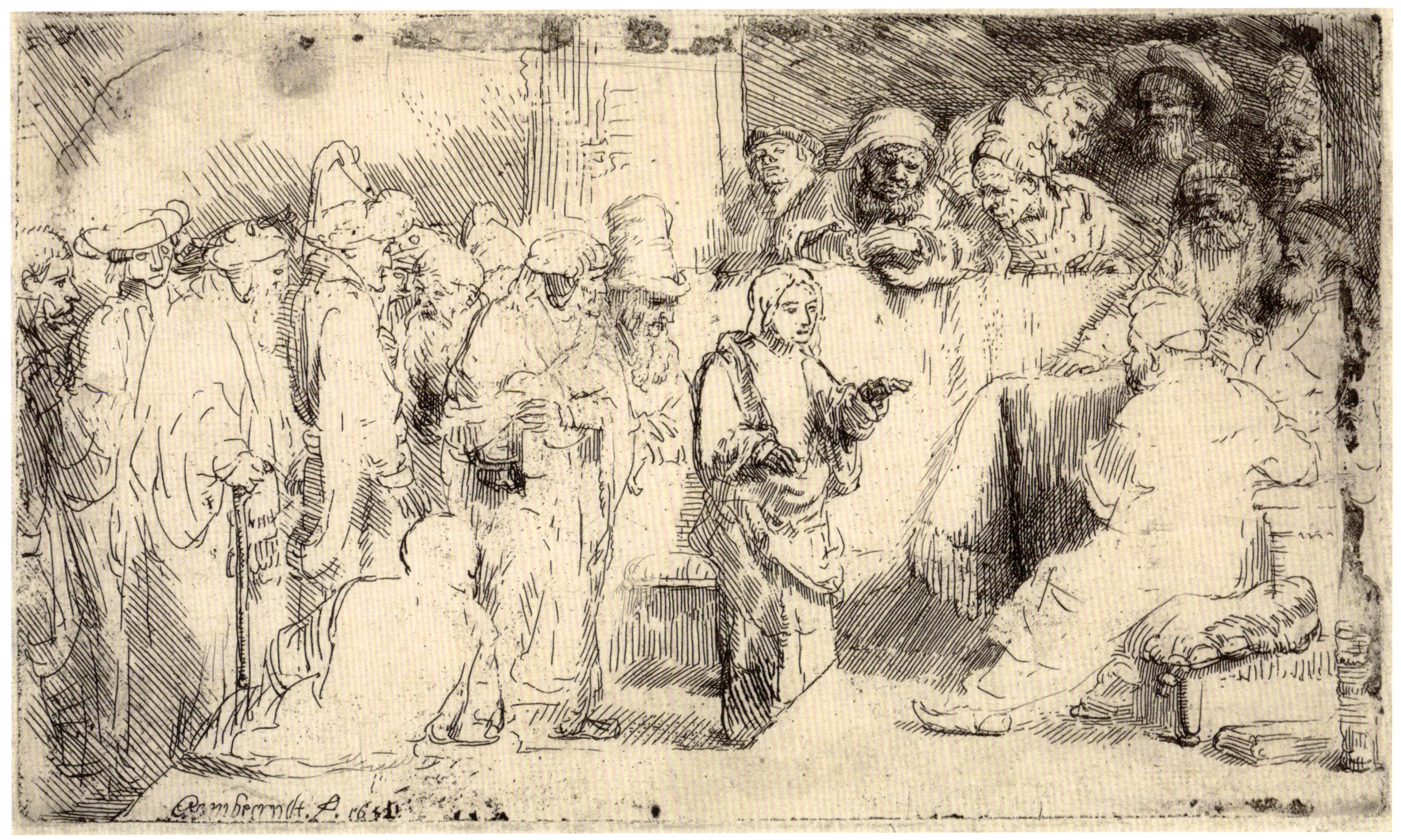

PLATE 38

39. *Christ Seated Disputing with the Doctors*

B. 64 (H. 277, Mz. 230, NHD 281)
Etching with some drypoint
Signed and dated in the plate: *Rembrandt f. 1654*
State I of I
Sheet: 9.5 × 14.4 cm, trimmed to the plate mark
Watermark: fragment of fleur-de-lis (?)
Verso: in graphite, *N°1/H64i/B277.1/Viscount Fitzharris*; collector's stamp, LL in a circle in red ink (Lugt 4796, Leslie E. Lancy)

Provenance:
Viscount Fitzharris, possibly James Earl Harris, 5th Earl of Malmesbury(1872–1950) (not in Lugt)
Leslie E. Lancy, Ellwood, PA (1911–96)
David Tunick Inc., New York, NY, 1977
Feddersen, Elkhart, IN, 1991
Snite Museum of Art
Acc. No.: 1991.025.035

Plate survives:
Noortman Master Paintings, Maastricht, The Netherlands (2007).

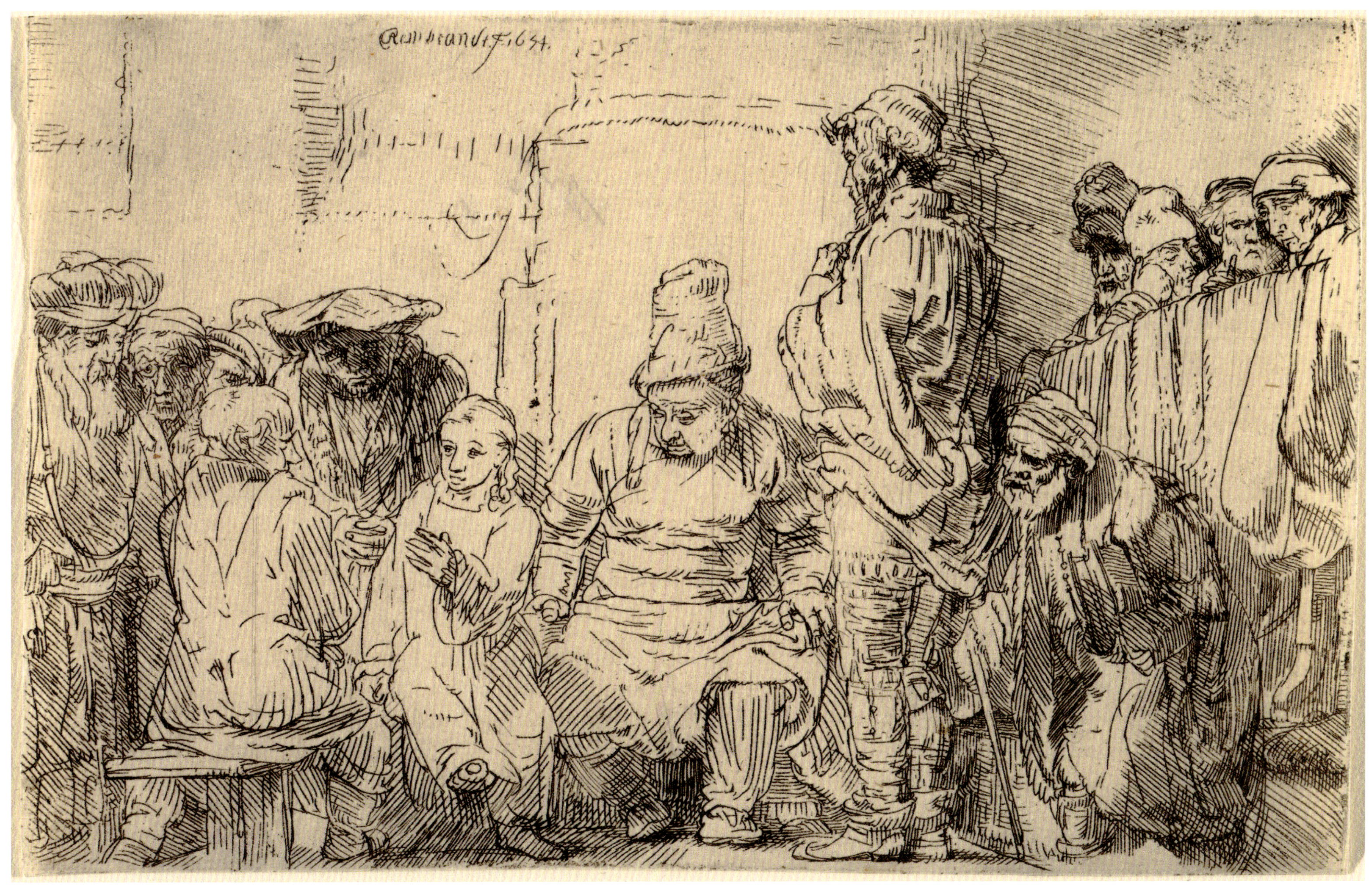

PLATE 39

The story of Jesus's disputation with the doctors in the Temple is told in Luke 2:41–50. Every year, Mary and Joseph traveled from Nazareth to Jerusalem for the feast of Passover. When Jesus was twelve, the family went to the holy city as was their custom, but afterward, when Mary and Joseph, along with relatives and other companions, were on their way home, they discovered that Jesus was missing; he had stayed behind. The holy couple returned to Jerusalem to find their son. After searching for three days, they finally found him "in the temple, sitting in the midst of the doctors [learned elders], both hearing them, and asking them questions. And all that heard him were astonished at his understanding and answers." When his parents asked Jesus why he had caused them such anguish, he replied, "How is it that you sought me? Did you not know that I was about my Father's business?" Puzzled by his reply, Mary and Joseph gathered up their son and returned home to Nazareth.

The story of Christ disputing with the doctors was portrayed regularly in the fifteenth and sixteenth centuries as part of a number of series variously dedicated to the Life of Christ, to the Passion, and to the Sorrows and Life of the Virgin. In most images, the young Jesus is shown seated, usually on a raised platform and occasionally at a desk or lectern. These types of compositions emphasize Jesus's role as a teacher who is instructing the elders,[1] implicitly asserting the superiority of the New Law over the Old. Rembrandt depicted the story three times in the course of his career, and in each instance, he eschewed this traditional type of hierarchical arrangement. In doing so, he may have been influenced by Calvin's commentary on Luke 2:45–46, in which the reformer emphasized Jesus's lowly station and noted that the scholars, who must have been inspired by their recognition of the child's divinity, allowed him to sit *among* them.[2] For Calvin, part of the miracle of this event was not just that Jesus could teach the elders, but that they treated him as an equal.[3] Rembrandt's compositional choices emphasize this sense of equality and, given Christ's divine nature, his humility.

Rembrandt's earliest print of Christ disputing with the doctors is a small etching (B. 66, cat. no. 37) done in a fine, miniaturist style. In its first two states, this print is signed and dated "*RHL* 1630" in the center of the lower margin of the plate.[4] In the third and final state, the one represented in the Snite Museum's collection, the plate was trimmed on three sides. The lower margin was cut off, as was a large area of unarticulated space at the top and a section along the left side of plate that had included a pair of seated figures. The trimmed and altered composition is much more compact, with the result that it is more narrowly focused on Christ's interaction with the scholars.

In this early etching of Christ Disputing with the Doctors, the encounter takes place on a low platform within the monumental, cavernous space of the Temple. A diminutive and very youthful Jesus, who appears to have just mounted the two steps at the right side of the image in order to join the elders on a circular dais, is bathed in a strong light coming from the rear of the chamber. His arms are raised in a rhetorical gesture of address, suggesting that he is not simply asking questions of the elders, but is actively engaged in a discussion or disputation. Three elderly turbaned Jews are seated in a semicircle before him, their heads inclined as they listen intently to his words. The men on Jesus's left and right lean forward into the light, straining to hear the young boy's words, while the third scholar, a man of substantial girth who is seated directly opposite Jesus, leans back in his seat in a relaxed fashion while gazing down at the extraordinary youth before him. In the left background, another scholar consults a large tome that lies open on a draped table, while immediately behind him, two other Pharisees appear to be engaged in discussing what they see and hear.[5] The theatrical quality of the scene is reinforced by strong chiaroscuro lighting and the scale of the architecture that looms behind the figures. As numerous scholars have noted, the manner in which Rembrandt constructs the space of the Temple—with massive columns, shadowy arches, and mysterious, cavernous depths—is based on the setting that the artist created for his 1629 painting *Judas Returning the Thirty Pieces of Silver* (England, private collection)[6] (fig. 1). Shelley Perlove and Larry Silver suggested that the setting depicted in both the painting and the etching is the Chamber of the Parhedrin, "the counselors' chamber used as a meeting place for the priests and elders who supervised the treasuries and nearly every aspect of the Temple cult."[7] During the late 1620s and early 1630s, theologians and scholars of Judaic studies in the city of Leiden were wrestling with the question of how the Temple in Jerusalem had actually looked, but it is not known whether the still quite youthful Rembrandt would have been privy to these debates and, therefore, might have been trying to recreate the specific geography of the Temple in these and other images.[8]

Mary and Joseph were typically included in representations of this biblical episode for two reasons: First, according to the narrative, they had returned to Jerusalem to find their son, and second, when they found him in the Temple, they bore witness to the miracle of his precociousness.[9] Calvin emphasized the testimonial role of the Virgin, in particular, observing that the event would have been forgotten had not Mary kept it "laid up in her heart."[10] Rembrandt included the holy couple in his 1630 etching, but just barely. They are presumably the tiny figures in the deep right background, approaching the dais from within the vast reaches of the Temple.

Rembrandt returned to the subject of the dispute in 1652, creating a larger, oblong etching, *Christ Disputing with the Doctors: A Sketch* (B. 65, cat. no 38). In contrast to the 1630 print, the architectural elements in this etching are kept to a minimum, the space is considerably more constricted, and the overall handling is much more cursory. Mary and Joseph are absent from both this etching and the final version (B. 64, 1654, cat. no. 40).[11] However, the number of figures has been greatly increased, and their reactions, postures, costumes, and ethnicity are more diverse, suggesting that Jesus is addressing not only the venerable elders in the Temple, but a much broader spectrum of mankind, including—at the extreme upper right-hand corner—a turbaned man with Moorish features.[12] This figure is one of a half dozen listeners who lean over a low wall along the back of the room, peering down at the youth below.[13] The onlookers are well-defined figures with distinctive attire and personalities.

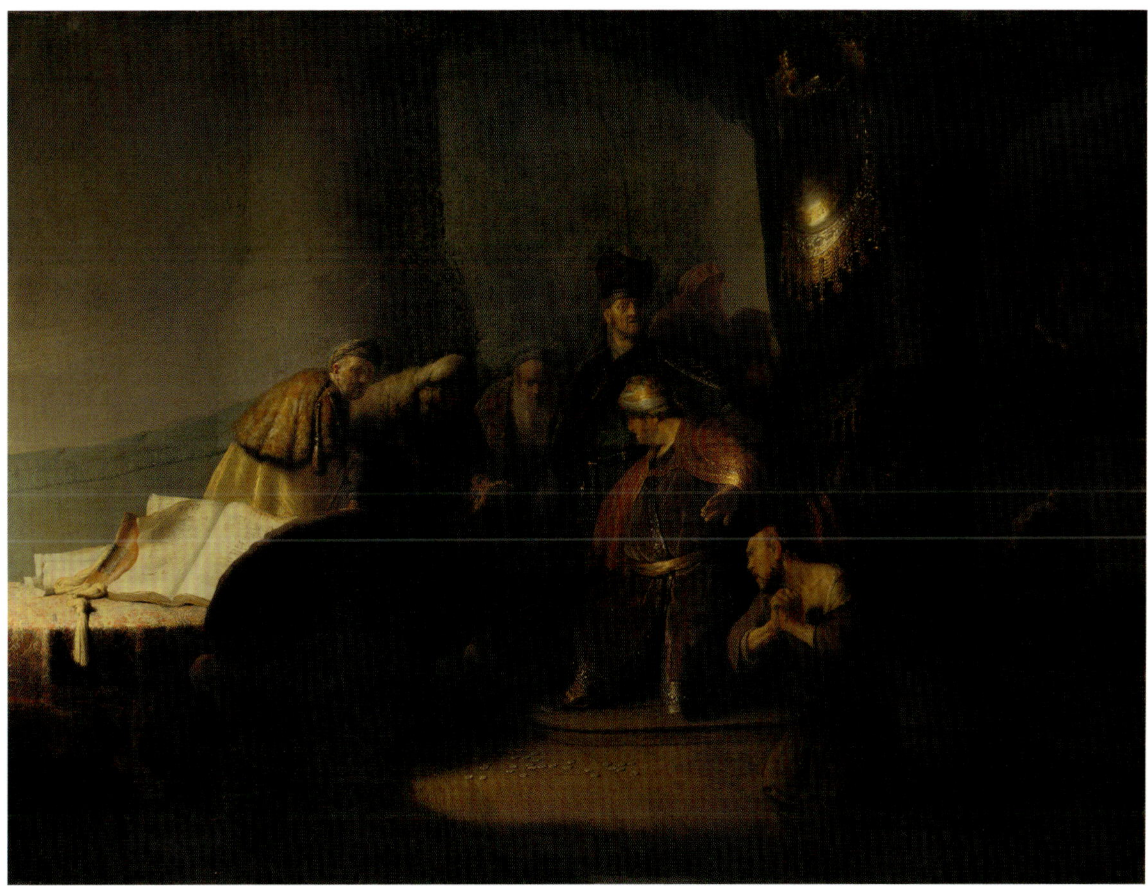

FIGURE 1. Rembrandt, *Judas Returning the Thirty Pieces of Silver*, oil on panel, 1629, private collection. *Photo: © Private Collection, Photography courtesy of the National Gallery, London, 2016.*

Executed during a period of extraordinary technical experimentation, the 1652 print demonstrates Rembrandt's remarkable range in the use of line and modeling. Many of the figures, such as the reclining man and diverse group of scholars on the left side of the print and the seated man in the right foreground, are just barely

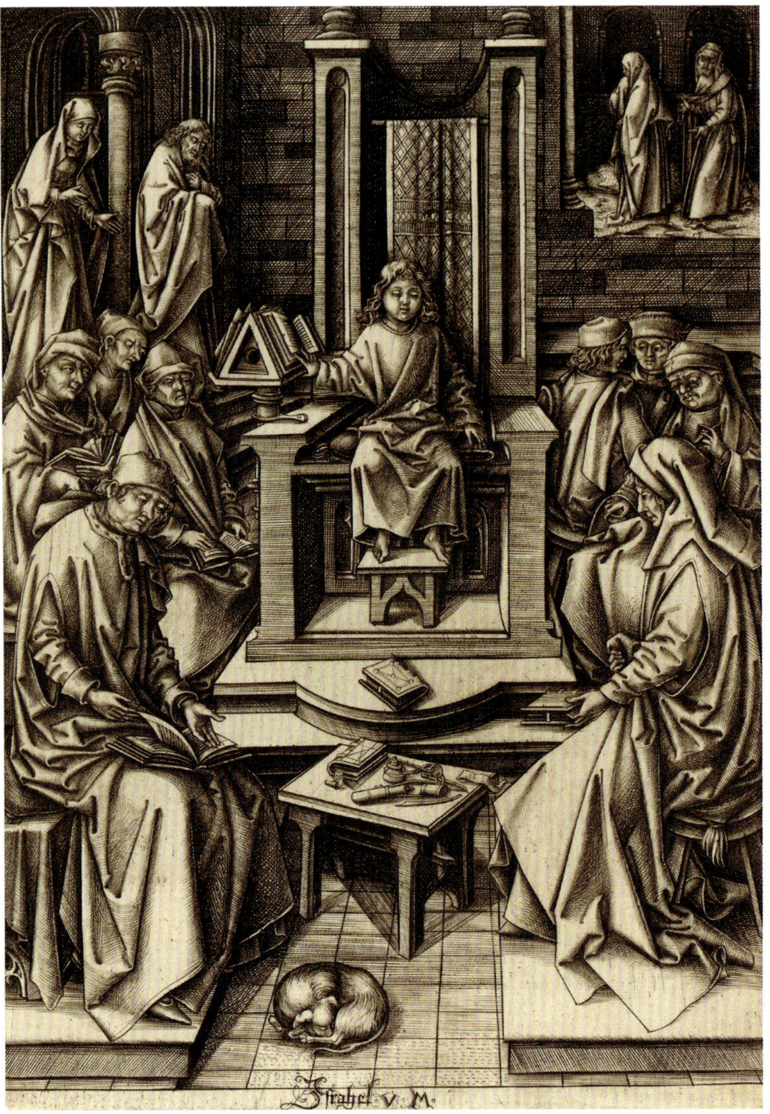

FIGURE 2. Israhel van Meckenem, *Christ Disputing with the Doctors*, engraving, c. 1490–1500. *Photo: Courtesy of the National Gallery of Art Washington, DC.*

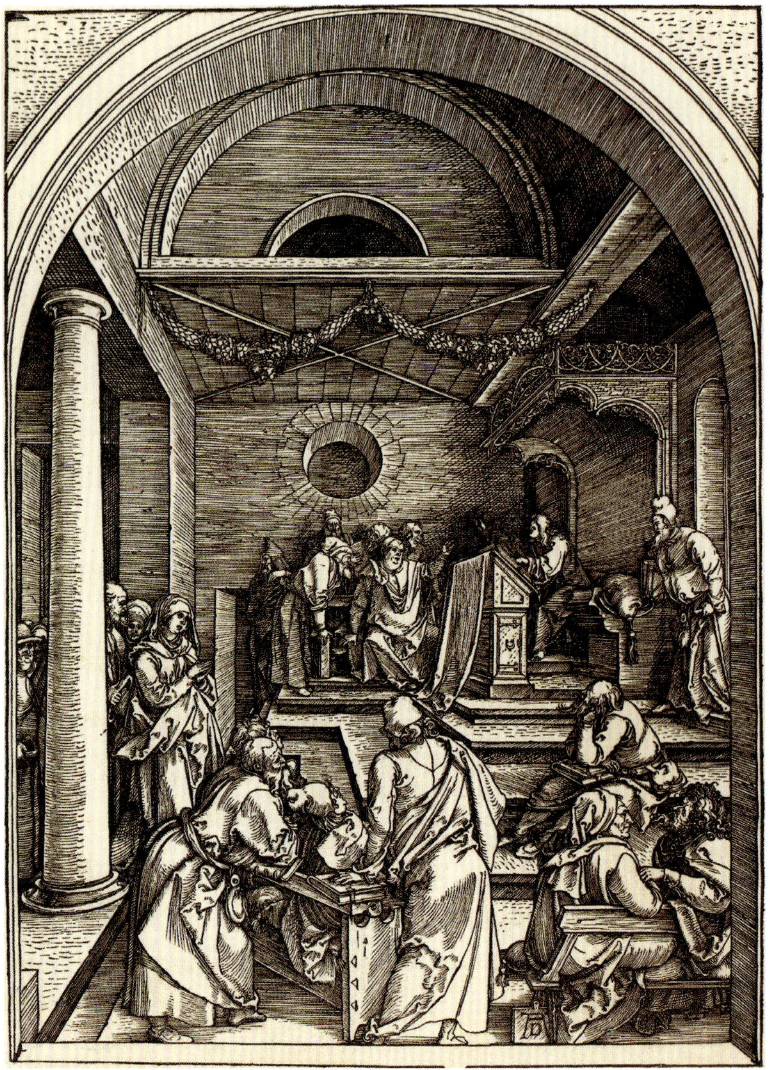

FIGURE 3. Albrecht Dürer, *Christ Disputing with the Doctors*, woodcut, from *Life of the Virgin*, 1503–4. *Photo: Courtesy of the National Gallery of Art, Washington, DC.*

defined through the use of thinly etched contour lines and patches of parallel hatching.[14] Jesus's hands and the contours of his tunic are more deeply etched, and in the first state of the print, touches of drypoint were added for emphasis, although by the second state, the drypoint burr is no longer visible.[15] Standing in the right center of the composition, almost in profile to the viewer, Jesus looks straight ahead, extending his arms as he addresses the scholars seated on a raised platform in front of him. His pose is more static than that of the younger orator in the 1630 print, who appears to exhort the wise men before him. On the floor in the right corner, beside the turbaned man whom Jesus addresses, is a closed book that identifies this as a place of study for the "people of the book" and suggests that the Old Law has been displaced by the New.

Unlike the earlier etching, in which Jesus has climbed up so that he is on an equal footing with the elders, the 1652 print shows a somewhat older youth who has ascended one level of the dais, but is still situated below the level of the three sages whom he addresses. He is isolated from the onlookers behind and above him, both in space and by virtue of the heaviness of the hatching that defines his robes and his gesturing hands. Whereas the light in the earlier print bursts out from the rear wall, narrowing to focus on the Christ Child, the light in the 1652 print spreads fairly evenly across the entire scene, except for the recess at the upper right. Although Rembrandt's use of illumination is less dramatic in the 1652 etching, the print appears more animated because of the many unique characters who seem mesmerized by Jesus's performance. The earlier print, by contrast, reads as a more serene, or even mystical, encounter, despite the more lively gestures of what appears to be an exuberantly engaged child.

Perlove and Silver suggested that the architecture in the 1652 print reflects that of the Beth Hammidrash, or divinity school, near the gathering place for the small Sanhedrin, or Jewish council. As they noted, this would be in keeping with Erasmus's description of the setting of the disputation as a synagogue or type of school. A similar architectural arrangement can be seen in Crispijn van den Broeck's illustration of Christ among the Doctors (fig. 5) created as the forty-second emblem in Benito Arias Montano's *Humanae Salutis Monumenta*, published in Antwerp in 1571. Unfortunately, it is not possible to determine whether the similarities between the architectural spaces in the Montano emblem and those in the Rembrandt print are the result of the artist's knowledge of the earlier van den Broeck image or of the fact that both derived from a common contemporary architectural type, the lecture hall or courtroom.

Rembrandt's final etching of Jesus speaking with the doctors dates from 1654 (B. 64, cat. no. 39). It is one of a series of six prints of that date that illustrate events from Christ's childhood.[16] Rectangular in format, the setting is similar to that of the 1652 version, but the composition has been simplified, and the number of actors reduced. Although there is still some variation in the rendering of the figures, the effect is not nearly as pronounced as in the 1652 version. The youthful Jesus, now somewhere in age between the young child of the first print (cat. no. 37) and the mature youth of the second (cat. no. 38), is seated on a low bench on the dais, amid the doctors. He appears to be addressing his remarks specifically to a seated elder who sits opposite him, straddling a low stool, with his back turned toward the viewer. In contrast to the 1652 print, Jesus is the most simply delineated of the actors. In this case, however, the simplicity of the image results in a kind of luminosity so that the precocious boy seems to be the source of light within the print. In effect, Rembrandt has expanded upon the tradition of representing the young Christ with a halo.[17] Here, the metaphor is not simply one of divinity, but also of enlightenment, both didactic and spiritual. As Perlove and Silver observed, the Pharisees and scribes who flank Jesus are clothed in a variety of costumes, reflecting contemporary Ashkenazi (Eastern European) and Sephardic (Portuguese and Spanish) dress. At the center, a very large man looms behind the young Jesus and inclines his head toward the boy, concentrating on the youth's words. By juxtaposing this massive figure and the slight boy seated nearby, Rembrandt emphasized Jesus's youth and human frailty, even as he has celebrated the miracle of the child's prescience and wisdom. Here, physical "might" defers to spiritual "light."

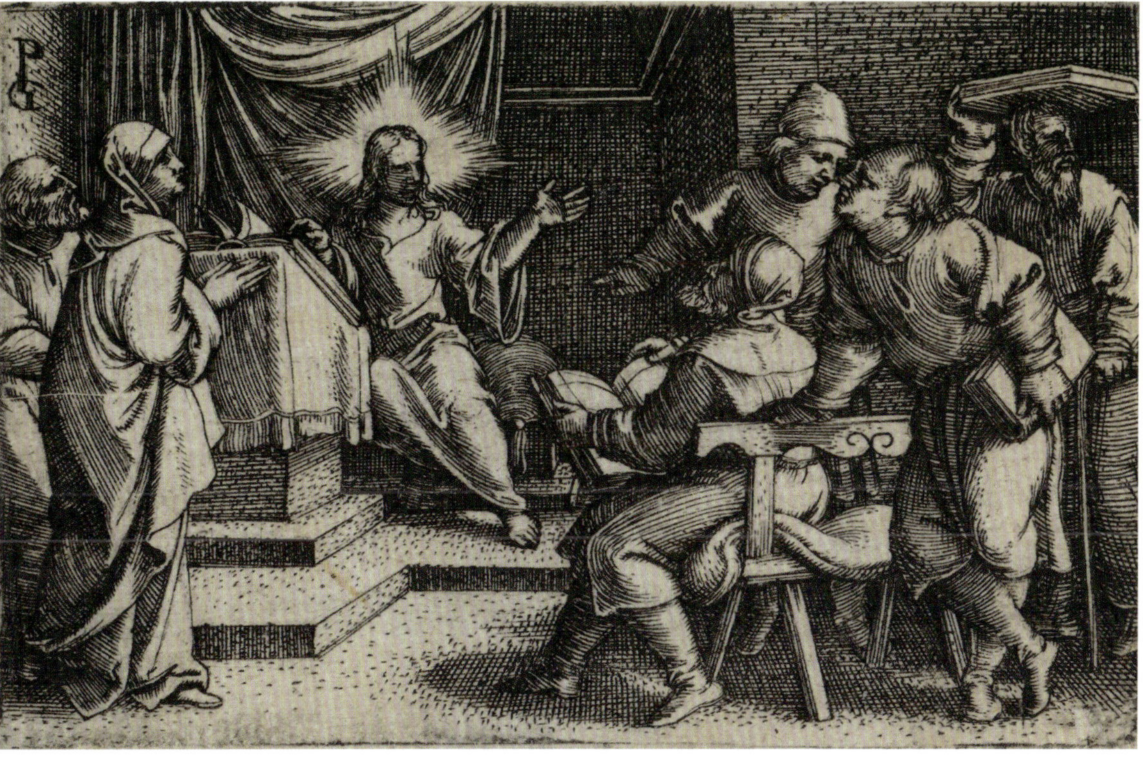

FIGURE 4. Georg Pencz, *Christ Disputing with the Doctors*, engraving, 1534–35. *The Metropolitan Museum of Art, New York, New York, Harris Brisbane Dick Fund, 1930.*

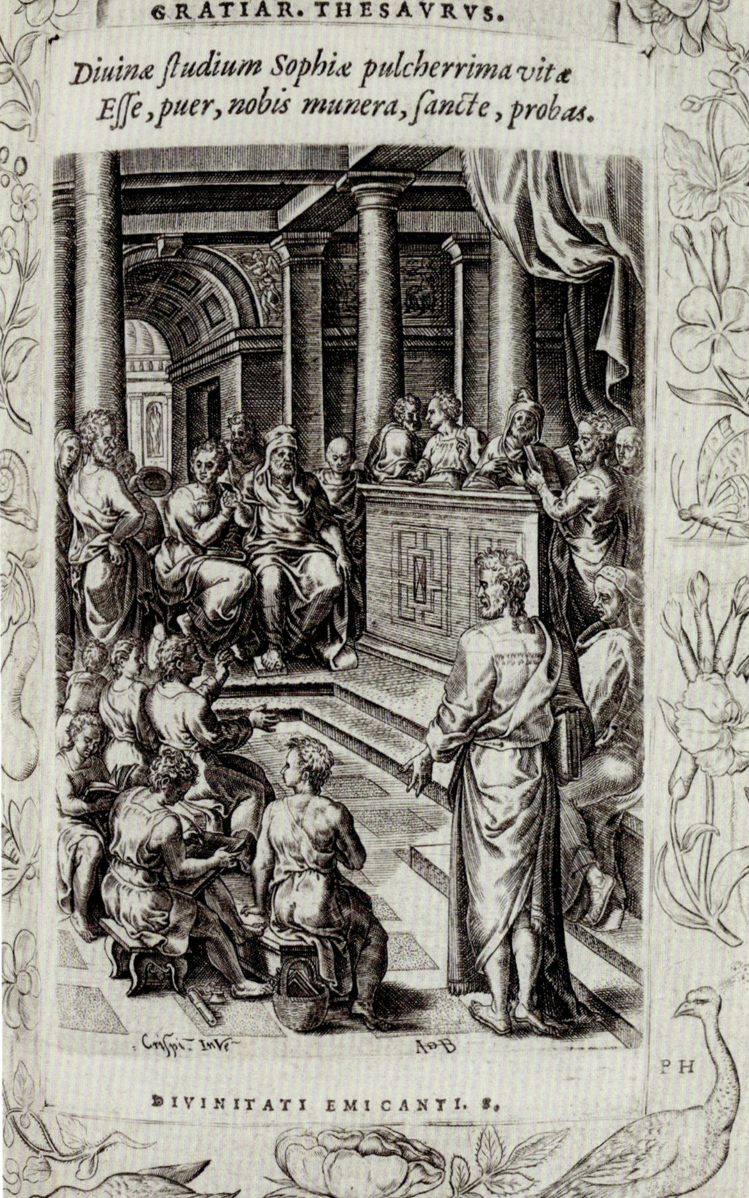

FIGURE 5. Abraham de Bruyn after Crispijn van den Broeck, *Christ Disputing with the Doctors*, engraving, in Benito Arias Montano, *Humanae Salutis Monumenta*, Antwerp, 1571. *Detroit Institute of Arts, Detroit, Michigan.*

The large seated man and the two men at Jesus's left constitute a noteworthy trio: a clean-shaven, middle-aged man wearing an apron and a high soft hat; a standing, younger man with a dark beard and sidelocks, clad in boots, slashed pantaloons, a tallit or prayer shawl, and a close-fitting cap; and a stooped, aged scholar with a white beard, who wears a tallit and a turban. The oldest man leans on a cane, which he holds with his right hand as he ascends the steps to the dais. Tucked under his left arm, he holds a large tome.[18] These three distinct figures—seated, standing, and walking; middle-aged, young and vigorous, and elderly and infirm—not only add variety to the composition, but also imply the universality of the audience ready to receive Christ's message, thus suggesting the susceptibility of all Jews to "enlightenment" and conversion.

Notes

1. Examples of these types of compositions include Lorenzo Ghiberti's bronze relief on the North Doors of the Baptistery, Florence (1404–24); Israhel van Meckenem's version in his engraved *Life of the Virgin* (1490–1500) (HG 59); an illustration for the Sixth Age of the World, in Hartman Schedel, *Liber Chronicarum*, f. 95v (Nuremberg, 1493); Albrecht Dürer's woodcut in his *Life of the Virgin* (1503–4), (TIB, woodcuts, 91); Albrecht Altdorfer's woodcut in his series *The Fall and Redemption of Man* (c. 1513) (NG, woodcuts, 14); Hans Schäufelein's woodcut illustration in *Das Plenarium oder Ewangely buoch* (Basel: Adam Petri, 1514) (HG 1063); Jacob Cornelisz. van Oostsanen's small woodcut Passion (c. 1523) (HD 10); Giovanni Battista Franco's engraving (1530–40) (TIB 9); Georg Pencz's engraved *Life of Christ* (1534–35) (HG 44); and Tobias Stimmer's woodcut illustration for Peter Canisius, *Commentariorum de verbi dei Corruptelis Tomi duo* (Ingolstadt: David Sartorius, 1583) (HG 1077).

2. Perlove and Silver (*Rembrandt's Faith,* 238) made this point in respect to the 1652 version of the print (B. 65, cat. no. 38).

3. John Calvin, *Commentary on a Harmony of the Evangelists: Matthew, Mark, and Luke,* 1 155–56, Commentary on Luke 2:40–47:

> 46. *Sitting in the midst of the doctors.* Rays of divine brightness must have evidently shone in this child: otherwise those haughty men would not have permitted him to sit along with them. Though it is probable that he occupied a lower seat, and not the rank of the doctors, yet such disdainful men would not have condescended to give him an audience in a public assembly, if some divine power had not constrained them. This was

a sort of prelude to his public calling, the full time of which had not yet arrived. In this way, however, he intended to give nothing more than a taste, which would immediately have faded from the recollection of men, had not Mary *kept* it for us *laid up in her heart,* (ver. 19, 51,) to bring it out afterwards, along with other treasures, for the use of all the godly.

47. *And all who heard him.* Two things here claim our attention. *All who heard him were astonished:* for they reckoned it a miracle, that a child should frame his questions with such correctness and propriety. Again, they *heard* Christ, and thus acted the part rather of scholars than of teachers. He had not yet been called by the Father, to avow himself a public teacher of the Church, and therefore satisfied himself with putting modest questions to the doctors. Yet there is no room to doubt that, in this first attempt, he already began to tax their perverse way of teaching: for what Luke afterwards says about *answers,* I consider as denoting, agreeably to the Hebrew idiom, any kind of discourse.

Accessed on July 18, 2014, http://www.ccel.org/ccel/calvin/calcom31.pdf. I am grateful to Prof. Randall Zachman for drawing this passage to my attention.

4. The first two states of the print measure about 10.8 × 7.8 cm. White and Boon, *Rembrandt's Etchings,* 1:33. It is quite possible that this print, along with *Presentation in the Temple with the Angel: Small Plate* (B. 51, 1630, cat. no. 25), the slightly later *Circumcision: Small Plate* (B. 48, c. 1633–34, cat. no. 23), and *Flight into Egypt: Small Plate* (B. 52, 1633, cat. no. 27) were conceived of as a "Childhood of Jesus" series, although there is no evidence that these etchings were actually distributed as such. Their small size means that they could have easily been pasted into a Bible to act as textual illustrations.

5. Rembrandt may be drawing a contrast between the written words of the Old Law and the spoken message of the New.

6. RRP, *Corpus,* A15. For a discussion of this painting, which was lavishly praised by the influential and very learned Constantijn Huygens, secretary to Stadtholder Frederik Hendrik, see Gary Schwartz, *Rembrandt, His Life, His Paintings* (London: Penguin, 1985), 73–76.

7. *Rembrandt's Faith,* 231–32. Perlove and Silver referred specifically to the plan of the Temple in Constantijn L'Empereur de Oppyck's translation and commentaries on the Mishnah Middoth of the Talmud, published in Leiden in 1630.

8. For information regarding seventeenth-century conceptions of the Temple's appearance and skepticism regarding any effort on Rembrandt's part to be archeologically correct in his settings, see the entry on *Peter and John Healing the Cripple at the Gate of the Temple* (B. 94, cat. no. 66).

9. See, for example, Israhel van Meckenem's engraved *Life of the Virgin* (1490–1500) (cited in note 1, above) (fig. 2), in which the holy couple appears twice, once seeking their son, and again listening to him speaking in the Temple. See also the illustration for the Sixth Age of the World in Hartman Schedel, *Liber Chronicarum,* f. 95v (Nuremberg, 1493) (cited in note 1, above), in which the Virgin peers into the Temple through a window on the left; Albrecht Dürer's woodcut *Life of the Virgin* (1503–4), (cited in note 1, above [fig. 3]), in which Mary stands beside a large column on the left, gazing intently up at Jesus; and Georg Pencz's engraved *Life of Christ* (1534–35) (cited in note 1, above [fig. 4]), in which Mary and Joseph are shown behind the lectern at which Jesus sits, as he turns away from them to address the "doctors."

10. See note 3, above.

11. Representing Christ among the doctors without Mary and Joseph is not without precedent. See, for example, the print by Giovanni Battista Franco executed between 1530 and 1540 (cited in note 1, above) and the illustration by Lucas van Doetecum after Gerard van Groeningen in Gerard de Jode's *Memorabilium Novi Testamenti in templo gestorum,* Antwerp, 1585 (Republished by Claes Jansz. Visscher in Amsterdam in 1639) (NHD 620 [the Van Doetecum Family]).

12. Perlove and Silver (*Rembrandt's Faith,* 239) related the presence of this Moorish figure to seventeenth-century texts that described Ethiopian Jews who made pilgrimages to Jerusalem and later converted to Christianity. They also cited the persistent legend of the Christian patriarch and king Prester John and the presence of a Christian community in Abyssinia. They drew particular attention to the contemporary Messianic writings of Menasseh ben Israel (see the discussion of the three prints for Menasseh's *Piedra gloriosa* [B. 36 A, C, and D, 1655, cat. nos. 8, 9, and 10] and the promised return of Jews from all over the world, including Africa, to Jerusalem in the Messianic age). Perlove and Silver noted, "Along these lines, the

African in Rembrandt's print of 1652 may represent a potential (even Jewish) convert to Christianity. . . . This exotic figure . . . seems to embody contemporary interest in conversion."

13. Once again, Rembrandt has provided an "audience" placed at somewhat of a remove from the main action.

14. In the eighteenth century, this plate was completely reworked and was "finished" in mezzotint. See Hinterding, *Copperplates,* fig. 13, 23.

15. The drypoint lines that are visible in the first state appear on Christ's upper torso, at the rear edge of the stool behind him, and around the tall hat of the Pharisee immediately behind him.

16. For an enumeration of the other prints in this series, see *The Adoration of the Shepherds: With the Lamp* (B. 45, cat. no. 20), esp. note 3.

17. See, for example, the version by Georg Pencz (cited in note 1, above) (fig. 4); Giulio Bonasone, from his Passion, c. 1555–65 (TIB 16); Virgili Solis, illustration for the *Hortulus Animae, Lustgarten der Seelen* (Nuremberg 1562) (HG, Book Illustrations, 20.63); Cornelis Cort after Michael Coxie, 1562 (NHD 43 and 44 [Cort]); and Jacques Callot, 1635 (Lieure, 1418).

18. Perlove and Silver (*Rembrandt's Faith*, 240–41) suggested that Rembrandt set this version of *Christ Seated Disputing with the Doctors* in the Beit Hillel, the School of Hillel. This school promoted a compassionate and flexible reading of the law and was particularly welcoming to the poor. In this context, they proposed that the elderly Jew with the book might be the grandson of Hillel Gamaliel, who taught St. Paul.

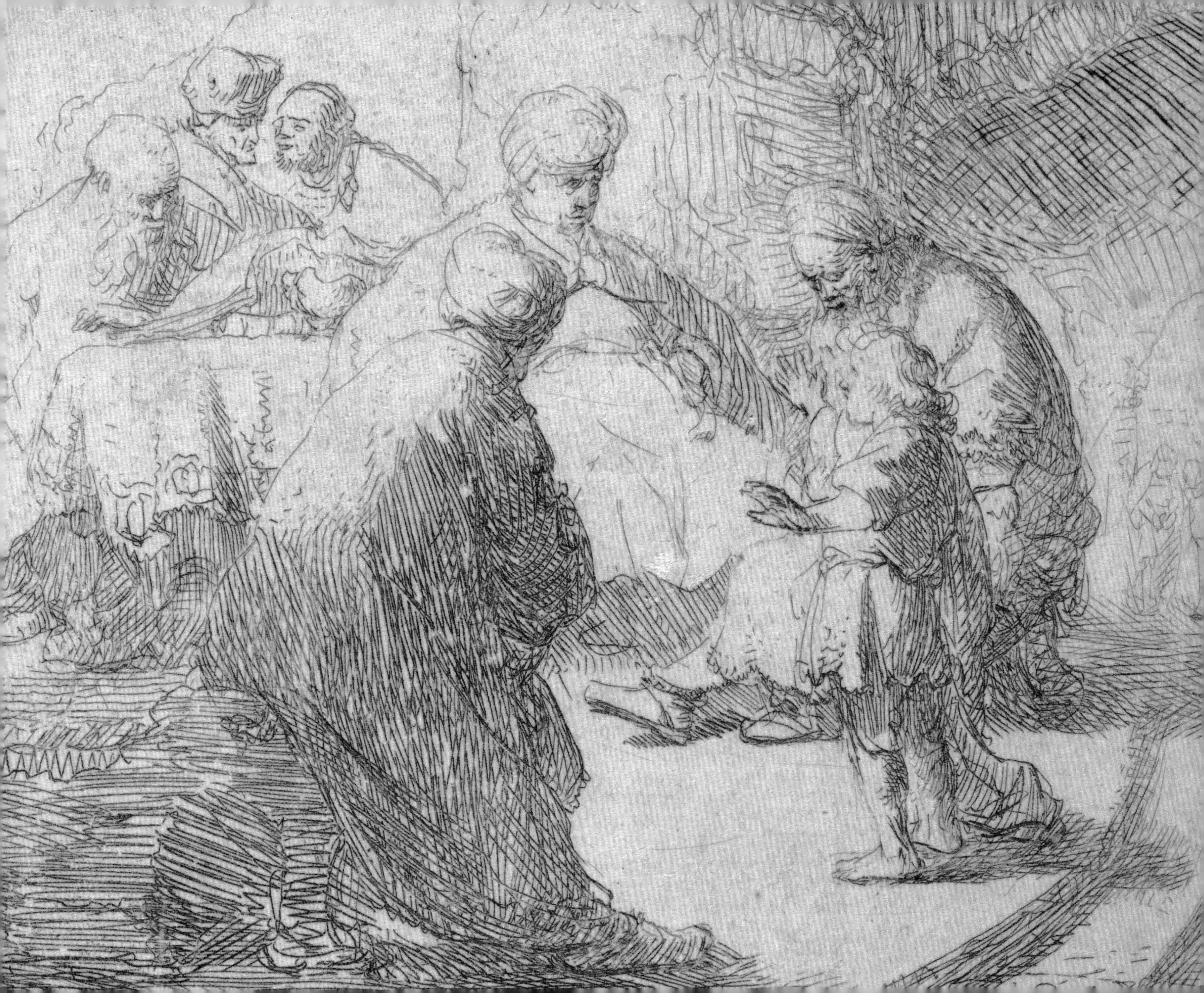

40. Christ Returning from the Temple with His Parents

B. 60 (H. 278, Mz. 231, NHD 276)
Etching and drypoint
Signed and dated in the plate: *Rembrandt f. 1654*
State I of I
Sheet: 9.5 × 14.4 cm, trimmed to the plate mark
Fragment of a watermark at top, possibly foolscap
Verso: in graphite, in center *64/*, bottom margin, *D7326–1200*
Label on mat: *Harlow, McDonald & Co., formerly Arthur H. Harlow & Co. / Etchings. Engravings. Paintings / 667 Fifth Avenue / New York;* stamped in red, *30353*, in graphite *Rembrant, in red pencil, 39* in a circle

Provenance:
Harlow, McDonald & Co., New York, NY
Feddersen, Elkhart, IN, 1991
Snite Museum of Art
Acc. No.: 1991.025.068

The plate does not survive.

Rembrandt's *Christ Returning from the Temple with His Parents* represents the last event of Christ's childhood to be depicted in the 1654 group of prints dedicated to Jesus's infancy and youth.[1] The subject of this print is without precedent and, as a result, has occasionally been misidentified. Edme-François Gersaint's catalog listed it as a representation of the Flight into Egypt, and Adam von Bartsch's catalog referred to it as *The Return from Egypt*.[2] The confusion is understandable, for the closest models for Rembrandt's image of a young Jesus walking with his parents are, in fact, to be found in engraved copies of, and variations on, Peter Paul Rubens's painting of *The Return from Egypt*, c. 1614.[3] However, Jesus's age and the absence of a donkey make it clear that neither of these more common themes is the subject of Rembrandt's print. Instead, Rembrandt's etching illustrates Jesus on the road home to Nazareth with Mary and Joseph after the boy's dispute with the doctors in the Temple in Jerusalem.[4] Mary and Joseph had previously set out for Nazareth only to discover that twelve-year-old Jesus had stayed behind. The worried couple returned to Jerusalem, where they found the boy at the Temple. The three of them then left Jerusalem together.[5]

Behind the three figures is a deep valley and rising mountainous plateaus. Although this background, which includes scattered architectural vignettes, a river, a mountaintop citadel, and a winding road with a procession of shepherds driving a herd of cattle to market, has been associated with Venetian landscape formulas, most notably those found in the prints of Domenico Campagnola,[6] it is considerably closer to a formula used by Rembrandt's teacher Pieter Lastman.[7]

In Rembrandt's etching, Jesus is portrayed as a youth walking between his parents.[8] The barefoot boy gazes upward, beyond his mother's modestly bowed head, and lays his right hand lightly upon her outstretched left hand, as if to gain her attention and understanding or to reassure her.[9] Joseph, by contrast, grasps Jesus's left arm firmly around the wrist, as if to convey the message that he does not intend to lose sight of the boy again. The elderly carpenter wears what appears to be an artisan's apron and holds a slender walking stick as he moves forward. He gazes out toward the viewer

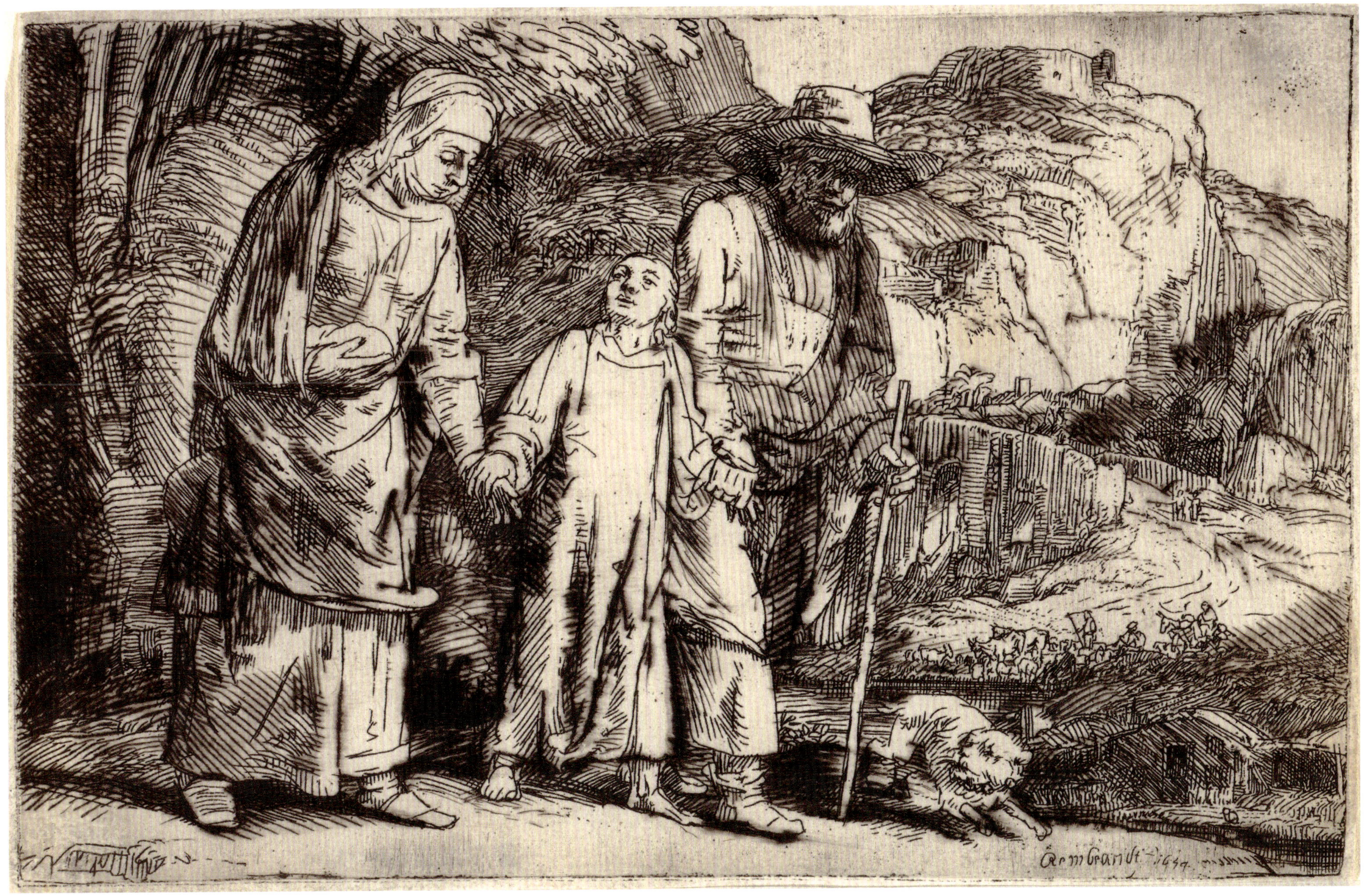

PLATE 40

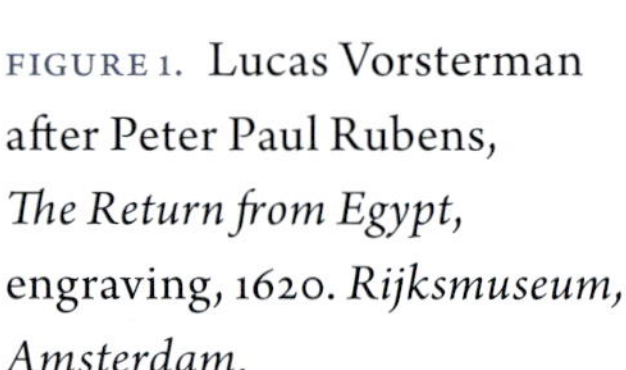

FIGURE 1. Lucas Vorsterman after Peter Paul Rubens, *The Return from Egypt*, engraving, 1620. *Rijksmuseum, Amsterdam.*

FIGURE 2. Schelte Adamsz. Bolswert after Peter Paul Rubens, *The Return from Egypt*, engraving, 1625–40. *Rijksmuseum, Amsterdam.*

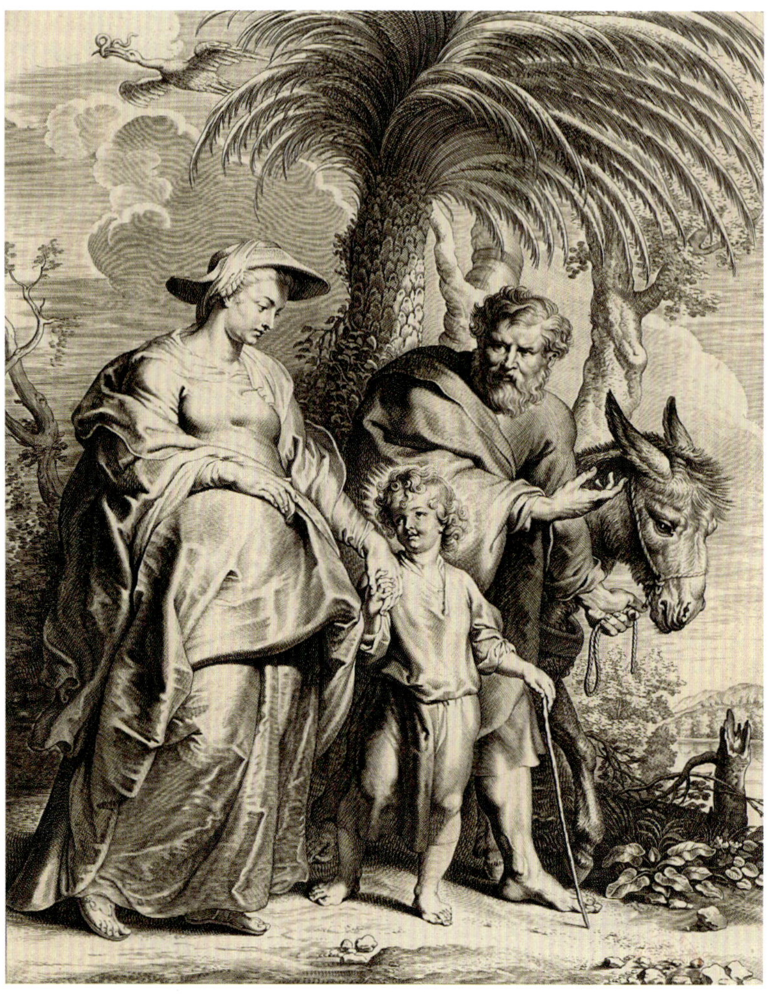

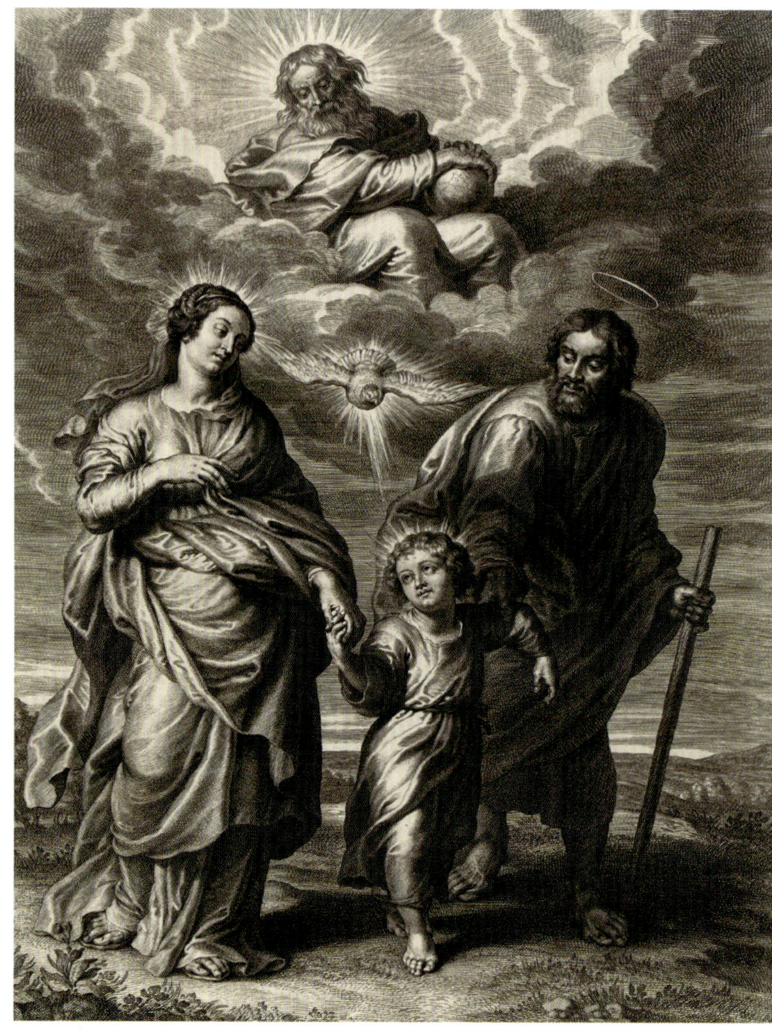

from beneath a broad-brimmed hat that casts his bearded face into deep shadow. Although he is walking side by side with Jesus as they go toward their home, the boy turns away from his earthly father to look upward toward his heavenly father. Indeed, despite the fact that the three figures are linked together, each seems lost in his or her own thoughts.[10] Mary cradles a bundle, perhaps food for their journey, in her right hand. As she walks, her forward movement is reinforced by the arc of her back and the canopy of leaves above her head. In the middle distance, the near wall of a bridge leads from the top of Joseph's staff toward the right side of the composition, adding to the forward momentum by leading the eye from left to right. The calm solemnity of this scene is relieved only by one of Rembrandt's ubiquitous dogs, a small, furry terrier that scampers innocently along just ahead of Joseph and turns its head to look back at the Holy Family.

The print projects an aura of tenderness in its depiction of the relationship between Jesus and his earthly parents, who are undoubtedly relieved to have found him, although perhaps puzzled by his ways. In its depiction of emotional and psychological connections, the etching resembles a few of the other prints in the 1654 childhood-of-Christ series in that it projects a particularly human vision of the Holy Family.[11] It may well be that Rembrandt's sympathetic depiction of familial relationships reflected circumstances in his own life at the time. His son, Titus, poised, like the etching's Jesus, on the brink of manhood, had turned twelve in September

1653, the year before the series was made, and in October 1654, Rembrandt's companion, Hendrickje Stoffels, gave birth to their daughter, Cornelia. The 1654 series of prints, then, could well have reflected the artist's recognition of the importance of family and his role as a father.

Notes

1. For a description of this series, see *Adoration of the Shepherds: With the Lamp* (B. 45, cat. no. 20), esp. note 3.

2. Hinterding, *Lugt Catalogue*, cat. 46. In the 1752 edition of Gersaint, the editors, Helle and Glomy, noted that Jesus is too old for this to be a representation of the Flight into Egypt and propose that it is a depiction of the Return from Egypt (40–41). According to Hinterding, it was Thomas Wilson who first identified the subject correctly in his catalog of 1836 (*A Descriptive Catalogue of the Prints of Rembrandt by an Amateur* [London: J. F. Setchel, 1836], cat. 64, 66), accessed January 21, 2013, http://catalog.hathitrust.org/api/volumes/oclc/3777539.html.

3. A copy of the original painting by Rubens (Roose 108) is in the Wadsworth Atheneum in Hartford, CT. In 1620, Lucas Vorsterman made an engraving (fig. 1) after the Rubens painting (HD 11). Other variations on the image include engravings by Schelte Adamsz. Bolswert (HD 183) (fig. 2) and Cornelius Galle II (BM 1891,0414.594). Both of these variations eliminated the donkey that appears in the Vorsterman engraving. Christian Tümpel (*Rembrandt legt,* cat. 68) identified the Bolswert print as a possible source for Rembrandt's image. The version by Galle is a bit closer, since it features a tree to the left of the Holy Family and a vista into a landscape with a river in the background, but it does not include the images of God the Father and the dove of the Holy Spirit (also absent in Rembrandt's *Christ Returning from the Temple*), which hover in the air above the Holy Family in the Bolswert engraving. None of these engravings, however, appears to be a credible source for Rembrandt's etching, which, aside from other details, features a much more mature figure of Jesus.

4. Rembrandt represented Christ's Disputing with the Doctors in the Temple three times. See cat. nos. 37–39 (*Christ Disputing . . .*) for a synopsis of the story of Jesus's experiences at the Temple and thereafter (Luke 2:41–50).

5. Luke 2:48–51.

6. The Venetian characteristics of the landscape have been remarked upon since the late nineteenth century. See B. P. J. Broos, *Index to the Formal Sources of Rembrandt's Art* (Maarssen, Netherlands: Schwatrz, 1977), 75. For Domenico Campagnola and the Venetian landscape, see David Rosand and Michelangelo Muraro, *Titian and the Venetian Woodcut: A Loan Exhibition* (Washington, DC: International Exhibitions Foundation, 1976), 139–71; and Elisabetta Saccomani, "Domenico Campagnola disegnatore di 'paesi' dagli esordi alla prima maturità," *Arte veneta* 36 (1982): 81–99.

7. See, for example, the background of the etching of the *Landscape with Tobit and the Angel* from 1600–20 by Simon Frisius after Lastman (NHD 192).

8. Perlove and Silver (*Rembrandt's Faith*, 242) suggested that there are hairs sprouting from Jesus's chin, a sign of his nascent maturity, and they related this detail to an instruction in the Mishnah (the compilation of oral Jewish traditions first written down around 200–220 CE) that prescribes that once a boy produces two hairs he must follow the Torah, and his father has an obligation to see that he does so. However, what Perlove and Silver read as hairs may simply be lines used to create shadows.

9. Perlove and Silver (*Rembrandt's Faith*, 241) read Jesus's gaze as being directed heavenward. In their interpretation, this is an allusion to his pursuit of his "Father's business" (Jesus's explanation to Mary and Joseph for why he had stayed behind), while the contemplative, downward gazes of Mary and Joseph suggest their concern with earthly matters.

10. Perlove and Silver (*Rembrandt's Faith*, 165) connected this print with the Seven Sorrows of the Virgin, since Christ disputing with the doctors is commonly held to be one of the events that is included in the list of Mary's sorrows. Although the Holy Family's return from Jerusalem is not specifically named as one of the sorrows, Perlove and Silver (241–2) noted that Calvin, in his commentary on the story in Luke, surmised that since the Virgin would not have upbraided her son in public, the conversation in which Jesus informed her that he was "in those things which belong to my Father," could well have taken place after they had left the temple. See Calvin, *Commentary on a Harmony of the Evangelists, Matthew, Mark, and Luke*, 1:157, Commentary on Luke 2:48, accessed July 18, 2014, http://www.ccel.org/ccel/Calvin/calcom31.pdf.

Christ's words to Mary prefigured the Passion, for they indicated his duty to God, a duty that would ultimately lead to his sacrifice upon the cross. Although Luke goes on to say that neither Mary nor Joseph understood what Christ had told them, he concludes that the Virgin retained the words in her heart. For Perlove and Silver, Rembrandt's print represented the "verbal exchange" between Mary and her son, an event that, arising as it does in the wake of the dispute with the doctors at the Temple, could be linked to the Seven Sorrows. In Rembrandt's print, Jesus appears to be speaking, whereas the Virgin seems to be listening or contemplating, with an expression that is serious or tranquil, rather than sad. There is no direct evidence in favor of the Seven Sorrows interpretation except, perhaps, for the solemnity of the group, Jesus's upturned face and parted lips, and Mary's thoughtful expression.

11. See, for example, the manner in which Joseph holds his infant son in the *Circumcision in the Stable* (B. 47, cat. no. 24), the way in which he seems to present the boy with pride in the *Adoration of the Shepherds: With the Lamp* (B. 45, cat. no. 20), and the extraordinarily loving vignette of Mary cradling her son in *Virgin and Child with the Cat and the Snake* (B. 63, cat. no. 36).

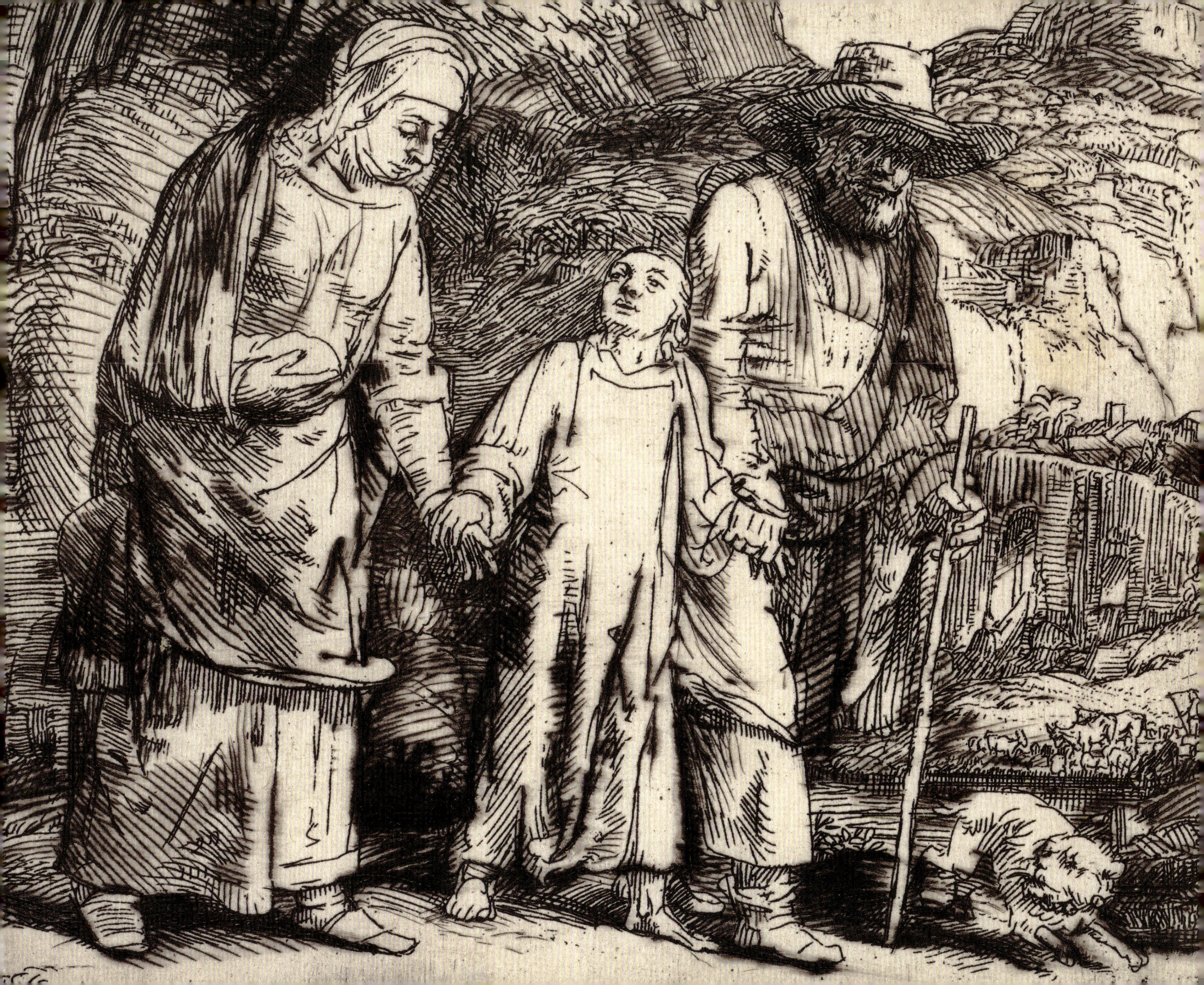

41. *Christ Preaching ("La petite Tombe")*

B. 67 (H. 256, Mz. 236, NHD 298)
Etching and drypoint
c. 1657 (1652?)
State I of II
Sheet: 16.6 × 22.0 cm; plate mark 15.3 × 20.6 cm
Watermark: unidentified fragment
Verso: in graphite, *45320 B. 67*

Provenance:
Harrods, London, 1973
Feddersen, Elkhart, IN, 1991
Snite Museum of Art
Acc. No.: 1991.025.038

The plate no longer survives.

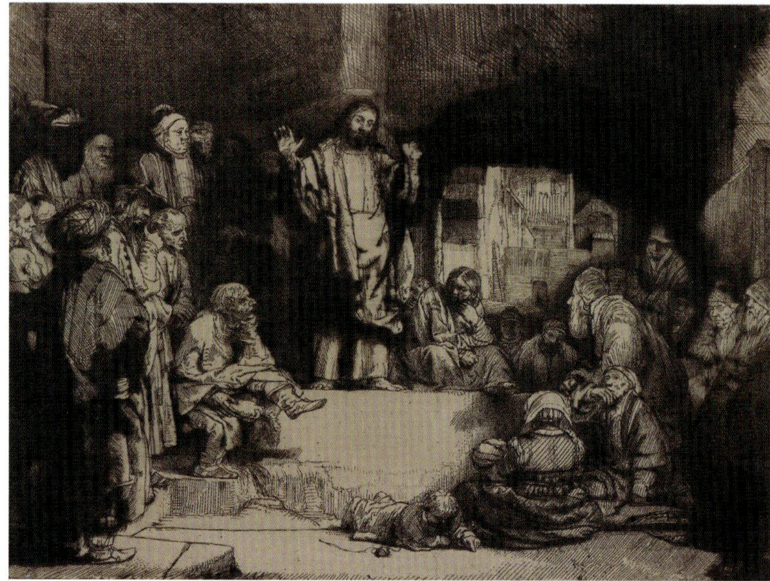

FIGURE 1. Rembrandt, *Christ Preaching* ("with the black sleeve"), etching and drypoint, c. 1657. *The Pierpont Morgan Library & Museum, New York, New York, RvR 104. Photography by Graham S. Haber.*

Rembrandt's print *Christ Preaching ("La petite Tombe")* is considered to be one of his more unusual works.[1] Dated to between 1652 and 1657,[2] the etching shares some elements with the earlier *Hundred Guilder Print* (B. 74, c. 1648, cat. no. 48). Both prints center on an image of Christ preaching to a diverse crowd. Jesus, who is emphasized not only through his central placement but also by means of light,[3] stands on a low riser or platform,[4] with the space in front of him open to the viewer. Both images place the action in front of a wall that is pierced by an archway located to Christ's left, although in the case of *Christ Preaching*, this opening offers a contrasting view into a brightly lit street or courtyard. The seated young man in *Christ Preaching* recalls the rich young man in the *Hundred Guilder Print*, and in both there is a woman cradling her baby, viewed from behind. The bent old man at Christ's left in *Christ Preaching* is reminiscent of the ailing man among the faithful at Christ's left in the earlier print, and both etchings are anchored at the lower left corner by a prominent, richly clad figure standing with his back to the viewer. Finally, the dog that ignores Jesus in the *Hundred Guilder Print* has been replaced by a young boy, who also lies on the ground at the front of the scene, facing away from Christ and paying no attention to him. Despite all of these similarities, however, there are also significant differences between the two prints in terms of composition and technique, as well as in subject matter. *Christ Preaching* is considerably more compact, static, and focused than the *Hundred Guilder Print*, and is less experimental in terms of its investigation of technical and tonal range.[5] Furthermore, unlike the *Hundred Guilder Print*, which was inspired by several specific

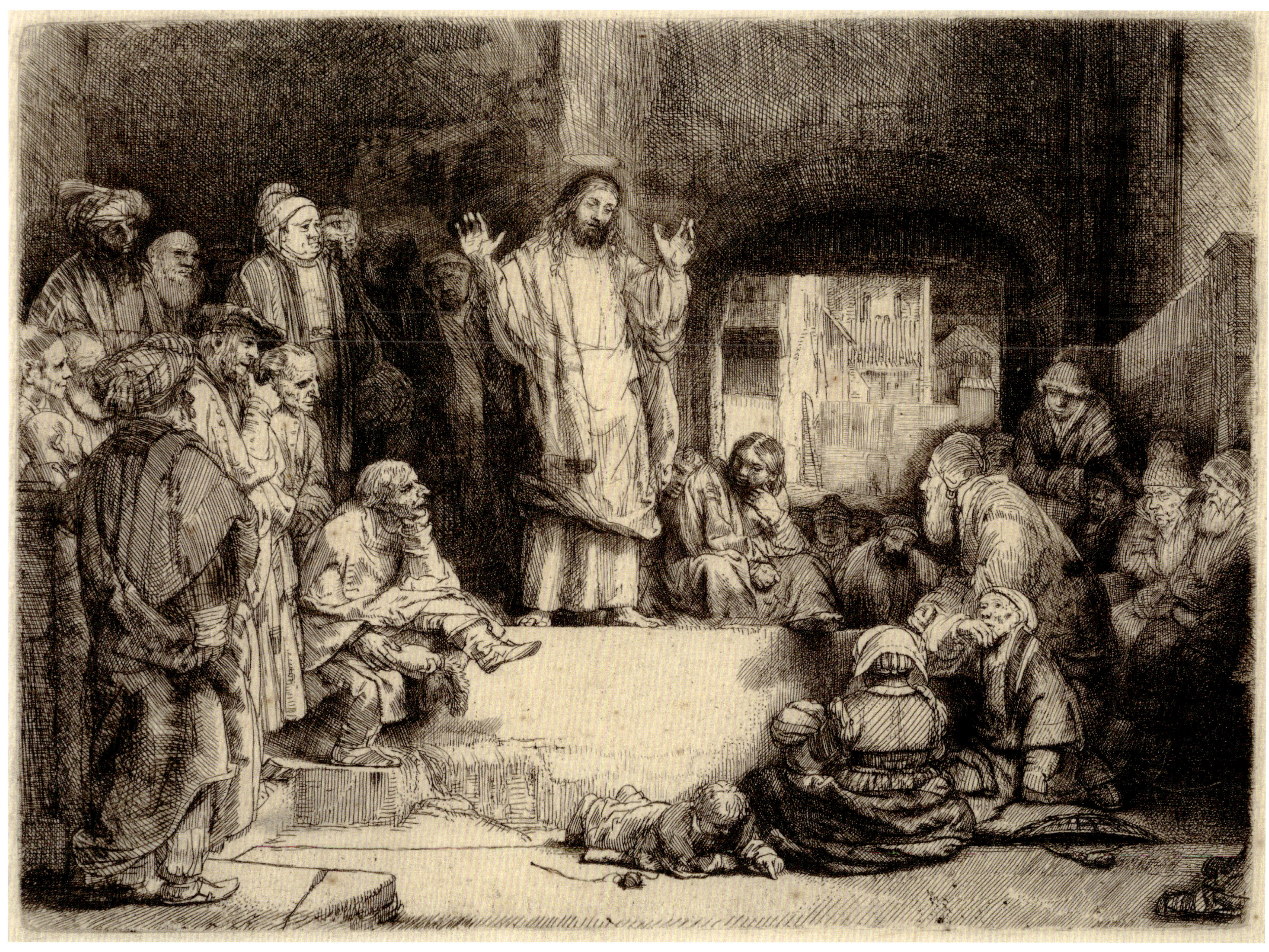

PLATE 41

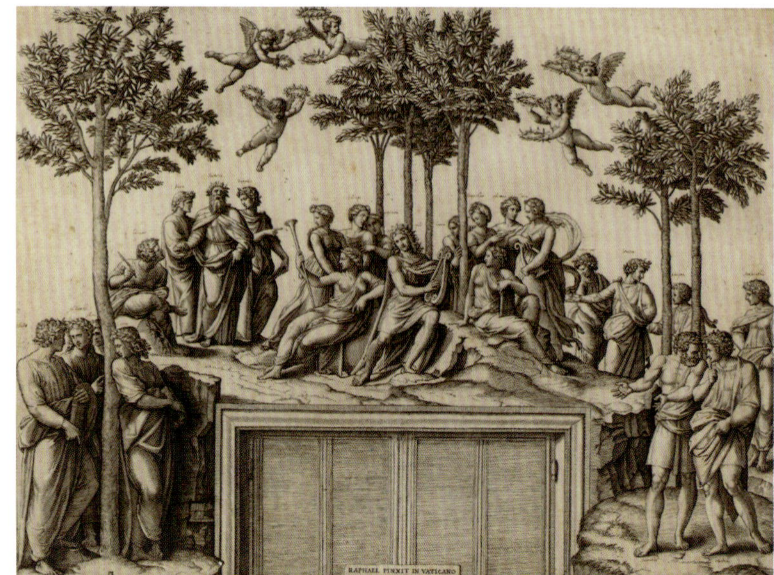

FIGURE 2. Marcantonio Raimondi after Raphael, *Parnassus*, engraving, c. 1510–20. *Photo: Courtesy of the National Gallery of Art, Washington, DC.*

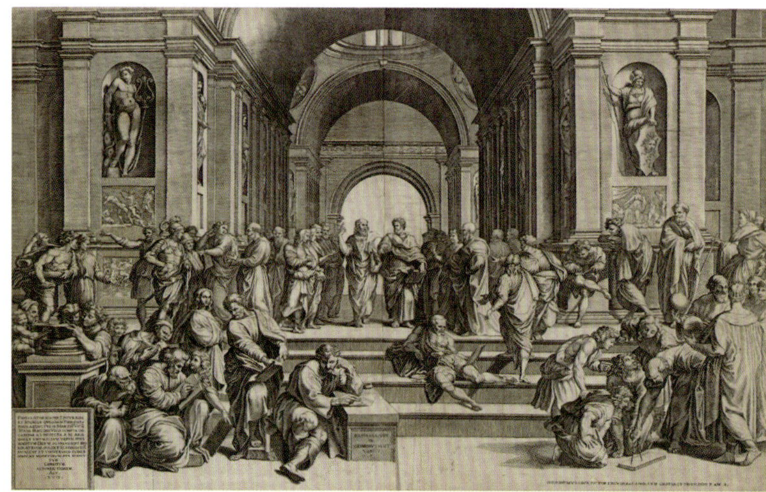

FIGURE 3. Giorgio Ghisi after Raphael, *The School of Athens*, engraving, 1550. *Yale University Art Gallery, New Haven, Connecticut.*

biblical passages, *Christ Preaching* concentrates solely on the act of preaching itself, something that, as Shelley Perlove and Larry Silver observed, reflects "one of the fundamental features of nearly all Protestant groups."[6] Unlike the Pharisees in the *Hundred Guilder Print*, most of the figures surrounding Jesus in *Christ Preaching* listen to the preacher's words with rapt attention.

The composition of *Christ Preaching* may have been inspired by Raphael's *Parnassus* or *The School of Athens* in the Vatican's Stanza della Segnatura. Rembrandt would have been familiar with the *Parnassus* through an engraving by Marcantonio Raimondi (fig. 2), an artist whom he greatly admired,[7] and the *School of Athens* through an engraving by Giorgio Ghisi (fig. 3) published by Hieronymus Cock in 1550. Raimondi's *Parnassus* has a compositional affinity with Rembrandt's own drawing of the blind Homer reciting his poetry (fig. 4),[8] an image created for the *album amicorum*[9] of his friend and patron Jan Six in 1652.[10] *Christ Preaching* is compositionally very closely related to the drawing of Homer,[11] particularly in regard to the semicircular distribution of the figures flanking Jesus and the specific poses of the two men seated to his right and left.

As he speaks, Jesus raises his hands slightly above his shoulders, palms facing forward.[12] John Bulwer, in his *Chirologia or the Natural Language of the Hand*, published in London in 1644, proposed a number of different interpretations for this type of gesture, including prayer and attestation, but the one that may be most pertinent in regard to Rembrandt's print comes from Bulwer's description of the Mass.[13] In his explanation of the gestures associated with the recitation of the *Oremus*, Bulwer noted that the priest first spreads his hands out and then joins them together, symbolizing the act of gathering in the hearts of the congregants and then uniting them as one (fig. 5). In this context, Christ's gesture may represent not solely his teaching, but also his welcoming and gathering of the souls before him.

In addition, Christ's display of his palms would probably have been associated with his crucifixion. In Raphael's *Disputa* in the Vatican's Stanza della Segnatura, which was also reproduced by Giorgio Ghisi (fig. 6),[14] Jesus's raised hands, displaying his wounds, clearly allude to Christ's sacrifice. Even if Rembrandt did not draw on Raphael as an inspiration for Jesus's gesture in his print, there were other well-established visual traditions of Jesus displaying his wounds in a similar fashion: artists' representations of Christ in the Mystic Mass of St. Gregory and as the Man of Sorrows.[15] Although no wounds are displayed on Christ's palms in the Rembrandt print because this event obviously takes place before the Crucifixion, a Catholic viewer familiar with this pose from images of the Man of Sorrows and the Mystic Mass of St. Gregory could easily have associated Jesus's pose with the Passion. Furthermore, in Rembrandt's etching, Christ stands before a vertical beam that

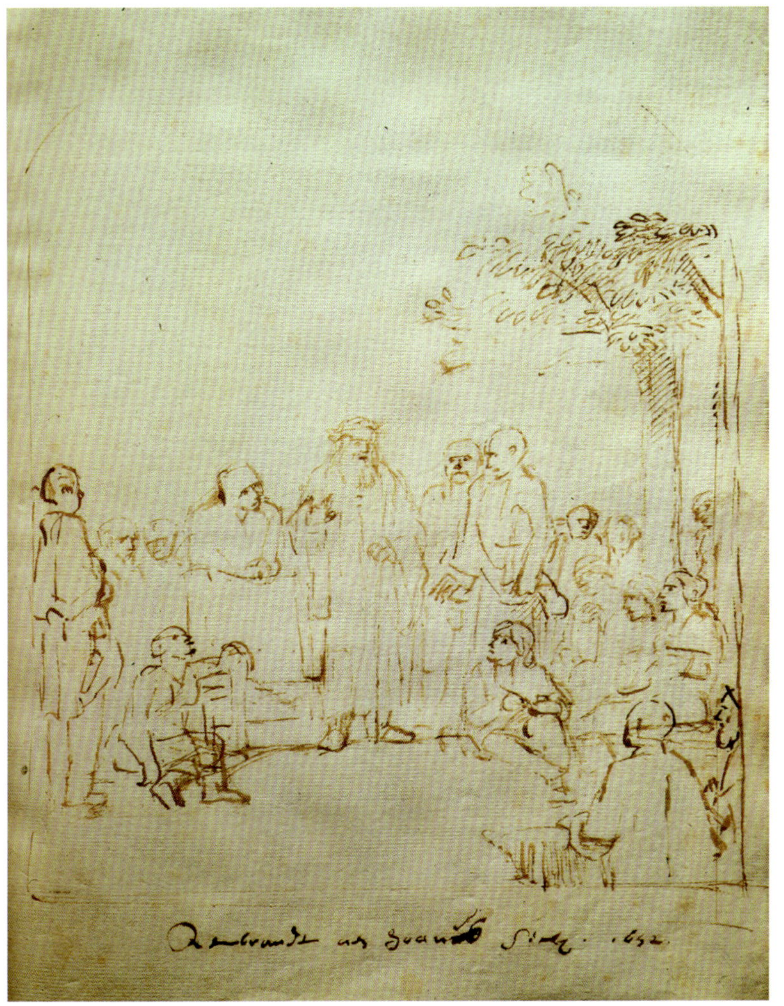

FIGURE 4. Rembrandt, *Homer Reciting Verses*, Ben., 913, pen and red bistre, 1652, *Album Amicorum of Jan Six: "Pandora." Six Collection, Amsterdam. Photo courtesy of Collectie Six, Amsterdam.*

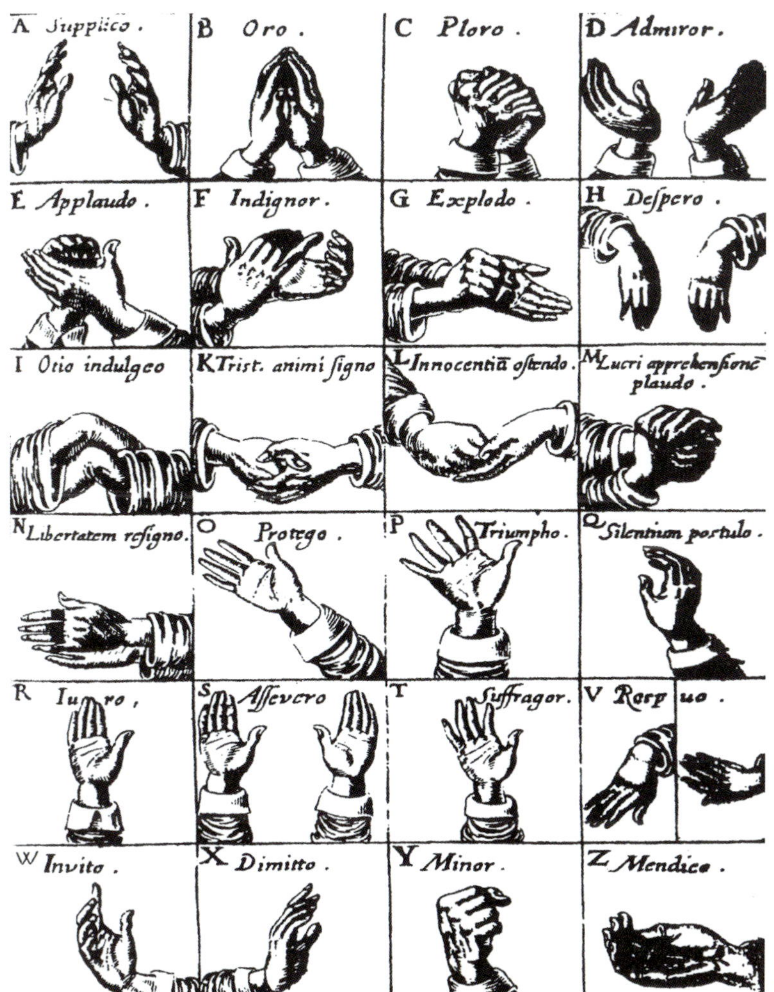

FIGURE 5. Hand gestures from John Bulwer, *Chirologia or the Natural Language of the Hand*, London, 1644.

may be read both as a column of light that draws the viewer's eye and implies divine inspiration and as an allusion to the cross on which he was martyred. In addition, there are visual precedents for the association between Christ preaching and his crucifixion: these events from his life and death were represented together in a woodcut illustration for the Epistle Reading for Palm Sunday by mid-sixteenth-century German printmaker Hans Brosamer (f. 1554).[16] In this woodcut, Jesus preaches to a crowd of men in the foreground, while the crucifixion of Christ and the two thieves takes place in the distant background. To the seventeenth-century viewer, then, Christ's raised hands could have suggested a broad spectrum of associations, ranging from the visual language of rhetorical address to the ritual of the Mass to a reminder of the Passion.

All of the figures in *Christ Preaching* except for the young boy sprawled out in the center foreground listen intently to Jesus's words. The reason for the inclusion of this distracted and unattended child,[17] whose top lies on the ground beside him and who appears to be amusing himself by writing or drawing in the dirt or dust, has been a matter of discussion. For some scholars, this boy represents innocence in the guise of a child who is too young to understand Christ's sermon, but is still embraced by Jesus's benevolent gaze and his words.[18] Still others view the boy as a symbol of inattentiveness. Curiously, no one has connected the boy's actions

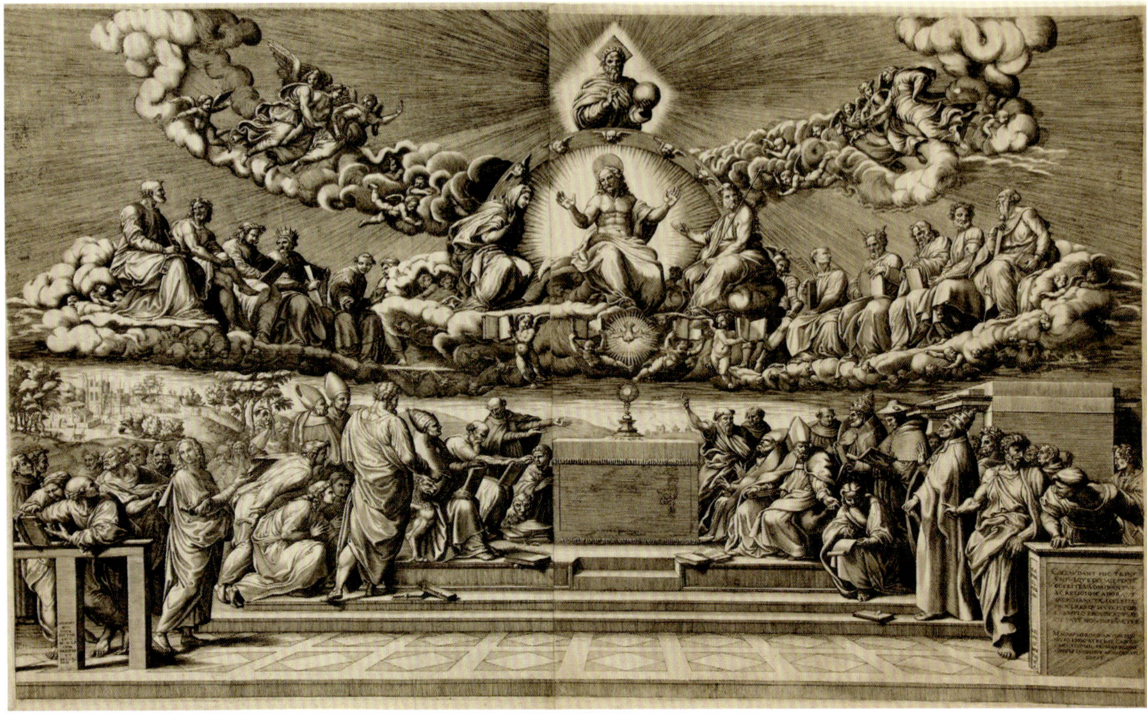

FIGURE 6. Giorgio Ghisi after Raphael, *The Disputa*, engraving, 1552. *Yale University Art Gallery, New Haven, Connecticut, Everett V. Meeks, B.A. 1901 Fund.*

FIGURE 7. Emblem XLIII, "Soo langh de Roe wanckt [How long the top spins]," from Roemer Visscher, *Sinnen-poppen*, III, Amsterdam, 1614.

with the idle top lying beside him. One of the emblems in Dutch merchant/writer Roemer Visscher's 1614 *Sinnen-poppen* (Moral emblems) was a spinning top being whipped by a hand coming out of the clouds (fig. 7). The motto for this well-known emblem reads "Soo langh de Roe wanckt" ("As long as [it is] whipped by the rod"), and the epigram explains that as the top turns only when it is struck, so men are pious only when they are in danger or distress. Wayne Franits drew attention to this emblem in his discussion of a painting by Caspar Netscher in which a mother combs a young boy's hair. In the painting, various toys lie discarded on the floor around them, including a top. Franits observed that in contrast to the image in the emblem, the top in Netscher's painting is no longer spinning. He noted that this image should perhaps be related to a passage in the Dutch poet and moralist Jacob Cats's *Kinderspel* (Children's Games).[19] According to Franits, Cats asserted that when the top "is no longer whipped [it] is symbolic of idleness, which overtakes men when their hardships cease."[20] In the poem, however, Cats actually suggested something even more ominous about human behavior, observing that when the rod is lifted, it is the devil who returns to light the way.[21] Perhaps, given contemporary Dutch interest in childrearing and religious instruction,[22] the child and his top in Rembrandt's etching were a reminder of children's natural inclination to be distracted from spiritual matters when parental guidance is lacking. The boy's mother, presumably the woman seated beside him holding an infant, is concentrating on Christ's message, but ignoring her son.

There are two less judgmental explanations for the boy's behavior. Christopher White suggested that the boy is concentrating hard and, possibly, writing down Jesus's words, in which case even "innocence" is touched by Christ's preaching.[23] In addition, given that Rembrandt was both a father and, as his art amply demonstrates, a careful observer of children, he would undoubtedly have been aware that when grownups gather for sober reflection, bored children try to find ways to amuse themselves. The boy may be just one more example of the artist's practice of leavening images of holy events with vignettes from everyday life.

Christ Preaching has also been popularly known as *La petite Tombe*, ever since Edme François Gersaint's catalogue raisonné of 1751. Gersaint took this nickname from the listing of Rembrandt plates sold by print dealer Clement de Jonghe in 1679. In the sale catalog, the plate was referred to as the "Latombish plaatjen."[24] Gersaint incorrectly thought that the name derived from the appearance of the platform on which Christ is standing, which he interpreted as resembling the mound of a tomb. This error was corrected by Pierre Yver in a 1756 supplement to the Gersaint catalog. Yver correctly inferred that "Latombish plaatjen" was actually a reference to the person who had owned the plate.[25] This observation was subsequently linked to a passage in Houbraken's brief biography of the Dutch painter Nicolaes de la Tombe. In this biography, Houbraken noted that Nicolaes had a brother who was a great lover of paintings and prints and had an etching made by Rembrandt that was called the "Tombe print."[26] Unfortunately, some confusion entered into the literature, and Nicolaes himself was assumed to be the "Tombe" in question, even though Houbraken clearly stated that it was Nicolaes's brother for whom the print was named. Nicolaes had three brothers, Pieter, Jacob, and Isaak, all of whom lived in Amsterdam, where they were book and art dealers and minor artists.[27] However, only the first of these, Pieter, is documented as having had a significant business relationship with Rembrandt: The artist made two portraits of Pieter de la Tombe; the two men jointly owned a painting of *Christ and the Samaritan Woman* attributed to Giorgione and a painting of the *Rich Man and Lazarus* by Jacopo Palma Vecchio; and in 1650, Rembrandt and Pieter de la Tombe were involved with a third party in the purchase of some drawings, possibly by one of Pieter's brothers.[28] It is most likely, therefore, that the owner of the plate and the one for whom it was named was not Nicolaes de la Tombe, but, rather, his brother Pieter.

Notes

1. Paul Crenshaw (*Rembrandt's Bankruptcy* [New York: Cambridge University Press, 2006], 100), claimed that Rembrandt's print is without precedent. In terms of its setting and cast of characters, this seems to be true. However, in sixteenth-century bibles and postils, there was a tradition of including illustrations of Christ preaching to the apostles or small groups of disciples. These scenes were usually set outside. See, for example, the woodcut illustrations by Hans Schaufelein in *Das Plenarium oder Ewangely buoch* (Basel, 1514) (HG 1080 and 1088); Lucas van Leyden's small woodcut *Christ's Sermon* (Mark 1:22) from the *Stomme Passye* published in Amsterdam around 1526 (NHD 283), which Christian Tümpel has specifically, though incorrectly, linked with Rembrandt's print (Tümpel, *Rembrandt legt*, cat. 88); Hans Sebald Beham's woodcuts in Johan von Eck, *Christenliche Auslegung* (Ingolstadt), 1530 (HG 715 and 724); and Hans Hersbach's more expansive woodcuts in Jacob Feucht, *Postilla Catholica Evangeliorum de Sanctis totius Anni* (Cologne, 1580) (British Museum, reg. nos. 1860,0114.382 and 1860,0114.370).

There are also independent prints of Christ preaching, one by Karolus after Lambert Lombard (c. 1550) (HD 52 under "Lombard") that, according to an inscription on the engraving, is an illustration of Christ preaching the Parable of the Sower (Luke 8:4–16); and another by Jacques Callot (1635) (Lieure, 1421), which is an etching illustrating the Sermon on the Mount.

2. The date of this unsigned, undated print remains a matter of discussion. White and Boon dated it to about 1652, while Ludwig Münz thought that it was more likely to have been produced around 1656. Most recently, Erik Hinterding (*Lugt Catalogue*, 141) suggested an even later date of c. 1657, based on the watermarks that appear on early impressions of the print.

3. In addition, Jesus's divinity is indicated by the small, flat halo that floats above his head. This literal halo contrasts with the one in *Hundred Guilder Print*, in which Rembrandt created an aura of light emanating from Christ's head.

4. Although it is unclear whether the scene takes place indoors or out, the platform appears to be a natural outcropping of rock, which might argue for an outdoor setting, possibly outside a city wall.

5. Although there is only a single state of the plate, there are two distinct versions of the print, which are distinguished by the shadows under Christ's upraised arms and on the clothing of the

turbaned man in the left front. In one version, these shadows are impenetrably black. These prints are known as "*Christ Preaching* with the black sleeve" (fig. 1). In the other, these shadows are described by open hatching, giving rise to the identification "*Christ Preaching* with the white sleeve." The Snite Museum impression is an example of the latter. Since Rembrandt used drypoint in these areas, it has been suggested that the difference in the quality of the shadows was due either to the artist's removal of the burr or simply to the natural wear of the plate. Hinterding, *Lugt Catalogue*, 141 and 143n13.

6. In their discussion of this print and the *Hundred Guilder Print,* Perlove and Silver (*Rembrandt's Faith*, 263–64) emphasized the importance of preaching as a means of creating a community and "inculcating and transforming daily lives on moral grounds" for almost all of the Protestant sects. For most Protestant viewers, the etching's emphasis on Christ's spoken message would have resonated with that philosophy.

Perlove and Silver (*Rembrandt's Faith*, 274) also proposed that the print "suggests" Matthew 18:1–14, a passage in which Christ admonishes his disciples to "become like children." This idea is supported by the fact that Christ's attention is generally directed toward the mother and child and the young distracted boy in the foreground. However, there may be other reasons for this emphasis on children. See the discussion of the "idle" and "inattentive" child, below.

Ludwig Münz (*Critical Catalogue,* vol. 1, cat. 236, 108) linked the Rembrandt image to a print by Adriaen Collaert after a composition by Maerten de Vos (HD 868 [Maerten de Vos]). Collaert's engraving of an apostle preaching (Münz incorrectly identifies the speaking figure as Christ), created around 1600, is one of a series of twelve illustrations of the Apostles' Creed. The image is labeled *Remissionem peccatorum* (remission of sins). On the basis of what is a very slight compositional relationship, Münz suggested that Rembrandt's print should be read as Christ preaching about the forgiveness of sin. Although there are some similarities—the man in a turban and cape in the left foreground, a woman with an infant toward the center foreground, and an urban landscape in the background—this is not a compelling argument.

7. According to Benesch and to Broos (*Index to the Formal Sources of Rembrandt's Art*, [Maarssen, Netherlands: Schwartz, 1970], 77), the connection between the images of *Parnassus* and *Christ Preaching* was first made by W. R. Valentiner in 1905 (*Rembrandt und seine Umgebung*). Ben. 913, 5:255: "Inspired by the composition of Raphael's *Parnassus,* known to Rembrandt through an engraving." For Rembrandt's particular attachment to the work of Raimondi, see the discussion of the *Hundred Guilder Print* (B. 74, cat. no. 48) in this catalog.

8. Ben. 913.

9. The Getty Institute online Art and Architecture thesaurus defines an *album amicorum* (literally a "book of friendship") as a "bound collection of autographs, writings, paintings, and drawings collected by the owner from his or her friends and acquaintances."

10. On Rembrandt's relationship with the merchant, writer, and art patron Jan Six, see Svetlana Alpers, *Rembrandt's Enterprise: The Studio and the Market* (Chicago: University of Chicago Press, 1988), 92–93; and Gary Schwartz, *Rembrandt: His Life, His Paintings* (London: Penguin, 1985), 259–60. On the album, which is labeled *Pandora 1651*, see George J. Möller, "Het album Pandora van Jan Six (1618–1700)," *Jaarboek van het Genootschap Amstelodamum* 76 (1984): 69–101.

11. This connection is one of the reasons why a date of 1652 has been proposed for the etching. The drawing in Jan Six's album is signed and dated 1652.

12. Perlove and Silver (*Rembrandt's Faith*, 274) noted that in Rembrandt's early painting of *Simeon and Hannah in the Temple* (c. 1628, Bredius 535, Kunsthalle, Hamburg), Hannah makes a similar gesture. In the context of this painting, the prophetess's pose implies that she is either bearing witness to the divinity of Christ or expressing her astonishment at the miracle of the Messiah. Perlove and Silver also related the gesture to that of the risen Christ in the *Ascension* that Rembrandt painted for Prince Frederik Hendrik (RRP, *Corpus*, A118, 1636, Alte Pinakothek, Munich). Here, the gesture, which is clearly derived from Titian's *Assumption of the Virgin*, serves a compositional as well as symbolic function: the upswept arms reinforce the upward movement of the figure and suggest Jesus's embrace of his heavenly fate. The pose in Rembrandt's *Ascension* is distinct from that of *Christ Preaching*, however, in that in the latter, Jesus's gaze is downward, toward his earthly listeners, not up toward heaven, and his elbows are drawn in toward his sides, with his hands extended as if in a rhetorical gesture or benediction, not thrown outward with upturned palms, as if to embrace the firmament above. Otto Pächt has suggested that the gesture was inspired by the figure of Christ

in Raphael's *Disputa*. Pächt, *Rembrandt* (Munich: Prestel Verlag, 1991), 184.

13. In Bulwer's *Chirologia: Or the Natural Language of the Hand* (London: Thomas Harper, 1644), the gesture of raising the hands was identified at first as signifying prayer (Gestures I and II, 14–26), and later as a form of declaration or affirmation (Gesture XVIII, 51–52). Bulwer specifically related the gesture to the celebration of the Mass. "In the Roman Church which doth superabound in the external adjuncts of Devotion, and where the Rubriques direct to varying forms of manuall expression, at the word *Oremus,* there is always annexed some emphatical behaviour of the Hand. Hence in the Masse when the Priest saith *Oremus,* he extendeth and then joyns his hand. By the extension of his Hands he gathered as it were the hearts of the people: by the joyning of his Hands together, he doth amasse them into one" (26–27).

14. Published by Hieronymus Cock in 1552.

15. See, for example, the engraving by Albrecht Dürer of the standing figure of Christ as the Man of Sorrows, c. 1500 (TIB 20), and his woodcut of the Mystic Mass of St. Gregory, 1511 (TIB, woodcuts, 123). It is also worth noting that Gregory mirrors Christ's gesture as the saint celebrates the Mass and witnesses the miracle.

16. Illustration for a Palm Sunday epistle, undescribed in Hollstein, BM 1927,0210.30.

17. Tümpel, *Rembrandt legt,* cat. 88, connected the motif to another distracted child, in Rembrandt's 1634 painting of *John the Baptist Preaching* (RRP, *Corpus*, A106, Gemäldegalerie, Berlin).

18. Christopher White, *Rembrandt as an Etcher: A Study of the Artist at Work*, 2nd ed. (New Haven, CT: Yale University Press, 1999), 69: "But even this action (the child's drawing in the dust) does not distract and such is the aura of concentration one feels he might even be spelling out Christ's words."

Perlove and Silver (*Rembrandt's Faith*, 274) connected the innocence of this boy with the Anabaptists' belief in the purity of children and their protection by God. They also drew attention to other instances in which Rembrandt represented children who remain unaware and distracted at significant spiritual moments, e.g., the *Presentation in the Temple with the Angel: Small Plate* of 1630 (B. 51, cat. no. 25) and the *Presentation in the Temple: Oblong Print* of 1639–40 (B. 49, cat. no. 26).

19. *Kinderspel* was published by Jacob Cats in his *Silenus Alcibiadis, sive Protevs, vitae humanae ideam, emblemate trifariàm variato, oculis subijciens* (Middelburgi: Ex officina typographica Iohannis Hellenij, 1618), accessed January 17, 2013, http://archive.org/details/silenusalcibiadioocats.

20. Wayne Franits, *Paragons of Virtue: Women and Domesticity in Seventeenth-Century Dutch Art* (Cambridge, UK: Cambridge University Press, 1993), 126. The Netscher painting is in the Rijksmuseum, Amsterdam, and is illustrated in Franits, fig. 103. Cats goes on to say that when the rod is lifted and we turn from God then we are on the devil's path.

21. *Kinderspel*, 277: "We have God as it were by the foot / As long as we are in a tight spot / But when the rod is off the arse / The devil's back holding the candle." I am grateful to Roger Kuin for this translation of the passage from Cats.

22. Perlove and Silver (*Rembrandt's Faith*, 274–75) also connected the boy to Dutch interests in the religious instruction of the young, but without commenting on his inattentiveness. See also Simon Schama, *The Embarassment of Riches: An Interpretation of Dutch Culture in the Golden Age* (Berkeley: University of California Press, 1987), chapter 7.

23. See note 18, above. In this case the abandoned top might mean that the boy has set aside childish pursuits for something more serious.

24. Hinterding, *Copperplates*, 16–17.

25. Pierre Yver, Edme François Gersaint, and Jean Baptiste Glomy, *Supplément au catalogue raisonné de MM. Gersaint, Helle et Glomy, de toutes les pièces qui forment l'œuvre de Rembrandt* (Amsterdam: Chez Pierre Yver, marchand de tableaux & d'estampes, 1756), 25, accessed January 15, 2013, http://www.archive.org/details/supplementaucataooyver.

26. Arnold Houbraken, *De Groote Schouburgh Der Nederlantsche Konstschilders . . .* (Amsterdam: Weduwe des Autheurs, 1718), 2:28, accessed January 11, 2013, http://www.dbnl.org/tekst/houboo5gr0001_01/houboo5groo01_01_0196.php: "Hy [Nicolaes] had ook een Broeder die een beminnaar van Schilderyen en Printkonst was, waar om 'er ook onder de Etskonst van *Rembrant* een printje uitgaat bekent by de naam van la Tombes printje."

27. For information regarding the de la Tombe family, see Isabella Henrietta van Eeghen, "De familie de la Tombe en Rembrandt," *Oud Holland* 71 (1956): 43–49.

28. For Rembrandt's relationship with Pieter de la Tombe, see Crenshaw, *Rembrandt's Bankruptcy*, 74, 100, and 105–6, and Charles M. Rosenberg, "Rembrandt's Religious Prints," in this catalog.

42. *The Tribute Money*

B. 68 (H. 124, Mz. 200, NHD 138)
Etching
c. 1635
State II of IV
Sheet: 7.3 × 10.3 cm, trimmed to the plate mark
Verso: in graphite, *PH.1*

Provenance:
Craddock & Barnard, London, 1977 (Catalogue 134, no. 223)
Feddersen, Elkhart, IN, 1991
Snite Museum of Art
Acc. No.: 1991.025.039

Plate survives:
Private collection, United Kingdom.

The Gospels of Matthew, Mark, and Luke all recount the story of Jesus's provocative response when he was challenged about the propriety of paying tribute to the ruling Roman government.[1] Preaching and working miracles, Jesus had traveled to Jerusalem, where he had driven the money changers out of the Temple and then, after spending the night in Bethany, had returned to the Temple, where he began to preach in parables.[2] The scholars, scribes, and priests who heard him feared that Jesus's teachings would turn the people against them, so they conspired to trick him into making his own words betray him. They sent a group of Pharisees and Herodians to question Jesus as he was preaching.[3] "Is it lawful to pay the imperial tax or not?" they asked him, knowing that either a "yes" or a "no" answer could have dire consequences. Jesus, aware of their ill will, responded, "Why are you trying to trap me?"[4] He asked them to bring him a denarius, one of the coins of the realm.[5] When they had done so, he pointed to the coin's face and asked, "Whose image and inscription do you see?" "Caesar's," they replied. To which Jesus responded, "Render unto Caesar what is Caesar's, and unto God what is God's." The conspirators were confounded and could offer no reply.

In creating an etching of the Tribute Money, Rembrandt set his scene in what Shelley Perlove and Larry Silver identified as the Temple's Court of the Gentiles.[6] In typical fashion, the artist divided the space into thirds by means of lighting and perspective. Jesus, dressed in a tunic and draped cloak, stands at the center of the composition, in front of a dimly lit corridor. A brilliant halo shines behind his head. His attention is focused on a coin being held out in front of him by a clean-shaven, pale-faced elderly Jew wearing a low turban and a heavy caftan. Christ's right hand is raised, pointing upward toward heaven, while his left hand reaches down toward the coin; his gestures indicate the distinction being made between spiritual and earthly obligations.[7]

To Jesus's left, a cluster of exotically dressed Jews are listening to the discussion.[8] Toward the right side of the composition, a bearded, hunched-over old man dressed in brocades stands stroking his chin as he contemplates Jesus's answer to the question that has been posed to him. The man's headdress throws the upper part of his face into shadow, and although he is facing forward, he casts a suspicious sideways glance at Christ from the corner of his eye. Perlove and Silver suggested that this man and the man seated in

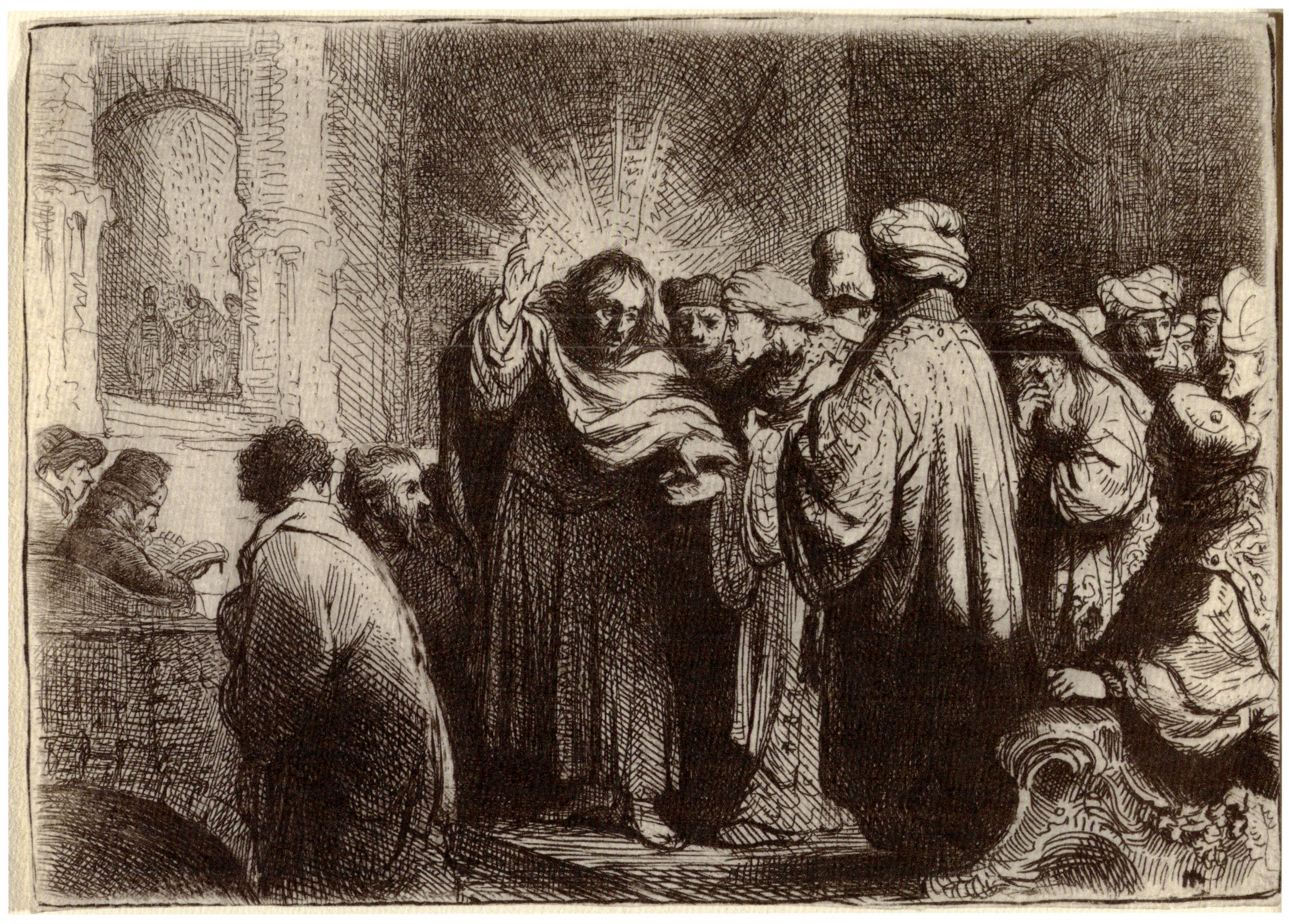

PLATE 42

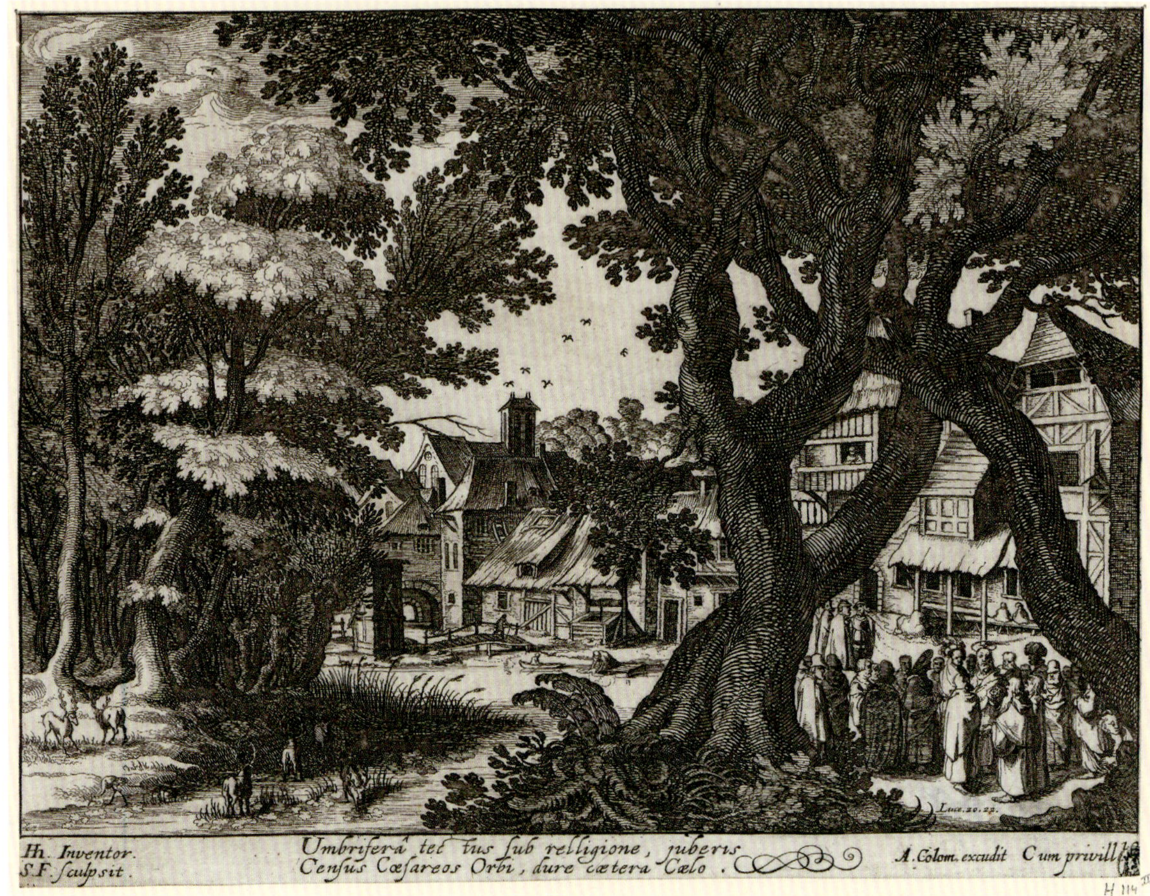

FIGURE 1 Simon Frisius after Hendrik Hondius, *The Tribute Money*, engraving, 1600–20. *Leiden University, Leiden.*

the decorative throne near him may be Herodians who are listening carefully for any hint of treason or sedition.[9] Behind this group, a densely shadowed wall with an arched niche or opening closes off the space on the right side. Directly across from Jesus is an imposing figure in heavy robes and a tall turban. With his back turned to the viewer, the man stands erect and watches Jesus's actions, as if he, too, is ready to judge him.

In the left foreground, a young man with a bushy head of hair is about to descend a staircase that appears to lead to the dark archway in the lower left corner of the scene. Wrapped in a cloak, he pauses and turns back to look at Christ. Nearby, two scholars are seated on benches above the arched passageway. One of them is absorbed in reading a text, and the other is thoughtfully stroking his chin. The scene opens up behind them, offering a view into a slightly raised, brightly illuminated arched opening, which in turn leads to a towering, brilliantly lit arcaded hall. Two men dressed in miters and copes, presumably high priests, and a third figure, wearing a turban, observe Christ's encounter with the Pharisees from afar. As they walk through a corridor bathed in light, these men may offer a contrast between those invested in spiritual matters and those who, like the Pharisees and the Herodians, have more worldly concerns. On the other hand, these may be the very priests who, concerned by Christ's preaching, dispatched conspirators to ensnare Jesus through casuistry. The space through which the distant figures move is also ambiguous. The priests' path appears first to descend and then to ascend as they approach the Court of the Gentiles.

Depictions of the Tribute Money are relatively rare.[10] Ludwig Münz suggested that Rembrandt was acquainted with an engraving of the story by Simon Frisius after a design by Hendrik Hondius (fig. 1).[11] However, it is difficult to find any connection between the Hondius composition, which sets the story in a very expansive landscape with diminutive, passive actors, and Rembrandt's etching, which is staged in a dramatically lit architectural space and is dominated by the actions and reactions of the figures.[12] Much more pertinent for Rembrandt's composition is an engraving from 1621 by Lucas Vorsterman (fig. 2) after a painting of the Tribute Money by Peter Paul Rubens.[13] The interior setting of the scene, the expanded crowd of spectators, and, most significant, Christ's rhetorical gestures, all suggest that Rembrandt was aware of the Vorsterman print and used it as a point of departure. However, Rembrandt characteristically rejected the heroic quality of Rubens's half-length figures and the classicizing details of his background in order to turn the encounter into a much more human moment enacted by figures on a much more human scale, within a dramatically resonant space.

As Perlove and Silver noted, the Mennonites of Rembrandt's day had cited Matthew 21:21 in the thirteenth article of their Confession of Faith, adopted in Dordrecht in 1632. This article dealt with the legitimacy of secular authorities and the obligations of the members of the church not only to respect their authority, but also to pay taxes,[14] a viewpoint that would certainly have provided a frame of reference for some contemporaries viewing Rembrandt's etching.[15]

Calvin's commentary on the same biblical passage offers an additional layer of significance to the tale. He began his commentary on Matthew 22:15 by noting that the Jews in question were embroiled in an argument over whether they should render tribute to the state or whether receiving such tributes was a right that should be reserved for God.[16] Like other commentators, Calvin construed Matthew 22:21, which deals with Christ's reference to Caesar's image on the coin, as a justification for a division of responsibility between secular and religious authorities. In addition, however, he noted that the Jews' use of coins with the imperial image and inscription on them effectively constituted tacit consent to Roman rule and meant that they were thereby obliged to pay tribute to their ruler.[17] This concept also had implications for the role of coinage in the Spanish Netherlands and the Dutch Republic during the sixteenth and seventeenth centuries. In the Spanish Netherlands, which was governed during the first few decades of the seventeenth century by Archduke Albert VII (1559–1621) and then jointly by Albert and his wife, the Archduchess Isabella (1566–1633), both gold and silver coins were struck with the likeness of the king or the Spanish governors, along with identifying legends.[18] In the Dutch Republic, by contrast, each province struck its own coinage. In Holland, a very few coins were minted with portraits of Robert Dudley, the earl of Leicester, who was the governor of the Netherlands from 1585 to 1587, or William the Silent, Prince of Orange, both heroes of the early revolt against the Dutch provinces' Spanish overlords. However, by the end of the second decade of the seventeenth century, these portrait types had been completely supplanted by generic images of a standing soldier in armor holding a sword and a bundle of arrows or a provincial shield, or an armed knight on horseback. Furthermore, these coins bore legends that specifically identified them as currency struck by an individual state (Holland, Gelderland, Vriesland, etc.) of the United Dutch Provinces.[19] Such coins, therefore, offered no numismatic implication that the user owed fealty to an overruling power, only to the individual province and the confederation of which it was a part. In the context of Calvin's commentary regarding the significance of tribute money being paid to Caesar, it could be argued that the use of coinage minted in the Spanish Netherlands, like that circulated in Roman Jerusalem, would have constituted a tacit recognition of the authority of the issuing ruling power, whereas the coins minted in the Dutch Republic would have attested to the free status of the Northern Provinces. This political interpretation of Rembrandt's etching is not likely to have been universally recognized. However, for an astute collector who was thoroughly familiar with Calvin's commentary and who as a merchant dealt with coins from all over Europe as well as the Dutch provinces on a daily basis, it might have provided the etching with an additional layer of meaning.

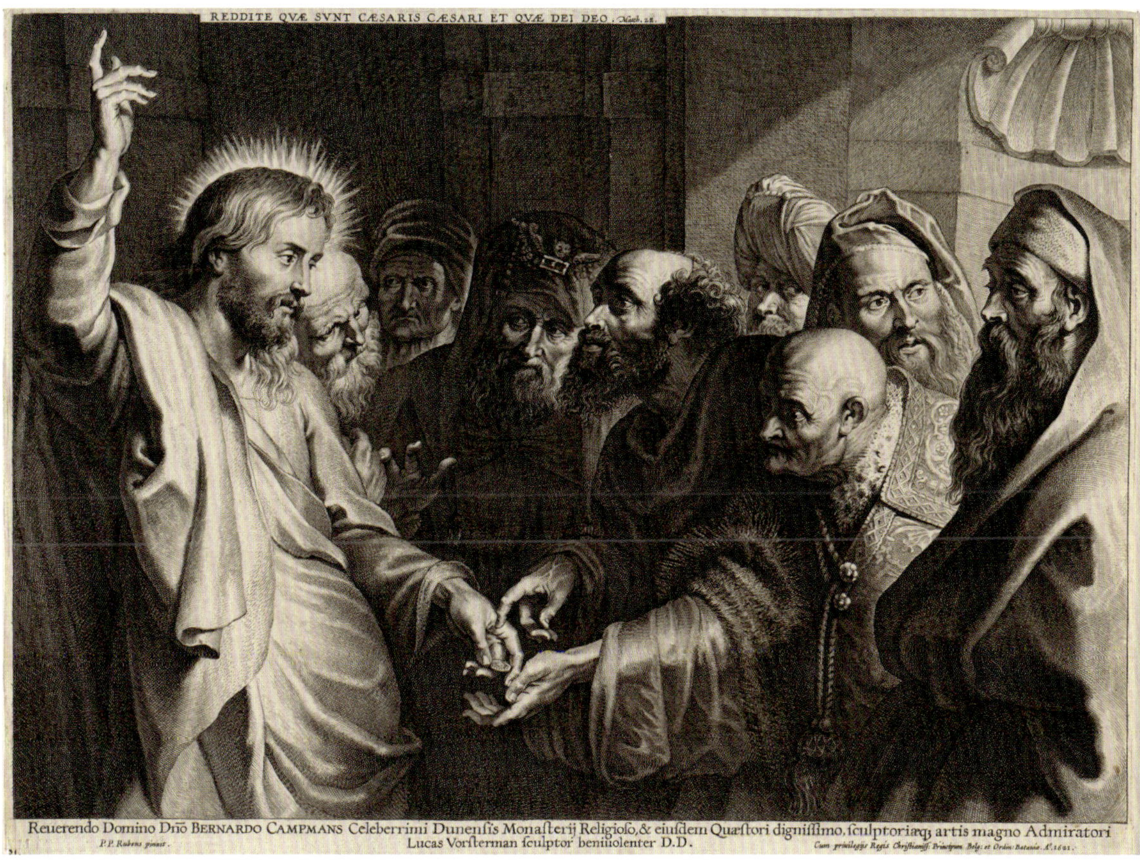

FIGURE 2. Lucas Vorsterman after Peter Paul Rubens, *The Tribute Money*, engraving, 1621. *Rijksmuseum, Amsterdam.*

Notes

1. Matthew 22:15–22, Mark 12:13–17, and Luke 20:20–26.

2. Rembrandt also made an etching of *Christ Driving the Money Changers from the Temple* (B. 69, 1635, cat. no. 43).

3. The Herodians were a religious party that was allied with Herod and the Romans. The apostles differed in their identification of those who actually questioned Jesus. According to Matthew and Mark, it was the Pharisees and the Herodians, while Luke simply referred to the interrogators as spies of the high priests and scribes.

4. Calvin explained the trap in his Commentary on Matthew 22: 15–21. "This trick of taking Christ by surprise is therefore continued by *the Pharisees,* that, in whatever way he reply as to *the tribute money,* they may lay snares for him. If he affirm that they ought not to pay, he will be convicted of sedition. If, on the contrary, he acknowledge it to be justly due, he will be held to be an enemy of his nation, and a betrayer of the liberty of his country. Their principal object is, to lead the people to dislike him." *A Commentary on a Harmony of the Evangelists: Matthew, Mark, and Luke,* 3:30, Commentary on Matthew 22:15, accessed July 21, 2014, http://www.ccel.org/ccel/calvin/calcom33.pdf.

5. A denarius was a small silver coin that typically bore an image of the emperor with an identifying inscription on its obverse and a symbolic image with or without a one- or two-word explanatory legend on its reverse.

6. *Rembrandt's Faith,* 255.

7. Perlove and Silver (*Rembrandt's Faith,* 256–57) specifically likened Christ's gesture to the pose in which he is typically shown in depictions of the Last Judgment. They suggested that the distinction between the damned and the saved implied by this gestural allusion is reinforced by the contrast between the brilliant light on Christ's right and the darkness at his left. Humble scholars appear at his right, but the arrogant, richly dressed Herodians and Pharisees are on his left.

8. The print exemplifies Rembrandt's penchant for "Eastern" (biblical) dress and a wide variety of hats and headdresses, exotic costumes that create a contrast with Jesus's own simple robes.

9. *Rembrandt's Faith,* 256.

10. Among the best-known examples of the Tribute Money are two works by Titian. One, from about 1516, is now in the Gemäldegalerie Alte Meister, Dresden, and the other, from the 1560s, is in the National Gallery, London. In both of these paintings, Christ is confronted by only a few conspirators. The figures are half-length and set close to the picture surface in a shallow, constricted space. The later Titian painting was reproduced in a slightly expanded version in an engraving by Cornelis I Galle sometime during the first half of the seventeenth century (HD 48).

11. Ludwig Münz, *Critical Catalogue,* vol. 2, cat. 200, 95. Frisius's etching is NHD 5.

12. There appear to be several light sources at play here, one from the front right side and one at the back left, in addition to the brightness that emanates from the halo behind Jesus's head.

13. Rubens's original painting, dated c. 1612, is in the California Palace of the Legion of Honor, San Francisco. The Louvre has a contemporary seventeenth-century copy of painting. There is also a later, expanded copy of the Vorsterman engraving after Rubens's *Tribute Money,* done by Claes Jansz. Visscher (second quarter of the seventeenth century), which is accompanied by an inscription in Dutch explaining the subject. HD 12 b (Lucas Vorsterman I).

14. *Dordrecht Confession of the Faith,* 1632, Article XIII, *Of the Office of the Secular Authority.*

> We believe and confess that God has ordained power and authority, and set them to punish the evil, and protect the good, to govern the world, and maintain countries and cities, with their subjects, in good order and regulation; and that we, therefore, may not despise, revile, or resist the same, but must acknowledge and honor them as the ministers of God, and be subject and obedient unto them, yea, ready for all good works, especially in that which is not contrary to the law, will, and commandment of God; also *faithfully pay custom, tribute, and taxes, and to render unto them their dues, even also as the Son of God taught and practiced, and commanded His disciples to do;* that we, moreover, must constantly and earnestly pray to the Lord for them and their welfare, and for the prosperity of the country, that we may dwell under its protection, earn our livelihood, and lead a quiet, peaceable life, with all godliness and honesty; and, furthermore, that the Lord would recompense unto them, here, and afterwards in eternity, all benefits, liberty, and favor which we enjoy here under their praiseworthy administration [emphasis added].

Rom. 13:1–7; Titus 3:1; I Pet. 2:17; Matt. 22:21; 17:27; 1 Tim. 2:1. Accessed July 21, 2014, http://www.bibleviews.com/Dordrecht.html.

15. There was a large Mennonite community in Amsterdam at this time, and some of Rembrandt's earliest clients belonged to this religious sect. He also had Mennonite relatives on his wife's side.

16. There was at that time, a great disputing among the Jews about the tribute-money; for, since the Romans had claimed for themselves the tribute-money, which God commanded to be paid to Himself under the Law of Moses, (Exodus 30:13,) the Jews everywhere complained that it was a shameful and intolerable crime for profane men to lay claim, in this manner, to a divine prerogative; besides that, as this payment of tribute, which was enjoined on them by the Law, was a testimony of their adoption, they looked upon themselves as deprived of an honor to which they had a just claim.

A Commentary on a Harmony of the Evangelists: Matthew, Mark, and Luke, 3:30, Commentary on Matthew 22:15, accessed July 21, 2014, http://www.ccel.org/ccel/calvin/calcom33.pdf.

17. "Christ reminds them that, as the subjection of their nation was attested by the coin, there ought to be no debate on that subject; as if he had said, 'If you think it strange to pay tribute, be not subjects of the Roman Empire. But the money (which men employ as the pledge of mutual exchanges) attests that Caesar rules over you; so that, by your own silent consent, the liberty to which you lay claim is lost and gone.'" *A Commentary on a Harmony of the Evangelists: Matthew, Mark, and Luke*, 3:32, Commentary on Matthew 22: 21, accessed July 21, 2014, http://www.ccel.org/ccel/calvin/calcom33.pdf.

18. Interestingly, this does not seem to have been the case for coins actually minted in Spain. Before the eighteenth century, the most common high value coins, *reales* and *escudos*, bore the arms of the king and an inscription with the ruler's name, but no likeness.

19. The customary legend on the silver coins struck in Holland was "MO ARG PROV CO_FOE BELG HOLL," an abbreviation for *Moneta Argentea Provinciarum Confoederati Belgii Hollandiae* (Silver currency of Holland of the Confederated Provinces of the Netherlands). Even when the coins bore the image of the earl of Leicester or William the Silent, the specific sitters were not identified in the accompanying legend.

43. *Christ Driving the Money Changers from the Temple*

B. 69 (H. 126, Mz. 206, NHD 139)
Etching
Signed and dated in the plate: *Rembrandt f. 1635*
State II of IV
Sheet: 14.7 × 17.9 cm; plate mark: 13.6 × 16.9 cm
Watermark: unreadable fragment
Verso: in graphite, *1200*—

Provenance:
Kennedy Galleries Inc., New York, NY, 1976
Feddersen, Elkhart, IN, 1991
Snite Museum of Art
Acc. No.: 1991.025.040

Plate survives:
Cabinet Cantonal des Estampes, Musée Jenisch,
Vevey, Switzerland (inv. DK r 23).

The story of Jesus's cleansing of the Temple is recounted in all four of the Gospels.[1] Immediately after Jesus and the apostles returned to Jerusalem from the Mount of Olives, he and his disciples visited the Herodian Temple. When Jesus discovered money changers and merchants who were selling animals for sacrifice carrying out their worldly business in the Temple, he was incensed. Brandishing a scourge, he drove the merchants and money changers and their clients from the Temple, admonishing them, "Is it not written, 'My house shall be called of all nations the house of prayer?' But ye have made it a den of thieves."[2] This act set the stage for the Passion, for "the scribes and chief priests heard [Jesus's words] and sought how they might destroy him: for they feared him, because all of the people were astonished at his doctrine."[3]

In the sixteenth century, artists represented this dramatic moment in several different contexts: as part of the Passion, as an independent event, or as a polemical allegory. In particular, as Shelley Perlove and Larry Silver observed, the subject of the cleansing of the Temple was often associated with church reform. Both Erasmus and Calvin commented on the passage, relating it in the first instance to the corruption of contemporary clergy, and in the second to the need for a program of doctrinal reform.[4] In 1521, when illustrating Luther's virulently anti-Catholic pamphlet *Passional Christi und Antichristi*, Lucas Cranach the Elder paired an image of the cleansing of the Temple with a woodcut depicting a papal Antichrist selling indulgences. In the early seventeenth-century Netherlands, the subject was invoked in the bitter controversy between the rigidly orthodox followers of Franciscus Gomarus (the Counter-Remonstrants, or Gomarists) and the more theologically tolerant followers of Jacob Arminius (the Remonstrants, or Arminians).[5] At the Synod of Dort in 1618, the Counter-Remonstrants successfully expelled the Remonstrants from the assembly, after which the Arminians endured a period of harsh persecution. In the course of the "pamphlet wars" that ensued, the actions of the Gomarists expelling the Remonstrants were likened to Christ's purification of the Temple, a characterization that the Arminians strongly rejected. As a consequence, in the broad context of the Reformation movements in the North and, more specifically, in the environment of the internecine doctrinal

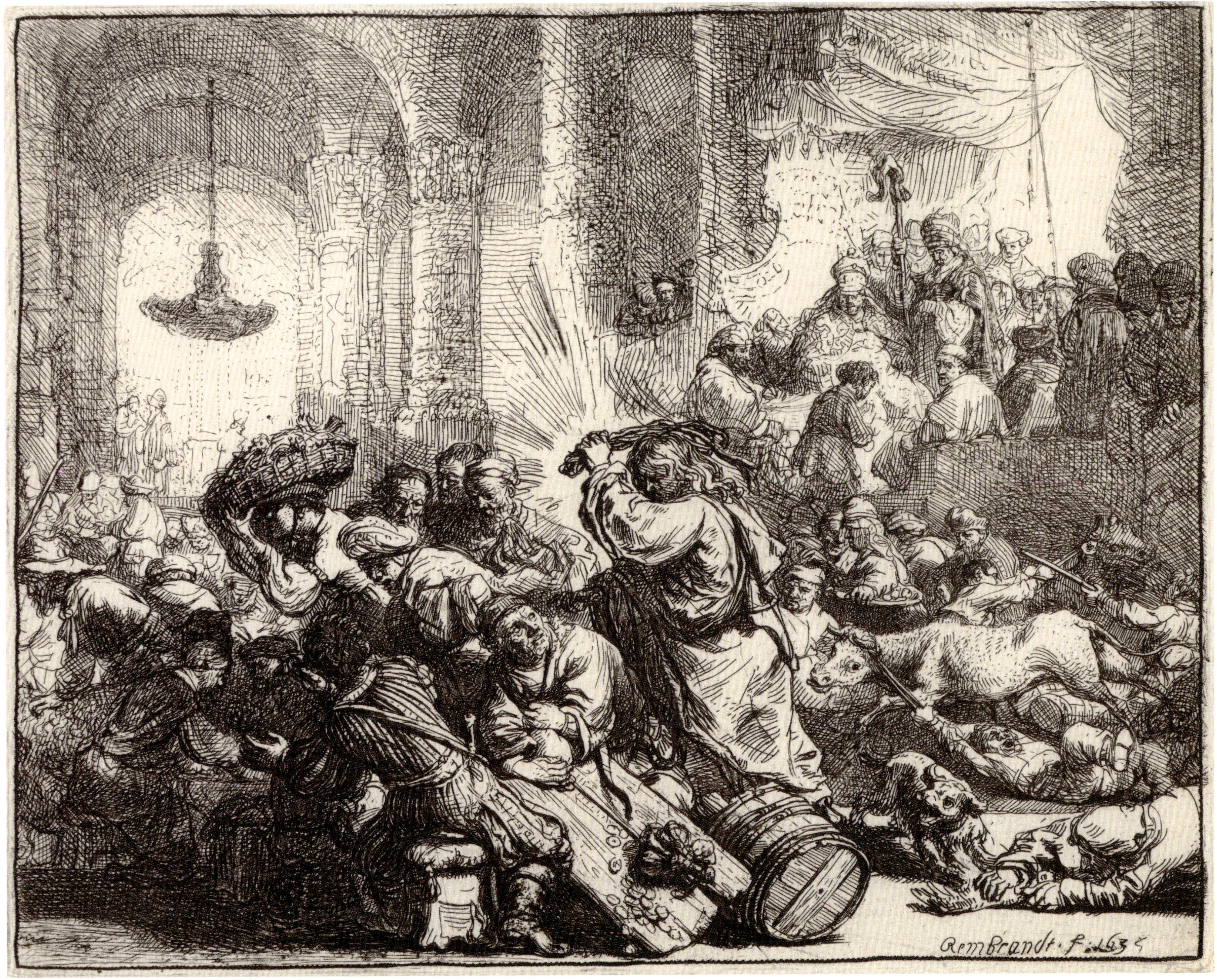

PLATE 43

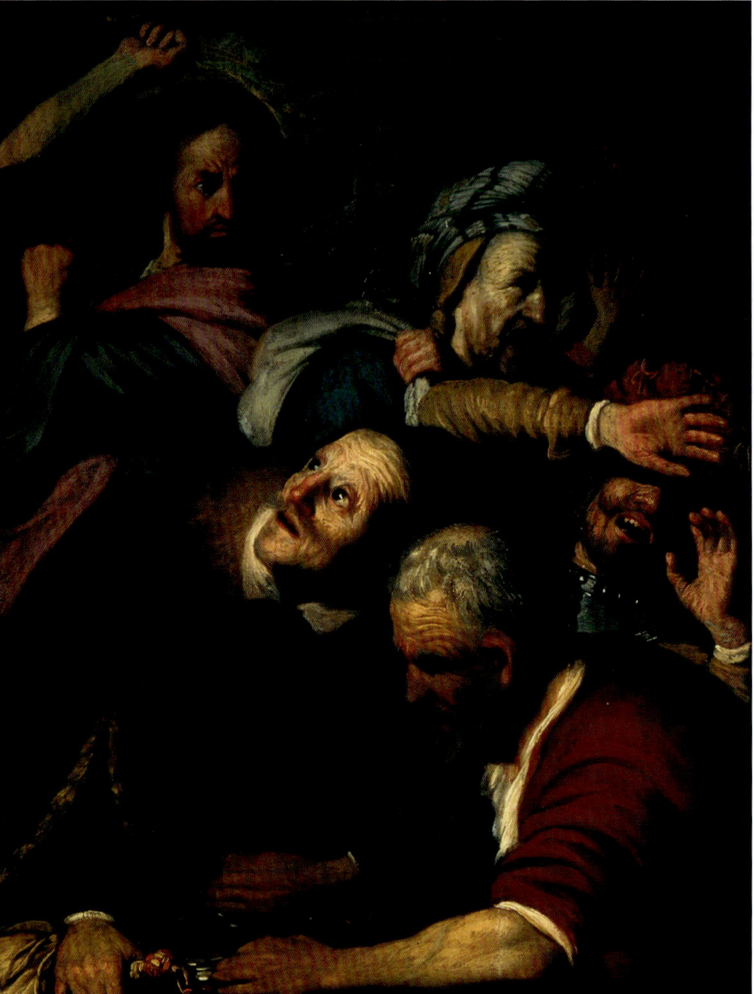

FIGURE 1. Rembrandt, *Christ Driving the Money Changers from the Temple,* oil on panel, c. 1626. *Pushkin Museum, Moscow. Photo: Scala/Art Resource.*

struggles in the Netherlands, images of the cleansing of the Temple would probably have been perceived as containing references to one or more contemporary theological conflicts.[6]

Rembrandt himself depicted the cleansing of the Temple twice, once in 1626, in a small oil panel painting (fig. 1),[7] and again in 1635, as an etching. In the oil painting, Rembrandt concentrated almost exclusively on the faces and actions of the angry Christ and a handful of frightened money changers and merchants.[8] The highly compressed space, providing a veritable "close-up" of the figures, provides few clues as to the setting. Only a fragment of architecture is visible in the immediate background.[9] The actors completely dominate the composition, with the result that the work becomes as much an investigation of *affetti,* that is, expressions and gestures as signs of emotion, as it is a narrative.[10]

The signed and dated 1635 etching is considerably more expansive than the 1626 painting in regard to both the setting and the cast of characters. Some scholars have suggested that this reflects Rembrandt's knowledge of early seventeenth-century painted versions of the story produced in the circle of the North Italian painter Jacopo Bassano.[11] Despite the similarities, however, it is not clear precisely how Rembrandt would have become familiar with this tradition.

In Rembrandt's print, the scene takes place in what Perlove and Silver described as "the unconsecrated ground within the columned cloister of the Gentiles near the Shushan Gate," which is within the Temple precinct.[12] In the right upper portion of the etching, a number of corpulent priests and elders are gathered under a baldachin.[13] One of the priests holds a staff symbolizing his authority,[14] and gazes down at a kneeling supplicant. Almost all of the scribes and members of the Sanhedrin ignore the turmoil before them, an insouciance that implies their indifference to the commercial desecration of the Temple, the practice to which Jesus reacts so violently. One seated elder, however, turns and looks over his shoulder with disapproval at the scene below, possibly foreshadowing the time when the priests and scribes who overheard Jesus's teachings would conspire against him. In the deep left background are a number of elderly Jews who appear to be unfazed by the chaotic scene being enacted nearby, although it may be the topic of conversation of the two men at the left.

In contrast to the static quality of the congregation of Jewish priests and elders, the lower half of the etching is a roiling sea of activity, with Christ wielding his scourge and attacking a cowering, bearded money changer and his clients. As numerous historians have observed, the figure of Christ was taken from Albrecht Dürer's representation of this biblical event in his *Small Woodcut Passion* of 1505–9 (fig. 3). However, the figure was reversed in the etching process, with the result that Rembrandt's Christ wields the scourge with his left hand.[15] The burst of light that seems to emanate from Jesus's hand suggests a spiritual source for, or emanation of, his anger.

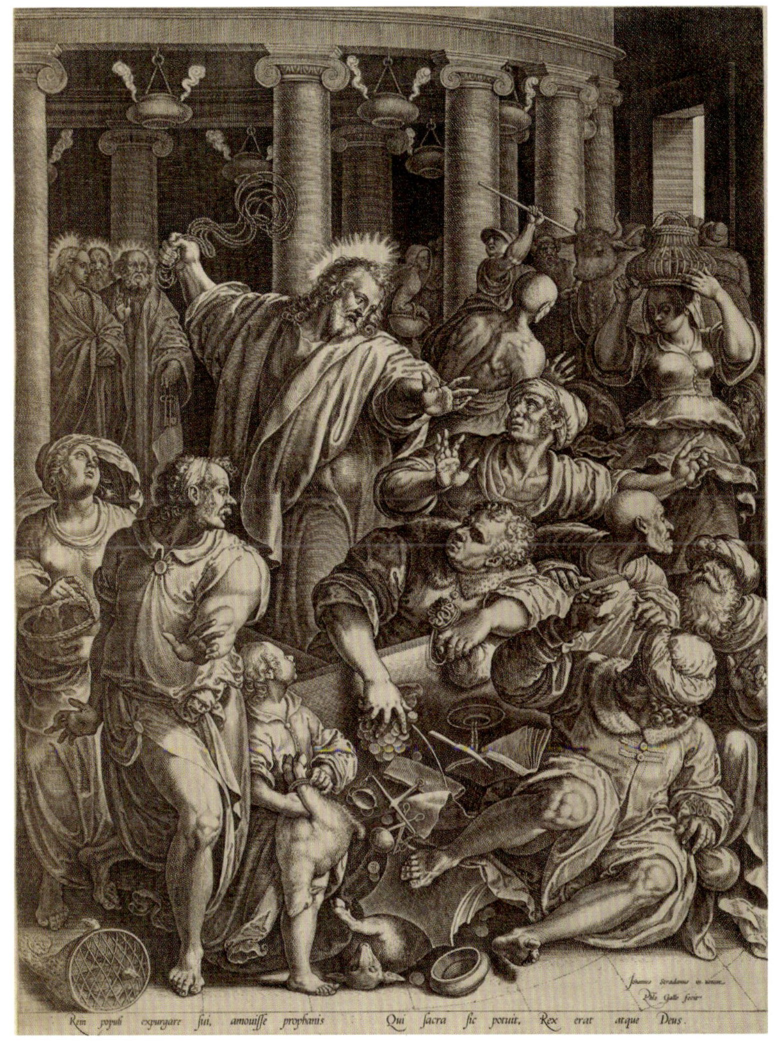

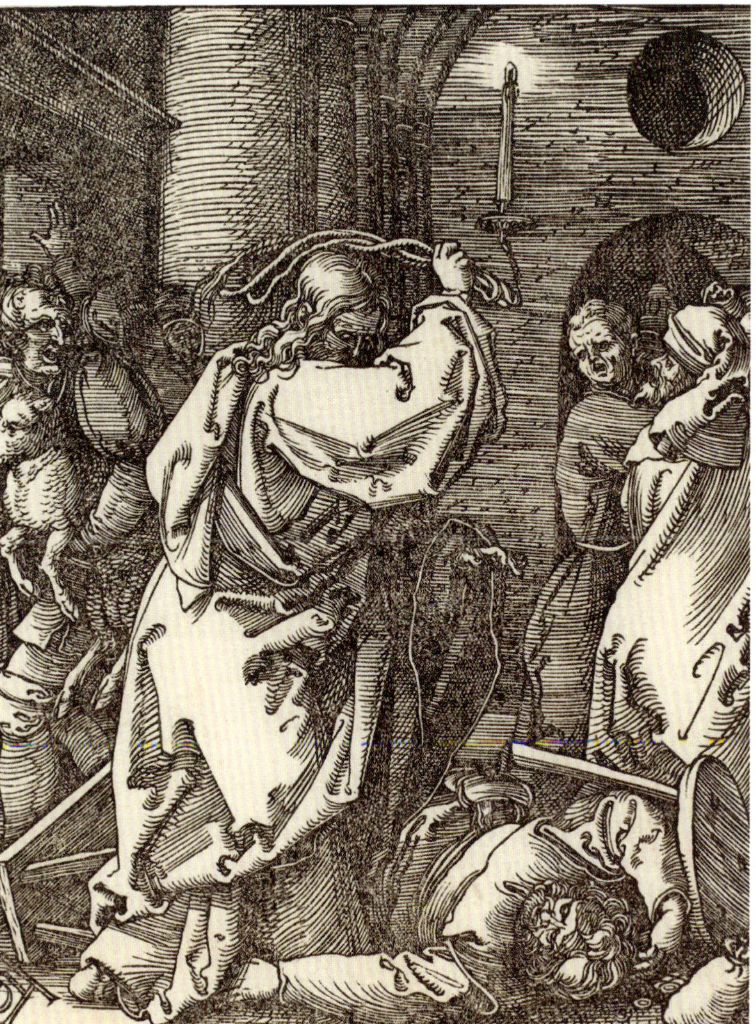

FIGURE 2. Philip Galle after Johannes Stradanus, *Christ Driving the Money Changers from the Temple*, engraving, c. 1575. *Albertina, Vienna.*

FIGURE 3. Albrecht Dürer, *Christ Driving the Money Changers from the Temple*, woodcut, 1505–9. *Photo: Courtesy of the National Gallery of Art, Washington, DC.*

Rembrandt filled the scene with numerous distinctive types. The money changer in the foreground, a figure emblematic of the sin of avarice, leans over a tipping table as he grasps a bag of coins to his chest.[16] At the same time, a young dandy, seen from the rear, falls over in his seat as he dodges Jesus's scourge. In contrast to the biblically robed Christ, this worldly young man wears a sword, boots, slashed breeches, and a pleated shirt with a soft ruff collar.[17] Near Jesus's raised hand are three unidentifiable elderly men who look on with concern. They may represent the Jews who will conspire against Jesus, or, more likely, they may be the apostles who accompanied Jesus on his visit to the Temple.[18] Just to their left, a woman balancing a basket of hens on her head[19] flees in the wake of an old man in a floppy peasant hat who is herding his sheep out of the temple courtyard. In the right foreground, absolute chaos reigns. Young boys and herdsmen struggle to control startled cattle, a dog barks hysterically, and a merchant who is grasping a struggling bird sprawls unceremoniously on the ground. These bits of naturalistic burlesque invest an otherwise sober theme of sin and righteous wrath with a strong element of comic relief.[20]

Notes

1. Matthew 21:12–14; Mark 11:15–17; Luke 19:45–46; and John 2:14–16.

2. Mark 11:17.

3. Mark 11:18.

4. *Rembrandt's Faith,* 254.

5. See the discussions of the Remonstrant/Counter-Remonstrant struggles in the entry for *Stoning of St. Stephen* (B. 97, cat. no. 67), an etching that was also created in 1635.

6. *Rembrandt's Faith,* 254.

7. RRP, *Corpus,* A4. The painting is now in the Pushkin Museum of Fine Arts, Moscow.

8. Rembrandt's contemporary pen-and-brush ink sketch of his own visage in the British Museum (Ben. 53) evinces a similar interest in facial expression.

9. Rembrandt's monogram, RHL, and the date, 1626, appear on the pier behind the figures.

10. Kurt Bauch (*Die frühe Rembrandt und seine Zeit* [Berlin: Verlag Gebr. Mann, 1960], 111) linked the painting to a print by Philip Galle (fig. 2) after a composition by Johannes Stradanus (NHD 44 [Johannes Stradanus], c. 1575). Among the common elements he cites are the figures of a money changer in the foreground who grasps a sack of coins as he looks over his shoulder at Christ, a man who raises his hands in a defensive gesture, and a woman in the right background carrying a basket of poultry on her head. Although Rembrandt may have been inspired by the Stradanus composition, he radically altered the image by stripping it of its setting, dramatically reducing the number of figures, and trimming away virtually all of its anecdotal details.

11. See, for example, Ludwig Münz, *Critical Catalogue,* vol. 2, no. 206, 96–97, "Here the main prototype was apparently one of Jacopo Bassano's representations of the same theme." Bassano's paintings of this theme do not seem to have circulated in the form of reproductive prints.

12. *Rembrandt's Faith,* 252.

13. Rembrandt's representation of the interior of the temple is reminiscent of the temple in his 1630 etching of *Presentation in the Temple with the Angel: Small Plate* (B. 51, cat. no. 25), in which columns divide a bright chamber at the left from a stairway at the right where a priest and his followers are arrayed on the steps leading up to the curtained Holy of Holies.

14. This staff is somewhat similar to the one that appears in Rembrandt's small *Circumcision in the Stable* of about 1630 (B. 47, cat. no. 24). Perlove and Silver equated this staff with the "scepter of Judah," a symbol of Jewish priestly authority (*Rembrandt's Faith,* 95 and 190), and, in a much more unlikely association, with the story of the brazen serpent that foreshadows the salvation of the Jews through the body of the Christ upon the cross (253–54).

15. Rembrandt's reversal of the figure of Jesus drawn from the Dürer print may actually have been intentional. Jesus uses his *left* hand to mete out justice to those who have disobeyed the Lord. This is the same hand—the "sinister" one—with which he will condemn sinners at the Last Judgment.

16. The money changer recalls a very similar figure in the foreground of Rembrandt's 1626 painting and, perhaps even more strongly, the figure grabbing for a pile of coins in the Stradanus print (fig. 2).

17. The man's costume is somewhat old-fashioned, resembling those that were worn in the middle of the sixteenth century. The print exemplifies Rembrandt's penchant for clothing his actors in an eclectic wardrobe that may include "biblical," anachronistic, and contemporary seventeenth-century garb, all featured in the same composition.
Perlove and Silver suggested that this figure resembles one of the *bravi* in Caravaggio's *Calling of St. Matthew* (*Rembrandt's Faith,* 251).

18. Peter, John, and a third nimbed apostle appear in the background of the Stradanus print (fig. 2). It is possible that they are the source of the three observers near Jesus in Rembrandt's print.

19. This motif appears in the background of Rembrandt's 1626 painting (fig. 1), as well as in the Stradanus print (fig. 2) and a 1593 print by Antonius Wierix after Bernardino Passeri (NHD 56.17.226 [the Wierix Family; Book Illustrations]).

20. Rembrandt achieved a similar comic effect with the frightened shepherds, dogs, and flocks in his etching of *Angel Appearing to the Shepherds* (B. 44, 1654, cat. no. 19). Regarding the animals that appear in Rembrandt's prints, see Rosenberg, "Rembrandt's Religious Prints," in this catalog.

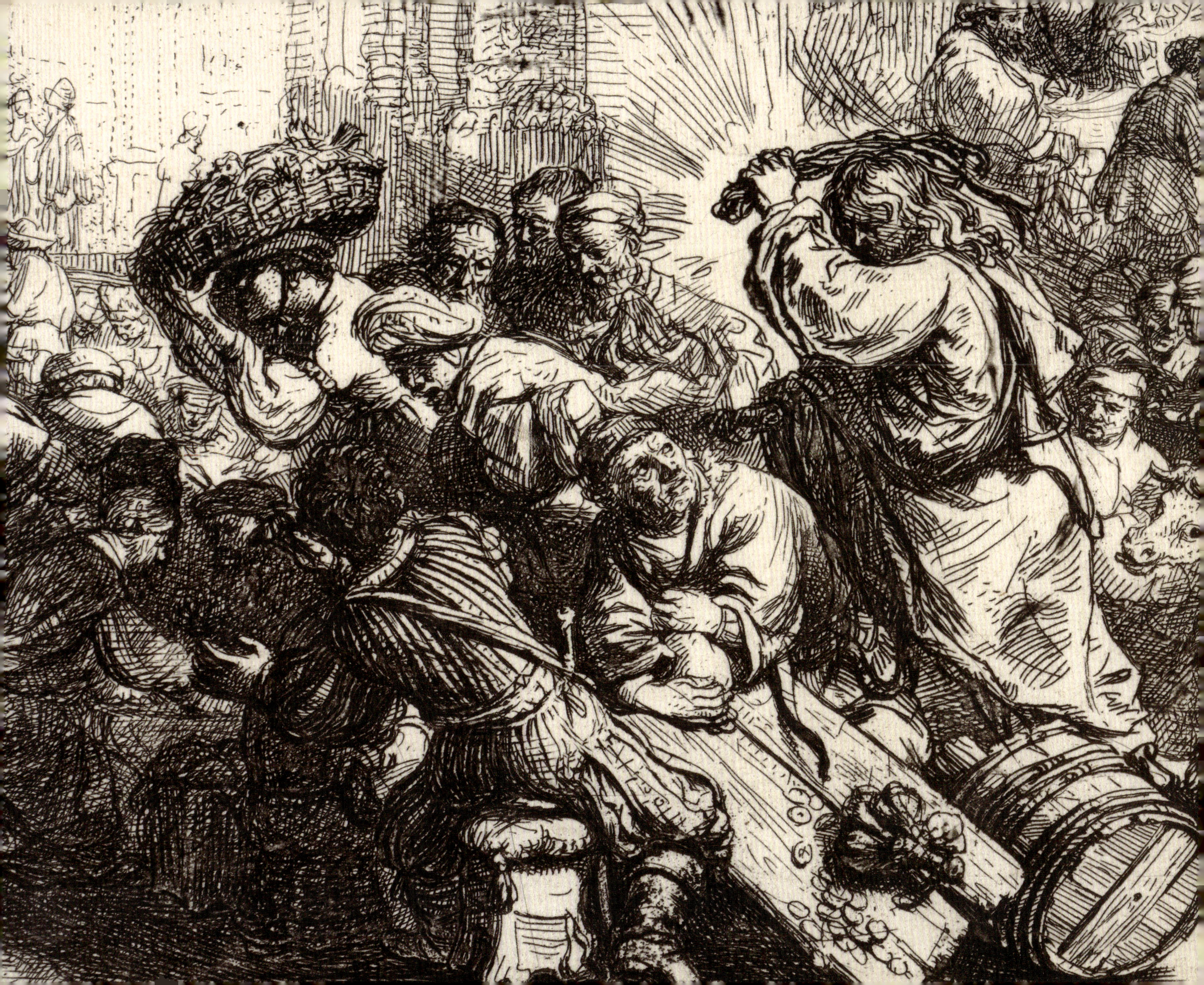

44–45. Christ and the Woman of Samaria

44. Christ and the Woman of Samaria among Ruins

B. 71 (H. 122, Mz. 201, NHD 127)
Etching
Sign and dated in the plate: *Rembrandt. f.1634*
State I of V[1]
Sheet: 12.3 × 10.6 cm, trimmed to the plate mark

Provenance:
Associated American Artists Inc., New York, NY, 1966
Feddersen, Elkhart, IN, 1991
Snite Museum of Art
Acc. No.: 1991.025.042

Plate survives (significantly reworked):
On the art market, USA, 2013.

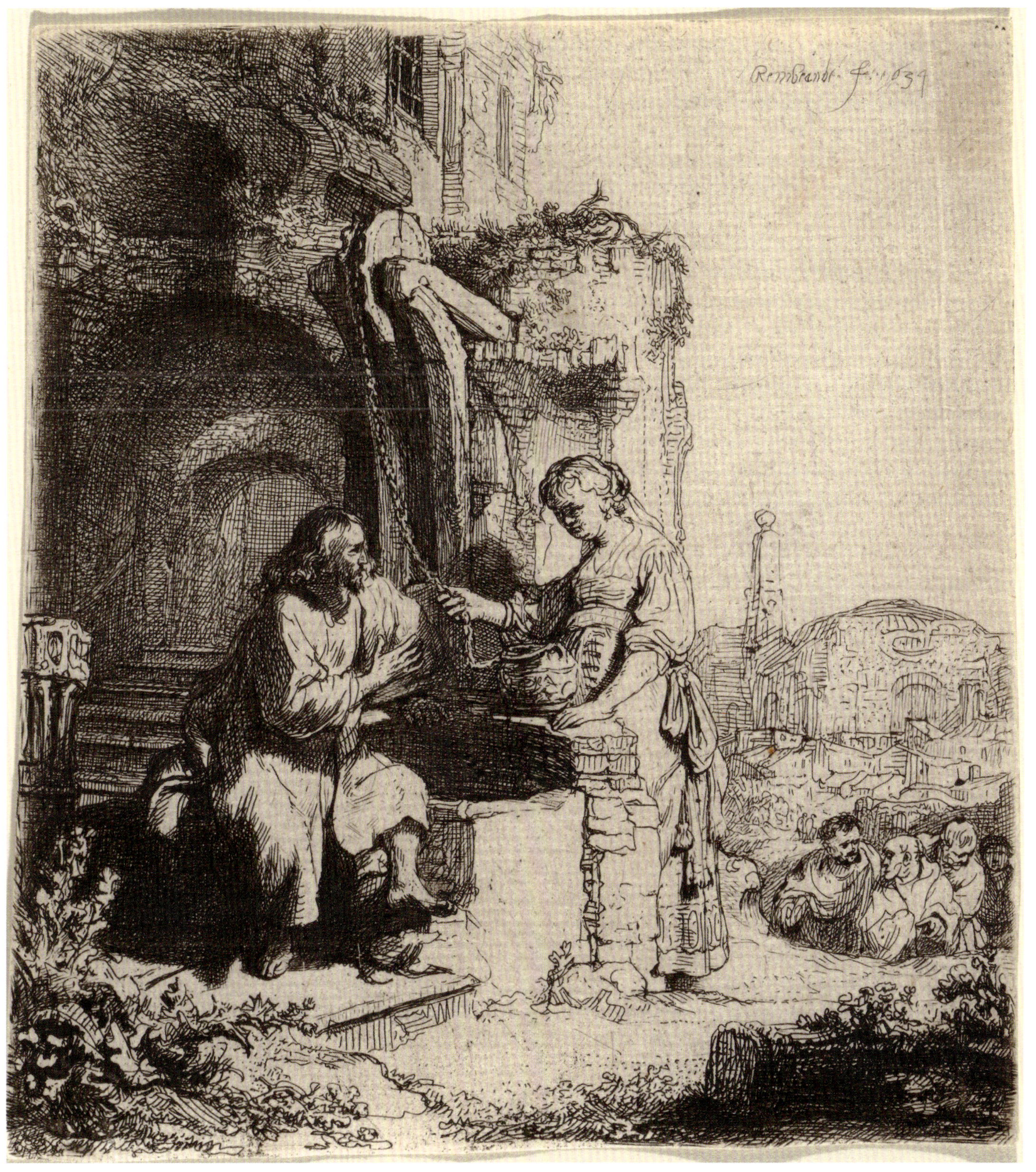

PLATE 44

45. Christ and the Woman of Samaria: An Arched Print

B. 70 (H. 294, Mz. 238, NHD 302)
Etching and drypoint
Signed and dated in the plate: *Rembrandt / f. 1658*[2] on State III
State IV of V
Sheet: 12.7 × 16.3 cm; plate mark: 12.5 × 16.0 cm
Watermark: arms of Amsterdam, unidentified
Verso: in brown ink, *21*

Provenance:
Associated American Artists Inc., New York, NY, 1974
Feddersen, Elkhart, IN, 1991
Snite Museum of Art
Acc. No.: 1991.025.041

Plate survives:
Worcester Art Museum, Worcester, MA.

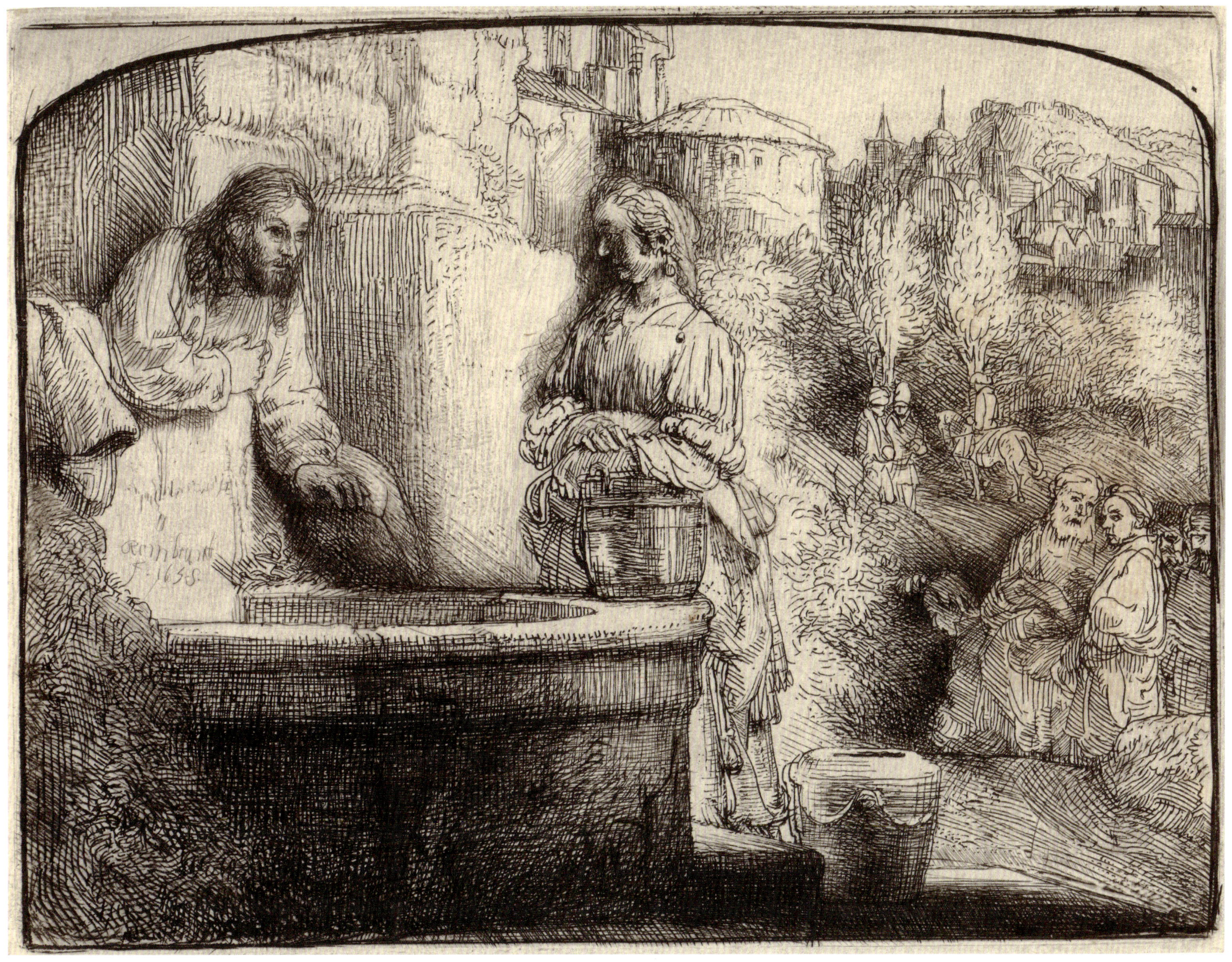

PLATE 45

Rembrandt created two etchings portraying the meeting of Jesus and the Samaritan woman, the first in 1634, and the second more than two decades later, in 1657–58.[3] The images derive from a story recounted in the fourth chapter of the Gospel of St. John:[4] When Jesus was travelling from Judea to Galilee, he passed through the Samaritan city of Sychar. Tired out from the journey, he stopped outside the city to rest beside an old well that had belonged to Jacob. Meanwhile, his disciples went back to Sychar to buy food. When a Samaritan woman came to the well to draw water, Jesus asked her for a drink. She asked him how he, a Jew, could ask her for water, since "Jews have no dealings with Samaritans." Jesus replied that if she had asked *him* for water, he would have complied, giving her "living water." Puzzled, the woman asked him how he would draw up water without a bucket, to which Jesus replied, "Everyone who drinks of this water will thirst again, but whoever drinks of the water that I shall give him will never thirst; the water that I shall give him will become in him a spring of water welling up to eternal life." The discussion continued until the Samaritan woman told Jesus, "I know that the Messiah is coming (he who is called Christ); when he comes, he will show us all things." Jesus responded "I who speak to you am he." Just then, Christ's disciples returned from their trip to Sychar, and the woman departed to carry the news of her encounter back to the city from which she had come.

The story of Jesus and the woman of Samaria would have appealed to sixteenth- and seventeenth-century viewers on several levels. First, for Christians, it was a direct affirmation by Jesus that he was the Messiah who would offer eternal life to the faithful. Second, the encounter between Jesus and the Samaritan represented paradigms of both the conversion of a nonbeliever through preaching and the establishment of a unified and universal church. Finally, for all viewers, it exemplified the possibility of peaceful reconciliation among enemies or strangers at a time when the people of northern Europe were enduring the protracted conflict of the Eighty Years War (1568–1648). As Shelley Perlove and Larry Silver observed, the vision of peace and unity inherent in this story would have had particular appeal in the 1650s, for in addition to offering an optimistic alternative for Dutch Protestants who saw their country continually wracked by internal doctrinal disputes, the appearance of the print coincided with the rising tide of millenarianism that characterized the decade.[5] As Perlove and Silver and also Michael Zell noted, the conversion of the Jews was seen as a crucial precondition for the return of the Messiah. Since Rembrandt had documented ties with proponents of the so-called philosemitic movement of the 1650s, a philosophy that promoted tolerance and persuasion, rather than persecution, as the proper path to the conversion of the Jews, his depiction of Jesus's encounter with the Samaritan woman would have served as an example of how unbelievers could become enlightened.[6]

Rembrandt's two etchings of the same subject illustrate a change in the artist's approach to the narrative in terms of both style and content. The 1634 etching is filled with anecdotal details. Two small patches of vegetation set in the lower corners of the foreground frame the dramatically lit scene of the encounter at the well, and in the lower right corner, a fragment of a fallen column is visible in the weeds. Jesus sits on the edge of the well, with his left leg dangling down and his feet facing the viewer. He twists back a bit to his left so as to face the Samaritan woman across the well mouth. As he leans slightly forward, he rests his weight on his left hand and gestures across his body with his right.[7] The woman has rolled up her sleeves, and she appears to have paused in the act of either lowering her bucket into the well or detaching a full bucket from the winch, before carrying it away. As she listens attentively to Jesus, her left hand lies casually on top of the low brick wall by the well, and her right hand grasps the slack rope attached to the bucket, which sits on the wall in front of her. Her head is inclined toward the stranger as she gazes intently at him.

The left side of the composition is taken up by a low flight of steps behind Jesus that leads into a darkly shadowed, vaulted passageway beneath a crumbling exterior. The vegetation growing out of the mortar joints indicates the decaying state of this mysterious fragment of architecture. The passage leads back to a two-story building that rises behind and beyond it. In back of the Samaritan woman, a massive brick and earthen buttress protrudes out from the side of the passageway. A fragment of a brick arch or a broad corbel supports a wooden structure that in turn holds the wheel of a pulley suspended out over the well. The collapsing ancient architecture—along with the fallen fragment of a column—may be a visual metaphor for the breakdown of past beliefs and the demise of a religion that will now, through Jesus's intercession, give way to the construction of a new theology.

The composition opens up dramatically on the right side. In the far distance, the city of Sychar is dominated by a large, low-domed building beside a high tower that is capped by an orb. This tower, perhaps an obelisk, lends an exotic "Eastern" air to the architecture, evoking a biblical landscape. The domed building beside the tower recalls the shape of Hagia Sophia and the Dome of the Rock. It is probably meant to suggest a temple and, hence, the seat of the idolatrous religion of the Samaritans. Halfway between the city and the foreground, the apostles can be seen conversing as they climb up the hill toward the well. Rembrandt manipulated line and shadow, along with perspective, to set off three distinct planes. The city, which is farthest away, is defined by lightly sketched lines. The apostles, in the middle distance, are more defined with some rudimentary shading. The niche where Jesus and the Samaritan woman converse is filled with exacting detail in areas such as the flowers, the woman's clothing, and the brickwork within the shaded well.

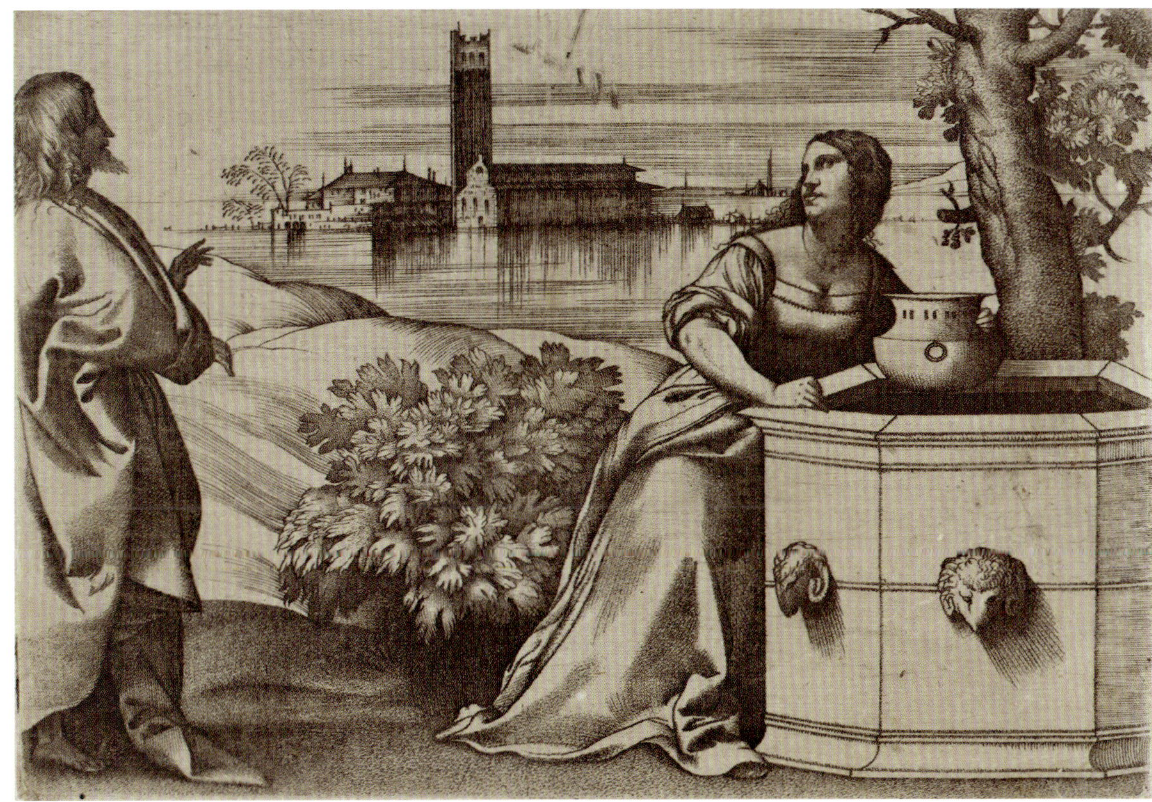

FIGURE 1. Giulio Campagnola, *Christ and the Woman of Samaria*, engraving, 1510–15. *Photo: Courtesy of the National Gallery of Art, Washington, DC.*

The composition of Rembrandt's 1657–58 etching is considerably more static and stately than that of the earlier version of the subject. The foreground is now dominated by a large cylindrical well, instead of the palpably textured one. In addition, the figures of Jesus and the Samaritan woman are brought much closer to the viewer and consequently have a greater psychological presence. At the far left, Jesus leans over a low, sunlit wall that rises out of the left side of the well. Only the upper part of his body in visible. His left hand rests on a stony protuberance beyond the well, while his right hand gestures toward his chest, as though to signify that what he says comes from within.[8] He seems almost to be a supplicant figure, rather than someone trying to proselytize or assert his authority. In contrast to the 1634 etching, Jesus does not face the Samaritan woman, but seems to look past her, into the distance. Hans Rotermund suggested that in this later print, Rembrandt intended Jesus's gaze to encompass the viewer, as well as the woman at the well, so that the message Jesus was preaching would be addressed directly to the beholder.[9] However, Jesus's gaze does not break the picture plane; rather, he appears to be listening to an inner voice, a view that is reinforced by his gesture toward his heart. Meanwhile, the Samaritan woman stands quietly beside the well. As in the earlier work, it is the woman, the incipient convert, who defines the central, vertical axis of the image. Her hands, which are folded primly across one another in front of her as one elbow rests on top of her bucket, suggest that she is closing herself off from the stranger's approach. Her eyes do not meet Jesus's, but are demurely lowered toward the well. Her face, shown in profile, is cast in shadow, possibly signifying her resistance to the message that Christ is delivering, an uncertainty that will be dispelled only when Jesus declares himself the Messiah. This etching is in stark contrast to the earlier print, in which Christ and the woman look at each other and lean toward one another with arms outstretched, as they gesture and converse.

Massive architectural forms close off the left side of the 1657–58 composition, but the picturesque and mysterious qualities of the structures behind Jesus in the 1634 etching have been abandoned in favor of much more simplified stereometric forms. The highly disciplined system of parallel hatching that the artist employed in his articulation of this more geometric architecture reinforces the ordered, classical character that pervades the print, a technique that typifies Rembrandt's late style. Although this print is the fourth state of five, it lacks the "finished" quality of the earlier print.

Like the 1634 print, the right half of the composition opens up into a landscape, but now, the progression back into space is more gradual and more clearly defined. Once again, the apostles appear in the middle distance as they approach the well. This time, however, they are more psychologically involved in the central action. Evidently, the sight of Jesus and the woman at the well has caused the disciples to stop and ponder the meaning of this encounter. While one of them eyes the meeting warily, his nearest companion, possibly St. Peter, leans in toward him, apparently commenting on the sight before them. In depicting the scene in this manner, Rembrandt anticipated the next part of the tale as it is related in scripture: when the apostles arrived at the well, they immediately challenged Jesus as to why he had been speaking to a Samaritan. Unlike Christ, who is ready to embrace all potential believers (as epitomized, possibly, by the gesture toward his heart), his disciples are still rooted in the mundane world of conflict and suspicion.

The landscape beyond the apostles reveals other travelers on the road to and from Sychar, as well as a two-story cylindrical building (possibly a remnant of the domed temple at the back of the 1634 etching), and, finally, the town itself, climbing up the side of a series of rolling hills that stretch off into the distance. The Venetian quality of this landscape, an aspect that has been noted by numerous scholars,[10] undoubtedly sprang from Rembrandt's familiarity with Venetian drawings and prints, including Giulio Campagnola's print of *Christ and the Woman of Samaria* (fig. 1). The 1656 inventory of Rembrandt's effects recorded a Giorgione painting of the Samaritan woman that hung in Rembrandt's house.[11] According to Wilhelm Valentiner, the painting in question was not actually a Giorgione, but a work by Moretto da Brescia, who also painted in the Venetian style.[12] Regardless of authorship, however, certain elements of Rembrandt's two etchings do seem to have been influenced by Moretto's work. Similarities to the painted work can be seen in Christ's pose in the 1634 print, and in the Samaritan woman's pose, the form of the well, and the handling of the distant townscape in the 1657–58 etching.[13]

Notes

1. Hinterding (*Lugt Catalogue*, cat. 57) considers State II a repair state, not by Rembrandt.

2. Signed and dated *Rembrandt f. 1657* on States I and II (on the rim of well).

3. There is also a pair of drawings of the subject attributed to Rembrandt (Ben. 611 and Ben. 978), as well as three painted versions of the story by either Rembrandt or his immediate circle (New York, Berlin, and St. Petersburg). All of these are dated to the 1650s. Walter Leidtke, Carolyn Logan, Nadine M. Orenstein, and Stephanie Dickey. *Rembrandt/Not Rembrandt in the Metropolitan Museum of Art:*

Aspects of Connoisseurship, exh. cat. (New York: Harry N. Abrams and Metropolitan Museum of Art, 1995), vol. 1, cat. 14, 100–104.

4. John 4:1–30.

5. *Rembrandt's Faith*, 41–45. Regarding these doctrinal disputes, see *The Stoning of Saint Stephen*, B. 97, cat. no. 64. Regarding millenarianism and Rembrandt's acquaintance with Menassah ben Israel, see Illustrations for Samuel Menasseh ben Israel, *Piedra gloriosa*, B. 36 A, B, and C, cat. nos. 8, 9, and 10, especially note 9, this catalog.

6. *Rembrandt's Faith*, 41–45; and Michael Zell, *Reframing Rembrandt: Jews and the Christian Image in Seventeenth-Century Amsterdam* (Berkeley: University of California Press, 2002), passim, esp. 144–55.

7. Jesus shows all five fingers on his right hand, and Peter van der Coelen (*Rembrandts passie: Het Nieuwe Testament in der Nederlandse prentkunst van de zestiende en zeventiende eeuw*, exh. cat. [Rotterdam: Museum Boijmans van Beuningen, 2007], 100) interpreted this gesture as signifying the moment when Jesus tells the Samaritan woman that she has had five husbands, a revelation that convinces her that Jesus is a prophet (John 4:18–19).

8. Perlove and Silver (*Rembrandt's Faith*, 44) interpreted the gesture in the context of Luke 4:20–24, where Christ declares that it does not matter where one worships, that he "wishes only to be adored 'in spirit and truth' within the heart." According to Perlove and Silver, Jesus's gesture toward his heart "would have had special meaning for Rembrandt's contemporaries, who advocated the primacy of the invisible church of the heart." It also seems reasonable to interpret the gesture as an illustration of Jesus's revelatory words, "I who speak to you am he [the Messiah]."

9. Hans Rotermund, *Rembrandt's Drawings and Etchings for the Bible*, trans. Shierry M. Weber (Philadelphia: Pilgrim Press, 1969), 186. Rotermund sees this as typical of the more "homiletic character" of Rembrandt's work from the end of the 1650s.

10. See, for example, the comments of Kenneth Clark in Clark, *Rembrandt and the Italian Renaissance* (New York: New York University Press, 1966), 111–14.

11. In the *cessio bonorum* inventory, the painting is described as being in the room behind the parlor: "A large picture of 'The Samaritan Woman' by Giorgione of which a half share belongs to Pieter [de] la Tombe." Walter L. Strauss and Marjon van der Meulen, eds. and trans., *The Rembrandt Documents* (New York: Abaris, 1979), 359, item no. 109. For a discussion of the possible ramifications of the joint ownership of this Venetian-style painting by Rembrandt and a member of de la Tombe family and the circumstances surrounding the commission of the 1657–58 etching, see Rosenberg, "Rembrandt's Religious Prints," in this catalog.

12. Tümpel, *Rembrandt legt*, cat. 77. Ludwig Münz (*Critical Catalogue*, vol. 1, cat. 238) identified the painting (today in the Accademia Carrara, Bergamo, inv. no. 58MR00032) as a work by Girolamo Olgiati, not Moretto. For a color reproduction of the painting, see the online catalog of the Accademia Carrara, accessed June 20, 2016, http://www.lacarrara.it/en/catalogo/58mr00032/.

13. Tümpel, *Rembrandt legt*, cat. 77.

46–47. The Raising of Lazarus

46. Raising of Lazarus: Larger Plate

B. 73 (H. 96, Mz. 192, NHD 113)
Etching and burin
Signed with a monogram on the rock in front of Christ in the plate: *RHL v Ryn f.*[1]
c. 1632
State IX of IX[2]
Trimmed to the arch, 37.0 × 26.0 cm
Watermark: fragment of a crown (unidentifiable)
Verso: in graphite, *H 96, B73, H7502, H*

Provenance:
Harrods, London, 1980
Feddersen, Elkhart, IN, 1991
Snite Museum of Art
Acc. No.: 1991.025.044

Plate survives: On the art market, USA, 2013.

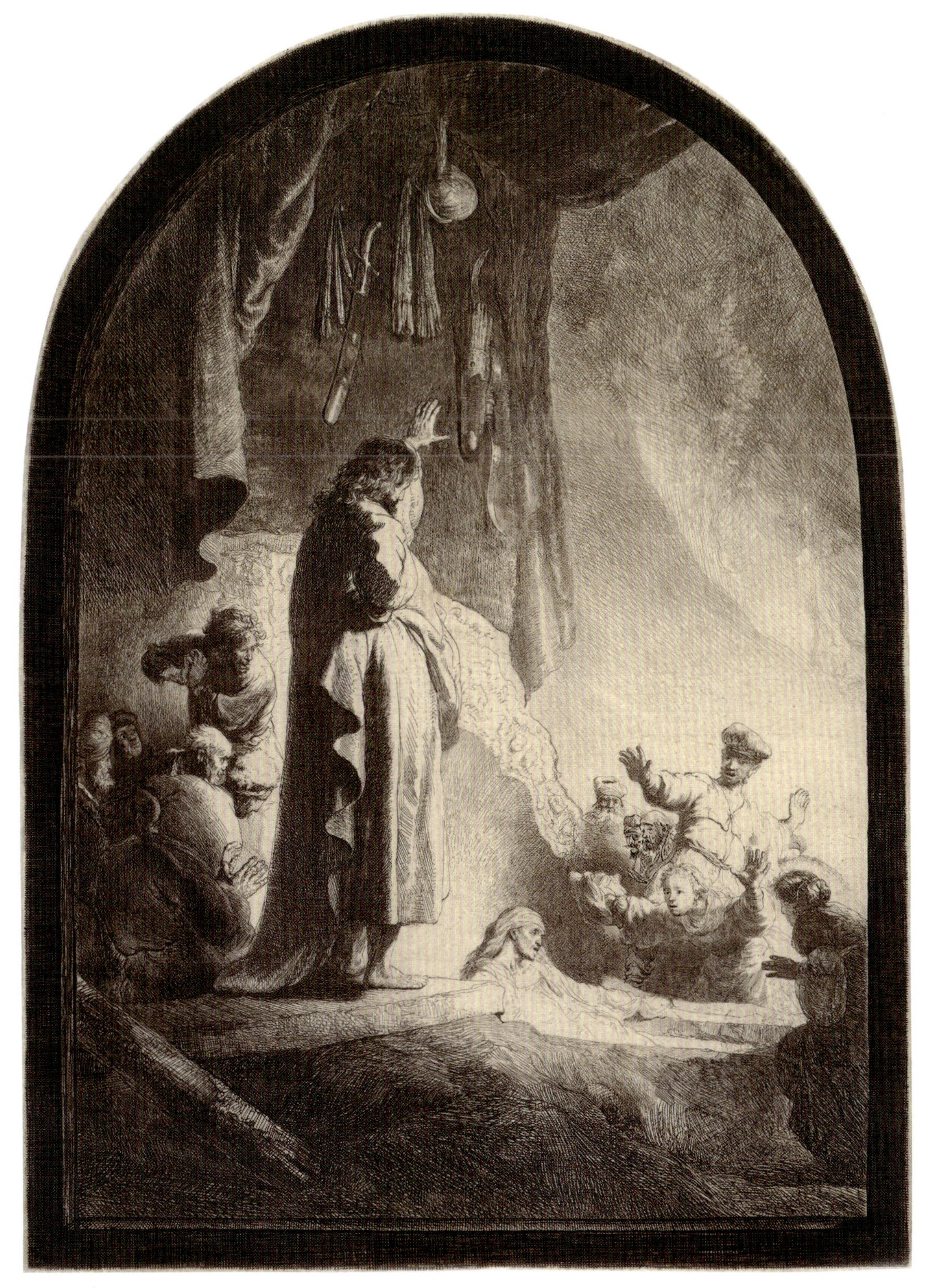

PLATE 46

47. Raising of Lazarus: Small Plate

B. 72 (H. 198, Mz. 214, NHD 206)
Etching
Signed and dated in the plate: *Rembrandt f 1642* ("2" reversed)
State I of II
Sheet 15.0 × 11.4 cm, trimmed to the plate mark
Watermark: fragment of arms of Amsterdam (Ash and Fletcher, D.c)
Verso: in graphite, *4*; collector's stamp: bleeding standing swan (Lugt 2820, unidentified)

Provenance:
Associated American Artists Inc., New York, NY, 1977
Feddersen, Elkhart, IN, 1991
Snite Museum of Art
Acc. No.: 1991.025.043

Plate survives:
Museum of Fine Arts, Boston (inv. 1993.92).

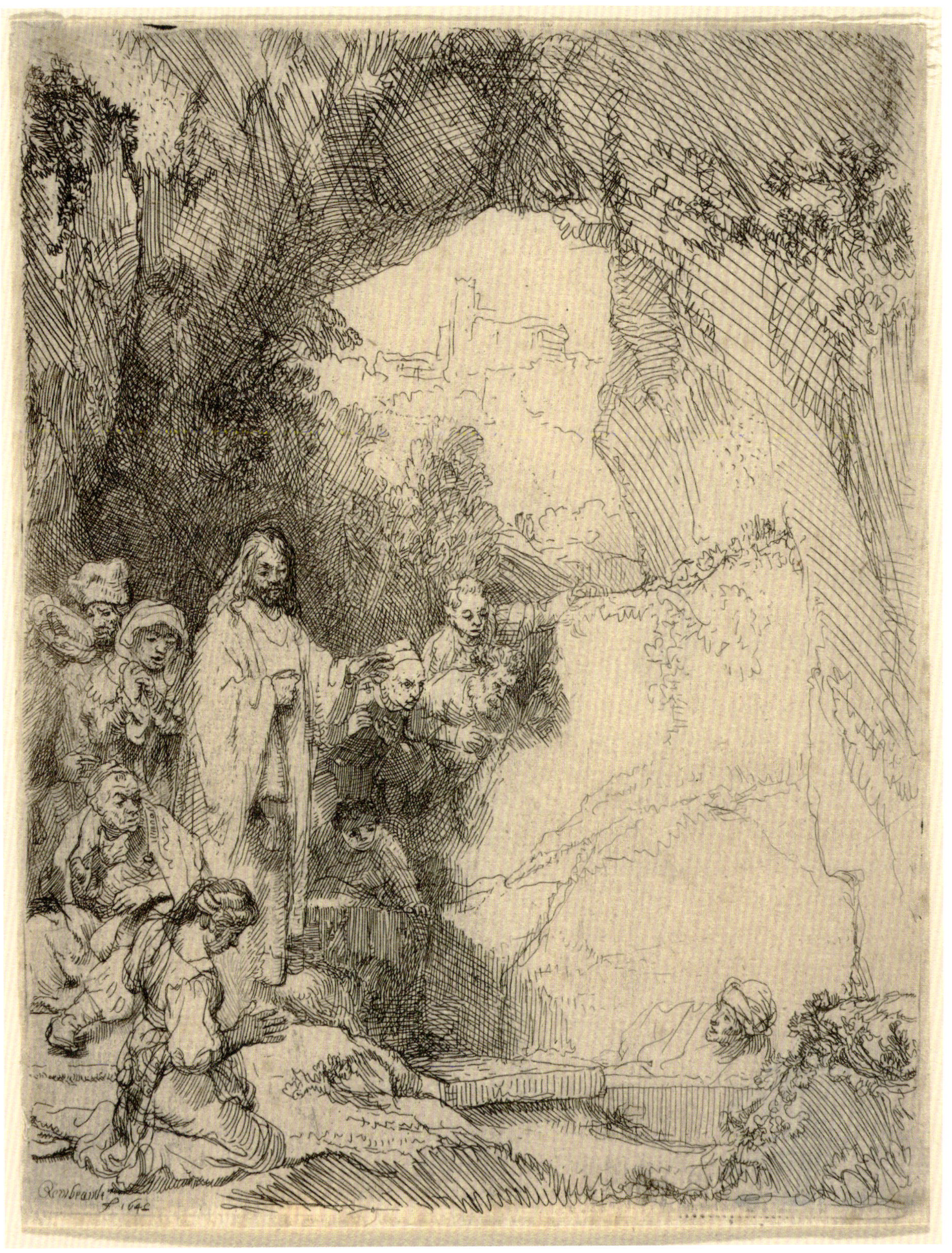

PLATE 47

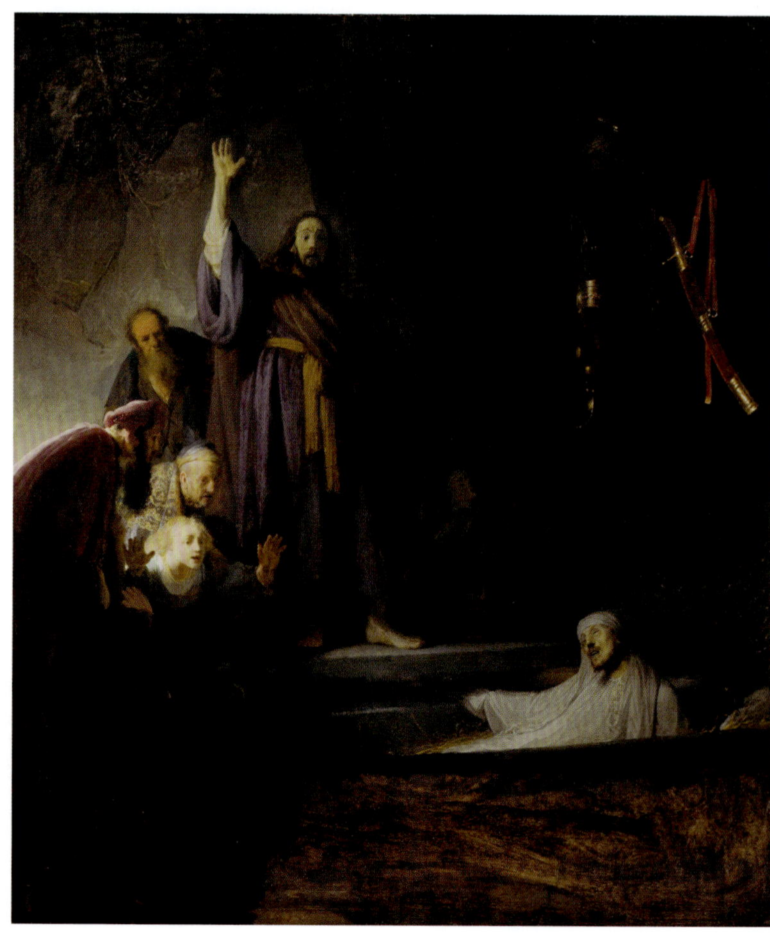

FIGURE 1. Rembrandt, *The Raising of Lazarus*, oil on panel, c. 1630. *Los Angeles County Museum, Los Angeles, California, Gift of H. F. Ahmanson and Company, in memory of Howard F. Ahmanson.*

The miracle of the raising of Lazarus is recounted in the Gospel of John.[3] When Lazarus became ill, his sisters, Mary and Martha, sent a messenger to Jesus, asking him to come to Bethany to heal their brother. By the time Jesus arrived, however, Lazarus had already died and had been buried for four days. Seeing the sisters' distress, Jesus asked that the stone be removed from the front of the cave in which Lazarus's body lay. At the gravesite, he prayed for God's assistance and then called out in a loud voice "Lazarus, come forth." At Jesus's command, the dead man, still wrapped in his winding cloth, rose from the grave. Jesus then commanded that Lazarus be unbound and allowed to depart.

The Raising of Lazarus, Christ's last miracle before the Passion, was a popular subject in Renaissance and Baroque art, quite possibly because it was the most transparent prefiguration of the Resurrection.[4] John Calvin specifically interpreted the miracle in this fashion,[5] and it is likely that Rembrandt's Calvinist contemporaries would have done the same. In addition, Calvin asserted that miracles in general served a larger twofold purpose: to prepare one for, or confirm one in, the faith.[6] In this context, Rembrandt's depictions of the Raising of Lazarus, visual reminders of one of Christ's most remarkable miracles, would have recalled and reaffirmed the foundations of the faith.

Rembrandt's earliest representation of the Raising of Lazarus was a painting that reflected the artist's engagement with expressive emotion and dramatic chiaroscuro (fig. 1).[7] Set inside a deeply shadowed and mysterious cavern, the drama is illuminated by a hidden source of light that penetrates the darkness from the left side, picking out a small cluster of Jewish observers at the foot of the grave; the face and arm of the commanding, frontal figure of Jesus, who raises his right hand as he summons Lazarus back from the dead;[8] Lazarus's reanimated corpse, which begins to rise from the tomb as if in a trance; and a still life consisting of a turban, bow and arrows, and a sheathed sword,[9] all suspended from the wall above the open grave. Lazarus's drawn face, with its sunken eyes, hollow cheeks, and gaping mouth, suggests his still liminal state between death and resurrection. Three elderly Jewish men, witnesses to the miracle, react with curiosity and amazement. Staring down at Lazarus, they are astounded by the scene before them. These are the witnesses who, according to Calvin, were assembled "by a secret decree of God . . . [so] that the resurrection of Lazarus might not remain unknown."[10] The miracle would not inspire all of these witnesses to belief and fealty, for, according to St. John (1:45–53), some of the observers would subsequently report Lazarus's resurrection to the Pharisees and scholars in the Temple, thus setting in motion the events of the Passion.

Lazarus's sisters exhibit very different reactions to their brother's resurrection. Martha, the more reserved of the two women, is a dark figure seen from behind as she kneels at the lower left corner of the painting. She raises her arms and draws back slightly, as if in amazement or fear. Although her head is turned in lost profile, the edge of her face is illuminated, as if by the light of faith. Mary Magdalen's reaction is more overtly demonstrative.[11] She leans forward toward Lazarus and thrusts out her arms in a gesture of astonishment. Her eyes are wide open and her mouth is agape, as if she is crying out.

Rembrandt made his first etching of the Raising of Lazarus (B. 73, cat. no. 46) sometime around 1632, about a year after his painted version of the subject. It was the largest print he had made to date,[12] and it was clearly much more ambitious and technically accomplished than the prints that he had produced in the late 1620s.[13] The fact that the etching has a broad black "frame" and is arched at the top makes it clear that Rembrandt conceived of this print as an independent work of art, presumably meant to be displayed on a wall, rather than kept in an album.[14] He retained few of the elements of his earlier painting. The composition has been rotated so that in lieu of a procession back through a series of planes parallel to the picture surface, there is a shallow diagonal that runs from the top left to the bottom right edge of the scene. Lazarus's tomb has been set somewhat farther back within the cave, bringing him into much closer proximity with Jesus. Lazarus's head is now directly in front of Christ's feet, but despite this, Jesus's gaze actually appears to be fixed not on the dead man, but on the brightly illuminated, standing man who is gesturing at the right. The Magdalen's pose remains essentially the same as in the painting, although now she and Martha appear on the opposite (right) side in the print. Jesus faces inward, so he is seen from the right, and much of his face is hidden.[15] As a result, Christ's gestures assume even greater importance. He raises his left hand in a commanding sign of address or command and places his right hand, akimbo, aggressively on his hip.[16] The rendition of his elbow, which protrudes out toward the viewer, is a tour de force of foreshortening. Bright light enters the tomb from the cave's opening at the back right side of the image, creating chiaroscuro contrasts that are even stronger than those of the painting. The illuminated mouth of the cave is a lofty space that dwarfs all of the mortals below, emphasizing the contrast between them and their savior, who towers above them.

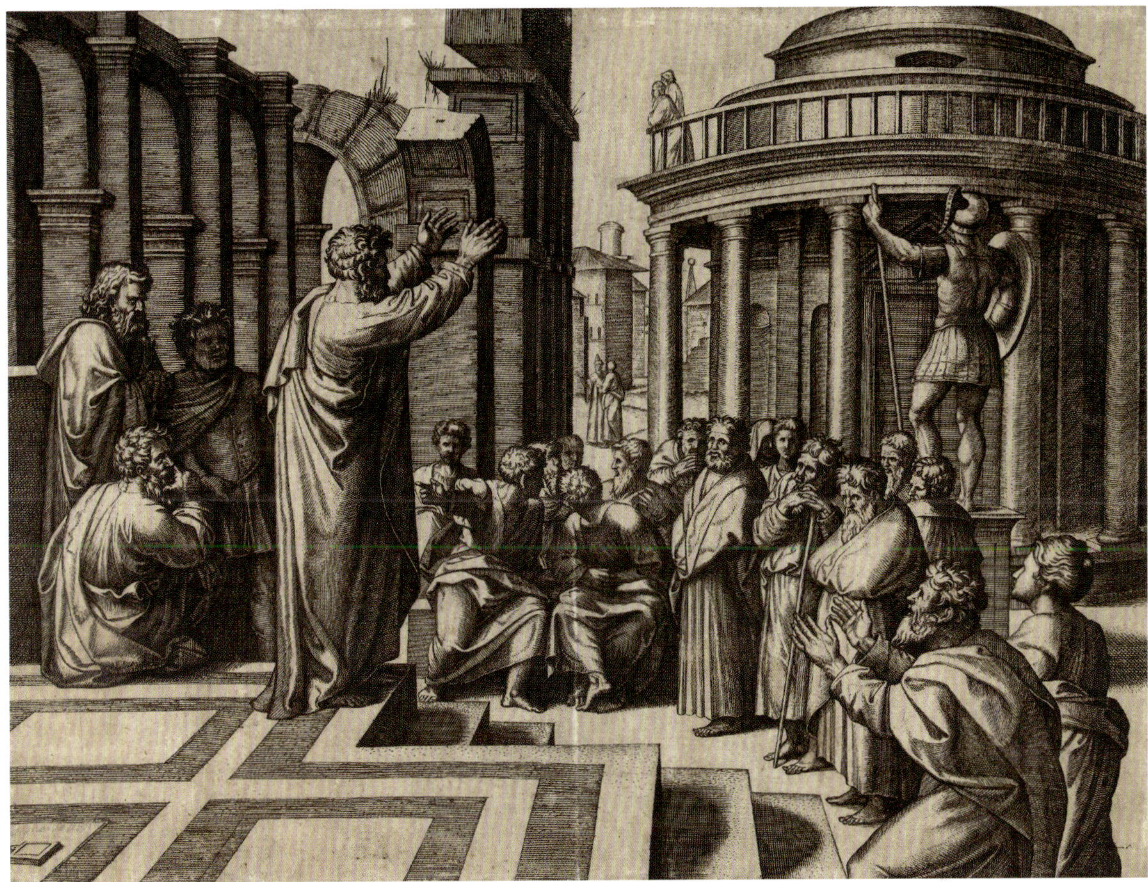

FIGURE 2. Marcantonio Raimondi after Raphael, *St. Paul Preaching at Athens*, engraving, c. 1520. *Rijksmuseum, Amsterdam.*

Above and beyond the figure of Christ, Rembrandt created another martial still life. Here, the objects are suspended from the

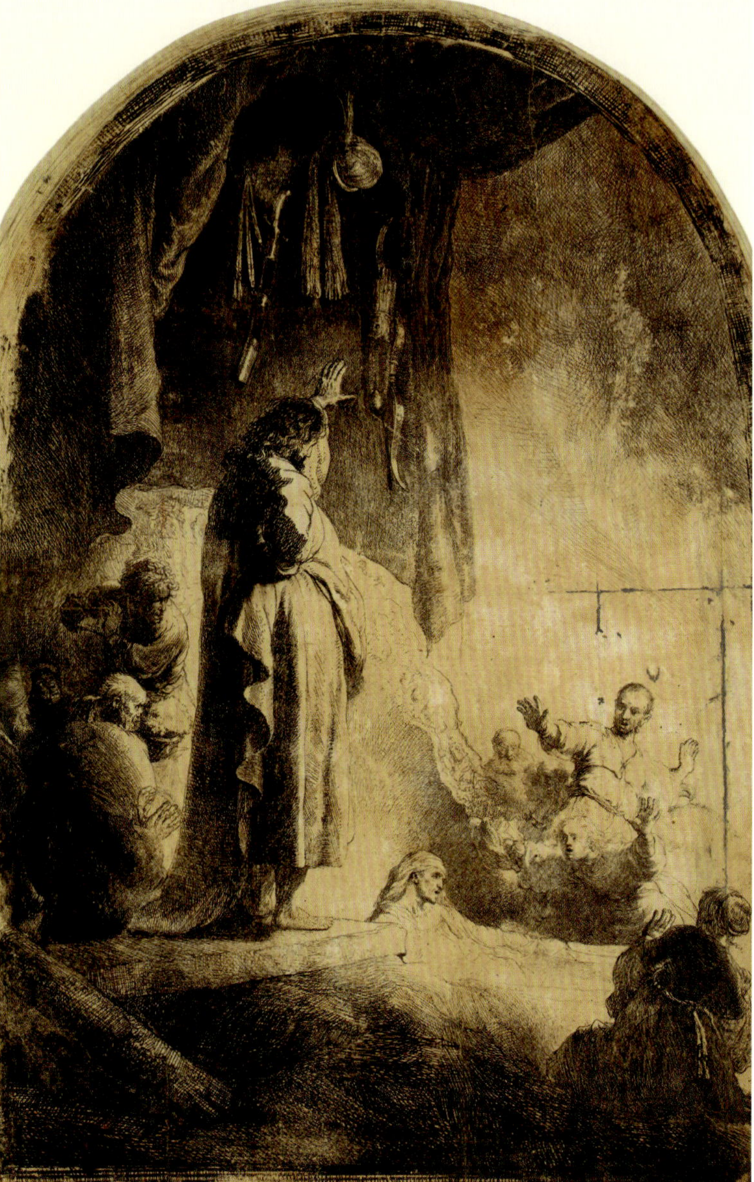

FIGURE 3. Rembrandt, *The Raising of Lazarus: The Larger Plate*, etching, State I, c. 1632. *Photo: © Trustees of the British Museum.*

ceiling of the cavern, just beyond the head of Lazarus's grave. This time, however, the sword, bow and arrow, and turban are enframed by drapery, suggesting a more regal or ceremonial setting.

Rembrandt seems to have invested a fair amount of time in this etching, for he carried it through several different states as he refined poses and details of costume.[17] The figure of Martha, for example, was significantly transformed during the course of this process. In the first state (fig. 3), Martha faces toward the tomb, with her back toward the viewer. She throws up her hands in amazement and pulls back, away from Lazarus, as though frightened or overwhelmed by the miracle before her. Beginning with the third state, however, Rembrandt turned Martha so that she was more in profile, the pose in which she appears in the Snite Museum impression. Now, she leans forward and seems to look directly into Lazarus's eyes. As in the painting, her dark form closes off the composition at one of the lower corners, this time at the right, and draws the viewer's eye back to the core of the miracle.

One of the most telling differences between the etching and the painting that preceded it is the dramatic increase in the number of witnesses observing Lazarus's resurrection, a change that gave Rembrandt an opportunity to depict a much broader range of reactions to the miracle through expression and gesture. A couple of years before the artist produced this print, Constantijn Huygens, the powerful and culturally sophisticated secretary of Prince Frederik Hendrik of Orange, the stadtholder of Holland, contrasted Rembrandt with the artist's slightly older rival, Jan Lievens, and singled out Rembrandt's ability to express "liveliness of emotion" as the young artist's particular strength.[18] Rembrandt had been in contact with Huygens since the late 1620s, and it is likely that the secretary was instrumental in Prince Frederik Hendrik's decision, around 1630–31, to commission the artist to create an important series of paintings dedicated to the Passion. Lievens may well have competed for the same commission. There is evidence that the two artists may have sought to outdo one another in other endeavors, as well. In 1631, Lievens produced his own painted and etched versions of *The Raising of Lazarus*, and it has been suggested that Lievens's painting was done as a response to Rembrandt's (figs. 4 and 5).[19] It is quite possible, then, that Rembrandt's 1632 etching was his response to Lievens's painting.[20] This might help to explain the scale of Rembrandt's print, as well as the work's pictorial framing and the amount of time that he devoted to it. Rembrandt's invention of an unusual pose for Christ and his expansion of the cast of characters in the composition, in comparison not only to his own painting but also to Lievens's, would have served to demonstrate his technical and creative virtuosity to both Huygens and

Prince Frederik Hendrik,[21] as well as to a much broader audience, strengthening his reputation as an imaginative narrative artist capable of depicting strong emotions.

Rembrandt returned to the subject of the Raising of Lazarus in 1642 (B. 72, cat. no. 47), a year that was one of both triumph and despair for the artist. In that year, *The Shooting Company of Frans Banning Cocq*, the monumental militia painting better known as *The Nightwatch*, was completed, and even Filippo Baldinucci, one of Rembrandt's harshest critics, admitted that it "brought him [Rembrandt] such fame as was scarcely ever achieved by any other painter in those parts."[22] In June of the same year, Rembrandt's wife, Saskia, died after an extended illness, a loss that could have influenced the artist's decision to return to the theme of Lazarus's miraculous resurrection. The 1642 etching, which is executed in a lighter, more linear graphic style, is considerably smaller, more introspective, and less rhetorically charged than the earlier print. The scene is set in the grotto in which Lazarus was entombed, and the martial still life of turban, sword, and bow and quiver has been eliminated. The figures are smaller in respect to the space of the cavern, and are disposed in a relatively shallow plane set almost parallel to the picture surface. The mouth of the cave is visible behind the figures and offers a view out to a lightly sketched landscape dominated by a distant, raised, towered building.[23] In spite of the fact that the opening of the cavern is behind the figures, there is a strong, undetermined light source at the front of the scene that picks out the figure of Christ against the darkened, arched wall of the cave and, to a somewhat lesser extent, the figures clustered around him at the left. This same light seems to grow in intensity at the right side of the cavern, bleaching out the figure of Lazarus and the rock wall behind him. It is, as Clifford Ackley has put it, as though the dead man has "returned to the light of day."[24]

Christ, clothed in biblical robes, is surrounded by Mary, Martha, and a group of other witnesses. Although slightly larger than the other figures, Jesus is now more integrated into the composition as a whole. The sculptural, monumental quality of the figure in the 1632 etching has been abandoned in favor of a figure of a more human scale. Jesus extends his left hand out toward Lazarus in a gesture that is much more restrained and sacramental than that of the powerful, commanding, raised-arm posture of the earlier painting and etching. His right hand, which is closed, is pressed to his heart.[25] In general, there is a sense that, as Christopher White observed, the miracle derives not from power, but from prayer.[26] The kneeling figure of Mary Magdalen[27] in the left foreground reflects Martha's pose in the 1632 etching, although Mary is not cast into shadow in the same way. The Magdalen's reaction is more subdued than that of either woman in the earlier etching, and, because of the lighting, her exotic costume is more fully described. Martha, who is more modestly dressed, is close to Christ's right side as she leans forward to see Lazarus. The witnesses react to the

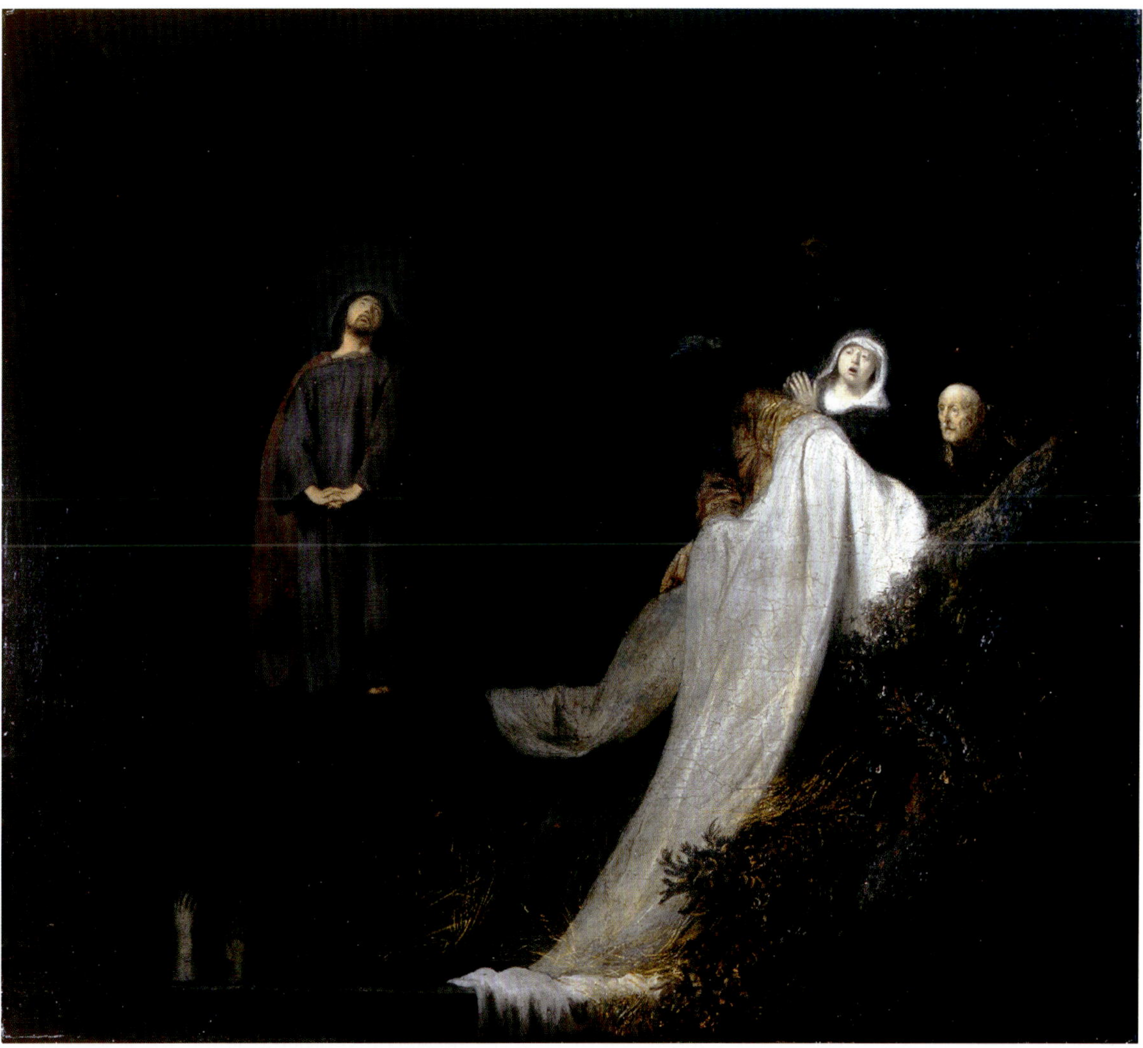

FIGURE 4. Jan Lievens, *The Raising of Lazarus*, oil on canvas, 1631. *Royal Pavilion & Museums, Brighton and Hove, England.*

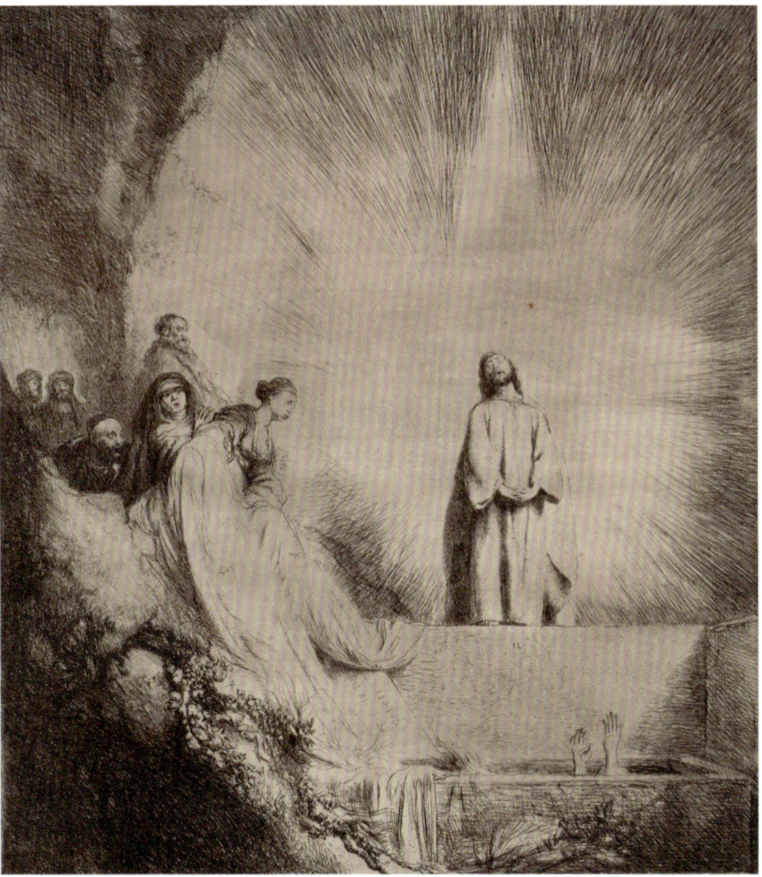

FIGURE 5. Jan Lievens, *The Raising of Lazarus*, etching, c. 1631. *Rijksmuseum, Amsterdam.*

miracle in a variety of ways, and while none of them exhibits the kind of uninhibited amazement shown by the standing, turbaned Jew at the right side of the earlier etching, they do represent an extensive array of emotions, ranging from shock (Mary) to rapture (Martha) and from curiosity (the child on the ledge at Christ's left) to consternation (the man beside Jesus's left hand). Nonetheless, the Baroque theatricality that characterized Rembrandt's approach to the subject in the 1630s has given way to a vision that is calmer, more solemn, and more static. The scene's aura of solemnity may foreshadow the next phase of Christ's earthly journey, his betrayal and condemnation. On the left side of the image, standing behind Martha, are two Jews who turn away from the miraculous resurrection and appear to be conversing.[28] The man wearing a turban is seen only from the rear, but his companion, who wears a high soft hat of the type worn by Temple elders in other Rembrandt prints,[29] faces forward, revealing Semitic features. He wears an expression not of joy or wonder, but of skepticism or disquiet. These two figures may represent the Jews who were not converted by the miracle they witnessed and who would later report Jesus's actions to the Pharisees. The Pharisees, along with the chief priests, would summon the council that would decree that Christ would have to die.[30]

Notes

1. The signature, which would read in full, "Rembrandus Hermanni Leidensis van Rijn fecit," is unique to this etching. Gary Schwartz, ed., *The Complete Etchings of Rembrandt* (New York: Dover Publications, 1988), under B. 46.

2. The original catalog of the Feddersen Collection (Snite Museum of Art, *Rembrandt Etchings from a Private Collection, Biblical Subjects: The Old and New Testaments,* Catalogue from the Exhibition of January 8 – March 29, 1981, exh. cat. [Notre Dame, IN: Snite Museum of Art, 1981], cat. 42, 19) incorrectly identified this as state IV of X and "a Watelet retouch." That identification was based on Harrods' description of the print.

The Snite Museum's impression is quite light, and certain details—most notably the crude rendering of the three figures to the left of the standing turbaned figure in the background—suggest that this print is an impression drawn from a plate that had been reworked after Rembrandt's death. Certain details, such as the black mark on the turban of the figure in the center back, do not appear in the NHD catalog description. Therefore, this may be a later undescribed state.

3. John 11:38–44.

4. Gertrud Schiller, *The Iconography of Christian Art,* trans. Janet Seligman (Greenwich, CT: New York Graphic Society, 1971), 1:186, cited in William H. Halewood, *Six Subjects of Reformation Art: A Preface to Rembrandt* (Toronto: University of Toronto Press, 1982), 36.

5. John Calvin, *Commentary on John,* 1:348 Commentary on John 11:1, "Not only did Christ give remarkable proof of his Divine power in raising Lazarus, but he likewise placed before our eyes a lively image of our future resurrection." Accessed July 21, 2014, http://www.ccel.org/ccel/calvin/calcom34.pdf.

6. Ibid., 1:366, Commentary on John 11:45, "Christ did not permit the miracle which he had wrought to be without fruit, for by means of it he drew some persons to the faith. For we ought to understand that miracles have a twofold use. They are intended either to prepare us for faith, or to confirm us in faith." Accessed July 21, 2014, http://www.ccel.org/ccel/calvin/calcom34.pdf.

7. Los Angeles County Museum of Art, Los Angeles, California. RRP, *Corpus*, A30.

8. This gesture has been associated with the classical pose known as *adlocutio*, a term that denotes the stance of an emperor addressing his troops or the public. It clearly carries with it a connotation of command.

9. Rembrandt's inclusion of these objects in a composition representing the Raising of Lazarus seems to have been unique. According to Christian Tümpel, *Rembrandt: Images and Metaphors* (London: Haus Books, 2006), 42, the weapons were inspired by a medieval legend that identified Lazarus as a knight. Their presence also lends a triumphal aura to the scene, since triumphal arches were often adorned with martial images including piles of arms and armor. See, for example, the arches designed by Rubens for the Joyous Entry of the Cardinal-Infante Ferdinand into Antwerp in 1635, illustrated in John Rupert Martin, *Corpus Rubenianum Ludwig Burchard: An Illustrated Catalogue Raisonné of the Work of Peter Paul Rubens Based on the Material Assembled by the Late Ludwig Burchard*, pt. 16, *The Decorations for the Pompa Introitus Ferdinandi* (London: Phaidon, 1972). The turban on the wall may have been intended to identify Lazarus as a Jew.

10. Calvin, *Commentary on John*, 1:354., Commentary on John 11:18, accessed July 21, 2014, http://www.ccel.org/ccel/calvin/calcom34.pdf.

11. Martha's sister Mary has traditionally been identified as Mary Magdalen.

12. Filippo Baldinucci reported that Rembrandt paid 50 scudi to buy back a copy of this print that was already in circulation, a practice he sometimes followed in order to help maintain the market value of his prints by making them scarcer. Baldinucci, "Life of Rembrandt," from *Cominciamento, e progresso dell'arte dell'intagliare in rame, colle vite di molti de'più eccellenti maestri della stessa professione*, in Joachim von Sandrart, Filippo Baldinucci, and Arnold Houbraken, *Lives of Rembrandt*, introd. Charles Ford (London: Pallas Athene, 2007), 46.

13. For a comparison, see, for example, the very early *Circumcision* (S. 328, c. 1626, cat. no. 22) and *Rest on the Flight into Egypt* (B. 59, c. 1626–27) (cat. nos. 32 and 33, fig. 1).

14. Barbara Welzel observed that this is the first time that Rembrandt made the case that one of his prints had a status equal to that of a painting. Welzel in Holm Bevers, Peter Schatborn, and Barbara Welzel, *Rembrandt: The Master and His Workshop*, vol. 2, *Drawings and Etchings*, exh. cat. (New Haven, CT; Yale University Press, 1991), cat. 7, 185.

15. Christian Tümpel (*Rembrandt legt*, cat. 73) suggested that the figure of Jesus, seen from behind, was inspired by Raphael's St. Paul in his tapestry of *St. Paul Preaching at Athens*, which Rembrandt could have known through Marcantonio Raimondi's print from the early 1520s inspired by the tapestry cartoon (TIB 44) (fig. 2).

16. This type of pose, standing with one arm akimbo, was associated with masculinity and strength. On the significance of this gesture, see Joaneath Spicer, "The Renaissance Elbow," in *A Cultural History of Gesture*, ed. Jan Bremmer and Herman Roodenburg (Ithaca, NY: Cornell University Press, 1991), 84–128.

17. See note 2, above, regarding the number of states.

18. Walter L. Strauss and Marjon van der Meulen, eds. and trans., *The Rembrandt Documents* (New York: Abaris, 1979), doc. 1630/5, 7. In a diary entry, Huygens noted, "I will dare to pronounce perfunctorily on each man as follows. Rembrandt is superior to Lievens in judgment and in the liveliness of emotion."

19. Jan Lievens produced a much more reserved painted version of the miracle (Brighton Art Gallery and Museum, Brighton, England, signed and dated 1631), which he then reproduced in an undated etching (HD 7). Gary Schwartz, *Rembrandt, His Life, His Paintings* (London: Penguin, 1985), 82–86.

20. Rembrandt may actually have owned Lievens's painting of the Raising of Lazarus. Christopher White, *Rembrandt as an Etcher*, 2nd ed. (New Haven, CT: Yale University Press, 1999), 27n15.

21. On the unusual qualities of Rembrandt's print and its rhetorical structure, see Rudolf Preimesberger, 'Die Erweckung des Lazarus' in Los Angeles und 'Die Reue des Judas' in englishem Privatebesitz," in *Rembrandt—Wissenschaft auf der Suche*, ed. Holm Bevers, Jan Kelch, Bernd Wolfgang Lindemann, and Christian Tico Seofert, *Jahrbuch der Berliner Museen*, N.F. 51 (2009) (Berlin: Gebr. Mann Verlag, 2009), 101–2.

22. Baldinucci, "Life of Rembrandt," 37. The *Cominciamento* was published in 1686. Despite his acknowledgment of Rembrandt's fame, Baldinucci condemned the painting, saying that except for the foreshortening of the spear held by Cocq's lieutenant, "the picture . . . was jumbled and confused to such a degree that other figures could scarcely be distinguished from one another."

23. Perlove and Silver specifically identified this as a view of the Temple Mount in Jerusalem, with the tower signifying the Temple. In their view, the juxtaposition of Jesus and the Temple was meant to associate Christ with the High Priest in the order of Melchizedek. *Rembrandt's Faith*, 275–76.

24. Clifford Ackley in *Rembrandt's Journey,* cat. 129–30, 199.

25. Later, Rembrandt would depict Christ in a similar pose in *Christ and the Woman of Samaria: An Arched Print* (B.70, 1658, cat. no. 45), as Jesus was counseling the woman at the well regarding God's miraculous gift of eternal life through Christ.

26. White, *Rembrandt as an Etcher,* 48.

27. This figure's clothing suggests that she is Mary, but it is not completely clear as to which woman is Mary Magdalen and which is Martha.

28. There are other instances in which Rembrandt included two disaffected Jews standing at the edge of a biblical scene, where they are set apart from the action (usually, at the left of the composition), and appear to be engaged in conversation, e.g., *Presentation in the Temple: Oblong Print* (B. 49, c. 1639–41, cat. no. 26); *Christ Appearing to the Apostles* (B. 89, 1650, cat. no. 61), with the figures on the right, instead of the left; and *Peter and John Healing the Cripple at the Gate of the Temple* (B. 94, 1659, cat. no. 66).

29. See, for example, all three examples of Christ Disputing with the Doctors (B. 66, cat. no. 37; B. 65, cat. no. 38; and B. 64, cat. no. 39).

30. John 11:45–53.

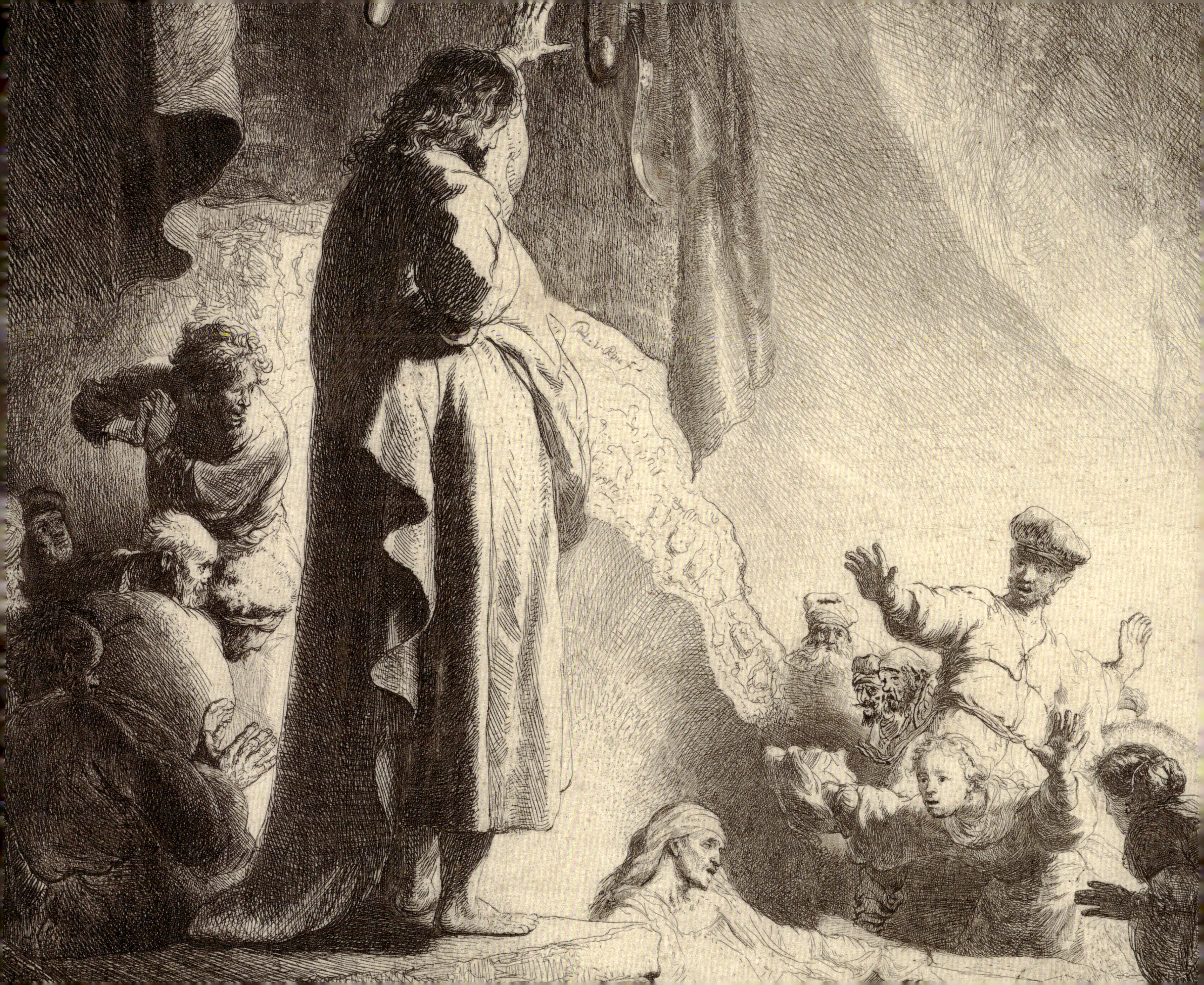

48. Hundred Guilder Print

B. 74 (H. 236, Mz. 217, NHD 239)
Etching, drypoint, and burin
c. 1648
State II of IV
Sheet: 27.8 × 38.8 cm, trimmed to the plate mark, fold down the center
Watermark: Churchill n. 463; "Pot"[1]
Verso: in graphite, *WATERMARK*

Provenance:
Harrods, London, 1973
Feddersen, Elkhart, IN, 1991
Snite Museum of Art
Acc. No.: 1991.025.045

The plate no longer survives.

The so-called *Hundred Guilder Print* is one of Rembrandt's most famous graphic works. The title refers to the extraordinarily high price that was paid for an impression of the print during Rembrandt's own lifetime.[2] On February 9, 1654, Flemish painter and printmaker Jan Meyssens of Antwerp wrote to Charles van den Bosch, bishop of Bruges, "Also here is the rarest print published by Rembrandt, in which Christ is healing the sick, and I know that in Holland [it] has been sold various times for 100 guilders and more; and it is as large as this sheet of paper, very fine and lovely, but ought to cost 30 guilders. It is very beautiful and pure."[3] The earliest record of the print being referred to as the "Hundred Guilder Print" is in an entry dated March 1, 1711, in Zacharias Conrad von Uffenbach's journal, *Noteworthy Journeys through the Netherlands, Holland, and England*:[4]

> We [Uffenbach and his brother] were at David Bramen's[5] to see his engravings as he has no time in the week to show them. He has a considerable number of them, among which the finest is a large lot by Rembrandt, yet he did not have the best, nor the so-called "Hundred Guilder Print." It is thus called because it once fetched as much at auction.[6] It shows the miracle of Christ healing a blind and deaf man. But Herr Bramen had the "Thirty Guilder" and "Twenty Guilder" prints which my brother in Holland also bought. The former is the *Ecce Homo*, the latter the *Taking of Christ from the Cross*.[7]

The *Hundred Guilder Print* is generally acknowledged to be one of Rembrandt's finest etchings. Praised for its technical mastery, range of tones, variety of costume, sensitive gestural language, and emotional expressiveness, the work is a virtuoso piece, utilizing all three intaglio techniques: etching, engraving, and drypoint.[8] The print is unique in the artist's graphic oeuvre because it illustrates not just one but several biblical incidents in a single unified field by means of a seamless interweaving of four narrative moments, presenting Christ as preacher, teacher, and miraculous healer.[9] Drawing on the Gospel of St. Matthew 19,[10] Rembrandt's image depicts different aspects of Jesus's ministry in Judea, including Christ's healing of the sick (19:1–2), his dispute with the Pharisees (19:3–12), his admonition to his disciples to "suffer the children" to come to him (19:13–15), and his response to a rich young man's inquiry about how to gain salvation (19:16–26).

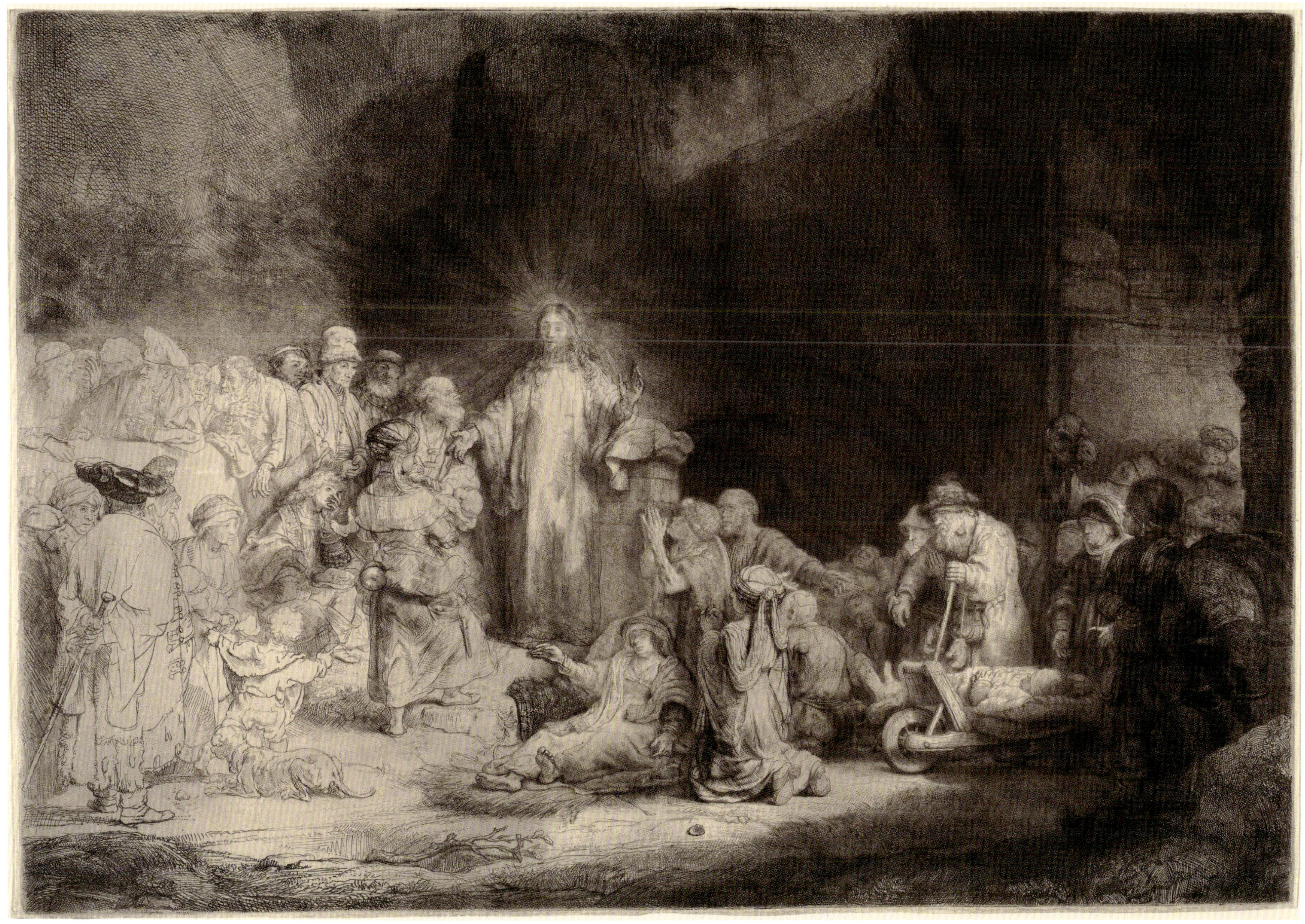

PLATE 48

In the print, Jesus serves as the vertical axis and unifying figure in a complex but carefully integrated composition. He stands on a low rise, with his head at the apex of a broad triangle that encompasses the crowds on each side of him. Delicately rendered rays of light appear to emanate from his head and upper body, while a much brighter light falls on his face and tunic, casting him into strong relief against dense, almost black shadows that enshroud the cavernous and mysterious space behind him. A fragment of a low wall stands to Christ's immediate left.[11] An emaciated old woman kneels in supplication just in front of the wall, and the shadow of her clasped hands falls on Jesus's white tunic, a detail that links him with the sick and pious believers who have gathered beside him.[12]

The manner in which Rembrandt describes each of the figures in the congregation of disciples at his left illustrates the artist's sympathetic engagement with the elderly, the ill, and the marginalized.[13] His compassion for those in need is exemplified by his sensitive rendering of an elderly couple—a shuffling, bearded, old blind man with a goiter who is tenderly supported by his aged wife—and an ailing woman who has collapsed on a woven mat, her dirty bare feet resting on a small pile of straw. One of this woman's hands is draped limply at her side, and the other is extended out as she reaches for help with what appears to be her last bit of strength. Through half-closed eyes, she gazes off into the distance, out of the picture plane at the left.

Another of Rembrandt's figures introduces a number of intriguing associations that broaden the implications of the print. An Ethiopian wearing a dangling earring and what appears to be a bandage over one eye stands in the shadows at the right of the procession of suffering believers, his head tilted up toward Jesus's face. This striking Moorish figure may serve to represent the universal reach of Christ's healing message, but he is also an example of Rembrandt's fascination with the exotic.[14] Beside the African man is a heavily laden donkey, and behind both of them, under an archway, stands a camel, its head turned toward the Moor. The camel is very likely a reference to the passage in Matthew 19:23 in which Jesus advises a wealthy young man that "it is easier for a camel to pass through the eye of a needle, than for a rich man to enter into the kingdom of God." Seated on the left side of the print, between two mothers holding their babies, is a luxuriously dressed young man who might well represent the one whose question elicited Jesus's response. The young man leans forward, resting his right hand on his knee while holding his face in his left hand. The youth looks upward, although not directly at Christ, while listening closely to Jesus's words.

Another richly clad figure stands at a farther remove from salvation, both spiritually and spatially: a large, portly figure stands at the far left of the scene, clad in soft leather boots and a fur-trimmed cape and carrying a knob-headed walking stick. The man presents his back to the viewer, and although his paunch faces Jesus, he has turned his head away from the preacher and his words. Unlike the figures who reach out toward Jesus or raise their hands in prayer, this well-dressed figure places his hands behind his back, clasping his walking stick. The elegant staff that completes his luxurious attire provides a stark contrast to the humble stick that the blind old man uses as a cane. In a visual commentary on the lack of humanity in those who would shun the word of God and his representative on earth, Rembrandt placed a dog near the wealthy man's feet. Like the Pharisees, the dog ignores Jesus's message and has turned its attention elsewhere.

The presence of the camel—along with the Ethiopian man—may have yet another significance. Placed in the midst of those who have come to seek succor and salvation, they recall another procession, that of the Magi, the three kings from the East who brought precious gifts to the infant Jesus. From at least the mid-fifteenth century on, it was customary to depict one of the Magi as Moorish, or African, and to include a camel or camels in the background in order to suggest the wise men's exotic, Eastern origins.[15] It is possible that the allusions to the theme of the Adoration of the Magi[16] in the *Hundred Guilder Print* would have provided seventeenth-century viewers with a somewhat ironic layer of meaning that went beyond the lessons found in Matthew 19. The Magi brought gifts of gold, frankincense, and myrrh—symbols of wealth and kingship—to Jesus. In the *Hundred Guilder Print*, by contrast, the rich and powerful (the Pharisees at the left) ignore Christ, while the powerless and the needy, including the Moor who evokes the Adoration story, bring their faith to Jesus, in the hopes of receiving from him the gifts of physical and spiritual healing.[17]

Because of Rembrandt's compassionate representation of the afflicted on the right side of the composition, this work has often been described as "Christ Healing the Sick."[18] However, Jesus's admonition to "suffer the children to come unto me" (Matthew 19:14) may actually have been the conceptual core of the print, since the figure of Christ is oriented primarily toward a mother and child.[19] Although Jesus's gaze seems somewhat unfocused, he does look out in the direction of a turbaned woman who approaches him from the left. She, in turn, gazes down at a swaddled infant cradled in her arms, while the child looks up toward Christ. Peter,[20] who stands immediately to Jesus's right, places a hand on the child, trying to prevent the woman from approaching, but Jesus raises his left hand, its palm turned forward in a gesture of benediction and inclusion, and reaches out with his right hand toward the woman and her infant, welcoming them. A little boy behind these figures rushes forward toward Jesus, pointing in his direction as he tugs at the skirt of his pensive, humbly dressed mother. Like the more centrally placed woman, she holds an infant in her arms. Her son looks back at her, as if trying to get her attention and encourage her to follow him.

The significance of Jesus's blessing of the children was a matter of dispute during the sixteenth and seventeenth centuries. Calvin interpreted the passage in Matthew as specifically sanctioning infant baptism,[21] a sacrament that was also supported by the Dutch Reformed Church. Anabaptist theologians, however, opposed the practice, subscribing instead to the principle that only adults were capable of making the spiritual commitment necessary to receive the sacrament of baptism. Indeed, sixteenth-century Dutch theologian Dirk Philips interpreted Matthew 19 as evidence that children were accepted into the kingdom of heaven by virtue of Christ's grace and mercy, not by reason of baptism. Closely parsing Matthew 18:3–4[22] and 19:14, Philips claimed that Christ had admonished believers to become like children, that is, to become simple and unassumingly humble, and therefore also worthy of his blessings.[23] Given the contentious arguments surrounding the question of infant baptism and the importance of Matthew 19 in the dispute, seventeenth-century viewers of the *Hundred Guilder Print* might well have read the image in the context of this contemporary theological discussion. Any interpretation would have depended on the confessional orientation of the viewer, although the print's emphasis on the grace that Christ was bestowing on the humble petitioners who came to him for healing might favor a more Anabaptist reading.[24]

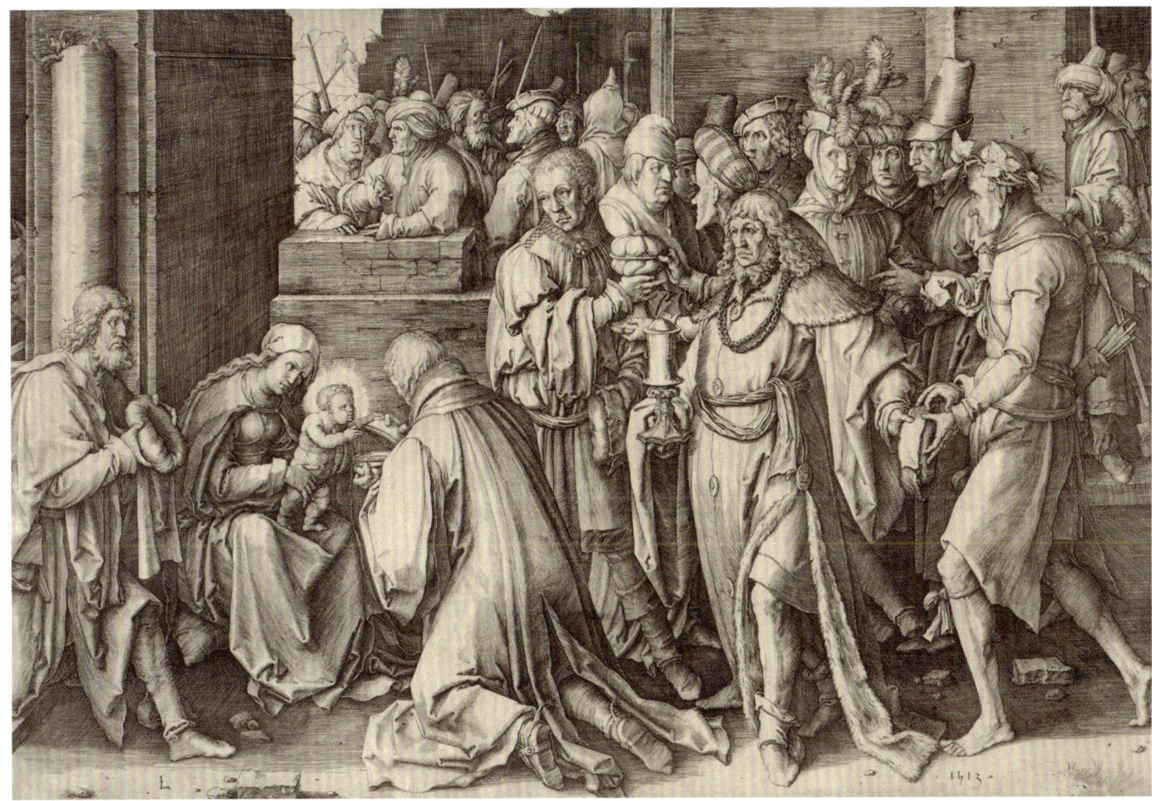

FIGURE 1. Lucas van Leyden, *The Adoration of the Magi*, engraving, 1513. *Snite Museum of Art, University of Notre Dame, Notre Dame, Indiana. Acquired with funds from the Fritz and Mildred Kaeser Endowment for Liturgical Art.*

At the left side of the etching, a group of Pharisees stands behind a waist-high wall.[25] In marked contrast to the believers gathered at the right side of the composition, these elders, who brazenly ignore Christ, are rendered in a very cursory manner, with little modeling or substance, and are flattened out by the light. For Arnold Houbraken, the author of *The Great Theater of Dutch Painters* (1718), the lightly sketched quality of these figures was characteristic of Rembrandt's tendency to leave work incomplete,[26] but there is no evidence that the artist abandoned the *Hundred Guilder Print* prematurely. On the contrary, from a purely technical perspective, the variation in handling between the two halves of the print is evidence of Rembrandt's graphic skill. It demonstrates his ability to render figures both with pure line and with extraordinary tonal modeling. It also suggests a kind of paradoxical conceptual difference between the two groups: Contrary to the traditional identification of light with divinity and spiritual enlightenment, it is the proud, unenlightened skeptics (the Pharisees) who are bathed in light, while the humble faithful (the poor and infirm) remain in half shadow. It seems that in this case, Rembrandt was employing a different metaphor, one that hinged on the concept of substantiality: faith invests believers with spiritual weight; doubt robs them of that substance. Placed between these two poles is the mother who offers her child to Jesus for his blessing. She and the infant have been limned with a degree of modeling that contrasts with the lightly sketched young boy who tugs at his mother's skirt and points to Jesus. This child seems to act more out of innocent curiosity than of spiritual commitment. He, his mother, and the baby she holds do not yet have the spiritual—and graphic—"weight" of those who have already professed their faith. Still, because of what Dirk Philips referred to as "simple, unassuming humility" and purity, they are poised to recognize Christ, gain his attention, and receive the full measure of his blessing.

Notes

1. W. A. Churchill, *Watermarks in Paper in Holland, England, France, etc. in XVII and XVIII Centuries and Their Interconnections* (Amsterdam: M. Hertzberger, 1935).

Erik Hinterding (*Lugt Catalogue*, 158) questioned whether any of the impressions of the second state on Western paper was actually done in Rembrandt's lifetime. He noted that although a significant number of impressions on Western paper survive, none of them has any of the watermarks that appear on Rembrandt's other prints. This is true of the fragment of the "Pot" watermark on the Snite impression.

2. Although this was a considerable sum to pay for a print, it is worth noting that in the seventeenth century, a rare copy of Lucas van Leyden's *Uilenspiegel* (The beggar family) sold for 400 guilders, and according to Samuel van Hoogstraten, one of Rembrandt's pupils, the artist himself paid 200 guilders for an impression of the *Uilenspiegel* print. In the same vein, Joachim von Sandrart reported that Rembrandt paid 1,400 guilders for fourteen prints by Lucas. William W. Robinson, "'This Passion for Prints': Collecting and Connoisseurship in Northern Europe during the Seventeenth Century," in Clifford S. Ackley, *Printmaking in the Age of Rembrandt*, exh. cat. (Boston: Boston Museum of Fine Arts, 1981), xliii.

3. Jan Meyssens, cited in Erik Hinterding, Ger Luijten, and Martin Royalton-Kisch, *Rembrandt the Printmaker*, exh. cat. (Chicago and London: Fitzroy Dearborn Publishers, 2000), cat. 61, 255.

4. Zacharias Conrad von Uffenbach, *Herrn Zacharias Conrad von Uffenbach Merkwürdige Reisen durch Niedersachsen, Holland und Engelland*, vol. 3 (Ulm and Memmingen: Gaum, 1754), accessed December 19, 2012, http://books.google.com/books?id=FUsHAAAAQAAJ&pg=PA2#v=onepage&q&f=false;.

5. Bramen was a clockmaker and print collector.

6. Edme-François Gersaint offered a different explanation for the name of the print. He reported that it derived from a bargain that Rembrandt struck with a Roman art dealer. According to Gersaint, the dealer had a number of prints by Marcantonio Raimondi for which he was asking 100 florins (or the equivalent of 100 Dutch guilders). Rembrandt offered Gersaint an impression of the *Hundred Guilder Print* in exchange for the Raimondi prints, and the dealer agreed. Gersaint, *Catalogue raisonné de toutes les pièces qui forment l'oeuvre de Rembrandt* (Paris: Chez Hochereau, 1751), cat. 75, 60.

There is yet another tradition that holds that Rembrandt did not sell any impressions of the etching, but gave them as gifts to his friends, instead. This idea derives from an eighteenth-century inscription in French on the verso of an impression from the first state of the etching, in Amsterdam. The author of the inscription comments on the rarity of the etching because "there were not but very few impressions made, of which not one was ever sold in Rembrandt's time, but distributed among his friends." Quoted in Michael Zell, "Rembrandt's Gift: A Case Study of Actor-Network-Theory," *Journal of Historians of Netherlandish Art* 3, no. 2 (Summer 2011): note 46, accessed December 26, 2012, http://www.jhna.org/index.php/past-issues/volume-3-issue-2/143-zell-rembrandts-gifts.

7. Münz, *Critical Catalogue*, 2:213–14.

8. Gersaint, for example, characterized the work as the finest that the artist ever produced: "Cette Estampe étant réellement la plus belle qui soit sortie de la pointe de ce Maître" (Gersaint, cat. 75, 60). Cited in Holm Bevers, Peter Schatborn, and Barbara Welzel, *Rembrandt: The Master and His Workshops*, vol. 2, *Drawings and Etchings* (New Haven, CT: Yale University Press, 1991), cat. 27, 242. Barbara Welzel characterizes the range of techniques evident in the print as "a deliberate sign of virtuosity" (ibid., 245).

9. The multiplicity of roles played by Christ in the print has been remarked on by Werner Weisbach (*Rembrandt* [Berlin: De Gruyter, 1926], 364), Otto Pächt (*Rembrandt* [Munich: Prestel Verlag, 1991], 184), and others. Cited in Nicola Suthor, "Ein Schattenspiel: Rembrandts 'Hundertguldenblatt,'" in *Kanon Kunstgeschichte: Einführung in Werke, Methoden und Epochen*, ed. Kristin Marek and Martin Schulz, vol. 2, *Neuzeit* (Paderborn: Wilhelm Fink, 2015), 351.

10. The interpretation of this print as illustrating Matthew 19 was first noted by Albrecht Jordan in 1893. "Bemerkungen zu Rembrandt's Radierungen," *Repertorium für Kunstgeschichte* 16 (1893): 296–302, esp. 299–301.

11. Holm Bevers interpreted this wall as a reference to the Petrine image of Christ as the living stone rejected by the builders that became the cornerstone of the faith (1 Peter 2: 4–7). Holm Bevers, "'Das Hunderguldenblatt'." cat. 57, in Bevers, Jasper Kettner, and Gudula Metze, *Rembrandt: Ein Virtuose der Druckgraphik* (Berlin: Dumont and Kupferstichkabinett, Staatliche Museen, 2006), 106.

12. The shadow does not precisely mirror the profile of the woman who appears to cast it, nor does the light on this woman's right side seem bright enough to have created so well-defined a silhouette. Furthermore, she also seems to cast a shadow on the fragment of wall immediately beside Christ. These anomalies suggest that the shadow is meant to reveal something more than literal spatial relationships or sources of light. Werner Weisbach interpreted the shadow on Christ's robes as signifying Christ's role as a miraculous healer. Cited in Suthor, "Ein Schattenspiel," 352.

The detail may also be meant to signify Christ's own identification with the plight of the suffering figures on his left, even though his attention seems to be focused in the other direction, toward the woman holding a child before him.

13. This group of unfortunates appears to have been of particular concern for Rembrandt, for virtually all of the preparatory drawings associated with this print address either the group as a whole or the poses of individual figures within it. See, for example, Ben. 188 (*Group Study*; Kupferstichkabinett, Berlin), 543 (*Group Study*; Louvre, Paris), 183 (*Sick Woman*;, Rijksmuseum,Amsterdam), 388 (*Supplicating Woman*; British Rail Pension Fund, London), and 185 (*Blind Old Man Guided by a Woman*; Louvre, Paris). The only preparatory image that has been associated with the print but is not related to the group of sufferers is a black chalk drawing of a Dutch woman seen from the back as she carries a child. That drawing (Ben. 1071), now in the Pushkin Museum, Moscow, should probably be dated to the mid-1630s, that is, considerably earlier than the *Hundred Guilder Print*. Barbara Welzel, in Holms Bevers, Peter Schatborn, and Barbara Welzel, *Rembrandt: The Master and his Workshops*, vol. 2, *Drawings and Etchings*, cat. 27, 245n19.

On the Protestant foundations of Rembrandt's representations of the poor and the dispossessed, see Robert W. Baldwin, "'On Earth We Art Beggars as Christ Himself Was': The Protestant Background of Rembrandt's Imagery of Poverty, Disability, and Begging," *Kunsthistorisk tidskrift* 54, no. 3 (1985): 122–35.

14. For other examples of Moorish figures in Rembrandt's etchings as emblems of universality and/or exoticism, see *Adoration of the Shepherds: With the Lamp* (B. 45, 1654, cat. no. 20); *Beheading of John the Baptist* (B. 93, 1631, cat. no. 64); *Christ Disputing with the Doctors: A Sketch* (B. 65, 1652, cat. no. 38); *Christ before Pilate: Large Plate* (B. 77, 1636, cat. no. 50), and *Baptism of the Eunuch* (B. 98, 1641, cat. no. 68).

15. For examples of Moorish, or African, Magi, see Albrecht Dürer's 1503 and 1511 woodcuts of the *Adoration of the Magi* from the *Life of the Virgin* series, and Hans Shaufelein's woodcut illustration for Johann Geiler von Kaisersberg, "Evangeli und Epistel," Augsburg: Schönsperger, 1512, in which the Magus wears an earring that is virtually identical to the one worn by the Moor in Rembrandt's print.

For graphic examples that incorporate camels as signifiers of the Eastern origins of the Magi, see, for example, Johannes Sadeler I's 1581 engraving of the *Adoration of the Magi* after Maerten de Vos (HD 165 [Johannes Sadeler I]), and Jacques Callot's *Adoration of the Magi* from between 1621 and 1635 (Lieure 671).

16. It should be noted that although representations of the Adoration of the Magi were quite common from the 1450s on, both north and south of the Alps, there are no undisputed examples of the theme by Rembrandt himself, in spite of the fact that he did

numerous representations of other scenes from the childhood of Christ. One would have thought that the possibility of staging a costume drama filled with exotic figures would have had special appeal for him. Given his country's recent history, however, it is possible that the contemporary tendency to emphasize the theme of kingship in interpretations of the Adoration dissuaded the Dutch artist from representing the subject. There are three painted representations of the theme that are now attributed to unidentified followers of Rembrandt (Konstmuseum, Göteborg, Sweden; State Hermitage Museum, St. Petersburg; and Buckingham Palace, London).

For Lucas van Leyden's engraved *Adoration of the Magi* (1513, NHD 37) (fig. 1) as a possible source for the figures on the left side of the print, see note 25, below.

17. See Baldwin, "On Earth," cited above, note 11, for a discussion of Protestant views on poverty and charity. Calvin, in his commentary on the story of the Magi in Matthew 2:1–12, emphasized the fact that the kings brought their gifts to the child when he was in a stable "amidst tokens not of honor, but of contempt," and without any worldly goods, and that the Magi paid homage to him there because God chose to inform mankind "that his kingdom was [not worldly, but] spiritual" (*Commentary on a Harmony of the Evangelists, Matthew, Mark, and Luke,* Commentary on Matthew 1:1, 1:123–24, accessed July 21, 2014, http//www.ccel.org/ccel/Calvin/calcom31.pdf). Such a message would also be in harmony with Jesus's advice to the rich young man that spiritual wealth outweighs temporal riches.

A branch and a cockleshell lie on the ground in front of the prostrate woman. These details may simply be spatial markers, but their prominence suggests that they may have had symbolic associations, as well. The branch is a traditional symbol for Christ himself (Isaiah 11:1 and Zechariah 6:12). In the commentary on Isaiah in the Dutch State Bible of 1637, the reference to the branch that comes from the root of the tree is interpreted as alluding to Christ's humble origins, to the fact that the house of Judah had declined, and to Christ's earthly father being a humble carpenter, not a king or sovereign, (accessed July 21, 2014, http://www.bijbelsdigitaal.nl/view/?bible=sv1637&page=692&sub=1-2). In his commentary on Zechariah, Calvin also linked the image of the branch to Christ's humble origins and his rejection by the heathens and the Jews: "We hence see that Christ is called Branch, because his beginning was contemptible, so that he was of hardly any repute among heathens; nay even among his own nation." In this way, the branch may be a commentary on the attitudes and actions of the print's Pharisees, who sought to discredit Jesus and rejected him as the Messiah.

The cockleshell was a common symbol of pilgrimage. In the context of the *Hundred Guilder Print,* a reference to pilgrimage conjures up both the arrival of the Magi and the journey of the infirm faithful.

18. See, for example, the 1654 letter from Jan Meyssens cited above and in note 3, and Gersaint, 61, as well as comments by Jonathan Richardson in *An Essay on the Theory of Painting,* 1725, in which he referred to the print as "Our Lord Healing the Sick" (cited in Seymour Slive, *Rembrandt and His Critics, 1630–1730* [New York: Hacker Art Books, 1998], 151). Münz (*Critical Catalogue,* 2:102 and 211–12) noted that seventeenth-century copies of the *Hundred Guilder Print* by Melchior Küsel in *Icones biblicae Veteris et Novi Testamenti* (Augsburg, 1679), and by Michael Wening in *Neue Himmels-Burg* (Munich, 1693), are labeled "Christ Heals Various (or All) Illnesses."

Paul Crenshaw ("Beyond Matthew 19: The Woman at Christ's Feet in Rembrandt's *Hundred Guilder Print,*" in *Midwestern Arcadia: Essays in Honor of Alison McNeil Kettering,* e-book, https://apps.carleton.edu/kettering/assets/Crenshaw.pdf; accessed February 23, 2017), drew attention to the fact that Meyssens actually referred to the print as "Christ healing the lepers." Crenshaw suggested that there is a compositional and thematic relationship between the *Hundred Guilder Print* and Marcantonio Raimondi's engraving after a design by Raphael that is known as *The Plague* (TIB 417). According to Crenshaw, the relationship between the two prints suggests that the primary theme of Rembrandt's etching was Christian healing, i.e. salvation. Crenshaw also argued that the woman at Christ's feet is a specific reference to the miraculous healing of the woman with the issue of blood (Matthew 9:18–26, Mark 5:21–43, and Luke 8:40–56). Although Crenshaw's identification of the suffering woman is convincing, his assertion of a compositional connection between the Raimondi and Rembrandt prints is not.

The image of Christ as healer and teacher may also have brought to mind the writings of the Netherlandish poet, printmaker, philosopher, and theologian Dirck Volkertsz. Coornhert (1522–90). Coornhert was a strong proponent of religious tolerance, opponent of the concept of predestination, promoter of the doctrine of human perfectibility, and advocate for the primacy of Christ's teachings as the sole source of religious and ethical beliefs. Coornhert's writings were an important inspiration for the Remonstrant movement. In particular, in his pamphlet critical of the Heidelberg catechism (*Proeve van de Nederlantche catechism* [1582]), Coornhert wrote, "Jesus Christ is the only true doctor of the soul. Thus his word is the true doctrine, and the only true medicine for the soul. Therefore, his doctrine is rightly called a healthy doctrine, because it makes the soul healthy" (quoted in Werner Weisbach, *Rembrandt*, 484). Rembrandt's depiction of Christ as teacher and healer in the *Hundred Guilder Print* seems to echo Coornhert's sentiment. For Coornhert's writings and his role in the politics of religious tolerance, see Marianne Roobol, *Disputation by Decree: The Public Disputations between Reformed Ministers and Dirck Volckertszoon Coornhert as Instruments of Religious Policy during the Dutch Revolt (1577–1583)* (Leiden: Brill, 2010).

19. Christian Tümpel (*Rembrandt legt*, cat. 86) suggested that "Christ blessing the Children" is, in fact, the main subject of this print.

The centrality of this theme is also supported by a *pentimento*, which indicates that at some point in the process of composing the scene, Rembrandt made Christ's left hand lower and more overtly directed toward the mother and her child, a position that would also explain the placement of a secondary shadow on Christ's tunic above the one cast by the hands of the praying woman. On alterations to the plate by Rembrandt prior to the first state, see Münz, *Critical Catalogue*, vol. 2, cat. no. 217, 101.

20. As several authors have noted, Peter's pug-nosed features are similar to those of traditional representations of Socrates (B. P. J. Broos, *Index to the Formal Sources of Rembrandt's Art* [Maarssen, Netherlands: Schwartz, 1977], 79–80). Rembrandt would have been familiar with images of Socrates, especially since he himself had a bust of the philosopher in his studio. Walter Strauss and Marjon van der Meulen, eds. and trans., *The Rembrandt Documents* (New York: Abaris, 1979), doc. 1656/12 (*Cessio bonorum* inventory), no. 162, "Een Socrates."

21. According to Calvin's *Commentary on A Harmony of the Evangelists: Matthew, Mark, Luke,* Commentary on Matthew 19: 14, 2:332–33:

> He declares that he wishes to receive *children*; and at length, *taking them in his arms,* he not only embraces, but *blesses* them by the *laying on of hand;* from which we infer that his grace is extended even to those who are of that age. And no wonder; for since the whole race of Adam is shut up under the sentence of death, all from the least even to the greatest must perish, except those who are rescued by the only Redeemer. To exclude from the grace of redemption those who are of that age would be too cruel; and therefore it is not without reason that we employ this passage as a shield against the Anabaptists. They refuse baptism to *infants*, because infants are incapable of understanding that mystery which is denoted by it. We, on the other hand, maintain that, since baptism is the pledge and figure of the forgiveness of sins, and likewise of adoption by God, it ought not to be denied to *infants*, whom God adopts and washes with the blood of his Son. Their objection, that repentance and newness of life are also denoted by it, is easily answered. *Infants* are renewed by the Spirit of God, according to the capacity of their age, till that power which was concealed within them grows by degrees, and becomes fully manifest at the proper time. Again, when they argue that there is no other way in which we are reconciled to God, and become heirs of adoption, than by faith, we admit this as to adults, but, with respect to *infants*, this passage demonstrates it to be false. Certainly, the *laying on of hands* was not a trifling or empty sign, and the prayers of Christ were not idly wasted in air. But he could not present the infants solemnly to God without giving them purity. And for what did he pray for them, but that they might be received into the number of the children of God? Hence it follows, that they were renewed by the Spirit to the hope of salvation. In short, by embracing them, he testified that they were reckoned by Christ among his flock. And if they were partakers of the spiritual gifts, which are represented by Baptism, it is unreasonable that they should be deprived of the outward sign.

Accessed July 21, 2014, http//www.ccel.org/ccel/Calvin/calcom32.pdf. Cited in *Rembrandt's Faith*, 273.

22. "Truly, I say to you, unless you turn and become like children, you will never enter the kingdom of heaven. Whoever humbles himself as this child, he is the greatest in the kingdom of heaven."

23. Cited in *Rembrandt's Faith*, 273. For the relevant passages by Dirk Philips (1504–68), see *The Writings of Dirk Philips,* trans. Cornelius J. Dyck, William E. Keeney, and Alvin J. Beachy (Scottdale, PA: Herald Press, 1992), 91–92.

24. In terms of Rembrandt's own position on the matter of infant baptism, the fact that Rembrandt's children were all baptized in the Reformed Church shortly after they were born would suggest that he personally believed in the practice. Filippo Baldinucci asserted that Rembrandt was a Mennonite: "This artist professed in those days the religion of the Mennonites, which, though false too, is yet opposed to that of Calvin, inasmuch as they do not practice the rite of baptism before the age of thirty." Baldinucci, "Life of Rembrandt," from *Cominciamento, e progresso dell'arte dell'intagliare in rame, colle vite di molti de'più eccellenti maestri della stessa professione*, in Joachim von Sandrart, Filippo Baldinucci, and Arnold Houbraken, *Lives of Rembrandt*, intro. Charles Ford (London: Pallas Athene, 2007), 4. However, there is no evidence to substantiate this view. For the arguments refuting the notion that Rembrandt was a Mennonite, see Willem Adolph Visser 't Hooft, *Rembrandt and the Gospel* (New York: Meridian Books, 1960), passim, and the extended discussion of Rembrandt's own confessional orientation in Rosenberg, "Rembrandt's Religious Prints," in this catalog.

25. Many authors (see the entry in Broos, *Index to the Formal Sources of Rembrandt's Art*, 79–80) have suggested that this grouping was inspired by Lucas van Leyden's representation of members of the Magi's entourage in his engraved *Adoration of the Magi* of 1513 (fig. 1). As in the *Hundred Guilder* print, two men, seemingly engaged in conversation, stand behind a waist-high wall. In both images, the man on the left has placed his right hand on top of the wall, and the man on the right rests his left forearm on it. If Rembrandt did, indeed, draw upon this source, which he certainly knew, it would suggest that he was thinking about the Magi's visit at the time he created the *Hundred Guilder Print*.

26. It is a pity, however, that he [Rembrandt] was so whimsical ... in his readiness to make so many alterations. Many works are only half completed, paintings and even more so his etched prints, those beginnings suggest to us the beauties we would have had from his hand if he had brought everything to fruition proportionate to the way he began them. This is especially to be seen in the so-called Hundred Guilder Print and others, the handling of which astonished us as we cannot understand how he was able to develop it from a preparatory rough sketch.

Arnold Houbraken, "Life of Rembrandt," in Sandrart, Baldinucci, and Houbraken, *The Lives of Rembrandt*, 64.

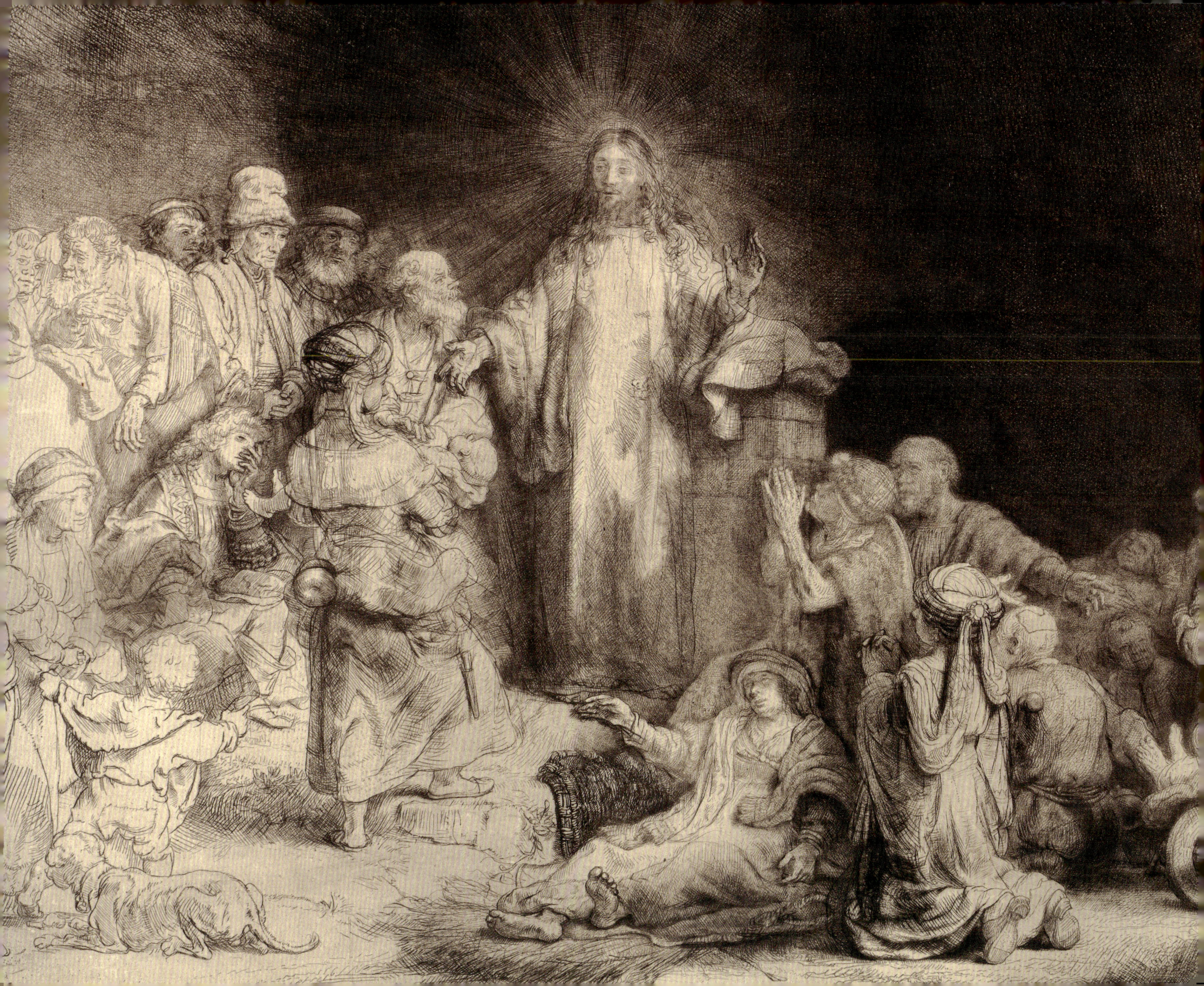

49. *Agony in the Garden*

B. 75 (H. 293, Mz. 225, NHD 269)
Etching and drypoint
Signed and date in the plate: *Rembrandt f. 165*[?].[1]
State III of III
Sheet: 11.9 × 9.0 cm; plate mark 11.1 × 8.4 cm, on wove paper
Verso: in graphite, *B75/H7955*

Provenance:
Harrods, London, 1980
Feddersen, Elkhart, IN, 1991
Snite Museum of Art
Acc. No.: 1991.025.046

The plate does not survive.

Christ's final moments of doubt on the Mount of Olives in the garden of Gethsemane are described in three of the four Gospels (Matthew 26:36–46; Mark 14:32–42; and Luke 22:40–46). All three accounts state that directly following the Last Supper and Christ's prediction of Peter's denial, he and the apostles went to Gethsemane. According to Matthew, Jesus instructed all of his disciples except Peter, John, and James, to stay behind as he walked on into the garden. While Jesus and his three companions continued on their way, he became troubled. He finally told the three apostles to halt and stand watch where they were. Jesus then walked on a bit further until, overcome by his emotions, he fell to the ground and prayed to God to "let this cup pass from me." Significantly, he added, "nevertheless, not as I will, but as thou wilt," thus affirming his obedience to God's will, even while questioning his fate. He then got up and returned to the place where he had left Peter, John, and James, only to find them fast asleep. He berated Peter for not having kept watch. Twice more, Jesus went off to pray, asking God to intervene, and twice more, he returned to find the three disciples sleeping. Finally, Jesus roused the slumbering apostles and warned them that the moment of his betrayal was at hand, but his warning came too late. While he was speaking, Judas and the soldiers arrived to arrest him.

Mark's account essentially repeats Matthew's, but Luke's is slightly different. In Luke's version, all of the disciples accompanied Christ when he went to the Mount of Olives. Once there, Jesus instructed them not to fall into temptation and then withdrew "about a stone's throw," knelt, and prayed. In this account, he prayed only once, and as he did, an angel appeared, "strengthening him." Despite the angel's ministrations, Jesus, "being in agony . . . prayed more earnestly; and his sweat became like great drops of blood falling down upon the ground" (Luke 22:44).[2] When Jesus had finished his prayers, he rose up and returned to the apostles, only to find them asleep.

For centuries, the Agony in the Garden had been an extremely popular subject for paintings and prints because of its devotional and theological implications. The pathos of the situation is clear. Jesus's anguish as he wrestles with the knowledge of his fate emphasizes his humanity, and the image offers the viewer an emotional model with which to identify. The scene also recalls the Last Supper's Eucharistic sacrifice and foreshadows Christ's physical suffering to come. In St. Paul's account of the Agony in the Garden in Hebrews 5:7–10, he emphasized Jesus's obedience to his Father's will. "In the days of his flesh, Jesus offered up prayers

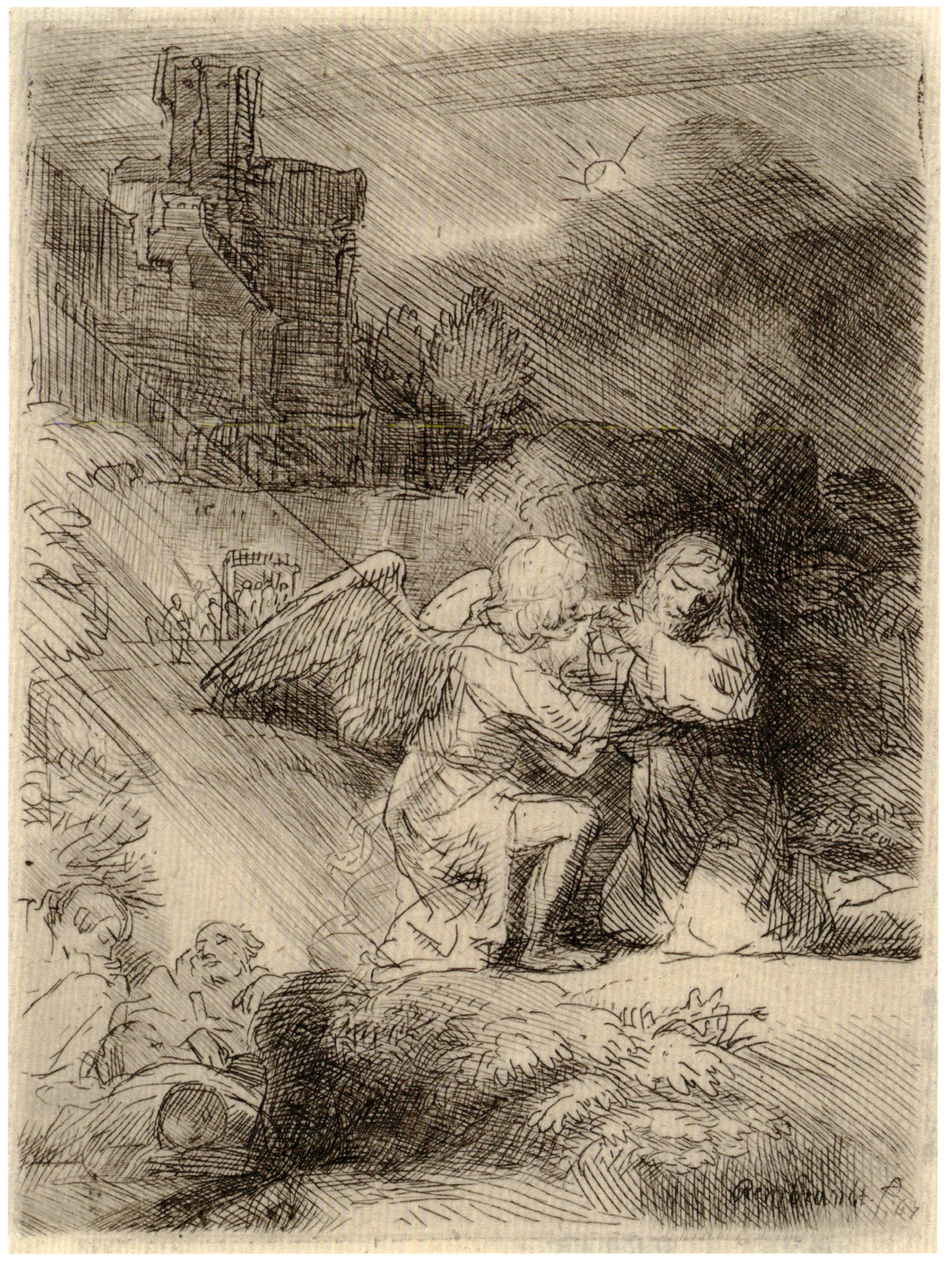

PLATE 49

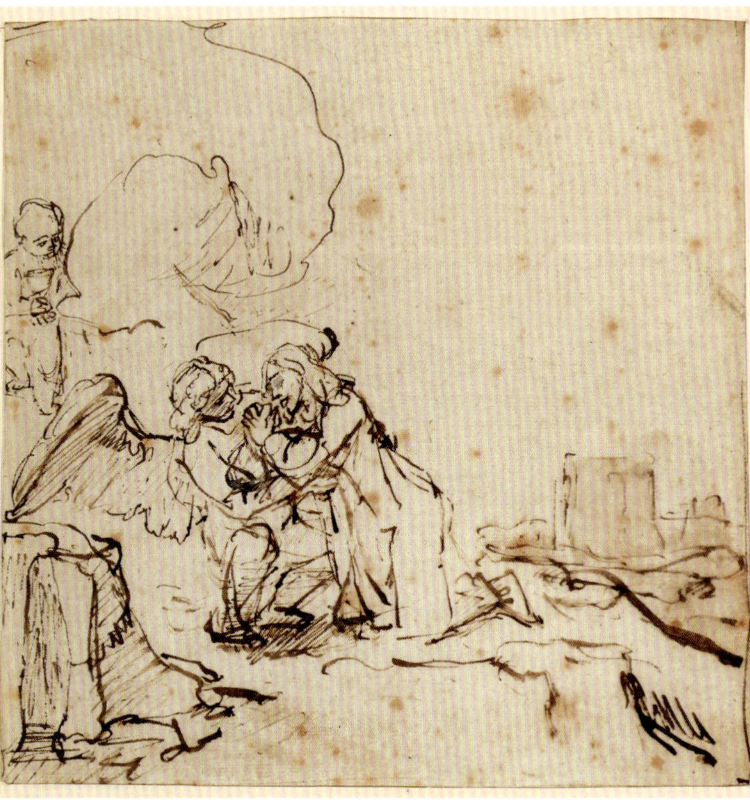

FIGURE 1. Rembrandt, *Christ Comforted by the Angel*, Ben. 626, pen and bistre with wash, c. 1648. *Fitzwilliam Museum, Cambridge, England. Fitzwilliam Museum Cambridge/Art Resource, New York.*

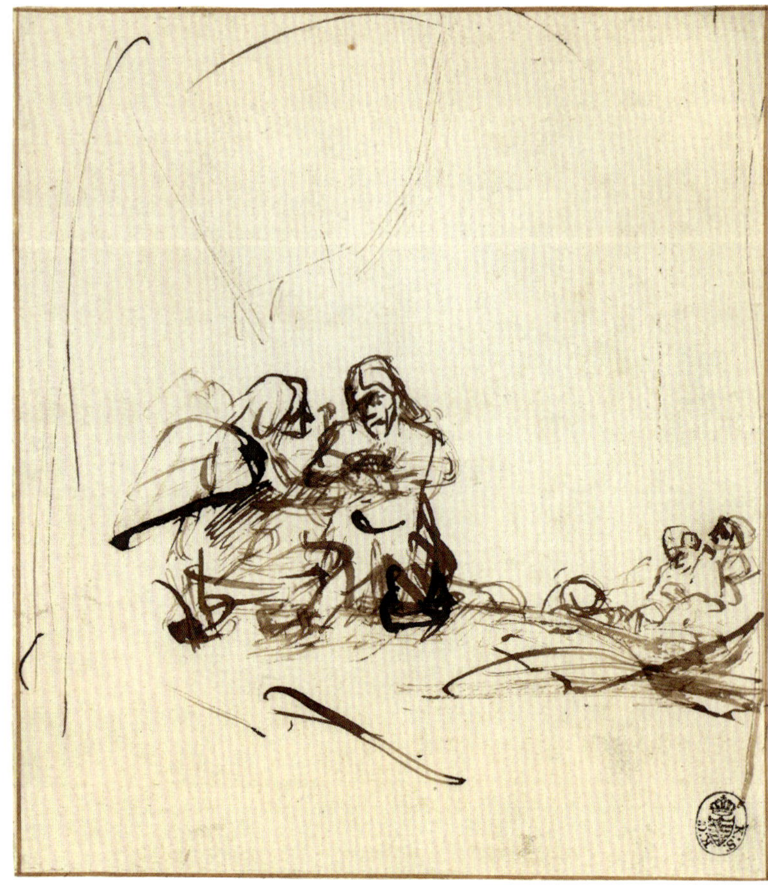

FIGURE 2. Rembrandt, *Christ Consoled by the Angel*, Ben. 898, pen and bistre, c. 1652. *Kupferstichkabinett, Dresden.*

and supplication, with loud cries and tears, to him who was able to save him from death, and he was heard for his godly fear. Although he was a son, he learned obedience through what he suffered; and being made perfect he became the source of eternal salvation to all who obey him, being designated by God a high priest after the order of Melchizedek." For Catholics, this reading stressed the authority of the priesthood and the need for obedience to the Church. For Protestants, and particularly Calvinists, Jesus's submission to his Father's will, even in the face of his fears, was interpreted as evidence of the inviolability of God's plan.

The iconography of the Agony in the Garden was fixed as early as the twelfth century.[3] Christ was usually shown kneeling in prayer on a mountainside, with Peter, James, and John asleep in the garden just below him. In most of the images, an angel appears above Jesus, holding a cross or chalice, but in some depictions, there is no angel, only the cross or a chalice. In a few examples, God's presence is indicated not by an angel, but by light streaming down out of a darkened sky.[4] As numerous critics have noted, Rembrandt deviated from these traditions. He chose to represent Luke's version of the event, with an angel "strengthening" the kneeling Jesus in his moment of doubt.[5] In the etching, God's emissary reaches out to Christ to offer comfort and support as Jesus becomes reconciled to the knowledge that there will be no divine reprieve from the Passion. Rembrandt's depiction of Jesus being nurtured by the angel offers a distinctly humanistic concept of the compassion of the divine.

There are several precedents for the way in which Rembrandt envisioned this moment. Ludwig Münz, for example, singled out a painting of the Agony by seventeenth-century Italian artist Orazio Borgianni in which the angel appears to comfort Christ.[6] In addition, a painting by Paolo Veronese and a late sixteenth-century print by Jacob Matham after a composition by Jacopo Palma Vecchio (fig. 3) both depict a swooning Christ physically supported by an angel.[7] It is not known whether Rembrandt was inspired by any of these models. What is more critical, as Clifford Ackley observed, is that Rembrandt's print reflects his own "tendency to represent the symbolic and spiritual in literal, physical terms."[8]

Nonetheless, Rembrandt did adhere to tradition in a couple of ways: he included the sleeping apostles in the lower left corner of the composition, and in the distant background, he depicted the figures of Judas and the soldiers emerging from the gates of Jerusalem. Although Rembrandt's scene is set at night, unlike some other representations of the subject, it is not a true nocturne.[9] The sky is darkened by parallel lines and tight cross-hatching, but it lacks the impenetrable blackness that enshrouds other nocturnal images by the artist, such as the *Flight into Egypt: A Night Piece* (B. 53, 1651, cat. no. 28) and *Adoration of the Shepherds: A Night Piece* (B. 46, c. 1652, cat. no. 21). In early impressions of the Agony, Rembrandt made extensive use of the drypoint needle in order to darken the scene. Billowing clouds partially obscured the silhouette of the Temple and the eclipsed moon. In the final state, however, the darkness was relieved by the creation of large areas of more open hatching. Jesus, highlighted, emerges from the densest area of shadow. While Rembrandt allowed the bare paper, itself, to describe the presence of light, he also employed the somewhat archaic device of describing rays of light by inscribing parallel lines. These rays form a wide swath of light pouring down from the upper left, as if they were describing the path that the angel took as it arrived from heaven. More rays are visible at the top of the picture, to the right of the Temple, as if to suggest a rain of heavenly illumination. The Snite Museum's example is a very late, possibly even posthumous, impression in which all of the drypoint burr has been lost, resulting in much less dramatic chiaroscuro.

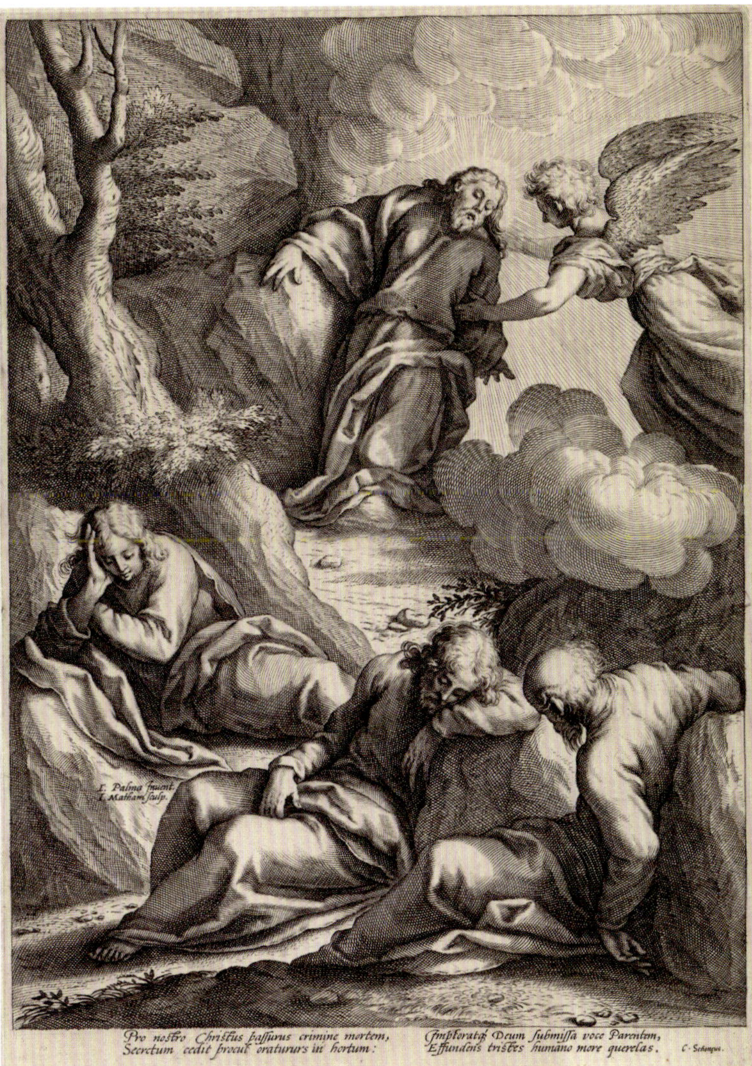

FIGURE 3. Jacob Matham after Palma Vecchio, *Christ on the Mount of Olives*, engraving, 1610. *Rijksmuseum, Amsterdam.*

Notes

1. Erik Hinterding (*Lugt Catalogue*, cat. 61, 161–62) dates the print to 1650–51 on the basis of watermarks.

2. The drops of blood in this description provide a clear link to the Passion and, hence, to the chalice and the Mass.

3. A representation of the Agony appears, for example, in the late twelfth-century mosaics in the south transept at Monreale, Sicily, although in this example, only Jesus and the angel appear, without a chalice or cross.

4. There were numerous images of the Agony in the Garden created in the fifteenth century. For example, there are sixty individual "Agony" prints in the volume of TIB dedicated to single-leaf German woodcuts before 1500 (vol. 161, nos. 184–213, 198–220). The vast majority of these simple compositions show Christ kneeling in front of a rocky platform or altar on which sits a chalice or a chalice with a cross. A few examples show an angel holding a chalice. An

anonymous Bohemian example (TIB 185) has only a rippling ribbon of light in the upper right corner, signifying God's presence. At the very end of the fifteenth century and in the early sixteenth century, Martin Schongauer included an Agony image in his Passion cycle (HG 19, c. 1480). Albrecht Dürer treated the subject four times: in his large and small woodcut Passions (TIB 6, 1497–1500; and TIB 26, 1510, respectively); in his engraved Passion (TIB 4, 1508); and in one of his few etchings (TIB 19, 1515). Lucas van Leyden depicted the subject twice as part of his two engraved Passion cycles (NHD 57, 1509; and NHD 44, 1521). In each of these examples, Christ prays before a chalice or an angel with a cross or a chalice. In 1582, Johannes Sadeler I (HD 222) did an engraving after a composition by Maerten de Vos in which God manifests his presence to Jesus only through a burst of light. Aegidius Sadeler (HD 44) did a similar representation, based on a painting by Johan of Aachen. Both of these late sixteenth-century examples are nocturnes.

5. There are two drawings by Rembrandt, one in Cambridge, England (Ben. 626) (fig. 1), and one in Hamburg, Germany (Ben. 898) (fig. 2), that are clearly related to the etching. In both of these, Rembrandt not only investigated the relationship between the angel and Jesus; he also included a cup. Shelley Perlove and Larry Silver suggested that Rembrandt might have decided to omit the cup or chalice from the print in order to avoid any allusion to the controversial subject of the Eucharist and the question of transubstantiation. Whereas Catholic dogma decreed that only a priest could administer the Eucharistic sacrament, Rembrandt's fellow Protestants saw the wine and the bread as a shared communal ritual that did not require the intercession of a priest. *Rembrandt's Faith*, 280–81.

6. *Critical Catalogue*, vol. 1, cat. 225, 105. Münz illustrated the painting by Borgianni on the same page as Rembrandt's *Agony in the Garden*. He also acknowledged that the connection between the painting and the print was first made by W. R. Valentiner. The Borgianni painting is in the Herzog Anton Ulrich-Museum, Braunschweig, Germany, cat. no. GG475. Sabine Jacob and Susanne König-Lein, *Die italienischen Gemälde des 16. bis 18. Jahrhunderts. Sammlungskataloge des Herzog Anton Ulrich-Museum Braunschweig* (Braunschweig and Munich: Hirmer, 2004), 13:29–31, and color plate 11.

7. TIB 187, Jacob Matham.

8. *Rembrandt's Journey*, 247n1.

9. Cf. the prints by Johannes Sadeler I and Aegidius Sadeler II cited in note 4, above, which are examples of nocturnes.

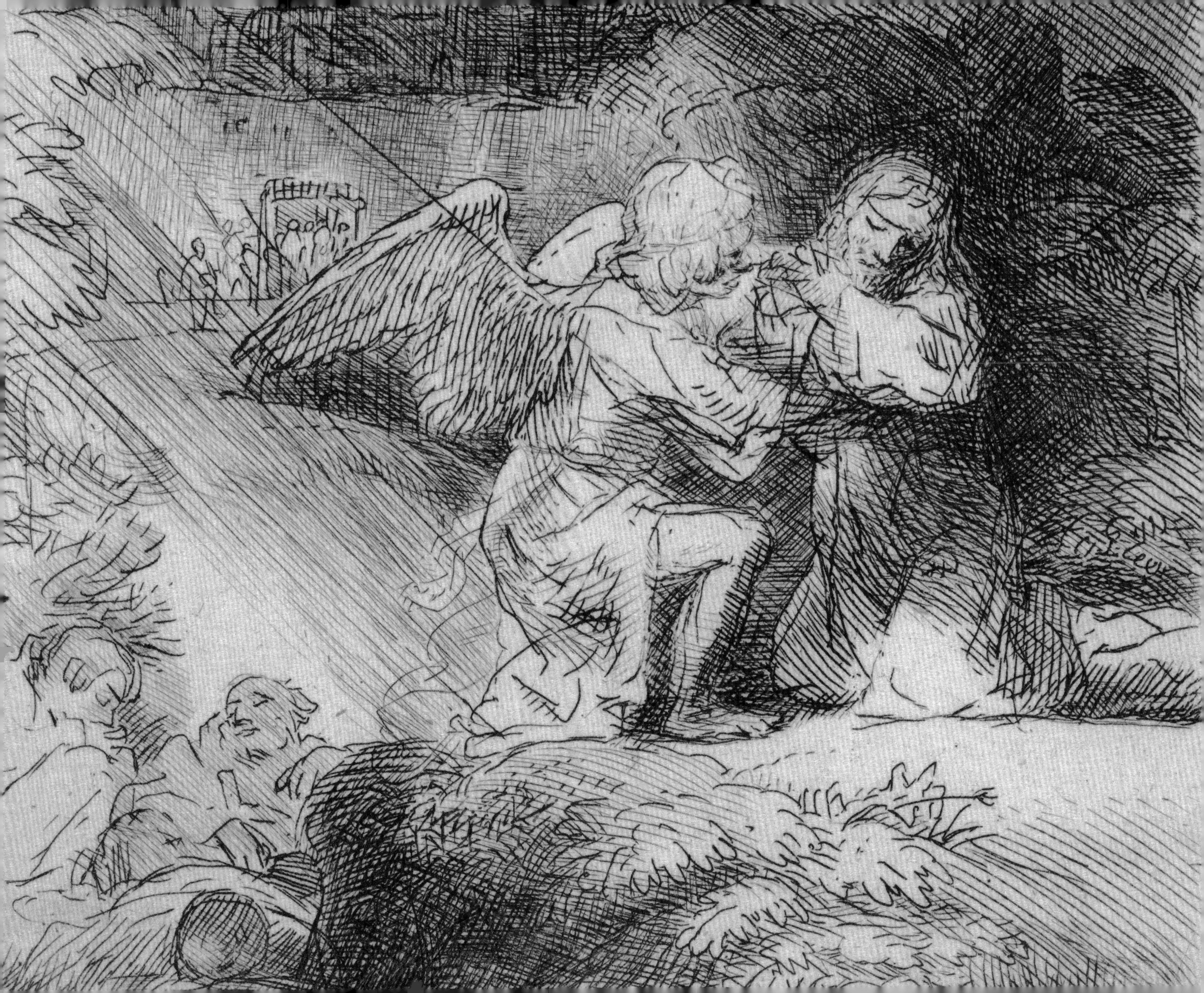

50. *Christ before Pilate: Large Plate*

B. 77 (II) (H. 143, Mz. 204, NHD 155)
Etching, engraving, and drypoint
Signed and date in the plate in the lower left margin: *Rembrandt f. 1636 cum privile*
IV of V states
Sheet: 55.4 × 44.9 cm; plate mark: 54.9 × 44.7 cm
Watermark: unidentified fragment

Provenance:
Craddock & Barnard, London, 1978
Feddersen, Elkhart, IN, 1991
Snite Museum of Art
Acc. no.: 1991.025.048

The plate does not survive.

Christ before Pilate, the largest print in Rembrandt's oeuvre, is unusual in that it concentrates on the moment before Pilate accedes to the crowd's demand to crucify Jesus.[1] By focusing on the Roman procurator's dilemma, Rembrandt deepened the psychological drama of the event, for even though the viewer knows how the story will eventually end, the question of Christ's fate is still unresolved in this striking image.

Populated with dozens of figures, Rembrandt's composition is powerfully and overtly theatrical.[2] On the right side of the print, Jesus, the high priests, Roman centurions, and Pilate are assembled on a raised platform. Although the eye may be drawn first to Pilate, the large robed figure in the right foreground, Rembrandt has bathed the captive Christ in light, and it is his figure that creates the central, vertical axis of the dominant triangular grouping, with his head at its apex. In the midst of the turmoil, Jesus stands erect, his hands clasped and bound in front of him. His upward gaze conveys both sorrowful resignation and an appeal to the heavens above.[3] Pilate, wearing a turban and dressed in a heavy, brocaded cloak, is at Jesus's left. In this nuanced representation, he is portrayed as a somewhat sympathetic figure, for he appears to be torn between his own sense of justice and the demands of the crowd and the conspiring high priests. Pilate hovers above the "seat of judgment," neither standing nor sitting, as he looks askance at the rod of judicial power that the priests are urging him to accept.[4] His left hand is raised as if to fend off the staff, and he gestures toward Jesus with his right hand. A tasseled baldachin, suspended over the judgment seat, closes off the upper right side of the composition.

The Roman guards standing behind Jesus wear clothing and armor drawn from a variety of periods, and they hold seventeenth-century weapons: halberds, spears, and partisans. Most of them seem more like curious spectators than menacing soldiers. The Jewish high priests and officers of the Temple cluster around Pilate, and one of them, kneeling before him, thrusts forward the rod of justice with his left hand, while pointing to it with his right. His companions speak and gesture animatedly as they press their case, anticipating that the procurator will give in to their arguments and the demands of the rabble. These priests and others, nearby, are individualized, with diverse features and exotic costumes. One of them faces away from Pilate as he addresses the large, restless crowd

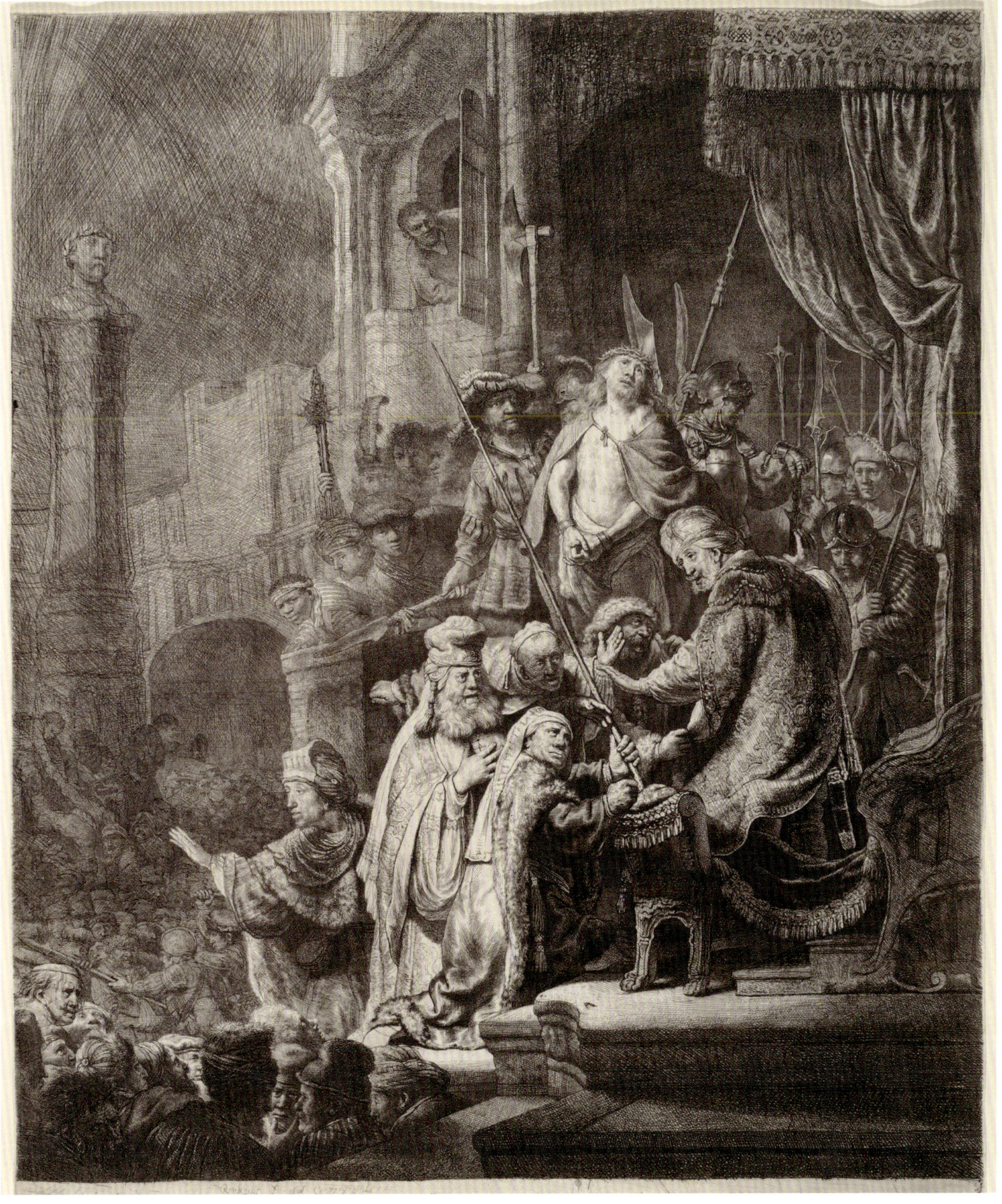

PLATE 50

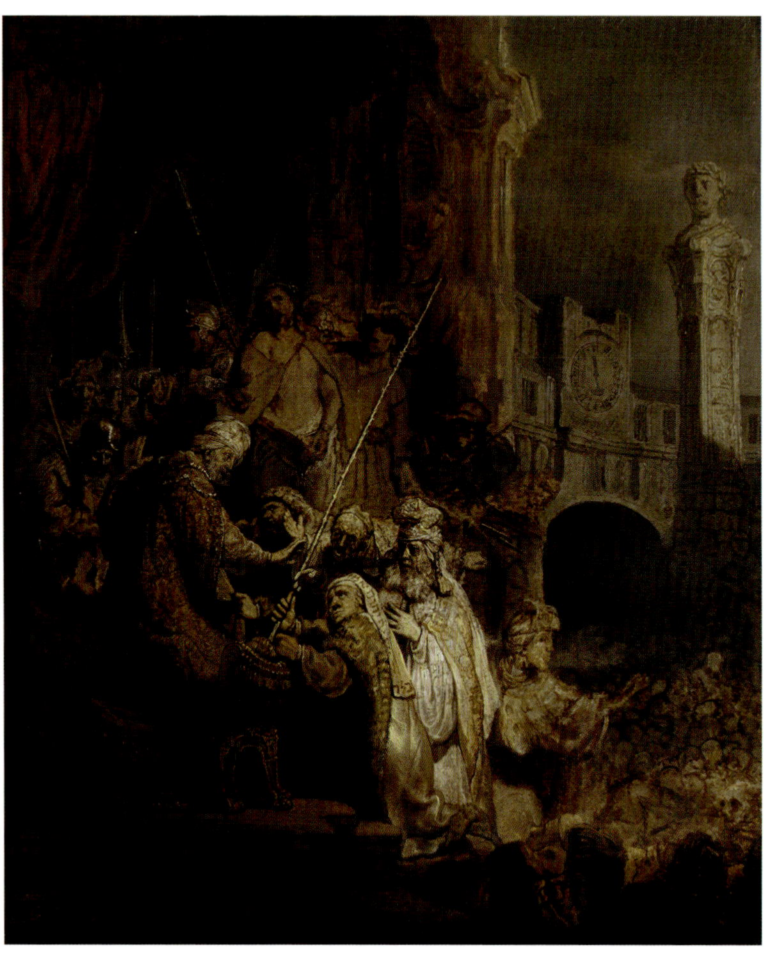

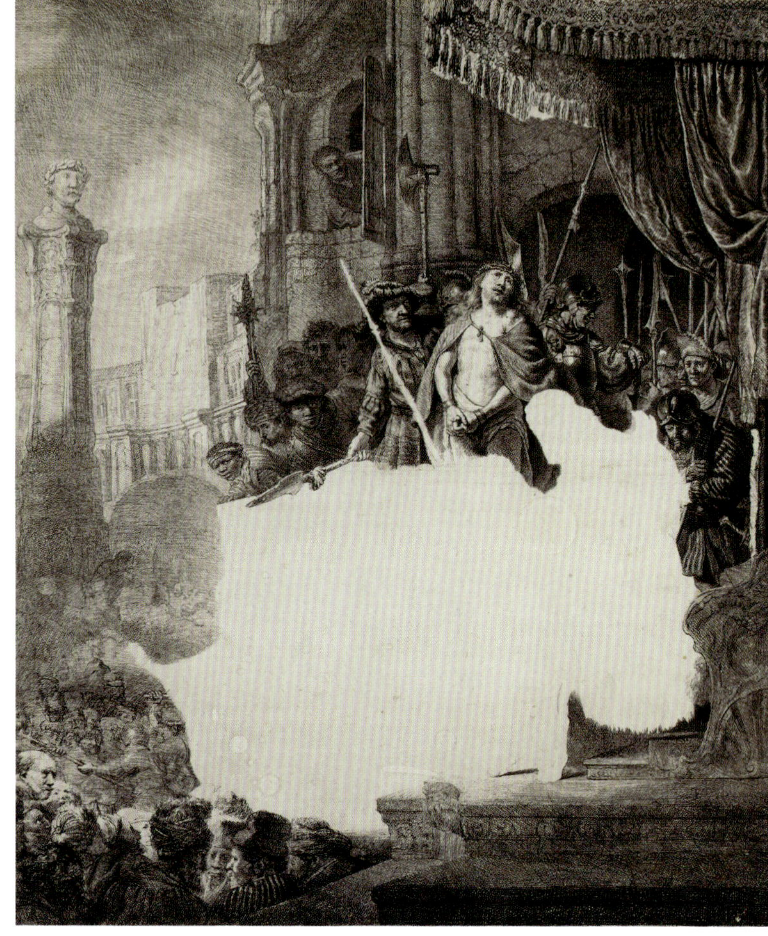

FIGURE 1. Rembrandt, *Christ before Pilate*, oil on paper, laid on canvas, 1635. *National Gallery, London. Photo: © National Gallery of Art, London/Art Resource.*

FIGURE 2. Rembrandt and van Vliet, *Christ before Pilate*, etching and engraving, State I, 1635–36. *Rijksmuseum, Amsterdam.*

that has gathered below the platform. He gestures out toward the throng, as if counseling patience to the masses awaiting Pilate's judgment.

In the left foreground, a group of four elderly men dressed in turbans and soft hats similar to those worn by the priests on the platform are engaged in conversation. Behind them, the unruly mob spreads out as far as the eye can see, back to a distant archway. Some have even scaled the base of a tall columnar monument crowned by an enormous bust of a bearded man, presumably a Roman emperor, in order to have a better view of the spectacle. Still others have climbed up onto the back edge of the platform to Christ's right. Some of them gaze out at the crowd; others lean forward, staring out at the viewer. One of these figures has Moorish features, and another—one with piercing eyes and the most well-defined visage—seems to have Rembrandt's own features. A stone tower, part of the Praetorium, rises up beyond these figures, and a man leans out of an open window, peering down at the drama unfolding below. The inclusion of the passive observers who represent a broad spectrum of times and places imparts a universally inclusive quality to this critical moment in biblical history. In this same spirit, Rembrandt composed the etching in such a way that the viewer, who sees the scene from a vantage point high above the rabble, can study the central figures of Pilate and Jesus in a manner not unlike that of some of the observers within the print. This device creates a psychological link between figures in the print and those viewing the image, since they are all witnesses to the judgment that will seal Christ's fate.

Size was not the only unusual aspect of this print. The process by which it was produced was also atypical; it was based on a unique, full-scale *en brunaille* oil sketch on paper of the composition in reverse that Rembrandt had made (fig. 1).[5] The contours of the figures and architecture in that large sketch are incised, indicating that the image was later transferred from the paper to the plate that was to be etched. There is no other example in Rembrandt's oeuvre of the artist producing a preparatory oil sketch of this scale for a print. Another curious aspect of this work is the existence of three impressions of an incomplete first state of the print dated 1635 (fig. 2).[6] In the first state, the center of the composition, including Pilate and the priests on the platform before him, that is, the psychological nexus of the narrative, is missing. As Thomas Rassieur observed, although it was not unusual for professional engravers to work from the outside of a composition in toward the center, this was not the norm for an etching.[7] The explanation for the evolution of this print may lie in the role played by a second artist. While it is generally agreed that this work was a collaboration between Rembrandt and Leiden printmaker Jan Georg van Vliet, the precise contribution of each man to the final form of the print has been a matter of some discussion.[8] The sketch and extant states of the print suggest that Rembrandt worked out the composition in the form of an oil sketch that he then turned over to van Vliet to execute as an etching. Then, as the image on the plate began to take shape, Rembrandt probably requested a proof from van Vliet. The fact that the most dramatic part of the composition is missing from the first state's "proof" suggests that Rembrandt may have wished to verify van Vliet's ability to render the image accurately before entrusting him with the task of translating the most complex part of the scene. It is likely that after van Vliet had completed the etched plate, Rembrandt himself added minor touches to the composition by means of a burin and a drypoint needle. It is also possible that he is the one who added the signature, the date (1636), and the claim that the print was issued *cum privile*, all in the lower margin of the plate beneath the image.[9] The phrase *cum privile* ("with privileges") referred to the receipt of exclusive rights to an image, rights that could be granted by a prince or, in the case of the Netherlands, the States General, to an artist or publisher. This was the seventeenth-century equivalent of copyrighting a work. Rubens, for example, received privileges from the rulers of the Spanish Netherlands for some of his prints and actually sought to receive privileges from the Dutch States General, as well. At a time when the art of reproductive engraving was flourishing, it made sense to try to forestall the production of unauthorized copies.[10] However, despite the claim written in the margin of *Christ before Pilate*, there is no documentary evidence that Rembrandt ever actually applied for or received such legal protection for any of his images.

By the beginning of the eighteenth century, *Christ before Pilate* was also known as the "thirty guilder print" and was often paired with artist's slightly earlier, but equally large, *Descent from the Cross: The Second Plate* (B. 81 II, 1633, cat. no. 55), which was popularly known as the "twenty guilder print."[11] While Rembrandt was producing these two prints, he was also actively engaged in painting part of a Passion cycle for the stadtholder, Prince Frederik Hendrik of Orange. It seems quite possible that *Descent* and *Christ before Pilate* were conceived of as part of a planned cycle of monumental Passion prints intended to rival those that Lucas Vorsterman had produced for Rubens.[12] It has been suggested that if such a cycle was, in fact, undertaken, it may have been dealer and entrepreneur Hendrik Uylenburgh, Rembrandt's relative by marriage and publisher of the fourth and fifth states of *Descent from the Cross*, who was responsible for the project, or who at least encouraged the artist to embark upon it.[13]

Notes

1. Pilate's reluctance to condemn Christ is recounted in all four of the Gospels (Matthew 27:15–26; Mark 15:6–16; Luke 23:13–24; John 19:1–16), but Rembrandt's image most closely illustrates the account in John. Only in John do the soldiers scourge Jesus and place a crown of thorns on his head and a purple cloak on his shoulders *before* Pilate passes his final judgment. Werner Hoffman and Martin Dierker, *Luther und die Folgen für die Kunst* (Munich: Prestel-Verlag, 1983), cat. 213, 344.

2. Kurt Bauch (*Die frühe Rembrandt und seine Zeit* [Berlin: Verlag Gebr. Mann, 1960], 192) compared the print's mise-en-scène to

the staging of rhetorician society plays that were regularly performed in the Netherlands from the sixteenth century on. Shelley Perlove and Larry Silver (*Rembrandt's Faith*, 283) linked the print to Hugo Grotius's 1627 Passion play *Tragoedia Christus Patiens*, in which Pilate blames his actions against Christ on his fear of the fury of the crowd.

3. Münz (*Critical Catalogue*, 2:96) drew a parallel between the expression on Christ's face and that which appears on Guido Reni's representations of Christ Crowned with Thorns. However, there is no evidence that Rembrandt ever knew any of Reni's paintings of the suffering Christ either directly or through copies.

4. Thomas Rassieur observed that this staff would have had significance for a Dutch viewer, since a similar rod was held by Dutch officials in the seventeenth century when they pronounced death sentences. It is also worth noting that in Renaissance depictions of the Ecce Homo, it is not unusual for Pilate to hold just such a staff as he stands at Jesus's side. Thomas Rassieur in *Rembrandt's Journey*, 118n3. See, for example, Albrecht Dürer's *Ecce Homo* of 1512 from the Small Engraved Passion (TIB 10), and Lucas van Leyden's *Ecce Homo* of the same date (NHD 70) and his engraving in his Passion of 1521 (NHD 50).

5. The oil sketch is now in the National Gallery, London.

6. One of these impressions is in the Rijksprentenkabinet in Amsterdam, and two are in the British Museum. One of the impressions in the British Museum has retouchings brushed on in brown oil paint. These are generally assumed to have been done by Rembrandt himself. Martin Royalton-Kisch in Christiaan Schuckman, Martin Royalton-Kisch, and Erik Hinterding, *Rembrandt and Van Vliet: A Collaboration on Copper* (Amsterdam: Museum het Rembrandthuis, 1996), cat. 6a, 68–69.

7. Rassieur in *Rembrandt's Journey*, 117.

8. Schuckman, Royalton-Kisch, and Hinterding (*Rembrandt and Van Vliet*) have assembled the basic biographical information on van Vliet's life and activity as a printmaker. Jan Georg van Vliet, also known as Jan Gillisz. van Vliet and Johannes van Vliet, was a painter and printmaker who was born in Leiden sometime between 1600 and 1610, and worked there all his life. His father was a grain trader. There is no information regarding Jan's training. There is some evidence that the printmaker visited Antwerp in 1634, which means that he would have been acquainted with Rubens's paintings of the *Raising of the Cross* and *Descent from the Cross* in that city. Van Vliet collaborated with Rembrandt from about 1631 to 1636, executing prints based on compositions by the master and, at least in the case of the *Christ before Pilate*, completing a plate that Rembrandt may have begun. Van Vliet apparently abandoned his career as a printmaker and painter sometime around 1637. In that year he married Susanna van Campen, the daughter of a wealthy and politically active man in Leiden, and it is possible that Susanna's dowry enabled van Vliet to pursue a more lucrative career. By 1640, documents referred to him as a vintner.

9. For one opinion as to what Rembrandt's specific additions to the plate may have been, see Royalton-Kisch in *Rembrandt and Van Vliet*, cat. 16b, 70–71.

10. For a discussion of "privileges" in the Netherlands, see Nadine Orenstein, *Hendrick Hondius and the Business of Prints in Seventeenth-Century Holland* (Rotterdam: Sound and Vision Interactive, 1996), 90–94.

11. Münz, *Critical Catalogue*, 2:213–14, citing an entry dated March 1, 1711, in Zacharias Conrad von Uffenbach's *Merkwürdige Reisen durch Niedersachsen, Holland und Engelland* (Ulm: Auf Kosten Johann Friedrich Gaum, 1753), 3:581. See the discussion of the *Hundred Guilder Print* (B. 74, cat. no. 48).

12. On the implicit rivalry between Rembrandt and Rubens, see Simon Schama, *Rembrandt's Eyes* (New York: Alfred Knopf, 1999), passim.

13. For a further discussion of this project, see the entry for *Descent from the Cross: The Second Plate* (B. 81 II, 1633, cat. no. 55).

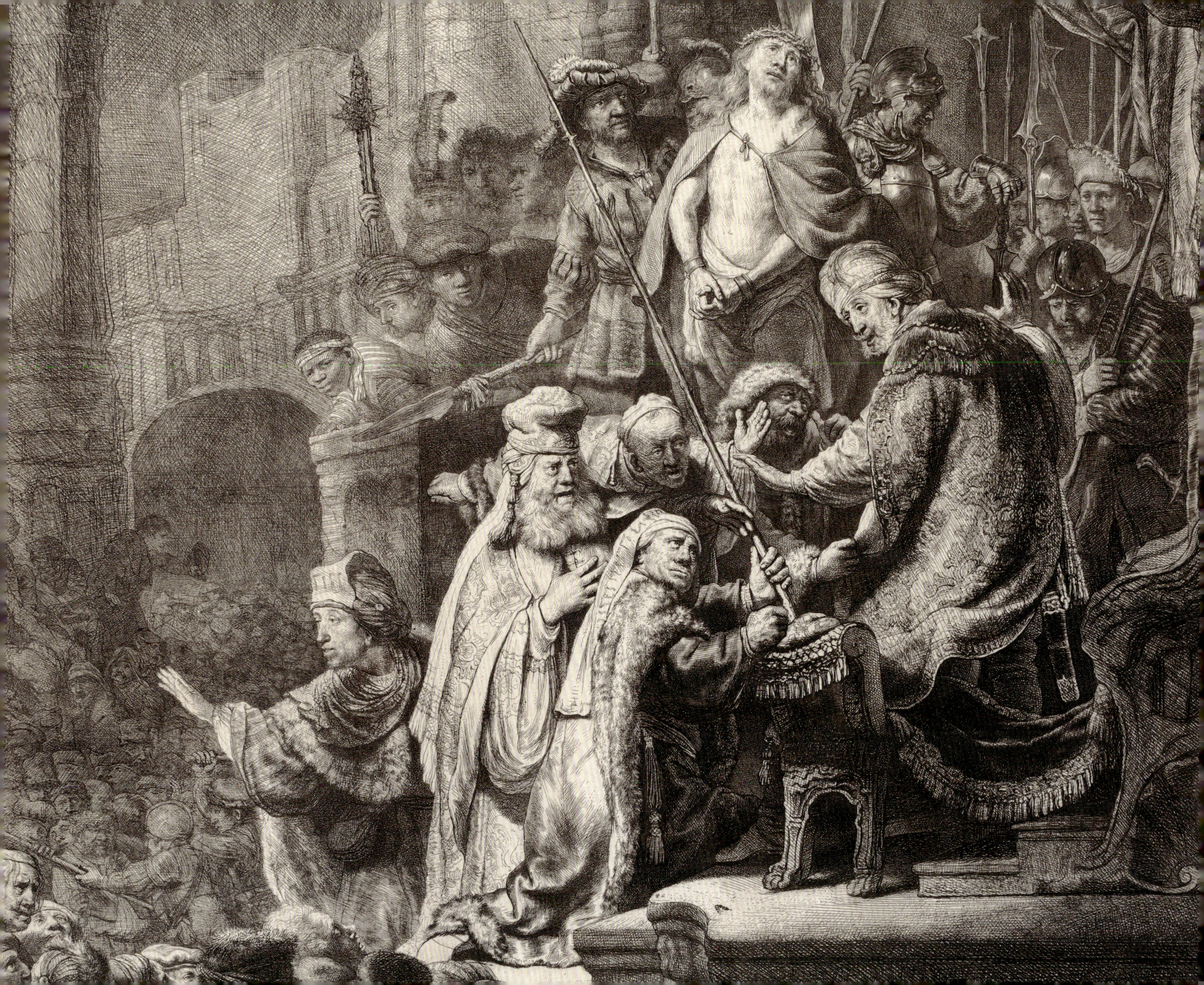

51. *Christ Presented to the People: Oblong Plate*

B. 76 (H. 271, Mz. 235, NHD 290)
Drypoint
Signed and dated in State VII in the plate: *Rembrandt f. 1655*
State VIII of VIII
Sheet: 35.8 × 45.5 cm, trimmed to the plate mark
Countermark: *ANH* (unidentified)
Verso: in graphite, *) 722*

Provenance:
Kennedy Galleries Inc., New York, NY, 1978
Feddersen, Elkhart, IN, 1991
Snite Museum of Art
Acc. No. 1991.025.047

The plate does not survive.

Rembrandt's drypoint prints *Christ Presented to the People: Oblong Plate* and *Christ Crucified between the Two Thieves: "The Three Crosses"* (B. 78, 1653–1655, cat. no. 54) are extraordinary images in terms of both scale and technique. Although the artist had employed drypoint as a means of embellishing his etched plates quite early in his career, neither he nor any other printmaker had ever executed an image of this magnitude entirely in that medium alone.[1] The appeal of drypoint was undoubtedly both its immediacy and the quality of the line that could be created. Drawing directly onto the plate with a drypoint needle produces a line with an accompanying burr, and because ink becomes caught up in this burr, the lines are softer and more velvety than those made by either etching or engraving.[2] *The Three Crosses* may have preceded *Christ Presented to the People* by as much as two years.[3] If so, then when Rembrandt created the later print, he already had experience with both the potential and the limitations of working in drypoint on this scale. If he had not judged the earlier experiment a success, it is doubtful that he would have undertaken so large and complex a project again. It is possible that Rembrandt began the two prints at about the same time. However, despite their similar scale and technique, certain stylistic differences—for example, the manner of rendering the figures in the two scenes—argue against a common date.

In his depiction of Christ Presented to the People, Rembrandt chose to illustrate the New Testament moment when Pilate asked the crowd before him which of the two prisoners, Jesus or the criminal Barabbas, he should pardon.[4] Rembrandt had already produced a work with a related theme some nineteen years earlier, the large collaborative etching *Christ before Pilate: Large Plate* (B. 77, 1635–36, cat. no. 50). However, in the earlier print, he had depicted a moment somewhat later in the story: the crowd has already condemned Jesus, and Pilate evinces his reluctance to carry out their wishes, hovering above the seat of judgment as he tries to reject the proffered staff that will confirm Jesus's condemnation and consignment to the cross. In terms of the artist's conception of both space and action, the earlier print is considerably more dramatic than *Christ Presented to the People*. The principal figures in *Christ before Pilate* are contained in a dense pyramid placed relatively close to the picture plane. Broadly gesticulating priests, Pharisees, and soldiers cluster around the central figure of Christ, with the entrance to

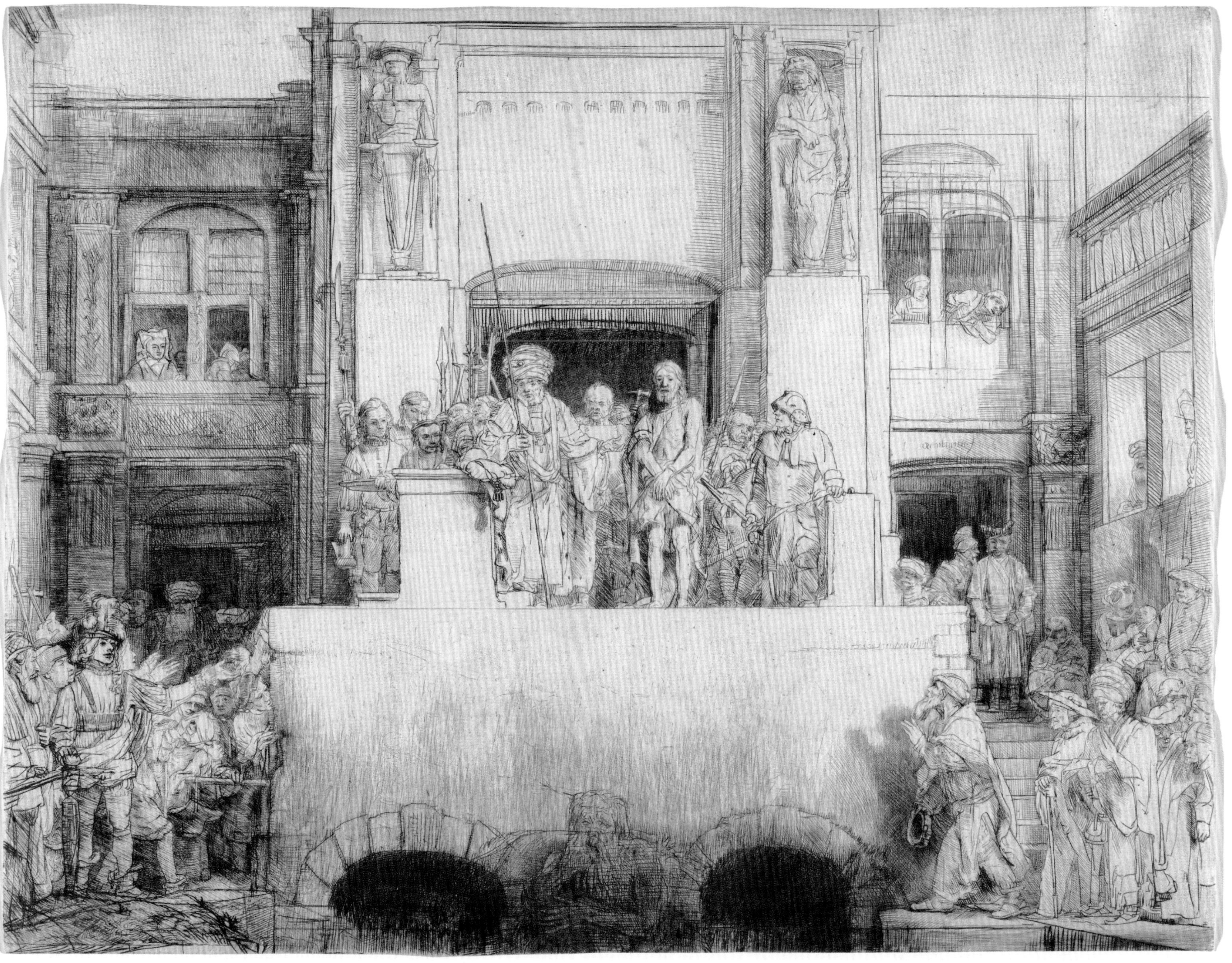

PLATE 51

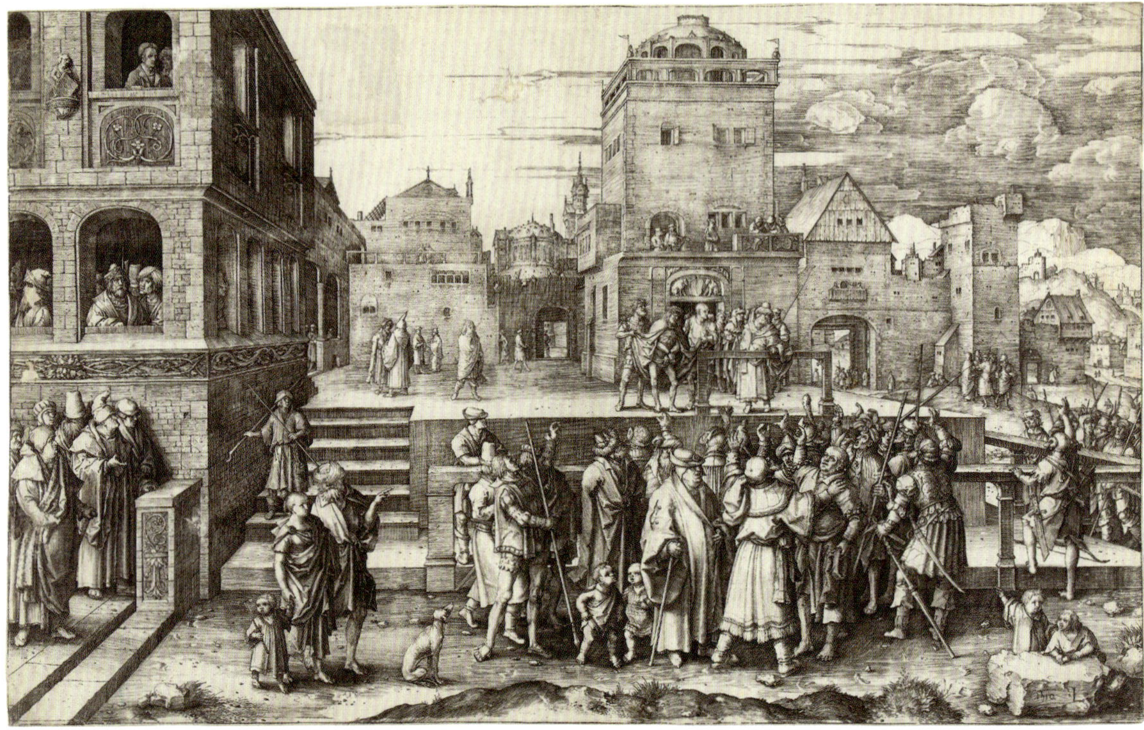

FIGURE 1. Lucas van Leyden, *Christ Presented to the People*, engraving, 1510. *Rijksmuseum, Amsterdam.*

Pilate's palace looming behind them. At the left, a shadowy, seething crowd of onlookers has gathered in a deep courtyard. The density of surface textures and detail in this print increases the sense of claustrophobic tumult and conflict swirling around the passive, long-suffering figure of Jesus.

By contrast, *Christ Presented to the People* is a much calmer, more classically structured image. Inspired by Lucas van Leyden's large engraving of the same subject from 1510 (fig. 1),[5] Rembrandt staged the presentation on a raised platform in the courtyard in front of Pilate's palace. In the first five states of his print, he placed a crowd of onlookers directly in front of the tribune as Lucas had done. Nonetheless, there are major differences in the ways in which the two artists conceived of the event. Lucas van Leyden's scene is set into a much deeper and broader urban space, one that is closed off by an elegant two-story palace on the left, but is open at the right. Also, in Lucas's print the prefect's palace is set back at a considerable distance from the crowd. As a result, the figures of Jesus and Pilate, who stand in front of the palace, are relatively small and inconspicuous. In fact, one has to look closely at the work in order to discern the theme of the print.

Rembrandt constructed a much shallower and more confined setting. He pulled the façade of Pilate's palace considerably closer to the foreground and added architectural wings that enframe the sides of the space. The result is highly scenographic: it is as though the event is taking place in a room from which the fourth wall has been removed. The façade of the prefect's palace is set parallel to the picture plane, as are an imposing projecting frontispiece and the tribune on which Pilate, his attendants, and the prisoners are arrayed. The prefect, Christ, and Barabbas stand out against the darkness of the low arched doorway behind them. Pilate, attired in a robe and turban, holds a long staff in his right hand as he gestures toward Jesus with his left. Jesus's hands are bound in front of him, and he is clad only in a loincloth and a cloak that covers one shoulder. He gazes pensively out into the space before him as he is presented to the throng below. A bald, Asiatic-looking figure who has been identified as Barabbas stands between and just behind the two principal figures.[6] On the tribune, to Pilate's right, are a scribe, seated behind a high desk, and a youth who holds a ewer, foreshadowing the dramatic moment when Pilate will wash his hands. Smooth, heavy stone piers flanking the doorway behind these figures act as supports for shallow niches containing herms. On the left is Justice, with her symbolic scales,[7] and on the right is Fortitude, wearing a lion-skin cape, leaning on a column, and holding a club in its left hand.[8] The wall between the niches is completely blank and is capped, in the first three states of the print, by a simple horizontal architrave (fig. 2).[9] Dark, secondary entrances that flank the central frontispiece are set into the stepped-back palace façade. Above these side doorways are partially arched windows that are open at the bottom. On the right side, a short flight of stairs leads up to the entrance, while on the left, a doorway seems to be directly accessible at ground level. There is a blank wall above the entrance on the right, while on the left, the space between the doorway and windows is ornamented. Figures bathed in sunlight peer out of the windows on the right, while on the left side, which is cast into dense shadow, a woman traditionally identified as Pilate's wife[10] stares impassively out from one side of the opening as a soldier passes behind the other. Only a sliver of architecture is visible at the far left edge of the print, but on the right, figures can be seen viewing the scene from two large rectangular openings.

In addition to the crowd that has gathered in front of the platform, a handful of priests, Pharisees, and temple elders has assembled at the right, some standing in shadow in the doorway, some on the steps, and some on the shallow earthen plane in front of the dais. They wear a variety of costumes, including turbans and the flat hats worn by Eastern European Jews in Rembrandt's own time. One bearded old man with a cap has moved forward and appears to be speaking as he looks up at Jesus and raises his left hand. Illuminated by a strong light, he casts a dense shadow on the face of the platform, the only figure to do so.[11] His approach, his shadow, his rapt attention, open mouth, uplifted gaze, and extended hand—as well as the attention to detail that Rembrandt employed in delineating this particular figure—all imply that the man has a special significance in the print. It is unclear, however, whether he is showing compassion for Jesus's plight or is one of the conspirators—a temple elder or a priest—who is responding to Pilate's question by calling for Jesus's condemnation. If the latter, then the dark shadow, a somewhat demonic shape, may be read as an omen, a black stain that foreshadows the evil and darkness to come.[12]

In each of the first five states of the print (fig. 2), a raggle-taggle assemblage of people stretches across the foreground from left to right in front of the tribune. In contrast to the Jewish figures in Rembrandt's earlier *Christ before Pilate*, the Pharisees here are no longer portrayed as Semitic caricatures. A substantial railing prevents the crowd from tumbling into what appears to be a steep incline or trench on the right. The crowd exhibits a great variety of actions, ages, and attire, and ranges from an old bearded patriarch and a young dandy with a plumed hat at the extreme left, to a heavily robed man with a walking stick in the middle, and a mother with her child near a middle-aged man with a sword and a high hat on the right. As was his wont, Rembrandt commingled time periods and styles. Some of the costumes appear to be ancient, some simply exotic, and still others contemporary. The implication is that all of humanity, from across the ages, has gathered to witness the moment of Christ's condemnation.

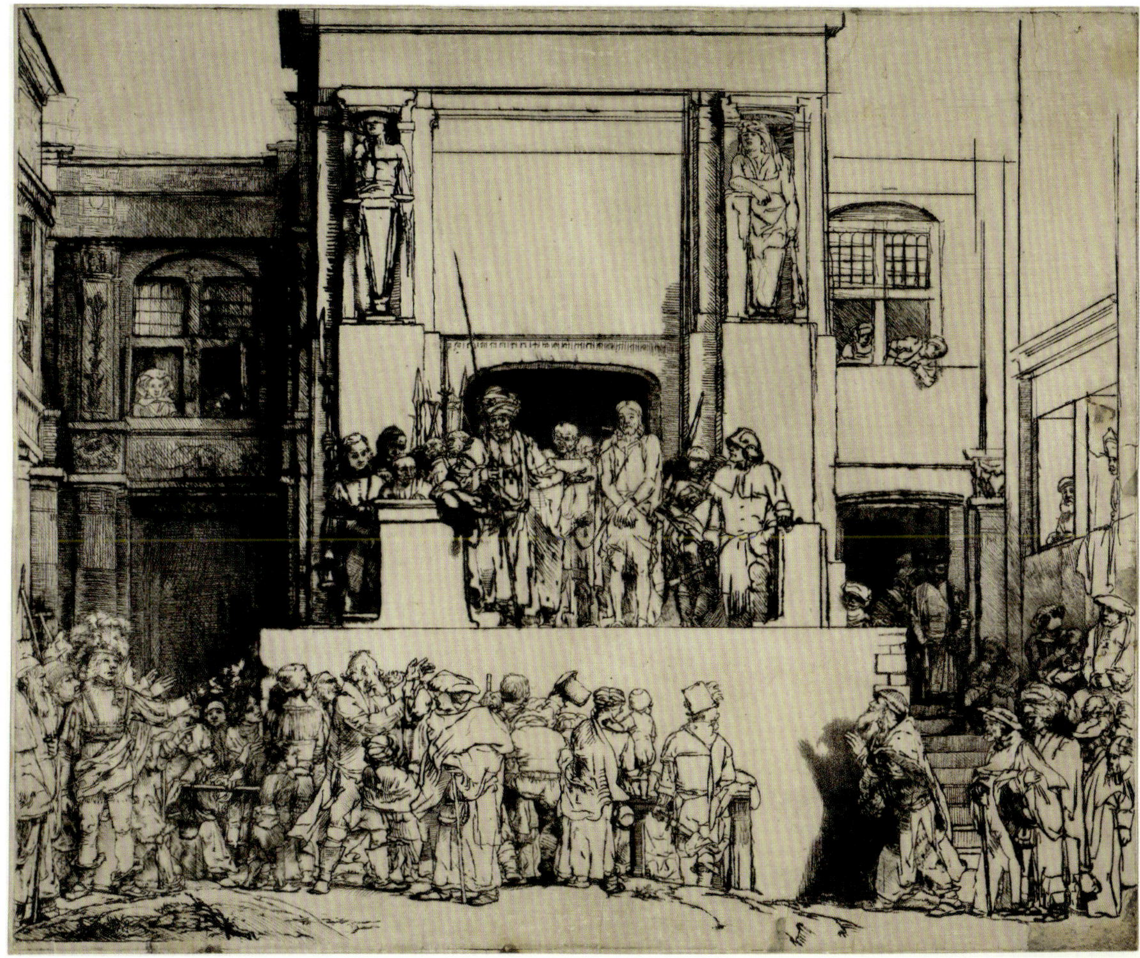

FIGURE 2. Rembrandt, *Christ Presented to the People: Oblong Plate*, drypoint, State III, 1655. *Photo: © Trustees of the British Museum.*

Beginning with the sixth state of the print, Rembrandt significantly transformed the image. He burnished out all of the spectators who had been standing in front of the tribune except for the old man whose shadow marks the face of the platform. The figures around the sides of the platform remained essentially unaltered, as did the figures on top of the tribune, but a rounded pediment was added to the archway enframing Pilate and Christ. Removing the throng of people at the forefront had the effect of making the figures on the tribune appear closer to the surface of the print and therefore more immediate. With no intermediaries, the viewer, in essence, replaced the crowd. Other modifications at this stage included a lightly sketched arch visible in the bottom center of the platform and a pair of ruled lines just above the lower edge of the print.[13]

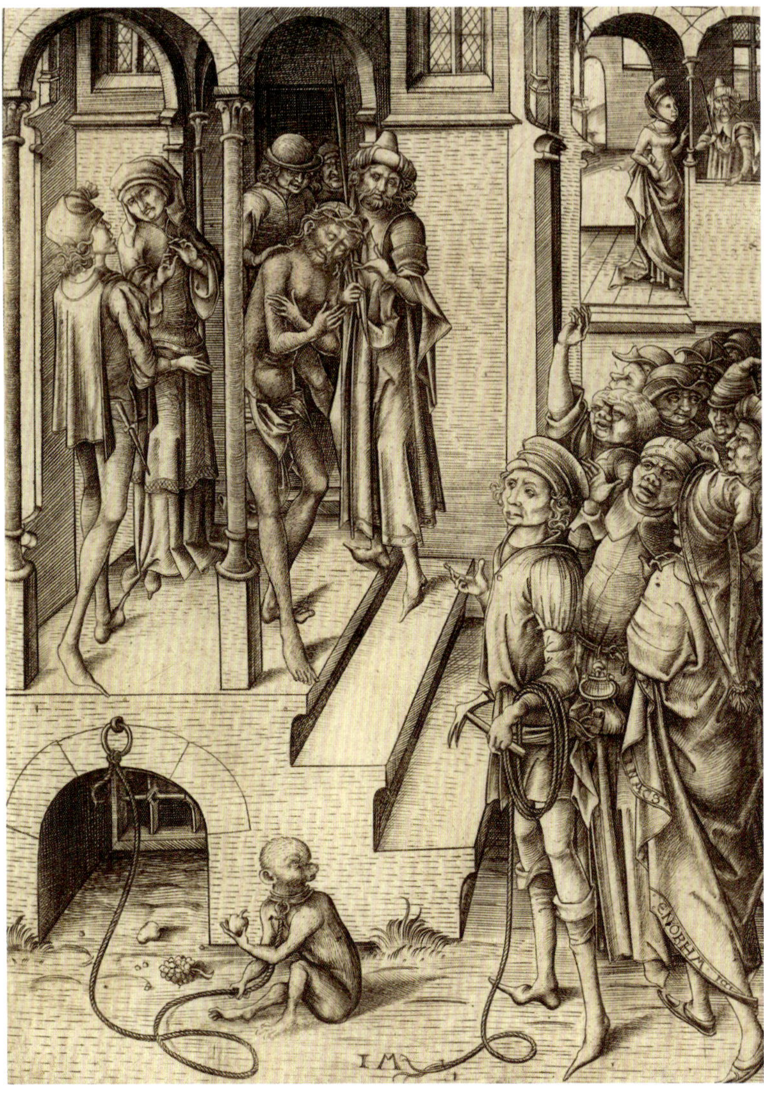

FIGURE 3. Israhel van Meckenem, *Christ Presented to the People*, engraving, c. 1475–85. *Photo: Courtesy of the National Gallery of Art, Washington, DC.*

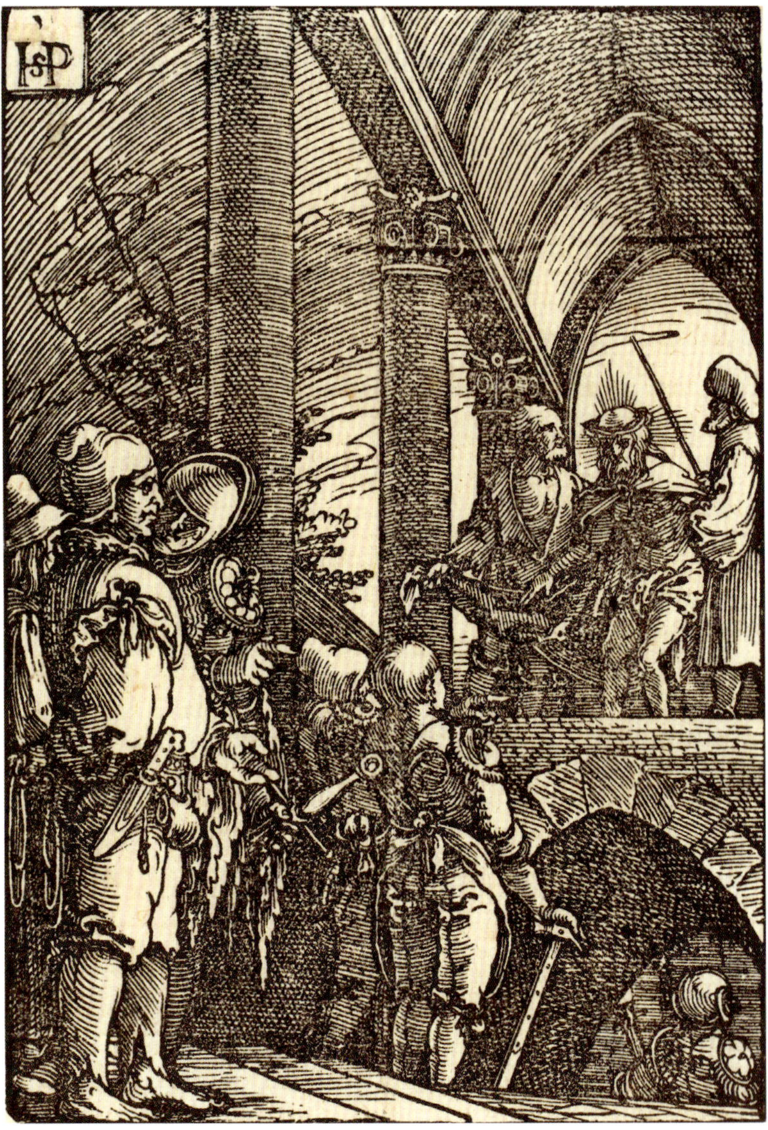

FIGURE 4. Hans Sebald Beham, *Christ Presented to the People*, woodcut, 1522. *Photo: Courtesy of the National Gallery of Art, Washington, DC.*

These lines may suggest that Rembrandt was considering adding a more regularized, paved space in front of the tribune, but he did not do so in this state nor in the final state, and as a result, the assembled elders, priests, and Pharisees at the right stand on a paved surface that seems to drop off precipitously at its left edge. The fact that only one impression from the sixth state of the composition, printed on Japanese paper, survives suggests that it was created purely as a transitional experiment.

In the next state, the seventh version of the work, Rembrandt signed and dated the plate just above the doorway on the right side of the palace facade. He also altered the windows above his signature, removing the mullions in the upper half of the arched openings; he deepened the shadows around the figures atop the tribune and on the left wing of the palace; and, most significant, he began to articulate the base of the tribune, introducing a large half-length statue of a haggard, bearded old man whose left arm rests on an urn and whose right hand fingers his beard.[14] He is flanked by two large, dark archways with heavily defined voussoirs. Rembrandt evidently considered this an intermediate stage in the creative process, for it seems that he pulled only a few impressions of the seventh state. In fact, only three examples survive. In the eighth and final state, of which the Snite Museum owns a light impression, Rembrandt drew horizontal lines through the sculpted old man at the base of the tribune and increased the density of the hatching in the arched openings that flank him. These alterations make the significance of the old man and the arches even more puzzling.

Historians have noted that the particular manner in which Rembrandt depicted Christ's presentation to the people derived not only from the artist's visual sources, but also from contemporary Netherlandish judicial practice. In capital cases, at the conclusion of a trial, the condemned criminal, accompanied by magistrates bearing the staff symbolic of their judicial office, was typically displayed to the public, either on a balcony or on a tribune in front the city hall. After the verdict and sentence were pronounced, the prisoner was immediately led to a "temporary stage . . . where the execution would take place."[15] If one of Rembrandt's purposes in removing the animated crowd from the space in front of the tribune was to encourage the print's viewer to take his or her own place as a spectator at this drama,[16] this effect would have been intensified by the inclusion of elements that related directly to seventeenth-century Dutch judicial practice.[17]

Certainly the most enigmatic elements in the last two states of the print are the half-length statue of the old man with a vessel and the two dark archways that flank him. There is one visual tradition that might explain the presence of the arches: in Israhel van Meckenem's engraving of the Ecce Homo, Christ and Pilate stand on a raised platform above a low vaulted arch and a barred window (fig. 3).[18] A similar motif appears in the Ecce Homo by Hans Sebald Beham from his small woodcut Passion of 1522 (fig. 4). In Beham's version, Christ and Pilate stand on an even higher platform, beneath which there is an arched opening that leads to a steeply descending vaulted passageway, at the bottom of which the head and shoulders of a soldier can be seen.[19] Pieter van der Borcht's depiction of the scene (fig. 5), which was used as an illustration in Benito Arias Montano's biblical emblem book, *Humanae Salutatis Monumenta*, published in Antwerp in 1571, actually includes the

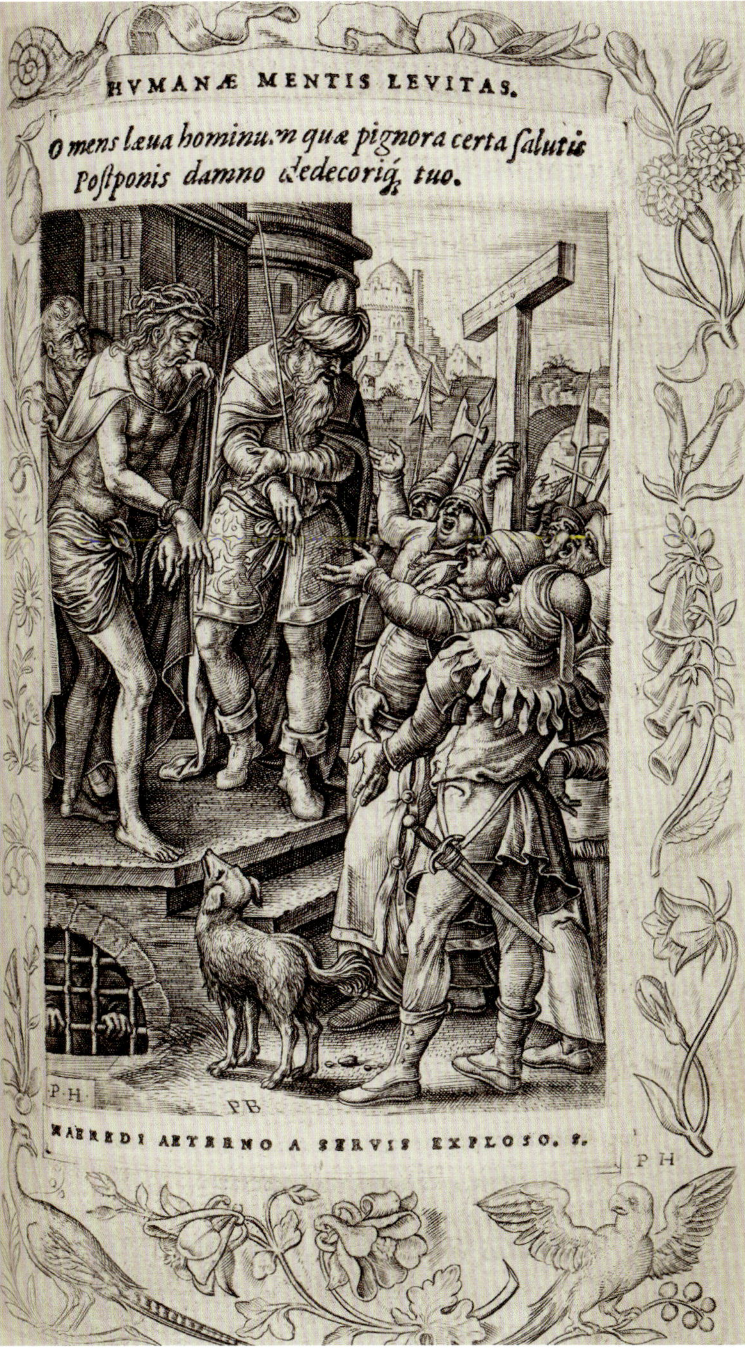

FIGURE 5. Peter Huys after Pieter van der Borcht, *Ecce Homo*, engraving, from Benito Arias Montano, *Humanae Salutatis Monumenta*, Antwerp, 1571. *Detroit Institute of Arts, Detroit, Michigan.*

faint image of a prisoner whose hands grasp the bars that cover an arched window at the base of the palace tribune.[20] Given this visual tradition, it is possible that a seventeenth-century viewer would have identified the darkened arches in Rembrandt's print as entrances to dungeons beneath Pilate's palace.[21]

Henri van de Waal, however, offered a different explanation for the two archways. He suggested that the downward-sloping ground in front of the platform represented the embankment of a canal, and that the archways represented openings for a watercourse running under the structure. In support of this idea, he cited the existence of a similar configuration in Leiden. The law court there was surrounded by a canal that disappeared under the building on one side.[22] According to van de Waal, Rembrandt might well have recalled this arrangement when he went to rework the plate. The statue of the enormous bearded man leaning on an open urn does seem to support the idea of a waterway, for the figure conforms to the traditional manner in which river gods have been represented since antiquity.[23] Unfortunately, van de Waal's account of the possible reasons for the reworked appearance of the tribune does not offer an explanation for the dramatic rethinking of the image or its relationship to the viewer that characterizes the final states of the print.

In yet another interpretation, Margaret Carroll offered a provocative theological explanation for Rembrandt's modifications. She suggested that the sloping ground and gloomy archways were meant to evoke images of death and the pit of Hell. Their juxtaposition with the presentation of Christ would remind the viewer of "the dire consequences of our condemning Christ."[24] In this context, Carroll identified the gloomy, pensive river god as a personification of Acheron, one of the three rivers in the underworld and the first to greet the dead when they descended into Hell.[25] In Carroll's view, the moment depicted in the etching signifies the end of the "tyranny" of the Old Law, which is replaced by grace through Christ's acceptance of his fate.[26]

Whether or not the specifics of Carroll's interpretation are valid, her assertion that in its final state this remarkable print is something more than a visualization of the events of Christ's trial is certainly correct. The enhanced immediacy of the image and the addition of the enigmatic, pensive figure of the river god and the ominous, yawning black arches would have challenged any viewer to examine his relationship to what he saw and to consider its implications for his own fate.

Because the Snite Museum's impression of *Christ Presented to the People* is very light, it is considerably easier to read the narrative and to discern individual details of the image, such as the gestures of the river god.

Notes

1. *Rembrandt's Journey*, 255.

2. Unlike the engraving process, in which the metal is literally carved out of the plate by a burin, producing a sharp-edged line, drypoint plates are incised by a needle that pushes the metal aside as it scratches the surface of the plate, thus raising a rough burr along one edge of the line. The principal disadvantage of this technique is that only a limited number of impressions can be pulled from a plate before the quality of the image begins to deteriorate significantly. Because of the shallowness of drypoint lines and the compression of the accompanying burr that occurs as the plate is run through the press, it is estimated that a maximum of only about fifty acceptable impressions can be pulled from a drypoint plate, whereas well over a hundred prints can be produced by an engraved or deeply etched plate.

3. As Christopher White observed, Rembrandt did not date the print of *Christ Presented* until he created the seventh state (1655). How long he had been working on the plate prior to this is not known. However, from White's perspective, the stylistic unity among all of the states of the *Christ Presented* print suggests a relatively short and continuous process. Thus, from his point of view, there is probably at most a two-year gap between the two large drypoint prints. White's analysis aside, it is not possible to determine whether the first states of *Christ Crucified* preceded those of *Christ Presented* or, if so, by how long. White, *Rembrandt as an Etcher*, 2nd ed. (New Haven, CT: Yale University Press, 1999), 102–4.

4. Matthew 27:15–23.

5. NHD 71. Certain details, such as the low staircase leading up to the platform on which Jesus and Pilate stand and the inclusion

of spectators viewing the scene through second-story windows in a structure off to the side, confirm the relationship between the van Leyden engraving and the Rembrandt print.

It has been suggested that in addition to the Lucas van Leyden print, Rembrandt drew on Nicolaes de Bruyn's two versions of the theme, one from 1604 and the other from 1618–19 (Eugene Winternitz, "Rembrandt's 'Christ Presented to the People'—1655: A Meditation on Justice and Collective Guilt," *Oud Holland* 84 [1969]: figs. 2 and 3); and from Jacques Callot's etching of *Christ Shown to the People* from the *Large Passion* published by Jean François Daumont in Paris between 1619 and 1624 (Lieure 285) (Münz, *Critical Catalogue*, 2:107–8). Callot's scene is also played out in a semi-enclosed stagelike setting.

6. Winternitz ("Rembrandt's 'Christ Presented to the People,'" 180–81.) identified this figure as Barabbas and noted that representations of the Ecce Homo that include Barabbas are very rare.

7. It is interesting to note that at the top of the print, Rembrandt depicted an ideal image of Justice with her balanced scales of unbiased judgment, while at the bottom of the print, in the midst of a throng offering up its own version of justice, he drew a man who balances two vessels on a stick as he covers one eye and turns away from both Pilate and Jesus, gazing instead at the nattily dressed man on the left.

8. Scholars have puzzled over the attributes and significance of this fierce figure. Henri van de Waal went so far as to suggest that it was actually supposed to represent Omphale, the seductress of Hercules. ("Some Possible Sources for Rembrandt's Etching [*sic*], *Ecce Homo* [1655]," in van de Waal, *Steps towards Rembrandt: Collected Articles 1937–1972*, ed. R. H. Fuchs; trans. Patricia Wardle and Alan Griffiths [Amsterdam: North-Holland, 1974], 186). Because Omphale was a "virile woman," van de Waal argued, she was often used to represent the world turned upside-down, i.e., a world in which the innocent Christ was condemned and the criminal Barabbas was set free. This idea has not been generally accepted. Winternitz ("Rembrandt's 'Christ Presented to the People'") suggested that the inclusion of the club, "a . . . brutal and vulgar weapon," was meant to suggest power and violence, rather than fortitude. According to his reading of the figures, the two statues characterize the presentation of Christ to the crowd as a miscarriage of justice, one in which the power of the crowd would prevail over Roman justice (ibid., 184).

There is, however, another possible interpretation. Fortitude's club and lion skin clearly link the statue, which is consistently referred to as female but whose gender is actually not clearly defined, with Hercules. There is a well-established tradition that associates the demigod with the virtue of fortitude because of the patience and strength he showed in the execution of his labors. For example, the fifth-century Roman author and philosopher Macrobius specifically identified Hercules with fortitude in his *Commentary on Cicero's Dream of Scipio* (Book I) and his *Saturnalia* (Book I, 20, 6). Macrobius was one of the sources for Vincenzo Cartari's popular sixteenth-century mythographic handbook, *Le imagini de I dei* (first published in 1556). In his section on Hercules, Cartari also cited the ancient lexicographer Suidas, who associated the demigod not only with fortitude, but also with prudence: (*Suida scrive che per dimostrare gli antichi che Ercole fu grande amatore di prudenza e virtù lo dipensero vestito di una pelle di lione, che significa la grandezza e generosità dell'animo, gli posero la mazza nella destra, che mostra desiderio di prudenza e di sapere*, 310). Although this might seem an obscure source for Rembrandt to draw on, Thijs Weststeijn noted that Samuel van Hoogstraten, a learned pupil of Rembrandt's, was quite familiar with Cartari. Weststeijn, *The Visible World: Samuel Van Hoogstraten's Art Theory and the Legitimation of Painting in the Dutch Golden Age* (Amsterdam: Amsterdam University Press, 2008), 48–49. It seems possible, then, that Rembrandt might also have had some familiarity with this source. It is also possible that the artist intended the statue to represent both fortitude *and* prudence. If this is so, then Rembrandt's statues would also have linked the print to the decorations of the Chamber of Justice in the newly constructed town hall in Amsterdam, for as Winternitz has noted ("Rembrandt's 'Christ Presented to the People,'" 181), the statues of Justice and Prudence were paired in this room. In this way, the etching's two herms, Justice and Fortitude/Prudence, would have been an easily recognized allusion to the traditional pairing of virtues in contemporary Netherlandish courtrooms. Rembrandt's decision to represent the second herm in such a way as to evoke Prudence, as well as Fortitude, would have offered a parallel to Christ's own virtues and his stoical acceptance of his fate.

9. The vast majority of impressions from the first three states of *Christ Presented to the People* were printed on Japanese or Chinese paper. The plate was so large, however, that a strip had to be attached

along the upper edge of the paper in order for the entire image to be accommodated. For the fourth state, in order to avoid this extra step, Rembrandt cut down the plate at the top so that the image could be printed on a single sheet. Other small alterations were also introduced at this point, although these dealt primarily with the distribution of shadows in the image and some adjustments to the architecture necessitated by the reduction in the size of the plate. White and Boon, 41.

10. Tümpel, *Rembrandt legt*, cat. 97; and Christopher White, *The Late Etchings of Rembrandt: A Study in the Development of a Print. An Arts Council Exhibition [at the] British Museum Gallery of Prints & Drawings, 20 March–11 May 1969*, exh. cat. (London: Arts Council, 1969), cat. XV, 23.

11. Samuel van Hoogstraten, one of Rembrandt's pupils, devoted an entire chapter in his theoretical treatise *An Introduction to the Great School of Painting* to a discussion of projected shadows and their use in the studio and in theatrical settings. Victor I. Stoichita, *A Short History of the Shadow* (London: Reaktion Books, 1997), 129–31. It is possible that Hoogstraten's interest arose from his experiences as a student in Rembrandt's studio.

12. On the demonic connotations of shadows, see Stoichita, *A Short History*, 127–34, and Ernst H. Gombrich, *Shadows: The Depiction of Cast Shadows in Western Art* (London: National Galley Publications, 1995), 57–58.

13. Margaret Deutsch Carroll, "Rembrandt as Meditational Printmaker," *Art Bulletin* 63, no. 4 (December 1981): 592: "To one familiar with town hall facades in other Dutch cities . . . it indicates that Rembrandt was toying with the idea of depicting a prison door or window in the podium wall."

14. Winternitz ("Rembrandt's 'Christ Presented to the People,'" 185 and 596n42) and others have suggested that this figure is a river god, and have noted that he is leaning on a pitcher or urn.

15. Carroll, "Rembrandt as Meditational Printmaker," 590.

16. Winternitz, "Rembrandt's 'Christ Presented to the People,'" 190, "Could it not be that, by that change (the erasure of the crowd) . . . Rembrandt meant to elevate the scene from a narration to a level of timeless significance? Whether we like it or not, we are all 'Jews.'"

17. See note 8, above, for a discussion of how the statues would also have been related to a mid-century Amsterdamer's experience of judicial procedures.

18. HG 148.

19. TIB 88.

20. Pieter Huys's engraving of Christ Presented to the People after a design by Pieter van der Borcht in Benito Arias Montano, *Humanae Salutis Monumenta,* "Humanae mentis levitas" (Antwerp, 1581), n.p., NHD 939 (Pieter van der Borcht, Book Illustrations).

21. H. van de Waal has noted that "the idea of a prison under a tribune would have been quite familiar to artists in the Low Countries, where, by tradition, the town lock-up was often located underneath the monumental steps and dais at the entrance to the town hall," van de Waal, "Some Possible Sources," 183.

22. Ibid.

23. Christopher White identified the figure as Neptune in the first edition of *Rembrandt as an Etcher: A Study of the Artist at Work* (London: A. Zwemmer, 1969, 90), but in the second edition (New Haven, CT: Yale University Press, 1999, 101), he modified that description, simply referring to the figure as a river god. Winternitz improbably identified the old man as Adam, asserting that Rembrandt was both alluding to the tradition of Jesus as the "new Adam," and commenting on a complex set of questions surrounding the issue of predestination. Winternitz, "Rembrandt's 'Christ presented to the People,'" 186–87.

24. Carroll, "Rembrandt as Meditational Printmaker," 593.

25. Ibid., 597–99. Carroll also suggested that the intimations of damnation that the openings introduce "serve as a proleptic allusion to that later moment in the Passion story when Christ descends into Hell." She noted that Calvin actually linked the trial of Jesus with the Harrowing of Hell, two events that indicate "Christ's acceptance of both the verdict and punishment that should be ours" (599–600).

26. "Perhaps . . . the imposing and incipiently ruinous architecture is intended to imply that Christ's condemnation marks the climax of the destructive power of the law—when Christ himself receives its curse—and at the same time the inauguration of its demise through Christ's redemptive sacrifice" (ibid., 601).

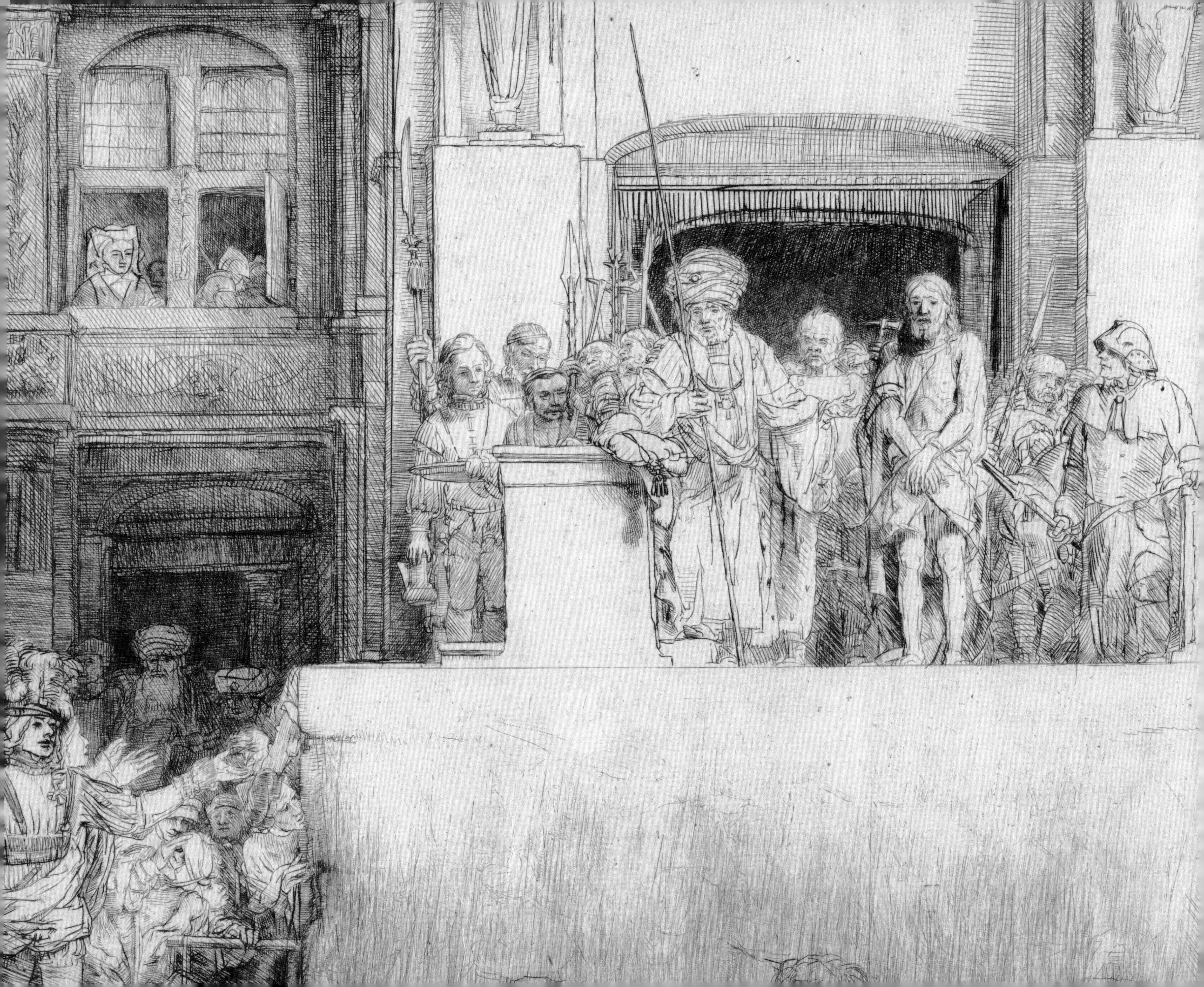

52–53. The Crucifixion

52. Crucifixion: Small Plate

B. 80 (H. 123 [1634], Mz. 202 [1634], NHD 143)
Etching (with plate tone)
Signed in the plate: *Rembrandt F.*
c. 1635
State I of III
Sheet: 10.7 × 7.2 cm; plate mark: 9.5 × 6.7 cm
Verso: in graphite, *Christus am Kreuz Kleine platt; B80; 56*

Provenance:
Associated American Artists Inc., New York, NY, 1969
Feddersen, Elkhart, IN, 1991
Snite Museum of Art
Acc. No.: 1991.025.051

Plate survives:
Private collection, USA

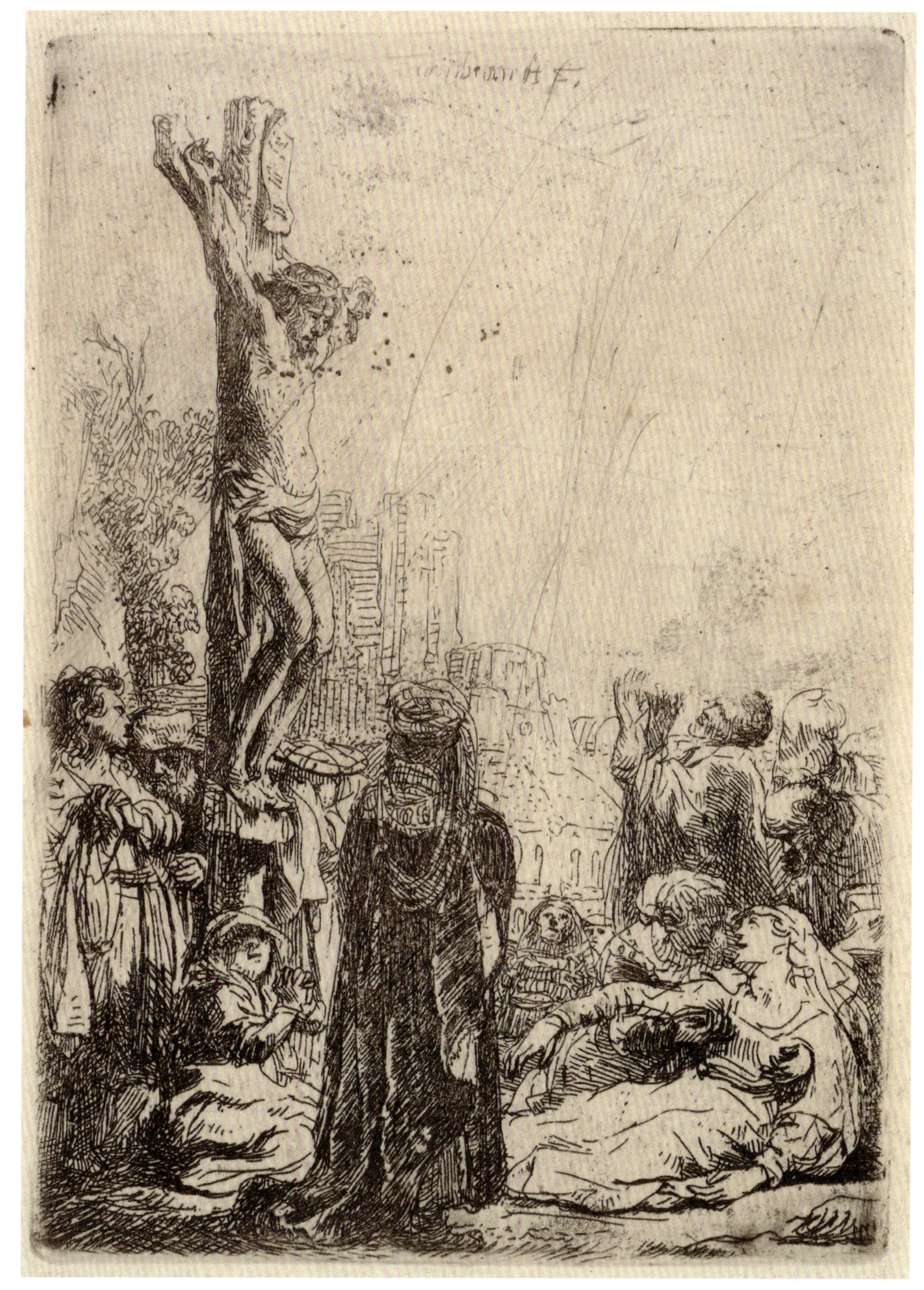

PLATE 52

53. *Christ Crucified between the Two Thieves: Oval Plate*

B. 79 (H. 173, Mz. 215, NHD 196)
Etching and drypoint
c. 1641
State I of III
Sheet: trimmed to rectangular sheet, 13.6 × 10.0 cm (height and width of the oval)
Verso: fragment of an unidentified collector's mark; and, in graphite, upper center, *B79II;* bottom, *N263; C/245; B79; 29.*

Provenance:
Kennedy Galleries Inc., New York, NY, 1976
Feddersen, Elkhart, IN, 1991
Snite Museum of Art
Acc. No.: 1991.025.050

The plate does not survive.

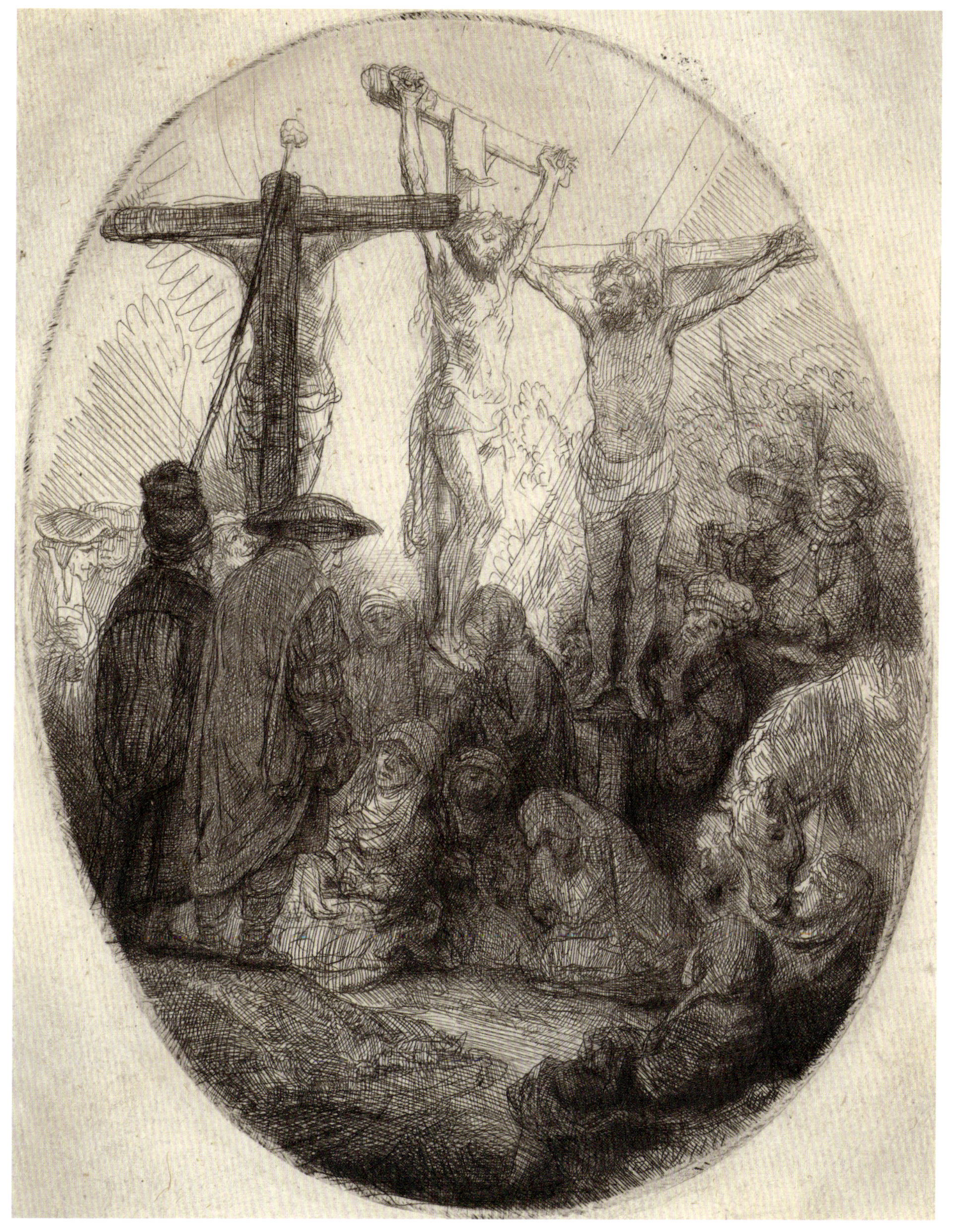

PLATE 53

Rembrandt made two etchings depicting the Crucifixion, as well as a very large drypoint print of the event (B. 78, 1653–55, cat. no. 54). The two smaller etchings, most likely meant for devotional purposes, exhibit significant differences in both form and content. The earlier *Crucifixion: Small Plate* (B. 80, c. 1635, cat. no. 52), the simpler of the two prints, is dominated by four figures. At the upper left corner of the image, Jesus is suspended from a cross set at a sharp angle to the picture plane. A strong diagonal extends down from the crucified Christ to the supine, swooning figure of the Virgin in the foreground at the lower right corner. Behind Mary, a man stands with his arms uplifted in prayer. Another man dominates the center of the composition, in the foreground. Dressed in a turban and long robes, he is seen from the back as he gazes at the events unfolding before him.

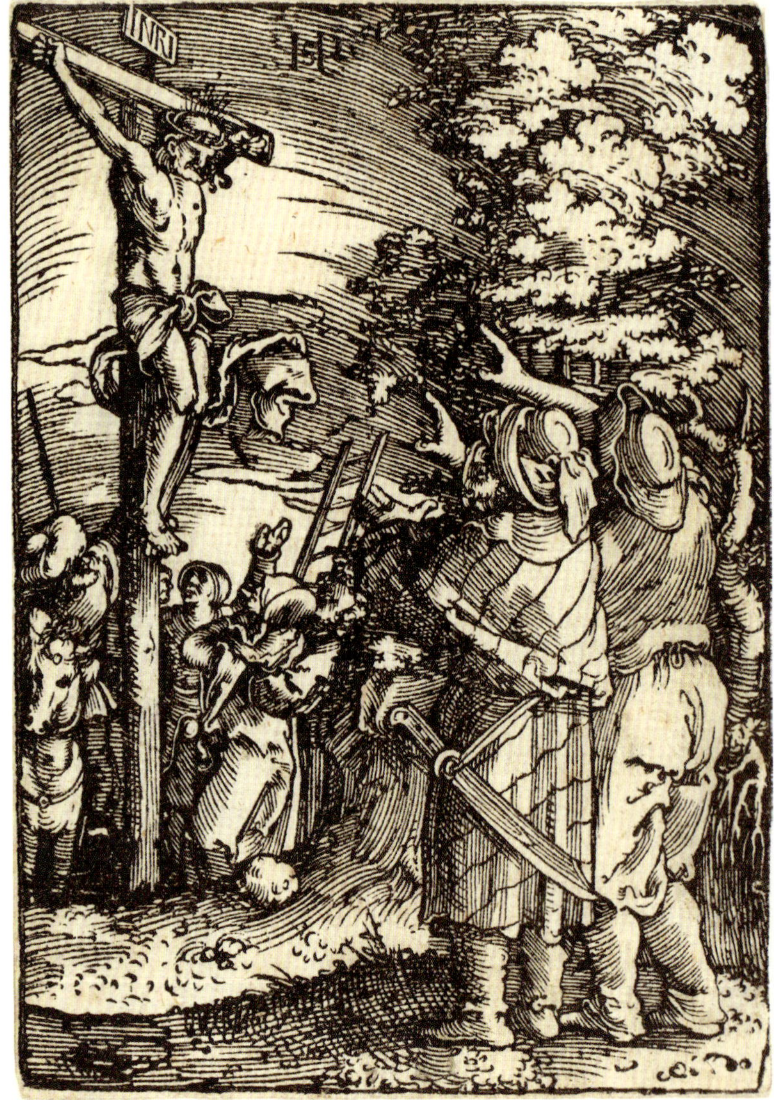

FIGURE 1. Hans Sebald Beham, *Crucifixion*, woodcut, 1520–35. *Photo: Courtesy of the National Gallery of Art, Washington, DC.*

Most of the scholarship regarding this etching has focused on possible sources for individual elements in the composition. Ludwig Münz proposed a woodcut of Calvary (B. 90) by Hans Sebald Beham (fig. 1) dating from the 1520s or 1530s as the thematic prototype for the print, but this idea has not found much support.[1] B. J. P. Broos's suggestion that Rembrandt drew upon a somewhat earlier woodcut representation of Calvary by Albrecht Altdorfer (fig. 2) has been more widely accepted, although that connection seems more generic than direct.[2] In fact, one aspect of Beham's print does relate to Rembrandt's etching in a way that the Altdorfer image does not: the touching portrayal of Christ and his grief-stricken mother as they look into each other's eyes. In the Altdorfer print, as in Rembrandt's *Crucifixion*, the Virgin has collapsed to the ground.[3] However, in Altdorfer's image, Mary's body is turned inward, and her face is hidden from the viewer. Furthermore, although Christ

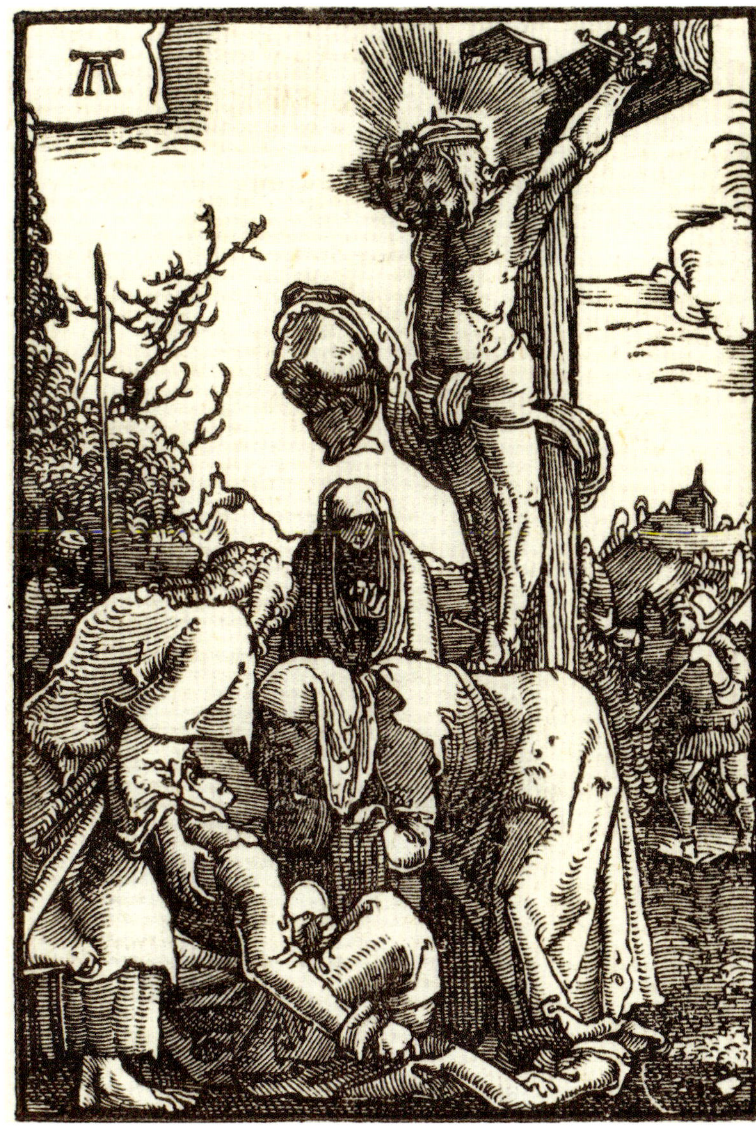

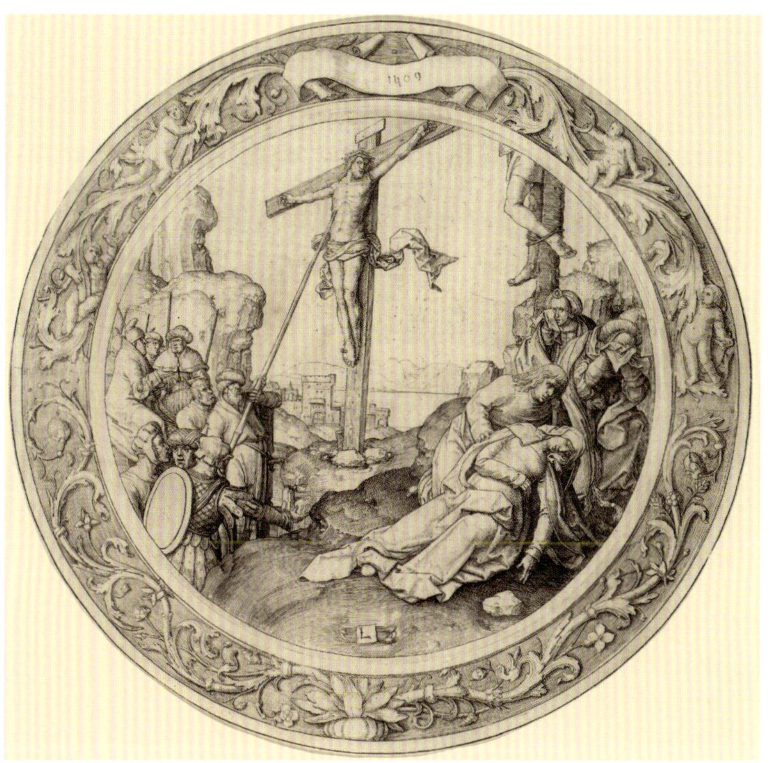

FIGURE 2. Albrecht Altdorfer, *Crucifixion*, woodcut, 1513. *Photo: Courtesy of the National Gallery of Art, Washington, DC.*

FIGURE 3. Lucas van Leyden, *Crucifixion*, engraving, 1509. *Photo: Courtesy of the National Gallery of Art, Washington, DC.*

looks downward, the Virgin's attendants block her view of her son. By contrast, in Beham's woodcut, the Virgin, supported by one of her companions, stands at the base of the cross and looks directly up at her son, who appears to return her gaze. One of the most poignant details in Rembrandt's print is a similarly intense visual link between Jesus and Mary, and it is this emotional bond between mother and son that was probably the basis for what Münz saw as a "thematic" link between the two devotional prints. In Rembrandt's print, of course, the connection is even more powerful than in Beham's, because the Virgin's face and her poignant expression are fully visible. Her lips are parted as if in lamentation or, possibly, to offer up words of comfort to her son during his last moments.

In the 1635 *Crucifixion*, Rembrandt created a remarkably powerful emotional drama on a very small stage. In addition to the tender, sorrowful exchange between Mary and Jesus, the artist presented a wide range of reactions in those gathered on the hilltop, from the solicitous concern of the woman and two elderly Jewish men bending over the Virgin to the soulful agony of the woman who stands at the foot of the cross and hides her face in sorrow, and from the anxious prayers of the disciple on the right who raises his hands toward heaven and the hand-wringing angst of the young St. John, at the left, to the troubled, inward gaze of the old bearded Jew beside him, possibly Nicodemus.

There is one figure, however, whose reaction remains hidden: the richly attired man seen from behind. This dark figure dominates the bottom half of the image, not only because of the dark shadows that cast him into silhouette against the ghostly image of the Temple

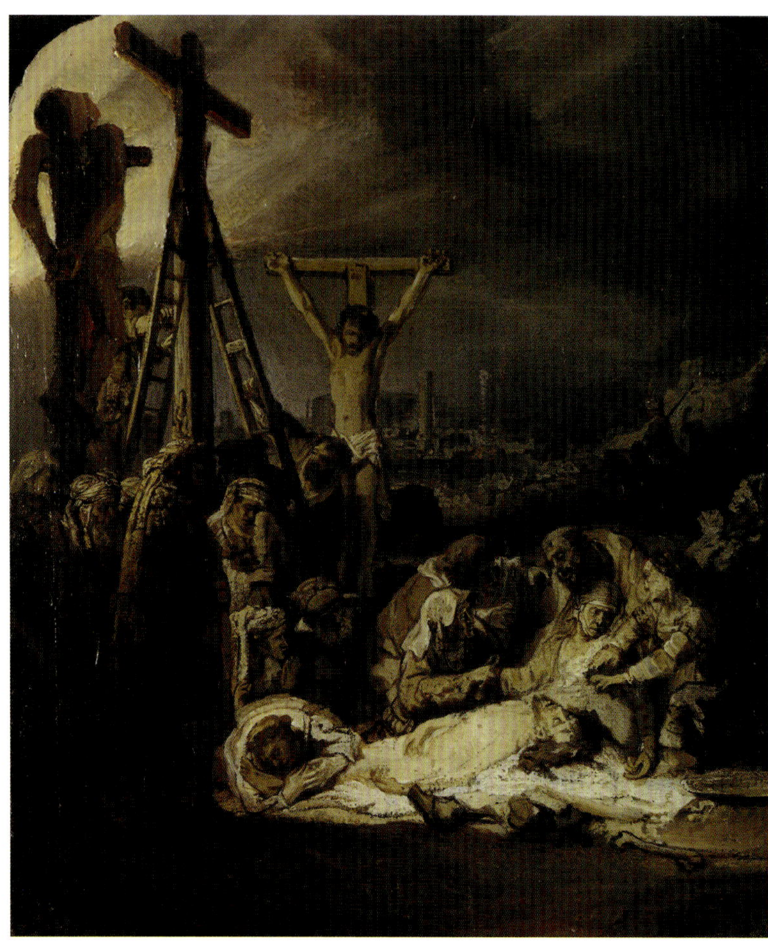

FIGURE 4. Rembrandt, *Lamentation at the Foot of the Cross*, oil on paper, mounted on panel, c. 1634–35. *National Gallery, London. Photo: ©National Gallery, London/ Art Resource, New York.*

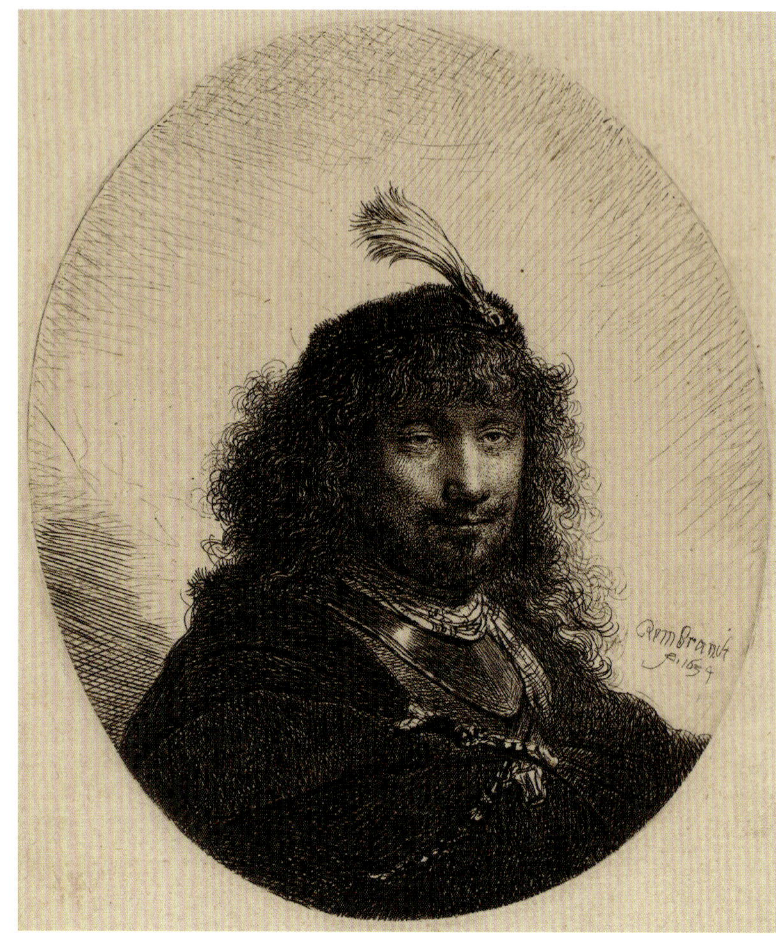

FIGURE 5. Rembrandt, *Self-Portrait with Plumed Cap and Lowered Sabre*, etching, State II, 1634. *Photo: Courtesy of the National Gallery of Art, Washington, DC.*

visible in the background, but also because the praying woman seated at the foot of the cross (possibly the Magdalen) gazes up at him, as does a woman in an ornate costume in the background, seen at a distance, to his right. This prominent man recalls the figure of Joseph of Arimathea in Rembrandt's 1634 painting of *The Descent from the Cross*.[4] Whatever the man's identity, his position in the foreground makes him a surrogate for the print's viewers, drawing them in as additional witnesses to the drama.

The format of Rembrandt's later etching of the subject, *Christ Crucified between the Two Thieves: Oval Plate* (B. 79, cat. no. 53), is an unusual one. Although there are a number of examples of earlier narrative woodcuts and engravings that are circular in design,[5] as well as some woodcuts and engravings that have an oval shape, there are extremely few other oval narrative etchings.[6] Rembrandt's novel use of the oval format for this print appears to have been an experiment that he did not repeat.

Unlike the earlier etching of the Crucifixion, which focused solely on Christ and those gathered around him, the oval etching includes the two thieves who were crucified alongside Jesus.[7] The nearest cross, set virtually parallel to the picture plane, is seen from the back. A long rod with a small sponge at its tip leans against it. The figure on this cross, viewed from behind, is illuminated only from the front, that is, from the area around and beyond Christ, who hangs from the center cross. The etching focuses attention on Jesus in several ways. His cross, which is turned at an angle to the picture plane, is taller than the two that bear the thieves,

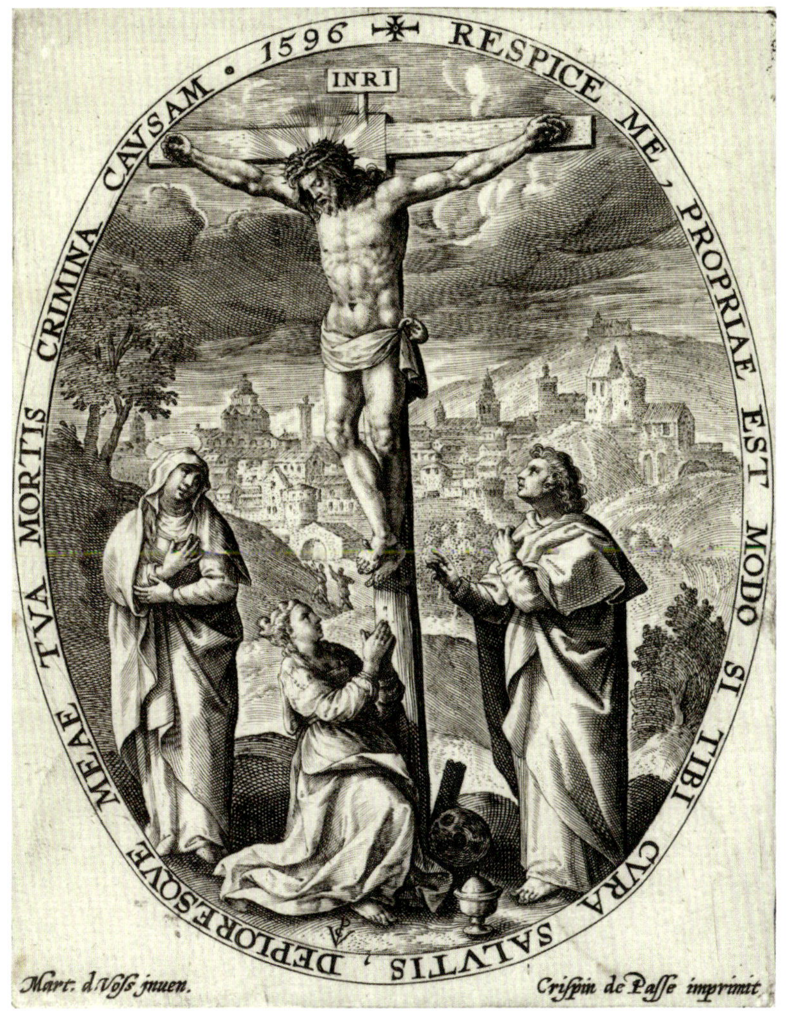

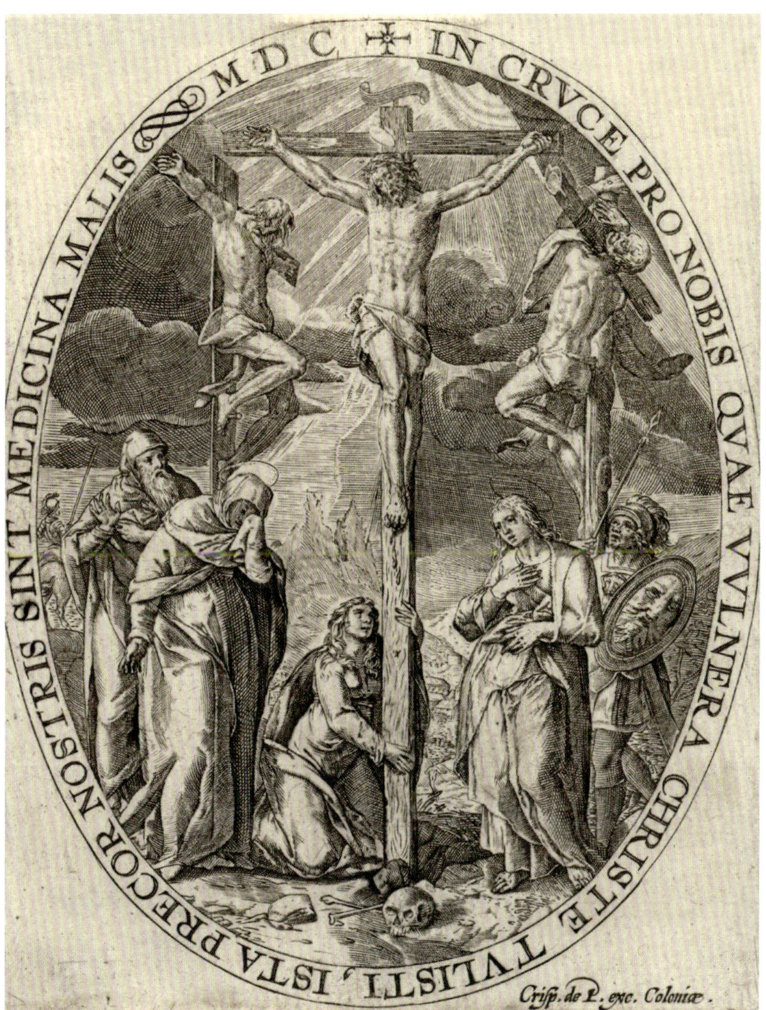

FIGURE 6. Crispijn de Passe the Elder after Maerten de Vos, *Crucifixion*, engraving, 1596. *Rijksmuseum, Amsterdam.*

FIGURE 7. Crispijn de Passe the Elder, *Crucifixion*, engraving, 1600–1601. *Rijksmuseum, Amsterdam.*

and provides the central vertical axis of the image. In addition, Christ's slender body is illuminated so brightly that it seems almost incandescent. Furthermore, although the figures gathered below the crosses face in various directions, the two thieves, hung on parallel crosses opposite each other, both face toward Jesus, reinforcing his central role in both the event and the composition.[8] In contrast to the thieves, Jesus's body hangs lower on his cross, with the result that his arms are stretched upward, forming a sharp "V" that frames his head and the crown of thorns, which presses down upon his brow. Jesus's eyes are closed, and his mouth is slightly open. It is difficult to tell whether he is speaking—either to the figures beside him or to those below him—or whether his closed eyes and slack mouth indicate that he has already succumbed to his fate. The third cross is placed slightly farther back in space, parallel to the picture plane, offering a clear view of the second thief. This man's lips are also parted, and he has turned his head in Jesus's direction. Nevertheless, the man's placement at Christ's left and the fact that his muscular body is cast in shadow suggests that he is the unrepentant thief, the one who mocked his savior.

In the center of the composition, four mourning women have gathered together in a triangular grouping at the foot of the cross. Three of them are seated, but one dark figure stands behind them,

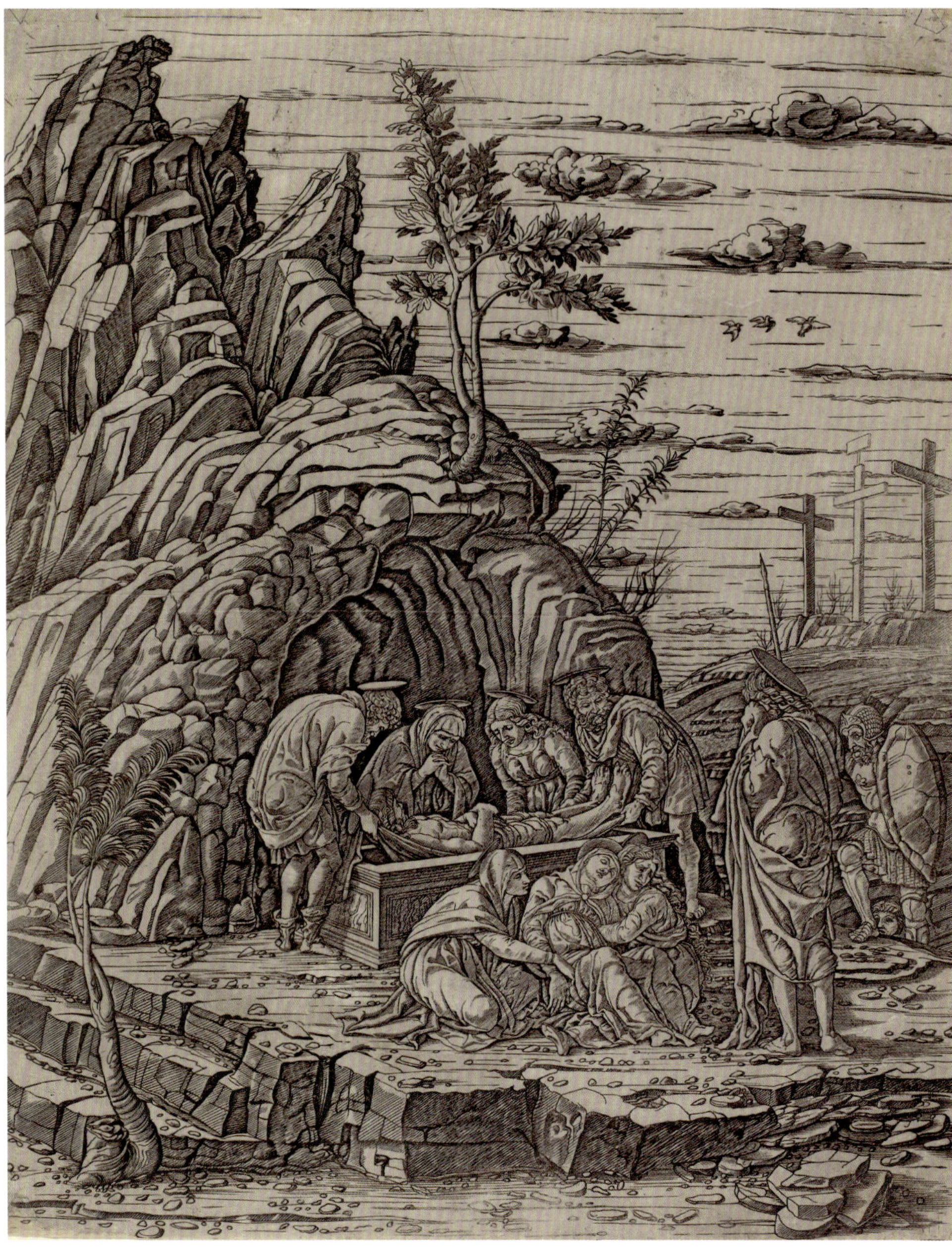

FIGURE 8. Andrea Mantegna, *The Entombment with Three Birds*, engraving, c. 1465. *Photo: Courtesy of the National Gallery of Art, Washington, DC.*

with her face near Jesus's pinioned feet. Her head, nearly hidden beneath a hood or scarf, forms the apex of the triangle. One of the seated women looks up, away from the three crosses, and appears to be speaking or praying. A fifth woman, facing forward, stands just beyond Christ's cross with a sorrowful expression on her face. Whereas the 1635 etching makes the distraught Virgin a major dramatic and compositional element in the scene, the later etching does not even distinguish which of the mourning woman is meant to represent Jesus's mother.

Two elderly Jews stand at the left foreground, their backs to the viewer.[9] While one of them looks up at the crucified men, the other looks over at the woman standing at the foot of the cross. Behind these figures, two other men, one with exaggerated Semitic features, confer; one speaks while the other listens attentively.[10]

Closing off the composition at the lower right side, another woman, a seated *repoussoir* figure in deep shadow, gazes up at Jesus, as does a young man wearing what looks like a keffiyeh.[11] A horse standing nearby bows its head as if to nuzzle or comfort this second observer. Farther back, several men stand just beyond the crucified thief at the right, creating a counterpart to the figures with their backs to the viewer, standing behind the thief at the left. Behind the figures on the right, a thin rod or spear, possibly a reference to the lance of Longinus, is faintly visible in front of some lightly sketched bits of foliage. This time, Rembrandt did not include the tower of the Temple that appeared in the distance in the etching of 1635. Unlike the mourners and observers in the earlier etching, most of the figures in the 1641 print are in shadow.[12] However, lightly sketched linear rays of light enter the scene from the upper right, and the radiance of the upper half of the oval—where the three men are being crucified—seems to create a small pool of light below Christ, where it reflects onto several of the mourning women, as well as the horse.

Although the later print's central focus is clearly the Crucifixion, Ludwig Münz suggested that it alludes to other events in Christ's life and death, as well, including Jesus's promise to the repentant thief that they will meet again in paradise.[13] Furthermore, the horse and attendant, as well as the faintly drawn spear, recall the biblical tale of the conversion of the centurion.[14] In addition, if the elderly Jews seen from behind are Nicodemus and Joseph of Arimathea, then their presence anticipates the descent from the cross and the entombment, events that are also evoked by the mourning women. It is not unlikely that Rembrandt left the narrative open-ended, encouraging viewers to meditate on the events of the Passion from the time of Christ's crucifixion through to the entombment, much as he did in his two etchings depicting the Descent from the Cross (B. 81 II, 1633, cat. no. 55; B. 83, 1654, cat. no. 56). This method of containing successive, related events within a single image was a narrative strategy that Rembrandt employed with some regularity, one that he also used in the later, much larger and more complex print of *The Three Crosses* (B. 78, 1653, cat. 54).

Notes

1. Ludwig Münz, *Critical Catalogue*, vol. 2, cat. 202, 95.

2. B. P. J. Broos, "Rembrandt Borrows from Altdorfer," *Simiolus: Netherlands Quarterly for the History of Art* 4, no. 2 (1970): 100–108. Broos published the Altdorfer print in reverse to illustrate the connection.

3. The swooning Virgin and those who attend her have been associated with a similar grouping in a circular engraving of the Crucifixion from 1509 by Lucas van Leyden (NHD 65) (fig. 3). Hinterding, *Lugt Catalogue*, cat. 66 and 66a, 175, citing J. P. Filedt Kok. However, the Lucas van Leyden print is not a very convincing precedent, especially since the Virgin in that engraving turns her head away from Christ.

Other works that have been linked to the etching are a Rembrandt drawing in the Kupferstichkabinet in Berlin (Inv. no. KdZ 12954; Ben. 108) and the artist's *Lamentation at the Foot of the Cross en brunaille* in the National Gallery, London (fig. 4) (RRP, *Corpus*, A107).

4. The State Hermitage Museum, St. Petersburg (RPP *Corpus*, C49). See the description of Joseph of Arimathea in this catalog's entry on *Descent from the Cross: The Second Plate* (B. 81 II, 1633, cat. no. 55).

5. Lucas van Leyden did a series of nine round engraved Passion prints in 1509, which culminated with the Crucifixion (NHD 57–65). These prints, which measure 29.5 cm across, enclose the narrative scenes in broad decorative borders. It has been suggested that these images could have been intended to serve as patterns for stained glass paintings. Ellen S. Jacobwitz and Stephanie Loeb Stepanek, *The Prints of Lucas van Leyden and His Contemporaries*, exh. cat. (Washington, DC: National Gallery of Art, 1983), cat. 20–22, 78–81, 269, and 270n2.

Dürer also depicted the Crucifixion in a circular print dated to about 1519 (TIB 23). This print has been associated with a letter of 1519 from Dürer to Georg Spalatin, a humanist and reformer, in which the artist reported sending Spalatin two prints of the Crucifixion pulled from an engraving in gold. The size of the print (only 3.7 cm across) and the documentation associated with it have led scholars to hypothesize that the print was pulled from an engraved gold medallion that was later incorporated into the ornamentation of the wheel pommel of a sword made for the Emperor Maximillian I. John Rowlands, *Drawings by German Artists and Artists from German-Speaking Regions of Europe in the Department of Prints and Drawings at the British Museum: The Fifteenth Century, and the Sixteenth Century by Artists Born before 1530* (London: British Museum Press, 1993), cat. 212, 95. This print was copied several times in the sixteenth century by members of the Wierix family.

For a sampling of other secular and religious subject matter produced in circular format prints in the sixteenth century, see the work of the so-called Master S (ac. 1500–25) (HD, vol. 13) and Allaert Claesz. (ac. 1520–30) (HD 10, 15, 68, 75, 116, 117, and 122). These circular engravings are quite small, 5–9 cm. in diameter, and were probably intended to serve as patterns for badges or the embellishment of metalwork, armor, or weapons.

6. By far the most common use of the oval format was for portrait engravings in which the sitter was depicted within an oval frame. Rembrandt himself made an etched oval self-portrait in 1634 (B. 23 II) (fig. 5).

Hendrick Goltzius, a printmaker who prided himself on his almost perverse inventiveness, made just a very few woodcuts and engravings in an oval format. These included a series of chiaroscuro woodcuts of the gods (1588–89, NHD 294–300) and engravings of Apollo (1588, NHD 151), Mars, and Venus (Jacob Matham after Goltzius, c. 1601, NHD [Goltzius] 597–98) and "The Four Disgracers" (NHD 325–28) after Cornelis Cornelisz. van Haarlem. These prints all measure about 35.5 × 26.5 cm, and are images of single or paired figures, not narratives. Goltzius also created a handful of considerably smaller oval engravings of single religious figures.

Two series of engravings by Crispijn de Passe the Elder represent an exception to the general principle that narratives were not presented in an oval format. The first is a series of twelve prints dedicated to the Life and Passion of Christ, created by Crispijn in 1596 after designs by Maerten de Vos (HD 68–79 [Crispijn de Passe

Oude]). The ovals are engraved on rectangular plates that measure about 13.5 × 10.3 cm. The second series, consisting of twenty plates dedicated to the Passion, was done in 1600–1601. These images, like the earlier ones, are engraved on rectangular plates, this time measuring about 14 × 11 cm. Crispijn signed all twenty of the plates as the publisher. In two cases, he credited other artists as the designers of the images (*The Entombment* is credited to Barocci, and *Three Women at the Tomb* is given to Jacques Bellange), and in seven others he claimed credit for engraving the plate. The 1596 series includes an image of Christ on the cross flanked by the Virgin and St. John, with the Magdalen praying at the base of the cross (HD 78) (fig. 6). The 1600 series includes a representation of Christ on the cross between the two thieves (HD 148) (fig. 7). In this image, the Magdalen grasps the base of Christ's cross, while the Virgin and Nicodemus stand to her right, and John the Evangelist and Longinus stand to her left.

Unlike the frame around the Rembrandt etching of *Christ Crucified*, the oval frames surrounding the individual scenes in Crispijn's series contain inscriptions that indicate the manner in which the narrative is to be approached. Also, Rembrandt's etching does not bear any real resemblance to either the Crucifixion in Crispijn's 1596 series or the Three Crosses from his 1600 series. It is therefore highly unlikely that Crispijn's engravings served as models or even significant inspirations for Rembrandt's etching.

7. In a later, larger drypoint (B. 78, 1653–1655, cat. no. 54) Rembrandt also depicted Christ crucified between the two thieves.

8. The alignment of the three crosses is similar to that in Rembrandt's *Lamentation at the Foot of the Cross en brunaille* of around 1635 (fig. 4).

9. Ludwig Münz (*Critical Catalogue*, vol. 2, cat. 215, 100) suggested that the image of the standing male with a broad flat hat, the figure turned toward the group of mourning women, could have been inspired by Mantegna's *Entombment with Three Birds* (TIB 2, c. 1465) (fig. 8).

10. The latter two figures recall Rembrandt's inclusion in other etchings of a pair of Jewish figures at the edge of a composition, at least one of whom is not fully engaged in the central event, but turns aside, instead, to remark on the events before them. See, for example, Rembrandt's etchings of *Presentation in the Temple: Oblong Print* (B. 49, ca. 1639–1641, cat. no. 26), *Christ Appearing to the Apostles* (B. 89, 1650, cat. no. 61), and *Peter and John Healing the Cripple at the Gate of the Temple* (B. 94, 1659, cat. no. 66).

11. In the first state of the print, this figure appears to be a boy. In the second state, the head covering looks more like a headscarf, and the figure could be read as a woman, a companion to the other woman shrouded in shadow at the right lower corner, in the foreground. If the horse is accompanying a woman, then any connection to the story of the conversion of the centurion seems unlikely.

12. The shadows on the first state and early impressions of the second state are considerably denser than those that appear in the Snite Museum's example. Although a great deal of the drypoint burr is absent from the Snite Museum's impression, the lines that remain are still quite crisp.

13. Luke 23:42–43: "Then he [one of the criminals on the side of Jesus] said, 'Jesus, remember me when you come into your kingdom.' Jesus answered him, 'I tell you the truth, today you will be with me in paradise.'"

14. Ludwig Münz (*Critical Catalogue,* vol. 2, cat. 215, 99–100) suggested that the print illustrates one of two possible moments: Christ's address to the two thieves (Luke 23:39–43) or the conversion of the centurion (Mark 15:39). In support of the latter, he notes the presence of the figure holding a horse in the right foreground, presumably the groom of the centurion who had been enlightened by Christ.

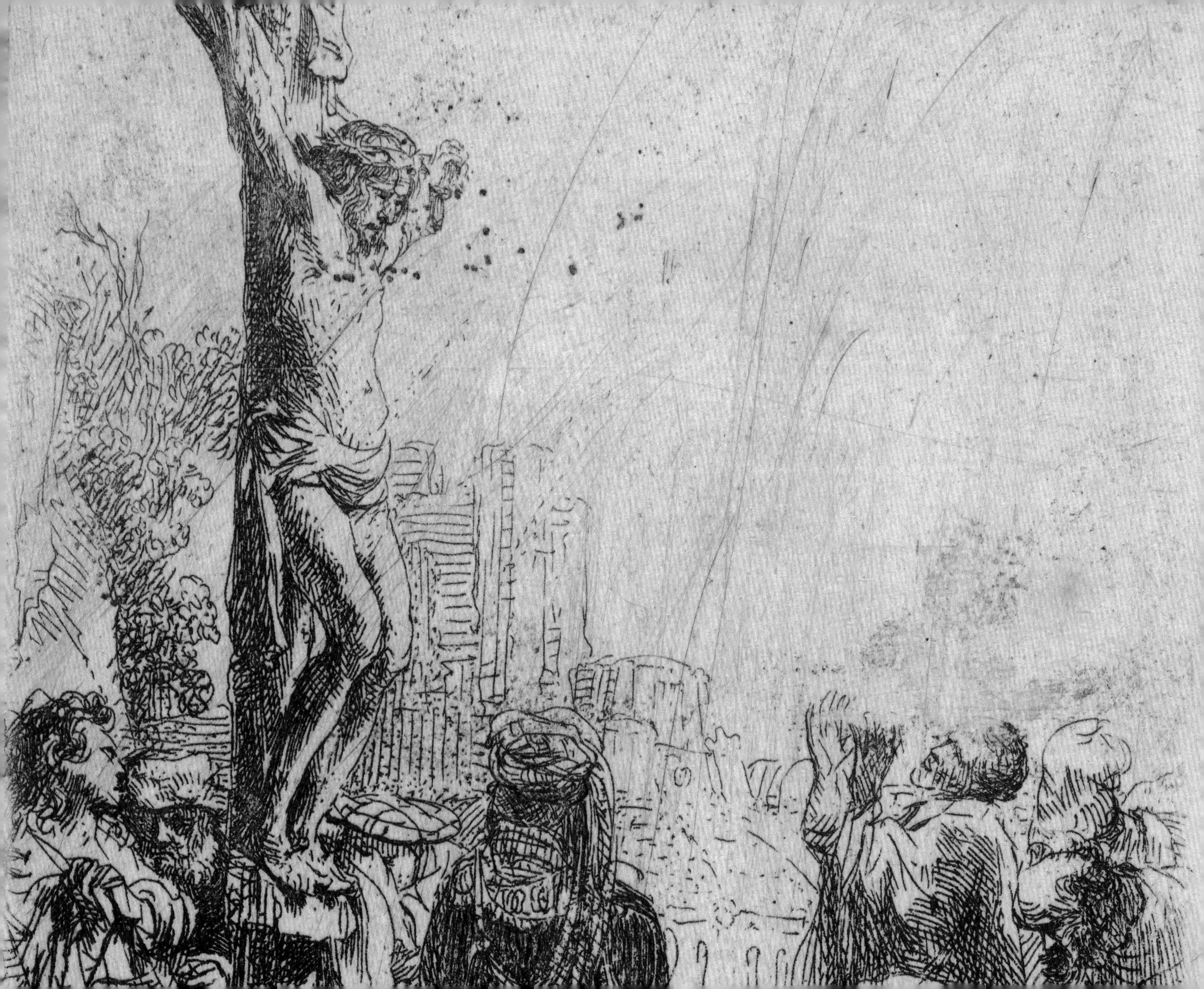

54. *Christ Crucified between the Two Thieves: "The Three Crosses"*

B. 78 (H. 270, Mz. 223, NHD 274)
Drypoint and burin
Signed in the plate: *Rembrandt f. 1653*[1]
c. 1653–55
State V of V
Sheet: 39.1 × 45.7 cm; plate mark: 38.6 × 45.2 cm
Recto: lower left corner, black ink, collector's stamp (Lugt 2849, George Hibbert)
Verso: collector's mark, in black ink, *JB* (Lugt 1419–1420, John Barnard); *major* (Thomas Major) (not in Lugt)
Written in the plate, bottom center: *Frans Carelse excudit*

Provenance:
John Barnard (1715–90)
Barnard Sale, London, May 7, 1798, lot 80 [for 10 shillings 6 pence][2]
Possibly Thomas Major (1720–99)[3]
George Hibbert (1757–1837)
Hibbert Sale, London, May 1, 1809, lot [for 2 pounds, 3 shillings]
Harrods, London, 1977
Feddersen, Elkhart, IN, 1991
Snite Museum of Art
Acc. No.: 1991.025.049

The plate does not survive.

Rembrandt's *Christ Crucified between the Two Thieves: "The Three Crosses"*[4] was created in the mid-1650s, a period of intense technical and spiritual exploration by the artist.[5] The large print was executed almost entirely in drypoint, an unusual medium for a work of this scale,[6] and Rembrandt carried the plate through four states, the first three of which are almost identical.[7] The work depicts the final moments of the Crucifixion:

> And it was now about the sixth hour, and there was darkness over the whole land until the ninth hour, while the sun's light failed; and the curtain of the temple was torn into two. Then Jesus, crying with a loud voice, said, "Father, into thy hands I commit my spirit!" And having said this, he breathed his last. Now when the centurion saw what had taken place, he praised God, and said, "Certainly this man was innocent!" And all the multitudes who assembled to see the sight, when they saw what had taken place, returned home beating their breasts. (Luke 23: 44–48)[8]

In the first three states of this print, which differ significantly from the fourth state and the Snite Museum's final fifth-state version of the scene, the biblical story of the conversion of the centurion Longinus plays a major role (fig. 2). The converted soldier kneels at the center of the composition, with his back turned toward the viewer. His arms are outstretched in a gesture of amazement as he gazes at the cross from which Jesus is suspended.[9] Behind the centurion, a small group of mounted soldiers holding lances and swords appears to be indifferent to the event taking place before them. Other figures mill about in the darkness in the left background.[10]

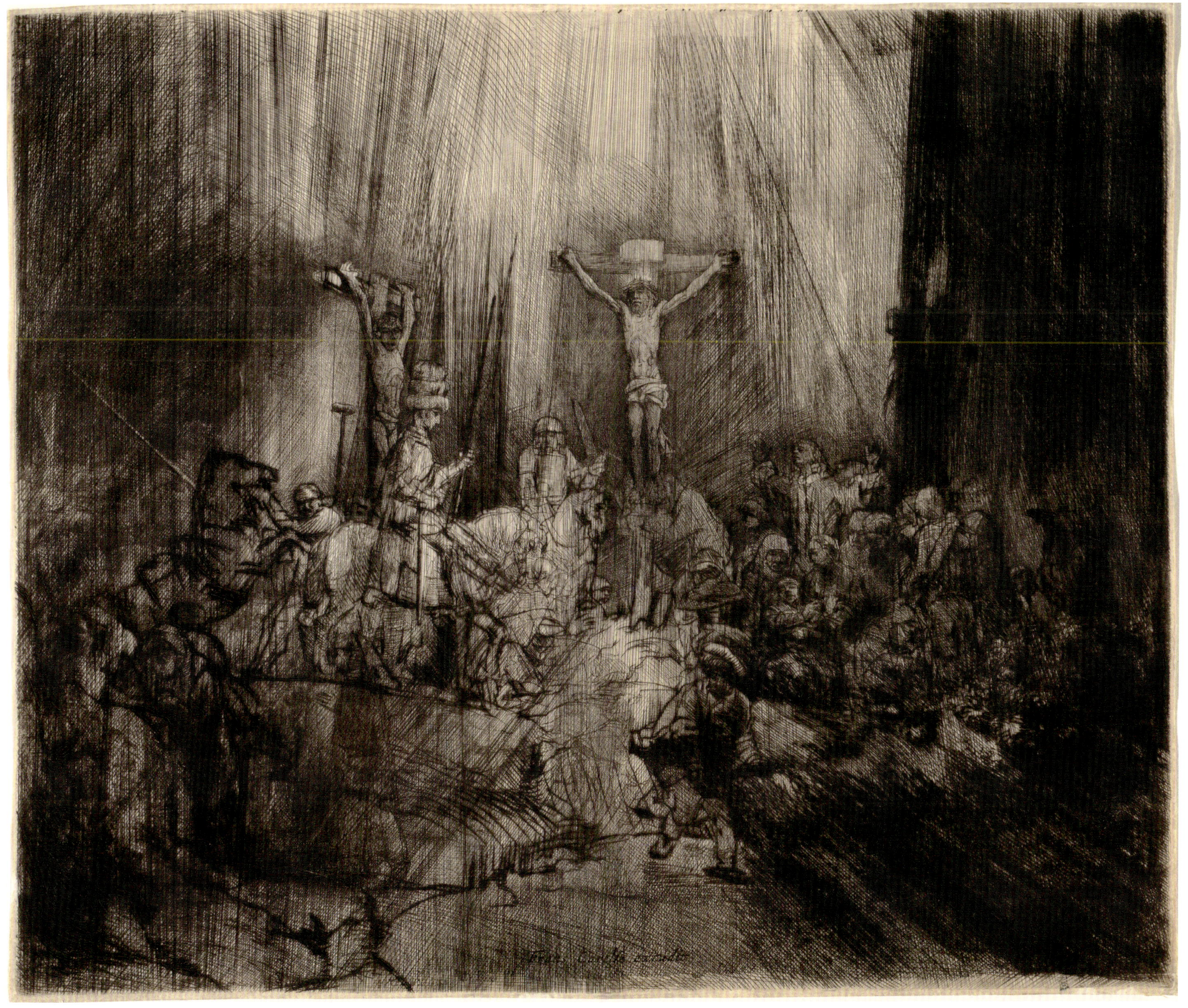

PLATE 54

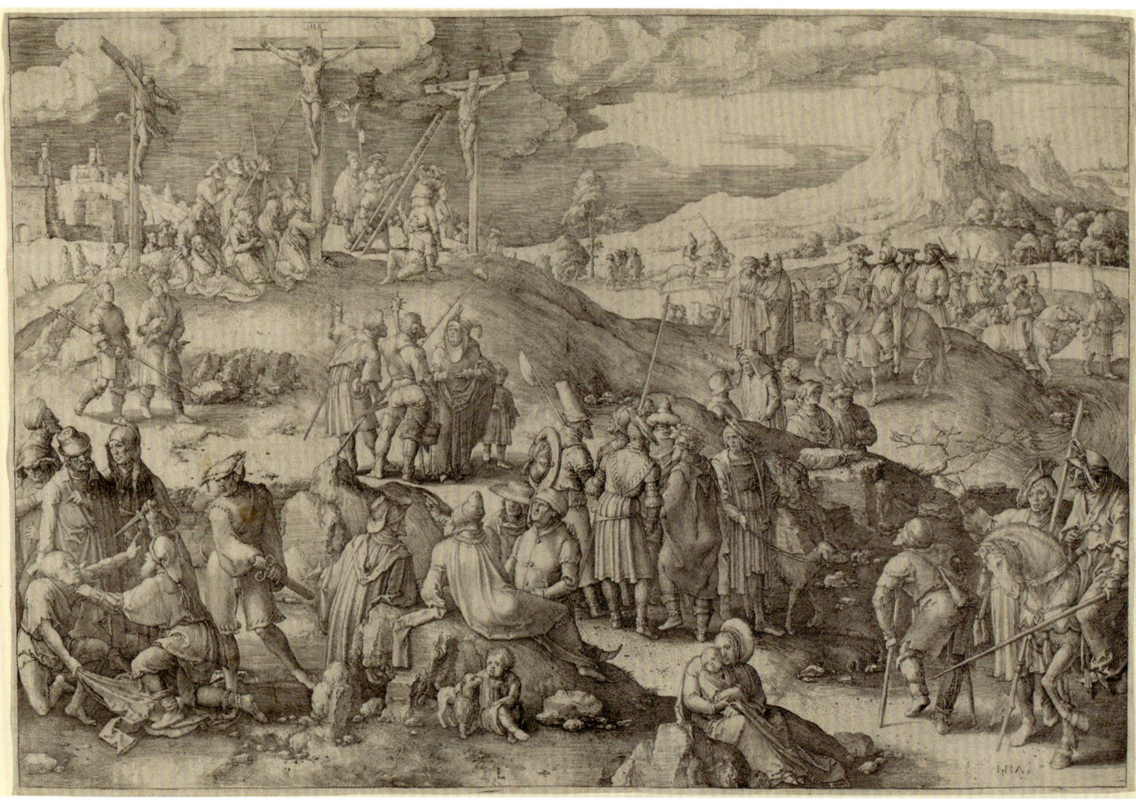

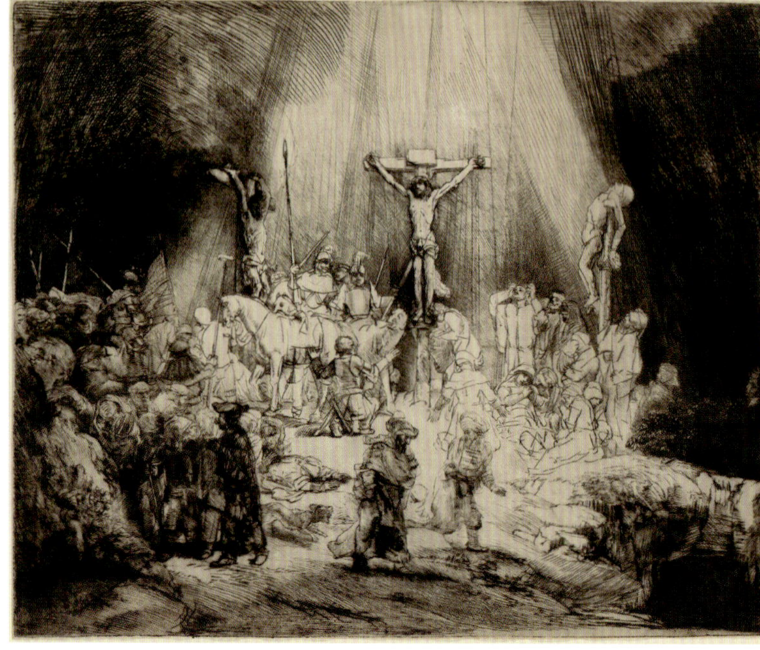

FIGURE 1. Lucas van Leyden, *Golgotha*, engraving, 1517. *Photo: Courtesy of the National Gallery of Art, Washington, DC.*

FIGURE 2. Rembrandt, *Christ Crucified between the Two Thieves: "The Three Crosses,"* drypoint, State II, 1653. *The Pierpont Morgan Library & Museum, New York, New York, RvR 123. Photography by Graham S. Haber.*

In front of this group, a cluster of mourning disciples, also cast into shadow, moves slowly away from the scene of the crucifixion.[11] Two of them cover their eyes in a classic gesture of grief. Right behind the group, a figure lies prostrate on the ground, overcome by sorrow. In the center foreground, two bearded and turbaned men converse as they walk to their left, and a small dog, looking back at the fallen mourner, follows after them.[12] Behind them, Mary, overcome by grief, has collapsed to the ground just to the right of the central cross. She is surrounded by disciples who stand and sit nearby, enclosing her in a semicircle of sorrow. She and her attendants face away from the cross on which her son has breathed his last. By contrast, John, who stands directly behind Mary, stares up at Jesus. The young disciple's arms are raised, his hands reaching for the sides of his head in a powerful gesture of grief. At the extreme right foreground of the print is a bush, and below it a dark, cave-like opening that may allude to one of the next stages of the Passion, that is, the Entombment or Christ's Harrowing of Hell.[13]

Within a cone of light, three shafts with rays formed by parallel lines illuminate the two thieves and the central focus of the composition, Jesus's slender body on the middle cross, the vertical axis of the composition. Deep shadows formed by dense cross-hatching fill the outer edges of the space.[14] The crosses that flank Jesus are turned at an angle to the picture surface so that the thieves who hang from them face inward, toward Jesus. The thief to Christ's left is bent backward over the top of the cross in such a way that his chest arches upward and his head hangs back; his face is turned toward the cascading light of heaven. By contrast, the thief to Christ's right in these early states of the print is partially shrouded in shadow, with his face mostly obscured by the darkness.[15] Curiously, Rembrandt has reversed the traditional placement of "good" (on the right side) and "evil" (on the left, or "sinister," side). Jesus himself hangs almost vertically from his cross, his arms raised above him, with his head tilted down. Because the central cross is set absolutely parallel to the picture surface, Jesus's body is presented directly to the viewer. His head, which is turned very slightly to his right, is settled down between his shoulders, and the crown of thorns sits low on his brow. The pertinent biblical

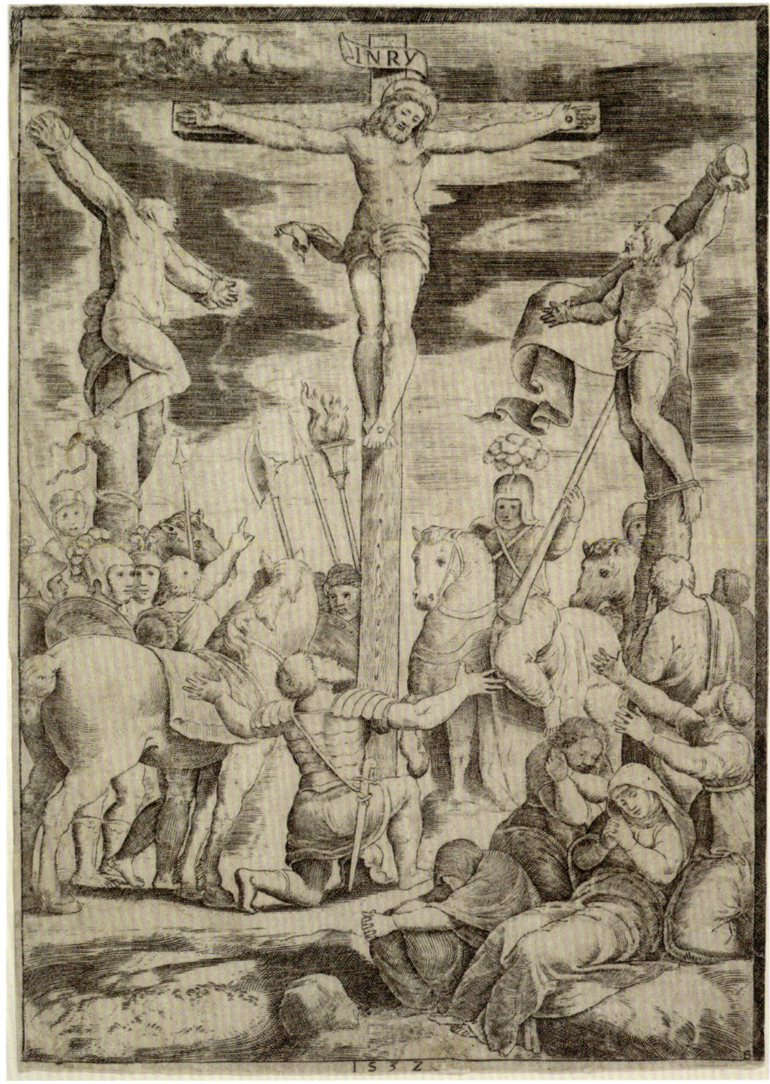

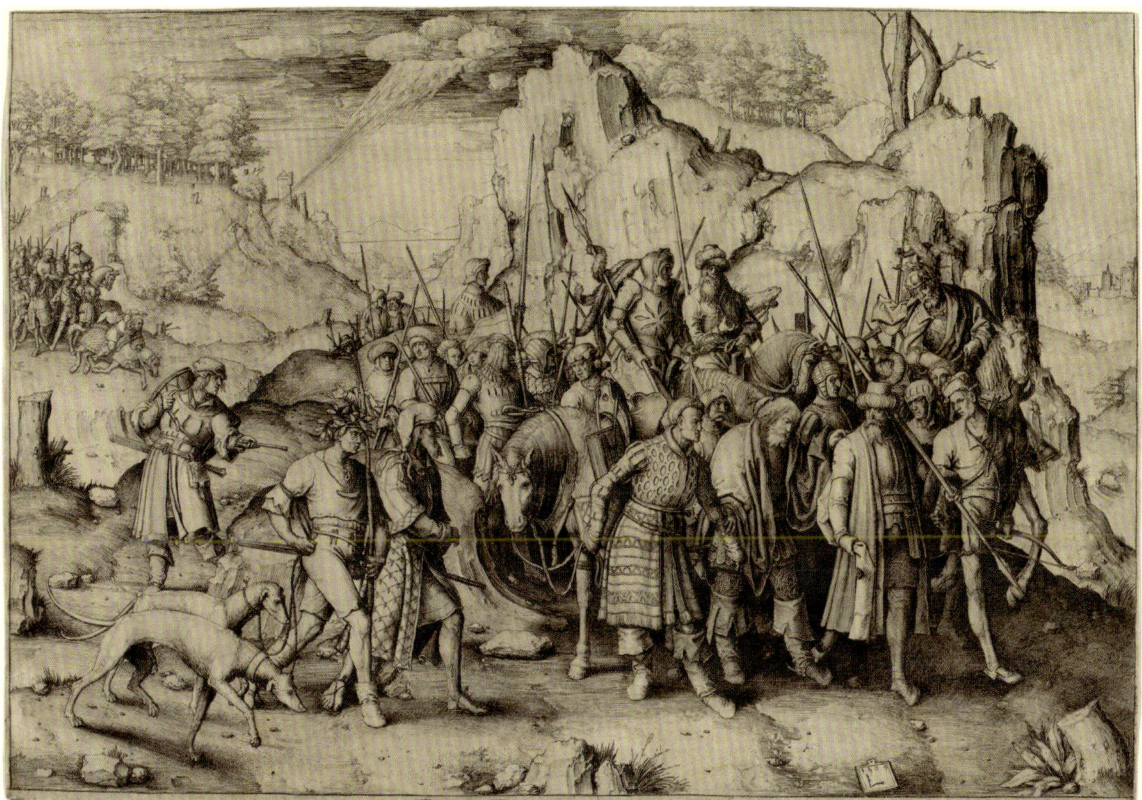

FIGURE 3. Master of the Die, *Conversion of the Centurion*, engraving, 1532. *The Metropolitan Museum of Art, New York, New York, the Elisha Whittelsey Collection.*

FIGURE 4. Lucas van Leyden, *Conversion of Saul*, engraving, 1509. *Photo: Courtesy of the National Gallery of Art, Washington, DC.*

text asserts that the centurion's epiphany occurred only after Jesus had expired, and his death is implied by the fact that many of the observers at the crucifixion have begun to depart.[16] Yet, because Christ's arms are stretched out and upward and his feet are planted firmly on the suppedaneum of the cross, there is a kind of tension in his body that suggests that there is still life within him. In either case, it is clear that the first three states of the print focus on three related subjects: Jesus's crucifixion, the pathos of the mourning disciples' reactions, and the spiritual enlightenment of the centurion.

Beginning with the fourth state, Rembrandt radically changed the appearance and conception of *The Three Crosses*. His reasons for doing so are unknown, but Christopher White speculated that practical considerations may have played a significant role in the decision. Because the plate was done entirely in drypoint, it would have been almost impossible to maintain the quality of the image over an extended run. The characteristic drypoint burr would have been worn down considerably after the first few dozen impressions, reducing the subtlety and depth of the lines and shadows. Accordingly, White proposed that Rembrandt decided not to try to retain the image as he had done when he reworked the plate after the first and second states, but rather to completely redo what was, finally, an exhausted plate, resulting in the radical changes seen in the fourth state.[17]

In order to salvage the plate, Rembrandt burnished out large areas of the plate, paring down the group in the left foreground to just a few crudely drawn figures[18] and eliminating the mounted

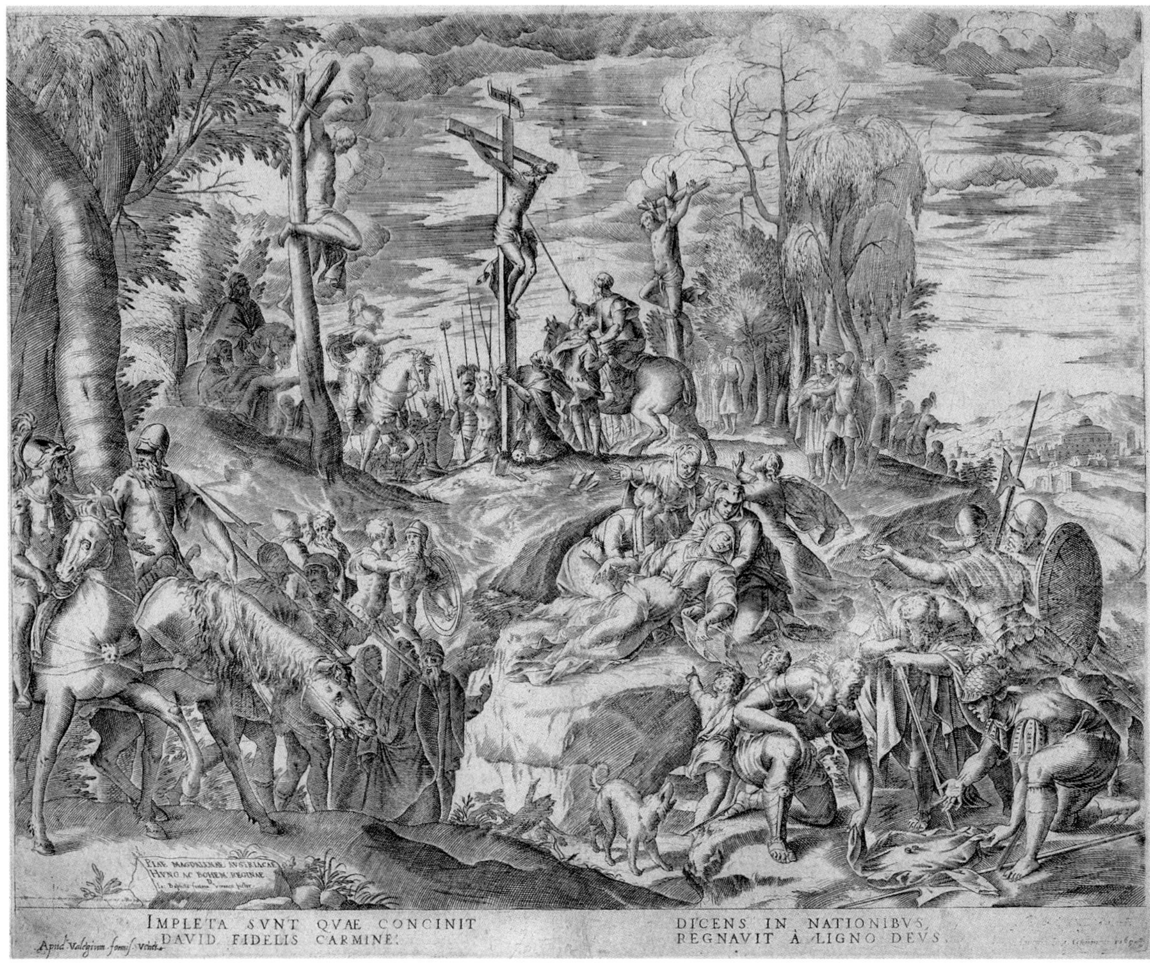

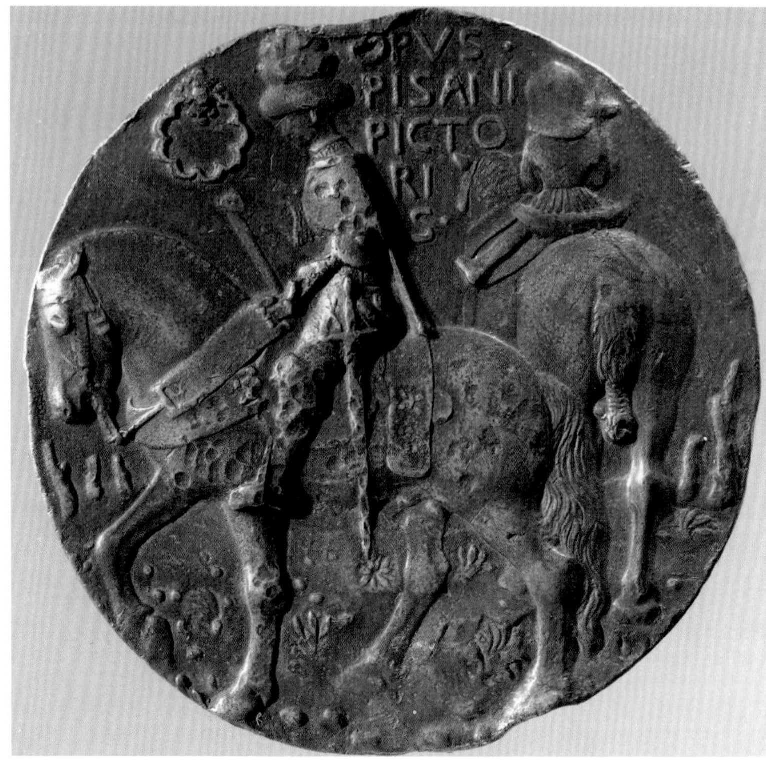

FIGURE 5. Giovanni Battista Fontana after Antonio Tempesta, *Calvary*, engraving, mid-sixteenth-century. *Photo: Gallery Bassenge, Berlin.*

FIGURE 6. Pisanello, *Medal of Gianfrancesco Gonzaga*, obverse, c. 1440. *The Metropolitan Museum of Art, New York, New York, Robert Lehman Collection.*

soldiers in the left background,[19] as well as the cave in the bottom right corner of the image. Most significant, he eliminated the pivotal figure of the centurion, replacing him with a very shadowy figure kneeling in prayer.[20] He added two enigmatic horsemen, both of whom were based on Italian models,[21] but erased one of the turbaned figures in the foreground. Whereas the two bearded figures in States 1–3 appear to be walking and talking, the one remaining figure in State IV (and State V) appears to be actually fleeing in haste from the horror of the crucified men behind him. Rembrandt also reworked the prostrate figure of the Virgin Mary and the mourners surrounding her, abandoning the light, linear style that he had used to describe them in the first three states in favor of a richer, darker, more modeled approach. Mary is depicted in a more frontal pose. St. John's gesture has also been modified; he now stands with his arms thrown wide open in an even more demonstrative gesture of grief.

Alterations to the figure of Jesus dealt chiefly with lighting effects: Rembrandt sharpened the silhouette of the crown of thorns against a small halo of light emanating from Christ's head, hollowed out his eyes, reinforced the contours of his body, intensified the shadows surrounding him, and cast his loincloth and legs into shadow. Finally, Rembrandt reconsidered the broader disposition of light and dark in the composition as a whole. The side shadows, which were primarily gathered into the upper corners of the print in the first three states, now press in toward the center, completely enveloping the cross and thief on Christ's left. In this way, Rembrandt returned to a more traditional representation of the "bad" thief: the criminal appears on Jesus's left and has now been denied the light of heaven.[22] As Michael Zell noted, these deep shadows seem to evoke the biblical vision of the curtain in the Temple torn asunder as the earth was plunged into darkness.[23] In its final incarnation, *The Three Crosses* seems to be more about pathos and uncertainty than enlightenment and hope. Although the body of Christ emerges from the shadows with an even greater clarity in the fourth state, the revelatory promise of salvation alluded to in the first three states by means of the spreading shower of heavenly light and the conversion of the centurion is absent. In its place are an oppressive cascade of darkness and the enigmatic equestrian, a figure that seems to do nothing more than wait impassively for whatever will ensue.

The Snite Museum's impression of this work is from the very rare fifth state. This version, which certainly dates from after Rembrandt's death, shows no significant alterations from the fourth state beyond the inclusion of the crudely scratched inscription *Frans Carelse excudit* ("Frans Carelse printed [this]") in the lower center section. Little is known about Carelse. He was a printer, publisher, and parchment seller who was born in Louvain, but who is recorded as living on Servetsteeg in Amsterdam by 1665.[24] In 1678, he was residing on Leyste Straet by the Koningsplein in Amsterdam.[25] He died in the city five years later, and was buried in the Oude Kerk.[26] *The Three Crosses* is the only Rembrandt plate known to be printed by Carelse. Although it is not known how the plate came into his possession, Carelse reprinted several plates by other artists that had initially been published by print seller and art lover Clement de Jonghe,[27] and de Jonghe had strong ties to Rembrandt, who had made an etched portrait of him in 1651.[28] Furthermore, at the time of de Jonghe's death in 1677, he owned seventy-four of Rembrandt's original plates.[29] He may also have purchased the plate for *The Three Crosses* from the artist and then sold it to Carelse, or de Jonghe may have acted as an intermediary between Rembrandt and Carelse.[30] However Carelse came to own the plate, it seems that he printed only a handful of impressions from it before disposing of it.[31]

Although the Snite Museum's print exhibits a prominent veil of plate tone, the etching as a whole is not a very dark impression. As a result, details that are lost in some of the most heavily inked examples of the fourth state are clearly visible in the fifth, for example, the man with the rearing horse in the left background. At the same time, some of the crispness of the cross-hatching in the shadows around the figure of Christ has broken down, suggesting that the plate was nearing the end of its useful life.

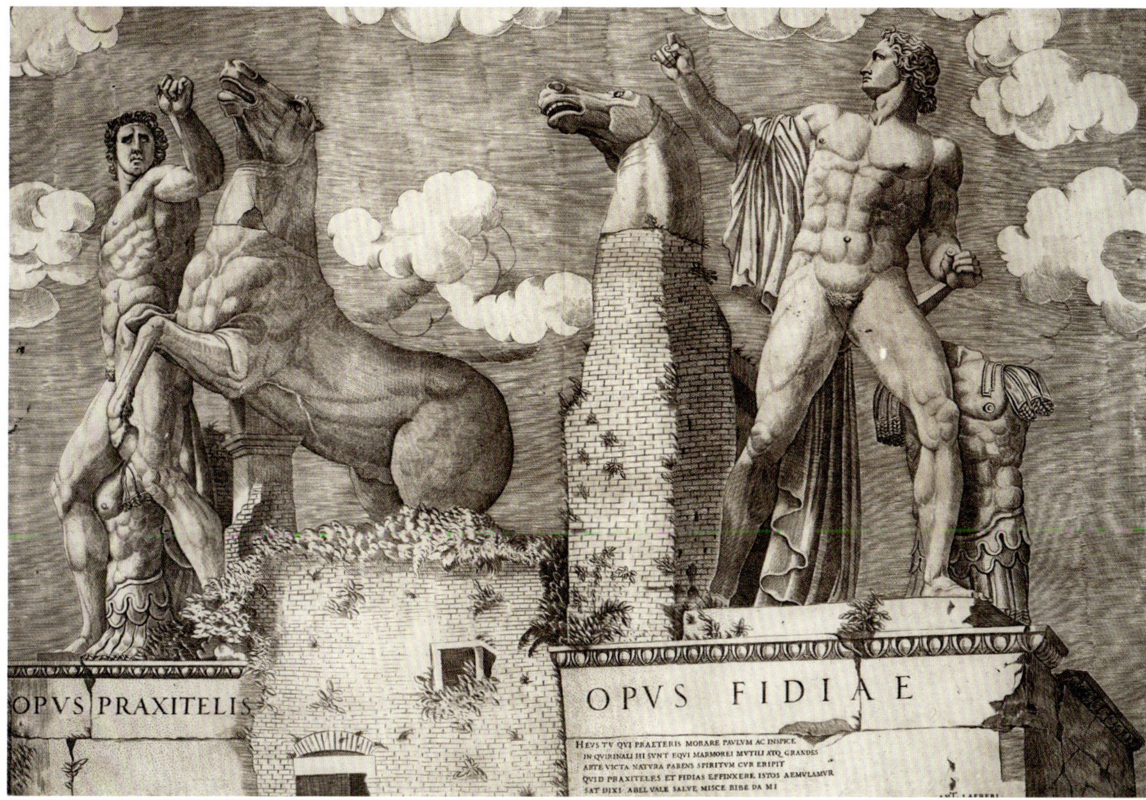

FIGURE 7. Anonymous, *The Horse Tamers*, engraving, 1538–45. *University of Chicago Library, Chicago, Illinois.*

Notes

1. Before Erik Hinterding's authoritative investigation of Rembrandt watermarks, it had been assumed on stylistic grounds that State IV of *The Three Crosses* was executed around 1660, that is, about seven years after the first three states (see, for example, White and Boon, 43). However, Hinterding was able to show that impressions of the greatly altered fourth state were printed on the same paper as the first three states. This suggests that the radical revisions that appear in the fourth state (and also in the fifth state) were actually carried out shortly after the completion of the third state, which would have

been prior to 1655, the date of the equally large *Christ Presented to the People* (B. 76, cat. no. 51). Hinterding, *Rembrandt as an Etcher: The Practice of Production and Distribution*, vol. 1 (Ouderkerk aan den IJssel, Netherlands: Sound and Vision Publishers, 2006), 128.

2. *Catalogue of the Superb and Entire Collection of Prints and Books of Prints of John Barnard, Esq . . . which will be sold by Auction under the Direction of Mr. Thomas Philipe . . . on Monday, the 16th of April, 1798, and Twenty-six days following, Sundays, Excluded* (London: G. Hayden, [1798]), unpaged., "Nineteenth Day's Sale. Rembrandt—New Testament." "110 Ditto [*The Three Crosses*]*—the fifth impression, or third from the second plate, with the name Frans Caralle* [*sic*], *excudit* __ 80." In the left margin "10.6," i.e., 10 shillings 6 pence. Accessed February 24, 2017, http://babel.hathitrust.org/cgi/pt?id=njp.32101066471283;view=1up;seq=126.

This print may have been purchased by Thomas Major, an English engraver, and later sold at the posthumous auction of his collection on January 30, 1801 (see note 3 below). Rembrandt prints were purchased at the Hibbert sale by dealer William Eisdaile and by the Duke of Buckingham. *Catalogue of a Superb Assemblage of Prints and Books of Prints, Formed by a Gentleman of Distinguished Taste and Judgment . . . Which Will Be Sold by Auction under the Direction of Mr. T. Philipe . . . Monday the 17th of April, 1809, and Fourteen following Days (Sundays Excepted),* (London: n.p., 1809), unpaged, "13th Day [May 1, 1809]. Rembrandt, 70. One—DITTO [Christ Crucified between two thieves, called THE THREE CROSSES], much varied in the composition, Frans Carelle [*sic*] excudit—rare 80." In left margin on f. 116, "2.3," i.e. £ 2 s. 3. Accessed August 9, 2013, http: //gallica.bnf.fr/ark:/12148/bpt6k990277p.

3. Thomas Major was an English engraver known primarily for his landscapes and views of ancient ruins. He was employed as the chief engraver of seals and had the distinction of becoming the first associate engraver of the Royal Academy in 1770. His collection of prints and drawings was sold in London in January 1801. Unfortunately, there is no mention of *The Three Crosses* in the sales catalog, but on January 30, the third day of the sale, 28 etchings by Rembrandt were sold. *A Catalogue of a Large and Valuable Collection of Drawings, Prints & Books of Prints, Belonging to Mr. Thos. Major, (Deceased) . . . to Which Will Be Added . . . Some Etchings & Proofs, by the Late Mr. B. T. Pouncy. Which will be Sold by Auction By Mr. King, at his Great Room, King Street, Covent-Garden . . .* (London: J Barker, 1801), accessed February 24, 2017, http://gallica.bnf.fr/ark:/12148/bpt6k990227z.

4. Two works, a print and a drawing, have been proposed as sources for elements in this composition. The first is the large 1517 engraving of *Golgotha* by Lucas van Leyden (NHD 74) (fig. 1). Lucas embeds the principal theme of the Crucifixion into a much larger landscape, one in which the foreground and middle ground are occupied by groups of onlookers and exotically costumed nonbelievers. The three crosses, the swooning Virgin, and the disciples, all lighter than the figures in the foreground, are set into the left background as if this critical event has already begun to fade into history. Although Rembrandt also included groups of peripheral figures in the early states of his print, his composition is dominated by the central figures of Christ and the two flanking thieves upon their crosses. In addition, Lucas van Leyden depicted a rocky vista at the right background of his composition, whereas Rembrandt did not expand the landscape, choosing instead to focus on Jesus's sacrifice.

Arthur Hind suggested another, even less likely, source of inspiration: a pen and bistre drawing by Antonio Tempesta that is now in the British Museum (BM 1935,1012.3). Hind, "Rembrandt and Recent Acquisitions," *British Museum Quarterly* 10, no. 3 (1936): 87, fig. XXVII. Beyond the placement of the three crosses in the middle distance and the introduction of dramatic chiaroscuro, the drawing and print have nothing in common.

5. During the mid-1650s, Rembrandt endured extraordinary personal and financial strains, but was nonetheless quite productive artistically. In addition to *The Three Crosses*, he created *The Presentation in the Temple in the Dark Manner* (B. 50, 1654), *Descent from the Cross by Torchlight* (B. 83, 1654, cat. no. 56), and *Entombment* (B. 86, 1654, cat. no. 58), all three of which represent powerful experiments in the use of exaggerated chiaroscuro for dramatic effect; the *Christ at Emmaus: Larger Plate* (B. 87, 1654, cat. no. 60), a much more sacramental investigation of this theme than the 1634 version (B. 88, cat. no. 59); the Childhood of Christ series (1654), which includes *Virgin and Child with the Cat and the Snake* (B. 63, cat. no. 36) and *Christ Returning from the Temple with His Parents* (B. 60, cat. no. 40), two unique images; and *Christ Presented to the People: Oblong Plate* (B. 76, 1655, cat. no. 51), a very large print done completely in drypoint. During this period, Rembrandt was also engaged in creating illustrations for Samuel Menasseh ben Israel's mystical, millenarianist

treatise, *Piedra gloriosa de la estatua de Nebuchadunezzar* (B. 36 A, C, and D, 1655, cat. nos. 8, 9, and 10).

6. There is agreement among Rembrandt scholars that the first three states of *The Three Crosses* were done entirely in drypoint. Christopher White (*Rembrandt as an Etcher: A Study of the Artist at Work*, 2nd ed. [New Haven, CT: Yale University Press, 1999], 86) found evidence of cross-hatching done with a burin in the fourth and fifth states of the print. Erik Hinterding (*Rembrandt as an Etcher*, 1:129), however, disputed this claim.

7. The publisher, Frans Carelse, created a fifth state after Rembrandt's death. For information about Carelse, see the text below.

8. Christ's crucifixion is also described in Matthew 27:45–58 and Mark 15:33–43.

9. As Ludwig Münz and many after him have suggested, this motif was inspired by a 1532 print of *The Conversion of the Centurion* (B. 3) by the so-called Master of the Die (fig. 3). Münz, *Critical Catalogue*, vol. 2, cat. 223, 103–4.

10. Münz linked the figure of a mounted soldier seen from the back on the left side of Rembrandt's print to Albrecht Dürer's engraving of *St. George on Horseback* (TIB 54). Although there are similarities between the figures, it seems likely that these are merely coincidental. Münz, *Critical Catalogue*, vol. 2, cat. 223, 103.

11. Münz proposed that this group might have been inspired by figures in Lucas van Leyden's *Conversion of Saul* (NHD 107, 1509) (fig. 4). Münz, *Critical Catalogue*, vol. 2, cat. 223, 104. The groupings, which are reversed, do not resemble each other very closely.

12. Christian Tümpel suggested that the two men in the foreground of *The Three Crosses* might have been inspired by the two soldiers at the center of Giovanni Battista Fontana's mid-sixteenth-century print after Antonio Tempesta's *Calvary*, since these soldiers are also walking toward the right and conversing (B. 14) (fig. 5). Tümpel, *Rembrandt legt*, cat. 103. This connection seems tenuous.

13. The rock tomb that served as Christ's grave was located on the slope of Calvary just below Golgotha. The relationship between the site of the Crucifixion and the tomb is clearly visible in Cornelius Galle's bird's-eye view of Calvary and its surroundings published in Antwerp in 1639. Francisco Quaresma, *Historica, theologica et moralis Terrae Sanctae elucidatio* (Antwerp, 1639), vol. 2, plate at 448, reproduced in Milan Pelc, "Representations and Descriptions of Jerusalem in the Printed Travelogues of the Early Modern Period," in *Visual Constructs of Jerusalem*, ed. Bianca Kühnel, Galit Noga-Banai, and Hanna Vorholts (Turnhout, Belgium: Brepols, 2014), 403, fig. 37.5.

14. Prints from heavily inked plates, such as the example in the Rijksmuseum in Amsterdam (White, *Rembrandt as an Etcher*, fig. 96), make the darkness close in more tightly around the central axis of the composition, investing the image with an ominous aura, while more lightly inked impressions, such as the one in the Teylers Museum, Haarlem (ibid., fig. 102), emphasize the power of spiritual light to dispel the surrounding darkness even at a moment of tragedy and despair, thus offering a more optimistic vision.

The first three states of *The Three Crosses* were printed on a variety of supports, including vellum, white paper, and oriental paper, and exhibit a wide range of inking. The relatively large number of impressions on vellum (14 out of 19 impressions of State I, and 2 out of 9 for State II, according to White and Boon) suggests that Rembrandt intended to market *The Three Crosses* as a luxury print, since vellum was considerably more expensive than paper. A dozen sheets of vellum cost as much as an entire ream of white paper. Erik Hinterding, "The Three Crosses," in Hinterding, Ger Luijten, and Martin Royalton-Kisch, *Rembrandt the Printmaker*, exh. cat. (Chicago and London: Fitzroy Dearborn Publishers, 2000), cat. 73, 302.

15. The good thief is ordinarily placed on Christ's right, and the bad one on his left, or "sinister," side. Rembrandt's inversion is unusual, but not without precedent. Similar lighting appears in Lucas van Leyden's *Golgotha* (fig. 1).

16. Luke 23:44–48.

17. White, *Rembrandt as an Etcher*, 83.

18. The less refined quality of these figures is characteristic of Rembrandt's late style.

19. As White observed, many of the details of the reworking of the plate are hidden, because Rembrandt typically printed very heavily inked impressions of the fourth state. It is only by examining the maculature, now in the British Museum, that one can see precisely how Rembrandt reworked the plate. White, *Rembrandt as an Etcher*, 84–85, fig. 106.

20. This praying figure cannot be the centurion of the previous states because he is not dressed in military garb.

21. As a number of historians have observed (e.g., White, *Rembrandt as an Etcher*, 85), the mounted figure wearing a soft high hat and approaching the crucified Christ from the left is based on the

reverse of Pisanello's mid-fifteenth-century medal of Gianfrancesco Gonzaga (fig. 6), while the figure holding the reins of a rearing horse just behind the mounted figure may have been inspired by the famous statues of the horse tamers on the Capitol (fig. 7) (although the latter seems less evident). Ben Broos speculated that Rembrandt might have actually possessed an example of the Pisanello medal. The 1656 *cessio bonorum* inventory notes that the artist owned a "small case of medallions." Ben Broos, "Rembrandt and his Picturesque Universe," in *Rembrandt's Treasures*, ed. Bob van den Boogert (Zwolle, Netherlands: Waanders, 1999), 123.

22. In his earlier work, *Christ Crucified between the Two Thieves: Oval Plate* (B. 79, 1641, cat. no. 53), Rembrandt situated the three crosses in such a way that the two thieves, placed across from one another, directed the viewer's eye toward Jesus, at the center of the composition. This is not true of the later states of *The Three Crosses*, where the deep shadows at the right of the print hide the bad thief and remove the symmetry of the earlier print.

23. Michael Zell, *Reframing Rembrandt: Jews and the Christian Image in Seventeenth-Century Amsterdam* (Berkeley: University of California Press, 2002), 142. In Zell's view, this reading would have signified the revelation of God's truth. The curtain-like effect is especially true at the right side of the print, where Rembrandt created a dense, vertical wall of shadow.

24. See Hinterding, *Copperplates*, 17n54.

25. Carelse's residence is described as "inde Leyse Straet by t Coninx pleyn inde gekroonde Kunst Pars" in an inscription on an engraving from 1678 commemorating the peace of Nijmegen. *Die vrede van Nijmegen*, RP-P-OB-82.495, Rijksmuseum, Amsterdam, accessed May 21, 2012, http://www.rijksmuseum.nl/collectie/RP-P-OB-82.495/de-vrede-van-nijmegen-1678. By 1683, he had moved to "op 't Water bij de Vrouwensteegh," François G. Waller and Willem R. Juynboll, *Biogaphisch Woordenboek van Noord Nederlandsche Graveurs* (Amsterdam: Israel, 1974), 436.

26. "Karelsz (Carelse), Frans," in M. M. Kleerkooper and W. P. van Stockum, *De boekhandel te Amsterdam voornamlijk in de 17e eeuw* ('s-Gravenhage: M. Nijhoff, 1914), 1:117.

27. White, *Rembrandt as an Etcher*, 266n23.

28. Although the sitter is not identified in the print (B. 272), it is generally agreed that this is a portrait of de Jonghe.

29. Seventy-four plates were cataloged in the 1679 inventory of Clement de Jonghe's possession. The relevant portion of the inventory was published by Dieuwke de Hoop Scheffer and Karel G. Boon, "De inventarislijst van Clement de Jonghe en Rembrandts etsplaten," *Kroniek van het Rembrandthuis* 25 (1971): 1–17.

30. Rembrandt sold some of his plates during his own lifetime. In 1637, for example, he sold the plate of *Abraham Casting Out Hagar and Ishmael* (B. 30, 1637, cat. no. 4) to the Portuguese painter Samuel d'Orta (Hinterding, *Copperplates*, 11). He may have sold a large number of plates to the print seller Clement de Jonghe as early as 1653 (see the discussion in Rosenberg, "Rembrandt's Religious Prints," in this catalog). In addition, the Amsterdam engraver and book, map, and print publisher and seller Dancker Danckerts. (f. 1666) "owned the copperplates of *The Descent from the Cross: Second plate* (B. 81, 1633, cat. no. 55) and an as yet unidentified print of St. Jerome" (Hinterding, *Copperplates*, 13). There are no copperplates listed in the 1656 *cessio bonorum* of Rembrandt's possessions. However, it does not seem likely that he had disposed of all of his plates prior to his bankruptcy. Rather, it is more likely that they were either exempted from the inventory as tools of his trade or had been "sold" to a third party as a means of keeping them out of the liquidation proceedings.

31. White, *Rembrandt as an Etcher*, 88: "It (the plate) must have soon been destroyed because no weak impressions are known." According to Hinterding and Jaco Rutgers, only three other examples of this state exist (NHD, cat. 274, 223).

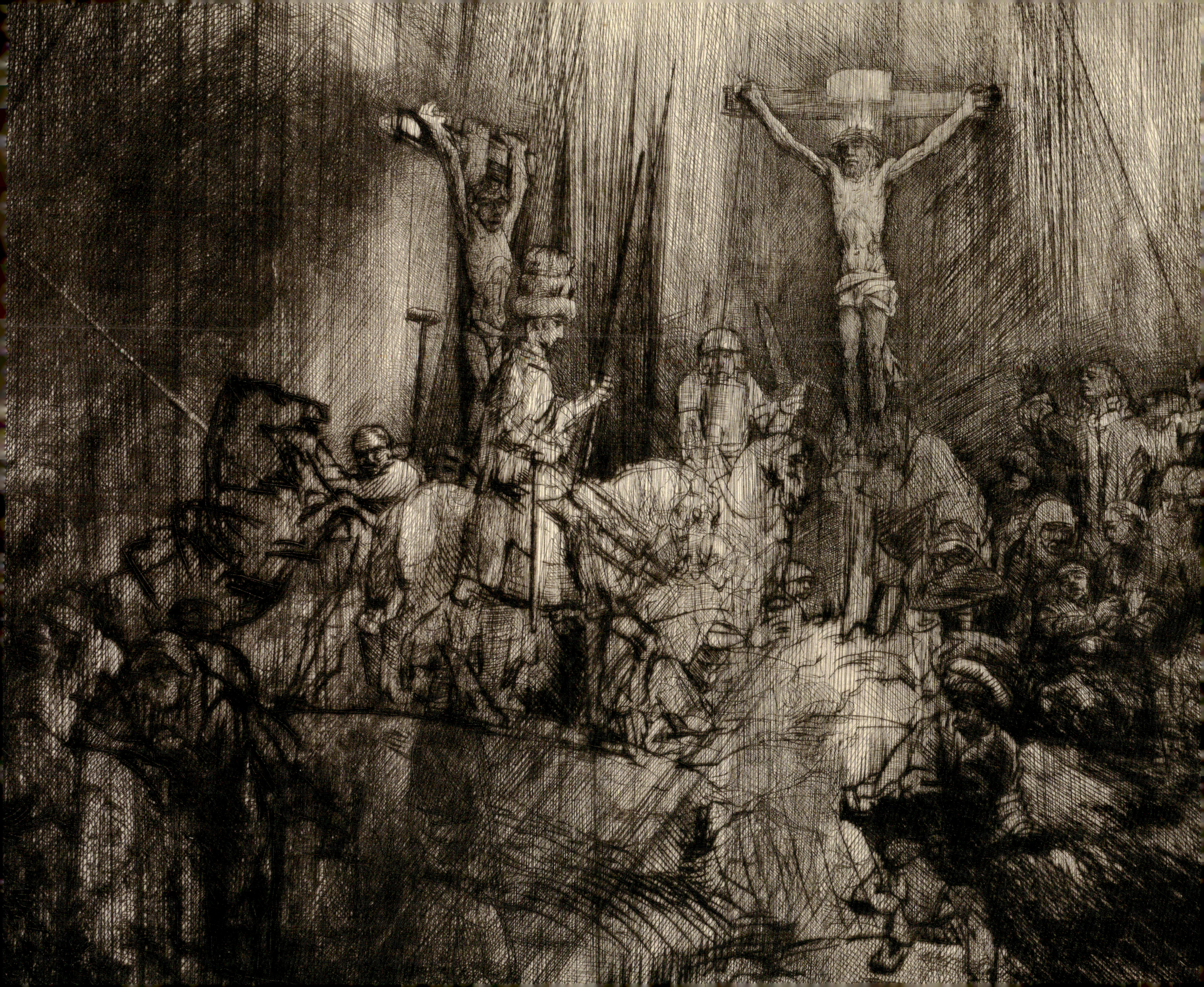

55. *Descent from the Cross: The Second Plate*

B. 81 II (H. 103, Mz. 198, NHD 119)
Etching and engraving (burin)
Signed and dated in the plate lower margin: *Rembrandt f. cum pryvlº 1633, Amstelodami Hendrikus Vlenburgensis Excudebat*
State IV of VIII
Sheet: 50.5 × 40.2 cm, trimmed inside the plate mark
Watermark: Strasbourg lily with *WR*
Recto: in graphite, lower right corner, *B 81 II*

Provenance:
Harrods, London, 1980
Feddersen, Elkhart, IN, 1991
Snite Museum of Art
Acc. No.: 1991.025.052

Plate survives:
Private collection, USA

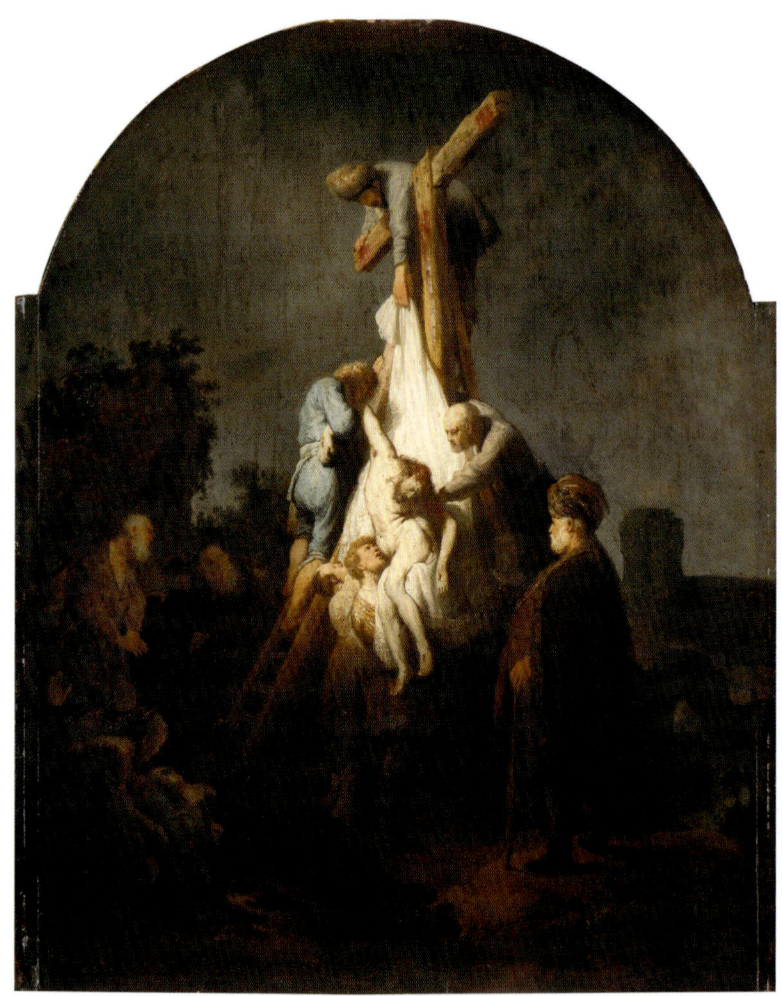

FIGURE 1. Rembrandt, *Descent from the Cross*, oil on panel, c. 1633, *Alte Pinakothek, Bayerische Staatsgemaeldesammlungen, Munich. Photo: bpk/Berlin/ Alte Pinakothek/Art Resource, New York.*

Rembrandt's *Descent from the Cross* is a problematic print that raises questions as to the etching's genesis and the artist's working process.[1] It is a variation on a painting of the same subject that Rembrandt produced in 1633 for Stadtholder Frederik Hendrik of Orange (fig. 1),[2] and was created in the same year as the painting. Rembrandt did very few reproductive etchings. It is now generally agreed that although it was designed by Rembrandt, it was executed in large part by Leiden printmaker Jan Georg van Vliet.[3] This print, along with the slightly later and slightly larger *Christ before Pilate: Large Plate* (B. 77, 1636, cat. no. 50), may have been intended to be part of an unrealized Passion series, a collaborative project between Rembrandt and van Vliet.[4] It has been suggested that Rembrandt and Hendrik Uylenburgh—the artist's landlord, dealer, and future

Rembrandt f. cum pryvl. ·1633· Amstelodami Hendrickus Vlenburgensis Excudebat.

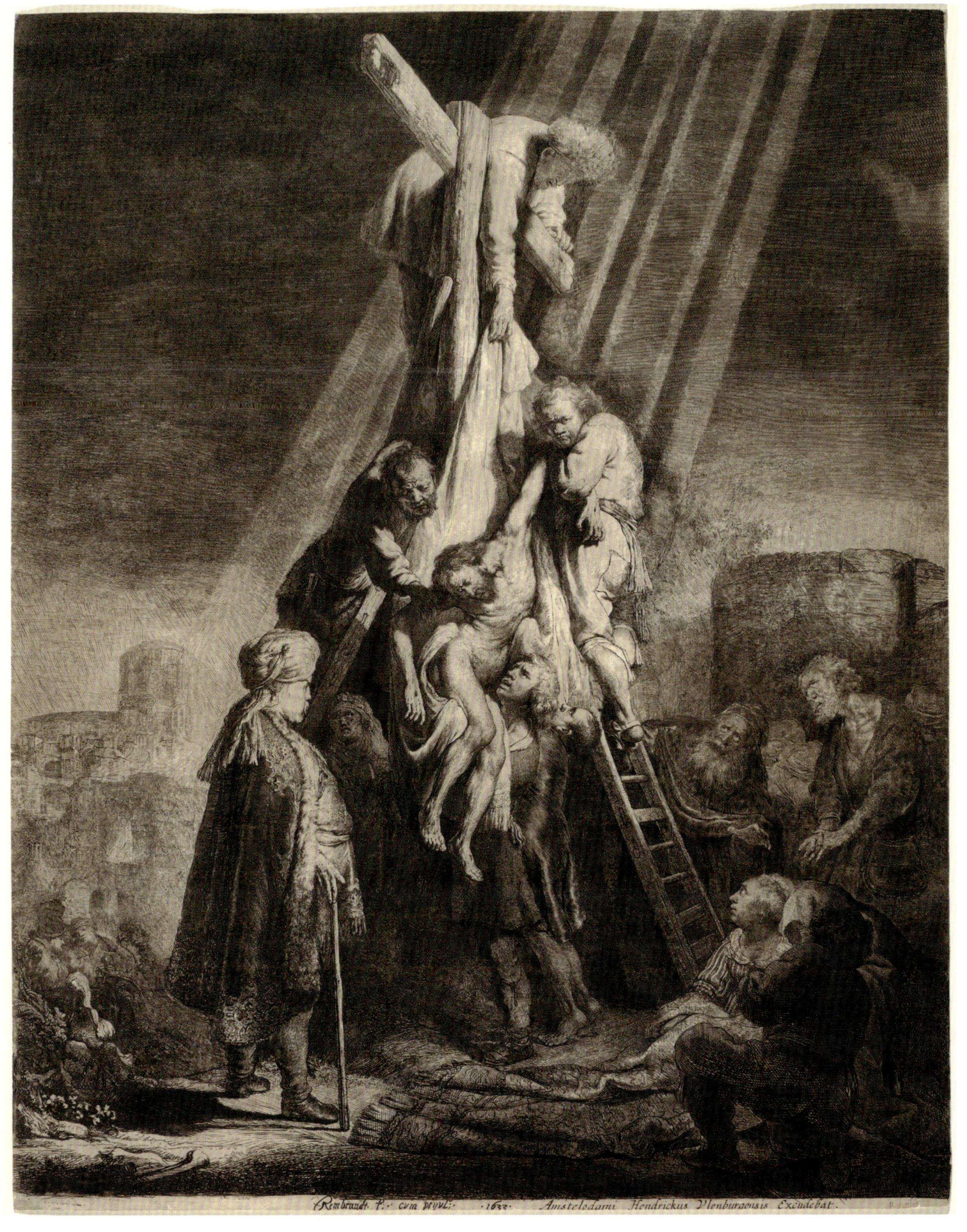

PLATE 55

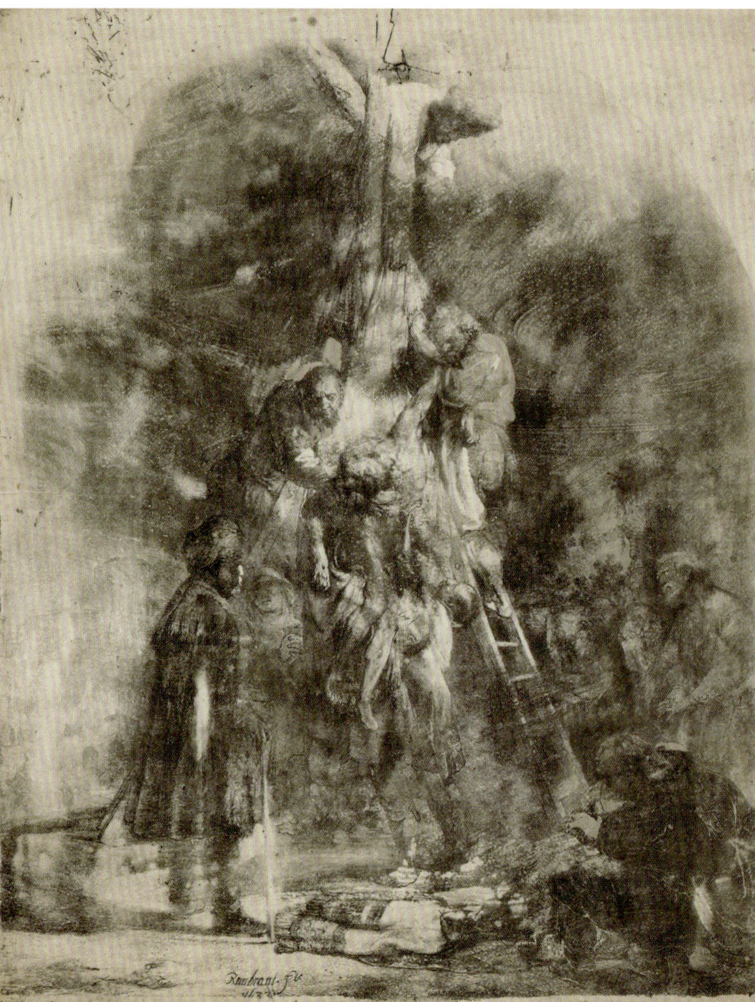

FIGURE 2. Rembrandt and van Vliet (?), *Descent from the Cross: First Plate*, B. 81 I, etching, 1633. *Photo: © Trustees of the British Museum.*

in-law—jointly conceived of the idea of producing such a series as a means of disseminating versions of the artist's painted images to a larger audience.[5] The fact that the third and fourth states of the *Descent* identify Uylenburgh as the publisher of the etching lends credence to this theory.[6] However, as Erik Hinterding observed, there is actually no direct evidence that Uylenburgh initiated the project, so the extent of his involvement in the creation of *The Descent* remains uncertain.[7]

Further complicating the history of this print is the existence of four impressions of a ruined first state of the image (B. 88 I) (fig. 2). This state reproduces the arched top of the 1634 painted version of the subject, suggesting that it was Rembrandt's first attempt at copying the painting, since other later states do not include the arch. Apparently, the ground on the plate broke down during the etching process, spoiling the image. The question of why four signed impressions of an obviously failed first state were printed remains a mystery.[8] Given the scale of this print, it seems very likely that the plate was not abandoned, but was simply burnished or scraped smooth and then reused for the second state of the *Descent*.

Although the etching of the *Descent* in the Snite Museum's Feddersen Collection is based on Rembrandt's Munich painting, the image was characteristically reversed in the printing process, and some elements were eliminated, while others were added. In this state, the etching has a rectangular format; the arch at the top is gone. Nonetheless, the central triangular grouping, which focuses on the broken and intensely human and vulnerable body of Christ, remains essentially the same. The dead weight of the lifeless body is clearly felt by the three men lowering Jesus into the cradling arms of the disciples below. A troubled workman is balanced on the rungs of the ladder at the right. In the painted version of the scene, this man's face is cast into shadow, but in the print, he looks sorrowfully out toward the viewer, and his features closely resemble those of Rembrandt himself. Two elderly male disciples, one of whom wrings his hands in despair while the other peers anxiously up at the body, also appear in both the painted and the etched version of the composition. In the print, however, additional turbaned figures have been introduced behind these mourners on the right.

Both the print and the painting feature an imposing figure at the left side of the composition. This man, probably Joseph of Arimathea, holds a staff and wears a turban and an exotic fur-lined cloak. He is a person of substance, in girth as well as dress. The man does not look up at the group laboring to lower Jesus from the cross. Instead, he seems to be lost in thought.

Rembrandt opted to create the same kind of dramatic lighting in the etching that he used in the Munich painting, and in good impressions of the print, he was fairly successful. At the same time, because of the translation from one medium to another and possibly as a result of the participation of van Vliet, some of the lighting effects in the print are rendered in a considerably less adept manner than in the painting. This lack of subtlety is most apparent in the strips of slanting rays of light descending from heaven behind the cross. As already noted, both the painting and the print feature a central triangular composition, and in both, Rembrandt highlighted the central action—the lowering of Christ's body from the cross—by illuminating the shroud and Jesus with brilliant light. In the print, however, the light is extended beyond the apex of the triangle, onto the figure of Joseph of Arimathea, who casts a very clear shadow on the ground behind him; and onto the two women in the right corner, who kneel by a lavishly embroidered pall laid out at the foot of the cross. As a result, while the painting has a singular focus on both action and illumination, the light in the etching is more dispersed, in effect highlighting more of the scene and more of the actions and reactions of the drama.

The print's background, with its view of the Temple in Jerusalem at the left and the rock-cut tomb at the right, is similar, though not identical, to that in the painting. In the etching, Rembrandt added yet another symbolic detail: the bone lying on the ground in the lower left-hand corner of the print. This is a traditional reference to Golgotha, the burial site that was also the scene of the Crucifixion.

Perhaps the most notable differences between the painted and etched versions of the *Descent* are Rembrandt's introduction of a pair of elderly Jews conversing in the left background of the print and a mysterious aged woman standing in the shadows beneath the ladder near Joseph of Arimathea, as well the reconfiguration of the group in the right foreground. The Jews in the background appear to be discussing the event unfolding before them. They may have been meant to represent the conspiring Pharisees who plotted Christ's demise, or possibly potential converts grappling with the significance of the event taking place before them. The identity of the old woman in the shadows beneath the ladder is also ambiguous.[9] Dressed in modest garb, she has an expression of great sorrow as she casts her eyes heavenward. It is not clear whether she represents the Virgin or simply another female mourner.

Finally, the left foreground corner of the painted version of the *Descent* is occupied by three women who gather around the prostrate figure of the Virgin Mary, who has fainted from grief. In the etching, three different figures are clustered in the right corner of the foreground: a kneeling male figure with his back to the viewer; a seated, hooded figure (possibly the Virgin) who gazes down toward the ground; and a seated, fashionably dressed younger woman who looks up toward Christ's body. In terms of both the distribution of light and the structure of the composition, they anchor the image. Spread out on the ground between them is a richly brocaded pall, ready to receive Christ's body.

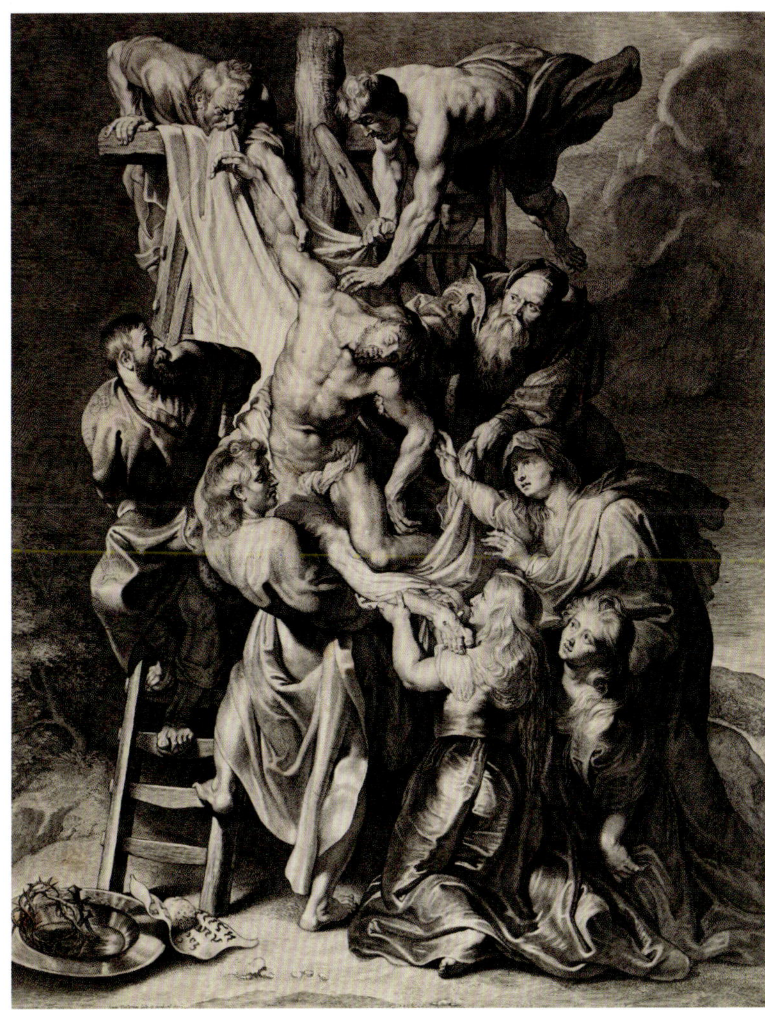

FIGURE 3. Lucas Vorsterman after Peter Paul Rubens, *Descent from the Cross*, engraving, 1620. *Philadelphia Museum of Art, Philadelphia, Pennsylvania, the Muriel and Philip Berman Gift, Object Number 1985–52–15165.*

The swooning Virgin of the painting has been eliminated in the etching, a change that was quite possibly motivated by a desire to make the print acceptable to as broad a denominational audience as possible. When Peter Paul Rubens was commissioned to paint a Descent from the Cross for the high altar of Antwerp Cathedral in

1611, he struggled with the question of how to represent the Virgin. In a preliminary drawing in St. Petersburg, he showed her collapsed on the ground, but in the painting, he repositioned the figure. The Council of Trent had insisted on an "accurate" representation of biblical events and, since the Gospel according to St. John specifically stated that "near the cross . . . stood his mother" (19:25), images that depicted her as lying on the ground were considered inappropriate. Probably in response to Tridentine strictures, Rubens finally decided to represent Mary as standing and reaching up toward her son.[10] When Lucas Vorsterman made an engraving after the painting in 1620, he copied that pose (fig. 3).[11] When Rembrandt painted *his* version of the Descent, however, he evidently wished to emphasize the pathos of the scene, for he opted to show the Virgin fainting with grief. That was how Mary was often represented in the fifteenth and sixteenth centuries, probably because it reinforced the theological parallel between the Virgin's compassionate suffering and Christ's Passion, one of the foundations of the argument for her rightful place as intercessor.[12] By leaving Mary's identity ambiguous in the etched version of the *Descent*, Rembrandt finessed the issue, allowing the viewer to draw whatever conclusions he or she wished about the Virgin's participation in the Passion.[13] He even provided two candidates for the bereaved mother, the woman gazing heavenward from her place in the shadows beneath the ladder, and the hooded figure crouched in the lower right-hand corner of the sheet, looking down at the pall before her.

It is has been suggested that Rembrandt's painting and print were both inspired by Lucas Vorsterman's engraved reproduction of Rubens's painted *Descent*.[14] The Vorsterman print, published in 1620, would certainly have been known to Rembrandt,[15] and Rubens's "privileges," or copyright protection, would have expired by the time that Rembrandt made his painting and print of the subject.[16] Rembrandt's creation of an image based on his own painting would have been a good marketing strategy, not only because of its intrinsic aesthetic and devotional merits, but also because it would have allowed connoisseurs to compare his work with that of his rival, Rubens. Rubens's vision of Christ is Herculean and exultant—a triumphalist image—whereas Rembrandt's actors are human and vulnerable, making palpable the personal, emotion-laden distress of those gathered to mourn Jesus's death and free his body from the cross.

Notes

1. In the eighteenth century, this etching was also known as the "twenty guilder print," and sometimes paired with *Christ before Pilate* (B. 77, 1636, cat. no. 50), which was referred to as the "thirty guilder print." Ludwig Münz, *Critical Catalogue*, 1:213, document of 1711.

2. The painting (RRP, *Corpus*, A65), which is now in the Alte Pinakothek, Munich, was the first in a series of Passion paintings that the artist produced for the prince's collection. Regarding the Passion cycle, see Gary Schwartz, *Rembrandt: His Life, His Paintings* (London: Penguin, 1985), 106–18.

3. Christopher White (*Rembrandt as an Etcher*, 2nd ed. [New Haven, CT: Yale University Press, 1999], 17) has summarized the discussion regarding this collaboration. See the entry for *Christ before Pilate* (B. 77, cat. no. 50) for a discussion of van Vliet's career and his collaboration with Rembrandt. The evidence in favor of van Vliet's role in the production of the print is both stylistic and technical. See Martin Royalton-Kisch in Christiaan Schuckman, Martin Royalton-Kisch, and Erik Hinterding, *Rembrandt and Van Vliet: A Collaboration on Copper* (Amsterdam: Museum het Rembrandthuis, 1996), cat. 18, 74. Erik Hinterding's investigation of the watermarks on impressions of the first and second states of the *Descent* also supports the assumption of a collaboration between the two artists. Hinterding, *Rembrandt as an Etcher: The Practice of Production and Distribution* (Ouderkerk aan den IJssel, Netherlands: Sound and Vision Publishers, 2006), 1:92–96.

For other examples of reproductive prints after Rembrandt made by van Vliet, see Schuckman, Royalton-Kisch, and Hinterding, *Rembrandt and Van Vliet*, and Ernst van de Wetering "Remarks on Rembrandt's Oil-sketches for Etchings," in Erik Hinterding, Ger Luijten, and Martin Royalton-Kisch, *Rembrandt the Printmaker*, exh. cat. (Chicago and London: Fitzroy Dearborn Publishers, 2000), 36–38.

4. Van de Wetering "Remarks," 52–56. Van de Wetering (52–53) suggested that an unrealized print of Joseph recounting his dreams may have been intended to be part of the series.

5. Gary Schwartz, cited in Hinterding, *Rembrandt as an Etcher*, 1:92.

6. Hinterding (*Rembrandt as an Etcher*, 1:92–93) noted that by 1641, Uylenburgh owned at least 125 plates, which suggests that he was a print publisher. On Hendrick Uylenburgh, see Friso Lammertse and Jaap van der Veen, *Uylenburgh & Son: Art and Commerce from Rembrandt to De Lairesse, 1625–1675* (Amsterdam: Het Rembrandthuis; Zwolle, Netherlands: Waanders, 2006), 13–59 and 126–60.

7. Hinterding, *Rembrandt as an Etcher*, 1:92–94. Ernst van de Wetering suggested that Uylenburgh may have been involved in another aspect of Rembrandt's work with prints: "One may justifiably wonder whether van Vliet's activity as an engraver of Rembrandt's prototypes was initiated by Uylenburgh rather than by Rembrandt himself." ("Remarks on Rembrandt's Oil-sketches," 51.)

8. The plate was signed, so all four first-state impressions bear Rembrandt's signature. Royalton-Kisch, *Rembrandt and Van Vliet*, cat. 17, believed that the signature was added to the plate by van Vliet and that he was responsible for the technical failure of the first state. If this is the case, then van Vliet might have pulled the four impressions because he thought that there would be a market for any print associated with Rembrandt's name, regardless of the quality of the image. However, it seems unlikely that in 1633, Rembrandt would already have enjoyed that kind of renown.

The watermark on each of these four early impressions is the same, and it corresponds to one that appears on paper used by van Vliet and Rembrandt in the early 1630s. Hinterding, *Rembrandt as an Etcher*, 2:153.

9. A similar figure is visible in the underpainting in the Munich composition.

10. For a discussion of this iconographic controversy, see Kristin Lohse Belkin, *Rubens* (London: Phaidon, 1998), 112.

11. See below in the text of this catalog entry for a discussion of the Vorsterman print.

12. Perhaps the most famous example of this identification of Mary's compassion and the Passion is Rogier van der Weyden's *Deposition* from 1435, now in the Prado Museum, Madrid. On the significance of the fainting Virgin, see Otto von Simson, "*Compassio* and *Co-redemptio* in Rogier van der Weyden's *Descent from the Cross*," *Art Bulletin* 35 (1953): 9–16.

13. Gary Schwartz (*Rembrandt*, 111) made this observation.

14. White, *Rembrandt as an Etcher*, 15–16: "There is little doubt that Rembrandt, following the example of Rubens, planned a series of reproductive prints . . . Once again pointing to the example of Rubens, the composition [of the *Descent*] was clearly influenced by Lucas Vorsterman's engraving reproducing, in reverse, the painting by Rubens in Antwerp Cathedral." Vorsterman's print was produced under Rubens's supervision and was based on the central panel in the Flemish painter's altarpiece in the Cathedral of Antwerp.

15. Van Vliet might also have been familiar with Rubens's original painting, since there is some evidence that the printmaker was in Antwerp in 1632. Van de Wetering, "Remarks on Rembrandt's Oil-sketches," 51.

16. "Privileges" were first issued to books in the early sixteenth century. They began to be applied to prints in the Dutch Republic at the end of the century. As Nadine Orenstein and others have observed, unlike the case of a modern copyright, the granting of a privilege for a print did not protect its intellectual content, but rather the "plate and the printing and selling of that plate." Nadine Orenstein, "Sleeping Caps, City Views, and State Funerals: Privileges for Prints in the Dutch Republic, 1597–1650," in *In His Milieu: Essays on Netherlandish Art in Memory of John Michael Montias*, ed. Amy Golahny, Mia M. Mochizuki, and Lisa Vergara (Amsterdam: Amsterdam University Press, 2006), 314.

As Gary Schwartz (*Rembrandt*, 111) noted, the "copyright" on Rubens's engraving would have expired in the North after seven years, i.e., in 1627, and in the South after twelve, i.e., in 1632. As a result, Rubens's image would have been "out of copyright" when Rembrandt and van Vliet published their *Descent*.

Although Rembrandt claims to have published his etching *cum pryvl*°, there is no record of the States General or the States of Holland having issued him such rights. In the article cited above, Nadine Orenstein includes a table of privileges issued by the States General. As she noted, the vast majority of privileges were issued for portraits and representations of political events. Therefore, if Rembrandt had obtained protection for his *Descent from the Cross*, a unique religious image, this would have been an anomaly.

56. Descent from the Cross by Torchlight

B. 83 (H. 280, Mz. 232, NHD 286)
Etching and drypoint
Signed and dated in the plate: *Rembrandt. f 1654*
State I of IV
Sheet: 23.9 × 18.9 cm; plate mark 21.0 × 16.1 cm
Watermark: fragment of unidentified watermark on right margin (scrolls)
Verso: in graphite, right corner, *LA 900553 H280 /~~100378~~*
Label on original mat: *LONDON ARTS GALLERY/ Rembrandt van Rijn/ 1606 1669/ "The Descent from the Cross by Torchlight"/ H. 280 only state BRS. 83/ B-B. 54 Gii/ii with full margins all around/#900/,* 553; in graphite, *UTXX*

Provenance:
London Arts Gallery, London, 1971
Feddersen, Elkhart, IN, 1991
Snite Museum
Acc. No.: 1991.025.053

Plate survives:
Pierpont Morgan Library, New York, NY

Rembrandt depicted the Deposition, or Descent from the Cross, four times. The painting he made in 1633 for Stadtholder Frederik Hendrik, the Prince of Orange, was probably the earliest.[1] That same year, working in collaboration with Leiden etcher Jan Georg van Vliet, Rembrandt reproduced the painting's image in reverse, in an etched and engraved print[2] (B. 81 II, cat. no. 55). In both of these early Depositions, the diminutive, lifeless body of Christ is being lowered from a towering cross placed almost directly on the central axis of the composition. Three men have climbed up on ladders in order to pass Jesus's body down into the arms of waiting disciples. One of them bends over the top of the cross as he grasps a white shroud that hangs behind the body. The other two men steady the body as it descends. At the side, Joseph of Arimathea, a large, imposing figure, stands like a wealthy Eastern pasha, gazing out across the scene. In the painting, the Virgin, overcome by grief, has fainted and fallen to the ground, where she is being attended by three women. In the etching, a brocaded pall is spread out on the ground in front of two women, ready to receive Christ's body. The hooded woman may be the Virgin, although this remains ambiguous. The silhouetted towers and walls of Jerusalem are visible in the distance. Christ's body, though unheroic in its pose and scale, is the focal point in both compositions, and it is highlighted by dramatic, supernatural light. In the painting, an enveloping darkness is broken by a brilliant white glow that seems to emanate from Christ himself. This light reflects off the white linen shroud suspended behind Christ and also picks out details of his followers. In the print, sharply defined shafts of celestial light pour down from heaven, illuminating the shroud and the figures clustered around Christ's body.

Rembrandt's third representation of the event, *Descent from the Cross, a Sketch* (B. 82) (fig. 1) is a print from 1642,[3] executed in etching and drypoint. In this version, the Deposition is pushed much closer to the picture surface, while the setting is almost totally suppressed; the figures now dominate the composition. A much larger, more muscular figure of Christ is being lowered down by a sling fashioned from the shroud, the ends of which have been

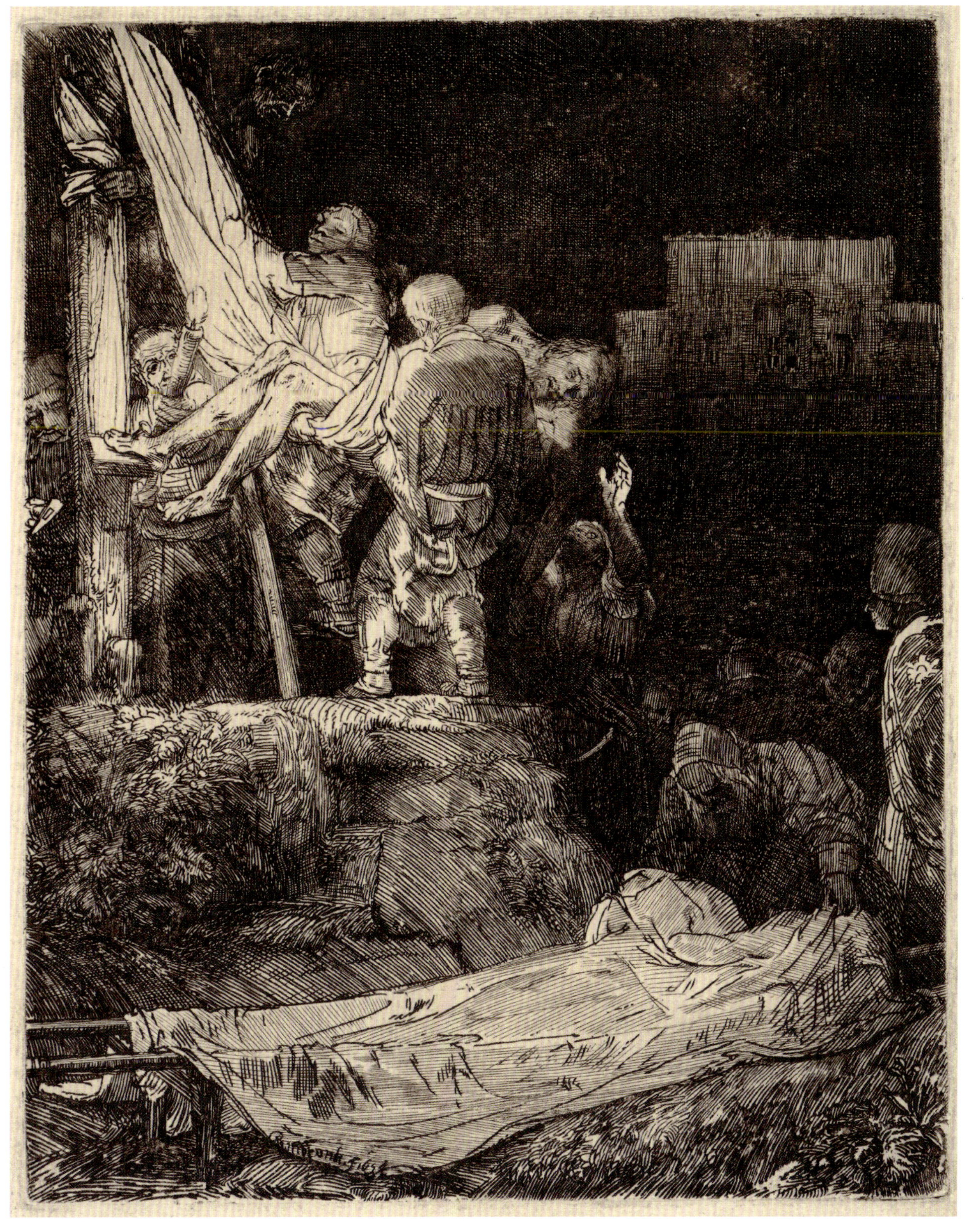

PLATE 56

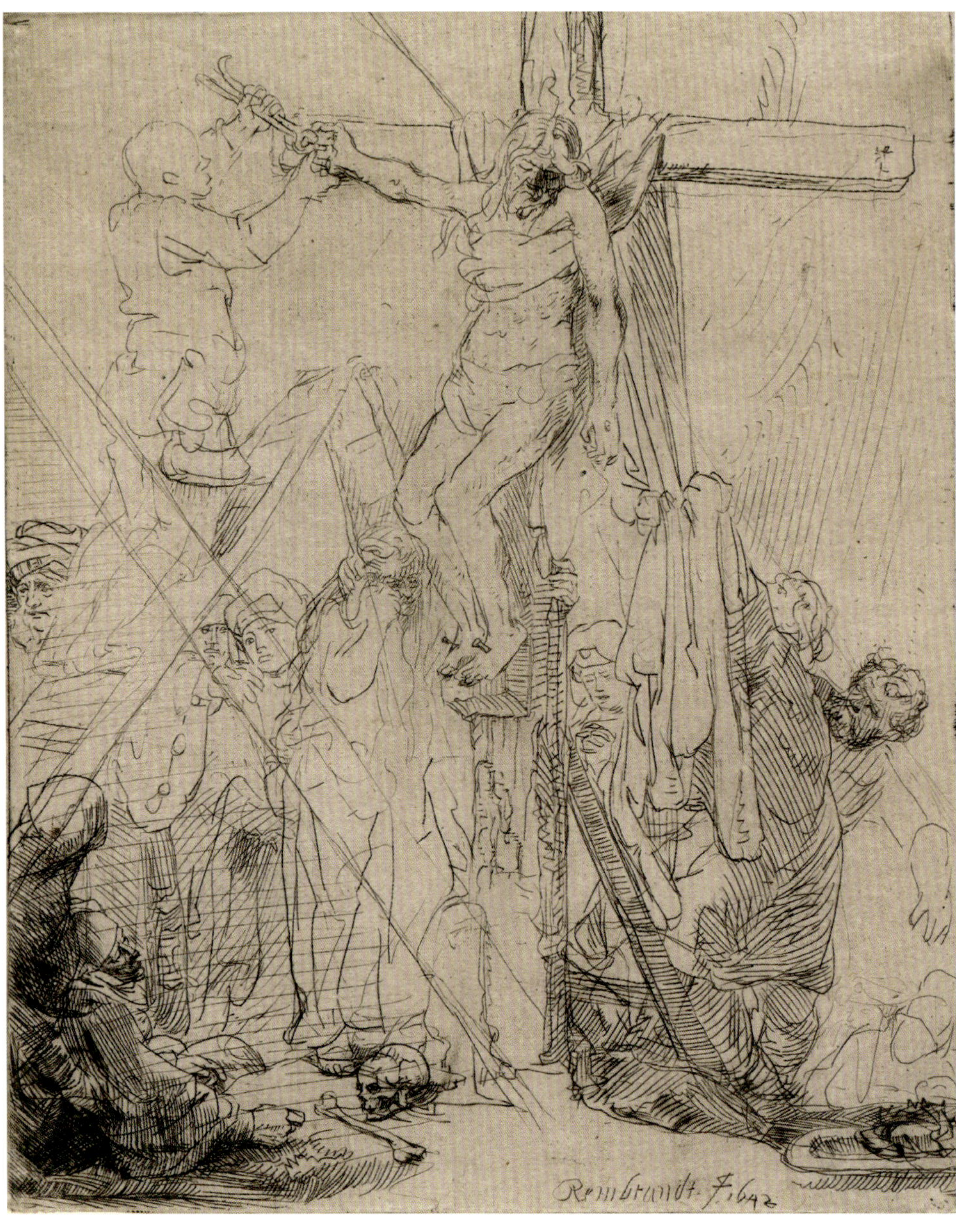

FIGURE 1. Rembrandt, *Descent from the Cross: A Sketch,* etching and drypoint, 1642. *The Pierpont Morgan Library & Museum, New York, New York, RvR 129. Photography by Janny Chiu, 2016.*

thrown over the top of a sturdy cross. Two disciples stand slightly behind the cross, holding on to the ends of the shroud and straining against the limp weight of Christ's body.[4] Jesus's feet are still nailed to the suppedaneum, and while his left arm hangs limply at his side, his right hand remains pinned to the cross. A disciple standing on a triangular ladder is in the process of prying the nail out of Jesus's pinioned hand. Other male and female followers are lightly drawn in the background. At the lower left corner of the print, the fainting Virgin is being supported by a female disciple. These women, two of the more finished figures in the sketch, sit in shadow, as though their grief has cast a veil of darkness over them. The skull and leg bone that lie on the ground beside Mary and her attendant evoke the name of the hill on which Jesus has died (Golgotha, "the place of the skull") and also man's mortality. Two diagonal lines cut across the image from the left side, suggesting a beam of light falling toward the base of the cross. These rays bisect the angled ladder at the left, creating a second large cross. As the descriptive title suggests, this print, which evinces a wide range of handling, looks more like a sketch than a fully realized work. In particular, the absence of any coherent system of modeling makes the print appear unfinished, even though the plate was signed and dated.

The Snite Museum's *Descent from the Cross by Torchlight,* dated 1654,[5] deviates from these earlier examples in a number of significant ways. This time, Rembrandt conceived of the scene as a nocturne, a night scene illuminated not by divine light but by a single blazing torch held in front of the shroud hanging from the cross. The lowering of the body, nominally the subject of the print, has been moved from the center to the upper left corner of the composition, and the cross, raised on a low hillock, has been truncated; only the lower part of its shaft and a tiny fragment of one of its arms are visible. A shadowy figure leans out over the top of the cross, holding on to one end of the white linen shroud, which he appears to have anchored by wrapping it around the upright of the cross. The winding cloth cascades down in a broad, descending diagonal and then goes under and around the body of Christ. In contrast to the earlier examples, Jesus's lowered body is supported by a disciple who has his back to the viewer, with the result that although it is possible to see Christ's lolling head and thin legs—and the disturbing image of one foot still nailed to the cross—Jesus's torso is hidden behind the man holding him; thus, direct access to the martyred Christ has been partially obscured. This change weakens the traditional associations of the scene with the Eucharist, in which an image of Christ's lifeless body, lowered from the cross, is exhibited in the same manner that the host is displayed to the congregation during the Mass.[6]

The light from the torch penetrates the night shadows just enough to illuminate the hand of a disciple who is standing on the ground below the man cradling Christ's body. As the man reaches up, his expressive gesture becomes another point in the downward trajectory that is described by the luminescent winding cloth and the figures beside the cross. The bright hand also serves to direct the viewer's eye up toward Jesus's face. At the bottom of the print, a bearded, elderly Jew, whose head is covered with a prayer shawl, kneels over a litter that has been set down upon the ground, filling much of the bottom quarter of the composition. He is busy arranging a white cloth over the stretcher, preparing it to receive Jesus's body.[7] The cloth is illuminated in such a way that this litter commands almost as much attention as the group engaged in lowering Jesus's body from the cross. Standing at the extreme right edge of the print is a man wearing a tall fur hat. The identities of this man and the kneeling figure are unclear. It is possible that one is Nicodemus and the other Joseph of Arimathea, since, according to the Gospel of St. John (19:38–42), they took charge of preparing Jesus's body for the tomb.[8] The Virgin is notably absent from the central grouping,[9] but other figures and a looming "spectral image" of what may be Pilate's palace[10] are faintly visible in the background.

In the 1654 *Descent from the Cross by Torchlight*, even more than in the much earlier etched and painted examples of the Descent, Rembrandt foreshadowed subsequent moments of the Passion: the pathos of the lamentation, the body's preparation for burial, and, as implied by the litter on which the bright cloth lies in the foreground, Christ's journey to the tomb. The viewer is thus led to contemplate not only the act of the Deposition, but also its aftermath, when Jesus's body has been released from the cross.[11] Representations of the Lamentation often show Mary, Mary Magdalen, and other distraught mourners gathered around the body of Christ as it lies on its shroud at the base of the cross.[12] Rembrandt's 1634–35 drawing of *The Lamentation at the Foot of the Cross*,[13] for example, portrays mourners gathered in just such a manner: Christ's body lies on a white shroud in the center of the composition, while on the left side, the bottoms of two of the crosses are visible. A seventeenth-century viewer of Rembrandt's *Descent from the Cross by Torchlight* who was familiar with the sequential images of the Passion might well have anticipated these subsequent actions unfolding in the emotion-laden narrative, envisioning the moment in which the Virgin Mary, the Magdalen, and Christ's followers would emerge out of the shadows in order to gather around Jesus's body and grieve before the litter was raised and borne to the tomb.

Notes

1. Alte Pinakothek, Munich, RPP, *Corpus*, A65. Illustrated in the entry for cat. no. 55, fig. 1. There is another version of the Descent, dated 1634, in the State Hermitage Museum, St. Petersburg, which has been rejected by the Rembrandt Research Project (C49) as an authentic by Rembrandt.

2. See the discussion of *Descent from the Cross: The Second Plate* (B. 81, cat. no. 55) in this catalog.

3. This print is not in the Snite Museum's Feddersen Collection.

4. This particular motif seems to derive from Dürer's *Descent from the Cross* from his small woodcut *Passion* of 1509–10 (TIB, woodcuts, 42).

5. The print is normally grouped with three other works of the same date and size, the *Entombment* (B. 86, cat. no. 58), the *Presentation in the Temple in the Dark Manner* (B. 50), and *Christ at Emmaus: Larger Plate* (B. 87, cat. no. 60). Two of these prints are nocturnes.

6. This divergence from the iconography of the Catholic Mass may have made Rembrandt's print more acceptable to a Protestant clientele. For the sacramental associations of the body of Christ in the Deposition and the Host, see Barbara Lane, *The Altar and the Altarpiece: Sacramental Themes in Early Netherlandish Painting* (New York: Harper & Row, 1984), 90–91.

7. Rembrandt showed the body being borne to the tomb on just such a litter in his etching from the mid-1640s, *Christ Carried to the Tomb* (B. 84, c. 1645, cat. no. 57), and in *Entombment* (B. 86, c. 1654, cat. no. 58), which is traditionally associated with this *Descent*.

8. Perlove and Silver (*Rembrandt's Faith*, 301–2) suggested that the costume of the man in the tall fur hat might identify him as an unconverted, blind Ashkenazi Jew.

The figure crouching by the litter is similar to the figure in biblical attire in Rembrandt's *Entombment* (B. 86, c. 1654, cat. no. 58), a man whom some have identified as Joseph of Arimathea. It could also be argued that the elderly Jew arranging the linens on the litter in *Descent from the Cross by Torchlight* is Nicodemus, and the well-dressed man at the far right is Joseph of Arimathea, a figure that would be more consistent with the appearance of the opulent Joseph in Rembrandt's 1633 *Descent from the Cross: The Second Plate* (B. 81 II, cat. no. 55), a composition in which the wealthy disciple also stands apart from the action and observes.

9. Although it is possible that, as Holm Bevers asserted, viewers are meant to assume that Mary is depicted among the virtually invisible followers hidden in the darkened background, this is not necessarily so. Bevers, "The Descent from the Cross by Torchlight," in Bevers, Peter Schatborn, and Barbara Welzel, *Rembrandt: The Master and His Workshop,* vol. 2, *Drawings and Etchings,* exh. cat. (New Haven, CT: Yale University Press, 1992), cat. 37, 272.

10. *Rembrandt's Journey,* 238. Perlove and Silver (*Rembrandt's Faith,* 301) identified this structure as the Temple, which is "aligned with the body of Christ . . . a further juxtaposition of the old faith and the new." It is interesting to note that in Rembrandt's three more finished versions of the Descent, he chose to include a substantial building in the background. This is true of his 1634–35 Lamentation, as well. The inclusion of this kind of structure is unusual for Deposition images in the early modern period, although it is not without precedent.

11. As Clifford Ackley stated, the "almost medieval tendency to suggest different moments in the story in a single scene is a familiar aspect of Rembrandt's religious narratives." *Rembrandt's Journey,* 109. Ackley noted that this characteristic was first acknowledged by Christian Tümpel in his introduction to the catalog *Rembrandt legt.*

12. See, for example, Dürer's Lamentation in his engraved *Passion* (1507, TIB, engravings, 14) and in his small woodcut *Passion* (1509–10, TIB, woodcuts, 43).

13. British Museum, London, Ben. 154.

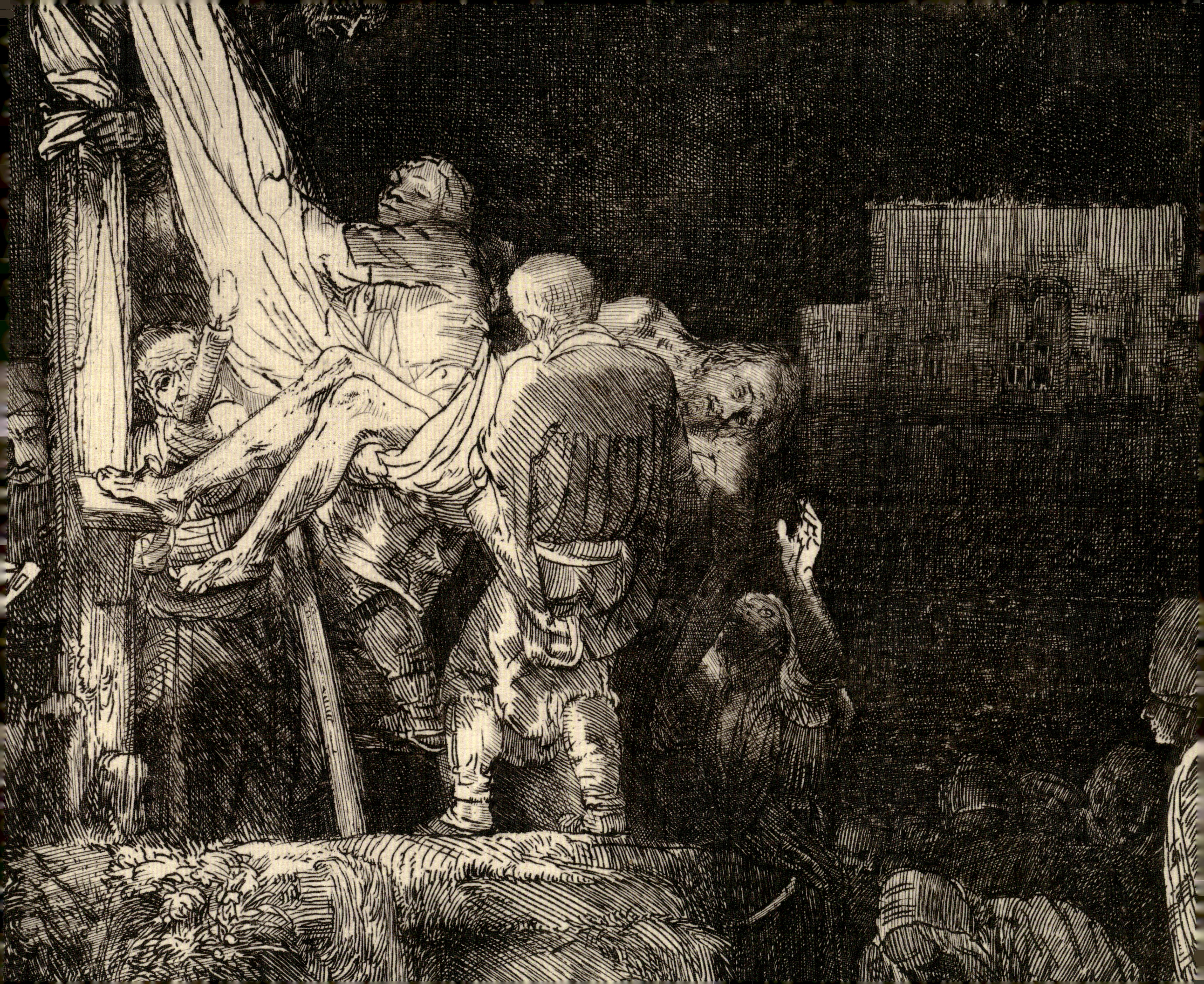

57. *Christ Carried to the Tomb*

B. 84 (H. 215, Mz. 224, NHD 223)
Etching and drypoint
Signed in the plate: *Rembrant* [*sic*]
c. 1645 (?)
State I of I
Sheet: 14.7 × 12.3 cm; plate mark: 13.1 × 10.8 cm
Verso: in graphite, *H-215/BB-45–3 o*

Provenance:
Associated American Artists Inc., New York, NY, 1968
Feddersen, Elkhart, IN, 1991
Snite Museum of Art
Acc. No.: 1991.025.054

The plate does not survive.

Rembrandt's etching of *Christ Carried to the Tomb* depicts a moment in the Passion that is rarely portrayed: mourning disciples bearing the body of Christ from his place of execution, Golgotha, to the rock-cut tomb carved into a hillside below. Representations of the Deposition, Lamentation, and the actual Entombment are not uncommon, but images of this transitional moment are.[1] In Rembrandt's print, four pallbearers move solemnly from right to left, bearing the litter with Jesus's body on it toward the dark, cavernous opening of the tomb. The litter consists of a shroud draped over two long poles. A length of cloth flows out behind the leading pallbearers, emphasizing the group's forward progress. Jesus has not yet been wrapped in his burial sheet,[2] but appears as he did in Rembrandt's images of the Crucifixion and the Descent, naked except for a loincloth. The pallbearers are accompanied by four additional somber figures. As Clifford Ackley observed, Rembrandt had originally placed a second cluster of mourners at the left, standing beside the opening to the rock tomb. Later, in the reworked plate, these figures disappeared into the shadows, possibly so as to not to distract from the funeral procession itself.[3]

The path that the cortege followed down from the site of the crucifixion rises up above it in the distance, and the lightly sketched hill with the tomb-cavern at its base looms large at the left side of the image. At the top of the hill on the right, a family gazes down at the procession below. The man's anachronistic flat Eastern European hat identifies them as Jews.[4] To their right, a figure thrusts both arms toward the sky in a traditional gesture of grief. Two additional, barely defined figures appear behind him. These onlookers presumably witnessed the tragic events that took place at the summit and then remained there in order to watch the funeral procession wend its way down from the hilltop. They represent a visual link between past and present events in the narrative of the Passion.[5]

Despite the powerful subject of this print, Rembrandt's mourners in the funeral procession do not display their grief in a dramatic fashion. Their movement toward the cave appears stately and measured. Unlike the diminutive figure gesturing above, they evince only muted expressions of sorrow: bowed heads and tender, sorrowful expressions. The pallbearers at the head of the procession exhibit a sort of melancholy resignation. The most prominent figure, the pallbearer toward the center of the group, gazes down at Jesus with compassion. He is singled out not only by his position, but also by virtue of the fact that he is the only mourner who faces

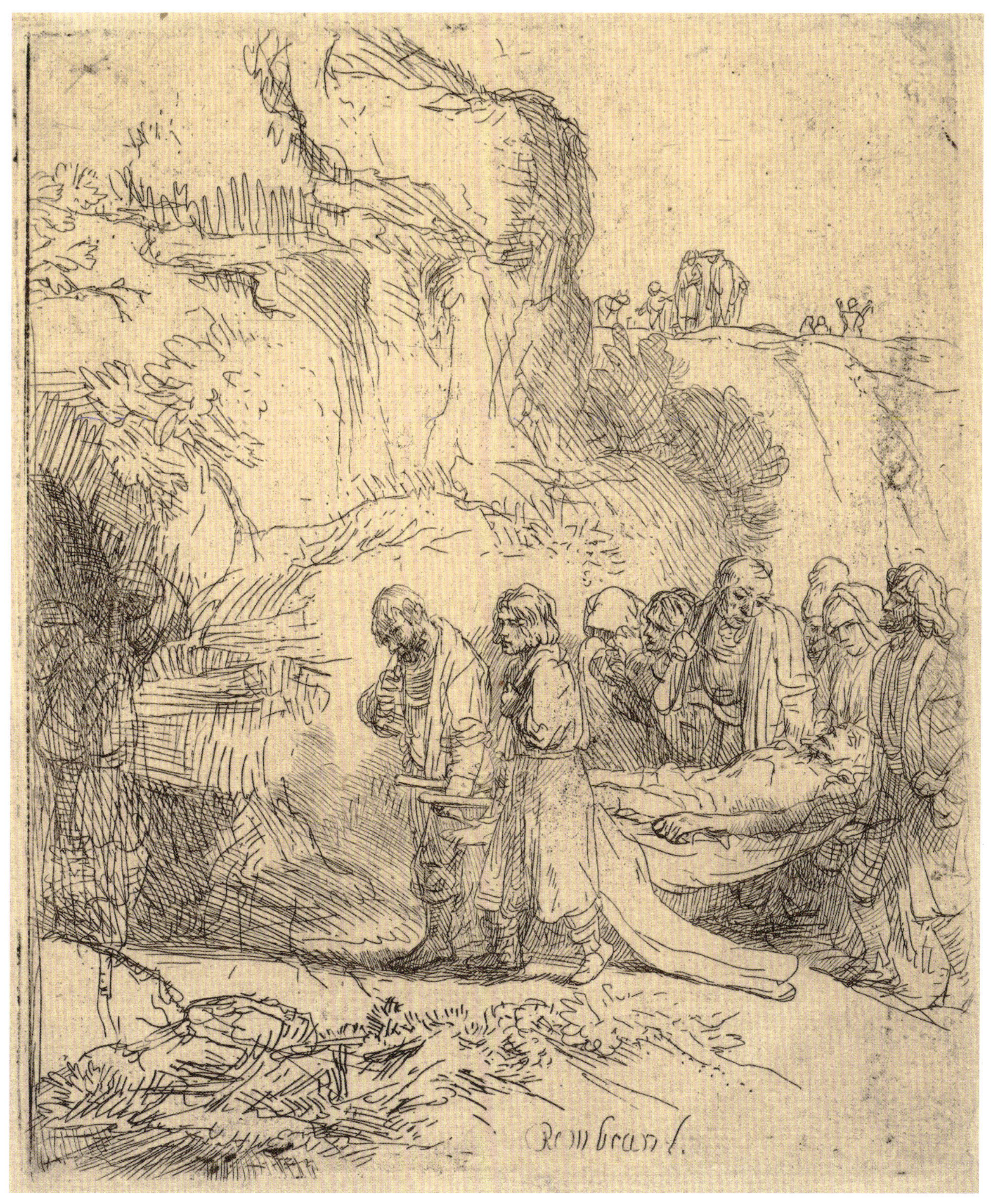

PLATE 57

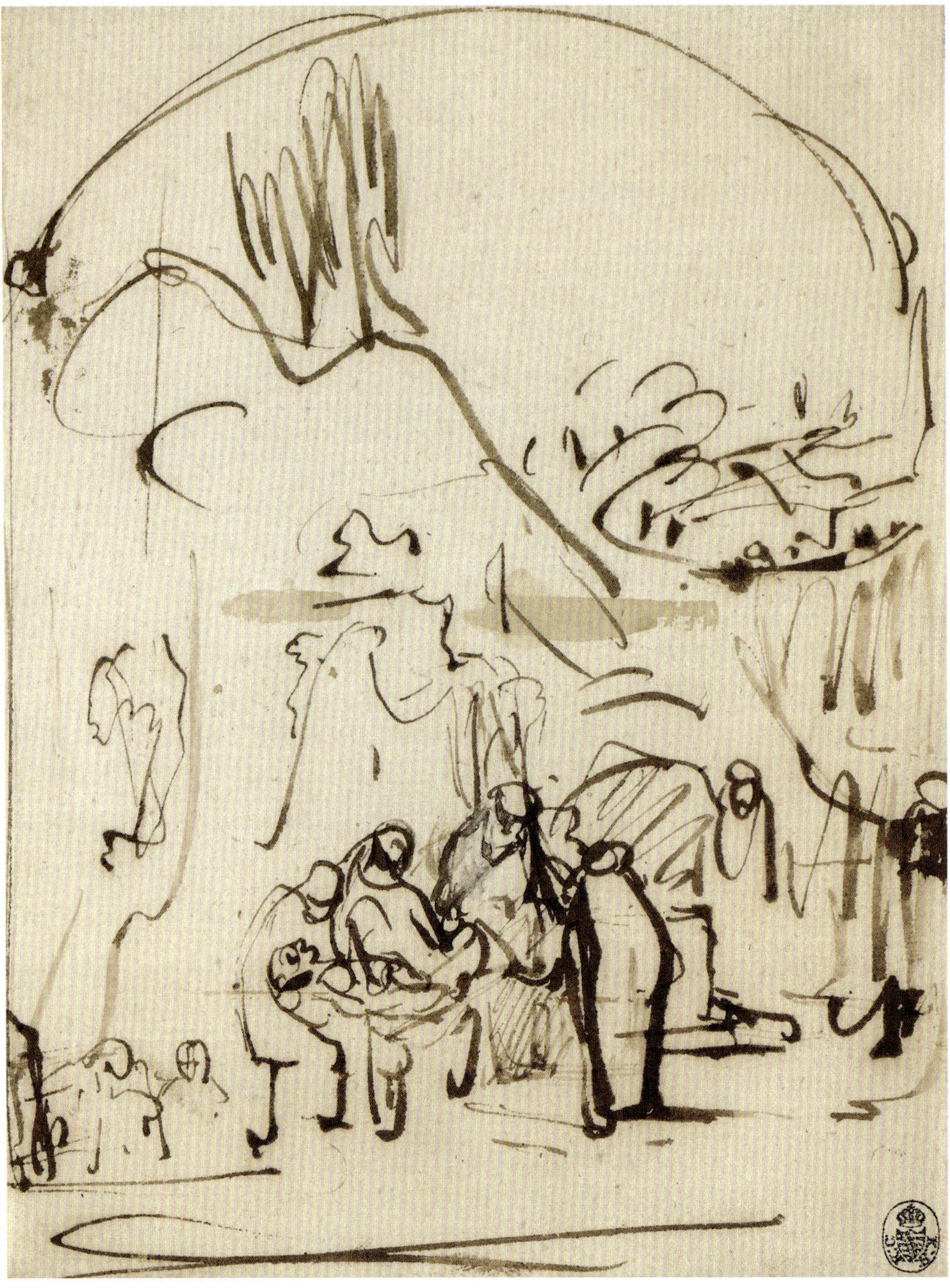

FIGURE 1. Rembrandt, *The Entombment of Christ*, pen and bistre, Ben. 483, c. 1640. *Kupferstichkabinett, Dresden.*

out toward the viewer. Walking near him, beside the burial party, is a woman whose hooded face is completely hidden from view. Like the hooded woman in Rembrandt's *Descent from the Cross: The Second Plate* (B. 81 II, 1633, cat. no. 55), this woman may be Mary, portrayed as a mother whose grief is too private and devastating to be witnessed.[6] However, the procession also includes another woman who may be identified as the Virgin. She follows along behind the litter and gazes directly down at the dead Christ's face.

The dating of this print has been a matter of some controversy. Ludwig Münz proposed a date of about 1653, while most other historians, including Arthur Hind, as well as Christopher White and Karel Boon, have suggested a date closer to 1645. As Erik Hinterding noted, the earlier date is supported by the etching's rather loose style of drawing, a technique that appears in some Rembrandt prints from the early and mid-1640s, such as the *Raising of Lazarus: Small Plate* (B. 72, cat. no. 47), which is signed and dated 1642. A drawing in Dresden (fig. 1) that Otto Benesch dates to 1641–42, and that is clearly related to the print of Christ Carried to the Tomb, is further evidence for an early date for this print.[7] The artist's signature on the plate, "Rembrant," is missing the "d" from the artist's name, and this same spelling appears on some prints from the mid-1640s, such as *Abraham and Isaac* (B. 34, cat. no. 6). Arguing against an early date is the existence of early impressions of the composition on Japanese paper, a support that Rembrandt used only after 1647, and also the presence of watermarks that appear on editions from 1651 and after.[8]

Notes

1. Rembrandt's choice of a transitional, rather than overtly dramatic, moment makes this print comparable to his depiction of *Abraham and Isaac* (B. 34, 1645, cat. no. 6), in which father and son have set out to fulfill God's command, but have not yet reached their destination.

2. Biblical accounts relate that after the Deposition, Joseph of Arimathea wrapped Jesus's body in a linen shroud and then buried him, but the Gospels do not describe the journey from the hilltop to the tomb. According to the Gospel of St. Matthew (27:59–60), "when Joseph had taken the body he wrapped it in a clean linen cloth, and laid it in his own new tomb, which he had hewn out in the rock." In St. Mark (15:46), "He [Joseph of Arimathea] bought fine linen, and took him [Jesus] down [from the cross], and wrapped him in the linen, and laid him in a sepulcher which was hewn out of rock." In

St. Luke (23:53), "he took [Jesus's body] down, and wrapped it in linen, and laid it in a sepulcher that was hewn in stone." In St. John's account (19:40–42), the destination seems quite different: "Then took they the body of Jesus, and wound it in linen clothes with the spices as the manner of the Jews is to bury. Now in the place where he was crucified there was a garden; and in the garden a new sepulcher, wherein was never man yet laid. There laid they Jesus therefore because of the Jews' preparation day; for the sepulcher was nigh at hand."

3. *Rembrandt's Journey*, 112.

4. *Rembrandt's Faith*, 308.

5. Shelley Perlove and Larry Silver (*Rembrandt's Faith*, 307) observed that when Golgotha appears in the background of an Entombment or Lamentation, as it does, for example, in Dürer's *Large Passion*, artists usually show the three crosses on the summit of the hill. Rembrandt has just barely suggested two of them.

6. The practice of representing extreme grief by including a figure whose features are shrouded from view was a common artistic device whose practice went back to the ancient artist Timanthes's painting of Agamemnon at the sacrifice of his daughter, Iphigenia. Pliny the Elder, *Natural History*, Book 35, 73: "As to Timanthes, he was an artist highly gifted with genius, and loud have some of the orators been in their commendations of his Iphigenia, represented as she stands at the altar awaiting her doom. Upon the countenance of all present, that of her uncle in particular, grief was depicted; but having already exhausted all the characteristic features of sorrow, the artist adopted the device of veiling the features of the victim's father [Agamemnon], finding himself unable adequately to give expression to his feelings."

7. Dresden Kupferstichkabinett (Ben. 483).

8. Hinterding (*Lugt Catalogue*, 186–87) summarized the arguments for and against the 1645 date and ultimately decided in favor of it.

58. *Entombment*

B. 86 (H. 281, Mz. 241, NHD 284)
Etching, drypoint, and burin
c. 1654
State IV of IV
Sheet: 21.1 × 16.1 cm, trimmed to the plate mark
Watermark: crowned single-headed Eagle with Basel crozier with a maker's mark, cross, *D*, three roundels (Petrus Düring?) below the tail (close to Briquet 1370)
Verso: collector's stamp, black ink, Delanglade (Lugt 660, Charles Delanglade)

Provenance:
Charles Delanglade (1870–1952)
Theodore B. Donson Ltd., New York, NY, 1980
Feddersen, Elkhart, IN, 1991
Snite Museum of Art
Acc. No.: 1991.025.055

The plate does not survive.

The events surrounding Christ's burial are recounted in all four of the Gospels.[1] After the Crucifixion, Joseph of Arimathea, a wealthy disciple of Christ, came to Pilate and asked that he be given Jesus's body. When Pilate granted him permission, Joseph took the body down from the cross and wrapped it in "a clean linen cloth" that he had brought with him. He then laid Christ's body "in his own [Joseph's] new tomb, which he had hewn out in the rock."[2] According to the Gospel of St. John, the secret convert Nicodemus joined Joseph in preparing the body, anointing it with myrrh and aloe before it was wrapped in the linen shroud. John also states that the tomb was located in a garden "in the place where [Christ] was crucified,"[3] that is, in Golgotha.

Because Christ's entombment was a traditional part of the Passion cycle, it was a popular subject during the Early Modern period. Martin Schongauer, for example, made an engraving of the scene as part of his Passion series from about 1480 (TIB 18) (fig. 1), and Albrecht Dürer included the episode in both his small woodcut *Passion* of 1497–98 (TIB 44) (fig. 2) and his engraved Passion of 1511–12 (TIB 15) (fig. 3). In all three of these examples, the scene is set in front of the entrance to a cave, and Christ's disciples, including Joseph of Arimathea and Nicodemus, are shown supporting Jesus's body on a white linen shroud as they lower it into an open stone sarcophagus. Female disciples, including, presumably, Mary Magdalen, who is specifically mentioned in Matthew's account, also bear witness to the entombment.[4] Numerous other sixteenth-century artists, including the virtuoso Dutch printmaker Hendrick Goltzius, created variations on this formula. In his engraving of 1596 (NHD 31) (fig. 4), however, Goltzius altered the setting. Although the core of the composition remained the same—Christ's body rests on a linen shroud as it is being used to lower him into a sarcophagus surrounded by numerous male and female disciples—the scene was moved inside the burial cave. Goltzius also added some curious onlookers: two children perched on a rocky ledge above the mourners, and a man and woman standing at the top of a short flight of steps leading up to the entrance of the cave. In the mid-1630s, Jan Georg van Vliet composed another variation on the entombment (HD 9) (fig. 5) as part of a series of six Passion prints.[5] In his engraving, van Vliet set the scene within a cave, but he narrowed the scope of the composition to the cavern itself, focusing on two female disciples and a few figures carrying

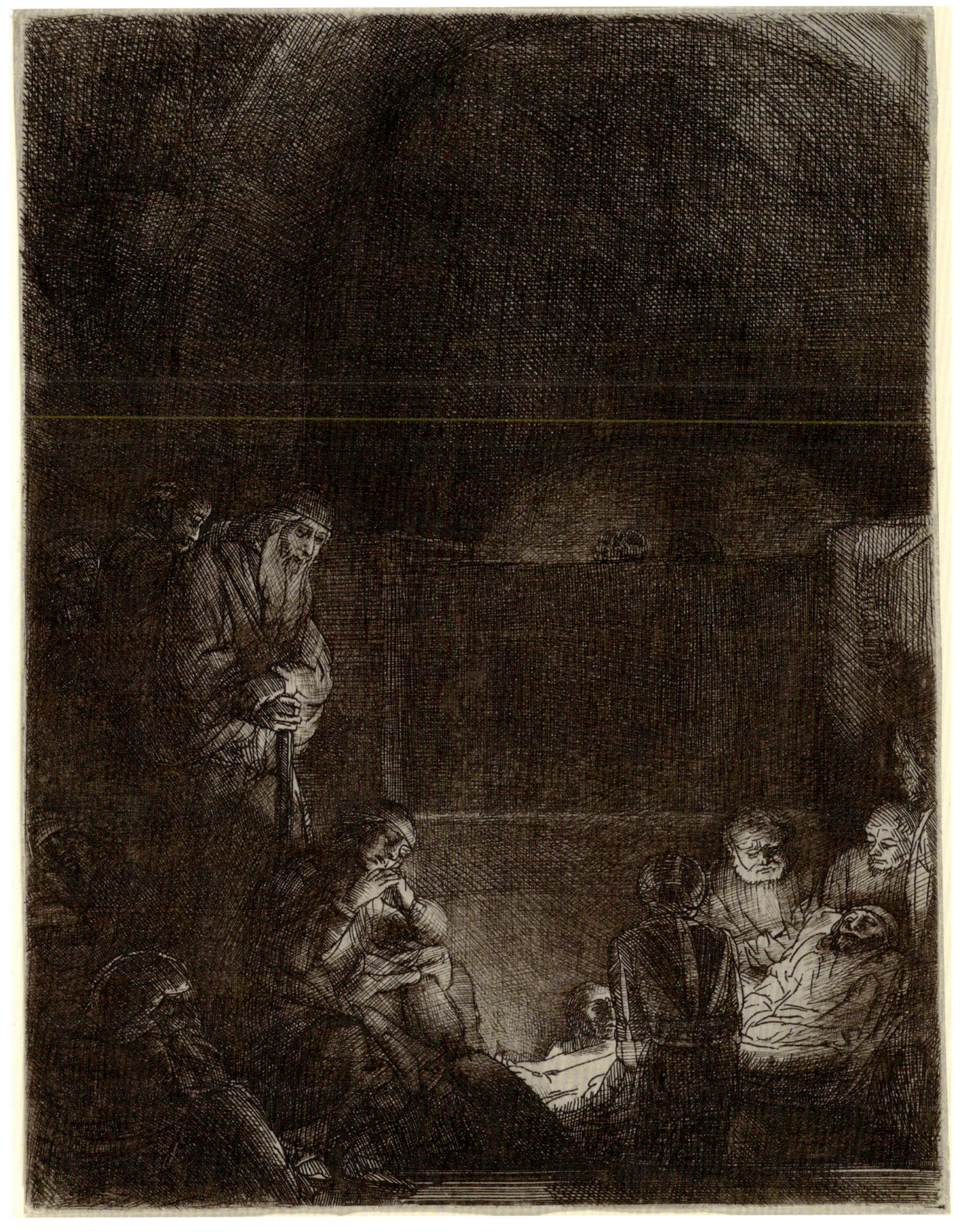

PLATE 58

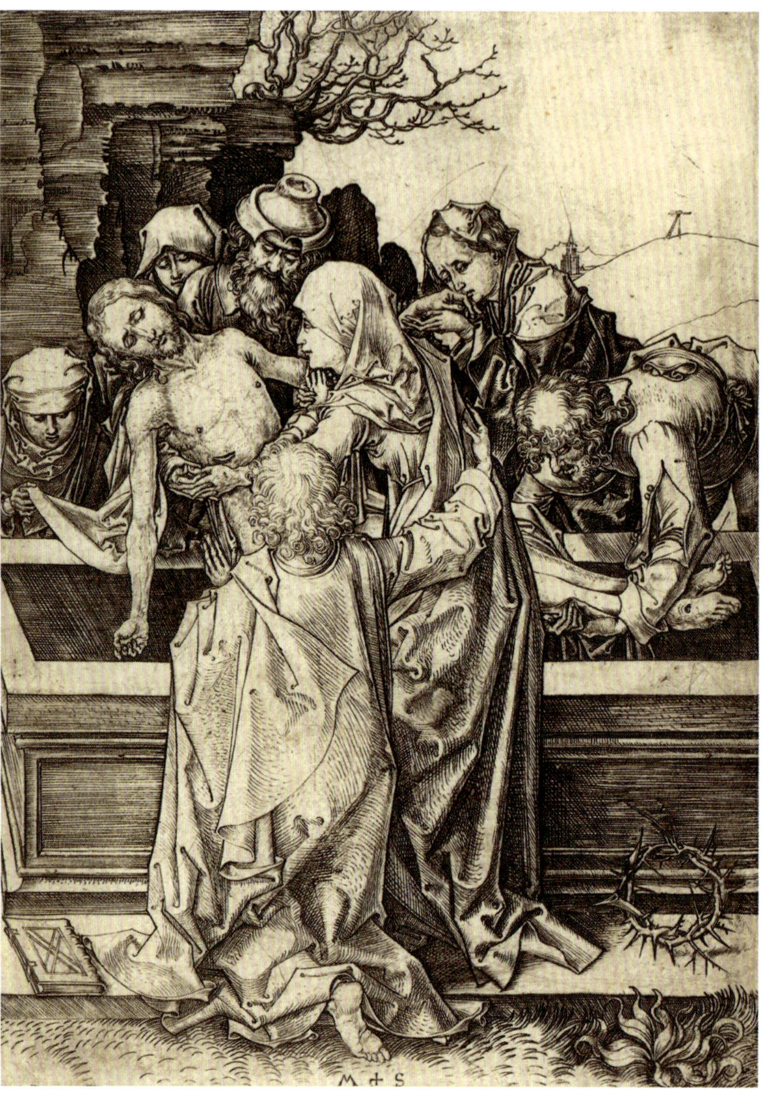

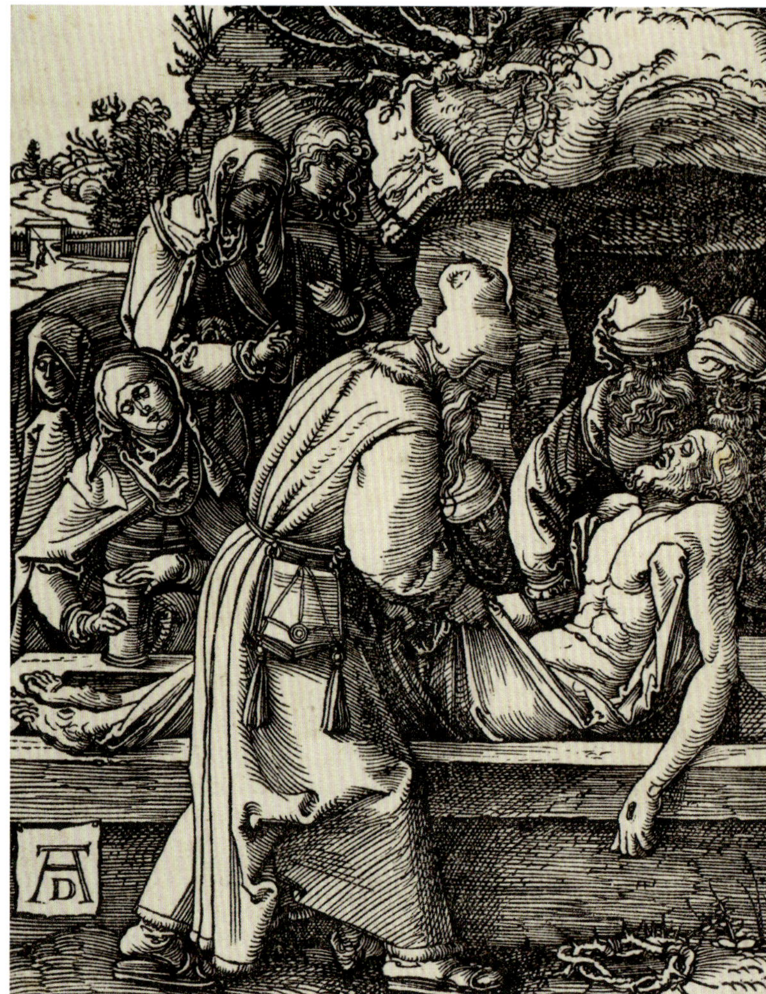

FIGURE 1. Martin Schongauer, *Entombment*, engraving, c. 1480. *Photo: Courtesy of the National Gallery of Art, Washington, DC.*

FIGURE 2. Albrecht Dürer, *Entombment*, woodcut, 1497–98. *The Metropolitan Museum of Art, New York, New York, Gift of Junius Spencer Morgan.*

Christ's body down a curving flight of steps toward a stone sarcophagus. In this engraving, van Vliet seems to have been considerably more interested in the volumetric rendering of the actors and the dramatic effects of light and shadow than in the setting.

Rembrandt painted two versions of the Entombment in the late 1630s, one an almost monochromatic oil sketch on panel, today in Glasgow (fig. 6),[6] and the other a more finished, and later heavily restored, oil on canvas, now in Munich (fig. 7).[7] In the oil sketch, the scene is set within a mysterious, dimly lit cavern. The incandescently pale body of Christ, cradled in a white linen winding cloth, is being gently lowered to the floor of the sepulchral cave by a young man. Joseph of Arimathea, leaning forward with an expression of anguish on his face, stands behind the young disciple. An elderly woman kneels beside Christ, holding a lit candle, the only source of light within the otherwise darkened cavern, while a bearded, white-haired, elderly man supports Jesus's head and shoulders and gazes down at the dead man's face. At the right, numerous other disciples, some wearing clothing typical of seventeenth-century Dutch Jews, peer down at the scene from the shadowy recesses of the cave.

The Munich painting, a larger, more finished version of the Entombment, was executed between 1636 and 1639, in conjunction with a commission for a series of paintings of the Passion that

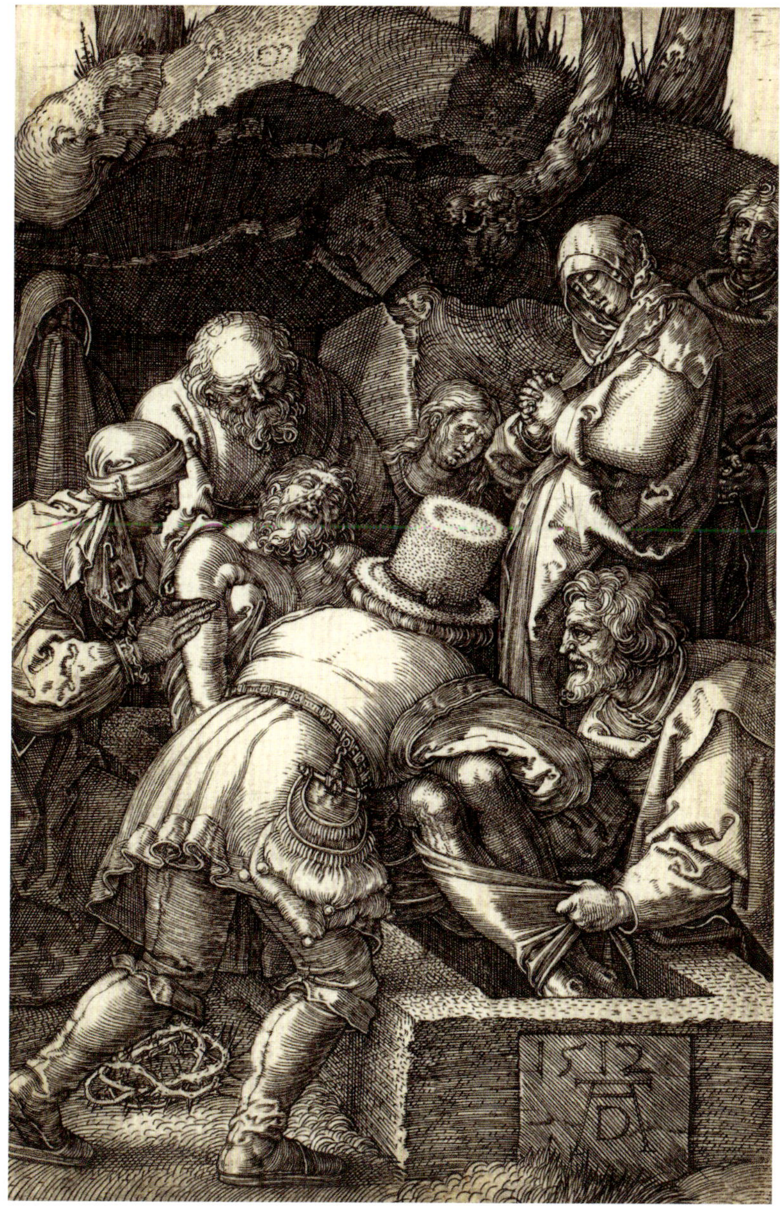

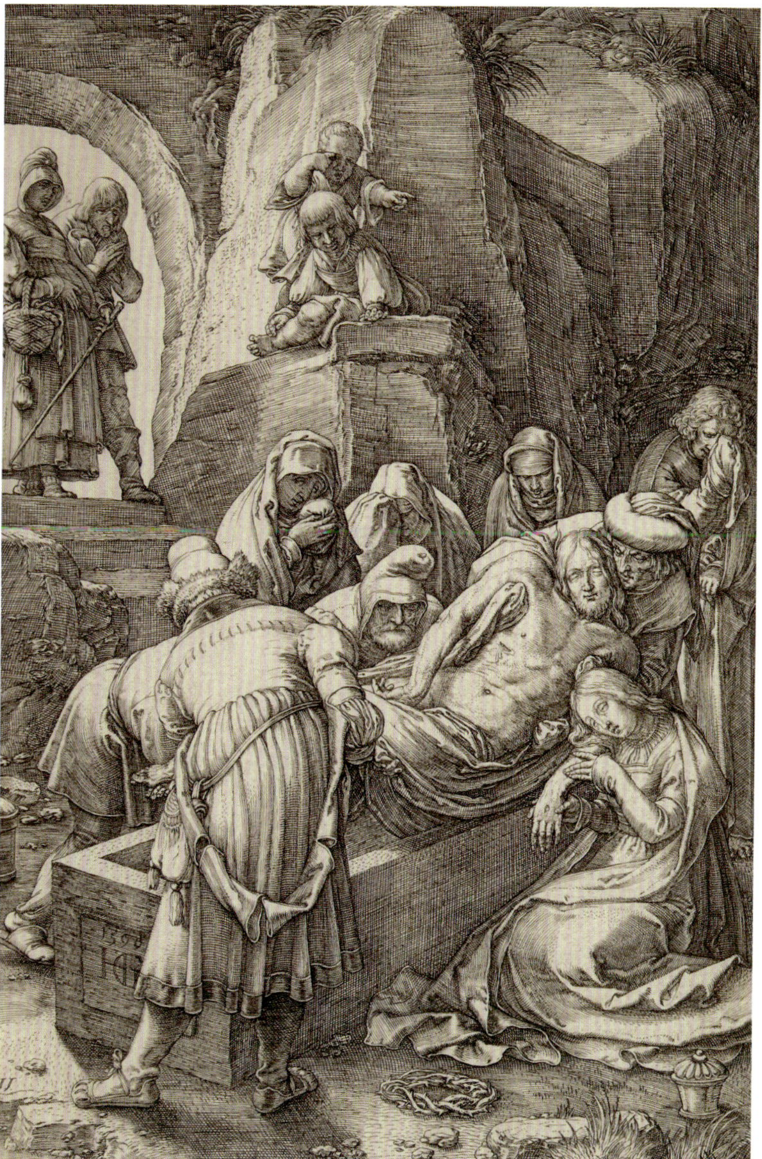

FIGURE 3. Albrecht Dürer, *Entombment*, engraving, 1512. *Photo: Courtesy of the National Gallery of Art, Washington, DC.*

FIGURE 4. Hendrick Goltzius, *Entombment*, engraving, 1596. *Yale University Art Gallery, New Haven, Connecticut, Gift of Edward B. Greene, B.A. 1900.*

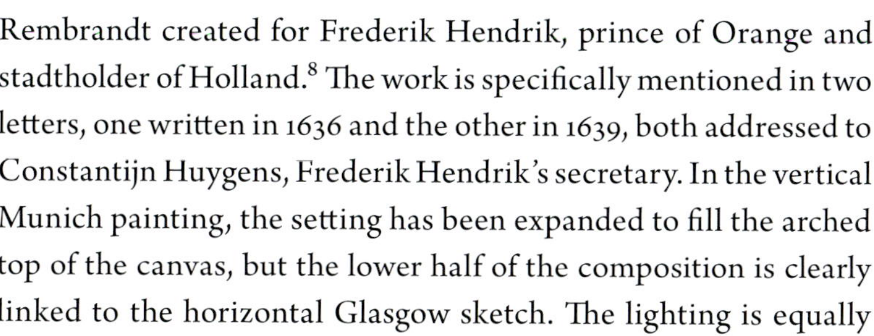

Rembrandt created for Frederik Hendrik, prince of Orange and stadtholder of Holland.[8] The work is specifically mentioned in two letters, one written in 1636 and the other in 1639, both addressed to Constantijn Huygens, Frederik Hendrik's secretary. In the vertical Munich painting, the setting has been expanded to fill the arched top of the canvas, but the lower half of the composition is clearly linked to the horizontal Glasgow sketch. The lighting is equally dramatic, with a powerful pool of light focused on the shroud, Christ's head and upper torso, and the followers who are clustered around him. In this version of the scene, Jesus's body is being lowered not onto the floor of the cavern, but into a stone sarcophagus set parallel to the picture plane. A shovel and woven basket lean against the face of the tomb. As in the Glasgow sketch, a young follower holds the sides of the shroud so as to make a sling, but in the Munich painting, in an added touch of realism, he strains backward

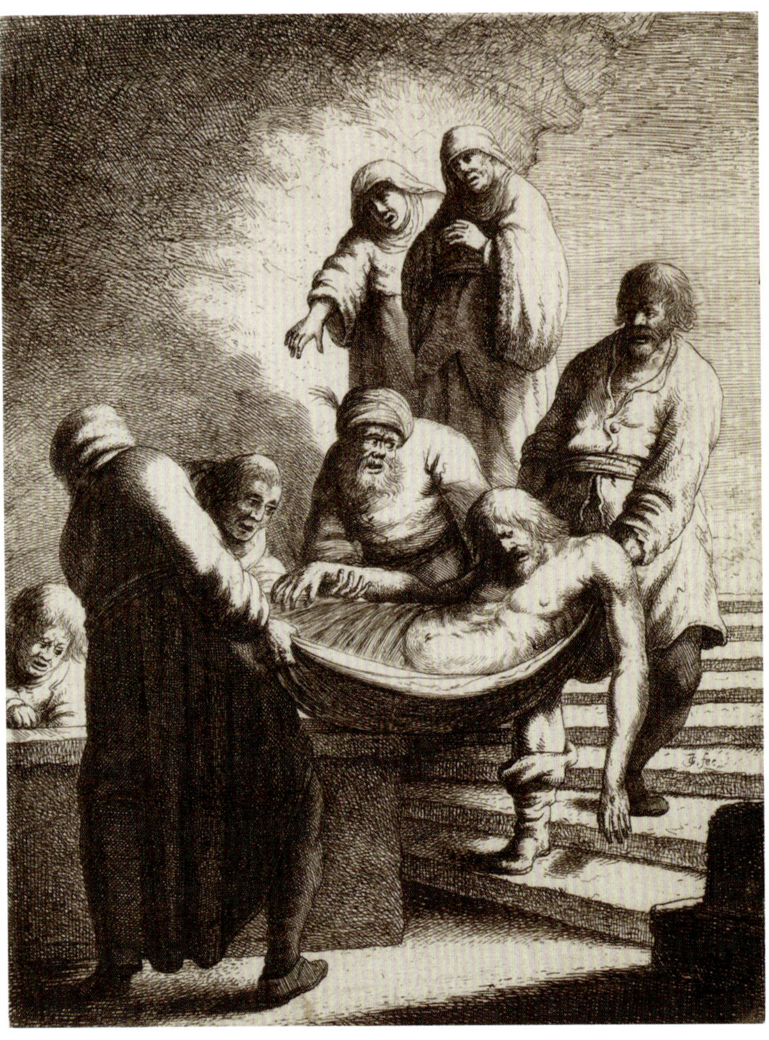

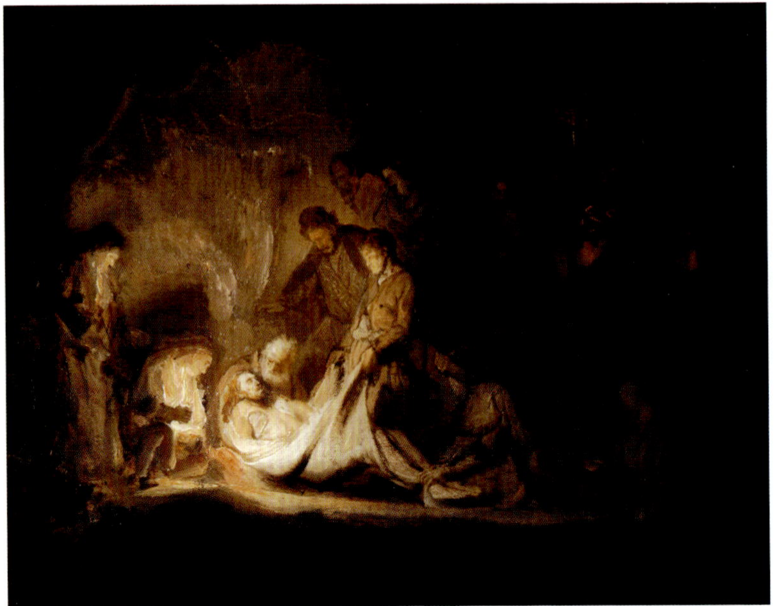

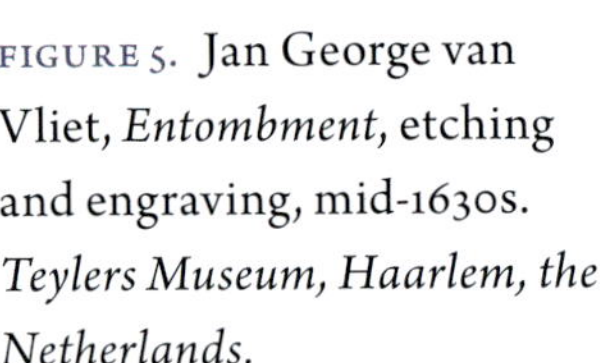

FIGURE 5. Jan George van Vliet, *Entombment*, etching and engraving, mid-1630s. *Teylers Museum, Haarlem, the Netherlands.*

FIGURE 6. Rembrandt, *Entombment*, oil on oak panel, 1633–35. *The Hunterian Art Gallery, University of Glasgow, Glasgow.*

so as to offset the weight of Jesus's body. Joseph of Arimathea stands beside him. One of the followers supports Christ's feet, and at the left side of the composition, another disciple supports Jesus's shoulders. The light from two candles illuminates the scene. One of these is held by a kneeling elderly woman who is backlit and in silhouette at the lower left corner. Behind her, a bearded old man holds the other candle, shielding its flame with his hand. To the right of the sarcophagus, three weeping women are seated upon the ground, and next to them—at the far right, in counterpoint to the shielded candle at the far left—hangs a glowing lantern, behind which additional figures are just barely visible in the darkness. Deep in the background, the mouth of the cave discloses an endless sky with clouds. That expanse seems all the more vast by virtue of its contrast with the miniaturized view of the hill of Golgotha, the crosses of the crucifixion, and a few tiny figures, in the distance.[9] This outdoor scene, glimpsed through the cave's opening, is dramatically illuminated by the crepuscular light of the setting sun. Another major departure from the Glasgow sketch is the inclusion of a draped niche crowned by an ornamented shield or hanging, located at the upper left corner of the composition. The addition of this niche and the significance of the heraldic-looking decoration have yet to be explained.

The Snite Museum's etching of the Entombment is clearly related to Rembrandt's two earlier painted versions, but it is also strongly influenced by a drawing of the subject attributed to Polidoro da Caravaggio (fig. 8),[10] a work that Rembrandt owned and closely copied at the end of the 1650s (fig. 9).[11] In both the original Polidoro drawing and Rembrandt's copy in pen and bistre, the Entombment takes place in a setting that suggests a familiarity with ancient catacombs and that is consequently much more architectural than that of either of the two painted versions. Three figures hold Christ's shroud-wrapped body suspended in front of a simple sarcophagus set under a low arch. A skull set into a small niche located just above the keystone of the arch may be a reference

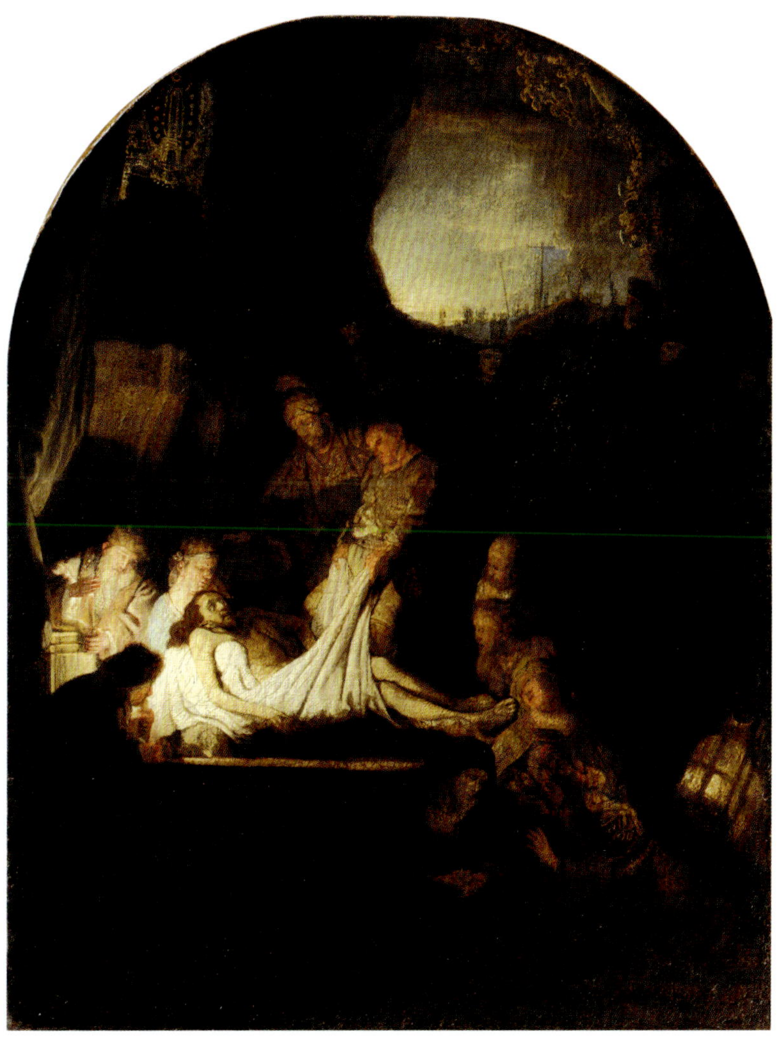

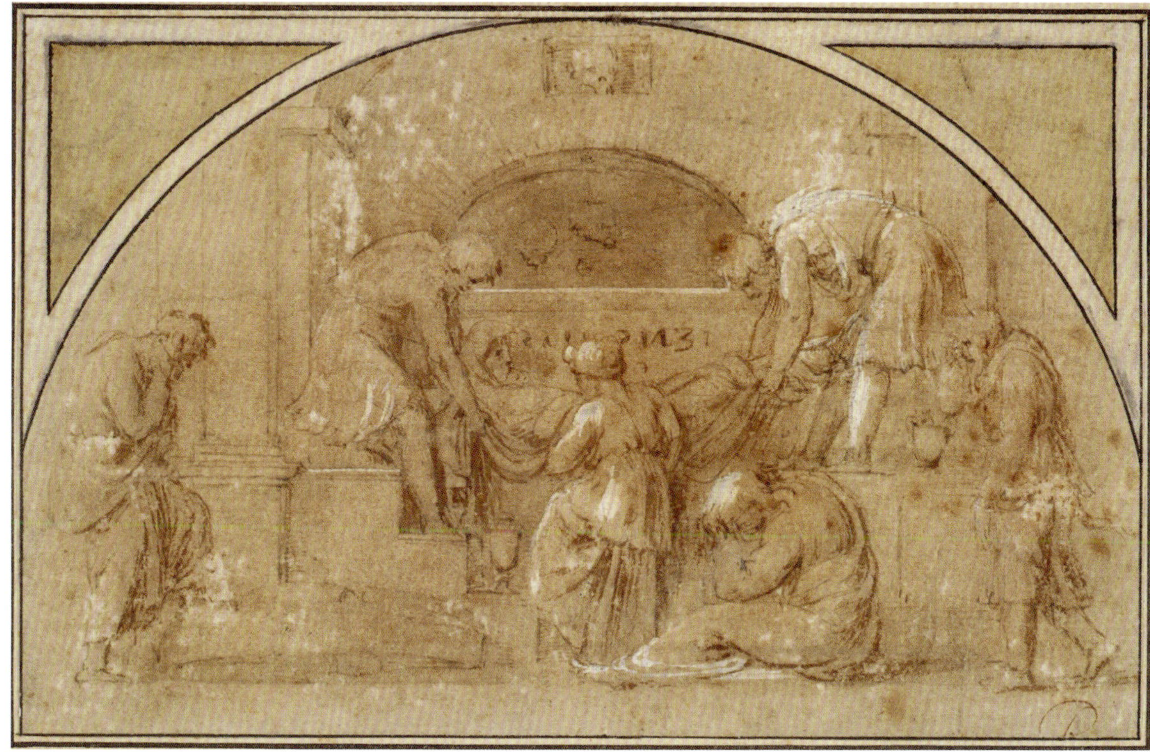

FIGURE 7. Rembrandt, *Entombment*, c. 1636–39. *Alte Pinakothek, Munich. Photo: bpk/Berlin/Alte Pinakothek, Munich/Art Resource, New York.*

FIGURE 8. Polidoro da Caravaggio, *Entombment*, brown ink and brown wash, heightened with white gouache, c. 1530–40. *Harvard Art Museums/ Fogg Art Museum, Bequest of Charles A. Loeser, Cambridge, Massachusetts. Photo: Imaging Department © President and Fellows of Harvard College.*

to both "Golgotha" ("skull" in Aramaic) and Adam, whose grave, according to tradition, was located there. Two men standing at the top of short staircases flanking the grave hold onto the ends of the shroud, and a figure in the center with her back to the viewer supports the middle of the draped body. This is probably meant to be Mary Magdalen, since in the original Polidoro drawing, a covered vessel, her attribute, appears beside her. A second woman, seated on the ground beside the Magdalen, rests her head on her left hand in a traditional pose of melancholy. An older man approaches the scene from the right, while another stands hunched over at the left, covering his face in a gesture of grief. Rembrandt's copy of the Polidoro original is extremely close in terms of both its composition and its cast of characters. He introduced small changes, such as the placement of the Magdalen's covered vessel, but the principal differences between the two images result from Rembrandt's personal style and his choice of medium. The contours of the figures are handled more loosely, the white highlights in Polidoro's drawing are eliminated, and the way in which the light is distributed is more dramatic.

In creating his etching of the Entombment, Rembrandt adopted Polidoro's device of an enframing arch, but abandoned compositional symmetry and placed the arch off-center. He chose to use a vertical format for the etching and also, through the use of light and shadow and the placement of the most prominent figures, carried the curve of the arch around until it completed an oval frame for the scene. In the print, massive cut stone blocks are set into the niche under the arch, and two ghoulish skulls sit on top of the center block. The background of the etching is cast into shadow, which in the first state of the print is rendered with narrowly spaced parallel lines of hatching. In the right foreground, five men

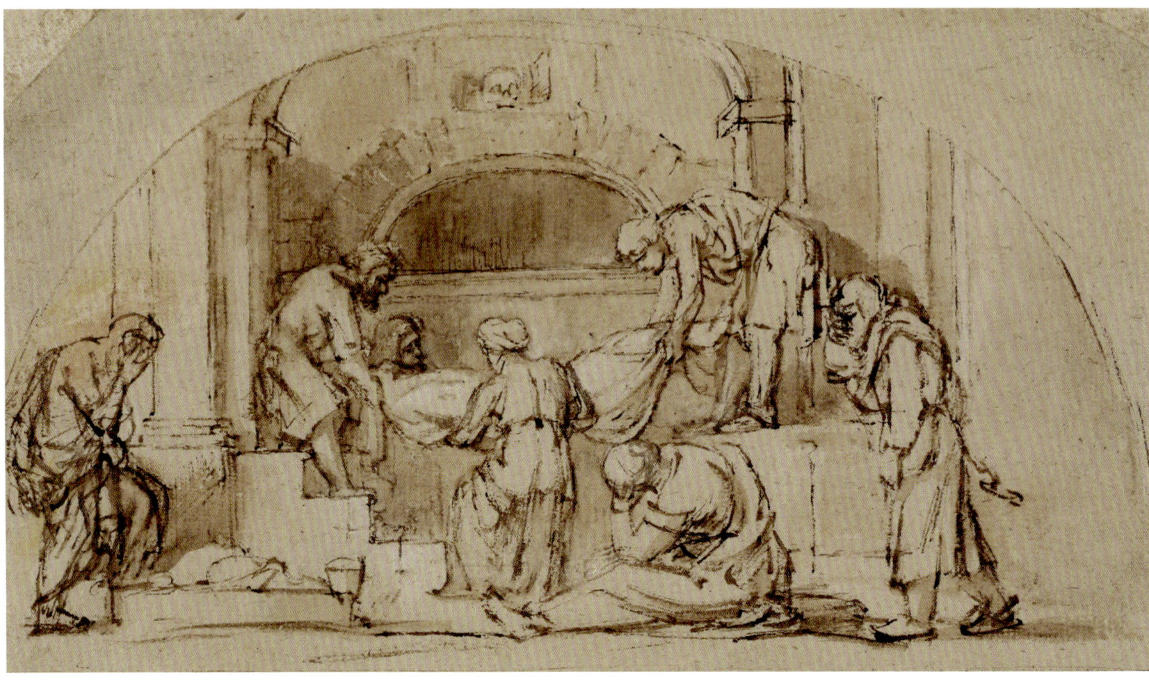

FIGURE 9. Rembrandt after Polidoro da Caravaggio, *Entombment*, pen and bistre with wash, Ben. 1208, c. 1657–58. *Teylers Museum, Haarlem, the Netherlands.*

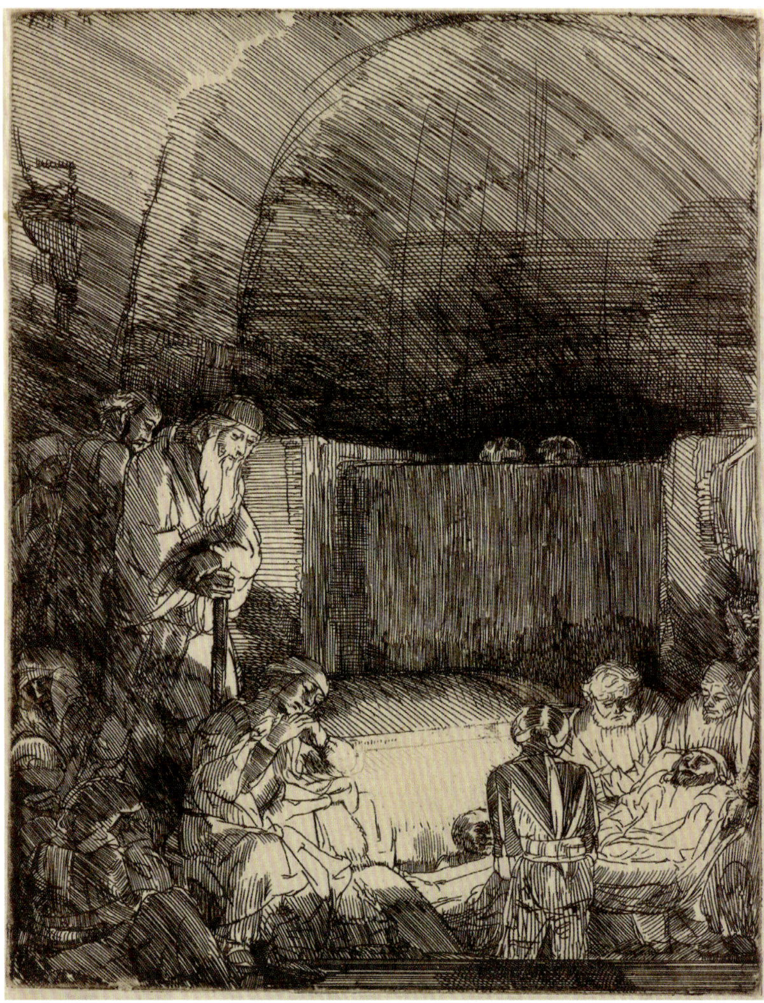

FIGURE 10. Rembrandt, *Entombment*, etching and drypoint, State I, c. 1654. *The Pierpont Morgan Library & Museum, New York, New York, RvR 133. Photography by Graham S. Haber.*

stand in or around the grave into which the body of Christ, partially wrapped in its winding cloth, is being carefully lowered. The figure with its back to the viewer recalls the placement of the Magdalen in the Polidoro drawing, while the bearded balding man and his companions who support Christ's head and upper torso recall similar figures in Rembrandt's Munich and Glasgow paintings. Bright white light seems to emanate from the body of Christ itself, most strongly from his bare legs, feet, and toes, which are not covered by the shroud. Dim light reveals the face of a very simple stone sarcophagus at the center of the print and illuminates a woman seated in front of the sarcophagus at the left. This disciple rests her head on her clasped hands, and her eyes appear to be shut in contemplation or repose.[12] An elderly, bearded man with a skullcap and shawl, possibly Joseph of Arimathea,[13] stands behind her, gazing down at Christ's body. These two figures recall the kneeling woman with a candle and the man standing beside her in Rembrandt's Glasgow oil sketch. A few additional mourners—two women and a man—are visible in the shadows beyond Joseph.

It has been hypothesized that *Entombment* was one of a series of four etchings of similar dimensions that Rembrandt created in the mid-1650s.[14] The other works are *The Presentation in the Temple in the Dark Manner* (B. 50), *Descent from the Cross by Torchlight* (B. 83, cat. no. 56), and *Christ at Emmaus: Larger Plate* (B. 87, cat. no. 60).[15] However, there is no evidence that Rembrandt ever intended the four prints to be sold as a series.

The first state of *Entombment* (fig. 10) is closely allied with the style that Rembrandt employed in other prints from the mid-1650s such as the *Adoration of the Shepherds: With the Lamp* (B. 45, cat. no. 20) and the *Circumcision in the Stable* (B. 47, cat. no. 24). In that early state, there is a broad variation in the manner in which form and light are described, ranging from the simple graphic outline of Christ's body to the dense shadows behind the skulls. Rembrandt was evidently not satisfied, however, for he radically reworked the plate, transforming it into a dramatic nocturne. Much of the surface was covered with a dense web of cross-hatching, with the result that the only light in the sepulchral cavern is that which seems to emanate from Christ himself. The niche, arch, and skulls in the background are also barely visible in the Stygian gloom of this etching. The effect of that change was to make the elegiac mood of this moment of great despair even more prominent. As Clifford Ackley so elegantly put it, "the extinguishing of the light becomes a metaphor for the extinction of life."[16]

In the 1650s, Rembrandt took a particularly experimental approach to printmaking, investigating various methods of inking and using different types of paper, printing impressions on Japanese, Chinese, and Western papers, and even vellum.[17] In the case of *Entombment*, he increased the sense of gloom by leaving a heavy plate tone on many of the impressions pulled from the second and third states of the print, creating monoprints. The Snite Museum's impression of *Entombment* was pulled from the fourth and final state, one that was printed on a laid cream paper with a dramatic spread-winged eagle watermark. There is only minimal plate tone on the surface, and as a result, the figures and setting remain clearly visible beneath the veil of cross-hatching.

Notes

1. Matthew 27:57–60; Mark 15:42–46; Luke 23:50–55; John 19:38–42.

2. Matthew 27:59–60.

3. John 19:40.

4. Lucas van Leyden's engraved *Entombment* of 1521 (NHD 54) follows the same basic formula, except that the lowering of the body into the sarcophagus is set in front of a dense screen of trees, with no cave visible in the background.

5. On Jan Georg van Vliet, a printmaker who collaborated with Rembrandt in the early 1630s, see also the entries on *Christ before Pilate: Large Plate* (B. 77, cat. no. 50) and *Descent from the Cross: The Second Plate* (B. 81 II, cat. no. 55).

6. Hunterian Art Gallery, Glasgow, Inv. GLAHA 43785; RRP, *Corpus,* A105. The dating of this painting and its relationship to the work in Munich has been a matter of some discussion. In the *Corpus,* the Glasgow painting is dated 1633–35 and considered to be a preliminary sketch for an unrealized series of Passion prints. Shelley Perlove and Larry Silver (*Rembrandt's Faith*, 438n43), however, suggested that the work should be dated to the 1640s or even 1650s. Recently, on the basis of a cleaning and close technical examination of the Hunterian panel, Peter Black suggested that the painting was initially done in the late 1630s, that is, after the Munich painting, and was then modified by the artist in the 1650s. Peter Black, *Rembrandt and the Passion* (Munich: Prestel Verlag, 2012), 93–99.

The authors of the *Corpus* have also suggested that this work may be the "sketch of the entombment of Christ" that Rembrandt had in his possession at the time of his bankruptcy sale of 1656. Walter Strauss and Marjon van der Meulen, eds. and trans., *The Rembrandt Documents* (New York: Abaris, 1979), doc. 1656/13, item no. 111, "schets van de begraeffenis Christ."

7. Munich, Bayerische Staatsgemäldesammlungen, Alte Pinakothek, Inv. No. 398. RRP, *Corpus*, A126.

8. On the Passion cycle that was expanded to include an *Adoration of the Shepherds* (Munich, Alte Pinakothek, and London, National Gallery) and *Circumcision* (copy after Rembrandt, Braunschweig, Herzog Anton Ulrich Museum), see Gary Schwartz, *Rembrandt: His Life, His Paintings* (London: Penguin, 1985), chapter 17, and 238–39.

9. There is a well-established visual tradition that associates Golgotha with Christ's tomb, as described in the Gospel of John. See, for example, Martin Schongauer, *Entombment*, c. 1480 (HG 28); Circle of Mantegna, *Entombment*, c. 1470–1500 (TIB 2); Dürer, *Entombment* from the *Large Woodcut Passion*, 1497–1500 (TIB, woodcuts, 13); and Giulio Bonasone after Titian, *Entombment,* 1563 (TIB 44). Peter Black (*Rembrandt and the Passion*, 93–99) suggested that Rembrandt might have been influenced by Johannes Sadeler I's engraving after Dirck Barendz's *Entombment* (HD 251, c. 1600), a print that shows a similar view of Golgotha through the mouth of the cave. Rembrandt also appears to have made this association between the two sites when he created the early states of *The Three Crosses* (B. 78, 1653–55, cat. no. 54), in which the mouth of a cave is visible in the right corner, and in *Christ Carried to the Tomb* (B. 84, c. 1645, cat. no. 57), where there is just the barest suggestion of crosses in the space between a

donkey and a group of figures on the distant hill of Golgotha, above the funeral procession wending its way toward the cave.

10. Fogg Art Museum, Cambridge, MA, Inv. 1932.348. Rembrandt probably believed that this drawing was by Raphael.

11. Ben. 1208. The drawing is in the Teylers Museum, Haarlem, Inv. o*49.

12. This woman may be the Magdalen, or perhaps even the Virgin, although the Gospels do not mention Jesus's mother as being present at the entombment.

13. This "biblical"-style Joseph of Arimathea provides a contrast to the wealthy, exotically costumed Joseph of Rembrandt's 1633 *Descent from the Cross: The Second Plate* (B. 81 II, cat. no. 55).

14. For this series, see Ernst van de Wetering, "Remarks on Rembrandt's Oil Sketches for Etchings," in Erik Hinterding, Ger Luijten, and Martin Royalton-Kisch, *Rembrandt the Printmaker,* exh. cat. (Chicago and London: Fitzroy Dearborn Publishers, 2000), 44–47; and *Rembrandt's Journey,* 232–39. The Snite Museum's collection includes an example of each print in the series with the exception of the *Presentation in the Temple in the Dark Manner.*

15. Although this may seem like a heterogeneous group of subjects, it should be remembered that the Passion cycle that Rembrandt produced for Frederik Hendrik in the late 1630s and early 1640s—scenes from the end of Jesus's life—was expanded to include two scenes from Christ's earliest days, *Adoration of the Shepherds* and *Circumcision.* See note 8, above.

16. *Rembrandt's Journey,* 238.

17. See the discussion of Rembrandt's supports in Rosenberg, "Rembrandt's Religious Prints," in this catalog.

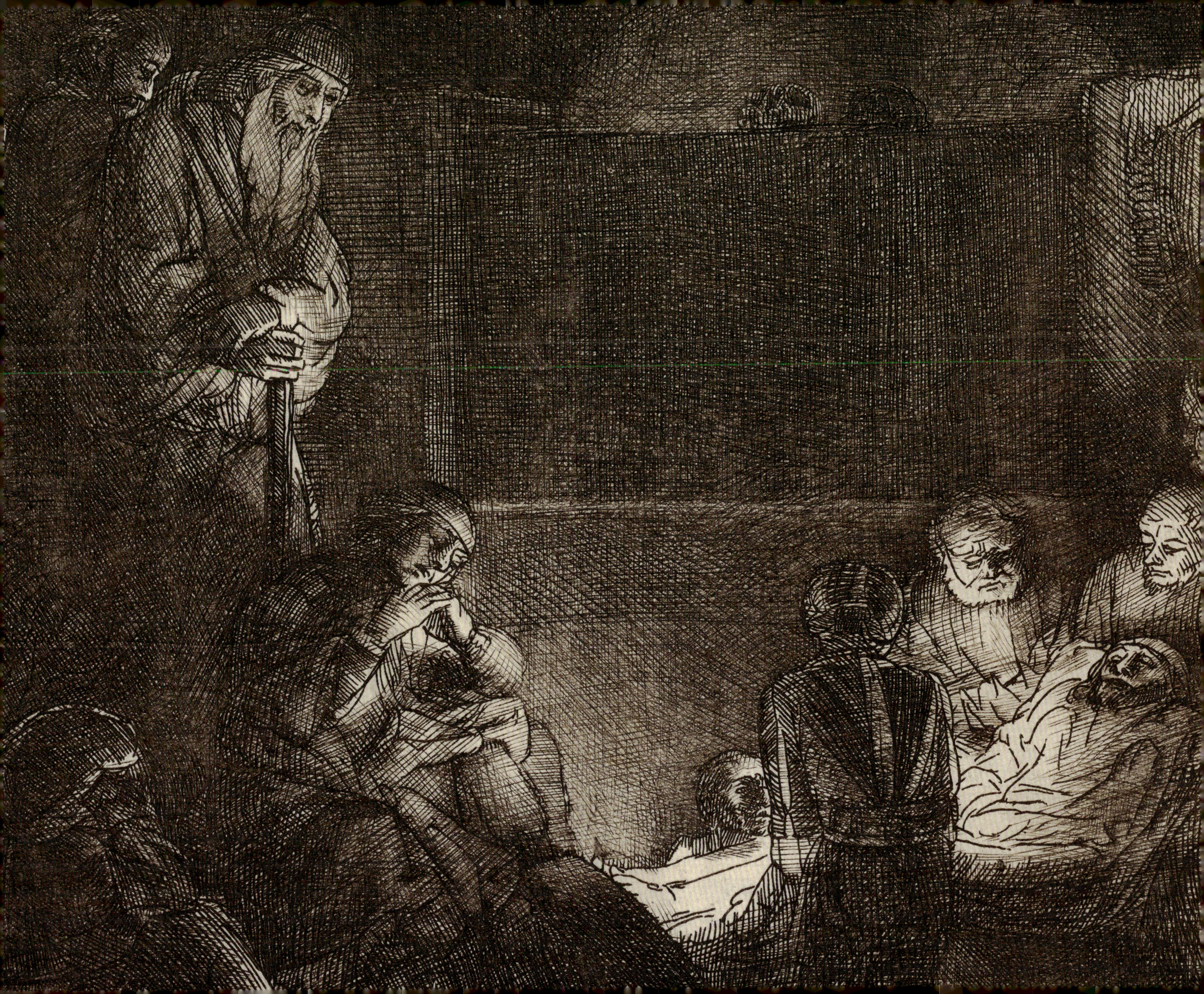

59–60. Christ at Emmaus

59. Christ at Emmaus: Small Plate

B. 88 (H. 237, Mz. 220, NHD 129)
Etching with touches of drypoint
Signed and dated in the plate: *Rembrandt f. 1634*
State I of I
Sheet: 10.5 × 7.6 cm; plate mark 10.2 × 7.3 cm

Provenance:
Craddock & Barnard, London, 1978
Feddersen, Elkhart, IN, 1991
Snite Museum of Art
Acc. No.: 1991.025.057

The plate does not survive.

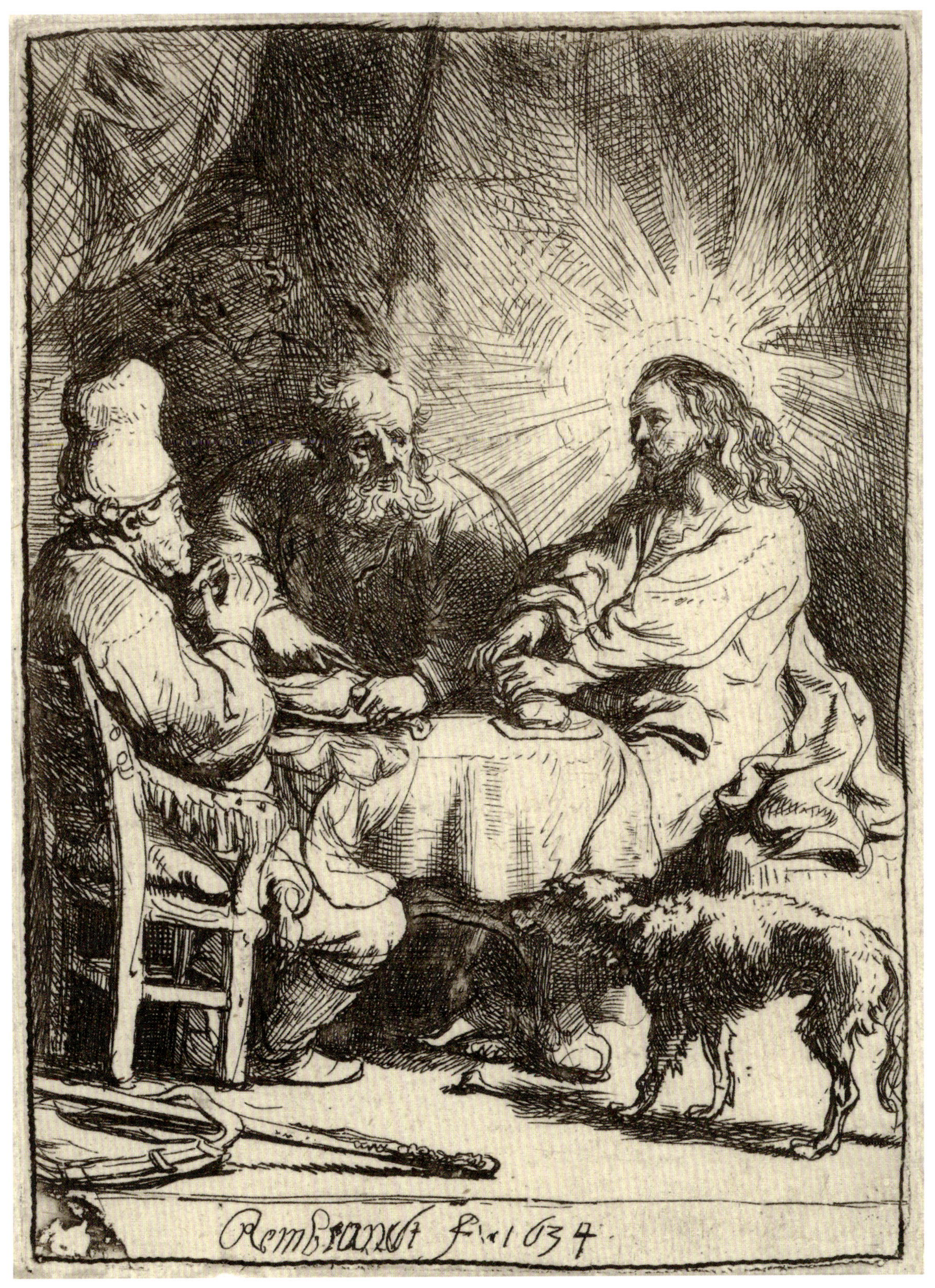

PLATE 59

60. Christ at Emmaus: Larger Plate

B. 87 (H. 282, Mz. 233, NHD 283)
Etching, burin (doubted by Hinterding), and drypoint
Signed and dated: *Rembrandt f. 1654*
State IV of V
Sheet: 23.5 × 17.9 cm; plate mark 21.1 × 16.0 cm
Verso: in graphite, *B87*

Provenance:
Associated American Artists, Inc., New York, NY, 1969
Feddersen, Elkhart, IN, 1991
Snite Museum of Art
Acc. No.: 1991.025.056

Plate survives:
Art Institute of Chicago, Chicago (inv. 1993.181).

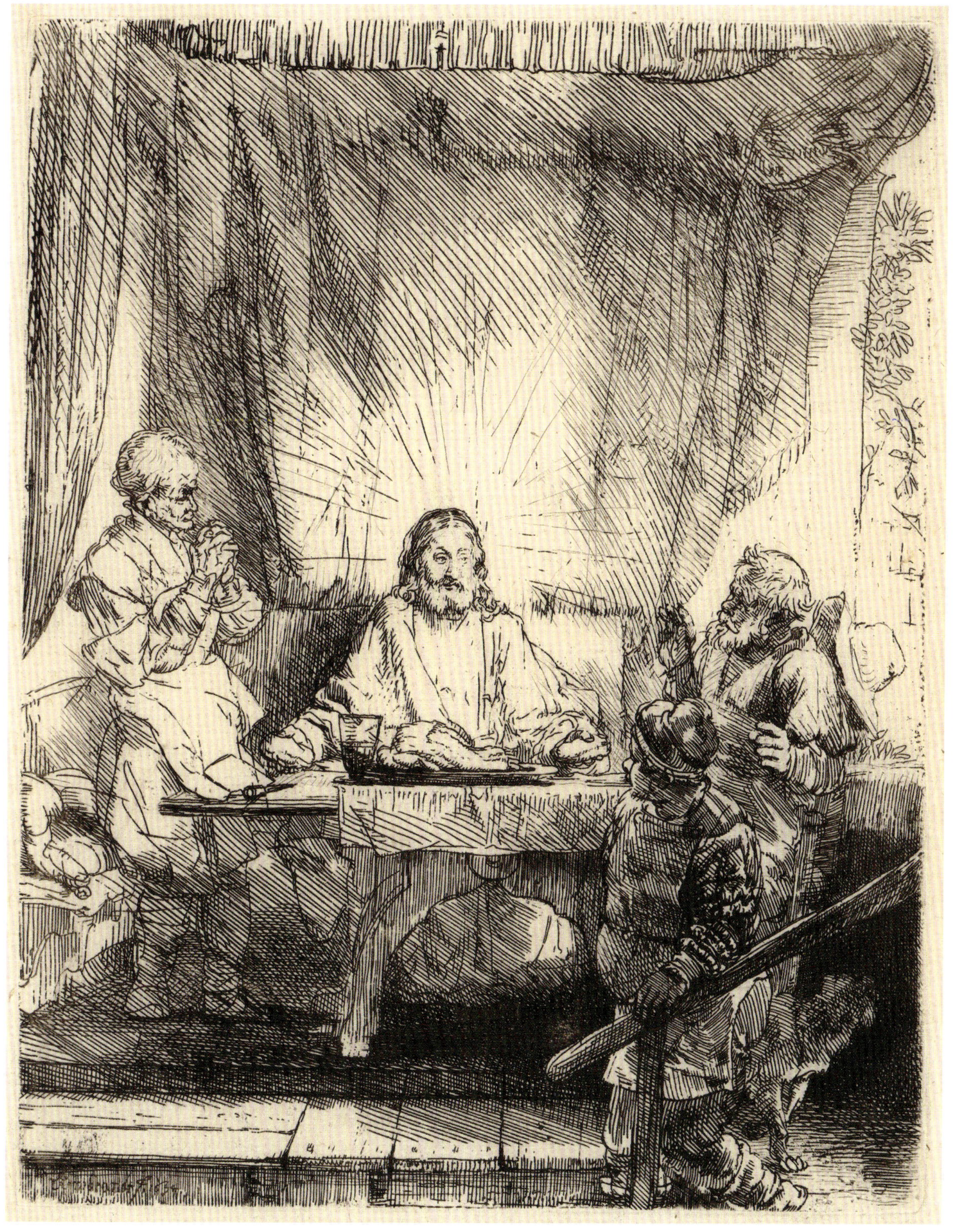

PLATE 60

FIGURE 1. Arnold Houbraken after a lost Rembrandt, *Disciples at Emmaus*, engraving, published 1718. *Rijksmuseum, Amsterdam.*

The Gospel of St. Luke describes the encounter between Jesus and two disciples on the road to Emmaus immediately after the account of the visit of the three Marys to Jesus's empty tomb and Peter's subsequent visit to the sepulcher. According to Luke,[1] the two disciples had been walking along, conversing, when Jesus joined them and asked them what they were discussing. Because Christ had altered his appearance, the men did not recognize him. They told the newcomer about Jesus's crucifixion and its aftermath, and they expressed their skepticism regarding the miracle reported by the Marys. Jesus reassured the two men, telling them that all the events that had been witnessed had been foretold by the prophets. By the time the three men reached Emmaus, the day was waning, and the disciples invited their companion to remain with them. He agreed, and they went to dine at an inn in town. When they sat down at the table, Jesus "took bread and blessed it, and broke it, and gave it to them. And their eyes were opened, and they recognized him; and he vanished from their eyes."[2]

The story of the Supper at Emmaus represents one of the earliest, and possibly the first, of Christ's appearances to his disciples after his entombment.[3] It was this encounter that confirmed the truth of Jesus's resurrection to his disciples and, later, to readers of the Gospels. In Rembrandt's time, when the conversion of Jews was a major question under debate,[4] this story of skeptical followers transformed into believers might well have had a special resonance. Rembrandt depicted the subject of the Supper at Emmaus at different times and in different media during his career.[5] In addition to two prints, examples of which are found in the Snite Museum's collection, Rembrandt made at least two paintings of the encounter.

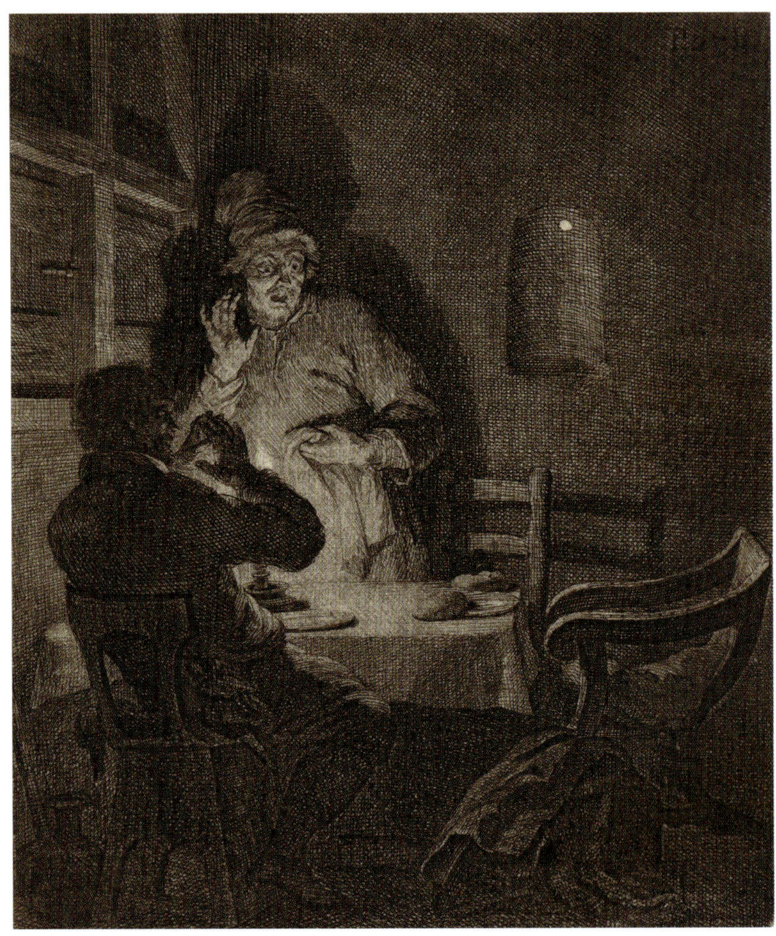

A lost work is reflected in a print by Arnold Houbraken and several seventeenth- and eighteenth-century drawings (figs. 1 and 2).[6] The earliest painted example, dated about 1629, is a small work executed in oil on paper[7] (fig. 3). A highly theatrical painting, it is a study in tenebristic lighting, facial expression, and the rhetoric of gesture.

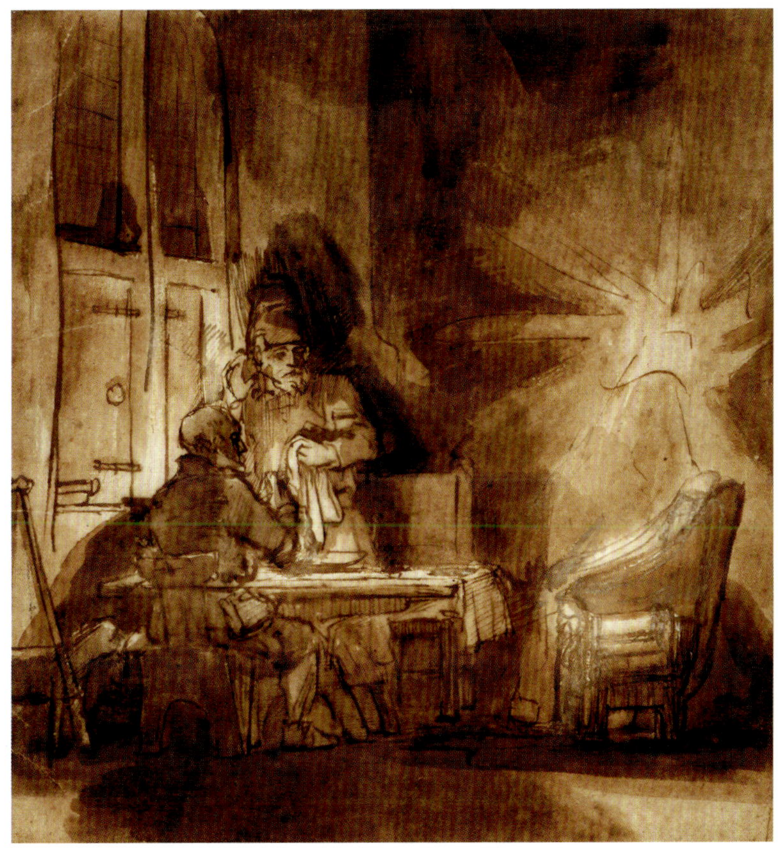

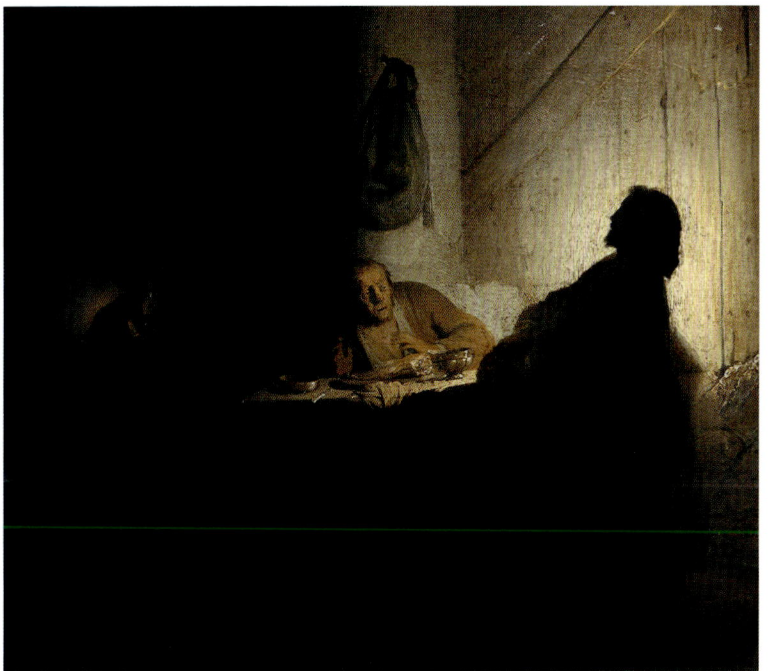

FIGURE 2. Copy after Rembrandt (?), *The Supper at Emmaus*, pen and India ink, bistre, and wash with white highlight, Ben. C47, c. 1640 with eighteenth-century additions. *Fitzwilliam Museum, Cambridge, England. Photo: © Fitzwilliam Museum/Art Resource, New York.*

FIGURE 3. Rembrandt, *Christ at Emmaus*, oil on paper mounted on panel, c. 1629. *Institut de France–Musée Jacquemart-André, Paris, France, P-848. Photo: © Institut de France–Musée Jacquemart-André, Paris, France.*

Christ and the two disciples are pictured in the right foreground. The moment of enlightenment is signified literally and metaphorically through a brilliant flash of light that washes across a wall of rough-cut boards at the rear of the room, casting the figure of Christ into dramatic silhouette. The reactions of the two pilgrims reflect the psychological power of the revelation: one of the disciples kneels in the dense shadows at Christ's feet. The man has risen from his seat so quickly that he has upset his chair, an indexical sign of the moment of epiphany. The other disciple is still seated at the table. Bathed in reflected light, he stares at Jesus and recoils as if fearful of what might happen next. On the other side of the room, the space opens out into a corridor that leads to a second room, where a woman can be seen attending to a cooking pot suspended over a dimly flickering fire. Spiritual, as well as visual, contrasts are created, between the pilgrims to whom the miracle of Christ has been revealed and the woman who attends to her tasks, unaware of the drama taking place; and between the dazzling light of Christ's divinity and the dim flicker of earthly illumination.

The earlier of the two etchings of the Supper at Emmaus (B. 88, cat. no. 59) is signed and dated 1634. Although the print is quite small, Rembrandt filled the space with large-scale figures, drawing the viewer's eye to the details of the event and their significance. The tiny print is considerably less theatrical than the 1629 Emmaus painting, and, in keeping with the work's intimate size, Rembrandt eschewed his earlier emphasis on expression and dramatic light effects in favor of a quiet consideration of the nature of spiritual enlightenment. Jesus, seated at the right side of the table, is dressed in soft, voluminous robes. He holds a loaf of bread in his left hand and prepares to break it with his right as he gazes intently at the man seated across from him. The painted version's aureola of light behind and above Jesus's head has been translated into a halo described by linear rays. The light dissolves the shadows above Jesus, but inexplicably leaves his far shoulder in darkness. A second, equally intense source of light enters the room from the right foreground,

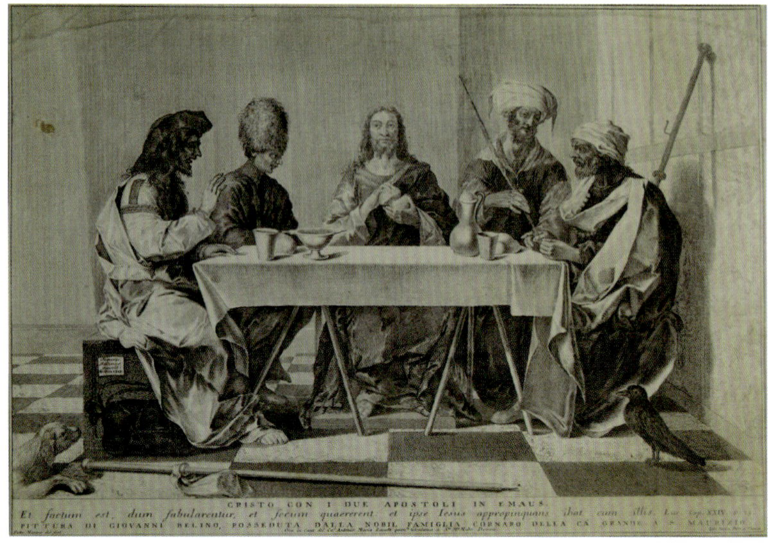

FIGURE 4. Pietro Monaco (1730–63) after Giovanni Bellini, *Christ at Emmaus*, engraving, eighteenth century. *Munich, Staatliche Graphische Sammlung. Photo: Courtesy of Fine Art Vienna.*

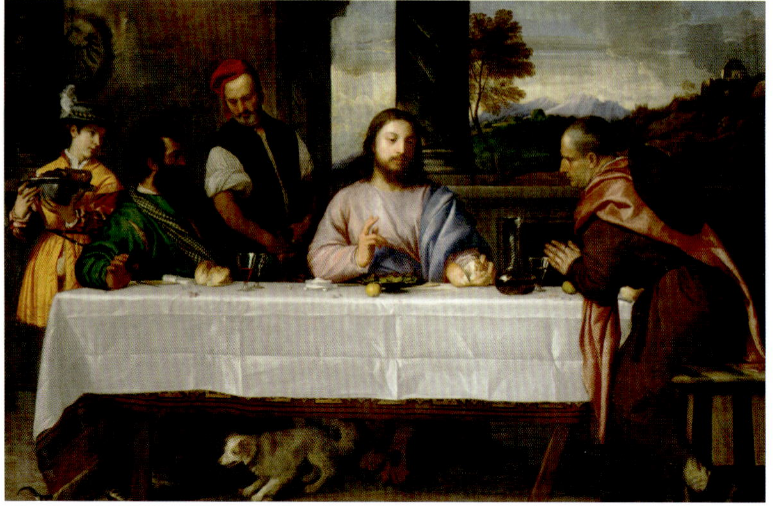

FIGURE 5. Titian, *Christ at Emmaus*, oil on canvas, c. 1530. *Louvre, Paris. Photo: Erich Lessing/Art Resource, New York.*

FIGURE 6. *Facing left*, Dirck Volkertsz. Coornhert after Maarten van Heemskerck, *Christ at Emmaus*, engraving, 1548. *Rijksmuseum, Amsterdam.*

illuminating Jesus's face, the left side of his body, the front of the tablecloth, and the right side of the pilgrim seated across the table from him, from the man's tall, soft hat to the toe of his boot.[8] The traveler's walking staff and bag[9] have been casually set down on the floor beside his chair. This elderly, somewhat jowly disciple returns Christ's gaze as he draws the fingertips of his cupped hands together in front of him, a pose that can be variously interpreted as an expression of contemplation or, perhaps a prelude to clasping his hands together in prayer, a sign of his dawning recognition of the identity of the stranger he has befriended. The second pilgrim is seated behind the table. Like the man at the center of the 1629 painting, he gazes quizzically at Jesus. He has paused in the act of carving the joint that is about to nourish them and that may be an allusion to the symbolic paschal lamb. This disciple's face and left shoulder are illuminated by the light emanating from Jesus, but the rest of his body remains in shadow, which suggests that the man is not yet fully "enlightened"; he is just becoming aware of the identity of the stranger beside him.

A thin, mangy dog stands in the lower right corner of the composition, its attention fixed on the disciple carving the joint. The dog, oblivious to the miracle taking place before him, is presumably waiting to be thrown a scrap of meat; the bone lying on the floor before him has already been picked clean. While irreverent dogs appear in a number of Rembrandt's etchings,[10] the inclusion of a dog in a depiction of the Supper of Emmaus was not unique to him. A number of earlier examples of the scene also featured a dog, most famously Giovanni Bellini's lost *Supper at Emmaus* of 1490 (fig. 4),[11] known from prints after the painting; Titian's version of the subject from about 1530, in which a dog and cat confront one another beneath the table (fig. 5);[12] and a 1548 print by Dirck Volkertsz. Coornhert after a design by Maarten van Heemskerck with a dog and cat seated on the floor in the foreground (fig. 6).[13] The attentiveness of Rembrandt's mongrel to the scene playing out before it, however, is unusual.[14] His dog also serves important compositional and narrative functions: it offers a visual entrée into the scene and adds a measure of anecdotal comic realism, a device that Rembrandt used to good effect in several other prints.[15] In addition, Larry Silver and Shelley Perlove have interpreted the dog as a symbol of carnality and a representation of the Old Law, that is, a covenant of the flesh, in contrast to the New, that is, a covenant of the spirit.[16]

A piece of drapery at the upper left-hand corner of the etching appears to have been pulled aside to allow access to and from the room where Jesus and his disciples dine. At the same time, this curtain helps to close off the space where the three men sit, imparting an air of intimate privacy to their meal. The motif of the drawn curtain may be an allusion to the act of revelation itself, a veil that

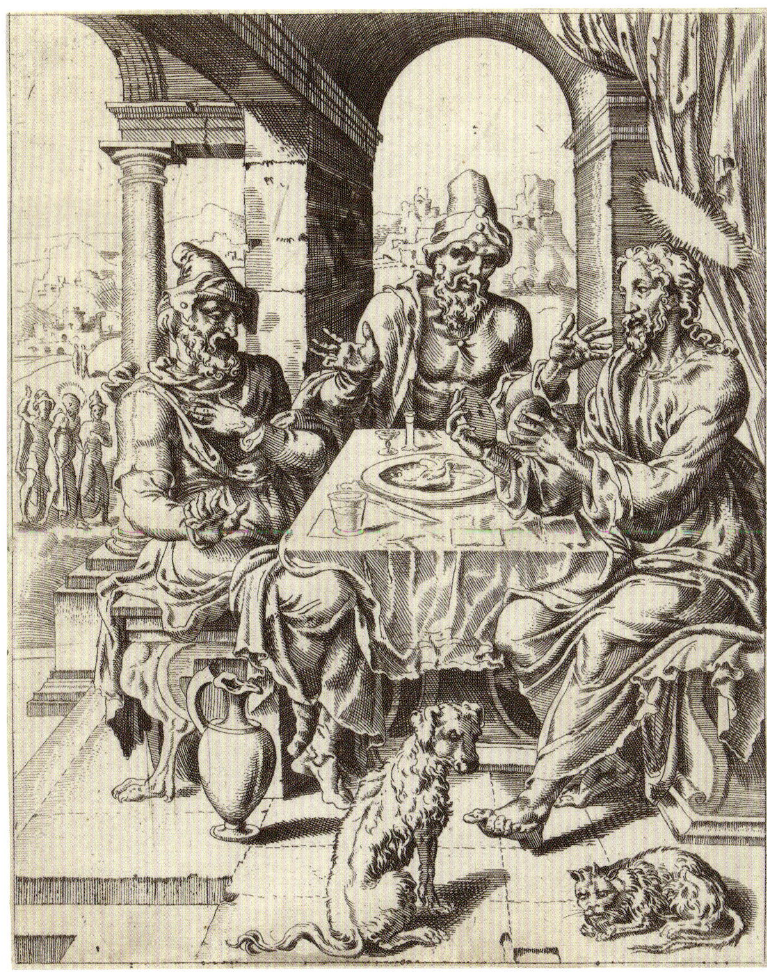

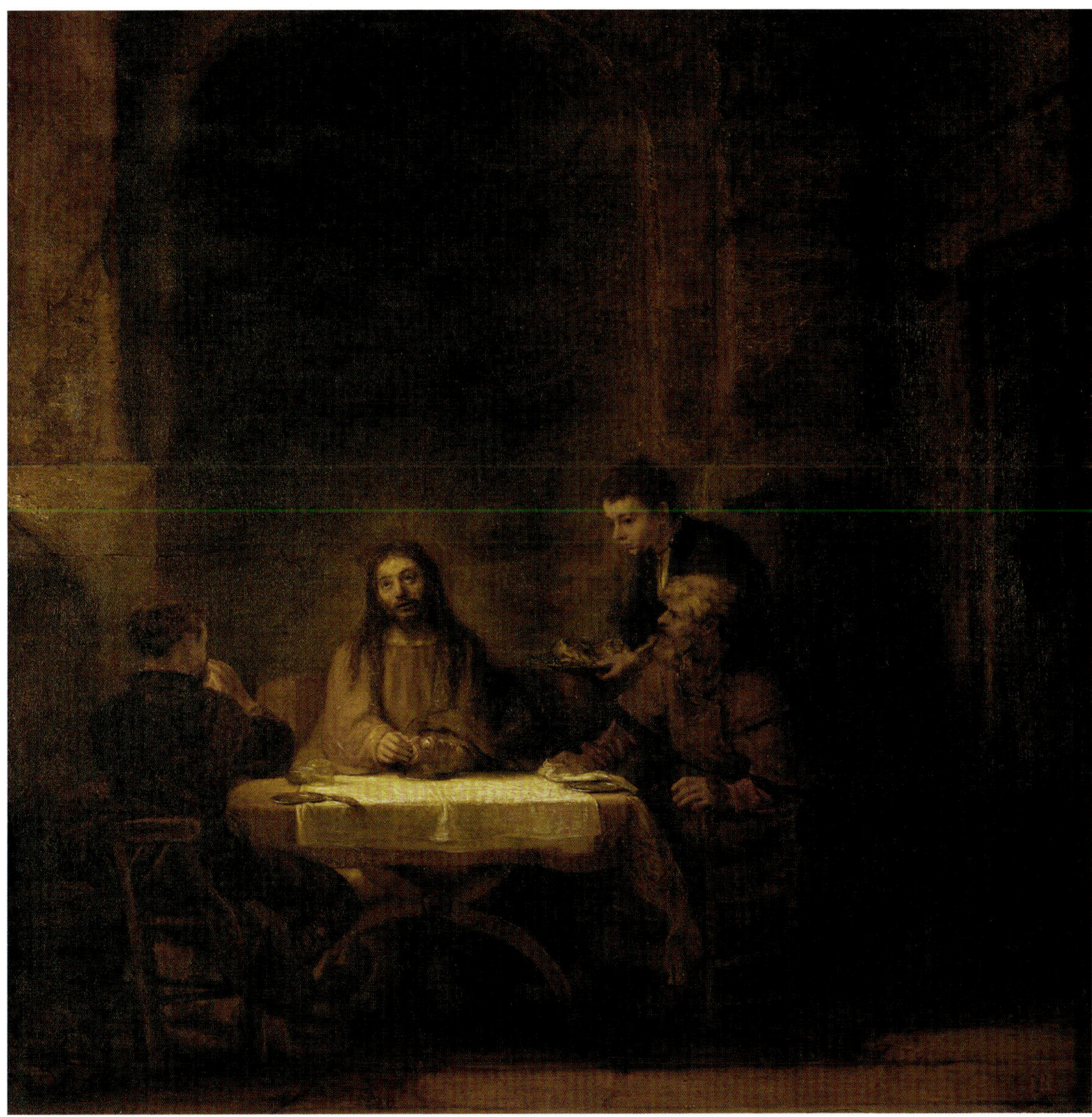

FIGURE 7. Rembrandt, *Christ at Emmaus*, oil on panel, 1648. *Louvre, Paris. Photo: Erich Lessing/Art Resource, New York.*

has been lifted from the eyes of the disciples and of the viewer. Just barely visible in the deep shadows to the right of the curtain is a fourth figure, presumably the innkeeper or a servant.[17] Shrouded almost completely in darkness, this dim figure may represent an unwitting bystander who has not yet seen the light, that is, the revelatory miracle taking place nearby.

Rembrandt returned to the Emmaus story again in 1648, creating a second painted version (fig. 7).[18] This time, he composed a work that was more sacramental, more akin to earlier examples of the revelation at Emmaus, such as Albrecht Dürer's woodcut from his small Passion[19] (fig. 8) and Titian's 1530 painting of the subject (fig. 5). Like those images, Rembrandt's new work more directly associated the event with traditional representations of the Last Supper. Christ, seated behind a table that is set parallel to the picture plane, holds a braided bread before him. The viewer now looks directly at him. The disciples are seated across from each other at the small, square folding table, one to each side of their new companion. The man at the right places his right hand on the table and stares intently at Jesus. The second disciple, a younger, clean-shaven man, is seen from the back. Like his counterpart in the 1634 etching, this figure brings his hands together in a gesture

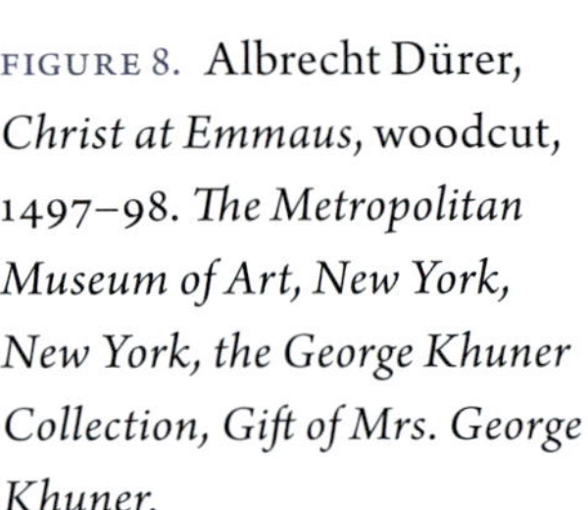

FIGURE 8. Albrecht Dürer, *Christ at Emmaus*, woodcut, 1497–98. *The Metropolitan Museum of Art, New York, New York, the George Khuner Collection, Gift of Mrs. George Khuner.*

FIGURE 9. Rembrandt after Giovanni Pietro Birago after Leonardo, *Last Supper*, red chalk, Ben. 443, c. 1635. *The Metropolitan Museum of Art, New York, New York, Robert Lehman Collection.*

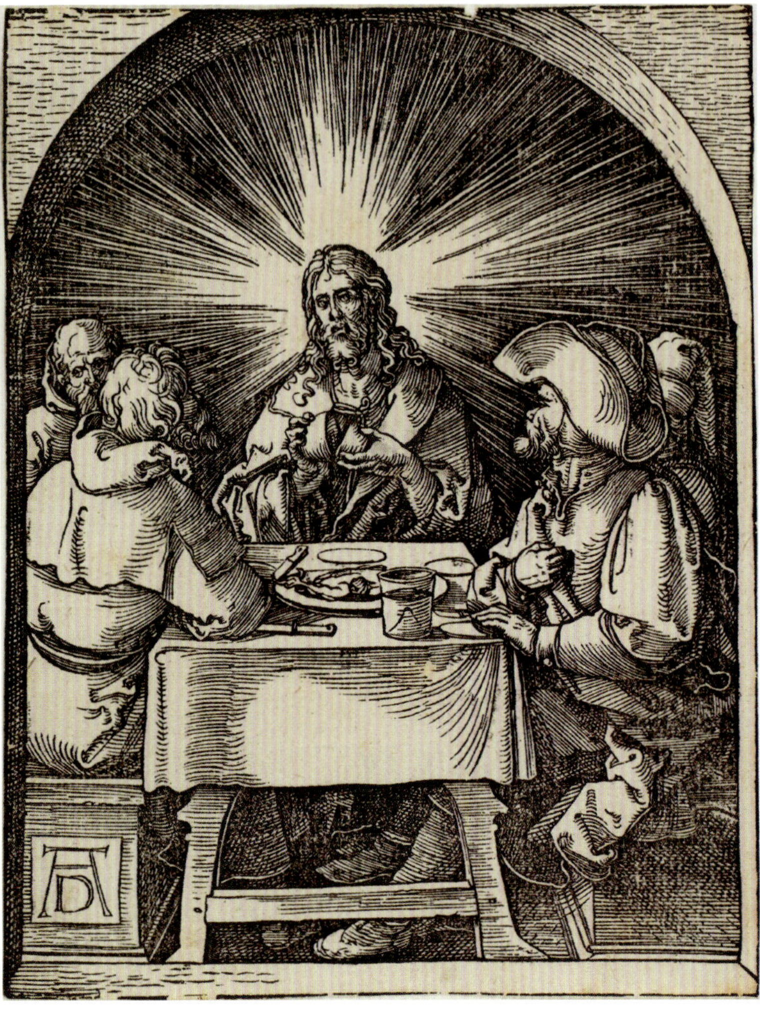

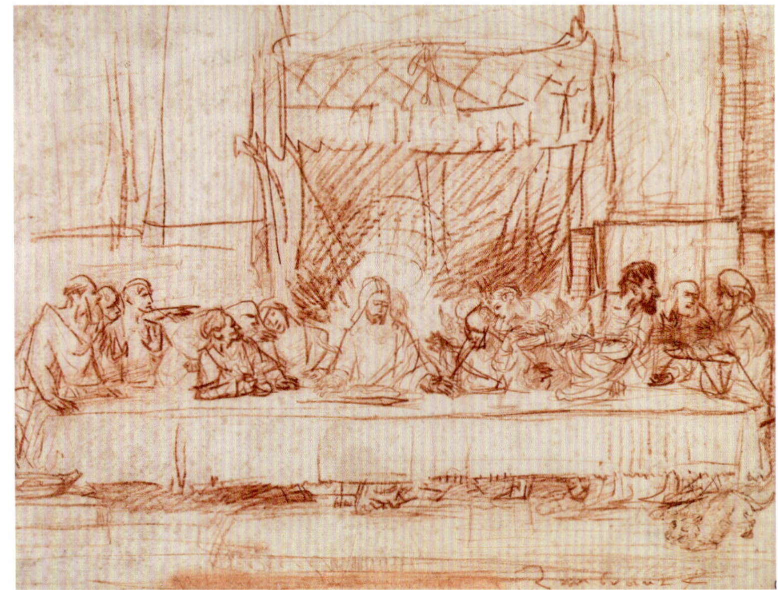

of contemplation or prayer. An innkeeper or young servant is in the act of placing a platter of meat on the table between Jesus and the bearded disciple. Christ's gaze seems unfocused; although his head is inclined toward the young man at his right, his eyes look upward, seemingly out beyond the confines of the room or hall where he is about to dine. A prominent aureola surrounds his head. Although the lighting in this painting is relatively even, the brightness emanating from Christ is strongly reflected off the snowy white tablecloth in front of him, making that surface and his body, behind it, the focus of the viewer's attention. Because Rembrandt placed the table and the ensemble of figures gathered around it close to the picture plane, there is no way to judge how deep a space this is meant to represent, but the area is clearly quite high and broad. It is an imposing venue, quite unlike the intimate space of the 1629 painting or the 1634 etching. A large arched niche, flanked by massive stone pilasters on raised socles, enframes the figure of Jesus, and a doorway is visible on the right side. These architectural elements evoke not only a monumental, ennobling, classical setting, but also an ecclesiastical one, with the table standing in for the altar, and Christ serving as the priest.

In Rembrandt's final depiction of the Supper at Emmaus, he returned to the print medium. In his 1654 etching (B. 87, cat. no. 60), he heightened the sacramental aspects of the meal that he had introduced in the 1648 painting. This time, Christ is seated on a draped bench behind a table partially covered with a cloth and set with a glass and a large platter bearing a meal that clearly evokes the symbolic paschal lamb. The table and cloth closely resemble those in the 1648 painting. Having already blessed and divided the bread, Jesus stretches out his arms and offers half of the loaf to each of his two companions. Both Christ's pose and the reaction of the disciple on his left are clearly allusions to Leonardo's *Last Supper*. Rembrandt's acquaintance with Leonardo's masterpiece is well documented: many years earlier (1634–35), Rembrandt had done a red chalk drawing (fig. 9) based on an engraving attributed to Giovanni Pietro Birago after the Leonardo fresco.[20] In that drawing, Rembrandt introduced a canopy over the central grouping, a decorative motif that he added to the 1654 print as well, investing the scene with a sense of regal grandeur. This drapery contrasts with the wide boards of the rustic flooring on which the folding table sits and the meal's ambiguous setting. It is unclear whether the meal at Emmaus takes place inside an inn or within a temporary shelter that is open on the right side, where some sort of stone wall and climbing greenery can be seen.[21] In Rembrandt's time, there were well-established traditions of depicting the Supper at Emmaus as taking place either on a veranda or in an interior room with a view to the outside (fig. 10),[22] and Rembrandt's composition allows for either of these interpretations.

The connection between the print and the Leonardo painting reinforces the association of the epiphany at Emmaus with the institution of the Eucharist. The disciples have already recognized their holy companion, and they react accordingly. The one on the left rises, clasping his hands together in prayer, and gazes down at the central figure of Christ, while the disciple on the right raises his hands in a traditional gesture of amazement. He stares intently at Jesus as though he is still digesting the startling revelation before him. Although the Gospel describes this as the moment in which Jesus "vanished from their eyes," Rembrandt's Jesus remains not just present, but monumental, so that the artist can dramatically depict the figures' varied reactions to the still unfolding miracle. Nonetheless, the print anticipates that epiphanic moment, for the scene's composition and lighting indicate a spectrum of solidity and spirituality: reading clockwise from the left, the eye moves from less densely modeled figures to more substantial ones and—both literally and spiritually—from light/enlightenment to dark/ignorance. In harmony with these distinctions, Jesus and the man at his right are clad in "biblical" attire, whereas the other disciple and the publican wear more contemporary clothing.

The apron-clad innkeeper, a figure who was barely visible in the 1634 etching, has now been placed prominently in the foreground. Unlike the servant in the 1648 painting, who stands behind the table to present the meal, this publican is at the front of the composition. As he holds onto a railing at the lower right-hand corner of

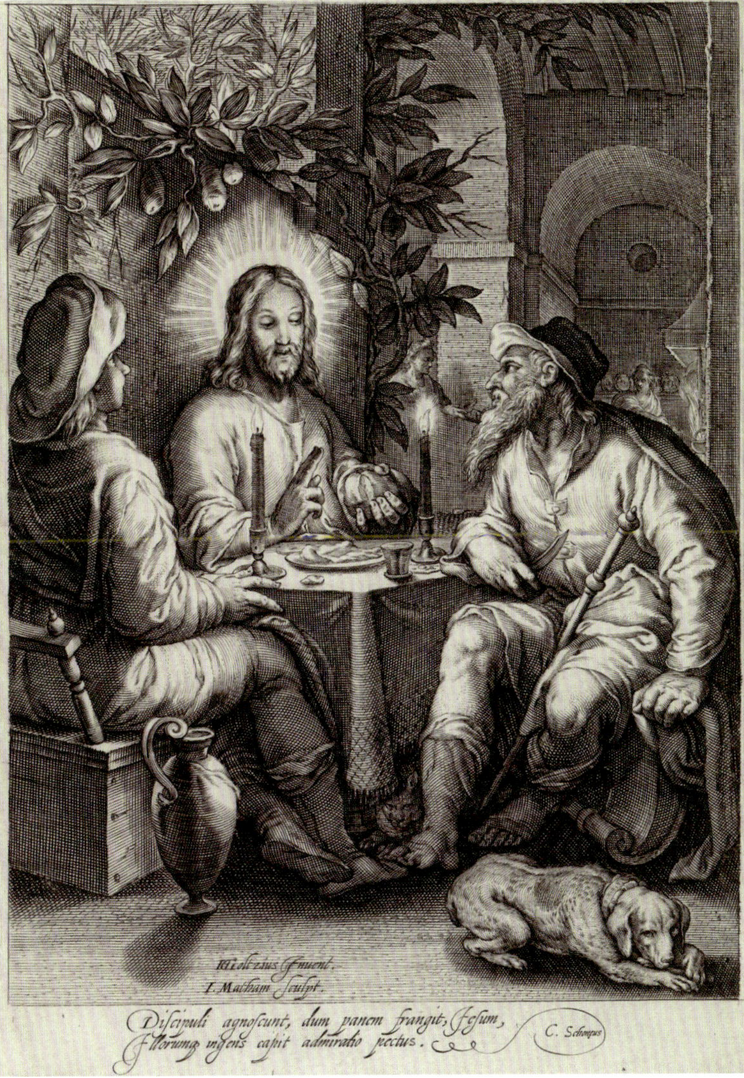

FIGURE 10. Jacob Matham after Hendrick Goltzius, *Christ at Emmaus*, engraving, c. 1590. *Rijksmuseum, Amsterdam.*

the picture, he appears to have paused on his way downstairs to the cellar, below. An outsider, perhaps representative of contemporary viewers of the print, he stares at the prayerful man who has risen to his feet in awed response to the risen Christ. These three men illustrate three different stages of enlightenment: curiosity (the innkeeper), amazement (the disciple at the right), and belief and acceptance (the prayerful disciple on the left).

The dog in the earlier etching reappears, but Rembrandt has given it a much less prominent position. Tucked behind the substantial figure of the innkeeper, the animal looks off into the darkness beyond the right edge of the picture, unaware of or uninterested in the revelatory miracle playing out beside it. It is probably no accident that Rembrandt placed the true believer at Christ's right, while those who are portrayed as questioning, ignorant, or unaware appear at his left.

Notes

1. Luke 24:13–31. Only one of the disciples, Cleopas, is named in the account. The encounter is also described in a much abbreviated form in Mark 16:12, but without a specific account of Christ's revelation to the disciples at the evening meal.

2. Luke 24:30–31.

3. There is some confusion in the Gospels as to whether Christ actually appeared to the Marys before or after his appearance on the road to Emmaus. In Luke, this is clearly the first appearance of Jesus after his resurrection. The account in Mark 1:9–12 states that he first appeared to Mary Magdalen, and only then to the two disciples on the road. Matthew makes no mention of the encounter with the disciples en route to Emmaus. Instead, he states that Jesus appeared to the three Marys as they were returning from their encounter with the angel (Matthew 28:8–10).

4. On the active debate in England and Holland concerning the second coming and the imminent conversion of the Jews, see Shelley Perlove, "Awaiting the Messiah: Christians, Jews and Muslims in the Late Work of Rembrandt," *Bulletin of the University of Michigan Museum of Art* 11 (1996): 84–113, and Stephen Nadler, *Rembrandt's Jews* (Chicago: University of Chicago Press, 2003), 110–12.

5. Arnold Houbraken singled out Rembrandt's multiple representations of this theme as exemplary of the artist's "thoughtful consideration of the great number of emotions which necessarily come into play in the subject he depicts." Arnold Houbraken, "Life of Rembrandt," from *De Groote Schouburgh der Nederlandtsche Schilderessen* (1718–21), trans. Charles Ford, in Joachim von Sandrart, Filippo Baldinucci, and Arnold Houbraken, *Lives of Rembrandt*, intro. by Charles Ford (London: Pallas Athene, 2007), 60.

6. In *Groote Schouburgh*, Houbraken published a print (fig. 1) after a lost painting or drawing by Rembrandt that carried the biblical story to its conclusion: Christ has vanished from the room, and the disciples react with astonishment to the empty chair where he had been sitting. The lighting in the print is as dramatic as that which appears in Rembrandt's earliest rendition of the subject, the painting of c. 1629, now in the Musée Jacquemart-André (fig. 3).

According to Otto Benesch (*The Drawings of Rembrandt: A Critical and Chronological Catalogue* [London: Phaidon, 1973], 4:223), Ignace-Joseph de Claussin identified three states of the Houbraken print, "of which the second carries the etched inscription: Rembrandt 1635. " For a reproduction of the print and a study for the disciples at Emmaus (Ben. 87), see Ernst Gombrich, *Art and Illusion* (Princeton, NJ: Princeton University Press, 1969), figs. 283 and 284.

Although the presence of the strongly focused light and powerful shadows in the Houbraken print are clearly attributable to a candle that is partially hidden by the foremost pilgrim, the effect is also to suggest that the light is a vestige of Christ's own divine aura. This effect is made even clearer in a pen and wash drawing (Ben. C47) in the Fitzwilliam Museum, Cambridge, England, where the vanished Christ is replaced by a brilliant burst of light (fig. 2). In the Fitzwilliam catalog, this drawing is dated to 1640–41 and attributed to Rembrandt, with washes added in the eighteenth century. Accessed July 9, 2014, http://www.fitzmuseum.cam.ac.uk/opac/search/cataloguedetail.html?&priref=5026&_function_=xslt&_limit_=50. Otto Benesch (*Drawings*, 4:223) rejected the drawing as an autograph Rembrandt and suggested that it was a copy after an original Rembrandt executed in the later 1640s. Martin Royalton-Kisch, in his online catalog of Rembrandt and Rembrandt school drawings in the British Museum, maintained that the Fitzwilliam drawing is authentic and offered a date of about 1650 for its creation. "Catalogue of Drawings by Rembrandt and His School in the British Museum," accessed July 9, 2014, http://www.britishmuseum.org/research/publications/online_research_catalogues/search_object_details.aspx?objectId=710449&partId=1&catparentPageId=27094&catalogueOnly=true&output=bibliography/!!/OR/!!/5806/!//!/Catalogue%20of%20Drawings%20by%20Rembrandt%20and%20his%20School%20in%20the%20British%20Museum/!//!!//!!!/;.

7. RRP, *Corpus*, A16. The work measures 37.4 × 42.3 cm. The painting is now in the Musée Jacquemart-André, Paris.

8. This hat may be a sign of the disciple's humble status, since many of Rembrandt's early beggars wear similar hats. See, for example, B. 162, B.163, B. 166, and B. 171.

9. These objects are also traditional symbols of pilgrimage.

10. See the discussion of dogs in Charles M. Rosenberg, "Rembrandt's Religious Prints," in this catalog.

11. Bellini's painting for Giorgio Cornaro was destroyed in a fire in the eighteenth century. However, there are several copies of this painting, including an eighteenth-century engraving by Pietro Monaco (fig. 4). In the Bellini composition, the dog lay on the ground at the very edge of the composition. In another parallel, Bellini's image included a pilgrim's staff and bag on the ground in front of the table. It is not known if or how Rembrandt would have been acquainted with this painting. Wolfgang Stechow, ("Rembrandts Darstellungen des Emmausmahles," *Zeitschrift für Kunstgeschichte* 3 [1934], 335), identified the Bellini *Supper* as the earliest example of the Emmaus scene to include a dog.

12. It is not likely that Rembrandt would have known the Titian painting, since apparently it was not reproduced until the middle of the seventeenth century. Harold Wethey, *The Paintings of Titian*, vol. 1, *Religious Paintings* (New York: Phaidon, 1969], cat. 153. Titian's painting is now in the Louvre, Paris.

13. NHD 302. Christian Tümpel (*Rembrandt legt,* cat. 115) suggested the Heemskerck composition as a source for the Rembrandt etching.

14. Some years later, Rubens adopted a similar pose for the dog in his painting of the Supper at Emmaus (1638), which is now in the Prado. The dog, holding a bone in its mouth, looks up at the table as if waiting for another morsel. Rubens's composition was engraved by Hans Witdoeck in 1638 (HD 7 [under Witdoeck]).

15. See, for example, *Angel Appearing to the Shepherds* (B. 44, 1634, cat. no. 19), *Christ Driving the Money Changers from the Temple* (B. 69, 1635, cat. no. 43), and *The Good Samaritan* (B. 90, 1633, cat. no. 62).

16. *Rembrandt's Faith*, 317.

17. Some scholars (e.g., Tümpel, *Rembrandt legt,* cat. 115; and Hinterding, *Lugt Catalogue,* cat. 73, 194) have suggested that Rembrandt intended to remove this figure by covering him up with a dense network of cross-hatching. This seems unlikely. Rembrandt would have been perfectly capable of completely erasing the figure if he had wished to. A print of this small size invites viewers to examine it carefully and at length, and the artist would most likely have expected the viewer to discover the shadowy figure as he scrutinized the etching. The figure's existence offers one more link to Rembrandt's previous *Supper,* the painted version of about 1629.

18. RRP, *Corpus,* V14. The painting is in the Louvre, Paris. Yet another painting of the Supper at Emmaus, this one in Copenhagen (RRP, *Corpus* V15), was attributed to Rembrandt by earlier scholars, including Abraham Bredius, Horst Gerson, and Gary Schwartz. Recently, however, the Rembrandt Research Project argued convincingly that the work should be attributed to Rembrandt's workshop, instead.

19. Albrecht Dürer, *Christ and the Disciples at Emmaus* (TIB, woodcuts, 48).

20. Hinterding, *Lugt Catalogue,* cat. 72, 192. Rembrandt's red chalk drawing (Ben. 443) after the engraving by Giovanni Pietro Birago is in the Robert Lehman Collection in the Metropolitan Museum of Art. For a reproduction of both the drawing and the engraving, see Walter Leidtke, Carolyn Logan, Nadine M. Orenstein, and Stephanie Dickey, *Rembrandt/Not Rembrandt in the Metropolitan Museum of Art: Aspects of Connoisseurship*, exh. cat. (New York: Harry N. Abrams and Metropolitan Museum of Art, 1995), cat. 56, 157.

21. *Rembrandt's Faith*, 319. Perlove and Silver have suggested that this bit of greenery may be symbolic of new life or the Branch of David prophesied by Jeremiah. Jeremiah 23:5: "Behold, the days come, saith the Lord, that I will raise unto David a righteous Branch, and a King shall reign and prosper, and shall execute judgment and justice in earth."

22. See, for example, the painting by Titian in the Louvre, the engraving after Heemskerck (fig. 6), the engraving by Jacob Matham after a design by Hendrick Goltzius (c. 1590) (NHD 46) (fig. 10), and the 1638 engraving by Witdoeck after Rubens (HD 7 [under Witdoeck]).

61. Christ Appearing to the Apostles

B. 89 (H. 237, M. 220, NHD 296)
Counterproof (etching)
Signed and dated in the plate: *Rembrandt f. 1656*
State I of I
Sheet: 16.2 × 21.0 cm, trimmed to the plate mark
Watermark: unidentified
Verso: in graphite, H8524/in script, *Besse Uberto* [illegible]*ien* (?)/*contre epreuve/ 0-W99; C193 CHH/ N094 Wilson*[1]/*B89/68 Daulby* (?)[2]/*4481*

Provenance:
Harrods, London, 1981
Feddersen, Elkhart, IN, 1991
Snite Museum of Art
Acc. No.: 1991.025.070

The plate does not survive.

The subject matter of this rare print now known as *Christ Appearing to the Apostles* has been a matter of some confusion.[3] In 1731, Valerius Röver described the print as "Christ giving the keys to Peter . . . lightly etched."[4] Twenty years later, in his catalogue raisonné of Rembrandt's prints, Edme-François Gersaint described the etching as *Our Lord Healing the Sick*,[5] but in 1797, Adam von Bartsch reverted to Röver's description ("Christ giving the keys . . ."). In the 1824 revision of Gersaint's catalog by J. J. de Claussin, the print acquired yet another title, *Christ among his Disciples*, though the image was actually described as a depiction of the incredulity of St. Thomas.[6] On the basis of this description, *The Incredulity of St. Thomas* became the title of choice until the 1930s. That is the title that appears, for example, in Arthur M. Hind's 1923 catalog of Rembrandt prints.[7] Finally, in 1936, Werner Weisbach reinterpreted the print as an illustration of Christ's first appearance to his disciples in Jerusalem after his encounter with the pilgrims at Emmaus.[8] It is now generally agreed that this is the most accurate interpretation of this etching.[9]

The Snite Museum's example of *Christ Appearing to the Apostles* is actually a counterproof, that is, a second impression pulled from a freshly printed impression while the ink is still wet.[10] By its very nature, a counterproof is considerably lighter and less distinct than a print drawn from the plate itself, and it also reverses the original etching in the same way that a normal impression reverses the image on the plate. In the case of *Christ Appearing to the Apostles*, the reduction in clarity and intensity that characteristically results from the counterproof process exaggerated qualities that were already inherent in the etching. In this print, Rembrandt was working in an extremely telegraphic style, pushing the limits of simple contour line to define form, and utilizing the whiteness of the paper to describe light. Shadows, defined by parallel lines and cross-hatching, are severely limited, appearing chiefly at Christ's feet and in the areas behind and beside the glowing, spectral figure. Jesus's sunken eyes are in shadow, and his body is barely visible, defined by a minimum number of strokes. Standing amid his disciples, Jesus addresses his followers, demonstrating his corporeal presence by thrusting one arm outward, toward the viewer, while pointing the other toward his chest, possibly a reference to the wound he received at the time of the crucifixion.[11] In his manipulation of the medium, Rembrandt was particularly successful in

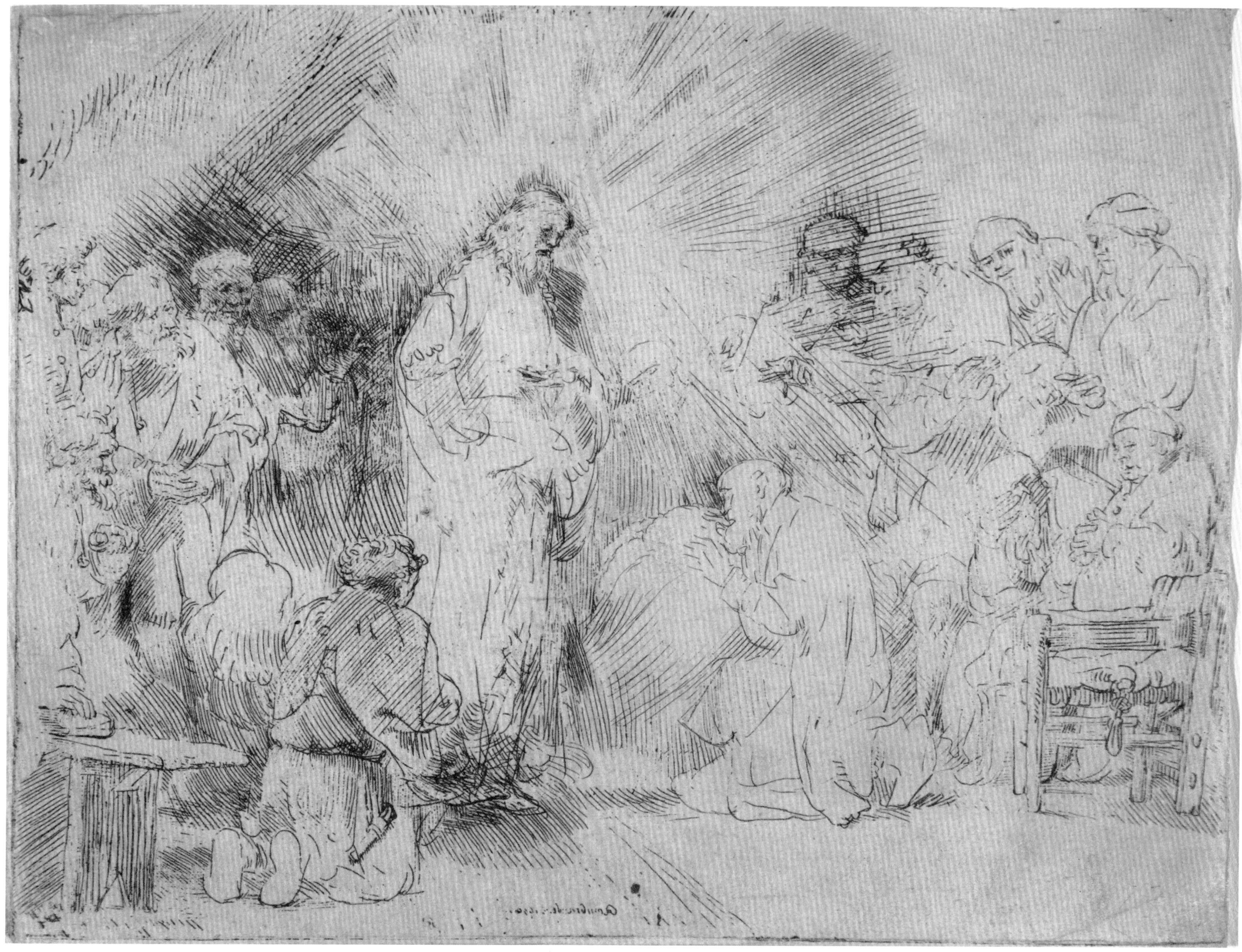

PLATE 61

FIGURE 1. Israhel van Meckenem, *Christ Appearing to the Apostles*, engraving, c. 1460–70. *Photo: Courtesy of the National Gallery of Art, Washington, DC.*

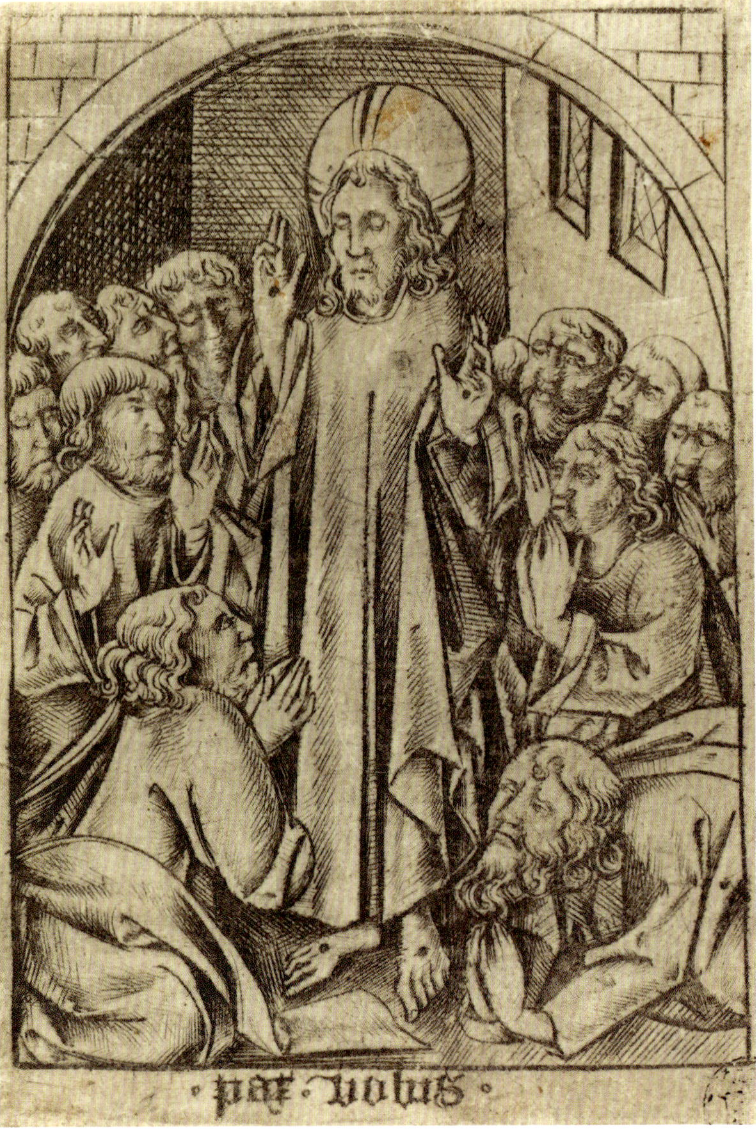

rendering the ambiguity of the corporeal and the spiritual, a theme that is the crux of this moment: the first manifestation of the risen Christ to his disciples.

Although the depiction of the disciples is handled with same economy of line as the figure of Jesus, each of his followers evinces a unique reaction, providing the viewer with a range of characters and psychological states with which to identify. Some followers kneel near Jesus, while others sit or stand, contemplating the significance of the miracle of the risen Christ and his charge to spread the gospel.[12] One man cowers; one raises an arm as if to deflect the strong rays of spiritual light; one peers forward from behind the crowd, as if to see better; and one, evidently a person of some stature, to judge from his garb and his comfortably cushioned chair, has the classic pose of someone who has drifted off to sleep, his hands folded over his ample belly.[13] It is as if Rembrandt is reminding the viewer that each person will receive the news and promise of Christ's resurrection in his own way, and that those who are rich in worldly goods are not necessarily rich in spiritual understanding.

Notes

1. This reference is to Thomas Wilson, *A Descriptive Catalogue of the Prints of Rembrandt by an Amateur* (London: J. F. Setchel, 1836), cat. 94, "Jesus Christ, in the Middle of His Disciples," accessed January 21, 2013, http://catalog.hathitrust.org/api/volumes/oclc/3777539.html.

2. This may be a reference to Daniel Daulby, the author of *A Descriptive Catalogue of the Works of Rembrandt, and of His Scholars, Bol, Livens, and Van Vliet, Compiled from the Original Etchings, and from the Catalogues of De Burgy, Gersaint, Helle and Glomy, Marcus, and Yver* (Liverpool: Printed by J. M'Creery, and sold by J. Edwards London, 1796). Daulby's is an expanded translation of Edme Gersaint's 1751 catalogue raisonné. See note 3, below.

3. In his 1751 catalogue raisonné, Edme Gersaint described the print as "rare": "On ne le trouve pas communément." Gersaint, *Catalogue raisonné de toutes les pièces qui forment l'oeuvre de Rembrandt* (Paris: Chez Hochereau, 1751), 62. In 1967, G. W. Nowell-Usticke classified the etching as one of Rembrandt's forty rarest prints. Nowell-Usticke, *Rembrandt's Etchings: States and Values* (Narberth, PA: Livingston Publishing, 1967), cat. B. 89 (*The Incredulity of Thomas*), rated RRRR (almost unobtainable).

4. Erik Hinterding, *Lugt Catalogue*, 195.

5. Gersaint, cat. 76, 61–62: "Une autre Morceau, gravé très-légerement [*sic*] presqu'au simple trait. Son sujet n'est pas facile à decider; il paroît cependant avoir du rapport à quelques miracles de J.C. Notre-Seigneur, dont la tête est environée de rayons, se trouve debout vers le milieu de l'Estampe en tirant sur la droite. On voit à ses pieds un homme à genoux."

6. *Catalogue raisonné de toutes les estampes qui forment l'oeuvre de Rembrandt . . . composé par Gersaint, Helle, Glomy et Yver. Nouvelle edition corrigée et considérablement augmentée par M. le Chevalier de Claussin* (Paris: Firmin Didot, 1824), cat. 93, 63: "Jésus-Christ au milieu de ses disciples. Morceau très-légèrement gravé et sans effet. On y voit Jésus-Christ apparaissant à ses disciples après sa mort. Il est debout au milieu de l'estampe, dirigé un peu vers la gauche, où Thomas est à genoux devant lui. Les autres disciples placés aux deux côtés, expriment leur étonnement des paroles de Jésus-Christ, qui semble dire à Thomas: *Vous avez cru, Thomas, parce que vous avez vu,* etc."

7. Arthur M. Hind, *A Catalogue of Rembrandt's Etchings*, 2nd ed. (London: Metheun, 1923), cat. 237, 103.

8. Hinterding, *Lugt Catalogue*, 195–96. The new title derives from the account of Jesus trying to persuade his disciples of his corporeality. See Luke 24:36–41, "As they were saying this, Jesus stood before them the two pilgrims from Emmaus, the eleven apostles, and "those who were there. But they were startled and frightened, and supposed that they saw a spirit. And he said to them, "Why are you troubled, and why do questionings rise in your hearts? See my hands and my feet, that it is I myself; handle me, and see; for a spirit has not flesh and bones as you see I have."

9. Images of Christ Appearing to the Apostles are relatively rare, but there are a few earlier examples. See, for example, the small engraving by Israhel van Meckenem (HG 113, c. 1485) (fig. 1).

10. The New Hollstein catalog of Rembrandt etchings (NHD) listed seven counterproofs. This is an unusually large number. Ordinarily, counterproofs were employed by an artist as an aid to working out changes on the etching plate, since the image produced in the process reproduces what is etched into the plate itself. In the case of this print, however, since Rembrandt only produced a single state, it is unlikely that he was concerned about modifications to the plate. He might have been curious to see how the etching would look if the strength of illumination in the print were diminished, as it would be in a counterproof. This would be in keeping with the experiments in plate tone and inking that occupied the artist in the 1650s, investigations that culminated in *The Three Crosses* (B. 78, 1653, cat. no. 54). In this instance, however, whether or not Rembrandt made the counterproof in order to examine light effects, the results apparently did not persuade him to rework the plate.

11. With the inclusion of these gestures, Rembrandt created an image of Christ Appearing to the Apostles that recalls the account in John 20: 9–23 rather than in Luke. This may explain why the print originally bore the title *The Incredulity of Thomas* when it was given to the Snite Museum.

12. Luke 24:44–49.

13. Gersaint provided a picturesque description of this figure: "Tout-à-fait à la gauche sur le devant, paroît une espèce d'hydropique assis dans une fauteuil." [All the way on the left, in the foreground, there is a dropsical man seated in an armchair.] Gersaint, 61–62.

62. The Good Samaritan

B. 90 (H. 101, Mz. 196, NHD 116)
Etching and burin
Signed and dated in the plate in the lower margin:
Rembrandt. Inventor et feecit [sic] 1633
State IV of IV
Sheet: 25.7 × 20.8 cm, trimmed to the plate mark
Watermark: partial foolscap
Verso: in graphite, *B90; D. 15; S.B. 41; H10460; B 90*; collector's stamp, blue ink, *GALICHON* in an oval (Lugt 1058, Emile Galichon)

Provenance:
Emile Galichon (1829–75)
Harrods, London, 1980
Feddersen, Elkhart, IN, 1991
Snite Museum of Art
Acc. No.: 1991.025.058

The plate does not survive.

The parable of the Good Samaritan is related in Luke 10: 25–37: When a skeptical lawyer asked Jesus how one might achieve eternal life, Christ responded that the man should love God with all his heart, soul, strength, and mind, and should love his neighbor as himself. The lawyer then asked, "And who is my neighbor?" In response, Jesus recounted the story of the Good Samaritan. A Jewish man traveling between Jerusalem and Jericho was beset by thieves who stole his clothing and wounded him, leaving him half-dead by the side of the road. First a priest and then a Levite passed right by the fallen man, ignoring his plight. Finally, a Samaritan who saw the stricken traveler stopped to tend to the man's wounds with wine and oil, even though the people of Samaria were sworn enemies of the Jews. The Samaritan then lifted the wounded man up onto his horse and brought him to a nearby inn where the victim could rest and recover. The next morning, before the Samaritan departed, he gave the innkeeper money to take care of the injured man and promised that if the ministrations should cost the innkeeper more than he had already received, he would be reimbursed for the additional expense when the Samaritan returned. After reciting this parable, Christ asked the lawyer which of the three passersby was a neighbor to the unfortunate man: the priest, the Levite, or the Samaritan. The lawyer replied that it was the one who had shown mercy. Christ responded, "Go, and do thou likewise."

Rembrandt's representation of the parable illustrates two of the Samaritan's acts combined into a single frame. In front of the inn, the wounded man is being helped down from the Samaritan's horse, and at the same time, the Samaritan is paying the innkeeper, an event that only occurred the following day. A young groom sporting a plumed hat and wearing a sword holds the reins of the horse as a more humbly clad servant struggles to lift the half-naked victim down from its back.[1] A flight of stone steps with a rough wooden railing ascends from the courtyard up to the inn's door, which is framed by an ornamental arch and a fragment of a worn pilaster. The turbaned Samaritan, seen from behind and therefore anonymous, stands on the raised stone porch at the top of the steps and

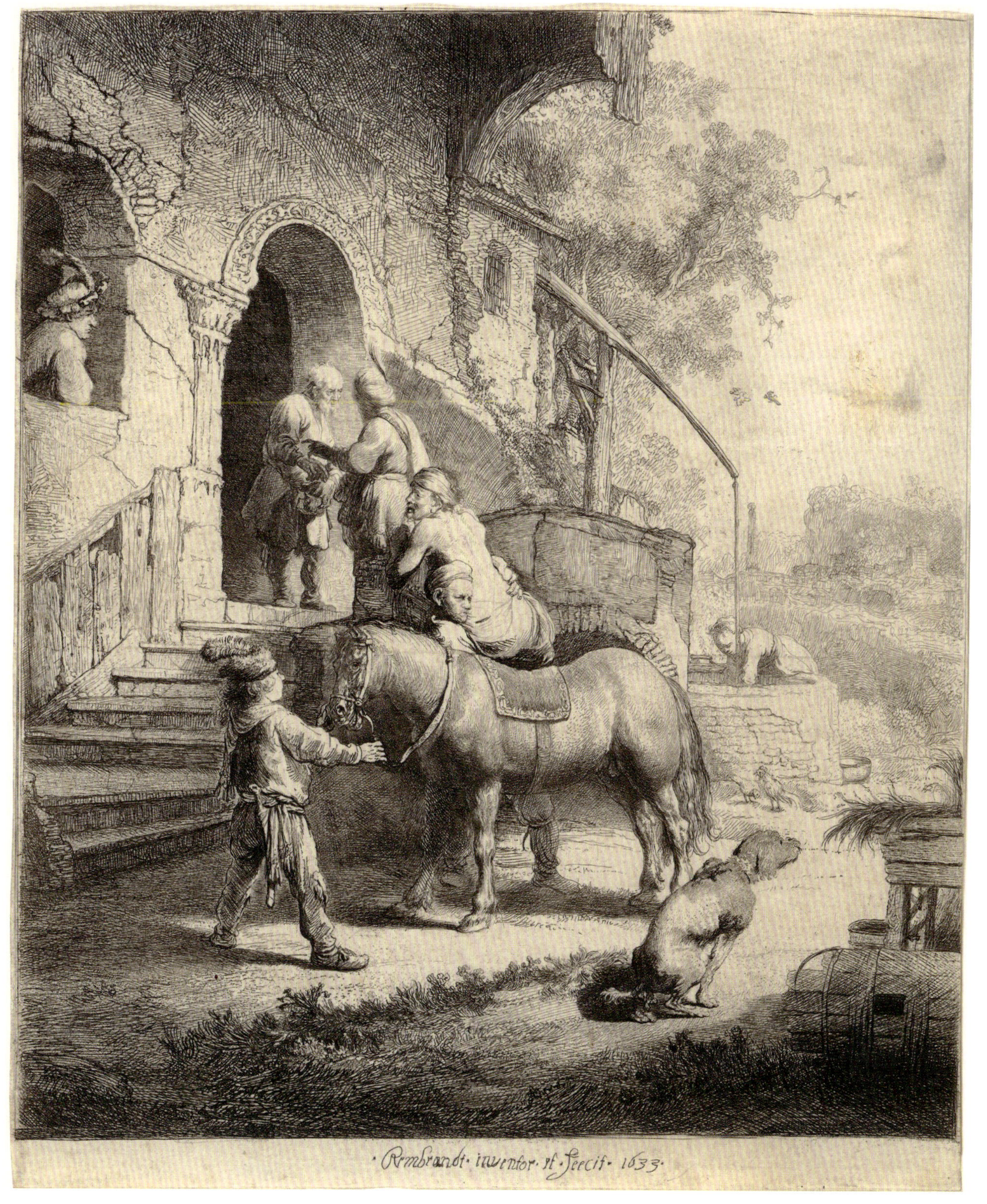

PLATE 62

FIGURE 1. Nicolas Beatrizet after Michelangelo, *Abduction of Ganymede*, engraving, 1542. *The Metropolitan Museum of Art, New York, New York, the Elisha Whittelsey Collection, the Elisha Whittelsey Fund.*

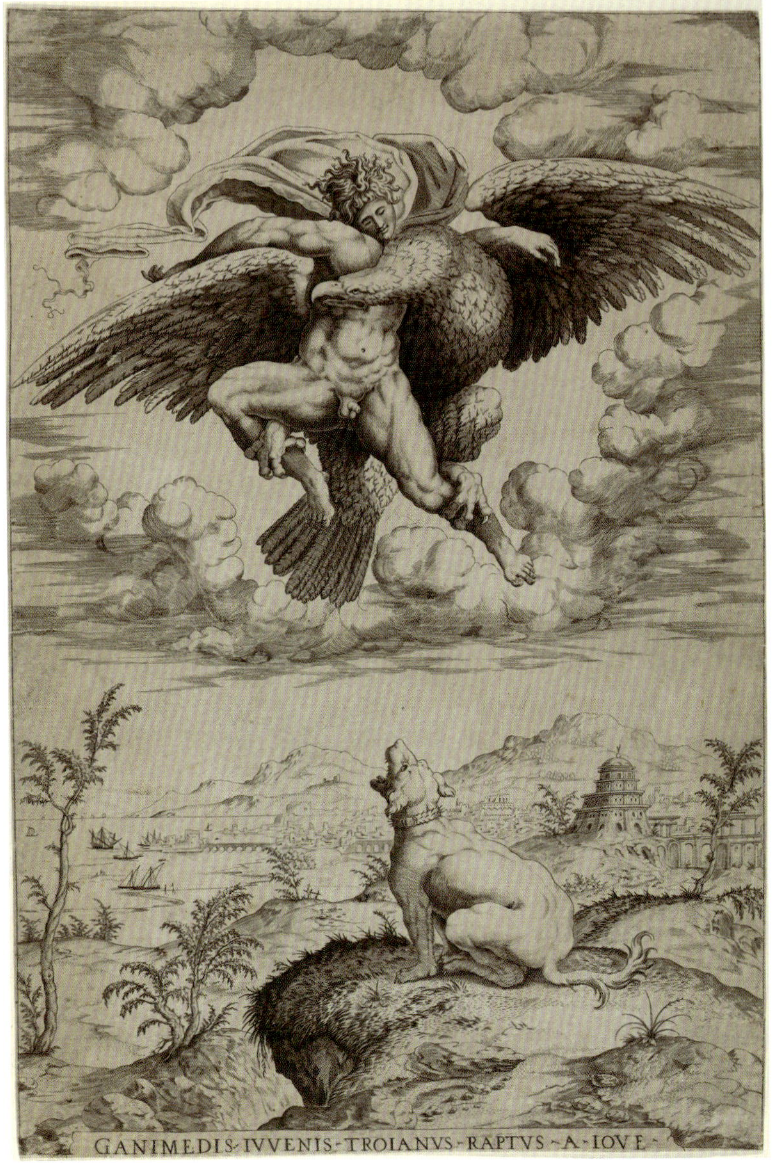

converses with the bearded, elderly innkeeper. The traveler's left hand is raised in a gesture of address or instruction, and the landlord listens attentively as he places the coins that he has received into a purse hanging from his belt. At the left, a young man wearing a plumed, slashed beret gazes out at the scene from an arched stone window.[2] The inn has clearly seen better days. Patches of plaster have flaked off its façade, revealing the brickwork beneath, and at the top of the building, the ragged remains of a stone buttress protrude from the wall, supporting an arch faced with rotting wooden panels.

Toward the right-hand side of the composition, a woman drawing water from a stone well seems completely oblivious to the plight of the wounded man, the kindness of his rescuer, or the negotiations being conducted with the innkeeper. Beyond the woman, the scene opens up to reveal a hazy landscape of trees, distant wild birds wheeling in the sky, and a few lightly sketched structures, including an obelisk, a reference to the ancient world of the parable and an anomaly in an otherwise very contemporary-looking scene.

What is most unusual about Rembrandt's version of the parable is his inclusion of a defecating dog prominently placed in the right foreground at the base of a strong diagonal that leads down from the doorway where the virtuous Samaritan and the innkeeper are illuminated by sunlight, to the lower right corner, where the dog sits in a shady area, squatting beside a broken barrel, a bucket, and a manger with some hay or grain lying on top of it. The animal's indecorous action has elicited a fair degree of comment in the Rembrandt literature, most of it negative.[3] Other, earlier representations of the Good Samaritan also include dogs,[4] but Rembrandt's is the only version in which the dog is engaged in such an unseemly act. Kenneth Clark suggested that Rembrandt borrowed the animal from an engraving by Nicolas Beatrizet after Michelangelo's *Rape of Ganymede* (fig. 1), but in that print, the shepherd's dog simply sits on its haunches, barking at the eagle that has abducted its young master. Although Clark sees Rembrandt's inclusion of the dog as an example of anticlassicism, of the artist "sticking his tongue out at the High Renaissance," he does allow that it may also have been a way of insisting that "if we are to practice Christian humility we must not avert our eyes from the humblest of natural functions."[5] Susan Donahue Kuretsky offered a more theologically based explanation for the appearance of this animal. In her view, the print sets up a contrast between the dog, representing bestial impurity and pollution, and the woman drawing water from the well, exemplifying purity. Kuretsky also noted that this woman calls to mind another biblical parable, the story of Christ meeting a Samaritan woman at a well, an encounter that Rembrandt illustrated in two later etchings (B. 71, 1634, cat. no. 44; and B. 70, 1658, cat. no. 45).[6] During that encounter, Jesus told the woman that the water that *he* offered was a source of eternal life, thus implying that the water was a source of spiritual purification.[7] Regardless of whether or not the dog was meant to contrast the impure and the pure and their theological and moral overtones, it is nonetheless reasonable to acknowledge, as Kuretsky did, that the dissonant detail of the dog is provocative. Of course, as she also pointed out, seventeenth-century audiences might not have been as easily offended by the dog's action as viewers from later centuries.[8]

Both Luther and Calvin commented on the parable of the Good Samaritan. Luther viewed it as an allegory of the healing power of Christ, whereas Calvin explicitly rejected such an allegorical reading and saw the story simply as a lesson about charity and mercy.[9] During the sixteenth and seventeenth centuries, visual representations of the parable laid out the story in three ways: as a series of prints that illustrated separate episodes; as a single print that highlighted one of the episodes but included others as secondary scenes; or as a print that, like Rembrandt's, focused exclusively on the conclusion of the story.[10] Rembrandt's conflation of the arrival of the Samaritan with his charge, and his payment to the innkeeper the following day, is quite unusual, though not completely without precedent. The same combination of events appears in a nocturnal rendering of the scene by Jan van de Velde II (c. 1593–1641) (fig. 2), a print that is generally agreed to have been the immediate inspiration for Rembrandt's etching.[11] What is especially intriguing about the two artists' compositions is that unlike the other examples of isolated incidents drawn from the story, their works do not focus on the Samaritan's rendering of direct aid to the wounded Jew, but instead highlight the delegation of responsibility for the man's care to the innkeeper in anticipation of the Samaritan's absence. This particular choice does not exclude the theme of personal responsibility for charity, but it does seem to place greater emphasis on the role of money, or alms, in enabling others to carry out the charitable acts of tending to the sick and/or needy. Such an interpretation of Rembrandt's etching might have had a special resonance for seventeenth-century Dutch viewers, given the significant presence of charitable institutions—hospitals, almshouses, and orphanages—in Holland and elsewhere in the Dutch Republic. The availability of such resources was sufficiently impressive as to elicit comment from foreign visitors.[12]

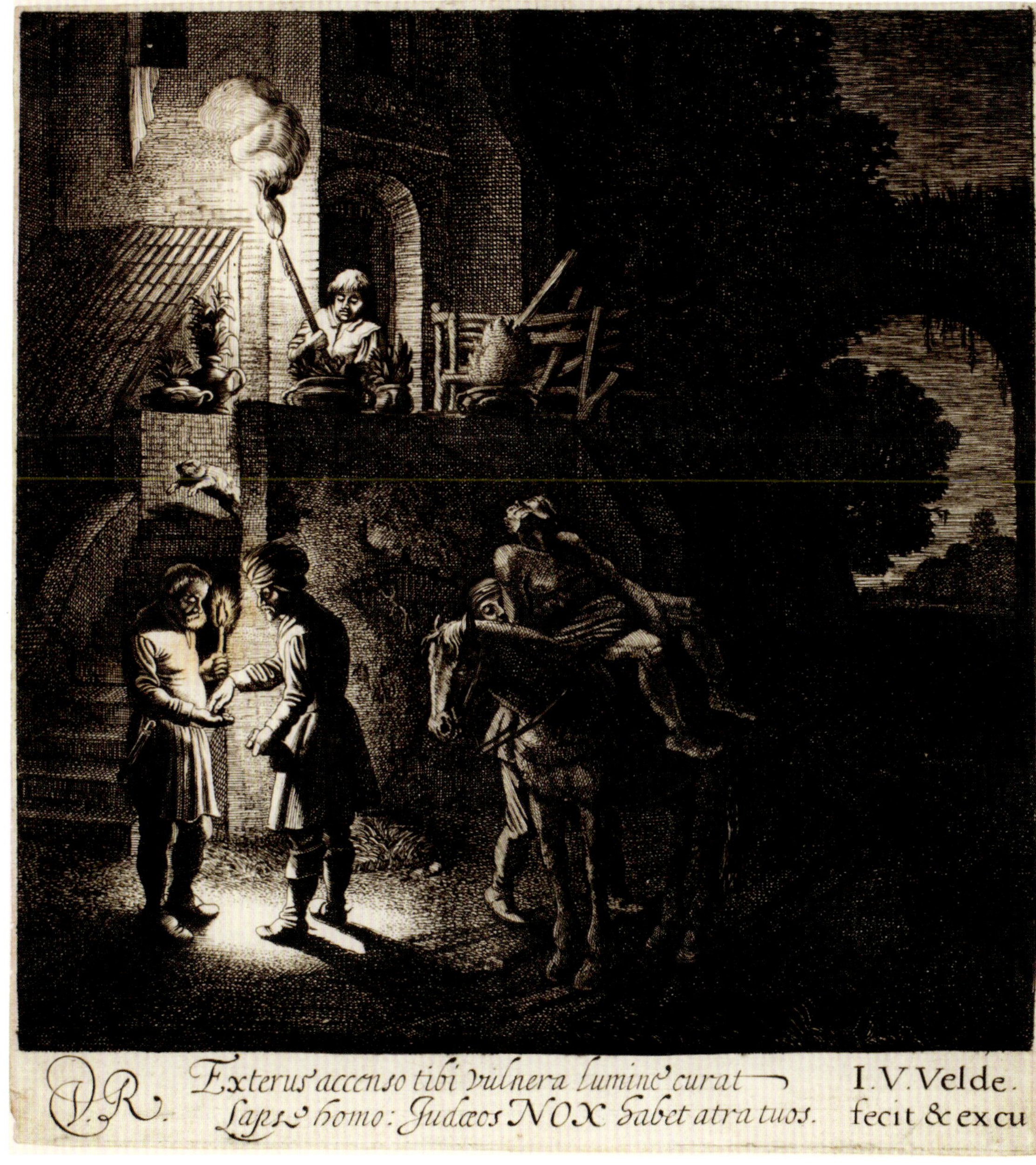

FIGURE 2. Jan van de Velde II, *The Good Samaritan*, etching, 1615–40. *Philadelphia Museum of Art, Philadelphia, Pennsylvania, the Muriel and Philip Berman Gift, Object Number, 1985-52-999.*

Notes

1. The wounded man's head is wrapped in some sort of cloth or bandage, evidence of the Samaritan's ministrations.

2. On the basis of the beret and the man's "blunt features" Susan Donahue Kuretsky identified this figure as Rembrandt himself, observing the scene from inside the inn. "Rembrandt's Good Samaritan Etching: Reflections on a Disreputable Dog," in *Shop Talk: Studies in Honor of Seymour Slive, Presented on His Seventy-Fifth Birthday*, ed. Cynthia P. Schneider, William W. Robinson, and Alice I. Davies (Cambridge, MA: Harvard University Art Museums, 1995), 150. It is difficult to see the resemblance of this figure to Rembrandt's self-portraits of the early 1630s, although he does wear a similar plumed bonnet in his self-portrait from 1638 (B. 20, cat. no. 1). Marieke de Winkel (*Fashion and Fancy: Dress and Meaning in Rembrandt's Paintings* [Amsterdam: Amsterdam University Press, 2006], 165–66) noted that although the plumed beret or bonnet was fashionable in the Netherlands in the 1520s, it had fallen out of favor by the seventeenth century. By Rembrandt's time, such hats were worn only by very young boys. In discussing the appearance of the plumed bonnet in Lucas van Leyden's print, *Young Man with a Skull* (1519), which Rembrandt used as a source for his 1638 etched self-portrait, de Winkel noted that this type of hat was probably not a common *vanitas* motif, but, rather, a detail meant to reinforce the significance of the van Leyden print through the beret's reference to current fashion. "It shows the young man to be a worldly and vain dandy and after all, fashion and youth only last for a very short time." In the context of Rembrandt's print of the Good Samaritan, the plumed bonnet worn by the figure in the window (as well as the one by the groom), not only provides an example of the artist's interest in archaic costumes, but also offers a contrast between the fashionable but passive dandy drawn to the window to observe what is happening outside and the modestly dressed Samaritan, who is engaged in charitable acts.

3. Kenneth Clark, *Rembrandt and the Italian Renaissance* (New York: New York University Press, 1966), 12, called the dog repulsive. Later on, when discussing a painting of *The Good Samaritan* in the Wallace Collection London (RRP, *Corpus*, 1630(?), C48), which mirrors the etching but omits the dog, Clark referred to the dog in the etched version as "shocking," and asserted that Rembrandt had included it in order to "jolt" the viewer. Clark, "Rembrandt's 'Good Samaritan' in the Wallace Collection," *Burlington Magazine* 118 (1976): 809.

4. There is a dog, for example, in Crispijn de Passe the Elder's print after a design by Hans Bol (HD 110), and in Jan van de Velde II's nocturnal rendering of the scene (fig. 2) (HD 12), a work that is generally acknowledged as an important source for Rembrandt's etching.

5. Clark, "Rembrandt's 'Good Samaritan,'" 809.

6. Kuretsky, "Rembrandt's Good Samaritan," 151.

7. Kuretsky (ibid.) also cites an exegetical passage from the third-century theologian Origen in which the "water" of Christ's teachings is said to "cleanse from defilements the soul which has been defiled by the pollution of sin."

8. In this regard, Kuretsky draws the reader's attention to Rembrandt's portrayal of urinating figures in such works as a painting of a frightened infant Ganymede (Staatliche Kunstsammlungen, Dresden, RRP, *Corpus*, 1635, A113) and etchings of a peasant man and woman (B. 190, 1631; and B. 191, 1631). (Kuretsky, "Rembrandt's Good Samaritan," 152n17). It should be noted, however, that unlike *The Good Samaritan*, none of these other examples appears in a work based on a lesson about morality. It is possible that even some contemporary viewers would have considered it a breach of decorum to include this kind of earthy detail in a work illustrating a parable about virtue.

9. Kuretsky, "Rembrandt's Good Samaritan," 151.

10. Examples of the parable depicted in a series include four prints by Dirck Coornhert after Maarten van Heemskerck (NHD 353 [Heemskerck]), 1549; four by Heinrich Aldegrever (HG 40-43), c. 1554–80; and six by Crispijn de Passe the Elder, based on designs by Hans Bol (HD 105-110), c. 1600. Examples of single prints with multiple episodes include Georg Pencz (HG 36), 1543 (the Samaritan tending the wounds of the Jew, with the robbers, the Levite and priest, and negotiations with the innkeeper in the background); Johannes Sadeler I after Maerten de Vos (HD 197 [Sadeler]), c. 1580–1600 (the Samaritan tending the victim's wounds, with the Levite and priest walking by in the background); and Philip Galle after Johannes Stradanus (NHD 47 [Stradanus]), f. 1612 (the Samaritan tending the man's wounds, with the Levite and priest walking in the background). Examples of single prints depicting a single incident

include Hanns Lautensack (HG 43), 1550–65 (the Samaritan helping the victim in the forest); Aegidius Sadeler after Jan Brueghel the Elder (HD 218), 1593–1625 (the Samaritan tending the wounded Jew in a landscape); and Wolfgang Kilian after Jacopo Bassano (HG 7), c. 1600–15 (the Samaritan tending the man's wounds).

11. HD 12. At least three different editions of this print were published, attesting to the etching's popularity. The first was issued by Jan van de Velde II, the second by Claes Jansz. Visscher (1587–1652), and the third by Frederik de Wit (1629–1706).

12. See, for example, the comments of James Howell (1594?–1666) in his letter from Amsterdam of May 1, 1619:

> It is a rare thing to meet with a Beggar here, as rare as to see a Horse, they say, upon the Streets of Venice; and this is held to be one of their best pieces of Government: for besides the strictness of their Laws against Mendicants, they have Hospitals of all sort for young and old, both for the relief of the one, and the employment of the other, so that there is no Object here to exercise any Act of Charity upon. (*Epistolae Hoe-Elianae: The Familiar Letters of James Howell*, vol. 1 [Boston: Houghton Mifflin, 1907], 20–21)

Sir William Temple was also moved to remark upon the Dutch emphasis on charitable institutions:

> Charity seems to be very National among them, though it be regulated by Orders of the Country, and not usually mov'd by the common Objects of Compassion. But it is seen in the admirable Provisions that are made out of it for all sort of Persons that can want, or ought to be kept in a Government. Among the many and various Hospitals that are in every Man's Curiosity and Talk that travels their Country, I was affected with none more than that of the aged Sea men at Enchusyen, which is contrived, finished, and ordered, as if it were done with a kind intention of some well-natur'd man, That those who had past their whole lives in the Hardships and Incommodities of the Sea, should find a Retreat stor'd with all the Eases and Conveniences that Old age is capable of feeling and enjoying.

Temple, *The Works of Sir William Temple, bart.*, vol. 1, *Observations upon the United Provinces of the Netherlands* (London: Printed for J. Brotherton, 1770; first pub. 1687), 159–60), accessed February 25, 2017, https://babel.hathitrust.org/cgi/pt?id=ucw.ark:/13960/t8x92t82q ;view=1up;seq=165.

63. Return of the Prodigal Son

B. 91 (H. 147, Mz. 207, NHD 159)
Etching
Signed and dated in the plate: *Rembrandt f. 1636*
State I of III
Sheet: 16.7 × 14.7 cm; plate mark: 15.6 × 13.6 cm
Verso: in graphite, in center, *Le Retour de l'enfant prodigue; Bartsch 91; B. 91*^{etat} I; at bottom right, *65*

Provenance:
Craddock & Barnard, London, 1972
Feddersen, Elkhart, IN, 1991
Snite Museum of Art
Acc. No.: 1991.025.059

Plate survives:
Museum het Rembrandthuis, Amsterdam. (On the reverse, an engraved geometrical figure illustrating squaring the circle.)

The story of the prodigal son as recounted in the Gospel of Luke is one of the most familiar of Jesus's parables.[1] It is the tale of "a certain man" who had two sons. The younger son asked his father, "give me the portion of goods that falleth to me," and the man did so, dividing his goods between his two sons.[2] Shortly thereafter, the younger son took all of his possessions and left home for a "distant country," where he "wasted his substance in riotous living."[3] Famine descended upon the country, and the young man, finding himself without means, hired himself out and was sent by his master into the fields to feed the pigs. Watching the pigs eat, he longed to fill his own stomach, but no one offered him anything to eat. Taking stock of his situation, the young man thought about the fact that his father's servants had plenty to eat and yet he was starving, and decided to return home, admit his sins, and ask his father to take him back as a servant. As he neared home, his father saw him and ran out to meet his errant son, embracing and kissing him. The boy told his father that he had sinned against him and against heaven and was no longer worthy to be called his son, but his father responded by instructing his servants "Bring forth the best robe, and put it on him; and put a ring on his hand and shoes on his feet; and bring hither the fatted calf and kill it; and let us eat and be merry. For this my son was dead, and is alive again; he was lost and is found. And they began to be merry."[4]

This parable, which the Dutch seventeenth-century philosopher and playwright Hugo Grotius described as "the most remarkable of all, full of emotions and the most beautiful painted colors,"[5] was an extremely popular subject in sixteenth- and seventeenth-century art and literature.[6] The story of the profligate son's sin, repentance, and forgiveness was often represented in print series that included anywhere from four to twelve images.[7] These series almost always ended with a depiction of the joyous reunion of the young man and his father,[8] the event that Rembrandt chose to illustrate in his print. The story of the reconciliation between father and son was interpreted by both Catholics and Protestants as reflecting God's mercy and willingness to forgive a repentant sinner.[9] Where Catholics and Protestants differed was on the question of whether God's forgiveness required any actions on the part of the sinner or whether forgiveness could be conferred by an act of grace alone.[10] Since Rembrandt's etching does not address this controversy, his

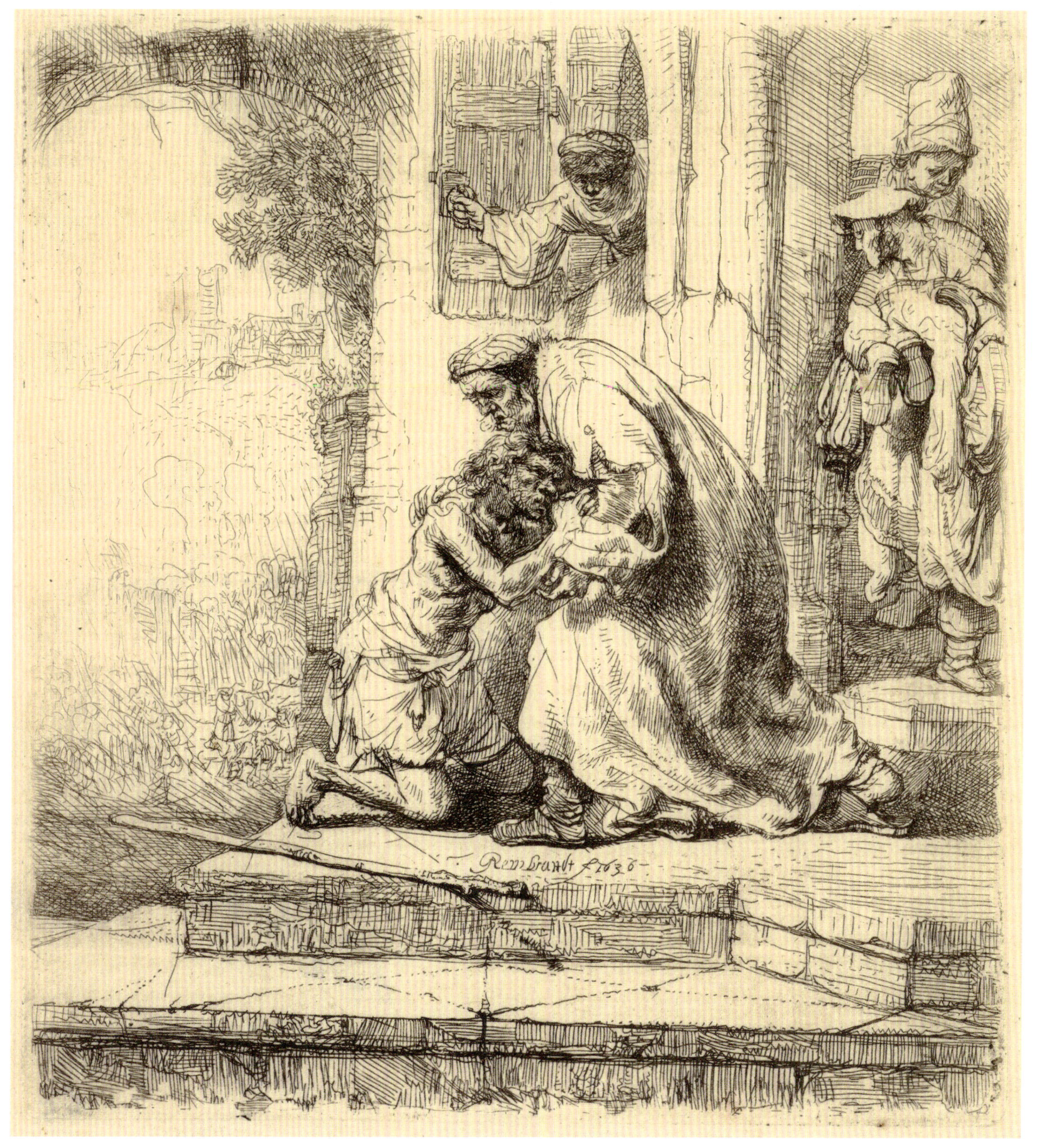

PLATE 63

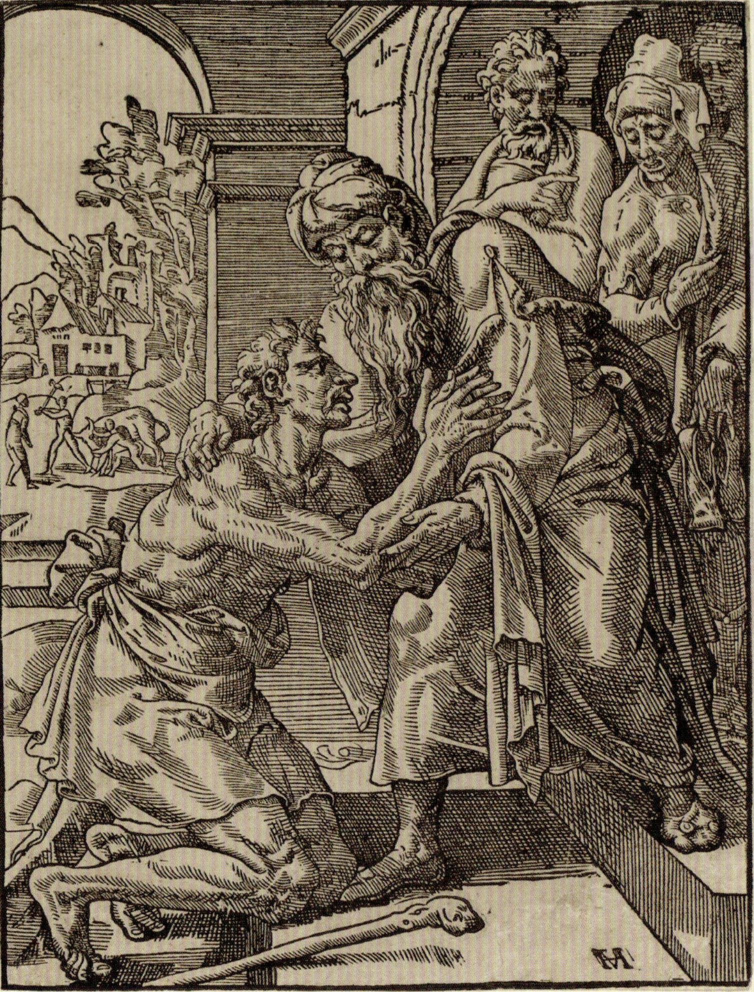

FIGURE 1. Dirck Volkertsz. Coornhert after Maarten van Heemskerk, *Return of the Prodigal Son*, woodcut, 1548. *Photo: Courtesy of the National Gallery of Art, Washington, DC.*

print would have been doctrinally neutral, acceptable to collectors of either persuasion.

Rembrandt derived his composition from a woodcut by Dirck Volckertsz. Coornhert (fig. 1) after a design by Maarten van Heemskerck from a series of four prints dedicated to the story of the prodigal son (c. 1548).[11] In both the Heemskerck woodcut and the Rembrandt etching, the reunion is set at the threshold of the father's house, an unusual location that, as Susan Donahue Kuretsky observed, deviates from the biblical text, which specifically states that the prodigal's father saw his son from afar and ran out to meet him.[12] She noted that this departure from tradition is especially significant since Calvin specifically drew "a parallel between the father's leaving the house to meet his son, even before hearing his apologies and regrets, with God's eternal willingness to meet the sinner at the very moment of repentance."[13] Kuretsky suggested that by placing the meeting on the home's threshold, both Heemskerck and Rembrandt were able to draw a clear contrast between the outsider (the son—near the archway that leads away from the house) and the insider (the father—near the door and window that lead into the house).[14] According to Kuretsky, this location, with its connotations of safety and homecoming, works as a metaphor for salvation and the spiritual passage from earth to Heaven through the entryway that is Christ.[15]

Although numerous elements show Rembrandt's dependence on Heemskerck's earlier woodcut—the prominent display of the prodigal son's walking staff on the step beside him;[16] the placement of the father's hands on his son's arm and back; the servants, poised in the doorway behind their master as they bear the shoes and clothing for the boy; the foliage in the archway; and the buildings visible on the distant hill in the background—there are also significant differences between the earlier print and Rembrandt's etching, all of which make the latter's interpretation more intimate and emotionally engaging. For example, Rembrandt introduced more space between the viewer and the action and also around the actors. As a result, his figures are less monumental and consequently more approachable than Heemskerck's. Rembrandt's descriptive technique—his less strident line and softer, more atmospheric lighting—reinforces the sense of the pathos of the reunion. Rembrandt's kneeling young prodigal is thinner than Heemskerck's muscular young man. The son's loincloth is more tattered, and his expression is more anguished.[17] In Heemskerck's woodcut, the father, whose body is turned slightly forward, is caught in mid-stride as he steps down to meet his kneeling son.[18] The old bearded man gazes down at the wayward boy and, with a look of tender compassion, reaches out to embrace him. The prodigal son, in turn, holds his hands up in front of him in a gesture of supplication. His mouth is slightly open as if he is reciting his speech of penitence. Even though the father touches his son and the boy speaks to his father, the two figures remain separated from one another, both spatially and psychologically. By contrast, the two men in Rembrandt's etching are visually and emotionally united in a single tender moment. This father is also caught in mid-stride, but he is now on the same level as his son. He bends over the youth, almost resting his chin on the young man's head, as if to shelter him with his own body. With his eyes closed, the old man expresses not joy, but rather a poignant sense of relief at the return of his lost child, while the penitent son, humbled before his father, rests his head on the old man's chest.

Overall, Rembrandt's scene exhibits a greater sense of picturesque naturalism than Heemskerck's starker, more stylized woodcut. The architecture, for example, is more rustic, showing its age, and the reactions and costumes of the servants who have brought the new shoes and a shirt to clothe the penitent wastrel are more varied. Also, Rembrandt's introduction of a curious maidservant leaning out of a window and gazing down at the scene adds a light, human dimension to the drama. Finally, Rembrandt altered the secondary scene that appears in the deep background through the archway on the left. A herd of cows—visible just beyond the prodigal son's right heel—can just be discerned in the faintly sketched landscape below. Whereas Heemskerck's print depicts the actual slaying of the fatted calf, Rembrandt's vignette leaves that aspect of the story to the viewer's imagination.

Return of the Prodigal Son, an early etching, is a clear illustration of the manner in which Rembrandt drew on earlier models—rather overtly, in this case—but significantly transformed them in order to create more psychologically complex works of art that would resonate with the viewer's own experience.

Notes

1. Luke 15:11–32
2. Luke 15:12.
3. Luke 15:13.
4. Luke 15:22–24.
5. Hugo Grotius, *Annotationes in Novum Testamentum* (Groningen, Netherlands: W. Zuidema, 1827), 3:368, "Inter omnes Christi parabolas haec sane eximia est, plena affectuum et pulcherrimis picta coloribus."
6. Ellen G. D'Oench went so far as to call it "the most frequently illustrated biblical parable in Western art," *Prodigal Son Narratives, 1480–1980*, exh. cat. (New Haven, CT: Yale University Art Gallery; Middletown, CT: Davison Art Center, Wesleyan University, 1995), 3. On the parable's popularity in the sixteenth and seventeenth centuries, see D'Oench, 3–7; Barbara Haeger, "The Religious Significance of Rembrandt's 'Return of the Prodigal Son': An Examination in the Context of the Visual and Iconographic Tradition," PhD diss., University of Michigan, Ann Arbor, 1983; and Haeger, "Cornelis Anthonsz's Representation of the Parable of the Prodigal Son: A Protestant Interpretation of the Biblical Text," *Netherlands kunsthistorisch jaarboek* 37 (1986): 133 and 146n5.
7. Smaller series are more common, but the so-called Monogrammist MT did a series of twelve prints (B. 3-14) and Jacques Callot did a series of ten plates and a frontispiece (Lieure 1404–14, 1635) dedicated to the story.
8. The exception to this rule was Philip Galle's engraved cycle of the parable after Maarten van Heemskerck (NHD 365 [Heemskerck]), which ends with the actual conclusion of the story, that is, the father upbraiding his elder son for his lack of charity toward his brother. On this cycle, see Barbara Haeger, "Philips Galle's Engravings after Maarten van Heemskerck's *Parable of the Prodigal Son*," *Oud Holland* 102, no. 2 (1988): 127–140.
9. For a summary of the medieval exegesis of the parable derived from the writings of the Church Fathers, see Philippe Verdier, "The Tapestry of the Prodigal Son," *Journal of the Walters Art Gallery* 18 (1955): 24–25.

Calvin was very explicit in interpreting the parable as an illustration of God's unconditional mercy and forgiveness:

> In the person of a young prodigal who, after having been reduced to the deepest poverty by luxury and extravagance, returns as a suppliant to his father, to whom he had been disobedient and rebellious, Christ describes all sinners who, wearied of their folly, apply to the grace of God. To the kind father, on the other hand, who not only pardons the crimes of his son, but of his own accord meets him when returning, he compares God, who is not satisfied with pardoning those who pray to him, but even advances to meet them with the compassion of a father.

Calvin's Commentaries: A Commentary on a Harmony of the Evangelists: Matthew, Mark, and Luke, Introduction to the Commentary of Luke, 2:293, accessed July 11, 2014, http://www.ccel.org/ccel/calvin/calcom32.pdf.

10. On the Catholic and Protestant positions, see Barbara Haeger, "The Prodigal Son in Sixteenth- and Seventeenth-Century Netherlandish Art: Depictions of the Parable and the Evolution of a Catholic Image," *Simiolus: Netherlands Quarterly for the History of Art* 16, nos. 2/3 (1986): 128–38, esp. 128.

11. NHD 356-59 (Heemskerck).

12. Susan Donahue Kuretsky, "Rembrandt at the Threshold," in *Rembrandt, Rubens, and the Art of Their Time: Recent Perspectives*, ed. Roland E. Fleisher and Susan Clare Scott (University Park: Pennsylvania State University Press, 1997), 64. In her 1983 dissertation on Rembrandt's painting of *The Return of the Prodigal Son* (Bredius 598) in the State Hermitage Museum, St. Petersburg, Barbara Haeger stated that "Van Heemkerck's woodcut representation of the return of the prodigal son differs from all other sixteenth-century Netherlandish renditions of the subject in one respect. It is the only such work that places the father's reception of his son on the threshold of the entrance to the house" ("The Religious Significance," 24). While this may be the case with Netherlandish examples, there is at least one sixteenth-century German example, a print by the Monogrammist MT (B. 13, 1543, BM 1842,1112.55), that also places the meeting in front of the father's house.

13. Kuretsky, "Rembrandt at the Threshold," 64. On Calvin's remarks on this passage, see *Calvin's Commentaries: A Commentary on a Harmony of the Evangelists*, 2:296, Commentary on Luke 15:20: "As this father, therefore, is not merely pacified by the entreaties of his son, but meets him when he is coming, and before he has heard a word, embraces him, filthy and ugly as he is, so God does not wait for long prayer, but of his own free will meets the sinner as soon as he proposes to confess his fault." Accessed July 1, 2014, http://www.ccel.org/ccel/calvin/calcom32.pdf.

14. Kuretsky, "Rembrandt at the Threshold," 64.

15. Ibid., 65. Kuretsky notes that in John 10:9, Christ declares, "I am the door: by me if any man enter in, he shall be saved."

16. The staff is probably simply a walking stick, possibly evoking, in this case, the recognition that the prodigal son was on a pilgrimage back to his home and his father, or that he may have needed a staff to lean on, since he was weak from hunger.

17. The prodigal son in Rembrandt's etching is actually quite homely, possibly a reflection of Calvin's comment that the father embraced his son, "filthy and ugly as he is." See note 13, above.

18. In Rembrandt's etching, it is the foremost servant who descends the steps, with one foot on one riser, and the other foot on another, like the father in Heemskerck's work.

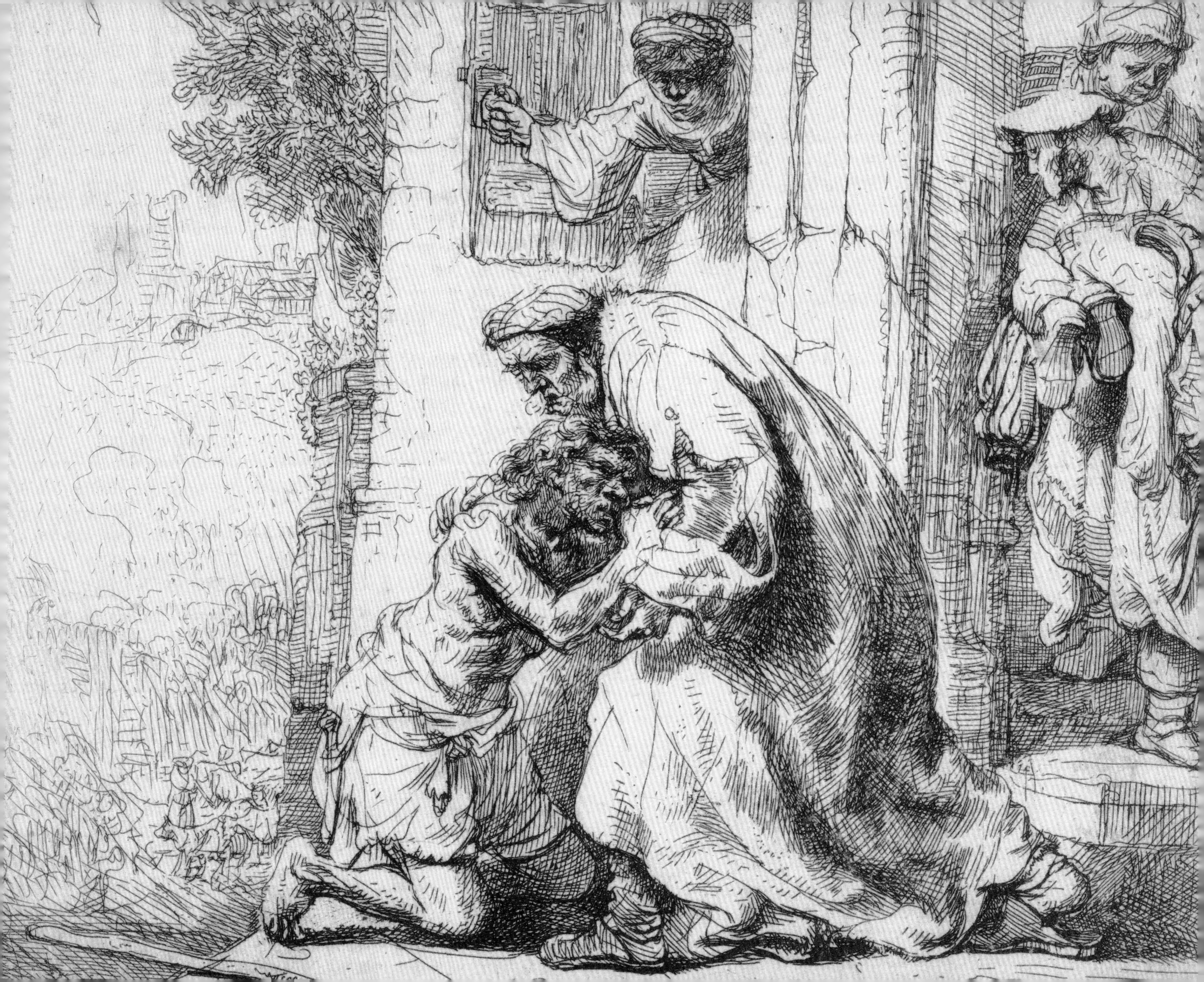

64–65. Beheading of John the Baptist

64. Beheading of John the Baptist

B. 93 (H. 308 [as van Vliet], Mz. 289 [Rembrandt, reworked by van Vliet], NHD 109)
Etching
Signed in the plate: *RHL*
c. 1631
State III of VII
Sheet: 15.7 × 12.4, trimmed to the plate mark
Verso: collector's stamp, black ink, a walrus or "morse" (Lugt 4320, Peter Morse); in graphite, *B 93*III *H308, DTMC CHK*

Provenance:
Peter Morse (1935–93)[1]
David Tunick Inc., New York, NY, 1977
Feddersen, Elkhart, IN, 1991
Snite Museum of Art
Acc. No.: 1991.025.061

The plate does not survive.

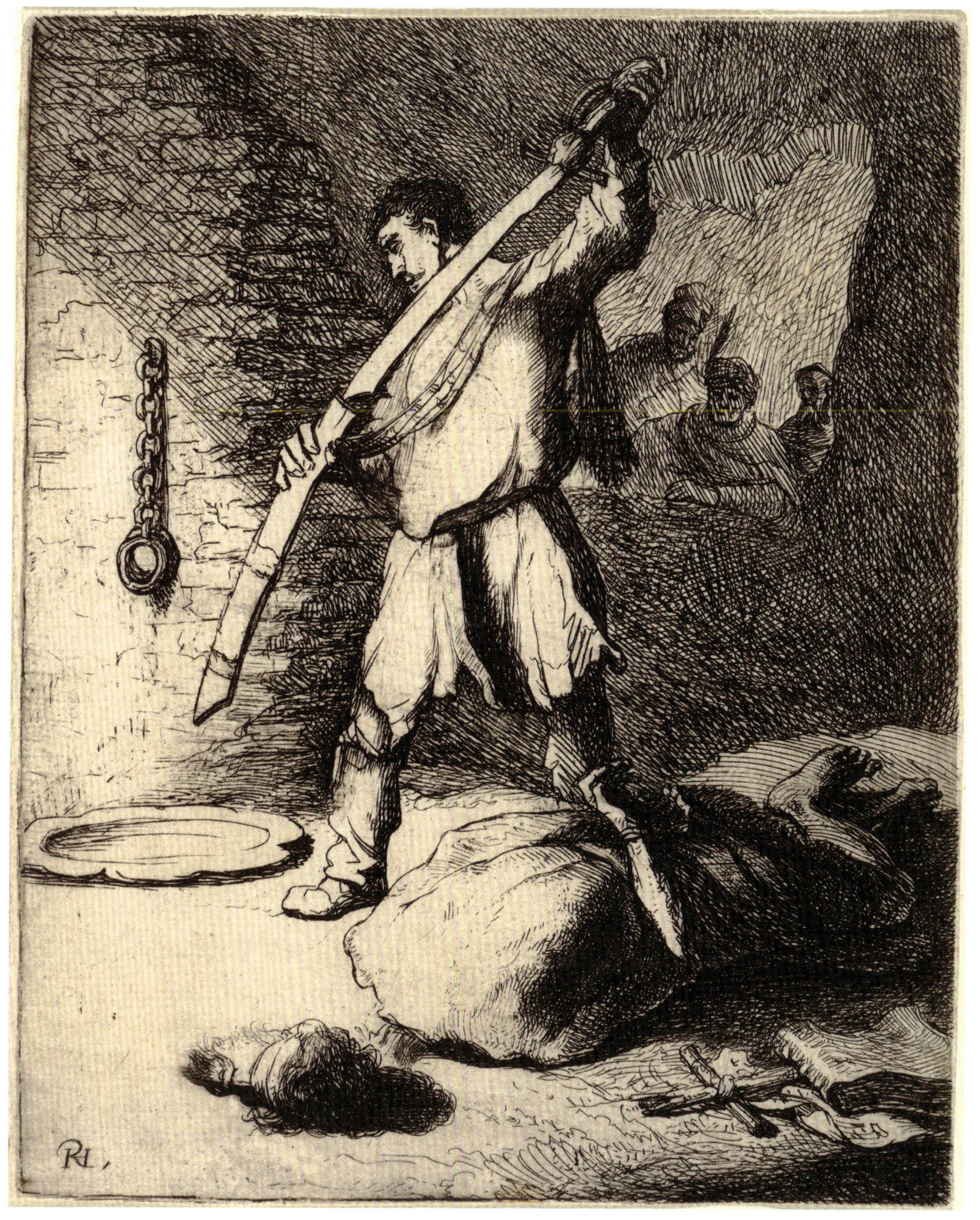

PLATE 64

65. Beheading of John the Baptist

B. 92 (H. 171, Mz. 209, NHD 183)
Etching and drypoint
Signed and dated in the plate: *Rembrandt f. 1640*
State I of III
Sheet: 13.1 × 11.0 cm; plate mark: 12.9 × 10.3 cm
Verso: in graphite, top *H6078, 163*, below "163" *3/56*, center left *317* in a circle, below "317" *B92, 781, 7016/45720, H.1711, II, H 6078, B92*

Provenance:
Harrods, London, 1980
Feddersen, Elkhart, IN, 1991
Snite Museum of Art
Acc. No.: 1991.025.060

Plate survives:
Private collection, USA

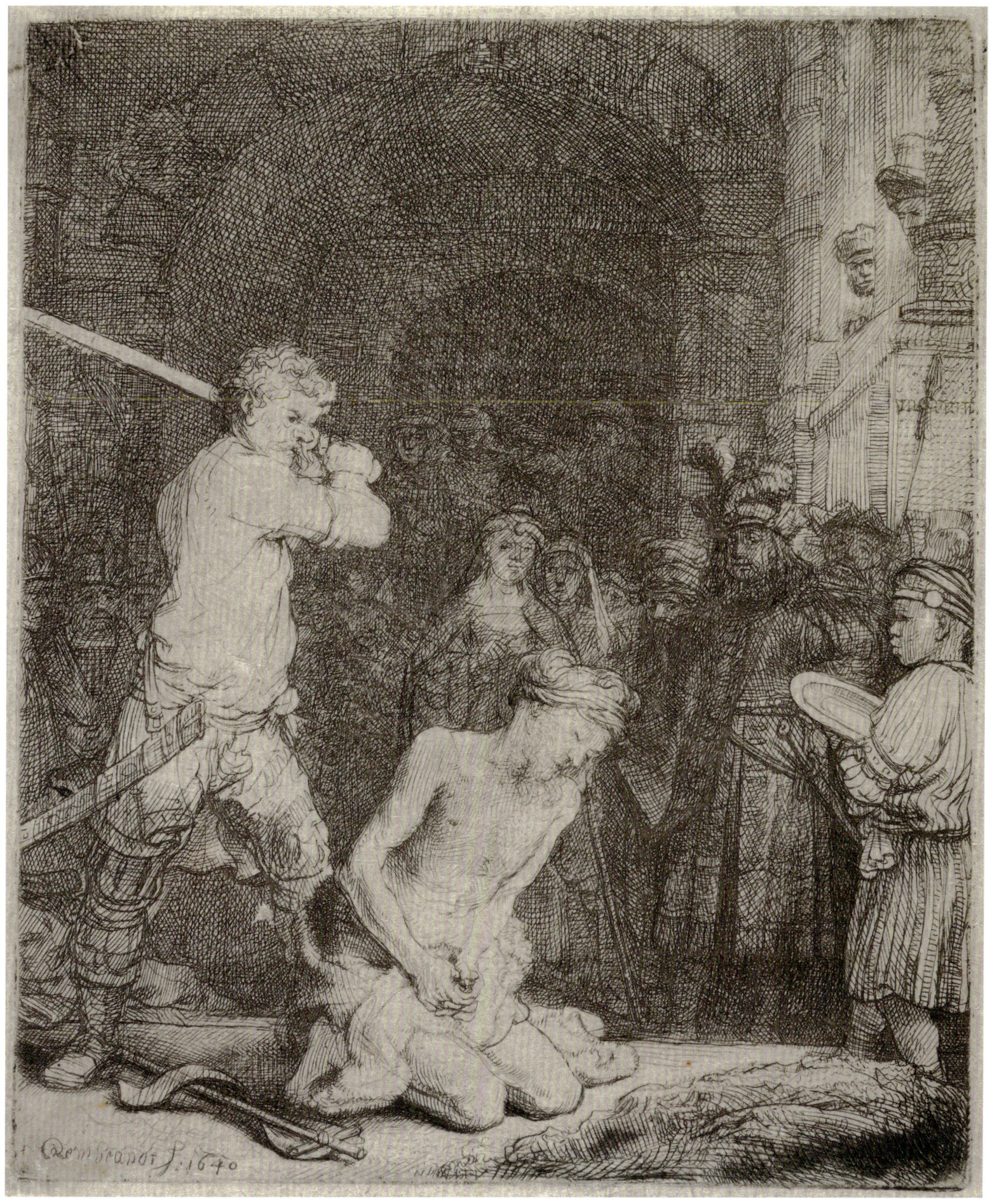

PLATE 65

The story of John the Baptist's execution is related in Matthew 14:3–11. Saint John had been preaching against King Herod's marriage to the king's sister-in-law, Herodias, and in order to silence the prophet, Herodias had John sent to prison. At a feast held in honor of Herod's birthday, Herodias's daughter, Salome, danced for the king and his guests, and her stepfather was so pleased with her that he promised to grant Salome one request. After consulting with her mother, Salome asked for the Baptist's head. John was immediately decapitated, and his head was placed on a platter and brought from the prison to the feast, where it was presented to Salome.

Rembrandt created two prints of the Beheading of John the Baptist, the first around 1631 (B. 93, cat. no. 64), and the second in 1640 (B. 92, cat. no. 65). The earlier print focuses on the moment after John is killed. The Baptist's body and severed head have fallen awkwardly to the ground at the feet of the executioner, who is in the process of sheathing his massive sword.[2] In the lower right corner are a crudely fashioned cross, a scrap of paper, and a closed book—objects that suggest that the Baptist was a man of faith whose last moments were spent in prayer. The salver on which the severed head is to be brought to the banquet hall lies on the floor to the soldier's right. The platter is bathed in light, and the soldier's scabbard acts as a directional arrow pointing down toward it. Shackles attached to the wall above the salver identify the space as a prison cell. The brick wall of the chamber behind the executioner has been breached, and three exotic, shadowy figures, one wearing a plumed turban,[3] peer into the cell through the rough opening.

The Snite Museum print is an impression from the third state of this etching. In the first two states, a short flight of stairs led up out of the composition to the left, beside the salver. In the third state, these distracting steps were burnished away, creating a patch of bright light whose source remains undefined, but that sets up a strong contrast between foreground and background. While the light on the soldier's sword and scabbard direct the viewer's eye to the salver, the light that illuminates the executioner's head and body and continues down along one of John's bound arms creates another bright diagonal, one that also divides the dramatic action from the murky background of the prison and the onlookers.

The authorship of this print has been disputed since the nineteenth century.[4] Despite the fact that the etching bears the monogram that Rembrandt used during his years in Leiden, "RHL" [Rembrandt Harmenz. van Leiden], the print was sometimes attributed to one of Rembrandt's collaborators, the printmaker Jan Georg van Vliet.[5] However, the existence of an autograph drawing in the Louvre (Ben. 101) (fig. 2) which may be a study for the executioner[6] suggests that Rembrandt was at least the designer of the print. If the print is, indeed, a work by Rembrandt, then it appears to be an example of his more tentative, youthful style. There are numerous awkward aspects of the etching, most notably the foreshortening of the body of the Baptist and the contour of his right shoulder, the relative sizes of John's head and body, the undecipherable area on which the saint's crossed legs rest, and the fractured space of the cell. Two other factors muddy the waters in terms of authorship: First, the date of the Louvre drawing is disputed, and if the drawing did not precede the etching, then it obviously does not provide evidence of Rembrandt's hand and intentions in the print. Second, as Erik Hinterding noted, there are stylistic anomalies in the execution of the etching, particularly in the use of the short

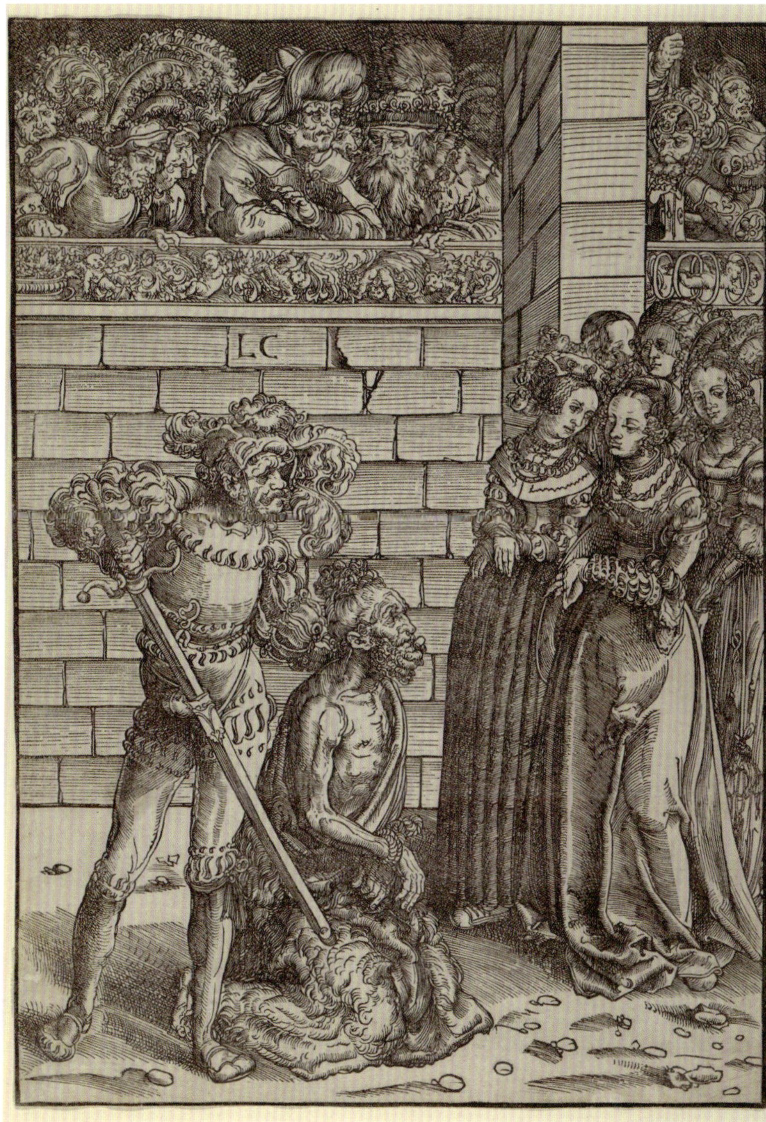

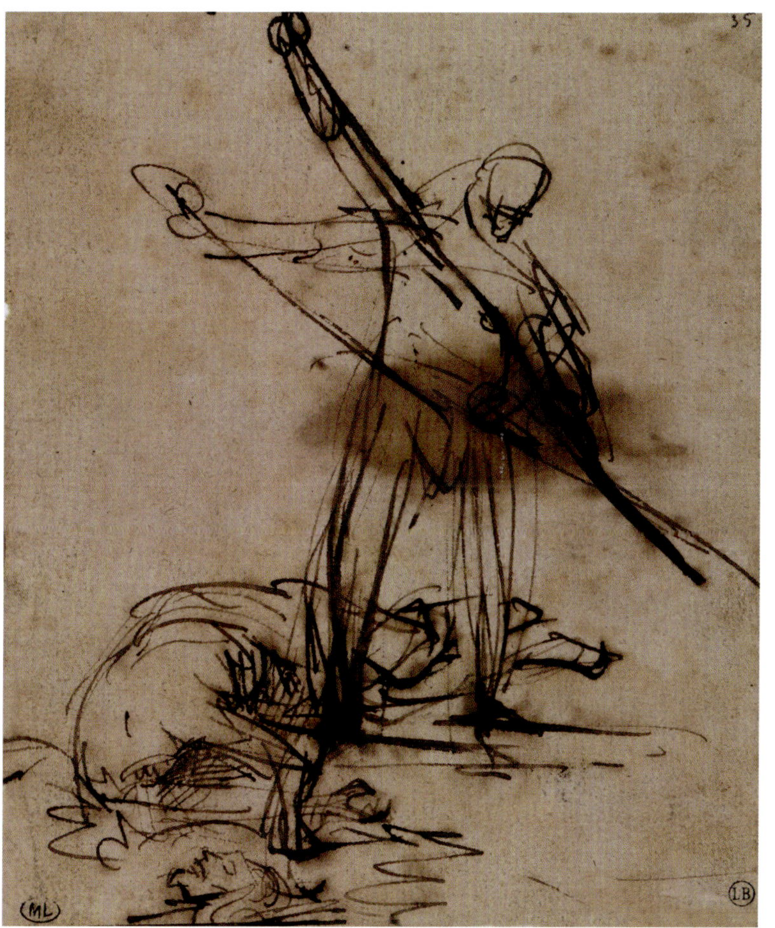

FIGURE 1. Lucas Cranach the Elder, *The Beheading of John the Baptist*, woodcut, c. 1505–10. *The Metropolitan Museum of Art, New York, New York, Gift of Felix M. Warburg, 1920.*

FIGURE 2. Rembrandt (?), *The Beheading of John the Baptist*, pen and ink, Ben. 101, 1635 (?). *Louvre, Paris, RF 4743. © RMN–Grand Palais/Art Resource, New York.*

linear strokes engraved with a burin in order to create shadows in the right background. This technique was not used by Rembrandt.[7] It may be that the print was a collaboration between Rembrandt and van Vliet, for they did work in tandem on other occasions, a partnership that is known to have produced much more successful, more sophisticated works.[8] It is possible that this Beheading was designed by Rembrandt, but primarily executed by van Vliet or reworked by a pupil.[9] The general consensus of scholars now is that despite the evidence of another hand at work, the etching does belong in Rembrandt's oeuvre.

The later print of the Beheading (B. 92, cat. no. 65), a work securely attributed to Rembrandt, represents an earlier moment in the biblical narrative, one that creates much more dramatic tension. The executioner has discarded his coat, rolled up his sleeves, and raised his sword. As he prepares to strike the fatal blow, he twists in a powerful contrapposto pose and glares down at the Baptist before him. John kneels on the dirt floor, his unbound hands clasped in front of him. His naked body, covered only by a hair shirt draped around his hips and lap, is slender and vulnerable. His head, wrapped in a turban, is bowed as he gazes down at the ground before him. As in the earlier print, the emblems of John's faith appear prominently

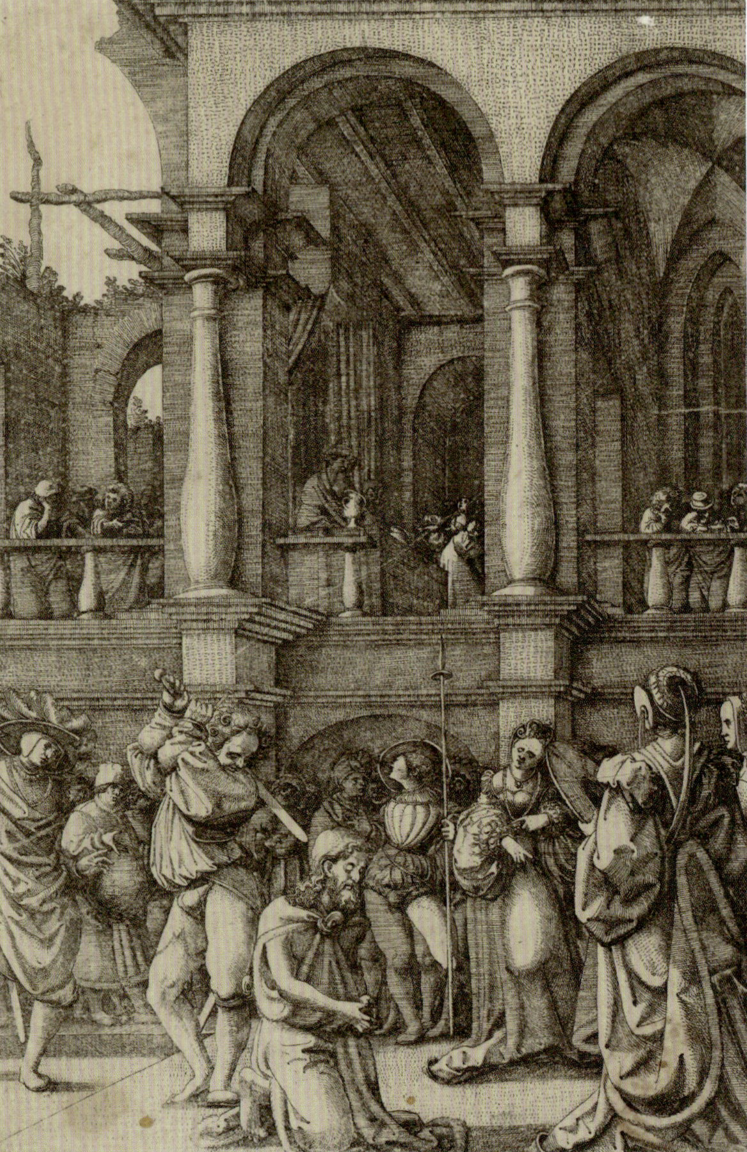

FIGURE 3. Frans Crabbe, *The Beheading of John the Baptist*, engraving, c. 1520–30. *Rijksmuseum, Amsterdam.*

in the foreground, with the reed cross and the scroll twined around it alluding to the Baptist's role as a prophet and disciple of Christ. At the right side of the print, a young Moorish servant stands by, impassively holding the salver on which the Baptist's head will be placed. This figure adds an element of exoticism and helps to situate the event in the "East" in biblical times.

Light falls primarily on the three figures in the foreground—executioner, martyr, and salver-bearer—focusing the viewer's attention on the brutal act about to take place. Because Rembrandt depicted the executioner just before he struck the blow, the print captures a moment of suspended time, even as the outcome of the action is foreshadowed by the presence of the servant with the platter, at the right. The illuminated diagonal that runs down the length of the sword at the far left, across the composition to the waiting platter at the right, leaves the viewer no doubt as to the fateful sequence of events that is about to occur. Set between the executioner and the Moor, the Baptist acts as the focal point of the narrative and a fulcrum for the composition.

The space behind the three principal figures opens up into a large, darkened, vaulted chamber that is crowded with figures who stand and watch. The complexity and weight of the architecture, including the raised gallery at the upper right with observers peering out of its openings, contributes to the theatrical quality of the print. Herod, bearded and dressed in sumptuous garments and an exotic plumed headdress, stands at the peak of a triangle anchored by the Baptist and the young Moor. Although Herod is in shadow, his size, location, and rich attire identify him as a man of consequence. Off to his right, reflected light falls on a woman, possibly Herodias, who wears a wimple and a cloak. The light also picks out the headdress of a younger woman, peering around from behind Herodias. Although this woman has no distinguishing features, she has been identified as Salome.[10] The Gospels do not place Herodias and Salome at the beheading, but it is they who set this execution in motion, and Rembrandt may have exploited this dramatic—and chilling—fact by inserting the two women into the space between executioner and martyr. The series of arches in the center of the background frames Herodias, Salome, and John—schemers and victim—at the center of the scene.

Representations of the beheading of the Baptist were not unusual in Rembrandt's time, but they normally focused on the actual act of decapitation or the moment when Salome received the severed head.[11] Jaco Rutgers identified a print of The Beheading[12] by the sixteenth-century artist Frans Crabbe[13] (fig. 3) that may have inspired Rembrandt to depart from these traditions. The Crabbe print has a complicated architectural setting, including a series of arches and a second-story gallery, and also includes crowds of spectators. Even more telling, the sixteenth-century print shows the executioner standing behind the Baptist, ready to strike John as the saint kneels, his hands clasped in front of him. Although Rembrandt's 1640 etching may have used Crabbe's print as a point of departure, his own image has much greater narrative and spiritual complexity.

It is possible that Rembrandt's depictions of the beheading of the Baptist, as well as numerous drawings that he made of executions had contemporary religious and political significance.[14] As Stephanie Dickey noted, Rembrandt had Mennonite acquaintances, and Mennonite martyrologies recounted instances of the persecution of Anabaptists in the sixteenth century. The Mennonites chronicled numerous beheadings of Anabaptists in Amsterdam and elsewhere, and drew parallels to the martyrdom of early Christians, including the death of the Baptist.[15]

Notes

1. Peter Morse (1935–93) was an art historian, collector, and writer who served as an associate curator in the Division of Graphic Arts, Smithsonian Institution, Museum of History and Technology from 1965 to 1967. In that capacity, he published a study of one of Rembrandt's landscape etchings (B. 224), *Rembrandt's Etching Technique: An Example, Contributions from the Museum of History and Technology*, paper no. 61 (Washington, DC: Smithsonian Institution, 1966). According to Roger S. Keyes, Morse was primarily a collector of prints by Japanese artist Katsushika Hokusai, but also owned some Rembrandt prints, including an impression of *The Three Crosses*. Morse sold these at auction in New York in the early or mid-1970s. Roger S. Keyes, personal communication, March 5, 2013.

2. Ludwig Münz (*Critical Catalogue*, vol. 2, cat. 289, 173) suggested that the artist might have been influenced by a sixteenth-century woodcut by Lucas Cranach (B. 61) of the same subject (fig. 1), since both compositions include the unusual image of an executioner sheathing his sword, but this seems like a tenuous connection.

3. According to Mariette de Winkel (*Fashion and Fancy: Dress and Meaning in Rembrandt's Paintings* [Amsterdam: Amsterdam University Press, 2006], 258), the turban with an aigrette was an authentic example of Ottoman dress, and was used by Rembrandt to indicate an Eastern setting. The artist portrayed himself wearing just such a headdress in a self-portrait from 1631 (RRP, *Corpus*, A40).

4. For a summary of attributions, see entry 109 in the Rembrandt volume of the NHD, 170.

5. For a discussion of van Vliet and his relationship to Rembrandt in the early 1630s, see the entry for *Christ before Pilate: Large Plate* (B. 77, 1636, cat. no. 50).

6. Although Frits Lugt dated the drawing to between 1625 and 1628, and Ed de Heer (*The Mystery of the Young Rembrandt* [Wolfratshausen, Germany: Edition Minerva, 2001] cat. 57, 290–93), dated it to about 1627, Otto Benesch (*The Drawings of Rembrandt: A Critical and Chronological Catalogue* [London: Phaidon, 1973] vol. 1, cat. 101, 30) dated it to about 1635. If Benesch's proposed chronology is correct, then the drawing cannot be considered a preparatory study for the print, since, as Hinterding noted (*Lugt Catalogue,* cat. 78, 206), impressions of the first state were produced on paper with a watermark that can be dated to between 1631–33. The 1635 date is repeated in the Rembrandt volume of the NHD, 170.

7. Hinterding, *Lugt Catalogue,* cat. 78, 206.

8. Examples include *Descent from the Cross: The Second Plate* (B. 81 II, 1633, cat. no. 55) and *Christ before Pilate: Large Plate* (B.77, 1636, cat. no. 50), in this catalog.

9. Arthur M. Hind (*Rembrandt's Etchings: An Essay and a Catalogue, with Some Notes on the Drawings*, 2nd ed., [London: Metheun; New York: Scribner, 1923], cat. 308, 121) classified the print as "probably by van Vliet." Ludwig Münz (*Critical Catalogue,* cat. 289, 173) identified the print as an image by Rembrandt that was reworked by van Vliet. Christopher White and Karel Boon (*Rembrandt's Etchings,* B. 93, 171) placed the print among those "prints by Rembrandt only known in later states reworked by a pupil." White and Boon seemed to accept the design as Rembrandt's, but remained somewhat uncertain as to the identity of the early pupil who reworked the plate. Ed de Heer, in the catalog *The Mystery of the Young Rembrandt* (cat. no. 57, 290–93), considered the etching to be by Jan van Vliet after Rembrandt. Hinterding (*Lugt Catalogue,* 205–6) seemed to favor Rembrandt as the inventor of the print, but with extensive reworkings of the final image by van Vliet or a pupil. Kurt Bauch proposed Jan Lievens as the author of the print. Kurt Bauch, "Rembrandt und Lievens," *Wallraf-Richartz-Jahrbuch* 11 (1939): 239–68.

10. Tümpel, *Rembrandt legt,* cat. 72.

11. See, for example, the 1510 woodcut by Albrecht Dürer (TIB, woodcuts, 125).

12. Jaco Rutgers, "A Source for Rembrandt's *Beheading of S. John the Baptist*," *Print Quarterly* 21, no. 2 (2004): 154–56.

13. HD 26.

14. There are at least seven drawings by Rembrandt that are related to the 1640 print and/or the more general theme of executions. See Ben. 477–482.

15. Stephanie S. Dickey, "Beheading of Prisoners," in Walter Leidtke, Carolyn Logan, Nadine M. Orenstein, and Stephanie Dickey, *Rembrandt/Not Rembrandt in the Metropolitan Museum of Art: Aspects of Connoisseurship*, exh. cat. (New York: Harry N. Abrams and Metropolitan Museum of Art, 1995), cat. 73, 2:180.

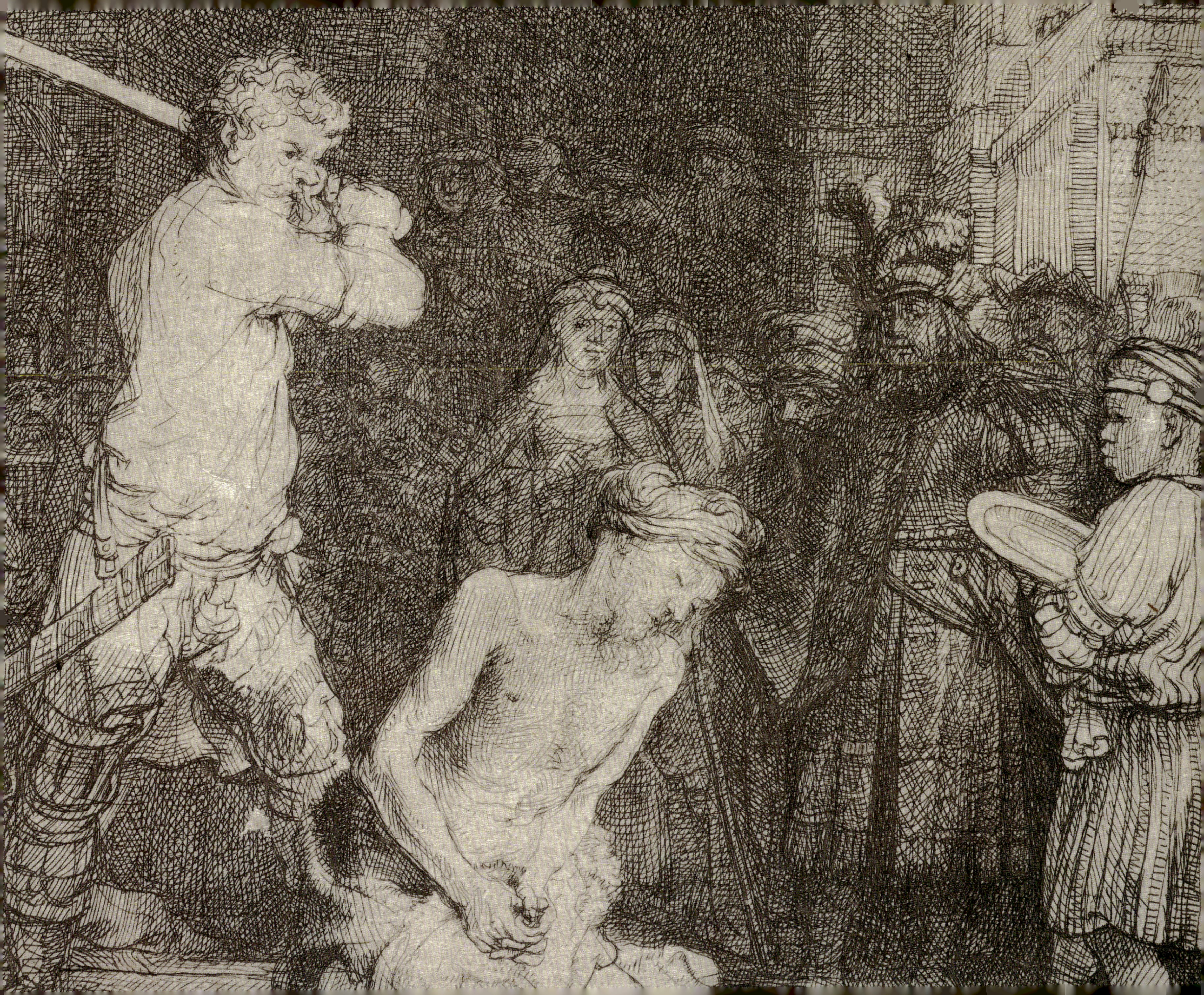

66. Peter and John Healing the Cripple at the Gate of the Temple

B. 94 (H. 301, Mz. 239, NHD 312)
Etching, drypoint, and burin
Signed and dated in the plate: *Rembrandt f. 1659*
State IV of VI
Sheet: 18.2 × 21.8 cm; plate mark: 18.0 × 21.5 cm
Watermark: Similar to Ash and Fletcher Miscellaneous, Late, A-a-d, and Hinterding, Miscellaneous A-d-z ("Paris 1680")
Countermark: *LAI* . . . [Illegible]
Verso: in graphite, *The rare 3rd* [*sic.*] *state before the alterations in the 4th and 5th states;* lower left corner, *7262;* lower right corner, collector's mark (?), handwritten in graphite *E* in a circle (not in Lugt)

Provenance:
Kennedy Galleries Inc., New York, NY, 1977
Feddersen, Elkhart, IN, 1991
Snite Museum of Art
Acc. No.: 1991.025.062

Plate survives:
Herzog Anton-Ulrich Museum, Braunschweig, Germany.

The story of Peter healing a lame man at the "Beautiful Gate" of the Temple in Jerusalem is recounted in Acts 3:1–8. It is the first miracle that Peter performed after Pentecost:

> Now Peter and John went up together into the temple at the hour of prayer, being the ninth hour. And a certain man lame from his mother's womb was carried, whom they laid daily at the gate of the temple which is called Beautiful, to ask alms of them that entered into the temple; Who, seeing Peter and John about to go into the temple asked alms. And Peter, fastening his eyes upon him with John, said, "Look on us." And he gave heed unto them, expecting to receive something of them. Then Peter said, "Silver and gold have I none; but such as I have given thee: In the name of Jesus Christ of Nazareth rise up and walk." And he took him by the right hand, and lifted him up: and immediately his feet and ankle bones received strength. And he leaping up stood, and walked, and entered with them into the temple, walking, and leaping, and praising God.

Rembrandt selected this story as the subject of one of his very first prints (B. 95, c. 1629) (Rosenberg, "Rembrandt's Religious Prints," fig. 9, in this catalog).[1] In that early, rather rough etching,[2] the three main actors, Peter, John, and the crippled man, are grouped together on what appears to be a landing or low platform at the top of a steep pathway or flight of steps. Pressed close to the picture surface, the figures dominate the space. The lame beggar, seated at the lower right corner of the composition, is seen from the side and back as he looks up at Peter and raises a hand, importuning the apostles for alms. His crutches, lying on the ground behind him, extend out over the edge of the platform as if entering the

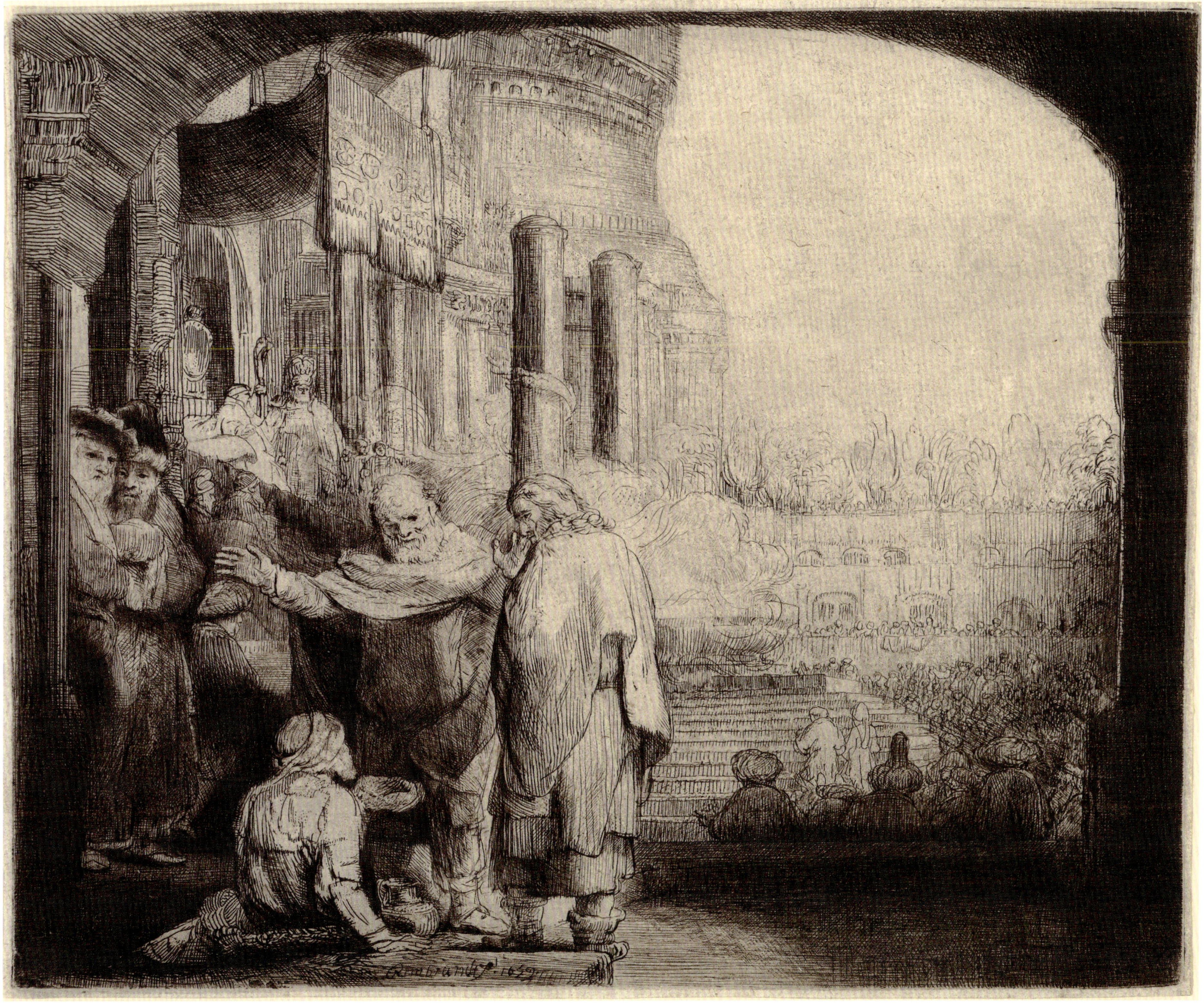

PLATE 66

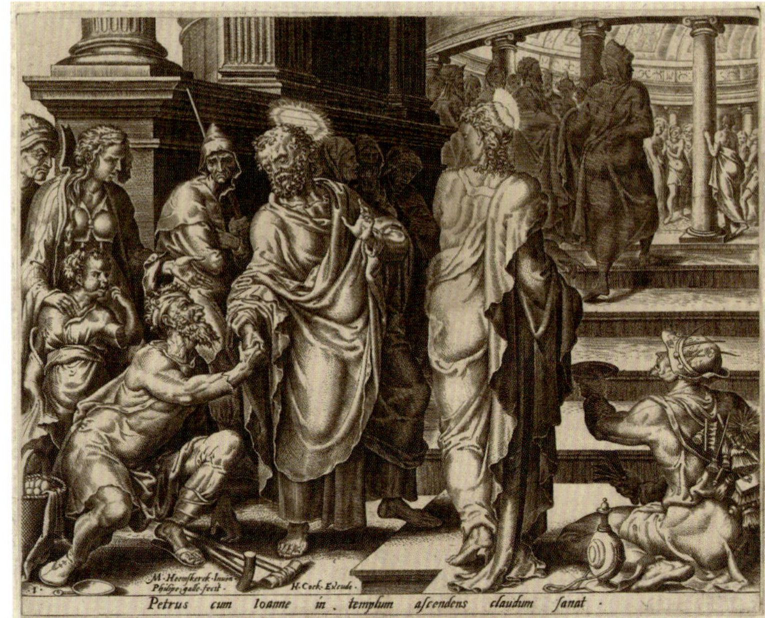

FIGURE 1. Philip Galle and Hieronymus Cock after Maarten van Heemskerck, *Peter and John Healing the Cripple*, engraving, 1558. *Rijksmuseum, Amsterdam.*

space of the viewer. For those familiar with the biblical tale, this simple tromp-l'oeil detail foreshadows the next stage of the story, the moment when the beggar will miraculously regain the use of his legs and be able to cast aside his crutches. Peter and John, seen from the front, are dark, looming presences standing over the beggar. John bends slightly forward, titling his head. His face, shrouded in dense shadow, is unreadable. Peter's mouth is open and his arms are spread wide apart in a gesture that is ambiguous in its intent; it is not clear whether Peter is speaking to the man on the ground, healing him, and/or blessing him.

The apostles are silhouetted in front of a white wall, and the setting beyond the central figures is described in a very cursory manner. The space drops away from them on the left, where, in the middle distance, Rembrandt depicted part of a high arched gateway, presumably the Beautiful Gate, leading up to the Temple forecourt. One diminutive turbaned figure stands by the gate, and two other men can be seen climbing up the slope of Mount Moriah, toward the apostles. One of the approaching figures wears a low-brimmed hat, while the other has a very tall peaked hat that identifies him as a Jewish elder or priest. A few minimally sketched buildings can be seen through the arch, in the distance. There is no attempt to reconstruct the historical appearance of the Temple or its surroundings.

Approximately thirty years after creating this early etching, Rembrandt returned to the subject. The 1659 etching of *Peter and John Healing the Cripple at the Gate of the Temple* was his final biblical narrative print. In this version, Rembrandt created a much more expansive narrative and a considerably richer setting than those that he had employed in his youthful version of the encounter. He shifted the orientation of his plate from vertical to horizontal, providing room to represent a vast cast of characters and a much more detailed background. The Beautiful Gate now serves to enframe both Rembrandt's narrative, in the foreground, and the Temple courtyard, in the background. Against this wide panorama, the two apostles and the lame beggar, placed close to the picture surface as before, loom large. The beggar has been turned even farther toward Peter and John, presenting his back to the viewer, and the three figures have been moved from the right side of the composition to the left. They are also weightier and more compact in their proportions, and their poses and interaction are clearer than in the earlier example. A radiant light falls on the ragged beggar's back, revealing the patches on his clothing as he holds out his beggar's bowl. On the ground beside him is an urn, possibly a water jug. Like the early etching, this print portrays the moment before Peter's miraculous act of healing has been completed. As before, Peter faces forward, his arms spread out above the beggar, as he looks down at the supplicant and opens his mouth to speak. John's pose however, is more ambiguous than it was in the earlier version. He looks as if he had been on his way to join the worshippers when something suddenly caught his attention and he turned back to look at Peter. This representation of John may have been inspired by an engraving of the scene by Philip Galle (fig. 1), after a design by Maarten van Heemskerck.[3] The significance of John's backward glance remains a mystery, but the pose does have the effect of suggesting the suspension or reversal of movement.[4]

In another significant change to the composition, Rembrandt added two observers to the scene.[5] The bearded men at the left are nearly as prominent in size and substance as the print's three central figures. In contrast to the apostles, who wear generic "ancient"

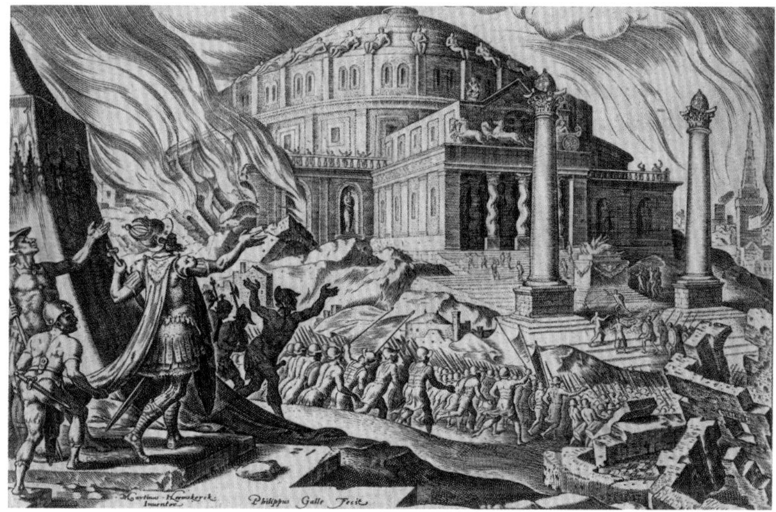

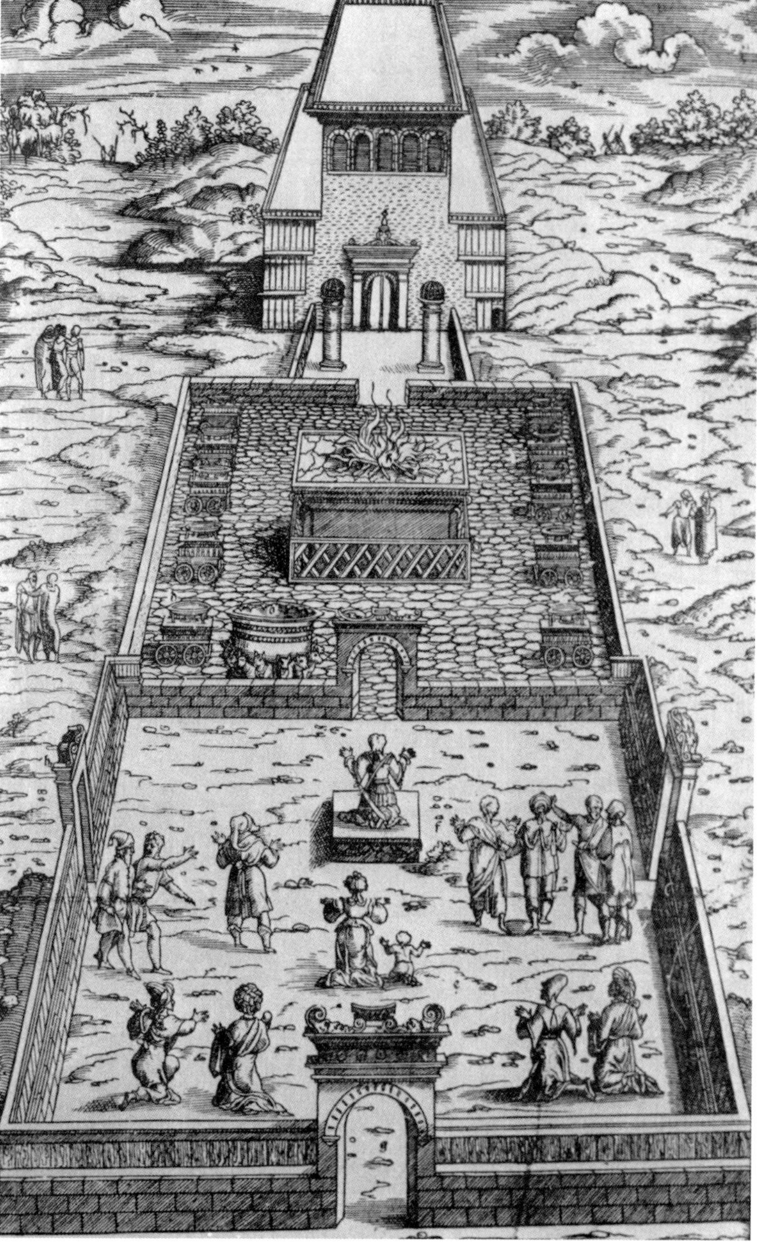

FIGURE 2. Philip Galle after Maarten van Heemskerck, *The Destruction of Jerusalem by Emperor Titus*, engraving, 1569. *Rijksmuseum, Amsterdam.*

FIGURE 3. Jost Amman, *The Exterior of Solomon's Temple*, from woodcut, from *Biblia. Das ist die ganzte heyliche schrifft Teutsch. D. Mart. Luther . . .*, 1 Kings 6, (Frankfurt am Main, 1565), f. 137r.

clothing, and the beggar and the masses of Jewish faithful gathering in the courtyard in the background, who sport exotic turbans, these two wear seventeenth-century clothing. On the basis of their costume, Michael Zell identified the two men as contemporary Jews, "the modern descendants of the ancient Hebrews," onlookers who apparently are not yet convinced of, or converted to, Christianity. The figure at the far left observes the scene with a look of distaste, as if repelled by the unfortunate mendicant. The man beside him looks directly out at the viewer while seeming to confide some observation to his companion. Whereas Peter reaches out to the beggar, these two men stand apart. Despite their apparent lack of sympathy, the men may represent the philosemitic hopes of millenarianists of Rembrandt's time for the imminent peaceful conversion of the Jews, unbelievers who simply need the evidence of their own eyes in order to accept Jesus as the Messiah, evidence that in the context of this print is about to be provided by Peter's miracle.[6]

The background of this scene has elicited considerable discussion. Scholars have debated what sources Rembrandt might have drawn on when he created the image of the courtyard and the Porch of Solomon seen through the arched opening of the Beautiful Gate. Certain details of the scene reflect biblical sources.[7] For example, the two columns that stand in front of the Temple porch represent "Jachin" and "Boaz," the two colossal pillars of bronze cast by Hiram of Tyre and erected by Solomon before the entrance to the Temple, which are described in both *Kings* and *Chronicles*.[8] Other details, however, such as the elaborately embellished draped canopy before the doorway into the Temple—the so-called Babylonian curtain[9]—and the enormous burnt-offerings altar in front of the entrance,[10] may have been drawn from descriptions of the Herodian Temple that appear in Josephus's *The Jewish*

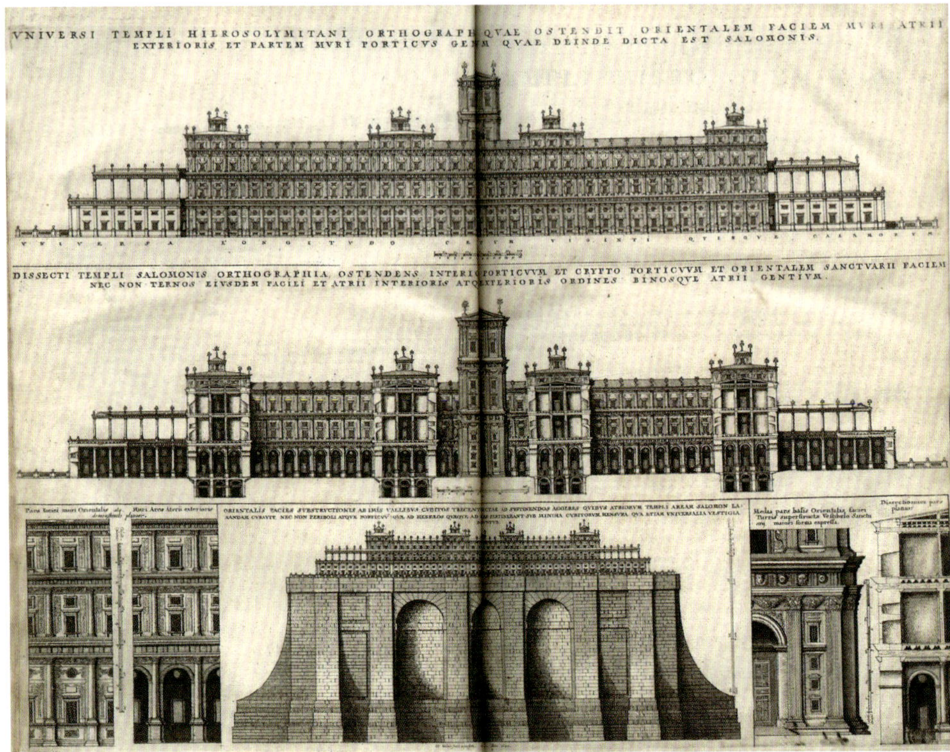

FIGURE 4. Wenceslas Hollar, *Solomon's Temple*, engraving, from Brian Walton, *Biblia Sacra Polyglotta* (London: Roycroft, 1657). *Bridwell Library Special Collections, Perkins School of Theology, Southern Methodist University, Dallas, Texas.*

Wars and Juan Bautista Villalpando's description of Solomon's Temple, *Exechielem Explanationes.*[11] In addition to such texts, various visual sources may also have been available to the artist, including seventeenth-century plans of the Temple by Constantijn L'Empereur de Oppyck and John Lightfoot,[12] a wooden model of the structure and its surroundings created for Rabbi Jacob Judah Leon,[13] and prints such as Philip Galle's *Destruction of Jerusalem by Emperor Titus* after a design by Maarten van Heemskerck, which shows the two bronze columns (fig. 2),[14] or Jost Amman's woodcut illustration for 1 Kings 6, which depicts the exterior of the Temple with the columns and a large rectangular altar for burnt offerings in the courtyard in front of them (fig. 3).[15] Still, as Shelley Perlove and Larry Silver observed, despite the enormous sixteenth- and early seventeenth-century interest in reconstructing the form of the Temple,[16] Rembrandt does not appear to have been interested in creating an archeologically precise representation of either the Solomonic or the Herodian Temple.[17] Instead, he incorporated just enough traditional details—the columns, the holocaust altar,[18] the vast flight of steps leading up to Solomon's porch, and the ceremonial curtain—to identify the space as the setting of the story, the courtyard of the Temple in Jerusalem. He then added elements that may have had some relationship to contemporary ideas about the appearance of the Temple and its surroundings, but that were liberally and imaginatively embellished, including the balcony on the far side of the scene, which runs in front of tiered walls pierced by windows set into low arches between massive buttresses;[19] and the massive, cylindrical citadel towering over the courtyard on the left side, possibly a reference to the tower of Antonia mentioned in Josephus's text.[20] Ultimately, as several scholars have observed, the contrast between the elaborate setting in which two of the high priests are officiating over the ceremonial sacrifices mandated by the Old Covenant and the simplicity of Peter's miracle illustrates the contemporary Christian distinction between the empty rituals of Old Law and the gift of healing grace of the New.[21] Rembrandt's use of the archway to separate the old and the new visually reinforces this divide. The two Jewish observers at the left are in the foreground, but are marginalized by being tucked just to the far side of one of the supports of the gateway arch.

The Snite Museum's example of *Peter and John Healing the Cripple at the Gate* has a "crown" watermark that also appears in some posthumous impressions of the print.[22] In their study of watermarks in Rembrandt's prints, Nancy Ash and Shelley Fletcher suggested that paper with this particular watermark may also have been used by Pierre-François Basan in his late eighteenth-century *Recueil.*[23]

Notes

1. This early etching is usually dated between 1629 and 1630. It is not included in the Snite Museum's Feddersen Collection.

2. The artist's inexperience in handling the medium is visible not only in the unsophisticated uniformity of the etched lines and crude system of modeling, but also in the intrusive surface scratches and prominent patches of unaddressed foul biting.

3. NHD 181 (Philip Galle). This engraving is one of a series of six illustrating the story of SS. Peter and Paul published by

Hieronymus Cock in 1558. Galle did another version of the same subject in 1575 (NHD 399 [Maarten van Heemskerck]), also based on a design by Heemskerck. This image was one of sixteen plates illustrating the *Acts of the Apostles*. In this later version, the entire story of the miracle is told in a single field, from the lame man being carried to his station near the Beautiful Gate to Peter's address to the people following the miracle. In both prints, Peter has taken the beggar's hand and the lame man has begun to rise, making the nature of the miracle much clearer. Neither of these prints describes the Temple precinct in as much detail as Rembrandt's 1659 etching, though the latter example does incorporate an altar at the top of a flight of steps.

4. Zell, *Reframing Rembrandt: Jews and the Christian Image in Seventeenth-Century Amsterdam* (Berkeley: University of California Press, 2002), 158, quoting Ulrich Keller, suggested that John "is caught between two opposing spiritual realms," that of the Old Law and servitude (the background) and that of the New Law and freedom (the miracle that is about to occur). Zell offered no explanation as to why John, a committed disciple of Christ, should embody this uncertainty. On a more mundane level, John's pose does invest the print with a sense of the momentary suspension of time, of what is happening in the "present" and what is about to happen, a strategy that Rembrandt employed in any number of narrative images.

5. There are also onlookers in Galle's 1558 engraving, a woman with her son and two men. The woman and child react to the miracle with curiosity and joy, while the two older men seem to be scowling.

6. Zell, *Reframing Rembrandt*, 158–59. Zell commented that "the onlookers' reaction certainly cannot be reconciled with the scriptural report of the Hebrews' jubilant response to the miracle." Although it is true that the bystanders look on disapprovingly, Zell's observation did not take into account the fact that the miracle has not yet taken place. He went on to suggest that the two men might be occupying a spiritually liminal space, suspended between the covenants of Abraham and Christ. Perlove and Silver (*Rembrandt's Faith*, 261) likened the two figures' costumes to those worn by the scholars in Rembrandt's *Christ Disputing with the Doctors* of 1654 (B. 64, cat. no. 39) and concluded that the men may have been meant to foreshadow the Jews who would subsequently arrest and question the apostles, as recounted in Acts 4:1–3.

7. Zell, *Reframing Rembrandt*, 156, asserted that the "human and architectural backdrop . . . reflects Rembrandt's comprehensive reading of the story in Acts."

8. 1 Kings 7:15–22; and 2 Chronicles 3:5–17; 4:1–6. The pillars are also described by Josephus in *Jewish Antiquities*, 83, 3, 4. Rembrandt owned a copy of *Jewish Antiquities*.

9. Josephus, *The Jewish War*, 5, 5, 4. Franz Landsberger ("Rembrandt and Josephus," *Art Bulletin* 36, no. 1 [March 1954]: 62–63), was a strong supporter of the proposal that Josephus's work influenced Rembrandt's imagery in this print, but Rachel Wischnitzer ("Rembrandt, Callot, and Tobias Stimmer, *Art Bulletin* 39, no. 3 [September 1957]: 226–28), was quite critical of Landsberger's conclusions. Christopher White, *Rembrandt as an Etcher*, 112, cited Wischnitzer, but stated that the mise-en-scène was "based on the description given by the Jewish historian, Flavius Josephus."

10. Josephus, *The Jewish War*, 5, 5, 6.

11. *Rembrandt's Faith*, 257: "Rembrandt's recreation of the site is indebted to Josephus and Juan Battista Villalpando." Juan Bautista Villalpando, *Juan Bautista Villalpando's* Ezechielem Explanationes*: A Sixteenth-Century Architectural Treatise*, trans. Tessa Morrison (Lewiston, NY: Mellen Press, 2009). Villalpando's treatise was published in Rome between 1596 and 1605.

12. Both of these plans are illustrated in *Rembrandt's Faith*, figs. 137 and 138, respectively.

13. The wooden model was constructed in 1641 or 1642 at the behest of Rabbi Jacob Judah Leon. The model was originally put on display in Middleburg, where Leon lived, but in about 1643 or 1644, he moved to Amsterdam, bringing the model with him. The miniature Temple, which was about 4¼' long × 4' wide × 2' high, was apparently portable, since Leon applied for permission to display it at a fair in The Hague in 1646. It appears that he charged admission to see the model. In 1642, a short tract written by the rabbi describing the Temple (*Afbeeldinghe van den Tempel Salomonis*) was published in Dutch and in Spanish in Middleburg. The following year, it was published in French, and in the 1660s and 1670s, Latin and German translations appeared. Finally, in 1778, an English translation was published in London, which was evidently the final home of the model, which is no longer extant. A. K. Offenberg, "Jacob Jehuda Leon (1602–1675) and His Model of the Temple," in *Jewish-Christian Relations in the Seventeenth Century, Studies and Documents*, ed. Johannes van den Berg and Ernestine G. E. van der Wall (Dordrecht: Kluwer Academic Publishers, 1988), 95–115. For Leon's model, see the illustrations in Helen Rosenau, "Jacob Judah Leon Templo's

Contribution to Architectural Imagery," *Journal of Jewish Studies* 23, no. 1 (Spring 1972): figs. 2 and 5.

14. Münz (*Critical Catalogue*, vol. 2, cat. 239, 110) suggested that Galle's print after Heemskerck's design was a possible source for the columns in Rembrandt's print. This print (NHD 258 [Heemskerck]) was one of a series of twenty-two prints dedicated to the disasters of the Jewish people and published in 1569. It should be noted, however, that Heemskerck gave the columns odd pinecone-shaped capitals, whereas Rembrandt's columns are completely devoid of capitals of any kind.

15. TIB, vol. 20, pt. 1, Jost Amman, woodcuts, 1.57.

16. For a brief overview of some of these projects, see the discussion of Rembrandt's 1630 print of *Presentation in the Temple with the Angel: Small Plate* (B. 51, cat. no. 25) in *Rembrandt's Faith*, 202–4.

17. *Rembrandt's Faith,* 208: "While various architectural elements within this space appear to be related to descriptions and plans of the Temple, this painting [*Simeon's Song of Praise*, The Hague, 1631]—and all of Rembrandt's Temple imagery—must not be viewed as an 'authentic' reconstruction. Rembrandt produced imaginative recreations inspired by bits and pieces of information mined from varied sources, by means of patrons and acquaintances. None of his Temple images follows texts with any consistency. Rembrandt chose to use details when it suited his purposes or the wishes of his learned patrons."

18. Rembrandt's altar does not correspond to the rectangular shape of the one illustrated by both Heemskerck and Amman and described by Josephus in *Jewish Antiquities*, 8, 3, 7: "He also made a brazen altar whose length was twenty cubits, and its breadth the same, and its height ten, for the burnt offerings." Instead, its basin-like form seems to relate more to the mysterious "molten sea" created by Hiram of Tyre as described in 1 *Kings* 7:23–26, and Josephus in *Jewish Antiquities*, 8, 3, 5.

19. This architecture does seem to bear some relationship to the way in which Rabbi Leon articulated the exterior walls of his model and also to Wenceslas Hollar's engraved image of the Temple based on Leon's model, a print published in Brian Walton's 1657 edition of the *Polyglot Bible* (fig. 4).

20. Josephus, *Jewish Antiquities*, 5, 11, 4, and *The Jewish War*, 5, 5, 8. Landsberger identified this structure as the Tower of Antonia ("Rembrandt and Josephus," 63). His identification was subsequently questioned by Wischsnitzer in "Rembrandt, Callot, and Tobias Stimmer," 227–28. She pointed out that Josephus describes the fortress as square, and Rembrandt's fortress is cylindrical.

21. As Zell, *Reframing Rembrandt*, 158, noted, "The pomp and theatricality surrounding the performance of an Old Testament rite contrast strikingly with the humble dress of the apostles preaching the faith in Christ's Resurrection, whose efficacy is proved by the beggar's miraculous healing." Similarly, Perlove and Silver (*Rembrandt's Faith*, 261) suggested that "visually, then, Rembrandt's *Peter and John* gathers and contrasts all of the components of the scene in order to offer the viewer a choice: New Testament against Old, healing faith against Temple ceremony."

Another interpretation can be found in Calvin's *Commentary on the Acts of the Apostles*, in which Calvin described Peter's initial interaction with the lame beggar as a form of mockery that was then transformed through the apostle's miracle. Calvin related this "horrible wickedness," i.e., the mockery, to the actions of the papacy. At the time of the pope's elevation, according to Calvin, he "shamelessly abuses this place [the biblical text regarding Peter and the beggar], making thereof a comical, or rather scoffing play" by first responding to the people's request for alms by quoting Peter and "casting crosses in the air with his fingers," and then moving off to a different location, where he is surrounded by bags of money that the Church offers as evidence of alms given to the poor. Calvin went on to state, "I have made mention hereof to the end that all men may see that Satan does questionless reign there, where they do so manifestly mock the sacred Word of God." John Calvin, *The Commentaries of M. John Calvin upon the Actes of the Apostles, Faithfully Translated out of Latin into English for the Great Profit of Our Countrymen, by Christopher Fetherstone* (London, 1585), 101, Commentary on Acts 3:6, accessed July 21, 2014, http://www.ccel.org/ccel/calvin/calcom36.pdf.

For a strict Dutch Calvinist contemporary of Rembrandt's, then, the contrasts within the artist's print might have had antipapal overtones. The rituals overseen by priests in the background, one of whom is attended by a man carrying a crosier-like staff, could be perceived as evoking not only the rites of the Old Law, but also the excesses of the Catholic Church.

22. Erik Hinterding (*Rembrandt as an Etcher: The Practice of Production and Distribution* [Ouderkerk aan den Ijssel, Netherlands: Sound and Vision Publishers, 2006],2:275), listed three other impressions of the fourth state of this print that have a variation of the same watermark.

23. Ash and Fletcher, 219.

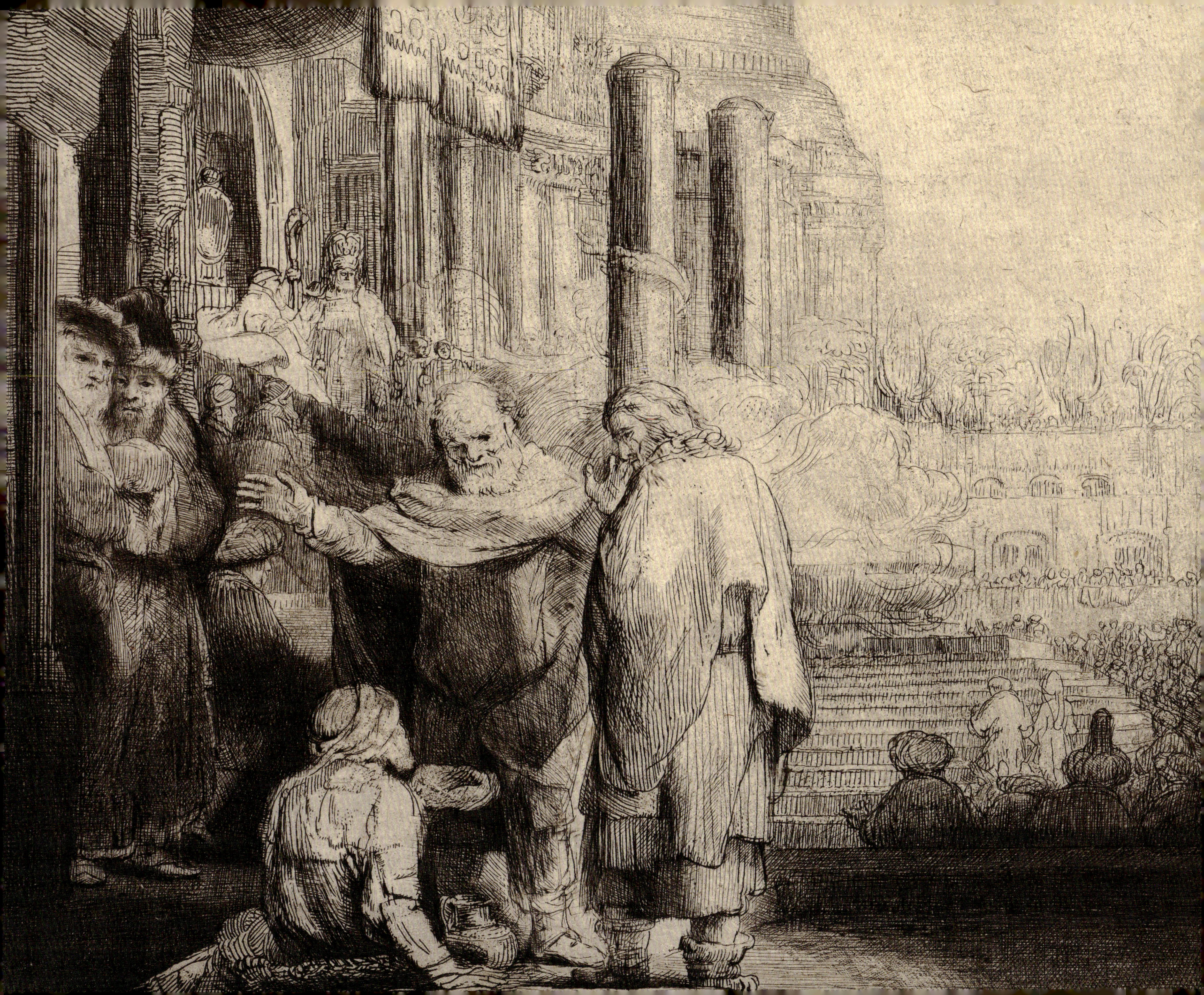

67. Stoning of St. Stephen

B. 97 (H. 125, Mz. 205, NHD 140)
Etching
Signed and dated in the plate: *Rembrandt f. 1635*
State III of IV
Sheet: 9.9 × 8.9 cm; plate mark: 9.5 × 8.5 cm
Verso: collector's stamp in lower left corner LAL overlapping in an oval, black ink (Lugt 3388, Sir Lionel Arthur Lindsay); in graphite, *DE1585; B 97; C33003; The Stoning of S. Stephen, H. 125*
Nineteenth-century (?) impression on wove paper.

Provenance:
Sir Lionel Arthur Lindsay (1874–1961)
Associated American Artists Inc., New York, NY, 1966
Feddersen, Elkhart, IN, 1991
Snite Museum of Art
Acc. No.: 1991.025.063

Plate survives:
Private collection, USA

The story of the martyrdom of St. Stephen, one of the first deacons of the Church, is told in the seventh chapter of the Acts of the Apostles.[1] When Stephen was preaching in Jerusalem, a group of Jews accused him of blaspheming against Moses and God. They had him seized and brought to the Temple, where he was made to defend himself before the Sanhedrin, the supreme religious court. False witnesses testified against him, and his own testimony further enraged the council's members. But, even as the Sanhedrin railed at him, Stephen, "full of the Holy Spirit, looked up steadfastly into heaven, and saw the glory of God, and Jesus standing on the right hand of God, and said, 'Behold, I see the heavens opened, and the Son of man standing on the right hand of God.'"[2] Unmoved by Stephen's vision, the judges cast him out of Jerusalem, where, as he knelt and prayed for his soul and for forgiveness for those who persecuted him, he was stoned to death, the punishment for blasphemy.

Rembrandt depicted the Stoning of St. Stephen two times, first as a painting (fig. 1) and then as an etching. He made the painting in 1625, while still residing in Leiden.[3] Gary Schwartz suggested that Petrus Scriverius, a prominent Dutch humanist and patron of the arts, commissioned the picture.[4] Schwartz and others proposed that for the pro-Remonstrant Scriverius, the painting contained a political subtext alluding to the martyrdom in 1619 of Johan van Oldenbarnevelt, Holland's pensionary, or chief legal officer, at the hands of Counter-Remonstrants.[5]

Rembrandt used light and shadow to divide his painting into two main parts. Stephen's martyrdom occupies the right half of the composition and is brilliantly illuminated. The saint, who has sunk to his knees, is dressed in a dalmatic and tunicella, the traditional robes of a deacon.[6] He gazes up toward an unseen source of light on the left as he spreads his arms in a gesture that implies not only prayer and submission, but also Christological suffering.[7] Stephen is surrounded by his tormentors, who prepare to stone him to death. Two groups of observers appear in the background, one made up of three elderly men, possibly the Sanhedrin, and

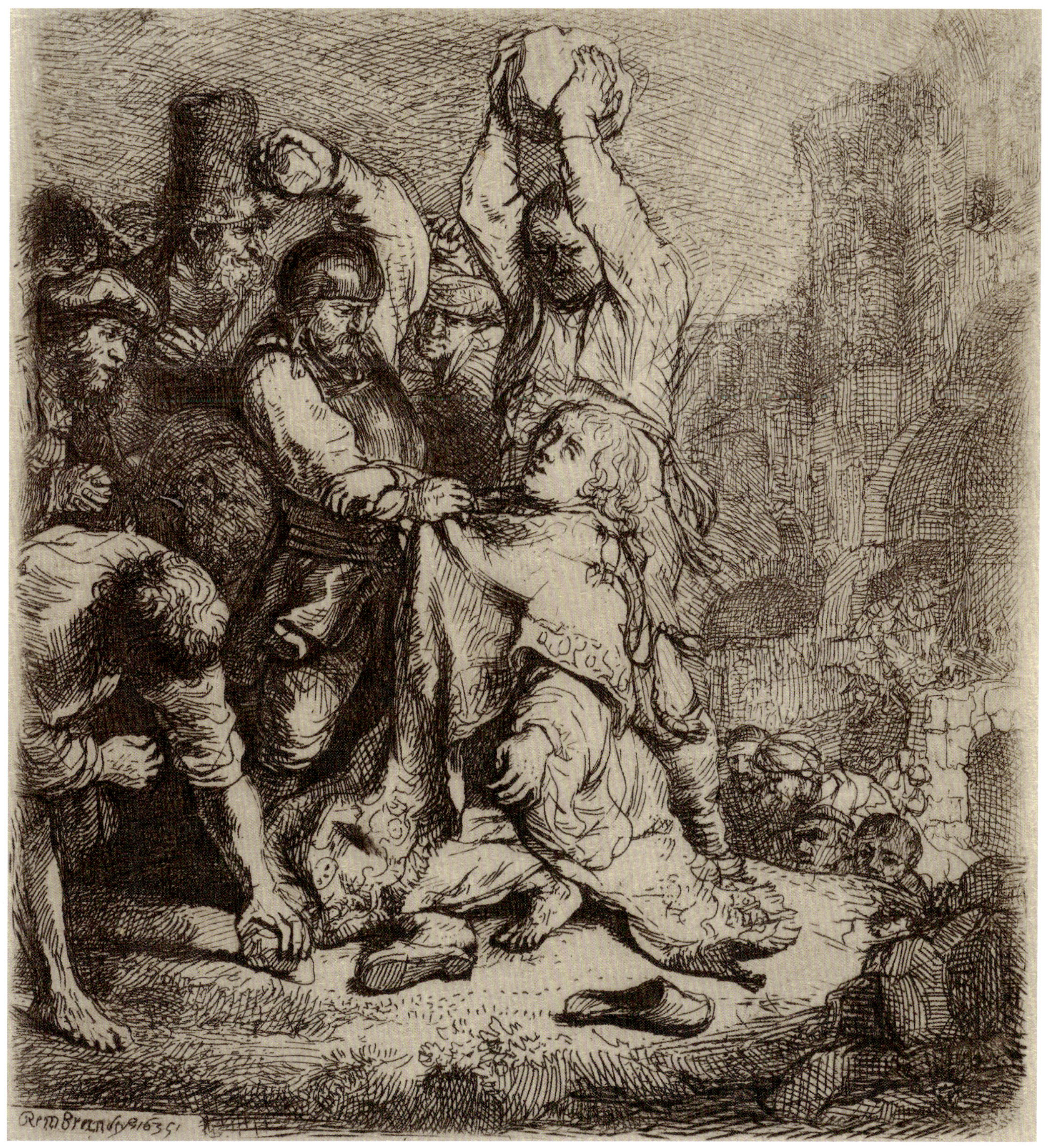

PLATE 67

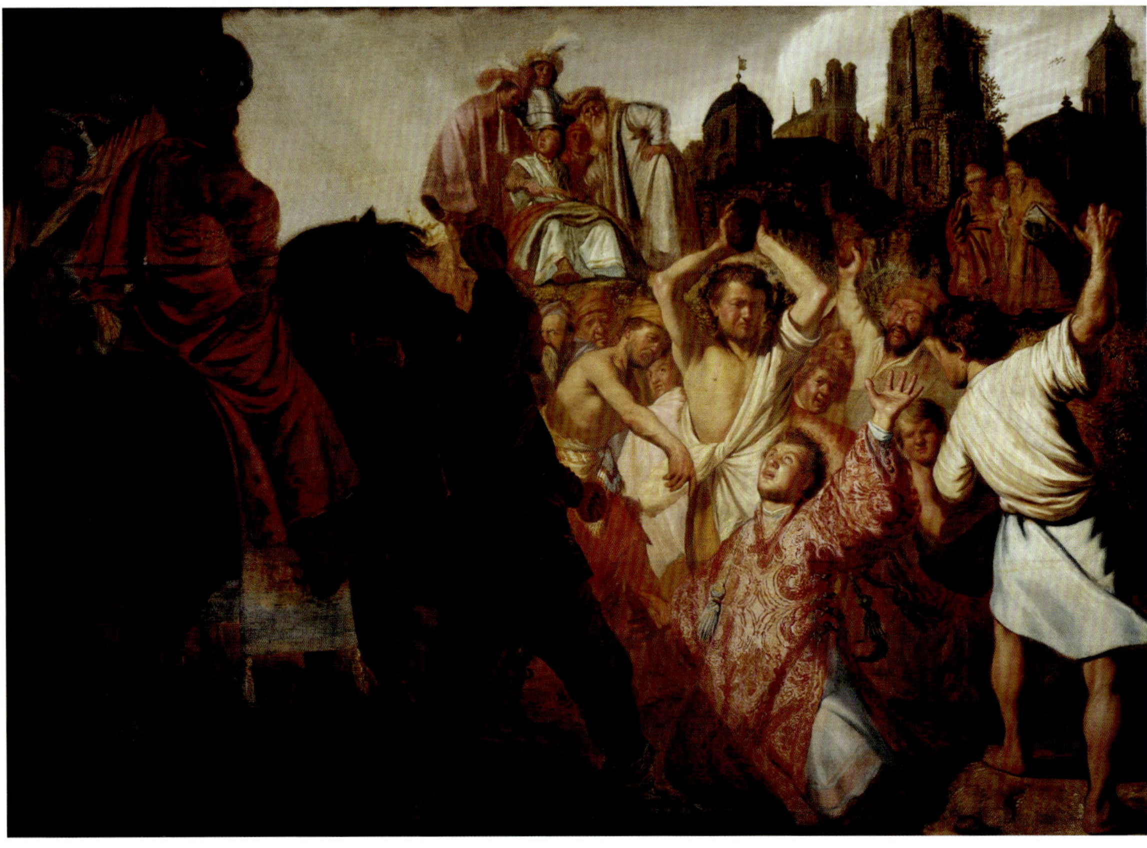

FIGURE 1. Rembrandt, *The Stoning of St. Stephen*, oil on panel, 1625. *Musée des Beaux-Arts, Lyons, France. Photo: Scala/White Images/Art Resources, New York.*

another consisting of four men clustered around a seated young man who discusses the action below with one of his companions. It is possible that this young man is meant to be Saul, the Pharisee who condoned Stephen's martyrdom but who would later convert to Christianity.[8] The towers of Jerusalem are visible in the right background. The left side of the painting is cast into deep shadow, a symbolic as well as a compositional device. This half of the work is dominated by the figure of a bearded Ottoman horseman who observes the martyrdom with an air of command. The equestrian figure, who is draped in a red cloak and wears a large turban, carries a war hammer, which may be a symbol of rank.[9] One of Stephen's executioners, also shrouded in shadow, stands just to the right of the horseman.

In the 1635 etching of *Stoning of St. Stephen* Rembrandt focused almost exclusively on the acts of violence against Stephen. He eliminated the prominent turban-wearing observer and the Pharisee Saul and his companions, and chose to concentrate even more compellingly on Stephen's suffering and the malevolence of his enemies. At the center of the composition, the saint, whose legs are collapsing under him, is held upright by a soldier who has grabbed the front of Stephen's dalmatic. This soldier, wearing a cuirass and a variation on a well-known military headdress, a "pot helmet" with earflaps,[10] holds a stone in his raised left hand, preparing to strike his helpless victim. The exhausted saint, described in Acts as having "the face of an angel,"[11] turns his head and gazes out at the viewer with melancholy resignation. Stephen's left arm hangs limply at his side, while his right hand is draped over the murderous soldier's arm. As in the earlier examples, one of the saint's tormentors stands behind the martyr, holding a large rock above Stephen's head, while another man bends over to pick up a stone.

Spectators have gathered to witness the brutal attack, and a crowd of people can be seen coming up an incline from the city of Jerusalem, which is depicted in the right background as a crumbling mass of arches and buttressed walls symbolic of the erosion of the old faith.[12] On the left side of the composition, the spectators who have already arrived press in tightly around the saint and his murderous tormentors. Three elderly men standing on the left side of this group seem particularly engaged. One, wearing the flat soft hat typical of the Dutch Ashkenazi Jews of Rembrandt's time, leans forward and wrings his hands. A second man, sporting a long, full beard and wearing a turban, has ducked down in order to get a better view; he is barely visible as he peers out of the shadows. Finally, a man with Semitic features and a tall stovepipe hat towers over the entire scene. This smirking observer seems to take particular delight in the beating that he is witnessing. The specific physiognomic indication of Jewish culpability for the murder of Stephen is one of the differences between this etching and Rembrandt's painting of 1625,[13] although it does recall Lastman's painting. In general, the pose and dress of the figures in Rembrandt's etching are less stylized and theatrically biblical than in his lost painting, giving it a decidedly more contemporary look. Rembrandt also included a small but significant detail in his print: one of Stephen's clogs has slipped off his foot and lies abandoned on the ground beside him. The lost shoe attests to the brutality of the attack on the suffering saint, adds to the pathos of the scene, and heightens the sense of Stephen's helplessness as he offers himself up to his faith and submits to his fate.

Rembrandt very rarely made prints depicting saints,[14] which raises the question of why he would choose to create an etching of the martyrdom of St. Stephen in 1635. One possible explanation lies in the artist's perception of the aptness of the print's subject matter as a commentary on the contemporary Remonstrant controversy, as noted above in regard to Rembrandt's 1625 painting of *The Stoning of St. Stephen.*[15] In 1635, the same year as the St. Stephen print, Rembrandt made a portrait etching of the Remonstrant preacher and scholar Jan Uytenbogaert (B. 279) (fig. 2). He had already done a three-quarter-length painting of Uytenbogaert two years earlier, for one of the preacher's followers.[16] Uytenbogaert, the author of the original *Remonstrance* that had been submitted to the State of Holland in 1610, was a vocal supporter of the Arminian/Remonstrant position. He had been forced to flee Holland following the arrest of fellow Remonstrance supporters Oldenbarnevelt and Hugo Grotius in 1618, and was subsequently banished by the stadtholder, Prince Maurits. Following the prince's death in 1625, Maurits's son, Frederik Hendrik, succeeded to the title of prince of Orange and the office of stadtholder. Primarily for political reasons, Frederik Hendrik was initially more tolerant of the Remonstrant position, and although there were still conflicts with the more orthodox Calvinists, the Remonstrants were allowed a more public presence. Rembrandt's future client Uytenbogaert, who had served as Frederik Hendrik's tutor, was able to secretly return to the Netherlands immediately following Maurits's death and, with the tacit approval of the new stadtholder, settled in The Hague, where he remained for the rest of his life. The theological-political situation in the Republic, however, was still in flux. After first actively negotiating for peace with the Southern Provinces and Spain, an outcome enthusiastically supported by the Dutch Remonstrants and opposed by the Counter-Remonstrants, Frederik Hendrik suddenly reversed his position at the end of 1633 and openly broke with the Arminian bloc that controlled Holland, realigning himself with the Counter-Remonstrant "war party."[17] As historian Jonathan Israel noted, the struggles that ensued between the stadtholder and his Counter-Remonstrant allies on one side and the Remonstrants on the other, for control of Holland and, subsequently, of the United Provinces, mirrored the conflicts of 1618, although the disagreement was now motivated more by overtly political, rather than theological, goals.

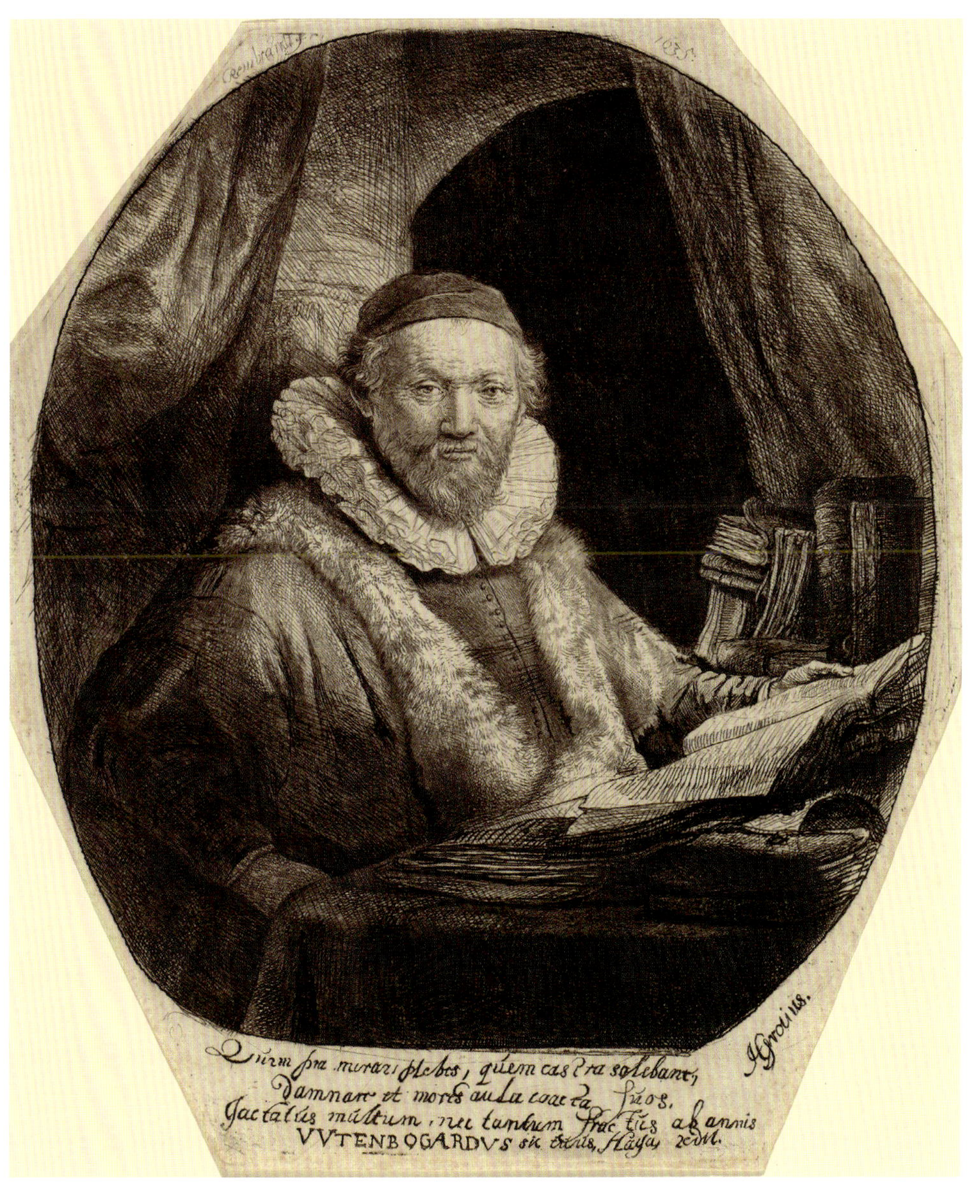

FIGURE 2. Rembrandt, *Jan Uytenbogaert*, B. 279, etching, 1635. *Photo: Courtesy of the National Gallery of Art, Washington, DC.*

In Rembrandt's oval etched portrait of Uytenbogaert, the preacher is dressed in a skullcap, a ruff collar, and a tabard with a fur lining. He is seated in his study and appears to have been interrupted in the midst of reading the book held open on the desk in front him. These details emphasize his role as scholar and preacher. In the third state of the portrait print, Rembrandt added a rather crudely lettered inscription below the oval. The fact that the artist did not employ a professional calligrapher to write the inscription led Stephanie Dickey to propose that Rembrandt might not have intended the print for general circulation, but, rather, might have undertaken the work on his own initiative for a restricted audience.[18] The inscription, translated below, is a Latin eulogy written by Hugo Grotius in honor of Uytenbogaert:

> The worldly court was forced to condemn the man so admired
> By the pious, the soldiers and the court itself, and to denounce
> his convictions.
> The Hague, after much wandering your fellow townsman
> Uytenbogaert
> Returns, withered, not by the years alone.—Hugo de Groot.[19]

This poem clearly refers to the persecution that Uytenbogaert suffered because of his role as a Remonstrant leader during the time of Prince Maurits, and possibly also to the betrayal of his cause at the hands of Frederik Hendrik and his new Counter-Remonstrant allies. Dickey suggested that in this context, the etched portrait and its accompanying inscription could well have been linked to the specific events that occurred in 1635, events that would have been familiar to informed viewers, particularly those residing in The Hague, the city addressed in the poem. Frederik Hendrik had used his new Counter-Remonstrant alliance to maneuver the States General into signing a treaty with France that bound them to act together in any military campaign against Spain. As a result, when France declared war on Spain and invaded the Spanish Netherlands, Frederik Hendrik invaded Flanders from the north, a strategy that ultimately proved ill conceived. According to Dickey, the portrait print would not only have commemorated Uytenbogaert and his Remonstrant position, but would also, by inference, have provided a subtle critique of the stadtholder and his actions.[20]

Given this historical context and the political parallels drawn between St. Stephen's martyrdom and contemporary theological and political persecutions, it seems likely that Rembrandt's small print of the Stoning of St. Stephen, like his earlier pro-Remonstrant painting of 1625 and the etched portrait of Jan Uytenbogaert, may have been intended as a pro-Remonstrant commentary on the continuing conflict. Several aspects of the print support this idea: the increased focus on the attack (the elimination of Stephen's vision and the absence of the turbaned spectator and "Saul"); the contemporary—as opposed to biblical—dress of the figures; and a possible allusion to the military events of 1635, given that one of the most prominent of the saint's tormentors—the soldier who has grabbed hold of Stephen's dalmatic—is dressed not in Roman armor or generically "antique" workmen's garb, but rather in what appears to be a variation of seventeenth-century armor.[21] For Rembrandt's contemporaries, such a figure might well have appeared to be a reference to the current military campaign being waged by Frederik Hendrik and his Counter-Remonstrant allies.

Rembrandt's etching of the Stoning of St. Stephen would certainly have appealed to a diverse audience. Its concentration on the sufferings of the saint meant that it could be appreciated as a narrative work, one rife with pathos. In this context, its diminutive size made it ideal for pasting into a connoisseur's album, where it could be perused as a precious example of Rembrandt's graphic skill. As a carefully edited biblical subject, the print could also serve to inspire Christians of different denominations, encouraging them to meditate upon the stirring illustration of a saint's sacrifice for his faith. Finally, for those who understood the ways in which the biblical tale of Stephen's martyrdom resonated with contemporary religious and political events, the etching could be perceived as both a condemnation of the persecution that the Remonstrants in general, and Uytenbogaert in particular, had suffered at the hands of their enemies and as an implicit critique of the military adventures of the pro–Counter-Remonstrant stadtholder Frederik Hendrik.

Notes

1. Acts 7:54–60.

2. Acts 7:55–56.

3. The painting (RRP, *Corpus*, A1) is now in the Musée des Beaux-Arts, Lyons, France. Rembrandt's painting has been compared with two earlier works, an oil-on-copper painting by the German artist Adam Elsheimer (Acc. no. NG 2281, National Gallery of Scotland, Edinburgh) and a lost work by Pieter Lastman known through a black chalk drawing now attributed to Salomon Koninck in Berlin (KdZ 10323, Kupferstichkabinett, Berlin) and a description by Simon Ingen (*De getrouwe Herderin* [Amsterdam, 1658]).

4. Gary Schwartz, *Rembrandt: His Life, His Paintings* (London: Penguin, 1991), 23–25. The identification of Scriverius as the patron of the painting is based on an entry in the auction catalog of the estate of Scriverius's son Willem Schrijver, from 1663. "Two imposing large pieces by Rembrandt" are said to have come from Petrus Scriverius's estate, and these have been identified by M. L. Wurfbain, Gary Schwartz, and others as *The Stoning of Stephen* and the enigmatic *History Piece* that is now in the Stedelijk Museum De Lakenhal, Leiden, RRP, *Corpus*, A6.

5. Petrus Scriverius, a supporter of the liberal Remonstrant movement, spent most of his life in Leiden. For an extended discussion of the Remonstrant/Counter-Remonstrant controversy and it consequences, see Jonathan Israel, *The Dutch Republic: Its Rise, Greatness and Fall, 1477–1806* (Oxford: Clarendon Press, 1995), 393–95 and 421–65. Regarding the controversy's implications, particularly for its relationship to Rembrandt's painting of *The Stoning of St. Stephen*, see Schwartz, *Rembrandt*, 14–15 and 35–36; and *Rembrandt's Faith*, 23–28.

Sebastian A. C. Dudok van Heel suggested that the theme of St. Stephen's martyrdom was used as a reference in the polemics generated by the contemporary Remonstrant controversy. In particular, he interpreted Jacob Pynas's 1617 painting of the Stoning of St. Stephen (Agnes Etherington Art Center, Kingston, ON, Canada) as a reflection of a confrontation between the Remonstrant and Counter-Remonstrant factions that occurred in Amsterdam in February 1617. At this violent encounter, the Counter-Remonstrants pummeled their Remonstrant opponents with rocks. Dudok van Heel, "De jonge Rembrandt onder tijdgenoten: godsdienst en schilderkunst in Leiden en Amsterdam," diss., Radboud Universiteit, Nijmegen, Netherlands, 2006, 142–43. Dudok van Heel also noted that in the 1627 satire "Rommel-pot van Hane-kot" by the famous Dutch poet and playwright Joost van den Vondel, the raiders of the Arminian congregation in Montelbaansburgwal were referred to as "sinte Stevens [beulen]," ("the murderers of St. Stephen"), ibid., 187.

6. In images as early as the 1493 woodcut of *The Stoning of St. Stephen* in the Nuremberg Chronicle, the saint is depicted in a dalmatic and tunicella.

7. The implication is that the light emanates from heaven and that it stands for the vision that is explicitly visible in the Elsheimer painting in Edinburgh.

8. A similar figure in the Koninck drawing was identified as Saul by Christian Tümpel. Christian Tümpel, "Pieter Lastman en Rembrandt/Pieter Lastman and Rembrandt," in Astrid Tümpel and Peter Schatborn, *Pieter Lastman leermeester van Rembrandt; Pieter Lastman, the Man Who Taught Rembrandt*, exh. cat. (Zwolle, Netherlands: Waanders Uitgevers; Amsterdam: Museum het Rembrandthuis, 1991), 55.

9. The turban identifies the figure as Eastern or Ottoman. As Marieke de Winkel observed, "Figures in oriental dress form an important component of Rembrandt's history paintings because the biblical world was equated with the East," *Fashion and Fancy: Dress and Meaning in Rembrandt's Paintings*, (Amsterdam: Amsterdam University Press, 2006), 255. Rembrandt frequently used the turban to identify Jewish figures in his biblical scenes, e.g., the two etchings of the Raising of Lazarus (B. 73, cat. no. 46, and B. 72, cat. no. 47) and two other etchings done during the period 1639–41, i.e., a few years after *Stoning of St. Stephen*: *The Presentation in the Temple: Oblong Print* (B. 49, cat. no. 26) and *Three Oriental Figures (Jacob and Laban?)* (B. 118, cat. no. 70). A similar "Turkish" horseman appears in the Elsheimer painting in Edinburgh.

For a discussion of the "war hammer" and its function as a sign of rank, see Leonard Slatkes, "The 'Polish' Rider," in Slatkes, *Rembrandt and Persia* (New York: Abaris, 1983), 75.

10. This type of armor, though somewhat old-fashioned, would have been familiar to seventeenth-century viewers, since it was based on the kind of helmet and cuirass worn by soldiers, including the Dutch forces, during the Thirty Years' War. The helmet, reminiscent of the type known as a *zischagge*, is a variation on an Ottoman helmet known as the *chichak*. For his etching, Rembrandt simplified the helmet. It would normally have included a nose guard, a visor, and a

"lobster tail" down the back, but Rembrandt omitted the first two, and the back of the helmet isn't visible in the print. For an illustration of the *zischagge*, see R. Ewart Oakeshott, *European Weapons and Armour: From the Renaissance to the Industrial Revolution* (Rochester, NY: Boydell Press, 2000), fig. 95. The soldier pulling on the base of the cross in Rembrandt's *The Raising of the Cross* (Alte Pinakothek, Munich, c. 1633, RRP, *Corpus,* A69) and two of the soldiers in Rembrandt's slightly later painting of *The Blinding of Samson* (Städelsches Kunstinstitut, Frankfurt-am-Main, 1636, RRP, *Corpus,* A116) wear similar helmets.

Rembrandt himself was a prodigious collector of armor and weapons. The 1656 inventory of his possessions (Walter L. Strauss and Marjon van der Meulen, eds. and trans., *The Rembrandt Documents* [New York: Abaris, 1979], doc. 1656/12) lists an impressive collection of armaments, including two iron helmets (Item 157); Japanese and Croatian helmets (Items 158 and 159); iron armor and another helmet (Item 167); 60 pieces of Indian hand weapons, arrows, shafts, javelins, and bows (Item 313); five antique helmets and shields (Item 320); twenty pieces including halberds, swords, and Indian fans (Item 339); and five cuirasses (Item 342).

11. Acts 6:18, "And all that sat in the council, looking steadfastly on him, saw his face as it had been the face of an angel."

12. Elsheimer's painting also shows Jerusalem in ruins. The city was usually depicted with sturdy walls, massive gates, towers, and domed buildings.

13. The heightened focus on the Jewish identity of the observers in the print may have been Rembrandt's reaction to contemporary demands for "accuracy" in illustrating biblical texts, but it may also simply reflect contemporary attitudes toward Jews in general. Gary Schwartz argued that Rembrandt's attitude toward Jews was not as sanguine as has normally been assumed. According to Schwartz, Rembrandt would more likely have held the same anti-Semitic biases as his contemporaries. Gary Schwartz, "Rembrandt's Hebrews," *Rembrandt—Wissenschaft auf der Suche,* ed. Holm Bevers, Jan Kelch, Bernd Wolfgang Lindemann, and Christian Tico Seofert. *Jahrbuch der Berliner Museen,* N.F. 51 (2009) (Berlin: Gebr. Mann Verlag, 2009), 33–38.

14. Rembrandt made seven etchings devoted to St. Jerome (B. 100–106). Since Jerome was one of the principal exemplars of penitence, these may have been intended to have devotional appeal, but they may also have appealed to scholarly collectors who would have identified with the studious Jerome. In addition to the St. Jerome prints and *Stoning of St Stephen,* the only other Rembrandt prints devoted to saints are *Beheading of John the Baptist* (B. 92, 1640, cat. no. 65; and B. 93, 1627/1631–32, cat. no. 64); *Peter and John Healing the Cripple at the Gate of the Temple* (B. 94, 1659, cat. no. 66); *St. Francis beneath a Tree Praying* (B. 107, c. 1657), and, possibly, *The Little Jewish Bride (Saskia as St. Catherine)* (B. 342, 1638).

15. See note 5, above.

16. The portrait (Rijksmuseum, Amsterdam, RRP, *Corpus,* A80) was created for Amsterdam merchant and candlemaker Abraham Anthonisz. Recht, a convert to Remonstrantism. Uytenbogaert noted in his diary that he sat for the portrait in The Hague on April 13, 1633. Stephanie S. Dickey, *Rembrandt Portraits in Print* (Amsterdam: John Benjamins Publishing, 2004), 36.

17. On Prince Frederik Hendrik's loss of sympathy with the Arminians' positions and his decision in 1633 to side with the Counter-Remonstrants instead, see Israel, *The Dutch Republic,* 523–25.

18. Dickey, *Portraits in Print,* 38. Erik Hinterding proposed that the print was intended to be distributed to Uytenbogaert's friends and admirers. Hinterding, Ger Luijten, and Martin Royalton-Kisch, *Rembrandt the Printmaker,* exh. cat., (Chicago and London: Fitzroy Dearborn Publishers, 2000), 148.

19. Dickey, *Portraits in Print,* 338.

20. Ibid., 40–41. Dickey noted that at the same time Rembrandt was doing the portrait of Uytenbogaert, he was also working on a painted Passion cycle commissioned by Frederik Hendrik. Although the artist may have been sympathetic to the antiwar Remonstrant faction that still dominated the political life of Amsterdam, he was also a pragmatist who evidently was not about to abandon a highly lucrative commission from the prince for political reasons.

21. Although soldiers dressed in Roman armor appear in some earlier representations of the Stoning of St. Stephen (cf. Virgil Solis, *Stoning of St. Stephen,* woodcut, c. 1550 [B. 175] and Johannes Sadeler I's engraving after a design by Maerten de Vos [HD 326]), there do not seem to be any precedents for figures wearing contemporary armor. Regarding the soldier's helmet, see note 10, above.

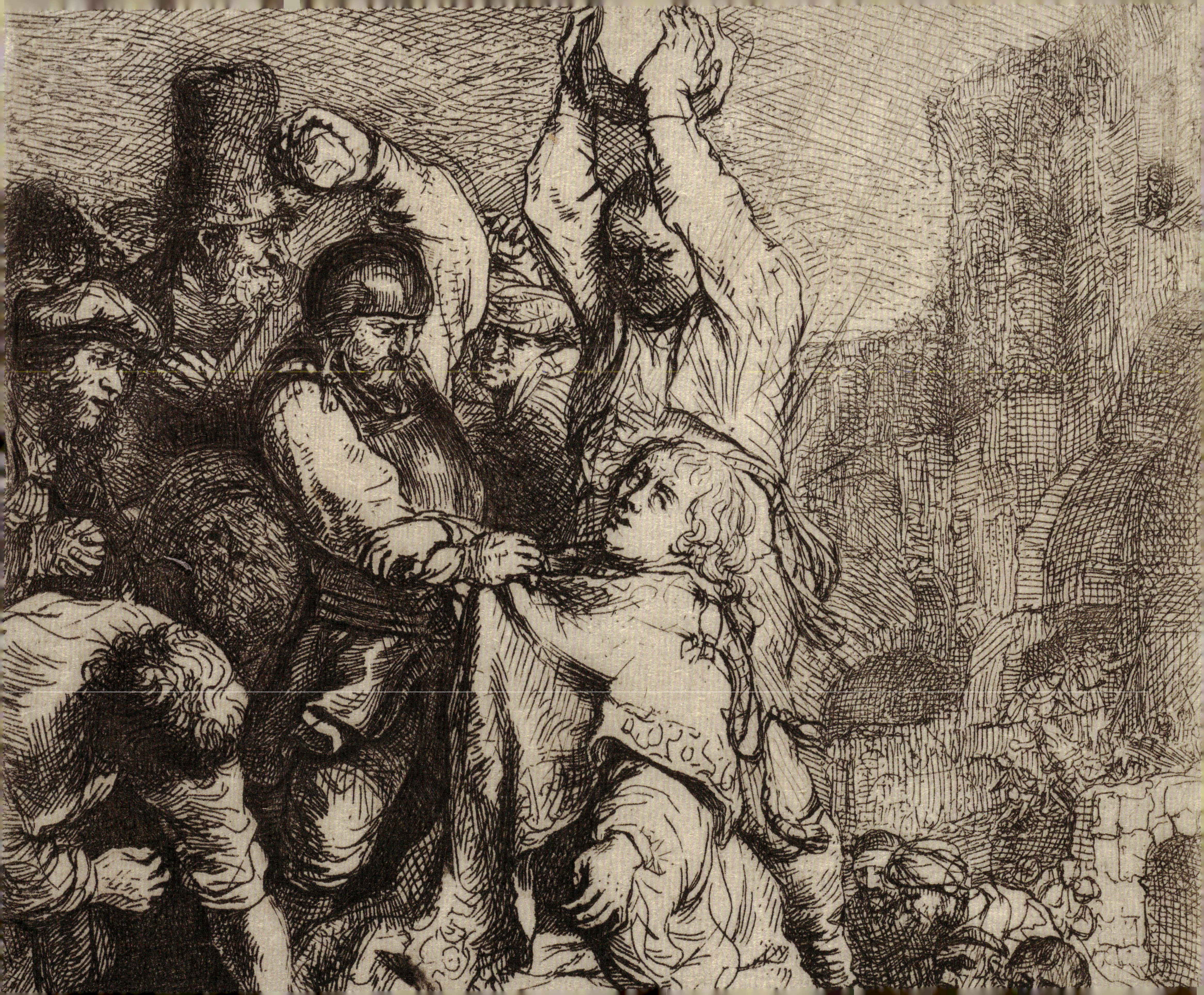

68. Baptism of the Eunuch

B. 98 (H. 182, Mz. 211, NHD 186)
Etching
Signed and dated in the plate: *Rembrandt f 1641*
State II of IV
Sheet: 17.9 × 21.6 cm; plate mark: 17.8 × 21.3 cm
Watermark: large unreadable watermark with countermark
Verso: collector's stamp, in blue ink, entwined script "C" and "S" (Lugt 636, Carl Schlosser); in graphite, *20 (-20)/ B 98/ 99.15/ a12729 B. 97/ ax M (xx)K/c. 11960/* /(script) *larx/ H7737*

Provenance:
Carl Schlosser, Elberfeld, Germany (1827–84)
Harrods, London, 1980
Feddersen, Elkhart, IN, 1991
Snite Museum of Art
Acc. No.: 1991.025.064

Plate survives:
Bibliothèque Nationale, Paris (inv. Rés-Musée-Pl).

The apostle Philip's act of converting and baptizing an Ethiopian eunuch is described in Acts 8:26–39. God ordered Philip, who had been in Jerusalem, to travel south to Gaza. On the way, Philip came across a man sitting in a chariot, reading the Book of Isaiah. He discovered that the stranger, a eunuch, was the treasurer of the queen of Ethiopia. When Philip heard the man reading scripture, he asked him if he understood it. The stranger replied that he needed help with the passage he had been reading, and asked Philip to sit with him and guide him. Philip responded by preaching the Gospel. The two men rode along together, and when they came to the edge of a pool of water, the Ethiopian asked if there was any reason why he could not be baptized right then and there. Philip replied that if the man believed in Christ with all his heart, he could be baptized. The treasurer affirmed his belief and commanded his driver to halt the chariot. Philip and the eunuch climbed down and approached the pool, where the apostle baptized the man. Afterward, God made Philip disappear, and the eunuch "went on his way rejoicing."

This somewhat obscure story of conversion was quite popular in the Netherlands in the seventeenth century, primarily because it focused on faith and the sacrament of baptism. For most Protestant parishioners, the Catholic cycle of seven sacraments had been reduced to just two principal ones, baptism and communion. These were interpreted not as conferring grace on the recipients but as signs of a covenant between the individual and the community. The fact that Philip insisted that the Ethiopian must first affirm his belief before he could be baptized was seen as an illustration of the primacy of faith. The sacrament that followed the affirmation served only as a confirmation of the recipient's spiritual commitment.[1] Depicting the eunuch's baptism as an adult may also have been Rembrandt's way of weighing in on contemporary disputes over the appropriateness of infant and adult baptism.[2] Odilia Bonebakker suggested that the subject of the baptism of the eunuch would have resonated with a broad Dutch audience. She pointed out the contrast commonly made in prints, poems, and biblical exegeses between the darkness of the Ethiopian's skin and the whiteness of his soul. Paintings on this theme, commonly referred to in Dutch inventories as images of the "baptism of the moor," were

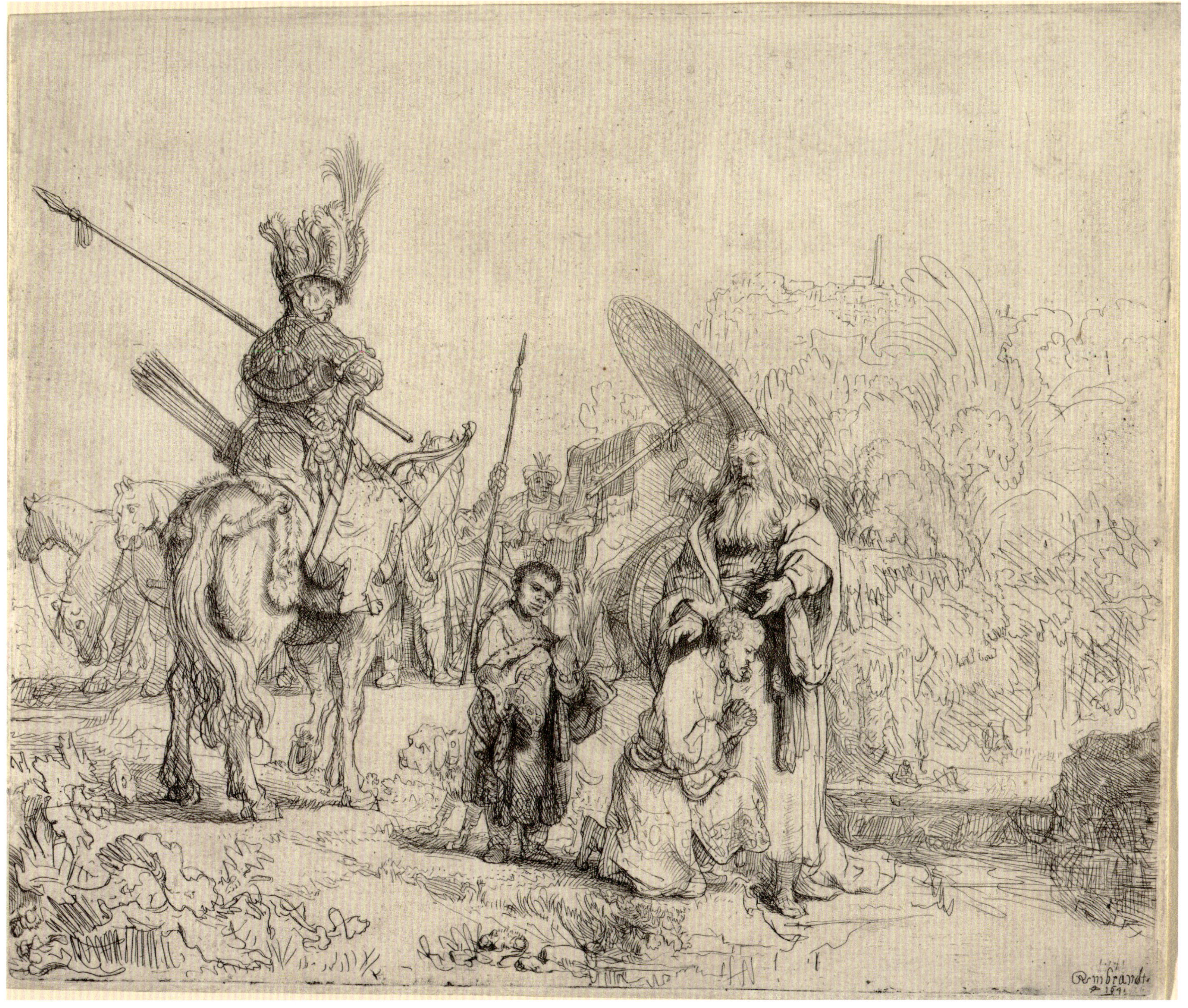

PLATE 68

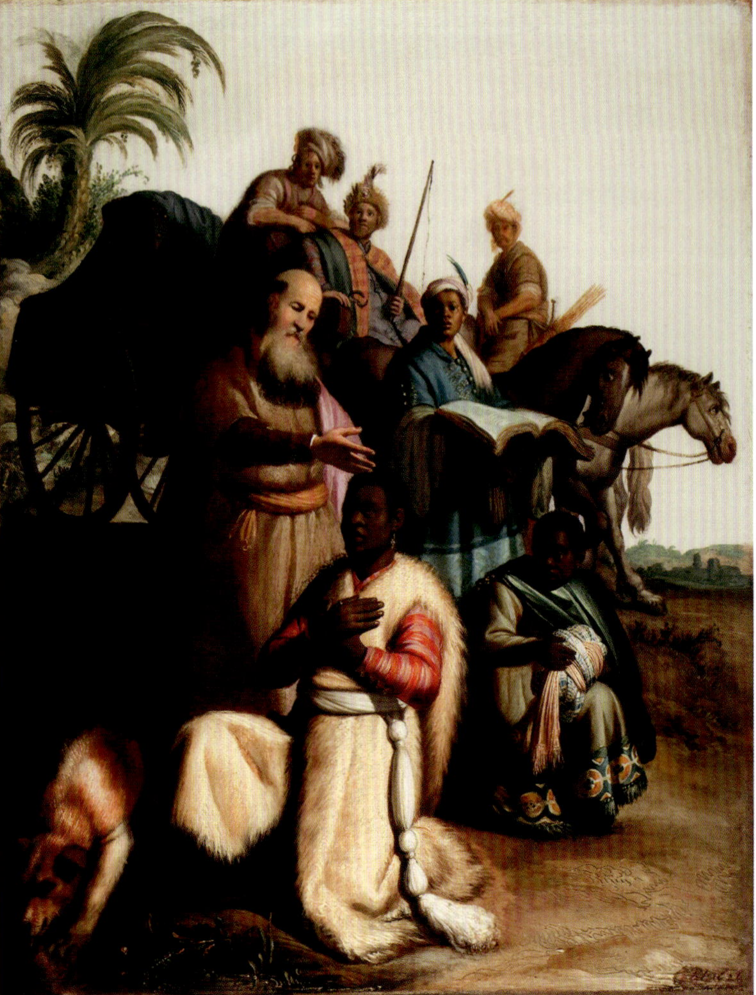

FIGURE 1. Rembrandt, *Baptism of the Eunuch*, oil on panel, 1626. *Rijksmuseum Het Catharijneconvent, Utrecht.*

interpreted as illustrating God's power: "while it was impossible to 'whiten' the eunuch's skin, God could 'whiten' his soul."[3] As Bonebakker observed, this was a theme that would have resonated not only with Dutch Calvinists, but with Christian audiences in general.[4]

Pieter Lastman, Rembrandt's mentor in Amsterdam, painted at least four versions of the Baptism of the Eunuch, and Rembrandt himself did three paintings of the subject, as well as the 1641 etching represented in the Snite Museum collection.[5] The best known and earliest of Rembrandt's paintings of the Baptism of the Eunuch (fig. 1)[6] was done in 1626, while the artist was still in Leiden. This sizable, vertical composition is rendered with highly saturated color in the liquid style of the artist's early career. Landscape motifs are reduced to a minimum; a distant view of the desert, the branch of a palm tree, and the edge of a pool of water suffice to set the scene. The large figures of Philip, the Ethiopian official, and two of the treasurer's five attendants dominate the composition. The exotically costumed figures are very stiffly posed, and the actors in this frozen tableau evince no real emotion. In fact, it appears that Rembrandt was as interested in painting exotic costumes as he was in relating the biblical tale.[7] One of the eunuch's servants, another dark-skinned Moor, holds his master's turban. A second attendant, standing beside the horse and carriage, holds open a very large tome, presumably the book of scripture that his master had been reading when Philip appeared. As the Ethiopian kneels at the very edge of the water in the foreground, Philip stands just behind him, sprinkling water on the convert's head. The eunuch wears a rich white fur cape over a crimson and gold chemise, and his hands are crossed over his chest. His dark, chestnut-colored face is somber as he casts his eyes heavenward. Nearby, a dog laps at the water in the pool, oblivious to the sacred event occurring beside him.[8]

Shelley Perlove and Larry Silver linked Rembrandt's painting and his 1641 etching of the same subject to the missionary activities of the Dutch in Africa during the first half of the seventeenth century. The Dutch West Indies Company had been actively involved in the slave trade from at least 1621 on, and its representatives had been charged with converting the Africans whom they encountered to Christianity, an enterprise not welcomed by the local population. In this context, the dark complexion of the Ethiopian and his young servant in the painting may refer not only to the biblical text, but also to the broader evangelical Calvinist mission in Africa.[9]

In the etching, which exists in four states, Rembrandt exchanged the vertical composition of the painting for a horizontal format, expanding the landscape to fill the space. Even so, in this lightly etched print, Rembrandt continued to focus on the main figures, now expanded to four: Philip, the eunuch, the eunuch's young servant, and a mounted soldier. The carriage, rocky landscape, small waterfall, and pool are very lightly delineated in the background, as are the Ethiopian's other servants. The wiry line and silvery tone of the ink used in impressions from the first state of the print suggest that Rembrandt was attempting to capture the qualities of a silverpoint drawing.[10]

In the 1641 etching, as in his 1626 painting, the artist gave both the convert and his servant Moorish features, alluding to their exotic origins and the universality of Philip's message. The costumes in the etching, however, have been simplified. The treasurer no longer sports a fur cape over his chemise; instead he is dressed in a simple belted garment, suggesting that he has already shed the emblems of his earthly rank in favor of his new spiritual identity. Shown in profile, he clasps his hands together in a gesture of prayer and leans forward in a pose evocative of piety and humility. As in Rembrandt's painting, the Ethiopian's young servant stands at a slight remove from Philip and the convert. Gazing at his master with his head cocked slightly to the side, the boy seems to be staring intently at the ritual taking place before him, just as his somewhat older counterpart did in the Utrecht painting. Rembrandt included a dog in the scene once again, but in the etching, the animal has been reduced to a faint image behind the servant boy. Once again, it looks away from the baptismal scene.

The mustachioed soldier on horseback is a notable addition to Rembrandt's cast of characters. A similar skeptical mounted guardsman appears in two previous versions of the subject: Pieter Lastman's painted version of the Baptism now in Munich,[11] and Rembrandt's own lost painting known through an engraving by Jan Georg van Vliet (fig. 2).[12] In Rembrandt's etching, the heavily armed rider is dressed in an elaborate, exotic costume and sports a high, plumed turban. He sits erect in the saddle, with his right arm aggressively akimbo as he looks down on Philip and the eunuch with an air of haughty aloofness.[13] The cavalryman's weapons and headdress have been associated with other Eastern types that Rembrandt regularly incorporated in his biblical narratives,[14] and the figure clearly reflects Rembrandt's fascination with foreign costumes and arms, objects that the artist collected. The rider's worldly finery and detachment provide a contrast with the Ethiopian's humble dress and piety, a contrast that distinguishes the nonbeliever from the believer.

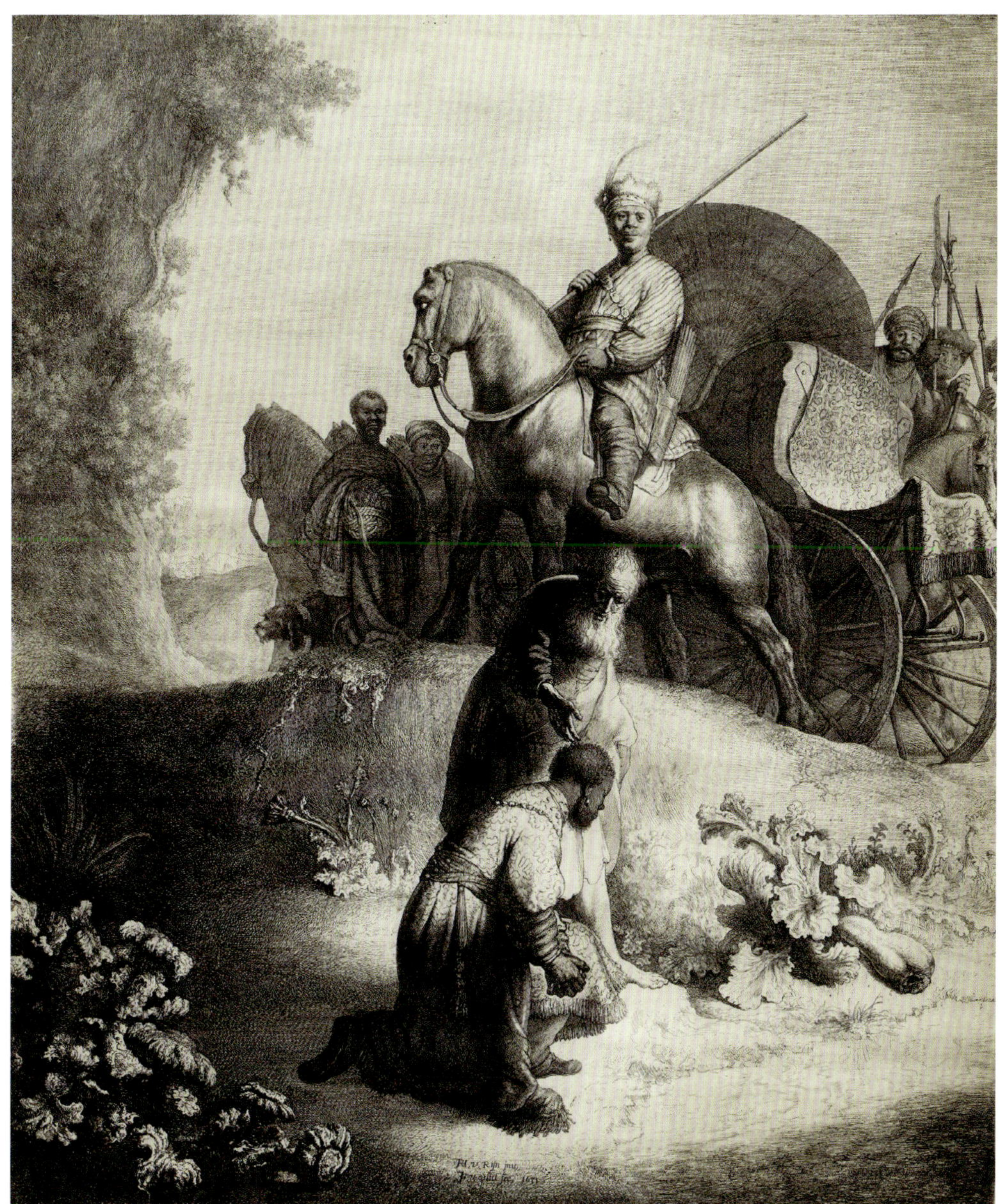

FIGURE 2. Jan Georg van Vliet after Rembrandt, *The Baptism of the Eunuch*, engraving, 1631. *Photo: © The Trustees of the British Museum, London.*

Notes

1. *Rembrandt's Faith*, 23.

2. Calvin addressed this issue directly in his commentary on Acts 8:37. Calvin, *The Commentaries of M. John Calvin upon the Actes of the Apostles, Faithfully Translated out of Latin into English for the Great Profit of Our Countrymen, by Christopher Fetherstone* (London, 1585), 273–74, Commentary on Acts 8:37:

> But frantic fellows do both unskillfully and also wickedly impugn baptizing of infants under color hereof. Why was it meet that faith should go before baptism in the eunuch? To wit, because seeing that Christ marketh those alone which are of the household of the Church with this note and mark, they must be ingrafted unto the Church who are to be baptized. And as it is certain that those who are grown up are ingrafted by faith, so I say that the children of the godly are born the children of the Church, and that they are accounted members of Christ from the womb, because God adopteth us upon this condition, that he may be also the Father of our seed.

Accessed July 21, 2014, http://www.ccel.org/ccel/calvin/calcom36.pdf. See also the discussion of contemporary Dutch views on baptism in the entry on the *Hundred Guilder Print* (B. 74, cat. no. 48).

3. Odilia Bonebakker, "Rembrandt's Drawing of the Baptism of the Eunuch in Munich: Style and Iconography," in *Symposion: Rembrandt-Zeichnungen in München,* edited by Thea Vignau-Wilberg (Munich: Staatliche Graphische Sammlung, 2003), 35–38.

4. Bonebakker, "Rembrandt's Drawing," 35.

5. Hinterding, *Lugt Catalogue,* cat. 82, 212.

6. RRP, *Corpus,* A5. The painting, which measures about 24" × 19", is in the Rijksmuseum Het Catharijneconvent, Utrecht.

7. *Rembrandt's Journey,* cat. 107, 176.

8. The dog is one of a number of examples of Rembrandt's use of the animal as an unwitting, unenlightened foil in a biblically inspired scene. Perlove and Silver (*Rembrandt's Faith,* 23) suggested that in the Utrecht painting, the dog drinking from the pool to satisfy its corporeal thirst signifies that the water itself is not intrinsically holy; it is only the agent by which Philip can attend to the spiritual needs of the Ethiopian.

9. *Rembrandt's Faith,* 20–23.

10. Erik Hinterding (*Lugt Catalogue,* 212) drew attention to the style of this print, noting that Rembrandt seems to have pursued this approach even more vigorously around 1645.

11. Bonebakker, "Rembrandt's Drawing," 33.

12. HD 12 (van Vliet)

13. On the significance of the so-called Renaissance elbow, see Joneath Spicer, "The Renaissance Elbow," in *A Cultural History of Gesture,* ed. Jan Bremmer and Herman Roodenburg (Ithaca, NY: Cornell University Press, 1991), 84–128.

14. Leonard Slatkes, (*Rembrandt and Persia* [New York: Abaris Books, 1983], 75–76), called the rider an "Eastern equestrian warrior" who displays the same type of bow and sheath as the figure in *The Polish Rider,* 1657 (Frick Collection, New York, Bredius 279). This was also noted by Julius S. Held in his article "The 'Polish' Rider" (in Held, *Rembrandt's* Aristotle *and Other Rembrandt Studies* [Princeton, NJ: Princeton University Press, 1969], 63n78 and 69n101), in which he referred to the figure as an Oriental rider. Two drawings are associated with this figure, Ben. 363v and 214.

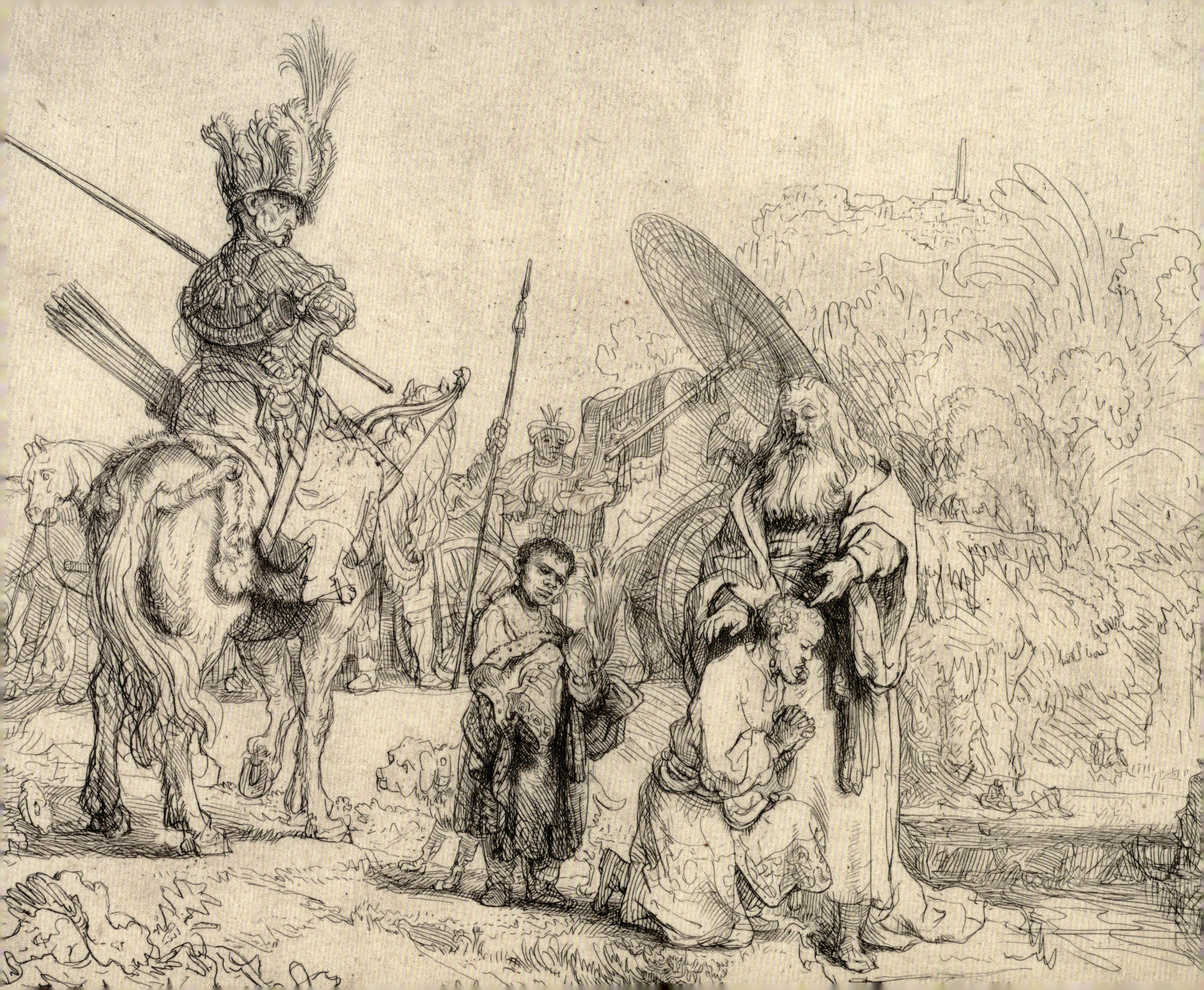

69. *Death of the Virgin*

B. 99 (H. 161, Mz. 208, NHD 173)
Etching and drypoint
Signed and dated in the plate: *Rembrandt f. 1639*
State IV of V
Sheet: 41.5 × 32.0 cm; plate mark: 41.2 × 31.6. cm
Watermark: four lines of undecipherable text, with a heart as the second letter on the second line. Similar to Hinterding, Words-C-a_MMA. Possibly eighteenth-century French paper.
Verso: in sepia ink, *10 Marz 840* (possibly 1840); unknown paraph; in graphite, *f. 10 sch; N°97; 465 (16); flis(?); B. 99 H. 161 B-B 39–17.*

Provenance:
Associated American Artists Inc., New York, NY, 1969
Feddersen, Elkhart, IN, 1991
Snite Museum of Art
Acc. No.: 1991.025.065

The plate does not survive.

The story of the death and assumption of the Virgin does not appear in the Bible. In Rembrandt's day, the most popular account of these events, one that would have been readily available to the artist and his contemporaries, is the version that appeared in Jacobus de Voragine's thirteenth-century compilation of the lives of the saints known as *The Golden Legend.*[1]

According to *The Golden Legend*, when the Virgin reached the age of seventy-two, an angel appeared to her bearing a palm branch, the symbol of martyrdom, and told her that she would soon die. Mary was ready to accept her death, but made two requests of the angel: that the apostles attend her when she died and that no demons be present when her soul left her body. When the time came, the angel granted both requests. All of the apostles were miraculously transported to Mary's doorstep. The first to arrive was St. John, to whom Christ had entrusted Mary's care.[2] Once all of the apostles had gathered, Mary sat down with them in "the midst of lighted lamps and candles."[3] Then, at the third hour of the night, Jesus came "with the ranks of the angels, the troop of the patriarchs, the host of the martyrs, the army of the confessors, and the choir of virgins."[4] Obsequies were performed, and Christ summoned his mother's soul to him. Christ then told the apostles to take Mary's body to a new tomb in the valley of Jehoshaphat and to wait there for three days, at which time he would come to them. Three virgins began to prepare Mary's body for burial. They removed her clothing to wash her, but "the body at once gave forth so dazzling a light that they could touch it indeed, but could not see it; and the light shone for as long as the virgins were washing the body."[5] Once Mary's body was prepared, the apostles had it placed upon a bier, and then, led by St. John bearing the palm that had been given to the Virgin, they took her to the tomb and laid her in it. On the third day, as promised, Christ appeared and, after addressing the apostles, summoned the Archangel Michael to bring Mary's soul to him. Then, in order to prevent the corruption of her body, Christ reunited it with her soul "and she came forth glorious from the tomb, and was assumed into the heavenly chamber, a multitude of angels mounting withal."[6]

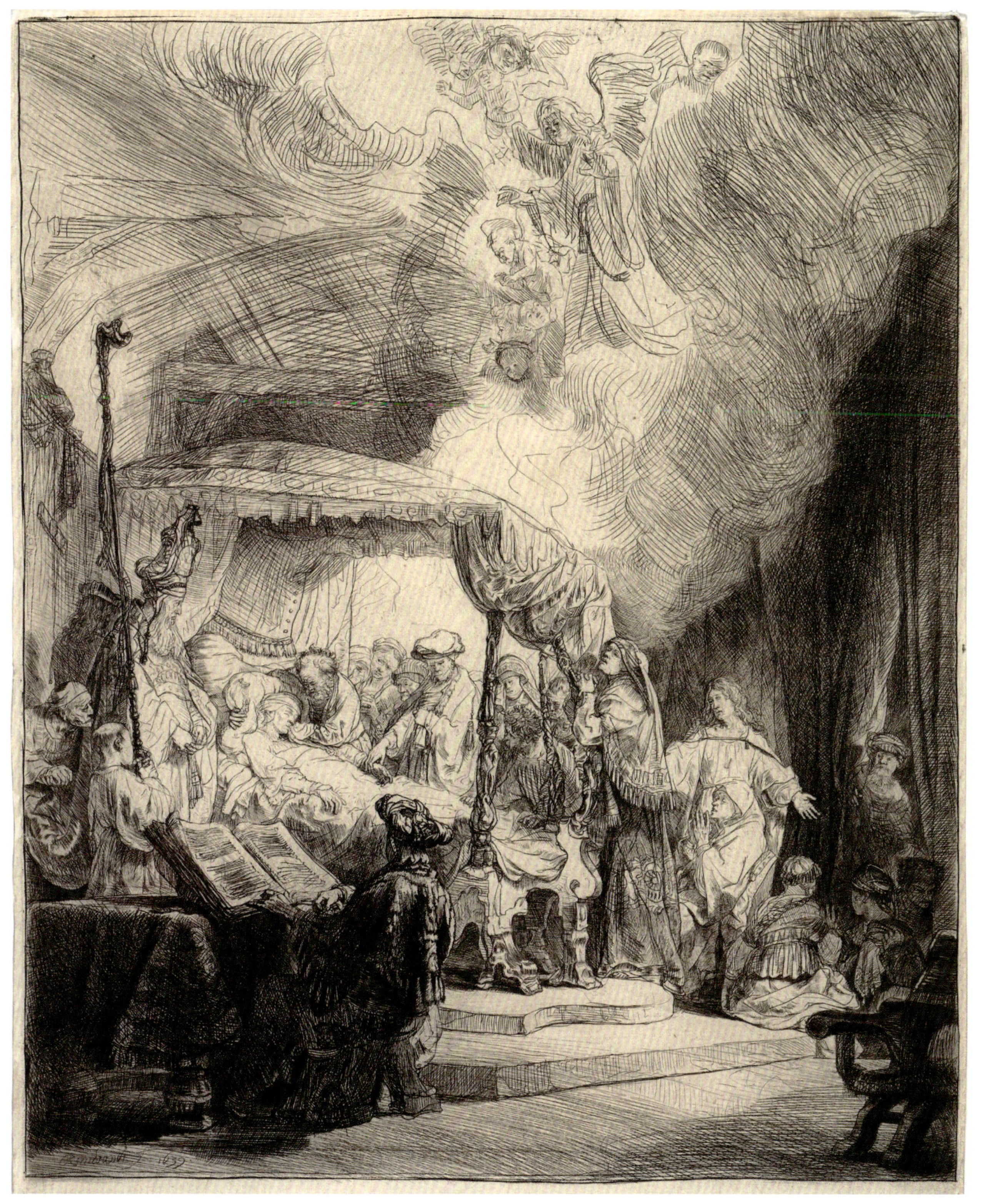

PLATE 69

Rembrandt's depiction of the Virgin's deathbed scene, one of his largest etchings, is one of his most theatrical and baroque. In it, he weds heaven and earth, the spiritual and the secular, in a seamless vision of an event that is simultaneously mournful and, in anticipation of the Assumption, triumphant. His Virgin Mary is a frail, elderly woman lying in a large, ornate, canopied bed, which stands on a low platform. Inspired by several different visual sources and, presumably, by a familiarity with *The Golden Legend*'s account of Mary's death, Rembrandt depicted the dying or just-deceased Virgin surrounded by a number of attendants and mourning figures, including the apostles who had been summoned to her deathbed. One of the apostles, probably Peter,[7] leans over the Virgin, raising her head as he gently wipes her mouth. Standing near him are a number of female mourners, possibly including the three virgins who are to wash Mary's body, or perhaps some of the "choir of virgins" who accompanied Christ when he first summoned his mother's soul to him.[8] A doctor, possibly St. Luke,[9] stands beside Peter. This elegantly dressed figure takes Mary's left wrist in his right hand as if to take her pulse, and he gazes down at her body with a solemn, pensive expression, attending to the state of her physical being.[10] A third man—a figure with coarse features, a ragged beard, and tousled hair—leans on the bed beside the doctor.

Standing near this leaning man are three women who express their grief in different ways. The most prominent member of the group, an elegantly dressed woman standing at the foot of the bed, is the most dramatic. She expresses her anguish by throwing back her head and clasping her hands in front of her. Although Mary Magdalen is not specifically named in Jacobus de Voragine's account of the death of the Virgin, it has been suggested that this figure may represent that archetypical repentant sinner. The woman's overt expression of grief would have recalled images of the distraught Magdalen as she was typically represented, especially in scenes of the Crucifixion, where she was often depicted mourning at the base of the cross.[11] A slightly older woman, seated in a chair beside the Magdalen, contributes to the ritualistic tenor of the scene as she closes her eyes, brings her hands together, and opens her mouth as if reciting a prayer. The third woman, standing beside the doctor, has brought a handkerchief to her face as if to wipe away her tears.[12] This last woman can also be viewed as a member of a different trio of female mourners. At the doctor's right side are a young woman and an elderly one, and at his left is the mature woman holding a handkerchief. It is possible that when composing a scene representing Mary's death, Rembrandt took the opportunity to represent three stages of a woman's life, as well.

Behind the women and at a slight remove from the bed stands an enigmatic figure. Bathed in light, this long-haired young man who wears a very simple tunic and cloak has been identified as either St. John or Jesus.[13] He spreads his arms wide in a gesture that may signify either the young apostle's grief, or Jesus's readiness to receive his mother's soul. Because the young man has a mournful expression as he gazes at the Virgin and is depicted in the bedchamber, along with other mortals, as opposed to above in the clouds, amid the heavenly host, it seems likely that this figure is, in fact, John, rather than Jesus.[14]

Although John's face is turned toward the Virgin, his outstretched arm directs the eye toward a circle of figures at the lower right side of the composition. Two exotically dressed women are seated near John's feet, one on the lowest step of the platform and one on the ground. These women, who are in shadow, appear to have turned away from the unfolding drama of Mary's death. One is seen only from the back, while the other has turned her head away from the dying Virgin, even though her torso faces forward. Mary Christine Barker suggested that these two women represent indifference and despair.[15] Beyond them, an elderly, bearded, patriarchal figure parts the heavy curtains that close off the back of the Virgin's chamber. The man's face and upper torso are bathed in light as he turns toward Mary and peers into the room. A younger man, a figure with narrow eyes and a heavy mustache, crouches or sits in front of him, his head resting on the curtain. This man's head is on a level with those of the two seated women nearby, and although he does not interact with them, Barker suggested that he, too, represents an unsavory attribute: evil. Shrouded in darkness, this somewhat sinister figure looks downward, away from the Virgin. In another interpretation, Shelley Perlove and Larry Silver tentatively identified the two men by the curtain as a converted (enlightened) Jew and an unconverted (unenlightened) Jew.[16]

Near these figures gathered at the right, an unoccupied Savonarola chair fills the lower front corner of the composition.[17] This detail, a large, dark presence, received special attention from the artist. In the second state of the print, Rembrandt went back to the plate and heightened the contours and shadows around the chair, using drypoint.[18] The empty chair's prominence adds poignancy to the scene as Rembrandt converted a realistic domestic detail into a symbol of loss.

The left side of the composition is occupied by only five figures. A man wearing a broad turban and heavy, ornate, tasseled shawl is seated before a ponderous table covered by a thick ornamental carpet. Seen from the back, he functions as a *repoussoir* figure, directing the viewer's eye up toward the Virgin, even though the darkness and detail of his modeling—a contrast to the lightness of the central image—initially captures the observer's attention. A large tome is propped open on the table in front of him. As Barker observed, although it is not possible to read what is actually written on the pages of this open book, strokes that suggest capital letters along the right margins of the pages indicate that the text is meant to be read from right to left, implying that the man is reading the scriptures in Hebrew.[19] The turbaned figure has interrupted his reading in order to look up toward the Virgin; he has left off contemplating the written words of the Old Testament in order to witness the miraculous event being played out before him.

Standing beside the bed on the left side is a lightly sketched, but nonetheless imposing, priestly figure. He folds his hands in front of his substantial stomach and gazes solemnly across at the physician, as though awaiting the moment when it will be his turn to officiate, that is, when the Virgin's needs are no longer corporeal, but spiritual. This priest wears heavy robes and a very tall miter-like hat with tasseled cords hanging down from it, as well as a bell suspended from its peak. His costume not only illustrates Rembrandt's flare for the theatrical, but also serves a symbolic, syncretistic function by evoking both Catholic ecclesiastical dress, through its allusions to the cope and miter, and ancient Jewish liturgical garments, through such exotic details as the bell and tassels.[20] The priest is assisted by a short, tonsured boy who holds a tall staff with a sculpted crown from which hangs an embroidered ribbon. This ceremonial staff calls to mind a bishop's crosier or processional cross, but since the rod corresponds to neither of these objects, it again suggests an oblique synthesis of Jewish and Christian rituals.

Two final figures close out the composition at the left. One is an elderly seated man who peers anxiously around the back of the priest in order to witness the Virgin's last moments. The other is a man who is almost completely hidden behind the priest. It is unclear whether this last figure, who is seen from the back, is looking at the Virgin or is in the process of leaving the chamber. Barker suggested that he might be turning to pass through an unseen portal, the doorway to Paradise (*porta coeli*) that has been reopened by the Virgin.[21] In either case, his long hair and flat cap suggest that he may be have been styled to look like a seventeenth-century figure, unlike the others in the chamber, who have been exotically costumed so as to evoke an earlier age.

Heaven itself intrudes into this scene of mourning, bringing with it the promise of Mary's assumption and dissolving the boundaries between indoors and out, between the earthly and the celestial. Above Mary's bed, light pours down into the room through masses of clouds that are populated by cherubim, seraphim, and an angel standing with outstretched arms.[22] The light, which also illuminates the Virgin and those who attend her, dramatically distinguishes the heavenly and earthly spheres. The luminosity of the Virgin not only signals her spiritual purity, but also anticipates the miraculous aura that, according to *The Golden Legend*, will blind the three virgins when they set out to bathe her body before its interment. Rembrandt also used line and modeling to reinforce the distinction between mortal and spiritual beings. In contrast to the clear three-dimensional chiaroscuro modeling that gives substance to those who attend the Virgin, the angelic beings and Mary herself are primarily described through contour lines; these figures have little weight or volume, and "appear" only after the viewer's eye has traveled up across the deathbed scene from the denser, more fully realized table and reader at the lower left-hand corner.

On February 13, 1638, Rembrandt purchased several copies of Albrecht Dürer's woodcut series of *The Life of the Virgin* at an estate sale in Amsterdam.[23] It is very likely that at least one copy of Dürer's *Death of the Virgin* from 1510 (fig. 1) was included in the purchase.

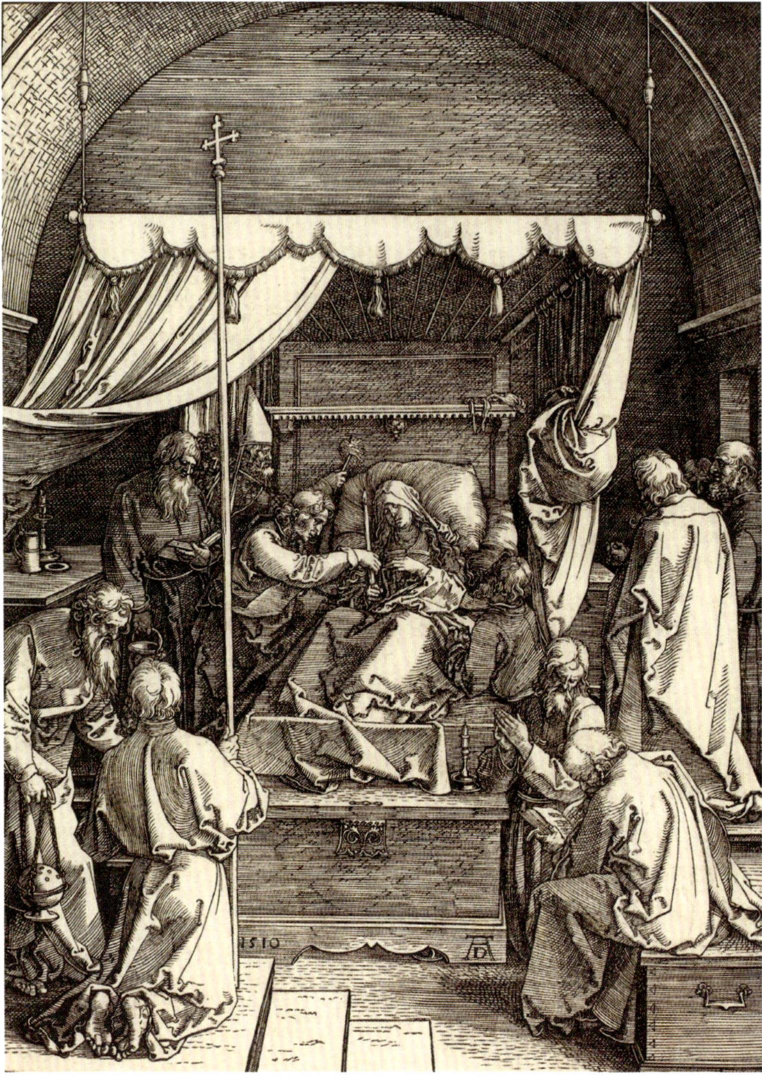

FIGURE 1. Albrecht Dürer, *Death of the Virgin*, woodcut, 1510. *Photo: Courtesy of the National Gallery of Art, Washington, DC.*

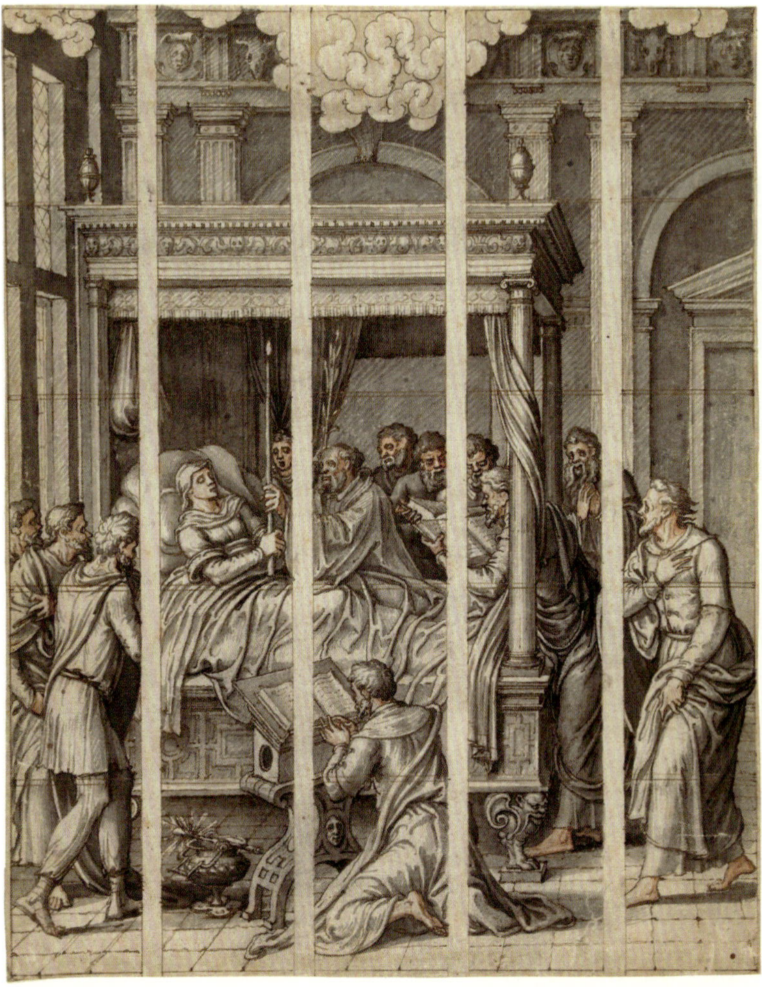

FIGURE 2. Dirck Crabeth, *Death of the Virgin*, gouache on paper, 1561–65. *Rijksmuseum, Amsterdam.*

Rembrandt greatly admired Dürer, and may have studied the German master's interpretation of this scene as he composed his own, perhaps even envisioning his creation as a sort of contemporary challenge to that of his artistic ancestor. Dürer's composition, like Rembrandt's, depicted a large canopied bed with its curtains drawn aside to reveal the Virgin, and a number of figures gathered around the bed.[24] In addition to this source, Rembrandt also drew on a stained-glass-window representation of the Death of the Virgin in the Oude Kerk in Amsterdam by sixteenth-century Dutch artist Dirck Crabeth (fig. 2).[25] Crabeth's composition for the window may have been the source of the seated figure reading scripture, in the foreground. Ultimately, though, it is not the associations with these prior examples, but the ways in which Rembrandt's version deviates from them, that is most intriguing. Although Crabeth included a small mass of clouds at the very top of his composition, they are considerably more modest than Rembrandt's baroque heavenly vision. Barker suggested an alternative source for this dramatic vision: Jacques Callot's small 1633 etching of *The Death of the Virgin* (fig. 3).[26] Certainly, Callot's print exhibits something of the same baroque sensibility as Rembrandt's, but the French artist's version, like several other fifteenth- and sixteenth-century examples, differs in that it places the figure of Christ awaiting the Virgin at the center

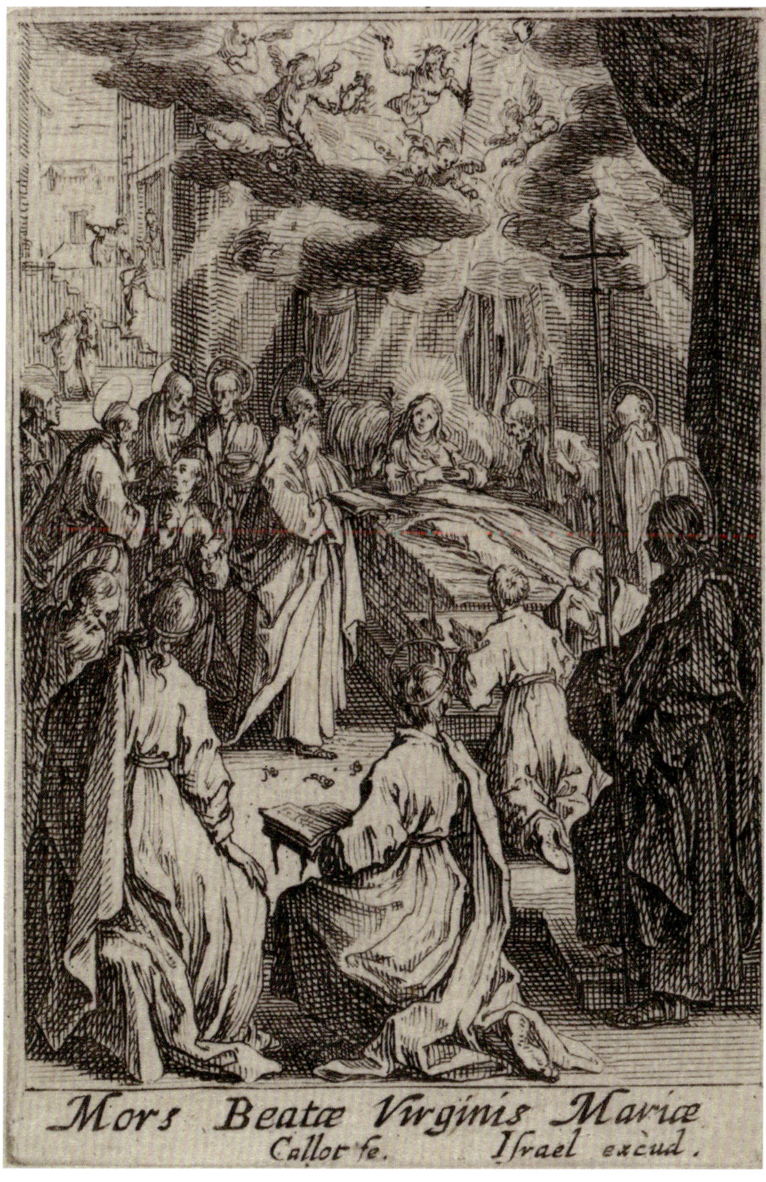

FIGURE 3. Jacques Callot, *Death of the Virgin*, etching, 1633. *Snite Museum of Art, University of Notre Dame, Notre Dame, Indiana, 1963 University of Notre Dame Purchase Fund.*

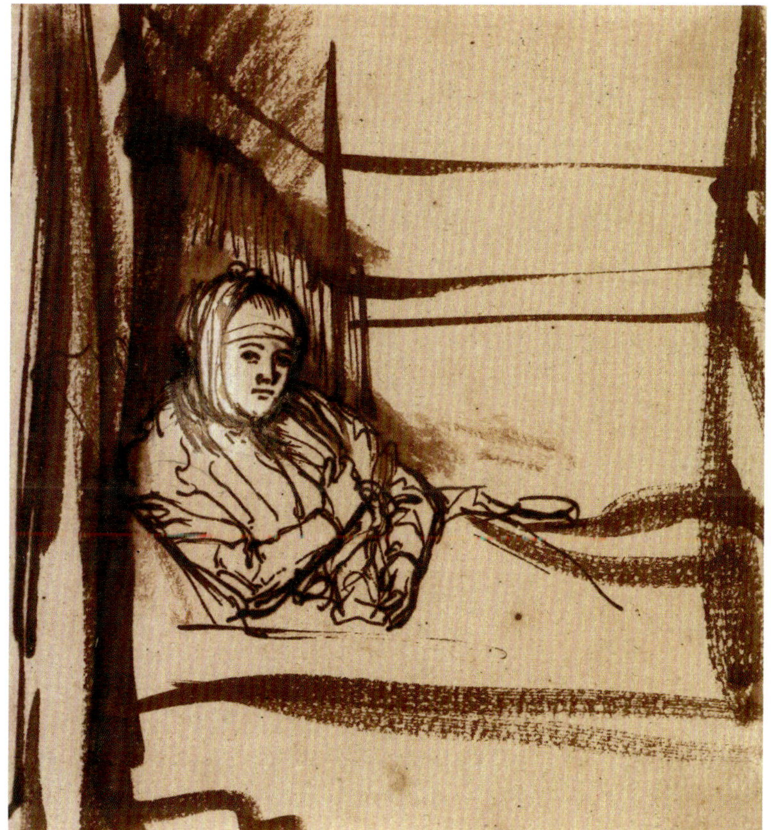

FIGURE 4. Rembrandt, *Saskia in Bed*, Ben. 255, pen and ink with wash, c. 1638, Kupferstichkabinett, Dresden. *Photo: bpk/Kupferstichkabinet/Herbert Boswank/Art Resource, New York.*

of the clouds, in order to foreshadow the ensuing assumption,[27] whereas Rembrandt's Christ is absent or, at best, may be in attendance as one of the bedside mourners. Both Dürer and Crabeth included explicit references to the Catholic sacrament of Last Rites. In Dürer's woodcut, Peter wears a bishop's miter and sprinkles holy water on the dying Virgin with an aspergillum, while another apostle holds the aspersorium. John hands the Virgin the candle that is required for the administration of Last Rites, while a fourth apostle, kneeling at the foot of the bed, holds up a tall, processional cross for Mary to gaze upon during her final moments. Although Crabeth eschewed the bishop's miter and the cross in his version of the scene, he did include the aspergillum, the aspersorium, and a candle in the Virgin's hand. Rembrandt eliminated all of these explicitly Catholic liturgical references from his composition.[28] In addition, Rembrandt greatly expanded the company of mourners to include not only a Jewish priest, but also a physician and a large number of women.

Because the doctrine of the Assumption of the Virgin was explicitly rejected by Calvinists, it has been suggested that Rembrandt must have made this print for a Catholic clientele. However, some scholars have noted that he not only excluded specific references to Catholic Last Rites in this print; he also chose to include a physician and other elements that emphasized Mary's corporeality.[29] What seems most likely is that Rembrandt sought to create a work that could be acceptable to those from diverse confessional traditions. On the one hand, the print incorporates elements that anchor the scene in reality and that would therefore have resonated with his Calvinist contemporaries.[30] In particular, Rembrandt clearly drew on his own experience to create a very human, emotional scene. He utilized sketches of his wife, Saskia, who was often bedridden during the period from 1635 until her death in 1642, as a source for the image of the exhausted Virgin in her last moments of life (fig. 4).[31] The presence of a physician at an ailing woman's bedside must have been a familiar sight in the artist's own home. Finally, the numerous women gathered in the Virgin's bedchamber would have harmonized with contemporary practices, for in seventeenth-century Amsterdam, modesty would have dictated that the attendants for a woman, particularly one who was ill or dying, would have been other women. On the other hand, Catholic viewers would have read the appearance of the angel and other celestial beings hovering above as an allusion not only to Mary's sanctity, but also to her imminent assumption. Barker suggested that the absence of specific Catholic liturgical elements from the scene could be explained by the fact that at the time of the Virgin's death, the Church and its rituals had not yet been fully systematized, a circumstance that offered Rembrandt the freedom to depict an imagined set of Jewish practices being performed by Jewish clergy.[32] In the end, Rembrandt's interpretation of the death of the Virgin is neither fully Protestant nor fully Catholic in nature. It remains open to both interpretations and acknowledges the confessional diversity of the marketplace within which the print would have circulated, a strategy that the pragmatic artist employed throughout his career.

Notes

1. For a summary of the early history of the legends surrounding the death and assumption of the Virgin, see Marina Warner, *Alone of All Her Sex: The Myth and the Cult of the Virgin Mary* (New York: Alfred Knopf, 1976), 81–90. *The Golden Legend* was translated into the Dutch dialect as early as the mid-fourteenth century. By 1492, it was available in a printed edition in Dutch *[Legenda aurea]: Dat Leuend der Hÿlghen, mit velen nÿen seer merckliken Hÿstorien doer ghemenghet*, Lübeck, 1492. Since this important source of hagiographical and Mariological lore is organized according to the liturgical calendar, the stories of Mary's death and assumption are recounted in the entry for August 15, the Feast of the Assumption.

2. John 19:26–27.

3. Jacobus de Voragine, *The Golden Legend*, trans. Granger Ryan and Helmut Ripperger (New York: Arno Press, 1969), 451.

4. Ibid.

5. Ibid., 452.

6. Ibid., 454.

7. It is difficult to identify any of the male figures in the etching as specific apostles, since they are not given clear attributes. Some scholars have identified this figure as St. John because of his charge to care for Mary. However, the man is depicted in the manner in which Peter was traditionally represented, that is, as an older, bearded, balding man with a round face. See, for example, Rembrandt's later representation of the saint in *Peter and John Healing the Cripple at the Gate of the Temple* (B. 94, cat. no. 66).

8. There were visual precedents for depicting women in attendance at the death of the Virgin. In Pieter Bruegel the Elder's mid-sixteenth-century painting of *The Death of the Virgin* (Upton House, Warwickshire, UK), for example, there are several women—including one who leans over to fluff up the pillow behind the Virgin's back—amid the vast ranks of mourners. Philip Galle did an engraving after the Bruegel painting in 1574 (NHD 229). Also, the illustration of the Death of the Virgin (*Transitus Matris Dei*) by Hieronymus Wierix for the 1593 edition of Jerome Nadal's *Evangelicae Historiae Imagines* (HD 339 [the Wierix Family, Book Illustrations]) includes a group of four mourning women standing by an open doorway within the chamber. What is unusual about Rembrandt's print is the large number of female mourners, possibly included as a means of anchoring this mystical event in contemporary experience, for although *The Golden Legend* relates that Mary requested that the apostles be present at her death, and physicians at that time were certainly male, the care of a sick or dying woman would doubtless have been entrusted to other women. The account in *The Golden Legend* acknowledged a sort of universal respect for the female body when it specified that the Virgin's body was to be washed and prepared for burial by three virgins and that when the cleansing took place, blinding light preserved her modesty during that ritual. It

should be noted that in Rembrandt's etching, although Peter is the one who most actively attends to Mary's physical comfort, he does not actually touch her. He uses a pillow to raise her head, and a cloth to wipe her face.

9. St. Luke is traditionally identified as a physician. In Colossians 4:14, St. Paul refers to him as "the most dear physician."

10. This figure's action identifies him as a physician. Taking a patient's pulse was a common practice dating back to ancient times, and had been depicted in such Renaissance works as the terra cotta reliefs of about 1535 by Giovanni della Robbia on the exterior of the Spedale del Ceppo in Pistoia, one of which portrays visiting the sick as one of the acts of mercy. On the history of measuring the pulse and its qualities as a means of diagnosing illness, see Stanley Joel Rieser, *Medicine and the Reign of Technology* (Cambridge, UK: Cambridge University Press, 1978), 95–97. In seventeenth-century Dutch art, the most common contexts for the depiction of a physician checking a patient's pulse were in misogynistic and satirical paintings of love sickness such as Jan Steen's *The Love Sick Girl* (Alte Pinakothek, Munich), and his *Doctor's Visit* (Mauritshuis, The Hague).

11. The identification of this figure as the Magdalen was first made by Gerard Brom, "De traditie in Rembrandt's *Dood van Maria*," *Oud Holland* 43 (1926): 114. The idea was recently revived by Mary Christine Barker, "Transcending Tradition: Rembrandt's 'Death of the Virgin' 1639: A Re-Vision," *Dutch Crossing* 34, no. 2 (2010): 154.

12. Stephanie S. Dickey, "'Met een wenende ziel . . . doch droge ogen': Women Holding Handkerchiefs in Seventeenth-Century Dutch Portraits," *Nederlands kunsthistorisch jaarboek* 46 (1995): 332–67.

13. Both Ronald Bernier ("The Economy of Salvation: Narrative and Liminality in Rembrandt's Death of the Virgin," *Religion and the Arts* 9, no. 3–4 [2005]: 196), and Elissa Auerbach ("Taking Mary's Pulse: Cartesianism and Modernity in Rembrandt's *The Death of the Virgin*," in *Power and Image in Early Modern Europe*, ed. Jessica Goethals, Valerie McGuire, and Gaoheng Zhang [Newcastle, UK: Cambridge Scholars, 2008], 100), tentatively identified this figure as Jesus. Barker, "Transcending Tradition," 153, identified him as John.

14. It could be posited that Jesus would be portrayed as rejoicing at his mother's triumphant assumption, whereas John, standing among those in Mary's bedchamber, would be mourning her earthly death.

15. Barker, "Transcending Tradition," 153.

16. *Rembrandt's Faith*, 49. Barker, "Transcending Tradition," 153, on the other hand, suggested that the figure emerging into the light could be Thomas, who, according to *The Golden Legend*, arrived late. She identified the sinister figure in shadow as a foul spirit, one who remains unseen by the Virgin, as Mary had requested. Coupled with the two women who are also in shadow, the trio would represent "indifference, despair and evil." According to Barker, the presence of these "demons" at the death of the Virgin associated Rembrandt's etching with representations of the so-called *ars moriendi*, or art of dying. In the popular Northern print cycles and block books from the fifteenth century that illustrated the process of achieving a good Christian death, the dying man was shown going through a series of trials and temptations in which demons tried to lure him into despair or denial. In the final image of the series, the forces of darkness were routed by saints and angels, and the diminutive soul of the deceased was carried up to heaven. According to Barker, Rembrandt envisioned a similar juxtaposition of triumphant angels and defeated demons. For the Art of Dying, see, for example, the engraved series by the Master E.S., and the block book *Ars Moriendi* illustrated in Alan Shestack, *Master E.S., Five Hundredth Anniversary Exhibition, September Fifth through October Third, Philadelphia Museum of Art*, exh. cat. (Philadelphia: Philadelphia Museum of Art, 1967), cat. 4–15. The presence of demons in Mary's bedchamber would have been a betrayal of the promise made to the Virgin by the angel who announced her impending death.

17. This chair, the heavy table topped by a rug, and the ornate bedstead are anachronistic details of contemporary life that Rembrandt casually combined with his own conception of how ancient, "biblical" objects and dress—both Jewish and early Christian—might have appeared.

18. Barker, "Transcending Tradition," 152, connected this empty chair with the Jewish rituals associated with mourning the dead known as *shiva*, during which mourners sit on low stools, close to the ground, for seven days. Whether or not this is the specific reference in Rembrandt's print, an empty chair certainly implies absence, which evokes the sense of loss that follows the death of a loved one. If the artist did indeed wish to allude to mourners sitting *shiva*, then perhaps the three figures in exotic dress seated at the far right represent the Jewish tradition, and the man crouching in shadow with an unfixed gaze personifies the darkness and heaviness of sorrow.

19. Ibid., 151.

20. Ibid., 152. A passage in Exodus (28:15–38) describes the garments that God instructed Aaron to wear when he presided as high priest and entered the Holy of Holies. Among other things, the Lord prescribed that bells should hang from the hem of Aaron's jeweled robes (his *ephod*); that he should wear a jeweled, golden breastplate; and that his head should be covered by a turban with a "plate of pure gold" fastened onto the front of it "by a lace of blue." Although Rembrandt did not recreate Aaron's priestly robes per se, he loosely evoked the opulence specified in Exodus by means of an ornate costume embellished with an embroidered panel across the priest's chest, a bell suspended from the top of the priest's "mitre," and tasseled laces hanging down from his headgear. On Rembrandt's evocation of this costume in another context, see *Rembrandt's Faith*, 193.

21. Barker, "Transcending Tradition," 152. Barker noted the prominent presence of doorways in other representations of the scene, e.g., Dürer's 1510 woodcut (TIB 93) and Dirck Crabeth's late sixteenth-century drawing for a stained glass window (RP-T-1905-73, Rijksmuseum, Amsterdam). See also the text, below.

22. Bernier, "The Economy of Salvation," 178, suggested that the prominent standing angel might be a reference to the angel who came to Mary to announce her imminent death. However, since this angel does not hold a palm frond, it is difficult to make such an assumption. Barker, "Transcending Tradition," 146, allowed that Bernier might be correct, but offered another possibility, that this figure is the Archangel Michael, sent by Christ to collect Mary's soul. In keeping with this latter hypothesis, Barker also suggested that the cherub standing in front of this angel might represent the Virgin's soul, already assumed into heaven (156).

23. Walter Strauss and Marjon van der Meulen, eds. and trans., *The Rembrandt Documents* (New York: Abaris, 1979), doc. 1638/2, 150. There are nine entries recording purchases of *The Life of the Virgin* (*'t vrou leven*) by Rembrandt on this date. The prices of the prints ranged from one guilder sixteen stivers apiece for seven of them, to two guilders seven stivers for one. Whether these were single prints from the series or complete or fragmentary series is not clear. Rembrandt purchased a number of other prints by Dürer at this same sale, including one copy of his *Passion* for sixteen guilders, and twelve copies of *St. Christopher* for a total of just ten stivers.

24. Similar motifs also appear in Martin Schongauer's very popular engraving of *The Death of the Virgin* (HG 16), which dates from the beginning of the third quarter of the fifteenth century. It is quite possible that Rembrandt knew this print, as well.

25. Brom, "De traditie," 113, first made the connection between Rembrandt's *Death of the Virgin* and this window, which he incorrectly identified as having been designed by Pieter Aersten. Ludwig Münz, *Critical Catalogue,* vol. 2, cat. 208, noted that in 1926, Benesch correctly identified the designer of the window as Dirck Crabeth.

26. Lieure 1367.

27. Barker, "Transcending Tradition," 147. For some other, earlier examples of the representation of heaven with Christ in the clouds appearing in the Virgin's bedchamber, see Hugo van der Goes, *Death of the Virgin,* c. 1475 (Groeningemuseum, Bruges); Hieronymus Wierix's illustration "Transitus Matris Dei," from Jerome Nadal, *Evangelicae Historiae Imagines,* Antwerp, 1595 (note 8 above); and Hieronymus Wierix, after a design by Otto van Veen, c. 1600 (HD 902 [the Wierix Family]).

28. Despite *The Golden Legend*'s description of Mary and the apostles seated in "the midst of lighted lamps and candles," Rembrandt included neither in his etching. Dutch Calvinism specifically forbade the burning of candles at the deathbed. Auerbach, "Taking Mary's Pulse," 107.

29. As John Knipping noted, such Catholic theologians as Johannes Molanus and Johannes Eck considered it inappropriate to portray the Virgin as a dying woman in bed. Knipping, *Iconography of the Counter Reformation in the Netherlands* (Nieuwkoop, Netherlands: De Graaf, 1974), 252.

30. Willem Adolph Visser 't Hooft, *Rembrandt and the Gospel* (New York: Meridian Books, 1960), 44, called the scene "a very simple one—the death of a beloved mother."

31. Münz, *Critical Catalogue,* 97; and Auerbach, "Taking Mary's Pulse," 107.

32. Barker, "Transcending Tradition," 151–52.

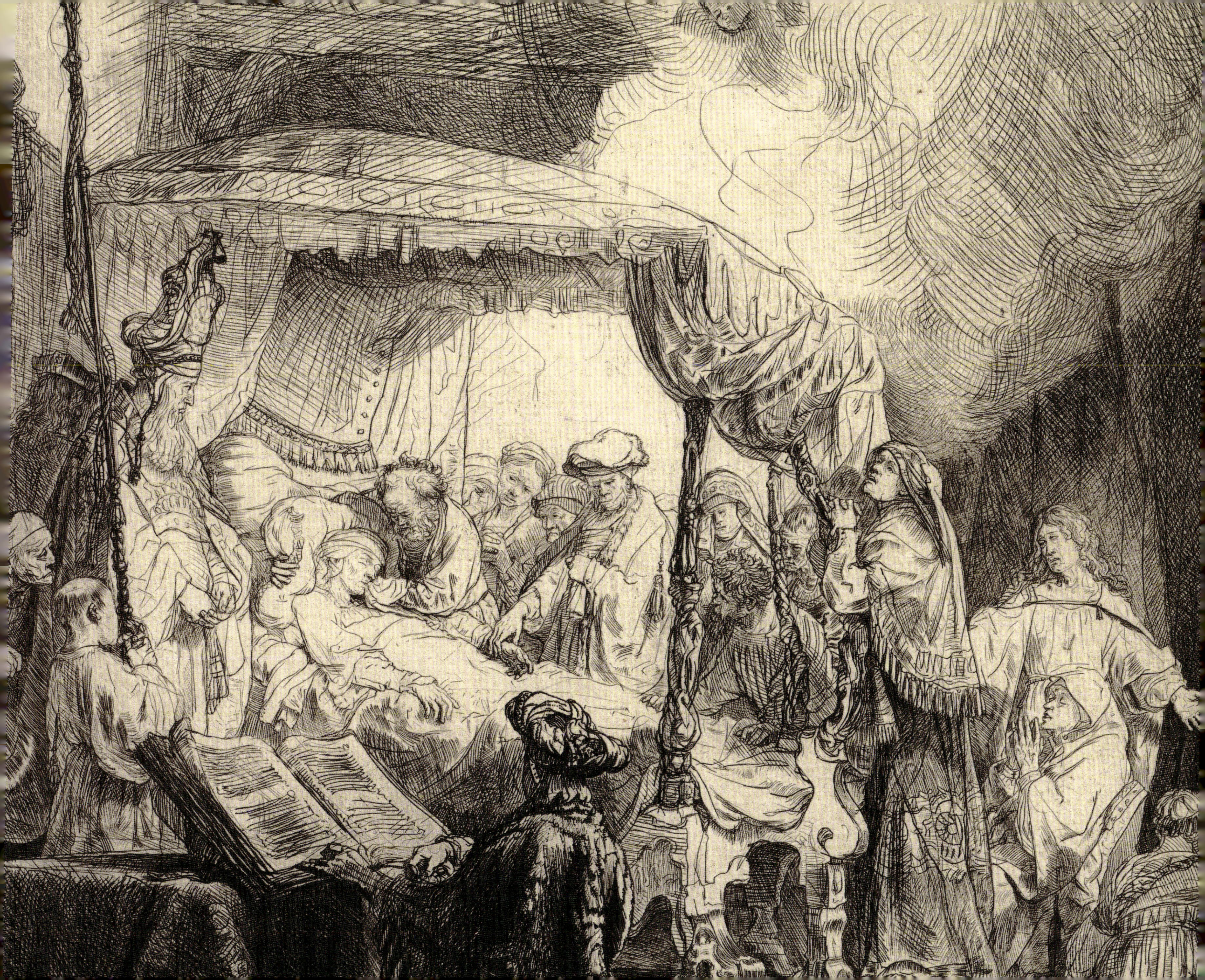

70. Three Oriental Figures (Jacob and Laban [?])

B. 118 (H. 183, Mz. 261, NHD 190)
Etching with touches of drypoint
Signed and dated in reverse in the plate: *Rembrandt f. 1641*
State II of II
Sheet: 14.8 × 11.8 cm; plate mark: 14.5 × 11.4 cm
Verso: in graphite, *10*

Provenance:
Craddock & Barnard, London, 1982
Feddersen, Elkhart, IN, 1991
Snite Museum of Art
Acc. No.: 1991.025.069

Plate survives:
Private collection, United Kingdom.

In the enigmatic etching that has come to be known as *Three Oriental Figures*, two men, a woman, and a dog stand before the threshold of a house.[1] A fourth figure stands just inside the entrance, his crossed arms resting on top of the bottom section of a Dutch door. It is unclear whether the man at the door is speaking to the three people standing before him or if one of them is addressing him. Although the man at the far right is gesturing, his finger points down toward the base of the doorway, not at the man standing within it. The central, patriarchal figure faces outward, toward the viewer, and seems somewhat detached from the others' interaction. The dog turns its head to stare down at the feet of the two visitors before him.

The etching is rendered in the loose, calligraphic style that was typical of Rembrandt's work in the early 1640s.[2] The shadows on the ground are created by a series of rapidly drawn parallel lines and undulating scribbles, and only the densest areas of darkness exhibit a more organized system of cross-hatching. In comparison with the three visitors, secondary details such as the dog, the architecture, and the background foliage are delineated with more open, freely drawn contours set against large expanses of white.

The identification of the subject represented in this etching has been a matter of discussion since the mid-nineteenth century. The earliest catalogers of Rembrandt's prints, Edme-François Gersaint (G. 114) and Adam von Bartsch, both described the print as a genre scene, referring to it simply as "Three Oriental Figures." However, in 1859, Charles Blanc suggested that the etching represents the confrontation between Laban and Jacob as described in Genesis 30:25–34:

> And it came to pass, when Rachel had born [*sic*] Joseph, that Jacob said unto Laban, "Send me away, that I may go unto mine own place, and to my country. Give me my wives and my children, for whom I have served thee, and let me go: for thou knowest my service which I have done thee." And Laban said unto him, "I pray thee, if I have found favour in thine eyes, tarry: for I have learned by experience that the Lord hath blessed me for thy sake." And he said, "Appoint me thy wages, and I will give it." And he said unto him, "Thou knowest how I have served thee, and how thy cattle was with me. For it was little which thou hadst before I came, and it is now increased unto a multitude;

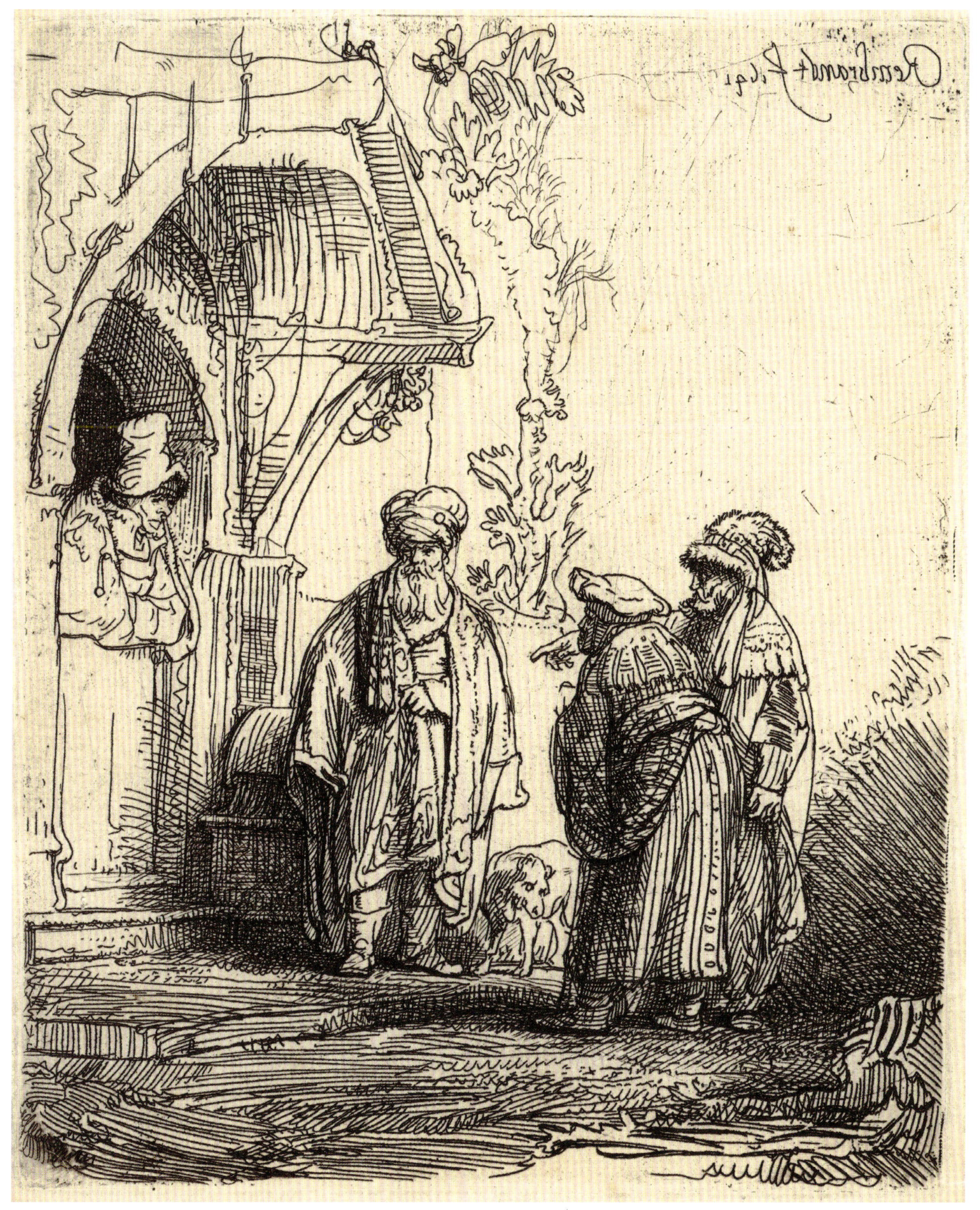

PLATE 70

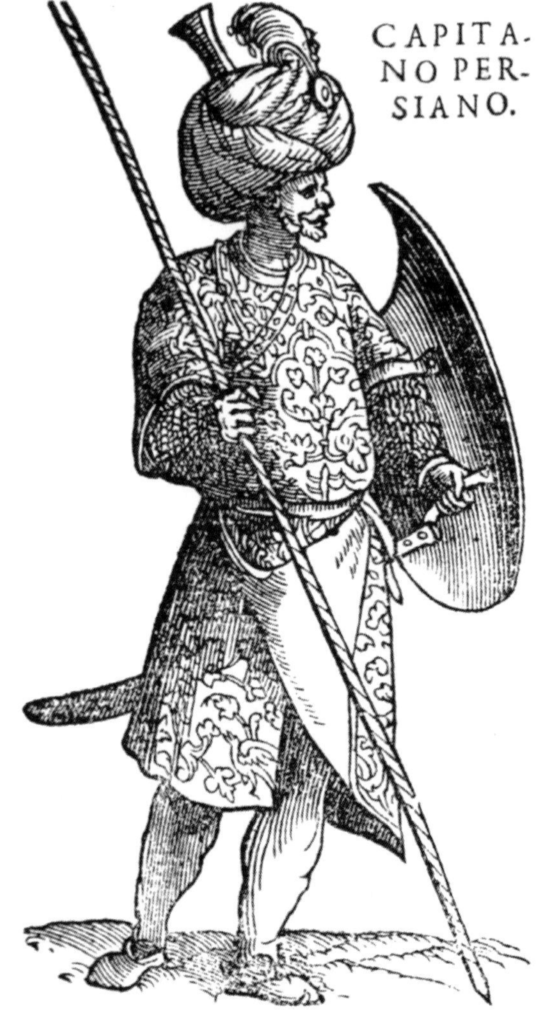

FIGURE 1. Cesare Vecellio, *Capitano ò Soldato Persiano,* woodcut, from *De gli Habiti Antichi et Moderni . . . , Libro Secondo: De Gli Habiti, Costumi, Et Usanze Dell'Asia Et Dell'Africa,* f. 449v, Venice, 1590.

> and the Lord hath blessed thee since my coming: and now when shall I provide for mine own house also?"

Blanc based his identification on the "biblical" character of the composition and what he interpreted as the angry demeanor of the man at the right addressing the figure in the house.[3] Most recent scholars, however, have rejected Blanc's proposal, noting that the ages of the protagonists do not correspond to the presumed ages of Jacob and Rachel. Furthermore, the biblical description of the encounter suggests that there were only two people conversing (Jacob and Laban), not four. While it is true that there are "biblical" aspects to the print, especially in regard to the costume of the bearded patriarchal figure with a turban,[4] the details of the etching do not support Blanc's specific identification of the story.

The more traditional descriptive title of the print, *Three Oriental Figures,* is based on the attire of the turbaned patriarch. However, beyond the biblical and Eastern associations of this figure,[5] the clothing worn by the other characters in the etching seems more fanciful than historically, ethnically, or geographically specific. Indeed, the clothing seems to attest more to Rembrandt's overall interest in depicting imaginative costumes as a means of imbuing his compositions with visual variety and an exotic atmosphere than to an effort to illustrate any particular narrative or place.[6] The subject of this print remains a mystery.

Notes

1. As Susan Donahue Kurestsky noted ("Rembrandt at the Threshold," in *Rembrandt, Rubens and the Art of Their Time: Recent Perspectives,* ed. Roland E. Fleischer and Susan Clare Scott [University Park: Pennsylvania State University Press, 1997], 60–105), setting a significant action at the threshold of a building often has symbolic significance. Such is the case in *Return of the Prodigal Son* (B. 91, cat. no. 63), *Abraham Casting out Hagar and Ishmael* (B. 30, cat. no. 4), *Abraham Entertaining the Angels* (B. 29, cat. no. 3), and the *Angel Departing from the Family of Tobias* (B. 43, cat. no. 18). In the case of *Three Oriental Figures,* however, no such significance has been discerned.

2. See, for example, *Triumph of Mordecai* (B. 40, cat. no. 14), *Angel Departing from the Family of Tobias* (B. 43, cat. no. 18), *Rest on the Flight into Egypt: Lightly Etched* (B. 58, cat. no. 33), *Virgin and Child in the Clouds* (B. 61, cat. no. 34), *Raising of Lazarus: Small Plate* (B. 72, cat. no. 47), *Christ Crucified between the Two Thieves: Oval Plate* (B. 79, cat. no. 53), *Christ Carried to the Tomb* (B. 84, cat. no. 57), *Baptism of the Eunuch* (B. 98, cat. no. 68), and *The Descent from the Cross: A Sketch* (B. 82, illus. in cat. no. 56).

3. Charles Blanc, *L'oeuvre de Rembrandt, décrit et commenté par Charles Blanc* (Paris: A. Quantin, 1880; 1st ed., Paris: Gide, 1859), cat. 7.

4. The fact that the central figure is quite similar to Rembrandt's Abraham in *Abraham Casting out Hagar and Ishmael* (B. 30,

cat. no. 4)—with the figure seen in reverse—adds weight to the view that *Three Oriental Figures* has biblical overtones, even if the latter image has not, to date, been linked to any specific text. Both men have the long white beards of biblical patriarchs and are clad in rich garments including a cloak, a turban, and boots. There are additional similarities between these two prints: an arched doorway in which a figure stands, peering out; an overhang resting on a curved support; and sketchily drawn greenery at the rear of each scene. It does appear likely that Rembrandt drew on one etching when creating the other.

5. Turbans were associated not only with biblical dress (see note 6), but also, more generally, with Persian, that is, Eastern, attire. See, for example, the representation of the captain or Persian soldier in Cesare Vecellio's *De gli Habiti Antichi et Moderni di Diverse Parti del Mondo* (Venice, 1590) (fig. 1).

6. The costume and appearance of the patriarchal man with the turban can be compared not only to Rembrandt's Abraham in *Abraham Casting out Hagar and Ishmael* (B. 30, cat. no. 4) and *Abraham and Isaac* on the way to Mount Moriah (B. 34, cat. no. 6), but also to Nicodemus in the *Descent from the Cross: The Second Plate* (B. 81 II, cat. no. 55) and Pilate in *Christ Presented to the People: Oblong Plate* (B. 76 cat. no. 51). For a discussion of the association of eastern dress with biblical times, see Marieke de Winkel, *Fashion and Fancy: Dress and Meaning in Rembrandt's Paintings* (Amsterdam: Amsterdam University Press, 2006), 255.

Appendix: Additional Rembrandt Prints at the Snite Museum of Art

THE SHEETS PRESENTED IN THIS APPENDIX SUPPLEMENT the catalog of the Feddersen Collection at the Snite Museum and provide a complete description of the University of Notre Dame's holdings of Rembrandt prints. In 1962 the university recognized the importance of having an example of the master printmaker's work for study and research and purchased Rembrandt's *Circumcision in the Stable*. When the Feddersens first exhibited their collection at the Snite Museum in 1981, a local doctor and his wife, Norval and Fern Green, generously donated their impression of *Joseph and Potiphar's Wife* to the museum. The Snite Museum enjoyed remarkable growth in the year 1991, receiving both the Feddersens' gift of their collection and a substantial endowment from the Humana Foundation. The Humana Endowment funded the acquisition of the Hayden-Hopkins Collection of prints, which included an additional example of Rembrandt's *Christ and the Woman of Samaria among the Ruins*. These important acquisitions offer alternate impressions of three plates represented in the Feddersen Collection—*Joseph and Potiphar's Wife*, discussed in catalog entry 13; *Circumcision in the Stable*, described in catalog entry 24; and *Christ and the Woman of Samaria among the Ruins*, considered in catalog entry 44.

These holdings and the Feddersens' gift continue to drive the growth of the University's print collection as new acquisitions that shed light on Rembrandt's sources, creative process, and legacy are added to enrich and advance future studies. Most recently, an alumnus and long-time Museum supporter donated a captivating portrait of Rembrandt's aging mother.

A1. The Artist's Mother, Head and Bust: Three Quarters Right

B. 354 (H. 1, Mz. 82, NHD 5)
Etching and drypoint
Signed and dated in the plate: *RHL 1628* ("2" reversed)
II of II states
Sheet: 7.0 × 6.8 cm; plate mark: 6.6 × 6.3 cm
Recto: Lower right corner, in graphite, *221*
Verso: Lower right, in graphite, *322/No. 322*; in sepia ink, collector's paraphe (?)"NA"or "MA" (not in Lugt). Lower left, *16/5107*

Provenance:

C. G. Boerner, New York, NY, 1995 (*Schongauer bis Whistler: die schönstenneuerwerbungen Graphik aus fünf Jahrhunderten. Neue Lagerliste 104*, [Düsseldorf, 1995], no. 33)
Dr. and Mrs. R. Stephen Lehman, Carmel, IN, 2006
Snite Museum of Art
Acc. No.: 2006.066.002
Gift of Dr. and Mrs. R. Stephen Lehman

The plate does not survive.

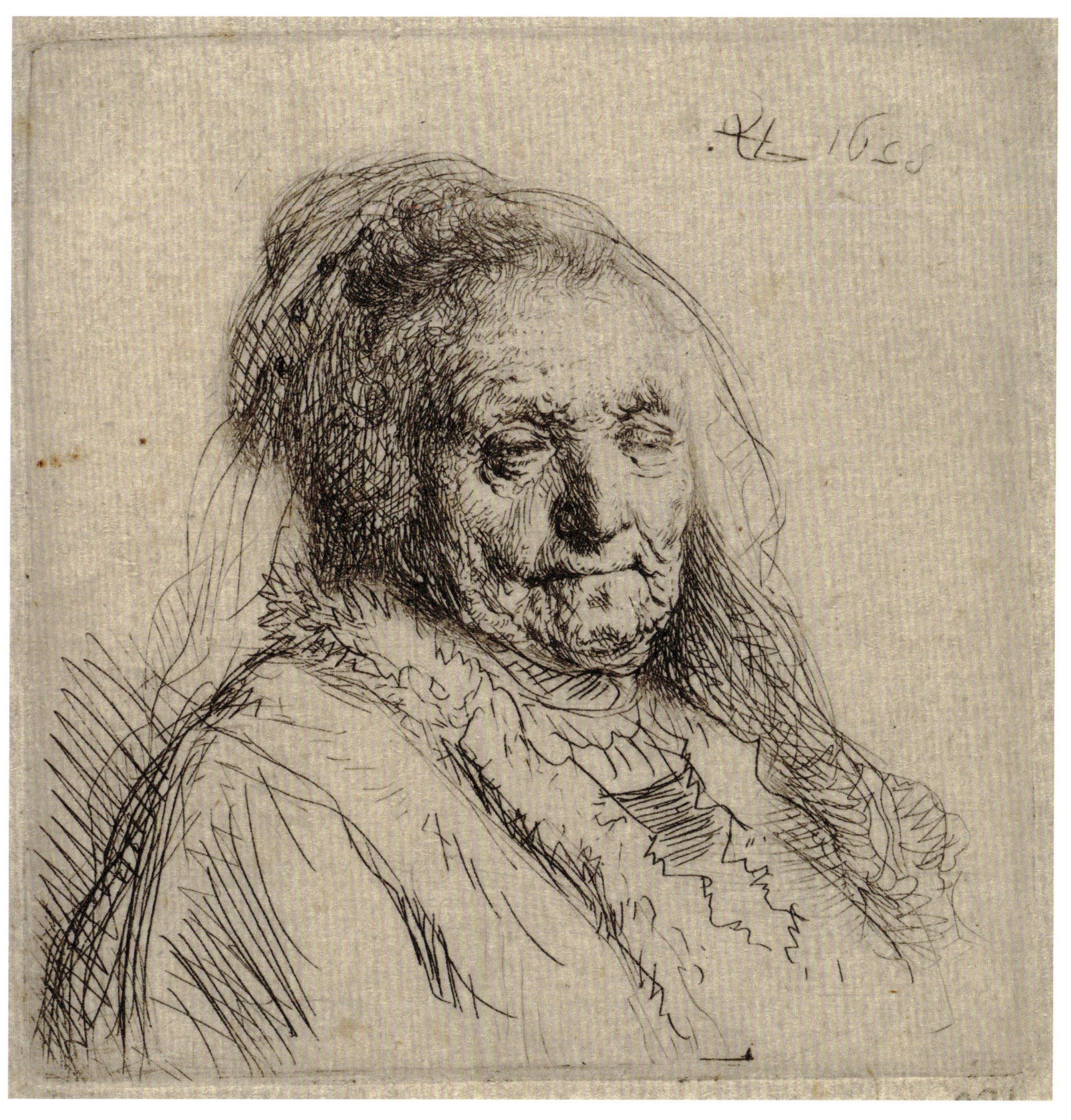

FIGURE 1. Rembrandt, *The Artist's Mother with Her Hand on Her Chest: Small Bust*, State II, etching, 1631. *Rijksmuseum, Amsterdam.*

Rembrandt made at least ten different images[1] of an elderly woman commonly identified as his mother, Neeltgen Willemsdochter van Zuytbrouck (c. 1568–1640). In the 1679 inventory of Rembrandt plates in the possession of Clement de Jonghe, one of these plates is specifically described as "*Rembrandts moeder.*"[2] It has been suggested that the plate referred to in the de Jonghe inventory is a later image, that of *The Artist's Mother with Her Hand on Her Chest* (1631, B. 349, State II, fig. 1). Since the late eighteenth century, the sitter in the etching in the Snite's collection (B. 354) has been identified as Rembrandt's mother as well.[3]

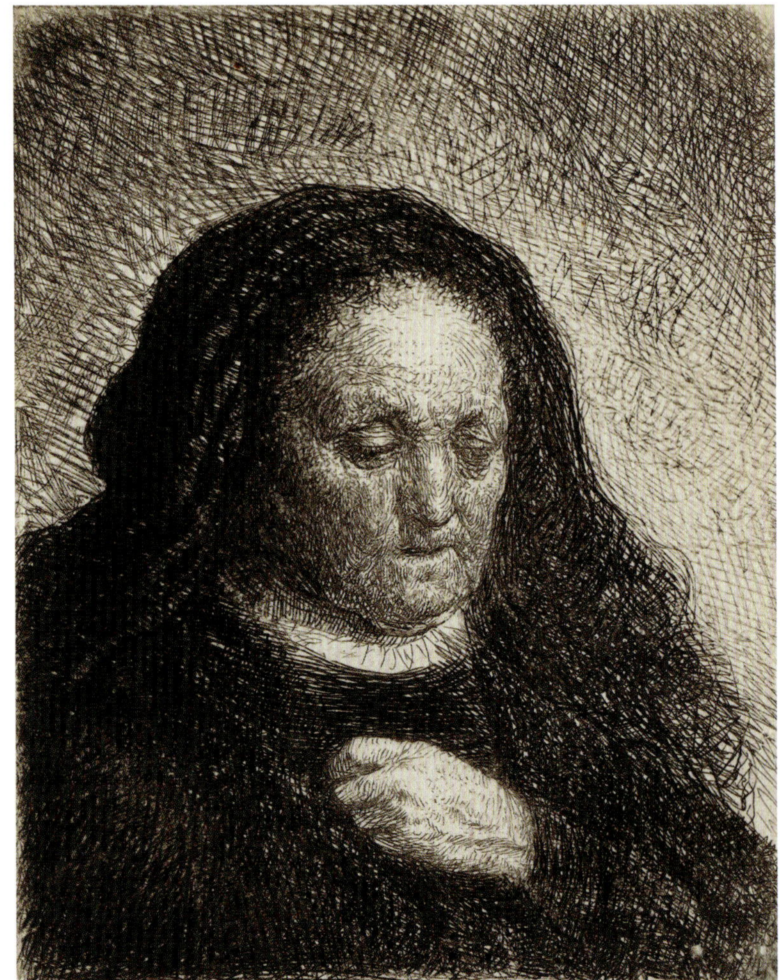

In the first state of this etching, Rembrandt depicted only the sitter's head capped by a veil that cascades down along her left shoulder and down her back. A few lightly sketched lines indicate the placement of her upper torso.[4] Neeltgen's mouth, eyes, wispy hair, and wrinkled visage are rendered with remarkable care and sympathy, suggesting that she was drawn directly from life. In the second state of the etching, Rembrandt filled in the figure's upper body, rendering her pleated blouse and fur-collared jacket in a much looser, more calligraphic style. He added dry point hatching along the left side of the figure, clarifying the direction of the light in the image and setting the somewhat flat figure in a shallow space. He also signed and dated the work in the plate. According to Roelof van Straten, this etching and a second one, also portraying the artist's mother (B. 352), are the first to be signed by the artist with his monogram *RHL* (Rembrandt Harmensz. Leydensis). The fact that the "2" in the date on the plate is backward has been interpreted as evidence of Rembrandt's incomplete control of the reversal of the plate that occurs in the printing process, but overall, the technical skill manifested in both the first and second states of this print is very high. The subtlety of modeling and the extensive vocabulary of descriptive strokes suggests an unexpected level of graphic sophistication for an etching of such an early date.[5]

Rembrandt may have produced this portrait of his mother as a character study and technical exercise. Since he was probably living at home at the time, Neeltgen would have been a convenient model.[6] Rembrandt imbued his sitter with an aura of quiet repose, while simultaneously recognizing the expressive potential of his mother's weathered features. This early work presages a career in which the artist would continue to evince a fascination with elderly figures and faces.

The fact that Rembrandt signed and dated this etching indicates that although he may have initially undertaken the project as an exercise, he ultimately decided to market it.[7] In spite of a growing demand for portraits of contemporary famous men, including artists and other virtuosi, it is very unlikely that in the late 1620s there would have been a market for a portrait of the mother of a relatively unknown young artist like Rembrandt.[8] Rather, the print was probably collected, at least at first, as a *tronie*.[9]

Notes

1. Thomas Rassieur noted that Rembrandt did at least six etchings, one drawing, and three paintings of this woman. *Rembrandt's Journey*, 85.

2. De Jonghe knew Rembrandt and was therefore likely to have known the identity of the sitter. D[ieuwke] de Hoop Scheffer and K[arel] G. Boon, "De inventaislijst van Clement de Jonghe en Rembrandts etsplaten," *Kroniek van het Rembrandthuis* 25 (1971): 6n10.

3. Edme-François Gersaint (*Catalogue raisonné de toutes les pièces qui forment l'œuvre de Rembrandt* [Paris: Chez Hochereau, 1751; London, 1752], cat. no. 321 [misnumbered as 221], 251) described the print as representing an old woman, "buste de vieille d'un beau caractère." According to Erik Hinterding (*Lugt Catalogue*, cat. no. 249, 593–94), this description was modified by Daniel Daulby in his English language version of Gersaint's catalog published in 1796 (*A Descriptive Catalogue of the Works of Rembrandt, and of His Scholars, Bol, Livens, and Van Vliet, Compiled from the Original Etchings, and from the Catalogues of De Burgy, Gersaint, Helle and Glomy, Marcus, and Yver* [Liverpool: Printed by J. M'Creery, and sold by J. Edwards London, 1796], cat. 321, 210). Daulby described the etching as having "a resemblance to Rembrandt's mother." Adam von Bartsch took up Daulby's identification in his catalogue raisonné, describing the print as "Tête de la mère de Rembrandt," and this denomination stuck.

4. Only a single impression of this state survives. It is in the British Museum (1848,0911.182).

5. The etching is contemporary with Rembrandt's much larger *Rest on the Flight into Egypt* (cat. nos. 22–24, fig. 1), a print that shows none of the technical mastery or subtlety of stroke seen in the elderly woman's portrait.

6. *Rembrandt's Journey*, 85.

7. Nearly fifty examples of the second state of this print are listed in the NHD, an extraordinarily large number. The size of the etching may have contributed to what is probably a high rate of survival. The etching's diminutive scale meant that it could very easily have been stored in the pages of a collector's album.

8. For bibliography on sixteenth- and seventeenth-century series of engraved portraits of famous men, see cat. no. 1, note 5.

9. For a definition and brief discussion of the term *tronie*, see the entry for cat. no. 1. Rassieur (*Rembrandt's Journey*, 86) notes that in seventeenth-century Holland, there was a growing taste for images of elderly men and women.

A2. *Joseph and Potiphar's Wife*

B. 39 (H. 118, Mz. 173, NHD 128, Cat. no. 13)
Etching
Signed and dated in the plate: *Rembrandt f. 1634*
II of IV states
Sheet: 9.0 × 11.5 cm, trimmed to the plate mark
Verso: lower left corner, in graphite, *60II*
Supporting sheet: Verso: upper right, *70-U33-CONOVX/XX*, upside down *P3312*

Provenance:
Radecki Galleries, South Bend, IN
Dr. and Mrs. Norval Green, South Bend, IN, 1981
Snite Museum of Art
Acc. No.: 1981.106
Gift of Dr. and Mrs. Norval Green

Plate survives:
On long-term loan to Museum het Rembrandthuis, Amsterdam.

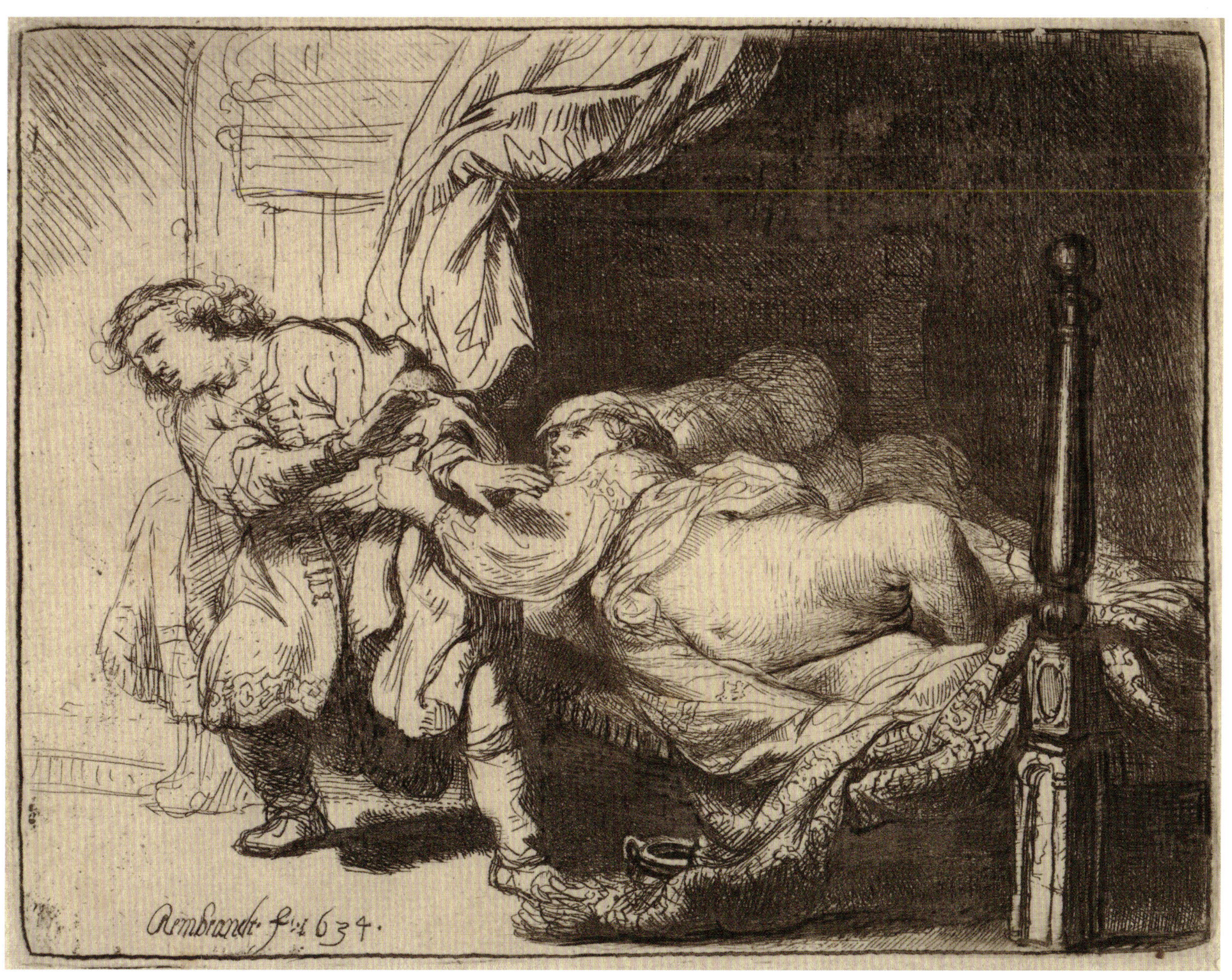
Rembrandt. f. 1634.

A3. Circumcision in the Stable

B. 47 (H. 274, Mz. 227, NHD 280, Cat. no. 24)
Signed and dated in the plate: *Rembrandt f. 1654*
Etching
State I of V
Sheet: 9.5 x 14.1 cm, trimmed within the plate mark.
Verso: lower right, in graphite, upside down: *B 47 ST/ KA 604/10*; top, in sepia, upside down, *Eugene Jantzen, Danzig*

Provenance:
Eugene Jantzen, Danzig (not in Lugt)
Roten Galleries, Baltimore, MD, 1962
Snite Museum of Art
Acc. No.: 1962.024.003
1962 University of Notre Dame Purchase Fund

The plate does not survive.

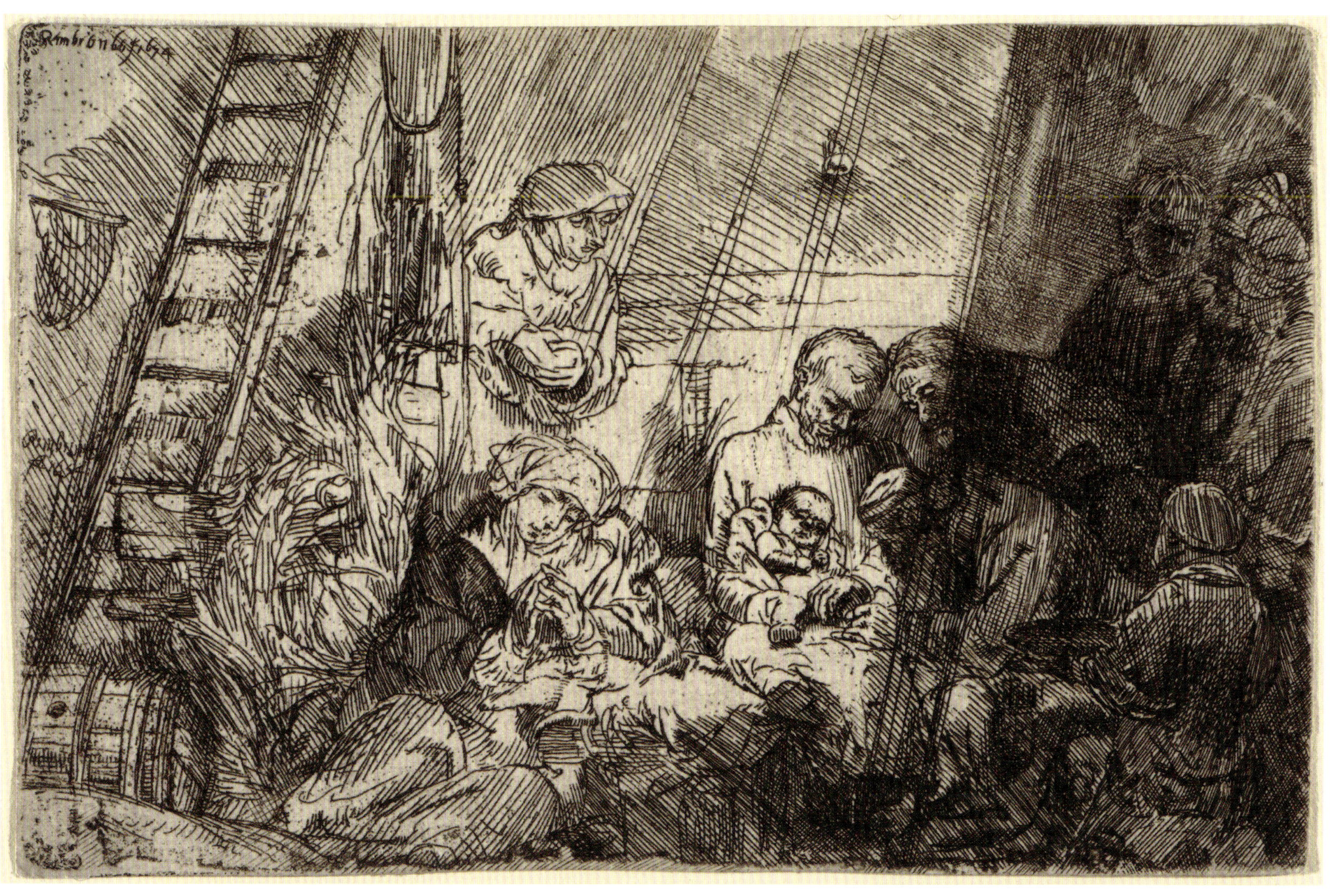

A4. Christ and the Woman of Samaria among Ruins

B. 71 (H. 122, Mz. 201, NHD 127, Cat. no. 44)
Etching
Sign and dated in the plate: *Rembrandt. f.1634*
State III of V
Sheet: 12.3 × 11.0 cm, trimmed to the plate mark
Verso: Lower left, in graphite, *36157/C17049/ amx—*, upper center, in sepia ink,*122/72*

Provenance:
Hayden-Hopkins Collection, 1991
Snite Museum of Art
Acc. No.: 1991.001.191
Acquired with funds provided by the Humana Endowment for American Art

Plate survives (significantly reworked):
On the art market, USA, 2013.

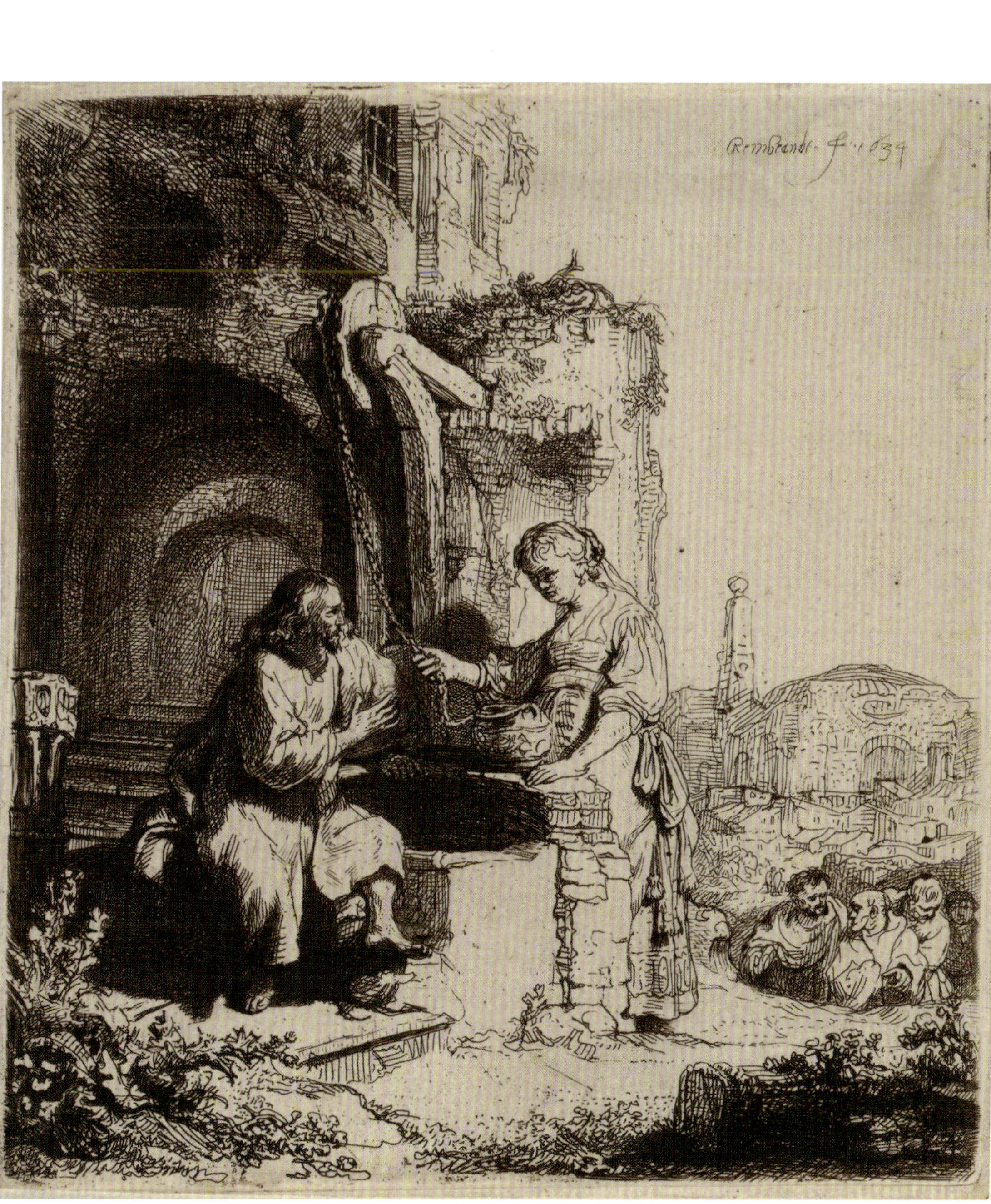
Rembrandt. f. 1634

GLOSSARY OF PRINT TERMS

Bistre A brown pigment made from chimney soot.

Burin A tool used for engraving. Its sharp tip is diamond-shaped, allowing the engraver to control the width of the line by varying the pressure on the tool. The burin generally produces a sharp, clean-edged line.

Burnishing A method of removing marks from a metal plate. The printmaker uses a smooth tool to rub out unwanted etched or engraved lines.

Burr The rough metal left around a drypoint line by the path of the needle. When the plate is inked, this metal traps ink and the burr prints a deep, velvety black.

Collector's Mark or stamp A stamp or inscription (paraph) left on a print by an owner to identify it as a work from his or her collection. It is generally found on the back of the printed sheet or on the front margin. A blind or dry stamp refers to a mark that is embossed onto the front or back of a print to identify the owner.

Countermark The initials or emblem of the printer created by wires woven into the mold on which the paper is formed. These are visible when the print is held up to the light. See also watermark.

Counterproof An impression made by laying a damp piece of paper on top of a freshly printed impression before the ink has dried. The resulting contact print "re-reverses" the image, creating an impression that corresponds to the one that is actually cut into the plate.

Designer The individual responsible for the design of an image. In the case of a reproductive print this is the artist responsible for the original image. The designer is often indicated by the abbreviation *in.* or *inv.*, or the word *invenit* or *inventor.* When the designer and the one who actually cuts the image into the plate are the same, this individual can be denoted by the abbreviation *fe.* or *fec.*, or the word *fecit* or *faciebat*. When the designer and the maker of the plate are different, the latter may be indicated by the abbreviation *sc.* or *sculpt.*, or the word *sculpsit.*

Drypoint An intaglio method in which the printmaker scratches lines directly on the plate with a drypoint needle. This action displaces copper, which is thrown up beside the furrow in the form of a rough ridge of metal or burr. If the burr is not scraped away, it will retain ink and will print as a dark, velvety accent. The burr wears down quickly under the pressure of printing.

Edition A set of identical prints. Impressions within a modern edition are normally identified by two numbers at the lower edge of the print. The first number indicates the place of the print in the order of all the prints in the edition. The second number indicates the size of the edition. Rembrandt's prints are not numbered.

Engraving An intaglio technique in which the printmaker cuts lines into a copper plate with a burin. The burin makes a neat V-shaped furrow in the soft copper.

Etching An intaglio technique. The etcher coats a copper plate with a ground, draws on the ground with a needle to reveal the metal beneath, and covers the plate's surface in acid or another mordant, which bites into the exposed metal lines. The longer the metal is exposed to the acid, the deeper the lines.

Foul Biting A problem in the etching process when the ground lifts partially, allowing acid to leak underneath and bite a light pattern into the copper where it wasn't intended.

Ground The waxy or resinous substance with which an etcher coats a plate to protect it in an acid bath.

Impression The image that is created each time a plate or block is printed. Impressions made from the same plate can vary widely.

Inking The application of ink to the plate. In the process of inking, an artist can vary both the color of ink used and the amount of ink left on the surface of the plate.

Intaglio A printmaking technique in which lines are cut into a plate. When ink is applied to the plate, the ink sinks into the channels and prints as black lines. Engraving, etching, and drypoint are intaglio processes.

Japanese paper A handmade paper imported from Japan by the Dutch East India Company in the mid-seventeenth century. This paper was made from various types of vegetable fibers, including the inner bark of the gampi, mitsumata, and mulberry trees. It varies in thickness, transparency, and color.[1]

Laid Paper A handmade paper cast from a mold with vertical wires and horizontal "chains." The marks made by the wires and chains are clearly visible when the paper is held up to the light.

Maculature A second impression pulled from a plate before the plate is re-inked. This normally results in a rather faint image.

Monoprints Impressions pulled from an etched plate that differ from one another because the artist adds pigment or other elements of design to the plate's surface.

Plate A piece of flat metal, usually copper, used for processes such as etching and engraving.

Plate Mark The impression made by the beveled edge of the plate as the plate and paper pass through a high-pressure printing press. The plate mark is generally seen as an embossed line that surrounds the composition.

Plate or Surface Tone A film of ink that is intentionally left by the printer on the surface of a plate as he wipes the plate prior to printing. This ink creates areas of tone or shading on the impression.

Privileges A copyright issued by a sovereign, city, or state. Privileges were intended to protect an image against unauthorized reproduction.

Publisher An individual or company that underwrites the production and/or distribution of a print. The publisher is sometimes indicated by the abbreviation *ex.* or *exc.,* or the word *excudit* or *excudebat.*

1. Deborah La Camera, Rhona Macbeth, and Kimberly Nichols, "Materials and Technique," in *Rembrandt's Journey*, 336.

Relief printing A printmaking process in which what is *not* cut away from the plate or block is what prints. Woodcuts are the most common type of relief prints.

Reproductive print A print that reproduces a work that was created in another medium, such as painting or drawing.

State Used to denote both major and minor changes made to a plate. Different states of the same print can feature the addition or elimination of lines, cross-hatching, or even figures and accessory details, signatures, and publisher's addresses and inscriptions.

Support The material on which an image is printed. In the seventeenth century, etchings were usually printed on European laid paper, but theoretically, impressions could be made on almost any material that would pass through a press, including cloth, parchment, or vellum.

Vellum A fine and expensive form of parchment made from the skins of young calves.

Watermark A hallmark identifying the manufacturer of a paper stock. Watermarks are visible when light is transmitted through a sheet of paper. They are created by wires attached in a pattern to the mold in which paper is formed. Such marks can be helpful in documenting the date and/or origin of a particular impression of a print.

Woodcut See relief printing. The matrix is a wood block or plank, and the design is carved along the grain.

Wove Paper Paper made from a mold in which the wires are so tightly woven that no wire lines are visible when the sheet is held up to the light. Wove paper was invented in the 1750s and became widely used by the 1790s.

BIBLIOGRAPHY

Ackley, Clifford S. *Printmaking in the Age of Rembrandt.* Exh. cat. Boston: Boston Museum of Fine Arts, 1981.

———. "Rembrandt as Actor and Dramatist: Gesture and Body Language in the Biblical Etchings." *Apollo* 157, no. 495 (2003): 34–38.

Ackley, Clifford S., Ronni Baer, Thomas Rassieur, and William W. Robinson. *Rembrandt's Journey: Painter, Draughtsman, Etcher.* Exh. cat. Boston: MFA Publications, 2003.

Adams, Ann Jensen. "Rembrandt f(ecit): The Italic Signature and the Commodification of Artistic Identity." In *Künstlerischer Austausch, Artistic exchange: Akten des XXVIII. Internationalen Kongresses für Kunstgeschichte, Berlin, 15.–20. Juli 1992,* edited by Thomas W. Gaehtgens, 581–94. Berlin: Akademie Verlag, 1993.

Alpers, Svetlana. *Rembrandt's Enterprise: The Studio and the Market.* Chicago: University of Chicago Press, 1988.

Ash, Nancy, Shelley Fletcher, and J. P. Filedt Kok. *Watermarks in Rembrandt's Prints.* Washington, DC: National Gallery of Art, 1998.

Auerbach, Elissa. "Taking Mary's Pulse: Cartesianism and Modernity in Rembrandt's *The Death of the Virgin.*" In *Power and Image in Early Modern Europe,* edited by Jessica Goethals, Valerie McGuire, and Gaoheng Zhang, 95–118 and 151–61. Newcastle, UK: Cambridge Scholars, 2008.

Baldinucci, Filippo. *Cominciamento, e progresso dell'arte dell'intagliare in rame, colle vite di molti de'più eccellenti maestri della stessa professione* [The origins and progress of the art of engraving on copper, with the lives of many of the most excellent masters of this same profession]. Florence: Stamperia di P. Matini, 1686.

Baldwin, Robert W. "A Bibliography of the Prodigal Son in Art and Literature." *Bulletin of Bibliography* 44 (September 1987): 167–71.

———. "'On Earth We Art Beggars as Christ Himself Was': The Protestant Background of Rembrandt's Imagery of Poverty, Disability, and Begging." *Kunsthistorisk tidskrift* 54, no. 3 (1985): 122–35.

———. "Rembrandt's Visual Sources in Italy and the Antique Reconsidered." *Source* 4, no. 1 (1984): 22–29.

Barker, Mary C. "Transcending Tradition: Rembrandt's 'Death of the Virgin' 1639: A Re-Vision." *Dutch Crossing* 34, no. 2 (2010): 138–61.

Bartsch, Adam von. *Le peintre-graveur.* 22 vols. in 4. Nieuwkoop, Netherlands: B. de Graaf, 1982. Reprinted with illustrations as *The Illustrated Bartsch (TIB),* New York: Abaris Books, 1978–2016.

Bartsch, Adam von, and Edme-François Gersaint. *Catalogue raisonné de toutes les estampes qui forment l'oeuvre de Rembrandt, et ceux de ses principaux imitateurs, composé par les Sieurs Gersaint, Helle, Glomy et P. Yver.* Vienna: Chez A. Blumauer, 1797.

Basan, François. *Dictionnaire des graveurs anciens et modernes.* Paris: De Lormel, 1767; 2nd ed., 1789.

Basan, Pierre François. *Recueil de quatre-vingt estampes originales, dessinées et gravées par Rembrandt.* Paris: Chez Basan, Rue et hotel Serpente, no. 14, [1789].

Bauch, Kurt. *Die frühe Rembrandt und seine Zeit*. Berlin: Verlag Gebr. Mann, 1960.

———. "Rembrandt und Lievens." *Wallraf-Richartz-Jahrbuch* 11 (1939): 239–68.

Baudis, Hela, Kornelia Röder, Horst Janssen, and Kornelia von Berswordt-Wallrabe. *Rembrandt fecit: 165 Rembrandt-Radierungen aus der Sammlung des Staatlichen Museums Schwerin: Ausstellung vom 28. Mai bis 6. August 1995*. Exh. cat. Schwerin, Germany: Das Museum, 1995.

Benesch, Otto. *Artistic and Intellectual Trends from Rubens to Daumier as Shown in Book Illustrations*. Cambridge, MA: Harvard College Library, 1943.

Benesch, Otto, and Eva Benesch. *The Drawings of Rembrandt: A Critical and Chronological Catalogue*. 6 vols. London: Phaidon, 1973.

Bernier, Ronald R. "The Economy of Salvation: Narrative and Liminality in Rembrandt's Death of the Virgin." *Religion and the Arts* 9, no. 3/4 (2005): 173–207.

Bevers, Holm. "Rembrandt as an Etcher." In Holm Bevers, Peter Schatborn, and Barbara Welzel, *Rembrandt: The Master and His Workshop*, vol. 2, *Drawings and Etchings*, 160–69.

Bevers, Holm, Peter Schatborn, and Barbara Welzel. *Rembrandt: The Master and His Workshop*. Vol. 2, *Drawings and Etchings*. Exh. cat. New Haven, CT: Yale University Press, 1991.

Bevers, Holm, Jasper Kettner, and Gudula Metze. *Rembrandt: Ein Virtuose der Druckgraphik*. Berlin: Dumont and Kupferstichkabinett, Staatliche Museen, 2006.

Biblia, dat is: De gantsche H. Schrifture, vervattende alle de canonijcke boecken des Ouden en des Nieuwen Testaments. Nu eerst, door last der hoogh-mog: heeren Staten Generael vande Vereenighde Nederlanden, en volgens het besluyt van de Synode Nationael, gehouden tot Dordrecht, inde jaeren 1618. ende 1619. uyt de oorspronckelijcke talen in onse Neder-landtsche tale getrouwelijck overgeset. Met nieuwe bij-gevoegde verklaringen op de duystere plastsen, aenteeckeningen vande ghelijck-luydende texten, ende nieuwe registers over beyde de Testamenten. Leyden: Gedruckt bij P.A. van Ravensteyn voor de weduwe ende erfgenamen van wijlen H.J. van Wouw, 1637. (Statenbijbel or Statenvertaling). Accessed January 17, 2013. http://www.bijbelsdigitaal.nl/view/?bible=sv1637.

Biörklund, George, and Osbert H. Barnard. *Rembrandt's Etchings: True or False: A Summary Catalogue in a Distinctive Chronological Order and Completely Illustrated by George Biörklund*. Stockholm: n.p., 1955; 2nd ed. with essay by Barnard, New York: n.p., 1968.

Black, Peter, and Erma Hermens. *Rembrandt and the Passion*. Exh. cat. Munich: Prestel Verlag, 2012.

Blanc, Charles. *L'oeuvre de Rembrandt, décrit et commenté par Charles Blanc*. Paris: A. Quantin, 1880; 1st ed., Paris: Gide, 1859.

Blankert, Albert. *Rembrandt: A Genius and His Impact*. Exh. cat. Melbourne: National Gallery of Victoria; Canberra: National Gallery of Australia; Zwolle, Netherlands: Waanders, 1997.

Blankert, Albert, et al. *Gods, Saints & Heroes, Dutch Painting in the Age of Rembrandt*. Exh. cat. Washington, DC: National Gallery of Art; Detroit: Detroit Institute of Arts; Amsterdam; Rijsmuseum, 1980.

Bonebakker, Odilia. "Rembrandt's Drawing of the Baptism of the Eunuch in Munich: Style and Iconography." In *Symposion, Rembrandt-Zeichnungen in München*, edited by Thea Vignau-Wilberg, 29–44. Munich: Staatliche Graphische Sammlung, München, 2003.

Boogert, Bob van den, ed. *Rembrandt's Treasures*. Exh. cat. Zwolle, Netherlands: Waanders, 1999.

Bredius, Abraham, and Horst Gerson. *Rembrandt: The Complete Edition of the Paintings*. London: Phaidon, 1969.

Bremmer, Jan, and Herman Roodenburg. *A Cultural History of Gesture*. Ithaca, NY: Cornell University Press, 1992.

Briquet, C.-M. [Charles-Moise]. *Les filigranes: dictionnaire historique des marques du papier*. Hildesheim, Germany: George Olms Verlag, 1991.

Brom, Gerard. "De traditie in Rembrandt's *Dood van Maria*." *Oud Holland* 43 (1926): 112–15.

Broos, B. P. J. *Index to the Formal Sources of Rembrandt's Art*. Maarssen, Netherlands: Schwartz, 1977.

———. "Rembrandt Borrows from Altdorfer." *Simiolus: Netherlands Quarterly for the History of Art* 4, no. 2 (1970): 100–108.

———. *Rembrandt en zijn Voorbeelden—Rembrandt and His Sources*. Amsterdam: Museum het Rembrandthuis, 1985.

———. "Review of Walter L. Strauss; Marjon van der Meulen, *The Rembrandt Documents*." *Simiolus: Netherlands Quarterly for the History of Art: Netherlands Quarterly for the History of Art* 12, no. 4 (1981–82): 245–62.

Brown, Christopher, Jan Kelch, and Pieter van Thiel. *Rembrandt: The Master and His Workshop*. 2 vols. Exh. cat. New Haven, CT: Yale University Press, 1991.

Bruyn, Josua. "Rembrandt and the Italian Baroque." *Simiolus: Netherlands Quarterly for the History of Art* 4 (1970): 28–48.

Bulwer, John. *Chirologia: Or the Natural Language of the Hand*. London: Thomas Harper, 1644.

Buxtorf, Johann. *The Jewish Synagogue, Or, An Historical Narration of the State of the Jews, at This Day Dispersed over the Face of the Whole Earth. Translated Out of the Learned Buxtor Fius by A.B., M.A. of Q. Col. in Oxford*. London: T. Roycroft for H.R. and Thomas Young, 1663. Accessed June 9, 2016. http://gateway.proquest.com.proxy.library.nd.edu/openurl?ctx_ver=Z39.88-2003&res_id=xri:eebo&rft_id=xri:eebo:citation:45504384.

Cafritz, Robert C. "Reverberations of Venetian Graphics in Rembrandt's Pastoral Landscapes." In Robert C. Cafritz, *Places of Delight: The Pastoral Landscape*, 130–47. Washington, DC: Phillips Collection and National Gallery of Art, 1988.

Carroll, Margaret Deutsch. "Rembrandt as Meditational Printmaker." *Art Bulletin* 63, no. 4 (December 1981): 585–610.

Casselle, Pierre. "Pierre-François Basan, marchand d'estampes à Paris (1723–1797)." *Paris et Ile-de-France* 33 (1982): 99–185.

Cayeux, J. "Watelet et Rembrandt." *Bulletin de la société de l'histoire de l'art français* (1965): 131–61.

Chapman, H. Perry. "Reclaiming the Inner Rembrandt: Passion and the Early Self-Portraits." In *The Passions in the Arts of the Early Modern Netherlands—De Hartstochten in de Kunst in de vroegmoderne Nederlanden*, edited by Stephanie S. Dickey and Herman Roodenburg, 233–61. *Nederlands Kunsthistorisch Jaarboek* 60. Zwolle, Netherlands: Waanders Uitgeverij, 2010.

——. *Rembrandt's Self-Portraits*. Princeton, NJ: Princeton University Press, 1990.

——. "Review of Golahny, *Rembrandt's Reading: The Artist's Bookshelf of Ancient Poetry and History* and Zell, *Reframing Rembrandt: Jews and the Christian Image in Seventeenth-Century Amsterdam*." *Art Bulletin* 87, no. 2 (June 2005): 346–52.

Churchill, W. A. *Watermarks in Paper in Holland, England, France, etc. in XVII and XVIII Centuries and Their Interconnections*. Amsterdam: M. Hertzberger, 1935.

Chong, Alan, and Michael Zell, eds. *Rethinking Rembrandt*. Zwolle, Netherlands: Waanders, 2002.

Clark, Kenneth. *Rembrandt and the Italian Renaissance*. New York: New York University Press, 1966.

——. "Rembrandt's 'Good Samaritan' in the Wallace Collection." *Burlington Magazine* 118 (1976): 806–9.

Coelen, Peter van der, ed. *Patriarchs, Angels and Prophets: The Old Testament in Netherlandish Printmaking from Lucas van Leyden to Rembrandt*. Exh. cat. Amsterdam: Rembrandt Information Centre, 1996.

——. *Rembrandts passie: Het Nieuwe Testament in der Nederlandse prentkunst van de zestiende en zeventiende eeuw*. Exh. cat. Rotterdam: Museum Boijmans van Beuningen, 2007.

Coppier, André-Charles. *Les eaux-fortes de Rembrandt*. Paris: Librairie Armand Colin, 1922.

Cornelis, Bart, and Jan Piet Filedt Kok. "The Taste for Lucas van Leyden Prints." *Simiolus: Netherlands Quarterly for the History of Art* 26, no. 1 / 2 (1998): 18–86.

Crenshaw, Paul. "Beyond Matthew 19: The Woman at Christ's Feet in Rembrandt's *Hundred Guilder Print*." In *Midwestern Arcadia: An E-festschrift in Honor of Alison McNeil Kettering*. 2014. Accessed February 23, 2017. https://apps.carleton.edu/kettering/assets/Crenshaw.pdf.

——. *Rembrandt's Bankruptcy*. New York: Cambridge University Press, 2006.

Daulby, Daniel. *A Descriptive Catalogue of the Works of Rembrandt, and of His Scholars, Bol, Livens, and Van Vliet, Compiled from the Original Etchings, and from the Catalogues of De Burgy, Gersaint, Helle and Glomy, Marcus, and Yver*. Liverpool: Printed by J. M'Creery, and sold by J. Edwards London, 1796.

DeWitt, Lloyd. *The Bader Collection; Dutch and Flemish Paintings*. Kingston, ON: Agnes Etherington Art Centre, 2008.

——, ed. *Rembrandt and the Face of Jesus*. Exh. cat. New Haven, CT: Yale University Press, 2011.

Dickey, Stephanie S[owa]. "Lievens and Printmaking." In Arthur Wheelock Jr., *Jan Lievens: A Dutch Master Rediscovered*, 54–67. Exh. cat. London and New Haven, CT: Yale University Press; Washington, DC: National Gallery of Art, 2008.

——. "Mennonite Martyrdom in Amsterdam and the Art of Rembrandt and His Contemporaries." In *Contemporary Explorations in the Culture of the Low Countries*, edited by William Shetter and Inge Van der Cruysse-Van Antwerpen, 81–103. Lanham, MD: University Press of America, 1995.

——. "'Met een wenende ziel . . . doch droge ogen': Women Holding Handkerchiefs in Seventeenth-Century Dutch Portraits." *Nederlands kunsthistorisch jaarboek* 46 (1995): 332–67.

——. "Prints, Portraits and Patronage in Rembrandt's Work around 1640." PhD diss., New York University, 1994.

——. *Rembrandt Portraits in Print*. Amsterdam: John Benjamins Publishing, 2004.

——. "Van Dyck in Holland: The Iconography and Its Impact on Rembrandt and Jan Lievens." In *Van Dyck 1599–1999: Conjectures and*

Refutations, edited by Hans Vlieghe, 289–302. Turnhout, Belgium: Brepols, 2001.

D'Oench, Ellen G. "'A Madness to Have His Prints,' Rembrandt and Georgian Taste, 1720–1800." In Christopher White, David Alexander, and Ellen D'Oench, *Rembrandt in Eighteenth Century England*, 63–81. New Haven, CT: Yale Center for British Art, 1983.

——. *Prodigal Son Narratives, 1480–1980*. Exh. cat. New Haven, CT: Yale University Art Gallery; Middletown, CT: Davison Art Center, Wesleyan University, 1995.

Döring, Thomas. *Ansichten vom Ich. 100 ausgewählte Blatter der Sammlung Künstler sehen sich selbst. Graphische Selbstbildnisse des 20. Jahrhunderts*. Exh. cat. Braunschweig, Germany: Herzog Anton-Ulrich-Museum, 1997.

Dudok van Heel, Sebastian A. C. "De jonge Rembrandt onder tijdgenoten: godsdienst en schilderkunst in Leiden en Amsterdam." Diss., Radboud Universiteit, Nijmegen, Netherlands, 2006.

Eck, Xander van. "Painting and Religious Toleration in the Golden Age." In *Traits of Tolerance: Religious Tolerance in the Golden Age*, edited by Xander van Eck, Beverly Jackson, and Ruud Priem, 33–75.

Eck, Xander van, Beverly Jackson, and Ruud Priem, eds. *Traits of Tolerance: Religious Tolerance in the Golden Age*. Zwolle, Netherlands: W Books, 2013.

Eeghen, Isabella Henrietta van. "De familie de la Tombe en Rembrandt." *Oud Holland* 71 (1956): 43–49.

Ekkart, Rudolf E. O., and M. L. Wurfbain. *Geschildert tot Leyden anno 1626: schilderijen, tekeningen en prenten van Van Goyen, De Heem, Lievens, Porcellis, Rembrandt e. a. [Tentoonstelling] 18 november 1976–9 januari 1977, Stedelijk Museum de Lakenhal, Leiden*. Exh. cat. Leiden: Stedelijk Museum de Lakenhal, 1977.

Ekserdjian, David. *Correggio*. New Haven, CT: Yale University Press, 1997.

Engammare, Max. "Le Figures de la Bible. Le destin oublié d'un genre littéraire en image (XVIe–XVIIe siècles)." *Mélanges de l'Ecole française de Rome. Italie et Méditerranée*. 106, no. 2 (1994): 549–91.

Evelyn, John. *Sculptura: Or the History and Art of Chalcography and Engraving in Copper*. London: Printed by J. C. for G. Beedle and T. Collins, 1662.

Filedt Kok, J. P. *Rembrandt Etchings and Drawings in the Rembrandt House: A Catalogue*. Maarssen, Netherlands: Gary Schwartz, 1972.

Fontaine Verwey, Herman de la. "Rembrandt as a Book-Illustrator." *Quaerendo* 3, no. 1 (1971): 3–19.

Forssman, Erik. "Rembrandt's Radierung 'Der Triumph des Mardochai.'" *Zeitschrift für Kunstgeschichte* 39, no. 4 (1976): 297–311.

Franits, Wayne. "On the Subject Matter of Rembrandt's Etching B. 33." *Marsyas* 21 (1981–82): 13–16.

——. *Paragons of Virtue: Women and Domesticity in Seventeenth-Century Dutch Art*. Cambridge, UK: Cambridge University Press, 1993.

Gaston, Robert W. "Prospero Fontana's Holy Family with Saints." *Art Bulletin of Victoria* 19 (1978): 28–45.

Gelder, J.G. van, and N.F. van Gelder-Schrijver. "De 'Memorie' van Rembrandts prenten in het bezit van Valerius Röver." *Oud Holland* 55 (1938): 1–16.

Gersaint, Edme-François. *Catalogue raisonné de toutes les pièces qui forment l'oeuvre de Rembrandt*. Paris: Chez Hochereau, 1751; London, 1752. [See also Yver, Pierre, Edme François Gersaint, and Jean Baptiste Glomy, below.]

Golahny, Amy. "The Disappearing Angel: Heemskerk's Departing Raphael in Rembrandt's Studio." *Canadian Journal of Netherlandic Studies. Revue canadienne d'études néerlandaises* 28 (2007): 38–52.

——. *Rembrandt's Reading: The Artist's Bookshelf of Ancient Poetry and History*. Amsterdam: Amsterdam University Press, 2003.

Goltzius, Hendrick. *Hendrik Goltzius (1558–1617): Drawings, Prints and Paintings*. Exh. cat. Zwolle, Netherlands: Waanders; Amsterdam: Rijksmuseum; New York: Metropolitan Museum of Art; Toledo, OH: Museum of Art, 2003.

Gombrich, Ernst H. "Aims and Limits of Iconology." In Ernst H. Gombrich, *Symbolic Images*, 1–22. Oxford: Clarendon Press, 1972.

——. *Shadows: The Depiction of Cast Shadows in Western Art*. London: National Gallery Publications, 1995.

Griffiths, Antony. "The Archaeology of the Print." In *Collecting Prints and Drawing in Europe, c. 1500–1750*, edited by Christopher Blake, Caroline Elam, and Genevieve Warwick, 9–27. Aldershot, UK: Ashgate, 2003.

Grotius, Hugo. *Annotationes in Novum Testamentum*. 9 vols. Groningen, Netherlands: W. Zuidema, 1827.

H. P. R. "Capt. William Baillie, 17th Dragoons and John Greenwood, of Boston." *Bulletin of the Museum of Fine Arts* 41, no. 244 (June 1943): 28–32.

Haak, Theodore. *The Dutch Annotations upon the Whole Bible, or, All the Holy Canonical Scriptures of the Old and New Testament: Together with and According to Their Own Translation of All the Text, As Both the One and the Other Were Ordered and Appointed by the Synod of Dort, 1618 and Published by Authority, 1618 and Published by Authority, 1637, Now Faithfully Communicated to the Use of Great Britain, in English: Whereunto Is Prefixed an Exact Narrative Touching the Whole*

Work, and This Translation. London: Printed by Henry Hills, for John Rothwell, Joshua Kirton, and Richard Tomlins, 1657. Accessed August 22, 2016. http://gateway.proquest.com/openurl?ctx_ver=Z39.88–2003&res_id=xri:eebo&rft_val_fmt=&rft_id=xri:eebo:image:61806.

Haeger, Barbara. "Cornelis Anthonisz's Representation of the Parable of the Prodigal Son: A Protestant Interpretation of the Biblical Text." *Nederlands kunsthistorisch jaarboek* 37 (1986): 133–50.

——. "Philips Galle's Engravings after Maarten van Heemskerk's *Parable of the Prodigal Son*." *Oud Holland*, 102. no. 2 (1988): 127–40.

——. "The Prodigal Son in Sixteenth- and Seventeenth-Century Netherlandish Art: Depictions of the Parable and the Evolution of a Catholic Image." *Simiolus: Netherlands Quarterly for the History of Art* 16, nos. 2/3 (1986): 128–38.

——. "The Religious Significance of Rembrandt's 'Return of the Prodigal Son': An Examination in the Context of the Visual and Iconographic Tradition." PhD diss., University of Michigan, 1983.

Halewood, William H. *Six Subjects of Reformation Art: A Preface to Rembrandt*. Toronto: University of Toronto Press, 1982.

Haverkamp-Begemann, Egbert. "The Etchings of Willem Buytewech." In Carl Zigrosser, *Prints*, 55–81. New York: Holt, Rinehart and Winston, 1962.

——. "Rembrandt Simeon och Jesusbarnet: Simeon and the Christ Child." In Görel Cavalli-Björkman and Mårten Snickare, *Rembrandt och Hans Tid: Rembrandt and His Age*, 30–40. Exh. cat. Stockholm: Nationalmuseum, 1992.

——. "Rembrandt's Night Watch and The Triumph of Mordecai." In *Album Amicorum J. G. van Gelder*, edited by Josua Bruyn, J. A. Emmons, E. De Jongh, and D. P. Snoep, 5–8. The Hague: Nijhoff, 1973.

——. "Review of Rotermund, *Rembrandts Handzeichenungen und Radierungen zur Bibel*." *Master Drawings* 4, no. 1 (Spring 1966): 49–52.

Haverkamp-Begemann, Egbert, K. G. Boon, and J. Verbeek. *Hercules Seghers, the Complete Etchings*. Amsterdam: Scheltema & Holkema, 1973.

Heawood, Edward. *Watermarks, Mainly of the 17th and 18th Centuries*. Hilversum, Netherlands: Paper Publications Society, 1950.

Held, Julius S. *Rembrandt's* Aristotle *and Other Rembrandt Studies*, 104–29. Princeton, NJ: Princeton University Press, 1969.

——. *Rembrandt Studies*. Princeton, NJ: Princeton University Press, 1991.

Hind, Arthur Mayger. *Rembrandt's Etchings: An Essay and a Catalogue, with Some Notes on the Drawings*. 2nd ed. London: Metheun; New York: Scribner, 1923; reprint, 2 vols. in 1, New York: Da Capo Press, 1967.

——. *Early Italian Engraving: A Critical Catalogue*. 7 vols. London: British Museum, 1938.

Hinterding, Erik. *The History of Rembrandt's Copperplates: With a Catalogue of Those That Survive*. Zwolle, Netherlands: Waanders, 1995. Originally in *Simiolus: Netherlands Quarterly for the History of Art* 22 (1993–94): 253–307.

——. *Rembrandt as an Etcher: The Practice of Production and Distribution*. 3 vols. Ouderkerk aan den IJssel, Netherlands: Sound and Vision Publishers, 2006.

——. *Rembrandt Etchings from the Frits Lugt Collection: Catalogue raisonné* and *Plates*. 2 vols. Bussum, Netherlands: Thoth Publishers; Paris: Fondation Custodia, 2008.

Hinterding, Erik, Ger Luijten, and Martin Royalton-Kisch. *Rembrandt the Printmaker*. Exh. cat. Chicago and London: Fitzroy Dearborn Publishers, 2000.

Hinterding, Erik, Jaco Rutgers, and Ger Luijten. *Rembrandt*. 5 vols. *The New Hollstein Dutch & Flemish Etchings, Engravings and Woodcuts, 1450–1700*. Ouderkerk aan den IJssel, Netherlands: Sound & Vision Publishers, 2013.

Hogan, Joan Mary. "The Iconography of Rembrandt's Depiction of the Holy Family (in a Domestic Setting)." MA diss., Queens University, Kingston, ON, 2008.

Hollstein, F[riedrich] W[ilhelm] H[einrich]. *Hollstein's Dutch and Flemish Etchings, Engravings, and Woodcuts, ca. 1450–1700*. Amsterdam: M. Hertzberger, 1949–2004. Expanded as *New Hollstein Dutch and Flemish Etchings, Engravings and Woodcuts, 1450–1700*, Rotterdam and Ouderwerk aan den IJssel, Netherlands: Sound & Vision Publishers; Amsterdam: in cooperation with the Rijksprentenkabinet, Rijksmuseum, 1993–.

——. *Hollstein's German Engravings, Etchings and Woodcuts, 1400–1700*. Amsterdam: M. Hertzberger, 1954–.

Hondius, Hendrik. *Pictorum aliquot celebrium praecipuae Germaniae effigies*. The Hague: Officina Henrici Hondii, 1610.

Hoofstede de Groote, Cornelis, ed. *Die Urkunden über Rembrandt (1575–1721)*. The Hague: Nijhoff, 1906. Accessed December 31, 2012. http://digi.ub.uni-heidelberg.de/diglit/hofstede_de_groot1906bd1.

Hoop Scheffer, D[ieuwke] de, and K[arel] G. Boon, "De inventaislijst van Clement de Jonghe en Rembrandts etsplaten." *Kroniek van het Rembrandthuis* 25 (1971): 1–17.

Houbraken, Arnold. *De Groote Schouburgh Der Nederlantsche Konstschilders En Schilderessen* [The great theater of Netherlandish painters and paintresses]. 3 vols. Amsterdam: Weduwe des Autheurs, 1718–21.

——. "Life of Rembrandt." In Joachim von Sandrart, Filippo Baldinucci, and Arnold Houbraken, *Lives of Rembrandt*, 89–91. London: Pallas Athene, 2007.

Howell, James. *Epistolæ Ho-Elianæ: The Familiar Letters of James Howell.* Boston: Houghton, Mifflin, 1907.

Isolani, Isidoro. *Summa de donis Sancti Ioseph*. Pavia, Italy: Iacob Paucidrapium, 1522.

Israel, Jonathan. *The Dutch Republic: Its Rise, Greatness, and Fall, 1477–1806*. Oxford: Clarendon Press, 1995.

Jacobowitz, Ellen S., and Sephanie Loeb Stepanek. *The Prints of Lucas van Leyden and His Contemporaries*. Exh. cat. Washington, DC: National Gallery of Art, 1983.

Jacobus de Voragine. *The Golden Legend of Jacobus de Voragine*. Translated by Granger Ryan and Helmut Rippinger. New York: Arno Press, 1969.

Jongh, Eddy de. "Erotica in vogelperspectief. De dubbelzinnigheid van een reeks 17de eeuwse genrevoorstellingen." *Simiolus: Netherlands Quarterly for the History of Art* 3, no. 1 (1968–69): 22–74.

——. "The Spur of Wit: Rembrandt's Response to an Italian Challenge." *Delta: A Review of Arts, Life and Thought in the Netherlands* 12, no. 2 (1969): 49–67.

Jongh, Eddy de, and Ger Luijten. *Mirror of Everyday Life: Genre Prints in the Netherlands 1550–1700*. Translated by Michael Hoyle. Amsterdam: Rijksmuseum; Ghent: Snoeck-Ducaju & Zoon, 1997.

Jordan, Albrecht. "Bemerkungen zu Rembrandt's Radierungen." *Repertorium für Kunstgeschichte* 16 (1893): 296–302.

Judson, J. Richard. "Jacob Isaacz van Swanenburgh and the Phelegraean Fields." In *Essays in Northern European Art Presented to Egbert Haverkamp-Begemann on His Sixtieth Birthday*, edited by Anne-Marie Logan, 119–22. Doornspijk, Netherlands: Davaco, 1983.

Kelly, Henry Ansgar. "The Metamorphoses of the Eden Serpent during the Middle Ages and Renaissance." *Viator* 2 (1971): 301–27.

Klipstein & Kornfeld. *Kupferstiche, Radierungen und Holzschnitte alter Meister: Teile der Sammlung Atherton Curtis, Doubletten der Albertina und anderer Museen, verschiedene Privatsammlungen, darunter die Sammlungen Dr. R. und George Björklund; Versteigerung in Bern, 4. Juni 1957 durch Klipstein et Kornfeld vorm. Gutekunst et Klipstein. Auktion 85*. Bern: Gutekunst & Klipstein, 1957.

Knipping, John. *Iconography of the Counter Reformation in the Netherlands*. Nieuwkoop, Netherlands: De Graaf, 1974.

Koerner, Joseph. "Rembrandt and the Epiphany of the Face." *RES: Anthropology and Aesthetics* 12 (Autumn 1986): 5–32.

Kooi, Christine. *Liberty and Religion: Church and State in Leiden's Reformation, 1572–1620*. Leiden: Brill, 2000.

Koslow, Susan. "Frans Hal's *Fisherboys*: Exemplars of Idleness." *Art Bulletin* 57, no. 3 (September 1975): 418–32.

Krönig, Wolfgang. "Cranach und Gossaert bei Rembrandt. Zu Rembrandts Darstellungen der Johannesenthauptung." In *Festschrift Dr. h.c. Eduard Trautscholdt zum siebzigsten Geburtstag am 13. Januar. 1963*, edited by Heinz Ladendorf and Eduard Trautscholdt. 100–108. Hamburg: E. Hauswedell, 1965.

Krüger, Peter. "'Adam und Eva'—Radierung. Eine Aemulatio mit Dürer." *Jahrbuch der Berliner Museen*, N. F. 35 (1993): 215–26.

Küp, Karl. "Some Early Costume Books." In Karl Küp, *Costume, Gothic & Renaissance: Some Early Costume Books*, 3–9. New York: New York Public Library, 1937.

Kuretsky, Susan Donahue. "Rembrandt at the Threshold." In *Rembrandt, Rubens, and the Art of Their Time: Recent Perspectives*, edited by Roland E. Fleischer and Susan Clare Scott, 60–105. University Park: Pennsylvania State University Press, 1997.

——. "Rembrandt's Cat." In *Aemulatio. Imitation, Emulation and Invention in Netherlandish Art from 1500 to 1800: Essays in Honor of Eric Jan Sluijter*, edited by Anton W. Boschloo, Jacquelyn N. Couttre, Stephanie S. Dickey, and Nicolette C. Sluijter-Seijffert, 263–76. Zwolle, Netherlands: Waanders, 2011.

——. "Rembrandt's Good Samaritan Etching: Reflections on a Disreputable Dog." In *Shop Talk: Studies in Honor of Seymour Slive, Presented on His Seventy-Fifth Birthday*, edited by Cynthia P. Schneider, William W. Robinson, and Alice I. Davies, 150–53, 351–53. Cambridge, MA: Harvard University Art Museums, 1995.

——. "Rembrandt's Tree Stump: An Iconographic Attribute of St. Jerome." *Art Bulletin* 56, no. 4 (December 1974): 571–80.

Labriola, Albert C., and John W. Smeltz. *The Bible of the Poor* [Biblia Pauperum], *a Facsimile and Edition of the British Library Blockbook C. 9 d. 2*. Pittsburgh, PA: Duquesne University Press, 1990.

Lammertse, Friso, and Jaap van der Veen. *Uylenburgh & Son: Art and Commerce from Rembrandt to De Lairesse, 1625–1675*. Amsterdam: Het Rembrandthuis; Zwolle, Netherlands: Waanders, 2006.

Lampsonius, Dominicus. *Pictorum aliquot celebrium Germaniae inferiors effigies.* Antwerp: apud viduam Hieronymi Cock, 1572.

Landau, David, and Peter Parshall. *The Renaissance Print: 1470–1550.* New Haven, CT: Yale University Press, 1994.

Landsberger, Franz. "Rembrandt and Josephus." *Art Bulletin* 36, no. 1 (March 1954): 62–63.

Lane, Barbara. *The Altar and the Altarpiece: Sacramental Themes in Early Netherlandish Painting.* New York: Harper & Row, 1984.

Laurentius, Th[eo]. *Etchings by Rembrandt: Reflections of the Golden Age.* Amsterdam: Van Rossum; Zwolle, Netherlands: Waanders, 1996.

Lehrs, Max. *Geschichte und kritischer Katalog des deutschen, niederländischen und französischen Kupferstichs im XV. Jahrhundert.* 9 vols. Wien: Gesellschaft für vervielfältigende Kunst, 1908–34.

Leidtke, Walter, Carolyn Logan, Nadine M. Orenstein, and Stephanie Dickey. *Rembrandt/Not Rembrandt in the Metropolitan Museum of Art: Aspects of Connoisseurship.* 2 vols. Exh. cat. New York: Harry N. Abrams and Metropolitan Museum of Art, 1995.

Lieure, Jules. *Jacques Callot.* 3 vols. Paris: Editions de la Gazette des Beaux-Arts, 1927.

Ludman, Joan, and Lauris Mason, compilers. *Fine Print References: A Selected Bibliography of Print-Related Literature.* Millwood, NY: Kraus International Publications, 1982.

Lugt, Frits. *Les marques de collections de dessins & d'estampes; marques estampillées et écrites de collections particulières et publiques. Marques de marchands, de monteurs et d'imprimeurs. Cachets de vente d'artistes décédés. Marques de graveurs apposées après le tirage des planches. Timbres d'édition. Etc. Avec des notices historiques sur les collectionneurs, les collections, les ventes, les marchands et éditeurs, etc.* 4 vols. Amsterdam: Vereenigde drukkerijen, 1921. Online database. Accessed July 18, 2014. http://www.marquesdecollections.fr/.

Luijten, Ger. "The *Iconography*: Van Dyck's Portraits in Print." In *Anthony van Dyck as a Printmaker,* edited by Carl Depauw and Ger Luijten, 75–91. Antwerp: distributed by Rizzoli, 1999.

Luther und die Folgen für die Kunst. Hamburger Kunsthalle, 11 November 1983–8 Januar 1984, edited by Werner Hofmann. Exh. cat. Munich: Prestel Verlag, 1983.

Maberly, Joseph. *The Print Collector: An Introduction to the Knowledge Necessary for Forming a Collection of Ancient Prints.* New York: Dodd, Mead, 1885; 1st ed., London: Saunders and Otley, 1844.

Manuth, Volker. "*'Are you a Mennonite, Papist, Arminian, or Beggar?'* Art, Religion and Rembrandt." In *Rembrandt, Quest of a Genius,* edited by Ernst de Wetering, 65–77. Exh. cat. Zwolle, Netherlands: Waanders and Museum het Rembrandthuis, 2006.

———. "Denomination and Iconography: The Choice of Subject Matter in the Biblical Paintings of the Rembrandt Circle." *Simiolus: Netherlands Quarterly for the History of Art* 22, no. 4 (1993–94): 235–52.

Mayor, A. Hyatt. "Rembrandt and the Bible." *Metropolitan Museum of Art Bulletin* 36, no. 3 (Winter 1978–79): 2–48.

McGrath, Elizabeth. "Rubens's *Susanna and the Elders* and Moralizing Inscriptions on Prints." In *Wort und Bild in der Niederländischen Kunst und Literatur des 16. und 17. Jahrhunderts,* edited by Herman Vekeman and Justus Müller Hofstede, 73–90. Erftstadt, Germany: Lukassen Verlag, 1984.

Meder, Joseph. *Dürer-Katalog; ein Handbuch über Albrecht Dürers Stiche, Radierungen, Holzschnitte, deren Zustände, Ausgaben und Wasserzeichen.* New York: Da Capo Press, 1971.

Meiers, Sarah. "Portraits in Print: Hieronymus Cock, Dominicus Lampsonius, and 'Pictorum aliquot celebrium Germaniae inferioris effigies.'" *Zeitschrift für Kunstgeschichte* 69, no. 1 (2006): 1–16.

Meiss, Millard. "Light as Form and Symbol in Some Fifteenth-Century Paintings." *Art Bulletin* 27, no. 3 (September 1945): 175–81.

———. "The Madonna of Humility." *Art Bulletin* 18, no. 4 (1936): 435–64.

Melion, Walter J. *The Meditative Art: Studies in Northern Devotional Prints, 1550–1625.* Philadelphia, PA: Saint Joseph's University Press, 2009.

Middleton-Wake, Charles Henry. *A Descriptive Catalogue of the Etched Work of Rembrandt Van Rhyn.* London: J. Murray, 1878.

Moerman, Ingrid W. L. "Leiden, City in Holland." In Roelof van Straten, *Young Rembrandt: The Leiden Years, 1606–1632.* Leiden: Foleor, 2005.

Moffit, John. "Mary as a 'Prophetic Seamstress' in Siglo de Oro Sevillian Painting." *Wallraf-Richartz-Jahrbuch* 54 (1993): 141–61.

———. "Rembrandt, Revelation and Calvin's Curtains." *Gazette des Beaux-Arts* 113–114 (April 1987): 175–84.

Möller, George J. "Het album Pandora van Jan Six (1618–1700)." *Jaarboek van het Genootschap Amstelodamum* 76 (1984): 69–101.

Montias, John Michael. *Art at Auction in 17th-Century Amsterdam.* Amsterdam: Amsterdam University Press, 2002.

———. "Works of Art in Seventeenth-Century Amsterdam: An Analysis of Subjects and Attributions." In *Art in History/History in Art: Studies in Seventeenth-Century Dutch Culture,* edited by David Freedberg and Jan de Vries, 331–72. Santa Monica, CA: Getty Center for the History of Art and the Humanities, 1991.

Mukerji, Chandra. *From Graven Images: Patterns of Modern Materialism.* New York: Columbia University Press, 1983.

Münz, Ludwig. *A Critical Catalogue of Rembrandt's Etchings and the Etchings of His School Formerly Attributed to the Master: With an Essay on Rembrandt's Technique and Documentary Sources.* 2 vols. London: Phaidon, 1952.

Nadler, Steven. *Rembrandt's Jews.* Chicago: University of Chicago Press, 2003.

Nieuwstraten, J[ohannes]. "Het werkelijke onderwerp van Aert de Gelders 'Heilige Familie' te Berlijn." *Oud Holland* 112 (1998): 157–68.

Nowell-Usticke, Gordon W. *Rembrandt's Etchings: States and Values.* Narbeth, PA: Livingston Publishing, 1967.

Nystad, S[aam]. "Joseph and Mary Find Their Son among the Doctors." *Burlington Magazine* 117, no. 864 (March 1975): 140–47.

Oakeshott, R. Ewart. *European Weapons and Armour: From the Renaissance to the Industrial Revolution.* Rochester, NY: Boydell Press, 2000.

Offenberg, A. K. "Jacob Jehuda Leon (1602–1675) and His Model of the Temple." In *Jewish-Christian Relations in the Seventeenth Century, Studies and Documents,* edited by Johannes van den Berg and Ernestine G. E. van der Wall, 95–115. Dordrecht, Netherlands: Kluwer Academic Publishers, 1988.

O'Neill, John P. *The Painterly Print: Monotypes from the Seventeenth to the Twentieth Century; [. . . Publ. in Connection with an Exhibition at the Metropolitan Museum of Art, New York, from October 16 to December 7, 1980, and at the Museum of Fine Arts, Boston, from January 24 to March 22, 1981].* Exh. cat. New York: Metropolitan Museum of Art, 1980.

Orenstein, Nadine. *Hendrick Hondius and the Business of Prints in Seventeenth-Century Holland.* Rotterdam: Sound and Vision Interactive, 1996.

——. "Marketing Prints to the Dutch Republic: Novelty and the Print Publisher." *Journal of Medieval & Early Modern Studies* 28, no. 1 (1998): 141–65.

——. "Rembrandt's Prints and the Question of Attribution." In Walter Leidtke, Carolyn Logan, Nadine M. Orenstein, and Stephanie Dickey, *Rembrandt/Not Rembrandt in the Metropolitan Museum of Art: Aspects of Connoisseurship,* 2: 201–3.

——. "Sleeping Caps, City Views, and State Funerals: Privileges for Prints in the Dutch Republic, 1597–1650." In *His Milieu: Essays on Netherlandish Art in Memory of John Michael Montias,* edited by Amy Golahny, Mia M. Mochizuki, and Lisa Vergara, 313–46. Amsterdam: Amsterdam University Press, 2006.

Orenstein, Nadine, Huigen Leeflang, Ger Luijten, and Christiaan Schuckman. "Print Publishers in the Netherlands, 1580–1620." In *Dawn of the Golden Age: Northern Netherlandish Art, 1580–1620,* edited by Ger Luijten and Ariane van Suchtelen, 167–99. Exh. cat. Amsterdam: Rijksmuseum; Zwolle, Netherlands: Waander, 1993.

Pächt, Otto. *Rembrandt.* Munich: Prestel Verlag, 1991.

Parente, James A., Jr. *Religious Drama and the Humanist Tradition: Christian Theater in Germany and in the Netherlands 1500–1680.* Leiden: E. J. Brill, 1987.

Parshall, Peter. "Art and the Theater of Knowledge: The Origins of Print Collecting in Northern Europe. " *Harvard University Museums Bulletin* 2, no. 3 (1994): 7–36.

——. "Prints as Objects of Consumption in Early Modern Europe." *Journal of Medieval & Early Modern Studies* 28, no. 1 (1998): 19–36.

Parshall, Peter, Stacey Sell, and Judith Brodie. *The Unfinished Print.* Exh. cat. Washington, DC: National Gallery of Art, 2001.

Pelc, Milan. "Representations and Descriptions of Jerusalem in the Printed Travelogues of the Early Modern Period." In *Visual Constructs of Jerusalem,* edited by Bianca Kühnel, Galit Noga-Banai, and Hanna Vorholts, 397–407. Turnhout, Belgium: Brepols, 2014.

Perlove, Shelley Karen. "Awaiting the Messiah: Christians, Jews and Muslims in the Late Work of Rembrandt." *Bulletin of the University of Michigan Museum of Art* 11 (1996): 84–113.

——. "The Ferocious Dragon and the Docile Elephant: The Unleashing of Sin in Rembrandt's *Garden of Eden.*" In *Religion, the Supernatural and Visual Culture in Early Modern Europe,* edited by Jennifer Spinks and Dagmar Eichberger, 283–301. Leiden: Brill, 2015.

——. "An Irenic Vision of Utopia: Rembrandt's 'Triumph of Mordecai' and the New Jerusalem." *Zeitschrift für Kunstgeschichte* 56, no. 1 (1993): 38–60.

Perlove, Shelley Karen, and Robert Baldwin. *Impressions of Faith: Rembrandt's Biblical Etchings.* Dearborn: University of Michigan-Dearborn, Mardigian Library, 1989.

Perlove, Shelley Karen, and Larry Silver. "Rembrandt and the Dutch Catholics." *Canadian Journal of Netherlandic Studies; Revue canadienne d'études néerlandaises* 28 (2007): 53–75.

——. *Rembrandt's Faith: Church and Temple in the Dutch Golden Age.* University Park: Pennsylvania State University Press, 2009.

Philips, Angel, Michael Hoyle, and Hessel Miedema. "Philips Angel, 'Praise of Painting.'" *Simiolus: Netherlands Quarterly for the History of Art* 24, nos. 2–3 (1996): 227–58.

Philips, Dirk. *The Writings of Dirk Philips*. Translated by Cornelius J. Dyck, William E. Keeney, and Alvin J. Beachy. Scottdale, PA: Herald Press, 1992.

Pol, Lotte van de. *The Burgher and the Whore: Prostitution in Early Modern Amsterdam*. Oxford: Oxford University Press, 2011.

Preimesberger, Rudolf. "'Inventio' in Rembrandts Frühwerk. 'Die Erweckung des Lazarus' in Los Angeles und 'Die Reue des Judas' in englishem Privatebesitz." In *Rembrandt—Wissenschaft auf der Suche*, edited by Holm Bevers, Jan Kelch, Bernd Wolfgang Lindemann, and Christian Tico Seofert, 97–112. *Jahrbuch der Berliner Museen*, N.F. 51 (2009). Berlin: Gebr. Mann Verlag, 2009.

Rassieur, Thomas E. "Looking over Rembrandt's Shoulder: The Printmaker at Work." In Clifford S. Ackley, Thomas Rassieur, and William Robinson, *Rembrandt's Journey: Painter, Draughtsman, Etcher*, 45–60.

Raupp, Hans-Joachim. *Untersuchungen zu Künstlerbildnis und Künstlerdarstellung in den Niederlanden im 17. Jahrhundert*. Hildesheim, Germany: Olms, 1984.

——. "Rembrandts Radierungen mit biblischen Themen 1640–1650 und das 'Hundertguldenblatt.'" *Zeitschrift für Kunstgeschichte* 57 (1994): 403–20.

Rembrandt Harmenszoon van Rijn. *Rembrandt, beyond the Brush: Master Prints from the Weil Collection*. Exh. cat. Montgomery, AL: Montgomery Museum of Fine Arts, 1999.

——. *Rembrandt: Experimental Etcher*. Prepared by Felice Stampfle, Eleanor Sayre, Sue W. Reed, and Clifford Ackley. Exh. cat. Boston: Museum of Fine Arts; distributed by New York Graphic Society, Greenwich, CT [1969].

——. *Rembrandt: The Master & His Workshop*. 2 vols. Exh. cat. New Haven, CT: Yale University Press; London: National Gallery Publications, 1991.

Rembrandt Harmenszoon van Rijn, and Rembrandt Research Project. *A Corpus of Rembrandt Paintings: Stichting Foundation Rembrandt Research Project*. 6 vols. The Hague: Nijhoff; Dordrecht, Netherlands: Springer, 1982–2015.

Renger, Konrad. *Graphik in Holland*. Exh. cat. Munich: Staatliche Graphische Sammlung, 1982.

Rice, Eugene F. *St. Jerome in the Renaissance*. Baltimore, MD: Johns Hopkins University Press, 1985.

Riggs, Timothy, and Larry Silver. *Graven Images: The Rise of Professional Printmakers in Antwerp and Haarlem, 1540–1640*. Exh. cat. Evanston, IL: Northwestern University Press, 1993.

Robinson, Frank. "Puns and Plays in Rembrandt's Etchings." *Print Collector's Newsletter* 11, no. 5 (November–December 1980): 165–68.

Robinson, William W. "'This Passion for Prints': Collecting and Connoisseurship in Northern Europe during the Seventeenth Century." In Clifford S. Ackley, *Printmaking in the Age of Rembrandt*, xxvii–l. Exh. cat. Boston: Boston Museum of Fine Arts, 1981.

Rogers, Charles. *A Collection of Prints in Imitation of Drawings: To Which Are Annexed Lives of Their Authors with Explanatory and Critical Notes by Charles Rogers Esq. F.R.S. and S.A.L.* 2 vols. London: Printed by J. Nichols, successor to Mr. Bowyer, and sold by John Boydell, engraver, No. 93, Cheapside. Benjamin White, at Horace's Head, Fleet-Street. Peter Molini, in Oxendon-Street, Hay-Market, 1778.

Roobol, Marianne. *Disputation by Decree: The Public Disputations between Reformed Ministers and Dirck Volckertszoon Coornhert as Instruments of Religious Policy during the Dutch Revolt (1577–1583)*. Leiden: Brill, 2010.

Rosenau, Helen. "Jacob Judah Leon Templo's Contribution to Architectural Imagery." *Journal of Jewish Studies* 23, no. 1 (Spring 1972): 72–81.

Rosenberg, Charles M. "A Rembrandt Self-Portrait and *Tronie*." In *Face to Face*, 6–11. Exh. cat. Notre Dame, IN: Snite Museum of Art, 2003.

——. "Rembrandt's Etching of *The Stoning of St. Stephen* and the Remonstrant Controversy." *Zeitschrift für Kunstgeschichte* 78, no. 1 (2015): 94–104.

Rosenberg, Jacob. *Rembrandt: Life & Work*. London: Phaidon, 1964.

——. "Rembrandt and Mantegna." *Art Quarterly* 19, no. 2 (1956): 153–61.

Rotermund, Hans. *Rembrandt's Drawings and Etchings for the Bible*. Translated by Shierry M. Weber. Philadelphia: Pilgrim Press, 1969.

Rovinski, Dimitri. *L'oeuvre gravé de Rembrandt: reproduction des planches originales dans tous leurs états successifs: 1000 phototypies sans retouches: avec un catalogue raisonné*. St. Petersburg, Russia: Imprimerie de l'Académie Impériale des Sciences, 1890.

Rowlands, John. *Drawings by German Artists and Artists from German-Speaking Regions of Europe in the Department of Prints and Drawings in the British Museum: The Fifteenth Century, and the Sixteenth Century by Artists Born before 1530*. 2 vols. London: British Museum Press, 1993.

Royalton-Kisch, Martin. *Drawings by Rembrandt and His Circle in the British Museum*. London: British Museum Press, 1992.

——. "Rembrandt: Two Passion Prints Reconsidered." *Apollo* 119 (February 1984): 130–32.

Rubin, Patricia. *Giorgio Vasari: Art and History*. New Haven, CT: Yale University Press, 1995.

Rutgers, Jaco. "A Source for Rembrandt's *Beheading of St. John the Baptist.*" *Print Quarterly* 21, no. 2 (2004): 154–56.

Salamon, Ferdinando. *The History of Prints and Printmaking from Dürer to Picasso: A Guide to Collecting.* New York: American Heritage Press, 1972.

Sandrart, Joachim von, and Jochen Becken. *Teutsche Academie der Bau-, Bild- und Mahlerey-Künste* [The German Academy of the Noble Art of Architecture, Sculpture, and Painting]. (Nüremberg, 1675); Nördlingen, Germany: Dr. Alfons Uhl, 1994.

Sandrart, Joachim von, Filippo Baldinucci, and Arnold Houbraken. Introduction by Charles Ford. *Lives of Rembrandt.* London: Pallas Athene, 2007.

Scallen, Catherine B. "Rembrandt, Emulation and the Northern Print Tradition." In *In Detail: New Studies of Northern Renaissance Art in Honor of Walter S. Gibson*, edited by Laurinda S. Dixon, 135–49. Turnhout, Belgium: Brepols, 1998.

——. "Rembrandt's Nocturne Prints." *On Paper* 1 (January–February 1997): 13–17

——. "Rembrandt's Reformation of a Catholic Subject: The Penitent and the Repentant Saint Jerome." *Sixteenth Century Journal* 30, no. 1 (1999): 71–88.

Schama, Simon. *The Embarrassment of Riches: An Interpretation of Dutch Culture in the Golden Age.* New York: Knopf, 1987.

——. *Rembrandt's Eyes.* New York: Knopf, 1999.

Schatborn, Peter. *Tekeningen van Rembrandt, zijn onbekende leerlingen en navoglers; Drawings by Rembrandt, His Anonymous Pupils and Followers.* Translated by Eric Wulfert and Patricia Wardle. The Hague: Staatsuitgeverij, 1985.

Schneider, Cynthia. *Rembrandt's Landscapes: Drawings and Prints.* Exh. cat. Washington, DC: National Gallery of Art, 1990.

Schuckman, Christiaan, Martin Royalton-Kisch, and Erik Hinterding. *Rembrandt and Van Vliet: A Collaboration on Copper.* Amsterdam: Museum het Rembrandthuis, 1996.

Schwartz, Gary. *Rembrandt: His Life, His Paintings.* London: Penguin, 1991.

——. *The Rembrandt Book.* New York: Abrams, 2006.

——. "Rembrandt's Hebrews." In *Rembrandt—Wissenschaft auf der Suche*, edited by Holm Bevers, Jan Kelch, Bernd Wolfgang Lindemann, and Christian Tico Seofert, 33–38. *Jahrbuch der Berliner Museen*, N.F. 51 (2009). Berlin: Gebr. Mann Verlag, 2009.

Schwartz, Sheila. "The Iconography of the Rest on the Flight into Egypt." PhD diss., New York University, 1975.

Sebkova Thaller, Suzana. "Il gatto nell'arte tardo Medioevo e del Rinascimento." In *Gatti nell'arte: il magico e il quotidiano: 3 giugno–19 luglio 1987, Palazzo Barberini, Galleria nazionale d'arte antica*, 27–34. Rome: Multigrafica, 1987.

Seidlitz, Woldemar von. *Kritisches Verzeichnis der Radierungen Rembrandts, zugleich eine Anleitung zu deren Studium.* Leipzig: E. A. Seeman, 1895.

Seigneur, Marie-Christine. "On Counterproofs." *Print Quarterly* 21 (2004): 115–27.

Sellin, Christine Petra. *Fractured Families and Rebel Maidservants: The Biblical Hagar in Seventeenth-Century Dutch Art and Literature.* New York: Continuum, 2006.

Siefert, Christian Tico. *Pieter Lastman, Studien zu Leben und Werk.* Petersberg, Germany: Michael Imhof Verlag, 2011.

Silver, Larry, and Shelley Perlove. "Rembrandt's Jesus." In *Rembrandt and the Face of Jesus*, edited by Lloyd Dewitt, 75–107. Exh. cat. New Haven, CT: Yale University Press, 2011.

——. "Rembrandt's Protestant Joseph." In *Joseph of Nazareth through the Centuries*, edited by Joseph F. Chorpenning, OSFS, 173–211. Philadelphia: Saint Joseph's University Press, 2011.

Simson, Otto Georg von, and Jan Kelch. *Neue Beiträge Zur Rembrandt-Forschung.* Berlin: Gebr. Mann, 1973.

Singer, Hans Wolfgang. *Rembrandt: des Meisters Radierungen.* Stuttgart: Dt. Verl.-Anst, 1906.

Slatkes, Leonard. *Rembrandt and Persia.* New York: Abaris Books, 1983.

——. "Rembrandt's Elephant." *Simiolus: Netherlands Quarterly for the History of Art* 11, no. 1 (1980): 7–13.

——. "Review of C. White and K. Boon, *Rembrandt's Etchings*, and C. White, *Rembrandt as an Etcher.*" *Art Quarterly* 36 (1973): 250–63.

Slive, Seymour. *Frans Hals.* 3 vols. London: Phaidon: 1970–74.

——. *Rembrandt and His Critics, 1630–1730.* New York: Hacker Art Books, 1998; original, The Hague: M. Nijhoff, 1953.

——. *Rembrandt Drawings.* Los Angeles: J. Paul Getty Museum, 2009.

Sluijter, Eric. *Rembrandt and the Female Nude.* Amsterdam: Amsterdam University Press, 2006.

Smith, David R. "Raphael's Creation, Rembrandt's Fall." *Zeitschrift für Kunstgeschichte* 50 (1987): 496–508.

——. "Rembrandt's Metaphysical Wit: *The Three Trees* and *The Omval*," *Word & Image: A Journal of Verbal/Visual Inquiry* 21, no. 1 (2005): 1–21.

——. "Towards a Protestant Aesthetics: Rembrandt's 1655 *Sacrifice of Isaac.*" *Art History* 8, no. 3 (1985): 290–302.

Snite Museum of Art. *Rembrandt Etchings from a Private Collection, Biblical Subjects: The Old and New Testaments.* Catalogue from the Exhibition of January 8 – March 29, 1981. Exh. cat. Notre Dame, IN: Snite Museum of Art, 1981.

Solomons, Israel. "The Second Series of Illustrations for the *Piedra Gloriosa* of Menasseh ben Israel." *Jewish Chronicle*, July 27, 1906, 31.

Spicer, Joaneath. "The Renaissance Elbow." In *A Cultural History of Gesture*, edited by Jan Bremmer and Herman Roodenburg, 84–128. Ithaca, NY: Cornell University Press, 1991.

Stechow, Wolfgang. "Rembrandts Darstellungen der Kreuzabnahme." *Jahrbuch der Preussischen Kunstsammlungen* 50 (1929): 217–32.

———. "Rembrandts Darstellungen des Emmausmahles." *Zeitschrift für Kunsgeschichte* 3 (1934): 329–41.

———. "Some Observations on Rembrandt and Lastman." *Oud Holland* 84 (1969): 148–62.

Steinberg, Leo. "Michelangelo's Florentine *Pietà*: The Missing Leg." *Art Bulletin* 50, no. 2 (1968): 343–53

Stogdon, Nicolas. "Captain Baillie and *The Hundred Guilder Print*." *Print Quarterly* 12 (1996): 53–56.

Stoichita, Victor I. *A Short History of the Shadow.* London: Reaktion Books, 1997.

Straten, Roelof van. "Rembrandt's 'Earliest Prints' Reconsidered." *Artibus et historiae* 23, no. 45 (2002): 167–77.

———. *Young Rembrandt: The Leiden Years, 1606–1632.* Leiden: Foleor, 2005.

Stratton, Suzanne. "Rembrandt's Beggars: Satire and Sympathy." *Print Collector's Newsletter* 17, no. 3 (July–August 1986): 77–81.

Strauss, Walter. "The Puzzle of Rembrandt's Plates." In *Essays in Northern European Art Presented to Egbert Haverkamp-Begemann on His Sixtieth Birthday*, edited by Anne-Marie Logan, 260–67. Doornspijk, Netherlands: Davaco, 1983.

Strauss, Walter, and Marjon van der Meulen, eds. and trans. *The Rembrandt Documents.* New York: Abaris, 1979.

Stronks, Els. *Negotiating Differences: Word, Image and Religion in the Dutch Republic.* Leiden: Brill, 2011.

Suthor, Nicola. "Ein Schattenspiel: Rembrandts 'Hundertguldenblatt'." In *Kanon Kunstgeschichte: Einführung in Werke, Methoden und Epochen.* Vol. 2: *Neuzeit*, edited by Kristin Marek and Martin Schulz, 345–67. Paderborn, Germany: Wilhelm Fink, 2015.

Temple, William. *The Works of Sir William Temple, bart.* Vol. 1. *Observations upon the United Provinces of the Netherlands.* London: Printed for J. Brotherton, 1770; first pub. 1687. Accessed February 25, 2017. https://babel.hathitrust.org/cgi/pt?id=ucw.ark:/13960/t8x92t82q;view=1up.

Thompson, John L. *Writing the Wrongs: Women of the Old Testament among Biblical Commentators from Philo through the Reformation.* New York: Oxford University Press, 2001. *Oxford Scholarship Online.* Oxford University Press. Accessed March 1, 2011. http://dx.doi.org/10.1093/0195137361.001.0001.

Topsell, Edward. *The Histoire of Four Footed Beastes and Serpents.* London: William Laggard, 1607.

Tümpel, Astrid. "Claes Cornelisz. Moeyaert." *Oud Holland* 88, no. 1–2 (1974): 1–164.

Tümpel, Astrid, and Peter Schatborn. *Pieter Lastman: leermeester van Rembrandt; The Man Who Taught Rembrandt.* Exh. cat. Zwolle, Netherlands: Waanders; Amsterdam: Museum het Rembrandthuis, 1991.

Tümpel, Christian. "The Iconography of the Pre-Rembrandtists." In Astrid Tümpel, *The Pre-Rembrandtists*, 127–50. Exh. cat. Sacramento, CA: E. B. Crocker Art Gallery, 1974.

———. "Religious History Painting." In Albert Blankert et al., *Gods, Saints and Heroes, Dutch Painting in the Age of Rembrandt*, 45–54. Exh. cat. Washington, DC: National Gallery of Art; Detroit: Detroit Institute of Arts; Amsterdam: Rijsmuseum, 1980.

———. *Rembrandt: Images and Metaphors.* London: Haus Books, 2006.

———. *Rembrandt mit Selbstzeugnissen und Bilddokumenten.* Reinbeck bei Hamburg, Germany: Rowohlt, 1977.

———. "Studien zur Ikonografie der Historien Rembrandts." *Nederlands Kunsthistorisch Jaarboek* 20 (1969): 107–98.

Tümpel, Christian, and Astrid Tümpel. *Rembrandt legt die Bibel aus. Zeichnungen und Radierungen aus dem Kupferstichkabinett der Staatlichen Museen Preussischer Kulturbesitz Berlin.* Exh. cat. Berlin: Verlag Bruno Hessling, 1970.

Turner, Jane, ed. *From Rembrandt to Vermeer: 17th-Century Dutch Artists.* Grove Dictionary of Art. New York: St. Martin's Press, 2000.

Uffenbach, Zacharias Conrad von. *Herrn Zacharias Conrad von Uffenbach Merkwürdige Reisen durch Niedersachsen, Holland und Engelland.* Vol. 3. Ulm and Memmingen: Gaum, 1754. Accessed December 19, 2012. http://books.google.com/books?id=FUsHAAAAQAAJ&pg=PA2#v=onepage&q&f=false.

Veldman, Ilja M. *Images for the Eye and Soul: Function and Meaning in Netherlandish Prints (1450–1650).* Leiden: Primavera Pers, 2006.

Verdi, Richard. *Rembrandt's Themes: Life into Art.* New Haven, CT: Yale University Press, 2014.

Verdier, Philippe. "The Tapestry of the Prodigal Son." *Journal of the Walters Art Gallery* 18 (1955): 8–58.

Villalpando, Juan Bautista. *Juan Bautista Villalpando's Ezechielem Explanationes: A Sixteenth-Century Architectural Treatise*, translated by Tessa Morrison. Lewiston, NY: Edwin Mellen Press, 2009.

Visscher, Roemer. *Sinnen-poppen*. Amsterdam: Willem Iansz, 1614; reprint, The Hague: Martinus Nijhoff, 1949.

Visser 't Hooft, Willem Adolph. *Rembrandt and the Gospel*. New York: Meridian Books, 1960.

Waal, Henri van de. *Steps towards Rembrandt: Collected Articles 1937–1972*. Edited by R. H. Fuchs; translated by Patricia Wardle and Alan Griffiths. Amsterdam: North-Holland, 1974.

Waiboer, Adriaan, and Michiel Franken. *Northern Nocturnes: Nightscapes in the Age of Rembrandt*. Dublin: National Gallery of Ireland, 2005.

Warner, Marina. *Alone of All Her Sex: The Myth and the Cult of the Virgin Mary*. New York: Alfred Knopf, 1976.

Weisbach, Werner. *Rembrandt*. Berlin: De Gruyter, 1926.

Westermann, Mariët. *Rembrandt*. London: Phaidon, 2000.

Weststeijn, Thijs. *The Visible World: Samuel Van Hoogstraten's Art Theory and the Legitimation of Painting in the Dutch Golden Age*. Amsterdam: Amsterdam University Press, 2008.

Wetering, Ernst van de. "The Multiple Functions of Rembrandt's Self Portraits." In *Rembrandt by Himself*, edited by Christopher White and Quentin Buvelot, 8–37. Exh. cat. London, The Hague, and New Haven, CT: distributed by Yale University Press, 1999.

——, ed. *Rembrandt, Quest of a Genius*. Exh. cat. Zwolle, Netherlands: Waanders; Amsterdam: Museum het Rembrandthuis, 2006.

Wetering, Ernst van de, Bernhard Schnackenburg, and Ed de Heer. *The Mystery of the Young Rembrandt*. Kassel, Germany: Staatliche Museen; Amsterdam: Rembrandthuis; Wolfratshausen, Germany: Edition Minerva, 2001.

Wheelock, Arthur K. "The Influence of Lucas van Leyden on Rembrandt's Narrative Etchings." In *Essays in Northern European Art Presented to Egbert Haverkamp-Begemann*, edited by Anne-Marie Logan, 291–96. Doornspijk, Netherlands: Davaco, 1983.

——. *Jan Lievens: A Dutch Master Rediscovered*. New Haven, CT: Yale University Press; Washington, DC: National Gallery of Art, 2008.

White, Christopher. *The Late Etchings of Rembrandt: A Study in the Development of a Print. An Arts Council Exhibition [at the] British Museum Gallery of Prints & Drawings, 20 March–11 May 1969*. Exh. cat. London: Arts Council, 1969.

——. *Rembrandt as an Etcher: A Study of the Artist at Work*. London: A. Zwemmer, 1969; 2nd ed., New Haven, CT: Yale University Press, 1999.

White, Christopher, David Alexander, and Ellen D'Oench. *Rembrandt in Eighteenth-Century England*. Exh. cat. New Haven, CT: Yale Center for British Art, 1983.

White, Christopher, and Karel G. Boon. *Rembrandt's Etchings: An Illustrated Critical Catalogue*. Amsterdam: Van Gendt; New York: Abner Schram, 1970.

White, Christopher, and Quentin Buvelot, eds. *Rembrandt by Himself*. Exh. cat. London, The Hague, and New Haven, CT: distributed by Yale University Press, 1999.

Wieck, Roger S. *Time Sanctified: The Book of Hours in Medieval Art and Life*. New York: George Braziller, 1988.

Williams, Julia Lloyd, ed. *Rembrandt's Women*. New York: Prestel Verlag, 2001.

Williamson, Beth. "Liturgical Image or Devotional Image? The London 'Madonna of the Firescreen.'" In *Objects, Images, and the Word*, edited by Colum Hourihane, 298–318. Princeton, NJ: Princeton University Press, 2003.

——. *The Madonna of Humility: Development, Dissemination & Reception, c. 1340–1400*. Woodbridge, UK: Boydell, 2009.

Wilson, Bronwen. *The World in Venice. Print, the City, and Early Modern Identity*. Toronto, ON: University of Toronto Press, 2005.

——. "*Foggie diverse di vestire de' Turchi*. Turkish Costume Illustration and Cultural Translation." *Journal of Medieval and Early Modern Studies* 31, no. 1 (Winter 2007): 97–139.

Wilson, Carolyn C. *St. Joseph in Italian Renaissance Society and Art: New Directions and Interpretations*. Philadelphia: St. Joseph's University Press, 2001.

——. "*Sanctus Joseph Nutritor Domini*: A Triptych Attributed to Jan Gossaert Considered as Evidence of Early Hapsburg Embrace of St. Joseph's Cult." In *Święty Józef -Patron na nasze czasy. Akta X Międzynarodowego Kongresu Józefologicznego; Saint Joseph: Patron for Our Times. Proceedings of the Tenth International Josephological Congress, Kalisz, Poland, September 27–October 4, 2009*, 499–524. Kalisz, Poland: Centrum Józefologiczne, 2010.

Wilson, Thomas. *A Descriptive Catalogue of the Prints of Rembrandt by an Amateur*. London: J. F. Setchel, 1836. Accessed January 21, 2013. http://catalog.hathitrust.org/api/volumes/oclc/3777539.html.

Wilson, William H. "'The Circumcision,' A Drawing by Romeyn de Hooghe." *Master Drawings* 13, no. 3 (Autumn 1975): 250–58, 320–21.

Winkel, Marieke de. "Costume in Rembrandt's Self-Portraits." In *Rembrandt by Himself*, edited by Christopher White and Quentin Buvelot, 58–74. Exh. cat. London, The Hague, and New Haven, CT: distributed by Yale University Press, 1999.

——. *Fashion and Fancy: Dress and Meaning in Rembrandt's Paintings.* Amsterdam: Amsterdam University Press, 2006.

Winner, Matthais. "Rembrandts 'Hundertguldenblatt' und Raffaels 'Schule von Athen.'" In *Rembrandt—Wissenschaft auf der Suche*, edited by Holm Bevers, Jan Kelch, Bernd Wolfgang Lindemann, and Christian Tico Seofert, 77–86. *Jahrbuch der Berliner Museen*, N.F. 51 (2009). Berlin: Gebr. Mann Verlag, 2009.

Winternitz, Emanuel. "A Rabbi with Wings: Remarks on Rembrandt's Etching 'Abraham Entertaining the Angels.'" *Metropolitan Museum Journal* 12 (1977): 101–6.

——. "Rembrandt's 'Christ Presented to the People'—1655: A Meditation on Justice and Collective Guilt." *Oud Holland* 84 (1969): 177–98.

Wischnitzer, Rachel. "Rembrandt, Callot and Tobias Stimmer." *Art Bulletin* 39, no. 3 (September 1957): 224–30.

Witcombe, Christopher L. C. E. "Dürer's *Prodigal Son*." *Source* 17, no. 3 (1998): 7–13.

Wyckoff, Elizabeth. "Innovation and Popularization: Printmaking and Print Publishing in Haarlem during the 1620s." PhD diss., Columbia University, 1998.

Yver, Pierre, Edme-François Gersaint, and Jean Baptiste Glomy. *Supplément au catalogue raisonné de MM. Gersaint, Helle et Glomy, de toutes les pièces qui forment l'œuvre de Rembrandt.* Amsterdam: Chez Pierre Yver, marchand de tableaux & d'estampes, 1756.

Zell, Michael. *Reframing Rembrandt: Jews and the Christian Image in Seventeenth-Century Amsterdam.* Berkeley: University of California Press, 2002.

——. "Rembrandt's Gift: A Case Study of Actor-Network-Theory." *Journal of Historians of Netherlandish Art* 3, no. 2 (Summer 2011). Accessed December 26, 2012. http://www.jhna.org/index.php/past-issues/volume-3-issue-2/143-zell-rembrandts-gifts.

Zumthor, Paul. *Daily Life in Rembrandt's Holland.* Translated by Simon Watson Taylor. London: Weidenfeld and Nicolson, 1962.

INDEX

Page numbers in italics refer to illustrations.

CHARLES M. ROSENBERG is Professor Emeritus of Art History at the University of Notre Dame. His publications on Renaissance and Baroque art include articles in the *Renaissance Quarterly, Art Bulletin, American Historical Review, Schifanoia, Zeitschrift für Kunstgeschichte,* and *Studies in the History of Art.* A recipient of NEH and ACLS fellowships, Rosenberg has been a fellow at the American Academy in Rome and at the Harvard Center for Renaissance Studies at the Villa I Tatti in Florence. He is author of *The Este Monuments and Urban Development in Renaissance Ferrara* and editor of *Art and Politics in Late Medieval and Early Renaissance Italy: 1250–1515* and *The Court Cities of Northern Italy.*

DIRECTOR	*Gary Dunham*
ASSISTANT ACQUISITIONS EDITOR	*Peggy Solic*
PROJECT MANAGER	*Nancy Lightfoot*
BOOK AND JACKET DESIGNER	*Leyla Salamova*
COMPOSITION COORDINATOR	*Tony Brewer*
TYPEFACES	*Arno, Bodoni, New Baskerville*